WOMEN'S VOICES

Visions and Perspectives

WOMEN'S VOICES
Visions and Perspectives

Pat C. Hoy II
U.S. Military Academy, West Point

Esther H. Schor
Princeton University

Robert DiYanni
Pace University, Pleasantville

McGRAW-HILL PUBLISHING COMPANY
New York St. Louis San Francisco Auckland Bogotá Caracas Hamburg Lisbon
London Madrid Mexico Milan Montreal New Delhi Oklahoma City Paris
San Juan São Paulo Singapore Sydney Tokyo Toronto

This book was developed by STEVEN PENSINGER, Inc.

WOMEN'S VOICES: VISIONS AND PERSPECTIVES

1 2 3 4 5 6 7 8 9 0 DOH DOH 8 9 4 3 2 1 0 9

ISBN 0-07-557732-1

This book was set in Electra by ComCom, Inc.
The editors were Steven Pensinger and Barbara Curialle Gerr;
the designer was Leon Bolognese;
the production supervisor was Dick Phillips. R. R. Donnelley & Sons Company was printer and
binder.

Top: *Downtown*, Georgia Mills Jessop, 1967. The National Museum of Women in the Arts, Gift
of Savannah Clark.
Middle: *Portrait of Anna Vaughan Hyatt*, Marion Boyd Allen, 1915. Maier Museum of Art,
Randolph-Macon Woman's College.
Bottom: *The Cradle*, Berthe Morisot, 1872. Musée d'Orsay, Paris photograph Art Resource.

Library of Congress Cataloging-in-Publication Data

Women's voices: visions and perspectives/[edited by] Pat C. Hoy II,
    Esther H. Schor, Robert DiYanni.
    p. cm.
    Includes index.
    ISBN 0-07-557732-1
    1. Feminism—History—Sources. 2. Feminist criticism—History—
Sources. 3. Feminism and literature—History—Sources. 4. Women
and literature—History—Sources. 5. Literature—Women authors—
History and criticism.   I. Hoy, Pat C.   II. Schor, Esther H.
III. DiYanni, Robert.
HQ1154.W936 1990
305.4'2—dc19   88-37567

FOR
Ann, Sandra, and Mary

Contents

PART I

Introduction: Rereading and Rewriting the World   *1*

Part II

Introduction: Positions and Perspectives　*439*

Source Notes

VIRGINIA WOOLF

Chapter One from *A Room of One's Own* by Virginia Woolf, copyright 1929 by Harcourt Brace Jovanovich, Inc. and renewed 1957 by Leonard Woolf, reprinted by permission of the publisher, and by permission of The Hogarth Press, London.

"Mary Wollstonecraft" and "Geraldine and Jane" from *The Second Common Reader* by Virginia Woolf, copyright 1932 by Harcourt Brace Jovanovich, Inc. and renewed 1960 by Leonard Woolf, reprinted by permission of the publisher, and by permission of The Hogarth Press, London.

"Montaigne" from *The Common Reader* by Virginia Woolf, copyright 1925 by Harcourt Brace Jovanovich, Inc. and renewed 1953 by Leonard Woolf, reprinted by permission of the publisher, and by permission of The Hogarth Press, London.

PART II

RIKA LESSER

"Degli Sposi" reprinted from *Etruscan Things* by Rika Lesser. Copyright © 1983 by Rika Lesser. Published by George Braziller, Inc. and used with permission.

MARY WOLLSTONECRAFT

"On Love" and "Women in Society," from *A Vindication of the Rights of Woman*, Penguin Books Ltd., 1986.

MARGARET FULLER

"A Woman at Forty," from *Woman in the Nineteenth Century*, W. W. Norton.

ELIZABETH CADY STANTON

Address to the New York State Legislature, 1860, and "Declaration of Sentiments and Resolutions" adopted by the Seneca Falls Convention, July 19–20, 1848. (both in the public domain)

OLIVE SCHREINER

"Woman and War," from *Woman and Labour*, 1911.

VIRGINIA WOOLF

"The Daughters of Educated Men" from *Three Guineas* by Virginia Woolf, copyright 1938 by Harcourt Brace Jovanovich, Inc. and renewed 1966 by Leonard Woolf, reprinted by permission of the publisher, and by permission of The Hogarth Press, London.

SIMONE DE BEAUVOIR

Introduction from *The Second Sex* by Simone de Beauvoir, translated and edited by H. M. Parshley. Copyright 1952 by Alfred A. Knopf, Inc. Reprinted by permission of the publisher.

HÉLÈNE CIXOUS

"The Laugh of the Medusa," translated by Keith Cohen and Paula Cohen, *Signs* 1 (Summer 1976): 875–94. Copyright © 1976 by the University of Chicago Press. All rights reserved.

LUCE IRIGARAY

"When Our Lips Speak Together," translated by Carolyn Baker, *Signs* 1 (Autumn 1980): 69–79. Copyright © 1980 by The University of Chicago Press. All rights reserved.

KATE SIMON

"Birthing," from *Bronx Primitive* by Kate Simon. Copyright © 1982 by Kate Simon. All rights reserved. Reprinted by permission of Viking Penguin, a division of Penguin Books USA, Inc.

MARY ANNE DOLAN

"When Feminism Failed," in *The New York Times* Magazine, June 26, 1988. Permission authorized by Mary Anne Dolan and M.A.D., Inc., Los Angeles, 1989.

ANGELA Y. DAVIS

"Racism, Birth Control and Reproductive Rights" from *Women, Race and Class* by Angela Davis. Copyright © 1981 by Angela Davis. Reprinted by permission of Random House, Inc.

SUSAN BROWNMILLER

"The Police-Blotter Rapist," from *Against Our Will* by Susan Brownmiller. Copyright © 1975 by Susan Brownmiller. Reprinted by permission of Simon & Schuster, Inc.

ZORA NEALE HURSTON

"How It Feels to Be Colored Me," in *The World Tomorrow*, May 11, 1928.

PAULE MARSHALL

excerpt from "The Poets in the Kitchen," from *Reena and Other Stories* by Paule Marshall, © 1983 by The Feminist Press. Reprinted by permission.

URSULA K. LE GUIN

"Is Gender Necessary Redux (1976–1987)." Copyright © 1976, 1989 by Ursula K. Le Guin; an earlier version, published as "Is Gender Necessary?" first appeared in *Aurora: Beyond Equality*, edited by Susan Janice Anderson and Vonda N. McIntyre; the revised text first appeared in *Dancing at the Edge of the World*, by Ursula K. Le Guin (Grove Press, 1989); reprinted by permission of the author and the author's agent, Virginia Kidd.

EVELYN FOX KELLER

"A World of Difference," from *Reflections on Gender and Science* by Evelyn Fox Keller. Reprinted by permission of Yale University Press.

LESLIE MARMON SILKO

"Landscape, History, and the Pueblo Imagination," © 1986 by Leslie Marmon Silko.

Editors' Acknowledgments

For generous assistance during the preparation of our book, we would like to thank a number of our friends and colleagues: Linda Bamber, Carol Barash, Malika Benlounes, Barbara Bowen, Diane Brodson, Abena Busia, Judith Butler, Carol Cook, Maria DiBattista, J. Ellen Gainor, Sandra Gilbert, Sally Goldfarb, Ellen Cronon Rose, Elaine Showalter, Valerie Smith, Claire Sprague, Joanne Wolfe, and Gordon Wolfe. We would also like to thank our reviewers: Jane Hedley, Bryn Mawr College; Nancy Sorkin Rabinowitz, Hamilton College; and Patricia Savoie, Pasadena City College.

A fine professional staff at McGraw-Hill encouraged us from the outset and gave us wise suggestions as we prepared the manuscript. We would like to thank especially Steve Pensinger for his confidence in the project, his spirited encouragement, and his recognition that these women's voices needed to be heard. Cynthia Ward and David Morris helped us refine our notions in the early stages, and Barbara Curialle Gerr kept us and the project on track during production. All shared our enthusiasm.

Finally, we would like to acknowledge our daughters and sons—Patrick and Tim Hoy, Daniel Greenblatt, Karen and Michael DiYanni—who were always on our minds, if not in our manuscripts. Ann Hoy, Walter Greenblatt, and Mary DiYanni offered encouragement, wisdom, and patience rare among even the best of spouses. We also want to thank Sandra Schor for all she contributed: her experience as a writer and as a teacher of writing, her candid responses to our selections, and even mother love.

Pat C. Hoy II
Esther H. Schor
Robert DiYanni

WOMEN'S VOICES
Visions and Perspectives

Part I

INTRODUCTION:
Rereading and Rewriting the World

If we continue to speak the same language to each other, we will reproduce the same story. Begin the same stories all over again. Don't you feel it? Listen: men and women around us all sound the same. Same arguments, same quarrels, same scenes. Same attractions and separations. Same difficulties, the impossibility of reaching each other. Same . . . same. . . . Always the same.
—LUCE IRIGARAY

But a decade later, a decade after Irigaray wrote those words, men and women talking and writing do not sound the same, and if the difficulties and even the impossibility of reaching one another still plague us, we have a much clearer sense of why. We have a clearer sense too of whether we want, always, to reach each other. All of us, women and men, are learning to cherish solitude, to make something of ourselves out of ourselves, alone as well as in community. The rules are changing—life's rules, the rules of language—and women, many women, seem to have heeded Irigaray's suggestion: "Stretching out, never ceasing to unfold ourselves, we must invent so many different voices to speak all of 'us,' including our cracks and faults, that forever won't be enough time. We will never travel all the way round our periphery: we have so many dimensions."

Women's Voices offers testimony to women's multiplicity, testimony that, in our time, women are unfolding themselves, never ceasing to invent different voices, writing urgently, writing beauti-

fully, as if forever won't be time enough.

Some time ago in a book about sexuality and the origins of culture, William Irwin Thompson predicted the "revolt of Lilith . . . the rising up from below of all that would be denied by the rational, male consciousness." What Thompson foresaw was a "destructuring of the old civilization,"* the one that would deny the feminine, the one that would privilege logic and order over intuition and imaginative circumlocution. Women seem to understand what Thompson meant, both actual women and women in fiction. Novelists as different as Virginia Woolf and D. H. Lawrence gave us some sense of women's unwillingness to accept the old patterns, their unwillingness to be dominated by men. And such critics as Sandra M. Gilbert and Susan Gubar have read similar subtexts in nineteenth-century women's fiction, revealing the complex issues related to women's development embedded in those texts. But complex works of fiction, even today, remain virtually inaccessible to a larger audience unskilled in the art of textual

The Time Falling Bodies Take to Light (New York: St. Martin's, 1981), pp. 17, 250–51.

1

interpretation. Now nonfiction sets the issues before all of us, makes those issues more accessible. Nonfiction even contains the new narratives, new stories, new possibilities for what Thompson called "the creative destructuring of the old civilization."

Women writers are setting before us the stories we have told ourselves in order to live, and they are finding the stories wanting. In their many voices, in their multiplicity and in their unity, these writers are urging us to reconsider those stories. They ask us whether we have become stuck in the patterns of yesteryear and forgotten the meaning behind the patterns. Fighting the beast, slaying it, winning wars, protecting the home, charting uncharted rivers, coloring the spaces on the map, bearing children, minding the home may once have been gender-related chores born of physical as well as psychological necessity. But what does the logic of the psyche ask of us when such patterns are no longer required by physical necessity? Do we have to persist in the old patterns? Must we submit? What about new relationships? Must we now go our separate ways, or might we seek to understand better the psychological necessity that lay beneath those old patterns and in so doing redirect our energies, retune our imaginations, enter into new and different relationships with one another, exploring otherness even as we consider new acts of union? The cards are still on the table. The game—the game that is no mere game—is still being played. Rules are being rewritten. Lives are in flux. Imaginations are active. The talking and the writing go on.

Women's Voices tries to capture the state of flux, tries to put before you the experience itself, the evolving struggle of women for self-definition and survival. It is a collection that freezes frames of experience without attempting to stop the moving picture show. Our aim is to present the dialogue between women and the world, to present many voices in concert, conflict, and community. What women writers are saying, at this moment, is reshaping the world, and we can all benefit from hearing them.

Jan Gordon, in an important essay about voice in E. M. Forster's fiction, tells us that when Forster's English characters fall victim to a single voice, they lose their ability to become "part of any dialogue because the sharing of voice is absent"; they become bound, victimized by a culture "that is defined only representationally, as the repository of letters, pictures, books." These characters rely on the received opinion; they stop thinking, and when they do, dialogue stops. The way out—the way back to life—comes not from reproducing voice "as a function of memory" but from developing one's own voice, from active listening. Forster's liberated characters, Gordon argues, ultimately become aware of the self as a "composite of voices." Hearing many voices, they must make choices, creating "a sense of self every day," freeing themselves from "the labels imposed by class." Choosing, Gordon seems to suggest, is a dialogic act of self-definition—one's inner voices mediating the collective voice of culture.

The strong voices in this anthology emerged out of cultures that have traditionally asked women to play secondary and subordinate roles. At worst, these cultures have silenced them. But we forget too often that women have gained strength from these various roles. They have always been workers and wives and mothers. Led astray, perhaps, by post-Renaissance notions of woman as a quiet, submissive, demure "angel in the house," we occasionally forget the truth. The pieces in this anthology remind us of women's strength and power.

All of the women in this anthology are critics; all understand the way criticism can change the direction of our lives. Some are angry; some conciliatory; some intimate; some ironic; some deliberately funny. But not one is indifferent; not one is content to let us see the world only on our own terms. We have chosen women of diverse national and ethnic backgrounds—

American, Canadian, British, French, South African, Black, West Indian, Asian-American, Jewish, and Native American. This diversity speaks against various patriarchal traditions that have attempted to limit women's development and muffle their voices. And so the academic critics, the culture critics, the naturalists, the sociologists, the psychologists—old and young, lesbian and heterosexual—the workers, mothers, and wives whose voices ring out from this anthology ask us to listen and to choose, to see, to think, and to reconsider. They call us into relation with one another, seeking not divisiveness but diversity, not uniformity but multiplicity. They call us together even when they celebrate differences; they make us see especially the urgent need to continue the work of revising.

The two sections of *Women's Voices* complement each other. The first section emphasizes writing, provides a sense of how writing renews the world, and invites us to think about gender, even when gender is not explicitly the issue. The multiple selections by these fifteen writers offer an opportunity to watch women exploring their own minds without the restraining influence of the old civilization. We have included three or four essays by each of these writers to provide a clear sense of how each writer's imagination orders and shapes experience. The essays themselves, as different as they are from one another, have this in common: Each is a powerful piece of writing, rich, many-layered, multidimensional. Each, moreover, can be experienced emotionally and reexperienced intellectually; each yields dividends on successive readings. Written in different voices, on different occasions, these essays speak nonetheless to one another. Indeed, part of the pleasure of reading them is the pleasure of discovering this dialogue.

One way of approaching these writers is to pair them. Angela Carter and Joan Didion take a whack at our culture. Both write about home and motherhood, women as artists, and social absurdities.

Annie Dillard and Gretel Ehrlich make an interesting pair of naturalists. Dillard's intense metaphysical speculations contrast nicely with Ehrlich's natural language and her submission to the landscape. June Jordan and Maxine Hong Kingston offer minority perspectives in voices that reflect their histories—Jordan's speechmaking tone against Kingston's personal reminiscences. Other pairs also present themselves for comparison: Audre Lorde and Nancy Mairs; Joyce Carol Oates and Cynthia Ozick; Virginia Woolf and Alice Walker. You will certainly discover other relationships as you read the anthology. You might, for example, want to consider the diversity among three Black writers: June Jordan, Alice Walker, and Audre Lorde—women who are friends, who have worked together over time to support each other and to change the world, but who retain personal visions and distinctive styles.

We selected the writers represented in Part I for the distinctive quality of their writing, the power of their voices, and the clarity of their visions. Their depth and diversity dazzle us. Moreover, because their writing encourages dialogue, we have provided a headnote for each writer which focuses on important characteristics of the selected essays. We have provided as well a series of questions that encourage you to think of these writers in relation to one another; these questions, placed at the end of each group of essays, explore relationships among essays and among writers; they also suggest ways in which you can bring Part I and Part II of the anthology together.

We have already suggested that the essays in Part I give all of us a sense of how writing renews the world, how such writing forces us to think about gender even when gender is not explicitly the issue. One way to get a clearer sense of what that promise means is to read the essays by Hélène Cixous and Luce Irigaray in Part II before you turn to an essay in Part I such as Gretel Ehrlich's "Spring." Irigaray's

"When Our Lips Speak Together" is, among many other things, a call to the blood, an appeal to women to awaken to the life of their bodies, to get back in touch with women. It is an appeal to undress, to take off the "images and appearances [that] separate us, one from another," to throw off the inhibiting shackles. Irigaray offers this promise: "One day we will learn to say ourselves. And what we say will be far more beautiful than our tears, totally fluent." Cixous's appeal in "The Laugh of the Medusa" is even more direct: "Write yourself. Your body must be heard. Only then will the immense resources of the unconscious spring forth. Our naphtha will spread, throughout the world, without dollars—black or gold—nonassessed values that will change the rules of the old game." If you think about these possibilities, put them to the side in memory, and consider these excerpts from Ehrlich's "Spring," something is bound to happen in your imaginations:

> Near town the river ice breaks up and lies stacked in industrial-sized hunks—big as railway cars—on the banks, and is flecked black by wheeling hurricanes of newly plowed topsoil. That's how I feel when winter breaks up inside me: heavy, onerous, up-ended, inert against the flow of water.

> Spring means restlessness.

> The sap rises in trees and in me and the hard knot of perseverance I cultivated to meet winter dissipates; I walk away from the obsidian of bitter nights.

> Last spring at this time I was coming out of a bout with pneumonia. I went to bed on January first and didn't get up until the end of February. . . . All engagements of mind—the circumlocutions of love-interest and internal gossip—appeared false. Only my body was true. And my body was trying to close down, go out the window without me.

> As I lay in bed, the black room was a screen through which some part of my body traveled, leaving the rest behind. I thought I was a sun flying over a barge whose iron holds soaked me up until I became rust, floating on a bright river.

> Spring jitterbugs inside me.

> At 5:03 the vernal equinox occurs. I go outside and stand in the middle of a hayfield with my eyes closed. The universe is restless but I want to feel celestial equipoise: twelve hours of daylight, twelve of dark, and the earth ramrod straight on its axis. In celebration I straighten my posture in an effort to resist the magnetic tilt back into dormancy, spiritual and emotional reticence. Far to the south I imagine the equatorial sash, now nose to nose with the sun, sizzling like a piece of bacon, then the earth slowly tilting again.

There is more, much more of this metaphorical seismography in the essay. And yet the point here is not to suggest that Ehrlich is under the influence of Irigaray or Cixous; she undoubtedly is not. Rather Ehrlich, in an independent act of creativity, renews the world for us, gives us a sense of what one woman's sensuous experience is like, turns the stir of blood into meaning, provides not just a new way of seeing but also a new way of feeling. She makes us want to step outside and feel the earth's forces acting on our bodies.

These controversial and provocative questions about bodies and feelings lead to other related questions. Is Ehrlich writing woman, or is she just writing very well? Are gender differences congenital or are they conditional? Are there in fact gender differences? Is the best writing genderless, as Joyce Carol Oates suggests, tentatively, in her essay "Literature as Pleasure, Pleasure as Literature"? Reflecting on her early reading in a bulky anthology of poetry, Oates makes this observation:

> If I noted the absence of women I have no memory of it and rather doubt that I did, since poetry even more than prose seemed to me then, and seemed to me for many years, a wholly neutral, or do I mean neuter, genderless activity. (I might have

thought—perhaps I still think—*That's the beauty of the enterprise!*) And it would have struck me as rude, vulgar, insipid, trivializing, a profanation of the very page, to read the poetry that excited me most as if it were the product, even, of a human being like myself; as if it were the product of what would one day be called a "female consciousness." For didn't it mean that, being a poet, having been granted the imprimatur of poet, Emily Dickinson had in fact transcended not only the "female" but the "human" categories?

Like Oates, Cynthia Ozick is troubled by the notion of a gendered imagination, and Virginia Woolf, who heralded a distinctive female literary tradition, wonders too whether the ideal literary imagination isn't incandescent or androgynous.

You will not have to read far in these pages to start asking yourself important questions about identity, gender, culture, writing. Reading, Oates reminds us, "is the sole means by which we slip, involuntarily, often helplessly, into another's skin; another's voice; another's soul. One might argue that serious reading is as sacramental an act as serious writing, and should therefore not be profaned. That, by way of a book, we have the ability to transcend what is immediate, what is merely personal, and to enter a consciousness not known to us, in some cases distinctly alien, *other.* . . ."

The voices of women writers, Oates's among them, should encourage us to reexamine the old stories and inspire us to imagine new ones so that we can find our way out of the old civilization into the new.

ANGELA CARTER
(b. 1940)

Angela Carter was born on the South Coast of England, in Eastbourne, but it was "not a place I'd have chosen," she said. She went there an "embryonic self" in the company of women; she went there to be born, safe from the ravages of war. But it is to South Yorkshire that she returns for her earliest memories, to her maternal grandmother's house. There during the first five years of her life her gran reared her "as a tough, arrogant and pragmatic Yorkshire child." She tells us that her "mother was powerless to prevent it." In "The Mother Lode" we glimpse the development of her own sensibility, see her in relation to family, begin to understand through the essay's subtle revelations why her tart tongue entices us, why it is repellingly fascinating. From that essay we get a sense of how it is that Carter has come to be one of the most productive and re-

spected English writers of her generation.

Two of her eight novels and one of her three collections of stories have won major awards: *The Magic Toyshop* (1967), the John Llewellyn Rhys Prize; *Several Perceptions* (1968), the Somerset Maugham Award; and *The Bloody Chamber* (1979), the Cheltenham Festival of Literature Award. She has published two works of nonfiction, *The Sadeian Woman: An Exercise in Cultural History* (1979) and *Nothing Sacred* (1982); translated the fairy stories of Charles Perrault; and written a film script of her story "The Company of Wolves" (with Neil Jordan). Carter lived two years in Japan, was Fellow in Creative Writing at Sheffield University from 1976 to 1978, and was Visiting Professor in the Writing Program at Brown University, 1980–1981. Her journalism has appeared in almost every major British publication and her work has been translated into all the major European languages.

In our first and third selections—"The Wound in the Face" and "People as Pictures"—Carter attacks the vanities, slices through the flesh of society, laying open the wound; language for her is a playground. Through piercing, biting understatement, she makes complex judgments about the commonplace in culture. "Wound" focuses on images, on women's faces as they have appeared (to Carter) for over two decades in fashion magazines. She describes and interprets those faces, sees them to some extent as manufacturers' cultural icons. "The sixties face had a bee-stung underlip, enormous eyes and a lot of disordered hair. It saw itself as a wild, sweet, gipsyish, vulnerable face. . . . The sixties look gloried in its open pores. . . ." Momentarily, it seemed, women had learned a valuable lesson from their rejection of pancake makeup; they had learned that the ungreased face does not erode. "A face is not a bicycle." Carter's judgments are layered: Judgment forms beneath judgment. As she uncovers the face, she uncovers darker psychic secrets: Even "naturalism [is] an ingenious form of artifice, it *was* a mask." The black lipstick and red eyeshadow that came after the natural look broke "ground for a whole new aesthetic of appearance," the possibility that women might get free from the "burden of having to look beautiful altogether." But it didn't work out, this "equivalent of Duchamp's moustache on the Mona Lisa." Carter loved it, but "most women could not resist keeping open a treacherous little corner on sex appeal." And so the mouth came "back as a bloody gash, a visible wound." What troubles Carter is just this: "We are so used to the bright red mouth we no longer see it as the wound it mimics, except in the treacherous lucidity of paranoia."

Beneath the underwear that women wear, or through the holes in it, Carter discovers other cultural secrets. In "Bridled Sweeties," a piece not included in this anthology, Carter exposes the "cultural taboo against nakedness," uncovers the complex standards inherent in that taboo. Again, one of her targets is capitalism: lingerie catalogues from Janet Reger and Frederick's of Hollywood show models "dressed up in undress, in a kind of clothing that is more naked than nudity." Carter sees these models as *"objets de luxe,"* and she is only too aware that in "hyper-culture" such nongarments—expensive underwear, some furs, evening dresses, gowns, real jewelry—are all "items of pure conspicious consumption" which "fulfill elaborate ritual functions." Carter's self-appointed business is to expose us to our own rituals, to make us see ourselves. It's okay to be nearly naked, dressed up but undressed in expensive "raunchy" lingerie. It's not okay to be nude. Partial dressing "fulfill[s], while it subvert[s], the conditions of the taboo against absolute nakedness."

"People as Pictures" examines the ancient art of *irezumi,* an elaborate, painful form of tattooing that covers the entire body. Behind this practice Carter senses something "verging on repugnance" in Japanese culture, something that doesn't like the sight of the human body unclothed, naked. Such tattooing dresses the body in an "intimate and gaily coloured" garment, but it also covers a "strong masochistic element" in a repressive culture. Carter believes that *irezumi* is "certainly one of the most exquisitely refined and skilful forms of sado-masochism the mind of man ever divined. It survives strangely but tenaciously in modern Japan."

Carter seems to rejoice in uncovering the truth, opening up for our inspection what might otherwise remain concealed beneath the fabric of our hectic daily lives. Occasionally, while uncovering others, she reveals herself. Colette is a woman she admires very much: "I must say, now, that this ineradicable quality of the fraud, the fake, of the unrepentant self-publicist, is one of the things about Colette I respect most; indeed, revere." She sees Colette's baring of her personal life, her appeal to the reader to become intimate, as "a familiar show-biz trick, the relationship of artificial intimacy the showgirl creates between her named self and the anonymous punter, with its intention to disarm." She likes Colette's courage, her ability to have the picaresque experience that is generally reserved for men, to have it "without putting herself in a state of hazard." "Magnificently she did not know her place." Carter gives us a sense of how a woman can celebrate femininity, "not only its physical glamour but its capacity to subvert and withstand the boredom of patriarchy." She is pleased with the way Colette "forged a career out of the kind of self-obsession which is supposed, in a woman, to lead only to tears before bedtime, in a man to lead to the peaks."

Carter's iconoclasm seems to have shaped itself from the curious elements of her family background, elements that she highlights in "The Mother Lode." Observing all her life the conflict between her mother and her maternal grandmother—a mother who "liked things to be nice" and a gran who "talked broad Yorkshire until the day she died" and otherwise complained about her "daughter's apparent weaknesses"—Carter learned to discriminate and to embrace differences. She loved both women, just as she loved her father, drawing from them sustenance and insight. She especially admires her father's end-of-life toughness, his ability to "cope with the ruins of Troy very well under his own steam." With him she shares a journalist's personal detachment. He taught her something about strength and independence which she did not get from the women. Yet in her biting iconoclastic wit there lurks a sentimentality that seems always to express itself as a contemptible kind of loving, a genuine concern for what she criticizes. Nowhere is her power as a writer more evident than in her closing tribute to her mother in "Mother Lode"; it is a tribute that reveals Carter's own complex sensibility.

The Wound in the Face

I spent a hallucinatory weekend, staring at faces I'd cut out of women's magazines, either from the beauty page or from the ads—all this season's faces. I stuck twenty or thirty faces on the wall and tried to work out from the evidence before me (a) what women's faces are supposed to be looking like, now; and (b) why. It was something of an exercise in pure form, because the magazine models' faces aren't exactly the face in the street—not low-style, do-it-yourself assemblages, but more a platonic, ideal face. Further, they reflect, as well as the mood of the moment, what the manufacturers are trying to push this year. Nevertheless, the *zeitgeist* works through the manufacturers, too. They do not understand their own imagery, any more than the consumer who demonstrates it does. I am still working on the nature of the imagery of cosmetics. I think it scares me.

Construing the imagery was an unnerving experience because all the models appeared to be staring straight at me with such a heavy, static quality of *being there* that it was difficult to escape the feeling they were accusing me of something. (How rarely women look one another in the eye.) Only two of the faces wear anything like smiles, and only one is showing a hint of her teeth. This season's is not an extravert face. Because there is not much to smile about this season? Surely. It is a bland, hard, bright face; it is also curiously familiar, though I have never seen it before.

The face of the seventies matches the fashions in clothes that have dictated some of its features, and is directly related to the social environment which produces it. Like fashions in clothes, fashions in faces have been stuck in pastiche for the past four or five years. This bankruptcy is disguised by ever more ingenious pastiche—of the thirties, the forties, the fifties, the Middle East, Xanadu, Wessex (those smocks). Compared with the short skirts and flat shoes of ten years ago, style in women's clothes has regressed. Designers are trying to make us cripple our feet again with high-heeled shoes and make us trail long skirts in dogshit. The re-introduction of rouge is part of this regression; rouge, coyly re-introduced under the nineteenth-century euphemism of 'blusher'.

The rather older face—the *Vogue* face, as opposed to the *Honey* face—is strongly under the 1930s influence, the iconographic, androgynous face of Dietrich and Garbo, with heavily emphasised bone structures, hollow cheeks and hooded eyelids. Warhol's transvestite superstars, too, and his magazine, *Interview*—with its passion for the tacky, the kitschy, for fake glamour, for rhinestones, sequins, Joan Crawford, Ann-Margaret—have exercised a profound influence. As a result, fashionable women now tend to look like women imitating men imitating women, an interesting reversal. The face currently perpetuated by the glossies aspires to the condition of that of Warhol's Candy Darling.

The main message is that the hard, bland face with which women brazened their way through the tough 1930s, the tough 1940s and the decreasingly tough 1950s (at the end of the 1950s, when things got less tough, they abandoned it) is back to sustain us through the tough 1970s. It recapitulates the glazed, self-contained look typical of times of austerity.

But what is one to make of the transvestite influence? Is it that the physical image of women took such a battering in the sixties that when femininity did, for want of anything better, return, the only people we could go to to find out what it had looked like were the dedicated male impersonators who had kept the concept alive in the sequined gowns, their spike-heeled shoes and their peony lipsticks? Probably. 'The feminine character, and the idea of femininity on which it is modelled, are products of masculine society,' says Theodore Adorno. Clearly a female impersonator knows more about his idea of the character he is mimicking than I do, because it is his very own invention, and has nothing to do with me.

Yet what about the Rousseauesque naturalism of the dominant image of women in the mid-1960s? Adorno can account for that, sociologically, too. 'The image of undistorted nature arises only in distortion, as its opposite.' The sixties face was described early in the decade by *Queen* (as it was then) as a 'look of luminous vacancy'.

The sixties face had a bee-stung underlip, enormous eyes and a lot of disordered hair. It saw itself as a wild, sweet, gipsyish, vulnerable face. Its very lack of artifice suggested sexual licence in a period that had learned to equate cosmetics, not with profligacy as in the nineteenth century, but with conformity to the standard social and sexual female norm. Nice girls wore lipstick, in the fifties.

When the sixties face used cosmetics at all, it explored imports such as kohl and henna from Indian shops. These had the twin advantages of being extremely exotic and very, very cheap. For purposes of pure decoration, for fun, it sometimes stuck sequins to itself, or those little gold and silver 'good conduct' stars. It bought sticks of stage make-up, and did extraordinary things around its eyes with them, at about the time of Flower Power. It was, basically, a low-style or do-it-yourself face. Ever in search of the new, the magazines eventually caught up with it, and high-style faces caught on to flowered cheeks and stars on the eyelids at about the time the manufacturers did. So women had to pay considerably more for their pleasures.

The sixties look gloried in its open pores and, if your eye wasn't into the particular look, you probably thought it didn't wash itself much. But it was just that, after all those years of pancake makeup, people had forgotten what the real colour of female skin was. This face cost very little in upkeep. Indeed, it was basically a most economical and serviceable model and it was quite a shock to realise, as the years passed, that all the beauty experts were wrong and, unless exposed to the most violent weather, it did not erode if it was left ungreased. A face is not a bicycle. Nevertheless, since this face had adopted naturalism as an ingenious form of artifice, it *was* a mask, like the grease masks of cosmetics, though frequently refreshingly eccentric.

At the end of that decade, in a brief period of delirium, there was a startling vogue of black lipstick and red eyeshadow. For a little while we were painting ourselves up just as arbitrarily as Larionov did before the Revolution. Dada in the boudoir! What a witty parody of the whole theory of cosmetics!

The basic theory of cosmetics is that they make a woman beautiful. Or, as the advertisers say, more beautiful. You blot out your noxious wens and warts and blemishes, shade your nose to make it bigger or smaller, draw attention to your good features by bright colours, and distract it from your bad features by more reticent tones. But those manic and desperate styles—leapt on and exploited instantly by desperate manufacturers—seemed to be about to break the ground for a whole new aesthetic of appearance, which would have nothing to do with the conformist ideology of 'beauty' at all. Might—ah, might—it be possible to use cosmetics to free women from the burden of having to look beautiful altogether?

Because black lipstick and red eyeshadow never 'beautified' anybody. They were the cosmetic equivalent of Duchamp's moustache on the Mona Lisa. They were cosmetics used as satire on cosmetics, on the arbitrary convention that puts blue on eyelids and pink on lips. Why not the other way round? The best part of the joke was that the look itself was utterly monstrous. It instantly converted the most beautiful women into outrageous grotesques; every face a work of anti-art. I enjoyed it very, very much.

However, it takes a helluva lot of guts to maintain oneself in a perpetual state of visual offensiveness. Most women could not resist keeping open a treacherous little corner on sex appeal. Besides, the joke went a little too near the bone. To do up your eyes so that they look like self-inflicted wounds is to wear on your face the evidence of the violence your environment inflicts on you.

Black paint around the eyes is such a familiar convention it seems natural; so does red paint on the mouth. We are so used to the bright red mouth we no longer see it as the wound it mimics, except in the treacherous lucidity of paranoia. But the shock of the red-painted eye recalls, directly, the blinding of Gloucester in *Lear*; or, worse and more aptly, the symbolic blinding of Oedipus. Women are allowed— indeed, encouraged—to exhibit the sign of their symbolic castration, but only in the socially sanctioned place. To transpose it upwards is to allow its significance to become apparent. We went too far, that time. Scrub it all off and start again.

And once we started again, red lipstick came back. Elizabeth I seems to have got a fine, bright carmine with which to touch up her far from generous lips. The Victorian beauty's 'rosebud mouth'—the mouth so tiny it was a wonder how it managed to contain her teeth—was a restrained pink. Flappers' lips spread out and went red again, and the 'generous mouth' became one of the great glamour conventions of the entire twentieth century and has remained so, even if its colour is modified.

White-based lipsticks, colourless glosses, or no lipstick at all, were used in the 1960s. Now the mouth is back as a bloody gash, a visible wound. This mouth bleeds over everything, cups, ice-cream, table napkins, towels. Mary Quant has a shade called (of course) 'Bloody Mary', to ram the point home. We will leave our bloody spoor behind us, to show we have been there.

In the thirties, that spoor was the trademark of the sophisticate, the type of Baudelairean female dandy Dietrich impersonated so well. Dietrich always transcended self-pity and self-destruction, wore the wound like a badge of triumph, and came out on top. But Iris Storm in Michael Arlen's *The Green Hat*, the heroines of Maurice Dekobra, the wicked film star in Chandler's *The Little Sister* who always dressed in black to offset her fire-engine of a mouth—they all dripped blood over everything as they stalked sophisticatedly to their dooms. In their wake, lipstick traces on a cigarette stub; the perfect imprint, like half a heart, of a scarlet lower lip on a drained Martini glass; the tell-tale scarlet letter. *A* for adultery, on a shirt collar . . . the kitsch poetry of it all!

Elizabeth Taylor scrawls 'Not for sale' on her bedroom mirror in her red, red lipstick in *Butterfield 8*. The generosity the mouth has given so freely will be spurned with brutal ingratitude. The open wound will never heal. Perhaps, sometimes, she will lament the loss of the tight rosebud; but it has gone forever.

The revival of red lipstick indicates, above all, I suppose, that women's sense of security was transient.

The Mother Lode

The first house in which I remember living gives a false impression of our circumstances. This house was part of the archaeology of my mother's mother's life and gran dug it up again and dived back within it when the times became precarious, that is, in 1940, and she took me with her, for safety's sake, with this result: that I always feel secure in South Yorkshire.

This first house of my memory was a living fossil, a two-up, two-down, red-brick, slate-tiled, terraced miners' cottage architecturally antique by the nineteenth-century standards of the rest of the village. There was a lavatory at the end of the garden beyond a scraggy clump of Michaelmas daisies that never looked well in themselves, always sere, never blooming, the perennial ghosts of themselves, as if ill-nourished by an exhausted soil. This garden was not attached to the cottage; the back door opened on to a paved yard, with a coal-hole beside the back gate that my grandmother topped up with a bit of judicious thieving, for, unlike the other coal-holes along the terrace, ours was not entitled to the free hand-out from the pits for miners' families. Nor did we need one. We were perfectly well-off. But gran couldn't resist knocking off a lump or two. She called this activity 'snawking', either a dialect or a self-invented word, I don't know which.

There was an access lane between the gate of the yard and the gate of the garden, so it was a very long trip out to the lavatory, especially in winter. We used chamber-pots a good deal—'jerries'—cause of much hilarity due to the hostilities. My mother had a pastel-coloured, Victorian indelicacy which she loved to repeat: 'When did the queen reign over China?' This whimsical and harmless scatalogical pun was my first introduction to the wonderful world of verbal transformations, and also a first perception that a joke need not be funny to give pleasure.

Beyond the brick-built lavatory, to which we used to light our way after dark with a candle lantern, was a red-brick, time-stained, soot-dulled wall that bounded an unkempt field; this field was divided by a lugubrious canal, in which old mattresses and pieces of bicycle used to float. The canal was fringed with willows, cruelly lopped, and their branches were always hung with rags tied in knots. I don't know why. It was a witchy, unpremeditated sight. Among the tips where we kids used to play were strange pools of oleaginous, clay-streaked water. A neighbor's child drowned in one of them.

The elements of desolation in the landscape give no clue to the Mediterranean extraversion and loquacity of the inhabitants. Similarly, all this grass-roots, working-class stuff, the miners' cottage and the bog at the end of the garden and all, is true, but not strictly accurate. The processes of social mobility had got under way long before I had ever been thought of, although my mother always assured me I had never been thought of as such, had simply arrived and, as I will make plain, somewhat inconveniently, too.

We took this trip back, not to my mother's but to *her* mother's roots because of the War. My grandmother had not lived in her native village herself since she was a girl and now she was an old woman, squat, fierce and black-clad like the granny in the Giles cartoons in the *Sunday Express*; because she, an old woman, took me back to her childhood, I think I became the child she had been, in a sense, for the first five years of my life. She reared me as a tough, arrogant and pragmatic Yorkshire child and my mother was powerless to prevent it.

My mother learned she was carrying me at about the time the Second World War was declared; with the family talent for magic realism, she once told me she had been to the doctor's on the very day. It must have been a distressing and agitated pregnancy. Shortly after she began to assemble all the birthing bric-à-brac, the entire child population of our part of South London was removed to the South Coast, away from the bombs, or so it was thought. My brother, then eleven, was sent away with them but my mother followed him because my father quickly rented a flat in a prosperous, shingle-beached resort. Which is why I was born in Eastbourne, not a place I'd have chosen, although my mother said that if Debussy had composed *La Mer* whilst sitting on Beachy Head, I should not turn my nose up at the place.

So off they all went, my mother and my embryonic self, my brother and my maternal grandmother went with them, to look after them all, while my father, in a reserved occupation, and who, besides, had served the whole term of the First World War, stayed behind in London to work but he came down whenever he could manage it and that was very often because he and my mother were very attached to each other.

My mother went into labour in Eastbourne but when she came out of it we were

on the front line because Dunkirk fell while I was shouldering my way into the world;
my grandmother said there was *one* place in the world the Germans would not dare
to bomb so we all shifted ourselves to a cottage that my father now rented for us
next door to the one in which my great-aunt, Sophia, my grandmother's sister, and
her brother, my great-uncle, Sydney, lived. And though the Germans bombed hell
out of the South Coast and also bombed the heart out of Sheffield, twenty-odd miles
away from where we had removed, not one bomb fell on us, just as she had predicted.

Uncle Syd worked down Manvers Main Colliery. He was a tall, gaunt man of a
beautiful, shy dignity, who had, I understand, originally wanted to be a bookie but
whose mother had not let him. I remember him all pigeon-coloured, soft greys
touched with beige, the colour of the clothes he was wearing when I last saw him,
when he came down south for my gran's funeral. And a pearl tie-pin. And a gold
watch-chain, across his camel-coloured waistcoat.

Sophie was a teacher. She had no formal qualifications at all, I think, had simply
never left school but stayed on to teach the babies the three R's and did so until
she retired in the 1950s, qualified eventually by experience, natural aptitude and,
probably, strength of character. Besides, by then she had taught several generations
of the village to read and write, probably taught most of the education committee
to read and write. She, too, had a great deal of formal dignity; I remember how,
unlike my grandmother, who had lived in London most of her life, Syd and Sophie
both had very soft voices, country voices. Though we could hear Syd's cough through
the wall, the dreadful, choking cough that all the men over forty in the village had.

The South Yorkshire coalfields are not half as ugly as they may seem at first glance.
Rather like the potteries, they are somehow time-locked, still almost a half-rural
society as it must have been in the early days of the Industrial Revolution. The
wounded and despoiled countryside remains lush and green around the workings;
sheep graze right up to the pit-heads, although the sheep I saw when I was a child
were all black with soot, and Doncaster Market is far richer in local agricultural
produce than the pretend-markets in Devon. There is a quite un-English preoccupation with food; the pig is dealt with in a bewildering and delicious variety of
ways but butter and cheese are good, too, and so is bread, the perfume of next
morning's loaves nightly flavouring the air around the corner bakery.

The streets of the red-brick villages are laid out in grid-like parallels, cheapest of
housing for working families, yet they manage to fold into the landscape with a
certain gritty reticence although it is one of gentle hills; there is none of the scenic
drama of West Yorkshire, instead, a bizarre sense of mucky pastoral. The colliers
were often famous poachers in their spare time. My granny taught me songs that
celebrated the wily fox, the poacher's comrade, and his depredations of bourgeois
farmyards:

> Old Mother Flipperty-flop jumped out of bed,
> Out of the window she stuck 'er 'ead—
> 'John, John, the grey goose is gone
> And the fox is off to his den, oh!'

It is almost the landscape of D. H. Lawrence, almost that of the Chatterleys, Mellors
was as tough on the poachers as only a true class-traitor could be. Lawrence ratted
on it all, of course, Lawrence, the great, guilty chronicler of English social mobility,

the classic, seedy Brit full of queasy, self-justificatory class shame and that is why they identify with him so much in British universities, I tell you. I know the *truth*. Him and his la-did-dah mother.

But I read *The Rainbow* a little while ago, searching for some of the flavour of the lives of my grandmother and her family eighty years ago, ninety years ago, in a village not unlike Eastwood, only a little more gritty, and there was Sophie, teaching school like Ursula Brangwen but making a much better job of it, I'm happy to say, perhaps since nobody sent her to Sheffield High School and taught her to give herself airs. At that, I hear my grandmother speaking in my head.

But Sophie *did* trek all the way to Leeds to go to art classes. Ruskin was a strong influence in these parts. To my knowledge, Sophie never drew or painted for pleasure when she was grown-up but she taught me the rudiments of perspective, and most of the alphabet, before I was five. Her father, my great-grandfather, had he owned a pub? At this point, they vanish into mist; there is a brewery in Sheffield with their family name, but it is a common enough name in South Yorkshire. Some connection was supposed to have been the cock-fighting king of the entire country but all this is irretrievable, now. I do not even know if they had seen better days, but I doubt it.

All the same, there was a beautiful parlour-organ in Sophie's pocket-handkerchief-sized front room and a grandfather clock so old it is now in the museum in Barnsley and a glass-fronted cabinet full of ancient blue-and-white china that must have been very fine because my mother always lusted after it but never managed to get her hands on it, in the end, because Sophie outlived her, to Sophie's grief. At night, the kitchen was lit by the dim, greenish, moth-like light of gas mantles; we took candles up the steep wooden stairs to bed. There was a coal range, that Sophie blacked; no hot water; a tin bath filled with kettles in which Syd washed off his pit dirt. There were no pit-head baths at Manvers Main until 1947, when the mines were national-ised.

Smelling of sweat and the sharp, mineral odour of coal dust, the miners came off the shift blacked up as for a minstrel show, their eyeballs and teeth gleaming, in their ragged jackets, braces, overalls, and I remember gangs of them exhaustedly swagger-ing home, so huge, so genial and so proudly filthy they seemed almost superhuman. I'm a sucker for the worker hero, you bet. I think most of them thought that nationalisation would mean workers' control and were justifiably pissed off when they found out it didn't, sold down the river by the Labour Party again, the old story.

Death was part of daily life, also; scarcely a family had not its fatality, its muti-lated, its grey-faced old man coughing his lungs out in the chair by the range. And everybody was, of course, very poor. It wasn't until the 1960s that miners were earning anything like a reasonable living wage and by then Sophie had electricity, and a bathroom, and a gas-stove, benefits she accepted from the Coal Board without gratitude, for they were no more than her due.

Of course I romanticise it. Why the hell not. I cry with pure anger when I pass the pits beside the railway-line from Sheffield to Leeds; the workings, grand and heartless monuments to the anonymous dead.

We are not a close-knit but nevertheless an obsessive family, sustained, as must be obvious, by a subjectively rich if objectively commonplace folk-lore. And claustro-phobic as a Jewish family, to which we have many similarities, even if we do not see one another often. I cannot escape them, nor do I wish to do so. They are the inhabitants of my heart, and the rhetoric and sentimentality of such a phrase is also built into me by the rich Highland sentimentality of my father's people that always made my mother embarrassed.

Since they were a matriarchal clan, my mother's side of the family bulked first and largest, if not finally most significantly.

My maternal grandmother seemed to my infant self a woman of such physical and spiritual heaviness she might have been born with a greater degree of gravity than most people. She came from a community where women rule the roost and she effortlessly imparted a sense of my sex's ascendancy in the scheme of things, every word and gesture of hers displayed a natural dominance, a native savagery, and I am very grateful for all that, now, although the core of steel was a bit inconvenient when I was looking for boyfriends in the South in the late fifties, when girls were supposed to be as soft and as pink as a nursuree.

Gran was ninety when she died ten years ago and wandering in her mind, so she'd talk about the miners' strikes of her girlhood, how they'd march in their pit dirt and rags with banners and music, they would play harmonicas, and she leaned out of the attics of the house where she worked as a chambermaid to watch. She would have made a bloody awful chambermaid, unnaturally servile until something inside her snapped.

My maternal grandfather, who died before I was born, originally hailed from East Anglia. There was no work on the farms so he joined the army and I think his regiment must have been sent to South Yorkshire to put down the strikes. Nobody ever told me this in so many words, but I can think of no other reason why he should have arrived there in time to meet my grandmother in the late 1880s or early nineties. He met her; they were engaged; and he was sent to India.

When we were clearing out my grandmother's effects, we found a little stack of certificates for exams my grandfather had passed in the army. In Baluchistan, in the Punjab, in Simla, he had become astoundingly literate and numerate. He must also have learned to argue like hell. Furthermore, he became radicalised, unless the seeds had already been sewn in the seething radicalism of the coalfields. He wrote to my grandmother once a week for seven years. Characteristically unsentimental, she threw away their letters, with their extraordinary fund of information about an NCO coming to consciousness through the contradictions inherent in the Raj, but she kept the stamps. What stamp albums my uncles had.

Of all the dead in my family, this unknown grandfather is the one I would most like to have talked to. He had the widest experience and perhaps the greatest capacity for interpreting it. There are things about him that give me great pleasure; for example, as a hobby, later in life, he enjoyed, though only in a modest, yet a not entirely unsuccessful way, playing the Stock Exchange, as if to prove to himself the childish simplicity with which the capitalist system operated. My grandmother thwarted this flair, she never trusted banks, she kept his money in mattresses, no really, in biscuit tins, on her person, in her big, black, leather bag.

When my mother's father came home, he married gran and joined the ILP and went to live in London, first Southwark, then Battersea, four children in a two-bedroom rabbit hutch. A yard, no garden. No bath. To the end of her life, my dotty aunt, who lived with gran, washed at the public slipper bath.

They were magnificently unbowed. There was a piano for the children, who played it; and did amateur dramatics; and went to see Shakespeare and Ibsen and

Sybil Thorndyke in *Saint Joan* at the Old Vic. He was a clerk in the War Department; he used his literacy to be shot of manual labour, first rung up the ladder of social mobility, then worked in one of the first of the clerical trades unions. (Which may have been down a snake.) He got out of the slums, feet first, in his coffin; gran stuck it out until the street was demolished in 1956. Before the First World War, he chaired a meeting at which Lenin spoke. He shook Lenin by the hand and he led my eldest uncle, then a small boy, up to shake Lenin's hand, also. This uncle, however, grew up to adopt a political stance somewhat, as the Americans say, to the right of Attila the Hun.

My maternal grandfather died of cirrhosis. A life-long teetotaller, the years in India had wrecked his liver. My grandmother's house was full of relics of the Empire, an ebony elephant, spears, a carved coconut shell representing the Hindu cosmogeny, beautiful shells from tropical seas, some with pierced messages: A Present From The Andaman Islands. Also enormous quantities of souvenir china, mugs, teapots and sugar basins commemorating every coronation from that of Edward VII to that of Elizabeth II; there was even a brace of scarlet enamelled tin trays from Victoria's Diamond Jubilee. Contradictions of English socialism. And enormous quantities of books, of course, some very strange: Foxe's *Books of Martyrs,* not one but three copies; Macchiavelli; *Twenty Thousand Leagues under the Sea.*

Their children were indefatigable self-educators, examination passers and prize-winners; those shelves were crammed with prizes for good conduct, for aptitude, for general excellence, for overall progress, though my gran fucked it all up for my mother. An intolerably bright girl, my mother won a scholarship to a ladies' grammar school, a big deal, in those days, from a Battersea elementary school. My gran attended prize-days to watch my mother score her loot with a huge Votes For Women badge pinned to her lapel and my mother, my poor mother, was ashamed because my gran was zapping the option her daughter had been given to be a lady just by standing up for her own rights not to be. (My mother used to sing The Internationale to me but only because she liked the tune.)

Perhaps my mother was ashamed of gran, as well, because gran talked broad Yorkshire until the day she died, all 'sithee' and 'thyssen' and ' 'e were runnin' like buggery'. When she gracelessly shoved a plate of food in front of you, she'd growl: 'Get it down thee,' with a dreadful menace. She taught me how to whistle. She hated tears and whining to no purpose; 'Don't be soft,' she'd say. Though she was often wrong, she was never silly. When I or anyone else was silly, she would wither me: 'Tha bloody fool,' making a broken dipthong out of the long 'o'. How to transcribe it: half-way between 'foo-ill' and 'foyle'.

When I was eighteen, I went to visit her rigged out in all the atrocious sartorial splendour of the underground high-style of the late fifties, black-mesh stockings, spike-heeled shoes, bum-hugging skirt, jacket with a black fox collar. She laughed so much she wet herself. 'You wait a few years and you'll be old and ugly, just like me,' she cackled. She herself dressed in dark dresses of heavy rayon crêpe, with grey Lisle stockings bound under the knee with two loops of knotted elastic.

Her personality had an architectonic quality; I think of her when I see some of the great London railway termini, especially St. Pancras, with its soot and turrets, and she overshadowed her own daughters, whom she did not understand—my mother, who liked things to be nice; my dotty aunt. But my mother had not the strength to put even much physical distance between them, let alone keep the old monster at an emotional arm's length. Although gran only actually lived with us in Yorkshire, and went back to her own house, five miles away, when we all went back to London at ceasefire, I remember her as always and ineradicably *there* until I was ten or eleven, by which time she was growing physically debilitated. I would have said 'frail', but that is quite the wrong word.

But my grandmother's toughness was a limitation of its own. There was to be no struggle for my mother, who married herself young to an adoring husband who indulged her, who was subject to ill-health, who spoke standard south London English, who continued to wear fancy clothes long after she was both wife and mother. My grandmother could have known of no qualities in herself she could usefully transmit to this girl who must have seemed a stranger to her. So, instead, she nagged her daughter's apparent weaknesses.

With the insight of hindsight, I'd have liked to have been able to protect my mother from the domineering old harridan, with her rough tongue and primitive sense of justice, but I did not see it like that, then. I did not see there was a drama between mother and daughter.

At my wedding, my grandmother spread brown sugar on her smoked salmon and ate it with relish. She did not approve of the man whom I married because he wore a belt to keep his trousers up instead of braces. She wore her hair in a bun on the very top of her head and secured it with giant, tortoiseshell pins.

When I lived in Japan, I learned to admire their tolerant acceptance of the involuntary nature of family life. Love in the sense of passionate attachment has nothing to do with it; the Japanese even have a different verb to define the arbitrary affection that grows among these chance juxtapositions of intimate strangers. There is also the genetic and environmental snare, of course; they are they and you are you but, nevertheless, alike. I would have defended my mother with my grandmother's weapons.

I also admire the Russian use of patronymics, although matronymics would do just as well. Aeneas carried his aged father on his back from the ruins of Troy and so do we all, whether we like it or not, perhaps even if we have never known them. But my own father recently resigned the post to go and live with his own brother and father, moving smartly out of our family back into his own, reverting, in his seventh decade, to the youthful role of sib. At an age when most parents become their children's children, he redefined himself as the equal of his son and daughter. He can cope with the ruins of Troy very well under his own steam. He will carry *me* out of them, I dare say.

When my father attached a plastic paraqueet he'd bought at Woolworth's, his favourite shop, to a disused gas fitting on the ceiling of our kitchen in south London, my mother said to him in a voice of weary petulance: 'Age cannot wither nor accustom stale your infinite variety.' They had then been married for thirty-five years.

My father has lined the walls of his own new home with pictures of my mother when she was young and beautiful; and beautiful she certainly was, with a broad, Slavonic jaw and high cheekbones like Anna Karenina, she took a striking photograph and had the talent for histrionics her pictures imply. They used to row dreadfully and pelt one another with household utensils, whilst shrieking with rage. Then my mother would finally break down and cry, possibly tears of sheer frustration that he was bigger than she, and my father, in an ecstasy of remorse—we've always been very good at remorse and its manifestations in action, emotional blackmail and irrational guilt—my father would go out and buy her chocolates.

The gift wiped away all resentment, as it happened, because he often bought her chocolates when they had not rowed at all. He really loved to buy her things. She herself liked Harrods, especially the sale, and sometimes Harvey Nichols; he could never see the difference between these places and Woolworth's except the restaurants but, since they very much enjoyed eating lunch out, he was happy to go with her, happy to carry the packages.

A morning's shopping was a major trip and they could indulge their taste for this diversion freely because my father worked from three o'clock in the afternoon until midnight most days. My mother was sometimes sorry for herself, to spend all her evenings alone, but he would come back in the middle of the night with the next day's newspapers and make her tea and bring her biscuits and they would chatter away for hours in the early morning. If I was awake, I could hear them through the wall.

Their life together was one of daytime treats and midnight feasts when I was usually at school or in bed. They spent more time alone with one another than do those parents who use children as an excuse for not talking to one another, and at times of the day when they were both rested and refreshed. No wonder they got on one another's nerves, sometimes. Then the storms were amazing. One could never rely on tranquillity, or not for long. But the rows were never conducted in hushed whispers—not of that 'pas devant les enfants' rubbish and were never about anything important, like money. Or me. At least, not yet. They were about nothing at all, a blocked-up lavatory, a blunt carving knife, my father's enthusiastic but not terribly scrupulous washing up. ('He'd like to wash up before we sat down to dinner.' 'He thinks we're going to want mustard all week.') Their rowing was the noisy music of compatibility.

It was a household in which midnight was early and breakfast merged imperceptibly into lunch. I can remember no rules, no punishments and I was expected to answer back. Once you were inside the door, a curious kind of dream-time operated; life passed at a languorous pace, everything was gently untidy, and none of the clocks ever told the right time, although they ticked away busily. We relied on the radio for the right time.

I went to look at this second house in which I lived last Christmas, the time for sentimental journeys. It was a good deal nicer than I had remembered it; a largish, even imposing Edwardian terrace house with a bay at the front and a little garden at the back, abutting on the Victoria-Brighton line. I had remembered it as smaller, poky, even. The entire street looked brighter and fresher than in the past; there were a few chocolate-brown doors and the glimpse of a Japanese paper lantern in some front-rooms. Hardly any net curtains, now. The whole area is clearly on the up, again, but my father sold the house five years ago, sold it for peanuts, glad to be shot of it now she was gone, and went off.

My father and mother had settled down, as I've said, only a few miles away from her own family if 500 miles away from his, in Balham, then, in the mid-twenties, a solid, middle-class suburb, lace curtains, privet hedges and so on. They planted roses in the arid soil of the back garden and, unfairly enough, for my father only entered the garden to brutally prune them, they bloomed lavishly every June. They furnished the house with mahogany sideboard, leather settee, oak Welsh dresser—

handsome furniture; I wouldn't mind some of it, now, only my father abandoned most of it there. He has no affection for possessions, unless they have only sentimental value. He keeps my wedding dress. Perhaps in case I need it again. No, he'd want to buy me a new one. But my mother loved nice things and said, when I told her I was leaving my husband, to be sure to take with me some silver-plated teaspoons she had recently given me. I did not and have often regretted it.

Here, when we came back from Yorkshire at the end of the War to a street that had had the residue of respectability bombed out of it, we settled into a curious kind of deviant middle-class life, all little luxuries and no small comforts, no refrigerator, no washing-machine, no consumer durables at all, but cream with puddings and terribly expensive soap and everything went to the laundry. And we were too messy for genuine discomfort. But our household became increasingly anachronistic as the neighborhood turned into a twilight zone. A social-realist family life for those first seminal five years, that I remember so well because the experience was finite; but the next ten years have a far more elusive flavour, it was as though we were stranded, somehow. A self-contained family unit with a curious, self-crafted life-style, almost but not quite an arty one, a very unself-conscious one, that flourished on its own terms but was increasingly at variance with the changes going on around it. My mother's passion for respectability in itself became a source of deviance; she actively encouraged me to wear black woollen stockings at a time when they were a positive sign of depravity. She forbade me lipstick in the days when only female beatniks did not wear lipstick. It was all very strange.

Since my father returned to his granite village beside its granite sea, returned not only to his native land—Scotland—but to the very house in which he grew up, triumphantly accomplishing the dearest dream of every migrant worker, I understand better how it was we were always somehow askew. I felt like a foreigner because my mother had married a foreigner, although neither she nor he himself ever realised it. Being a Scot, he never fully comprehended the English class system, nor did he realise he might have been socially upwardly mobile within it; he only thought he had not done badly, which is a different perspective upon it. He had seen what Dr. Johnson, one of my mother's favourites, called the finest thing a Scotsman can see, the high road to England, and he took it; did well enough; married happily; ushered into the world two satisfactory children. And then he went home, a symmetric life. He was a journalist until he retired and, of course, journalists have a curious marginality of their own, a professional detachment. If he had pretensions, they would have been to style as such, I think. He remains something of a dandy. He has always enjoyed walking sticks, bow ties, selects a different form of headgear for different hours of the day.

So we did not quite fit in, thank goodness; alienated is the only way to be, after all. After the War, my mother was always trying to persuade him to move to a posher neighborhood, as if she thought *that* was the problem, and a house big enough to have my gran live with us, as though the presence of my gran would not have cancelled the whole thing out. Mum fancied Streatham; she had her eye on one house after another and sometimes we were so near to moving that she would pack all the books up in cardboard boxes, but, when it came to the point, my father wouldn't budge.

He entered into the fantasy of the thing wholeheartedly, of course; estate agent after estate agent was led up the garden path by him, but, when the crunch came, he could not do it. I don't think it was the idea of living with gran that put him off; they recognised that, in their ways, they were a match for one another and treated one another with deference. But he was himself utterly oblivious of the way the neighborhood was growing seedy, the way the house was falling down. 'Nothing wrong with the old shack,' he'd say, as the woodworm gnawed the rafters and the defective wiring ignited small conflagrations hither and thither. 'Nothing wrong with the old shack.' Not defensively—rather, with the air of a man startled that anyone might think otherwise.

No. He hated the idea of a big mortgage. He liked to have the odd bob in his pocket, for chocolates, for ice-cream, for lunches out, for nice things for my mother, for his own modest dandyism, for occasional taxis that turned into taxis everywhere after my mother grew ill. Also, he particularly enjoyed travelling first-class on the railways—oh, those exquisite night-trains to Scotland! We could not afford a nicer house and all those luxuries besides; he did elaborate sums on the backs of envelopes to regretfully prove it—and then would climb back happily to the little eyrie he'd made for himself in the attic, where he would lie on his bed listening to obscure continental stations on his radio, smoking his pipe. 'What are you *doing?*' she'd shout from the bottom of the stairs. 'Contemplating the futility of it all,' he'd say. 'Contemplating the futility of it all, you old trout.'

When she told him how much she hated being called an old trout, he'd riposte: 'The trout is the most beautiful of fish.'

Charm is our curse.

So they stayed put. After he retired from work, maybe the only move he really wanted to make was back to Scotland but she would not hear of that, to put herself at the tender mercies of his kin and of the deathly climate. After I left home, they turned increasingly in on themselves; a good deal of the joy evaporated from their lives with my mother's illness and there was her own mother's death, a great blow since the umbilical cord had been ill-severed. But that was later, when I was no longer a child.

My mother and father were well on in their marriage when I was born, so there is a great deal about them I do not know and I do not remember them when they were young. My father was older when I was born than I am now. But he loved to take snaps in those unknown-to-me days and there are dozens of albums of pictures of my mother. My mother in wonderfully snappy clothes with my brother in his photogenic babyhood; with a black and white dog they had; in an open tourer my father subsequently crashed; on beaches; in fields among cornstooks; at the piano; playing at typing on my father's typewriter, every inch the dimpled twenties child-bride. My mother would often say what a lovely time she and my dad had before the War and there is the proof of it, trapped in the amber of the perpetual summer of the amateur photographer, redolent of a modest yet authentic period glamour.

I was not in any way part of that life, which had ended with the War; and the War ended with the onset of their middle-age. After the War, everything became drab, and drabness, I think, instinctively repelled them both. Chaos, even mayhem, yes; but a drab, an austere time, no, even if my mother paid a lot of lip-service to respectability. Love and money only bought me lousy toys in the 1940s and I acceded to my brother's generation, I loved best his plush Micky Mouse and his books, *Alice* and *Pooh*. Times grew less hard; then, at last, I acquired in full measure all the impedimenta of a bourgeois childhood, a dolls' house, toy sewing-machine, red patent-leather shoes with silver buckles, organdie dresses and so on, but these were all a little spooky in a twilight zone and the Cold War was a curious time during which to recreate a snug, privileged, thirties childhood for their daughter. I went to primary school with apprentice used-car dealers and my best friend was a girl whose uncle trained greyhounds, whose mother was an office-cleaner. Not that my parents thought there was anything odd about that. And always, when I came home, the dream-time engulfed me, a perpetual Sunday afternoon in which you could never trust the clocks, until, when I was fifteen, she was ill. And never fully recovered, was never really well again, always an invalid now. And the music of their rowing died to a soft *obbligato*.

She once warned me: 'Children wreck marriages.' I had not realised how essentially satisfied they had been with one another until then; not that I think she meant my brother and I had wrecked *her* marriage. If anything, we were too much loved, I don't think she resented us. I do not think she was registering a specific complaint, but making a grand generalisation based on observation, insight yet also, perhaps, she felt a dissatisfaction that was also generalised, had nothing to do with any of us, did not even exist as an 'if only', but as if, perhaps unconsciously, she felt she might have mislaid something important, in the eccentric, noisy trance of that rambling, collapsing house.

But then, I do not think you ever know you are happily married until you have been unhappily married, first.

She once gave me a rose tree.

It was for my tenth or eleventh birthday. I forget precisely which. It was a miniature rose tree, in a pot. I found it on my breakfast table, beside the other presents, of which there were a tremendous many, I was spoiled rotten. It was no more than a foot high and covered with pink blossom. I was a little disappointed with it, at first; I could not eat it, wear it or read it and I was a practical child and could not really see the use of it, though I could see it had been chosen with the greatest loving care.

I misunderstood my mother's subtleties. I did not realise this rose tree was not a present for my tenth birthday, but for my grown self, a present not for now, but to remember. Of all the presents of all the birthdays of a petted childhood, the rose tree is the one I remember best and it is mixed up, now, with my memory of her, that, in spite of our later discords, our acrimonious squabblings, once she gave me a perennial and never-fading rose tree, the outlines of which, crystallized in the transforming well of memory, glitter as if with properties she herself may not have been at all aware of, a present like part of herself she did not know about that she could still give away to me.

People as Pictures

Japanese tattooing, *irezumi*, bears the same relation to the floral heart on the forearm of a merchant seaman as does the Sistine Chapel to the graffiti on a lavatory wall. *Irezumi* is tattooing *in toto*. It transforms its victim into a genre masterpiece. He suffers the rigorous and ineradicable cosmetology of the awl and gouge (for the masters of the art do not use the needle) until, unique and glorious in his mutilation, he becomes a work of art as preposterous as it is magnificent.

He is a work of art with an authenticity peculiarly Japanese. He is visually superb; he exudes the weird glamour of masochism; and he carries upon his flesh an immutable indication of caste. Bizarre beauties blossom in the programmed interstices of repression. The puppets of the Bunraku theatre are the most passionate in the world; *ikebana* is the art of torturing flowers. *Irezumi* paints with pain upon a canvas of flesh.

During Japan's first encounter with the West in the 1880s, *irezumi* was banned, but the practice continued to flourish and the laws were later rescinded. Though the art is now in its decline—due, perhaps, to the bourgeoisification of the Japanese working class—the ultimate pictorial man may still be seen in his rococo but incontestable glory on summer beaches around Tokyo; on construction sites; in the public baths of certain quarters; anywhere, in fact, where members of the urban proletariat take off their clothes in public.

Those who traditionally wore tattoos—carpenters, scaffolding workers, labourers, gamblers, gangsters—wear them still, almost as an occupational badge. Among gangsters and the underworld, the practice still has elements of an initiation rite since it is extraordinarily painful, extremely lengthy and also exceedingly costly. It is often carried out at puberty.

There is an active appreciation of the art, which extends to other styles of tattooing. An Australian prisoner of war among the Japanese happened to have been extensively tattooed in the occidental style. He was often called out from among his comrades to exhibit himself to high-ranking visiting military and received many small gifts of candy, biscuits and cigarettes from his fascinated and admiring guards. This tattoo fancy extends to the collection of skins. In Tokyo there is a private museum, devoted to the display of particularly fine specimens. It is said that, in the heyday of *irezumi,* some enthusiasts would buy the pictures off a man's very back, making an initial down-payment and waiting for the demise of the bearer of the masterpiece to collect it. So, for the poor workmen, tattooing may have been a form of investment or even of life insurance.

The origins of the practice are lost, like the origins of the Japanese themselves, in the mists of antiquity. Tattooing is endemic to Oceania. One recalls Melville's 'living counterpane', Queequeg; and the English word, 'tattoo', is derived from the Tahitian. In the third century A.D. the custom was ascribed to the Wo, the aboriginal inhabitants of Kyushu, the southernmost of Japan's islands, by the Chinese chronicle, *The Records of Wei:* 'Men, great and small, all tattoo their faces and decorate their bodies with designs. . . . They are fond of diving in the water to get fish and shells and originally decorated their bodies in order to keep away large fish and waterfowl. Later, however, these designs became merely ornamental.'

Irezumi has recently been primarily the pursuit of the lower classes but the Edo era (1603–1867) was the classical age. Even the great artist Utamaro forsook his woodblock prints in order to design a great number of tattoos. Tattoo contests were held, where firemen, artisans, palanquin-bearers, and dandies of both the merchant and the samurai class vied in the display of their colours. The geishas of the pleasure quarters were often tattooed with remarkable finesse, especially on the back. In one of his short stories, the modern novelist Junichiro Tanizaki, with characteristic acumen, ascribes a socially acceptable, but extremely active, sadism to a tattoo artist of the period: 'His pleasure lay in the agony men felt. . . . The louder they screamed, the keener was Seikichi's strange delight.'

Today's favourite designs are still based on those popular in the eighteenth and nineteenth centuries. They include the Dragon, giver of strength and sagacity; the Carp (perseverance); folk heroes like the infant prodigy Kintaro, who stands for success; Chinese sages and Japanese deities. If there are relics of superstitions behind these choices, they are as tenuous as those behind the names of Japanese baseball teams—the Hiroshima Toyo Carp, the Chunichi Dragons, the Osaka Tigers. Many designs have no such significance but are chosen only for their intrinsic beauty. Flowers. The sea. Lightning. Famous lovers. Young ladies astonished by snakes.

Traditionally, the Japanese have always felt a lack of interest, verging on repugnance, at the naked human body. Lady Murasaki, the eleventh-century novelist, wrote with a shudder of distaste: 'Unforgettably horrible is the sight of the naked body. It really does not have the slightest charm.' Even the erotic actors in the pictorial sex-instruction manuals of the Edo era rarely doff their kimono. The genitalia, bared, are rendered explicitly enough, but the remainder of the human form is heavily draped, either because it was considered irrelevant to the picture's purpose or because nobody ever told the Japanese the human form was supposed to be divine.

Modern Japanese men have come to terms with the female nude, to a certain extent, in that there is now an active appreciation of its erotic quality—as though they said, with Donne: 'Oh, my America! My new found land!' But the indifference of 2000 years, whatever created this indifference, lends a peculiarly borrowed quality to the reaction to, for example, a strip-show.

Now, a man who has been comprehensively tattooed—and the *irezumi* artist is nothing if not comprehensive—can hardly be said to be naked, for he may never remove this most intimate and gaily coloured of garments. Stark he may be, but always decent, and therefore never ashamed. He will never look helplessly, defencelessly, indelicately nude. This factor may or may not be important in the psychological bases of *irezumi*—which provides the potentially perhaps menacing human form with an absolute disguise. In Japan, the essence is often the appearance.

A tattooed Japanese has, in effect, been appliquéd with a garment somewhat resembling a snugly fitting Victorian bathing costume. The finished ensemble covers the back, the buttocks, both arms to the elbow and the upper thigh. The middle of the chest, the stomach and the abdomen are usually left in the natural state. This enhances rather than detracts from the 'dressed' look, because the bare skin, incorporated into the overall design, acquires an appearance of artificiality.

This is the method of *irezumi*. First, the design is selected, possibly from a chapbook of great antiquity. Then the design is drawn on the skin with black Chinese ink, or *sumi*, which gives its name to the technique. *Irezumi* is derived from *sumi* and *ireru*, which means 'put'. The dye is then applied, following these outlines. A series of triangular-shaped gouges or chisels are used. The full-dye brush is kept steady by the little finger of the left hand, while the gouge is held in the right, rubbed against the brush, then pushed under the skin. This is repeated, until a thick, clear line is achieved. To keep the working surface clean, the master must wipe away blood all the time. Finally, using the full, traditional palette, he works the design into the epidermis.

The traditional palette remains that of the Edo era. The primary tint is, again, *sumi,* which turns an ineffable blue under Japanese skin. Green is also used, together with a light blue and a very subtle red of such extraordinarily excruciating properties that the client can tolerate only a few new square inches of it a week. The brush, and the human form on which it works, together dictate a curvilinear technique. The design flows around the body with the amorous voluptuousness of Art Nouveau. There can be no straight lines in *irezumi.* The effect is that of coarse lace. It is an overall, total and entire transformation.

It is this absolute sense of design that is unique to *irezumi.* Not the eclectic variety of the tattoo produced by the needle—a dragon here, a tombstone marked 'Mother' there, and, on the biceps, the name 'Mavis' surrounded by rosebuds. The master-pieces of the European tattooist are essentially imitative of painting. If they utilise the nature of the body on which they are depicted, it is by way of a happy accident— as when a tattooed hunt follows, in full cry down a man's back, the fox which is about to disappear into his anus. There is nothing whimsical about *irezumi.* No slogans. No skulls or daggers.

It may take as long as a year of weekly visits to a tattooist before the *œuvre* is complete. These visits will last as long as the customer can endure them, perhaps several hours. The process of covering large areas of skin with a single pigment can be extremely painful. Soreness and itching are concomitant with the growth of the garden on one's skin. *Il faut souffrir pour être belle.*

The tattoo-masters themselves tend to inherit the art from their fathers. The apprenticeship is long and arduous, and requires a high degree of artistic skill. They are conscious of the archaic dignity of their profession and may be found in the old-fashioned quarters of Tokyo, where they still cultivate the hobbies of ancient Edo (Tokyo's name before the Meiji restoration), such as keeping crickets in cages and breeding songbirds.

Irezumi is a favourite motif in popular art. Japan produces, for her domestic market, a number of leisurely sagas about the native gangster, the *yakusa.* The word 'gangster', with its overtones of Capone, does not do full justice to these racketeers, who wear kimonos and often fight with swords. Even today they possess a strange kind of outmoded respectability. The *yakusa* films are usually set in the thirties, though the only indications of period may be the occasional western-style suit, pick-up truck or revolver. The heroes will display handsome, though greasepaint, *irezumi* as a simple indication of *yakusa* status.

The motif of the tattooed bride, the girl from the gangster class or the brothel, who has successfully 'passed' and tearfully reveals the evidence of her past on her wedding night, is not infrequent. Involuntary tattooing, for both men and women, is also a recurring motif. They may be tattooed as punishment for the infringement of group rules, or from revenge. Women are also stripped and lengthily tattooed in certain kinds of blue movie. The tattoo-master, with madly glittering eye, and awl poised above the luscious flesh of his defenceless prey, appears in many stills in the series of publications called *Adult Cinema—Japan,* among pictures of young ladies hanging upside down from ceilings during operations for amputation of the breast.

Masochism and sadism are different sides of the same coin, and perhaps a repres-sive culture can only be maintained by a strong masochistic element among the repressed. In Japan it is rare to hear a voice raised in anger, and rarer still to see a fight in public. It is considered subtly offensive to show the teeth when smiling, for a public display of teeth may be mistaken for a menacing snarl. If I am angry with my friend, not only do I never tell him so, I probably never speak to him again. More Japanese die of apoplexy than from anything else, as though they have bottled up their passions and bottled them up and bottled them up . . . until one day they just explode.

Perhaps one must cultivate masochism in depth if one is to endure a society based on constant expressions of the appearance of public goodwill, let alone try to maintain it. And, though it is difficult to ascertain the significance of *irezumi,* it is almost certainly one of the most exquisitely refined and skilful forms of sado-masochism the mind of man ever divined. It survives strangely but tenaciously in modern Japan.

Colette

Colette is one of the few, possibly the only, well-known woman writer of modern times who is universally referred to simply by her surname, *tout court.* Woolf hasn't made it, even after all these years; Rhys without the Jean is incognito, Nin without the Anais looks like a typo. Colette, Madame Colette, remains, in this as much else, unique.

However, Colette did not acquire this distinction because she terrorised respect language out of her peers, alas; by a happy accident, her family name also doubles as a girlish handle and a very ducky one, too. One could posit 'Bonny' or 'Rosie' as some kind of English equivalent. It was by a probably perfectly unconscious sleight of hand that Colette appropriated for herself the form of address of both masculine respect and masculine intimacy of her period, a fact that, in a small way, reflects the whole message of her career. This is: if you can't win, change the rules of the game.

Her career was a profoundly strange one and necessarily full of contradictions, of which her uncompromising zeal for self-exploitation is one. Madame Colette, though never quite Madame Colette de l'Académie Française—one game she couldn't crack—was accorded a state funeral by the French government; this was the woman whose second husband's aristocratic family dismissed her as a cunning little strip-tease artist over-eager for the title of Baroness. As Madame Colette, she first appeared on pin-up pictures of 'Our pretty actresses: Madame Colette of the Olympia'. And, in these pictures, taken in her late thirties, she is very beautiful and sexy indeed; she looks out at you with all the invitation of the stripper, '*you* can call me Colette', a familiar show-biz trick, the relationship of artificial intimacy the showgirl creates between her named self and the anonymous punter, with its intention to disarm.

This artificial creation of a sense of intimacy with Colette herself is one of the qualities that gives her writing its seductiveness; Colette certainly wasn't on the halls all those years for nothing, although the extent to which a wilful exhibitionism kept her on the boards against the advice of the majority of her critics well into her fifties may be connected with a certain capacity to embarrass that often frays the edges of her writing.

Because '*you* can call me Colette' isn't a statement of the same order as 'Call me

Ishmael.' The social limitations to experience in a woman's life still preclude the kind of unselfconscious picaresque adventuring that formed the artistic apprentice-ships of Melville, Lowry, Conrad, while other socio-economic factors mean that those women who see most of the beastly backside of the world, that is, prostitutes, are least in a position to utilise this invaluable experience as art. Somewhere, Norman Mailer says there won't be a *really* great woman writer, one, you understand, *con cojones* and everything, until the first call-girl tells her story. Though it's reasonable to assume that, when she does, Mailer won't like it at all, at all, the unpleasant truth in this put-down is that most women don't have exposure to the kind of breadth of experience that, when digested, produces great fiction. (Okay, so what about the Brontës? Well, as vicar's daughters in a rural slum parish, peripatetic international governesses and terminal consumptives, they *did* have such a variety of experience. So.) But the life of Colette was as picaresque as a woman's may be without putting herself in a state of hazard.

Her first novel, *Claudine at School,* and its sequels appeared with the name of her husband on the title page. This man, the peculiar Willy, one of the best-publicised Bohemians of the Belle Époque, ensured that the little Burgundian village girl, Colette's favourite disguise, encountered not only numerous whores of both sexes at an impressionable age but also *everybody,* Proust, Debussy, Ravel, you name them. When Willy left her, his wife found herself in the unusual position of having written a number of best-sellers whilst being unable to take any financial or artistic credit for them. To earn a living in the years before the First World War, she felt she had no alternative but to go on the halls. Since she could neither sing nor dance, she performed as a sex-object and subject of scandal, and not a particularly up-market sex object, either. Since Willy had enjoyed sexually humiliating her, no doubt there was a special pleasure in exploiting her sexuality whilst herself secure and unavaila-ble; after Willy, she took refuge in the bosom of the lesbian Establishment of the period. Our pretty actress had an aristocratic protector, the Marquise de Mornay; nothing unusual, not even the sex of the Marquise, about this in those permissive times.

Then came a Cinderellaesque marriage to (Baron) Henry de Jouvenal, editor of *Le Matin,* later a politician of considerable distinction. One thing about Colette interests me; when did she stop lying about her age? The voluptuous dancer was pushing forty when she married de Jouvenal; 'But the registry office has to know your age!' she complained to a friend. There comes a time when a woman freely publicises her age so people can say: 'How young you look!' It seems to have come later than most to Colette, but when it did, she gloried in it, as in all else.

In tandem with this characteristically if rather Hollywood Edwardian career, not one but two writers are growing within Colette. One writes *La Vagabonde* in 1910, a novel which is still one of the most truthful expositions of the dilemma of a free woman in a male-dominated society. Perhaps because Colette, having the trium-phant myopia of a vain woman, refused to acknowledge her society as male-domina-ted, she sees no dilemma; there is no real choice. One *is* free. In the same year, the other writer, the one more nearly related to our pretty actress, began work as a journalist for *Le Matin,* which is how she met its editor. Renée Néré, music-hall artiste, prefers to go it alone in *La Vagabonde,* but Colette, Colette married and married well. Her marriage also sealed her fate as a journalist, which in turn sealed her fate as a novelist, because the professions are mutually exclusive, even if simultaneously conducted.

Colette became literary editor of *Le Matin* in 1919 and thereafter was to work almost continuously in newspapers and magazines in one way and another, whilst continuing to write fiction and, from time to time, to act. In 1924, after her divorce from de Jouvenal, she started signing her work, for the first time, neither Colette Willy nor Colette de Jouvenal but simply 'Colette'. Her third marriage, some ten years later, would never make her dwindle into Colette Goudeket, even if Colette was not her own but her father's name. You can't subvert patriarchy *that* easily, after all, even if your father's name might be roughly analogous to 'Darling', and he so weak and feckless you have only acquired the very haziest grasp of the power of patriarchy. However, now 'Colette' she was, for all seasons.

As a writer, both of journalism and of some of her fiction, Colette exploits this intimacy of the stripper with her reader quite remorselessly. She trades on the assumption that you are going to care about Maman because this is the unique Colette's unique Maman. The details of her Burgundian childhood, endlessly recapitulated and, one suspects, endlessly elaborated over the years, are purveyed with a child-like sense of self-importance, such a naïve expectation that the smallest details of the Colette family diet and customs are worth recounting that it seems churlish to ask: 'What is the point of all this?'

She puts herself into much of her actual fiction. Not so much that all her fiction tends to draw on childhood, on the music-hall, on the sad truths distilled from unhappy marriages as that whole short novels—*Chance Acquaintances, Break of Day*—and many short stories are recounted in the first person of a Colette very precisely realised as subject and object at the same time. In the collection Penguin publish under the title *The Rainy Moon,* most of the stories feature Colette herself, if not as a major character then never as passive narrator. She always gives herself a part, as though she could not bear to leave herself out, must always be on stage.

She stopped writing fiction altogether after *Gigi,* in 1942, a Belle Époque fable of the apparent triumph of innocence that would be nauseating were it not so cynical. Her later work, until her death in 1954, is mostly a series of extended autobiographical reveries, among them *The Blue Lantern, The Evening Star.* These, and the volumes of autobiographical journalism that preceded them, *My Mother's House* (given this curious biblical title in English—in French, *La Maison de Claudine*), *Sido, My Apprenticeships, Music-Hall Sidelights,* etc., are a peculiar kind of literary striptease in themselves, a self-exploitation that greedily utilises every scrap of past experience in an almost unmediated form.

Yet there is no sense of the confessional about this endless flow of memory. Colette never tells you about herself. Instead, she describes herself. Few writers have described their own physicality so often; 'savage' child, with the long, blond plaits; bride with the 'splash of red carnations on the bodice of her white wedding gown'; in dinner jacket and monocle; pregnant, looking like 'a rat dragging a stolen egg'. And so on.

But she gives the impression of telling all, in a literary form unclassifiable except as a version of what television has accustomed us to call 'fictionalised documentary'. Robert Phelps was able to construct a perfectly coherent autobiography from Colette's scattered reminiscences, and present *The Earthly Paradise* as if it were not an imaginative parallel to her real life but the real thing. All Colette's biographers rely heavily on the sources she herself provides, even Michèle Sarde's recent, exhaustive, lengthy life, as if Colette could be trusted not to keep her fingers crossed when she was talking about herself, even when remembering events across a great gulf of years. Also, as if her sincerity was in itself important. Such is the sense of intimacy Colette creates; you feel you know her, because she has said 'you can call me Colette', although she says this to everybody who pays.

And yet these memories, this experience, are organized with such conscious art, such lack of spontaneity! She must have acquired from Balzac her taste for presenting those she loved best and admired most, including herself, as actors in *tableaux vivants,* as beings complete in themselves, as if unmodified by the eyes of an observer who is herself part of the tableau; she describes finished objects in a perfect perspective, almost *trompe l'oeil,* stuck fast in the lucid amber of her prose. Her portrait of her friend, the poet Renée Vivian, in *The Pure and the Impure,* has the finite quality of nineteenth-century fiction. 'I remember Renée's gay laughter, her liveliness, the faint halo of light trembling in her golden hair all combined to sadden me, as does the happiness of blind children who laugh and play without the help of light.' All that Colette has left out of this portrait is the possibility of some kind of inner life beyond Colette's imagining which belongs to Renée Vivian alone. This holds true for all the dazzling galaxy of heterogeneous humanity in Colette's fictionalised documentaries. The apparent objectivity of her prose is a device to seal these people in her own narrative subjectivity.

The portraits, of Renée Vivian, of actresses like La Belle Otéro and Polaire, even of Willy and, later, of her own daughter, are exemplary because of their precision and troubling because of their detachment. Even in the accounts of her beloved mother, Colette's actual prose implicitly invites the reader to admire both the quality of the observation and the skill with which a different time and place are recreated; then, with a shock, you realise you have been seduced into applauding not so much a remarkable woman as the quality of Colette's love for her. Colette's actual prose is itself narcissistic.

So her apparently total lack of reticence tells us, in the end, nothing about her real relationships and her self-absorption becomes a come-on, a device like a mask behind which an absolute privacy might be maintained. Her obsessive love of make-up, of the stage, of disguises, suggests a desire, if not to conceal, then to mystify. The daughter of Captain Jules-Joseph Colette of the Zouaves could die happy in the notion she had never been on first-name terms with anyone outside her immediate family, not even, least of all, with any of her three husbands.

Since she appears to have been a profoundly disingenuous person, there seems no reason to think she did *not* die happy in this respect. The best lie is the truth, after all. Colette was indeed her name. Her childhood *was* a Burgundian idyll, even if one sister later killed herself, while a brother burned all of Colette's two thousand letters to her mother, as if to ensure that some things, at least, would remain sacrosanct from the daughter's guzzling, inordinate rapacity for material. Because the demands of journalism made Colette desperate for material; once a journalist has established the power-base of a cult of personality, he or she is positively encouraged to trot out their own opinions and anecdotes over and over again.

Colette's novels are of a different order of reality than her autobiographical pieces, because her novels are fiction and hence the truth; the rest is journalism and so may bear only the most peripheral relation to truth, even if a journalist tells you every single thing that actually happened.

In Colette's first novel, *Claudine at School,* she kills off Claudine's mother before the action begins. Claudine, her first *alter ego.* This is a far more interesting fact than all the obsessive gush about her own real mother that spills out later in *La Maison de Claudine, Sido* and *Break of Day.* In this last novel, in fact a transparently fictionalised documentary using real Provençale locations and some real persons, Colette virtually apotheosises her dead mother, but leaves out altogether her third husband, Maurice Goudeket, who was happily ensconced by her side as she scribbled: 'I have paid for my folly, shut away the heady young wine that intoxicated me, and folded up my big, floating heart.'

The extent to which Colette came to believe her own mythology of herself is, of course, another question. Goudeket himself entered into the spirit of the thing wholeheartedly. His memoir of her last twenty years with him, *Close to Colette,* celebrates her peasant wisdom, her child-like enthusiasm. To him we owe the anecdote of her encounter with the cat in New York: 'At last someone who speaks French!' Michèle Sarde repeats this unblushingly, as if it told us something about the wit and wisdom of Colette. Michèle Sarde has swallowed the mythology whole; but the anecdote *does* tell us a good deal about Colette. It shows how wisely she picked her last companion, her Boswell, her PRO faithful beyond the grave.

Goudeket rhapsodies: 'There were so many arts which she had not lost. With her the art of living came before the art of writing. She knew a receipt for everything, whether it was for furniture polish, vinegar, orange-wine or quince-water, for cooking truffles or preserving linen and materials.' French, he says—she was French to her fingertips, and provincial to boot, even after sixty years' total immersion in the heady whirlpool of Parisian artistic life. French and provincial as Elizabeth David's *French Country Cooking,* and just as much intended for publication.

I must say, now, that this ineradicable quality of the fraud, the fake, of the unrepentant self-publicist, is one of the things about Colette I respect most; indeed, revere. Michèle Sarde's biography, however besotted, however uncritical, however willing to draw illegimate parallels between art and life, nevertheless demonstrates how it was the passionate integrity of Colette's narcissism that rendered her indestructible.

It's possible to see her entire career as a writer, instigated as it was by Willy, who robbed her of the first fruits of her labours, as an act of vengeance on him. A certain kind of woman, a vain woman, that is to say, a woman with self-respect, is spurred on by spite. Had the Rev. Brontë supported and encouraged his daughters' ambitions, what would the poor things have done then? I don't think Leonard Woolf did his wife a favour by mothering her. After Colette met kind, sweet, intelligent, loving Goudeket, she wrote very little major fiction.

In Simone de Beauvoir's memoirs, there's a description of a dinner party de Beauvoir attended with Sartre, at which Colette, already the frizzed and painted sacred cow of French letters, babbling away to *les gars,* as was her wont, about dogs, cats, knitting, *le bon vin, les bons fromages* and so on, offered de Beauvoir only the meagre attention of an occasional, piercing stare. De Beauvoir thought Colette disliked women. Possibly Colette, never a one to be *bouleversée* by a great mind, and, perhaps, privately relishing boring a great mind into the ground with nuggets of earthy Burgundian wisdom, was no more than contemplating the question every thinking woman in the western world must have posed herself one time or other: why is a nice girl like Simone wasting her time sucking up to a boring old fart like J.-P.? Her memoirs will be mostly about him; he will scarcely speak of her. Colette would have *known* so, intuitively.

Of course, Colette could no more have written *The Second Sex* than de Beauvoir could have danced naked on a public stage, which precisely defines the limitations of both these great ladies, and it is this very self-exploitative, stripper quality that earths most of Colette's later writing. However, it is hard to imagine Colette, had she attended the Sorbonne, getting any kind of buzz out of coming second to Sartre in her final examinations, or, indeed, out of coming second to anybody. She had to be number one, even if she had to reinvent a whole genre of literature, and herself included, to do so.

Even after all these years, de Beauvoir still appears to be proud that only Sartre achieved higher marks in those first exams than she. What would have happened, one wonders, if she had come top? What would it have done to Sartre? Merely to think of it makes the mind reel. Only love can make you proud to be an also-ran. Would love have made J.-P. proud like that?

But Colette simply did not believe that women *were* the second sex. One of Goudeket's anecdotes from her declining years is very revealing. He carried her in her wheelchair into a holiday hotel; the lobby filled with applauding, cheering fans; she was a national institution in France, after all. Colette seemed touched: 'They've remembered me from last year.' This isn't modesty, though Goudeket pretends to think so; it's irony, I hope, because, if it isn't irony, then what is it? What monstrous vanity would think it was perfectly natural for a little old lady to receive a tumultuous welcome from her hotel staff? Of course she didn't believe she was really famous, towards the end. She knew she wasn't famous enough to gratify her unappeasable ego. Magnificently she did not know her place.

But to believe women are not the second sex is to deny a whole area of social reality, however inspiriting the toughness and resilience of Colette and most of her heroines may be, especially after the revival of the wet and spineless woman-as-hero which graced the seventies. (The zomboid creatures in Joan Didion's novels, for example; the resurrected dippy dames of Jean Rhys, so many of whom might have had pathetic walk-on parts in Colette's own stories of Paris in the twenties.) Colette celebrated the status quo of femininity, not only its physical glamour but its capacity to subvert and withstand the boredom of patriarchy. This makes her an ambivalent ally to the Women's Movement. She is like certain shop-stewards who devote so much time to getting up management's nose that they lose sight of the great goals of socialism.

Her fiction, as opposed to her journalism, is dedicated to the proposition of the battle of the sexes—'love, the bread and butter of my pen', she observes in a revealing phrase. But, in Colette's battles, the results are fixed, men can never win, unless, as in the short story 'The Képi', the woman is foolish enough to believe a declaration of love is tantamount to a cessation of hostilities.

In the brief, fragile, ironic novels that are Colette's claim to artistic seriousness, *Ripening Seed, The Vagabond, Chéri* and *The Last of Chéri,* the men are decorative but useless. The delicious adolescent Phil, in *Ripening Seed,* lolls at ease on the beach while little Vinca arranges their picnic, her role is to serve, but this role makes him a parasite. The beautiful (and economically self-sufficient, as so many of Colette's heroines) lady who seduces him, whom he calls his 'master', is not really Vinca's rival at all, but her fellow conspirator in the ugly plot to 'make a man' of Phil with all that implies of futility and arrogance and complacency.

Renée Néré, the vagabond, tenderly consigns her rich suitor to the condition of a fragrant, unfulfilled memory since that is the only way she can continue to think kindly of him; she knows quite well the truth of the fairy tale is, kiss Prince Charming and he instantly turns into a frog. Léa simply grows out of Chéri, which is tough on Chéri.

The two Chéri novellas probably form Colette's masterpieces, although they are now so 'period' in atmosphere that the luxurious Edwardian décor blurs their hard core of emotional truth. As they recede into history, the décor will disappear; we will be left with something not unlike *Les Liaisons Dangereuses*. They are her masterpieces because they transcend the notion of the battle between the sexes by concentrating on an exceptionally rigorous analysis of the rules of war. Léa's financial independence is, of course, taken for granted; otherwise, in Colette's terms, there would be no possibility of a real relationship.

Julie de Carneilhan, published in 1941, a brief novel about upper-class alimony, is interesting in this respect because it deals specifically with a woman as an economically contingent being. I suspect this is what Colette meant when she said it was as close a reckoning with the elements of her second marriage as she ever allowed herself, since de Jouvenal was theoretically in control of their joint finances for the duration of their relationship. Without financial resources of her own, Julie is duped and stripped of self-respect by her husband, finally taking refuge with her brother and father, an obvious fantasy ending to which the shadow of approaching war promises an appropriately patriarchal resolution. Curiously enough, another war, the First World War, provides the watershed between the two *Chéri* novellas; released from the maternal embrace of Léa, anyone but Colette would have thought the trenches would make a *real* man of Chéri. But she knew it wasn't as simple as that.

The Chéri novels are about the power politics of love, and Léa and Chéri could be almost any permutation of ages or sexes. It is not in the least like *Der Rosenkavalier*, although we first meet Léa in her graceful late forties, some twenty-five years older than her boy lover. But they could both as well be men; or both women. Psychologically, Chéri could just as well be Chérie and Léa, Léo, except that we are socially acclimatised to the sexual vanity of middle-aged men; a handsome, successful, rich, fifty-year-old Léo might well feel that Chéri, at twenty-five, after an affair of six years, was getting a touch long in the tooth for his tastes. But even the age difference is not the point of the stories; the point is that Léa holds the reins. The only person who could film these novels with a sufficiently cold and dialectical eye is Fassbinder and he is the contemporary artist whom Colette most resembles. Not that she was a political person at all, in the Fassbinder sense, but she watched with a beady eye and drew the correct conclusions.

Given the thrust towards an idealised past of the major part of Colette's work, it is disconcerting to find that the moral of the *Chéri* novellas is: memory kills. When Chéri goes to see his ageing mistress, after the war and an absence of seven years, he finds, not the faded, touching ghost of love and beauty—no Miss Havisham, she—but a fat, jolly, altogether unrecognisable old lady quite unprepared to forgive him for once having flinched from her wrinkles. No tender scene of a visit to Juliet's tomb ensues, but a brisk invitation to grow up and forget, which Chéri is temperamentally incapable of accepting. A bullet in the brain is the only way out for Chéri. Léa was forced to reconstruct herself as a human being in order to survive the pain of Chéri's first rejection of her; the reconstructed Léa inevitably destroys Chéri by her very existence.

Colette's 'personal' voice is altogether absent from this parable. All the leading characters are either whores or the children of whores. They are all rich. If Colette set in motion the entire Colette industy in order to create for herself the artistic freedom and privacy to construct this chilling account of libido and false consciousness, then it was all abundantly worthwhile.

Penguin continue to reissue translations of most of Colette by a variety of hands, some of them, especially Antonia White's (the *Claudine* books), conspicuously handier than others. These slim volumes are currently dressed up in melting pinks, tones of pink, mauve and almond green not unlike the colour of Léa's knickers drawer. The exquisitely period photographs on the covers often turn out to depict Colette's own foxy mask, done up in a variety of disguises—a sailor suit for *Gigi*; full drag for *The Pure and the Impure.* The Women's Press put a charcoal drawing of the geriatric Colette, foxier than ever, on their edition of *Break of Day.* The cult of the personality of Colette, to which Michèle Sarde's biography, *Colette,* is a votive tribute, continues apace although it detracts attention from the artist in her, turns her more and more into a figure of historic significance, the woman who *did,* who occupied a key position in a transitional period of social history, from 1873 to 1954, and noted down most of what happened to her.

Apart from the *Chéri* novels and one or two others, her achievement as a whole *was* extraordinary though not in a literary sense; she forged a career out of the kind of self-obsession which is supposed, in a woman, to lead only to tears before bedtime, in a man to lead to the peaks. Good for her. I've got a god-daughter named after her. Or rather, such are the contradictions inherent in all this, named after Captain Jules-Joseph Colette, one-legged tax-gatherer and bankrupt.

Considerations for Thinking and Writing

1. Angela Carter does for British culture what Tom Wolfe does for American. She attacks the vanities, slices through the flesh of society, laying open the wound. But Carter is less likely than Wolfe to hide her fine mind in typography, in the elaborate jokes language concocts as it lays itself out on the printed page. Carter relies a great deal on piercing, biting understatement. Can you find examples of such understatement in her essay on faces? Go to the library and read an essay from one of Tom Wolfe's collections. Which writer do you prefer? Explain.

2. Compare Carter's portrayal of her mother in "The Mother Lode" with Maxine Hong Kingston's presentation of her mother in "No Name Woman." What can you learn of cultural values from such a comparison? What do these two mothers have in common with the mother that Patricia Berry discusses in "What's the Matter With Mother?"—an essay in Part II of this anthology?

3. Why does Carter like Colette so much that she has a "god-daughter named after her"? Read Joyce Carol Oates's essays on Simone Weil and Flannery O'Connor. What do you think Oates would think of Colette, given what you know of Colette from Carter's essay? Explain.

4. "People as Pictures" seems to be a process piece that explains in great detail the historical background and the procedure for *irezumi,* Japanese tattooing. But as Carter concludes her essay, she makes some strong assertions about a repressive culture and its sadomasochistic

tendencies. What are those assertions? What might they tell us about our own culture?

5. Go to the library and look at women's faces in the advertisements in *Cosmopolitan*, *Vogue*, and the *New York Times Magazine*. Using "The Wound in the Face" as a model, develop your own analysis of what advertisers are trying to project. What do those images tell you about "women's sense of security" in the 1980s? Do you find the images true to life? Are they exploitive or authentic? If you are a woman, what is the relationship between you and the advertisers who are trying to reach you and represent you with their products? If you are a man, to what extent do those images satisfy your notion of what women ought to look like? Has the advertiser matched the image of the woman in your head? What might your expectations and the manufacturer's images have to do with the relationships you try to develop with women?

6. Take a careful, thoughtful look at the relationship between you and your mother and your grandmother. Develop an essay that accounts for those relationships as you understand them. Do you think your assessment will change over time? Explain. Are relationships with mothers and grandmothers more problematic for women than for men? If we made fathers and grandfathers the subject of the essay, would that alter your response to the last question?

7. Read Susan Sontag's essay "Woman's Beauty: Put-Down or Power Source?" Imagine a conversation between her and Carter on the subject. See if you can sketch out the dialogue.

8. Consider Alice Walker's "Beauty: When the Other Dancer Is the Self." How might Carter's sense of beauty and Walker's differ?

JOAN DIDION
(b. 1934)

Joan Didion writes to impose her views on us. For Didion, writing is *"the act of saying listen to me, see it my way, change your mind."* Writing, for Didion, is an aggressive act, at times a hostile one. Such a view appears with vigor and forthrightness in her essay "Why I Write," whose title, she reminds us, she stole from George Orwell. What's interesting here is not only that she took Orwell's title but that she characterizes her appropriation as a theft. What is important, however, is the use to which she puts the title, the way she makes it hers, especially the reason she offers for taking it: she likes the sound of "I" in it. "Why I Write" is another way of saying "I," "I," "I." It's a way of asserting the self, of "imposing oneself on other people." And it's also Didion's way of suggesting that her writing is decisively personal.

Like Susan Sontag and Angela Carter, among others, Joan Didion writes about culture and society, about the way we live,

about our values, beliefs, attitudes—in short, about the way we act out our images of ourselves. Unlike Sontag and Carter, however, Didion writes as a reporter who is personally involved in what she writes about. Hers is not the detachment of the conventional reporter. She does not attempt to present neutral facts, whether she is writing about the political situation in El Salvador, the weather in Los Angeles, or the art of Georgia O'Keeffe. The facts she presents are filtered through her particular way of seeing things; she presents not the bare facts but a set of details selected and shaped by her distinctive judgments, attitudes, and values. Didion is thus less a reporter than a thoughtful observer, interpreter, and critic of contemporary society.

What does Didion criticize, and conversely, what does she value? She is critical of brutality ("Salvador"), dishonesty ("On Self-Respect"), injustice ("Georgia

O'Keeffe"). She laments the loss of stability traditionally provided by home, church, and family. But she is also aware of the dangerous limitations imposed by the traditional shapers of culture and character. Since familial, social, and religious ideals no longer serve their character-building purposes, Didion looks to the virtues of self-respect and integrity to anchor and sustain the self. Hence she values honesty, courage, discipline, character. Her essays, whatever their ostensible subjects, consistently celebrate versions of these old-fashioned virtues.

Didion celebrates Georgia O'Keeffe's "hardness," turning that hardness into something intriguing and affecting. O'Keeffe is tough-minded just as Didion is, and her character is reflected in her artistic style. While Didion suggests at the outset that "every brush stroke laid or not laid down—betrayed one's character," she writes less about the brush strokes than about the character behind them. She is enamored of the woman herself, the woman who refused to listen to "the men" who wanted her to learn to paint on their terms. Two things seem most important about this essay's style: the understated but powerful argument against "the men" Didion wages with O'Keeffe's words, and the repetition of words and phrases for rhetorical effect. " 'The men' believed it impossible to paint New York, so Georgia O'Keeffe painted New York. 'The men' didn't think much of her bright color, so she made it brighter." "The men" didn't . . . so Georgia O'Keeffe did.

The toughness exhibited in Didion's essay on Georgia O'Keeffe also inhabits "On Self-Respect." There too we find insistent sentence rhythms. Didion hammers home the point that if we are to have self-respect, we must "eventually lie down alone in that notoriously uncomfortable bed, the one we make ourselves." We, in short, are responsible for who we are and for what we become. But that's not all; we must also develop "character—the willingness to accept responsibility for one's own life"; we need to learn "discipline, a habit of mind that can never be faked but can be developed, trained, coaxed forth." And we are also shown to require the solace of ritual, which deepens and sustains the small daily disciplines enacted in our lives.

Didion is a West Coast woman. She was born in Sacramento, California, in 1934, and she was educated at the University of California at Berkeley. And although she has traveled widely around the world and has lived for a time on the East Coast, mostly in New York City, she is happiest in California, whose atmosphere, spirit, and mood she captures in such essays as "Los Angeles Notebook" and "Goodbye to All That."

She has been an associate editor at *Vogue,* has taught creative writing, and has contributed stories, articles, and reviews to numerous periodicals, including *Esquire, Mademoiselle, The National Review,* and *The American Scholar.* In addition, she has written four novels: *Run River* (1963), *Play It as It Lays* (1970), *A Book of Common Prayer* (1976), and *Democracy* (1983). Her essays, better known and generally more highly regarded than her fiction, have been collected in two volumes: *Slouching towards Bethlehem* (1968) and *The White Album* (1979). Her most recent books of nonfiction are *Salvador* (1983) and *Miami* (1987).

These mere facts, however, do not reveal Joan Didion the woman and writer. For that revelation we must turn to her prose pieces, especially to her sharply etched, often incisive essays.

Los Angeles Notebook

There is something uneasy in the Los Angeles air this afternoon, some unnatural stillness, some tension. What it means is that tonight a Santa Ana will begin to blow, a hot wind from the northeast whining down through the Cajon and San Gorgonio Passes, blowing up sandstorms out along Route 66, drying the hills and the nerves to the flash point. For a few days now we will see smoke back in the canyons, and hear sirens in the night. I have neither heard nor read that a Santa Ana is due, but I know it, and almost everyone I have seen today knows it too. We know it because we feel it. The baby frets. The maid sulks. I rekindle a waning argument with the telephone company, then cut my losses and lie down, given over to whatever it is in the air. To live with the Santa Ana is to accept, consciously or unconsciously, a deeply mechanistic view of human behavior.

I recall being told, when I first moved to Los Angeles and was living on an isolated beach, that the Indians would throw themselves into the sea when the bad wind blew. I could see why. The Pacific turned ominously glossy during a Santa Ana period, and one woke in the night troubled not only by the peacocks screaming in the olive trees but by the eerie absence of surf. The heat was surreal. The sky had a yellow cast, the kind of light sometimes called "earthquake weather." My only neighbor would not come out of her house for days, and there were no lights at night, and her husband roamed the place with a machete. One day he would tell me that he had heard a trespasser, the next a rattlesnake.

"On nights like that," Raymond Chandler once wrote about the Santa Ana, "every booze party ends in a fight. Meek little wives feel the edge of the carving knife and study their husbands' necks. Anything can happen." That was the kind of wind it was. I did not know then that there was any basis for the effect it had on all of us, but it turns out to be another of those cases in which science bears out folk wisdom. The Santa Ana, which is named for one of the canyons it rushes through, is a *foehn* wind, like the *foehn* of Austria and Switzerland and the *hamsin* of Israel. There are a number of persistent malevolent winds, perhaps the best known of which are the mistral of France and the Mediterranean sirocco, but a *foehn* wind has distinct characteristics: it occurs on the leeward slope of a mountain range and, although the air begins as a cold mass, it is warmed as it comes down the mountain and appears finally as a hot dry wind. Whenever and wherever a *foehn* blows, doctors hear about headaches and nausea and allergies, about "nervousness," about "depression." In Los Angeles some teachers do not attempt to conduct formal classes during a Santa Ana, because the children become unmanageable. In Switzerland the suicide rate goes up during the *foehn,* and in the courts of some Swiss cantons the wind is considered a mitigating circumstance for crime. Surgeons are said to watch the wind, because blood does not clot normally during a *foehn.* A few years ago an Israeli physicist discovered that not only during such winds, but for the ten or twelve hours which precede them, the air carries an unusually high ratio of positive to negative ions. No one seems to know exactly why that should be; some talk about friction and others suggest solar disturbances. In any case the positive ions are there, and what an excess of positive ions does, in the simplest terms, is make people unhappy. One cannot get much more mechanistic than that.

Easterners commonly complain that there is no "weather" at all in Southern

California, that the days and the seasons slip by relentlessly, numbingly bland. That is quite misleading. In fact the climate is characterized by infrequent but violent extremes: two periods of torrential subtropical rains which continue for weeks and wash out the hills and send subdivisions sliding toward the sea; about twenty scattered days a year of the Santa Ana, which, with its incendiary dryness, invariably means fire. At the first prediction of a Santa Ana, the Forest Service flies men and equipment from northern California into the southern forests, and the Los Angeles Fire Department cancels its ordinary non-firefighting routines. The Santa Ana caused Malibu to burn the way it did in 1956, and Bel Air in 1961, and Santa Barbara in 1964. In the winter of 1966–67 eleven men were killed fighting a Santa Ana fire that spread through the San Gabriel Mountains.

Just to watch the front-page news out of Los Angeles during a Santa Ana is to get very close to what it is about the place. The longest single Santa Ana period in recent years was in 1957, and it lasted not the usual three or four days but fourteen days, from November 21 until December 4. On the first day 25,000 acres of the San Gabriel Mountains were burning, with gusts reaching 100 miles an hour. In town, the wind reached Force 12, or hurricane force, on the Beaufort Scale; oil derricks were toppled and people ordered off the downtown streets to avoid injury from flying objects. On November 22 the fire in the San Gabriels was out of control. On November 24 six people were killed in automobile accidents, and by the end of the week the Los Angeles *Times* was keeping a box score of traffic deaths. On November 26 a prominent Pasadena attorney, depressed about money, shot and killed his wife, their two sons, and himself. On November 27 a South Gate divorcée, twenty-two, was murdered and thrown from a moving car. On November 30 the San Gabriel fire was still out of control, and the wind in town was blowing eighty miles an hour. On the first day of December four people died violently, and on the third the wind began to break.

It is hard for people who have not lived in Los Angeles to realize how radically the Santa Ana figures in the local imagination. The city burning is Los Angeles's deepest image of itself: Nathanael West perceived that, in *The Day of the Locust*; and at the time of the 1965 Watts riots what struck the imagination most indelibly were the fires. For days one could drive the Harbor Freeway and see the city on fire, just as we had always known it would be in the end. Los Angeles weather is the weather of catastrophe, of apocalypse, and, just as the reliably long and bitter winters of New England determine the way life is lived there, so the violence and the unpredictability of the Santa Ana affect the entire quality of life in Los Angeles, accentuate its impermanence, its unreliability. The wind shows us how close to the edge we are.

2

"Here's why I'm on the beeper, Ron," said the telephone voice on the all-night radio show. "I just want to say that this *Sex for the Secretary* creature—whatever her name is—certainly isn't contributing anything to the morals in this country. It's pathetic. Statistics *show.*"

"It's *Sex and the Office,* honey," the disc jockey said. "That's the title. By Helen Gurley Brown. Statistics show what?"

"I haven't got them right here at my fingertips, naturally. But they *show.*"

"I'd be interested in hearing them. Be constructive, you Night Owls."

"All right, let's take *one* statistic," the voice said, truculent now. "Maybe I haven't read the book, but what's this business she recommends about *going out with married men for lunch?*"

So it went, from midnight until 5 A.M., interrupted by records and by occasional calls debating whether or not a rattlesnake can swim. Misinformation about rattlesnakes is a leitmotiv of the insomniac imagination in Los Angeles. Toward 2 A.M. a man from "out Tarzana way" called to protest. "The Night Owls who called earlier must have been thinking about, uh, *The Man in the Gray Flannel Suit* or some other book," he said, "because Helen's one of the few authors trying to tell us what's really going *on.* Hefner's another, and he's also controversial, working in, uh, another area."

An old man, after testifying that he "personally" had seen a swimming rattlesnake, in the Delta-Mendota Canal, urged "moderation" on the Helen Gurley Brown question. "We shouldn't get on the beeper to call things pornographic before we've read them," he complained, pronouncing it porn-ee-oh-graphic. "I say, get the book. Give it a chance." The original *provocateur* called back to agree that she would get the book. "And then I'll burn it," she added.

"Book burner, eh?" laughed the disc jockey good-naturedly.

"I wish they still burned witches," she hissed.

3

It is three o'clock on a Sunday afternoon and 105° and the air so thick with smog that the dusty palm trees loom up with a sudden and rather attractive mystery. I have been playing in the sprinklers with the baby and I get in the car and go to Ralph's Market on the corner of Sunset and Fuller wearing an old bikini bathing suit. That is not a very good thing to wear to the market but neither is it, at Ralph's on the corner of Sunset and Fuller, an unusual costume. Nonetheless a large woman in a cotton muumuu jams her cart into mine at the butcher counter. *"What a thing to wear to the market,"* she says in a loud but strangled voice. Everyone looks the other way and I study a plastic package of rib lamb chops and she repeats it. She follows me all over the store, to the Junior Foods, to the Dairy Products, to the Mexican Delicacies, jamming my cart whenever she can. Her husband plucks at her sleeve. As I leave the check-out counter she raises her voice one last time: *"What a thing to wear to Ralph's,"* she says.

4

A party at someone's house in Beverly Hills: a pink tent, two orchestras, a couple of French Communist directors in Cardin evening jackets, chili and hamburgers from Chasen's. The wife of an English actor sits at a table alone; she visits California rarely although her husband works here a good deal. An American who knows her slightly comes over to the table.

"Marvelous to see you here," he says.

"Is it," she says.

"How long have you been here?"

"Too long."

She takes a fresh drink from a passing waiter and smiles at her husband, who is dancing.

The American tries again. He mentions her husband.

"I hear he's marvelous in this picture."

She looks at the American for the first time. When she finally speaks she enunciates every word very clearly. "He . . . is . . . also . . . a . . . fag," she says pleasantly.

5

The oral history of Los Angeles is written in piano bars. "Moon River," the piano player always plays, and "Mountain Greenery." "There's a Small Hotel" and "This Is Not the First Time." People talk to each other, tell each other about their first wives and last husbands. "Stay funny," they tell each other, and "This is to die over." A construction man talks to an unemployed screenwriter who is celebrating, alone, his tenth wedding anniversary. The construction man is on a job in Montecito: "Up in Montecito," he says, "they got one square mile with 135 millionaires."

"Putrescence," the writer says.

"That's all you got to say about it?"

"Don't read me wrong, I think Santa Barbara's one of the most—Christ, *the* most—beautiful places in the world, but it's a beautiful place that contains a . . . *putrescence*. They just live on their putrescent millions."

"So give me putrescent."

"No, no," the writer says. "I just happen to think millionaires have some sort of lacking in their . . . in their elasticity."

A drunk requests "The Sweetheart of Sigma Chi." The piano player says he doesn't know it. "Where'd you learn to play the piano?" the drunk asks. "I got two degrees," the piano player says. "One in musical education." I go to a coin telephone and call a friend in New York. "Where are you?" he says. "In a piano bar in Encino," I say. "Why?" he says. "Why not," I say.

Georgia O'Keeffe

"Where I was born and where and how I have lived is unimportant," Georgia O'Keeffe told us in the book of paintings and words published in her ninetieth year on earth. She seemed to be advising us to forget the beautiful face in the Stieglitz photographs. She appeared to be dismissing the rather condescending romance that had attached to her by then, the romance of extreme good looks and advanced age and deliberate isolation. "It is what I have done with where I have been that should be of interest." I recall an August afternoon in Chicago in 1973 when I took my daughter, then seven, to see what Georgia O'Keeffe had done with where she had been. One of the vast O'Keeffe "Sky Above Clouds" canvases floated over the back stairs in the Chicago Art Institute that day, dominating what seemed to be several stories of empty light, and my daughter looked at it once, ran to the landing, and kept on looking. "Who drew it," she whispered after a while. I told her. "I need to talk to her," she said finally.

My daughter was making, that day in Chicago, an entirely unconscious but quite basic assumption about people and the work they do. She was assuming that the glory she saw in the work reflected a glory in its maker, that the painting was the painter as the poem is the poet, that every choice one made alone—every word chosen or rejected, every brush stroke laid or not laid down—betrayed one's character. *Style is character.* It seemed to me that afternoon that I had rarely seen so instinctive an application of this familiar principle, and I recall being pleased not only that my daughter responded to style as character but that it was Georgia O'Keeffe's particular style to which she responded: this was a hard woman who had imposed her 192 square feet of clouds on Chicago.

"Hardness" has not been in our century a quality much admired in women, nor in the past twenty years has it even been in official favor for men. When hardness surfaces in the very old we tend to transform it into "crustiness" or eccentricity, some tonic pepperiness to be indulged at a distance. On the evidence of her work and what she has said about it, Georgia O'Keeffe is neither "crusty" nor eccentric. She is simply hard, a straight shooter, a woman clean of received wisdom and open to what she sees. This is a woman who could early on dismiss most of her contemporaries as "dreamy," and would later single out one she liked as "a very poor painter." (And then add, apparently by way of softening the judgment: "I guess he wasn't a painter at all. He had no courage and I believe that to create one's own world in any of the arts takes courage.") This is a woman who in 1939 could advise her admirers that they were missing her point, that their appreciation of her famous flowers was merely sentimental. "When I paint a red hill," she observed coolly in the catalogue for an exhibition that year, "you say it is too bad that I don't always paint flowers. A flower touches almost everyone's heart. A red hill doesn't touch everyone's heart." This is a woman who could describe the genesis of one of her most well-known paintings—the "Cow's Skull: Red, White and Blue" owned by the Metropolitan—as an act of quite deliberate and derisive orneriness. "I thought of the city men I had been seeing in the East," she wrote. "They talked so often of writing the Great American Novel—the Great American Play—the Great American Poetry. . . . So as I was painting my cow's head on blue I thought to myself, "I'll make it an American painting. They will not think it great with the red stripes down the sides—Red, White and Blue—but they will notice it.' "

The city men. The men. They. The words crop up again and again as this astonishingly aggressive woman tells us what was on her mind when she was making her astonishingly aggressive paintings. It was those city men who stood accused of sentimentalizing her flowers: "I made you take time to look at what I saw and when you took time to really notice my flower you hung all your associations with flowers on my flower and you write about my flower as if I think and see what you think and see—and I don't." *And I don't.* Imagine those words spoken, and the sound you hear is *don't tread on me.* "The men" believed it impossible to paint New York, so Georgia O'Keeffe painted New York. "The men" didn't think much of her bright color, so she made it brighter. The men yearned toward Europe so she went to Texas, and then New Mexico. The men talked about Cézanne, "long involved remarks about the 'plastic quality' of his form and color," and took one another's long involved remarks, in the view of this angelic rattlesnake in their midst, altogether too seriously. "I can paint one of those dismal-colored paintings like the men," the woman who regarded herself always as an outsider remembers thinking one day in 1922, and she did: a painting of a shed "all low-toned and dreary with the tree beside the door." She called this act of rancor "The Shanty" and hung it in her next show. "The men seemed to approve of it," she reported fifty-four years later, her contempt undimmed. "They seemed to think that maybe I was beginning to paint. That was my only low-toned dismal-colored painting."

Some women fight and others do not. Like so many successful guerrillas in the war between the sexes, Georgia O'Keeffe seems to have been equipped early with an immutable sense of who she was and a fairly clear understanding that she would be required to prove it. On the surface her upbringing was conventional. She was a child on the Wisconsin prairie who played with china dolls and painted watercolors with cloudy skies because sunlight was too hard to paint and, with her brother and sisters, listened every night to her mother read stories of the Wild West, of Texas, of Kit Carson and Billy the Kid. She told adults that she wanted to be an artist and was embarrassed when they asked what kind of artist she wanted to be: she had no idea "what kind." She had no idea what artists did. She had never seen a picture that interested her, other than a pen-and-ink Maid of Athens in one of her mother's books, some Mother Goose illustrations printed on cloth, a tablet cover that showed a little girl with pink roses, and the painting of Arabs on horseback that hung in her grandmother's parlor. At thirteen, in a Dominican convent, she was mortified when the sister corrected her drawing. At Chatham Episcopal Institute in Virginia she painted lilacs and sneaked time alone to walk out to where she could see the line of the Blue Ridge Mountains on the horizon. At the Art Institute in Chicago she was shocked by the presence of live models and wanted to abandon anatomy lessons. At the Art Students League in New York one of her fellow students advised her that, since he would be a great painter and she would end up teaching painting in a girls' school, any work of hers was less important than modeling for him. Another painted over her work to show her how the Impressionists did trees. She had not before heard how the impressionists did trees and she did not much care.

At twenty-four she left all those opinions behind and went for the first time to live in Texas, where there were no trees to paint and no one to tell her how not to paint them. In Texas there was only the horizon she craved. In Texas she had her sister Claudia with her for a while, and in the late afternoons they would walk away from town and toward the horizon and watch the evening star come out. "That evening star fascinated me," she wrote. "It was in some way very exciting to me. My sister had a gun, and as we walked she would throw bottles into the air and shoot as many as she could before they hit the ground. I had nothing but to walk into nowhere and the wide sunset space with the star. Ten watercolors were made from that star." In a way one's interest is compelled as much by the sister Claudia with the gun as by the painter Georgia with the star, but only the painter left us this shining record. Ten watercolors were made from that star.

On Self-Respect

Once, in a dry season, I wrote in large letters across two pages of a notebook that innocence ends when one is stripped of the delusion that one likes oneself. Although now, some years later, I marvel that a mind on the outs with itself should have nonetheless made painstaking record of its every tremor, I recall with embarrassing clarity the flavor of those particular ashes. It was a matter of misplaced self-respect.

I had not been elected to Phi Beta Kappa. This failure could scarcely have been more predictable or less ambiguous (I simply did not have the grades), but I was unnerved by it; I had somehow thought myself a kind of academic Raskolnikov, curiously exempt from the cause-effect relationships which hampered others. Although even the humorless nineteen-year-old that I was must have recognized that the situation lacked real tragic stature, the day that I did not make Phi Beta Kappa nonetheless marked the end of something, and innocence may well be the word for it. I lost the conviction that lights would always turn green for me, the pleasant certainty that those rather passive virtues which had won me approval as a child automatically guaranteed me not only Phi Beta Kappa keys but happiness, honor, and the love of a good man; lost a certain touching faith in the totem power of good manners, clean hair, and proven competence on the Stanford-Binet scale. To such doubtful amulets had my self-respect been pinned, and I faced myself that day with the nonplused apprehension of someone who has come across a vampire and has no crucifix at hand.

Although to be driven back upon oneself is an uneasy affair at best, rather like trying to cross a border with borrowed credentials, it seems to me now the one condition necessary to the beginnings of real self-respect. Most of our platitudes notwithstanding, self-deception remains the most difficult deception. The tricks that work on others count for nothing in that very well-lit back alley where one keeps assignations with oneself: no winning smiles will do here, no prettily drawn lists of good intentions. One shuffles flashily but in vain through one's marked cards—the kindness done for the wrong reason, the apparent triumph which involved no real effort, the seemingly heroic act into which one had been shamed. The dismal fact is that self-respect has nothing to do with the approval of others—who are, after all, deceived easily enough; has nothing to do with reputation, which, as Rhett Butler told Scarlett O'Hara, is something people with courage can do without.

To do without self-respect, on the other hand, is to be an unwilling audience of one to an interminable documentary that details one's failings, both real and imagined, with fresh footage spliced in for every screening. *There's the glass you broke in anger, there's the hurt on X's face; watch now, this next scene, the night Y came back from Houston, see how you muff this one.* To live without self-respect is to lie awake some night, beyond the reach of warm milk, phenobarbital, and the sleeping hand on the coverlet, counting up the sins of commission and omission, the trusts betrayed, the promises subtly broken, the gifts irrevocably wasted through sloth or cowardice or carelessness. However long we postpone it, we eventually lie down alone in that notoriously uncomfortable bed, the one we make ourselves. Whether or not we sleep in it depends, of course, on whether or not we respect ourselves.

To protest that some fairly improbable people, some people who *could not possibly respect themselves,* seem to sleep easily enough is to miss the point entirely, as surely as those people miss it who think that self-respect has necessarily to do with not having safety pins in one's underwear. There is a common superstition that "self-respect" is a kind of charm against snakes, something that keeps those who have it locked in some unblighted Eden, out of strange beds, ambivalent conversations, and trouble in general. It does not at all. It has nothing to do with the face of things, but concerns instead a separate peace, a private reconciliation. Although the careless, suicidal Julian English in *Appointment in Samarra* and the careless, incurably dishonest Jordan Baker in *The Great Gatsby* seem equally improbable candidates for self-respect, Jordan Baker had it, Julian English did not. With that genius for accommodation more often seen in women than in men, Jordan took her own measure, made her own peace, avoided threats to that peace: "I hate careless people," she told Nick Carraway. "It takes two to make an accident."

Like Jordan Baker, people with self-respect have the courage of their mistakes. They know the price of things. If they choose to commit adultery, they do not then go running, in an access of bad conscience, to receive absolution from the wronged parties; nor do they complain unduly of the unfairness, the undeserved embarrassment, of being named co-respondent. In brief, people with self-respect exhibit a certain toughness, a kind of moral nerve; they display what was once called *character*, a quality which, although approved in the abstract, sometimes loses ground to other, more instantly negotiable virtues. The measure of its slipping prestige is that one tends to think of it only in connection with homely children and United States senators who have been defeated, preferably in the primary, for reelection. Nonetheless, character—the willingness to accept responsibility for one's own life—is the source from which self-respect springs.

Self-respect is something that our grandparents, whether or not they had it, knew all about. They had instilled in them, young, a certain discipline, the sense that one lives by doing things one does not particularly want to do, by putting fears and doubts to one side, by weighing immediate comforts against the possibility of larger, even intangible, comforts. It seemed to the nineteenth century admirable, but not remarkable, that Chinese Gordon put on a clean white suit and held Khartoum against the Mahdi; it did not seem unjust that the way to free land in California involved death and difficulty and dirt. In a diary kept during the winter of 1846, an emigrating twelve-year-old named Narcissa Cornwall noted coolly: "Father was busy reading and did not notice that the house was being filled with strange Indians until Mother spoke about it." Even lacking any clue as to what Mother said, one can scarcely fail to be impressed by the entire incident: the father reading, the Indians filing in, the mother choosing the words that would not alarm, the child duly recording the event and noting further that those particular Indians were not, "fortunately for us," hostile. Indians were simply part of the *donnée*.

In one guise or another, Indians always are. Again, it is a question of recognizing that anything worth having has its price. People who respect themselves are willing to accept the risk that the Indians will be hostile, that the venture will go bankrupt, that the liaison may not turn out to be one in which *every day is a holiday because you're married to me.* They are willing to invest something of themselves; they may not play at all, but when they do play, they know the odds.

* * *

That kind of self-respect is a discipline, a habit of mind that can never be faked but can be developed, trained, coaxed forth. It was once suggested to me that, as an antidote to crying, I put my head in a paper bag. As it happens, there is a sound physiological reason, something to do with oxygen, for doing exactly that, but the psychological effect alone is incalculable: it is difficult in the extreme to continue fancying oneself Cathy in *Wuthering Heights* with one's head in a Food Fair bag. There is a similar case for all the small disciplines, unimportant in themselves; imagine maintaining any kind of swoon, commiserative or carnal, in a cold shower.

But those small disciplines are valuable only insofar as they represent larger ones. To say that Waterloo was won on the playing fields of Eton is not to say that Napoleon might have been saved by a crash program in cricket; to give formal dinners in the rain forest would be pointless did not the candlelight flickering on the liana call forth deeper, stronger disciplines, values instilled long before. It is a kind of ritual, helping us to remember who and what we are. In order to remember it, one must have known it.

To have that sense of one's intrinsic worth which constitutes self-respect is potentially to have everything: the ability to discriminate, to love and to remain indifferent. To lack it is to be locked within oneself, paradoxically incapable of either love or indifference. If we do not respect ourselves, we are on the one hand forced to despise those who have so few resources as to consort with us, so little perception as to remain blind to our fatal weaknesses. On the other, we are peculiarly in thrall to everyone we see, curiously determined to live out—since our self-image is untenable—their false notions of us. We flatter ourselves by thinking this compulsion to please others an attractive trait: a gist for imaginative empathy, evidence of our willingness to give. *Of course* I will play Francesca to your Paolo, Helen Keller to anyone's Annie Sullivan: no expectation is too misplaced, no role too ludicrous. At the mercy of those we cannot but hold in contempt, we play roles doomed to failure before they are begun, each defeat generating fresh despair at the urgency of divining and meeting the next demand made upon us.

It is the phenomenon sometimes called "alienation from self." In its advanced stages, we no longer answer the telephone, because someone might want something; that we could say *no* without drowning in self-reproach is an idea alien to this game. Every encounter demands too much, tears the nerves, drains the will, and the specter of something as small as an unanswered letter arouses such disproportionate guilt that answering it becomes out of the question. To assign unanswered letters their proper weight, to free us from the expectations of others, to give us back to ourselves—there lies the great, the singular power of self-respect. Without it, one eventually discovers the final turn of the screw: one runs away to find oneself, and finds no one at home.

Salvador

The three-year-old El Salvador International Airport is glassy and white and splendidly isolated, conceived during the waning of the Molina "National Transformation" as convenient less to the capital (San Salvador is forty miles away, until recently a drive of several hours) than to a central hallucination of the Molina and Romero regimes, the projected beach resorts, the Hyatt, the Pacific Paradise, tennis, golf, water-skiing, condos, *Costa del Sol*; the visionary invention of a tourist industry in yet another republic where the leading natural cause of death is gastrointestinal infection. In the general absence of tourists these hotels have since been abandoned, ghost resorts on the empty Pacific beaches, and to land at this airport built to service them is to plunge directly into a state in which no ground is solid, no depth of field reliable, no perception so definite that it might not dissolve into its reverse.

The only logic is that of acquiescence. Immigration is negotiated in a thicket of automatic weapons, but by whose authority the weapons are brandished (Army or National Guard or National Police or Customs Police or Treasury Police or one of a continuing proliferation of other shadowy and overlapping forces) is a blurred point. Eye contact is avoided. Documents are scrutinized upside down. Once clear of the airport, on the new highway that slices through green hills rendered phosphorescent by the cloud cover of the tropical rainy season, one sees mainly underfed cattle and mongrel dogs and armored vehicles, vans and trucks and Cherokee Chiefs fitted with reinforced steel and bulletproof Plexiglas an inch thick. Such vehicles are a fixed feature of local life, and are popularly associated with disappearance and death. There was the Cherokee Chief seen following the Dutch television crew killed in Chalatenango province in March of 1982. There was the red Toyota three-quarter-ton pickup sighted near the van driven by the four American Catholic workers on the night they were killed in 1980. There were, in the late spring and summer of 1982, the three Toyota panel trucks, one yellow, one blue, and one green, none bearing plates, reported present at each of the mass detentions (a "detention" is another fixed feature of local life, and often precedes a "disappearance") in the Amatepec district of San Salvador. These are the details—the models and colors of armored vehicles, the makes and calibers of weapons, the particular methods of dismemberment and decapitation used in particular instances—on which the visitor to Salvador learns immediately to concentrate, to the exclusion of past or future concerns, as in a prolonged amnesiac fugue.

Terror is the given of the place. Black-and-white police cars cruise in pairs, each with the barrel of a rifle extruding from an open window. Roadblocks materialize at random, soldiers fanning out from trucks and taking positions, fingers always on triggers, safeties clicking on and off. Aim is taken as if to pass the time. Every morning *El Diario de Hoy* and *La Prensa Gráfica* carry cautionary stories. *"Una madre y sus dos hijos fueron asesinados con arma cortante (corvo) por ocho sujetos desconocidos el lunes en la noche"*: A mother and her two sons hacked to death in their beds by eight *desconocidos*, unknown men. The same morning's paper: the unidentified body of a young man, strangled, found on the shoulder of a road. Same morning, different story: the unidentified bodies of three young men, found on another road, their faces partially destroyed by bayonets, one faced carved to represent a cross.

It is largely from these reports in the newspapers that the United States embassy compiles its body counts, which are transmitted to Washington in a weekly dispatch referred to by embassy people as "the grimgram." These counts are presented in a kind of tortured code that fails to obscure what is taken for granted in El Salvador, that government forces do most of the killing. In a January 15 1982 memo to Washington, for example, the embassy issued a "guarded" breakdown on its count of 6,909 "reported" political murders between September 16 1980 and September 15 1981. Of these 6,909, according to the memo, 922 were "believed committed by security forces," 952 "believed committed by leftist terrorists," 136 "believed committed by rightist terrorists," and 4,889 "committed by unknown assailants," the famous *desconocidos* favored by those San Salvador newspapers still publishing. (The figures actually add up not to 6,909 but to 6,899, leaving ten in a kind of official limbo.) The memo continued:

> "The uncertainty involved here can be seen in the fact that responsibility cannot be fixed in the majority of cases. We note, however, that it is generally believed in El Salvador that a large number of the unexplained killings are carried out by the security forces, officially or unofficially. The Embassy is aware of dramatic claims that have been made by one interest group or another in which the security forces figure as the primary agents of murder here. El Salvador's tangled web of attack and vengeance, traditional criminal violence and political mayhem make this an impossible charge to sustain. In saying this, however, we make no attempt to lighten the responsibility for the deaths of many hundreds, and perhaps thousands, which can be attributed to the security forces. . . ."

The body count kept by what is generally referred to in San Salvador as "the Human Rights Commission" is higher than the embassy's, and documented periodically by a photographer who goes out looking for bodies. These bodies he photographs are often broken into unnatural positions, and the faces to which the bodies are attached (when they are attached) are equally unnatural, sometimes unrecognizable as human faces, obliterated by acid or beaten to a mash of misplaced ears and teeth or slashed ear to ear and invaded by insects. *"Encontrado en Antiguo Cuscatlán el día 25 de Marzo 1982: camisón de dormir celeste,"* the typed caption reads on one photograph: found in Antiguo Cuscatlán March 25 1982 wearing a sky-blue nightshirt. The captions are laconic. Found in Soyapango May 21 1982. Found in Mejicanos June 11 1982. Found at El Playón May 30 1982, white shirt, purple pants, black shoes.

The photograph accompanying that last caption shows a body with no eyes, because the vultures got to it before the photographer did. There is a special kind of practical information that the visitor to El Salvador acquires immediately, the way visitors to other places acquire information about the currency rates, the hours for the museums. In El Salvador one learns that vultures go first for the soft tissue, for the eyes, the exposed genitalia, the open mouth. One learns that an open mouth can be used to make a specific point, can be stuffed with something emblematic; stuffed, say, with a penis, or, if the point has to do with land title, stuffed with some of the dirt in question. One learns that hair deteriorates less rapidly than flesh, and that a skull surrounded by a perfect corona of hair is a not uncommon sight in the body dumps.

All forensic photographs induce in the viewer a certain protective numbness, but dissociation is more difficult here. In the first place these are not, technically, "forensic" photographs, since the evidence they document will never be presented in a court of law. In the second place the disfigurement is too routine. The locations are too near, the dates too recent. There is the presence of the relatives of the disappeared: the women who sit every day in this cramped office on the grounds of the archdiocese, waiting to look at the spiral-bound photo albums in which the photographs are kept. These albums have plastic covers bearing soft-focus color photographs of young Americans in dating situations (strolling through autumn foliage on one album, recumbent in a field of daisies on another), and the women, looking for the bodies of their husbands and brothers and sisters and children, pass them from hand to hand without comment or expression.

> One of the more shadowy elements of the violent scene here [is] the death squad. Existence of these groups has long been disputed, but not by many Salvadorans. . . . Who constitutes the death squads is yet another difficult question. We do not believe that these squads exist as permanent formations but rather as ad hoc vigilante groups that coalesce according to perceived need. Membership is also uncertain, but in addition to civilians we believe that both on- and off-duty members of the security forces are participants. This was unofficially confirmed by right-wing spokesman Maj. Roberto D'Aubuisson who stated in an interview in early 1981 that security force members utilize the guise of the death squad when a potentially embarrassing or odious task needs to be performed.
>
> *—From the confidential but later*
> *declassified January 15, 1982 memo*
> *previously cited, drafted for the State*
> *Department by the political section at the*
> *embassy in San Salvador.*

The dead and pieces of the dead turn up in El Salvador everywhere, every day, as taken for granted as in a nightmare, or a horror movie. Vultures of course suggest the presence of a body. A knot of children on the street suggests the presence of a body. Bodies turn up in the brush of vacant lots, in the garbage thrown down ravines in the richest districts, in public rest rooms, in bus stations. Some are dropped in Lake Ilopango, a few miles east of the city, and wash up near the lakeside cottages and clubs frequented by what remains in San Salvador of the sporting bourgeoisie. Some still turn up at El Playón, the lunar lava field of rotting human flesh visible at one time or another on every television screen in America but characterized in June of 1982 in the *El Salvador News Gazette,* an English-language weekly edited by an American named Mario Rosenthal, as an "uncorroborated story . . . dredged up from the files of leftist propaganda." Others turn up at Puerta del Diablo, above Parque Balboa, a national *Turicentro* described as recently as the April–July 1982 issue of *Aboard TACA,* the magazine provided passengers on the national airline of El Salvador, as "offering excellent subjects for color photography."

I drove up to Puerta del Diablo one morning in June of 1982, past the Casa Presidencial and the camouflaged watch towers and heavy concentrations of troops and arms south of town, on up a narrow road narrowed further by landslides and deep crevices in the roadbed, a drive so insistently premonitory that after a while I began to hope that I would pass Puerta del Diablo without knowing it, just miss it, write it off, turn around and go back. There was however no way of missing it. Puerta del Diablo is a "view site" in an older and distinctly literary tradition, nature as lesson, an immense cleft rock through which half of El Salvador seems framed, a site so romantic and "mystical," so theatrically sacrificial in aspect, that it might be a cosmic parody of nineteenth-century landscape painting. The place presents itself as pathetic fallacy: the sky "broods," the stones "weep," a constant seepage of water weighting the ferns and moss. The foliage is thick and slick with moisture. The only sound is a steady buzz, I believe of cicadas.

Body dumps are seen in El Salvador as a kind of visitors' must-do, difficult but worth the detour. "Of course you have seen El Playón," an aide to President Alvaro Magaña said to me one day, and proceeded to discuss the site geologically, as evidence of the country's geothermal resources. He made no mention of the bodies. I was unsure if he was sounding me out or simply found the geothermal aspect of overriding interest. One difference between El Playón and Puerta del Diablo is that most bodies at El Playón appear to have been killed somewhere else, and then dumped; at Puerta del Diablo the executions are believed to occur in place, at the top, and the bodies thrown over. Sometimes reporters will speak of wanting to spend the night at Puerta del Diablo, in order to document the actual execution, but at the time I was in Salvador no one had.

The aftermath, the daylight aspect, is well documented. "Nothing fresh today, I hear," an embassy officer said when I mentioned that I had visited Puerta del Diablo. "Were there any on top?" someone else asked. "There were supposed to have been three on top yesterday." The point about whether or not there had been any on top was that usually it was necessary to go down to see bodies. The way down is hard. Slabs of stone, slippery with moss, are set into the vertiginous cliff, and it is down this cliff that one begins the descent to the bodies, or what is left of the bodies, pecked and maggoty masses of flesh, bone, hair. On some days there have been helicopters circling, tracking those making the descent. Other days there have been militia at the top, in the clearing where the road seems to run out, but on the morning I was there the only people on top were a man and a woman and three small children, who played in the wet grass while the woman started and stopped a Toyota pickup. She appeared to be learning how to drive. She drove forward and then back toward the edge, apparently following the man's signals, over and over again.

We did not speak, and it was only later, down the mountain and back in the land of the provisionally living, that it occurred to me that there was a definite question about why a man and a woman might choose a well-known body dump for a driving lesson. This was one of a number of occasions, during the two weeks my husband and I spent in El Salvador, on which I came to understand, in a way I had not understood before, the exact mechanism of terror.

. . . .

During the week before I flew down to El Salvador a Salvadoran woman who works for my husband and me in Los Angeles gave me repeated instructions about what we must and must not do. We must not go out at night. We must stay off the street whenever possible. We must never ride in buses or taxis, never leave the capital, never imagine that our passports would protect us. We must not even consider the hotel a safe place: people were killed in hotels. She spoke with considerable vehemence, because two of her brothers had been killed in Salvador in August of 1981, in their beds. The throats of both brothers had been slashed. Her father had been cut but stayed alive. Her mother had been beaten. Twelve of her other relatives, aunts and uncles and cousins, had been taken from their houses one night the same August, and their bodies had been found some time later, in a ditch. I assured her that we would remember, we would be careful, we would in fact be so careful that we would probably (trying for a light touch) spend all our time in church.

She became still more agitated, and I realized that I had spoken as a *norte-americana*: churches had not been to this woman the neutral ground they had been to me. I must remember: Archbishop Romero killed saying mass in the chapel of the Divine Providence Hospital in San Salvador. I must remember: more than thirty people killed at Archbishop Romero's funeral in the Metropolitan Cathedral in San Salvador. I must remember: more than twenty people killed before that on the steps of the Metropolitan Cathedral. CBS had filmed it. It had been on television, the bodies jerking, those still alive crawling over the dead as they tried to get out of range. I must understand: the Church was dangerous.

I told her that I understood, that I knew all that, and I did, abstractly, but the specific meaning of the Church she knew eluded me until I was actually there, at the Metropolitan Cathedral in San Salvador, one afternoon when rain sluiced down its corrugated plastic windows and puddled around the supports of the Sony and Phillips billboards near the steps. The effect of the Metropolitan Cathedral is immediate, and entirely literary. This is the cathedral that the late Archbishop Oscar Arnulfo Romero refused to finish, on the premise that the work of the Church took precedence over its display, and the high walls of raw concrete bristle with structural rods, rusting now, staining the concrete, sticking out at wrenched and violent angles. The wiring is exposed. Fluorescent tubes hang askew. The great high altar is backed by warped plyboard. The cross on the altar is of bare incandescent bulbs, but the bulbs, that afternoon, were unlit: there was in fact no light at all on the main altar, no light on the cross, no light on the globe of the world that showed the northern American continent in gray and the southern in white; no light on the dove above the globe, *Salvador del Mundo.* In this vast brutalist space that was the cathedral, the unlit altar seemed to offer a single ineluctable message: at this time and in this place the light of the world could be construed as out, off, extinguished.

In many ways the Metropolitan Cathedral is an authentic piece of political art, a statement for El Salvador as *Guernica* was for Spain. It is quite devoid of sentimental relief. There are no decorative or architectural references to familiar parables, in fact no stories at all, not even the Stations of the Cross. On the afternoon I was there the flowers laid on the altar were dead. There were no traces of normal parish activity. The doors were open to the barricaded main steps, and down the steps there was a spill of red paint, lest anyone forget the blood shed there. Here and there on the cheap linoleum inside the cathedral there was what seemed to be actual blood, dried in spots, the kind of spots dropped by a slow hemorrhage, or by a woman who does not know or does not care that she is menstruating.

There were several women in the cathedral during the hour or so I spent there, a young woman with a baby, an older woman in house slippers, a few others, all in black. One of the women walked the aisles as if by compulsion, up and down, across and back, crooning loudly as she walked. Another knelt without moving at the tomb of Archbishop Romero in the right transept. "LOOR A MONSEÑOR ROMERO," the crude needlepoint tapestry by the tomb read, "Praise to Monsignor Romero from the Mothers of the Imprisoned, the Disappeared, and the Murdered," the *Comité de Madres y Familiares de Presos, Desaparecidos, y Asesinados Políticos de El Salvador.*

The tomb itself was covered with offerings and petitions, notes decorated with motifs cut from greeting cards and cartoons. I recall one with figures cut from a Bugs Bunny strip, and another with a pencil drawing of a baby in a crib. The baby in this drawing seemed to be receiving medication or fluid or blood intravenously, through the IV line shown on its wrist. I studied the notes for a while and then went back and looked again at the unlit altar, and at the red paint on the main steps, from which it was possible to see the guardsmen on the balcony of the National Palace hunching back to avoid the rain. Many Salvadorans are offended by the Metropolitan Cathedral, which is as it should be, because the place remains perhaps the only unambiguous political statement in El Salvador, a metaphorical bomb in the ultimate power station.

Considerations for Thinking and Writing

1. Compare the way Didion uses her personal experience in these essays with the ways Phyllis Rose and Alice Walker use theirs. Develop a set of terms to describe the differing manner each writer employs to bring her personal self into her written world.

2. Compare Didion's treatment of Georgia O'Keeffe with Adrienne Rich's approach to Emily Dickinson. How does each essay writer use the older, more famous artist to advance her own cause? Why do O'Keeffe and Dickinson appeal so strongly to Didion and Rich?

3. After reading Alice Walker's "Beauty" and Adrienne Rich's "What Does a Woman Need to Know?" consider how Walker and Rich would respond to Didion's "On Self-Respect." Would they like the essay? Dislike it? Explain.

4. In "Los Angeles Notebook" Didion makes an argument about how such external realities as weather affect our moods, our behavior, our lives. Using your own experience and the details in Didion's essay, develop an argument on the subject. Consider whether you agree with Didion that "to live with the Santa Ana is to accept, consciously or unconsciously, a deeply mechanistic view of human behavior."

5. In an essay not included among our selections in this book, "On Keeping a Notebook," Didion says that "the point of my keeping a notebook has never been, nor is it now, to have an accurate factual record of what I have been doing or thinking." Her instinct, as she explains it, is neither for reality nor for history. It is rather, she insists, a personal impulse—a desire to remember who she was at different points in her life, an urge to recall how things felt, what they seemed like then.

With these ideas in mind, do the following: Begin your own notebook or journal and keep it for at least a week, preferably for a month or longer. Try to make it a reacting notebook, a book of notes on your thoughts and feelings, your ideas and attitudes about the things you do, see, hear, read, and otherwise encounter.

6. Compare Didion's "On Self-Respect" with Cynthia Ozick's "On Excellence." Apply the perspectives of both Didion and Ozick to Nancy Mairs's views in "On Being a Cripple."

ANNIE DILLARD
(b. 1945)

Annie Dillard's is a fascinating and expansive imagination that takes wings from the natural world around us. She sees what we cannot see, or will not see, and by hook and by crook, she pulls us out into the open, into nature, where she instructs us about seeing with our eyes as well as our senses. A meditative observer, Dillard tells us what she sees around her as well as in her mind's eye; she lets us in on her most secret moments, moments when she's trying to see through pain and beauty to an unfathomable God, moments when she's squinting, trying to catch sight of the wind, moments when she breaks through, sees connections and experiences the sheer joy of living, of "opening a life and feeling it touch—with an electric hiss and cry— this speckled mineral sphere, our present world."

The range of Dillard's imagination is matched by the range of her writing: a collection of poems, *Tickets for a Prayer Wheel* (1974); works of philosophical speculation, *Holy the Firm* (1977), and of literary theory, *Living by Fiction* (1979); and most recently, two collections of essays, *Teaching a Stone to Talk* (1982) and *Encounters with Chinese Writers* (1984), and an autobiography, *An American Childhood* (1987). Her first book, *Pilgrim at Tinker Creek* (1974), was a best seller and won a Pulitzer Prize. Nowhere is the range of her prose more evident than in that book, where meditative, expansive passages become taut and poetic, where incantatory rhythms draw us spellbound beneath the roots of sycamore trees, where she entices us to join the dance of the universe.

In "Heaven and Earth in Jest," Dillard describes herself as an "explorer" and a "stalker"—both of the natural world and of the meanings locked within it. She searches in and through nature for transcendent truths, and her intense scrutiny of nature is fueled by a passion for meaning. To go with Dillard to Tinker Creek or to any of her other haunts is to go on a journey into the heartland. But it is also to go beyond the heartland into uncharted regions of the mind and the spirit. We find in the heartland and in those uncharted regions both terror and ecstasy. "Jest" gives us glimpses of Dillard's mind trying to fathom the unfathomable, trying to come to terms with a creator who could place pain and beauty in close proximity. Her speculations push us beyond simplicity: "It could be that God has not absconded but spread, as our vision and understanding of the universe have spread,

to a fabric of spirit and sense so grand and subtle, so powerful in a new way, that we can only feel blindly of its hem."

"On a Hill Far Away," from *Stone*, suggests her impatience with more simplistic, less courageous explorations into mysteries. The essay recounts Dillard's encounter with Christian witnesses, a mother and her son, who live just on the other side of Tinker Creek not so far distant from her own "anchor-hold"; but as her title suggests, the hill they live on seems much farther away, the hill with an "eight-foot aluminum cross" encircled by honeysuckle, announcing that CHRIST THE LORD IS OUR SALVATION. Talking to the boy across a barbed-wire fence, Dillard grows impatient but cannot leave him abruptly; she senses his loneliness, his need to hold her there. A year earlier she had also felt an uneasy sympathy with the boy's mother. They make her uncomfortable, and so she pulls away from the boy even as he tells his story about stepping on a snake while knee-deep in honeysuckle, turns back across the creek: "It was dark, it was cold, and I had a roast in the oven, lamb, and I don't like it too well done."

"The Deer at Providencia," also from *Stone*, gives us an unusual chance to see Dillard describing dispassionately the slow, painful death of a deer, an event that would seem to demand sympathy and compassion. In clear and transparent prose, she renders a report of her encounter with the deer and with the others who also witness the death. As she does so, she includes her own self-conscious reaction. We get to observe her observing the deer; we also get glimpses of the men who are watching her on the scene. Just as we think we have sized up this Dillard, she reverses the terms of the argument, offers a different view of the same woman from another room. She ends on a note of philosophical and theological speculation, shocking us with her piercing insight and her implied questions about God's mercy. It is a prose performance that makes us reconsider "Heaven and Earth in Jest."

The selections from *An American Childhood* give us glimpses of a younger Dillard as she breaks into consciousness, but they give us as well insight into the development of her meditative, speculative mind. These pieces, taut and clear rather than expansive and exploratory, record Dillard's early stalking. In "Football and Snowballs" she is caught up in boy's business, traveling as she is in the company of three young male friends with whom she plays football and baseball. On the day of this story, during the Christmas season, their sport is more appropriate for the season. They get caught pelting cars with snowballs, caught and chased all over the neighborhood. Thrilled, absolutely thrilled by the chase, wanting it to last forever, Dillard nevertheless learns a significant lesson about the chaser, an adult male: "It was an immense discovery, pounding into my hot head with every sliding, joyous step, that this ordinary adult evidently knew what I thought only children who trained at football knew: that you have to fling yourself at what you're doing, you have to point yourself, forget yourself, aim, dive." Not only that, such diving is joyous, compensatory, fulfilling. "If in that snowy backyard the driver of the black Buick had cut off our heads, Mikey's and mine, I would have died happy. . . ."

"Joy" shows a ten-year-old Dillard making other discoveries about the world's riches. In a very general sense she is learning about "joy in concentration," about "joy in effort." She discovers that "the world resisted effort to just the right degree, and yielded to it at last." But that is not the importance of this piece; the importance lies in the way Dillard chooses to show us how she learned these important lessons, how she tested the premise that "with faith all things are possible." She tested it by flying down Penn Avenue: "Just once I wanted a task that required all the joy I had." The man she meets during her flight doesn't understand what she is doing; the "linen-suited woman in her fif-ties" does: "The woman's smiling, deep glance seemed to read my own awareness from my face, so we passed on the sidewalk—a beautiful upright woman walking in her tan linen suit, a kid running and flapping her arms—we passed on the sidewalk with a look of accomplices who share a humor just beyond irony." It was a lesson against dignity, a lesson about the kinship between foolishness and freedom.

"Mother," a piece about an older Dillard, is a haunting tribute to the female mind making something contiguous out of the "discrete dots" of its daily life, a female mind suggestively akin to Virginia Woolf's. This older Dillard attempts a more mature leap of faith than that required for "flying," a leap of faith essential to sanity, a belief "that those apparently discrete dots of you were contiguous: that little earnest dot, so easily amused; that alien, angry adolescent; and this woman with loosening skin on bony hands, hands now fifteen years older than your mother's hands when you pinched their knuckle skin into mountain ridges on an end table. You must take it on faith that these severed places cohered, too . . . if only through the motion and shed molecules of the traveler." The way back through memory, Dillard claims, is finally lost to all of us. We can never go all the way back, but moments, exquisite moments, nevertheless remain. "And still [even in my present bewildering age] I break up through the skin of awareness a thousand times a day, as dolphins burst through seas, and dive again, and rise, and dive." Through yet another act of intellection, Dillard cinches up, faces the void, finds a pattern—a pattern, Woolf would say, behind the cotton wool of daily life.

These autobiographical pieces complement the other essays, show us the formative stages in the evolution of a mind so finely honed that it cuts through the veil to reveal the mysteries, a mind so restless that it continues to push into the darkness, a mind so inviting it compels us to get into the boat as Dillard rows us out into the "thick darkness" toward a different kind of light. With her we sense both terror and ecstasy.

The Deer at Providencia

There were four of us North Americans in the jungle, in the Ecuadorian jungle on the banks of the Napo River in the Amazon watershed. The other three North Americans were metropolitan men. We stayed in tents in one riverside village, and visited others. At the village called Providencia we saw a sight which moved us, and which shocked the men.

The first thing we saw when we climbed the riverbank to the village of Providencia was the deer. It was roped to a tree on the grass clearing near the thatch shelter where we would eat lunch.

The deer was small, about the size of a whitetail fawn, but apparently full-grown. It had a rope around its neck and three feet caught in the rope. Someone said that the dogs had caught it that morning and the villagers were going to cook and eat it that night.

This clearing lay at the edge of the little thatched-hut village. We could see the villagers going about their business, scattering feed corn for hens about their houses, and wandering down paths to the river to bathe. The village headman was our host; he stood beside us as we watched the deer struggle. Several village boys were interested in the deer; they formed part of the circle we made around it in the clearing. So also did four businessmen from Quito who were attempting to guide us around the jungle. Few of the very different people standing in this circle had a common language. We watched the deer, and no one said much.

The deer lay on its side at the rope's very end, so the rope lacked slack to let it rest its head in the dust. It was "pretty," delicate of bone like all deer, and thin-skinned for the tropics. Its skin looked virtually hairless, in fact, and almost translucent, like a membrane. Its neck was no thicker than my wrist; it was rubbed open on the rope, and gashed. Trying to paw itself free of the rope, the deer had scratched its own neck with its hooves. The raw underside of its neck showed red stripes and some bruises bleeding inside the muscles. Now three of its feet were hooked in the rope under its jaw. It could not stand, of course, on one leg, so it could not move to slacken the rope and ease the pull on its throat and enable it to rest its head.

Repeatedly the deer paused, motionless, its eyes veiled, with only its rib cage in motion, and its breaths the only sound. Then, after I would think, "It has given up; now it will die," it would heave. The rope twanged; the tree leaves clattered; the deer's free foot beat the ground. We stepped back and held our breaths. It thrashed, kicking, but only one leg moved; the other three legs tightened inside the rope's loop. Its hip jerked; its spine shook. Its eyes rolled; its tongue, thick with spittle, pushed in and out. Then it would rest again. We watched this for fifteen minutes.

Once three young native boys charged in, released its trapped legs, and jumped back to the circle of people. But instantly the deer scratched up its neck with its hooves and snared its forelegs in the rope again. It was easy to imagine a third and then a fourth leg soon stuck, like Brer Rabbit and the Tar Baby.

We watched the deer from the circle, and then we drifted on to lunch. Our palm-roofed shelter stood on a grassy promontory from which we could see the deer tied to the tree, pigs and hens walking under village houses, and black-and-white cattle standing in the river. There was even a breeze.

Lunch, which was the second and better lunch we had that day, was hot and fried. There was a big fish called *doncella,* a kind of catfish, dipped whole in corn flour and beaten egg, then deep fried. With our fingers we pulled soft fragments of it from its sides to our plates, and ate; it was delicate fish-flesh, fresh and mild. Someone found the roe, and I ate of that too—it was fat and stronger, like egg yolk, naturally enough, and warm.

There was also a stew of meat in shreds with rice and pale brown gravy. I had asked what kind of deer it was tied to the tree; Pepe had answered in Spanish, *"Gama."* Now they told us this was *gama* too, stewed. I suspect the word means merely game or venison. At any rate, I heard that the village dogs had cornered another deer just yesterday, and it was this deer which we were now eating in full sight of the whole article. It was good. I was surprised at its tenderness. But it is a fact that high levels of lactic acid, which builds up in muscle tissues during exertion, tenderizes.

After the fish and meat we ate bananas fried in chunks and served on a tray; they were sweet and full of flavor. I felt terrific. My shirt was wet and cool from swimming; I had had a night's sleep, two decent walks, three meals, and a swim— everything tasted good. From time to time each one of us, separately, would look beyond our shaded roof to the sunny spot where the deer was still convulsing in the dust. Our meal completed, we walked around the deer and back to the boats.

That night I learned that while we were watching the deer, the others were watching me.

We four North Americans grew close in the jungle in a way that was not the usual artificial intimacy of travelers. We liked each other. We stayed up all that night talking, murmuring, as though we rocked on hammocks slung above time. The others were from big cities: New York, Washington, Boston. They all said that I had no expression on my face when I was watching the deer—or at any rate, not the expression they expected.

They had looked to see how I, the only woman, and the youngest, was taking the sight of the deer's struggles. I looked detached, apparently, or hard, or calm, or focused, still. I don't know. I was thinking. I remember feeling very old and energetic. I could say like Thoreau that I have traveled widely in Roanoke, Virginia. I have thought a great deal about carnivorousness; I eat meat. These things are not issues; they are mysteries.

Gentlemen of the city, what surprises you? That there is suffering here, or that I know it?

We lay in the tent and talked. "If it had been my wife," one man said with special vigor, amazed, "she wouldn't have cared *what* was going on; she would have dropped *everything* right at that moment and gone in the village from here to there to there, she would not have *stopped* until that animal was out of its suffering one way or another. She couldn't *bear* to see a creature in agony like that."

I nodded.

Now I am home. When I wake I comb my hair before the mirror above my dresser. Every morning for the past two years I have seen in that mirror, beside my sleep-softened face, the blackened face of a burnt man. It is a wire-service photograph clipped from a newspaper and taped to my mirror. The caption reads: "Alan McDonald in Miami hospital bed." All you can see in the photograph is a smudged triangle of face from his eyelids to his lower lip; the rest is bandages. You cannot see the expression in his eyes; the bandages shade them.

The story, headed MAN BURNED FOR SECOND TIME, begins:

"Why does God hate me?" Alan McDonald asked from his hospital bed.

"When the gunpowder went off, I couldn't believe it," he said. "I just couldn't believe it. I said, 'No, God couldn't do this to me again.'"

He was in a burn ward in Miami, in serious condition. I do not even know if he lived. I wrote him a letter at the time, cringing.

He had been burned before, thirteen years previously, by flaming gasoline. For years he had been having his body restored and his face remade in dozens of operations. He had been a boy, and then a burnt boy. He had already been stunned by what could happen, by how life could veer.

Once I read that people who survive bad burns tend to go crazy; they have a very high suicide rate. Medicine cannot ease their pain; drugs just leak away, soaking the sheets, because there is no skin to hold them in. The people just lie there and weep. Later they kill themselves. They had not known, before they were burned, that the world included such suffering, that life could permit them personally such pain.

This time a bowl of gunpowder had exploded on McDonald.

"I didn't realize what had happened at first," he recounted. "And then I heard that sound from 13 years ago. I was burning. I rolled to put the fire out and I thought, 'Oh God, not again.'

"If my friend hadn't been there, I would have jumped into a canal with a rock around my neck."

His wife concludes the piece, "Man, it just isn't fair."

* * *

I read the whole clipping again every morning. This is the Big Time here; every minute of it. Will someone please explain to Alan McDonald in his dignity, to the deer at Providencia in his dignity, what is going on? And mail me the carbon.

When we walked by the deer at Providencia for the last time, I said to Pepe, with a pitying glance at the deer, *"Pobrecito"*—"poor little thing." But I was trying out Spanish. I knew at the time it was a ridiculous thing to say.

On a Hill Far Away

In Virginia, late one January afternoon while I had a leg of lamb in the oven, I took a short walk. The idea was to exercise my limbs and rest my mind, but these things rarely work out as I plan.

It was sunset by the time I crossed Tinker Creek by hopping from stone to stone and inching up a fallen tree trunk to the bank. On the far side of the creek I followed a barbed-wire fence through steers' pasture and up to a high grassy hill. I'd never been there before. From the hill the distant creek looked still and loaded with sky.

On the hilltop, just across the barbed-wire fence, were three outbuildings: a fenced horse barn, around which a dun mare and a new foal were nervously clattering; a cyclone-fenced dog pen with a barking shepherd and a barking bird dog; and a frame toolshed under whose weedy eaves a little boy was pretending to write with a stone.

The little boy didn't see me. He looked to be about eight, thin, wearing a brown corduroy jacket with darker brown pile on the collar and a matching beaked corduroy cap with big earflaps. He alternated between pretending to write big letters on the toolshed wall and fooling with the dogs from outside their pen. The dogs were going crazy at their fence because of me, and I wondered why the boy didn't turn around; he must be too little to know much about dogs. When he did see me, by accident, his eyebrows shot up. I smiled and hollered and he came over to the barbed wire.

We watched the horses. "How old's the foal?" I asked him. The golden foal looked like a test model in a patent office—jerky, its eyes not set quite right, a marvel. It ran to keep from falling.

"That one is just one. You'd have to say he was *one*. . . ."

Boy, I thought. I sure don't know anything about horses.

". . . he was just *born* six days ago."

The foal wanted to approach. Every time it looked at us, the mare ran interference and edged the foal away.

The boy and I talked over the barbed wire. The dogs' names were Barney and Duke. "Luke?" I said. The boy was shocked. "Duke," he said. He was formal and articulate; he spoke in whole sentences, choosing his words. "I haven't yet settled on a name for the foal, although Father says he is mine." When he spoke this way, he gazed up at me through meeting eyebrows. His dark lips made a projecting circle.

He looked like a nineteenth-century cartoon of an Earnest Child. This kid is a fraud, I thought. Who calls his father "Father"? But at other times his face would loosen; I could see then that the accustomed gesture of his lips resembled that of a person trying not to cry. Or he would smile, or look away shyly, like now: "Actually, I've been considering the name Marky Sparky."

"Marky Sparky," I repeated, with as much warmth as I could muster. The sun was down. What was I doing chatting with a little kid? Wasn't there something I should be reading?

Then he paused. He looked miserably at his shoetops, and I looked at his brown corduroy cap. Suddenly the cap lifted, and the little face said in a rush, "Do you know the Lord as your personal savior?"

"Not only that," I said, "I know your mother."

It all came together. She had asked me the same question.

Until then I had not connected this land, these horses, and this little boy with the woman in the big house at the top of the hill, the house I'd approached from the other direction, to ask permission to walk the land. That was about a year ago. There had been a very long driveway from the highway on the other side of the hill. The driveway made a circle in front of the house, and in the circle stood an eight-foot aluminum cross with a sign underneath it reading CHRIST THE LORD IS OUR SALVA- TION. Spotlights in the circle's honeysuckle were trained up at the cross and the sign. I rang the bell.

The woman was very nervous. She was dark, pretty, hard, with the same trembling lashes as the boy. She wore a black dress and one brush roller in the front of her hair. She did not ask me in.

My explanation of myself confused her, but she gave permission. Yes, I could walk their property. (She did not add, as others have, "But I don't want no kids in here roughhousing.") She did not let me go; she was worried about something else. She worked her hands. I waited on the other side of the screen door until she came out with it:

"Do you know the Lord as your personal savior?"

My heart went out to her. No wonder she had been so nervous. She must have to ask this of everyone, absolutely everyone, she meets. That is Christian witness. It makes sense, given its premises. I wanted to make her as happy as possible, reward her courage, and run.

She was stunned that I knew the Lord, and clearly uncertain whether we were referring to the same third party. But she had done her bit, bumped over the hump, and now she could relax. She told me about her church, her face brightening. She was part of the Reverend Jerry Falwell's congregation. He is the powerful evangelist in Lynchburg, Virginia, who has recently taken to politics. She drove, I inferred, 120 miles round trip to go to church. While I waited behind the screen door she fetched pamphlets, each a different color. I thanked her kindly; I read them later. The one on the Holy Spirit I thought was good.

So this was her son. She had done a good job. He was a nice little kid. He was glad now his required speech was over; he was glad that I was talking easily, telling about meeting his mother. That I had met her seemed to authenticate me to him and dissolve some wariness.

The wind that follows sunset was blowing from the western ridge, across our hill and down. There had been ice in the creek. The boy moved closer to the barbed-wire fence; he jammed his fists in his pockets. Whenever I smiled or laughed he looked at me disbelieving, and lifted his eyes from beneath his cap's bill again and again to my face.

He never played at the creek, he said. Because he might be down there, and Father might come home not knowing he was there, and let all the horses out, and the horses would trample him. I had noticed that he quailed whenever the mare in her pen jerked his way.

Also there were snakes down there—water moccasins, he said. He seemed tired, old even, weary with longings, solemn. Caution passes for wisdom around here, and this kid knew all the pitfalls. In fact, there are no water moccasins this far north, except out on the coast, but there are some copperheads; I let it go. "They won't hurt you," I said. "I play at the creek," I said. "Lots." How old are you? Eight? Nine? How could you not play at the creek? Or: Why am I trying to force this child to play at the creek? What do I do there alone that he'd want to do? What do I do there at all?

The distant creek looked like ice from the hill, lightless and unmoving. The bare branches of sycamores on its banks met soundlessly. When was spring coming? The sky was purpling. Why would anyone in his right mind play at the creek?

"You're cold," I said to the boy. His lips were blue. He tried to keep his corduroy shoulders against his bare neck. He pretended not to hear. "I have to go," I said.

"Do you know how to catch a fish when you haven't got a rod, or a line, or a hook?" He was smiling, warming up for a little dialect, being a kid in a book. He must read a lot. "First, you get you a *stick*. . . ." He explained what sort of stick. "Then you pull you a thread of honey-suckle . . . and if you need you a *hook* . . ."

We talked about fishing. "I've got a roast in the oven," I said. "I've got to go." He had to go too; Father would be home, and the boy had to set the table for dinner. His mother was fasting. I said so long, so long, and turned. He called, "One more thing!" I looked back; he hesitated a second and began loudly, "Did you ever step on a big old snake?"

All right, then. I thanked God for the sisters and friends I had had when I was little; I have not been lonely yet, but it could come at any time. I pulled my jacket collar up as high as I could.

He described stepping on the snake; he rolled his eyes and tried to stir me. "I felt it just . . . *move* under my foot. It was so . . . *slimy*. . . ." I bided my time. His teeth were chattering. "We were walking through the field beneath the cemetery. I called, 'Wait, Father, wait!' I couldn't lift my foot." I wondered what they let him read; he spoke in prose, like *le bourgeois gentilhomme*.

"Gee," I kept saying, "you must have been scared."

"Well, I was *about* knee-deep in honeysuckle."

Oh! That was different. Probably he really *had* stepped on a snake. I would have been plenty scared myself, knee-deep in honeysuckle, but there was no way now to respond to his story all over again, identically but sincerely. Still, it was time to go. It was dark. The mare had nosed her golden foal into the barn. The creek below held a frail color still, the memory of a light that hadn't yet been snuffed.

We parted sadly, over the barbed-wire fence. The boy lowered his enormous, lighted eyes, lifted his shoulders, and went into a classic trudge. He had tried again to keep me there. But I simply had to go. It was dark, it was cold, and I had a roast in the oven, lamb, and I don't like it too well done.

Heaven and Earth in Jest

I used to have a cat, an old fighting tom, who would jump through the open window by my bed in the middle of the night and land on my chest. I'd half-awaken. He'd stick his skull under my nose and purr, stinking of urine and blood. Some nights he kneaded my bare chest with his front paws, powerfully, arching his back, as if sharpening his claws, or pummeling a mother for milk. And some mornings I'd wake in daylight to find my body covered with paw prints in blood; I looked as though I'd been painted with roses.

It was hot, so hot the mirror felt warm. I washed before the mirror in a daze, my twisted summer sleep still hung about me like sea kelp. What blood was this, and what roses? It could have been the rose of union, the blood of murder, or the rose of beauty bare and the blood of some unspeakable sacrifice or birth. The sign on my body could have been an emblem or a stain, the keys to the kingdom or the mark of Cain. I never knew. I never knew as I washed, and the blood streaked, faded, and finally disappeared, whether I'd purified myself or ruined the blood sign of the passover. We wake, if we ever wake at all, to mystery, rumors of death, beauty, violence. . . . "Seem like we're just set down here," a woman said to me recently, "and don't nobody know why."

These are morning matters, pictures you dream as the final wave heaves you up on the sand to the bright light and drying air. You remember pressure, and a curved sleep you rested against, soft, like a scallop in its shell. But the air hardens your skin; you stand; you leave the lighted shore to explore some dim headland, and soon you're lost in the leafy interior, intent, remembering nothing.

I still think of that old tomcat, mornings, when I wake. Things are tamer now; I sleep with the window shut. The cat and our rites are gone and my life is changed, but the memory remains of something powerful playing over me. I wake expectant, hoping to see a new thing. If I'm lucky I might be jogged awake by a strange birdcall. I dress in a hurry, imagining the yard flapping with auks, or flamingos. This morning it was a wood duck, down at the creek. It flew away.

I live by a creek, Tinker Creek, in a valley in Virginia's Blue Ridge. An anchorite's hermitage is called an anchor-hold; some anchor-holds were simple sheds clamped to the side of a church like a barnacle to a rock. I think of this house clamped to the side of Tinker Creek as an anchor-hold. It holds me at anchor to the rock bottom of the creek itself and it keeps me steadied in the current, as a sea anchor does, facing the stream of light pouring down. It's a good place to live; there's a lot to think about. The creeks—Tinker and Carvin's—are an active mystery, fresh every minute. Theirs is the mystery of the continuous creation and all that providence implies: the uncertainty of vision, the horror of the fixed, the dissolution of the present, the intricacy of beauty, the pressure of fecundity, the elusiveness of the free, and the flawed nature of perfection. The mountains— Tinker and Brushy, McAfee's Knob and Dead Man—are a passive mystery, the oldest of all. Theirs is the one simple mystery of creation from nothing, of matter itself, anything at all, the given. Mountains are giant, restful, absorbent. You can heave your spirit into a mountain and the mountain will keep it, folded, and not throw it back as some creeks will. The creeks are the world with all its stimulus and beauty; I live there. But the mountains are home.

The wood duck flew away. I caught only a glimpse of something like a bright torpedo that blasted the leaves where it flew. Back at the house I ate a bowl of oatmeal; much later in the day came the long slant of light that means good walking.

If the day is fine, any walk will do; it all looks good. Water in particular looks its best, reflecting blue sky in the flat, and chopping it into graveled shallows and white chute and foam in the riffles. On a dark day, or a hazy one, everything's washed-out and lackluster but the water. It carries its own lights. I set out for the railroad tracks, for the hill the flocks fly over, for the woods where the white mare lives. But I go to the water.

Today is one of those excellent January partly cloudies in which light chooses an unexpected part of the landscape to trick out in gilt, and then shadow sweeps it away. You know you're alive. You take huge steps, trying to feel the planet's roundness arc between your feet. Kazantzakis says that when he was young he had a canary and a globe. When he freed the canary, it would perch on the globe and sing. All his life, wandering the earth, he felt as though he had a canary on top of his mind, singing.

West of the house, Tinker Creek makes a sharp loop, so that the creek is both in back of the house, south of me, and also on the other side of the road, north of me. I like to go north. There the afternoon sun hits the creek just right, deepening the reflected blue and lighting the sides of trees on the banks. Steers from the pasture across the creek come down to drink; I always flush a rabbit or two there; I sit on a fallen trunk in the shade and watch the squirrels in the sun. There are two separated wooden fences suspended from cables that cross the creek just upstream from my tree-trunk bench. They keep the steers from escaping up or down the creek when they come to drink. Squirrels, the neighborhood children, and I use the downstream fence as a swaying bridge across the creek. But the steers are there today.

I sit on the downed tree and watch the black steers slip on the creek bottom. They are all bred beef: beef heart, beef hide, beef hocks. They're a human product like rayon. They're like a field of shoes. They have cast-iron shanks and tongues like foam insoles. You can't see through to their brains as you can with other animals; they have beef fat behind their eyes, beef stew.

I cross the fence six feet above the water, walking my hands down the rusty cable and tightroping my feet along the narrow edge of the planks. When I hit the other bank and terra firma, some steers are bunched in a knot between me and the barbed-wire fence I want to cross. So I suddenly rush at them in an enthusiastic sprint, flailing my arms and hollering, "Lightning! Copperhead! Swedish meatballs!" They flee, still in a knot, stumbling across the flat pasture. I stand with the wind on my face.

When I slide under a barbed-wire fence, cross a field, and run over a sycamore trunk felled across the water, I'm on a little island shaped like a tear in the middle of Tinker Creek. On one side of the creek is a steep forested bank; the water is swift and deep on that side of the island. On the other side is the level field I walked through next to the steers' pasture; the water between the field and the island is shallow and sluggish. In summer's low water, flags and bulrushes grow along a series of shallow pools cooled by the lazy current. Water striders patrol the surface film, crayfish hump along the silt bottom eating filth, frogs shout and glare, and shiners and small bream hide among roots from the sulky green heron's eye. I come to this island every month of the year. I walk around it, stopping and staring, or I straddle the sycamore log over the creek, curling my legs out of the water in winter, trying to read. Today I sit on dry grass at the end of the island by the slower side of the creek. I'm drawn to this spot. I come to it as to an oracle; I return to it as a man years later will seek out the battlefield where he lost a leg or an arm.

A couple of summers ago I was walking along the edge of the island to see what I could see in the water, and mainly to scare frogs. Frogs have an inelegant way of taking off from invisible positions on the bank just ahead of your feet, in dire panic, emitting a froggy "Yike!" and splashing into the water. Incredibly, this amused me, and, incredibly, it amuses me still. As I walked along the grassy edge of the island, I got better and better at seeing frogs both in and out of the water. I learned to recognize, slowing down, the difference in texture of the light reflected from mud-bank, water, grass, or frog. Frogs were flying all around me. At the end of the island I noticed a small green frog. He was exactly half in and half out of the water, looking like a schematic diagram of an amphibian, and he didn't jump.

He didn't jump; I crept closer. At last I knelt on the island's winterkilled grass, lost, dumbstruck, staring at the frog in the creek just four feet away. He was a very small frog with wide, dull eyes. And just as I looked at him, he slowly crumpled and began to sag. The spirit vanished from his eyes as if snuffed. His skin emptied and drooped; his very skull seemed to collapse and settle like a kicked tent. He was shrinking before my eyes like a deflating football. I watched the taut, glistening skin on his shoulders ruck, and rumple, and fall. Soon, part of his skin, formless as a pricked balloon, lay in floating folds like bright scum on top of the water: it was a monstrous and terrifying thing. I gaped bewildered, appalled. An oval shadow hung in the water behind the drained frog; then the shadow glided away. The frog skin bag started to sink.

I had read about the giant water bug, but never seen one. "Giant water bug" is really the name of the creature, which is an enormous, heavy-bodied brown beetle. It eats insects, tadpoles, fish, and frogs. Its grasping forelegs are mighty and hooked inward. It seizes a victim with these legs, hugs it tight, and paralyzes it with enzymes injected during a vicious bite. That one bite is the only bite it ever takes. Through the puncture shoot the poisons that dissolve the victim's muscles and bones and organs—all but the skin—and through it the giant water bug sucks out the victim's body, reduced to a juice. This event is quite common in warm fresh water. The frog

I saw was being sucked by a giant water bug. I had been kneeling on the island grass; when the unrecognizable flap of frog skin settled on the creek bottom, swaying, I stood up and brushed the knees of my pants. I couldn't catch my breath.

Of course, many carnivorous animals devour their prey alive. The usual method seems to be to subdue the victim by downing or grasping it so it can't flee, then eating it whole or in a series of bloody bites. Frogs eat everything whole, stuffing prey into their mouths with their thumbs. People have seen frogs with their wide jaws so full of live dragonflies they couldn't close them. Ants don't even have to catch their prey: in the spring they swarm over newly hatched, featherless birds in the nest and eat them tiny bite by bite.

That it's rough out there and chancy is no surprise. Every live thing is a survivor on a kind of extended emergency bivouac. But at the same time we are also created. In the Koran, Allah asks, "The heaven and the earth and all in between, thinkest thou I made them *in jest?*" It's a good question. What do we think of the created universe, spanning an unthinkable void with an unthinkable profusion of forms? Or what do we think of nothingness, those sickening reaches of time in either direction? If the giant water bug was not made in jest, was it then made in earnest? Pascal uses a nice term to describe the notion of the creator's, once having called forth the universe, turning his back to it: *Deus Absconditus.* Is this what we think happened? Was the sense of it there, and God absconded with it, ate it, like a wolf who disappears round the edge of the house with the Thanksgiving turkey? "God is subtle," Einstein said, "but not malicious." Again, Einstein said that "nature conceals her mystery by means of her essential grandeur, not by her cunning." It could be that God has not absconded but spread, as our vision and understanding of the universe have spread, to a fabric of spirit and sense so grand and subtle, so powerful in a new way, that we can only feel blindly of its hem. In making the thick darkness a swaddling band for the sea, God "set bars and doors" and said, "Hitherto shalt thou come, but no further." But have we come even that far? Have we rowed out to the thick darkness, or are we all playing pinochle in the bottom of the boat?

Cruelty is a mystery, and the waste of pain. But if we describe a world to compass these things, a world that is a long, brute game, then we bump against another mystery: the inrush of power and light, the canary that sings on the skull. Unless all ages and races of men have been deluded by the same mass hypnotist (who?), there seems to be such a thing as beauty, a grace wholly gratuitous. About five years ago I saw a mockingbird make a straight vertical descent from the roof gutter of a four-story building. It was an act as careless and spontaneous as the curl of a stem or the kindling of a star.

The mockingbird took a single step into the air and dropped. His wings were still folded against his sides as though he were singing from a limb and not falling, accelerating thirty-two feet per second per second, through empty air. Just a breath before he would have been dashed to the ground, he unfurled his wings with exact, deliberate care, revealing the broad bars of white, spread his elegant, white-banded tail, and so floated onto the grass. I had just rounded a corner when his insouciant step caught my eye; there was no one else in sight. The fact of his free fall was like the old philosophical conundrum about the tree that falls in the forest. The answer must be, I think, that beauty and grace are performed whether or not we will or sense them. The least we can do is try to be there.

Another time I saw another wonder: sharks off the Atlantic coast of Florida. There is a way a wave rises above the ocean horizon, a triangular wedge against the sky. If you stand where the ocean breaks on a shallow beach, you see the raised water in a wave is translucent, shot with lights. One late afternoon at low tide a hundred big sharks passed the beach near the mouth of a tidal river in a feeding frenzy. As each green wave rose from the churning water, it illuminated within itself the six- or eight-foot-long bodies of twisting sharks. The sharks disappeared as each wave rolled toward me; then a new wave would swell above the horizon, containing in it, like scorpions in amber, sharks that roiled and heaved. The sight held awesome wonders: power and beauty, grace tangled in a rapture with violence.

We don't know what's going on here. If these tremendous events are random combinations of matter run amok, the yield of millions of monkeys at millions of typewriters, then what is it in us, hammered out of those same typewriters, that they ignite? We don't know. Our life is a faint tracing on the surface of mystery, like the idle, curved tunnels of leaf miners on the face of a leaf. We must somehow take a wider view, look at the whole landscape, really see it, and describe what's going on here. Then we can at least wail the right question into the swaddling band of darkness, or, if it comes to that, choir the proper praise.

At the time of Lewis and Clark, setting the prairies on fire was a well-known signal that meant, "Come down to the water." It was an extravagant gesture, but we can't do less. If the landscape reveals one certainty, it is that the extravagant gesture is the very stuff of creation. After the one extravagant gesture of creation in the first place, the universe has continued to deal exclusively in extravagances, flinging intricacies and colossi down aeons of emptiness, heaping profusions on profligacies with ever-fresh vigor. The whole show has been on fire from the word go. I come down to the water to cool my eyes. But everywhere I look I see fire; that which isn't flint is tinder, and the whole world sparks and flames.

I have come to the grassy island late in the day. The creek is up; icy water sweeps under the sycamore log bridge. The frog skin, of course, is utterly gone. I have stared at that one spot on the creek bottom for so long, focusing past the rush of water, that when I stand, the opposite bank seems to stretch before my eyes and flow grassily upstream. When the bank settles down I cross the sycamore log and enter again the big plowed field next to the steers' pasture.

The wind is terrific out of the west; the sun comes and goes. I can see the shadow on the field before me deepen uniformly and spread like a plague. Everything seems so dull I am amazed I can even distinguish objects. And suddenly the light runs across the land like a comber, and up the trees, and goes again in a wink: I think I've gone blind or died. When it comes again, the light, you hold your breath, and if it stays you forget about it until it goes again.

It's the most beautiful day of the year. At four o'clock the eastern sky is a dead stratus black flecked with low white clouds. The sun in the west illuminates the ground, the mountains, and especially the bare branches of trees, so that everywhere silver trees cut into the black sky like a photographer's negative of a landscape. The air and the ground are dry; the mountains are going on and off like neon signs. Clouds slide east as if pulled from the horizon, like a tablecloth whipped off a table. The hemlocks by the barbed-wire fence are flinging themselves east as though their backs would break. Purple shadows are racing east; the wind makes me face east, and again I feel the dizzying, drawn sensation I felt when the creek bank reeled.

At four-thirty the sky in the east is clear; how could that big blackness be blown? Fifteen minutes later another darkness is coming overhead from the northwest; and it's here. Everything is drained of its light as if sucked. Only at the horizon do inky black mountains give way to distant, lighted mountains—lighted not by direct illumination but rather paled by glowing sheets of mist hung before them. Now the blackness is in the east; everything is half in shadow, half in sun, every clod, tree, mountain, and hedge. I can't see Tinker Mountain through the line of hemlock, till it comes on like a streetlight, ping, *ex nihilo*. Its sandstone cliffs pink and swell. Suddenly the light goes; the cliffs recede as if pushed. The sun hits a clump of sycamores between me and the mountains; the sycamore arms light up, and *I can't see the cliffs*. They're gone. The pale network of sycamore arms, which a second ago was transparent as a screen, is suddenly opaque, glowing with light. Now the sycamore arms snuff out, the mountains come on, and there are the cliffs again.

I walk home. By five-thirty the show has pulled out. Nothing is left but an unreal blue and a few banked clouds low in the north. Some sort of carnival magician has been here, some fast-talking worker of wonders who has the act backwards. "Something in this hand," he says, "something in this hand, something up my sleeve, something behind my back . . ." and abracadabra, he snaps his fingers, and it's all gone. Only the bland, blank-faced magician remains, in his unruffled coat, bare-handed, acknowledging a smattering of baffled applause. When you look again the whole show has pulled up stakes and moved on down the road. It never stops. New shows roll in from over the mountains and the magician reappears unannounced from a fold in the curtain you never dreamed was an opening. Scarves of clouds, rabbits in plain view, disappear into the black hat forever. Presto chango. The audience, if there is an audience at all, is dizzy from head-turning, dazed.

Like the bear who went over the mountain, I went out to see what I could see. And, I might as well warn you, like the bear, all that I could see was the other side of the mountain: more of same. On a good day I might catch a glimpse of another wooded ridge rolling under the sun like water, another bivouac. I propose to keep here what Thoreau called "a meteorological journal of the mind," telling some tales and describing some of the sights of this rather tamed valley, and exploring, in fear and trembling, some of the unmapped dim reaches and unholy fastnesses to which those tales and sights so dizzyingly lead.

I am no scientist. I explore the neighborhood. An infant who has just learned to hold his head up has a frank and forthright way of gazing about him in bewilderment. He hasn't the faintest clue where he is, and he aims to learn. In a couple of years, what he will have learned instead is how to fake it: he'll have the cocksure air of a squatter who has come to feel he owns the place. Some unwonted, taught pride diverts us from our original intent, which is to explore the neighborhood, view the landscape, to discover at least *where* it is that we have been so startlingly set down, if we can't learn why.

So I think about the valley. It is my leisure as well as my work, a game. It is a fierce game I have joined because it is being played anyway, a game of both skill and chance, played against an unseen adversary—the conditions of time—in which the payoffs, which may suddenly arrive in a blast of light at any moment, might as well come to me as anyone else. I stake the time I'm grateful to have, the energies I'm glad to direct. I risk getting stuck on the board, so to speak, unable to move in any direction, which happens enough, God knows; and I risk the searing, exhausting nightmares that plunder rest and force me face down all night long in some muddy ditch seething with hatching insects and crustaceans.

But if I can bear the nights, the days are a pleasure. I walk out; I see something, some event that would otherwise have been utterly missed and lost; or something sees me, some enormous power brushes me with its clean wing, and I resound like a beaten bell.

I am an explorer, then, and I am also a stalker, or the instrument of the hunt itself. Certain Indians used to carve long grooves along the wooden shafts of their arrows. They called the grooves "lightning marks," because they resembled the curved fissure lightning slices down the trunks of trees. The function of lightning marks is this: if the arrow fails to kill the game, blood from a deep wound will channel along the lightning mark, streak down the arrow shaft, and spatter to the ground, laying a trail dripped on broadleaves, on stones, that the barefoot and trembling archer can follow into whatever deep or rare wilderness it leads. I am the arrow shaft, carved along my length by unexpected lights and gashes from the very sky, and this book is the straying trail of blood.

Something pummels us, something barely sheathed. Power broods and lights. We're played on like a pipe; our breath is not our own. James Houston describes two young Eskimo girls sitting cross-legged on the ground, mouth on mouth, blowing by turns each other's throat cords, making a low, unearthly music. When I cross again the bridge that is really the steers' fence, the wind has thinned to the delicate air of twilight; it crumples the water's skin. I watch the running sheets of light raised on the creek's surface. The sight has the appeal of the purely passive, like the racing of light under clouds on a field, the beautiful dream at the moment of being dreamed. The breeze is the merest puff, but you yourself sail headlong and breathless under the gale force of the spirit.

An American Childhood

Football and Snowballs

Some boys taught me to play football. This was fine sport. You thought up a new strategy for every play and whispered it to the others. You went out for a pass, fooling everyone. Best, you got to throw yourself mightily at someone's running legs. Either you brought him down or you hit the ground flat out on your chin, with your arms empty before you. It was all or nothing. If you hesitated in fear, you would miss and get hurt: you would take a hard fall while the kid got away, or you would get kicked in the face while the kid got away. But if you flung yourself wholeheartedly at the back of his knees—if you gathered and joined body and soul and pointed them diving fearlessly—then you likely wouldn't get hurt, and you'd stop the ball. Your fate, and your team's score, depended on your concentration and courage. Nothing girls did could compare with it.

Boys welcomed me at baseball, too, for I had, through enthusiastic practice, what was weirdly known as a boy's arm. In winter, in the snow, there was neither baseball nor football, so the boys and I threw snowballs at passing cars. I got in trouble throwing snowballs, and have seldom been happier since.

On one weekday morning after Christmas, six inches of new snow had just fallen. We were standing up to our boot tops in snow on a front yard on trafficked Reynolds Street, waiting for cars. The cars traveled Reynolds Street slowly and evenly; they were targets all but wrapped in red ribbons, cream puffs. We couldn't miss.

I was seven; the boys were eight, nine, and ten. The oldest two Fahey boys were there—Mikey and Peter—polite blond boys who lived near me on Lloyd Street, and who already had four brothers and sisters. My parents approved Mikey and Peter Fahey. Chickie McBride was there, a tough kid, and Billy Paul and Mackie Kean too, from across Reynolds, where the boys grew up dark and furious, grew up skinny, knowing, and skilled. We had all drifted from our houses that morning looking for action, and had found it here on Reynolds Street.

It was cloudy but cold. The cars' tires laid behind them on the snowy street a complex trail of beige chunks like crenellated castle walls. I had stepped on some earlier; they squeaked. We could have wished for more traffic. When a car came, we all popped it one. In the intervals between cars we reverted to the natural solitude of children.

I started making an iceball—a perfect iceball, from perfectly white snow, perfectly spherical, and squeezed perfectly translucent so no snow remained all the way through. (The Fahey boys and I considered it unfair actually to throw an iceball at somebody, but it had been known to happen.)

I had just embarked on the iceball project when we heard tire chains come clanking from afar. A black Buick was moving toward us down the street. We all spread out, banged together some regular snowballs, took aim, and, when the Buick drew nigh, fired.

A soft snowball hit the driver's windshield right before the driver's face. It made a smashed star with a hump in the middle.

Often, of course, we hit our target, but this time, the only time in all of life, the car pulled over and stopped. Its wide black door opened; a man got out of it, running. He didn't even close the car door.

He ran after us, and we ran away from him, up the snowy Reynolds sidewalk. At the corner, I looked back; incredibly, he was still after us. He was in city clothes: a suit and tie, street shoes. Any normal adult would have quit, having sprung us into flight and made his point. This man was gaining on us. He was a thin man, all action. All of a sudden, we were running for our lives.

Wordless, we split up. We were on our turf; we could lose ourselves in the neighborhood backyards, everyone for himself. I paused and considered. Everyone had vanished except Mikey Fahey, who was just rounding the corner of a yellow brick house. Poor Mikey, I trailed him. The driver of the Buick sensibly picked the two of us to follow. The man apparently had all day.

He chased Mikey and me around the yellow house and up a backyard path we knew by heart: under a low tree, up a bank, through a hedge, down some snowy steps, and across the grocery store's delivery driveway. We smashed through a gap in another hedge, entered a scruffy backyard and ran around its back porch and tight between houses to Edgerton Avenue; we ran across Edgerton to an alley and up our own sliding woodpile to the Halls' front yard; he kept coming. We ran up Lloyd Street and wound through mazy backyards toward the steep hilltop at Willard and Lang.

He chased us silently, block after block. He chased us silently over picket fences, through thorny hedges, between houses, around garbage cans, and across streets. Every time I glanced back, choking for breath, I expected he would have quit. He must have been as breathless as we were. His jacket strained over his body. It was an immense discovery, pounding into my hot head with every sliding, joyous step, that this ordinary adult evidently knew what I thought only children who trained at football knew: that you have to fling yourself at what you're doing, you have to point yourself, forget yourself, aim, dive.

Mikey and I had nowhere to go, in our own neighborhood or out of it, but away from this man who was chasing us. He impelled us forward; we compelled him to follow our route. The air was cold; every breath tore my throat. We kept running, block after block; we kept improvising, backyard after backyard, running a frantic course and choosing it simultaneously, failing always to find small places or hard places to slow him down, and discovering always, exhilarated, dismayed, that only bare speed could save us—for he would never give up, this man—and we were losing speed.

He chased us through the backyard labyrinths of ten blocks before he caught us by our jackets. He caught us and we all stopped.

We three stood staggering, half blinded, coughing, in an obscure hilltop backyard: a man in his twenties, a boy, a girl. He had released our jackets, our pursuer, our captor, our hero: he knew we weren't going anywhere. We all played by the rules. Mikey and I unzipped our jackets. I pulled off my sopping mittens. Our tracks multiplied in the backyard's new snow. We had been breaking new snow all morning. We didn't look at each other. I was cherishing my excitement. The man's lower pants legs were wet; his cuffs were full of snow, and there was a prow of snow beneath them on his shoes and socks. Some trees bordered the little flat backyard, some messy winter trees. There was no one around: a clearing in a grove, and we the only players.

It was a long time before he could speak. I had some difficulty at first recalling why we were there. My lips felt swollen; I couldn't see out of the sides of my eyes; I kept coughing.

"You stupid kids," he began perfunctorily.

We listened perfunctorily indeed, if we listened at all, for the chewing out was redundant, a mere formality, and beside the point. The point was that he had chased us passionately without giving up, and so he had caught us. Now he came down to earth. I wanted the glory to last forever.

But how could the glory have lasted forever? We could have run through every backyard in North America until we got to Panama. But when he trapped us at the lip of the Panama Canal, what precisely could he have done to prolong the drama of the chase and cap its glory? I brooded about this for the next few years. He could only have fried Mikey Fahey and me in boiling oil, say, or dismembered us piecemeal, or staked us to anthills. None of which I really wanted, and none of which any adult was likely to do, even in the spirit of fun. He could only chew us out there in the Panamanian jungle, after months or years of exalting pursuit. He could only begin, "You stupid kids," and continue in his ordinary Pittsburgh accent with his normal righteous anger and the usual common sense.

If in that snowy backyard the driver of the black Buick had cut off our heads, Mikey's and mine, I would have died happy, for nothing has required so much of me since as being chased all over Pittsburgh in the middle of winter—running terrified, exhausted—by this sainted, skinny, furious redheaded man who wished to have a word with us. I don't know how he found his way back to his car.

Joy

What can we make of the inexpressible joy of children? It is a kind of gratitude, I think—the gratitude of the ten-year-old who wakes to her own energy and the brisk challenge of the world. You thought you knew the place and all its routines, but you see you hadn't known. Whole stacks at the library held books devoted to things you knew nothing about. The boundary of knowledge receded, as you poked about in books, like Lake Erie's rim as you climbed its cliffs. And each area of knowledge disclosed another, and another. Knowledge wasn't a body, or a tree, but instead air, or space, or being—whatever pervaded, whatever never ended and fitted into the smallest cracks and the widest space between stars.

Any way you cut it, colors and shadows flickered from multiple surfaces. Just enough work had already been done on everything—moths, say, or meteorites—to get you started and interested, but not so much there was nothing left to do. Often I wondered: was it being born just now, in this century, in this country? And I thought: no, any time could have been like this, if you had the time and weren't sick; you could, especially if you were a boy, learn and do. There was joy in concentration, and the world afforded an inexhaustible wealth of projects to concentrate on. There was joy in effort, and the world resisted effort to just the right degree, and yielded to it at last. People cut Mount Rushmore into faces; they chipped here and there for years. People slowed the spread of yellow fever; they sprayed the Isthmus of Panama puddle by puddle. Effort alone I loved. Some days I would have been happy to push a pole around a threshing floor like an ox, for the pleasure of moving the heavy stone and watching my knees rise in turn.

I was running down the Penn Avenue sidewalk, revving up for an act of faith. I was conscious and self-conscious. I knew well that people could not fly—as well as anyone knows it—but I also knew the kicker: that, as the books put it, with faith all things are possible.

Just once I wanted a task that required all the joy I had. Day after day I had noticed that if I waited long enough, my strong unexpressed joy would dwindle and dissipate inside me, over many hours, like a fire subsiding, and I would at last calm down. Just this once I wanted to let it rip. Flying rather famously required the extra energy of belief, and this, too, I had in superabundance.

There were boxy yellow thirties apartment buildings on those Penn Avenue blocks, and the Evergreen Café, and Miss Frick's house set back behind a wrought-iron fence. There were some side yards of big houses, some side yards of little houses, some streetcar stops, and a drugstore from which I had once tried to heist a five-pound box of chocolates, a Whitman sampler, confusing "sampler" with "free sample." It was past all this that I ran that late fall afternoon, up old Penn Avenue on the cracking cement sidewalks—past the drugstore and bar, past the old and new apartment buildings and the long dry lawn behind Miss Frick's fence.

I ran the sidewalk full tilt. I waved my arms ever higher and faster; blood balled in my fingertips. I knew I was foolish. I knew I was too old really to believe in this as a child would, out of ignorance; instead I was experimenting as a scientist would, testing both the thing itself and the limits of my own courage in trying it miserably self-conscious in full view of the whole world. You can't test courage cautiously, so I ran hard and waved my arms hard, happy.

Up ahead I saw a business-suited pedestrian. He was coming stiffly toward me down the walk. Who could ever forget this first test, this stranger, this thin young man appalled? I banished the temptation to straighten up and walk right. He flattened himself against a brick wall as I passed flailing—although I had left him plenty of room. He had refused to meet my exultant eye. He looked away, evidently embarrassed. How surprisingly easy it was to ignore him! What I was letting rip, in fact, was my willingness to look foolish, in his eyes and in my own. Having chosen this foolishness, I was a free being. How could the world ever stop me, how could I betray myself, if I was not afraid?

I was flying. My shoulders loosened, my stride opened, my heart banged the base of my throat. I crossed Carnegie and ran up the block waving my arms. I crossed Lexington and ran up the block waving my arms.

A linen-suited woman in her fifties did meet my exultant eye. She looked exultant herself, seeing me from far up the block. Her face was thin and tanned. We converged. Her warm, intelligent glance said she knew what I was doing—not because she herself had been a child but because she herself took a few loose aerial turns around her apartment every night for the hell of it, and by day played along with the rest of the world and took the streetcar. So Teresa of Avila checked her unseemly joy and hung on to the altar rail to hold herself down. The woman's smiling, deep glance seemed to read my own awareness from my face, so we passed on the sidewalk—a beautifully upright woman walking in her tan linen suit, a kid running and flapping her arms—we passed on the sidewalk with a look of accomplices who share a humor just beyond irony. What's a heart for?

I crossed Homewood and ran up the block. The joy multiplied as I ran—I ran never actually quite leaving the ground—and multiplied still as I felt my stride begin to fumble and my knees begin to quiver and stall. The joy multiplied even as I slowed bumping to a walk. I was all but splitting, all but shooting sparks. Blood coursed free inside my lungs and bones, a light-shot stream like air. I couldn't feel the pavement at all.

I was too aware to do this, and had done it anyway. What could touch me now? For what were the people on Penn Avenue to me, or what was I to myself, really, but a witness to any boldness I could muster, or any cowardice if it came to that, any giving up on heaven for the sake of dignity on earth? I had not seen a great deal accomplished in the name of dignity, ever.

Mother

A dream consists of little more than its setting, as anyone knows who tells a dream or hears a dream told:
 We were squeezing up the stone street of an Old World village.
 We were climbing down the gangway of an oceangoing ship, carrying a baby.
 We broke through the woods on the crest of a ridge and saw water; we grounded our blunt raft on a charred point of land.
 We were lying on boughs of a tree in an alley.
 We were dancing in a darkened ballroom, and the curtains were blowing.

 The setting of our urgent lives is an intricate maze whose blind corridors we learn one by one—village street, ocean vessel, forested slope—without remembering how or where they connect in space.
 You travel, settle, move on, stay put, go. You point your car down the riverside road to the blurred foot of the mountain. The mountain rolls back from the flood plain and hides its own height in its trees. You get out, stand on gravel, and cool your eyes watching the river move south. You lean on the car's hot hood and look up at the old mountain, up the slope of its green western flank. It is September; the goldenrod is out, and the asters. The tattered hardwood leaves darken before they die. The mountain occupies most of the sky. You can see where the route ahead through the woods will cross a fire scar, will vanish behind a slide of shale, and perhaps reemerge there on that piny ridge now visible across the hanging valley— that ridge apparently inaccessible, but with a faint track that fingers its greenish spine. You don't notice starting to walk; the sight of the trail has impelled you along it, as the sight of the earth moves the sun.
 Before you the mountain's body curves away backward like a gymnast; the mountain's peak is somewhere south, rolled backward, too, and out of sight. Below you lies the pale and widening river; its far bank is forest now, and hills, and more blue hills behind them, hiding the yellow plain. Overhead and on the mountain's side, clouds collect and part. The clouds soak the ridges; the wayside plants tap water on your legs.
 Now: if here while you are walking, or there when you've attained the far ridge and can see the yellow plain and the river shining through it—if you notice unbidden that you are afoot on this particular mountain on this particular day in the company of these particular changing fragments of clouds—if you pause in your daze to connect your own skull-locked and interior mumble with the skin of your senses and sense, and notice you are living—then will you not conjure up in imagination a map or a globe and locate this low mountain ridge on it, and find on one western slope the dot which represents you walking here astonished?
 You may then wonder where they have gone, those other dim dots that were you: you in the flesh swimming in a swift river, swinging a bat on the first pitch, opening a footlocker with a screwdriver, inking and painting clowns on celluloid, stepping out of a revolving door into the swift crowd on a sidewalk, being kissed and kissing till your brain grew smooth, stepping out of the cold woods into a warm field full of crows, or lying awake in bed aware of your legs and suddenly aware of all of it, that the ceiling above you was under the sky—in what country, what town?

You may wonder, that is, as I sometimes wonder privately, but it doesn't matter. For it is not you or I that is important, neither what sort we might be nor how we came to be each where we are. What is important is anyone's coming awake and discovering a place, finding in full orbit a spinning globe one can lean over, catch, and jump on. What is important is the moment of opening a life and feeling it touch—with an electric hiss and cry—this speckled mineral sphere, our present world.

On your mountain slope now you must take on faith that those apparently discrete dots of you were contiguous: that little earnest dot, so easily amused; that alien, angry adolescent; and this woman with loosening skin on bony hands, hands now fifteen years older than your mother's hands when you pinched their knuckle skin into mountain ridges on an end table. You must take on faith that those severed places cohered, too—the dozens of desks, bedrooms, kitchens, yards, landscapes—if only through the motion and shed molecules of the traveler. You take it on faith that the multiform and variously lighted latitudes and longitudes were part of one world, that you didn't drop chopped from house to house, coast to coast, life to life, but in some once comprehensible way moved there, a city block at a time, a highway mile at a time, a degree of latitude and longitude at a time, carrying a fielder's mitt and the Penguin *Rimbaud* for old time's sake, and a sealed envelope, like a fetish, of untouchable stock certificates someone one hundred years ago gave your grandmother, and a comb. You take it on faith, for the connections are down now, the trail grown over, the highway moved; you can't remember despite all your vowing and memorization, and the way back is lost.

Your very cells have been replaced, and so have most of your feelings—except for two, two that connect back as far as you can remember. One is the chilling sensation of lowering one foot into a hot bath. The other, which can and does occur at any time, never fails to occur when you lower one foot into a hot bath, and when you feel the chill spread inside your shoulders, shoot down your arms and rise to your lips, and when you remember having felt this sensation from always, from when your mother lifted you down toward the bath and you curled up your legs: it is the dizzying overreal sensation of noticing that you are here. You feel life wipe your face like a big brush.

You may read this in your summer bed while the stars roll westward over your roof as they always do, while the constellation Crazy Swan nosedives over your steaming roof and into the tilled prairie once again. You may read this in your winter chair while Orion vaults over your snowy roof and over the hard continent to dive behind a California wave. "O'Ryan," Father called Orion, "that Irishman." Any two points in time, however distant, meet through the points in between; any two points in our atmosphere touch through the air. So we meet.

I write this at a wide desk in a pine shed as I always do these recent years, in this life I pray will last, while the summer sun closes the sky to Orion and to all the other winter stars over my roof. The young oaks growing just outside my windows wave in the light, so that concentrating, lost in the past, I see the pale leaves wag and think as my blood leaps: Is someone coming?

Is it Mother coming for me, to carry me home? Could it be my own young, my own glorious Mother, coming across the grass for me, the morning light on her skin, to get me and bring me back? Back to where I last knew all I needed, the way to her two strong arms?

And I wake a little more and reason, No, it is the oak leaves in the sun, pale as a face. I am here now, with this my own dear family, up here at this high latitude, out here at the farthest exploratory tip of this my present bewildering age. And still I break up through the skin of awareness a thousand times a day, as dolphins burst through seas, and dive again, and rise, and dive.

Considerations for Thinking and Writing

1. What do you think of Dillard's reaction to the slow death in "The Deer at Providencia"? Why do you think she closes the essay the way she does? Would your reaction to this essay be different if Dillard had been in the company of women instead of men? How might that change affect the way she develops her essay?

2. If the boy in "On a Hill Far Away" tried to keep Dillard there with him as she suspects, why do you think he did? What kind of relationship do you think there is in his mind among the three adults in his life: his father, his mother, and Dillard?

3. Near the end of "Heaven and Earth in Jest," Dillard describes herself as an "explorer" and a "stalker." Obviously, she thinks of herself too as a writer. Read Gretel Ehrlich's "Looking for a Lost Dog." Ehrlich claims this is an essay about writing. Judging from these two essays, how do you think Dillard's and Ehrlich's self-appointed writing tasks differ? Point to their interests and to their writing habits to illustrate your answer.

4. Read "Joy" and write a short piece of your own about the "inexpressible joy of childhood."

5. In an essay not included in this anthology, Dillard claims that it's "a privilege to muck about in sentences all morning. It's a challenge to bring off a powerful effect, or to tell the truth about something." Find evidence in one of her essays in *Women's Voices* that Dillard has brought off a powerful effect. Come to class prepared to talk about and illustrate from your own writing that it is indeed a privilege to muck about in sentences all morning.

GRETEL EHRLICH
(b. 1946)

Born in California, educated at Bennington, the UCLA Film School, and the New School for Social Research, Gretel Ehrlich went to Wyoming in 1976 to film a documentary on sheepherders. The spirit of the place captured her, and after a brief stint of wandering following the loss of a loved one, she returned to stay. The essays in this anthology give us a sense of a woman who has indeed found her place—her place on an "end-of-the-road ranch," under the changing hues of a Wyoming sky, in a marriage, among a community of loving and lovable misfits, among the Plains Indians. She is at home in the Wyoming landscape, and she is content to work there and wander, content to surrender, "stripping down, taking away every veil, every obstacle between [herself] and earth." To bow to the earth is, for Ehrlich, a "gesture of respect, of dignity, of mutuality."

Her respect for the earth and her fascination with the life around her are reflected in her first book of essays, *The*

Solace of Open Spaces (1985), and in her short stories in *City Tales, Wyoming Stories* (1986), a collection she published with Edward Hoagland. Other prose pieces have appeared in *Harper's*, the *New York Times, Atlantic Monthly, Time*, and *New Age Journal*. Her first novel (*Heart Mountain*), published in 1988, will be followed by a second collection of essays (*Islands, Universe, and Home*) in 1989. She won the Harold B. Vurcell Memorial Award for *Solace*, a Whiting Foundation grant for "Spring," and a Guggenheim fellowship.

Ehrlich claims that when she went to Wyoming to make the documentary film, she "had the experience of waking up not knowing where I was, whether I was a man or a woman, or which toothbrush was mine." In the face of a personal tragedy, she says she "*had* lost (at least for a while) . . . my appetite for the life I had left: city surroundings, old friends, familiar comforts." She made her way through that fairly desperate stage, somehow getting round the roadblocks: "The detour, of course, became the actual path; the digressions in my writing, the narrative." She did precisely what she set out to do; she set out to "give the page the same qualities as earth: weather would land on it harshly; light would elucidate the most difficult truths; wind would sweep away obtuse padding." Weather, light, and wind also land on Ehrlich's body; she becomes earth—at once full, barren, contradictory, acted upon, changed, and charged. When she finds beauty and sadness in the changing seasons, it is because she feels so intensely what is happening to her. And like Persephone, she knows the price one pays for being alive. Hers is a sensuous delight tinged with sadness.

"Looking for a Lost Dog" gives us a sense of Ehrlich's unorthodox methodology, her way of momentarily subordinating mind to impulse and intuition. It is a curious subordination of mind to body. At the beginning of "Lost Dog" she alludes to Thoreau, suggesting that her most valuable thoughts "are anything but what *I* thought." The essay—ostensibly a narrative account of her search for a lost dog—actually abandons the dog in favor of the "peregrine saunterings of the mind." What Ehrlich finds as she follows those alien saunterings of her mind's underside is space, space to "walk with a purpose but no destination," space in which to "find what is lost" in a culture that lives too much under the influence of logic and rationality. She surrenders momentarily to seemingly impossible "longings," to a powerful but latent desire to "live multiple lives," to an impulse that would locate her life and ours somewhere within the struggle that takes place between "impulse and reason, logic and passion." "Lost Dog," she told a group of teachers last year, "is a piece about writing."

"Just Married" records Ehrlich's discovery "of love gone deep into a friendship." But within the peace of even a marriage so right, she detects "a premonition of death—the deathbed calm we're supposed to feel after getting our affairs in order." She acknowledges her and her husband's mutual concern about the "proprietary impulse," the impulse that can bring out the worst in us: ownership, possessiveness, power, greed. But she finds promise in the hard life of ranch work and in the land itself, promise in the kind of "impermanence [that] take[s] a long time" to manifest itself. She finds perhaps her greatest satisfaction in being possessed by the land itself, by the joint human partnership that is born of such possession: "Mowing hayfields feels like mowing myself. I wake up mornings expecting to find my hair shorn. . . . Later in the year, feeding the bales of hay we've put up is a regurgitative act: thrown down from a high stack on chill days they break open in front of the horses like loaves of hot bread." Theirs is a communion.

"To Live in Two Worlds" and "Spring" give substance to Ehrlich's claim in "Married" that she is a "culture straddler." These two far-ranging essays suggest her concern about culture and cosmos, about the rituals that sustain us and about our bodies that press "matter into relation to matter," bodies that make us aware of our relationship with the vast forces that work in and through our lives. In the Indian cultures that Ehrlich visits to observe a Sun Dance and to attend a Crow Fair, she finds solace, finds evidence—even in the face of mixed marriages, Indians in pickups and Corvettes, and young warriors under the influence of new wave music—of a cultural stability that other Americans have lost. She laments that, for the most part, her culture has "lost its memory," and she yearns for and finds in her life on the ranch the binding rituals that can sustain us, rituals that give pattern and purpose to life, bind us to each other and to the earth. She finds something of what the Indians have not lost.

Yet Ehrlich's is no naive nature lover's view of such deep relationships. The complexity of her vision is nowhere more evident than in "Spring," an essay that calls into account human perceptions of cosmic interactions; it is yet another of her efforts to find solace in impermanence: "What I see as order and stillness—the robust, time-bound determinacy of my life—is really a mirage suspended above chaos." But such randomness, interaction, indeterminacy ultimately please Ehrlich. She wants nothing more than to feel the universe's restlessness during the vernal equinox as she yearns "to resist the magnetic tilt back into dormancy, spiritual and emotional reticence." Her resistance is not defiance but rather an effort to sense more fully the force itself: feeling as celebration, celebration as feeling. Ehrlich takes us beyond the linearity of time to a more profound sense of things, and in the face of her discovery—"that I am a random multiple; that the many fit together like waves; that my swell is a collision of particles"—she remains undaunted, alive and alert. That she also remains human and a woman, we never forget.

Ehrlich's work invites comparison with Dillard's. Theirs is an inquiry into Nature, but their visions are very different. Ehrlich's surrender to the body stands in marked contrast to Dillard's sheer intellectuality. Dillard does occasionally "fill up like a new wineskin" as she opens up to Nature's show, but she is more often "abstracted and dazed," "stunned into stillness," she claims on one occasion. And those occasions lead to intense metaphysical speculation, dazzling moments of insight. They also lead us away from this earth into disembodied spiritual excursions. Ehrlich, on the other hand, invites us into the stream of time with her, asks us to watch her strip bare, exposing herself to the elements, to time and chance. Hers is an act of submission amounting to respect, and her language is as natural and as changeable as the seasons playing on her nakedness. It is above all a language of intimacy, a call to relationship.

Spring

We have a nine-acre lake on our ranch and a warm spring that feeds it all winter. By mid-March the lake ice begins to melt where the spring feeds in, and every year the same pair of mallards come ahead of the others and wait. Though there is very little open water they seem content. They glide back and forth through a thin estuary, brushing watercress with their elegant, folded wings, then tip end-up to eat and after, clamber onto the lip of ice that retreats, hardens forward, and retreats again.

Mornings, a transparent pane of ice lies over the meltwater. I peer through and see some kind of waterbug—perhaps a leech—paddling like a sea turtle between green ladders of lakeweed. Cattails and sweetgrass from the previous summer are bone-dry, marked with black mold spots, and bend like elbows into the ice. They are swords which cut away the hard tenancy of winter. At the wide end a mat of dead waterplants has rolled back into a thick, impregnable breakwater. Near it, bubbles trapped under the ice are lenses focused straight up to catch the coming season.

It's spring again and I wasn't finished with winter. That's what I said at the end of summer too. I stood on the twenty-foot-high haystack and yelled, "No!" as the first snow fell. We had been up since four in the morning picking the last bales of hay from the oatfield by hand, slipping under the weight of them in the mud, and by the time we finished the stack, six inches of snow had fallen.

It's spring but I was still cataloguing the different kinds of snow: snow that falls dry but is rained on; snow that melts down into hard crusts; wind-driven snow that looks blue; powder snow on hardpack on powder—a Linzertorte of snow. I look up. The troposphere is the seven-to-ten-mile-wide sleeve of air out of which all our weather shakes. A bank of clouds drives in from the south. Where in it, I wonder, does a snowflake take on its thumbprint uniqueness? Inside the cloud where schools of flakes are flung this way and that like schools of fish? What gives the snowflake its needle, plate, column, branching shapes—the battering wind or the dust particles around which water vapor clings?

Near town the river ice breaks up and lies stacked in industrial-sized hunks—big as railway cars—on the banks, and is flecked black by wheeling hurricanes of newly plowed topsoil. That's how I feel when winter breaks up inside me: heavy, onerous, up-ended, inert against the flow of water. I had thought about ice during the cold months too. How it is movement betrayed, water seized in the moment of falling. In November, ice thickened over the lake like a cataract, and from the air looked like a Cyclops, one bad eye. Under its milky spans over irrigation ditches, the sound of water running south was muffled. One solitary spire of ice hung noiselessly against dark rock at the Falls as if mocking or mirroring the broom-tail comet on the horizon. Then, in February, I tried for words not about ice, but words hacked from it—the ice at the end of the mind, so to speak—and failed.

Those were winter things and now it is spring, though one name can't describe what, in Wyoming, is a three-part affair; false spring, the vernal equinox, and the spring when flowers come and the grass grows.

Spring means restlessness. The physicist I've been talking to all winter says if I look more widely, deeply, and microscopically all at once I might see how springlike the whole cosmos is. What I see as order and stillness—the robust, time-bound determinacy of my life—is really a mirage suspended above chaos. "There's a lot of random jiggling going on all the time, everywhere," he tells me. Winter's tight sky hovers. Under it, the hayfields are green, then white, then green growing under white. The confinement I've felt since November resembles the confinement of subatomic particles, I'm told. A natural velocity finally shows itself. The particle moves; it becomes a wave.

The sap rises in trees and in me and the hard knot of perseverance I cultivated to meet winter dissipates; I walk away from the obsidian of bitter nights. Now, when snow comes, it is wet and heavy, but the air it traverses feels light. I sleep less and dream not of human entanglements, but of animals I've never seen: a caterpillar fat as a man's thumb, made of linked silver tubes, has two heads—one human, one a butterfly's.

Last spring at this time I was coming out of a bout with pneumonia. I went to bed on January first and didn't get up until the end of February. Winter was a cocoon in which my gagging, basso cough shook the dark figures at the end of my bed. Had I read too much Hemingway? Or was I dying? I'd lie on my stomach and look out. Nothing close up interested me. All engagements of mind—the circumlocutions of love-interests and internal gossip—appeared false. Only my body was true. And my body was trying to close down, go out the window without me.

I saw things out there. Our ranch faces south down a long treeless valley whose vanishing point is two gray hills, folded one in front of the other like two hands, and after that—space, cerulean air, clouds like pleated skirts, and red mesas standing up like breeching whales in a valley three thousand feet below. Afternoons, our young horses played, rearing up on back legs and pawing oh so carefully at each other, reaching around, ears flat back, nipping manes and withers. One of those times their falsetto squeals looped across the pasture and hung on frozen currents of air. But when I tried to ingest their sounds of delight, I found my lungs had no air.

It was thirty-five below zero that night. Our plumbing froze and because I was very weak my husband had to bundle me up and help me to the outhouse. Nothing close at hand seemed to register with me: neither the cold nor the semi-coziness of an uninsulated house. But the stars were lurid. For a while I thought I saw the horses, dead now, and eating each other, and spinning round and round in the ice of the air.

My scientist friends talk with relish about how insignificant we humans are when placed against the time-scale of geology and the cosmos. I had heard it a hundred times, but never felt it truly. As I lay in bed, the black room was a screen through which some part of my body traveled, leaving the rest behind. I thought I was a sun flying over a barge whose iron holds soaked me up until I became rust, floating on a bright river.

A ferocious loneliness took hold of me. I felt spring-inspired desire, a sense of trajectory, but no interception was in sight. In fact, I wanted none. My body was a parenthetical dash laid against a landscape so spacious it defied space as we know it—space as a membrane—and curved out of time. That night a luscious, creamy fog rolled in, like a roll of fat, hugging me, but it was snow.

Recuperation is like spring: dormancy and vitality collide. In any year I'm like a bear, a partial hibernator. During January thaws I stick my nose out and peruse the frozen desolation as if reading a book whose language I don't know. In March I'm ramshackle, weak in the knees, giddy, dazzled by broken-backed clouds, the passing of Halley's comet, the on-and-off strobe of sun. Like a sheepherder I "X" out each calendar day as if time were a forest through which I could clearcut a way to the future. My physicist friend straightens me out on this point too. The notion of "time passing," like a train through a landscape, is an illusion, he says. I hold the Big Ben clock taken from a dead sheepherder's wagon and look at it. The clock measures intervals of time, not the speed of time, and the calendar is a scaffolding we hang as if time were rushing water we could harness. Time-bound I hinge myself to a linear bias—cause and effect all laid out in a neat row—and in this we learn two things: blame and shame.

Julius Caesar had a sense of humor about time. The Roman calendar with its Kalends. Nones, and Ides—counting days—changed according to who was in power. Caesar serendipitously added days, changed the names of certain months, and when he was through, the calendar was so skewed that January fell in autumn.

Einsteinian time is too big for even Julius Caesar to touch. It stretches and shrinks and dilates. In fact, it is the antithesis of the mechanistic concept we've imposed on it. Time, indecipherable from space, is not one thing, but an infinity of space-times, overlapping, interfering, wavelike. There is no future that is not now, no past that is not now. Time includes every moment.

It's the Ides of March today.

I've walked to a hill a mile from the house. It's not really a hill but a mountain slope that heaves up, turns sideways, and comes down again, straight down to a foot-wide creek. Everything I can see from here used to be a flatland covered with shallow water. "Used to be" means several hundred million years ago, and the land itself was not really "here" at all, but part of a continent floating near Bermuda. On top is a fin of rock, a marine deposition created during Jurassic times by small waves moving in and out slapping the shore.

I've come here for peace and quiet and to see what's going on in this secluded valley, away from ranch work and sorting corrals, but what I get is a slap on the ass by a prehistoric wave, gains and losses in altitude and aridity, outcrops of mud composed of rotting volcanic ash which fell continuously for ten thousand years a hundred million years ago. The soils are a geologic flag—red, white, green, and gray. On one side of the hill, mountain mahogany gives off a scent like orange blossoms, on the other, colonies of sagebrush root wide in ground the color of Spanish roof tiles. And it still looks like the ocean to me. "How much truth can a man stand, sitting by the ocean, all that perpetual motion," Mose Allison, the jazz singer, sings.

The wind picks up and blusters. Its fat underbelly scrapes the uneven ground, twisting like taffy towards me, slips up over the mountain and showers out across the Great Plains. The sea smell it carried all the way from Seattle has long since been absorbed by pink grus—the rotting granite that spills down the slopes of the Rockies. Somewhere over the Midwest the wind slows, tangling in the hair of hardwood forests, and finally drops into the corridors of the cities, past Manhattan's World Trade Center, ripping free again as it crosses the Atlantic's green swell.

Spring jitterbugs inside me. Spring *is* wind, symphonic and billowing. A dark cloud pops like a blood blister over me, letting hail down. It comes on a piece of wind that seems to have widened the sky, comes so the birds have something to fly on.

A message reports to my brain but I can't believe my eyes. The sheet of wind had a hole in it: an eagle just fell out of the sky. It fell as if down the chute of a troubled airplane. Landed, falling to one side as if a leg were broken. I was standing on the hill overlooking the narrow valley that had been a seashore 170,000,000 years ago, whose sides had lifted like a medic's litter to catch up this eagle now.

She hops and flaps seven feet of wing and closes them down and sways. She had come down (on purpose?) near a dead fawn whose carcass had recently been feasted upon. When I walked closer, all I could see of the animal was a ribcage rubbed red with fine tissue and the decapitated head lying peacefully against sagebrush, eyes closed.

At twenty yards the eagle opened her wings halfway and rose up, her whole back lengthening and growing stiff. At forty feet she looked as big as a small person. She craned her neck, first to one side, then the other, and stared hard. She's giving me "the eagle eye," I thought.

Friends who have investigated eagles' nests have literally feared for their lives. It's not that they were in danger of being pecked to death but, rather, grabbed. An eagle's talons are a powerful jaw. Their grip is so strong the talons can slice down through flesh to bone in one motion.

But I had come close only to see what was wrong, to see what I could do. An eagle with a bum leg will starve to death. Was it broken, bruised, or sprained? How could I get close enough to know? I approached again. She hopped up in the air dashing the critical distance between us with her great wings. Best to leave her alone, I decided. My husband dragged a road-killed deer up the mountain slope so she could eat, and I brought a bucket of water. Then we turned towards home.

A golden eagle is not golden but black with yellow spots on the neck and wings. Looking at her, I had wondered how feathers came to be, how their construction— the rachis, vane, and quill—is unlike anything else in nature.

Birds are glorified flying lizards. The remarkable feathers which, positioned together, are like hundreds of smaller wings evolved from reptilian scales. Ancestral birds had thirteen pairs of cone-shaped teeth that grew in separate sockets like a snake's, rounded ribs, and bony tails. Archaeopteryx was half bird, half dinosaur who glided instead of flying: Ichthyornis was a fish-bird, a relative of the pelican; Diatryma was a giant, seven feet tall with a huge beak and wings so absurdly small they must have been useless, though later the wingbone sprouted from them. *Aquila chrysaëtos,* the modern golden eagle, has seven thousand contour feathers, no teeth, and weighs about eight pounds.

I think about the eagle. How big she was, how each time she spread her wings it was like a thought stretching between two seasons.

Back at the house I relax with a beer. At 5:03 the vernal equinox occurs. I go outside and stand in the middle of a hayfield with my eyes closed. The universe is restless but I want to feel celestial equipoise: twelve hours of daylight, twelve of dark, and the earth ramrod straight on its axis. In celebration I straighten my posture in an effort to resist the magnetic tilt back into dormancy, spiritual and emotional reticence. Far to the south I imagine the equatorial sash, now nose to nose with the sun, sizzling like a piece of bacon, then the earth slowly tilting again.

In the morning I walk up to the valley again. I glass both hillsides, back and forth through the sagebrush, but the eagle isn't there. The hindquarters of the road-killed deer have been eaten. Coyote tracks circle the carcass. Did they have eagle for dinner too?

Afternoon. I return. Far up on the opposite hill I see her, flapping and hopping to the top. When I stop, she stops and turns her head. Her neck is the plumbline on which earth revolves. Even at two hundred yards, I can feel her binocular vision zeroing in; I can feel the heat of her stare.

Later, I look through my binoculars at all sorts of things. I'm seeing the world with an eagle eye. I glass the crescent moon. How jaded I've become, taking the moon at face value only, forgetting the charcoal, shaded backside, as if it weren't there at all.

That night I dream about two moons. One is pink and spins fast; the other is an eagle's head, farther away and spinning in the opposite direction. Slowly, both moons descend and then it is day.

At first light I clamber up the hill. Now the dead deer my husband brought is only a hoop of ribs, two forelegs, and hair. The eagle is not here or along the creek or on either hill. I go to the hill and sit. After a long time an eagle careens out from the narrow slit of the red-walled canyon whose creek drains into this valley. Surely it's the same bird. She flies by. I can hear the bone-creak and whoosh of air under her wings. She cocks her head and looks at me. I smile. What is a smile to her? Now she is not so much flying as lifting above the planet, far from me.

Late March. The emerald of the hayfields brightens. A flock of gray-capped rosy finches who overwintered here swarms a leafless apple tree, then falls from the smooth boughs like cut grass. The tree was planted by the Texan who homesteaded this ranch. As I walk past, one of the boughs, shaped like an undulating dragon, splits off from the trunk and falls.

Space is an arena in which the rowdy particles that are the building blocks of life perform their antics. All spring, things fall; the general law of increasing disorder is on the take. I try to think of what it is to be a cause without an effect, an effect without a cause. To abandon time-bound thinking, the use of tenses, the temporally related emotions of impatience, expectation, hope, and fear. But I can't. I go to the edge of the lake and watch the ducks. Like them, my thinking rises and falls on the same water.

Another day. Sometimes when I'm feeling small-minded I take a plane ride over Wyoming. As we take off I feel the plane's resistance to accepting air under its wings. Is this how an eagle feels? Ernst Mach's principle tells me that an object's resistance against being accelerated is not the intrinsic property of matter, but a measure of its interaction with the universe; that matter only has inertia because it exists in relation to other matter.

Airborne, then, I'm not aloof but in relation to everything—like Wallace Stevens's floating eagle for whom the whole, intricate Alps is a nest. We fly southeast from Heart Mountain across the Big Horn River, over the long red wall where Butch Cassidy trailed stolen horses, across the high plains to Laramie. Coming home the next day, we hit clouds. Turbulence, like many forms of trouble, cannot always be seen. We bounce so hard my arms sail helplessly above my head. In evolution, wingbones became arms and hands: perhaps I'm de-evolving.

From ten thousand feet I can see that spring is only half here: the southern part of the state is white, the northern half is green. Land is also time. The greening of time is a clock whose hands are blades of grass moving vertically, up through the fringe of numbers, spreading across the middle of the face, sinking again as the sun moves from one horizon to the other. Time doesn't go anywhere; the shadow of the plane, my shadow, moves across it.

To sit on a plane is to sit on the edge of sleep where the mind's forge brightens into incongruities. Down there I see disparate wholenesses strung together and the string dissolving. Mountains run like rivers; I fly through waves and waves of chiaroscuro light. The land looks bare but is articulate. The body of the plane is my body, pressing into spring, pressing matter into relation with matter. Is it even necessary to say the obvious? That spring brings on surges of desire? From this disinterested height I say out loud what Saint Augustine wrote: "My love is my weight. Because of it I move."

Directly below us now is the fine old Wyoming ranch where Joel, Mart, Dave, Hughy, and I have moved thousands of head of cattle. Joel's father, Smokey, was one of two brothers who put the outfit together. They worked hard, lived frugally, and even after Fred died, Smokey did not marry until his late fifties. As testimony to a long bachelorhood, there is no kitchen in the main house. The cookhouse stands separate from all the other buildings. In back is a bedroom and bath which has housed a list of itinerant cooks ten pages long.

Over the years I've helped during roundup and branding. We'd rise at four. Smokey, now in his eighties, cooked flapjacks and boiled coffee on the wood cook-stove. There was a long table. Joel and Smokey always sat at one end. They were look-alikes, both skin-and-bones tall with tipped-up dark eyes set in narrow faces. Stern and vigilant, Smokey once threw a young hired hand out of the cookhouse because he hadn't grained his saddle horse after a long day's ride. "On this outfit we take care of our animals first," he said. "Then if there's time, we eat."

Even in his early twenties, Joel had his father's dignity and razor-sharp wit. They both wore white Stetsons identically shaped. Only their hands were different: Joel had eight fingers and one thumb—the other he lost while roping.

Eight summers ago my parents visited their ranch. We ate a hearty meal of homemade whiskey left over from Prohibition days, steaks cut from an Angus bull, four kinds of vegetables, watermelon, ice cream, and pie. Despite a thirteen-year difference in our ages, Smokey wanted Joel and me to marry. As we rose from the meal, he shook my father's hand. "I guess you'll be my son's father-in-law," he said. That was news to all of us. Joel's face turned crimson. My father threw me an astonished look, cleared his throat, and thanked his host for the fine meal.

One night Joel did come to my house and asked me if I would take him into my bed. It was a gentlemanly proposition—doffed hat, moist eyes, a smile almost grimacing with loneliness. "You're an older woman. Think of all you could teach me," he said jauntily, but with a blush. He stood ramrod straight waiting for an answer. My silence turned him away like a rolling wave and he drove to the home ranch, spread out across the Emblem Bench thirty-five miles away.

The night Joel died I was staying at a writer's farm in Missouri. I had fallen asleep early, then awakened suddenly, feeling claustrophobic. I jumped out of bed and stood in the dark. I wanted to get out of there, drive home to Wyoming and I didn't know why. Finally, at seven in the morning, I was able to sleep. I dreamed about a bird landing, then lifting out of a tree along a river bank. That was the night Joel's pickup rolled. He was found five hours after the accident occurred—just about daylight—and died on the way to the hospital.

Now I'm sitting on a fin of Gypsum Springs rock looking west. The sun is setting. What I see are three gray cloud towers letting rain down at the horizon. The sky behind these massifs is gilded gold, and long fingers of land—benches where the Hunt Oil Company's Charolais cattle graze—are pink. Somewhere over Joel's grave the sky is bright. The road where he died shines like a dash in a Paul Klee painting. Over my head, it is still winter: snow so dry it feels like styrofoam when squeezed together, tumbles into my lap. I think about flying and falling. The place in the sky where the eagle fell is dark, as if its shadow had burned into the backdrop of rock—Hiroshima style. Why does a wounded eagle get well and fly away; why do the head wounds of a young man cut him down? Useless questions.

Sex and death are the riddles thrown into the hopper, thrown down on the planet like hailstones. Where one hits the earth, it makes a crater and melts, perhaps a seed germinates, perhaps not. If I dice life down into atoms, the trajectories I find are so wild, so random, anything could happen: life or nonlife. But once we have a body, who can give it up easily? Our own or others'? We check our clocks and build our beautiful narratives, under which indeterminacy seethes.

Sometimes, lying in bed, I feel like a flounder with its two eyes on one side pointing upward into nothingness. The casings of thought rattle. Then I realize there are no casings at all. Is it possible that the mind, like space, is finite, but has no boundaries, no center or edge? I sit cross-legged on old blankets. My bare feet strain against the crotch of my knees. Time is between my toes, it seems. Just as morning comes and the indigo lifts, the leaflessness of the old apple tree looks ornate. Nothing in this world is plain.

"Every atom in your body was once inside a star," another physicist says, but he's only trying to humor me. Not all atoms in all kinds of matter are shared. But who wouldn't find that idea appealing? Outside, shadows trade places with a sliver of sun which trades places with shadow. Finally the lake ice goes and the water—pale and slate blue—wears its coat of diamonds all day. The mallards number twenty-six pairs now. They nest on two tiny islands and squabble amicably among themselves. A Pacific storm blows in from the south like a jibsail reaching far out, backhanding me with a gust of something tropical. It snows into my mouth, between my breasts, against my shins. Spring teaches me what space and time teach me: that I am a random multiple; that the many fit together like waves; that my swell is a collision of particles. Spring is a kind of music, a seething minor, a twelve-tone scale. Even the odd harmonies amassed only lift up to dissolve.

Spring passes harder and harder and is feral. The first thunder cracks the sky into a larger domain. Sap rises in obdurateness. For the first time in seven months, rain slants down in a slow pavanne—sharp but soft—like desire, like the laying of hands. I drive the highway that crosses the wild-horse range. Near Emblem I watch a black studhorse trot across the range all alone. He travels north, then turns in my direction as if trotting to me. Now, when I dream of Joel, he is riding that horse and he knows he is dead. One night he rides to my house, all smiles and shyness. I let him in.

To Live in Two Worlds:
Crow Fair and a Sun Dance

June. Last night, alone on the ranch, I tried to pull a calf in a rainstorm. While attempting to hold a flashlight in one hand and a six-foot-long winchlike contraption called a "calf puller" in the other, I slipped in the mud and fell against the cow's heaving flank. I yelled apologies to her over thunder so concussive that friends at a neighboring ranch claimed "it shook the handles loose from the coffee cups." On my feet again, I saw rain undulate down hay meadows and three theaters of lightning making simultaneous displays: over Red Basin's tipped-up mesas a thick root of lightning drilled straight down; closer, wide shoals of it flashed like polished car hoods all being lifted at once; and in the pasture where I fumbled with a chain, trying to fasten it around the calf's emerging front feet, lightning snapped sideways like flowered vines shot from a cannon over my shoulders. In that cadaverous refulgence, the calf was born dead. The next morning, clear and cool after a rainless month of hundred-degree heat, I tightened my lariat around his hocks and, from the rubbery, purplish afterbirth they had impaled, dragged him behind the pickup out of the pasture.

Implicated as we westerners are in this sperm, blood, and guts business of ranching, and propelled forward by steady gusts of blizzards, cold fronts, droughts, heat, and wind, there's a ceremonial feel to life on a ranch. It's raw and impulsive but the narrative thread of birth, death, chores, and seasons keeps tugging at us until we find ourselves braided inextricably into the strand. So much in American life has had a corrupting influence on our requirements for social order. We live in a culture that has lost its memory. Very little in the specific shapes and traditions of our grandparents' pasts instructs us how to live today, or tells us who we are or what demands will be made on us as members of society. The shrill estrangement some of us felt in our twenties has been replaced a decade or so later by a hangdog, collective blues. With our burgeoning careers and families, we want to join up, but it's difficult to know how or where. The changing conditions of life are no longer assimilated back into a common watering trough. Now, with our senses enlivened—because that's the only context we have to go by—we hook change onto change ad nauseam.

On a ranch, small ceremonies and private, informal rituals arise. We ride the spring pasture, pick chokecherries in August, skin out a deer in the fall, and in the enactment experience a wordless exhilaration between bouts of plain hard work. Ritual—which could entail a wedding or brushing one's teeth—goes in the direction of life. Through it we reconcile our barbed solitude with the rushing, irreducible conditions of life.

For the fifth consecutive year I helped my neighbors Stan and Mary move their cattle through four 6,000-acre pastures. The first morning we rode out at three. A new moon grew slimmer and slimmer as light ballooned around us. I came on two burly Hereford bulls sniffing the cool breeze through the needles of a white pine, shaded even from moonlight as if the severe sexual heat of their bodies could stand no excess light. All week we moved cows, calves, and bulls across washes of ocher earth blooming with purple larkspur, down sidehills of gray shale that crumbled under our processional weight like filo pastry. Just before we reached the last gate, six hundred calves ran back; they thought their mothers, who had loped ahead, were behind them. Four of us galloped full tilt through sagebrush to get around and head off this miniature stampede, but when we did catch up, the calves spilled through us in watery cascades, back to the last pasture, where we had to start the gather all over again. This midseason roundup lasted six days. We ate together, slept, trailed cattle, and took turns bathing in the big galvanized tub at cow camp. At the end of the week, after pairing off each cow with the proper calf, then cutting them out of the herd—a job that requires impeccable teamwork and timing between rider and rider and rider and horse—we knew an intimacy had bloomed between us. It was an old closeness that disappears during other seasons, and each year, surprised afresh by the slightly erotic tint, we welcomed it back.

July. Last night from one in the morning until four, I sat in the bed of my pickup with a friend and watched meteor showers hot dance over our heads in sprays of little suns that looked like white orchids. With so many stars falling around us I wondered if daylight would come. We forget that our sun is only a star destined to someday burn out. The time scale of its transience so far exceeds our human one that our unconditional dependence on its life-giving properties feels oddly like an indiscretion about which we'd rather forget.

The recent news that astronomers have discovered a new solar system in-the-making around another sun-star has startled us out of a collective narcissism based on the assumption that we dominate the cosmic scene. Now we must make room for the possibility of new life—not without resentment and anticipation—the way young couples make room in their lives for a baby. By chance, this discovery came the same day a Kiowa friend invited me to attend a Sun Dance.

I have Indian neighbors all around me—Crow and Cheyenne to the north, Shoshone and Arapaho to the south—and though we often ranch, drink, and rodeo side by side, and dress in the same cowboy uniforms—Wrangler jeans, tall boots, wide-brimmed, high-crowned hats—there is nothing in our psyches, styles, or temperaments that is alike.

Because Christians shaped our New World culture we've had to swallow an artificial division between what's sacred and what's profane. Many westerners, like Native Americans, have made a life for themselves out in the raw wind, riding the ceremony of seasons with a fine-tuned eye and ear for where the elk herd is hidden or when in fall to bring the cattle down. They'll knock a sage hen in the head with a rock for dinner and keep their bearings in a ferocious storm as ably as any Sioux warrior, but they won't become visionaries, diviners, or healers in the process.

On a Thursday I set off at two in the morning and drove to the reservation. It was dark when I arrived and quiet. On a broad plain bordered in the west by mountains, the families of the hundred men who were pledging the dance had set up camps: each had a white canvas tipi, a wall tent, and a rectangular brush arbor in a circle around the Lodge, where for the next four days the ceremony would take place. At 5 A.M. I could still see stars, the Big Dipper suspended in the northwest as if magnified, and to the east, a wide band of what looked like blood. I sat on the ground in the dark. Awake and stirring now, some of the "dancers" filed out of the Lodge, their star quilts pulled tightly over their heads. When they lined up solemnly behind two portable johns, I thought I was seeing part of the dance. Then I had to laugh at myself but at the same time understood how the sacredness of this ceremony was located not just in the Lodge but everywhere.

Sun Dance is the holiest religious ceremony of the Plains tribes, having spread from the Cheyenne to the Sioux, Blackfoot, Gros Ventre, Assiniboine, Arapaho, Bannock, and Shoshone sometime after the year 1750. It's not "sun worship" but an inculcation of regenerative power that restores health, vitality, and harmony to the land and all tribes.

For the hundred dancers who have volunteered to dance this year (the vow obligates them to dance four times during their lives) Sun Dance is a serious and painful undertaking; called "thirsty standing," they eat no food and drink no water for four days. This year, with the hundred-degree heat we've been having, their suffering will be extreme. The ceremonies begin before dawn and often last until two or three in the morning. They must stay in the Lodge for the duration. Speaking to or making eye contact with anyone not dancing is forbidden, and it's considered a great disgrace to drop out of the dance before it is over.

Sun Dance was suppressed by the government in the 1880s, and its full revival has only been recent. Some tribes practiced the ceremony secretly, others stopped. George Horse Capture, a Gros Ventre who lives near me and has completed one Sun Dance, has had to read the same sources I have—Dorsey, Kroeber, and Peter Powell—to reeducate himself in his tradition.

"Did you sleep here last night?" an old man, one of the elders of the tribe, asked. Shrunken and hawk-nosed, he wore a blue farmer's cap and walked with a crudely carved pine cane. "No, I drove from Shell," I answered, sounding self-conscious because I seemed to be the only white person around. "Oh . . . you have a very good spirit to get up so early and come all this way. That's good . . . I'm glad you are here," he said. His round eyes narrowed and he walked away. On the other side of the shed where the big drum was kept he approached three teenage girls. "You sober?" he asked. "Yes," they replied in unison. "Good," he said. "Don't make war on anyone. If you're not drunk, there's peace." He hobbled past me again out into the parched field between the circle of tents and the Lodge. Coleman lanterns were being lighted and the tipis behind him glowed. He put both hands on top of the cane and, in a hoarse voice that carried far across the encampment, sang an Arapaho morning song: "Get up, Everyone get up . . . ," it began, followed by encouragements to face the day.

The sky had lightened; it was a shield of pink. The new moon, white when I had arrived, now looked blue. Another voice—sharp, gravelly, and less patient, boomed from the north, his song overlapping that of the first Crier's. I looked: he was a younger man but bent at the shoulders like a tree. He paced the hard ground as he sang, and the tweed jacket he wore, which gave him a Dickensian look, hung from him and swayed in the breeze. Now I could hear two other Criers to the south and west. The four songs overlapped, died out, and started again. The men, silhouetted, looked ghostlike against the horizon, almost disembodied, as though their age and authority were entirely in the vocal cords.

First light. In the Lodge the dancers were dressing. Over gym shorts (the modern substitute for breechclouts), they pulled on long, white sheath skirts, to which they fastened, with wide beaded belts, their dance aprons: two long panels, front and back, decorated with beads, ribbons, and various personal insignias. Every man wore beaded moccasins, leaving legs and torso bare. Their faces, chests, arms, and the palms of their hands were painted yellow. Black lines skittered across chests, around ankles and wrists, and encircled each face. Four bundles of sage, which represents healing and breath, were tucked straight up in the apron fronts; thin braided wreaths of it were slipped onto the dancer's wrists and ankles, and a crown of sage ending in two loose sprays looked like antennae.

Light begets activity—the Lodge began filling up. It's a log arbor, forty yards across, covered with a thatchwork of brush. Its sixteen sides radiate from a great center pole of cottonwood—the whole trunk of a hundred-year-old tree whose forked top looked like antlers. A white cloth was tied with rope around the bark, and overhead, on four of the pine stringers, tribal members had hung bandannas, silk cowboy scarves, and shawls that all together form a loose, trembling hieroglyph spelling out personal requests for health and repair.

Alongside the dancers, who stood in a circle facing east, a group of older men filed in. These were the "grandfathers" (ceremonially related, not by blood) who would help the younger dancers through their four-day ordeal.

The little shed against which I had leaned in the premorning light opened and became an announcer's stand. From it the drum was rolled out and set up at the entrance to the Lodge.

Light begets activity begets light. The sky looked dry, white, and inflammable. Eleven drummers who, like "the grandfathers," were probably ranchers sat on metal folding chairs encircling the drum. A stream of announcements in both Arapaho and English flooded the air. Friends and relatives of the dancers lined up in front of the Lodge. I found myself in a group of Indian women. The drumming, singing, and dancing began all at once. It's not really a dance with steps but a dance of containment, a dance in place. Facing east and blowing whistles made of eagle wing bones in shrill unison, the men bounced up and down on their heels in time to the drumbeat. Series after series of songs, composed especially for Sun Dance, were chanted in high, intense voices. The ropey, repeating pulse was so strong it seemed to pull the sun up.

There were two important men at the back of the Lodge I hadn't noticed. That their faces were painted red, not yellow, signified the status of Instructor, Pledger, or Priest. The taller of the two held a hoop (the sun) with eagle feathers (the bird of day) fastened around it. The "grandfather" standing in back of him raised the hoop-holding hand and, from behind, pushed the arm up and down in a wide, swinging arc until it took flight on its own.

I felt warmth on my shoulder. As the sun topped the horizon, the dancers stretched their arms straight out, lifting them with the progress of the sun's rising. Songs pushed from the backs of the drummers' throats. The skin on the dancers' chests bounced as though from some interior tremor. When the light hit their faces, they looked as if they were made of sun.

The sunrise ceremony ended at eight. They had danced for nearly two hours and already the heat of the day was coming on. Pickups rambled through camps, children played quietly everywhere. Walking to a friend's camp, I began to understand how the wide ampleness of the Indian body stands for a spirit of accommodation. In the ceremony I had just witnessed, no one—dancer, observer, child, priest, or drummer—had called attention to himself. There was no applause, no frivolousness. Families ambled back to their camps as though returning from a baseball game. When I entered my friend's brush arbor (already a relief from the sun) and slid behind the picnic table bench she handed me the cup of coffee I'd been hoping for. "They're dancing for all of us," she said. Then we drained our cups in silence.

Though I came and went from the Sun Dance grounds (it was too hot to stand around in the direct sun) the ceremonies continued all day and most of each night. At nine the "runners" drove to the swamp to cut reeds from which they fashioned beds for the dancers. The moisture in the long, bladelike leaves helped cool the men off. At ten, special food eaten by the dancers' families was blessed in the Lodge, and this was surely to become one of the dancers' daily agonies: the smell of meat, stew, and fry bread filling the space, then being taken away. The sunrise drummers were spelled by new ones, and as the songs began again those dancers who could stood in their places and danced. Each man was required to dance a certain number of hours a day. When he was too weak or sick or reeling from hallucination, he was allowed to rest on his rush mat.

"What happens if it rains during Sun Dance?" I asked my Kiowa friend. "It doesn't," she answered curtly. By eleven, it was ninety-nine degrees. We drove west away from the grounds to the land she owned and went skinny-dipping in the river. Her brown body bobbed up and down next to my white one. Behind us a wall of colored rock rose out of the water, part of a leathery bluff that curved for miles. "That's where the color for the Sun Dance paints comes from," my friend's husband said, pointing to a cave. He'd just floated into view from around an upstream bend. With his big belly glinting, he had the complacent look of a man who lords over a houseful of women: a wife, two daughters, a young tutor for his girls. The night before, they'd thrown an anniversary party at this spot. There were tables full of Mexican food, a five-piece Mexican band whose members looked like reformed Hell's Angels, a charro with four skinny horses and a trick-riding act, two guests who arrived from the oil fields by helicopter, and a mutual friend who's Jewish and a Harvard professor who popped bikini-clad out of a giant plywood cake.

The men in the Rabbit Lodge danced as late as the partygoers. The next morning when I arrived at four-thirty the old man with the cane walked directly to me. "Where's your coat? Aren't you cold?" he asked gruffly, though I knew he was welcoming me. The dancers spit bile and shuffled back and forth between the johns and the Lodge. A friend had asked one of them how he prepared for Sun Dance. He replied, "I don't. There's no way to prepare for pain." As the dancers began to look more frail, the singing became raucous. The astounding volume, quick rises in pitch, and forays into falsetto had an enlivening effect on all of us. Now it was the drummers who made the dancers make the sun rise.

Noon. In the hottest midday sun the dancers were brought out in front of the Lodge to be washed and freshly painted. The grandfathers dipped soft little brooms of sage in water and swabbed the men down; they weren't allowed to drink. Their families gathered around and watched while the dancers held their gaze to the ground. I couldn't bring myself to stand close. It seemed a violation of privacy. It wasn't nudity that rendered the scene so intimate (they still had their gym shorts on), but the thirst. Behind me, someone joked about dancing for rain instead of sun.

I was wrong about the bathing scene. Now the desolation of it struck me as beautiful. All afternoon the men danced in the heat—two, eight, or twenty of them at a time. In air so dry and with their juices squeezed out, the bouncing looked weightless, their bodies thin and brittle as shells. It wasn't the pain of the sacrifice they were making that counted but the emptiness to which they were surrendering themselves. It was an old ritual: separation, initiation, return. They'd left their jobs and families to dance. They were facing physical pain and psychological transformation. Surely, the sun seared away preoccupation and pettiness. They would return changed. Here, I was in the presence of a collective hero. I searched their faces and found no martyrs, no dramatists, no antiheroes either. They seemed to pool their pain and offer it back to us, dancing not for our sins but to ignite our hearts.

Evening. There were many more spectators tonight. Young Indian women cradling babies moved to the front of the Lodge. They rocked them in time with the drums and all evening not one child cried. Currents of heat rose from the ground; in fact, everything seemed to be rising: bone whistles, arms, stars, penises, the yeast in the fry bread, the smell of sage. My breasts felt full. The running joke in camp was about "Sun Dance Babies." Surely the expansive mood in the air settled over the tipis at night, but there was more to it than that. Among some tribes a "Sacred Woman" is involved in the ceremony. The sun is a "man power" symbol. When she offers herself to the priest, their union represents the rebirth of the land, water, and people. If by chance a child is conceived, he or she is treated with special reverence for a lifetime.

Dawn. This morning I fainted. The skinny young man dancing in front of me appeared to be cringing in pain. Another dancer's face had been painted green. I'm not saying they made me faint—maybe I fainted for them. With little ado, the women behind me picked me up. Revived and feeling foolish, I stood through to the end. "They say white people don't have the constitution to go without water for so many days," a white friend commented later. It sounded like a racist remark to me. She'd once been offered a chance to fast with a medicine man and refused. "I think it has more to do with one's concepts of hope and fear," I mumbled as she walked through the field to her car.

Afternoon. At five, only two dancers were standing. Because of the heat, the smell of urine had mixed with the sage.

Later in the evening I stood next to two teenage boys from Oklahoma. Not realizing I was old enough to be their mother, they flirted with me, then undercut the dares with cruelty. "My grandmother hates white tourists," the one who had been eyeing my chest said to me. "You're missing the point of this ceremony," I said to him. "And racism isn't a good thing anywhere." They walked away, but later, when I bumped into them, they smiled apologetically.

When I had coffee in a friend's brush arbor during a break in the dancing, the dancer's wife looked worried. "He looks like death warmed over," she said. A young man with black braids that reached his belt buckle was dangling a baby on each knee; I've never seen men so gentle and at ease with children. A fresh breeze fanned us. The round-the-clock rhythm of drumbeats and dancing made day and night seem the same. Sleeping became interchangeable with waiting, until, finally, there was no difference between the two.

Sunday. Two American flags were raised over the Lodge today—both had been owned by war veterans. The dance apron of a man near me had U.S. Navy insignias sewn into the corners. Here was a war hero, but he'd earned his medal far from home. Now the ritual of separation, initiation, and return performed in Vietnam, outside the context of community, changes into separation, benumbment, and exile.

Throughout the afternoon's dancing there was a Give-Away, an Indian tradition to honor friends, relatives, and admirers with a formal exchange of gifts. In front of the announcer's stand there was a table chock-full of food and another stacked high with Pendleton blankets, shawls, and beadwork. The loudspeaker overwhelmed the drumming until all the gifts were dispersed. Pickups streamed through the camps and a layer of dust muted the hard brightness of the day. After his first Sun Dance one old man told me he had given nearly everything he owned away: horse, wagons, clothes, winter blankets. "But it all comes back," he said, as if the day and night rhythm of this ceremony stood for a bigger tidal cadence as well.

Evening. They've taken the brush away from the far side of the Lodge. Now the dancers face west. All hundred men, freshly painted with a wild dappling of dots, stripes, and crooked lines, bounced up and down vigorously and in short strokes waved eagle fans in front of their bodies as if to clear away any tiredness there.

When I asked why the Sun Dance ended at night, my friend said, "So the sun will remember to make a complete circle, and so we'll always have night and day." The sun drained from the dancers' faces and sank into a rack of thunderclouds over the mountains. Every movement coming from the Lodge converged into a single trajectory, a big "V" like a flock of birds migrating toward me. This is how ritual speaks with no words. The dancing and whistling surged; each time a crescendo felt near, it ebbed. In the southwest, the first evening star appeared, and the drumming and singing, which had begun to feel like a hard dome over my head, stopped.

Amid cries of relief and some clapping I heard hoarse expulsions of air coming from dancers, like whales breaching after being under water too long. They rushed forward to the front of the Lodge, throwing off the sage bracelets and crowns, knelt down in turn by wooden bowls of chokecherry juice, and drank their first liquid in four days.

The family standing next to me approached the Lodge cautiously. "There he is," I heard the mother say. They walked toward the dancer, a big, lumbering man in his thirties whose waist, where rolls of fat had been, now looked concave. The man's wife and father slid their arms around his back, while his mother stood in front and took a good look at him. He gave her the first drink of sweet water from his bowl. "I tried to be there as much as possible today. Did you see me?" his wife asked. He nodded and smiled. Some of the young children had rushed into the Lodge and were swinging the flattened reeds that had been the dancers' beds around and around in the air. One of the drummers, an energetic man with an eccentric, husky voice, walked up to a group of us and started shaking our hands. He didn't know us but it didn't matter. "I'm awfully glad you're here," he kept saying, then walked away laughing ecstatically. The dancer I had been watching was having trouble staying on his feet. He stumbled badly. A friend said he worked for Amoco and tomorrow he'd be back in the oil fields. Still supporting him with their arms, his family helped him toward their brush arbor, now lit with oil lamps, where he would vomit, then feast.

It's late August. Wind swings down the hay meadows from high cornices of rimrock above the ranch like guffaws of laughter. Since Sun Dance several images recur: the shaded, shell-like bodies of the dancers getting smaller and smaller; the heated, expanding spectators surrounding them. At the point of friction, a generosity occurs. The transition to autumn is a ritual like that: heat and cold alternate in a staccato rhythm. The magnetizing force of summer reverses itself so that every airplane flying over me seems to be going away. Heat lightning washes over and under clouds until their coolness drops down to us and then flotillas of storms bound through as though riding the sprung legs of a deer. I feel both emptied and brimming over.

A week later. I'm camped on a hill next to an anthropologist and his wife. He's Indian, she's white, and they drove here on what he calls his "iron pony"—a motorcycle—to attend Crow Fair. "You see I had to marry one of these skinny white women so we could both fit here," he explained as they squeezed onto the seat. He was as round and cheerful as the chrome gas tank his belly rested on. Surrounding us were the rolling grasslands that make up the middle Yellowstone Valley, site of the summer councils held by the warring Crow, Sioux, Blackfoot, and Cheyenne. The Wolf Mountains to the south step up into pitched rises, crowned with jack pines. The dark creases in the hills are dry washes, now blackened with such an abundance of ripe chokecherries they look clotted with blood. On a knob nearby, recently singed with fire, is Custer's battlefield. "If there was any yellow hair left on that sonofabitch, it's gone now," a Crow friend who had fought the fire said. The Crows, of course, were the ones scouting for Custer, but it seems to have been a temporary alliance, having more to do with their animosity toward other tribes than a love for any white man.

Crow Fair is a five-day country fair—Indian style. It's different from ours because their roots are nomadic, not agricultural. Instead of the horse pulls, steer judging, and cake stands, they have all-night sessions of Indian dancing, a traditional dress parade, and a lengthy rodeo augmented by horse racing and betting. Looking down from the hill where I pitched our borrowed tent, the encampment of well over five hundred tipis could have been a summer council at the turn of the nineteenth century except for the pickups, loudspeakers, and the ubiquitous aluminum folding chairs. Inside the sprawl of tipis, tents, and arbors was a circle of concession stands, at the center of which stood the big open-air dance arbor.

My young friend Ursula, who was visiting from Cambridge, asked if these Indians lived here all the time. Indians don't, of course, still live in tipis, but the encampment looked so well-worn and amiable she wasn't wrong in thinking so. Part of the "wholeness" of traditional Indian life that the tipi and circular dance arbor signify is the togetherness at these powwows. Indians don't go home at night; they camp out where the action is, en masse, whole extended families and clans spanning several generations. It's a tradition with them the way sending our kids to summer camp is with us.

Two days before the fair started, the pickups began to roll in with tipi poles slung over the tailgates. Brush was cut, canvas unrolled, and in twelve hours a village had been made. Tipis and tents, reserved mainly for sleeping, were often as plush as an Arab's. Inside were wall-to-wall rugs, hanging lanterns, and ceremonial drums. Outdoor kitchens were arranged under canvas flies or inside a shady brush arbor with packing crates turned on end for shelves, and long picnic tables were loaded with food. With barely any elbow room between camps, even feuding tribes took on a congenial air, their children banding together and roving freely.

At the morning parade you could see the splendors of traditional beadwork, elk tooth shirts, buckskin dresses, and beaded moccasins, but what interested me more were the contradictions: the Sioux boy in warrior dress riding the hood of a Corvette; vans with smokey windows covered with star quilts and baskets; the roar of new wave music coming from the cars. John Whiteman, the last surviving Custer scout, rode on the back of a big ton truck with his tiny wife, who had hoisted up a brown-and-white-striped umbrella to shade herself from the sun. They were both, someone said, well past 110 years old.

Ursula and I were the first ones at the rodeo because everyone else seemed to know it would start late. The young, cigar-smoking man who sold us our tickets turned out to be an Eskimo from Barrow, Alaska. He'd come south to live with what he called "these mean Plains Indians."

The Crow crossed into this valley in the late 1700s and fought off the Shoshone to claim territory that spread between the Big Horns, the Badlands, and the Wind River Mountains. Trappers, like Osborne Russell, who hunted right along with them, described the Crow as tall, insolent, and haughty, but submissive when cornered. Russell met one chief who had hair eleven feet long, and said their beadwork was "excessively gaudy." The Crows were so pinched geographically by raiding Sioux and Blackfeet they adopted a militaristic style, still evident in the way they zipped around camp in police cars with "Executive Security Force" emblazoned on the doors. Endowed with a natural horse-handling ability, they became famous horse thieves.

The rodeo got under way after an off-key rendition of "God Bless America" (instead of the national anthem). A local band, aptly named "The Warriors," warmed up on the stand in front of us. While the rough stock was run into the bucking chutes they played "He's Just a Coca-Cola Cowboy." As testimony to their enthusiasm for horses, the rodeo, usually a two- or three-hour affair, lasted seven hours.

Before the all-night session of dancing began we made the circuit of concession stands. Between the corn dogs and Indian tacos—fry bread topped with beans and hot sauce—was an aisle of video games. Between the menudo and the caramel apples were two gambling tents—one for bingo, the other for poker. You could eat corn barbecued in the husk Navajo style and a hunk of Taos bread, or gulp down a buffalo burger and a Coke, the one cooked by a Navajo from Shiprock, the other by an Ogalalla Sioux. Ursula had her ears pierced and bought a pair of opalescent earrings; I bought a T-shirt with the words "Crow Fair" across the front, and around and around we went until the dancing began.

Dark. Instead of the tamping, rigid, narcotic bounce of Sun Dance that seemed to set into motion a chronic tremor, one that radiated out of the Lodge to knock against our legbones and temples, the dances at Crow Fair were show-offish and glittering. These Society, War, Animal, and Contest Dances served no direct purpose these days, the way some religious dances do. "What you're seeing out there is a lot of dyed turkey feathers and plastic elk teeth, and kids doing the Indian disco," a friend commented. He's an Italian from Saint Louis who married a Kiowa woman when he was sixteen and together they moved to Wyoming to live with the Shoshone. Incongruity delights him as much as tradition. "We assimilate a little this way, and a little that way. Life is only mutation."

The dance arbor was lit by mercury vapor lamps hung from one forty-foot power pole at the center—no bonfires or Coleman lanterns here. The ceremonies started with a long prayer in English during which a Crow child in front of me shot off a toy gun, aiming first at the preacher, then at himself, then at me. Six separate drum groups set up around the periphery with names like Night Hawks, Whistling Elk, Plenty Coups, Magpie, and Salt Lake Crows. Although participants had come from a great number of tribes—Assiniboine, Apache and Shoshone, Sioux, Kiowa, and Arapaho—what we saw was only Plains Indian dancing. Performed in a clockwise motion, as if following the sun, the dancers moved in long lines like spokes on a wheel. Anyone could dance, and it seemed at times as if everyone did. Families crowded in around the dance space with their folding chairs and Pendleton blankets—babies and grandmothers, boys and fathers, mothers and daughters, all dressed fit to kill. The long succession of dances began: Girls' Fancy Shawl, Boys' Traditional, Fast and Slow War Dance, a Hoop Dance, a Hot Dance, and a Grass Dance. Intertribal dances—open to anyone—alternated with contest dances that were judged. Participants wore Coors numbers pinned to their backs the way bronc riders do. The costumes were elaborate. There were feathers dyed magenta and lime green, then fluffed at the tips; great feather bustles attached to every backside; and long straps of sleighbells running from ankles to hips. The Hot Dancers wore porcupine-hair roaches on their heads, the War Dancers carried straight and crooked lances, the Society Dancers wore wolf heads with little pointed ears, and the women in fringed buckskin dresses carried elegant eagle fans. One young man, who seemed to be a loner, had painted black stripes across his face and chest so thickly the paint ran together into a blackface. Later, we discovered he was white. A good many white people danced every night. One couple had flown in from Germany; they were Hot Dance aficionados, and when I tried to talk to them I found out they spoke only German and Crow. A blond boy of ten said he had driven north from Arizona with his adopted Apache parents. After eating a cheesy, dripping box of nachos, he went out to win his contest.

I squeezed through the delicious congestion of bodies, feathers brushing my cheeks, and circled under the eaves of the arbor. One boy, who couldn't have been older than three, in war bonnet and bells, shuffled out into the dance circle. The Mylar balloon tied to his hand was shaped like a fish. Four boys dancing near the power pole crouched low, jerking their heads and shoulders in the Prairie Chicken Dance. The Fast Dancers spun by, like wheels of fireworks, orbiting at twice the speed of the others.

Outside the arbor was a residual flux: crowds of Indian teenagers ambled past the bright concession stands, behind which a ribbon of headlights streamed, and behind them glowed rows of tents and tipis.

The arbor closed at 3 A.M., and we walked up our hill and went to bed. A couple of drunks stumbled by. "Hey. What's this? A tombstone?" one of them said as he kicked the tent. When no one answered, he disappeared in the brush. Later, the 49ers, a roving group of singers, began their encampment serenade. They sang until dawn every night of the fair so that even sleep, accompanied by their drumbeats, felt like a kind of dancing.

Crow Fair days are hot; Crow Fair nights are cold. A rumbling truck woke me. It was the septic tank man (he was white) pumping the outhouses. Some Livingston, Montana, friends who had arrived late were scattered around on the ground in sleeping bags. I brushed my teeth with water I'd brought for the radiator. The dance arbor, abandoned and dreary at midday, was getting a facelift from a cleanup crew. All the action was elsewhere: when I walked toward the bluffs behind the camp, I discovered two hundred children splashing in the Little Big Horn River.

That afternoon I visited Gary Johnson's camp. He's a bright, sly Crow drummer. Over some beadwork repairs he was swatting flies. "You killed our buffalo, I'll kill your flies," he said with a sardonic grin as I pulled up a chair. A small boy had taken Gary's drumstick and had beaten the metal top of a beer cooler until it was covered with dents. "Let him play, let him play," Gary admonished the boy's mother. "That's how we learn to make music." To be a drummer is to be a singer too, the voice used as percussively as the drum is musically. "I'd like to steal this boy. He and I would sing every night."

Every turn of the nomadic Crow life was once marked by movement and music. There were dances to celebrate birth, puberty, marriage, or death. There were healing dances and hunters' dances and contrary dances, in which all movement was done in reverse. There were dances to count coup, welcome strangers, honor guests, to cement alliances and feuds. Songs weren't composed but received whole from animals, plants, or storms. Antelope gave mothers lullabies, thunder and wind gave medicine songs, bears taught hunting songs.

Carlos Castaneda gave us talking bushes, but few of us realized how common these transmissions had become in aboriginal America. When I asked Gary about his pink-and-red-striped tipi—the only one of its kind in camp—he explained: "That's a medicine tipi. Somehow I inherited it. The creek water rose up and told the guy living in it to dress and live like a woman. That was to be his medicine. So he became a *berdache* [a transvestite]." He gave me a serious look. "I'll do anything in that tipi, but I'll be damned if I'm going to sleep in it."

D. H. Lawrence described the Apache ceremonies he saw as "the feet of birds treading a dance" and claimed the music awakened in him "new root-griefs, old root-richnesses." In the next three nights I saw the quick, addled movements of blue grouse, feet that worked the ground like hooves, or else massaged it erotically with moccasins. One of the nights, when almost everyone had gone, I thought I heard women singing. It turned out to be teenage boys whose strange, hoarse voices convulsed and ululated in a falsetto. Gary was there and he drummed and danced and his son and wife danced, all the repetitions redoubled by multiple generations. How affectionately the shimmering beadwork traced the shapes of their dreams and threaded them back to the bodies that dreamed them.

It had been raining on and off all evening. The spectators and all but a few dancers had left. Shoals of garbage—pop cans, hot-dog wrappers, corn husks, and pieces of fry bread—drifted up against the wooden benches. I knew I had been riding an ebb tide here at Crow Fair. I'd seen beadworkers' beadwork, dancers' dance steps, Indianness for the sake of being Indian—a shell of a culture whose spontaneous force had been revived against great odds and was transmitting weak signals. But transmitting nonetheless. The last intertribal dance was announced. Already, three of the drum groups had packed up and were leaving the arbor when five or six Crow men, dressed like cowboys, walked onto the grass. In boots, not moccasins, and still smoking cigarettes, they formed a long line and shuffled around and around. The shrill, trembling song that accompanied them could empower anyone listening to turn away from distraction and slide their hands across the buttocks of the world— above and beyond the ceremonial decor that was, after all, the point of all this. At the last minute, a young boy jumped up and burst into a boiling, hot-stepping Fast Dance, his feathered headdress shaking down his back like lightning. I wondered how much of this culture-straddling he could take and what in it would finally be instructive to him. Almost under his bounding feet a row of young children were sleeping on blankets laid out for them. Their feather bustles were bent and askew and a couple of moccasins were missing. A very tall Crow man with long braids but skin so light he might actually have been white began picking up the children. One by one, and so gently none of them woke, he carried them away.

Looking for a Lost Dog

The most valuable thoughts which I entertain are anything but what I thought.
Nature abhors a vacuum, and if I can only walk with sufficient carelessness I am
sure to be filled.
—HENRY DAVID THOREAU

I started off this morning looking for my lost dog. He's a red heeler, blotched brown and white, and I tell people he looks like a big saddle shoe. Born at Christmas on a thirty-below-zero night, he's tough, though his right front leg is crooked where it froze to the ground.

It's the old needle-in-the-haystack routine: small dog, huge landscape, and rugged terrain. While moving cows once, he fell in a hole and disappeared. We heard him whining but couldn't see him. When we put our ears to the ground, we could hear the hole that had swallowed him.

It's no wonder human beings are so narcissistic. The way our ears are constructed, we can only hear what's right next to us or else the internal monologue inside. I've taken to cupping my hands behind my ears—mule-like—and pricking them all the way forward or back to hear what's happened or what's ahead.

"Life is polyphonic," a Hungarian friend in her eighties said. She was a child prodigy from Budapest who had soloed on the violin in Paris and Berlin by the time she was twelve. "Childishly, I once thought hearing had mostly to do with music," she said. "Now that I'm too old to play the fiddle, I know it has to do with the great suspiration of life everywhere."

But back to the dog. I'm walking and looking and listening for him, though there is no trail, no clue, no direction to the search. Whimsically, I head north toward the falls. They're set in a deep gorge where Precambrian rock piles up to ten thousand feet on either side. A raven creaks overhead, flies into the cleft, glides toward a panel of white water splashing over a ledge, and comes out cawing.

To find what is lost is an art in some cultures. The Navajos employ "hand tremblers," usually women, who go into a trance and "see" where the lost article or person is located. When I asked one such diviner what it was like when she was in trance, she said, "Lots of noise, but noise that's hard to hear."

Near the falls the ground flattens into a high-altitude valley before the mountains rise vertically. The falls roar, but they're overgrown with spruce, pine, willow, and wild rose, and the closer I get, the harder it is to see the water. Perhaps that is how it will be in my search for the dog.

We're worried about Frenchy because last summer he was bitten three times by rattlesnakes. After the first bite he walked toward me, reeled dramatically, and collapsed. I could see the two holes in his nose where the fangs went in, and I felt sure he was dying. I drove him twenty miles to the vet; by the time we arrived, Frenchy resembled a monster. His nose and neck had swollen as though a football had been sewn under the skin.

I walk and walk. Past the falls, through a pass, toward a larger, rowdier creek. The sky goes black. In the distance snow on the Owl Creek Mountains glares. A blue ocean seems to stretch between, and the black sky hangs over like a frown. A string of cottonwoods whose new, tender leaves are the color of limes pulls me downstream. I come into the meadow with the abandoned apple orchard. The trees have leaves but have lost most of their blossoms. I feel as if I had caught strangers undressed.

The sun comes back, and the wind. It brings no dog, but ducks slide overhead. An Eskimo from Barrow, Alaska, told me the reason spring has such fierce winds is so birds coming north will have something to fly on.

To find what's lost; to lose what's found. Several times I've thought I might be "losing my mind." Of course, minds aren't literally misplaced—on the contrary, we live too much under them. As with viewing the falls, we can lose sight of what is too close. It is between the distant and close-up views that the struggle between impulse and reason, logic and passion takes place.

The feet move; the mind wanders. In his journals Thoreau wrote: "The saunterer, in the good sense, is no more vagrant than the meandering river, which is all the while sedulously seeking the shortest course to the sea."

Today I'm filled with longings—for what I'm not, for what is impossible, for people I love who can't be in my life. Passions of all sorts struggle soundlessly, or else, like the falls, they are all noise but can't be seen. My hybrid anguish spends itself as recklessly and purposefully as water.

Now I'm following a game trail up a sidehill. It's a mosaic of tracks—elk, deer, rabbit, and bird. If city dwellers could leave imprints in cement, it would look this way: tracks would overlap, go backward and forward like the peregrine saunterings of the mind.

I see a dog's track, or is it a coyote's? I get down on my hands and knees to sniff out a scent. What am I doing? I entertain expectations of myself as preposterous as when I landed in Tokyo—I felt so at home there that I thought I would break into fluent Japanese. Now I sniff the ground and smell only dirt. If I spent ten years sniffing, would I learn scents?

The tracks veer off the trail and disappear. Descending into a dry wash whose elegant, tortured junipers and tumbled boulders resemble a Japanese garden, I trip on a sagebrush root. I look. Deep in the center of the plant there is a bird's nest, but instead of eggs, a locust stares up at me.

Some days I think this one place isn't enough. That's when nothing is enough, when I want to live multiple lives and be allowed to love without limits. Those days, like today, I walk with a purpose but no destination. Only then do I see, at least momentarily, that everything is here. To my left a towering cottonwood is lunatic with birdsong. Under it I'm a listening post while its great gray trunk—like a baton or the source of something—heaves its green symphony into the air.

I walk and walk: from the falls, over Grouse Hill, to the dry wash. Today it is enough to make a shadow.

Just Married

I met my husband at a John Wayne film festival in Cody, Wyoming. The film series was a rare midwinter entertainment to which people from all over the state came. A mutual friend, one of the speakers at the festival, introduced us, and the next morning when *The Man Who Shot Liberty Valance* was shown, we sat next to each other by chance. The fact that he cried during sad scenes in the film made me want to talk to him so we stayed in town, had dinner together, and closed down the bars. Here was a man who could talk books as well as ranching, medieval history and the mountains, ideas and mules. Like me he was a culture straddler. Ten months later we were married.

He had planned to propose while we were crossing Cougar Pass—a bald, ten-thousand-foot dome—with twenty-two head of loose horses, but a front was moving through, and in the commotion, he forgot. Another day he loped up to me: "Want to get hitched?" he said. Before I could respond there was horse trouble ahead and he loped away. To make up for the unceremonious interruption, he serenaded me that night with the wistful calls sandhill cranes make. A cow elk wandered into the meadow and mingled with the horses. It snowed and in the morning a choir of coyotes howled, "Yes."

After signing for our license at the county courthouse we were given a complimentary "Care package," a Pandora's box of grotesqueries: Midol, Kotex, disposable razors, shaving cream, a bar of soap—a summing up, I suppose, of what in a marriage we could look forward to: blood, pain, unwanted hair, headaches, and dirt. "Hey, where's the champagne and cigars?" I asked.

We had a spur-of-the-moment winter wedding. I called my parents and asked them what they were doing the following Saturday. They had a golf game. I told them to cancel it. "Instead of waiting, we've decided to get married while the bloom is still on," I said.

It was a walk-in wedding. The road crew couldn't get the snow plowed all the way to the isolated log cabin where the ceremony was to be held. We drove as far as we could in my pickup, chaining up on the way.

In the one hushed moment before the ceremony started, Rusty, my dog, walked through the small crowd of well-wishers and lay down at my feet. On his wolfish-wise face was a look that said, "What about me?" So the three of us were married that day. Afterward we skated on the small pond in front of the house and drank from open bottles of champagne stuck in the snow.

"Here's to the end of loneliness," I toasted quietly, not believing such a thing could come true. But it did and nothing prepared me for the sense of peace I felt—of love gone deep into a friendship—so for a while I took it to be a premonition of death—the deathbed calm we're supposed to feel after getting our affairs in order.

A year later while riding off a treeless mountain slope in a rainstorm I was struck by lightning. There was a white flash. It felt as though sequins had been poured down my legs, then an electrical charge thumped me at the base of my skull as if I'd been mugged. Afterward the crown of my head itched and the bottoms of my feet arched up and burned. "I can't believe you're still alive," my husband said. The open spaces had cleansed me before. This was another kind of scouring, as when at the end of a painful appointment with the dentist he polishes your teeth.

Out across the Basin chips of light on waterponds mirrored the storm that passed us. Below was the end-of-the-road ranch my husband and I had just bought, bumped up against a nine-thousand-foot-high rockpile that looks like a Sung Dynasty painting. Set off from a series of narrow rambling hayfields which in summer are cataracts

of green is the 1913 poor-man's Victorian house—uninsulated, crudely plumbed—
that is now ours.

A Texan, Billy Hunt, homesteaded the place in 1903. Before starting up the
almost vertical wagon trail he had to take over the Big Horns to get there, he married
the hefty barmaid in the saloon where he stopped for a beer. "She was tough as a
piece of rawhide," one old-timer remembered. The ten-by-twenty cabin they built
was papered with the editorial and classified pages of the day; the remnants are still
visible. With a fresno and a team of horses, Hunt diverted two mountain creeks
through a hundred acres of meadows cleared of sagebrush. Across the face of the
mountain are the mossed-over stumps of cedar and pine trees cut down and axed
into a set of corrals, sheds, gates, and hitchrails. With her first child clasped in front
of the saddle, Mrs. Hunt rode over the mountains to the town of Dayton—a trip
that must have taken fifteen hours—to buy supplies.

Gradually the whole drainage filled up with homesteaders. Twenty-eight children
attended the one-room schoolhouse a mile down the road; there were a sawmill and
blacksmith's shop, and once-a-month mail service by saddle horse or sleigh. Now the
town of Cloverly is no more; only three families live at the head of the creek.
Curiously, our friends in the valley think it's crazy to live in such an isolated
place—thirty miles from a grocery store, seventy-five from a movie theater. When
I asked one older resident what he thought, he said, "Hell almighty . . . God didn't
make ranchers to live close to town. Anyway, it was a better town when you had
to ride the thirty miles to it."

We moved here in February: books, tables, and a rack of clothes at one end of
the stock truck, our horses tied at the back. There was a week of moonless nights
but the Pleiades rose over the ridge like a piece of jewelry. Buying a ranch had sent
us into spasms of soul-searching. It went against the bachelor lives we had grown
used to: the bunkhouse-bedroll-barroom circuit; it meant our chronic vagrancy
would come to an end. The proprietary impulse had dubious beginnings anyway—
we had looked all that up before getting married: how ownership translates into
possessiveness, protection into xenophobia, power into greed. Our idea was to rescue
the ranch from the recent neglect it had seen.

As soon as the ground thawed we reset posts, restrung miles of barbed wire, and
made the big ranch gates—hung eighty years ago between cedar posts as big around
as my hips—swing again.

Above and around us steep canyons curve down in garlands of red and yellow
rimrock: Precambrian, Madison, Chugwater formations, the porous parts of which
have eroded into living-room-sized caves where mountain lions lounge and feast on
does and snowshoe rabbits. Songbirds fly in and out of towering cottonwoods the
way people throng office buildings. Mornings, a breeze fans up from the south;
evenings, it reverses directions, so there is a streaming of life, a brushing back and
forth like a massage. We go for walks. A friend told us the frosting of limestone that
clings to the boulders we climb is all that's left of the surface of the earth a few
million years ago. Some kinds of impermanence take a long time.

The seasons are a Jacob's ladder climbed by migrating elk and deer. Our ranch
is one of their resting places. If I was leery about being an owner, a possessor of land,
now I have to understand the ways in which the place possesses me. Mowing

hayfields feels like mowing myself. I wake up mornings expecting to find my hair shorn. The pastures bend into me; the water I ushered over hard ground becomes one drink of grass. Later in the year, feeding the bales of hay we've put up is a regurgitative act: thrown down from a high stack on chill days they break open in front of the horses like loaves of hot bread.

Considerations for Thinking and Writing

1. In "Spring" Ehrlich claims, "Nothing in this world is plain." In what ways does she convince you that her claim is reliable? At the end of the essay, Ehrlich says that she dreams of Joel "riding that horse and he knows he is dead. One night he rides to my house, all smiles and shyness. I let him in." Why do you suppose she would let him in? What has made her change her mind?

2. Read Leslie Marmon Silko's "Landscape, History, and the Pueblo Imagination." In what ways might her essay help you understand what Ehrlich is saying about ritual and ceremony in "To Live in Two Worlds"? What do you think Silko's reaction would be to Ehrlich's essay?

3. In "Two Worlds" Ehrlich says that we "live in a culture that has lost its memory." What does she mean? Find evidence from your own life and the life of your community that contradicts Ehrlich's judgment.

4. What happens to the "Lost Dog"? In terms of what Ehrlich is trying to tell us about thinking, does it matter? Explain.

5. Read Phyllis Rose's prologue to *Parallel Lives* and Ehrlich's "Just Married." Compare the nineteenth-century lives and relationships Rose discusses with Ehrlich's marriage. Which kind of marriage would you prefer? Why?

6. If Joan Didion were to compare Georgia O'Keeffe and Gretel Ehrlich, what do you think she would say about these two women? Would she consider Ehrlich a "hard" woman? Elaborate.

7. How do you think Luce Irigaray and Hélène Cixous would react to Ehrlich's writing? Before you answer that question, you might want to read another of Ehrlich's essays—"A Storm, the Cornfield, and Elk," in *The Solace of Open Spaces.* Do you think that Ehrlich is writing woman, or do you think she is simply writing well?

JUNE JORDAN
(b. 1936)

June Jordan, born in Harlem and raised in the Bedford-Stuyvesant section of Brooklyn, has one of the most powerful and authentic voices in modern letters. In addition to the two volumes of political essays—*Civil Wars* (1981) and *On Call* (1985)—represented in this anthology, Jordan has published fourteen volumes of poetry, drama, and biography. Her essays and poems have appeared in such publica-tions as the *New York Times,* the *Village Voice,* the *New Republic, Ms., Essence, Newsday, New Black Poetry,* and *Partisan Review.* Her awards include a Rockefeller Grant in Creative Writing, the American Library Association's award for the best book of the year, the *New York Times* award for outstanding book of the year, and the Prix de Rome in Environmental Design. She has also been a National Book

Award finalist and a fellow of the National Education Association. Jordan is a member of the Board of Directors for Poets and Writers, Inc., and of the Center for Constitutional Rights. She has taught at City College of the City University of New York, Sarah Lawrence College, and Yale University. She is Professor of English at State University of New York, Stony Brook.

The essays we have chosen represent the range of Jordan's mind and the complexity of her vision. She is a combative, powerful woman whose urgent, insistent voice never lacks compassion, never fails to express, even in moments of anger, the love she prescribes as antidote to hatred, injustice, and political ineptitude. Her strength and her clarity of vision come always from her fundamental insistence on human rights, on dignity and freedom for individuals regardless of color, creed, or gender. Hers is not a self-righteous solipsistic view of the world, but she does put self-respect and self-love at the very center of that world view. Jordan argues forcefully in "Where Is the Love?" that the struggle for self-respect and for self-love is at bottom a struggle against "suicide," against the death of the individual in the collective. But her argument is nevertheless a call to unity, a movement toward collective strength that will engender individual rights; it is above all a rousing appeal by a Black feminist to those at the 1978 National Black Writers Conference to unite in love rather than divide over issues of sexuality. The difficult task she sets for herself—to "say things that people believe they don't want to hear, without having to kick ass and without looking the fool for holding out your hand"—calls for a compassionate activist. Jordan fills the bill, insisting that "a steady-state deep caring and respect for every other human being, a love that can only derive from a secure and positive self-love," overshadows less important, divisive issues.

In "Many Rivers to Cross" we get some sense of how difficult it may have been for Jordan to earn her own self-respect, some sense of the enormous price she and the rest of us have to pay for a regenerative kind of self-love. On the surface, "Rivers" is simply a narrative about her mother's death, but in the telling it becomes a powerful essay shaped around a complex tale of family struggle, of failure, of loss, and finally of Jordan's discovery of strength and resolve in the aftermath of her mother's suicide. But suicide is not the focal point of this essay; betrayal is—her mother's betrayal of her own self, of her own life, a betrayal so significant that it transcends the merely personal, representing all such acts of self-denial. And it is also a story of a father who at the very end of his wife's life could not determine whether she was living or dead; it is a bitter story of his indifference, a story in which we discover the dire necessity of self-love when no other love is available. The essay's power comes as much from a single image—an image of her mother frozen at the moment of death, trying to rise from her bed, trying to stand up—as it does from the haunting and tangled tale of Jordan's family life. That image of her mother informs all that Jordan has to tell us about her own resolve to live her life "so that people would know unmistakably that I am alive, so that when I finally die people will know the difference for sure between my living and my death." Jordan turns her mother's weakness into her own strength, shows us something about her own "steady-state deep caring" for her self and for her son.

"Report from the Bahamas," an essay about "consciousness of race and class and gender identity," complicates the politics of loving, shows us how difficult it is to put theory into practice. On vacation in the Bahamas, Jordan finds herself in a culture that requires Blacks to play the fool for whites, finds something troubling about bargaining with the Black woman for Bahamian gifts to take back to the United States, finds herself caught in a strange relationship with "Olive," the Black woman who cleans her hotel room, finds herself thinking about the inadequacy of courses in Black History and Women's Studies, finds that something important is missing from all the formal, academic schemes for unity, something essential. She doubts that the "usual race and class concepts of connection, or gender assumptions of unity, . . . apply well." When the "deal turns real," those concepts and assumptions can't bear the burden. Jordan denies that "the enemy" (the oppressor) is the "ultimate connection" between those in need. "The ultimate connection must be the need that we find between us. It is not only who you are, in other words, but what we can do for each other that will determine the connection." Jordan turns again to love, shows us finally how a young white woman befriended a young South African in need, shows us how her theory of unity works in the real world.

In "Nobody Mean More to Me Than You and the Future Life of Willie Jordan," Jordan herself is the actor, working to solve the world's problems but doing so in the context of her daily life, her work. "Willie Jordan" attacks police brutality and indifference. It is an essay that tells us finally how Willie Jordan, one of June Jordan's students at Stony Brook, comes to terms with the death of his brother. But this essay, like most of Jordan's essays, does not take shape out of a single narrative account. Willie Jordan's life and his brother's death at the hands of the police constitute the emotional center of an essay that develops out of a sense of community that Jordan creates in her classroom. Although she never suggests it, that classroom is a microcosm, a world within a world, a showcase for what we might do to change our lives and the lives of our students. Teaching a new course, "In Search of the Invisible Black Woman," she dis-covered while discussing *The Color Purple* that her students, male and female, Black and white, had no appreciation for the Black language of the novel. They were intimidated by it, didn't like it, had no sense of its power. So out of the context of their common misunderstanding, under Jordan's wise tutelage, they taught each other a language, a Black language, a language of power and clarity and community, a language that always "assumes the living and active participation of at least two human beings, the speaker and the listener," a language in which no passive construction is possible. Willie Jordan was in that class, learning that language, developing a sense of community, trying desperately to come to terms with injustice in South Africa while facing even more severe forms of injustice at home. So while teaching her students to talk plain and live "connected" lives, she shows us how to teach, how to use two languages in the same essay, how to weave two stories together, how to create an essay so powerful that it may change other lives.

To read June Jordan's essays is to be taxed, to be caught short, to be called into action. Her essays are indeed political, even meditational. They are smart, very smart, but they are not written to afford us quiet relaxed evenings in our studies. They demand something more of us. Because Jordan looks around corners, opens doors and drawers that others prefer to leave closed, because she likes to attack giants who have roamed the earth unmolested, we find too often that she has found us. She gets under our skin. Holding nothing sacred except life itself, she finds power in her own voice when she finds life violated, any life. And when she writes, she speaks, speaks directly to us in a language that stirs us out of our complacency into action.

Where Is the Love?

The 1978 National Black Writers Conference at Howard University culminated with an extremely intense public seminar entitled *Feminism and the Black Woman Writer*. This was an historic, unprecedented event tantamount to conceding that, under such a heading, there might be something to discuss! Acklyn Lynch, Sonia Sanchez, Barbara Smith, and myself were the panelists chosen to present papers to the standing room only audience. I had been asked, also, to moderate the proceedings and therefore gave the opening statement, *Where Is the Love?*, which was later published in *Essence* magazine.

From phone calls and other kinds of gossip, I knew that the very scheduling of this seminar had managed to divide people into camps prepared for war. Folks were so jumpy, in fact, that when I walked into the theater I ran into several Black feminists and then several Black men who, I suppose, just to be safe, had decided not to speak to anyone outside the immediate circle of supportive friends they had brought with them.

The session was going to be hot. Evidently, feminism was being translated into lesbianism, into something interchangeable with lesbianism, and the taboo on feminism, within the Black intellectual community, had long been exceeded in its orthodox severity only by the taboo on the subject of the lesbian. I say within the intellectual Black community, because, minus such terms as *feminist* and *lesbian*, the phenomena of self-directed Black women or the phenomena of Black women loving other women have hardly been uncommon, let alone unbelievable, events to Black people not privy to theoretical strife about correct and incorrect Black experience.

This blurring of issues seemed to me incendiary and obnoxious. Once again, the Black woman writer would be lost to view as issues of her sex life claimed public attention at the expense of intellectual and aesthetic focus upon her work. Compared to the intellectual and literary criticism accorded to James Baldwin and Richard Wright, for example, there is damned little attention paid to their bedroom activities. In any case, I do not believe that feminism is a matter, first or last, of sexuality.

The seminar was going to be a fight. It was not easy to prepare for this one. From my childhood in Brooklyn I knew that your peers would respect you if you could hurt somebody. Much less obvious was how to elicit respect as somebody who felt and who meant love.

I wanted to see if it was possible to say things that people believe they don't want to hear, without having to kick ass and without looking the fool for holding out your hand. Was there some way to say, to insist on, each, perhaps disagreeable, individual orientation and nonetheless leave the union of Black men and Black women, as a people, intact? I felt that there had to be: If the individual cannot exist then who will be the people?

I expected that we, Black panelists and audience, together, would work out a way to deal, even if we didn't want to deal. And that's what happened, at Howard. We did. Nobody walked out. Nobody stopped talking. The session ended because we ran out of time.

* * *

As I think about anyone or any thing—whether history or literature or my father or political organizations or a poem or a film—as I seek to evaluate the potentiality, the life-supportive commitment/possibilities of anyone or any thing, the decisive question is, always, *Where is the love?* The energies that flow from hatred, from negative and hateful habits and attitudes and dogma do not promise something good, something I would choose to cherish, to honor with my own life. It is always the love, whether we look to the spirit of Fannie Lou Hamer, or to the spirit of Agostinho Neto, it is always the love that will carry action into positive new places, that will carry your own nights and days beyond demoralization and away from suicide.

I am a feminist, and what that means to me is much the same as the meaning of the fact that I am Black: it means that I must undertake to love myself and to respect myself as though my very life depends upon self-love and self-respect. It means that I must everlastingly seek to cleanse myself of the hatred and the contempt that surrounds and permeates my identity, as a woman, and as a Black human being, in this particular world of ours. It means that the achievement of self-love and self-respect will require inordinate, hourly vigilance, and that I am entering my soul into a struggle that will most certainly transform the experience of all the peoples of the earth, as no other movement can, in fact, hope to claim: because the movement into self-love, self-respect, and self-determination is the movement now galvanizing the true, the unarguable majority of human beings everywhere. This movement explicitly demands the testing of the viability of a moral idea: that the health, the legitimacy of any status quo, any governing force, must be measured according to the experiences of those who are, comparatively, powerless. Virtue is not to be discovered in the conduct of the strong vis-à-vis the powerful, but rather it is to be found in our behavior and policies affecting those who are different, those who are weaker, or smaller than we. How do the strong, the powerful, treat children? How do we treat the aged among us? How do the strong and the powerful treat so-called minority members of the body politic? How do the powerful regard women? How do they treat us?

Easily you can see that, according to this criterion, the overwhelming reality of power and government and tradition is evil, is diseased, is illegitimate, and deserves nothing from us—no loyalty, no accommodation, no patience, no understanding— except a clear-minded resolve to utterly change this total situation and, thereby, to change our own destiny.

As a Black woman, as a Black feminist, I exist, simultaneously, as part of the powerless and as part of the majority peoples of the world in two ways: I am powerless as compared to any man because women, per se, are kept powerless by men/by the powerful; I am powerless as compared to anyone white because Black and Third World peoples are kept powerless by whites/by the powerful. I am the majority because women constitute the majority gender. I am the majority because Black and Third World peoples constitute the majority of life on this planet.

And it is here, in this extreme, inviolable coincidence of my status as a Black feminist, my status as someone twice stigmatized, my status as a Black woman who is twice kin to the despised majority of all the human life that there is, it is here, in that extremity, that I stand in a struggle against suicide. And it is here, in this extremity, that I ask, of myself, and of any one who would call me sister, *Where is the love?*

The love devolving from my quest for self-love and self-respect and self-determination must be, as I see it, something you can verify in the ways that I present myself to others, and in the ways that I approach people different from myself. How do I reach out to the people I would like to call my sisters and my brothers and my children and my lovers and my friends? If I am a Black feminist serious in the undertaking of self-love, then it seems to me that the legitimate, the morally defensible character of that self-love should be such that I gain and gain and gain in the socio-psychic strength needed so that I may, without fear, be able and willing to love and respect women, for example, who are not like me: women who are not feminists, women who are not professionals, women who are not as old or as young as I am, women who have neither job nor income, women who are not Black.

And it seems to me that the socio-psychic strength that should follow from a morally defensible Black feminism will mean that I become able and willing, without fear, to love and respect all men who are willing and able, without fear, to love and respect me. In short, if the acquirement of my self-determination is part of a worldwide, an inevitable, and a righteous movement, then I should become willing and able to embrace more and more of the whole world, without fear, and also without self-sacrifice.

This means that, as a Black feminist, I cannot be expected to respect what somebody else calls self-love if that concept of self-love requires my suicide to any degree. And this will hold true whether that somebody else is male, female, Black, or white. My Black feminism means that you cannot expect me to respect what somebody else identifies as the Good of The People, if that so-called Good (often translated into *manhood* or *family* or *nationalism*) requires the deferral or the diminution of my self-fulfillment. We *are* the people. And, as Black women, we are most of the people, any people, you care to talk about. And, therefore, nothing that is Good for The People is good unless it is good for me, as I determine myself.

When I speak of Black feminism, then, I am speaking from an exacerbated consciousness of the truth that we, Black women, huddle together, miserably, on the very lowest levels of the economic pyramid. We, Black women, subsist among the most tenuous and least likely economic conditions for survival.

When I speak of Black feminism, then, I am not speaking of sexuality. I am not speaking of heterosexuality or lesbianism or homosexuality or bisexuality; whatever sexuality anyone elects for his or her pursuit is not my business, nor the business of the state. And, furthermore, I cannot be persuaded that one kind of sexuality, as against another, will necessarily provide for the greater happiness of the two people involved. I am not talking about sexuality. I am talking about love, about a steady-state deep caring and respect for every other human being, a love that can only derive from a secure and positive self-love.

As a Black woman/feminist, I must look about me, with trembling, and with shocked anger, at the endless waste, the endless suffocation of my sisters: the bitter sufferings of hundreds of thousands of women who are the sole parents, the mothers of hundreds of thousands of children, the desolation and the futility of women trapped by demeaning, lowest-paying occupations, the unemployed, the bullied, the beaten, the battered, the ridiculed, the slandered, the trivialized, the raped, and the sterilized, the lost millions and multimillions of beautiful, creative, and momentous lives turned to ashes on the pyre of gender identity. I must look about me and, as a Black feminist, I must ask myself: *Where is the love?* How is my own lifework serving to end these tyrannies, these corrosions of sacred possibility?

As a Black feminist poet and writer I must look behind me with trembling, and with shocked anger, at the fate of Black women writers until now. From the terrible graves of a traditional conspiracy against my sisters in art, I must exhume the works of women writers and poets such as Georgia Douglas Johnson (who?).

In the early flush of the Harlem Renaissance, Georgia Johnson accomplished an astonishing, illustrious life experience. Married to Henry Lincoln Johnson, U.S. Recorder of Deeds in Washington, D.C., the poet, in her own right, became no less than Commissioner of Conciliation for the U.S. Department of Labor *(who was that again? Who?)*. And she, this poet, furthermore enjoyed the intense, promotional attention of Dean Kelley Miller, here at Howard, and W. E. B. Du Bois, and William Stanley Braithwaite, and Alain Locke. And she published three volumes of her own poetry and I found her work in Countee Cullen's anthology, *Caroling Dusk,* where, Countee Cullen reports, she, Georgia Douglas Johnson, thrived as a kind of Gwendolyn Brooks, holding regular Saturday night get-togethers with the young Black writers of the day.

And what did this poet of such acclaim, achievement, connection, and generosity, what did this poet have to say in her poetry, and who among us has ever heard of Georgia Douglas Johnson? And is there anybody in this room who can tell me the name of two or three other women poets from the Harlem Renaissance? And why did she die, and why does the work of all women die with no river carrying forward the record of such grace? How is it the case that whether we have written novels or poetry or whether we have raised our children or cleaned and cooked and washed and ironed, it is all dismissed as "women's work"; it is all, finally, despised as nothing important, and there is no trace, no echo of our days upon the earth?

Why is it not surprising that a Black woman as remarkably capable and gifted and proven as Georgia Douglas Johnson should be the poet of these pathetic, beggarly lines:

> I'm folding up my little dreams
> within my heart tonight
> And praying I may soon forget
> the torture of their sight
> *"My Little Dreams"*

How long, how long will we let the dreams of women serve merely to torture and not to ignite, to enflame, and to ennoble the promise of the years of every lifetime? And here is Georgia Douglas Johnson's poem "The Heart of a Woman":

> The heart of a woman goes forth with the dawn,
> As a lovebird, softwinging, so restlessly on,
> Afar o'er life's turrets and vales does it roam
> In the wake of those echoes the heart calls home.
>
> The heart of a woman falls back with the night
> And enters some alien cage in its plight,
> And tries to forget it has dreamed of the stars,
> While it breaks, breaks, breaks on the sheltering bars.

And it is against such sorrow, and it is against such suicide, and it is against such deliberated strangulation of the possible lives of women, of my sisters, and of powerless peoples—men and children—everywhere, that I work and live, now, as a feminist trusting that I will learn to love myself well enough to love you (whoever you are), well enough so that you will love me well enough so that we will know exactly where is the love: that it is here, between us, and growing stronger and growing stronger.

Many Rivers to Cross

When my mother killed herself I was looking for a job. That was fifteen years ago. I had no money and no food. On the pleasure side I was down to my last pack of Pall Malls plus half a bottle of J & B. I needed to find work because I needed to be able fully to support myself and my eight-year-old son, very fast. My plan was to raise enough big bucks so that I could take an okay apartment inside an acceptable public school district, by September. That deadline left me less than three months to turn my fortunes right side up.

It seemed that I had everything to do at once. Somehow, I must move all of our things, mostly books and toys, out of the housing project before the rent fell due, again. I must do this without letting my neighbors know because destitution and divorce added up to personal shame, and failure. Those same neighbors had looked upon my husband and me as an ideal young couple, in many ways: inseparable, doting, ambitious. They had kept me busy and laughing in the hard weeks following my husband's departure for graduate school in Chicago; they had been the ones to remember him warmly through teasing remarks and questions all that long year that I remained alone, waiting for his return while I became the "temporary," sole breadwinner of our peculiar long-distance family by telephone. They had been the ones who kindly stopped the teasing and the queries when the year ended and my husband, the father of my child, did not come back. They never asked me and I never told them what that meant, altogether. I don't think I really knew.

I could see how my husband would proceed more or less naturally from graduate school to a professional occupation of his choice, just as he had shifted rather easily from me, his wife, to another man's wife—another woman. What I could not see was how I should go forward, now, in any natural, coherent way. As a mother without a husband, as a poet without a publisher, a freelance journalist without assignment, a city planner without a contract, it seemed to me that several incontestable and conflicting necessities had suddenly eliminated the whole realm of choice from my life.

My husband and I agreed that he would have the divorce that he wanted, and I would have the child. This ordinary settlement is, as millions of women will testify, as absurd as saying, "I'll give you a call, you handle everything else." At any rate, as my lawyer explained, the law then was the same as the law today; the courts would surely award me a reasonable amount of the father's income as child support, but the courts would also insist that they could not enforce their own decree. In other words, according to the law, what a father owes to his child is not serious compared to what a man owes to the bank for a car, or a vacation. Hence, as they say, it is extremely regrettable but nonetheless true that the courts cannot garnish a father's salary, nor freeze his account, nor seize his property on behalf of his children, in our society. Apparently this is because a child is not a car or a couch or a boat. (I would suppose this is the very best available definition of the difference between an American child and a car.)

Anyway, I wanted to get out of the projects as quickly as possible. But I was going to need help because I couldn't bend down and I couldn't carry anything heavy and I couldn't let my parents know about these problems because I didn't want to fight with them about the reasons behind the problems—which was the same reason I couldn't walk around or sit up straight to read or write without vomiting and acute abdominal pain. My parents would have evaluated that reason as a terrible secret compounded by a terrible crime; once again an unmarried woman, I had, nevertheless, become pregnant. What's more I had tried to interrupt this pregnancy even though this particular effort required not only one but a total of three abortions—each of them illegal and amazingly expensive, as well as, evidently, somewhat poorly executed.

My mother, against my father's furious rejections of me and what he viewed as my failure, offered what she could; she had no money herself but there was space in the old brownstone of my childhood. I would live with them during the summer while I pursued my crash schedule for cash, and she would spend as much time with Christopher, her only and beloved grandchild, as her worsening but partially undiagnosed illness allowed.

After she suffered a stroke, her serenely imposing figure had shrunk into an unevenly balanced, starved shell of chronic disorder. In the last two years, her physical condition had forced her retirement from nursing, and she spent most of her days on a makeshift cot pushed against the wall of the dining room next to the kitchen. She could do very few things for herself, besides snack on crackers, or pour ready-made juice into a cup and then drink it.

In June, 1966, I moved from the projects into my parents' house with the help of a woman named Mrs. Hazel Griffin. Since my teens, she had been my hairdresser. Every day, all day, she stood on her feet, washing and straightening hair in her crowded shop, the Arch of Beauty. Mrs. Griffin had never been married, had never finished high school, and she ran the Arch of Beauty with an imperturbable and contagious sense of success. She had a daughter as old as I who worked alongside her mother, coddling customer fantasy into confidence. Gradually, Mrs. Griffin and I became close; as my own mother became more and more bedridden and demoralized, Mrs. Griffin extended herself—dropping by my parents' house to make dinner for them, or calling me to wish me good luck on a special freelance venture, and so forth. It was Mrs. Griffin who closed her shop for a whole day and drove all the way from Brooklyn to my housing project apartment in Queens. It was Mrs. Griffin who packed me up, so to speak, and carried me and the boxes back to Brooklyn, back to the house of my parents. It was Mrs. Griffin who ignored my father standing hateful at the top of the stone steps of the house and not saying a word of thanks and not once relieving her of a single load she wrestled up the stairs and past him. My father hated Mrs. Griffin because he was proud and because she was a stranger of mercy. My father hated Mrs. Griffin because he was like that sometimes: hateful and crazy.

My father alternated between weeping bouts of self-pity and storm explosions of wrath against the gods apparently determined to ruin him. These were his alternating reactions to my mother's increasing enfeeblement, her stoic depression. I think he was scared; who would take care of him? Would she get well again and make everything all right again?

This is how we organized the brownstone: I fixed a room for my son on the top floor of the house. I slept on the parlor floor in the front room. My father slept on the same floor, in the back. My mother stayed downstairs.

About a week after moving in, my mother asked me about the progress of my plans. I told her things were not terrific but that there were two different planning jobs I hoped to secure within a few days. One of them involved a study of new towns in Sweden and the other one involved an analysis of the social consequences of a huge hydro-electric dam under construction in Ghana. My mother stared at me uncomprehendingly and then urged me to look for work in the local post office. We bitterly argued about what she dismissed as my "high-falutin" ideas and, I believe, that was the last substantial conversation between us.

From my first memory of him, my father had always worked at the post office. His favorite was the night shift, which brought him home usually between three and four o'clock in the morning.

It was hot. I finally fell asleep that night, a few nights after the argument between my mother and myself. She seemed to be rallying; that afternoon, she and my son had spent a long time in the backyard, oblivious to the heat and the mosquitoes. They were both tired but peaceful when they noisily re-entered the house, holding hands awkwardly.

But someone was knocking at the door to my room. Why should I wake up? It would be impossible to fall asleep again. It was so hot. The knocking continued. I switched on the light by the bed: 3:30 A.M. It must be my father. Furious, I pulled on a pair of shorts and a t-shirt. "What do you want? What's the matter?" I asked him, through the door. Had he gone berserk? What could he have to talk about at that ridiculous hour?

"OK, all right," I said, rubbing my eyes awake as I stepped to the door and opened it. "What?"

To my surprise, my father stood there looking very uncertain.

"It's your mother," he told me, in a burly, formal voice. "I think she's dead, but I'm not sure." He was avoiding my eyes.

"What do you mean," I answered.

"I want you to go downstairs and figure it out."

I could not believe what he was saying to me. "You want me to figure out if my mother is dead or alive?"

"I can't tell! I don't know!!" he shouted angrily.

"Jesus Christ," I muttered, angry and beside myself.

I turned and glanced about my room, wondering if I could find anything to carry with me on this mission; what do you use to determine a life or a death? I couldn't see anything obvious that might be useful.

"I'll wait up here," my father said. "You call up and let me know."

I could not believe it; a man married to a woman more than forty years and he can't tell if she's alive or dead and he wakes up his kid and tells her, "You figure it out."

I was at the bottom of the stairs. I halted just outside the dining room where my mother slept. Suppose she really was dead? Suppose my father was not just being crazy and hateful? "Naw." I shook my head and confidently entered the room.

"Momma?!" I called, aloud. At the edge of the cot, my mother was leaning forward, one arm braced to hoist her body up. She was trying to stand up! I rushed over. "Wait. Here, I'll help you!" I said.

And I reached out my hands to give her a lift. The body of my mother was stiff. She was not yet cold, but she was stiff. Maybe I had come downstairs just in time! I tried to loosen her arms, to change her position, to ease her into lying down.

"Momma!" I kept saying. "Momma, listen to me! It's OK! I'm here and everything. Just relax. Relax! Give me a hand, now. I'm trying to help you lie down!"

Her body did not relax. She did not answer me. But she was not cold. Her eyes were not shut.

From upstairs my father was yelling, "Is she dead? Is she dead?"

"No!" I screamed at him. "No! She's not dead!"

At this, my father tore down the stairs and into the room. Then he braked.

"Milly?" he called out, tentative. Then he shouted at me and banged around the walls. "You damn fool. Don't you see now she's gone. Now she's gone!" We began to argue.

"She's alive! Call the doctor!"

"No!"

"Yes!"

At last my father left the room to call the doctor.

I straightened up. I felt completely exhausted from trying to gain a response from my mother. There she was, stiff on the edge of her bed, just about to stand up. Her lips were set, determined. She would manage it, but by herself. I could not help. Her eyes fixed on some point below the floor.

"Momma!" I shook her hard as I could to rouse her into focus. Now she fell back on the cot, but frozen and in the wrong position. It hit me that she might be dead. She might be dead.

My father reappeared at the door. He would not come any closer. "Dr. Davis says he will come. And he call the police."

The police? Would they know if my mother was dead or alive? Who would know?

I went to the phone and called my aunt. "Come quick," I said. "My father thinks Momma has died but she's here but she's stiff."

Soon the house was weird and ugly and crowded and I thought I was losing my mind.

Three white policemen stood around telling me my mother was dead. "How do you know?" I asked, and they shrugged and then they repeated themselves. And the doctor never came. But my aunt came and my uncle and they said she was dead.

After a conference with the cops, my aunt disappeared and when she came back she held a bottle in one of her hands. She and the police whispered together some more. Then one of the cops said, "Don't worry about it. We won't say anything." My aunt signalled me to follow her into the hallway where she let me understand that, in fact, my mother had committed suicide.

I could not assimilate this information: suicide.

I broke away from my aunt and ran to the telephone. I called a friend of mine, a woman who talked back loud to me so that I could realize my growing hysteria, and check it. Then I called my cousin Valerie who lived in Harlem; she woke up instantly and urged me to come right away.

I hurried to the top floor and stood my sleeping son on his feet. I wanted to get him out of this house of death more than I ever wanted anything. He could not stand by himself so I carried him down the two flights to the street and laid him on the backseat and then took off.

At Valerie's, my son continued to sleep, so we put him to bed, closed the door, and talked. My cousin made me eat eggs, drink whiskey, and shower. She would take care of Christopher, she said. I should go back and deal with the situation in Brooklyn.

When I arrived, the house was absolutely full of women from the church dressed as though they were going to Sunday communion. It seemed to me they were, every one of them, wearing hats and gloves and drinking coffee and solemnly addressing invitations to a funeral and I could not find my mother anywhere and I could not find an empty spot in the house where I could sit down and smoke a cigarette.

My mother was dead.

Feeling completely out of place, I headed for the front door, ready to leave. My father grabbed my shoulder from behind and forcibly spun me around.

"You see this?" He smiled, waving a large document in the air. "This am insurance paper for you!" He waved it into my face. "Your mother, she left you insurance, see?"

I watched him.

"But I gwine burn it in the furnace before I give it you to t'row away on trash!"

"Is that money?" I demanded. "Did my mother leave me money?"

"Eh-heh!" he laughed. "And you don't get it from me. Not today, not tomorrow. Not until I dead and buried!"

My father grabbed for my arm and I swung away from him. He hit me on my head and I hit back. We were fighting.

Suddenly, the ladies from the church bustled about and pushed, horrified, between us. This was a sin, they said, for a father and a child to fight in the house of the dead and the mother not yet in the ground! Such a good woman she was, they said. She was a good woman, a good woman, they all agreed. Out of respect for the memory of this good woman, in deference to my mother who had committed suicide, the ladies shook their hats and insisted we should not fight; I should not fight with my father.

Utterly disgusted and disoriented, I went back to Harlem. By the time I reached my cousin's place I had begun to bleed, heavily. Valerie said I was hemorrhaging so she called up her boyfriend and the two of them hobbled me into Harlem Hospital.

I don't know how long I remained unconscious, but when I opened my eyes I found myself on the women's ward, with an intravenous setup feeding into my arm. After a while, Valerie showed up. Christopher was fine, she told me; my friends were taking turns with him. Whatever I did, I should not admit I'd had an abortion or I'd get her into trouble, and myself in trouble. Just play dumb and rest. I'd have to stay on the ward for several days. My mother's funeral was tomorrow afternoon. What did I want her to tell people to explain why I wouldn't be there? She meant, what lie?

I thought about it and I decided I had nothing to say; if I couldn't tell the truth then the hell with it.

I lay in that bed at Harlem Hospital, thinking and sleeping. I wanted to get well.

I wanted to be strong. I never wanted to be weak again as long as I lived. I thought about my mother and her suicide and I thought about how my father could not tell whether she was dead or alive.

I wanted to get well and what I wanted to do as soon as I was strong again, actually, what I wanted to do was I wanted to live my life so that people would know unmistakably that I am alive, so that when I finally die people will know the difference for sure between my living and my death.

And I thought about the idea of my mother as a good woman and I rejected that, because I don't see why it's a good thing when you give up, or when you cooperate with those who hate you or when you polish and iron and mend and endlessly mollify for the sake of the people who love the way that you kill yourself day by day silently.

And I think all of this is really about women and work. Certainly this is all about me as a woman and my life work. I mean I am not sure my mother's suicide was something extraordinary. Perhaps most women must deal with a similar inheritance, the legacy of a woman whose death you cannot possibly pinpoint because she died so many, many times and because, even before she became your mother, the life of that woman was taken; I say it was taken away.

And really it was to honor my mother that I did fight with my father, that man who could not tell the living from the dead.

And really it is to honor Mrs. Hazel Griffin and my cousin Valerie and all the women I love, including myself, that I am working for the courage to admit the truth that Bertolt Brecht has written; he says, "It takes courage to say that the good were defeated not because they were good, but because they were weak."

I cherish the mercy and the grace of women's work. But I know there is new work that we must undertake as well: that new work will make defeat detestable to us. That new women's work will mean we will not die trying to stand up: we will live that way: standing up.

I came too late to help my mother to her feet.

By way of everlasting thanks to all of the women who have helped me to stay alive I am working never to be late again.

Nobody Mean More to Me Than You and the Future Life of Willie Jordan

Black English is not exactly a linguistic buffalo; as children, most of the thirty-five million Afro-Americans living here depend on this language for our discovery of the world. But then we approach our maturity inside a larger social body that will not support our efforts to become anything other than the clones of those who are neither our mothers nor our fathers. We begin to grow up in a house where every true mirror shows us the face of somebody who does not belong there, whose walk and whose talk will never look or sound "right," because that house was meant to shelter a family that is alien and hostile to us. As we learn our way around this environment, either we hide our original word habits, or we completely surrender our own voice, hoping to please those who will never respect anyone different from themselves: Black English is not exactly a linguistic buffalo, but we should understand its status as an endangered species, as a perishing, irreplaceable system of community intelligence, or we should expect its extinction, and, along with that, the extinguishing of much that constitutes our own proud, and singular identity.

What we casually call "English" less and less defers to England and its "gentlemen." "English" is no longer a specific matter of geography or an element of class privilege; more than thirty-three countries use this tool as a means of "intranational communication." Countries as disparate as Zimbabwe and Malaysia, or Israel and Uganda, use it as their non-native currency of convenience. Obviously, this tool, this "English," cannot function inside thirty-three discrete societies on the basis of rules and values absolutely determined somewhere else, in a thirty-fourth other country, for example.

In addition to that staggering congeries of non-native users of English, there are five countries, or 333,746,000 people, for whom this thing called "English" serves as a native tongue. Approximately 10% of these native speakers of "English" are Afro-American citizens of the U.S.A. I cite these numbers and varieties of human beings dependent on "English" in order, quickly, to suggest how strange and how tenuous is any concept of "Standard English." Obviously, numerous forms of English now operate inside a natural, an uncontrollable, continuum of development. I would suppose "the standard" for English in Malaysia is not the same as "the standard" in Zimbabwe. I know that standard forms of English for Black people in this country do not copy those of whites. And, in fact, the structural differences between these two kinds of English have intensified, becoming more Black, or less white, despite the expected homogenizing effects of television and other mass media.

Nonetheless, white standards of English persist, supreme and unquestioned, in these United States. Despite our multi-lingual population, and despite the deepening Black and white cleavage within that conglomerate, white standards control our official and popular judgements of verbal proficiency and correct, or incorrect, language skills, including speech. In contrast to India, where at least fourteen languages co-exist as legitimate Indian languages, in contrast to Nicaragua, where all citizens are legally entitled to formal school instruction in their regional or tribal languages, compulsory education in America compels accommodation to exclusively white forms of "English." White English, in America, is "Standard English."

This story begins two years ago. I was teaching a new course, "In Search of the Invisible Black Woman," and my rather large class seemed evenly divided between young Black women and men. Five or six white students also sat in attendance. With unexpected speed and enthusiasm we had moved through historical narratives of the 19th century to literature by and about Black women, in the 20th. I had assigned the first forty pages of Alice Walker's *The Color Purple,* and I came, eagerly, to class that morning:

"So!" I exclaimed, aloud. "What did you think? How did you like it?"

The students studied their hands, or the floor. There was no response. The tense, resistant feeling in the room fairly astounded me.

At last, one student, a young woman still not meeting my eyes, muttered something in my direction:

"What did you say?" I prompted her.

"Why she have them talk so funny. It don't sound right."

"You mean the language?"

Another student lifted his head: "It don't look right, neither. I couldn't hardly read it."

At this, several students dumped on the book. Just about unanimously, their criticisms targeted the language. I listened to what they wanted to say and silently marvelled at the similarities between their casual speech patterns and Alice Walker's written version of Black English.

But I decided against pointing to these identical traits of syntax; I wanted not to make them self-conscious about their own spoken language—not while they clearly felt it was "wrong." Instead I decided to swallow my astonishment. Here was a negative Black reaction to a prize-winning accomplishment of Black literature that white readers across the country had selected as a best seller. Black rejection was aimed at the one irreducibly Black element of Walker's work: the language—Celie's Black English. I wrote the opening lines of *The Color Purple* on the blackboard and asked the students to help me translate these sentences into Standard English:

> *You better not never tell nobody but God. It'd kill your mammy.*
> Dear God,
>   I am fourteen years old. I have always been a good girl. Maybe you can give me a sign letting me know what is happening to me.
>   Last spring after Little Lucious come I heard them fussing. He was pulling on her arm. She say it too soon, Fonso. I aint well. Finally he leave her alone. A week go by, he pulling on her arm again. She say, Naw, I ain't gonna. Can't you see I'm already half dead, an all of the children.

Our process of translation exploded with hilarity and even hysterical, shocked laughter: The Black writer, Alice Walker, knew what she was doing! If rudimentary criteria for good fiction includes the manipulation of language so that the syntax and diction of sentences will tell you the identity of speakers, the probable age and sex and class of speakers, and even the locale—urban/rural/southern/western—then Walker had written, perfectly. This is the translation into Standard English that our class produced:

> *Absolutely, one should never confide in anybody besides God. Your secrets could prove devastating to your mother.*
> Dear God,
>   I am fourteen years old. I have always been good. But now, could you help me to understand what is happening to me?
>   Last spring, after my little brother, Lucious, was born, I heard my parents fighting. My father kept pulling at my mother's arm. But she told him, "It's too soon for sex, Alfonso. I am still not feeling well." Finally, my father left her alone. A week went by, and then he began bothering my mother again: pulling her arm. She told him, "No, I won't! Can't you see I'm already exhausted from all of these children?"

(Our favorite line was "It's too soon for sex, Alphonso.")

Once we could stop laughing, once we could stop our exponentially wild improvisations on the theme of Translated Black English, the students pushed me to explain their own negative first reactions to their spoken language on the printed page. I thought it was probably akin to the shock of seeing yourself in a photograph for the first time. Most of the students had never before seen a written facsimile of the way they talk. None of the students had ever learned how to read and write their own verbal system of communication: Black English. Alternatively, this fact began to baffle or else bemuse and then infuriate my students. Why not? Was it too late? Could they learn how to do it, now? And, ultimately, the final test question, the one testing my sincerity: Could I teach them? Because I had never taught anyone Black English and, as far as I knew, no one, anywhere in the United States, had ever offered such a course, the best I could say was "I'll try."

He looked like a wrestler.

He sat dead center in the packed room and, every time our eyes met, he quickly nodded his head as though anxious to reassure and encourage, me.

Short, with strikingly broad shoulders and long arms, he spoke with a surprisingly high, soft voice that matched the soft bright movement of his eyes. His name was Willie Jordan. He would have seemed even more unlikely in the context of Contemporary Women's Poetry, except that ten or twelve other Black men were taking the course, as well. Still, Willie was conspicuous. His extreme fitness, the muscular density of his presence underscored the riveted, gentle attention that he gave to anything anyone said. Generally, he did not join the loud and rowdy dialogue flying back and forth, but there could be no doubt about his interest in our discussions. And, when he stood to present an argument he'd prepared, overnight, that nervous smile of his vanished and an irregular stammering replaced it, as he spoke with visceral sincerity, word by word.

That was how I met Willie Jordan. It was in between "In Search of the Invisible Black Women" and "The Art of Black English." I was waiting for Departmental approval and I supposed that Willie might be, so to speak, killing time until he, too, could study Black English. But Willie really did want to explore Contemporary Women's Poetry and, to that end, volunteered for extra research and never missed a class.

Towards the end of that semester, Willie approached me for an independent study project on South Africa. It would commence the next semester. I thought Willie's writing needed the kind of improvement only intense practice will yield. I knew his intelligence was outstanding. But he'd wholeheartedly opted for "Standard English" at a rather late age, and the results were stilted and frequently polysyllabic, simply for the sake of having more syllables. Willie's unnatural formality of language seemed to me consistent with the formality of his research into South African apartheid. As he projected his studies, he would have little time, indeed, for newspapers. Instead, more than 90% of his research would mean saturation in strictly historical, if not archival, material. I was certainly interested. It would be tricky to guide him into a more confident and spontaneous relationship with both language and apartheid. It was going to be wonderful to see what happened when he could catch up with himself, entirely, and talk back to the world.

September, 1984: Breezy fall weather and much excitement! My class, "The Art of Black English," was full to the limit of the fire laws. And, in Independent Study, Willie Jordan showed up, weekly, fifteen minutes early for each of our sessions. I was pretty happy to be teaching, altogether!

I remember an early class when a young brother, replete with his ever-present pork-pie hat, raised his hand and then told us that most of what he'd heard was "all right" except it was "too clean." "The brothers on the street," he continued, "they mix it up more. Like 'fuck' and 'motherfuck.' Or like 'shit.' " He waited. I waited. Then all of us laughed a good while, and we got into a brawl about "correct" and "realistic" Black English that led to Rule 1.

Rule 1: *Black English is about a whole lot more than mothafuckin.*

As a criterion, we decided, "realistic" could take you anywhere you want to go. Artful places. Angry places. Eloquent and sweetalkin places. Polemical places. Church. And the local Bar & Grill. We were checking out a language, not a mood or a scene or one guy's forgettable mouthing off.

It was hard. For most of the students, learning Black English required a fallback to patterns and rhythms of speech that many of their parents had beaten out of them. I mean *beaten.* And, in a majority of cases, correct Black English could be achieved only by striving for *incorrect* Standard English, something they were still pushing at, quite uncertainly. This state of affairs led to Rule 2.

Rule 2: *If it's wrong in Standard English it's probably right in Black English, or, at least, you're hot*.

It was hard. Roommates and family members ridiculed their studies, or remained incredulous. "You *studying* that shit? At school?" But we were beginning to feel the companionship of pioneers. And we decided that we needed another rule that would establish each one of us as equally important to our success. This was Rule 3.

Rule 3: *If it don't sound like something that come out somebody mouth then it don't sound right. If it don't sound right then it ain't hardly right. Period.*

This rule produced two weeks of compositions in which the students agonizingly tried to spell the sound of the Black English sentence they wanted to convey. But Black English is, preeminently, an oral/spoken means of communication. *And spelling don't talk.* So we needed Rule 4.

Rule 4: *Forget about the spelling. Let the syntax carry you.*

Once we arrived at Rule 4 we started to fly because syntax, the structure of an idea, leads you to the world view of the speaker and reveals her values. The syntax of a sentence equals the structure of your consciousness. If we insisted that the language of Black English adheres to a distinctive Black syntax, then we were postulating a profound difference between white and Black people, *per se.* Was it a difference to prize or to obliterate?

There are three qualities of Black English—the presence of life, voice, and clarity—that testify to a distinctive Black value system that we became excited about and self-consciously tried to maintain.

1. Black English has been produced by a pre-technocratic, if not anti-technological, culture. More, our culture has been constantly threatened by annihilation or, at least, the swallowed blurring of assimilation. Therefore, our language is a system constructed by people constantly needing to insist that we exist, that we are present. Our language devolves from a culture that abhors all abstraction, or anything tending to obscure or delete the fact of the human being who is here and now/the truth of the person who is speaking or listening. Consequently, *there is no passive voice construction possible in Black English.* For example, you cannot say, "Black English is being eliminated." You must say, instead, "White people eliminating Black English." The assumption of the presence of life governs all of Black English. Therefore, overwhelmingly, *all action takes place in the language of the present*

indicative. And every sentence assumes the living and active participation of at least two human beings, the speaker and the listener.

2. A primary consequence of the person-centered values of Black English is the delivery of voice. If you speak or write Black English, your ideas will necessarily possess that otherwise elusive attribute, *voice.*

3. One main benefit following from the person-centered values of Black English is that of *clarity.* If your idea, your sentence, assumes the presence of at least two living and active people, you will make it understandable because the motivation behind every sentence is the wish to say something real to somebody real.

As the weeks piled up, translation from Standard English into Black English or vice versa occupied a hefty part of our course work.

Standard English (hereafter S.E.): "In considering the idea of studying Black English those questioned suggested—"
(What's the subject? Where's the person? Is anybody alive in there, in that idea?)
Black English (hereafter B.E.): "I been asking people what you think about somebody studying Black English and they answer me like this:"

But there were interesting limits. You cannot "translate" instances of Standard English preoccupied with abstraction or with nothing/nobody evidently alive, into Black English. That would warp the language into uses antithetical to the guiding perspective of its community of users. Rather you must first change those Standard English sentences, themselves, into ideas consistent with the person-centered assumptions of Black English.

Guidelines For Black English

1. Minimal number of words for every idea: This is the source for the aphoristic and/or poetic force of the language; eliminate every possible word.
2. Clarity: If the sentence is not clear it's not Black English.
3. Eliminate use of the verb *to be* whenever possible. This leads to the deployment of more descriptive and therefore more precise verbs.
4. Use *be* or *been* only when you want to describe a chronic, ongoing state of things.
   He *be* at the office, by 9. (He is always at the office by 9.)
   He *been* with her since forever.
5. Zero copula: Always eliminate the verb *to be* whenever it would combine with another verb, in Standard English.
   S.E.: She is going out with him.
   B.E.: She going out with him.
6. Eliminate *do* as in:
   S.E.: What do you think? What do you want?
   B.E.: What you think? What you want?

Rules number 3, 4, 5, and 6 provide for the use of the minimal number of verbs per idea and, therefore, greater accuracy in the choice of verb.

7. In general, if you wish to say something really positive, try to formulate the idea using emphatic negative structure.
   S.E.: He's fabulous.
   B.E.: He bad.

8. Use double or triple negatives for dramatic emphasis.
   S.E.: Tina Turner sings out of this world.
   B.E.: Ain nobody sing like Tina.

9. Never use the *-ed* suffix to indicate the past tense of a verb.
   S.E.: She closed the door.
   B.E.: She close the door. Or, she have close the door.

10. Regardless of intentional verb time, only use the third person singular, present indicative, for use of the verb *to have,* as an auxiliary.
    S.E.: He had his wallet then he lost it.
    B.E.: He have him wallet then he lose it.
    S.E.: We had seen that movie.
    B.E.: We seen that movie. Or, we have see that movie.

11. Observe a minimal inflection of verbs. Particularly, never change from the first person singular forms to the third person singular.
    S.E.: Present Tense Forms: He goes to the store.
    B.E.: He go to the store.
    S.E.: Past Tense Forms: He went to the store.
    B.E.: He go to the store. Or, he gone to the store. Or, he been to the store.

12. The possessive case scarcely ever appears in Black English. Never use an apostrophe ('s) construction. If you wander into a possessive case component of an idea, then keep logically consistent: *ours, his, theirs, mines.* But, most likely, if you bump into such a component, you have wandered outside the underlying world-view of Black English.
    S.E.: He will take their car tomorrow.
    B.E.: He taking they car tomorrow.

13. Plurality: Logical consistency, continued: If the modifier indicates plurality, then the noun remains in the singular case.
    S.E.: He ate twelve doughnuts.
    B.E.: He eat twelve doughnut.
    S.E.: She has many books.
    B.E.: She have many book.

14. Listen for, or invent, special Black English forms of the past tense, such as: "He losted it. That what she felted." If they are clear and readily understood, then use them.

Do not hesitate to play with words, sometimes inventing them; e.g., "astropotomous" means huge like a hippo plus astronomical and, therefore, signifies real big.

15. In Black English, unless you keenly want to underscore the past tense nature of an action, stay in the present tense and rely on the overall context of your ideas for the conveyance of time and sequence.

16. Never use the suffix -*ly* form of an adverb in Black English.
    S.E.: The rain came down rather quickly.
    B.E.: The rain come down pretty quick.

17. Never use the indefinite article *an* in Black English.
    S.E.: He wanted to ride an elephant.
    B.E.: He want to ride him a elephant.

18. In variant syntax: In correct Black English it is possible to formulate an imperative, an interrogative, and a simple declarative idea with the same syntax:
    B.E.: You going to the store?
          You going to the store.
          You going to the store!

Where was Willie Jordan? We'd reached the mid-term of the semester. Students had formulated Black English guidelines, by consensus, and they were now writing with remarkable beauty, purpose, and enjoyment:

I ain hardly speakin for everybody but myself so understan that.

—Kim Parks

Samples from student writings:

"Janie have a great big ole hole inside her. Tea Cake the only thing that fit that hole. . . .

"That pear tree beautiful to Janie, especial when bees fiddlin with the blossomin pear there growin large and lovely. But personal speakin, the love she get from starin at that tree ain the love what starin back at her in them relationship." (Monica Morris)

"Love is a big theme in *They Eye Was Watching God*. Love show people new corners inside theyself. It pull out good stuff and stuff back bad stuff. . . . Joe worship the doing uh his own hand and need other people to worship him too. But he ain't think about Janie that she a person and ought to live like anybody common do. Queen life not for Janie." (Monica Morris)

"In both life and writin, Black womens have varietous experience of love that be cold like a iceberg or fiery like a inferno. Passion got for the other partner involve, man or woman, seem as shallow, ankle-deep water or the most profoundest abyss." (Constance Evans)

"Family love another bond that ain't never break under no pressure." (Constance Evans)

"You know it really cold/When the friend you/Always get out the fire/Act like they don't know you/When you in the heat." (Constance Evans)

"Big classroom discussion bout love at this time. I never take no class where us have any long arguin for and against for two or three day. New to me and great. I find the class time talkin a million time more interestin than detail bout the book." (Kathy Esseks)

*   *   *

As these examples suggest, Black English no longer limited the students, in any way. In fact, one of them, Philip Garfield, would shortly "translate" a pivotal scene from Ibsen's *Doll House,* as his final term paper:

NORA: I didn't gived no shit. I thinked you a asshole back then, too, you make it so hard for me save mines husband life.

KROGSTAD: Girl, it clear you ain't any idea what you done. You done exact what once done, and I losed my reputation over it.

NORA: You asks me believe you once act brave save you wife life?

KROGSTAD: Law care less why you done it.

NORA: Law must suck.

KROGSTAD: Suck or no, if I wants, judge screw you wid dis paper.

NORA: No way, man. (Philip Garfield)

But where was Willie? Compulsively punctual, and always thoroughly prepared with neatly typed compositions, he had disappeared. He failed to show up for our regularly scheduled conference, and I received neither a note nor a phone call of explanation. A whole week went by. I wondered if Willie had finally been captured by the extremely current happenings in South Africa: passage of a new constitution that did not enfranchise the Black majority, and militant Black South African reaction to that affront. I wondered if he'd been hurt, somewhere. I wondered if the serious workload of weekly readings and writings had overwhelmed him and changed his mind about independent study. Where was Willie Jordan?

One week after the first conference that Willie missed, he called: "Hello, Professor Jordan? This is Willie. I'm sorry I wasn't there last week. But something has come up and I'm pretty upset. I'm sorry but I really can't deal right now."

I asked Willie to drop by my office and just let me see that he was okay. He agreed to do that. When I saw him I knew something hideous had happened. Something had hurt him and scared him to the marrow. He was all agitated and stammering and terse and incoherent. At last, his sadly jumbled account let me surmise as follows: Brooklyn police had murdered his unarmed, twenty-five-year-old brother, Reggie Jordan. Neither Willie nor his elderly parents knew what to do about it. Nobody from the press was interested. His folks had no money. Police ran his family around and around, to no point. And Reggie was really dead. And Willie wanted to fight, but he felt helpless.

With Willie's permission I began to try to secure legal counsel for the Jordan family. Unfortunately Black victims of police violence are truly numerous while the resources available to prosecute their killers are truly scarce. A friend of mine at the Center for Constitutional Rights estimated that just the preparatory costs for bringing the cops into court normally approaches $180,000. Unless the execution of

Reggie Jordan became a major community cause for organizing and protest, his murder would simply become a statistical item.

Again with Willie's permission, I contacted every newspaper and media person I could think of. But the William Bastone feature article in *The Village Voice* was the only result from that canvassing.

Again with Willie's permission, I presented the case to my class in Black English. We had talked about the politics of language. We had talked about love and sex and child abuse and men and women. But the murder of Reggie Jordan broke like a hurricane across the room.

There are few "issues" as endemic to Black life as police violence. Most of the students knew and respected and liked Jordan. Many of them came from the very neighborhood where the murder had occurred. All of the students had known somebody close to them who had been killed by police, or had known frightening moments of gratuitous confrontation with the cops. They wanted to do everything at once to avenge death. Number One: They decided to compose personal statements of condolence to Willie Jordan and his family, written in Black English. Number Two: They decided to compose individual messages to the police, in Black English. These should be prefaced by an explanatory paragraph composed by the entire group. Number Three: These individual messages, with their lead paragraph, should be sent to *Newsday*.

The morning after we agreed on these objectives, one of the young women students appeared with an unidentified visitor, who sat through the class, smiling in a peculiar, comfortable way.

Now we had to make more tactical decisions. Because we wanted the messages published, and because we thought it imperative that our outrage be known by the police, the tactical question was this: Should the opening, group paragraph be written in Black English or Standard English?

I have seldom been privy to a discussion with so much heart at the dead heat of it. I will never forget the eloquence, the sudden haltings of speech, the fierce struggle against tears, the furious throwaways and useless explosions that this question elicited.

That one question contained several others, each of them extraordinarily painful to even contemplate. How best to serve the memory of Reggie Jordan? Should we use the language of the killers—Standard English—in order to make our ideas acceptable to those controlling the killers? But wouldn't what we had to say be rejected, summarily, if we said it in our own language, the language of the victim, Reggie Jordan? But if we sought to express ourselves by abandoning our language, wouldn't that mean our suicide on top of Reggie's murder? But if we expressed ourselves in our own language, wouldn't that be suicidal to the wish to communicate with those who, evidently, did not give a damn about us/Reggie/police violence in the Black community?

At the end of one of the longest, most difficult hours of my own life, the students voted, unanimously, to preface their individual messages with a paragraph composed in the language of Reggie Jordan. *"At least we don't give up nothing else. At least we stick to the truth: Be who we been. And stay all the way with Reggie."*

It was heartbreaking to proceed, from that point. Everyone in the room realized that our decision in favor of Black English had doomed our writings, even as the distinctive reality of our Black lives always has doomed our efforts to "be who we been" in this country.

I went to the blackboard and took down this paragraph, dictated by the class:

> . . . You Cops!
> We the brother and sister of Willie Jordan, a fellow stony brook student who the brother of the dead Reggie Jordan. Reggie, like many brother and sister, he a victim of brutal racist police, October 25, 1984. Us appall, fed up, because that another senseless death what occur in our community. This what we feel, this, from our heart, for we ain't stayin' silent no more.

With the completion of this introduction, nobody said anything. I asked for comments. At this invitation, the unidentified visitor, a young Black man, ceaselessly smiling, raised his hand. He was, it so happens, a rookie cop. He had just joined the force in September and, he said, he thought he should clarify a few things. So he came forward and sprawled easily into a posture of barroom, or fireside, nostalgia:

"See," Officer Charles enlightened us, "most times when you out on the street and something come down you do one of two things. Over-react or under-react. Now, if you under-react then you can get yourself kilt. And if you over-react then maybe you kill somebody. Fortunately it's about nine times out of ten and you will over-react. So the brother got kilt. And I'm sorry about that, believe me. But what you have to understand is what kilt him: over-reaction. That's all. Now you talk about Black people and white police but see, now, I'm a cop myself. And [big smile] I'm Black. And just a couple months ago I was on the other side. But see it's the same for me. You a cop, you the ultimate authority: the Ultimate Authority. And you on the street, most of the time you can only do one of two things: over-react or under-react. That's all it is with the brother. Over-reaction. Didn't have nothing to do with race."

That morning Officer Charles had the good fortune to escape without being boiled alive. But barely. And I remember the pride of his smile when I read about the fate of Black policemen and other collaborators in South Africa. I remember him, and I remember the shock and palpable feeling of shame that filled the room. It was as though that foolish, and deadly, young man had just relieved himself of his foolish, and deadly, explanation, face to face with the grief of Reggie Jordan's father and Reggie Jordan's mother. Class ended quietly. I copied the paragraph from the blackboard, collected the individual messages, and left to type them up.

Newsday rejected the piece.

The Village Voice could not find room in their "Letters" section to print the individual messages from the students to the police.

None of the tv news reporters picked up the story.

Nobody raised $180,000 to prosecute the murder of Reggie Jordan.

Reggie Jordan is really dead.

I asked Willie Jordan to write an essay pulling together everything important to him from that semester. He was still deeply beside himself with frustration and amazement and loss. This is what he wrote, un-edited, and in its entirety:

> Throughout the course of this semester I have been researching the effects of oppression and exploitation along racial lines in South Africa and its neighboring countries. I have

become aware of South African police brutalization of native Africans beyond the extent of the law, even though the laws themselves are catalyst affliction upon Black men, women and children. Many Africans die each year as a result of the deliberate use of police force to protect the white power structure.

Social control agents in South Africa, such as policemen, are also used to force compliance among citizens through both overt and covert tactics. It is not uncommon to find bold-faced coercion and cold-blooded killings of Blacks by South African police for undetermined and/or inadequate reasons. Perhaps the truth is that the only reason for this heinous treatment of Blacks rests in racial differences. We should also understand that what is conveyed through the media is not always accurate and may sometimes be construed as the tip of the iceberg at best.

I recently received a painful reminder that racism, poverty, and the abuse of power are global problems which are by no means unique to South Africa. On October 25, 1984 at approximately 3:00 P.M. my brother, Mr. Reginald Jordan, was shot and killed by two New York City policemen from the 75th precinct in the East New York section of Brooklyn. His life ended at the age of twenty-five. Even up to this current point in time the Police Department has failed to provide my family, which consists of five brothers, eight sisters, and two parents, with a plausible reason for Reggie's death. Out of the many stories that were given to my family by the Police Department, not one of them seems to hold water. In fact, I honestly believe that the Police Department's assessment of my brother's murder is nothing short of ABSOLUTE BULLSHIT, and thus far no evidence had been produced to alter this perception of the situation.

Furthermore, I believe that one of three cases may have occurred in this incident. First, Reggie's death may have been the desired outcome of the police officer's action, in which case the killing was premeditated. Or, it was a case of mistaken identity, which clarifies the fact that the two officers who killed my brother and their commanding parties are all grossly incompetent. Or, both of the above cases are correct, i.e., Reggie's murderers intended to kill him and the Police Department behaved insubordinately.

Part of the argument of the officers who shot Reggie was that he had attacked one of them and took his gun. This was their major claim. They also said that only one of them had actually shot Reggie. The facts, however, speak for themselves. According to the Death Certificate and autopsy report, Reggie was shot eight times from point-blank range. The Doctor who performed the autopsy told me himself that two bullets entered the side of my brother's head, four bullets were sprayed into his back, and two bullets struck him in the back of his legs. It is obvious that unnecessary force was used by the police and that it is extremely difficult to shoot someone in his back when he is attacking or approaching you.

After experiencing a situation like this and researching South Africa I believe that to a large degree, justice may only exist as rhetoric. I find it difficult to talk of true justice when the oppression of my people both at home and abroad attests to the fact that inequality and injustice are serious problems whereby Blacks and Third World people are perpetually short-changed by society. Something has to be done about the way in which this world is set up. Although it is a difficult task, we do have the power to make a change."

—Willie J. Jordan Jr.
EGL 487, Section 58, November 14, 1984

It is my privilege to dedicate this book to the future life of Willie J. Jordan Jr.

August 8, 1985

Report from the Bahamas

I am staying in a hotel that calls itself the Sheraton British Colonial. One of the photographs advertising the place displays a middle-aged Black man in a waiter's tuxedo, smiling. What intrigues me most about the picture is just this: while the Black man bears a tray full of "colorful" drinks above his left shoulder, both of his feet, shoes and trouser legs, up to ten inches above his ankles, stand in the also "colorful" Caribbean salt water. He is so delighted to serve you he will wade into the water to bring you Banana Daquiris while you float! More precisely, he will wade into the water, fully clothed, oblivious to the ruin of his shoes, his trousers, his health, and he will do it with a smile.

I am in the Bahamas. On the phone in my room, a spinning complement of plastic pages offers handy index clues such as CAR RENTAL and CASINOS. A message from the Ministry of Tourism appears among these travellers tips. Opening with a paragraph of "WELCOME," the message then proceeds to "A PAGE OF HISTORY," which reads as follows:

> New World History begins on the same day that modern Bahamian history begins— October 12, 1492. That's when Columbus stepped ashore—British influence came first with the Eleutherian Adventurers of 1647—After the Revolutions, American Loyalists fled from the newly independent states and settled in the Bahamas. Confederate blockade-runners used the island as a haven during the War between the States, and after the War, a number of Southerners moved to the Bahamas. . . .

There it is again. Something proclaims itself a legitimate history and all it does is track white Mr. Columbus to the British Eleutherians through the Confederate Southerners as they barge into New World surf, land on New World turf, and nobody saying one word about the Bahamian people, the Black peoples, to whom the only thing new in their island world was this weird succession of crude intruders and its colonial consequences.

This is my consciousness of race as I unpack my bathing suit in the Sheraton British Colonial. Neither this hotel nor the British nor the long-ago Italians nor the white Delta airline pilots belong here, of course. And every time I look at the photograph of that fool standing in the water with his shoes on I'm about to have a West Indian fit, even though I know he's no fool; he's a middle-aged Black man who needs a job and this is his job—pretending himself a servile ancillary to the pleasures of the rich. (Compared to his options in life, I am a rich woman. Compared to most of the Black Americans arriving for this Easter weekend on a three nights four days' deal of bargain rates, the middle-aged waiter is a poor Black man.)

We will jostle along with the other (white) visitors and join them in the tee shirt shops or, laughing together, learn ruthless rules of negotiation as we, Black Americans as well as white, argue down the price of handwoven goods at the nearby straw market while the merchants, frequently toothless Black women seated on the concrete in their only presentable dress, humble themselves to our careless games:

"Yes? You like it? Eight dollar."

"Five."

"I give it to you. Seven."

And so it continues, this weird succession of crude intruders that, now, includes me and my brothers and my sisters from the North.

This is my consciousness of class as I try to decide how much money I can spend on Bahamian gifts for my family back in Brooklyn. No matter that these other Black women incessantly weave words and flowers into the straw hats and bags piled beside them on the burning dusty street. No matter that these other Black women must work their sense of beauty into these things that we will take away as cheaply as we dare, or they will do without food.

We are not white, after all. The budget is limited. And we are harmlessly killing time between the poolside rum punch and "The Native Show on the Patio" that will play tonight outside the hotel restaurant.

This is my consciousness of race and class and gender identity as I notice the fixed relations between these other Black women and myself. They sell and I buy or I don't. They risk not eating. I risk going broke on my first vacation afternoon.

We are not particularly women anymore; we are parties to a transaction designed to set us against each other.

"Olive" is the name of the Black woman who cleans my hotel room. On my way to the beach I am wondering what "Olive" would say if I told her why I chose the Sheraton British Colonial; if I told her I wanted to swim. I wanted to sleep. I did not want to be harassed by the middle-aged waiter, or his nephew. I did not want to be raped by anybody (white or Black) at all and I calculated that my safety as a Black woman alone would best be assured by a multinational hotel corporation. In my experience, the big guys take customer complaints more seriously than the little ones. I would suppose that's one reason why they're big; they don't like to lose money any more than I like to be bothered when I'm trying to read a goddamned book underneath a palm tree I paid $264 to get next to. A Black woman seeking refuge in a multinational corporation may seem like a contradiction to some, but there you are. In this case it's a coincidence of entirely different self-interests: Sheraton/cash = June Jordan's short-run safety.

Anyway, I'm pretty sure "Olive" would look at me as though I came from someplace as far away as Brooklyn. Then she'd probably allow herself one indignant query before righteously removing her vacuum cleaner from my room; "and why in the first place you come down you without your husband?"

I cannot imagine how I would begin to answer her.

My "rights" and my "freedom" and my "desire" and a slew of other New World values; what would they sound like to this Black woman described on the card atop my hotel bureau as "Olive the Maid"? "Olive" is older than I am and I may smoke a cigarette while she changes the sheets on my bed. Whose rights? Whose freedom? Whose desire?

And why should she give a shit about mine unless I do something, for real, about hers?

It happens that the book that I finished reading under a palm tree earlier today was the novel *The Bread Givers*, by Anzia Yezierska. Definitely autobiographical. Yezierska lays out the difficulties of being both female and "a person" inside a traditional Jewish family at the start of the 20th century. That any Jewish woman became anything more than the abused servant of her father or her husband is really an improbable piece of news. Yet Yezierska managed such an unlikely outcome for her own life. In *The Bread Givers*, the heroine also manages an important, although partial, escape from traditional Jewish female destiny. And in the unpardonable, despotic father, the Talmudic scholar of that Jewish family, did I not see my own and hate him twice, again? When the heroine, the young Jewish child, wanders the streets with a filthy pail she borrows to sell herring in order to raise the ghetto rent and when she cries, "Nothing was before me but the hunger in our house, and no bread for the next meal if I didn't sell the herring. No longer like a fire engine, but like a houseful of hungry mouths my heart cried, 'herring—herring! Two cents apiece!" who would doubt the ease, the sisterhood of conversation possible between that white girl and the Black women selling straw bags on the streets of paradise because they do not want to die? And is it not obvious that the wife of that Talmudic scholar and "Olive," who cleans my room here at the hotel, have more in common than I can claim with either one of them?

This is my consciousness of race and class and gender identity as I collect wet towels, sunglasses, wristwatch, and head towards a shower.

I am thinking about the boy who loaned this novel to me. He's white and he's Jewish and he's pursuing an independent study project with me, at the State University where I teach whether or not I feel like it, where I teach without stint because, like the waiter, I am no fool. It's my job and either I work or I do without everything you need money to buy. The boy loaned me the novel because he thought I'd be interested to know how a Jewish-American writer used English so that the syntax, and therefore the cultural habits of mind expressed by the Yiddish language, could survive translation. He did this because he wanted to create another connection between us on the basis of language, between his knowledge/his love of Yiddish and my knowledge/my love of Black English.

He has been right about the forceful survival of the Yiddish. And I had become excited by this further evidence of the written voice of spoken language protected from the monodrone of "standard" English, and so we had grown closer on this account. But then our talk shifted to student affairs more generally, and I had learned that this student does not care one way or the other about currently jeopardized Federal Student Loan Programs because, as he explained it to me, they do not affect him. He does not need financial help outside his family. My own son, however, is Black. And I am the only family help available to him and that means, if Reagan succeeds in eliminating Federal programs to aid minority students, he will have to forget about furthering his studies, or he or I or both of us will have to hit the numbers pretty big. For these reasons of difference, the student and I had moved away from each other, even while we continued to talk.

My consciousness turned to race, again, and class.

Sitting in the same chair as the boy, several weeks ago, a graduate student came to discuss her grade. I praised the excellence of her final paper; indeed it had seemed to me an extraordinary pulling together of recent left brain/right brain research with the themes of transcendental poetry.

She told me that, for her part, she'd completed her reading of my political essays. "You are so lucky!" she exclaimed.

"What do you mean by that?"

"You have a cause. You have a purpose to your life."

I looked carefully at this white woman; what was she really saying to me?

"What do you mean?" I repeated.

"Poverty. Police violence. Discrimination in general."

(Jesus Christ, I thought: Is that her idea of lucky?)

"And how about you?" I asked.

"Me?"

"Yeah, you. Don't you have a cause?"

"Me? I'm just a middle-aged woman: a housewife and a mother. I'm a nobody."

For a while, I made no response.

First of all, speaking of race and class and gender in one breath, what she said meant that those lucky preoccupations of mine, from police violence to nuclear wipe-out, were not shared. They were mine and not hers. But here she sat, friendly as an old stuffed animal, beaming good will or more "luck" in my direction.

In the second place, what this white woman said to me meant that she did not believe she was "a person" precisely because she had fulfilled the traditional female functions revered by the father of that Jewish immigrant, Anzia Yezierska. And the woman in front of me was not a Jew. That was not the connection. The link was strictly female. Nevertheless, how should that woman and I, another female, connect, beyond this bizarre exchange?

If she believed me lucky to have regular hurdles of discrimination, then why shouldn't I insist that she's lucky to be a middle-class white Wasp female who lives in such well-sanctioned and normative comfort that she even has the luxury to deny the power of the privileges that paralyze her life?

If she deserts me and "my cause" where we differ, if, for example, she abandons me to "my" problems of race, then why should I support her in "her" problems of housewifely oblivion?

Recollection of this peculiar moment brings me to the shower in the bathroom cleaned by "Olive." She reminds me of the usual Women's Studies curriculum because it has nothing to do with her or her job: you won't find "Olive" listed anywhere on the reading list. You will likewise seldom hear of Anzia Yezierska. But yes, you will find, from Florence Nightingale to Adrienne Rich, a white procession of independently well-to-do women writers (Gertrude Stein/Virginia Woolf/Hilda Doolittle are standard names among the "essential" women writers).

In other words, most of the women of the world—Black and First World and white who work because we must—most of the women of the world persist far from the heart of the usual Women's Studies syllabus.

Similarly, the typical Black History course will slide by the majority experience it pretends to represent. For example, Mary McLeod Bethune will scarcely receive as much attention as Nat Turner, even though Black women who bravely and efficiently provided for the education of Black people hugely outnumber those few Black men who led successful or doomed rebellions against slavery. In fact, Mary McLeod Bethune may not receive even honorable mention because Black History too often apes those ridiculous white history courses which produce such dangerous gibberish as the Sheraton British Colonial "history" of the Bahamas. Both Black and white history courses exclude from their central consideration those people who neither killed nor conquered anyone as the means to new identity, those people who took care of every one of the people who wanted to become "a person," those people who still take care of the life at issue: the ones who wash and who feed and who teach and who diligently decorate straw hats and bags with all of their historically unrequired gentle love: the women.

Oh the old rugged cross
on a hill far away
Well I cherish the old rugged cross

It's Good Friday in the Bahamas. Seventy-eight degrees in the shade. Except for Sheraton territory, everything's closed.

It so happens that for truly secular reasons I've been fasting for three days. My hunger has now reached nearly violent proportions. In the hotel sandwich shop, the Black woman handling the counter complains about the tourists; why isn't the shop closed and why don't the tourists stop eating for once in their lives. I'm famished and I order chicken salad and cottage cheese and lettuce and tomato and a hard boiled egg and a hot cross bun and apple juice.

She eyes me with disgust.

To be sure, the timing of my stomach offends her serious religious practices. Neither one of us apologizes to the other. She seasons the chicken salad to the peppery max while I listen to the loud radio gospel she plays to console herself. It's a country Black version of "The Old Rugged Cross."

As I heave much chicken into my mouth tears start. It's not the pepper. I am, after all, a West Indian daughter. It's the Good Friday music that dominates the humid atmosphere.

Well I cherish the old rugged cross

And I am back, faster than a 747, in Brooklyn, in the home of my parents where we are wondering, as we do every year, if the sky will darken until Christ has been buried in the tomb. The sky should darken if God is in His heavens. And then, around 3 P.M., at the conclusion of our mournful church service at the neighborhood St. Philip's, and even while we dumbly stare at the black cloth covering the gold altar and the slender unlit candles, the sun should return through the high gothic windows and vindicate our waiting faith that the Lord will rise again, on Easter.

How I used to bow my head at the very name of Jesus: ecstatic to abase myself in deference to His majesty.

My mouth is full of salad. I can't seem to eat quickly enough. I can't think how I should lessen the offense of my appetite. The other Black woman on the premises, the one who disapprovingly prepared this very tasty break from my fast, makes no remark. She is no fool. This is a job that she needs. I suppose she notices that at least I included a hot cross bun among my edibles. That's something in my favor. I decide that's enough.

I am suddenly eager to walk off the food. Up a fairly steep hill I walk without hurrying. Through the pastel desolation of the little town, the road brings me to a confectionary pink and white plantation house. At the gates, an unnecessarily large statue of Christopher Columbus faces me down, or tries to. His hand is fisted to one hip. I look back at him, laugh without deference, and turn left.

It's time to pack it up. Catch my plane. I scan the hotel room for things not to forget. There's that white report card on the bureau.

"Dear Guests:" it says, under the name "Olive." I am your maid for the day. Please rate me: Excellent. Good. Average. Poor. Thank you."

I tuck this momento from the Sheraton British Colonial into my notebook. How would "Olive" rate *me*? What would it mean for us to seem "good" to each other? What would that rating require?

But I am hastening to leave. Neither turtle soup nor kidney pie nor any conch shell delight shall delay my departure. I have rested, here, in the Bahamas, and I'm ready to return to my usual job, my usual work. But the skin on my body has changed and so has my mind. On the Delta flight home I realize I am burning up, indeed.

So far as I can see, the usual race and class concepts of connection, or gender assumptions of unity, do not apply very well. I doubt that they ever did. Otherwise why would Black folks forever bemoan our lack of solidarity when the deal turns real. And if unity on the basis of sexual oppression is something natural, then why do we women, the majority people on the planet, still have a problem?

The plane's ready for takeoff. I fasten my seatbelt and let the tumult inside my head run free. Yes: race and class and gender remain as real as the weather. But what they must mean about the contact between two individuals is less obvious and, like the weather, not predictable.

And when these factors of race and class and gender absolutely collapse is whenever you try to use them as automatic concepts of connection. They may serve well as indicators of commonly felt conflict, but as elements of connection they seem about as reliable as precipitation probability for the day after the night before the day.

It occurs to me that much organizational grief could be avoided if people understood that partnership in misery does not necessarily provide for partnership for change: *When we get the monsters off our backs all of us may want to run in very different directions.*

And not only that: even though both "Olive" and "I" live inside a conflict neither one of us created, and even though both of us therefore hurt inside that conflict, I may be one of the monsters she needs to eliminate from her universe and, in a sense, she may be one of the monsters in mine.

I am reaching for the words to describe the difference between a common identity that has been imposed and the individual identity any one of us will choose, once she gains that chance.

That difference is the one that keeps us stupid in the face of new, specific information about somebody else with whom we are supposed to have a connection because a third party, hostile to both of us, has worked it so that the two of us, like it or not, share a common enemy. *What happens beyond the idea of that enemy and beyond the consequences of that enemy?*

I am saying that the ultimate connection cannot be the enemy. The ultimate connection must be the need that we find between us. It is not only who you are, in other words, but what we can do for each other that will determine the connection.

I am flying back to my job. I have been teaching contemporary women's poetry this semester. One quandary I have set myself to explore with my students is the one of taking responsibility without power. We had been wrestling ideas to the floor for several sessions when a young Black woman, a South African, asked me for help, after class.

Sokutu told me she was "in a trance" and that she'd been unable to eat for two weeks.

"What's going on?" I asked her, even as my eyes startled at her trembling and emaciated appearance.

"My husband. He drinks all the time. He beats me up. I go to the hospital. I can't eat. I don't know what/anything."

In my office, she described her situation. I did not dare to let her sense my fear and horror. She was dragging about, hour by hour, in dread. Her husband, a young Black South African, was drinking himself into more and more deadly violence against her.

Sokutu told me how she could keep nothing down. She weighed 90 lbs. at the outside, as she spoke to me. She'd already been hospitalized as a result of her husband's battering rage.

I knew both of them because I had organized a campus group to aid the liberation struggles of Southern Africa.

Nausea rose in my throat. What about this presumable connection: this husband and this wife fled from that homeland of hatred against them, and now what? He was destroying himself. If not stopped, he would certainly murder his wife.

She needed a doctor, right away. It was a medical emergency. She needed protection. It was a security crisis. She needed refuge for battered wives and personal therapy and legal counsel. She needed a friend.

I got on the phone and called every number in the campus directory that I could imagine might prove helpful. Nothing worked. There were no institutional resources designed to meet her enormous, multifaceted, and ordinary woman's need.

I called various students. I asked the Chairperson of the English Department for advice. I asked everyone for help.

Finally, another one of my students, Cathy, a young Irish woman active in campus IRA activities, responded. She asked for further details. I gave them to her.

"Her husband," Cathy told me, "is an alcoholic. You have to understand about alcoholics. It's not the same as anything else. And it's a disease you can't treat any old way."

I listened, fearfully. Did this mean there was nothing we could do?

"That's not what I'm saying," she said. "But you have to keep the alcoholic part of the thing central in everybody's mind, otherwise her husband will kill her. Or he'll kill himself."

She spoke calmly. I felt there was nothing to do but to assume she knew what she was talking about.

"Will you come with me?" I asked her, after a silence. "Will you come with me and help us figure out what to do next?"

Cathy said she would but that she felt shy: Sokutu comes from South Africa. What would she think about Cathy?

"I don't know," I said. "But let's go."

We left to find a dormitory room for the young battered wife.

It was late, now, and dark outside.

On Cathy's VW that I followed behind with my own car was the sticker that reads BOBBY SANDS FREE AT LAST. My eyes blurred as I read and reread the words. This was another connection: Bobby Sands and Martin Luther King Jr. and who would believe it? I would not have believed it; I grew up terrorized by Irish kids who introduced me to the word "nigga."

And here I was following an Irish woman to the room of a Black South African. We were going to that room to try to save a life together.

When we reached the little room, we found ourselves awkward and large. Sokutu attempted to treat us with utmost courtesy, as though we were honored guests. She seemed surprised by Cathy, but mostly Sokutu was flushed with relief and joy because we were there, with her.

I did not know how we should ever terminate her heartfelt courtesies and address, directly, the reason for our visit: her starvation and her extreme physical danger.

Finally, Cathy sat on the floor and reached out her hands to Sokutu.

"I'm here," she said quietly, "because June has told me what has happened to you. And I know what it is. Your husband is an alcoholic. He has a disease. I know what it is. My father was an alcoholic. He killed himself. He almost killed my mother. I want to be your friend."

"Oh," was the only small sound that escaped from Sokutu's mouth. And then she embraced the other student. And then everything changed and I watched all of this happen so I know that this happened: this connection.

And after we called the police and exchanged phone numbers and plans were made for the night and for the next morning, the young South African woman walked down the dormitory hallway, saying goodbye and saying thank you to us.

I walked behind them, the young Irish woman and the young South African, and I saw them walking as sisters walk, hugging each other, and whispering and sure of each other and I felt how it was not who they were but what they both know and what they were both preparing to do about what they know that was going to make them both free at last.

And I look out the windows of the plane and I see clouds that will not kill me and I know that someday soon other clouds may erupt to kill us all.

And I tell the stewardess No thanks to the cocktails she offers me. But I look about the cabin at the hundred strangers drinking as they fly and I think even here and even now I must make the connection real between me and these strangers everywhere before those other clouds unify this ragged bunch of us, too late.

Considerations for Thinking and Writing

1. Consider Jordan's appeal for collective strength in "Where Is the Love?" against Adrienne Rich's appeal for a "lesbian continuum" in "Compulsory Heterosexuality and Lesbian Existence." How are the two arguments related? Look carefully at the way in which the two women present their arguments. Is one more effective than the other? Which do you prefer? Why? In what way might audiences have influenced these writers?

2. In what ways do the needs of Black feminists differ from those of other feminists? Consider Audre Lord's essays in Part I and Angela Y. Davis's essay in Part II. Think too of what Alice Walker says about Virginia Woolf in her essay "In Search of Our Mothers' Gardens." Why does Walker have to change Woolf's language? Why would she quote Woolf even though she has to change some of Woolf's words?

3. In "Many Rivers to Cross" Jordan lets us see her mother, sitting on the side of her cot trying to get up, locked in a position somewhere between life and death. How does Jordan use this image later in her essay? Compare Jordan's picture of her mother and father with Phyllis Rose's "Mothers and Fathers." What does such a comparison tell you about class and racial differences?

4. Why does Jordan begin "Nobody Mean More to Me" with a statistical survey about "Standard English"? How does the tone of her essay change after the first four paragraphs? What point do you think Jordan finally makes about "Standard English"? Does she convince you that Black English is effective? Why? If you live in a neighborhood or in a community with a language of its own, see if you can write down a few of the rules governing usage.

5. At the very beginning of "Report from the Bahamas," what rhetorical use does Jordan make of the Black man carrying daquiris? How does she go on to complicate the problem of race in this essay? How does she implicate herself? Does she redeem herself? Why do you think Jordan includes the story about the Irish woman and the South African woman?

6. Read through all of Jordan's essays looking at how she manages to express her anger and love simultaneously. While urging her audiences to unite in love, she shows anger and outrage. Does her anger diminish or strengthen the power of her appeal? Explain.

7. In "Report from the Bahamas" Jordan expresses some doubt about "gender assumptions of unity." Do you see more signs of unity or disunity among the women you know? How might individual differences, racial differences, and class differences complicate the question of unity? What about bodily differences? Do they divide women? What differences does Evelyn Fox Keller identify in "A World of Difference"? Are the differences significant? Explain.

MAXINE HONG KINGSTON
(b. 1940)

The first voice we hear in Maxine Hong Kingston's *Woman Warrior* is her mother's: " 'You must not tell anyone,' my mother said, 'what I am about to tell you.' " Ironically, the mother admonishes her daughter to silence even as she nourishes her with stories of her Chinese forebears. This memorable opening signals both the complexity of Kingston's identity as a Chinese-American woman writer and the complexity of the writing itself, a stunning blend of autobiography, history, myth, folklore, and legend.

One cannot read very far in either of Kingston's books without confronting the difficulty of telling fact from fiction. In "No Name Woman," for example, she supposes that her pregnant aunt had been raped, then considers who the rapist might have been. Finally, she wonders "whether he masked himself when he joined the raid on her family." Similarly, in "The Father from China," in *China Men*, Kingston narrates five different versions of her father's entry into the United States. We cannot be sure whether he entered at New York or at San Francisco, as a stowaway or through immigration at Angel Island, illegally or legally. Instead of facts about her family, Kingston recreates for us the spell of the "talk-story," a Cantonese tradition kept alive mainly by women. (Even the stories told in *China Men*, Kingston claims, were told to her by women.) The story-talkers of Kingston's childhood tell stories in multiple versions, sometimes with graphic, startling details, sometimes in whispers. Like the powerful account of her aunt's pregnancy, childbirth, and suicide, the stories contain silences that compel the listener to venture imaginatively into the dangerous world of the story. Kingston's suppositions—"I wonder," "perhaps," "may have"—enable us to witness the writer taking up her voice among the story-talkers of her childhood.

Though Kingston has won major awards for nonfiction—the National Book Critics Circle Award for *The Woman Warrior* and the American Book Award for *China Men*—her writing teases out a cultural bias in the very existence of such delimiting categories as fiction and nonfiction. By bringing to the surface the discrepancies in her own narratives, Kingston forces us to perceive unaccustomed relations between fact and fiction in our own lives. For this reason—and because of its savage poetry— her writing challenges and unsettles us. Her two books about her family also explore a family resemblance between fiction and nonfiction, between stories and histories. Kingston wants us to be aware that what she knows of the past is partly what she has needed to tell herself about it. Conversely, not to remake the past is to risk its forfeiture. Kingston's books meditate not on the difference between facts and fictions but on how we relate to them in ways that are at once real and imaginary.

In an interview, Kingston once called China "a country I made up." At times Kingston suggests that the China her parents left behind seems unreal to her: "Those of us in the first American generations have had to figure out how the invisible world the emigrants built around our childhoods fits in solid America." The story of Mad Sao dramatizes the fierce grip of the ghostly past on the present. The mother's letters from China describe a ferocious and elemental hunger that contrasts starkly with her son's tales of mortgage payments, new cars, and American daughters. Like the vengeful, restless spirit of the "No Name Woman," Mad Sao's mother becomes a demon whose demands persist with new intensity after her death. Ultimately her ghostly powers prevail over the complacency of her son's American life, hurling him into madness and torment until he returns to Chinese soil and appeases her. On the other hand, Kingston shows that the American world, for all its apparent solidity, often seems ghostly and inscrutable to the child of immigrants. We find that Caucasians are called demons— the "newsboy-demon," the "Mexican demons"—because the shades of their skin give them the appearance of Chinese ghosts. Because both American and Chinese culture seem spectral to the Chinese-American child, each is easily and frequently penetrated by the other. Kingston's account of her Chinese-American girlhood in California features disruptions in the "roundness" of family life which awaken her to self-consciousness.

In "Imagined Life," an essay on teaching writing, Kingston considers *The Woman Warrior* the book of her mother, calling *China Men* her "father-book." But both books, while dominated by the experiences of her mother and father, respectively, move outward to dwell on her male and female relatives. *The Woman Warrior* gives voice to the women who have shaped Kingston's imagination even as it gives shape to these women on the page. The woman warrior of the title is the heroic Fa Mu Lan, warrior, wife, and mother, whose legend Kingston had been told by her mother: "She said I would grow up a wife and a slave, but she taught me the song of the warrior woman, Fa Mu Lan." As though challenged by her mother, Kingston tells in the first person the story of Fa Mu Lan's rescue of her village. Having vowed to grow up a warrior woman, Kingston finds that America comes between her and her ambition: "I could not figure out what was my village." Though Kingston names her book for Fa Mu Lan, she tells first the suppressed story of her nameless aunt, whose catastrophe resulted in her family's ruin and her death (and that of her nameless child). The two stories provide an uneasy counterpoint against which Kingston tells the story of her mother's training as a midwife in China and that of her aunt's doomed attempt to confront the husband who had left her for America years before. Only in the final section of *The Woman Warrior* does Kingston tell her own story. Here the young Maxine (Ting Ting) tries mercilessly to wring speech from a silent classmate. As in "No Name Woman," Kingston displays her intuitive childhood awareness of the desperate importance of speech.

While Kingston has insisted that her two books were written "more or less simultaneously," *China Men* reveals several developments in Kingston's autobiographical art. First, Kingston intersperses brief, stark Chinese legends among lengthy narratives about her father, grandfather, great-grandfather, and brother. In "On Discovery" Kingston renders legendary material in an attenuated, suggestive, parabolic style. We sense an odd kinship between Kingston's impulse to concentrate a story and her impulse to vary a story. She is out to convince us that memorable stories owe as great a debt to the imagination and skill of the teller as they do to experience. "On Discovery" assaults the reader with the knowledge that beautiful women, like beautiful writing, arise by dint of pain and effort. In the extreme world of the parable, even a man can become a woman; Tang Ao, having submitted to the rigors of femininity, becomes disarmingly beautiful. But unlike texts, women suffer when they submit to rigorous standards that are not of their making. While "On Discovery" fantasizes a female revenge, it also probes the irony of using power to recapitulate one's own oppression.

Perhaps because Kingston's wildness is focused in such fierce parables, the narratives in *China Men* are freer than those in *The Woman Warrior* to acknowledge the hardness of American life for Chinese immigrants. Here Kingston tells the story of her Chinese grandfather, who blasted through solid rock so that railroads might be built; and that of her great-grandfather, who, together with thousands of other Chinese immigrants lured to Hawaii by false promises, hacked out the wilderness so that sugarcane might be grown. *China Men* seems the more politically engaged of the two books; in "The Brother in Vietnam," of which she gives us a glimpse in "Imagined Life," Kingston criticizes harshly the ways in which American economic and military might are put to use.

Since winning national acclaim with her two books, Kingston has become free to write full-time. Born in Stockton, California, in 1940, she has lived in Hawaii for twenty years with her husband and son, and is now writing a novel. Of the nameless aunt whose story she commits to the page, Kingston remarks, "Unless I see her life branching into mine, she gives me no ancestral help." In the mother-book and the father-book Kingston bears witness to the branchings of the lives of those who come before us in our own. By doing so, she both speaks in ancestral voices and transforms the story-talkers' rich, haunting inheritance into her own memorable and lasting art.

No Name Woman

"You must not tell anyone," my mother said, "what I am about to tell you. In China your father had a sister who killed herself. She jumped into the family well. We say that your father has all brothers because it is as if she had never been born.

"In 1924 just a few days after our village celebrated seventeen hurry-up weddings—to make sure that every young man who went 'out on the road' would responsibly come home—your father and his brothers and your grandfather and his brothers and your aunt's new husband sailed for America, the Gold Mountain. It was your grandfather's last trip. Those lucky enough to get contracts waved good-bye from the decks. They fed and guarded the stowaways and helped them off in Cuba, New York, Bali, Hawaii. 'We'll meet in California next year,' they said. All of them sent money home.

"I remember looking at your aunt one day when she and I were dressing; I had not noticed before that she had such a protruding melon of a stomach. But I did not think, 'She's pregnant,' until she began to look like other pregnant women, her shirt pulling and the white tops of her black pants showing. She could not have been pregnant, you see, because her husband had been gone for years. No one said anything. We did not discuss it. In early summer she was ready to have the child, long after the time when it could have been possible.

"The village had also been counting. On the night the baby was to be born the villagers raided our house. Some were crying. Like a great saw, teeth strung with lights, files of people walked zigzag across our land, tearing the rice. Their lanterns doubled in the disturbed black water, which drained away through the broken bunds. As the villagers closed in, we could see that some of them, probably men and women we knew well, wore white masks. The people with long hair hung it over their faces. Women with short hair made it stand up on end. Some had tied white bands around their foreheads, arms, and legs.

"At first they threw mud and rocks at the house. Then they threw eggs and began slaughtering our stock. We could hear the animals scream their deaths—the roosters, the pigs, a last great roar from the ox. Familiar wild heads flared in our night windows; the villagers encircled us. Some of the faces stopped to peer at us, their eyes rushing like searchlights. The hands flattened against the panes, framed heads, and left red prints.

"The villagers broke in the front and the back doors at the same time, even though we had not locked the doors against them. Their knives dripped with the blood of our animals. They smeared blood on the doors and walls. One woman swung a chicken, whose throat she had slit, splattering blood in red arcs about her. We stood together in the middle of our house, in the family hall with the pictures and tables of the ancestors around us, and looked straight ahead.

"At that time the house had only two wings. When the men came back, we would build two more to enclose our courtyard and a third one to begin a second courtyard. The villagers pushed through both wings, even your grandparents' rooms, to find your aunt's, which was also mine until the men returned. From this room a new wing for one of the younger families would grow. They ripped up her clothes and shoes and broke her combs, grinding them underfoot. They tore her work from the loom. They scattered the cooking fire and rolled the new weaving in it. We could hear them in the kitchen breaking our bowls and banging the pots. They overturned the great waist-high earthenware jugs; duck eggs, pickled fruits, vegetables burst out and mixed in acrid torrents. The old woman from the next field swept a broom through the air and loosed the spirits-of-the-broom over our heads. 'Pig.' 'Ghost.' 'Pig,' they sobbed and scolded while they ruined our house.

"When they left, they took sugar and oranges to bless themselves. They cut pieces from the dead animals. Some of them took bowls that were not broken and clothes that were not torn. Afterward we swept up the rice and sewed it back up into sacks. But the smells from the spilled preserves lasted. Your aunt gave birth in the pigsty that night. The next morning when I went for the water, I found her and the baby plugging up the family well.

"Don't let your father know that I told you. He denies her. Now that you have started to menstruate, what happened to her could happen to you. Don't humiliate us. You wouldn't like to be forgotten as if you had never been born. The villagers are watchful."

Whenever she had to warn us about life, my mother told stories that ran like this one, a story to grow up on. She tested our strength to establish realities. Those in the emigrant generations who could not reassert brute survival died young and far from home. Those of us in the first American generations have had to figure out how the invisible world the emigrants built around our childhoods fits in solid America.

The emigrants confused the gods by diverting their curses, misleading them with crooked streets and false names. They must try to confuse their offspring as well, who, I suppose, threaten them in similar ways—always trying to get things straight, always trying to name the unspeakable. The Chinese I know hide their names; sojourners take new names when their lives change and guard their real names with silence.

Chinese-Americans, when you try to understand what things in you are Chinese, how do you separate what is peculiar to childhood, to poverty, insanities, one family, your mother who marked your growing with stories, from what is Chinese? What is Chinese tradition and what is the movies?

If I want to learn what clothes my aunt wore, whether flashy or ordinary, I would have to begin, "Remember Father's drowned-in-the-well sister?" I cannot ask that. My mother has told me once and for all the useful parts. She will add nothing unless powered by Necessity, a riverbank that guides her life. She plants vegetable gardens rather than lawns; she carries the odd-shaped tomatoes home from the fields and eats food left for the gods.

Whenever we did frivolous things, we used up energy; we flew high kites. We children came up off the ground over the melting cones our parents brought home from work and the American movie on New Year's Day—*Oh, You Beautiful Doll* with Betty Grable one year, and *She Wore a Yellow Ribbon* with John Wayne another year. After the one carnival ride each, we paid in guilt; our tired father counted his change on the dark walk home.

Adultery is extravagance. Could people who hatch their own chicks and eat the embryos and the heads for delicacies and boil the feet in vinegar for party food, leaving only the gravel, eating even the gizzard lining—could such people engender a prodigal aunt? To be a woman, to have a daughter in starvation time was a waste enough. My aunt could not have been the lone romantic who gave up everything for sex. Women in the old China did not choose. Some man had commanded her to lie with him and be his secret evil. I wonder whether he masked himself when he joined the raid on her family.

Perhaps she had encountered him in the fields or on the mountain where the daughters-in-law collected fuel. Or perhaps he first noticed her in the marketplace. He was not a stranger because the village housed no strangers. She had to have dealings with him other than sex. Perhaps he worked an adjoining field, or he sold her the cloth for the dress she sewed and wore. His demand must have surprised, then terrified her. She obeyed him; she always did as she was told.

When the family found a young man in the next village to be her husband, she had stood tractably beside the best rooster, his proxy, and promised before they met that she would be his forever. She was lucky that he was her age and she would be the first wife, an advantage secure now. The night she first saw him, he had sex with her. Then he left for America. She had almost forgotten what he looked like. When she tried to envision him, she only saw the black and white face in the group photograph the men had had taken before leaving.

The other man was not, after all, much different from her husband. They both gave orders: she followed. "If you tell your family, I'll beat you. I'll kill you. Be here again next week." No one talked sex, ever. And she might have separated the rapes from the rest of living if only she did not have to buy her oil from him or gather wood in the same forest. I want her fear to have lasted just as long as rape lasted so that the fear could have been contained. No drawn-out fear. But women at sex hazarded birth and hence lifetimes. The fear did not stop but permeated everywhere. She told the man, "I think I'm pregnant." He organized the raid against her.

On nights when my mother and father talked about their life back home, sometimes they mentioned an "outcast table" whose business they still seemed to be settling, their voices tight. In a commensal tradition, where food is precious, the powerful older people made wrongdoers eat alone. Instead of letting them start separate new lives like the Japanese, who could become samurais and geishas, the Chinese family, faces averted but eyes glowering sideways, hung on to the offenders and fed them leftovers. My aunt must have lived in the same house as my parents and eaten at an outcast table. My mother spoke about the raid as if she had seen it, when she and my aunt, a daughter-in-law to a different household, should not have been living together at all. Daughters-in-law lived with their husbands' parents, not their own; a synonym for marriage in Chinese is "taking a daughter-in-law." Her husband's parents could have sold her, mortgaged her, stoned her. But they had sent her back to her own mother and father, a mysterious act hinting at disgraces not told me. Perhaps they had thrown her out to deflect the avengers.

She was the only daughter; her four brothers went with her father, husband, and uncles "out on the road" and for some years became western men. When the goods were divided among the family, three of the brothers took land, and the youngest, my father, chose an education. After my grandparents gave their daughter away to her husband's family, they had dispensed all the adventure and all the property. They expected her alone to keep the traditional ways, which her brothers, now among the barbarians, could fumble without detection. The heavy, deep-rooted women were to maintain the past against the flood, safe for returning. But the rare urge west had fixed upon our family, and so my aunt crossed boundaries not delineated in space.

The work of preservation demands that the feelings playing about in one's guts not be turned into action. Just watch their passing like cherry blossoms. But perhaps my aunt, my forerunner, caught in a slow life, let dreams grow and fade and after some months or years went toward what persisted. Fear at the enormities of the forbidden kept her desires delicate, wire and bone. She looked at a man because she liked the way the hair was tucked behind his ears, or she liked the question-mark line of a long torso curving at the shoulder and straight at the hip. For warm eyes or a soft voice or a slow walk—that's all—a few hairs, a line, a brightness, a sound, a pace, she gave up family. She offered us up for a charm that vanished with tiredness, a pigtail that didn't toss when the wind died. Why, the wrong lighting could erase the dearest thing about him.

It could very well have been, however, that my aunt did not take subtle enjoyment of her friend, but, a wild woman, kept rollicking company. Imagining her free with sex doesn't fit, though. I don't know any women like that, or men either. Unless I see her life branching into mine, she gives me no ancestral help.

To sustain her being in love, she often worked at herself in the mirror, guessing at the colors and shapes that would interest him, changing them frequently in order to hit on the right combination. She wanted him to look back.

On a farm near the sea, a woman who tended her appearance reaped a reputation for eccentricity. All the married women blunt-cut their hair in flaps about their ears or pulled it back in tight buns. No nonsense. Neither style blew easily into heart-catching tangles. And at their weddings they displayed themselves in their long hair for the last time. "It brushed the backs of my knees," my mother tells me. "It was braided, and even so, it brushed the backs of my knees."

At the mirror my aunt combed individuality into her bob. A bun could have been contrived to escape into black streamers blowing in the wind or in quiet wisps about her face, but only the older women in our picture album wear buns. She brushed her hair back from her forehead, tucking the flaps behind her ears. She looped a piece of thread, knotted into a circle between her index fingers and thumbs, and ran the double strand across her forehead. When she closed her fingers as if she were making a pair of shadow geese bite, the string twisted together catching the little hairs. Then she pulled the thread away from her skin, ripping the hairs out neatly, her eyes watering from the needles of pain. Opening her fingers, she cleaned the thread, then rolled it along her hairline and the tops of her eyebrows. My mother did the same to me and my sisters and herself. I used to believe that the expression "caught by the short hairs" meant a captive held with a depilatory string. It especially hurt at the temples, but my mother said we were lucky we didn't have to have our feet bound when we were seven. Sisters used to sit on their beds and cry together, she said, as their mothers or their slave removed the bandages for a few minutes each night and let the blood gush back into their veins. I hope that the man my aunt loved appreciated a smooth brow, that he wasn't just a tits-and-ass man.

Once my aunt found a freckle on her chin, at a spot that the almanac said predestined her for unhappiness. She dug it out with a hot needle and washed the wound with peroxide.

More attention to her looks than these pullings of hairs and pickings at spots would have caused gossip among the villagers. They owned work clothes and good clothes, and they wore good clothes for feasting the new seasons. But since a woman combing her hair hexes beginnings, my aunt rarely found an occasion to look her best. Women looked like great sea snails—the corded wood, babies, and laundry they carried were the whorls on their backs. The Chinese did not admire a bent back; goddesses and warriors stood straight. Still there must have been a marvelous freeing of beauty when a worker laid down her burden and stretched and arched.

Such commonplace loveliness, however, was not enough for my aunt. She dreamed of a lover for the fifteen days of New Year's, the time for families to exchange visits, money, and food. She plied her secret comb. And sure enough she cursed the year, the family, the village, and herself.

Even as her hair lured her imminent lover, many other men looked at her. Uncles, cousins, nephews, brothers would have looked, too, had they been home between journeys. Perhaps they had already been restraining their curiosity, and they left, fearful that their glances, like a field of nesting birds, might be startled and caught. Poverty hurt, and that was their first reason for leaving. But another, final reason for leaving the crowded house was the never-said.

She may have been unusually beloved, the precious only daughter, spoiled and mirror gazing because of the affection the family lavished on her. When her husband left, they welcomed the chance to take her back from the in-laws; she could live like the little daughter for just a while longer. There are stories that my grandfather was different from other people, "crazy ever since the little Jap bayoneted him in the head." He used to put his naked penis on the dinner table, laughing. And one day he brought home a baby girl, wrapped up inside his brown western-style greatcoat. He had traded one of his sons, probably my father, the youngest, for her. My grandmother made him trade back. When he finally got a daughter of his own, he doted on her. They must have all loved her, except perhaps my father, the only brother who never went back to China, having once been traded for a girl.

Brothers and sisters, newly men and women, had to efface their sexual color and present plain miens. Disturbing hair and eyes, a smile like no other, threatened the ideal of five generations living under one roof. To focus blurs, people shouted face to face and yelled from room to room. The immigrants I know have loud voices, unmodulated to American tones even after years away from the village where they called their friendships out across the fields. I have not been able to stop my mother's screams in public libraries or over telephones. Walking erect (knees straight, toes pointed forward, not pigeon-toed, which is Chinese-feminine) and speaking in an inaudible voice, I have tried to turn myself American-feminine. Chinese communication was loud, public. Only sick people had to whisper. But at the dinner table, where the family members came nearest one another, no one could talk, not the outcasts nor any eaters. Every word that falls from the mouth is a coin lost. Silently they gave and accepted food with both hands. A preoccupied child who took his bowl with one hand got a sideways glare. A complete moment of total attention is due everyone alike. Children and lovers have no singularity here, but my aunt used a secret voice, a separate attentiveness.

She kept the man's name to herself throughout her labor and dying; she did not accuse him that he be punished with her. To save her inseminator's name she gave silent birth.

He may have been somebody in her own household, but intercourse with a man outside the family would have been no less abhorrent. All the village were kinsmen, and the titles shouted in loud country voices never let kinship be forgotten. Any man within visiting distance would have been neutralized as a lover—"brother," "younger brother," "older brother"—one hundred and fifteen relationship titles. Parents researched birth charts probably not so much to assure good fortune as to circumvent incest in a population that has but one hundred surnames. Everybody has eight million relatives. How useless then sexual mannerisms, how dangerous.

As if it came from an atavism deeper than fear, I used to add "brother" silently to boys' names. It hexed the boys, who would or would not ask me to dance, and made them less scary and as familiar and deserving of benevolence as girls.

But, of course, I hexed myself also—no dates. I should have stood up, both arms waving, and shouted out across libraries, "Hey, you! Love me back." I had no idea, though, how to make attraction selective, how to control its direction and magnitude. If I made myself American-pretty so that the five or six Chinese boys in the class fell in love with me, everyone else—the Caucasian, Negro, and Japanese boys—would too. Sisterliness, dignified and honorable, made much more sense.

Attraction eludes control so stubbornly that whole societies designed to organize relationships among people cannot keep order, not even when they bind people to one another from childhood and raise them together. Among the very poor and the wealthy, brothers married their adopted sisters, like doves. Our family allowed some romance, paying adult brides' prices and providing dowries so that their sons and daughters could marry strangers. Marriage promises to turn strangers into friendly relatives—a nation of siblings.

In the village structure, spirits shimmered among the live creatures, balanced and held in equilibrium by time and land. But one human being flaring up into violence could open up a black hole, a maelstrom that pulled in the sky. The frightened villagers, who depended on one another to maintain the real, went to my aunt to show her a personal, physical representation of the break she had made in the "roundness." Misallying couples snapped off the future, which was to be embodied in true offspring. The villagers punished her for acting as if she could have a private life, secret and apart from them.

If my aunt had betrayed the family at a time of large grain yields and peace, when many boys were born, and wings were being built on many houses, perhaps she might have escaped such severe punishment. But the men—hungry, greedy, tired of planting in dry soil—and had been forced to leave the village in order to send food-money home. There were ghost plagues, bandit plagues, wars with the Japanese, floods. My Chinese brother and sister had died of an unknown sickness. Adultery, perhaps only a mistake during good times, became a crime when the village needed food.

The round moon cakes and round doorways, the round tables of graduated size that fit one roundness inside another, round windows and rice bowls—these talismans had lost their power to warn this family of the law: a family must be whole, faithfully keeping the descent line by having sons to feed the old and the dead, who in turn look after the family. The villagers came to show my aunt and her lover-in-hiding a broken house. The villagers were speeding up the circling of events because she was too shortsighted to see that her infidelity had already harmed the village, that waves of consequences would return unpredictably, sometimes in disguise, as now, to hurt her. This roundness had to be made coin-sized so that she would see its circumference: punish her at the birth of her baby. Awaken her to the inexorable. People who refused fatalism because they could invent small resources insisted on culpability. Deny accidents and wrest fault from the stars.

After the villagers left, their lanterns now scattering in various directions toward home, the family broke their silence and cursed her. "Aiaa, we're going to die. Death is coming. Death is coming. Look what you've done. You've killed us. Ghost! Dead ghost! Ghost! You've never been born." She ran out into the fields, far enough from the house so that she could no longer hear their voices, and pressed herself against the earth, her own land no more. When she felt the birth coming, she thought that she had been hurt. Her body seized together. "They've hurt me too much," she thought. "This is gall, and it will kill me." With forehead and knees against the earth, her body convulsed and then relaxed. She turned on her back, lay on the ground. The black well of sky and stars went out and out and out forever; her body and her complexity seemed to disappear. She was one of the stars, a bright dot in blackness, without home, without a companion, in eternal cold and silence. An agoraphobia rose in her, speeding higher and higher, bigger and bigger; she would not be able to contain it; there would be no end to fear.

Flayed, unprotected against space, she felt pain return, focusing her body. This pain chilled her—a cold, steady kind of surface pain. Inside, spasmodically, the other pain, the pain of the child, heated her. For hours she lay on the ground, alternately body and space. Sometimes a vision of normal comfort obliterated reality: she saw the family in the evening gambling at the dinner table, the young people massaging their elders' backs. She saw them congratulating one another, high joy on the mornings the rice shoots came up. When these pictures burst, the stars drew yet further apart. Black space opened.

She got to her feet to fight better and remembered that old-fashioned women gave birth in their pigsties to fool the jealous, pain-dealing gods, who do not snatch piglets. Before the next spasms could stop her, she ran to the pigsty, each step a rushing out into emptiness. She climbed over the fence and knelt in the dirt. It was good to have a fence enclosing her, a tribal person alone.

Laboring, this woman who had carried her child as a foreign growth that sickened her every day, expelled it at last. She reached down to touch the hot, wet, moving mass, surely smaller than anything human, and could feel that it was human after all—fingers, toes, nails, nose. She pulled it up on to her belly, and it lay curled there, butt in the air, feet precisely tucked one under the other. She opened her loose shirt and buttoned the child inside. After resting, it squirmed and thrashed and she pushed it up to her breast. It turned its head this way and that until it found her nipple. There, it made little snuffling noises. She clenched her teeth at its preciousness, lovely as a young calf, a piglet, a little dog.

She may have gone to the pigsty as a last act of responsibility: she would protect this child as she had protected its father. It would look after her soul, leaving supplies on her grave. But how would this tiny child without family find her grave when there would be no marker for her anywhere, neither in the earth nor the family hall? No one would give her a family hall name. She had taken the child with her into the wastes. At its birth the two of them had felt the same raw pain of separation, a wound that only the family pressing tight could close. A child with no descent line would not soften her life but only trail after her, ghostlike, begging her to give it purpose. At dawn the villagers on their way to the fields would stand around the fence and look.

Full of milk, the little ghost slept. When it awoke, she hardened her breasts against the milk that crying loosens. Toward morning she picked up the baby and walked to the well.

Carrying the baby to the well shows loving. Otherwise abandon it. Turn its face into the mud. Mothers who love their children take them along. It was probably a girl; there is some hope of forgiveness for boys.

"Don't tell anyone you had an aunt. Your father does not want to hear her name. She has never been born." I have believed that sex was unspeakable and words so strong and fathers so frail that "aunt" would do my father mysterious harm. I have thought that my family, having settled among immigrants who had also been their neighbors in the ancestral land, needed to clean their name, and a wrong word would incite the kinspeople even here. But there is more to this silence: they want me to participate in her punishment. And I have.

In the twenty years since I heard this story I have not asked for details nor said my aunt's name; I do not know it. People who can comfort the dead can also chase after them to hurt them further—a reverse ancestor worship. The real punishment was not the raid swiftly inflicted by the villagers, but the family's deliberately forgetting her. Her betrayal so maddened them, they saw to it that she would suffer forever, even after death. Always hungry, always needing, she would have to beg food from other ghosts, snatch and steal it from those whose living descendants give them gifts. She would have to fight the ghosts massed at crossroads for the buns a few thoughtful citizens leave to decoy her away from village and home so that the ancestral spirits could feast unharassed. At peace, they could act like gods, not ghosts, their descent lines providing them with paper suits and dresses, spirit money, paper houses, paper automobiles, chicken, meat, and rice into eternity—essences delivered up in smoke and flames, steam and incense rising from each rice bowl. In an attempt to make the Chinese care for people outside the family, Chairman Mao encourages us now to give our paper replicas to the spirits of outstanding soldiers and workers, no matter whose ancestors they may be. My aunt remains forever hungry. Goods are not distributed evenly among the dead.

My aunt haunts me—her ghost drawn to me because now, after fifty years of neglect, I alone devote pages of paper to her, though not origamied into houses and clothes. I do not think she always means me well. I am telling on her, and she was a spite suicide, drowning herself in the drinking water. The Chinese are always very frightened of the drowned one, whose weeping ghost, wet hair hanging and skin bloated, waits silently by the water to pull down a substitute.

Imagined Life

One summer in Hawai'i, John Hawkes and I taught writing seminars in adjoining classrooms. I told my students: Don't worry about form; write any old thing, and it will naturally take shape. It will be a classical shape—a sonnet, an essay, a novel, a short story, a play—of its own accord. Do you think that Petrarch cooked up fourteen lines and an *abbaabbacdcdcd* rhyme scheme capriciously? After stating a problem, the human mind inevitably mulls on it, looks at its complexities, and comes to a new understanding. At its most efficient, the mind does this in fourteen lines, and when the resolution is especially neat, it makes a couplet. Like a computer program, a sonnet is one of the natural patterns of the brain. And iambic pentameter is the normal rhythm of the English language. I told the students to copy and tack over their desks some advice from Lew Welch:

> When I write, my only concern is accuracy. I try to write accurately from the poise of mind which lets us see that things are exactly what they seem. I never worry about beauty; if it is accurate there is always beauty. I never worry about form; if it is accurate there is always form.

Write about any old thing that has been obsessing you for years, then step back and see what shape the words are tending toward; then use that recognizable structure for guidance as you rewrite. For example, if some of the lines are iambic tetrameter with a syllable left over, see what happens if you push the line out another half a foot. Maybe there will be a concomitant extending of thought. Or shorten the line and see if you like the closer, thicker effect. You short story writers, sustain a scene for one more page; the characters may have to perform a culminating deed, and the scene then must yield its drama.

* * *

Meanwhile, in John Hawkes's seminar, I imagined wonderful goings on. Better goings on. In college, my husband and I had written a series of papers on Hawkes's *The Beetle Leg, The Blood Oranges, The Cannibal, The Lime Twig,* and *Second Skin.* And I had just read *Travesty* in preparation for meeting Hawkes. He must be telling his students miraculous things that I didn't dare fool with. That I didn't even know about. While I dealt with form, he must be counselling imaginations. I could almost hear him speaking like the narrator in *Travesty: "Imagined life is more exhilarating than remembered life."* In Italics. Repeating. *"Imagined life is more exhilarating than remembered life."*

> Somewhere there still must be
> Her face not seen, her voice not heard.

I picture John Hawkes listening to students' lives, their loves, figuring out how to strengthen them, probing at sources of power. Helping people find bottomless pitchers of cream and the other sides of walls.

Every time I have taught a class or a workshop, the most forbidding student in there has been somebody who signs up for the course because she's "blocked." That summer, there was again such a woman. It's always a woman, and she is always too nicely dressed. I tried talking her into switching from my course to John Hawkes's, but she wouldn't go. It was too late anyway; she'd already handed me her IBM card, which I'd turned in to the office. Also, it was at the last of the course that she admitted to being "blocked." Like other troubled writers in previous classes, she had shown me work she had done years ago, and fooled me. If I come across such a woman again, I will pretend to be John Hawkes and tell her to wear wanton dresses and to brush her hair more loosely. Then I am going to tell her that what's wrong with her is that she believes that a writer only exposes lives—when what a writer really does is imagine lives. To imagine a life means to take such an interest in someone that you suppose about him. You conjecture about him. You care what he eats and about whatever he is doing. "Stands he or sits he? Or does he walk? Or is he on his horse?"

"But—," says the "blocked" lady, who begins too many of her sentences with "but." "But I don't have a problem with romantic fantasizing." No, her problem is in the real world, and it is with real people. Each one of my "blocked" ladies has said she can't write because she is afraid of hurting her friends and relatives. "What does your mother think about your book?" she keeps asking me. "What does your father think?" Well, like everybody else of my generation who majored in English, I was trained in the New Criticism, and I didn't like that kind of question.

All right. To make your mother and your scandalous friends read about themselves and still like you, you have to be very cunning, very crafty. Don't commit yourself. Don't be pinned down. Give many versions of events. Tell the most flattering motives. Say: "Of course, it couldn't have been money that she was after." In *The Woman Warrior,* my mother-book, the No Name Woman might have been raped;

she might have had a love affair; she might have been "a wild woman, and kept rollicking company. Imagining her free with sex . . ." Imagining many lives for her made me feel free. I have so much freedom in telling about her, I'm almost free even from writing itself, and therefore obeying my mother, who said, "Don't tell."

Forget "definitive." The reason that John Hawkes finds imagined life more exhilarating than remembered life is that imagined life is not set.

The blocks that my father put in my way took more craftiness to break than my mother's. A consequence for my mentioning immigration papers could be his deportation. The Immigration and Naturalization Service demands consistency in the life story of a China Man. So, in my father-book, *China Men,* I used the very techniques that the men developed over a hundred years. They made themselves citizens of this country by telling American versions of their lives. My father has three or four stories about how he happens to be in America in spite of the Exclusion Laws and history and common sense. In "The Father from China," the illegal father sailed to Cuba, where he had his friends nail him up in a crate to stow away to New York Harbor. The last sentence of that story goes like this: "Of course, my father could not have come that way. He came a legal way." The legal father landed at the immigration station on Angel Island, where the imprisoned men wrote poems on the walls. They spent their time memorizing stories to tell at hearings. Some even had paper and wood models of the village they had supposedly come from so that all the people from that village could describe it the same way. Those who bought papers from American citizens memorized other men's lives.

In a third story, my father was born here. If you're born in America, you're automatically a citizen. So, my grandfather ran out of the San Francisco Earthquake and Fire with a newborn baby in his arms. It was a magical birth since my grandmother was in China at the time. Coincidentally, this happened when the San Francisco Hall of Records burned to the ground. That means that everyone who wants a birth certificate can say, "All records of my birth were burned in the San Francisco Earthquake and Fire." "Every China Man was reborn out of that fire an American."

A fourth way that my father is legal is that his father had bought for a bag of Sierra gold a Citizenship Paper from a Citizenship Judge. So, we are Americans many times over. Even more times over: The brothers in Vietnam got top security clearances.

You see how people have imaginations out of necessity. I didn't have to make up ways for telling immigration stories.

My father doesn't say, "Don't tell." He doesn't say much at all. The way to end the silence he gave me was to write this sentence: "I'll tell you what I suppose from your silences and few words, and you can tell me that I'm mistaken." You may use that sentence yourself if you like. Copy it down and see what comes next.

My father is answering me by writing poems and commentary in the margins of my books. The pirated translations have wide margins. Writing commentary is a traditional Chinese literary form. You can break reader's block by writing well.

Yes, the imagined life is so exhilarating that householders go in quest of new lands—the Gold Mountain and China. The Gold Mountain is a land of gold-cobbled streets, and it is also a country with no war and no taxes; it is governed by women. Most of us are here in America today because somebody in our families imagined the Gold Mountain vividly enough to come looking for it. I guess most people think they've found it, and "Gold Mountain" is synonymous with "United States of America." But we aren't peaceful; taxes are due the day after tomorrow; and women aren't in charge. You see how much work we have ahead of us—we still have that country to find, and we still have its stories to tell. Maybe those "blocked" ladies don't know: There is work that belongs to all of us, and they can't quit.

I haven't seen China yet. I didn't want to go there before finishing my two books because I was describing the place that we Americans imagine to be China. The mythic China has its own history, smells, flowers, one hundred birds, long-lived people, dialects, music. We can taste its sweetness when our grandmother sends us invisible candy. The place is so real that we talk about it in common, and we get mail from there. As real as the Brontës' childhood cities. As real as Dungeons and Dragons. If I had gotten on a plane and flown to the China that's over there, I might have lost the imagined land.

I have a Boston cousin, and a Foster City cousin who went back to our home village. They report separately that there were hardly any people about. It's like Roanoke. What to make of such "airy nothing"?

Now, I don't want to leave you with the impression that to imagine life means that you only invent ways to befuddle and blur and to find what is not there. To live a true human life today, we have to imagine what really goes on when we turn on the machines. "The Brother in Vietnam" warns about how easy it is to operate an instrument panel and not see the people far away dying horribly. That story is grey like an aircraft carrier—no red, green, and gold dragons in the riggings. No red blood. We deliberately weaken and divert our imaginations to be able to bear a world with bombs.

We went to a movie where the attendants gave each kid a free picture of an atomic bomb explosion. Smoke boiled in a yellow and orange cloud like a brain on a column. It was a souvenir to celebrate the bombing of Japan. Since I did not own much, I enjoyed the ownership of the V-J picture. At the base of the explosion, where the people would have been, the specks didn't resolve into bodies. I hid the picture so the younger children could not see it, to protect them against the fear of such powerful evil, not to break the news to them too soon. Occasionally, I took it out to study. I hid it so well, I lost it. I drew billows and shafts of light, and almost heard the golden music of it, the gold trumpets and drums of it.

The yearning for beauty can prettify reality, and sometimes imagination has to restore us to terror.

(Do you have any friends—I do—who believe that they are poets because they have imagination and poetic feelings even though they don't write at all? I don't like telling them so, but it seems to me that imagination is one thing and writing is something else, a putting-into-words. Words pin down the once-seen, and reproduce it for readers. That's why I'm quoting from my books so much—I need those words to call forth other realities. The New Critics seem to be breathing over my shoulders and saying, "Cut it out." The work is supposed to be a self-contained whole, speaking for itself. There's not supposed to be an imagination apart from the work. But I know there is one. Words are only the known world—La Terra Conosciuta—beyond which the old maps showed Arabia Deserta, the Great American Desert, Red Cloud's Country, the unattached Territories, the Badlands, Barbaria, the Abode of Emptiness, the Mountains of the White Tigers, the Sea of Darkness— sea serpents and mermaids swam there—"strange beasts be here."—Nada ou Nouvel, whence the four winds blew. And the space maps show the Hyperspace Barrier, areas of Giants, Supergiants, Dwarfs, Protogalaxies, Black Holes—infinite areas named with a word or two.)

The Brother in Vietnam, who has some imagination left, refuses to go to language school because he can picture scenes in which he would use the *Vietnamese Phrase Book*:

Welcome, Sir. Glad to meet you.
How many are with you? Show me on your fingers.
Are you afraid of the enemy? Us?
Do you believe in
  (1) U.S. victory?
  (2) annihilation of Bolshevism?
Are you afraid? Why?
If we cannot trust a man,
  (1) wink your eye
  (2) place your left hand on your stomach
  (3) move your hand to the right, unnoticed, until we note your signal.

And because he knows languages, the brother cannot go wholeheartedly to war against people who have the same words as the Chinese for "happiness," "contentment," "bliss," "orchid," the same pun on "lettuce" and "life," the same words for things that matter, "study," "university," "love." The young men in the Vietnam story have reader's block.

*   *   *

As a passenger on a bombing run, the Brother in Vietnam tries his best to see.

Even using binoculars, he did not see much of the shore. Hanoi was an hour away by plane. He did not see the bombs drop out of the plane, whether they turned and turned, flashing in the sun. During loading, when they were locked into place, they looked like neatly rolled joints; they looked like long grains of rice; they looked like pupae and turds. He never heard cries under the bombing.

We approach the truth with metaphors.

All that he witnessed was heavy jungle and, in the open skies, other planes that seemed to appear and disappear quickly, shiny planes and their decals and formations. The bombs must have gone off behind them. Some air turbulence might have been a bomb ejected.

When a pilot did not show up in the chow line, it was up to the other men to imagine his death.

John Hawkes approaches God with metaphor:

. . . and I heard what she was saying: "God snapping him fingers," she said, and that sudden moment of waking was just what she said, "God snapping him fingers," though it was probably Edward breaking a twig or one of the birds bounding a bright seed off the smooth green back of a resounding calabash.

Now, I have told you those things about imagination that I'm sure of, and I have shown ways that words hold the imaginary; the book opens like hands parting, presenting you a surprise. But there are properties of the imagination which I don't understand at all. I hope that one of you will delve into the following, and let the rest of us know:

How is it possible that the writer can suddenly and effortlessly become now this character and now that one, see through his eyes, her eyes, speak with his voice, her voice, make the reader view the world with the soul of another? I can see a room, a forest, a street, from a very particular character's angle of vision, and there are details as definite as if I were watching a movie with point-of-view camera directions. What is the process that makes this—what is it? empathy? voodoo?—happen? If the "blocked" writer can't do this anymore, how can I show her how it's done? In voodoo, creatures exchange souls. But there are exercises and rites in voodoo, whereas in writing, the inhabiting of another person seems to happen spontaneously. Would it do us good to study with voodoo priestesses?

What about interest? How is it that interest is an emotion in me, and, I presume, in other writers? There are things, people, images that seem to have no significance in the world but are obsessionally interesting to me. And there are major current events, wars, assassinations that you would think every informed person should care about, and I cannot work up an interest. For about thirty-five years, I glimpsed a sharp white triangle. It looked like a shark's tooth or a corner of paper or a creased pantleg. I felt great fear and energy whenever I beheld it. I beheld it and beheld it until I found the story of it. That white triangle turned out to be *China Men*, and appears contained in that book as the creased pantleg of a Navy officer looking for the stowaway father. Where did that image come from? Why is it full of radiation—stories ramifying from it? How do you recognize this white triangle when it appears? How do you evoke one?

And that snap—God's fingers? a bird? a twig?—how and why did John Hawkes hear that snap?

Perhaps it does some good just to be aware of these writer's figments. Wanting them and wanting to write well may help them come.

Voodoo and white triangles. No wonder Shakespeare compared the lunatic, the lover, and the poet.

> The lunatic, the lover, and the poet
> Are of imagination all compact;
> One sees more devils than vast hell can hold,
> That is, the madman; the lover, all as frantic,
> Sees Helen's brow in a brow of Egypt.
> The poet's eye in a fine frenzy rolling,
> Doth glance from heaven to earth, from earth to heaven;
> And as imagination bodies forth
> The forms of things unknown, the poet's pen
> Turns them to shapes and gives to airy nothing
> A local habitation and a name.

Everybody knows about being a lover, so I'll just talk about madness. Haven't you tried to go mad? What a relief it would be. You could act any way you please. Say anything to anybody. But don't give in to madness. It binds too tightly. Moon Orchid, who couldn't speak English, imagined that the Mexicans plotted against her. She was talking-story as fast as she could, putting into words what the people around her were doing. And she kept repeating the same crazy stories over and over.

The lunatic exaggerates evil, and the lover exaggerates beauty. The poet, though, makes things real. I like that plain word "local"—and take it to mean the mundane, the ordinary. In the formless universe, the poet makes us at home.

Here's how John Hawkes ends *Second Skin:*

Now I sit at my long table in the middle of my loud wandering night and by the light of a candle—one half-burned candle saved from last night's spectacle—I watch this final flourish of my own hand and muse and blow away the ashes and listen to the breathing among the rubbery leaves and the insects sweating out the night. Because now I am fifty-nine years old and I knew I would be, and now there is the sun in the evening, the moon at dawn, the still voice. That's it. The sun in the evening. The moon at dawn. The still voice.

What's it? What still voice? We have to learn to hear it.

Finally, remember the most common use of imagination, its fantastic and magical power to turn the order of things upside down. I wrote about a tribe of musical barbarians, who played reed flutes and fought with bows and arrows. So I invented for them a nock whistle to attach to their arrows; the archers shot terrifying sounds through the air. Then, my book finished, I went to a Chinese archaeological exhibit, and there, in the last case before the exit—I was just about to leave but turned back—behind the glass was a nock whistle. I believe that I caused it to appear on earth. Just as, because my husband and I wrote many papers about him, one day John Hawkes appeared at our door and said, "Hello, my name is Jack. And this is my wife, Sophie."

On Discovery

Once upon a time, a man, named Tang Ao, looking for the Gold Mountain, crossed an ocean, and came upon the Land of Women. The women immediately captured him, not on guard against ladies. When they asked Tang Ao to come along, he followed; if he had had male companions, he would've winked over his shoulder.

"We have to prepare you to meet the queen," the women said. They locked him in a canopied apartment equipped with pots of makeup, mirrors, and a woman's clothes. "Let us help you off with your armor and boots," said the women. They slipped his coat off his shoulders, pulled it down his arms, and shackled his wrists behind him. The women who kneeled to take off his shoes chained his ankles together.

A door opened, and he expected to meet his match, but it was only two old women with sewing boxes in their hands. "The less you struggle, the less it'll hurt," one said, squinting a bright eye as she threaded her needle. Two captors sat on him while another held his head. He felt an old woman's dry fingers trace his ear; the long nail on her little finger scraped his neck. "What are you doing?" he asked. "Sewing your lips together," she joked, blackening needles in a candle flame. The ones who sat on him bounced with laughter. But the old women did not sew his lips together. They pulled his earlobes taut and jabbed a needle through each of them. They had to poke and probe before puncturing the layers of skin correctly, the hole in the front of the lobe in line with the one in back, the layers of skin sliding about so. They worked the needle through—a last jerk for the needle's wide eye ("needle's nose" in Chinese). They strung his raw flesh with silk threads; he could feel the fibers.

The women who sat on him turned to direct their attention to his feet. They bent his toes so far backward that his arched foot cracked. The old ladies squeezed each foot and broke many tiny bones along the sides. They gathered his toes, toes over and under one another like a knot of ginger root. Tang Ao wept with pain. As they wound the bandages tight and tighter around his feet, the women sang footbinding songs to distract him: "Use aloe for binding feet and not for scholars."

During the months of a season, they fed him on women's food: the tea was thick with white chrysanthemums and stirred the cool female winds inside his body; chicken wings made his hair shine; vinegar soup improved his womb. They drew the loops of thread through the scabs that grew daily over the holes in his earlobes. One day they inserted gold hoops. Every night they unbound his feet, but his veins had shrunk, and the blood pumping through them hurt so much, he begged to have his feet re-wrapped tight. They forced him to wash his used bandages, which were embroidered with flowers and smelled of rot and cheese. He hung the bandages up to dry, streamers that drooped and draped wall to wall. He felt embarrassed; the wrappings were like underwear, and they were his.

One day his attendants changed his gold hoops to jade studs and strapped his feet to shoes that curved like bridges. They plucked out each hair on his face, powdered him white, painted his eyebrows like a moth's wings, painted his cheeks and lips red. He served a meal at the queen's court. His hips swayed and his shoulders swiveled because of his shaped feet. "She's pretty, don't you agree?" the diners said, smacking their lips at his dainty feet as he bent to put dishes before them.

In the Women's Land there are no taxes and no wars. Some scholars say that that country was discovered during the reign of Empress Wu (A.D. 694–705), and some say earlier than that, A.D. 441, and it was in North America.

Mad Sao*

Third Grandfather had a grandson whom we called Sao Elder Brother to his face, but for a while behind his back, Mad Sao, which rhymes in our dialect. Sao firmly established his American citizenship by serving in the U.S. Army in World War II, then sent for a wife from China. We were amazed at how lovely and kind she was even though picked sight unseen. The new couple, young and modern *(mo-dang)*, bought a ranch house and car, wore fashionable clothes, spoke English, and seemed more American than us.

But Sao's mother sent him letters to come home to China. "I'm growing old," she said or the letter writer said. "If you don't come home now you'll never see me again. I remember you, my baby. Don't wait until you're old before coming back. I can't bear seeing you old like me." She did not know how American he had looked in his army uniform. "All you're doing is having fun, aren't you?" she asked. "You're spending all the money, aren't you? This is your own mother who rocked you to sleep and took care of you when you were sick. Do you remember your mother's face? We used to pretend our rocker was a boat like a peapod, and we were peas at sea. Remember? Remember? But now you send paper boats into my dreams. Sail back

*Excerpted from "The Making of More Americans," *China Men.*

to me." But he was having his own American babies yearly, three girls and a boy. "Who will bury me if you don't come back?" his mother asked.

And if she wasn't nagging him to return, she was asking for money. When he sent photographs of the family with the car in the background, she scolded him: "What are you doing feeding these girls and not your mother? What is this car, and this radio? A new house. Why are you building a new house in America? You have a house here. Sell everything. Sell the girls, and mail the profits to Mother. Use the money for ship fare. Why are you spending money on photographs of girls? Send me the money you give the photographers so I can send you *my* picture, the face you've forgotten." She did not know that he owned his own camera. His family was one of the first to own a shower, a lawn, a carport, and a car for passengers rather than for hauling.

"You're doing everything backward," his mother wrote. "I'm starving to death. In the enclosed picture, you can see my bones poking through the skin. You must be turning into a demon to treat a mother so. I have suffered all my life; I need to rest now. I'll die happy if you come home. Why don't you do your duty? I order you to come back. It's all those daughters, isn't it? They've turned your head. Leave them. Come back alone. You don't need to save enough money to bring a litter of females. What a waste to bring girls all the way back here to sell anyway. You can find a second wife here too. A Gold Mountain Sojourner attracts ten thousand rich fat women. Sell those girls, apprentice the boy, and use the money for your passage." Of course, though Mad Sao favored his son, there was no question but that, being very American, he would raise and protect his daughters.

"Let me tell you about hunger," wrote his mother. "I am boiling weeds and roots. I am eating flowers and insects and pond scum. All my teeth have fallen out. An army drafted the ox, and soldiers took the pigs and chickens. There are strangers in the orchard eating the fruit in its bud. I tried to chase them away. 'We're hungry. We're hungry,' they kept explaining. The next people through here will gnaw the branches. The sly villagers are hoarding food, begging it, and hiding it. You can't trust the neighbors. They'd do anything. I haven't eaten meat for so long, I might as well have been a nun who's taken a vegetable vow. You'd think I'd be holy by now and see miracles. What I see are the hungry, who wander lost from home and village. They live by swindling and scheming. Two crazed villagers are stealing a Dragon King statue from each other. It goes back and forth and whoever's doorstep it lands on has to pay for a party. There's no goodness and wisdom in hunger. You're starving me. I see you for what you are—an unfaithful son. Oh, what blame you're incurring. All right, don't bring yourself to me. I don't need a son. But send money. Send food. Send food. I may have been exaggerating before, but don't punish me for playing the boy who cried wolf. This time there really is a wolf at the door." He shut his heart and paid his house mortgage. He did nothing for her, or he did plenty, and it was not enough.

"Now we're eating potato leaves," she wrote. "We pound rice hulls into paste and eat it. At least send money to bury me." (Sao felt the terror in *bury*, the dirt packing the nose, plugging the eyes and mouth.) "I've wasted my life waiting, and what do I get for my sacrifices? Food and a fat old age? No. I'm starving to death alone. I hold you responsible. How can you swallow when you know of me?" Some letters were long and some short. "The beggar children who came to the door on your sister's wedding day were the worst-looking beggars in many years," she wrote. "Give them food? Huh. I should have kidnapped them and sold them. Except that people don't buy children any more, not even boys. There's a baby on the rich family's doorstep every morning. Oh, it's so pathetic. The mother hides behind bushes to watch the rich lady bring the baby inside. There are people eating clay balls and chewing bark. The arbor we sat under is gone, eaten. No more fish in the rivers. Frogs, beetles, all eaten. I am so tired. I can't drive the refugees off our property. They eat the seeds out of the dirt. There'll not be harvest again."

Other relatives wrote letters about their hunger: "We'd be glad to catch a rat but they're gone too," a cousin wrote. "Slugs, worms, bugs, all gone. You think we're dirty and depraved? Anything tastes good fried, but we can't buy oil." "We're chewing glue from hems and shoes," wrote another cousin. "We steal food off graves if people are rich enough to leave some. But who tends the dead any more?" "Starving takes a long time." "No more dogs and cats. No more birds. No mice. No grasshoppers." "We've burned the outhouse for fuel. Didn't need it anyway. Nothing comes out because nothing goes in. What shall we do? Eat shit and drink piss? But there isn't any coming out." "I can't sleep for the hunger. If we could sleep, we'd dream about food. I catch myself opening cupboards and jars even though I know they're empty. Staring into pots." "I searched under my own children's pillows for crumbs." "Soon I won't be able to concentrate on writing to you. My brain is changing. If only the senses would dull, I wouldn't feel so bad. But I am on the alert for food." "There are no children on some streets." "We know which weeds and berries and mushrooms and toads are poisonous from people eating them and dying." "Fathers leave in the middle of the night, taking no food with them." "The dead are luckier."

When the relatives read and discussed one another's hunger letters, they said, "Perhaps it's more merciful to let them die fast, starve fast rather than slow." "It's kinder either to send a great deal of money or none at all," they said. "Do you think people really go into euphoria when they die of hunger? Like saints fasting?"

"How can you leave me to face famine and war alone?" wrote Mad Sao's mother. "All I think about is you and food. You owe it to me to return. Advise me. Don't trick me. If you're never coming home, tell me. I can kill myself then. Easily stop looking for food and die." "The neighbors heard rumors about food inland to the north," she wrote next. "Others are following an army their sons joined. The villagers are moving. Tell me what to do. Some people are walking to the cities. Tin miners are coming through here, heading for the ocean. They spit black. They can't trade their tin or money for food. Rich people are throwing money into the crowds. I've buried the gold. I buried the money and jewels in the garden. We were almost robbed. The bandit used the old trick of sticking a pot like his head bulging against the curtain, and when I clubbed it, it clanged. At the alarm he fled. I had nothing to steal anyway." Hearing that money couldn't buy food relieved Mad Sao of feeling so guilty when he did not send money.

"Since everyone is traveling back and forth, I might as well stay put here," wrote his mother. "I'm frightened of these hungry eaters and killer soldiers and contagious lepers. It used to be the lepers and the deformed who hid; now the fat people hide."

"Shall I wait for you? Answer me. How would you like to come home and find an empty house? The door agape. You'll not find me waiting when you get here. It would serve you right. The weather has changed; the world is different. The young aren't feeding the old any more. The aunts aren't feeding me any more. They're keeping the food for their own children. Some slaves have run away. I'm chasing my slaves away. Free people are offering themselves as soldiers and slaves."

"I'm too old. I don't want to endure any more. Today I gave my last handful of rice to an old person so dried up, I couldn't tell whether it was man or woman. I'm ready to die." But she wrote again, "The fugitives are begging for burial ground and make a cemetery out of our farm. Let them bury their skinny bodies if they give me a little funeral food. They ask if Jesus demons have settled nearby; they leave the children with them. If you don't have stories that are equally heart-rending, you have nothing better to do with your money than send it to me. Otherwise, I don't want to hear about your mortgage payment or see photographs of your new car. What do you mean mortgage payment? Why are you buying land there when you have land here?"

"If only I could list foods on this paper and chew it up, swallow, and be full. But if I could do that, I could write your name, and you'd be here."

"I keep planning banquets and menus and guests to invite. I smell the food my mother cooked. The smell of puffed rice cookies rises from tombs. The aunts have left me here with the babies. The neighbors took their children with them. If they find food, they can decide then what to do with the children, either feed them or trade them for the food. Some children carry their parents, and some parents carry their children."

Mad Sao wished that his mother would hurry up and die, or that he had time and money enough to pay his mortgage, raise all his children, and also give his mother plenty.

Before a letter in a white envelope reached us saying that Sao Brother's mother had died, she appeared to him in America. She flew across the ocean and found her way to him. Just when he was about to fall asleep one night, he saw her and sat up with a start, definitely not dreaming. "You have turned me into a hungry ghost," she said. "You did this to me. You enjoyed yourself. You fed your wife and useless daughters, who are not even family, and you left me to starve. What you see before you is the inordinate hunger I had to suffer in my life." She opened her mouth wide, and he turned his face away not to see the depths within.

"Mother," he said. "Mother, how did you find your way across the ocean and here?"

"I am so cold. I followed the heat of your body like a light and fire. I was drawn to the well-fed."

"Here, take this, Mother," he cried, handing her his wallet from the nightstand.

"Too late," she said. "Too late."

With her chasing him he ran to the kitchen. He opened the refrigerator. He shoved food at her.

"Too late."

Curiously enough, other people did not see her. All they saw was Mad Sao talking to the air, making motions to the air, talking to no voice, listening to someone who moved about, someone very tall or floating near the ceiling. He yelled and argued, talked, sobbed. He lost weight from not eating; insomnia ringed his eyes. That's when people began to call him Mad Sao.

He knew how his grandfather had helped Fourth Grandfather by scolding him on his way. "Go home, Mother!" he was heard to scold, very firm, his face serious and his voice loud. "Go home! Go back to China. Go home to China where you belong." He went on with this scolding for days and nights, but it did not work. She never left him for a moment.

"I'm hungry," she cried. "I'm hungry." He threw money at her; he threw food at her. The money and food went through her. She wept continually, most disturbingly loud at night; though he pulled the covers over his ears and eyes, he heard her. "Why didn't you come home? Why didn't you send money?"

"I did send money."

"Not enough."

"It's against the law to send money," he told her—a weak excuse. "But even so, I sent it."

"I'm not a rich man," he said. "It isn't easy in this country either."

"Don't lie to me," she said. She pointed toward the kitchen, where the refrigerator and freezer were filled with food, and at the furniture, the radio, the TV. She pointed with her chin the way Chinese people point.

"Since you're here, Mother," he tried to bribe her, "you may have all the food I have. Take it. Take it."

She could see her surroundings exactly, but though she could see food, she could not eat it.

"It's too late," she mourned, and passed her hand through the footboard of his bed. He drew his feet up. He could not bear it if she should pass her hand through his feet. His wife beside him saw him gesturing and talking, sleepwalking and sleeptalking, and could not calm him.

"I died of starvation," his mother said. She was very thin, her eye sockets hollow like a Caucasian's. "I died of starvation while you ate."

He could not sleep because she kept talking to him. She did not fade with the dawn and the rooster's crowing. She kept a watch on him. She followed him to work. She kept repeating herself. "You didn't come home. You didn't send money."

She said, "I've got things to tell you that I didn't put in letters. I am going to tell them to you now. Did you know that when children starve, they grow coarse black hairs all over their bodies? And the heads and feet of starving women suddenly swell up. The skin of my little feet split open, and pus and blood burst out; I saw the muscles and veins underneath.

"One day there was meat for sale in the market. But after cooking and eating it, the villagers found out it was baby meat. The parents who had sold their children regretted it. 'We shouldn't have sold her,' they said. The rich people had bought the babies and resold them to butchers."

"Stop it, Mother," he said to the air. "I can't stand any more."

Night after night, she haunted him. Day after day. At last he drove to the bank. She sat in the back seat directly behind him. He took a lump of money out of his savings. Then he ran to a travel agency, his mother chasing him down the street, goading him. "Look, Mother," he was heard to say, sounding happier as he showed her the money and papers. "I'll take you home myself. You'll be able to rest. I'll go with you. Escort you. We're going home. I'm going home. I'm going home at last, just as you asked. I'll take you home. See? Isn't it a wonderful idea I have? Here's a ticket. See all the money I spent on a ticket, Mother? We're going home together."

He had bought an oceanliner ticket for one, so it was evident that he knew she was a ghost. That he easily got his passport proves that he was indeed an American citizen and in good standing with the Immigration and Naturalization Service. It was strange that at a time when Americans did not enter China, he easily got a visa also. He became much calmer. He did not suddenly scream any more or cry or throw food and money.

The family told him that there were no such things as ghosts, that he was wasting an enormous amount of savings, that it was dangerous to go to China, that the bandits would hold him hostage, that an army would draft him. The FBI would use our interest in China to prove our un-Americanness and deport all of us. The family scolded him for spending a fortune on a dead person. Why hadn't he mailed her the money when she was alive if he was going to spend it anyway? Why hadn't he gone to see her earlier? "Why don't you give the money to some wretch instead of wasting it on a vacation for yourself, eh?" He reminded them of a ghost story about a spirit that refused ghost money but had to have real money. They shook their heads. When my father saw that Mad Sao would not be swayed, he bought two Parker 51 fountain pens for fifty-five dollars, kept one for himself, and told Mad Sao to deliver the other to a most loved relative in China.

Mad Sao packed a small bag, all the time talking. "See, Mother? We're on our way home now. Both of us. Yes, I'm going home too. Finally going home. And I'm taking you home. We're together again, Mother." He hardly heard the live people around him.

All the way up the gangway, he was waving her on, "This way, Mother," leading her by the hand or elbow. "This way, Mother. This way." He gave her his bed and his deck chair. "Are you comfortable, Mother?" "Yes, Mother." He talked to no other passenger, and did not eat any of the ship's meals, for which he had already paid. He walked the decks day and night. "Yes, Mother. I'm sorry. I am sorry I did that. Yes, I did that, and I'm sorry."

He returned his mother to the village. He went directly to her grave, as if led by her. "Here you are, Mother," he said, and the villagers heard him say it. "You're home now. I've brought you home. I spent passage fare on you. It equals more than the food money I might have sent. Travel is very expensive. Rest, Mother. Eat." He heaped food on her grave. He piled presents beside it. He set real clothes and real shoes on fire. He burned mounds of paper replicas and paper money. He poured wine into the thirsty earth. He planted the blue shrub of longevity, where white carrier pigeons would nest. He bowed his forehead to the ground, knocking it hard in repentance. "You're home, Mother. I'm home too. I brought you home." He set off firecrackers near her grave, not neglecting one Chinese thing. "Rest now, heh, Mother. Be happy now." He sat by the grave and drank and ate for the first time since she had made her appearance. He stepped over the fires before extinguishing them. He boarded the very same ship sailing back. He had not spent any time sightseeing or visiting relatives and old friends except for dropping off the Parker 51. He hurried home to America, where he acted normal again, continuing his American life, and nothing like that ever happened to him again.

Considerations for Thinking and Writing

1. Why does Kingston begin "No Name Woman" by quoting her mother? Why does she want us to know that her telling of this story is transgressive? Imagine how Kingston might respond to Audre Lorde's essay "The Transformation of Silence into Language and Action." Do you consider language itself a mode of action?

2. Kingston writes unceasingly about "the roundness of family life," but she also treats the violent forces that break the family "circle." Consider the visions of family life offered in June Jordan's "Many Rivers to Cross," Phyllis Rose's "Mothers and Fathers," and Alice Walker's "In Search of Our Mothers' Gardens." What do these visions of family have in common with Kingston's?

3. In "Imagined Life" Kingston writes, "To imagine a life means to take such an interest in someone that you suppose about him." Clearly her fascination with her ghostly aunt involves a dense web of suppositions. How do other essayists in this volume interweave facts and suppositions when they imagine lives? Consider Angela Carter on Colette; Cynthia Ozick on Leonard Woolf, Virginia Woolf, and Edith Wharton; Alice Walker on Zora Neale Hurston; Virginia Woolf on Mary Wollstonecraft; Joyce Carol Oates on Flannery O'Connor. Or compare, if you wish, Oates and Susan Sontag on Simone Weil.

4. One of Kingston's preoccupations is the "necessity" of imagination. What social forces might make imagination a necessity? In what sense does Kingston's mingling of fact and fiction argue for the necessity of imagination?

5. We might read Kingston's "On Discovery" as a parable about gender. How does "On Discovery" support Simone de Beauvoir's observation that "one is not born a woman; one becomes a woman"? What difference does it make that a *man* becomes a woman?

6. Like many of the immigrants whose stories Kingston tells in *The Woman Warrior* and *China Men,* Mad Sao resides in two worlds at once. How does Kingston's own experience of living in two worlds compare with Mad Sao's? Compare Kingston's versions of Chinese-American identity with other representations of double identities, say, Jordan's concept of a Black feminist, or Ehrlich's discussion of rituals among the Kiowa and Crow tribes in "Living in Two Worlds."

7. Angela Carter's "Mother Lode" puns on the notion of mother as rich origin and mother as burden. How does Kingston's story "Mad Sao" express a similar ambivalence toward the mother? What part does Mad Sao's masculinity play in his relationship with his mother?

8. What role do female ghosts play in Kingston's imagination? After reading Annie Dillard's "Mother" from *An American Childhood,* would you consider Dillard haunted?

AUDRE LORDE
(b. 1934)

In an essay titled "Age, Race, Class, and Sex: Women Redefining Difference," Audre Lorde comments on her identity:

As a Black lesbian feminist comfortable with the many different ingredients of my identity, and a woman committed to racial and sexual freedom from oppression, I find I am constantly being encouraged to pluck out some one aspect of myself and present this as the meaningful whole, eclipsing or denying the other parts of self. But this is a destructive and fragmenting way to live. My fullest concentration of energy is available to me only when I integrate all the parts of who I am, openly. . . . Only then can I bring myself and my energies as a whole to the service of those struggles which I embrace as part of my living.

Black, lesbian, feminist; poet, essayist, teacher, activist; Audre Lorde embraces many struggles in her life and work. Born of Grenadian parents in New York City, Lorde has published seven volumes of poetry, one of which, *From a Land Where Other People Live* (1974), was nominated for the National Book Award. Her prose works include *The Cancer Journals* (1980); *Zami: A New Spelling of My Name* (1982), a "biomythography"; and *Sister Outsider* (1984), a collection of essays and addresses. The mother of two children,

Lorde has been a librarian and taught at City College, Lehman College, and John Jay College of Criminal Justice, all of the City University of New York. Since 1980 she has been Professor of English at Hunter College (CUNY) in New York City.

Among the struggles that Lorde writes about is her struggle with breast cancer. In 1977, a year before discovering that she had a malignancy, Lorde's sense of vocation was sharpened by the threat of cancer. The earliest of the essays included here is "The Transformation of Silence into Language and Action," written in 1977, when Lorde learned, after surgery, that a growth in her breast was benign. The essay dwells on her anguish before surgery, on "a three-week period of the agony of an involuntary reorganization of my entire life." The knowledge that "I was going to die, if not sooner then later, whether or not I had ever spoken myself," evokes in Lorde a new dedication to speaking out. For Lorde, to realize that death "is the final silence" is to realize that living silences are also mortal. Lorde dedicates herself in this brief essay to transforming silence into "language and action."

Lorde's notion of speech as transformative helps us to understand that her writing—including the poetry; especially the poetry—is a kind of activism. The essays reprinted here show that a range of styles may serve a conviction that language enables us to act in and upon the world. In "Breast Cancer: Power vs. Prosthesis," Lorde attacks the assumptions governing the treatment of breast cancer in the United States. By moving flexibly from exposition to narrative and back again, Lorde develops her attack into two hard-hitting arguments. First, she argues for the urgency of thinking about and preventing cancer for all women, particularly those living on "the underside of this society," whose survival rates are poorest. At times one feels that her account of her mastectomy is directed with particular force toward other postmastectomy patients: "For

as we open ourselves more and more to the genuine conditions of our lives, women become less and less willing to tolerate those conditions unaltered, or to passively accept external and destructive controls over our lives and our identities." But in the course of the essay, Lorde insists that the "genuine conditions of our lives" put all women at risk of breast cancer and the institutions that treat it.

Revealingly, it is not surgery but prosthesis that Lorde calls "an assault on my right to define and to claim my own body." We read of her decision to confront the "changed landscape" of her body, demanding that others confront it too. She knows that her decision is not right for all women, and she knows that she is making tough demands. Lorde responds, systematically but respectfully, to those who insist on prostheses. For Lorde, it is vital to live as a changed, bodily self both in private and in public; she takes up her stance as a "warrior," marked, different, heroic. But the issue, Lorde acknowledges, is not heroism so much as freedom, the freedom to "come to terms with [one's] altered life, not to transform it into another level of dynamic existence."

This powerful indictment of prosthesis is the stronger for Lorde's decision to treat prosthesis both literally and metaphorically: "We are equally destroyed by false happiness and false breasts and the passive acceptance of false values which corrupt our lives and distort our experience." Lorde's second argument is that we need not be complicit in what she calls "Cancer Inc." Whether or not one chooses literally to reject prosthesis, one can refuse the prosthesis of complacency. Since Lorde wrote this essay in 1979, "lumpectomy," a less disfiguring type of surgery than mastectomy, has gained in acceptance; in 1987 the American Cancer Society published its first nutritional guidelines for the prevention of cancer. But Lorde's grim assessment of the problem still hits hard: "We live in a profit economy and there is no profit in the prevention of cancer."

As this essay argues, the struggle against cancer is really many struggles. It is Audre Lorde's particular gift to be able to explain to those who struggle for various causes what their ordeals have in common. Perhaps she owes this gift to her identity as an outsider: she speaks as a feminist to Blacks, and as a Black lesbian to feminists. Perhaps her gift owes much to her ability to voice anger. If these are angry essays, it is because Lorde respects anger for articulating chaos and expressing an urgency that compels attention. In "Feminism & Black Liberation: The Great American Disease" Lorde responds heatedly to a Black sociologist who theorizes about why many Black men are hostile to feminism. Her reply is warm with both anger and compassion: anger for those Blacks who "repeat white america's mistakes"; compassion for those whose lives are damaged by anger that can find expression only in violence. She has special disgust for what she regards as the use of social theory to legitimize oppression; to Lorde, the privilege of articulation demands social responsibility. She closes the essay by appealing to Black men to view feminism as "central" to their own struggle: "the Black male consciousness must be raised to the realization that sexism and woman-hating are critically dysfunctional to his liberation . . . because they arise out of the same constellation that engenders racism and homophobia."

Audre Lorde is as undeterred by her audience's anger as she is by her own. "The Uses of Anger: Women Responding to Racism" was delivered as the keynote address to the National Women's Studies Association Conference in 1981. The essay begins with definitions and anecdotes, as Lorde vows not to theorize: "We are not here as women examining racism in a political and social vacuum. We operate in the teeth of a system for which racism and sexism are primary, established, and necessary props of profit." Lorde's metaphor—

"the teeth of a system"—is indeed carefully chosen. She speaks often of "this dragon we call america," a devourer of mythic proportions. Such a move is risky in the presence of an enemy described as monolithic and evil, an enemy that must be hacked apart rather than changed. But while Lorde states that racism victimizes all women (just as antifeminism defeats Black men), she demands that women realize their complicity with their oppressors. Her own questions bite the dragon back: "What woman here is so enamoured of her own oppression that she cannot see her heelprint upon another woman's face?" Lorde is not a seducer of audiences but a writer and speaker whose purposes require that she be demanding of her audience.

The rhetorical power of Audre Lorde's essays and speeches may make us forget that she can speak with a more inward voice. In "Poetry Is Not a Luxury" she identifies poetry with feeling, with dreams, with power. As a type of birth, poetry witnesses the emergence of sense from chaos. For Lorde, poetry is not a luxury because it is "a way we help give name to the nameless so it can be thought." An essay titled "Uses of the Erotic" suggests that the erotic also makes such figurative births possible: "The erotic is a measure between the beginnings of our sense of self and the chaos of our strongest feelings. It is an internal sense of satisfaction to which, once we have experienced it, we know we can aspire." The erotic, to Lorde, is a sharing of power that empowers both sharers.

By calling her volume of essays *Sister Outsider,* Audre Lorde declares her writing to be both intimate and alienated. Indeed, this seems a prescient title: in the major university library where we sought this book, it had been relegated to an annex—"Annex II"—several miles from the main library. To learn that there are institutions that cannot yet spare room for her would not surprise Audre Lorde, whose voice will surely carry.

Breast Cancer: Power vs. Prosthesis

On Labor Day, 1978, during my regular monthly self-examination, I discovered a lump in my right breast which later proved to be malignant. During my following hospitalization, my mastectomy and its aftermath, I passed through many stages of pain, despair, fury, sadness and growth. I moved through these stages, sometimes feeling as if I had no choice, other times recognizing that I could choose oblivion— or a passivity that is very close to oblivion—but did not want to. As I slowly began to feel more equal to processing and examining the different parts of this experience, I also began to feel that in the process of losing a breast I had become a more whole person.

After a mastectomy, for many women including myself, there is a feeling of wanting to go back, of not wanting to persevere through this experience to whatever enlightenment might be at the core of it. And it is this feeling, this nostalgia, which is encouraged by most of the post-surgical counseling for women with breast cancer. This regressive tie to the past is emphasized by the concentration upon breast cancer as a cosmetic problem, one which can be solved by a prosthetic pretense. The American Cancer Society's Reach For Recovery Program, while doing a valuable service in contacting women immediately after surgery and letting them know they are not alone, nonetheless encourages this false and dangerous nostalgia in the mistaken belief that women are too weak to deal directly and courageously with the realities of our lives.

The woman from Reach For Recovery who came to see me in the hospital, while quite admirable and even impressive in her own right, certainly did not speak to my experience nor my concerns. As a 44 year old Black Lesbian Feminist, I knew there were very few role models around for me in this situation, but my primary concerns two days after mastectomy were hardly about what man I could capture in the future, whether or not my old boyfriend would still find me attractive enough, and even less about whether my two children would be embarrassed by me around their friends.

My concerns were about my chances for survival, the effects of a possibly short- ened life upon my work and my priorities. Could this cancer have been prevented, and what could I do in the future to prevent its recurrence? Would I be able to maintain the control over my life that I had always taken for granted? A lifetime of loving women had taught me that when women love each other, physical change does not alter that love. It did not occur to me that anyone who really loved me would love me any less because I had one breast instead of two, although it did occur to me to wonder if they would be able to love and deal with the new me. So my concerns were quite different from those spoken to by the Reach For Recovery volunteer, but not one bit less crucial nor less poignant.

Yet every attempt I made to examine or question the possibility of a real integra- tion of this experience into the totality of my life and my loving and my work was ignored by this woman, or uneasily glossed over by her as not looking on "the bright side of things." I felt outraged and insulted, and weak as I was, this left me feeling even more isolated than before.

In the critical and vulnerable period following surgery, self-examination and self-evaluation are positive steps. To imply to a woman that yes, she can be the 'same' as before surgery, with the skillful application of a little puff of lambswool, and/or silicone gel, is to place an emphasis upon prosthesis which encourages her not to deal with herself as physically and emotionally real, even though altered and traumatized. This emphasis upon the cosmetic after surgery reinforces this society's stereotype of women, that we are only what we look or appear, so this is the only aspect of our existence we need to address. Any woman who has had a breast removed because of cancer knows she does not feel the same. But we are allowed no psychic time or space to examine what our true feelings are, to make them our own. With quick cosmetic reassurance, we are told that our feelings are not important, our appearance is all, the sum total of self.

I did not have to look down at the bandages on my chest to know that I did not feel the same as before surgery. But I still felt like myself, like Audre, and that encompassed so much more than simply the way my chest appeared.

The emphasis upon physical pretense at this crucial point in a woman's reclaiming of her self and her body-image has two negative effects:

1. It encourages women to dwell in the past rather than a future. This prevents a woman from assessing herself in the present, and from coming to terms with the changed planes of her own body. Since these then remain alien to her, buried under prosthetic devices, she must mourn the loss of her breast in secret, as if it were the result of some crime of which she were guilty.

2. It encourages a woman to focus her energies upon the mastectomy as a cosmetic occurrence, to the exclusion of other factors in a constellation that could include her own death. It removes her from what that constellation means in terms of her living, and from developing priorities of usage for whatever time she has before her. It encourages her to ignore the necessity for nutritional vigilance and psychic armament that can help prevent recurrence.

I am talking here about the need for every woman to live a considered life. The necessity for that consideration grows and deepens as one faces directly one's own mortality and death. Self scrutiny and an evaluation of our lives, while painful, can be rewarding and strengthening journeys toward a deeper self. For as we open ourselves more and more to the genuine conditions of our lives, women become less and less willing to tolerate those conditions unaltered, or to passively accept external and destructive controls over our lives and our identities. Any short-circuiting of this quest for self-definition and power, however well-meaning and under whatever guise, must be seen as damaging, for it keeps the post-mastectomy woman in a position of perpetual and secret insufficiency, infantilized and dependent for her identity upon an external definition by appearance. In this way women are kept from expressing the power of our knowledge and experience, and through that expression, developing strengths that challenge those structures within our lives that support the Cancer Establishment. For instance, why hasn't the American Cancer Society publicized the connections between animal fat and breast cancer for our daughters the way it has publicized the connection between cigarette smoke and lung cancer? These links between animal fat, hormone production and breast cancer are not secret. (See G. Hems, in *British Journal of Cancer*, vol. 37, no. 6, 1978.)

Ten days after having my breast removed, I went to my doctor's office to have the stitches taken out. This was my first journey out since coming home from the hospital, and I was truly looking forward to it. A friend had washed my hair for me and it was black and shining, with my new grey hairs glistening in the sun. Color was starting to come back into my face and around my eyes. I wore the most opalescent of my moonstones, and a single floating bird dangling from my right ear in the name of grand assymmetry. With an African kente-cloth tunic and new leather boots, I knew I looked fine, with that brave new-born security of a beautiful woman having come through a very hard time and being very glad to be alive.

I felt really good, within the limits of that grey mush that still persisted in my brain from the effects of the anesthesia.

When I walked into the doctor's office, I was really rather pleased with myself, all things considered, pleased with the way I felt, with my own flair, with my own style. The doctor's nurse, a charmingly bright and steady woman of about my own age who had always given me a feeling of quiet no-nonsense support on my other visits, called me into the examining room. On the way, she asked me how I was feeling.

"Pretty good," I said, half-expecting her to make some comment about how good I looked.

"You're not wearing a prosthesis," she said, a little anxiously, and not at all like a question.

"No," I said, thrown off my guard for a minute. "It really doesn't feel right," referring to the lambswool puff given to me by the Reach For Recovery volunteer in the hospital.

Usually supportive and understanding, the nurse now looked at me urgently and disapprovingly as she told me that even if it didn't look exactly right, it was "better than nothing," and that as soon as my stitches were out I could be fitted for a "real form."

"You will feel so much better with it on," she said. "And besides, we really like you to wear something, at least when you come in. Otherwise it's bad for the morale of the office."

I could hardly believe my ears! I was too outraged to speak then, but this was to be only the first such assault on my right to define and to claim my own body.

Here we were, in the offices of one of the top breast cancer surgeons in New York City. Every woman there either had a breast removed, might have to have a breast removed, or was afraid of having to have a breast removed. And every woman there could have used a reminder that having one breast did not mean her life was over, nor that she was less a woman, nor that she was condemned to the use of a placebo in order to feel good about herself and the way she looked.

Yet a woman who has one breast and refuses to hide that fact behind a pathetic puff of lambswool which has no relationship nor likeness to her own breasts, a woman who is attempting to come to terms with her changed landscape and changed timetable of life and with her own body and pain and beauty and strength, that woman is seen as a threat to the "morale" of a breast surgeon's office!

Yet when Moishe Dayan, the Prime Minister of Israel, stands up in front of parliament or on TV with an eyepatch over his empty eyesocket, nobody tells him to go get a glass eye, or that he is bad for the morale of the office. The world sees him as a warrior with an honorable wound, and a loss of a piece of himself which he has marked, and mourned, and moved beyond. And if you have trouble dealing with Moishe Dayan's empty eye socket, everyone recognizes that it is your problem to solve, not his.

Well, women with breast cancer are warriors, also. I have been to war, and still am. So has every woman who has had one or both breasts amputated because of the cancer that is becoming the primary physical scourge of our time. For me, my scars are an honorable reminder that I may be a casualty in the cosmic war against radiation, animal fat, air pollution, McDonald's hamburgers and Red Dye No. 2, but the fight is still going on, and I am still a part of it. I refuse to have my scars hidden or trivialized behind lambswool or silicone gel. I refuse to be reduced in my own eyes or in the eyes of others from warrior to mere victim, simply because it might render me a fraction more acceptable or less dangerous to the still complacent, those who believe if you cover up a problem it ceases to exist. I refuse to hide my body simply because it might make a woman-phobic world more comfortable.

As I sat in my doctor's office trying to order my perceptions of what had just occurred, I realized that the attitude towards prosthesis after breast cancer is an index of this society's attitudes towards women in general as decoration and externally defined sex object.

Two days later I wrote in my journal:

I cannot wear a prosthesis right now because it feels like a lie more than merely a costume, and I have already placed this, my body under threat, seeking new ways of strength and trying to find the courage to tell the truth.

For me, the primary challenge at the core of mastectomy was the stark look at my own mortality, hinged upon the fear of a life-threatening cancer. This event called upon me to re-examine the quality and texture of my entire life, its priorities and commitments, as well as the possible alterations that might be required in the light of that re-examination. I had already faced my own death, whether or not I acknowledged it, and I needed now to develop that strength which survival had given me.

Prosthesis offers the empty comfort of "Nobody will know the difference." But it is that very difference which I wish to affirm, because I have lived it, and survived it, and wish to share that strength with other women. If we are to translate the silence surrounding breast cancer into language and action against this scourge, then the first step is that women with mastectomies must become visible to each other.* For silence and invisibility go hand in hand with powerlessness. By accepting the mask of prosthesis, one-breasted women proclaim ourselves as insufficients dependent upon pretense. We reinforce our own isolation and invisibility from each other, as well as the false complacency of a society which would rather not face the results of its own insanities. In addition, we withhold that visibility and support from one another which is such an aid to perspective and self-acceptance. Surrounded by other women day by day, all of whom appear to have two breasts, it is very difficult sometimes to remember that I AM NOT ALONE. Yet once I face death as a life process, what is there possibly left for me to fear? Who can ever really have power over me again?

As women, we cannot afford to look the other way, nor to consider the incidence

*Particular thanks to Maureen Brady for the conversation which developed this insight.

of breast cancer as a private nor secret personal problem. It is no secret that breast cancer is on the increase among women in America. According to the American Cancer Society's own statistics on breast cancer survival, of the women stricken, only 50% are still alive after three years. This figure drops to 30% if you are poor, or Black, or in any other way part of the underside of this society. We cannot ignore these facts, nor their implications, nor their effect upon our lives, individually and collectively. Early detection and early treatment is crucial in the management of breast cancer if those sorry statistics of survival are to improve. But for the incidence of early detection and early treatment to increase, american women must become free enough from social stereotypes concerning their appearance to realize that losing a breast is infinitely preferable to losing one's life. (Or one's eyes, or one's hands. . . .)

Although breast self-examination does not reduce the incidence of breast cancer, it does markedly reduce the rate of mortality, since most early tumors are found by women themselves. I discovered my own tumor upon a monthly breast exam, and so report most of the other women I know with a good prognosis for survival. With our alert awareness making such a difference in the survival rate for breast cancer, women need to face the possibility and the actuality of breast cancer as a reality rather than as myth, or retribution, or terror in the night, or a bad dream that will disappear if ignored. After surgery, there is a need for women to be aware of the possibility of bilateral recurrence, with vigilance rather than terror. This is not a spread of cancer, but a new occurrence in the other breast. Each woman must be aware that an honest acquaintanceship with and evaluation of her own body is the best tool of detection.

Yet there still appears to be a conspiracy on the part of Cancer Inc. to insist to every woman who has lost a breast that she is no different from before, if with a little skillful pretense and a few ounces of silicone gel she can pretend to herself and the watching world—the only orientation toward the world that women are supposed to have—that nothing has happened to challenge her. With this orientation a woman after surgery is allowed no time or space within which to weep, rage, internalize, and transcend her own loss. She is left no space to come to terms with her altered life, nor to transform it into another level of dynamic existence.

The greatest incidence of breast cancer in american women appears within the ages of 40 to 55. These are the very years when women are portrayed in the popular media as fading and desexualized figures. Contrary to the media picture, I find myself as a woman of insight ascending into my highest powers, my greatest psychic strengths, and my fullest satisfactions. I am freer of the constraints and fears and indecisions of my younger years, and survival throughout these years has taught me how to value my own beauty, and how to look closely into the beauty of others. It has also taught me to value the lessons of survival, as well as my own perceptions. I feel more deeply, value those feelings more, and can put those feelings together with what I know in order to fashion a vision of and pathway toward true change. Within this time of assertion and growth, even the advent of a life-threatening cancer and the trauma of a mastectomy can be integrated into the life-force as knowledge and eventual strength, fuel for a more dynamic and focussed existence. Since the supposed threat of self-actualized women is one that our society seeks constantly to protect itself against, it is not coincidental that the sharing of this knowledge among women is diverted, in this case by the invisibility imposed by an insistence upon prosthesis as a norm for post-mastectomy women.

There is nothing wrong, per se, with the use of prostheses, if they can be chosen freely, for whatever reason, after a woman has had a chance to accept her new body. But usually prostheses serve a real function, to approximate the performance of a missing physical part. In other amputations and with other prosthetic devices, function is the main point of their existence. Artificial limbs perform specific tasks, allowing us to manipulate or to walk. Dentures allow us to chew our food. Only false breasts are designed for appearance only, as if the only real function of women's breasts were to appear in a certain shape and size and symmetry to onlookers, or to yield to external pressure. For no woman wearing a prosthesis can even for one moment believe it is her own breast, any more than a woman wearing falsies can.

Yet breast prostheses are offered to women after surgery in much the same way that candy is offered to babies after an injection, never mind that the end effect may be destructive. Their comfort is illusory; a transitional period can be provided by any loose-fitting blouse. After surgery, I most certainly did not feel better with a lambs-wool puff stuck in the front of my bra. The real truth is that certain other people feel better with that lump stuck into my bra, because they do not have to deal with me nor themselves in terms of mortality nor in terms of difference.

Attitudes toward the necessity for prostheses after breast surgery are merely a reflection of those attitudes within our society towards women in general as objectified and depersonalized sexual conveniences. Women have been programmed to view our bodies only in terms of how they look and feel to others, rather than how they feel to ourselves, and how we wish to use them. We are surrounded by media images portraying women as essentially decorative machines of consumer function, constantly doing battle with rampant decay. (Take your vitamins every day and he *might* keep you, if you don't forget to whiten your teeth, cover up your smells, color your grey hair and iron out your wrinkles. . . .) As women, we fight this depersonalization every day, this pressure toward the conversion of one's own self-image into a media expectation of what might satisfy male demand. The insistence upon breast prostheses as 'decent' rather than functional is an additional example of that wipe-out of self in which women are constantly encouraged to take part. I am personally affronted by the message that I am only acceptable if I look 'right' or 'normal,' where those norms have nothing to do with my own perceptions of who I am. Where 'normal' means the 'right' color, shape, size, or number of breasts, a woman's perception of her own body and the strengths that come from that perception are discouraged, trivialized, and ignored. When I mourn my right breast, it is not the appearance of it I mourn, but the feeling and the fact. But where the superficial is supreme, the idea that a woman can be beautiful and one-breasted is considered depraved, or at best bizarre, a threat to 'morale.'

In order to keep me available to myself, and able to concentrate my energies upon the challenges of those worlds through which I move, I must consider what my body means to me. I must also separate those external demands about how I look and feel to others from what I really want for my own body and how I feel to my selves. As women we have been taught to respond with a guilty twitch at any mention of the particulars of our own oppression, as if we are ultimately guilty of whatever has been done to us. The rape victim is accused of enticing the rapist. The battered wife is accused of having angered her husband. A mastectomy is not a guilty act that must be hidden in order for me to regain acceptance or protect the sensibilities of others. Pretense has never brought about lasting change or progress.

Every woman has a right to define her own desires, make her own choices. But prostheses are often chosen, not from desire, but in default. Some women complain it is too much effort to fight the concerted pressure exerted by the fashion industry. Being one-breasted does not mean being unfashionable; it means giving some time and energy to choosing or constructing the proper clothes. In some cases, it means making or remaking clothing or jewelry. The fact that the fashion needs of one-breasted women are not currently being met doesn't mean that the concerted pressure of our demands cannot change that.*

There was a time in America not long ago when pregnant women were supposed to hide their physical realities. The pregnant woman who ventured forth into public had to design and construct her own clothing to be comfortable and attractive. With the increased demands of pregnant women who are no longer content to pretend non-existence, maternity fashion is now an established, flourishing and particular sector of the clothing field.

The design and marketing of items of wear for one-breasted women is only a question of time, and we who are now designing and wearing our own asymmetrical patterns and New Landscape jewelry are certainly in the vanguard of a new fashion!

Some women believe that a breast prosthesis is necessary to preserve correct posture and physical balance. But the weight of each breast is never the same to begin with, nor is the human body ever exactly the same on both sides. With a minimum of exercises to develop the habit of straight posture, the body can accommodate to one-breastedness quite easily, even when the breasts were quite heavy.

Women in public and private employment have reported the loss of jobs and promotions upon their return to work after a mastectomy, without regard to whether or not they wore prostheses. The social and economic discrimination practiced against women who have breast cancer is not diminished by pretending that mastectomies do not exist. Where a woman's job is at risk because of her health history, employment discrimination cannot be fought with a sack of silicone gel, nor with the constant fear and anxiety to which such subterfuge gives rise. Suggesting prosthesis as a solution to employment discrimination is like saying that the way to fight race prejudice is for Black people to pretend to be white. Employment discrimination against post-mastectomy women can only be fought in the open, with head-on attacks by strong and self-accepting women who refuse to be relegated to an inferior position, or to cower in a corner because they have one breast.

When post-mastectomy women are dissuaded from any realistic evaluation of themselves, they spend large amounts of time, energy, and money in following any will-o-the-wisp that seems to promise a more skillful pretense of normality. Without the acceptance of difference as part of our lives, and in a guilty search for illusion, these women fall easy prey to any shabby confidence scheme that happens along. The terror and silent loneliness of women attempting to replace the ghost of a breast leads to yet another victimization.

The following story does not impugn the many reputable makes of cosmetic breast forms which, although outrageously overpriced, can still serve a real function for the

---

*Particular thanks to Frances Clayton for the conversations that developed this insight.

woman who is free enough to choose when and why she wears one or not. We find the other extreme reported upon in *The New York Times,* December 28, 1978:

ARTIFICIAL BREAST CONCERN CHARGED WITH CHEATING

A Manhattan concern is under inquiry for allegedly having victimized cancer patients who had ordered artificial breasts after mastectomies. . . . The number of women allegedly cheated could not be determined. The complaints received were believed to be "only a small percentage of the victims" because others seemed *too embarrassed to complain* [italics mine].

Although the company in question, Apres Body Replacement, founded by Mrs. Elke Mack, was not a leader in the field of reputable makers of breast forms, it was given ample publicity on the ABC-TV program "Good Morning, America" in 1977, and it is here that many women first heard of Apres. What was so special about the promises of this product that it enticed such attention, and so much money out of the pockets of women from New York to Maine? To continue from the *New York Times* article:

Apres offered an "individually designed product that is a total duplicate of the remaining breast," and "worn on the body by use of a synthetic adhesive" supposedly formulated by a doctor.

It is reported that in some cases, women paid up to $600, sight unseen, for this article which was supposedly made from a form cast from their own bodies. When the women arrived to pick up the prosthesis, they received something having no relation or kinship to their own breasts, and which failed to adhere to their bodies, and which was totally useless. Other women received nothing at all for their money.

This is neither the worst nor the most expensive victimization, however. Within the framework of superficiality and pretense, the next logical step of a depersonalizing and woman-devaluating culture is the advent of the atrocity euphemistically called "breast reconstruction." This operation is now being pushed by the plastic surgery industry as the newest "advance" in breast surgery. Actually it is not new at all, being a technique previously used to augment or enlarge breasts. It should be noted that research being done on this potentially life-threatening practice represents time and research money spent—not on how to prevent the cancers that cost us our breasts and our lives—but rather upon how to pretend that our breasts are not gone, nor we as women at risk with our lives.

The operation consists of inserting silicone gel implants under the skin of the chest, usually shortly after a mastectomy and in a separate operation. At an approximate cost of $1500 to $3000 an implant (in 1978), this represents a lucrative piece of commerce for the cancer and plastic surgery industries in this country. There are now plastic surgeons recommending the removal of the other breast at the same time as the mastectomy is done, even where there is no clinically apparent reason.

It is important when considering subcutaneous mastectomy to plan to do both breasts at the same time. . . . it is extremely difficult to attain the desired degree of symmetry under these circumstances with a unilateral prosthesis.

—R. K. Snyderman, M.D.
in *"What the Plastic Surgeon Has to Offer
in the Management of Breast Tumors"*

In the same article appearing in *Early Breast Cancer, Detection and Treatment,* edited by H. Stephen Gallegher, M.D., the author states:

> The companies are working with us. They will make prostheses to practically any design we desire. Remember that what we are doing in the reconstruction of the female breast is by no means a cosmetic triumph. What we are aiming for is to *allow women to look decent in clothes* [italics mine]. . . . The aim is for the patient to *look normal and natural when she has clothes on her body.*

Is it any coincidence that the plastic surgeons most interested in pushing breast reconstruction and most involved in the superficial aspects of women's breasts speak the language of sexist pigs? What is the positive correlation?

The American Cancer Society, while not openly endorsing this practice, is doing nothing to present a more balanced viewpoint concerning the dangers of reconstruction. In covering a panel on breast reconstruction held by the American Society of Plastic and Reconstructive Surgeons, the Spring 1978 issue of the ACS *Cancer News* commented:

> Breast reconstruction will not recreate a perfect replica of the lost breast, but it will enable many women who have had mastectomies *to wear a normal bra or bikini* [italics mine].

So, even for the editor of the ACS *Cancer News,* when a woman has faced the dread of breast cancer and triumphed, for whatever space of time, her primary concern should still be whether or not she can wear a *normal bra or bikini.* With unbelievable cynicism, one plastic surgeon reports that for patients with a lessened likelihood of cure—a poor prognosis for survival—*he waits two years before implanting silicone gel into her body.* Another surgeon adds,

> Even when the patient has a poor prognosis, she wants a *better quality of life* [italics mine].

In his eyes, obviously, this better quality of life will come, not through the woman learning to come to terms with her living and dying and her own personal power, but rather through her wearing a 'normal' bra.

Most of those breast cancer surgeons who oppose this practice being pushed by the American Society of Plastic and Reconstructive Surgeons either are silent, or tacitly encourage its use by their attitude toward the woman whom they serve.

On a CBS-TV Evening News Special Report on breast reconstruction in October, 1978, one lone doctor spoke out against the use of silicone gel implantations as a potentially carcinogenic move. But even he spoke of women as if their appearance and their lives were equally significant. "It's a real shame," he said, "when a woman has to choose between her life or her femininity." In other words, with a sack of silicone implanted under her skin, a woman may well be more likely to die from another cancer, but without that implant, according to this doctor, she is not 'feminine.'

While plastic surgeons in the service of 'normal bras and bikinis' insist that there is no evidence of increase in cancer recurrence because of breast reconstructions, Dr. Peter Pressman, a prominent breast cancer surgeon at Beth Israel Medical Center in New York City, has raised some excellent points. Although silicone gel implants have been used in enough nonmalignant breast augmentations to say that the material probably is not, in and of itself, carcinogenic, Dr. Pressman raises a number of questions which still remain concerning these implants after breast cancer.

1. There have been no large-scale studies with matched control groups conducted among women who have had post-mastectomy reconstruction. Therefore, we cannot possibly have sufficient statistics available to demonstrate whether reconstruction has had any negative effect upon the recurrence of breast cancer.

2. It is possible that the additional surgery necessary for insertion of the prosthesis could stir up cancer cells which might otherwise remain dormant.

3. In the case of a recurrence of breast cancer, the recurrent tumor can be masked by the physical presence of the implanted prosthesis under the skin. When the nipple and skin tissue is preserved to be used later in 'reconstruction,' minute cancer cells can hide within this tissue undetected.

Any information about the prevention or treatment of breast cancer which might possibly threaten the vested interests of the american medical establishment is difficult to acquire in this country. Only through continuing scrutiny of various non-mainstream sources of information, such as alternative and women's presses, can a picture of new possibilities for prevention and treatment of breast cancer emerge.

Much of this secrecy is engineered by the American Cancer Society, which has become "the loudest voice of the Cancer Establishment."[1] The ACS is the largest philanthropic institution in the United States and the world's largest non-religious charity. Peter Chowka points out that the National Information Bureau, a charity watchdog organization, listed the ACS among the groups which do not meet its standards. During the past decade, the ACS collected over $1 billion from the american public.[2] In 1977 it had a $176 million fund balance, yet less than 15% of its budget was spent on assisting cancer patients.[3]

Any holistic approach to the problem of cancer is viewed by ACS with suspicion and alarm. It has consistently focussed upon treatment rather than prevention of cancer, and then only upon those treatments sanctioned by the most conservative branches of western medicine. We live in a profit economy and there is no profit in the prevention of cancer; there is only profit in the treatment of cancer. In 1976, 70% of the ACS research budget went to individuals and institutions with whom ACS board members were affiliated.[4] And of the 194 members of its governing board, one is a labor representative and one is Black. Women are not even mentioned.

The ACS was originally established to champion new research into the causes and the cure of cancer. But by its blacklisting of new therapies without testing them, the ACS spends much of its remaining budget suppressing new and unconventional ideas and research.[5] Yet studies from other countries have shown interesting results from treatments largely ignored by ACS. European medicine reports hopeful experiments with immunotherapy, diet, and treatment with hormones and enzymes such as trypsin.[6] Silencing and political repression by establishment medical journals keep much vital information about breast cancer underground and away from the women whose lives it most affects. Yet even in the United States, there are clinics waging alternative wars against cancer and the medical establishment, with varying degrees of success.[7]

Breast cancer is on the increase, and every woman should add to her arsenal of information by inquiring into these areas of 'underground medicine.' Who are its leaders and proponents, and what are their qualifications? Most important, what is their rate of success in the control of breast cancer,[8] and why is this information not common knowledge?

The mortality for breast cancer treated by conventional therapies has not decreased in over 40 years.[9] The ACS and its governmental partner, the National Cancer Institute, have been notoriously indifferent, if not hostile, to the idea of general environmental causes of cancer and the need for regulation and prevention.[10] Since the american medical establishment and the ACS are determined to suppress any cancer information not dependent upon western medical bias, whether this information is ultimately useful or not, we must pierce this silence ourselves and aggressively seek answers to these questions about new therapies. We must also heed the unavoidable evidence pointing toward the nutritional and environmental aspects of cancer prevention.

Cancer is not just another degenerative and unavoidable disease of the aging process. It has distinct and identifiable causes, and these are mainly exposures to chemical or physical agents in the environment.[11] In the medical literature, there is mounting evidence that breast cancer is a chronic and systemic disease. Post-mastectomy women must be vigilantly aware that, contrary to the 'lightning strikes' theory, we are the most likely of all women to develop cancer somewhere else in the body.[12]

Every woman has a militant responsibility to involve herself actively with her own health. We owe ourselves the protection of all the information we can acquire about the treatment of cancer and its causes, as well as about the recent findings concerning immunology, nutrition, environment, and stress. And we owe ourselves this information *before* we may have a reason to use it.

It was very important for me, after my mastectomy, to develop and encourage my own internal sense of power. I needed to rally my energies in such a way as to image myself as a fighter resisting rather than as a passive victim suffering. At all times, it felt crucial to me that I make a conscious commitment to survival. It is physically important for me to be loving my life rather than to be mourning my breast. I believe it is this love of my life and myself, and the careful tending of that love which was done by women who love and support me, which has been largely responsible for my strong and healthy recovery from the effects of my mastectomy. But a clear distinction must be made between this affirmation of self and the superficial farce of "looking on the bright side of things."

Like superficial spirituality, looking on the bright side of things is a euphemism used for obscuring certain realities of life, the open consideration of which might prove threatening or dangerous to the status quo. Last week I read a letter from a doctor in a medical magazine which said that no truly happy person ever gets cancer. Despite my knowing better, and despite my having dealt with this blame-the-victim thinking for years, for a moment this letter hit my guilt button. Had I really been guilty of the crime of not being happy in this best of all possible infernos?

The idea that the cancer patient should be made to feel guilty about having had cancer, as if in some way it were all her fault for not having been in the right psychological frame of mind at all times to prevent cancer, is a monstrous distortion of the idea that we can use our psychic strengths to help heal ourselves. This guilt trip which many cancer patients have been led into (you see, it *is* a shameful thing because you could have prevented it if only you had been more . . .) is an extension of the blame-the-victim syndrome. It does nothing to encourage the mobilization of our psychic defenses against the very real forms of death which surround us. It is easier to demand happiness than to clean up the environment. The acceptance of illusion and appearance as reality is another symptom of this same refusal to examine the realities of our lives. Let us seek 'joy' rather than real food and clean air and a saner future on a livable earth! As if happiness alone can protect us from the results of profit-madness.

Was I wrong to be working so hard against the oppressions afflicting women and Black people? Was I in error to be speaking out against our silent passivity and the cynicism of a mechanized and inhuman civilization that is destroying our earth and those who live upon it? Was I really fighting the spread of radiation, racism, woman-slaughter, chemical invasion of our food, pollution of our environment, the abuse and psychic destruction of our young, merely to avoid dealing with my first and greatest responsibility—to be happy? In this disastrous time, when little girls are still being stitched shut between their legs, when victims of cancer are urged to court more cancer in order to be attractive to men, when 12-year-old Black boys are shot down in the street at random by uniformed men who are cleared of any wrong-doing, when ancient and honorable citizens scavenge for food in garbage pails, and the growing answer to all this is media hype or surgical lobotomy; when daily gruesome murders of women from coast to coast no longer warrant mention in *The N.Y. Times*, when grants to teach retarded children are cut in favor of more billion-dollar airplanes, when 900 people commit mass suicide rather than face life in america, and we are told it is the job of the poor to stem inflation; what depraved monster could possibly be always happy?

The only really happy people I have ever met are those of us who work against these deaths with all the energy of our living, recognizing the deep and fundamental unhappiness with which we are surrounded, at the same time as we fight to keep from being submerged by it. But if the achievement and maintenance of perfect happiness is the only secret of a physically healthy life in america, then it is a wonder that we are not all dying of a malignant society. The happiest person in this country cannot help breathing in smokers' cigarette fumes, auto exhaust, and airborne chemical dust, nor avoid drinking the water, and eating the food. The idea that happiness can insulate us against the results of our environmental madness is a rumor circulated by our enemies to destroy us. And what Woman of Color in america over the age of 15 does not live with the knowledge that our daily lives are stitched with violence and with hatred, and to naively ignore that reality can mean destruction? We are equally destroyed by false happiness and false breasts, and the passive acceptance of false values which corrupt our lives and distort our experience.

The idea of having a breast removed was much more traumatic for me before my mastectomy than after the fact, but it certainly took time and the loving support of other women before I could once again look at and love my altered body with the warmth I had done before. But I did. In the second week after surgery, on one of those tortuous night rounds of fitful sleep, dreams, and exercises, when I was moving in and out of physical pain and psychic awareness of fear for my life and mourning for my breast, I wrote in my journal:

> In a perspective of urgency, I want to say now that I'd give anything to have done it differently—it being the birth of a unique and survival-worthy, or survival-effective, perspective. Or I'd give anything not to have cancer and my beautiful breast gone, fled with my love of it. But then immediately after I guess I have to qualify that—there really are some things I wouldn't give. I wouldn't give my life, first of all, or else I wouldn't have chosen to have the operation in the first place, and I did. I wouldn't give Frances, or the children, or even any one of the women I love. I wouldn't give up my poetry, and I guess when I come right down to it I wouldn't give my eyes, nor my arms. So I guess I do have to be careful that my urgencies reflect my priorities.

> Sometimes I feel like I'm the spoils in a battle between good and evil, right now, or that I'm both sides doing the fighting, and I'm not even sure of the outcome nor the terms. But sometimes it comes into my head, like right now, what would you really give? And it feels like, even just musing, I could make a terrible and tragic error of judgement if I don't always keep my head and my priorities clear. It's as if the devil is really trying to buy my soul, and pretending that it doesn't matter if I say yes because everybody knows he's not for real anyway. But I don't know that. And I don't think this is all a dream at all, and no, I would not give up love.

> Maybe this is the chance to live and speak those things I really do believe, that power comes from moving into whatever I fear most that cannot be avoided. But will I ever be strong enough again to open my mouth and not have a cry of raw pain leap out?

I think I was fighting the devil of despair within myself for my own soul.

When I started to write this article, I went back to the books I had read in the hospital as I made my decision to have a mastectomy. I came across pictures of women with one breast and mastectomy scars, and I remembered shrinking from these pictures before my surgery. Now they seemed not at all strange or frightening to me. At times, I miss my right breast, the actuality of it, its presence, with a great and poignant sense of loss. But in the same way, and just as infrequently, I sometimes miss being 32, at the same time knowing that I have gained from the very loss I mourn.

Right after surgery I had a sense that I would never be able to bear missing that great well of sexual pleasure that I connected with my right breast. That sense has completely passed away, as I have come to realize that that well of feeling was within me. I alone own my feelings. I can never lose that feeling because I own it, because it comes out of myself. I can attach it anywhere I want to, because my feelings are a part of me, my sorrow and my joy.

I would never have chosen this path, but I am very glad to be who I am, here.

Notes

1. Peter Chowka, "Checking Up on the ACS," *New Age Magazine*, April 1980, p. 22.

2. Ibid.

3. Samuel Epstein, *The Politics of Cancer* (Anchor Books, New York, 1979), p. 456.

4. Ibid.

5. Chowka, p. 23.

6. Wayne Martin, "Let's Cut Cancer Deaths in Half," *Let's Live Magazine*, August 1978, p. 356.

7. Gary Null, "Alternative Cancer Therapies," *Cancer News Journal* 14, no. 4 (December 1979) (International Association of Cancer Victims and Friends, Inc. publication).

8. Ibid., p. 18.

9. Rose Kushner, *Breast Cancer* (Harcourt Brace Jovanovitch, New York, 1975), p. 161.

10. Epstein, p. 462.

11. Ibid., pp. xv–xvi.

12. Kushner, p. 163.

Feminism & Black Liberation:
The Great American Disease*

In Robert Staples' attack upon black feminists, there are saddening and obvious fallacies and errors.

Despite the economic gains made by black women recently, we are still the lowest paid group in the nation by sex and race. This should give the reader some idea of the inequality from which we started. In Staples' own words, black women now only "threaten to overtake black men" by the "next century" in education, occupation, and income. In other words, the inequality is self-evident; but how is it justifiable?

Furthermore, if Shange and Wallace are, as Staples suggests, unqualified to speak for black women merely because of their middle-class backgrounds, how does that reflect upon Staples' qualifications to speak for black men?

Black feminists speak as women because we are women, and do not need others to speak for us. It is for black men to speak up and tell us why their manhood is so threatened, and by what, that we should be the prime targets of their justifiable rage. What correct analysis of this rotten capitalist dragon within which we live will legitimize the wholesale rape of black women by black men that goes on within every city of this land?

At least black women, and black feminists other than Shange and Wallace,†have begun this much-needed dialogue, however bitter our words. At least we are not mowing down our brothers in the street, nor beating them to death with hammers. Yet.

Staples pleads his cause by saying capitalism has left the black man only his penis for fulfillment, and a "curious rage." Is this rage any more legitimate than the rage of black women? And why are black women supposed to absorb that male rage in silence? Why isn't that male rage turned upon our oppressors? Staples sees in Shange's play a "collective appetite for black male blood." But my female children and my black sisters lie bleeding all around me, victims of the appetites of their brothers.

Into what theoretical analysis would Staples fit Pat Cowan? She was a young black actress in Detroit, 22 years old and a mother. She answered an ad last spring for a black actress to audition in a play called "Hammer." As she acted out an argument scene, watched by the playwright's brother and her son, the black male playwright picked up a sledgehammer and bludgeoned her to death from behind. Will Staples'

*Published in *The Black Scholar*, vol. 10, no. 9 (May–June 1979) in response to "The Myth of Black Macho: A Response to Angry Black Feminists" by Robert Staples in *The Black Scholar*, vol. 10, no. 8 (March–April 1979).

†Ntozake Shange, *For Colored Girls Who Have Considered Suicide/When the Rainbow Is Enuf: A Choreopoem* (New York: Macmillan, 1977); Michele Wallace, *Black Macho and the Myth of the Superwoman* (New York: Dial, 1979).

"compassion for misguided black men" bring this young mother back, or make her senseless death more acceptable?

Black men's feelings of nobodiness and their fear of vulnerability must indeed be talked about, but not by black women any more, at the expense of our own "curious rage."

If society ascribes roles to black men which they are not allowed to fulfill, is it black women who must bend and alter our lives to compensate, or is it society that needs changing? And what about the blanket acceptance on the part of black men that these roles are correct ones, or anything other than a narcotic promise extended to them to encourage them to accept other facets of their own oppression?

One aspect of the Great American Disease has been always to blame the victim for the oppressor's victimization: black people are said to invite lynching by not knowing their place; black women are said to invite rape and murder and abuse by not being submissive enough, or by being too seductive, or too etc.

Staples' "fact" that black women get their sense of fulfillment from having children is only a "fact" stated out of the mouth of black men, and any black person in this country, even "happily married women" who "have no pent-up frustrations that need release" (!) is either a fool or insane. This smacks of the oldest sexist canard of all time, that all a woman needs to "keep her quiet" is a "good man."

Instead of beginning the much-needed dialogue between black men and black women, Staples retreats to a passive and defensive stance, sadly mirroring the fallacy of white liberals of the '60s, who saw any statement of black pride and self-assertion as an automatic threat to their own identity, as an attempt to wipe them out. Here we have an intelligent black man believing—or at least saying—that a call to black women to love ourselves (and no one said 'only') is a denial of, or threat to, his male identity!

In this country, black women traditionally have had compassion for everybody else except ourselves. We cared for whites because we had to for pay or survival; we cared for our children and our fathers and our brothers and our lovers. We need to also learn to care for ourselves. Our history and popular culture, as well as our personal lives, are full of tales of black women who had "compassion for misguided black men." Our scarred, broken, battered and dead daughters and sisters are a mute testament to that.

Shange's exhortation to black women at the end of her play is for us to extend that compassion and love at least to ourselves. In the light of what black women sacrifice for their children and their men, this is a much needed exhortation, no matter in what illegitimate manner the white media sees fit to use it. And this call for self-value, self-love, is quite different from narcissism, as Staples must certainly realize. The black man's well-documented narcissism comes, not out of self-love, but out of self-hatred.

The lack of a reasonable and articulate male viewpoint on these questions is not the responsibility of black women. We have too often been expected to be all things to all people, and speak everyone else's position but our very own. But black men do not need to be so passive under their veneer of macho, that they must have black women to speak for them. Even my 14 year old son knows that. It is for black men themselves to examine and articulate their own position, and to stand by the conclusions thereof. Unfortunately, the Staples article does not do this. It merely whines at the absence of his viewpoint in women's work. But oppressors have always expected the oppressed to extend to them the understanding and moral forebearance so lacking in themselves.

For Staples to suggest, for instance, that black men leave their families as a form of male protest against female decision-making in the home is in direct contradiction to his own observations in "The Myth of The Black Matriarchy."

Now it is quite true that many black men with middle-class aspirations frequently turn to white women, who they feel better fit the model of "femininity" set forth in this country. But for Staples to justify the act in terms of the reason is not only another error in reasoning, it also is akin to justifying the actions of a lemming who follows its companions over the cliff to sure death. Because it happens does not mean it should happen, nor that it is functional for the well-being of the individual or the group.

As I have said elsewhere, it is not the destiny of black America to repeat white America's mistakes. But we will, if we mistake the trappings of success in a sick society for the signs of a meaningful life. If black men continue to do so, defining 'femininity' in its archaic European terms, this augurs ill for our survival as a people, let alone our survival as individuals. Freedom and future for blacks does not mean absorbing the dominant white male disease.

As black people, we cannot begin our dialogue by denying the oppressive nature of male privilege. And if black males choose to assume that privilege, for whatever reason, raping, brutalizing, and killing women, then we cannot ignore black male oppression. One oppression does not justify another.

Staples states that black men cannot be denied their personal choice of the woman who meets their need to dominate. In that case, black women also cannot be denied our personal choices, and those choices are increasingly self-assertive ones, and female-oriented. "Personal choice" and "ontological" reasoning are knives that cut both ways.

As a people, we should most certainly work together to end our common oppression, and toward a future which is viable for us all. In that context, it is short-sighted to believe that black men alone are to blame for the above situations, in a society dominated by white male privilege. But the black male consciousness must be raised so that he realizes that sexism and woman-hating are critically dysfunctional to his liberation as a black man, because they arise out of the same constellation that engenders racism and homophobia, a constellation of intolerance for difference serving a profit motivation. And until this is done, black men like Staples will view sexism and the destruction of black women only as tangential to the cause of black liberation, rather than as central to that struggle. So long as this occurs, we will never be able to embark upon that dialogue between black women and black men that is so essential to our survival as a people. And this continued blindness between us can only serve the oppressive system within which we live.

Men avoid women's observations by accusing us of not being 'global', or of being too 'visceral'. But no amount of understanding the roots of black sexism and woman-hating will bring back Patricia Cowan, nor mute her family's loss. Pain is never global, it is very visceral, particularly to the people who are hurting. And as the poet McAnally said, "pain teaches us to take our hands *out* the fucking fire!"

If the problems of black women are derivatives only of a larger contradiction between capital and labor, then so is racism, and both must be equally fought against by all of us, since the capitalist structure is a many-headed monster. I might add here that in no socialist country that I have visited have I found absence of racism nor of sexism, so the eradication of both of these diseases seems to involve more than the abolition of capitalism as an institution.

No reasonable black man can possibly condone or excuse the rape and slaughter of black women by black men as any fitting response to capitalist oppression. And that destruction of black women by black men clearly cuts across all class lines at this point.

Whatever the "structural underpinnings" for sexism in the black community may be, it is obviously black women who are bearing the brunt of that sexism, and so it is in our vested interest to abolish it. We invite our black brothers to join us, since ultimately that destruction is in their best interests also. But since it is black women who are being abused, and our female blood that is being shed, it is for black women to decide whether or not sexism in the black community is pathological, not Staples. And we do not approach that question theoretically, as Staples does, who evidently cannot recognize how he himself is diminished by that sexism. Those "creative relationships" of which he speaks within the community are almost invariably to the benefit of black males, given the sex ratio of males to females and the implied power balance therein within a supply and demand situation. This is much the same as how "creative relationships" between master and slave were to the benefit of the master.

The occurrence of woman-hating in the black community is a tragedy which diminishes all black people. It must be seen in the context of the systematic devaluation of black women by this total society, for it is within this context that we become an acceptable target for black male rage, so acceptable that even a man of Staples' stature does not even question the depersonalizing abuse.

What black women are saying is that this abuse is no longer acceptable in the name of solidarity nor of black liberation. Any dialogue between black women and black men must begin there, no matter where it ends.

The Uses of Anger: Women Responding to Racism

Racism. The belief in the inherent superiority of one race over all others and thereby the right to dominance, manifest and implied.

Women respond to racism. My response to racism is anger. I have lived with that anger, ignoring it, feeding upon it, learning to use it before it laid my visions to waste, for most of my life. Once I did it in silence, afraid of the weight. My fear of anger taught me nothing. Your fear of that anger will teach you nothing, also.

Women responding to racism means women responding to anger; the anger of exclusion, of unquestioned privilege, of racial distortions, of silence, ill-use, stereotyping, defensiveness, misnaming, betrayal, and co-optation.

My anger is a response to racist attitudes and to the actions and presumptions that arise out of those attitudes. If your dealings with other women reflect those attitudes, then my anger and your attendant fears are spotlights that can be used for growth in the same way I have used learning to express anger for my growth. But for corrective surgery, not guilt. Guilt and defensiveness are bricks in a wall against which we all flounder; they serve none of our futures.

Because I do not want this to become a theoretical discussion, I am going to give a few examples of interchanges between women that illustrate these points. In the interest of time, I am going to cut them short. I want you to know there were many more.

For example:

- I speak out of direct and particular anger at an academic conference, and a white woman says, "Tell me how you feel but don't say it too harshly or I cannot hear you." But is it my manner that keeps her from hearing, or the threat of a message that her life may change?

- The Women's Studies Program of a southern university invites a Black woman to read following a week-long forum on Black and white women. "What has this week given to you?" I ask. The most vocal white woman says, "I think I've gotten a lot. I feel Black women really understand me a lot better now; they have a better idea of where I'm coming from." As if understanding her lay at the core of the racist problem.

- After fifteen years of a women's movement which professes to address the life concerns and possible futures of all women, I still hear, on campus after campus, "How can we address the issues of racism? No women of Color attended." Or, the other side of that statement, "We have no one in our department equipped to teach their work." In other words, racism is a Black women's problem, a problem of women of Color, and only we can discuss it.

- After I read from my work entitled "Poems for Women in Rage,"* a white woman asks me: "Are you going to do anything with how we can deal directly with *our* anger? I feel it's so important." I ask, "How do you use *your* rage?" And then I have to turn away from the blank look in her eyes, before she can invite me to participate in her own annihilation. I do not exist to feel her anger for her.

- White women are beginning to examine their relationships to Black women, yet often I hear them wanting only to deal with little colored children across the roads of childhood, the beloved nursemaid, the occasional second-grade classmate—those tender memories of what was once mysterious and intriguing or neutral. You avoid the childhood assumptions formed by the raucous laughter at Rastus and Alfalfa, the acute message of your mommy's handkerchief spread upon the park bench because I had just been sitting there, the indelible and dehumanizing portraits of Amos 'n' Andy and your daddy's humorous bedtime stories.

- I wheel my two-year-old daughter in a shopping cart through a supermarket in Eastchester in 1967, and a little white girl riding past in her mother's cart calls out excitedly, "Oh look, Mommy, a baby maid!" And your mother shushes you, but she does not correct you. And so fifteen years later, at a conference on racism, you can still find that story humorous. But I hear your laughter is full of terror and dis-ease.

- A white academic welcomes the appearance of a collection by non-Black women of Color.† "It allows me to deal with racism without dealing with the harshness of Black women," she says to me.

*One poem from this series is included in *Chosen Poems: Old and New* (W. W. Norton and Company, New York, 1978), pp. 105–108.
†*This Bridge Called My Back: Writings by Radical Women of Color,* edited by Cherríe Moraga and Gloria Anzaldua (Kitchen Table: Women of Color Press, New York, 1984), first published in 1981.

- At an international cultural gathering of women, a well-known white american woman poet interrupts the reading of the work of women of Color to read her own poem, and then dashes off to an "important panel."

If women in the academy truly want a dialogue about racism, it will require recognizing the needs and the living contexts of other women. When an academic woman says, "I can't afford it," she may mean she is making a choice about how to spend her available money. But when a woman on welfare says, "I can't afford it," she means she is surviving on an amount of money that was barely subsistence in 1972, and she often does not have enough to eat. Yet the National Women's Studies Association here in 1981 holds a conference in which it commits itself to responding to racism, yet refuses to waive the registration fee for poor women and women of Color who wished to be present and conduct workshops. This has made it impossible for many women of Color—for instance, Wilmette Brown, of Black Women for Wages for Housework—to participate in this conference. Is this to be merely another case of the academy discussing life within the closed circuits of the academy?

To the white women present who recognize these attitudes as familiar, but most of all, to all my sisters of Color who live and survive thousands of such encounters— to my sisters of Color who like me still tremble their rage under harness, or who sometimes question the expression of our rage as useless and disruptive (the two most popular accusations)—I want to speak about anger, my anger, and what I have learned from my travels through its dominions.

*Everything can be used/except what is wasteful/(you will need/to remember this when you are accused of destruction.)**

Every woman has a well-stocked arsenal of anger potentially useful against those oppressions, personal and institutional, which brought that anger into being. Focused with precision it can become a powerful source of energy serving progress and change. And when I speak of change, I do not mean a simple switch of positions or a temporary lessening of tensions, nor the ability to smile or feel good. I am speaking of a basic and radical alteration in those assumptions underlining our lives.

I have seen situations where white women hear a racist remark, resent what has been said, become filled with fury, and remain silent because they are afraid. That unexpressed anger lies within them like an undetonated device, usually to be hurled at the first woman of Color who talks about racism.

But anger expressed and translated into action in the service of our vision and our future is a liberating and strengthening act of clarification, for it is in the painful process of this translation that we identify who are our allies with whom we have grave differences, and who are our genuine enemies.

Anger is loaded with information and energy. When I speak of women of Color, I do not only mean Black women. The woman of Color who is not Black and who charges me with rendering her invisible by assuming that her struggles with racism are identical with my own has something to tell me that I had better learn from, lest we both waste ourselves fighting the truths between us. If I participate, know-

*From "For Each of You," first published in *From A Land Where Other People Live* (Broadside Press, Detroit, 1973), and collected in *Chosen Poems: Old and New* (W. W. Norton and Company, New York, 1982), p. 42.

ingly or otherwise, in my sister's oppression and she calls me on it, to answer her anger with my own only blankets the substance of our exchange with reaction. It wastes energy. And yes, it is very difficult to stand still and to listen to another woman's voice delineate an agony I do not share, or one to which I myself have contributed.

In this place we speak removed from the more blatant reminders of our embattlement as women. This need not blind us to the size and complexities of the forces mounting against us and all that is most human within our environment. We are not here as women examining racism in a political and social vacuum. We operate in the teeth of a system for which racism and sexism are primary, established, and necessary props of profit. Women responding to racism is a topic so dangerous that when the local media attempt to discredit this conference they choose to focus upon the provision of lesbian housing as a diversionary device—as if the Hartford *Courant* dare not mention the topic chosen for discussion here, racism, lest it become apparent that women are in fact attempting to examine and to alter all the repressive conditions of our lives.

Mainstream communication does not want women, particularly white women, responding to racism. It wants racism to be accepted as an immutable given in the fabric of your existence, like eveningtime or the common cold.

So we are working in a context of opposition and threat, the cause of which is certainly not the angers which lie between us, but rather that virulent hatred leveled against all women, people of Color, lesbians and gay men, poor people—against all of us who are seeking to examine the particulars of our lives as we resist our oppressions, moving toward coalition and effective action.

Any discussion among women about racism must include the recognition and the use of anger. This discussion must be direct and creative because it is crucial. We cannot allow our fear of anger to deflect us nor seduce us into settling for anything less than the hard work of excavating honesty; we must be quite serious about the choice of this topic and the angers entwined within it because, rest assured, our opponents are quite serious about their hatred of us and of what we are trying to do here.

And while we scrutinize the often painful face of each other's anger, please remember that it is not our anger which makes me caution you to lock your doors at night and not to wander the streets of Hartford alone. It is the hatred which lurks in those streets, that urge to destroy us all if we truly work for change rather than merely indulge in academic rhetoric.

This hatred and our anger are very different. Hatred is the fury of those who do not share our goals, and its object is death and destruction. Anger is a grief of distortions between peers, and its object is change. But our time is getting shorter. We have been raised to view any difference other than sex as a reason for destruction, and for Black women and white women to face each other's angers without denial or immobility or silence or guilt is in itself a heretical and generative idea. It implies peers meeting upon a common basis to examine difference, and to alter those distortions which history has created around our difference. For it is those distortions which separate us. And we must ask ourselves: Who profits from all this?

Women of Color in america have grown up within a symphony of anger, at being silenced, at being unchosen, at knowing that when we survive, it is in spite of a world that takes for granted our lack of humanness, and which hates our very existence outside of its service. And I say *symphony* rather than *cacophony* because we have had to learn to orchestrate those furies so that they do not tear us apart. We have had to learn to move through them and use them for strength and force and insight within our daily lives. Those of us who did not learn this difficult lesson did not survive. And part of my anger is always libation for my fallen sisters.

Anger is an appropriate reaction to racist attitudes, as is fury when the actions arising from those attitudes do not change. To those women here who fear the anger of women of Color more than their own unscrutinized racist attitudes, I ask: Is the anger of women of Color more threatening than the woman-hatred that tinges all aspects of our lives?

It is not the anger of other women that will destroy us but our refusals to stand still, to listen to its rhythms, to learn within it, to move beyond the manner of presentation to the substance, to tap that anger as an important source of empowerment.

I cannot hide my anger to spare you guilt, nor hurt feelings, nor answering anger; for to do so insults and trivializes all our efforts. Guilt is not a response to anger; it is a response to one's own actions or lack of action. If it leads to change then it can be useful, since it is then no longer guilt but the beginning of knowledge. Yet all too often, guilt is just another name for impotence, for defensiveness destructive of communication; it becomes a device to protect ignorance and the continuation of things the way they are, the ultimate protection for changelessness.

Most women have not developed tools for facing anger constructively. CR groups in the past, largely white, dealt with how to express anger, usually at the world of men. And these groups were made up of white women who shared the terms of their oppressions. There was usually little attempt to articulate the genuine differences between women, such as those of race, color, age, class, and sexual identity. There was no apparent need at that time to examine the contradictions of self, woman as oppressor. There was work on expressing anger, but very little on anger directed against each other. No tools were developed to deal with other women's anger except to avoid it, deflect it, or flee from it under a blanket of guilt.

I have no creative use for guilt, yours or my own. Guilt is only another way of avoiding informed action, of buying time out of the pressing need to make clear choices, out of the approaching storm that can feed the earth as well as bend the trees. If I speak to you in anger, at least I have spoken to you: I have not put a gun to your head and shot you down in the street; I have not looked at your bleeding sister's body and asked, "What did she do to deserve it?" This was the reaction of two white women to Mary Church Terrell's telling of the lynching of a pregnant Black woman whose baby was then torn from her body. That was in 1921, and Alice Paul had just refused to publicly endorse the enforcement of the Nineteenth Amendment for all women—by refusing to endorse the inclusion of women of Color, although we had worked to help bring about that amendment.

The angers between women will not kill us if we can articulate them with precision, if we listen to the content of what is said with at least as much intensity as we defend ourselves against the manner of saying. When we turn from anger we turn from insight, saying we will accept only the designs already known, deadly and safely familiar. I have tried to learn my anger's usefulness to me, as well as its limitations.

For women raised to fear, too often anger threatens annihilation. In the male construct of brute force, we were taught that our lives depended upon the good will of patriarchal power. The anger of others was to be avoided at all costs because there was nothing to be learned from it but pain, a judgment that we had been bad girls, come up lacking, not done what we were supposed to do. And if we accept our powerlessness, then of course any anger can destroy us.

But the strength of women lies in recognizing differences between us as creative, and in standing to those distortions which we inherited without blame, but which are now ours to alter. The angers of women can transform difference through insight into power. For anger between peers births change, not destruction, and the discomfort and sense of loss it often causes is not fatal, but a sign of growth.

My response to racism is anger. That anger has eaten clefts into my living only when it remained unspoken, useless to anyone. It has also served me in classrooms without light or learning, where the work and history of Black women was less than a vapor. It has served me as fire in the ice zone of uncomprehending eyes of white women who see in my experience and the experience of my people only new reasons for fear or guilt. And my anger is no excuse for not dealing with your blindness, no reason to withdraw from the results of your own actions.

When women of Color speak out of the anger that laces so many of our contacts with white women, we are often told that we are "creating a mood of hopelessness," "preventing white women from getting past guilt," or "standing in the way of trusting communication and action." All these quotes come directly from letters to me from members of this organization within the last two years. One woman wrote, "Because you are Black and Lesbian, you seem to speak with the moral authority of suffering." Yes, I am Black and Lesbian, and what you hear in my voice is fury, not suffering. Anger, not moral authority. There is a difference.

To turn aside from the anger of Black women with excuses or the pretexts of intimidation is to award no one power—it is merely another way of preserving racial blindness, the power of unaddressed privilege, unbreached, intact. Guilt is only another form of objectification. Oppressed peoples are always being asked to stretch a little more, to bridge the gap between blindness and humanity. Black women are expected to use our anger only in the service of other people's salvation or learning. But that time is over. My anger has meant pain to me but it has also meant survival, and before I give it up I'm going to be sure that there is something at least as powerful to replace it on the road to clarity.

What woman here is so enamoured of her own oppression that she cannot see her heelprint upon another woman's face? What woman's terms of oppression have become precious and necessary to her as a ticket into the fold of the righteous, away from the cold winds of self-scrutiny?

I am a lesbian woman of Color whose children eat regularly because I work in a university. If their full bellies make me fail to recognize my commonality with a woman of Color whose children do not eat because she cannot find work, or who has no children because her insides are rotted from home abortions and sterilization; if I fail to recognize the lesbian who chooses not to have children, the woman who remains closeted because her homophobic community is her only life support, the woman who chooses silence instead of another death, the woman who is terrified lest my anger trigger the explosion of hers; if I fail to recognize them as other faces of myself, then I am contributing not only to each of their oppressions but also to my own, and the anger which stands between us then must be used for clarity and mutual empowerment, not for evasion by guilt or for further separation. I am not free while any woman is unfree, even when her shackles are very different from my own. And I am not free as long as one person of Color remains chained. Nor is any one of you.

I speak here as a woman of Color who is bent not upon destruction but upon survival. No woman is responsible for altering the psyche of her oppressor, even when that psyche is embodied in another woman. I have suckled the wolf's lip of anger and I have used it for illumination, laughter, protection, fire in places where there was no light, no food, no sisters, no quarter. We are not goddesses or matriarchs or edifices of divine forgiveness; we are not fiery fingers of judgment or instruments of flagellation; we are women forced back always upon our woman's power. We have learned to use anger as we have learned to use the dead flesh of animals, and bruised, battered, and changing, we have survived and grown and, in Angela Wilson's words, we *are* moving on. With or without uncolored women. We use whatever strengths we have fought for, including anger, to help define and fashion a world where all our sisters can grow, where our children can love, and where the power of touching and meeting another woman's difference and wonder will eventually transcend the need for destruction.

For it is not the anger of Black women which is dripping down over this globe like a diseased liquid. It is not my anger that launches rockets, spends over sixty thousand dollars a second on missiles and other agents of war and death, slaughters children in cities, stockpiles nerve gas and chemical bombs, sodomizes our daughters and our earth. It is not the anger of Black women which corrodes into blind, dehumanizing power, bent upon the annihilation of us all unless we meet it with what we have, our power to examine and to redefine the terms upon which we will live and work; our power to envision and to reconstruct, anger by painful anger, stone upon heavy stone, a future of pollinating difference and the earth to support our choices.

We welcome all women who can meet us, face to face, beyond objectification and beyond guilt.

The Transformation of Silence into Language and Action

I have come to believe over and over again that what is most important to me must be spoken, made verbal and shared, even at the risk of having it bruised or misunderstood. That the speaking profits me, beyond any other effect. I am standing here as a Black lesbian poet, and the meaning of all that waits upon the fact that I am still alive, and might not have been. Less than two months ago I was told by two doctors, one female and one male, that I would have to have breast surgery, and that there was a 60 to 80 percent chance that the tumor was malignant. Between that telling and the actual surgery, there was a three-week period of the agony of an involuntary reorganization of my entire life. The surgery was completed, and the growth was benign.

But within those three weeks, I was forced to look upon myself and my living with a harsh and urgent clarity that has left me still shaken but much stronger. This is a situation faced by many women, by some of you here today. Some of what I experienced during that time has helped elucidate for me much of what I feel concerning the transformation of silence into language and action.

In becoming forcibly and essentially aware of my mortality, and of what I wished and wanted for my life, however short it might be, priorities and omissions became strongly etched in a merciless light, and what I most regretted were my silences. Of what had I *ever* been afraid? To question or to speak as I believed could have meant pain, or death. But we all hurt in so many different ways, all the time, and pain will either change or end. Death, on the other hand, is the final silence. And that might be coming quickly, now, without regard for whether I had ever spoken what needed to be said, or had only betrayed myself into small silences, while I planned someday to speak, or waited for someone else's words. And I began to recognize a source of power within myself that comes from the knowledge that while it is most desirable not to be afraid, learning to put fear into a perspective gave me great strength.

I was going to die, if not sooner then later, whether or not I had ever spoken myself. My silences had not protected me. Your silence will not protect you. But for every real word spoken, for every attempt I had ever made to speak those truths for which I am still seeking, I had made contact with other women while we examined the words to fit a world in which we all believed, bridging our differences. And it was the concern and caring of all those women which gave me strength and enabled me to scrutinize the essentials of my living.

The women who sustained me through that period were Black and white, old and young, lesbian, bisexual, and heterosexual, and we all shared a war against the tyrannies of silence. They all gave me a strength and concern without which I could not have survived intact. Within those weeks of acute fear came the knowledge—within the war we are all waging with the forces of death, subtle and otherwise, conscious or not—I am not only a casualty, I am also a warrior.

What are the words you do not yet have? What do you need to say? What are the tyrannies you swallow day by day and attempt to make your own, until you will sicken and die of them, still in silence? Perhaps for some of you here today, I am the face of one of your fears. Because I am woman, because I am Black, because I am lesbian, because I am myself—a Black woman warrior poet doing my work— come to ask you, are you doing yours?

And of course I am afraid, because the transformation of silence into language and action is an act of self-revelation, and that always seems fraught with danger. But my daughter, when I told her of our topic and my difficulty with it, said, "Tell them about how you're never really a whole person if you remain silent, because there's always that one little piece inside you that wants to be spoken out, and if you keep ignoring it, it gets madder and madder and hotter and hotter, and if you don't speak it out one day it will just up and punch you in the mouth from the inside."

In the cause of silence, each of us draws the face of her own fear—fear of contempt, of censure, or some judgment, or recognition, of challenge, of annihilation. But most of all, I think, we fear the visibility without which we cannot truly live. Within this country where racial difference creates a constant, if unspoken, distortion of vision, Black women have on one hand always been highly visible, and so, on the other hand, have been rendered invisible through the depersonalization of racism. Even within the women's movement, we have had to fight, and still do, for that very visibility which also renders us most vulnerable, our Blackness. For to survive in the mouth of this dragon we call america, we have had to learn this first and most vital lesson—that we were never meant to survive. Not as human beings. And neither were most of you here today, Black or not. And that visibility which makes us most vulnerable is that which also is the source of our greatest strength. Because the machine will try to grind you into dust anyway, whether or not we speak. We can sit in our corners mute forever while our sisters and our selves are wasted, while our children are distorted and destroyed, while our earth is poisoned; we can sit in our safe corners mute as bottles, and we will still be no less afraid.

In my house this year we are celebrating the feast of Kwanza, the African-american festival of harvest which begins the day after Christmas and lasts for seven days. There are seven principles of Kwanza, one for each day. The first principle is Umoja, which means unity, the decision to strive for and maintain unity in self and community. The principle for yesterday, the second day, was Kujichagulia—self-determination—the decision to define ourselves, name ourselves, and speak for ourselves, instead of being defined and spoken for by others. Today is the third day of Kwanza, and the principle for today is Ujima—collective work and responsibility—the decision to build and maintain ourselves and our communities together and to recognize and solve our problems together.

Each of us is here now because in one way or another we share a commitment to language and to the power of language, and to the reclaiming of that language which has been made to work against us. In the transformation of silence into language and action, it is vitally necessary for each one of us to establish or examine her function in that transformation and to recognize her role as vital within that transformation.

For those of us who write, it is necessary to scrutinize not only the truth of what we speak, but the truth of that language by which we speak it. For others, it is to share and spread also those words that are meaningful to us. But primarily for us all, it is necessary to teach by living and speaking those truths which we believe and know beyond understanding. Because in this way alone we can survive, by taking part in a process of life that is creative and continuing, that is growth.

And it is never without fear—of visibility, of the harsh light of scrutiny and perhaps judgment, of pain, of death. But we have lived through all of those already, in silence, except death. And I remind myself all the time now that if I were to have been born mute, or had maintained an oath of silence my whole life long for safety, I would still have suffered, and I would still die. It is very good for establishing perspective.

And where the words of women are crying to be heard, we must each of us recognize our responsibility to seek those words out, to read them and share them and examine them in their pertinence to our lives. That we not hide behind the mockeries of separations that have been imposed upon us and which so often we accept as our own. For instance, "I can't possibly teach Black women's writing—their experience is so different from mine." Yet how many years have you spent teaching Plato and Shakespeare and Proust? Or another, "She's a white woman and what could she possibly have to say to me?" Or, "She's a lesbian, what would my husband say, or my chairman?" Or again, "This woman writes of her sons and I have no children." And all the other endless ways in which we rob ourselves of ourselves and each other.

We can learn to work and speak when we are afraid in the same way we have learned to work and speak when we are tired. For we have been socialized to respect fear more than our own needs for language and definition, and while we wait in silence for that final luxury of fearlessness, the weight of that silence will choke us.

The fact that we are here and that I speak these words is an attempt to break that silence and bridge some of those differences between us, for it is not difference which immobilizes us, but silence. And there are so many silences to be broken.

Considerations for Thinking and Writing

1. In "Breast Cancer: Power vs. Prosthesis," Lorde writes: "Women have been programmed to view our bodies only in terms of how they look and feel to others, rather than how they feel to ourselves, and how we wish to use them." How does Lorde use her experience as a postmastectomy patient to substantiate this claim?

2. Compare Lorde's notion of beauty with other discussions of beauty in this book: Alice Walker's in "Beauty: When the Other Dancer Is the Self"; Susan Sontag's in "Woman's Beauty: Put-Down or Power Source?"; and Phyllis Rose's in "Tools of Torture: An Essay on Beauty and Pain." When is the beauty of women considered an aesthetic issue? When is it considered a political, feminist issue?

3. Lorde describes herself as a "warrior" against breast cancer. In what ways is she embattled? What images of heroism does she offer? How does Lorde's "wound"—her refusal to wear a prosthesis—enhance her identity as warrior?

4. "It is not the destiny of Black america to repeat white america's mistakes," Lorde writes in "Feminism & Black Liberation: The Great American Disease." Why does Lorde capitalize "Black" and not "america"? What larger purpose does this practice serve? In what ways is sexism among Black men different from sexism generally?

5. Several of these essays by Lorde were delivered as speeches, but in all of her writing she is keenly aware of her audience. What different audiences does she address in "Feminism," "The Transformation of Silence into Language and Action," and "The Uses of Anger"? Does she ever extend or narrow her audience within a given speech or essay? Compare Lorde's approach to her audience with that of Adrienne Rich in "What Does a Woman Need to Know?"

6. In "The Uses of Anger," Lorde takes pains to define her terms. How does she distinguish between anger and hatred? What is her definition of guilt? Does she define her terms theoretically or pragmatically? Compare her pairing of anger and hatred with Jordan's pairing of anger and love in "Where Is the Love?"

7. Lorde views silence in political terms in "The Transformation of Silence into Language and Action"; Sontag views silence in aesthetic terms in "The Aesthetics of Silence." Are there ways in which these two essays speak to each other? How do these views of silence compare with Gloria Steinem's notion of "listening" in "Men and Women Talking"?

NANCY MAIRS
(b. 1943)

"I spend my mornings writing essays," writes Nancy Mairs toward the end of her first book, *Plaintext*, "then turn without disruption to the other tasks of inscribing a life. None of the writing is easy, but I no longer refuse to do it for fear that I'll fail to get it right. It can never be right, I know; it can only be done. Life as scribble. And the reverse." Nancy Mairs's essays articulate the scribble of life with eloquence, candor, and generosity. Hers are searching, provisional essays that are more, not less, accomplished for their reluctance to resolve the tough issues they explore: chronic illness, loss, sex, parenting, loving, writing. With a sharp tongue and a ready wit, Mairs shows that the writing of essays is hard, serious work, as hard and serious, say, as the work of living with depression and multiple sclerosis. Unlike essayists who equate verbal artistry with the seeming absence of toil, Mairs meets us in her essays as a working writer, for she wants us to understand that for her the work of writing and the work of surviving are one and the same.

Born in California and raised in New England, Nancy Mairs lives in Tucson with her husband and two children. She has a Ph.D. in English from the University of Arizona and has published an award-winning volume of poems, *In All the Rooms of the Yellow House.* Recently confined to a motorized wheelchair, she writes, "My world has, of necessity, been circumscribed by my losses, but the terrain left me has been ample enough for me to continue many of the activities that absorb me: writing, teaching, raising children and cats and plants and snakes, reading, speaking publicly about MS and depression, even playing bridge." Yet Mairs begins "On Being a Cripple" by showing us how easily she is thrown off balance. We may be surprised that she has chosen to start this particular essay by taking up a comic stance. But we soon discover that Mairs is skeptical of stances, compelled instead by the surprises that life throws us. This masterful opening shows us how being thrown off guard provides Mairs with an oblique view of her predicament, and it is that obliqueness which opens a space for laughter. Pointedly, Mairs has begun her essay in a space both public and private—a public toilet. Though her essay unfolds by deepening its concerns rather than by extending them, it fulfills this rich opening by showing how Mairs's private ordeal reaches into the public sphere: "In search-

ing for and shaping a stable core in a life wrenched by change and loss, change and loss, I must recognize the same process, under individual conditions, in the lives around me." Mairs moves us because she keeps the particularity of her disease in tension with the universal fact of change and loss. Her knowledge of the particular authorizes her knowledge of the general.

If Mairs's essays are undeniably personal, they are just as concerned with the public sphere. As Mairs interprets the "scribble of life," she shows how deeply the lineaments of culture are etched in our thinking. She is, by her own account, "a perfectly good if unsystematic feminist," and her essays examine frankly her submission to the expectations of women which she was raised to meet. In "On Being Raised by a Daughter," Mairs writes wryly of the "fond approving gaze" that followed her from the altar (at nineteen, while a college student) to the nursery, then came to rest relentlessly on her children as reflections of their mother. Mairs is keenly aware that she was one of the gazers; her own self-criticism is an essential component of a lifelong tendency to depression. "On Being Raised by a Daughter" subtly shifts the focus from mother to daughter. Under Mairs's unwavering gaze, the conventional wisdom about mothering yields a threatening pair of premises: that mothers are destined to be dangerous; that daughters are destined to be their victims. Mairs insists that being a mother is something she had to learn from scratch. Her position, for all its understatement, is politically shrewd: to think of mothers and daughters as cooperating in the art of "living together well" may well be to shape a world in which symbiosis is the rule rather than the exception.

For Nancy Mairs, the alternative to being possessed by the "fond adoring gaze" is to be self-possessed. In her essays, she takes possession of her self by naming herself. One such name is "cripple": "I choose this word to name me," writes Mairs, demanding that we recognize a "tough customer" when we meet one. This act of self-naming, Mairs soon informs us, was not a conscious choice, and the burden of her essay is partly to understand how she came to call herself (and not others) a "cripple." The essay moves deliberately inward, from daily life with a disability to the "struts in the framework of my existence"—husband and children—to the "violent self-loathing" that flows and ebbs. By committing herself even to these strong currents of feeling, Mairs comes to acknowledge that "what I hate is not me but a disease. I am not a disease." To speak of "adjustment" to disease, Mairs decides, is to cling to illusion; better to speak of "a lesson in losses" learned "one at a time." When we read this essay, we witness such learning; it begins with words, with names.

In an essay not included here, "On Living behind Bars," Mairs tries on another name—"madwoman"—and finds that it does not fit. She writes trenchantly here of her six-month incarceration in a state mental hospital shortly after her first child was born. Looking back nearly twenty years later, she writes, "If in fact I was, as I now believe, not crazy but a sort of cultural prisoner, Met State certainly made a madwoman of me." The essay finds Mairs poring over her own journals to decipher what she elsewhere calls "metaphors, codes in the cultural text in which I am embedded." Reading the text of her life, Mairs shows us, is an act of revision that enables her to see:

> The terms of my existence: sickness, isolation, timidity, desire for death. They lie black as bars across the amazingly sunny landscape of a privileged life: good family, good education, good marriage, good jobs, good children. . . . But I'm not mad. You can take that as axiomatic. I've spent many years arriving at it, and it works. However comfortable an explanation madness might be, I can't have it.

Mairs refuses to be a hostage even to her own texts.

Perhaps the most convincing proof of this refusal lies in the extraordinary essay "On Not Liking Sex." Mairs surpasses her bold choice of topic by brazenly letting us watch her in the private act of revision. She begins by quoting an earlier, "brittle, glittery" attempt at the same topic. As she considers her own words, her voice becomes deeper, quieter, more tentative; she leads us from our seats at a performance of thinking into the dark spaces of thought itself. Her first thoughts are about having written "an exercise in making careful statements that would ensure that I never said what I really had to say." But this realization is only a step toward finding out what one did have to say. The true drama of the essay, which returns again and again to the earlier text, is Mairs's brave discovery that what she "really" had to say about sex was not bold and glib and free but profoundly self-defeating. But if revision provides an opportunity for self-criticism, Mairs insists that it is also, triumphantly, an occasion for forgiveness.

The brief essay "Happiness," written for the "Hers" column of the *New York Times*, reveals the craft that makes such brooding, experimental essays possible. Framed by her daughter's commencement procession and recession, the essay compares Mairs's present emotions with the desolation she felt at her own graduation: "Although surrounded by a proud and loving family, I was lonely for the one person who made my survival seem worthwhile, my husband, who was sailing in large aimless circles on a radar ship in the North Atlantic." Knowing nostalgia to be impossible, Mairs faces the momentous losses she has survived and finds herself suddenly "pierced by joy." A less stringent essayist might have left herself yearning to share her epiphany with the graduates, but Mairs puts her wisdom to the test, repeating her words of encouragement to a self that she will inevitably leave behind. Repeated to herself, the same happy words become austere and troubling.

Like "On Not Liking Sex," "Happiness" closes by opening and deepening. We understand why Mairs's emblem of happiness is not a sunny smile but a photograph of a young woman, "her mouth an oval of surprise." Her essays seem to surprise her as they surprise us. We trust her because she trusts her writing to surprise her, by both succeeding and failing, by being right and by being wrong. At the end of an essay on the trials of raising a teenage foster son, Mairs writes:

> That's how we get wise, by taking on in ignorance the tasks we would never later dare to do.
> No. Yes.

On Being a Cripple

To escape is nothing. Not to escape is nothing.
—LOUISE BOGAN

The other day I was thinking of writing an essay on being a cripple. I was thinking hard in one of the stalls of the women's room in my office building, as I was shoving my shirt into my jeans and tugging up my zipper. Preoccupied, I flushed, picked up my book bag, took my cane down from the hook, and unlatched the door. So many movements unbalanced me, and as I pulled the door open I fell over backward, landing fully clothed on the toilet seat with my legs splayed in front of me: the old beetle-on-its-back routine. Saturday afternoon, the building deserted, I was free to laugh aloud as I wriggled back to my feet, my voice bouncing off the yellowish tiles from all directions. Had anyone been there with me, I'd have been still and faint and hot with chagrin. I decided that it was high time to write the essay.

First, the matter of semantics. I am a cripple. I choose this word to name me. I choose from among several possibilities, the most common of which are "handicapped" and "disabled." I made the choice a number of years ago, without thinking, unaware of my motives for doing so. Even now, I'm not sure what those motives are, but I recognize that they are complex and not entirely flattering. People—crippled or not—wince at the word "cripple," as they do not at "handicapped" or "disabled." Perhaps I want them to wince. I want them to see me as a tough customer, one to whom the fates/gods/viruses have not been kind, but who can face the brutal truth of her existence squarely. As a cripple, I swagger.

But, to be fair to myself, a certain amount of honesty underlies my choice. "Cripple" seems to me a clean word, straightforward and precise. It has an honorable history, having made its first appearance in the Lindisfarne Gospel in the tenth century. As a lover of words, I like the accuracy with which it describes my condition: I have lost the full use of my limbs. "Disabled," by contrast, suggests any incapacity, physical or mental. And I certainly don't like "handicapped," which implies that I have deliberately been put at a disadvantage, by whom I can't imagine (my God is not a Handicapper General), in order to equalize chances in the great race of life. These words seem to me to be moving away from my condition, to be widening the gap between word and reality. Most remote is the recently coined euphemism "differently abled," which partakes of the same semantic hopefulness that transformed countries from "undeveloped" to "underdeveloped," then to "less developed," and finally to "developing" nations. People have continued to starve in those countries during the shift. Some realities do not obey the dictates of language.

Mine is one of them. Whatever you call me, I remain crippled. But I don't care what you call me, so long as it isn't "differently abled," which strikes me as pure verbal garbage designed, by its ability to describe anyone, to describe no one. I subscribe to George Orwell's thesis that "the slovenliness of our language makes it easier for us to have foolish thoughts." And I refuse to participate in the degeneration of the language to the extent that I deny that I have lost anything in the course of this calamitous disease; I refuse to pretend that the only differences between you and me are the various ordinary ones that distinguish any one person from another. But call me "disabled" or "handicapped" if you like. I have long since grown accustomed to them; and if they are vague, at least they hint at the truth. Moreover, I use them myself. Society is no readier to accept crippledness than to accept death, war, sex, sweat, or wrinkles. I would never refer to another person as a cripple. It is the word I use to name only myself.

I haven't always been crippled, a fact for which I am soundly grateful. To be whole of limb is, I know from experience, infinitely more pleasant and useful than to be crippled; and if that knowledge leaves me open to bitterness at my loss, the physical soundness I once enjoyed (though I did not enjoy it half enough) is well worth the occasional stab of regret. Though never any good at sports, I was a normally active child and young adult. I climbed trees, played hopscotch, jumped rope, skated, swam, rode my bicycle, sailed. I despised team sports, spending some of the wretchedest afternoons of my life, sweaty and humiliated, behind a field-hockey stick and under a basketball hoop. I tramped alone for miles along the bridle paths that webbed the woods behind the house I grew up in. I swayed through countless dim hours in the arms of one man or another under the scattered shot of light from mirrored balls, and gyrated through countless more as Tab Hunter and Johnny Mathis gave way to the Rolling Stones, Creedence Clearwater Revival, Cream. I walked down the aisle. I pushed baby carriages, changed tires in the rain, marched for peace.

When I was twenty-eight I started to trip and drop things. What at first seemed my natural clumsiness soon became too pronounced to shrug off. I consulted a neurologist, who told me that I had a brain tumor. A battery of tests, increasingly disagreeable, revealed no tumor. About a year and a half later I developed a blurred spot in one eye. I had, at last, the episodes "disseminated in space and time" requisite for a diagnosis: multiple sclerosis. I have never been sorry for the doctor's initial misdiagnosis, however. For almost a week, until the negative results of the tests were in, I thought that I was going to die right away. Every day for the past nearly ten years, then, has been a kind of gift. I accept all gifts.

Multiple sclerosis is a chronic degenerative disease of the central nervous system, in which the myelin that sheathes the nerves is somehow eaten away and scar tissue forms in its place, interrupting the nerves' signals. During its course, which is unpredictable and uncontrollable, one may lose vision, hearing, speech, the ability to walk, control of bladder and/or bowels, strength in any or all extremities, sensitivity to touch, vibration, and/or pain, potency, coordination of movements—the list of possibilities is lengthy and, yes, horrifying. One may also lose one's sense of humor. That's the easiest to lose and the hardest to survive without.

In the past ten years, I have sustained some of these losses. Characteristic of MS are sudden attacks, called exacerbations, followed by remissions, and these I have not had. Instead, my disease has been slowly progressive. My left leg is now so weak that I walk with the aid of a brace and a cane; and for distances I use an Amigo, a variation on the electric wheelchair that looks rather like an electrified kiddie car. I no longer have much use of my left hand. Now my right side is weakening as well. I still have the blurred spot in my right eye. Overall, though, I've been lucky so far. My world has, of necessity, been circumscribed by my losses, but the terrain left me has been ample enough for me to continue many of the activities that absorb me: writing, teaching, raising children and cats and plants and snakes, reading, speaking publicly about MS and depression, even playing bridge with people patient and honorable enough to let me scatter cards every which way without sneaking a peek.

Lest I begin to sound like Pollyanna, however, let me say that I don't like having MS. I hate it. My life holds realities—harsh ones, some of them—that no right-minded human being ought to accept without grumbling. One of them is fatigue. I know of no one with MS who does not complain of bone-weariness; in a disease that presents an astonishing variety of symptoms, fatigue seems to be a common factor. I wake up in the morning feeling the way most people do at the end of a bad day, and I take it from there. As a result, I spend a lot of time *in extremis* and, impatient with limitation, I tend to ignore my fatigue until my body breaks down in some way and forces rest. Then I miss picnics, dinner parties, poetry readings, the brief visits of old friends from out of town. The offspring of a puritanical tradition of exceptional venerability, I cannot view these lapses without shame. My life often seems a series of small failures to do as I ought.

I lead, on the whole, an ordinary life, probably rather like the one I would have led had I not had MS. I am lucky that my predilections were already solitary, sedentary, and bookish—unlike the world-famous French cellist I have read about, or the young woman I talked with one long afternoon who wanted only to be a jockey. I had just begun graduate school when I found out something was wrong with me, and I have remained, interminably, a graduate student. Perhaps I would not have if I'd thought I had the stamina to return to a full-time job as a technical editor; but I've enjoyed my studies.

In addition to studying, I teach writing courses. I also teach medical students how to give neurological examinations. I pick up freelance editing jobs here and there. I have raised a foster son and sent him into the world, where he has made me two grandbabies, and I am still escorting my daughter and son through adolescence. I go to Mass every Saturday. I am a superb, if messy, cook. I am also an enthusiastic laundress, capable of sorting a hamper full of clothes into five subtly differentiated piles, but a terrible housekeeper. I can do italic writing and, in an emergency, bathe an oil-soaked cat. I play a fiendish game of Scrabble. When I have the time and the money, I like to sit on my front steps with my husband, drinking Amaretto and smoking a cigar, as we imagine our counterparts in Leningrad and make sure that the sun gets down once more behind the sharp childish scrawl of the Tucson Mountains.

This lively plenty has its bleak complement, of course, in all the things I can no longer do. I will never run again, except in dreams, and one day I may have to write that I will never walk again. I like to go camping, but I can't follow George and the children along the trails that wander out of a campsite through the desert or into the mountains. In fact, even on the level I've learned never to check the weather or try to hold a coherent conversation: I need all my attention for my wayward feet. Of late, I have begun to catch myself wondering how people can propel themselves without canes. With only one usable hand, I have to select my clothing with care not so much for style as for ease of ingress and egress, and even so, dressing can be laborious. I can no longer do fine stitchery, pick up babies, play the piano, braid my hair. I am immobilized by acute attacks of depression, which may or may not be physiologically related to MS but are certainly its logical concomitant.

These two elements, the plenty and the privation, are never pure, nor are the delight and wretchedness that accompany them. Almost every pickle that I get into as a result of my weakness and clumsiness—and I get into plenty—is funny as well as maddening and sometimes painful. I recall one May afternoon when a friend and I were going out for a drink after finishing up at school. As we were climbing into opposite sides of my car, chatting, I tripped and fell, flat and hard, onto the asphalt parking lot, my abrupt departure interrupting him in mid-sentence. "Where'd you go?" he called as he came around the back of the car to find me hauling myself up by the door frame. "Are you all right?" Yes, I told him, I was fine, just a bit rattly, and we drove off to find a shady patio and some beer. When I got home an hour or so later, my daughter greeted me with "What have you done to yourself?" I looked down. One elbow of my white turtleneck with the green froggies, one knee of my white trousers, one white kneesock were blood-soaked. We peeled off the clothes and inspected the damage, which was nasty enough but not alarming. That part wasn't funny: The abrasions took a long time to heal, and one got a little infected. Even so, when I think of my friend talking earnestly, suddenly, to the hot thin air while I dropped from his view as though through a trap door, I find the image as silly as something from a Marx Brothers movie.

I may find it easier than other cripples to amuse myself because I live propped by the acceptance and the assistance and, sometimes, the amusement of those around me. Grocery clerks tear my checks out of my checkbook for me, and sales clerks find chairs to put into dressing rooms when I want to try on clothes. The people I work with make sure I teach at times when I am least likely to be fatigued, in places I can get to, with the materials I need. My students, with one anonymous exception (in an end-of-the-semester evaluation), have been unperturbed by my disability. Some even like it. One was immensely cheered by the information that I paint my own fingernails; she decided, she told me, that if I could go to such trouble over fine details, she could keep on writing essays. I suppose I became some sort of bright-fingered muse. She wrote good essays, too.

The most important struts in the framework of my existence, of course, are my husband and children. Dismayingly few marriages survive the MS test, and why should they? Most twenty-two- and nineteen-year-olds, like George and me, can vow in clear conscience, after a childhood of chickenpox and summer colds, to keep one another in sickness and in health so long as they both shall live. Not many are equipped for catastrophe: the dismay, the depression, the extra work, the boredom that a degenerative disease can insinuate into a relationship. And our society, with its emphasis on fun and its association of fun with physical performance, offers little encouragement for a whole spouse to stay with a crippled partner. Children experience similar stresses when faced with a crippled parent, and they are more helpless, since parents and children can't usually get divorced. They hate, of course, to be different from their peers, and the child whose mother is tacking down the aisle of a school auditorium packed with proud parents like a Cape Cod dinghy in a stiff breeze jolly well stands out in a crowd. Deprived of legal divorce, the child can at least deny the mother's disability, even her existence, forgetting to tell her about recitals and PTA meetings, refusing to accompany her to stores or church or the movies, never inviting friends to the house. Many do.

But I've been limping along for ten years now, and so far George and the children are still at my left elbow, holding tight. Anne and Matthew vacuum floors and dust furniture and haul trash and rake up dog droppings and button my cuffs and bake lasagne and Toll House cookies with just enough grumbling so I know that they don't have brain fever. And far from hiding me, they're forever dragging me by racks of fancy clothes or through teeming school corridors, or welcoming gaggles of friends while I'm wandering through the house in Anne's filmy pink babydoll pajamas. George generally calls before he brings someone home, but he does just as many dumb thankless chores as the children. And they all yell at me, laugh at some of my jokes, write me funny letters when we're apart—in short, treat me as an ordinary human being for whom they have some use. I think they like me. Unless they're faking. . . .

Faking. There's the rub. Tugging at the fringes of my consciousness always is the terror that people are kind to me only because I'm a cripple. My mother almost shattered me once, with that instinct mothers have—blind, I think, in this case, but unerring nonetheless—for striking blows along the fault-lines of their children's hearts, by telling me, in an attack on my selfishness, "We all have to make allowances for you, of course, because of the way you are." From the distance of a couple of years, I have to admit that I haven't any idea just what she meant, and I'm not sure that she knew either. She was awfully angry. But at the time, as the words thudded home, I felt my worst fear, suddenly realized. I could bear being called selfish: I am. But I couldn't bear the corroboration that those around me were doing in fact what I'd always suspected them of doing, professing fondness while silently putting up with me because of the way I am. A cripple. I've been a little cracked ever since.

Along with this fear that people are secretly accepting shoddy goods comes a relentless pressure to please—to prove myself worth the burdens I impose, I guess, or to build a substantial account of goodwill against which I may write drafts in times of need. Part of the pressure arises from social expectations. In our society, anyone who deviates from the norm had better find some way to compensate. Like fat people, who are expected to be jolly, cripples must bear their lot meekly and cheerfully. A grumpy cripple isn't playing by the rules. And much of the pressure is self-generated. Early on I vowed that, if I had to have MS, by God I was going to do it well. This is a class act, ladies and gentlemen. No tears, no recriminations, no faint-heartedness.

One way and another, then, I wind up feeling like Tiny Tim, peering over the edge of the table at the Christmas goose, waving my crutch, piping down God's blessing on us all. Only sometimes I don't want to play Tiny Tim. I'd rather be Caliban, a most scurvy monster. Fortunately, at home no one much cares whether I'm a good cripple or a bad cripple as long as I make vichyssoise with fair regularity. One evening several years ago, Anne was reading at the dining-room table while I cooked dinner. As I opened a can of tomatoes, the can slipped in my left hand and juice spattered me and the counter with bloody spots. Fatigued and infuriated, I bellowed, "I'm so sick of being crippled!" Anne glanced at me over the top of her book. "There now," she said, "do you feel better?" "Yes," I said, "yes, I do." She went back to her reading. I felt better. That's about all the attention my scurviness ever gets.

Because I hate being crippled, I sometimes hate myself for being a cripple. Over the years I have come to expect—even accept—attacks of violent self-loathing. Luckily, in general our society no longer connects deformity and disease directly with evil (though a charismatic once told me that I have MS because a devil is in me) and so I'm allowed to move largely at will, even among small children. But I'm not sure that this revision of attitude has been particularly helpful. Physical imperfection, even freed of moral disapprobation, still defies and violates the ideal, especially for women, whose confinement in their bodies as objects of desire is far from over. Each age, of course, has its ideal, and I doubt that ours is any better or worse than any other. Today's ideal woman, who lives on the glossy pages of dozens of magazines, seems to be between the ages of eighteen and twenty-five; her hair has body, her teeth flash white, her breath smells minty, her underarms are dry; she has a career but is still a fabulous cook, especially of meals that take less than twenty minutes to prepare; she does not ordinarily appear to have a husband or children; she is trim and deeply tanned; she jogs, swims, plays tennis, rides a bicycle, sails, but does not bowl; she travels widely, even to out-of-the-way places like Finland and Samoa, always in the company of the ideal man, who possesses a nearly identical set of characteristics. There are a few exceptions. Though usually white and often blonde, she may be black, Hispanic, Asian, or Native American, so long as she is unusually sleek. She may be old, provided she is selling a laxative or is Lauren Bacall. If she is selling a detergent, she may be married and have a flock of strikingly messy children. But she is never a cripple.

Like many women I know, I have always had an uneasy relationship with my body. I was not a popular child, largely, I think now, because I was peculiar: intelligent, intense, moody, shy, given to unexpected actions and inexplicable notions and emotions. But as I entered adolescence, I believed myself unpopular because I was homely: my breasts too flat, my mouth too wide, my hips too narrow, my clothing never quite right in fit or style. I was not, in fact, particularly ugly, old photographs inform me, though I was well off the ideal; but I carried this sense of self-alienation with me into adulthood, where it regenerated in response to the depredations of MS. Even with my brace I walk with a limp so pronounced that, seeing myself on the videotape of a television program on the disabled, I couldn't believe that anything but an inchworm could make progress humping along like that. My shoulders droop and my pelvis thrusts forward as I try to balance myself upright, throwing my frame into a bony S. As a result of contractures, one shoulder is higher than the other and I carry one arm bent in front of me, the fingers curled into a claw. My left arm and leg have wasted into pipe-stems, and I try always to keep them covered. When I think about how my body must look to others, especially to men, to whom I have been trained to display myself, I feel ludicrous, even loathsome.

At my age, however, I don't spend much time thinking about my appearance. The burning egocentricity of adolescence, which assures one that all the world is looking all the time, has passed, thank God, and I'm generally too caught up in what I'm doing to step back, as I used to, and watch myself as though upon a stage. I'm also too old to believe in the accuracy of self-image. I know that I'm not a hideous crone, that in fact, when I'm rested, well dressed, and well made up, I look fine. The self-loathing I feel is neither physically nor intellectually substantial. What I hate is not me but a disease.

I am not a disease.

And a disease is not—at least not singlehandedly—going to determine who I am, though at first it seemed to be going to. Adjusting to a chronic incurable illness, I have moved through a process similar to that outlined by Elizabeth Kübler-Ross in *On Death and Dying.* The major difference—and it is far more significant than most people recognize—is that I can't be sure of the outcome, as the terminally ill cancer patient can. Research studies indicate that, with proper medical care, I may achieve a "normal" life span. And in our society, with its vision of death as the ultimate evil, worse even than decrepitude, the response to such news is, "Oh well, at least you're not going to *die.*" Are there worse things than dying? I think that there may be.

I think of two women I know, both with MS, both enough older than I to have served me as models. One took to her bed several years ago and has been there ever since. Although she can sit in a high-backed wheelchair, because she is incontinent she refuses to go out at all, even though incontinence pants, which are readily available at any pharmacy, could protect her from embarrassment. Instead, she stays at home and insists that her husband, a small quiet man, a retired civil servant, stay there with her except for a quick weekly foray to the supermarket. The other woman, whose illness was diagnosed when she was eighteen, a nursing student engaged to a young doctor, finished her training, married her doctor, accompanied him to Germany when he was in the service, bore three sons and a daughter, now grown and gone. When she can, she travels with her husband; she plays bridge, embroiders, swims regularly; she works, like me, as a symptomatic-patient instructor of medical students in neurology. Guess which woman I hope to be.

At the beginning, I thought about having MS almost incessantly. And because of the unpredictable course of the disease, my thoughts were always terrified. Each night I'd get into bed wondering whether I'd get out again the next morning, whether I'd be able to see, to speak, to hold a pen between my fingers. Knowing that the day might come when I'd be physically incapable of killing myself, I thought perhaps I ought to do so right away, while I still had the strength. Gradually I came to understand that the Nancy who might one day lie inert under a bedsheet, arms and legs paralyzed, unable to feed or bathe herself, unable to reach out for a gun, a bottle of pills, was not the Nancy I was at present, and that I could not presume to make decisions for that future Nancy, who might well not want in the least to die. Now the only provision I've made for the future Nancy is that when the time comes—and it is likely to come in the form of pneumonia, friend to the weak and the old—I am not to be treated with machines and medications. If she is unable to communicate by then, I hope she will be satisfied with these terms.

Thinking all the time about having MS grew tiresome and intrusive, especially in the large and tragic mode in which I was accustomed to considering my plight. Months and even years went by without catastrophe (at least without one related to MS), and really I was awfully busy, what with George and children and snakes and students and poems, and I hadn't the time, let alone the inclination, to devote myself to being a disease. Too, the richer my life became, the funnier it seemed, as though there were some connection between largesse and laughter, and so my tragic stance began to waver until, even with the aid of a brace and a cane, I couldn't hold it for very long at a time.

After several years I was satisfied with my adjustment. I had suffered my grief and fury and terror, I thought, but now I was at ease with my lot. Then one summer day I set out with George and the children across the desert for a vacation in California. Part way to Yuma I became aware that my right leg felt funny. "I think I've had an exacerbation," I told George. "What shall we do?" he asked. "I think we'd better get the hell to California," I said, "because I don't know whether I'll ever make it again." So we went on to San Diego and then to Orange, up the Pacific Coast Highway to Santa Cruz, across to Yosemite, down to Sequoia and Joshua Tree, and so back over the desert to home. It was a fine two-week trip, filled with friends and fair weather, and I wouldn't have missed it for the world, though I did in fact make it back to California two years later. Nor would there have been any point in missing it, since in MS, once the symptoms have appeared, the neurological damage has been done, and there's no way to predict or prevent that damage.

The incident spoiled my self-satisfaction, however. It renewed my grief and fury and terror, and I learned that one never finishes adjusting to MS. I don't know now why I thought one would. One does not, after all, finish adjusting to life, and MS is simply a fact of my life—not my favorite fact, of course—but as ordinary as my nose and my tropical fish and my yellow Mazda station wagon. It may at any time get worse, but no amount of worry or anticipation can prepare me for a new loss. My life is a lesson in losses. I learn one at a time.

And I had best be patient in the learning, since I'll have to do it like it or not. As any rock fan knows, you can't always get what you want. Particularly when you have MS. You can't for example, get cured. In recent years researchers and the organizations that fund research have started to pay MS some attention even though it isn't fatal; perhaps they have begun to see that life is something other than a quantitative phenomenon, that one may be very much alive for a very long time in a life that isn't worth living. The researchers have made some progress toward understanding the mechanism of the disease: It may well be an autoimmune reaction triggered by a slow-acting virus. But they are nowhere near its prevention, control, or cure. And most of us want to be cured. Some, unable to accept incurability, grasp at one treatment after another, no matter how bizarre: megavitamin therapy, gluten-free diet, injections of cobra venom, hypothermal suits, lymphocytopharesis, hyperbaric chambers. Many treatments are probably harmless enough, but none are curative.

The absence of a cure often makes MS patients bitter toward their doctors. Doctors are, after all, the priests of modern society, the new shamans, whose business is to heal, and many an MS patient roves from one to another, searching for the "good" doctor who will make him well. Doctors too think of themselves as healers, and for this reason many have trouble dealing with MS patients, whose disease in its intransigence defeats their aims and mocks their skills. Too few doctors, it is true, treat their patients as whole human beings, but the reverse is also true. I have always tried to be gentle with my doctors, who often have more at stake in terms of ego than I do. I may be frustrated, maddened, depressed by the incurability of my disease, but I am not diminished by it, and they are. When I push myself up from my seat in the waiting room and stumble toward them, I incarnate the limitation of their powers. The least I can do is refuse to press on their tenderest spots.

This gentleness is part of the reason that I'm not sorry to be a cripple. I didn't have it before. Perhaps I'd have developed it anyway—how could I know such a thing?—and I wish I had more of it, but I'm glad of what I have. It has opened and enriched my life enormously, this sense that my frailty and need must be mirrored in others, that in searching for and shaping a stable core in a life wrenched by change and loss, change and loss, I must recognize the same process, under individual conditions, in the lives around me. I do not deprecate such knowledge, however I've come by it.

All the same, if a cure were found, would I take it? In a minute. I may be a cripple, but I'm only occasionally a loony and never a saint. Anyway, in my brand of theology God doesn't give bonus points for a limp. I'd take a cure; I just don't need one. A friend who also has MS startled me once by asking, "Do you ever say to yourself, 'Why me, Lord?' " "No, Michael, I don't," I told him, "because whenever I try, the only response I can think of is 'Why not?' " If I could make a cosmic deal, who would I put in my place? What in my life would I give up in exchange for sound limbs and a thrilling rush of energy? No one. Nothing. I might as well do the job myself. Now that I'm getting the hang of it.

On Not Liking Sex

"The other day, sitting in a tweed chair with my knees crossed, drinking a cup of coffee and smoking a cigarette, I looked straight at my therapist and said, 'I don't like sex.' I have known this man for years now. I have told him that I don't like my husband, my children, my parents, my students, my life. I may even have said at some time, 'I don't like sex very much.' But the difference between not liking sex very much and not liking sex is vast, vaster even than the Catholic Church's gulf between salvation and damnation, because there's no limbo, no purgatory. An irony here: For in another age (perhaps in this age within the bosom of the Holy Mother Church) I would be the woman whose price is above rubies, pure and virtuous, purity and virtue having always attached themselves, at least for women, to the matter of sex. As it is, I am, in my metaphor, one of the damned. My therapist has a homelier metaphor. I have, he says, what our society considers 'the worst wart.' In 1981 in the United States of America one cannot fail to like sex. It's not normal. It's not nice."

This paragraph opened a brief essay I wrote a couple of years ago entitled "On Not Liking Sex." The essay, which I have preserved here in quotation marks, was a brittle, glittery piece, a kind of spun confection of the verbal play I'd like to engage in at cocktail parties but can muster only at a solitary desk with a legal-size yellow pad in front of me. It was, in fact, as you can see if you read it straight through, cocktail party chatter. And yet it was true, insofar as any truth can be translated into words. That is, it said some things, and suggested others, about me and the times I live in which were accurate enough as far as they went.

But they certainly didn't go very far. Hardly to the end of the block. Certainly not across the street. This essay is an almost perfect example of a phenomenon I've only recently become aware of, though clearly at a deeper level I've understood its workings for a very long time, a kind of pretense at serious writing which I use to keep busy and out of trouble: the kind of trouble you get when you run smack into an idea so significant and powerful that the impact jars you to the bone. It's a way of staying out of the traffic. It is not babble, and it is not easy. On the contrary, it requires painstakingly chosen diction, deliberately controlled syntax, and seamless organization. A rough spot is a trouble spot, a split, a crack, out of which something dreadful (probably black, probably with a grin) may leap and squash you flat.

If this essay was an exercise in making careful statements that would ensure that I never said what I really had to say, then what did I have to say? I don't know. If I'd known then, I couldn't have written such a piece in the first place. And the only progress I've made since then is to have gained a little courage in the face of things that leap out of cracks in the pavement. If I look at the essay again closely, if I listen for the resonances among the words with the not-yet-words, perhaps I can discover some portion of the significance—for the woman just turned forty in the 1980s in the United States of America—of not liking sex.

The title and the first paragraph, by using words as though, like algebraic notation, they had fixed meanings in the context of a given problem, claim to have signified an attitude they have in fact obscured. Even if *on* and *not* may be allowed a certain fixity as they function here, *liking* and *sex* may not. *Sex,* in its most general sense, is simply the way one is: male or female just as black or brown, blue- or hazel-eyed, long- or stubby-fingered, able or not to curl one's tongue into a tube. The genes take care of it. One may dislike one's sex, apparently, just as my daughter dislikes her nose, which is round and tends toward rosy under the sun; some people, thanks to the technological genius of modern medicine, even change theirs. But I like my sex. I suffer from penis envy, of course, to the extent that freedom and privilege have attached themselves to this fleshy sign; I've never wished for the actual appendage, however, except on long car trips through sparsely populated areas. In fact, looked at this way, *not liking sex* doesn't make sense to me at all, any more than do *having sex, wanting sex, demanding sex, refusing sex.* Such phrases clarify the specialized use of the word as shorthand for sexual activity, particularly sexual intercourse.

So I don't like sexual activity. But *like* can mean both to take pleasure in, enjoy, and to wish to have, want; and wanting something seems to me quite a different matter from enjoying it. The former is volitional, a reaching out for experience, whereas the latter is a response to an experience (whether sought for or not) already in progress. In these terms I can and often do enjoy sex. But I do not necessarily want to engage in sexual activity even though I may enjoy doing so.

"The human psyche being the squirmy creature that it is, I have trouble pinning down my objections to sex. I do not seem to object to the act itself which, if I can bring myself to commit it, I like very well. I object to the idea. My objections are undoubtedly, in part, Puritanical. Not for nothing did John Howland, Stephen Hopkins, Thomas Rogers, and Elder William Brewster brings on the Mayflower the seed that would one day bloom in me. If it feels good, it's bad. Sex feels good. My objections may also be aesthetic: It's a sweaty, slimy business. Certainly they are mythic, Eros and Thanatos colliding in the orgasm to explode the frail self back into the atoms of the universe. Love is Death."

*   *   *

The human psyche squirms indeed, especially when it is striving to distance itself
from its desires by creating platonic distinctions between things in themselves and
the ideas of things. I don't object to the idea of sex. In fact, I don't feel any particular
response one way or the other to the idea of sex. Sex for me as for most, I should
think, is not ideational but sensual, and it is this distinction that gives me trouble,
a distinction that resembles that between wanting and enjoying. I don't object to
the *idea* of sex: I object to the *sense* of sex. An act is a sign. Directly apprehended,
it has always at least one meaning and usually a multiplicity of meanings. These I
must sort out—their implications, their resonances—in order to understand how I,
with a singularly human perversity, can not want what I enjoy.

Puritanism, aesthetics, and myth all play a part in this response, no doubt, though
the reference to the Mayflower is misleading (the Pilgrims were not Puritans, though
many of their descendants were), and as far as I know, the Puritans did not prohibit
the sex act—no matter what it felt like—so long as it was confined to the marriage
bed. The kind of puritanism that has dogged me is more diffuse than that of my
foremothers, perhaps the inevitable legacy of their hard-scrabble existence in tiny
communities clinging to the flinty, bitter-wintered New England coast, no longer
a religion but still a code of conduct, close-mouthed, grudging of joy, quick to judge
and reject. We conducted ourselves at all levels with restraint. Our disapproval of
Catholics was not particularly theological; rather, we thought them primitive, childishly taken with display, with their candles and crosses and croziers, play-acting at
religion. We painted our houses white with black or green shutters, grey with blue
shutters, sometimes soft yellow or dark brown, and we shuddered at the pink and
turquoise and lime green on the little capes and ranches that belonged, we assumed,
to the Italians. When we met, we greeted one another with a nod, perhaps a small
smile, a few words, a firm handshake, even a kiss on the cheek, depending on the
degree of our intimacy, but we did not fall into each other's arms with loud
smackings, everybody jabbering at once. As a child I was given to fits of weeping
and outbursts of delight which to this day my mother refers to with a sigh as
"Nancy's dramatics"; I do not, of course, have them now.

Here is the real aesthetics of the matter: the refinement of decoration and gesture
to a state so etiolated that voices pierce, perfumes smother, colors clash and scream
and shout. I still dislike wearing red and certain shades of pink and orange. The
entire sensory world impinges—presses, pinches, pummels—unless one keeps a
distance. Touch comes, eventually, to burn. Sex isn't bad so much because it feels
good as because it's poor form—the kind of rowdy, riotous behavior one squelches
in children as they become young ladies (honest to God, I was never permitted to
refer to female human beings as women but only as ladies) and gentlemen. Sex is
indecorous.

As for the sweat and slime, the basis for this objection strikes me as more medical
than aesthetic. After all, one can get a good deal grubbier on a hike up a small
mountain, which is just good clean fun. But the body itself is not clean. It is,
according to pathologists like my ancestor Rudolf Virchow, a veritable pesthouse.
I grew up knowing that my breath was pestilent ("cover your mouth when you
sneeze"), that my mouth was pestilent ("don't kiss me—you've got a cold"). And
then along came men, themselves crawling with germs, who breathed on me, who

wanted to put their mouths on mine and make me sick. Rudolf may have done wonders for German public health, but he sure put a kink in my private sex life. Oddly enough, this phobia of germs did not include my genitalia, perhaps because they lay untouched and unpondered until long after it had been formed. Nowadays, with the threat of venereal disease widely publicized, I don't suppose one can be so insouciant. The germs lurk at every orifice, and sex is simply contrary to good sanitary practices.

Poor sanitary practices may give you a cold or a stomach flu or herpes, but they are not, in Tucson in 1983, likely to do you in. The equation of sex with death is of another order altogether, though not the less dreadful for not being literal. As late as the Renaissance *to die* was used as we use *to come* to signify orgasm; and although we have abandoned the explicit connection, we have not lost the construct that underlies it. Orgasm shares, briefly, the characteristics we imagine death to have, the annihilation (or at least the transmogrification) of consciousness, the extinction of the *I* that forms and controls being. The loss of my hard-won identity, even for an instant, risks forfeiture of self: not perhaps the death that ends in the coffin but certainly the death that ends in the cell: I am afraid of going away and never coming back.

"But most strongly, my objections are what I reluctantly term 'political.' My reluctance stems from the sense that 'political' in this context implies the kind of radical lesbianism that suggests that medical technology is sufficiently advanced to permit the elimination of the male entirely. I learned, in one of the most poignant affairs of my life, that I am not lesbian. Nor am I even a good feminist, since I seldom think abstractly and tend to run principles together like the paints on a sloppy artist's palette, the results being colorful but hardly coherent. No, when I say 'political,' I mean something purely personal governing the nature of the relationship between me and a given man. In this sense, sex is a political act. In it, I lose power, through submission or, in one instance, through force. In either case, my integrity is violated; I become possessed."

Here's the heart of the matter—politics—and I've dashed it off and done it up with ribbons of lesbianism and feminism so that the plain package hardly shows. True, I'm not lesbian, but thanks to the fundamental heterosexual bias of our culture no one would be likely to assume that I was. And I am, in fact, a perfectly good if unsystematic feminist. Who in my audience, I wonder, was I worried about when I made that self-deprecatory moue, as if to say, "Don't expect too much of me; I'm just a nonradical heterosexual little woman, a bit daffy perhaps, but harmless"? And what the hell (now that I've got the ribbons off) is in the box that made me wrap it up so tight?

Politics. Power. Submission. Force. Violation. Possession. Sex is not merely a political act; it is an act of war. And no act is ever "purely personal." It is a nexus that accretes out of earlier and other acts older than memory, older than dreams: the exchange of women, along with goods, gestures, and words, in the creation of allies; the ascription to women of all that lurks terrible in the darkened brain; the protection and penetration of the maidenhead in rituals for ensuring paternity and perpetuating lineage; the conscription of women's sons for the destruction of human beings, of women's daughters for their reproduction; enforcement of silence; theft of subjectivity; immurement; death. If I think that what I do, in or out of bed, originates in me, I am a much madder woman that I believe myself to be. I am no original but simply a locus of language in a space and time that permits one—in politics as in sex—to fuck or get fucked. Aggression is the germ in all the words.

From such an angle, sex is always rape, and indeed I tangle the two words at the level just below articulation. Perhaps I do so because my first sexual intercourse was a rape. At least it occurred in the safety of my own bed by someone I knew intimately, so that although I was furious, I was never in fear for my life. We were both nineteen, had been high-school sweethearts grown apart, and he had come to spend a weekend at the Farm, where I was working as a mother's helper for the summer. We spent the evening deep in conversation, I remember, and after I went to bed, he came into my room, jumped on top of me, deflowered me, and went away again. I don't believe we ever exchanged a word or an embrace. I felt some pain, and in the morning I found blood on my thighs and on the sheets, which I had secretly to wash, so I know that all of this really happened, but I never permitted myself the least feeling about it, not as much as I might have given a nightmare. I *knew* that I was furious, but I *felt* nothing. I don't know what response he expected, but he got none at all. He left the next day, without my ever having spoken to him, and we never met again.

Nor do I know what effect he intended his act to have. I'm sure that he was marking me, for we grew up at the tail end of the time when virginity had real significance, and in defloration he claimed me in only a slightly more subtle manner than incising his initials into some hidden area of my flesh. He knew that I was in love with another man, that I planned to be married within a year, and for a long time I believed that he was trying, through some sort of magical thinking, to force me to marry him instead. We really did believe that a woman belonged to the man who first "had" her. But now I think that he wasn't marking me for himself so much as spoiling me for George. Whatever its true interpretation, his act makes clear my absence from the transaction. The business was between him and George, the item of exchange one tarnished coin.

To sense myself such a cipher robs me of power. In sex, as in many other instances, I feel powerless. Part of this feeling arises from the fact that, as new symptoms of multiple sclerosis appear and worsen, my power literally drains away. But to what extent is multiple sclerosis merely the physical inscription of my way of being in the world? In sex, as in the rest of my life, I am acted upon. I am the object, not the agent. I live in the passive voice. The phallus penetrates me; I do not surround, engulf, incorporate the phallus. No wonder Caleb raped me. Rape was his only grammatical option.

Thus, I see that in a queer and cruel way I raped him by forcing him to rape me. I always made myself the object of his desire. How many times, I remember now, we came to the brink of intercourse, and always at the last I turned him away, pretending that I couldn't overcome my moral scruples. What I really couldn't overcome was a barrier so ludicrous that I don't expect you to believe it: my underpants. I couldn't figure out how to get rid of them. The women in films and romantic novels, where I'd gotten my impressions of the mechanics of intercourse, didn't struggle with underpants. Did I think they just melted away? After all, I took my underpants off every day as matter-of-factly as I kicked them under the bed to drive my mother wild with despair over my inability to keep some man a decent house. Why then could I not just take them off an extra time? The gesture seemed too overt, too clumsy and pedestrian for the occasion. I couldn't bear to look a fool. So I lay in bondage to the concept of woman as image, not agent, kept a virgin till I was nineteen by Carter Lollipop Pants, red ones and navy ones, their combed cotton grim as iron through my crotch. But for Caleb, who knew nothing of my quandary, I was withholding a treasure that must have seemed of great worth, since I guarded it so jealously. I think I can understand his fury when I threatened to give it to someone else.

Ah, but I'm so old now. I can't blame myself for having been a fool, or him for having believed me a pearl of great price instead of a human being, for whatever she was worth. We were both too young to give tongue to the grammar of our intercourse. All I can do now is use the leverage of my understanding to pry open the box I have stripped and look at the contents squarely. In sex, that political act, I lose power because I have still not learned what it might be and how to claim it.

"For this reason, I have preferred casual lovers to a permanent, long-term partner. They have fewer expectations, thus minimizing possession and obligation. Less is at stake. With them, I can concentrate on the act itself without worrying about its implications. They will be gone long before they learn enough about me to threaten my privacy or come to consider sexual access a right or even a privilege. But even lovers, the romantic ones at least, are risky. They can be more interested in being in love than in bed. My latest lover pitched me out on the grounds that he wasn't in love with me (don't ask me why he took me in—life is complicated enough as it is); and with the irony that won't work in fiction but does splendidly in life, I had fallen in love with him, only the second time that I have done so and the only time that doing so was a mistake. The experience was so nearly disastrous that I learned precipitously the lesson that had long been floating just outside the periphery of my vision: Celibacy is power."

An agoraphobe, a depressive, I have long since learned that avoidance is the most comfortable way to cope with situations that make me uneasy, and God knows sex makes me uneasy. In the playfulness of the opening of a sexual relationship, the issue of power is eclipsed by curiosity, exhilaration, voluptuousness. I find my delight in the process chronicled in my journal: "I sit beside Richard. It is terribly hot—I can feel the steam from both our bodies. We play the touching game—arms touch, knees brush, shoulders press together—at first by 'accident,' testing for response, then deliberately. I love this game, as often as I've played it and as silly as it is; it has a kind of rhythm and elegance when played properly, with good humor, without haste. Richard is very good at it. When, at one point, we have looked at one another for a long moment, he smiles a little and I say, 'What?' He starts to say something, then breaks off: 'You know.' I laugh and say, 'I've been wondering what would happen if I leaned over and kissed you.' It is a dumb idea—I don't know most of the people there very well, but Richard does, and they all know that I'm married. 'I think we'd better wait to do that on our own,' he replies. 'Soon.' 'Yes,' I say, 'Yes, soon.' If I hadn't driven my own car, it could have been right then. Wasn't. The kiss is yet to come."

But in truth I do not like sex, even in brief affairs. In the rush of excitement I think I do, but afterwards I am always embarrassed by it. If I could stay balanced in the delicious vertigo of flirtation, I might not feel ashamed, but I can't. I always want to tumble dizzily into bed. And after I've been there, even once, my privacy has been not merely threatened but ruptured. My privacy I carry around me as a bubble of space. Quite literally. I hate to be touched. I hate to be known. If the bubble is pricked, I may disintegrate, leaking out vaporously and vanishing on the wind. The man who has even once seen me up close, naked and transported, knows more about me than I can bear for him to know. For this reason, I have not, in fact, preferred casual lovers to a permanent, long-term partner; if I had, I wouldn't still be married after twenty years. I have taken a casual lover every now and then in the hope that I can reduce sex to pure, unfreighted fun; but the baggage always catches up with me.

One of the cases, of course, carries love. Lovers and husbands alike are risky to a woman who cannot bear to be loved any more than to be touched. I can feel love creep around me, pat me with soft fingers, and I stiffen and struggle for breath. By contrast, I quite readily fall in love and have loved, in some way, all but one of the men I've slept with. So what all the bobbing and weaving about my "latest lover" might mean I'm not sure. I hadn't, at the time I wrote the essay, got over him, and my immediate judgment now is that one oughtn't to try to write the truth while in the kind of turmoil that at that time was threatening my sanity and therefore my life. But on second thought I see that here are simply two truths. I wrote the truth when I said that I'd fallen in love with only two lovers in my life, though I can't think now who I had in mind; I write the truth when I say that I've fallen in love with all but one. Quod scripsi, scripsi. Anyway, I must have learned some lesson from the bitterness the last one brought me, for I have not taken another.

All the same, celibacy is not power. Celibacy is celibacy: the withholding of oneself from sexual union. When it is actively chosen as a means of redirecting one's attention, as it is by some religious, it may both reflect and confer personal power. But when it is clutched at as a means of disengaging oneself from the tentacles of human conflict, it is simply one more technique for avoiding distress. As I stay at home to avoid agoraphobic attacks, I stay out of bed to avoid claustrophobic ones. I am celibate not for the love of God but for the fear of love.

"Avoiding sex altogether is not difficult. You must simply rent a tiny apartment, large enough only for yourself and possibly a very small black cat, and let no one into it. If you want friends, meet them at their houses, if they'll have you, at bars and restaurants, at art galleries, poetry readings, concerts. But don't take them home with you. Keep your space inviolate. During attacks of loneliness and desire, smoke cigarettes. Drink Amaretto. Throw the I Ching. Write essays. Letting someone into your space is tantamount to letting him between your legs, and more dangerous, since you risk his touching the inner workings of your life, not merely your body. Ask him if he wouldn't rather drive into the country for a picnic."

* * *

This advice is sound. I have tested all of it. Then I swallowed a handful of Elavil one Hallowe'en and almost succeeded in avoiding sex altogether.

"All this I have learned. What I haven't learned is what to do with the grief and guilt that not liking sex inevitably arouses. The grief is so protean and private that I will not attempt to articulate it. But the guilt is a decidedly public matter, since it could not exist—not in its present form anyway—in the absence of post-Freudian social pressure to regard sex as the primary source not of joy (I doubt that contemporary society knows much about joy) but of satisfaction. If I don't like sex, I am abnormal, repressed, pathetic, sick—the labels vary but the significance is consistent—I do not belong in the ranks of healthy human beings, health requiring as one of its terms sexual activity and fulfillment."

By separating out grief from the complex of responses I feel to not wanting sex, and by tying it off as a "private" matter, I hoped perhaps that, like a vestigial finger or toe, it would drop away. But the dissociation is not authentic, because in fact all my responses are private insofar as the construct they form is my peculiar *I*, and all are public insofar as that *I* is a linguistic product spoken by a patriarchal culture that insists that my God-created function is to rejoice, through my person, the heart of a man. Moreover, failure to do so results not in guilt, as I have stated it, but in shame, which is a truly protean (and, say some feminists, distinctively feminine) emotion, pervasive and inexpiable. About guilt one can do something: Like a wound in the flesh, with proper cleansing it will heal, the scar, however twisted and lumpy, proof against infection. Shame, like the vaginal wound always open to invasion, is an inoperable state. My tongue has given me these distinctions. With it I must acknowledge my shame.

Shamelessness, like shame, is not a masculine condition. That is, there is no *shameless man* as there is a *shameless woman* or, as my grandmother used to say, a *shameless hussy*. A man without shame is in general assumed simply to have done nothing he need feel guilty about. A woman without shame is a strumpet, a trollop, a whore, a witch. The connotations have been, immemorially, sexual. Here is the thirteenth-century author of the *Ancrene Riwle*, a priest instructing three anchoresses in the correct manner of confession: "A woman will say, 'I have been foolish' or 'I had a lover,' whereas she should confess, 'I am a stud mare, a stinking whore.' " And somewhat later, in the *Malleus Maleficarum*, a warning to Inquisitors: "All witchcraft comes from carnal Lust which is in Women insatiable." My sexuality has been the single most powerful disruptive force mankind has ever perceived, and its repression has been the work of centuries.

Now, suddenly, the message has changed. Now, after ages of covering my face and my genitals—St. Paul's veil over my hair, my breasts bound, my waist girded in whalebone, my face masked with kohl and rouge, my length swathed in white cambric pierced by a lace-edged buttonhole through which to guide the erect penis to my hidden treasure—I am supposed to strip to the skin and spread my legs and strive for multiple orgasm.

Knowing what The Fathers have given me to know of the dangers of female sexuality, how could I dare?

"If I got this message from one person at a time, I might be able to deal with it with rationality, distance, even amusement. But I get it impersonally, from all sides, in a barrage so relentless that the wonder is that I survive my guilt, let alone cope with it. I get the message from the bookshelves, where I find not only *The Joy of Sex* but also *More Joy of Sex*, written by a man whose very name promises physical contentment. (I have read some of these books. They contain many instructions on how to do it well. I know how to do it well. I just don't know whether I want to do it at all.) The message comes with my jeans, which I may buy no longer merely for durability and comfort but for the ache they will create in some man's crotch. It foams in my toothpaste, my bath soap, even my dish detergent. It follows me through the aisles of the supermarket and the drugstore. It ridicules my breastless body, my greying hair."

Or has the message really changed? The body swaddled has become the body naked but it is, all the same, the female body, artifice of desire, still inscribed after stripping with the marks of straps cut into the shoulders, underwires into the breasts, zipper into the belly, squeezed and shaved and deodorized until it is shapely and sanitary enough to arouse no dread of its subjective possibilities. The mechanics of its eroticism have been altered so that, instead of receiving male desire as a patient vessel, it is supposed to validate male performance by resonating when it is played upon. Nonetheless, it remains a thing, alien, "other," as Simone de Beauvoir has pointed out, to the man who dreams of it—and also to the woman who wears it, sculpturing it to the specifications of the male-dominated advertising, publishing, fashion, and cosmetic industries.

An object does not know its own value. Even a sentient being, made into an object, will feel uncertain of her worth except as it is measured by the standards of the agora, the market place, which will reflect whatever male fantasies about women are current. Thanks to astonishing technological advances in the broadcasting of these standards, almost everyone in the world knows what they are and can weigh his object or her self against them, no matter how bizarre the means for their attainment may be. Somewhere I read that it takes the concerted pushing and pulling of three people to get a high-fashion model zipped into her jeans and propped into position for photographing. We all see the photographs, though not the three laborers behind them, and believe that the ideal woman looks like that. Thus a standard has been fixed, and most of us, lacking the appropriate sturdy personnel, won't meet it.

Through such manipulation I have learned to despise my body. I have, perhaps, more reason than most for doing so, since my body is not merely aging but also crippled. On the fair market, its value is slipping daily as the musculature twists and atrophies, the digestive system grinds spasmodically, the vision blurs, the gait lurches and stumbles. But long before I knew I had multiple sclerosis, I hadn't much use for it. Nor have I had much use for the man who desires it. He lacks taste, it seems to me: the kind of man who prefers formica to teak, Melmac to Limoges, canned clam chowder to bouillabaisse. Who wants to have sex with a man who can't do better than you?

"Were I living in the Middle Ages, my difficulty could be quickly solved. I would become an anchoress, calling from my cell, 'And all shall be well, and all manner of thing shall be well.' God would love me. My fellow creatures would venerate me. But the wheel has turned and tipped me into a time when God has been dead for a century and my fellow creatures are likely to find me more pitiable than venerable. I shall no doubt be lonelier than any anchoress.

Nonetheless, my bed will stay narrow."

I love closure. Especially in any kind of writing. I like to tie off the tale with some statement that sounds as though nothing further can be said. Never mind the Princess's hysterical weeping on the morning after her wedding night, her later infidelities, the first son's cleft palate, the Prince's untimely death during an ill-advised raid on a neighboring kingdom, the old King's driveling madness: They lived happily ever after, or, if the tale is a modern one like mine, unhappily ever after. But their development ceased. I love closure enough to pretend that quick resolution lies along the length of a cell (in which I might prostrate myself praying not "All shall be well" but "I am a stud mare, a stinking whore"), enough to believe that virtue lies easy in a narrow bed. True, at the time I wrote the essay I was sleeping alone in a narrow bed, but it's widened again now to queen size, with George in one half, or sometimes two thirds, and often Vanessa Bell and Lionel Tigress too.

My sexuality is too complicated a text to be truncated neatly at any point. What has woven it together until now, I see, to prevent it from being a mere tangle of random terror and revulsion, has been my coherent inverse equation of autonomy with physical violation. Such a connection is predicated upon the denial of my own subjectivity in sexual experience. Afraid of being reduced by another to an object, I have persisted in seeing myself as such. Why did I lie, limp as a doll, while Caleb butted at me? Why didn't I writhe, scratch, bite? Why didn't I at least give him a thorough tongue-lashing the next morning before he left my life forever? Over and over I have demanded that I be raped and have then despised both the rapist and myself.

I understand now some of the teachings that helped me compose such a tale of invasion, illness, self-immolation. And I will not close it off with an *ever after,* happy or unhappy. Tomorrow the Princess gets out of bed again: She washes her hair, drinks her coffee, scribbles some pages, tells a joke to her son, bakes a spinach quiche. And the day after. And the day after that. All the while she is telling herself a story. In it, she is aging now, and she drags one foot behind her when she walks. These are changes she can scrutinize in her mirror. They tell her that the true texts are the ones that do not end but revolve and reflect and spin out new constellations of meaning day after day, page after page, joke after joke, quiche after quiche. She has been learning much about vision and revision. She has been learning much about forgiveness. In this story, she is the writer of essays. She has a black typewriter and several reams of paper. One day, she thinks, she could find herself writing an essay called "On Liking Sex." There's that to consider.

Happiness

My daughter has always been slight and compact, but she plants her feet firmly, heels first, as she walks. She has little hands and a small, slightly pointed face, now framed by a tumble of reddish curls. In her slim-waisted white cotton dress, trimmed with lace on the wide collar and flounced skirt, and her black ankle boots, she might be graduating in her great-great-grandmother's class of 1901. She has shrugged her heavy black gown over her dress and set her mortarboard square on her curls, and she strides by us looking solemn and steamy. She doesn't know where we are sitting, and when we speak her name she turns with a start, her mouth an oval of surprise captured forever by a Polaroid.

The weather and the campus provide a flawless setting. Despite a freak late-April snowstorm not three weeks ago, the vegetation is burgeoning. Dogwood, lilac, rhododendron and azalea stain the atmosphere with colors and scents that stun my senses, which are now tuned to Arizona's more muted spring. Far from needing the light woolen jacket I brought to thaw my desert-thinned blood, I'm grateful for the spotty shade of a nearby tree. I watch the women—687 of them—file to their seats and the Sheriff of Hampshire County in Massachusetts, his face wet and ruddy beneath his top hat, declare the proceedings open.

My own graduation, though it took place on a campus just as picturesque, I don't remember as half so lovely. My dress wasn't quite right, for one thing. (This is the surviving memory of most of the significant events of my life: that my dress wasn't quite right.) Our dresses were supposed to be white, but mine, made for me by my mother for some other occasion, was embroidered with tiny yellow flowers. The day was overcast and damp, and my spirits were equally gray. College had seemed one long survival test, which I had passed, but without distinction. Although surrounded by a proud and loving family, I was lonely for the one person who made my survival seem worthwhile, my husband, who was sailing in large aimless circles on a radar ship in the North Atlantic.

I knew I would immediately go on to travel to New Mexico for a friend's wedding, and in the fall teach school, and eventually have children. But these ventures all required leaps into unknown territory—the desert, the classroom, the nursery—and I was afraid that they, too, would turn out aimless and undistinguished. These feelings are symptomatic of depression, I know now. But I don't think they're unusual, even for people who aren't clinically depressed, at such radical junctures as leaving college, entering marriage, changing jobs, leaving one house for another. The comfortably familiar past slides away and leaves one gasping at the vertiginous brink of what can seem, to the inexperienced, a void. But in reality it is only the leading edge of what will become, and surprisingly soon, the comfortably familiar past.

Now, 23 years later, I am watching my daughter's commencement exercises from a wheelchair. My multiple sclerosis has gotten much worse in recent months, and I'm safe only if I stay put. A couple of days ago, trying to walk and read a letter at the same time, I fell flat on my face and shattered the edges of three front teeth, which are now painted on temporarily in plastic. Beside me, holding my hand, my husband (the same one), is recovering from the removal of a second melanoma. A few months ago his father died, reminding us that there is nothing that now stands between ourselves and death, and we are trying to help his mother settle into her grief as well as into her new apartment.

At this sweet moment, waiting to hear my daughter's name announced, I am suddenly perfectly happy, in a way I could not have dreamed at my own graduation. If anyone had told me then that by the time I was 43 I would be crippled and George would have cancer and my beloved family would have begun to die, I would have cried out (I did a lot of crying out in those days): "Oh no! I could never survive such pain!" But if anyone had told me that, in the presence of these realities, I would find myself, without warning, pierced by joy, I would have been stunned speechless, certain that my informant was either perverse or outright mad.

I wish that I could jump up (a move that would probably result in the loss of the rest of my teeth) and hug my daughter and all her classmates and shout to them: "Listen! No matter how happy you think you are today, you will be happier, I promise you. You can't imagine the women you will grow into, how large your spirits will become, stretching and stretching to encompass the challenges your lives will proffer. Take all these challenges as gifts, no matter how dubious their value seems at the time. They'll come in handy one day—you'll see. They'll open you up for joy."

But if I started jumping and hugging and shouting, the director of security, who happens to be hovering several feet to my right (Why here? What does he know?), would undoubtedly carry me off to the ambulance parked just outside the archway back there, and my daughter would be mortified at having my perversity and madness go public. Better I should bow my head politely for the benediction and whisper my message to myself. My own life promises to grow more complicated and difficult still, and I will need my own words of encouragement: you don't yet know the woman you will become, Nancy; you will be happier, in ways wholly new to you, than you now dream.

"God save the Commonwealth of Massachusetts!" shouts the Sheriff, and the pipers stomp and skirl at the head of the recession. This time Anne knows where we are, and she lights her sunny smile straight at the lens. We give this proper composition to her grandmother and keep the round-mouthed one for ourselves: Anne entering the future in the only way any of us can, unfocused and surprised.

On Being Raised by a Daughter

Mothering. I didn't know how to do it. Does anyone? If there really were a maternal instinct, as a good many otherwise quite responsible human beings have claimed, then would we need men like Dr. Alan Guttmacher and Dr. Benjamin Spock to teach us how to mother, and would we be forever scrambling to keep up with the shifts in their child-bearing and child-rearing theories? Would we turn, shaken by our sense of our female incapacity, to the reassuring instructive voices of the fathers, who increasingly come in both sexes, murmuring how much weight to gain or lose, how long to offer the breast, how soon to toilet train, to send to school? Does the salmon ask for a map to the spawning ground? Does the bee send to the Department of Agriculture for a manual on honeymaking?

No, I came with no motherly chromosomes to pattern my gestures comfortably. Not only did I not know how to do it, I'm not even sure now that I wanted to do it. These days people choose whether or not to have children. I am not so very old—my forty-first birthday falls this month—yet I can say with the verity of a wrinkled granny that we did things differently in my day. I no more chose to have children than I had chosen to get married. I simply did what I had been raised to do. Right on schedule (or actually a little ahead of schedule, since I hadn't yet finished college) I wrapped myself in yards of white taffeta and put orange blossoms in my hair and marched myself, in front of the fond, approving gaze of a couple of hundred people, into the arms of a boy in a morning coat who was doing what he had been raised to do. After a year or so, the fond, approving gaze shifted to my belly, which I made swell to magnificent proportions before expelling an unpromising scrap of human flesh on whom the gaze could turn. This was Anne, created in a heedless gesture as close to instinctual as any I would ever perform: satisfaction of the social expectation that I, young, vigorous, equipped with functioning uterus and ovaries and breasts, would sanctify my union with George by bringing forth a son. (I missed, though I had better luck next time.)

The birth of Anne was dreadful, and at the beginning I hated her, briefly, more fiercely than I had ever hated anyone. My doctor, a small round elderly GP who delivered whatever babies came along in Bath, Maine, told me that my protracted pelvis might necessitate a Caesarian section, but he never instructed me what to do during this birth by whatever means. I guess I was supposed not to do but to endure. I remember, hours into a lengthy and complicated labor that ended in Dr. Fichtner's extracting Anne with forceps like a six-pound thirteen-ounce wisdom tooth, twisting my fingers through my hair, yanking, raking my face with my nails, shrieking at the nurse beside me, "Get this thing out of me! I hate it!" Until then I had rather liked Anne, as she humped up bigger and bigger each night under the bedsheet, her wriggles and thumps giving a constant undertone of companionship to my often solitary daily activities. But now I was sure she was killing me. The nurse loosened my fingers and soothed, "You'll feel differently in a little while."

She was right. In a rather long while I did feel differently. I was no longer in pain. But I didn't feel motherly. In fact, Anne on the outside wasn't half so companionable as Anne on the inside, and I think I felt a little lonely. And frightened. I hadn't the faintest idea what I was doing with this mite with the crossed blue eyes and the whoosh of hair sticking straight up. And now, more than eighteen years later, I still have the frequent sense that I don't know what I'm doing, complicated now, of course, by the guilt that I don't know what I've done and the terror that I don't know what I'm going to do. How, I wonder when a young woman comes into my room and speaks to me, her hair blown dry to casual elegance and her eyes uncrossed behind round brown frames, how did you get here? And where, when you turn and walk out of here, out of my house and out of the dailiness of my life, where will you go?

I have been mystified by motherhood largely because motherhood itself has been mystified. Perhaps before Freud I might have raised my children without knowing consciously my power to damage their spirits beyond human repair, but the signs have always been there: the Good Mother and the Terrible Mother; the dead saint and the wicked stepmother waiting to offer disguised poisons, shoes of hellfire. The one is as alien as the other. If you live in a culture where all children are raised by mothers, Nancy Chodorow points out in *The Reproduction of Mothering,* and if half those children are males who must separate with some violence from the mother in order to establish their different gender, and if the males have the power to determine, through the creation of symbolic systems like language and art, what culture itself is, then you will get a cultural view of mothers as others, on whom are projected traits that even they (who speak some form of the language, who look at the pictures even if they don't paint them) come to assume are their own. We live in a culture of object-mothers. The subject-mothers, culturally silenced for millennia, are only just beginning to speak.

The voices of authority tell me I may harm, even ruin my daughter (in large measure by spoiling her for the pleasurable uses of men). At first they issue from the eminences of science, in measured tones like those of Carl Jung: "Thus, if the child of an over-anxious mother regularly dreams that she is a terrifying animal or a witch, these experiences point to a split in the child's psyche that predisposes it to a neurosis." I am the stuff of my daughter's nightmares. Gradually the pronouncements trickle down into the market place and are reformulated for popular consumption by voices like Nancy Friday's in that long whine of sexual anxiety *My Mother/My Self,* which was on the bestseller list some years back: "When mother's silent and threatening disapproval adds dark colors to the girl's emergent sexuality, this fear becomes eroticized in such strange forms as masochism, love of the brute, rape fantasies—the thrill of whatever is most forbidden." I make of my daughter's life a waking nightmare as well. A book like *My Mother/My Self,* in dealing with our earliest relationship, out of which our ability to form all other relationships grows, taps a rich subterranean vein of desire and disappointment, but it does so only to portray daughter as victim.

The real danger these voices pose lies not so much in what they say as in what they leave out about motherhood, whether through ignorance or through incapacity. Jung was not a woman at all, at least socially speaking (archetypally, of course, he had an anima, which doesn't seem to have caused him much trouble). And Friday refused to have children on the grounds that if she chanced to have a daughter, she'd ruin her child just as her mother had ruined her (such an assumption suggests that her choice was a wise one). But neither these two nor the vast crowd of fellow motherhood-mystifiers between them take into adequate account the persistence of human development, which keeps the personality malleable indefinitely, if it is allowed to, or the implacable power of six pounds thirteen ounces of human flesh from the moment it draws a breath and wails its spirit out into the world.

Among all the uncertainties I have experienced about myself as a mother, of one point I feel sure: that I am not today the woman I would have been had Anne not been born one September evening almost nineteen years ago. I cannot prove this hypothesis, there being no control in this experiment, no twenty-two-year-old Nancy Mairs that night who had a son instead, whose baby died, who had had a miscarriage, who had not been able to get pregnant at all, who never married and lives now in a small, well-appointed apartment on the Marina in San Francisco, walking her Burmese cats on leashes in Golden Gate Park. There is only this Nancy Mairs who, for nearly half her life, has in raising been raised by a daughter.

Anne can't have found her job an easy one. Raising a mother is difficult enough under the best of circumstances. But when you get one who's both crippled and neurotic—who doesn't do her fair share of the housework, who lurches around the house and crashes to the floor in front of your friends, whose spirits flag and crumple unpredictably, who gets attacks of anxiety in the middle of stores and has to be cajoled into finishing simple errands—then you have your work cut out for you. Of all the things Anne has taught me, perhaps the most important is that one can live under difficult circumstances with a remarkable amount of equanimity and good humor. It's a lesson I need daily.

My education began, no doubt, from the moment of her birth. Perhaps even before. Perhaps from the moment I perceived her presence in the absence of my period, or from the instant (Christmas Eve, I'm convinced) of her conception, or even from the time I began to dream her. But then she was anonymous. As soon as she appeared, she took me firmly in diminutive hand and trained me much as I've come to see that my cats have trained me, rewarding my good behavior (what difference a smile or a purr?) and punishing my bad (they've both tended to bite). But I don't think of my education as being under way till about nine months later when one day she heaved herself up in her car-bed, raised one arm in a stiff wave, and called, "Hi there!" A baby who could talk with me was beyond my ken. After all, I was raised before the days when dolls had electronic voice-boxes in their tummies and quavered "Hi there!" when you pulled the string. And anyway, Anne didn't have a string. *She* chose to speak to *me*.

I've never been the same.

Birth is, I think, an attenuated process, though we tend to use the word to describe only the physical separation of the baby from the mother. Fortunately, those first hours of birth were the worst, in terms of pain, or I don't think I'd have lasted. Each phase of the process involves separation, which may or may not be physical but always carries heavy psychic freight. For me, Anne's speech was a major step. It set her apart from me, over there, an entity with whom I could, literally, have a dialogue. It made her an other.

Feminist psychologists note that psychical birth, the process of differentiating self from other, is particularly problematic for female children. As Chodorow writes,

> Because they are the same gender as their daughters and have been girls, mothers of daughters tend not to experience these infant daughters as separate from them in the same way as do mothers of infant sons. . . . Primary identification and symbiosis with daughters tend to be stronger and cathexis of daughters is more likely to retain and emphasize narcissistic elements, that is, to be based on experiencing a daughter as an extension or double of a mother herself, with cathexis of the daughter as a sexual other usually remaining a weaker, less significant theme.

The consequence of this feeling of continuity between mother and daughter is that "separation and individuation remain particularly female developmental issues." But "problematic" doesn't mean "bad," a leap that Friday makes when she lifts "symbiosis" out of the psychoanalytic context in which Chodorow uses it and applies it to noninfantile relationships, giving it then not its full range of meaning but that portion of meaning which suits her program: symbiosis as a kind of perverse parasitism: a large but weak organism feeding on a smaller but strong host, which, as it grows, weakens until the two are evenly matched in size and incapacity. According to Friday, the mother limits her daughter's autonomy and independence, extinguishes her sexuality, terrifies her witless of men, then packages her in Saran Wrap to keep her fresh and hands her over to some man who, if she's not careful, will get on her a daughter on whom she will perform the same hideous rites.

I'm not saying that no mother does such things. Apparently Nancy Friday's mother did, and I recognize any number of my own experiences in hers. Nor am I saying that, through some virtue or miracle, I have avoided doing them to Anne. Of course I would want to think so; but God and Anne alone know what horrors I've perpetrated. All I can be sure of is that if Anne handed me a list of grievances, most of them would probably surprise me. If they didn't, I'd be a monster, not a mother.

What I am saying is that such things are not intrinsic to the mother-daughter relationship. As Chodorow notes in her study "Family Structure and Female Personality," women in societies as various as those in Atjeh, Java, and East London, where their "kin role, and in particular the mother role, is central and positively valued," have experiences and develop self-images very different from those of Western middle-class women:

> There is another important aspect of the situation in these societies. The continuing structural and practical importance of the mother-daughter tie not only ensures that a daughter develops a positive personal and role identification with her mother, but also requires that the close psychological tie between mother and daughter become firmly grounded in real role expectations. These provide a certain constraint and limitation upon the relationship, as well as an avenue for its expression through common spheres of interest based in the external social world.

Thus, although the problem of differentiation exists wherever mothers mother daughters, its implications vary from one social setting to another. If a woman like Friday's mother teaches her daughter that sex is risky at best and in general downright nasty, she does so not because she is a mother but because she is the product of a patriarchal order that demands that its women be chaste and compliant so that men may be sure of their paternity. In fact, such a concern is extrinsic to the mother-daughter relationship, which exists in essence outside the sphere of men. As soon as one can identify it for what it is, the concern of a particular group of human beings for maintaining a particular kind of power, one is free to choose whether or not to perpetuate it.

Thus, Friday's rationale for refusing to bear children, that she would inevitably visit upon her daughter the same evils her mother visited upon her, is off the mark, rooted in a sense of powerlessness in the face of the existing social order which seems to stem from belief in a biologically predetermined parasitism. Mothers, inexorably, must eat out the hearts of their daughters alive. Neither a mother nor a daughter has the power to avoid the dreadful outcome. They are only helpless women. But if we step outside socially imposed injunctions, then Friday is wrong, and daughters and their mothers wield powers for one another's help as well as harm. They may even make of one another revolutionaries.

Symbiosis is a spacious word. It may encompass parasitism and helotism (though the *Shorter Oxford Dictionary* disallows this meaning by requiring that the entities involved be mutually supportive). But it also—even chiefly—means commensalism, mutualism, "the intimate living together," says *Webster's Third*, "of two dissimilar organisms in any of various mutually beneficial relationships." The crux is the living-withness the word demands: We may live with one another well or badly. To live together reciprocally, each contributing to the other's support, in the figurative sense in which symbiosis represents human relationship, requires delicate balance, difficult to establish and to maintain. Both partners must give to it and take from it. Both must flourish under its influence, or it is no longer symbiotic. For these reasons, a symbiotic relationship between a mother and her growing daughter—or between any other two people, for that matter—may be rather rare. For these reasons, also, emotional symbiosis is not an ascribed characteristic of a relationship; rather, it is the outcome of the dynamics of some relationships between some people some of the time.

Symbiosis as I am now using the word—not like Chodorow to represent the phase of total infantile dependence or like Friday to suggest emotional vampirism but rather as a metaphor for the interdependence characteristic of living together well— does not result in identity. On the contrary, every definition I've found requires the difference of the entities involved. Thus, after the demands of infancy have been made and met, individuation is necessary if a true symbiotic system is to be maintained. Otherwise you get something else, some solid lump of psychic flesh whose name I do not know.

All the analyses I've read of mother-daughter relationships fail to account for my experience of Anne's power in our mutual life. The assumption seems to be that I'm the one in control, not just because I'm older than she is and, until recently, bigger and stronger, but because I have society's acknowledgment and support in the venture and she doesn't. I'm engaged in the honorable occupation of child-rearing, and if I can't figure the procedures out for myself, I can find shelves of manuals in any bookstore or library. No one even notices that Anne is engaged in mother-rearing, much less offers her any hot tips; indeed, books like *My Mother/My Self* only reinforce her powerlessness, making her out a victim of maternal solicitude and submerged rage, whose only recourse is more rage, rebellion, rejection: not an actor but a reactor. Such lopsided accounts arise, I suppose, from the premise—the consequence of a hierarchical view of human development—that adulthood signifies completion. But the fluidity, the pains and delights, the spurts of growth and sluggish spells of childhood never cease, though we may cease to acknowledge them in an effort to establish difference from, and hence authority over, our children. Out of the new arrivals in our lives—the odd word stumbled upon in a difficult text, the handsome black stranger who bursts in one night through the cat door, the telephone call out of a friend's silence of years, the sudden greeting from the girl-child— we constantly make of ourselves our selves.

When Anne waved and called out to me, she made an other not only of herself but of me. Language is the ultimate alienator. When she spoke she created for herself a self so remote from me that it could communicate with me only—imprecisely, imperfectly—through words. Shortly thereafter she named me, and went on naming me, into place, a slowish process. When she was not quite two, I left the world. I went into a state mental hospital and stayed there six months. During that time Anne lived with my mother, another Anne, and the two of them built a life around a space that they both expected me to come back to and fill. One afternoon, sitting in a basket in the checkout line at the IGA, Anne struck up a conversation with the man behind her who, gesturing toward Mother, said something about her mummy. "That's not my Mummy," Anne informed him, drawing herself high and fixing him with one crossed eye. "It's my Grandma. My Mummy is in the hospital." When Mother told me this story, I heard the message as I've heard it ever since: I'm the Mummy, the only Mummy (though I've grown up to be Mom, that hearty jokey apple-pie name, for reasons known only to my children), and that's who I've got to be.

As Mummy I have emphatically never been permitted to be Anne. Whatever fantasies I may have had, at some subliminal level, of my new daughter as a waxen dolly that I could pinch and pat into my likeness, Anne scotched them early, probably when she first spat puréed liver into my face (not to mention when she became the only one in the family who today eats liver in any form), certainly by the time she shouted out "Hi there!" (not "Mama" or "Dada," no private communiqué, but a greeting to all the world). Nor can I ever make her me. She wouldn't let me. Hence the possibility for our symbiosis, a state that demands two creatures for its establishment and maintenance. Anne has schooled me in the art of living well together by letting go.

Like any daughter's, hers hasn't been a simple task, but I don't think that the kind of gritty spirit it's called up in her will stand her in bad stead. She has been hampered by my own terror of separation, brought on perhaps by my early separation from my mother because of illness or my somewhat later permanent separation from my father through death. She has been helped, I think, by my curiosity to see what she would do next and by the fact that I've worked at jobs I enjoy since she was nine months old and that I've remained married, in considerable contentment, to her father, for as Chodorow points out, when "women do meaningful productive work, have ongoing adult companionship while they are parenting, and have satisfying emotional relationships with other adults, they are less likely to overinvest in children." And at least I've always *wanted* to let go. I just haven't always known how or when. Anne, through her peculiar quiet stubborn self-determination, has time after time peeled my white-knuckled fingers loose and shrugged away from my grasp.

Neither of us has had a whole lot of help from the world at large. We live in a society that still expects, even demands, that mothers control and manipulate their children's actions right into adulthood; that judges them according to the acceptability or unacceptability of their children's appearance and behavior; and that ensures their dependence on maternity for a sense, however diffuse, of self by giving them precious little else of interest to do. The mother who does let go, especially of a daughter, is still often considered irresponsible at best, unnatural at worst.

When Anne was sixteen, for instance, she decided to join a volunteer organization called Amigos de las Americas, training in Spanish and public health for several months and then going to Honduras to vaccinate pigs against hog cholera. United States policies in Central America hadn't yet created thoroughgoing chaos, and George and I thought this a wonderful way for her to begin inserting herself into the world. But George's parents, on a visit during her preparations, challenged me about Anne's plans. She ought not to be allowed to go, they said. It would be too much for her. The shock of entering a new culture would make her emotionally ill. "Ugh," Mum Mairs shuddered, "girls shouldn't have to dig latrines." (At that time, Anne hadn't yet received her assignment, but I presume that girls shouldn't have to slog around in pigshit either.) I was so startled by this attack, in terms I had not thought of before, that I doubt I said much to allay their fears, though I did ask Anne to tell them about her training in order to reassure them that she wasn't being thrust into the jungle naked and naive. Meanwhile, I thought about those terms, those feminine terms, forgotten at least momentarily by me, foreign as a source of motivation to Anne: nicety, physical and emotional frailty, passivity: all rolled into that statement that girls shouldn't have to dig latrines. (The logical extension of this attitude, I suppose, is that if a girl is all you've got, then you don't get a latrine. Ugh.)

Later, comparing notes with George, I learned that his parents had never mentioned the matter to him. I was at first hurt, angry, feeling picked on; later I came to understand that I was the natural target of their misgivings. George couldn't be counted on to know what girls should or shouldn't do, or to communicate his knowledge if he did. But I could. I was Anne's mother. And in letting her go to Latin America to live, if only briefly, in poverty, perhaps in squalor, and to perform manual labor, I was derelict in my duty.

Thus challenged, I had to rethink this duty. To Mum and Dad Mairs, obviously, it entailed the same protection I received growing up: keeping Anne safe and comfortable, even keeping her pure, at bottom probably protecting her maidenhead, though this mission is buried so deep in our cultural unconscious that I think they would be shocked at the mention of it. I recognized a different duty, a harsher one: to promote Anne's intellectual and spiritual growth even if it meant her leaving me. I didn't think that safety and comfort tended to lead to growth. As for protecting her maidenhead, I figured that was her responsibility, since she was the one who had it, or didn't have it, as the case might be. My duty, I saw, might in fact *be* dereliction, in the form of releasing her into the flood of choice and chance that would be her life. I thought she could swim. More important, she thought she could swim. Nonetheless, while she was gone I ran around distracted and stricken with guilt, mumbling primitive prayers to Our Lady of Guadalupe to take up the watch I had left off. Then she came home, bearing rum and machetes wide-eyed right through customs, with a new taste for mangoes and a new delight in hot showers but without even the lice and dysentery and other gruesome manifestations of tropical fauna she had been promised.

She came back but never, of course, all the way back. Each departure contains an irrevocable element of private growth and self-sufficiency. For the most part I have thought her departures thrilling: the month she spent in New England with her grandparents when she was eight, flying back to Tucson alone; her first period; the first night she spent (quite chastely) with a boy, and later her first lover; her excellence at calculus; her choice to leave lover and family and lifelong friends to go to college on the other side of the country. As long as her new flights give her joy, I rejoice. Where I balk—and balk badly—is at those junctures where the growing hurts her.

One night a couple of winters ago, I woke from heavy early sleep to a young man standing in the dark by my bed: David, Anne's boyfriend. "Mrs. Mairs," he whispered, "I think you'd better come. Anne is drunk and she's really sick and I think you should take care of her." Clearly David wasn't drunk, hadn't been at the same party, he explained, but had met up with Anne afterward. He'd taken her to a friend's house, and though Chris wasn't at home, his mother had kindly taken them in, given them some tea, let Anne throw up in her toilet. But it was getting late, and David had a deadline. He had to bring Anne home, but he didn't dare leave her alone.

I hauled myself out of bed and padded to the other end of the cold house, where Anne was in her bathroom washing her face. When she heard my voice, she hissed, "David, I'll kill you," then came out and burst into tears. I sent David along as I held and rocked her, listening to her wretched tale. She certainly was drunk. The fumes rising from my sodden lap were enough to make me tiddly. Gradually I got her quieted and tucked into bed. The next day she felt suitably miserable. To this day she prefers milk to alcohol.

The children were surprised that I wasn't angry about this episode. In a way I was surprised myself. After all, I had forbidden Anne to drink alcohol outside our house, and she had disobeyed me. Wasn't anger the appropriate response to a disobedient child? But though I specialize in appropriate responses, I did not feel angry. Instead, I felt overwhelmingly sad. For days I was stabbed to the heart by the thought of Anne reeling and stumbling along a darkened street, her emotions black and muddled, abandoned by the group of nasty little boys who had given her beer and vodka and then gone off to have some other fun.

By that one act she stripped me of whatever vestiges of magical thinking I was clinging to about mothers and daughters. Until then, I think, I had still believed that through my wisdom and love I could protect her from the pains I had endured as a child. Suddenly my shield was in tatters. It was a thing of gauze and tissue anyway. She has taught me the bitterest lesson in child-rearing I've yet had to learn: that she will have pain, must have it if she is to get to—and through—this place I am now and the places to which I have yet to go. For, as Juliet Mitchell writes, "pain and lack of satisfaction are the point, the triggers that evoke desire," that essential longing which marks our being in the world, both Anne's and mine, as human.

In teaching me to be her mother, Anne has, among all her other gifts, given me my own mother in ways that have often surprised me. For, as the French theorist Julia Kristeva writes in *Desire in Language*, "By giving birth, the woman enters into contact with her mother; she becomes, she is her own mother; they are the same continuity differentiating itself." Old rebellions have softened, old resentments cooled, now that I see my mother stereoscopically, the lens of motherhood superimposed on that of daughterhood. Every child, I'm sure, takes stern and secret vows along these lines: "When I grow up, I'm never going to make my child clean her room every Saturday, wear orange hair ribbons, babysit her sister, eat pea soup . . ."; and every mother must experience those moments of startlement and sometimes horror when she opens her mouth and hears issue forth not her own voice but the voice of her mother. Surprisingly often, I have found, my mother's voice speaks something that I, as a mother, want to say. I can remember that, when I had accepted a date with Fred—squat, chubby, a little loud, a French kisser, the bane of my high-school love life—and then got a better offer, Mother told me I had only two choices, to go with Fred or to stay home. I vowed then that I would never interfere with my child's social life. But I have had occasion to issue the same injunction, not because I can't tell where my mother ends and I begin, nor because I want Anne to suffer the same horrors I endured in the course of becoming a woman, but because I believe that the habit of courtesy toward one's fellow creatures is more durable than a fabulous night at the prom. Mother may have thought so too.

I gave Mother more trouble throughout my years at home than Anne has given me because, through some psychic and/or biochemical aberration, I was a depressive, though neither she nor I knew so at the time. I recognized that my behavior was erratic and that she got very angry with me for it. What I didn't see, and maybe she didn't either, was that behind her anger lay the anxiety and frustration caused by her helplessness to protect me from my pain. When, finally, I cracked up sufficiently to be sent to a mental hospital, I sensed that she was blaming herself for my troubledness (and no wonder in the disastrous wake of Freud), and I felt impatient with her for believing such silliness. But she was only exhibiting that reflexive maternal guilt which emerges at the infant's first wail: "I'm sorry. I'm sorry. I'm sorry I pushed you from this warm womb into the arms of strangers, me among them. I'm sorry I can't keep you perfectly full, perfectly dry, perfectly free from gas and fear, perfectly, perfectly happy." Any mother knows that if she could do these things, her infant would die more surely than if she covered its face with a rose-printed pillow. Still, part of her desire is to prevent the replication of desire.

Because I knew I had so often infuriated and wearied her, when I left for college I thought only of Mother's relief, never of the possibility that she might miss me. Why should she? The house was still crammed without me, my sister Sally still there, and my stepfather and the babies, and my grandmother too, not to mention an elderly Irish setter and a marmalade cat. As soon as I'd gone, Mother bought a dishwasher, and I figured that took care of any gap I'd left. Not until Anne began the process of selecting a college, finding a summer job in Wisconsin, packing away her mementoes, filling her suitcases did I think that Mother's first-born daughter (and not just a pair of hands in the dishpan) had once left her, and she must have grieved at the separation too. I love to visit her now because I know at last that she is delighted to have me there—not just glad of the company, but warmed and entertained by *me*, one of the daughters who raised her.

I am aware, too, that she once raised a mother, Granna, who lived with us for many years. And Granna raised a mother, Grandma Virchow, with whom she and Mother lived for many years. And Grandma must have raised a mother as well, left behind in Germany in the 1890s, who must herself have raised a mother. "For we think back through our mothers if we are women," writes Virginia Woolf in *A Room of One's Own.* Anne has helped me in that backward dreaming. When she tells me that she doesn't plan to have children, I feel sad, but not because I won't have grandchildren. I mean, I'd welcome them, but I have quite enough characters populating my life to keep me entertained. Rather, I would like her to have this particular adventure, this becoming that a daughter forces.

Overall, I think Anne has done a pretty good job with me. Even without encouragement, in a society that doesn't consider her task authentic, she's done her share of leaning and hauling, shaping me to her needs, forcing me to learn and practice a role I have often found wearing and frightening. Maybe some women are mothers by nature, needing only an infant in their arms to bloom. I'm not. I've needed a lot of nurture. And still I hate it sometimes, especially when she makes me into an authoritarian ogre rumbling disapproval (just as I did to Mother, oh, how many times?). But she's firm and often fair. She doesn't coddle me. Years ago, before I got my brace, I used to have a lot of trouble putting on my left shoe and she would help me with it; the right shoe she'd hand me, saying, "You can do this one yourself." But on my birthday she bakes me lemon bread and, when I ask her what

I smell, tells me she's washing dishes in lemon-scented detergent. I believe her and so am surprised by my birthday party. She is tolerant when I stamp my feet (figuratively speaking—if I really stamped my feet I'd fall in a heap and then we'd both get the giggles) and refuse to let her take my peach-colored gauze shirt to Honduras. But she is severe about suicide attempts. She has no use for my short stories, in which she says nothing ever happens, but she likes my essays, especially the ones she appears in, and sometimes my poems. She admires my clothing (especially my peach-colored gauze shirt), my hair, my cooking, but not my taste in music or in men. When my black cat, Bête Noire, the beast of my heart, was killed, she let me weep, hunched over, my tears splashing on the linoleum, and she never said, "Don't cry."

Before long Anne will have to consider the job done. A daughter can't spend a lifetime raising her mother any more than a mother can spend a lifetime raising her daughter; they both have other work to get on with. I can remember the liberating moment when I recognized that it was no longer my task to educate my mother in the ways of the real world; she'd just have to make the best of what she'd learned and muddle along on her own. Mother muddles well, I like to think because I gave her a good start. Anne deserves such a moment.

And I deserve her having it. It's what we've come this way for. Last summer, when George was visiting his parents, his mother sighed, "Life is never so good after the children have gone." George is her only child, and he's been gone for twenty-five years. I can't imagine sustaining a quarter of a century of anticlimax. Anne and I both confront transformation into women with wholly new sets of adventures as we learn to live well apart. I feel pretty well prepared now for muddling along on my own.

Considerations for Thinking and Writing

1. How does Mairs's account of her struggle with multiple sclerosis compare with Lorde's account of her "war" with cancer? Is Mairs also a "warrior"? What metaphors does she use to identify herself as a person with multiple sclerosis?

2. In "The Transformation of Silence," Lorde attributes her awareness of the danger of remaining silent to the knowledge that she is threatened by cancer. In "Breast Cancer," she claims that living with cancer has taught her other lessons about women's bodies, about self-respect, about American society. What lessons has Mairs learned from living with multiple sclerosis and depression? Do these writers expect us to learn from them what their illnesses have taught them? If not, then why write about the lessons their lives have taught them?

3. Compare Mairs's sly caricature of female beauty in "On Being a Cripple" with Kingston's description of the Chinese notion of female beauty in "No Name Woman." What does Kingston mean by "American-pretty"? How does Mairs's body shape her notion of beauty?

4. Why do Didion's "On Self-Respect" and Mairs's "On Not Liking Sex" both begin with rereadings of the author's earlier writing? What function does revision serve in Mairs's thinking about sex? In what way is a single endeavor to write an act of revision?

5. In "On Not Liking Sex," Mairs becomes aware of an ascetic strain within herself, a desire to avoid or deny sensuous experience. What stances on asceticism are taken by Oates and Sontag in their respective essays on the ascetic mystic Simone Weil? What is Mairs's stance on her asceticism?

6. What does Mairs mean when she calls the female body an "artifice of desire"? Compare the discussion of bodily artifice in "On Not Liking Sex" with Angela Carter's "Wound in the Face." Does Mairs's detailed treatment of the eroticized female body help you to read

between the lines of Carter's more oblique, provocative account? How do their differing approaches determine your understanding of the issue?

7. "On Being Raised by a Daughter" surprises our expectations of an essay on mothers and daughters by switching the roles. How does Mairs make the notion of surprise—of the unexpected—central to the essay? Compare the relationship between mother and daughter in this essay with that in Jordan's "Many Rivers to Cross." Which figure—mother or daughter—slips away in each essay?

8. How does Mairs handle the problem of closure in "Happiness"?

JOYCE CAROL OATES
(b. 1938)

Joyce Carol Oates has a public mind; it is continuously on display in the nation's finest magazines, offering penetrating insights into other writers' work. But in any given year she will almost certainly produce a novel of her own as well as plays, collected essays, and poetry. Somewhere too she will be meeting publicly with colleagues to discuss her work, and she will be teaching students, keeping her feet planted firmly on this earth, where she minds her share of the earth's business. Seemingly indefatigable, she performs these prodigious feats without losing her life to them. Friends, such as Elaine Showalter, offer written portraits that attest to her humanity. But Oates's texts, especially her essays, make the same claim without making it their business to do so. There in the text—clearheaded, independent, and lively—she affords us more than the considerable pleasures of her very fine mind. She affords us insight into one of those interesting personalities that T. S. Eliot detected at the back of Yeats's finest poems, "a unique personality which makes one sit up in excitement and eagerness to learn more about the author's mind and feelings." Hers is not a severed head.

In "Literature as Pleasure, Pleasure as Literature" Oates entices us as she reveals her own pleasures of reading and gives us an evolving sense of herself as reader, as seeker of pleasure. Reading, like writing, is for Oates a "sacramental" act. She tells us that reading "is the sole means by which we slip, involuntarily, often helplessly, into another's skin; another's voice; another's soul." She convinces us because she provides for our edification so many of her own pleasurable moments, whether they be from reading Walt Whitman, Emily Dickinson, or Nietzsche, or from helping a student savor a "perfectly honed and seemingly immortal prose" passage from Ernest Hemingway—her pleasure and her student's derived somehow from that "unfathomable mystery of personality," "personality transcribed and made permanent into art." Oates pushes us into the realm of both mystery and pleasure, into a realm of religion "that offers none of the vatic promises of religion," but makes us consider nevertheless our deeply felt relationship with the texts themselves and with those who create them. But as important as a writer's voice and personality are to Oates, she discerned once—and perhaps still does, by her own account—that the best literature derives from a "neuter, genderless activity," that such a poet as Dickinson "transcend[s] not only the 'female' but the 'human' as categories." However complex her critical conclusions, Oates makes it quite clear that reading, the act itself, is a loving pleasure.

" 'May God Grant that I Become Nothing' " adds another dimension to our reading of "Literature as Pleasure" and enriches our sense of Oates as reader. In

" 'God Grant,' " she sets out to examine the mysticism of Simone Weil by placing Weil's life and her ideas side by side, letting each serve as context for the other. Such a comparison yields a number of striking, intriguing paradoxes—*Misery is joy. Death is life. Affliction is a blessing. God's cruelty assures His tenderness*—paradoxes that Oates ultimately undermines when she assesses the value of Weil's texts outside the context of the life. "If the essays are examined without reference to the life . . . they rarely rise above the commonplace." Oates tells us why. And finally, she turns to the life without the texts, finding there in Weil's "grimly gloating obsession with starvation" the source both of her paradoxes and of her failure as a writer. At the end of the essay, it is not Weil herself who comes under Oates's scrutiny but those who admire her with "unquestioned loyalty." Oates sees Weil's life and career as "exemplary of the spiritual vacuum of our century: the hunger to believe in virtually anyone who makes a forthright claim to be divinely guided." " 'God Grant' " reminds us that Oates's fine, discriminating judgment turns not on personality or gender or social cause but on the quality of the texts themselves—on their coherence.

On Boxing seems to have been written as a "sacramental" act, as an attempt to do nothing less than set before her readers the essence of masculinity. Boxing is the vehicle for this excursion into the primitive, because boxing is "a remnant of another, earlier era when the physical being was primary and the warrior's masculinity its highest expression"; boxing is all that is left in our time of brute, face-to-face confrontation. In "Stories" Oates shows us that every bout is a "wayward story, one in which anything can happen" in a split second, even death. These wayward stories, very much a matter of style, depend on the boxers' intuition, training, relationships—all those experiences that influence what happens in the ring where the stories evolve. Oates sees that "boxing as performance is more clearly akin to dance or music

than narrative" because even the "narrative unity" provided by the ringside announcer leaves something out. In what Oates calls her "mosaic-like essay" she tries to recover what others have left out—"Pain," "Eroticism," "Woman"—tries to tell the rest of the story. Each piece of her mosaic about boxing gives us as well glimpses into Oates's art of writing, lets us think, if we are willing, of how she assembles her collected data, shaping them, creating tiny fragments of insight that, when taken together, give us a clearer sense of *machismo* than we have ever had before, lets us see too, as an aside, that the boxer and the writer partake of similar rituals.

In "Flannery O'Connor" Oates gives us additional glimpses of herself as reader while providing insight into a fairly complex topic: the relationship between a writer's public selves and the fiction she creates. In O'Connor's letters Oates finds "at least five distinctly different Flannery O'Connors," but she does not find there the O'Connor of the fiction. Having made this observation, Oates goes on to set some of those "different" O'Connors against the one who exists "supremely" in the fiction, affording penetrating insight into the relationship between that one and the others and into the rich complexity of O'Connor's fiction. Oates could see that O'Connor, in presenting herself to friends, often seemed unaware of the contradictions between the naive, sometimes bigoted, conservative views reflected in her letters and her more complex artistic vision. But even O'Connor would, on occasion, acknowledge something ironic about her own relationship to the fiction. To a man in Nashville who told her *Wise Blood* was a profound book and that she didn't "look like" she could have written it, O'Connor, after "muster[ing] up [her] squintiest expression . . . snarled, 'Well I did,' but at the same time [she] had to recognize he was right." At bottom, Oates writes about the art of writing, about the way O'Connor " 'discovered' the truth of her stories in the writing of them." It is a loving but probing examination of a "very beautiful record of a highly complex woman artist whose art was, perhaps, too profound for even the critic in her to grasp."

These essays suggest something of the complexity and subtlety of Oates's imagination. We see her theorizing about the pleasure of reading; we see her reading pleasurably two complex writers, offering penetrating analyses of the texts and the personalities that produced them; and we see her creating, in the pieces from *On Boxing,* texts of her own—we see her reading life itself out of the boxing ring. Oates is perhaps our most prolific living writer. Already she has given us eighteen novels, fourteen volumes of short stories, five books of literary criticism, and two books of plays. Hundreds of her published stories have not yet been collected, and she has written several novels that are yet to be published. Her work is important; her mind discriminating; her style clean, compelling, and enticing. Her lively essays show us how mind and personality can converge in texts that please us even as they explore life's mysteries. Hers is an imagination grounded in this life, but it is open to possibilities not yet unearthed.

Literature as Pleasure, Pleasure as Literature

I have always come to life after coming to books.
—JORGE LUIS BORGES

It might be argued that reading constitutes the keenest, because most secret, sort of pleasure. And that it's a pleasure best savored by night: by way of an ideal insomnia. At such times, lamplight illuminating the page but not much else, the world is writ small, deliciously small, and words, another's voice, come forward. *What I love about wakefulness* the insomniac says *is being alone, and reading.*

Insomnia is a predilection, a skill, a way of being, best cultivated young: in early adolescence if possible. To begin in adulthood would be a pity since, at the very least, so much precious solitude (i.e., occasions for reading) has already been lost.

You know it's poetry, Emily Dickinson says, when it takes the top of your head off. Or when, to use Randall Jarrell's metaphor, you're struck by lightning—as a reader. All great poetry is enhanced by the occasion of its discovery, and by the occasion of its savoring: a poem by night is far more powerful than a poem by day. And there are certain mysterious poems, like this by Walt Whitman—atypical Whitman, it should be noted—that can only be read by night.

A Clear Midnight

This is thy hour O soul,
    thy free flight into the wordless,
Away from books, away from art,
    the day erased, the lesson done,
Thee fully forth emerging, silent, gazing,
    pondering the themes thou lovest best:
Night, sleep, death and the stars.

Love at first sight/hearing—however delusory in human romantic terms it is nearly always reliable, in fact irresistible, in literary terms. A certitude that darts into the soul by way of the eye; provokes an involuntary visceral effect. Not always "pleasant" in the most benign sense of that ambiguous word but always, always exciting.

When you haven't realized you have memorized another's words, poetry or prose, and then, as if unbidden, the words assert themselves. Coleridge's "knowledge returning as power . . ." As, one evening in Princeton, a poet-friend and I discovered that we could recite in unison an early poem of Yeats' most admirers of Yeats would consider marginal, if, in its angry percussive rhythms, it could have been written by no one else—

To a Friend Whose Work Has Come to Nothing

Now all the truth is out,
Be secret and take defeat
From any brazen throat,
For how can you compete,
Being honour bred, with one
Who, were it proved he lies,
Were neither shamed in his own
Nor in his neighbours' eyes?
Bred to a harder thing
Than Triumph, turn away
And like a laughing string
Whereon mad fingers play
Amid a place of stone,
Be secret and exult,
Because of all things known
That is most difficult.

This too is a poem best savored, perhaps uniquely savored, by night. Like other great poems of Yeats'—"The Magi," "The Circus Animals' Desertion," "The Cold Heaven," "The Wild Swans at Coole," the Crazy Jane poems—to name only a few—which I first discovered in protracted, headachey, but utterly ravishing insomniac spells of reading in my late teens. How hard to maintain the keenest degree of consciousness after having been awake most of the night; how hard, how *willful* the task, to take daylight as seriously as night—! Yeats' magisterial imperatives have the authority, shading into contempt, of words engraved in stone: tombstone, maybe. Like those famous lines at the end of "Under Ben Bulben"—

Cast a cold eye
On life, on death.
Horseman, pass by!

"A book is an ax," Franz Kafka once said, "for the frozen sea within." Curious metaphors—particularly the ax. But we know what he means.

There are pleasures in reading so startling, so intense, they shade into pain. The realization that one's life has been irrevocably altered by . . . can it be mere words? Print on a page? The most life-rending discoveries involve what has in fact never been thought, never given form, until another's words embody them. Recall the ingenuous Dorian Gray of whom it is said he was "seduced by a book." (The book being Huysmans' masterwork of decadence, *A Rebours.*) And have there been innumerable others who were seduced by that book, and Wilde's own masterwork, *The Picture of Dorian Gray?* And what, at a morbid extreme, of the young killers Leopold and Loeb, who, having read Nietzsche as undergraduates, decided in the manner of Dostoyevsky's Raskolnikov to experiment with taking a human life— having ascended, as they thought, to the level of absolute moral freedom Nietzsche's Zarathustra preached? Is this pathology, or the greatest possible empathy? The least resistance to the "pleasure" of being overcome by another's voice?

Consider the phenomenon of reading, that most mysterious of acts. It is the sole means by which we slip, involuntarily, often helplessly, into another's skin; another's voice; another's soul. One might argue that serious reading is as sacramental an act as serious writing, and should therefore not be profaned. That, by way of a book, we have the ability to transcend what is immediate, what is merely personal, and to enter a consciousness not known to us, in some cases distinctly alien, *other* ... This morning I open a new hardcover book, of moderate size, modestly packaged, not guessing how, within minutes, in fact within seconds, my heart will be beating more quickly; my senses alert to the point of pain; an excitement coursing through me that makes it virtually impossible to stay seated. The book is *The Collected Poems of William Carlos Williams,* volume I, 1909–1939, edited by A. Walton Litz and Christopher MacGowen (New Directions, 1986), the poem I begin to read is "Paterson: Episode 17" with its haunting, percussive refrain "Beautiful Thing"— first read how many years ago? and reread how many times?—yet still possessed of its uncanny original power. And there are the great "raw" poems we all know, and have memorized, "By the road to the contagious hospital," "The pure products of America/go crazy," "The Widow's Lament at Springtime," that poem in honor/ awe/terror of America—

> The crowd at the ball game
> is moved uniformly
>
> by a spirit of uselessness
> which delights them—
>
> all the exciting detail
> of the chase
>
> and the escape, the error
> the flash of genius—
>
> all to no end save beauty
> the eternal—
>
> So in detail they, the crowd,
> are beautiful
>
> for this
> to be warned again
>
> saluted and defied—
> It is alive, venomous
>
> it smiles grimly
> its words cut—

The flashy female with her
mother, gets it—

The Jew gets it straight—it
is deadly, terrifying—

It is the Inquisition, the
Revolution

It is beauty itself
that lives

day by day in them
idly—

This is
the power of their faces

It is summer, it is the solstice
the crowd is

cheering, the crowd is laughing
in detail
permanently, seriously
without thought
(from Spring and All, 1923)

Elsewhere—

What are these elations I have
at my own underwear?

I touch it and it is strange
upon a strange thigh.
(from *The Descent of Winter,* 1928)

And: I enter an empty classroom in the old Hall of Languages Building, Syracuse University, sometime in the fall of 1956, discover a lost or discarded book on ethics, an anthology of sorts, open it at random, and begin reading . . . and reading . . . so that the class that begins in a few minutes, whatever remarks, long-forgotten, by whatever professor of philosophy, also, alas, long-forgotten, is a distraction and an interruption. How profoundly excited I am by this unknown new voice, this absolutely new and unique and enchanging voice!—though I am familiar, I suppose, with some of the writers *he* read, and from whom *he* learned (Shakespeare, Dostoyevsky, Emerson), I am not at all familiar with Nietzsche himself—only the name, the word, the sound, mysterious and forbidding. This philosopher who is an anti-philosopher; a poet; a mystic (and anti-mystic); whose genius expresses itself in aphorism and riddle—"philosophy with a hammer." To have read Nietzsche, aged eighteen, when one's senses are most keenly and nervously alert, the very envelope of the skin dangerously porous, to have heard, and been struck to the heart, by that astonishing voice—what ecstasy! what visceral unease!—as if the very floor were shifting beneath one's feet. Late adolescence is the time for love, or, rather, for passion—the conviction that *within the next hour* something can happen, will happen, to irrevocably alter one's life. (*"The danger in happiness:* Now everything I touch turns out to be wonderful. Now I love any fate that comes along. Who feels like being my fate?") Whatever books of Nietzsche's I then bought in paperback or took out of the university library—*The Birth of Tragedy, Human, All-Too-Human, The Gay Science, Thus Spake Zarathustra, Beyond Good and Evil, Twilight of the Idols*—I must have read, or devoured, quickly and carelessly and with no sense of their historical context; under the spell of an enchantment I had every reason to think was unique. And for me Nietzsche *was* unique—one of those voices out of a densely populated world that define themselves so brilliantly, in a way so poignantly, against that world, they become—almost—assimilated into one's very soul.

(Nietzsche died mad. But, mad, lived for a long time—eleven years. In January 1899 on a Turin street he saw a coachman flogging a horse, ran to protect the horse, flung his arms around it and collapsed; and never recovered. And in his madness, even, what radiance, what bizarre and heartrending poetry—signing himself "The Crucified" and "Dionysus"—writing letters like this one, to Jacob Burckhardt: ". . . In the end I would much rather be a Basel professor than God; but I have not dared push my private egoism so far as to desist for its sake from the creation of the world. You see, one must make sacrifices however and wherever one lives. . . . What is disagreeable and offends my modesty is that at bottom I am every name in history. With the children I have put into the world too, I consider with some mistrust whether it is not the case that all who come *into* the kingdom of God also come *out* of God. This fall I was blinded as little as possible when I twice witnessed my funeral. . . . We artists are incorrigible." And, in a postscript: "I go everywhere in my student's coat, and here and there slap somebody on the shoulder and say, 'Are we content? I am the god who has made this caricature.' ")

And: I leaf through a bulky anthology of poetry, too many years ago to calibrate though I was probably still in junior high school, and the names are mostly new, mysterious, lacking all associations, therefore talismanic, pure. No mere opinionizing went into the assemblage of this book—no literary politics—surely not!—so far as a thirteen-year-old might guess. If I noted the absence of women I have no memory of it and rather doubt that I did, since poetry even more than prose seemed to me then, and seemed to me for many years, a wholly neutral, or do I mean neuter, genderless activity. (I might have thought—perhaps I still think—*That's the beauty of the enterprise!*) And it would have struck me as rude, vulgar, insipid, trivializing, a profanation of the very page, to read the poetry that excited me most as if it were the product, even, of a human being like myself; as if it were the product of what would one day be called a "female consciousness." For didn't it mean that, being a poet, having been granted the imprimatur of poet, Emily Dickinson had in fact transcended not only the "female" but the "human" as categories?

> I hide myself within my flower,
> That fading from your Vase,
> You, unsuspecting, feel for me—
> Almost a loneliness.

I don't remember the first Dickinson poems I read except to know that this exquisite verse was not among them: it wasn't then, and isn't now, one of the anthology items. Very likely they were the same poems we all read, and reread, and were puzzled and haunted by, as by a child's riddle of such evident simplicity you feel you must understand it—yet can't, quite. Of the frequently anthologized poems it was the darker and more mysterious ones that struck me as embodying poetry's very essence. (Cheerfulness, even the cheerfulness of genius, has always bored me, since who needs it?—we have enough of our own.) The Dickinson who fascinates most is the Dickinson of the great elegiac poems, the poems of "madness," the terse elliptical statement poems that carry with them an air very nearly of belligerence, they are so short, and complete—

> The competitions of the sky
> Corrodeless ply.

And:

> Fame's Boys and Girls, who never die
> And are too seldom born—

And:

> We outgrow love, like other things
> And put it in the Drawer—
> Till an Antique fashion shows—
> Like Costumes Grandsires wore.

All good poets resist paraphrase; Emily Dickinson frequently resists simple comprehension. And should we "sense" her meaning we are inevitably excluded from her technique, marveling at the rightness of certain images, sounds, strategies of punctuation—the ellipses of a mind accustomed to thinking slantwise—yet unable to grasp the poem's ineluctable essence. (And the identity of the poem's narrative "I," shifting as it does from poem to poem.) When we read Dickinson the nerves tighten in sympathy, and wonder. Fragments leap out at us as powerfully as fully realized poems—

> It is the Past's supreme italic
> Makes this Present mean—
>   *
> Silence is all we dread.
> There's Ransom in a Voice—
> But Silence is Infinity.
> Himself have not a face.
>   *
> Oh Life, begun in fluent Blood
> And consummated dull!
>   *
> The Brain, within its Groove
> Runs evenly—and true—
> But let a Splinter swerve—
> 'Twere easier for You—
>
> To put a Current back—
> When Floods have slit the Hills—
> And scooped a Turnpike for Themselves—
> And trodden out the Mills—

Franz Kafka in his stories, parables, fragments, and journal entries rather more than
in his incompletely realized novels . . . Virginia Woolf in her diary and letters, in
which her voice sounds forth quicksilver and inimitable, rather more than in her
frequently stilted, always self-conscious prose fiction . . . Henry James when he is
most Jamesian (as in *The Wings of the Dove*) and then again least Jamesian (as in
the unabridged *Notebooks* in which he addresses himself without artifice, sometimes
in melancholy, sometimes in triumph, speaking to his muse whom he calls "mon
bon" as if he, or it, were a lover) . . . William James in that great work *The Varieties
of Religious Experience* in which you will find yourself in one or another chapter
("The Religion of Healthy-Mindedness," "The Sick Soul," "The Divided Self, and
the Process of Its Integration") . . . Hardy's great novels, prose-poetry as narrative,
Tess of the D'Urbervilles and *Jude the Obscure* in particular . . . Robert Frost despite
the distracting regularity of certain of his rhymes (which militate against, in the ears
of many admirers, the deeper music of his art) . . . D. H. Lawrence in his poetry
no less than in his prose, and in such "minor" work as *The Lost Girl* as well as in
the "major" novels . . . James Joyce in the very excess of his genius, word-maddened,
besotted, not so much crossing the line between sanity and craziness as erasing it—at
least in art. And there are the others, the many others, the flood of others, the voices
of strangers closer to us than the voices of friends, more intimate, in some instances,
than our own. Literature grants us few of the consolations and none of the vatic
promises of religion but *is* our religion nonetheless.

The expression on the young man's face—I am haunted by it, not envious (of it,
or of its cause) but wondering, bemused: was it simple surprise, at the masterpiece
of short prose fiction we had taken up in our workshop; was it awe?—sheer *interest*?
And his eagerness to read more by Hemingway, more of these short tight perfect
narratives, written when Hemingway was (as I tell my students gently) not much
older than they. The story is "A Very Short Story," one and a half pages of laconic
prose, bitten-back rage, "One hot evening in Padua they carried him up onto the
roof and he could look over the top of the town. . . ." and it's perfection of a kind,
of a kind Hemingway himself only infrequently achieved. It is a young man's record
of being wounded, the death of romance, of hope, as powerful in its way as the novel
it would later become, and far less sentimental. And the young, very young writers
in my workshop to whom "Ernest Hemingway" has always been a name or a
reputation are allowed to see that there was a Hemingway who did not know himself
Hemingway, could not, so young, have guessed it would turn out as in his most
aggressive childlike fantasies he'd dreamt it would: he *was* the real thing, wasn't he.
And one of them remains after class wanting to say something further, not wanting
the talk of Hemingway to end, or the talk, in any case, of *this* Hemingway to end,
this page and a half of perfectly honed and seemingly immortal prose; wanting to
ask me something but not knowing what to ask, as at all crucial moments in our lives
we want to speak without knowing what to say. What can I tell him of the
unfathomable mystery of personality? Of personality transcribed and made permanent in art?—in mere finite *words*? Perhaps the young man wants to ask, Can I do
it too? Can I try, too? but he would not ask such a thing, would not expose himself
so rawly, that isn't Princeton's style. He says, the book still open in his hands, his
voice rather vague, searching, "It's so short. It does so much." And I'm thinking,

yes, this is the real thing, this is love, that look on your face, again, always, what pleasure.

Nietzsche never married, had no child. It is believed his madness was caused by syphilitic infection contracted when he was a student or while nursing wounded soldiers in 1870. (The translation used here is by Walter Kaufmann.)

"May God Grant That I Become Nothing": The Mysticism of Simone Weil

André Gide spoke of her as "the most spiritual writer of this century"; Albert Camus called her "the only great spirit of our time." T. S. Eliot seems to have been the first person to speak of her in terms of sainthood, declaring moreover that she was "a woman of genius." Weil herself, in speaking of the fallen condition of humanity *here below* (her curious expression for the phenomenal world), declared that in our present era it is not enough even to be a saint: "We must have the saintliness demanded by the present moment, a new saintliness, itself also without precedent."

Simone Weil had the apparent modesty to exempt herself from this "new saintliness" because she believed herself a hopeless sinner; in fact, she considered herself more reprehensible than the greatest of criminals, for reasons that are not altogether clear. She set forth, however, with an air of remarkable authority, the means by which one might purify the self and approach the ultimate communion with God: which is to say, a systematic surrender of the world; a joyous acceptance of the Infinite; and an active embracing of the doctrine of "decreation" or "disincarnation." Weil's prayer echoes that of the ancient sect of Cathars, whom she admired above all orthodox followers of Christianity: "May God grant that I become nothing."

Since Catharism allowed for a form of indirect suicide by way of starvation, it is not surprising that Weil was attracted to its teachings. What more "saintly" project than to starve oneself to death in the ostensible service of a religious ideal? What more forthright and determined way to renounce the "fallen" world and the demanding flesh and the ubiquitous Devil?—and, not least, the torments of consciousness itself? No anorexic clinging defiantly to his or her representation of an ideal fleshless self has ever defined the terms of such saintliness (or delusion) more forcibly than Weil, in whom the instinct to die clearly preceded theory. In her impassioned essay "Decreation" she asserts that we can return to the divine only by way of "liberating" a trapped energy: and that this energy can be liberated only by actual death. "We must become nothing, we must go down to the vegetative level," Weil declares. "It is then that God becomes bread."

Weil the much-admired "saint," or Weil the self-deluded anorexic, possessed of a ferociously inviolate will even as she claims to possess no self: how is she to be judged, several decades after her death? Reading George A. Panichas's reverently edited collection of Simone Weil's writings, one is inclined to wonder if both Weil and her numerous admirers are not touched with a pernicious kind of madness: mad because Weil's "ideas" are so clearly without substance, mere vaporous and platitudinous musings; pernicious because, couched in an archetypal (or stereotypical) religious vocabulary, they cannot fail to exert a powerful appeal, even to the skeptic. Sacrifice, renunciation, asceticism, fasting, returning again to God (who then becomes "bread"): these are inclinations fueled as much by instinct as by religious idealism.

Then again, the puzzled reader thinks, is Weil speaking in parables? And is the body of her multifarious prose pieces really a kind of poem or extended metaphor, not to be taken literally? Weil herself, however, took it literally, and fasted to death in 1943, at the age of thirty-four, for political and religious reasons.

No one who knew Simone Weil could doubt that she was, from girlhood onward, an exceptional person. At least for some years she impressed observers as a brilliant and original thinker, in her long meditative essays "Analysis of Oppression," "The *Iliad,* Poem of Might," and "Uprootedness and Nationhood," in which she addressed, from a very different angle, those tragic aspects of contemporary civilization that so obsessed writers as dissimilar as D. H. Lawrence and Albert Camus. Weil seems to have believed that the social order in itself—perhaps because it is established *here below*—is intrinsically evil; and that there is a "diabolism" about the twentieth century in particular. Weil was clearly a person who came alive in conflict and combative argument: *give me something to oppose,* she might have said, *and I will know who I am.*

When Weil was twenty-eight years old, however, she experienced what might be called a conversion; and, after this, began to write passionately about religious and mystical matters. Retaining much of her authoritarian bias, and surrendering, it seems, virtually nothing of her misanthropic sentiments, she "discovers" the most remarkable of truths: God is love; appearance clings to being; God can only love Himself; affliction is the most precious evidence of God's "tenderness" for man; Christ is the key; all geometry proceeds from the Cross; all men bear an animal nature within them; life *here below* is sinful and fallen. Though Weil is often spoken of with reverence by liberals, she made it clear that, in her opinion, literature and "immorality" are inseparable and that literature should most certainly be censored— but only by "saints." Or, if no saints are forthcoming, by priests of the Roman Catholic Church who are empowered to speak for them.

Nietzsche speculated that the humble in spirit, the most adamantly "Christian" of persons, secretly wish to be exalted above their fellows and that their public humility is an inversion of their own thwarted will to power—or their timidity in claiming that will. Where humbleness is the characteristic pose, pride covertly reigns. The reiterated claim for selflessness is based upon the shaky proposition that such persons have underdeveloped or inferior selves: their spiritual "love" is really a form of resentment. ("A resentment experienced by creatures," Nietzsche says in *The Genealogy of Morals,* "who, deprived as they are of the proper outlet of action, are forced to find their compensation in an imaginary revenge." Hence, heaven is their proper abode; and hell that of their enemies.) Simone Weil's lifelong preoccupation with her "inferiority," her "worthlessness," her "sinfulness," does not contradict but in fact complements her inflated sense of knowing what God *really* intends for mankind.

According to the essay "A Spiritual Autobiography," Weil was so jealous of an older, and evidently brilliant, brother that she seriously thought of suicide, at least in theory, and became obsessed from that point onward with her characteristic attitude of rigorous self-loathing. The "resentment" of which Nietzsche speaks— and which, indeed, he saw as a central psychological reflex of Christianity in its orthodox forms—is closely linked with self-abasement and misdirected, or denied, anger. One affirms one's self by way of harsh denial: by way, in fact, of disintegration. "May God grant that I become nothing," the ascetic prays, as if to anticipate and, in a sense, overcome the ineluctable plan of godless Nature that, with the simple passage of time, he *must* become nothing.

I will myself *not to be*: therefore, *I am*.

While Simone Weil's political essays are rigorously impersonal, those on other subjects, particularly religious experience, are punctuated by the motif of "inferiority." Weil flagellates herself as a "poor unsatisfactory creature," a "beggar," a "slave," a "worthless object." It is her hope that she will be sent to prison and might become impoverished. (She was born of a well-to-do Jewish family.) So filled with self-loathing is Weil that she cannot imagine the possibility that any human being could feel simple friendship, let alone love, for her. Is it altogether surprising, then, that she one day discovers that God has, for His own inscrutable purpose, chosen *her* as a means by which His thoughts might be directly expressed, through the very pen she holds? A delicious paradox, absurdity with the true Kierkegaardian twist! "I would never dare speak to you like this if all these thoughts were the product of my own mind," Weil says to an acquaintance, in a letter of May 1942; but the thoughts are not Simone Weil's, of course: they are God's. And though Weil is a poor, unsatisfactory creature these thoughts, because they are God's and not hers, must be authentic. For, as Weil asserts, it does not matter if the consecrated host is made of the poorest quality of flour, not even if it is three parts rotten.

This phenomenon is all the more miraculous in that the vessel for God's wisdom knows herself unworthy of *that very salvation* she might aid others in attaining. As Weil remarks in a letter to a Catholic priest, her imagination, "mutilated by over-long and uninterrupted suffering," cannot conceive of salvation as a possibility for her. She alone is an outcast, a beggar, a slave. In fact, when she examines her conscience closely she is forced to the conclusion that she, more than any criminal, has just cause to fear God's wrath; for what would be a trivial sin in another person is a mortal sin in Weil.

This curious self-inflation is never questioned by any of Weil's admirers, who seem willing to accept her at her own estimation. In "A Spiritual Autobiography" even God becomes a participant in Weil's dramatization of the self, when, it seems, He deliberates for some time about whether Weil should be baptized in the Catholic Church and finally comes to the tentative conclusion that she should not. If God should change His mind, however, Weil would obey with alacrity. She would, in fact, "joyfully obey the order to go to the very center of hell and to remain there eternally." (Unless God is capricious or perverse, this is highly unlikely: for Weil is forced to admit that, after rigorous self-examination, she cannot discover any particular, *serious* faults in her behavior. And of course she has dedicated herself to a nunlike life of purity, for the very thought of carnal appetite is repulsive.)

God's magnificent anger, however, though it might be directed toward a faultless young woman who has suffered violent headaches and other disabilities without complaint for years, is not unjust or unwelcome—not at all. "By a strange twist," Weil says, "the thought of God's anger only arouses love in me." Affliction is, after all, a marvel of "divine technique." And though it is wrong to desire it one can be permitted to love its *possibility*. For, consider, our flesh is fragile; it can be pierced or torn or crushed, or one of its internal mechanisms can be permanently deranged, by any piece of matter in motion. We are not condemned, it seems, to eternal earthly happiness. Such is God's mercy that our fragility as creatures will ensure our decreation someday, and we may contemplate it with love and gratitude, stimulated by the occasion of "any suffering, whether great or small" ("The Love of God and Affliction"). It only seems that God is angry at us when we are afflicted or when thousands or millions of us are destroyed. In fact God loves us at such times. At such times, perhaps, more than others. Isn't our very misery proof of our special election? *"Malheur,"* says Weil, "is necessary so that the human creature may un-create itself."

Like Dostoyevsky Weil seems to have convinced herself that the suffering of mankind is an unqualified good, and woe to those who meddle with it. Imagine wanting to alter God's will . . . ! Isn't it a vicious sin, even, to feel sorry for sufferers? In a refugee camp in Casablanca Weil wrote that she sometimes felt moved when she saw afflicted people and that, for a certain space of time, her usual unqualified love of the merciful God was suspended; and this caused her grief because she must have offended God. "I hope he will forgive me my compassion," she says with absolute sincerity.

Yet it is doubtful that she was at heart a very compassionate person, or even a Christian in the usual sense of the word. She seems to have been charged with a self-righteous zeal that is, at times, rather chilling. In "The Responsibility of Writers" and "Morality and Literature" she blames writers of recent years for the disaster of the time—not only World War II but the "disaster" of the whole world so far as Western influence has penetrated. ("In recent years there have been some unbelievable degradations; for example, advice on love affairs by well-known writers. . . . Such easy morals in literature, such tolerance of baseness, involve our most eminent writers in responsibility for demoralizing country girls. . . .") Dadaism and Surrealism are, of course, totally unacceptable: they represent the "intoxication of license." But less extreme writers are equally guilty in undermining the morals of the time by their emphasis upon such qualities as spontaneity, sincerity, richness, etc., and their pointed ignoring of the age-old values of good and evil. Bergson is suspect in that he values Life itself; Proust is more concerned with beauty than with the Good; all "psychological" literature is reprehensible. In the seventeenth century, Weil asserts with approval, there were people with the "courage" to declare all writers immoral and to act upon their judgment, by sending them to prison or executing them.

It is not only imaginative literature, however, that is dangerous. It is the act of imagining itself. Daydreaming. And why is daydreaming so immoral? *Because it allows the afflicted person a respite from his condition and by such a way is God's will thwarted, however temporarily.* Only "reality," unsoftened by the wishes of a dreaming, yearning mind, is to be tolerated.

In the essay "Friendship" Weil states dogmatically that there can be no friendship when distance is not kept and respected. Erotic love is "unlawful" if the lovers imagine that they form a single entity; in fact, their relationship is "what might be called an adulterous union, even though it comes about between husband and wife." Elsewhere she speaks critically of carnal desires of all kinds (even hunger and thirst) because such desire is an orientation of the body toward the future, while a true detachment, an awareness of the "point of eternity" in one's soul, would be timeless. It is not surprising that Weil should speak with enthusiasm of the Gnostics, the Manichaeans, and the Cathars, and that she should speak contemptuously of the "coarseness of mind" that characterizes orthodox religion.

It has always been puzzling that Simone Weil's forthright anti-Semitism has been ignored, especially by her Jewish admirers. But how is it possible to extract her "saintliness" from her bigotry? The most chilling single entry in *The Simone Weil Reader* is a letter of November 1940 that Weil wrote to the French Ministry of Education, demanding her teaching job back because she did not consider herself a Jew. (The Vichy government had recently passed a statute denying the rights of Jews and persons of Jewish descent.) Step by step, with a precise Kafkan logic, Weil takes up the popular definitions of Judaism and declares herself outside them. She is careful not to attack the statute itself; she is not at all concerned with her Jewish colleagues' fate; she only wants to establish Simone Weil officially as a *non-Jew*. Proudly and desperately she states: "Mine is the Christian, French, Greek tradition. The Hebraic tradition is alien to me. . . . If, nevertheless, the law insists that I consider the term, 'Jew,' whose meaning I don't know, as applying to me, I am inclined to submit, as I would to any law. . . . If the Statute does not apply to me, then I should like to enjoy those rights which I am given by the contract implied in my title of 'professor.' " One waits in vain for Weil to protest the injustice of the statute, or to defend the rights of other Jews who have been persecuted.

Despite Weil's mystical emphasis upon the "point of eternity," her life was characterized by furious bursts of energy. Born in Paris in 1909, to Jewish parents, she became involved at an early age with Marxism, pacifism, and the trade union movement. Though evidently not temperamentally suited for teaching, she taught at various girls' schools and even worked for a while in a factory—but was dismissed for incompetence. She gave away most of her money to "worthy" causes. Posing as a journalist, she joined the Republican Front in the Spanish Civil War but was disabled after two months by an accident, and later wrote a letter to Georges Bernanos denouncing her former comrades for their cruelty. ("What do I care that you are a royalist . . . ?" she asks. "You are incomparably nearer to me than my comrades of the Aragon militias—and yet I loved them.") Increasingly disillusioned and embittered, and grown chronically ill, Weil withdrew from an active involvement with the world and became increasingly—and perhaps idiosyncratically— religious. She studied Greek and Hindu philosophy and, in the years 1940–1942, engaged in intense mystical contemplation and fasting. Displaced by the war, she went to London in 1942, where, to protest the starvation of persons in German-occupied territories, she refused to eat; once hospitalized, she refused all medical treatment and nourishment; she died in 1943, at the age of thirty-four, of starvation and pulmonary tuberculosis, leaving behind a considerable oeuvre: eleven volumes of essays, notebooks, and letters on such subjects as philosophy, literature, history, art, classics, politics, education, economics, and religion. She seems to have known virtually everything; or, at the very least, to have had an opinion on it. The continuous posthumous publication of her works has assured her a place in twentieth-century letters, but it seems to be her mystical writings, and her self-determined death, that have made her famous.

If the essays are examined without reference to the life, however, they rarely rise above the commonplace. "Factory Work," for instance, suffers from its author's predilection for abstraction and analysis without regard for the specific: Weil shows virtually no interest in workers as members of families, as lovers or friends, as *human beings* with a multiplicity of identities and relationships. She is apparently ignorant of the writings of Dickens, Zola, and Lawrence, among others; and she makes no reference to other sociological studies of the effects of urban industrialization upon the "masses." In such essays as "Analysis of Oppression" and "Uprootedness and Nationhood," the possibility of individual happiness is never allowed: "mankind" is imagined as a sort of Platonic essence despoiled by an increasingly mechanized and organized state. (By contrast, see D. H. Lawrence's subtle discussion of the "bonding" between miners, in his little-known essay "Nottingham and the Mining Countryside," in *The New Adelphi,* June–August 1930.) "Reflections on the Right Use of School Studies" has been called by one of Weil's loyal admirers "marvelous foolishness of which one believes every word": but it is doubtful that we can take seriously an educational theory in which school studies of virtually any subject, *no matter how tedious or irrelevant,* might be employed as a means of acquiring the virtues of humility and attentiveness necessary to the love of God. Indeed, can any such theory be justified as "educational" at all? Even Weil's most famous essay, "The *Iliad,* Poem of Might," advances a relatively simple theory, which is expanded at great length: war is brutal and brutalizing. And Weil's concluding diatribe against what she sees as the "Roman" and the "Hebraic" influence in the West is shrilly unconvincing. The melancholy poetic vision of a great work is here made to yield to polemics.

As for Weil's famous mystical essays—"Beauty," "Contemplation of the Divine," "Last Thoughts," "A Spiritual Autobiography"—since they belong to that subspecies of literature Aldous Huxley has called the perennial philosophy, they do not differ in substance or in expression from the writings of numerous other mystics. Writing of the divine, one cannot be original unless, like Kafka or St. John of the Cross, one *is* original in his imagination. Otherwise, a Buddhist saint sounds very much like a Christian saint; Sufism speaks in the accents of the Maitrayana Upanishad; Eckhart and St. Theresa are brother and sister. And Weil, if one can judge fairly by these representative essays, sounds as if she has steeped herself in them all. Her vocabulary consists almost exclusively of nonreferential terms like *good* and *evil, beauty, eternity, the world, the divine, the universe, God.* Her early and abiding infatuation with Platonism underlies this predilection for the abstract at the expense of the specific, but since Weil is no poet, and evidently possessed a fairly limited imagination, her mystical writings are curiously argumentative and flat.

Now that much is known of Weil's life and her obsession with the mortification of the flesh (primarily by way of fasting), it is difficult to take her "visions" seriously. From the age of sixteen Weil evidently felt an extraordinary disgust for the physical life, which must have taken its secret revenge upon her in various ways: not least, in her susceptibility to conversion. She speaks of Christ in embarrassingly girlish terms, wondering if he loves her or not; at the age of twenty-nine, she was so deeply impressed by a young English Catholic (gifted with an "angelic radiance") that, not long afterward, Christ himself came to her one day and "possessed" her. She speaks frankly of the soul's "virginity" being taken by God, and of the soul's "sleeping with God." One of the most curious selections in the *Reader* is an hallucinatory sequence in which Christ comes to Weil like a lover. He is mysterious and abrupt and resolutely masculine. He gives her bread and wine (Weil has been systematically starving herself at this time); they stretch out on the floor together and sleep; they talk of various things, like old friends; then Christ drives her from him, for unclear reasons, and throws her out into the street. This unabashed masochistic fantasy was recorded during the last months of Weil's life, when she was in a severe and possibly irreversible anorexic state.

Virginia Woolf once said that unless she weighed a certain weight she saw visions and heard voices. Thus with us all. It is a fact of physiological life, as anyone who has experimented with fasting, even minimally, knows. At a certain point, simply by not eating, by assuming control of the body's "natural" appetite, one can experience both euphoria and a marvelous and unquestioned sense of certainty. Hence the grimly gloating obsession with starvation that characterizes the sufferer of anorexia nervosa: hence the inclination to "believe" with great passion. (For, it seems, the skepticism of ordinary consciousness, as well as the psychological balance assured by a sense of humor, is lost in these odd "euphoric" states.) So light-headed, so exhausted, one is particularly susceptible to simple explanations of complex matters, and to the most extraordinary incursions from the unconscious: *Misery is joy. Death is life. Affliction is a blessing. God's cruelty assures His tenderness.* In this deranged state, induced by fasting and sleeplessness, Simone Weil made it a practice to repeat, continuously, the Lord's Prayer in Greek: with unsurprising "mystical" results.

It has been said that Weil resembles Kafka's Hunger Artist. But the analogy is false, for Kafka's Artist dies with a realization of his own egoism and spite, and Simone Weil died with her defenses and delusions intact. She more accurately resembles D. H. Lawrence's autobiographical portrait of a Christlike figure in *The Escaped Cock,* who, before his graphic resurrection in the flesh, preached love for all of mankind while being incapable of touching, or tolerating the touch, of a single human being.

The contemporary reader is puzzled, finally, less by Weil herself than by the unquestioned loyalty of her admirers. Do they so crave "saintliness" (in others, if not in themselves) that they will transform a sick, desperate, broken woman into a model of spiritual health; do they so crave "wisdom" that they will accept the speculations of a greatly troubled mind as if these speculations were superior, in fact, to their own? Simone Weil's life and posthumous career are fascinating, and doubtless exemplary of the spiritual vacuum of our century: the hunger to believe in virtually anyone who makes a forthright claim to be divinely guided. *Here below,* we must make do with what we have.

On Boxing

Stories

*Why are you a boxer, Irish featherweight
champion Barry McGuigan was asked. He said:
"I can't be a poet. I can't tell stories. . . ."*

Each boxing match is a story—a unique and highly condensed drama without words. Even when nothing sensational happens: then the drama is "merely" psychological. Boxers are there to establish an absolute experience, a public accounting of the outermost limits of their beings; they will know, as few of us can know of ourselves, what physical and psychic power they possess—of how much, or how little, they are capable. To enter the ring near-naked and to risk one's life is to make of one's audience voyeurs of a kind: boxing is so intimate. It is to ease out of sanity's consciousness and into another, difficult to name. It is to risk, and sometimes to realize, the agony of which *agon* (Greek, "contest") is the root.

In the boxing ring there are two principal players, overseen by a shadowy third. The ceremonial ringing of the bell is a summoning to full wakefulness for both boxers and spectators. It sets into motion, too, the authority of Time.

The boxers will bring to the fight everything that is themselves, and everything will be exposed—including secrets about themselves they cannot fully realize. The physical self, the maleness, one might say, underlying the "self." There are boxers possessed of such remarkable intuition, such uncanny prescience, one would think they were somehow recalling their fights, not fighting them as we watch. There are boxers who perform skillfully, but mechanically, who cannot improvise in response to another's alteration of strategy; there are boxers performing at the peak of their talent who come to realize, mid-fight, that it will not be enough; there are boxers— including great champions—whose careers end abruptly, and irrevocably, as we watch. There has been at least one boxer possessed of an extraordinary and disquieting awareness not only of his opponent's every move and anticipated move but of the audience's keenest shifts in mood as well, for which he seems to have felt personally responsible—Cassius Clay/Muhammad Ali, of course. "The Sweet Science of Bruising" celebrates the physicality of men even as it dramatizes the limitations, sometimes tragic, more often poignant, of the physical. Though male spectators identify with boxers no boxer behaves like a "normal" man when he is in the ring and no combination of blows is "natural." All is style.

Every talent must unfold itself in fighting. So Nietzsche speaks of the Hellenic past, the history of the "contest"—athletic, and otherwise—by which Greek youths were educated into Greek citizenry. Without the ferocity of competition, without, even, "envy, jealousy, and ambition" in the contest, the Hellenic city, like the Hellenic man, degenerated. If death is a risk, death is also the prize—for the winning athlete.

In the boxing ring, even in our greatly humanized times, death is always a possibility—which is why some of us prefer to watch films or tapes of fights already past, already defined as history. Or, in some instances, art. (Though to prepare for writing this mosaic-like essay I saw tapes of two infamous "death" fights of recent times: the Lupe Pintor–Johnny Owen bantamweight match of 1982, and the Ray Mancini–Duk Koo-Kim lightweight match of the same year. In both instances the boxers died as a consequence of their astonishing resilience and apparent indefatigability—their "heart," as it's known in boxing circles.) Most of the time, however, death in the ring is extremely unlikely; a statistically rare possibility like your possible death tomorrow morning in an automobile accident or in next month's headlined airline disaster or in a freak accident involving a fall on the stairs or in the bathtub, a skull fracture, subarachnoid hemorrhage. Spectators at "death" fights often claim afterward that what happened simply seemed to happen—unpredictably, in a sense accidentally. Only in retrospect does death appear to have been inevitable.

If a boxing match is a story it is an always wayward story, one in which anything can happen. And in a matter of seconds. Split seconds! (Muhammad Ali boasted that he could throw a punch faster than the eye could follow, and he may have been right.) In no other sport can so much take place in so brief a period of time, and so irrevocably.

Because a boxing match is a story without words, this doesn't mean that it has no text or no language, that it is somehow "brute," "primitive," "inarticulate," only that the text is improvised in action; the language a dialogue between the boxers of the most refined sort (one might say, as much neurological as psychological: a dialogue of split-second reflexes) in a joint response to the mysterious will of the audience which is always that the fight be a worthy one so that the crude paraphernalia of the setting—ring, lights, ropes, stained canvas, the staring onlookers themselves—be erased, forgotten. (As in the theater or the church, settings are erased by way, ideally, of transcendent action.) Ringside announcers give to the wordless spectacle a narrative unity, yet boxing as performance is more clearly akin to dance or music than narrative.

To turn from an ordinary preliminary match to a "Fight of the Century" like those between Joe Louis and Billy Conn, Joe Frazier and Muhammad Ali, Marvin Hagler and Thomas Hearns is to turn from listening or half-listening to a guitar being idly plucked to hearing Bach's *Well-Tempered Clavier* perfectly executed, and that too is part of the story's mystery: so much happens so swiftly and with such heart-stopping subtlety you cannot absorb it except to know that something profound is happening and it is happening in a place beyond words.

Pain

I hate to say it, but it's true—I only like it better when pain comes.
—FRANK "THE ANIMAL" FLETCHER,
FORMER MIDDLEWEIGHT CONTENDER

Years ago in the early 1950s when my father first took me to a Golden Gloves boxing tournament in Buffalo, New York, I asked him why the boys wanted to fight one another, why they were willing to get hurt. As if it were an explanation my father said, "Boxers don't feel pain quite the way we do."

Pain, in the proper context, is something other than pain.

Consider: Gene Tunney's single defeat in a thirteen-year career of great distinction was to a notorious fighter named Harry Greb who seems to have been, judging from boxing lore, the dirtiest fighter in history. Greb was infamous for his fouls—low blows, butting, "holding and hitting," rubbing his laces against an opponent's eyes, routine thumbing—as well as for a frenzied boxing style in which blows were thrown from all directions. (Hence, "The Human Windmill.") Greb, who died young, was a world middleweight champion for three years but a flamboyant presence in boxing circles for a long time. After the first of his several fights with Greb the twenty-two-year-old Tunney was so badly hurt he had to spend a week in bed; he'd lost an astonishing two quarts of blood during the fifteen-round fight. Yet, as Tunney said some years later:

> Greb gave me a terrible whipping. He broke my nose, maybe with a butt. He cut my eyes and ears, perhaps with his laces. . . . My jaw was swollen from the right temple down the cheek, along under the chin and partway up the other side. The referee, the ring itself, was full of blood. . . . But it was in that first fight, in which I lost my American light-heavyweight title, that I knew I had found a way to beat Harry eventually. I was fortunate, really. If boxing in those days had been afflicted with the Commission doctors we have today—who are always poking their noses into the ring and examining superficial wounds— the first fight with Greb would have been stopped before I learned how to beat him. It's possible, even probable, that if this had happened I would never have been heard of again.

Tunney's career, in other words, was built upon pain. Without it he would never have moved up into Dempsey's class.

Tommy Loughran, light-heavyweight champion in the years 1927–29, was a master boxer greatly admired by other boxers. He approached boxing literally as a science—as Tunney did—studying his opponents' styles and mapping out ring strategy for each fight, as boxers and their trainers commonly do today. Loughran rigged up mirrors in his basement so that he could watch himself as he worked out, for, as he said, no boxer ever sees himself quite as he appears to his opponent. He sees the opponent but not himself as an opponent. The secret of Loughran's career was that his right hand broke easily so that he was forced to use it only once each fight: for the knockout punch or nothing. "I'd get one shot then the agony of the thing would hurt me if the guy got up," Loughran said. "Anybody I ever hit with a left hook I knocked flat on his face, but I would never take a chance for fear if my [left hand] goes, I'm done for."

Both Tunney and Loughran, it is instructive to note, retired from boxing well before they were forced to retire. Tunney became a highly successful businessman, and Loughran a highly successful sugar broker on the Wall Street commodities market. (Just to suggest that boxers are not invariably stupid, illiterate, or punch-drunk.)

Then there was Carmen Basilio!—much loved for his audacious ring style, his hit-and-be-hit approach. Basilio was world middle- and welterweight champion 1953–57, stoic, determined, a slugger willing to get hit in order to deal powerful counter-punches of his own. Onlookers marveled at the punishment Basilio seemed to absorb though Basilio insisted that he didn't get hit the way people believed. And when he was hit, and hit hard—

> People don't realize how you're affected by a knockout punch when you're hit on the chin. It's nerves is all it is. There's no real concussion as far as the brain is concerned. I got hit on the point of the chin [in a match with Tony DeMarco in 1955]. It was a left hook that hit the right point of my chin. What happens is it pulls your jawbone out of your socket from the right side and jams it into the left side and the nerve there paralyzed the whole left side of my body, especially my legs. My left knee buckled and I almost went down, but when I got back to my corner the bottom of my foot felt like it had needles about six inches high and I just kept stamping my foot on the floor, trying to bring it back. And by the time the bell rang it was all right.

Basilio belongs to the rough-and-tumble era of LaMotta, Graziano, Zale, Pep, Saddler; Gene Fullmer, Dick Tiger, Kid Gavilan. An era when, if two boxers wanted to fight dirty, the referee was likely to give them license, or at least not to interfere.

Of Muhammad Ali in his prime Norman Mailer observed, "He worked apparently on the premise that there was something obscene about being hit." But in fights in his later career, as with George Foreman in Zaire, even Muhammad Ali was willing to be hit, and to be hurt, in order to wear down an opponent. Brawling fighters—those with "heart" like Jake LaMotta, Rocky Graziano, Ray Mancini—have little choice but to absorb terrible punishment in exchange for some advantage (which does not in any case always come). And surely it is true that some boxers (see Jake LaMotta's autobiographical *Raging Bull*) invite injury as a means of assuaging guilt, in a Dostoyevskian exchange of physical well-being for peace of mind. Boxing is about being hit rather more than it is about hitting, just as it is about feeling pain, if not devastating psychological paralysis, more than it is about winning. One sees clearly from the "tragic" careers of any number of boxers that the boxer prefers physical pain in the ring to the absence of pain that is ideally the condition of ordinary life. If one cannot hit, one can yet be hit, and know that one is still alive.

It might be said that boxing is primarily about maintaining a body capable of entering combat against other well-conditioned bodies. Not the public spectacle, the fight itself, but the rigorous training period leading up to it demands the most discipline, and is believed to be the chief cause of the boxer's physical and mental infirmities. (As a boxer ages his sparring partners get younger, the game itself gets more desperate.)

The artist senses some kinship, however oblique and one-sided, with the professional boxer in this matter of training. This fanatic subordination of the self in terms of a wished-for destiny. One might compare the time-bound public spectacle of the boxing match (which could be as brief as an ignominious forty-five seconds—the record for a title fight!) with the publication of a writer's book. That which is "public" is but the final stage in a protracted, arduous, grueling, and frequently despairing period of preparation. Indeed, one of the reasons for the habitual attraction of serious writers to boxing (from Swift, Pope, Johnson to Hazlitt, Lord Byron,

Hemingway, and our own Norman Mailer, George Plimpton, Ted Hoagland, Wilfrid Sheed, Daniel Halpern, et al.) is the sport's systematic cultivation of pain in the interests of a project, a life-goal: the willed transposing of the sensation we know as pain (physical, psychological, emotional) into its polar opposite. If this is masochism—and I doubt that it is, or that it is simply—it is also intelligence, cunning, strategy. It is an act of consummate self-determination—the constant reestablishment of the parameters of one's being. To not only accept but to actively invite what most sane creatures avoid—pain, humiliation, loss, chaos—is to experience the present moment as already, in a sense, past. *Here* and *now* are but part of the design of *there* and *then*: pain now but control, and therefore triumph, later. And pain itself is miraculously transposed by dint of its context. Indeed, it might be said that "context" is all.

The novelist George Garrett, an amateur boxer of some decades ago, reminisces about his training period:

> I learned something . . . about the brotherhood of boxers. People went into this brutal and often self-destructive activity for a rich variety of motivations, most of them bitterly antisocial and verging on the psychotic. Most of the fighters I knew of were wounded people who felt a deep, powerful urge to wound others at real risk to themselves. In the beginning. What happened was that in almost every case, there was so much self-discipline required and craft involved, so much else besides one's original motivations to concentrate on, that these motivations became at least cloudy and vague and were often forgotten, lost completely. Many good and experienced fighters (as has often been noted) become gentle and kind people. . . . They have the habit of leaving all their fight in the ring. And even there, in the ring, it is dangerous to invoke too much anger. It can be a stimulant, but is very expensive of energy. It is impractical to get mad most of the time.

Of all boxers it seems to have been Rocky Marciano (still our only undefeated heavyweight champion) who trained with the most monastic devotion; his training methods have become legendary. In contrast to reckless fighters like Harry "The Human Windmill" Greb, who kept in condition by boxing all the time, Marciano was willing to seclude himself from the world, including his wife and family, for as long as three months before a fight. Apart from the grueling physical ordeal of this period and the obsessive preoccupation with diet and weight and muscle tone, Marciano concentrated on one thing: the upcoming fight. Every minute of his life was defined in terms of the opening second of the fight. In his training camp the opponent's name was never mentioned in Marciano's hearing, nor was boxing as a subject discussed. In the final month Marciano would not write a letter since a letter related to the outside world. During the last ten days before a fight he would see no mail, take no telephone calls, meet no new acquaintances. During the week before the fight he would not shake hands. Or go for a ride in a car, however brief. No new foods! No dreaming of the morning after the fight! For all that was not *the fight* had to be excluded from consciousness. When Marciano worked out with a punching bag he saw his opponent before him, when he jogged he saw his opponent close beside him, no doubt when he slept he "saw" his opponent constantly—as the cloistered monk or nun chooses by an act of fanatical will to "see" only God.

Madness?—or merely discipline?—this absolute subordination of the self. In any case, for Marciano, it worked.

Eroticism

Tommy Hearns was a little cocky, and I had something for him.
—Marvin Hagler

No sport is more physical, more direct, than boxing. No sport appears more power-fully homoerotic: the confrontation in the ring—the disrobing—the sweaty heated combat that is part dance, courtship, coupling—the frequent urgent pursuit by one boxer of the other in the fight's natural and violent movement toward the "knock-out": surely boxing derives much of its appeal from this mimicry of a species of erotic love in which one man overcomes the other in an exhibition of superior strength and will. The heralded celibacy of the fighter-in-training is very much a part of boxing lore: instead of focusing his energies and fantasies upon a woman the boxer focuses them upon an opponent. Where Woman has been, Opponent must be.

As Ali's Bundini Brown has said: "You got to get the hard-on, and then you got to keep it. You want to be careful not to lose the hard-on, and cautious not to come."

Most fights, however fought, end with an embrace between the boxers after the final bell—a gesture of mutual respect and apparent affection that appears to the onlooker to be more than perfunctory. Rocky Graziano sometimes kissed his oppo-nents out of gratitude for the fight. One might wonder if the boxing match leads irresistibly to this moment: the public embrace of two men who otherwise, in public or in private, could never approach each other with such passion. Though many men are loudly contemptuous of weakness (as if eager to dissociate themselves from it: as during a boxing match when one or both boxers are unwilling to fight) a woman is struck by the admiration, amounting at times to awe, they will express for a man who has exhibited superior courage while losing his fight. And they will express tenderness for injured boxers, even if it is only by way of commentary on photo-graphs: the picture of Ray Mancini after his second defeat by Livingstone Bramble, for instance, when Mancini's face was hideously battered (photographs in *Sports Illustrated* and elsewhere were gory, near-pornographic); the much-reprinted photo-graph of the defeated Thomas Hearns being carried to his corner in the arms of an enormous black man (a bodyguard, one assumes) in solemn formal attire—Hearns the "Hit Man" now helpless, semiconscious, looking very like a black Christ taken from the cross. These are powerful, haunting, unsettling images, cruelly beautiful, inextricably bound up with boxing's primordial appeal.

Yet to suggest that men might love and respect one another directly, without the violent ritual of combat, is to misread man's greatest passion—for war, not peace. Love, if there is to be love, comes second.

In Place of Woman

What time is it?—"Macho Time"!
—Hector "Macho Man" Camacho,
WBC LIGHTWEIGHT CHAMPION

I don't want to knock my opponent out. I want to hit him, step away, and watch
him hurt. I want his heart.
—Joe Frazier,
FORMER HEAVYWEIGHT CHAMPION OF THE WORLD

A fairy-tale proposition: the heavyweight champion is the most dangerous man on earth: the most feared, the most manly. His proper mate is very likely the fairy-tale princess whom the mirrors declare the fairest woman on earth.

Boxing is a purely masculine activity and it inhabits a purely masculine world. Which is not to suggest that most men are defined by it: clearly, most men are not. And though there are female boxers—a fact that seems to surprise, alarm, amuse—women's role in the sport has always been extremely marginal. (At the time of this writing the most famous American woman boxer is the black champion Lady Tyger Trimiar with her shaved head and theatrical tiger-striped attire.) At boxing matches women's role is limited to that of card girl and occasional National Anthem singer: stereotypical functions usually performed in stereotypically zestful feminine ways—for women have no natural place in the spectacle otherwise. The card girls in their bathing suits and spike heels, glamour girls of the 1950s, complement the boxers in their trunks and gym shoes but are not to be taken seriously: their public exhibition of themselves involves no risk and is purely decorative. Boxing is for men, and is about men, and *is* men. A celebration of the lost religion of masculinity all the more trenchant for its being lost.

In this world, strength of a certain kind—matched of course with intelligence and tirelessly developed skills—determines masculinity. Just as a boxer is his body, a man's masculinity is his use of his body. But it is also his triumph over another's use of his body. The Opponent is always male, the Opponent is the rival for one's own masculinity, most fully and combatively realized. Sugar Ray Leonard speaks of coming out of retirement to fight one man, Marvin Hagler: "I want Hagler. I need that man." Thomas Hearns, decisively beaten by Hagler, speaks of having been obsessed with him: "I want the rematch badly . . . there hasn't been a minute or an hour in any day that I haven't thought about it." Hence women's characteristic repugnance for boxing per se coupled with an intense interest in and curiosity about men's fascination with it. Men fighting men to determine worth (i.e., masculinity) excludes women as completely as the female experience of childbirth excludes men. And is there, perhaps, some connection?

In any case, raw aggression is thought to be the peculiar province of men, as nurturing is the peculiar province of women. (The female boxer violates this stereo-type and cannot be taken seriously—she is parody, she is cartoon, she is monstrous. Had she an ideology, she is likely to be a feminist.) The psychologist Erik Erikson discovered that, while little girls playing with blocks generally create pleasant interior spaces and attractive entrances, little boys are inclined to pile up the blocks as high as they can and then watch them fall down: "the contemplation of ruins," Erikson observes, "is a masculine specialty." No matter the mesmerizing grace and beauty of a great boxing match, it is the catastrophic finale for which everyone waits, and hopes: the blocks piled as high as they can possibly be piled, then brought spectacularly down. Women, watching a boxing match, are likely to identify with the losing, or hurt, boxer; men are likely to identify with the winning boxer. There is a point at which male spectators are able to identify with the fight itself as, it might be said, a Platonic experience abstracted from its particulars; if they have favored one boxer over the other, and that boxer is losing, they can shift their loyalty to the winner—or, rather, "loyalty" shifts, apart from conscious volition. In that way the ritual of fighting is always honored. The high worth of combat is always affirmed.

Boxing's very vocabulary suggests a patriarchal world taken over by adolescents. This world is young. Its focus is youth. Its focus is of course *macho—machismo* raised beyond parody. To enter the claustrophobic world of professional boxing even as a spectator is to enter what appears to be a distillation of the masculine world, empty now of women, its fantasies, hopes, and stratagems magnified as in a distorting mirror, or a dream.

Here, we find ourselves through the looking-glass. Values are reversed, evaginated: a boxer is valued not for his humanity but for being a "killer," a "mauler," a "hit-man," an "animal," for being "savage," "merciless," "devastating," "ferocious," "vicious," "murderous." Opponents are not merely defeated as in a game but are "decked," "stiffed," "starched," "iced," "destroyed," "annihilated." Even the veteran sportswriters of so respectable a publication as *The Ring* are likely to be pitiless toward a boxer who has been beaten. Much of the appeal of Roberto Durán for intellectual boxing *aficionados* no less than for those whom one might suppose his natural constituency was that he seemed truly to want to kill his opponents: in his prime he was the "baby-faced assassin" with the "dead eyes" and "deadpan" expression who once said, having knocked out an opponent named Ray Lampkin, that he hadn't trained for the fight—next time he would kill the man. (According to legend Durán once felled a horse with a single blow.) Sonny Liston was another champion lauded for his menace, so different in spirit from Floyd Patterson as to seem to belong to another subspecies; to watch Liston overcome Patterson in tapes of their fights in the early 1960s is to watch the defeat of "civilization" by something so elemental and primitive it cannot be named. Masculinity in these terms is strictly hierarchical—two men cannot occupy the same space at the same time.

At the present time twenty-year-old Mike Tyson, Cus D'Amato's much-vaunted protégé, is being groomed as the most dangerous man in the heavyweight division. He is spoken of with awe as a "young bull"; his strength is prodigious, at least as demonstrated against fairly hapless, stationary opponents; he enters the arena robeless—"I feel more like a warrior"—and gleaming with sweat. He does not even wear socks. His boxing model is not Muhammad Ali, the most brilliant heavyweight of modern times, but Rocky Marciano, graceless, heavy-footed, indomitable, the man with the massive right-hand punch who was willing to absorb five blows in the hope of landing one. It was after having broken Jesse Ferguson's nose in a recent match that Tyson told reporters that it was his strategy to try to drive the bone back into the brain. . . .

*   *   *

The names of boxers! *Machismo* as sheer poetry.

Though we had, in another era, "Gentleman Jim" Corbett (world heavyweight champion, 1892–97); and the first black heavyweight champion, Jack Johnson (1908–15) called himself "Li'l Arthur" as a way of commenting playfully on his powerful physique and savage ring style. (Johnson was a white man's nightmare: the black man who mocked his white opponents as he humiliated them with his fists.) In more recent times we had "Sugar Ray" Robinson and his younger namesake "Sugar Ray" Leonard. And Tyrone Crawley, a thinking man's boxer, calls himself "The Butterfly." But for the most part a boxer's ring name is chosen to suggest something more ferocious: Jack Dempsey of Manassa, Colorado, was "The Manassa Mauler"; the formidable Harry Greb was "The Human Windmill"; Joe Louis was, of course, "The Brown Bomber"; Rocky Marciano, "The Brockton Blockbuster"; Jake LaMotta, "The Bronx Bull"; Tommy Jackson, "Hurricane" Jackson; Roberto Durán, "Hands of Stone" and "The Little Killer" variously. More recent are Ray "Boom-Boom" Mancini, Thomas "Hit-Man" Hearns, James "Hard Rock" Green, Al "Earthquake" Carter, Frank "The Animal" Fletcher, Donald "The Cobra" Curry, Aaron "The Hawk" Pryor, "Terrible" Tim Witherspoon, "Bonecrusher" Smith, Johnny "Bump City" Bumphus, Lonnie "Lightning" Smith, Barry "The Clones Cyclone" McGuigan, Gene "Mad Dog" Hatcher, Livingstone "Pit Bull" Bramble, Hector "Macho Man" Camacho. "Marvelous" Marvin Hagler changed his name legally to Marvelous Marvin Hagler before his fight with Thomas Hearns brought him to national prominence.

It was once said by José Torres that the *machismo* of boxing is a condition of poverty. But it is not, surely, a condition uniquely of poverty? Or even of adolescence? I think of it as the obverse of the feminine, the denial of the feminine-in-man that has its ambiguous attractions for all men, however "civilized." It is a remnant of another, earlier era when the physical being was primary and the warrior's masculinity its highest expression.

Flannery O'Connor:
A Self-Portrait in Letters

Profundity, Nietzsche said, loves the mask. And so it will be no surprise to admirers of Flannery O'Connor's enigmatic, troubling, and highly idiosyncratic fiction to learn that there were, behind the near-perfect little rituals of violence and redemption she created, not one but several Flannery O'Connors. And how wildly they differed. . . . The experience of reading these collected letters (which are, in fact, rigorously *selected* letters) is a disturbing one: but tonic, provocative, intriguing. For while it cannot be said of Flannery O'Connor's fiction that she revealed herself anywhere within it—her strategy was to submerge herself, to "correct" emotion by means of art—it must be said of the letters that they give life to a wonderfully warm, witty, generous, and complex personality, surely one of the most gifted of contemporary writers. At the same time they reveal a curiously girlish, childlike, touchingly timid personality, so conventional that the very idea of allowing James Baldwin to visit her in Milledgeville, Georgia, in 1959 frightened her into saying that she observed the traditions of the society she fed upon (which was, in most respects, defiantly untrue)—and that the meeting, "innocent" elsewhere, would cause her the "greatest trouble and disturbance and disunion" in Georgia. The letters give voice, on one side, to a hilariously witty observer of the grotesque, the vulgar, and the merely silly in this society, and in the rather limited world of the Catholic imagination; and then they reveal a Catholic intellectual so conservative and docile that she will write to a priest-friend for permission to read Gide and Sartre (at that time on the Church's Index of forbidden writers)—and she will remark, to another friend, that the Church is correct in "warning" believers against Teilhard de Chardin since his work is "incomplete and unclear on the subject of grace." Her view of "Cathlicks" was by no means a sentimental one; she knew that, as she said so succinctly, "The silence of the Catholic critic is so often preferable to his attention." (She did indeed endure ignorant misinterpretations of her work.) But then she will piously condemn the film of Tennessee Williams's *Baby Doll* as a "dirty little piece of trash"—without having seen it.

A brief review is not the place to count, even to categorize, aspects of personality: masks, voices, disingenuous roles. But I counted at least five distinctly different Flannery O'Connors here, in these pages, and it struck me as highly interesting that the O'Connor of the fiction is nowhere present. She simply doesn't exist—in the letters. She exists, as she must, only—and supremely—in the fiction. One should not read *The Habit of Being* with the hope of penetrating the "secret" of Flannery O'Connor's art, or even with the hope of learning more about her intentions and habits of composition than is already available in her posthumous collection of essays, *Mystery and Manners.* She wrote slowly, so slowly that it took her the same length of time (seven years) to write the brief, spare *The Violent Bear It Away* that it took Joyce to write *Ulysses.* (And Joyce too suffered ill-health.) Each paragraph, each sentence, each word was written with great deliberation, and rewritten, and rewritten, so that the final product—austere, "comic," allegorical, parable-like—was inevitably somewhat artificial, and inevitably profound. The person, the woman, the gracious, rather shy Southern girl Flannery, certainly could not embody such high seriousness in her being. She says in a letter to Elizabeth Hardwick and Robert Lowell, in 1954: ". . . I don't look very intelligent. I was in Nashville . . . and met a man who looked at me a while and said (of *Wise Blood*), 'That was a profound book. You don't look like you wrote it.' I mustered up my squintiest expression and snarled, 'Well I did,' but at the same time I had to recognize he was right." Apart from such rare remarks she seems not to have been troubled in the slightest by the contradictory, even warring aspects of her personality. If something disturbed her enough it found its way, no doubt, into her art: it did not touch her life. Or so it would seem, judging from the evidence of *The Habit of Being.*

The first letter in the collection was written in 1948, when Flannery was "up north" at Yaddo, the writers' colony in Saratoga Springs. (I am following Sally Fitzgerald in referring to Flannery O'Connor as *Flannery*: the full name seems inappropriately formal.) The last letter, a heartbreaking one, was written just before her death on August 3, 1964, when she knew she was dying (she had already taken the Sacrament of the Sick a month earlier) of complications following an operation for the removal of a tumor. The years between 1948 and 1964 were rich, full ones, despite the fact that Flannery's debilitating condition (lupus) kept her at home, and frequently bedridden, for long periods of time. She was not at all a solitary, reclusive person; she had a wide circle of friends and acquaintances, and clearly loved seeing them, and writing to them often. Among her "literary" and "interleteckchul" friends were Caroline Gordon and Allen Tate; Elizabeth Hardwick and Robert Lowell; Richard Stern; Robie Macauley; Elizabeth Bishop; Granville Hicks; John Hawkes; Walker Percy; J. F. Powers; Marion Montgomery; Robert Giroux (her editor); Andrew Lytle; and of course Sally and Robert Fitzgerald, at whose home in Connecticut she stayed. (She was evidently friendly with James Dickey as well, but for some reason no letters of hers to Dickey are reprinted here.) All the letters are warm, frank, bright, and courteous; only a few exhibit impatience with asinine questions about the deep symbolic meaning of her stories, put to her by "professors of English" and their students, and indefatigable pseudo-Freudians given to hallucinating phallic imagery on every page. (Perhaps Flannery was too kind, and wasted her tragically limited energies . . .? It is a pity that she felt obliged to reply to people who clearly misunderstood her work, or who took offense at it, as if she felt, despite her confidence in her art, that she must defend it. Her sharpest remark—which is very much justified—is made in response to a "litterary" person's queries about Freudian imagery in *The Violent Bear It Away:* "I'm sorry the book didn't come off for you but I think it is no wonder it didn't since you see everything in terms of sex symbols. . . . My Lord, Billy, recover your simplicity. You ain't in Manhattan. Don't inflict that stuff on the poor students there; they deserve better."

The most unanticipated, and perhaps the most unsettling, of the various Flannerys is the disingenuous hick, the self-conscious, self-mocking bumpkin who emerges in certain letters with great zest. This is the Flannery who never hesitates to make bad jokes and puns, to misspell words in a coyly illiterate way, to tell outrageous tales about Georgia doings; she refers to her *Opus nauseous,* she alludes to the tragedy of *Edipus,* she sprinkles her comments freely with "aint," "it don't," "yestiddy," "naw," "bidnis," "Cathlicks," "pilgrumidge," "litterary." The affectation of a sub-Socratic irony may strike some readers as embarrassing, particularly when it is overdone; and despite Sally Fitzgerald's insistence in her excellent introduction that Flannery loved and respected her mother, Regina, it is difficult to know how to interpret the numerous comic sketches in which Regina appears, often as a good-natured, bumbling idiot. The portrait is funny but cruel. But it *is* funny:

> My mamma and I have interesting literary discussions like the following which took place over some Modern Library books I had just ordered:
>
> SHE: *"Mobby Dick.* I've always heard about that."
>
> ME: *"Mow-by Dick."*
>
> SHE: *"Mow-by Dick. The Idiot.* You would get something called *Idiot.* What's it about?"
>
> ME: "An idiot." (From a letter of February 1953)

> Regina is getting very literary. "Who is this Kafka?" she says. "People ask me." A German Jew, I says, I think. He wrote a book about a man who turns into a roach. "Well, I can't tell people *that,*" she says. "Who is this Evalin Wow?"

Poor hapless Regina struggles with stray mules and with her hired help, who are every bit as grotesque as the poor whites in Flannery's stories; she despairs over her daughter's diction and her evident disdain for the more explicit Southern graces. She tells Flannery in exasperation, "You talk just like a nigger and someday you are going to be away from home and do it and people are going to wonder WHERE YOU CAME FROM." Certainly Flannery was hiding behind this mask, and yet one must assume that it *did* express her feelings, for there is a consistency about her country-cousinish persona that suggests the shrewd simplicity of a number of her characters. From a letter to Richard Stern, July 1963:

> What you ought to do is get you a Fullbright to Georgia and quit messing around with all those backward places you been at. Anyhow, don't pay a bit of attention to the Eyetalian papers. . . . All us niggers and white folks over here are just getting along grand—at least in Georgia and Mississippi. I hear things are not so good in Chicago and Brooklyn but you wouldn't expect them to know what to do with theirself there.

Then there is the conservative Catholic, who would seem, in my imagination at least, to seriously underestimate the artist: as if Flannery the docile, "good" little girl, schooled by nuns, were incapable of comprehending the other Flannery's gifts. Again and again she insists that "I write the way I do because and only because I am a Catholic. I feel that if I were not a Catholic, I would have no reason to write, no reason to see, no reason ever to feel horrified or even to enjoy anything." Of the novella *Wise Blood:* "The book was not agin free-will . . . which all the characters had plenty of and exercised. . . . The thought is all Catholic, perhaps overbearingly so." The celebration of the Mass, the taking of the Eucharist (which Flannery believed to *be* Christ's actual body and blood, and not "merely" a symbol), were for Flannery the "center of existence"; "all the rest of life is expendable." Though Flannery's ill-health must have caused her untold suffering, she insists upon the fact that such suffering, coming from personal *experience,* is less significant than the Church's teachings. If one gains in insight it is primarily through the Church: "simply from listening to what the Church teaches." God is Love, and all good, all complete, all powerful. That children may suffer hideous deaths is of course a mystery, not to be comprehended by mortal man, but there is never any doubt that God is All Good. Flannery, unlike her marvelous comic creation Hulga (who believes defiantly in nothing, and has a wooden leg), *believes* and *accepts* without the faintest protest.

The piety is touching, if sometimes implausible, and certainly it tells us nothing about the art to which Flannery devoted herself. The conservatism is rather more unpleasant, suggesting, as conservatism so frequently does, a refusal to examine one's beliefs, even one's vocabulary. I was saddened to read, and could not help interpreting in the context of the speaker's debilitating illness, and the small likelihood of *her* ever conceiving an unwanted child, such remarks as these:

> The Church's stand on birth control is the most absolutely spiritual of all her stands and with all of us being materialists at heart, there is little wonder that it causes unease. I wish various [priests] would quit trying to defend it by saying that the world can support 40 billion. I will rejoice in the day when they say: This is right, whether we all rot on top of each other or not, dear children. . . . Either practice restraint or be prepared for crowding. . . . [June 1959]

By twisting words about Flannery can convince herself that the Church's stand on birth control is "liberal"! Though she is well aware of the Church's history of persecution, she nevertheless insists in an ongoing debate with one of her closest friends, "A," that one cannot connect the Church with a belief in the use of force. "The Church is a mystical body which cannot, does not, believe in the use of force (in the sense of forcing conscience, denying the rights of conscience, etc.). I know all her hair-raising history . . . but principle must be separated from policy" (September 1955). In such circumspect, sophistic ways have the meek always aligned themselves with the bullies, allowing the organization, the hierarchy, to be their conscience for them, and to commit those crimes the meek would never dare entertain, even in fantasy. One has the feeling, in reading these passages, that the imaginative, artistic Flannery O'Connor had been nearly silenced by the bigot—and would have to take her revenge in art.

Though she had, evidently, no more than a conventional critical sensibility—she dismissed Randall Jarrell's marvelous *Pictures from an Institution* as bad fiction, she referred to Virginia Woolf as a "nut," and declared that she couldn't tell Mozart from Spike Jones, and despised the piano "and all its works"—she did possess a highly reliable talent for assessing her own work. She seems always to have known that she wrote well; that she *was* gifted. She saw how *Wise Blood* failed, she saw how certain of her stories—"Revelation," "Judgment Day," "Parker's Back"— succeeded beautifully. Having spent months on the long story *The Lame Shall Enter First,* she saw that it simply didn't come off, and tried—too late, as it happened—to stop its publication in *Sewanee Review.* Her instincts about her own fiction were always right. She wrote ingenious parables of the spiritual life, and her characters were drawn with broad, slashing strokes—"I am not one of the subtle sensitive writers like Eudora Welty," she says—meant to suggest, but not to embody, "reality." A creator of romances, like Hawthorne, or even Poe; but one with a fine, sharp eye for the absurd. (It is not surprising that she first wanted to be a cartoonist, and sent off cartoons, week after week, to *The New Yorker,* where they were invariably rejected.) Though she could not resist traveling to writers' conferences and to universities, where, in her words, "clichés are swapped" about the art of writing, she always knew that the process of creation was subjected to no rules, and that, as an artist, she "discovered" the truth of her stories in the writing of them. She enjoyed writing—perhaps it is not an exaggeration to say that she lived for it, and in it. Easily exhausted, she forced herself to work two or three hours every day, in the morning, and managed by this discipline to write about one story a year during the worst periods. During the final year of her life, 1964, when everything seemed to go wrong (tumor, operation, infections, reactivation of lupus, side effects of cortisone) she was completing the volume that would be her finest achievement, *Everything That Rises Must Converge,* which would be published, to wide critical acclaim, after her death. (One cannot imagine an ailing person less given to self-pity. When, as a fairly young woman, she learned that she would probably be on crutches the rest of her life, she says merely, "So, so much for that. I will henceforth be a structure with flying buttresses. . . ." Writing to a friend, Louise Abbot, in 1964, she says that she must submit to an operation because "I have a large tumor and if they don't make haste and get rid of it, they will have to remove me and leave it." It is only near the very end of her life that she says, briefly, to the same friend: "Prayers requested. I am sick of being sick.")

Partly because of her condition, and partly because of her temperament, Flannery O'Connor seems to have lived one of the most circumscribed lives ever lived by a distinguished artist. In a sense she enjoyed a prolonged childhood which was never ravaged by adolescence or the complications of "adult" life. (Judging by the collected letters and by Sally Fitzgerald's remarks, Flannery did not, evidently, write a single love letter, and there are no allusions to romantic relationships in her letters to friends. At the age of thirty-seven she writes defiantly to a friend, "I've usually had my own room but it's always been subject to intrusion. The only thing in mine that is not subject to intrusion is my desk. Nobody lays a hand on that, boy." Nobody meaning, of course, her mother, Regina.)

"As for biographies," Flannery said in 1958, "there won't be any biographies of me because, for only one reason, lives spent between the house and the chicken yard do not make exciting copy." But we measure an artist by the quality and depth of interior vision, and by the magnitude of achievement: and by these standards Flannery O'Connor is one of our finest writers. *The Habit of Being* is a deeply moving, deeply disturbing, and ultimately very beautiful record of a highly complex woman artist whose art was, perhaps, too profound for even the critic in her to grasp.

Considerations for Thinking and Writing

1. What do you think of the way Oates develops her argument about the pleasures of reading? Do all of those personal anecdotes convince you, or would you prefer a more formal presentation, something more objective? Explain.

2. Read Oates's " 'May God Grant that I Become Nothing' " and Susan Sontag's "Simone Weil." Look especially at the concluding paragraphs of each essay. Characterize what you think are the differences between Oates's and Sontag's views of Weil and her life's work. Think too about the differences in the way the two women present their views. Explain why you think they develop their essays in different ways. Might Oates be responding to Sontag in her essay? Explain.

3. In her essays on Weil and O'Connor, Oates looks carefully at two eccentric women. Why does she admire one and raise serious questions about the reliability of the other? To what extent do you think you can find Oates as a person in her own essays? Explain.

4. Oates calls her book *On Boxing* a "mosaic-like essay." Why do you think she chose that description? In the four pieces of the mosaic included in this anthology, you can see that Oates is trying to recover something mysterious behind the boxing bouts; she's not just reporting from the outside. What is she trying to reveal to us? Reading her other essays in this volume, can you see additional signs of Oates probing beneath life's surfaces? What do you think are her primary interests? Speculate a bit.

5. Do you think, after reading these selections, that Oates is a feminist? Explain.

6. Oates is a teacher; so is June Jordan. Read the final section of "Literature as Pleasure," and read Jordan's "Nobody Mean More to Me than You and the Future Life of Willie Jordan." Which woman would you prefer as a teacher? Explain.

CYNTHIA OZICK
(b. 1928)

Cynthia Ozick's essays are complex because while she is always herself, she is always many: a novelist, an essayist, a woman, a Jew. Born in New York City, she traces her literary ardor to a "big green truck"—a traveling library—that stopped often at her parents' Bronx pharmacy. According to her essay "The Lesson of the Master," writing a master's thesis on Henry James led her to spend "seven fruitless years" on a novel that remains unfinished and unpublished. This Jamesian apprenticeship was a hard one; in the end, Ozick had to teach herself "the true Lesson of the Master,"

> simply, never to venerate what is complete, burnished, whole, in its grand organic flowering or finish—never to look toward the admirable and dazzling end; never to be ravished by the goal; never to worship ripe Art or the ripened artist; but instead to seek to be young while young, primitive while primitive, ungainly when ungainly—to look for crudeness and rudeness, to husband one's own stupidity or ungenius.

The author of three novels—*Trust* (1983), *The Cannibal Galaxy* (1983), and *The Messiah of Stockholm* (1987)—and as many collections of short fiction, Ozick shows us that writing, at its best, is an act of ripening, not the erection of monuments. Her moral seriousness and intellectual rigor are animated by a wild and sometimes rude imagination, unafraid of its own energies.

In the foreword to *Art and Ardor* (1983), her collection of essays, Cynthia Ozick contrasts the wondrous journey of writing fiction with the essay writer's "journey of obligation": "No essay carrying its bundle of information, subject matter, 'field,' theme, argument, intent, no essay carrying its armful of context, point

of view, explicit history and explicit culture, can equal that. Essays know too much." But in the next breath, Ozick argues with herself:

> Except sometimes. Knowledge is not made out of knowledge. Knowledge swims up from invention and imagination—from ardor—and sometimes even an essay can invent, burn, guess, try out, dig up, hurtle forward, succumb to that flood of sign and nuance that adds up to intuition, disclosure, discovery. The only nonfiction worth writing—at least for me—lacks the summarizing gift, is heir to nothing, and sets out with empty pockets from scratch. Sensibility (or intellect, or susceptibility) is most provoked when most deprived of scaffolding; then it has to knot sheets for the climb.

The pages of Ozick's essays are often knotted sheets. She writes about difficulties, the knots of experience and thinking that measure out "the perilous span between birth and death," and her essays are often difficult. But they are essays in which craft and passion and wisdom make strange yet comfortable bedfellows.

As an essayist, Ozick broods often on the relation between life and letters. In biography she sees a commitment of life to letters and letters to life which many writers of contemporary fiction have relegated to the nineteenth century. "A good biography is itself a kind of novel," writes Ozick of R. B. Lewis's biography of Edith Wharton. In "Mrs. Virginia Woolf: A Madwoman and Her Nurse" Ozick discovers and retells a hidden story in Quentin Bell's biography of Virginia Woolf: the enigmatic story of the "outsider," Leonard Woolf, and his pursuit of a daughter of the illustrious Stephen family. Ozick's gift for asking unflinching questions serves her well here: "Whether Leonard Woolf fell in love with a young woman of beauty and intellect, or more narrowly with a Stephen of beauty and intellect, will always be a formidable . . . question." It is no more formidable than another question that Ozick asks: why Leonard Woolf decided that the couple would remain childless. And why, Ozick wants to know, did Leonard Woolf make the gargantuan and often thankless effort to keep his wife sane? Such questions merit manifold answers: "For her sake, for art's sake, for his own sake." Ozick senses that fairness to Leonard Woolf demands acknowledgment that "to keep her sane was, ultimately, to keep her writing." But finally it is Virginia Woolf's writing that Ozick asks us to take as an "antidote" to the biographical tales told by Woolf's widower and her nephew.

Paradoxically, Ozick's fascination with the interplay of life and letters stands beside her conviction that a writer's mind—a writer's "true" and "secret" self—is essentially private and mysterious. As she boldly declared in the pages of *Ms.*, "I am, as a writer, whatever I wish to become. I can think myself into a male, or a female, or a stone, or a raindrop, or a block of wood, or a Tibetan, or the spine of a cactus." If Ozick does not hear her own voice as a woman's voice, it may be for two reasons. First, as this quotation shows, she chafes at limiting the imagination to a single voice. Second, she is frankly disturbed by what she views among contemporary feminists as a betrayal of classical feminism. It was the agenda of classical feminism, according to Ozick, to defeat the "Great Multiple Lie": the assumption of a psychology, temperament, cluster of preoccupations, sensibility, and literary style peculiar to women. For Ozick, the label "woman writer"—whether used by men or by women—retains the bitter taint of the Lie, and she resists it vehemently: "In the absence of a women's movement, the term 'woman writer' had shut out, damaged, and demeaned writers; with the emergence of the movement and the direction it has taken, there are now no allies any-

where against reductiveness, and the language of clarity falls more and more into rubble." Ozick knows well that hers is a dissenting voice, that her views are unpopular with feminists who believe that the study of sexual difference will lead to a fairer, richer, and truer sense of human diversity. Perhaps some of this resentment stems from the fact that while Ozick voices her position on feminism resolutely, she seldom engages in dialogue with feminists.

But despite her claim that "when I write, I am free," Ozick realizes that "in life, I am not free." Her writings, whether fantastic or earthbound, identify her life as that of a woman and a Jew. Of the twenty-three essays in *Art and Ardor*, nine treat writing by women (including herself); ten others treat Jewish writers and issues. On being a Jew in America, Ozick writes:

> Paul's tactical "Be all things to all men" cannot apply; my own striving is . . . to speak in the same voice to every interlocutor, Gentile or Jew; not to have one attitude or subject matter (or imagining or storytelling) for one kind of friend and another for another kind. To be inwardly inhibited from this openness is mental abasement.

In "The Riddle of the Ordinary," Ozick considers the prohibition of idolatry, the crux of Mosaic law, against the matrix of culture. Originally written for a Jewish audience, this essay begins with a seemingly familiar contrast: that between the Extraordinary and the Ordinary. Soon we realize that this essay is not about two distinct categories but about how the Ordinary becomes the Extraordinary when our vision exalts it. Swiftly and naturally, Ozick's subject flowers into two ways of viewing the Ordinary. Her homely terms generate others more resonant—Image and Deed, aesthetic and moral, Greek and Hebrew. By the end, the Hebraic No—the prohibition of idolatry—meets the "shower of Yeses" that Jewish blessings rain on creation. "The Riddle of the Ordinary" is a tour de force that depends equally on inspiration and on craft.

Ozick's essays often derive their energy from her skilled pairing of ideas or people. In "Mrs. Virginia Woolf" Ozick observes dramatically that the two Woolfs are mutually exclusive: "Wherever Leonard Woolf is, there Virginia Woolf is not." More often, comparison and contrast result in a dialogue: between novel and biography, between domestic and demonic writers, between the Extraordinary and the Ordinary. Ozick is fond of using parables and anecdotes to dramatize her arguments. As a stylist, she has a gift for varied sentence structures, interspersing long, graceful, periodic sentences among sharp questions and blunt, aphoristic conclusions. Perhaps her meticulous craft, which brings to mind Woolf and Hazlitt, results from her apprenticeship to James, or from her readings of Latin poets; perhaps it is a happy freak of nature; most likely it is the sweet fruit of her hard labor. Whatever the secrets of her talent, the essays are ours to savor. As we read and reread them, we might say of Ozick what she says of Woolf: "She becomes easier to read, more complex to consider."

The Riddle of the Ordinary

Though we all claim to be monotheists, there is one rather ordinary way in which we are all also dualists: we all divide the world into the Ordinary and the Extraordinary. This is undoubtedly the most natural division the mind is subject to—plain and fancy, simple and recondite, commonplace and awesome, usual and unusual, credible and incredible, quotidian and intrusive, natural and unnatural, regular and irregular, boring and rhapsodic, secular and sacred, profane and holy: however the distinction is characterized, there is no human being who does not, in his own everydayness, feel the difference between the Ordinary and the Extraordinary.

The Extraordinary is easy. And the more extraordinary the Extraordinary is, the easier it is: "easy" in the sense that we can almost always recognize it. There is no one who does not know when something special is happening: the high, terrifying, tragic, and ecstatic moments are unmistakable in any life. Of course the Extraordinary can sometimes be a changeling, and can make its appearance in the cradle of the Ordinary; and then it is not until long afterward that we become aware of how the visitation was not, after all, an ordinary one. But by and large the difference between special times and ordinary moments is perfectly clear, and we are never in any doubt about which are the extraordinary ones.

How do we respond to the Extraordinary? This too is easy: by paying attention to it. The Extraordinary is so powerful that it commands from us a redundancy, a repetition of itself: it seizes us so undividedly, it declares itself so dazzlingly or killingly, it is so deafening with its LOOK! SEE! NOTICE! PAY ATTENTION! that the only answer we can give is to look, see, notice, and pay attention. The Extraordinary sets its own terms for its reception, and its terms are inescapable. The Extraordinary does not let you shrug your shoulders and walk away.

But the Ordinary is a much harder case. In the first place, by making itself so noticeable—it is around us all the time—the Ordinary has got itself in a bad fix with us: we hardly ever notice it. The Ordinary, simply by *being* so ordinary, tends to make us ignorant or neglectful; when something does not insist on being noticed, when we aren't grabbed by the collar or struck on the skull by a presence or an event, we take for granted the very things that most deserve our gratitude.

And this is the chief vein and deepest point concerning the Ordinary: that it *does* deserve our gratitude. The Ordinary lets us live out our humanity; it doesn't scare us, it doesn't excite us, it doesn't distract us—it brings us the safe return of the school bus every day, it lets us eat one meal after another, put one foot in front of the other. In short, it is equal to the earth's provisions; it grants us life, continuity, the leisure to recognize who and what we are, and who and what our fellows are, these creatures who live out their everydayness side by side with us in their own unextraordinary ways. Ordinariness can be defined as a breathing-space: the breathing-space between getting born and dying, perhaps; or else the breathing-space between rapture and rapture; or, more usually, the breathing-space between one disaster and the next. Ordinariness is sometimes the *status quo*, sometimes the slow, unseen movement of a subtle but ineluctable cycle, like a ride on the hour hand of the clock; in any case the Ordinary is above all *what is expected.*

And what is expected is not often thought of as a gift.

The second thing that ought to be said about the Ordinary is that it is sometimes extraordinarily dangerous to notice it. And this is strange, because I have just spoken of the gratitude we owe to the unnoticed foundations of our lives, and how careless we always are about this gratitude, how unthinking we are to take for granted the humdrum dailiness that is all the luxury we are ever likely to know on this planet. There are ways to try to apprehend the nature of this luxury, but they are psychological tricks, and do no good. It is pointless to contemplate, only for the sake of feeling gratitude, the bitter, vicious, crippled, drugged, diseased, deformed, despoiled, or corrupted lives that burst against their own mortality in hospitals, madhouses, prisons, all those horrendous lives chained to poverty and its variegated spawn in the long, bleak wastes on the outer margins of Ordinariness, mired in the dread of a ferocious Extraordinariness that slouches in insatiably every morning and never departs even in sleep—contemplating this, who would deny gratitude to our own Ordinariness, though it does not come easily, and has its demeaning price? Still, comparison confers relief more often than gratitude, and the gratitude that rises out of reflection on the extraordinary misfortune of others is misbegotten.—You remember how in one of the Old English poets we are told how the rejoicing hosts of heaven look down at the tortures of the damned, feeling the special pleasure of their own exemption. The consciousness of Ordinariness *is* the consciousness of exemption.

That is one way it is dangerous to take special notice of the Ordinary.

The second danger, I think, is even more terrible. But before I am ready to speak of this new, nevertheless very ancient, danger, I want to ask this question: If we are willing to see the Ordinary as a treasure and a gift, what are we to *do* about it? Or, to put it another way, what is to be gained from noticing the Ordinary? Morally and metaphysically, what are our obligations to the Ordinary? Here art and philosophy meet with a quizzical harmony unusual between contenders. "Be one of those upon whom nothing is lost," Henry James advised; and that is one answer, the answer of what would appear to be the supreme aesthetician. For the sake of the honing of consciousness, for the sake of becoming sensitive, at every moment, *to* every moment, for the sake of making life as superlatively polished as the most sublime work of art, we ought to notice the Ordinary.

No one since the Greek sculptors and artisans has expressed this sense more powerfully than Walter Pater, that eloquent Victorian whose obsession with attaining the intensest sensations possible casts a familiar light out toward the century that followed him. Pater, like Coleridge before him and James after him, like the metaphysicians of what has come to be known as the Counterculture, was after all the highs he could accumulate in a lifetime. "We are all under sentence of death," he writes, ". . . we have an interval, and then our place knows us no more. Some spend this interval in listlessness, some in high passions, the wisest . . . in art and song. For our only chance lies in expanding that interval, in getting as many pulsations as possible into the given time. Great passions may give us this quickened sense of life. . . . Only be sure it is passion—that it does yield you this fruit of a quickened, multiplied consciousness. . . . Of this wisdom, the poetic passion, the desire for beauty, the love of art for art's sake, has most; for art comes to you professing frankly to give nothing but the highest quality to your moments as they pass, and simply for those moments' sake." And like a Zen master who seizes on the data of life only to transcend them, he announces: "Not the fruit of experience, but experience itself, is the end."

What—in this view, which once more has the allegiance of the *Zeitgeist*—what is Art? It is first noticing, and then sanctifying, the Ordinary. It is making the Ordinary into the Extraordinary. It is the impairment of the distinction between the Ordinary and the Extraordinary.

The aestheticians—the great Experiencers—can be refuted. I bring you a Hebrew melody to refute them with. It is called "The Choice"; the poet is Yeats; and since the poem is only eight lines long I would like to give over the whole of it. It begins by discriminating between essence and possession: life interpreted as *doing* beautiful things or *having* beautiful things:

> The intellect of man is forced to choose
> Perfection of the life, or of the work,
> And if it take the second must refuse
> A heavenly mansion, raging in the dark.
> When all that story's finished, what's the news?
> In luck or out the toil has left its mark:
> That old perplexity an empty purse,
> Or the day's vanity, the night's remorse.

Our choice, according to Yeats, is the choice between pursuing the life of Deed, where acts have consequences, where the fruit of experience is more gratifying than the experience itself, and pursuing the life of Art, which signifies the celebration of shape and mood. Art, he tells us, turns away from the divine preference, and finishes out a life in empty remorse; in the end the sum of the life of Art is nothing. The ironies here are multitudinous, for no one ever belonged more to the mansion of Art than Yeats himself, and it might be said that in this handful of remarkable lines Yeats condemned his own passions and his own will.

But there is a way in which the Yeats poem, though it praises Deed over Image, though it sees the human being as a creature to be judged by his acts rather than by how well he has made something—there is a way in which this poem is after all *not* a Hebrew melody. The Jewish perception of how the world is constituted also tells us that we are to go in the way of Commandment rather than symbol, goodness rather than sensation: but it will never declare that the price of Art, Beauty,

Experience, Pleasure, Exaltation is a "raging in the dark" or a loss of the "heavenly mansion."

The Jewish understanding of the Ordinary is in some ways very close to Pater, and again very far from Yeats, who would punish the "perfection of the work" with an empty destiny.

With David the King we say, "All that is in the heaven and the earth is thine," meaning that it is all there for our wonder and our praise. "Be one of those upon whom nothing is lost"—James's words, but the impulse that drives them is the same as the one enjoining the observant Jew (the word "observant" is exact) to bless the moments of this world at least one hundred times a day. One hundred times: but Ordinariness is more frequent than that, Ordinariness crowds the day, we swim in the sense of our dailiness; and yet there is a blessing for every separate experience of the Ordinary.

Jewish life is crammed with such blessings—blessings that take note of every sight, sound, and smell, every rising-up and lying-down, every morsel brought to the mouth, every act of cleansing. Before he sits down to his meal, the Jew will speak the following: "Blessed are You, O Lord our God, Ruler of the Universe, whose Commandments hallow us, and who commands us to wash our hands." When he breaks his bread, he will bless God for having "brought forth bread from the earth." Each kind of food is similarly praised in turn, and every fruit in its season is praised for having renewed itself in the cycle of the seasons. And when the meal is done, a thanksgiving is said for the whole of it, and table songs are sung with exultation.

The world and its provisions, in short, are *observed*—in the two meanings of "observe." Creation is both noticed and felt to be sanctified. Everything is minutely paid attention to, and then ceremoniously praised. Here is a Talmudic saying: "Whoever makes a profane use of God's gifts"—which means partaking of any worldly joy without thanking God for it—"commits a theft against God." And a Talmudic dispute is recorded concerning which is the more important Scriptural utterance: loving your neighbor as yourself, or the idea that we are all the children of Adam. The sage who has the final word chooses the children-of-Adam thesis, because, he explains, our common creatureliness includes the necessity of love. But these celebrations through noticing are not self-centered and do not stop at humanity, but encompass every form of life and non-life. So there are blessings to rejoice in on smelling sweet woods or barks, fragrant plants, fruits, spices, or oils. There is a blessing on witnessing lightning, falling stars, great mountains and deserts: "Blessed are You . . . who fashioned Creation." The sound of thunder has its praise, and the sight of the sea, and a rainbow; beautiful animals are praised, and trees in their first blossoming of the year or for their beauty alone, and the new moon, and new clothing, and sexual delight. The sight of a sage brings a blessing for the creation of human wisdom, the sight of a disfigured person praises a Creator who varies the form of his creatures. From the stone to the human being, creatureliness is extolled.

This huge and unending shower of blessings on our scenes and habitations, on all the life that occupies the planet, on every plant and animal, and on every natural manifestation, serves us doubly: in the first place, what you are taught to praise you will not maim or exploit or destroy. In the second place, the categories and impulses of Art become the property of the simplest soul: because it is all the handiwork of the Creator, everything Ordinary is seen to be Extraordinary. The world, and every moment in it, is seen to be sublime, and not merely "seen to be," but brought home to the intensest part of consciousness.

Come back with me now to Pater: "The service of philosophy," he writes, "of speculative culture, toward the human spirit is to rouse, to startle it into sharp and eager observation. Every moment some form grows perfect in hand or face; some tone on the hills or the sea is choicer than the rest; some mood of passion or insight or intellectual excitement is irresistibly real and attractive to us—for that moment only." And now here at last is Pater's most celebrated phrase, so famous that it has often been burlesqued: "To burn always with this hard, gemlike flame, to maintain this ecstasy, is success in life."

But all this is astonishing. An idolator singing a Hebrew melody? I call Pater an idolator because he is one; and so is every aesthetician who sees the work of art as an end in itself. Saying "Experience itself is the end" is the very opposite of blessing the Creator as the source of all experience.

And just here is the danger I spoke of before, the danger Yeats darkly apprehended—the deepest danger our human brains are subject to. The Jew has this in common with the artist: he means nothing to be lost on him, he brings all his mind and senses to bear on noticing the Ordinary, he is equally alert to Image and Experience, nothing that passes before him is taken for granted, everything is exalted. If we are enjoined to live in the condition of noticing all things—or, to put it more extremely but more exactly, in the condition of awe—*how can we keep ourselves from sliding off from awe at God's Creation to worship of God's Creation?* And does it matter if we do?

The difference, the reason it matters, is a signal and shattering one: the difference is what keeps us from being idolators.

What is an idol? Anything that is allowed to come between ourselves and God. Anything that is *instead of* God. Anything that we call an end in itself, and yet is not God Himself.

The Mosaic vision concerning all this is uncompromisingly pure and impatient with self-deception, and this is the point on which Jews are famously stiff-necked— nothing but the Creator, no substitute and no mediator. The Creator is not contained in his own Creation; the Creator is incarnate in nothing, and is free of any image or imagining. God is not any part of Nature, or in any part of Nature; God is not any man, or in any man. When we praise Nature or man or any experience or work of man, we are worshiping the Creator, and the Creator alone.

But there is another way of thinking which is easier, and sweeter, and does not require human beings to be so tirelessly uncompromising, or to be so cautious about holding on to the distinction between delight in the world and worship of the world.

Here is a story. A Buddhist sage once rebuked a person who excoriated an idolator: "Do you think it makes any difference to God," he asked, "whether this old woman gives reverence to a block of wood? Do you think God is incapable of taking the block of wood into Himself? Do you think God will ignore anyone's desire to find Him, no matter where, and through whatever means? All worship goes up to God, who is the source of worship."

These are important words; they offer the most significant challenge to purist monotheism that has ever been stated. They tell us that the Ordinary is not merely, when contemplated with intensity, the Extraordinary, but more, much more than that—that the Ordinary is also the divine. Now there are similar comments in Jewish sources, especially in Hasidism, which dwell compassionately on the nobility of the striving for God, no matter through what means. But the striving is always toward the Creator Himself, the struggle is always toward the winnowing-out of every mediating surrogate. The Kotzker Rebbe went so far in his own striving that he even dared to interpret the command against idols as a warning not to make an idol out of a command of God.—So, in general, Jewish thought balks at taking the metaphor for the essence, at taking the block of wood as symbol or representation or mediator for God, despite the fact that the wood and its worshiper stand for everything worthy of celebration: the tree grew in its loveliness, the carver came and fashioned it into a pleasing form, the woman is alert to holiness; the tree, the carver, the woman who is alert to holiness are, all together, a loveliness and a reason to rejoice in the world. But still the wood does not mean God. It is instead of God.

It is not true, as we so often hear, that Judaism is a developmental religion, that there is a progression upward from Moses to the Prophets. The Prophets enjoined backsliders to renew themselves through the Mosaic idea, and the Mosaic idea is from then to now, and has survived unmodified: "Take heed to yourselves, that your heart be not deceived, and ye turn aside, and serve other gods, and worship them." (Deut. 11:16.) This perception has never been superseded. To seem to supersede it is to transgress it.

So it is dangerous to notice and to praise the Ordinariness of the world, its inhabitants and its events. We want to do it, we rejoice to do it, above all we are commanded to do it—but there is always the easy, the sweet, the beckoning, the lenient, the *interesting* lure of the *Instead Of:* the wood of the tree instead of God, the rapture-bringing horizon instead of God, the work of art instead of God, the passion for history instead of God, philosophy and the history of philosophy instead of God, the state instead of God, the shrine instead of God, the sage instead of God, the order of the universe instead of God, the prophet instead of God.

There is no Instead Of. There is only the Creator. God is alone. That is what we mean when we utter the ultimate Idea which is the pinnacle of the Mosaic revolution in human perception: God is One.

The child of a friend of mine was taken to the Egyptian galleries of the Museum. In a glass case stood the figure of a cat resplendent in the perfection of its artfulness—long-necked, gracile, cryptic, authoritative, beautiful, spiritual, autonomous, complete in itself. "I understand," said the child, "how they wanted to bow down to this cat. I feel the same." And then she said a Hebrew word: *asur*—forbidden—the great hallowed No that tumbles down the centuries from Sinai, the No that can be said only after the world is no longer taken for granted, the No that can rise up only out of the abundant celebrations and blessings of Yes, Yes, Yes, the shower of Yeses that praise fragrant oils, and wine, and sex, and scholars, and thunder, and new clothes, and falling stars, and washing your hands before eating.

Mrs. Virginia Woolf:
A Madwoman and Her Nurse

No recent biography has been read more thirstily by readers and writers of fiction than Quentin Bell's account of the life of his aunt Virginia. Reviewing it, Elizabeth Hardwick speaks of "the present exhaustion of Virginia Woolf," and compares the idea of Bloomsbury—it "wearies"—to a pond run out of trout. But for most American writers, bewildered by the instability of what passes for culture and literature, envious of the English sense of place and of being placed, conscious of separations that yet lack the respectability of "schools" or even the interest of alien perspectives, stuck mainly with the crudity of being either For or Against Interpretation, the legend of Bloomsbury still retains its inspiriting powers. Like any Golden Age, it promises a mimetic future: some day again, says Bloomsbury of 1905, there will be friends, there will be conversation, there will be moods, and they will all again *really matter,* and fall naturally, in the way of things that matter, into history.

Part of the special history of the Bloomsbury of mood is pictorial—and this has nothing to do with the art critic Roger Fry, or the painter Duncan Grant. It is not what the painters painted or what the writers wrote about painting that hangs on: it is the photographs, most of them no more official than snapshots, of the side of a house, two people playing checkers on an old kitchen chair set out in the yard, three friends and a baby poking in the sand. The snapshots are all amateur. Goblets of brightness wink on eaves, fences, trees, and wash out faces in their dazzle; eyes are lost in blackened sockets. The hem of a dress is likely to be all clarity, but the heads escape—under hat brims, behind dogs, into mottled leaf-shade. And out of the blur of those hopeless poses, cigarettes, hands on knees, hands over books, anxious little pups held up to the camera, walking sticks, long grotesque nose-shadows, lapels, outdoor chairs and tables, there rises up—no, leaks down—so much tension, so much ambition, so much fake casualness, so much heartbreaking attention to the momentariness of the moment. The people in the snapshots knew, in a way we do not, who they were. Bloomsbury was self-conscious in a way we are not. It sniffed at its own perceptions, even its own perceived posterity. Somewhere early in the course of her diaries, Virginia Woolf notes how difficult it would be for a biographer to understand her—how little biographers can know, she said—only from the evidence of her journals. Disbelieving in the probity of her own biography, she did not doubt that she would have her own biographer.

She did not doubt; she knew; they knew. Hatched from the last years of the reign of Victoria, Bloomsbury was still a world where things—if not people, then ideas—could be said to reign. Though old authority might be sneered at (or something worse even than a sneer—Virginia Woolf declared her certainty that she could not have become a writer had her father lived), though proprieties might be outrageously altered ("Semen?" asked Lytton Strachey, noticing a stain on Vanessa Bell's skirt one afternoon), though sex was accessible and often enough homoerotic, though freedom might be proclaimed on Gordon Square, though livings were earned, there was nonetheless a spine of authority to support Bloomsbury: family, descent, class and community—the sense of having-in-common. Bloomsbury, after all, was an inheritance. Both E. M. Forster's and Virginia Woolf's people were associated with the liberal and intellectual Clapham Sect of the century before. Cambridge made a kind of cousinship—the staircase at Trinity that drew together Clive Bell, Saxon Sydney-Turner, and Virginia Woolf's brother Thoby Stephen was the real beginning of the gatherings at Gordon Square. Bloomsbury was pacifist and busy with gossip about what it always called "buggery," but it was not radical and it did not harbor rebels. Rebels want to make over; the Bloomsburyites reinforced themselves with their like. The staircase at Trinity went on and on for the rest of their lives, and even Virginia Woolf, thinking to make over the form of the novel, had to have each newly completed work ratified by Morgan Forster and sometimes Maynard Keynes before she could breathe at ease again. The authority of one's closest familiars is the unmistakable note of Bloomsbury. It was that sure voice she listened for. "Virginia Woolf was a Miss Stephen," Quentin Bell begins, in the same voice; it is an opening any outsider could have written, but not in that sharp cadence. He is not so much biographer as a later member of the circle—Virginia Woolf's sister's son, the child of Vanessa and Clive Bell. He knows, he does not doubt. It is the note of self-recognition; of confidence; of inheritance. Everything is in his grip.

And yet—as she predicted—Virginia Woolf's biographer fails her. He fails her, in fact, more mournfully than any outsider could. It is his grip that fails her. This is not only because, sticking mainly to those matters he has sure authority over, he has chosen to omit a literary discussion of the body of work itself. "I have found the work of the biographer sufficiently difficult without adventuring in other directions," he tells us, so that to speak of Quentin Bell's "sure authority" is not to insinuate that all his data are, perhaps, out of childhood memory or family reminiscence, or that he has not mined library after library, and collection after collection of unpublished papers. He is, after all, of the next generation, and the next generation is always in some fashion an outsider to the one before. But what *is* in his grip is something more precise, curiously, than merely data, which the most impersonal research can reliably throw up: it is that particular intimacy of perspective—of experience, really—which characterizes not family information, but family bias. Every house has its own special odor to the entering guest, however faint—it sticks to the inhabitants, it is in their chairs and in their clothes. The analogy of bias to scent is chiefly in one's unconsciousness of one's own. Bell's Woolf is about Virginia, but it has the smell of Vanessa's house. The Virginia Woolf that comes off these pages is a kind of emanation of a point of view, long settled, by now, into family feeling. Stephens, Pattles, Fishers—all the family lines—each has its distinct and legendary scent. The Stephens are bold, the Pattles are fair, the Fishers are self-righteous. And Virginia is mad.

She was the family's third case of insanity, all on the Stephen side. Leslie Stephen, Virginia Woolf's celebrated father—a man of letters whose career was marked not least by the circumstance that Henry James cherished him—was married twice, the second time to Julia Duckworth, a widow with children. Together they produced Vanessa and Virginia, Thoby and Adrian. A child of Leslie Stephen's first marriage, the younger of Virginia's two half-sisters, was born defective—it is not clear whether backward or truly insane—and was confined to an asylum, where she died old. Virginia's first cousin—the child of her father's brother—went mad while still a young man, having struck his head in an accident. But one wonders, in the retrograde and rather primitive way one contemplates families, whether there might not have been a Stephen "taint." In a family already accustomed to rumor of aberration, Virginia Woolf, in any case, was incontrovertibly mad. Her madness was distinguished, moreover, by a threatening periodicity: at any moment it could strike, disabling everyone around her. Vanessa had to leave her children and come running, nurses had to be hired, rest homes interviewed, transport accomplished. The disaster was ten times wider than its victim.

And just here is the defect in writing out of family authority. The odor is personal, hence partial. Proust says somewhere that the artist brings to the work his whole self, to his familiars only those aspects that accommodate them. The biographer close to his subject has the same difficulty; the aspect under which Quentin Bell chiefly views his aunt Virginia is not of accommodation but of a still narrower partiality: discommodity, the effect on family perspective of Virginia Woolf's terrible and recurrent insanity. It was no mere melancholia, or poetic mooning—as, reading Leonard Woolf's deliberately truncated edition of her diary, we used to guess. A claustrophilic though inspired (also self-inspiring) document, it made us resent the arbitrary "personal" omissions: was it the madness he was leaving out? Certainly we wanted the madness too, supposing it to be the useful artistic sort: grotesque moods, quirks—epiphanies really. But it was not that; it was the usual thing people get put away for, an insanity characterized by incoherent howling and by violence. She clawed her attendants and had to be restrained; she would not touch food; she was suicidal. Ah, that cutting difference: not that she longed for death, as poets and writers sometimes do for melancholy's sake, but that she wanted, with the immediacy of a method, to be dead.

Bell's Woolf, then, is not about the Virginia Woolf of the diaries, essays, and novels—not, in the Proustian sense, about the writer's whole self. And surely this is not simply because literary criticism is evaded. Bell's Woolf is not about a writer, in fact; it is about the smell of a house. It is about a madwoman and her nurse.

The nurse was Leonard Woolf. Upon him Quentin Bell can impose no family aspects, rumors, characteristics, old experience, inherited style. He does not trail any known house-scent, like Stephens, Pattles, Fishers. Though he shared the Cambridge stairs—Thoby Stephen, Saxon Sydney-Turner, Clive Bell, Lytton Strachey, and Leonard Woolf together briefly formed the Midnight Society, a reading club that met on Saturday evenings in Clive Bell's rooms—he was not an inheritor of Cambridge. Cambridge was not natural to him, Bloomsbury was not natural to him, even England was not natural to him—not as an inheritance; he was a Jew. Quentin Bell has no "authority" over Leonard Woolf, as he has over his aunt; Leonard is nowhere in the biographer's grip.

The effect is unexpected. It is as if Virginia Woolf escapes—possessing her too selectively, the biographer lets her slip—but Leonard Woolf somehow stays to become himself. Which is to say, Bell's Virginia Woolf can be augmented by a thousand other sources—chiefly by her own work—but we learn as much about Leonard Woolf here as we are likely to know from any other source. And what we learn is a strange historical judgment, strange but unfragmented, of a convincing wholeness: that Leonard Woolf was a family sacrifice. Without him—Quentin Bell's clarity on this point is ineffaceable—Virginia Woolf might have spent her life in a mental asylum. The elder Stephens were dead, Thoby had died at twenty-six, Adrian married a woman apparently indifferent to or incompatible with the Bloomsburyites; it was Vanessa on whom the grimness fell. Leonard Woolf—all this is blatant—got Vanessa off the hook. He was, in fact, deceived: he had no inkling he was being captured for a nurse.

Neither Vanessa nor Adrian gave him a detailed and explicit account of Virginia's illnesses or told him how deadly serious they might be. . . . Her insanity was clothed, like some other painful things in that family, in a jest. . . . Thus, in effect if not in intention, Leonard was allowed to think of Virginia's illnesses as something not desperately serious, and he was allowed to marry her without knowing how fearful a care such a union might be. In fairness to all parties it must be said that, even if Virginia's brother and sister had been as explicit and circumstantial as they ought to have been, Leonard would certainly not have been deflected from his purpose of marrying Virginia. . . . As it was, he learnt the hard way and one can only wonder, seeing how hard it was, and that he had for so long to endure the constant threat of her suicide, to exert constant vigilance, to exercise endless persuasive tact at mealtimes and to suffer the perpetual alternations of hope and disappointment, that he too did not go mad.

In fact he nearly did, although he does not mention it.

"He does not mention it." There was in Leonard Woolf an extraordinary silence, a containment allied to something like concealment, and at the same time open to a methodical candor. This is no paradox; candor is often the mode of the obtuse person. It is of course perilous to think of Leonard Woolf as obtuse: he was both activist and intellectual, worldly and introspective; his intelligence, traveling widely and serenely over politics and literature, was reined in by a seriousness that makes him the most responsible and conscientious figure among all the Bloomsburyites. His seriousness was profound. It was what turned a hand press "small enough to stand on a kitchen table" into the Hogarth Press, an important and innovative publishing house. It was what turned Leonard Woolf himself from a highly able agent of colonialism—at the age of twenty-four he was an official of the British ruling apparatus in Ceylon—into a convinced anti-imperialist and a fervent socialist. And it was what turned the Jew into an Englishman.

Not that Leonard Woolf is altogether without ambivalence on this question; indeed, the word "ambivalence" is his own. Soon after his marriage to Virginia Stephen, he was taken round on a tour of Stephen relations—among them Virginia's half-brother, Sir George Duckworth, in his large house in Dalingridge Place, and "Aunt Anny," who was Lady Ritchie, Thackeray's daughter, in St. George's Square. He suffered in these encounters from an "ambivalence in my attitude to the society which I found in Dalingridge Place and St. George's Square. I disliked its respectability and assumptions while envying and fearing its assurance and manners." And: "I was an outsider to this class, because, although I and my father before me belonged to the professional middle class, we had only recently struggled up into it from the stratum of Jewish shopkeepers. We had no roots in it." This looks like candor—"we had no roots"—but it is also remarkably insensible. Aware of his not belonging, he gives no evidence anywhere that the people he moved among were also aware of it. It is true that his own group of self-consciously agnostic Cambridge intellectuals apparently never mentioned it to his face. Thoby Stephen in a letter to Leonard in Ceylon is quick enough to speak of himself, mockingly, as a nonbelieving Christian—"it's no good being dainty with Christians and chapel's obviously rot"—but no one seems ever to have teased Leonard about his being an agnostic Jew. In the atmosphere of that society, perhaps, teasing would have too dangerously resembled baiting; levity about being a Christian was clearly not interchangeable with levity about being a Jew. Fair enough: it never is. But Virginia, replying to a letter in which Leonard implores her to love him, is oddly analytical: ". . . of course, I feel angry sometimes at the strength of your desire. Possibly, your being a Jew comes in also at this point. You seem so foreign." Was he, like all those dark lubricious peoples whose origins are remote from the moderating North, too obscurely other? She corrects herself at once, with a kind of apology: "And then I am fearfully unstable. I pass from hot to cold in an instant, without any reason; except that I believe sheer physical effort and exhaustion influence me." The correction—the retraction—is weak, and fades off; what remains is the blow: "You seem so foreign."

274

We do not know Leonard's response to this. Possibly he made none. It would have been in keeping had he made none. Foreignness disconcerted him—like Virginia he was at moments disturbed by it and backed away—and if his own origins were almost never mentioned to his face, his face was nevertheless *there,* and so, in those striking old photographs, were the faces of his grandparents. Leonard Woolf is bemused in his autobiography by his paternal grandfather, "a large, stern, black-haired, and black-whiskered, rabbinical Jew in a frock coat." Again he speaks of this "look of stern rabbinical orthodoxy," and rather prefers the "round, pink face of an incredibly old Dutch doll," which was the face of his Dutch-born maternal grand-mother—about whom he speculates that it was "possible that she had a good deal of non-Jewish blood in her ancestry. Some of her children and grandchildren were fair-haired and facially very unlike the 'typical' Jew." Her husband, however, was a different case: "No one could have mistaken him for anything but a Jew. Although he wore coats and trousers, hats and umbrellas, just like those of all the other gentlemen in Addison Gardens, he looked to me as if he might have stepped straight out of one of those old pictures of caftaned, bearded Jews in a ghetto. . . ." Such Jews, he notes, were equipped with "a fragment of spiritual steel, a particle of passive and unconquerable resistance," but otherwise the character, and certainly the his-tory, of the Jews do not draw him. "My father's father was a Jew," he writes, exempting himself by two generations. "I have always felt in my bones and brain and heart English and, more narrowly, a Londoner, but with a nostalgic love of the city and civilization of ancient Athens." He recognizes that his "genes and chromo-somes" are something else; he is a "descendant" of "the world's official fugitives and scapegoats."

But a "descendant" is not the same as a member. A descendant shares an origin, but not necessarily a destiny. Writing in his eighties, Leonard Woolf recollects that as a schoolboy he was elected to an exclusive debating society under the thumb of G. K. Chesterton and his brother, and "in view of the subsequent violent anti-Semitism of the Chestertons" he finds this "amusing"; he reports that he was "surprised and flattered." Sixty-three years afterward he is still flattered. His descrip-tion of the public school that flattered him shows it to be a detestable place, hostile to both intellect and feeling: "I got on quite well with the boys in my form or with whom I played cricket, football, and fives, but it would have been unsafe, practically impossible, to let them know what I really thought or felt about anything which seemed to me important." *Would have been unsafe.* It was a risk he did not take—unlike Morgan Forster, who, in the same situation in a similar school, allowed himself to be recognized as an intellectual and consequently to suffer as a schoolboy pariah. Leonard Woolf did not intend to take on the role of pariah, then or later. Perhaps it was cowardice; or perhaps it was the opposite, that "fragment of spiritual steel" he had inherited from the ghetto; or perhaps it was his sense of himself as exempt from the ghetto.

Certainly he always thought of himself as wholly an Englishman. In the spring of 1935 he and Virginia drove to Rome. "I was astonished then (I am astonished still)," Quentin Bell comments, "that Leonard chose to travel by way of Germany." They were on German soil three days; near Bonn they encountered a Nazi demon-stration but were unharmed, and entered Italy safely. What prompted Leonard Woolf to go into Germany in the very hour Jews were being abused there? Did he expect Nazi street hoodlums to distinguish between an English Jewish face and a

German Jewish face? He carried with him—it was not needed and in the event of street hoodlumism would anyhow have been useless—a protective letter from an official of the German embassy in London. More than that, he carried—in his "bones and brain and heart"—the designation of Englishman. It was a test, not of the inherited fragment of spiritual steel, but of the strength of his exemption from that heritage. If Quentin Bell is twice astonished, it may be because he calculated the risk more closely than Leonard; or else he is not quite so persuaded of the Englishness of Leonard Woolf as is Leonard Woolf.

And, superficially at least, it is difficult to be persuaded of it. One is drawn to Leonard's face much as he was drawn to his grandfather's face, and the conclusion is the same. What Leonard's eyes saw was what the eyes of the educated English classes saw. What Leonard felt on viewing his grandfather's face must have been precisely what Clive Bell and Thoby Stephen would have felt. There is an arresting snapshot—still another of those that make up the pictorial history of Bloomsbury—of Leonard Woolf and Adrian Stephen. They are both young men in their prime; the date is 1914. They are standing side by side before the high narrow Gothic-style windows of Asham House, the Sussex villa Leonard and Virginia Woolf owned for some years. They are dressed identically (vests, coats, ties) and positioned identically—feet apart, hands in pockets, shut lips gripping pipe or cigarette holder. Their shoes are lost in the weedy grass, and the sunlight masks their faces in identical skull-shadows. Both faces are serene, holding back amusement, indulgent of the photographer. And still it is not a picture of two cultivated Englishmen, or not only that. Adrian is incredibly tall and Vikinglike, with a forehead as broad and flat as a chimney tile; he looks like some blueblood American banker not long out of Princeton; his hair grows straight up like thick pale straw. Leonard's forehead is an attenuated wafer under a tender black forelock, his nose is nervous and frail, he seems younger and more vulnerable than his years (he was then thirty-four) and as recognizably intellectual as—well, how does one put the contrast? Following Leonard, one ought to dare to put it with the clarity of a certain cultural bluntness: he looks like a student at the yeshiva. Leonard has the unmistakable face of a Jew. Like his grandfather—and, again like him, despite his costume—Leonard Woolf might have stepped out of one of those pictures of caftaned Jews in the ghetto.

The observation may be obvious and boring but it is not insignificant, if only because it is derived from Leonard himself; it is his own lesson. What can be learned from it is not merely that he was himself conscious of all that curious contrast, but that his fellows could not have been indifferent to it. In a 1968 review of the penultimate volume of Leonard Woolf's memoirs, Dan Jacobson wonders, "Did his being a Jew never affect . . . his career or social life in the several years he spent as a colonial officer in Ceylon, his only companions during that time being other colonial civil servants—not in general the most enlightened, tolerant, or tactful of British social groups? Did it not arise in the political work he carried out later in England, especially during the rise of Nazism?" On all these matters Leonard is mute; he does not mention it. Not so Virginia. "He's a penniless Jew," she wrote in a letter to a friend announcing her marriage, and we know that if she had married a poor man of her own set she would not have called him a penniless Englishman. She called Leonard a Jew not to identify or explain him, but because, quite simply, that is how she saw him; it was herself she was explaining. And if she wrote light-heartedly, making a joke of marriage without inheritance, it was also a joke in general about unaccoutered Jews—from her point of view, Leonard had neither inheritance nor heritage. He was—like the Hogarth Press later on—self-created.

Of course, in thinking about Leonard Woolf, one is plainly not interested in the question of the acculturated Jew (". . . nearly all Jews are both proud and ashamed of being Jews," Leonard writes—a model of the type); it is not on the mark. What *is* to the point is the attitude of the class Leonard aspired to join. "Virginia for her part," Quentin Bell notes—and it is unnecessary to remind oneself that he is her nephew—

> had to meet the Woolf family. It was a daunting experience. Leonard himself was suffi- ciently Jewish to seem to her disquietingly foreign; but in him the trait was qualified. He had become so very much a citizen of her world. . . . But Leonard's widowed mother, a matriarchal figure living with her large family in Colinette Road, Putney, seemed very alien to Virginia. No place could have been less like home than her future mother-in-law's house.
>
> And how did the Woolfs regard her? Did they perceive that she thought their furniture hideous? Did she seem to them a haughty goy thinking herself too good for the family of their brilliant son? I am afraid that they probably did.
>
> [Here follows an account of Virginia's response—aloof and truculent—upon learning the character of the dietary laws, which Mrs. Woolf observed.]
>
> Virginia was ready to allow that Mrs. Woolf had some very good qualities, but her heart must have sunk as she considered what large opportunities she would have for discovering them.
>
> "Work and love and Jews in Putney take it out of me," she wrote, and it was certainly true.

This aspect of Virginia Stephen's marriage to Leonard Woolf is usually passed over in silence. I have rehearsed it here at such length not to emphasize it for its own sake—there is nothing novel about upper-class English distaste for Jews—but to make a point about Leonard. He is commonly depicted as, in public, a saintly socialist, and, in private, a saintly husband. He was probably both; but he also knew, like any percipient young man in love with a certain segment of society, how to seize vantage ground. As a schoolboy he was no doubt sincerely exhilarated by the playing field, but he hid his intellectual exhilarations to make it look as if the playing field were all there was to esteem; it was a way, after all, of buying esteem for himself. And though he was afterward no doubt sincerely in love with Virginia Stephen (surely a woman less intelligent would not have satisfied him), it would be a mistake to suppose that Virginia herself—even given her brilliance, her splendid head on its splendid neck, the radiance of her first appearance in Thoby's rooms in Cambridge wearing a white dress and round hat and carrying a parasol, astonishing him, Leonard says, as when "in a picture gallery you suddenly come face to face with a great Rembrandt or Velasquez"—it would be ingenuous, not to say credulous, to think that Virginia alone was all there was to adore. Whether Leonard Woolf fell in love with a young woman of beauty and intellect, or more narrowly with a Stephen of beauty and intellect, will always be a formidable, and a necessary, question.

It is a question that, it seems to me, touches acutely on Leonard Woolf in his profoundly dedicated role as nurse. He was dedicated partly because he was earnestly efficient at everything, and also because he loved his wife, and also because he was a realist who could reconcile himself to any unlooked-for disaster. He came to the situation of Virginia's health determinedly and unquestioningly, much as, years later, when the German bombings had begun, he joined up with the Local Defence Volunteers: it was what had to be done. But in the case of Virginia more than merely courage was at issue; his "background" had equipped him well to be Virginia Stephen's nurse. When things were going badly he could take on the burden of all those small code-jottings in his diary—"V.n.w.," "b.n.," "V.sl.h."—and all the crises "Virginia not well," "bad night," "Virginia slight headache" horrendously implied, for the simple reason that it was worth it to him. It was worth it because she was a genius; it was worth it because she was a Stephen.

The power and allure of the Stephen world lay not in its distance from the Jews of Putney—Bloomsbury was anyhow hardly likely to notice the Jews of Putney, and if Virginia did notice, and was even brought to tea there, it was through the abnormal caprice of a freakish fate—but in its illustriousness. Virginia was an illustrious young woman: had she had no gift of her own, the luster of her father's situation, and of the great circle of the aristocracy of intellect into which she was born, would have marked her life. It was additionally marked by her double fortune of genius and insanity, and though her primary fortune—the circle into which she was born—attracted, in the most natural way, other members of that circle, the biting and always original quality of her mind put the less vivid of them off. Her madness was not public knowledge, but her intellect could not be hidden. Her tongue had a fearful and cutting brilliance. "I was surprised to find how friendly she made herself appear," said Walter Lamb, another of Thoby Stephen's Cambridge friends, amazed on one occasion to have been undevoured. He courted her for a time, pallidly, asking frightened questions: "Do you want to have children and love in the normal way?"—as if he expected nothing usual from Virginia Stephen. "I wish," she wrote to Lytton Strachey, after reporting Lamb's visits, "that earth would open her womb and let some new creature out." The courtship was brief and ended in boredom. Lamb's offer was one of at least four proposals of marriage from differing sources; Strachey himself had tendered her one. Since he preferred stableboys to women, a fact they both understood very well, it was a strange mistake. Sydney Waterlow, still another Cambridge name, was a suitor; she regarded him as "amiable." Hilton Young, a childhood friend—cast, says Quentin Bell, from a "smooth and well-proportioned mould"—might have been an appropriate match, mixing politics with poetry and gaining a peerage; he was merely "admirable." Meanwhile, Virginia was thoughtfully flirting with her sister's husband. At twenty-nine, despite all these attentions, she was depressed at being still unmarried; she was despondent, as she would be for the rest of her life, over her childlessness. Not one of those triflings had turned to infatuation, on either side.

It was fortunate. There was lacking, in all these very intelligent men, and indeed in their type in general, the kind of sexual seriousness that is usually disparaged as uxoriousness. It was a trait that Leonard invincibly possessed and that Clive Bell despised as "provincial and puritanical, an enemy to all that was charming and amusing in life." Clive was occupied by a long-standing affair and lived apart from Vanessa, who, at various times, lived with Roger Fry and with Duncan Grant—who was (so closely was this group tied) Lytton Strachey's cousin, and who may have been (so Quentin Bell allows us to conjecture) the father of Quentin's sister, Angelica. Vanessa typed and distributed copies of Lytton Strachey's indecent verse; once at a party she did a topless dance; it was legendary that she had at another party fornicated with Maynard Keynes *"coram publico"*—the whole room looking on. It may have been in honor of these last two occasions that Virginia Woolf, according to Quentin Bell, pronounced human nature to have been "changed in or about December 1910."

It was not a change Leonard Woolf approved of. Four years after this crucial date in human history he published a novel critical of "unnatural cultured persons" given to "wild exaggerated talk" and frivolous behavior; it was clearly an assault on Vanessa and Clive Bell and their circle. The novel, called *The Wise Virgins,* was about *not* marrying Virginia. Instead the hero is forced to marry a Putney girl, and lives unhappily ever after—only because, having been infected with Bloomsbury's licentious notions, he has carelessly gotten her with child. The fictional Leonard loses the heroine who represents Virginia, and is doomed to the drabness of Putney; in the one act he both deplores Bloomsbury and laments his deprivation of it. The real Leonard tried to pick his way between these soul-cracking contradictions. He meant to have the high excitement of Bloomsbury—and certainly "frivolity" contributed to Bloomsbury's dash and éclat—without the frivolity itself. He meant to be master of the full brilliant breadth of all that worldliness, and at the same time of the more sober and limiting range of his native seriousness.

That he coveted the one while requiring the other was—certainly in her biographer's eyes—the salvation of Virginia. No one else in that milieu could have survived—surely not as husband—her illnesses. Roger Fry, for instance, put his own mad wife away and went to live with Vanessa. As for Lamb, Waterlow, Young—viewed in the light of what Virginia Woolf's insanity extracted from her caretaker, their possibilities wither. Of all her potential husbands, only Leonard Woolf emerged as fit. And the opposite too can be said: of Bloomsbury's potential wives, only Virginia emerged as fit for Leonard. He was fit for her because her madness, especially in combination with her innovative genius, demanded the most grave, minutely persevering and attentive service. She was fit for him not simply because she represented Bloomsbury in its most resplendent flowering of originality and luminousness; so, after all, did Vanessa, an accomplished painter active with other painters in the revolutionary vitality of the Post-Impressionists. But just as no marriage could survive Vanessa for long, so Leonard married to Vanessa would not have survived Bloomsbury for long. What Leonard needed in Virginia was not so much her genius as her madness. It made possible for him the exercise of the one thing Bloomsbury had no use for: uxoriousness. It allowed him the totality of his seriousness unchecked. It *used* his seriousness, it gave it legitimate occupation, it made it both necessary and awesome. And it made *her* serious. Without the omnipresent threat of disintegration, freed from the oppression of continuous vigil against breakdown, what might Virginia's life have been? The flirtation with Clive hints at it: she might have lived, at least outwardly, like Vanessa. It was his wife's insanity, in short, that made tenable the permanent—the secure—presence in Bloomsbury of Leonard himself. Her madness fed his genius for responsibility; it became for him a corridor of access to her genius. The spirit of Bloomsbury was not Leonard's, his temperament was against it—Bloomsbury could have done without him. So could a sane Virginia.

The whole question of Virginia's sexuality now came into Leonard's hands. And here too he was curiously ambivalent. The honeymoon was not a success; they consulted Vanessa, Vanessa the sexual creature—when had she had her first orgasm? Vanessa could not remember. "No doubt," she reflected, "I sympathised with such things if I didn't have them from the time I was 2." "Why do you think people make such a fuss about marriage & copulation?" Virginia was writing just then; ". . . certainly I find the climax immensely exaggerated." Vanessa and Leonard put their heads together over it. Vanessa said she believed Virginia "never had understood or sympathised with sexual passion in men"; this news, she thought, "consoled" Leonard. For further consolation the two of them rehearsed (and this was before England had become properly aware of Freud) Virginia's childhood trauma inflicted by her elder half-brother George Duckworth, who had, under cover of big-brotherly affection, repeatedly entered the nursery at night for intimate fondlings, the nature of which Virginia then hardly comprehended; she knew only that he frightened her and that she despised him. Apparently this explanation satisfied Leonard—the "consolation" worked—if rather too quickly; the ability to adjust speedily to disappointment is a good and useful trait in a colonial officer, less so in a husband. It does not contradict the uxorious temperament, however, and certainly not the nursing enterprise: a wife who is seen to be frigid as well as mad is simply taken for that much sicker. But too ready a reconcilement to bad news is also a kind of abandonment, and Leonard seems very early to have relinquished, or allowed Virginia to relinquish, the sexual gratifications of marriage. All the stranger since he repeatedly speaks of himself as "lustful." And he is not known to have had so much as a dalliance during his marriage.

On the other hand, Quentin Bell suggests—a little coyly, as if only blamelessly hinting—that Virginia Woolf's erotic direction was perhaps toward women rather than men. The "perhaps" is crucial: the index to the first volume lists "passion for Madge Vaughan," "passion for Violet Dickinson," but the corresponding textual passages are all projections from the most ordinary sort of data. Madge Vaughan was a cousin by marriage whom Virginia knew from the age of seven; at sixteen she adored her still, and once stood in the house paralyzed by rapture, thinking, "Madge is here; at this moment she is actually under this roof"—an emotion, she once said, that she never equaled afterward. Many emotions at sixteen are never equaled afterward. Of Virginia's intense letter-writing to Violet Dickinson—a friend of her dead half-sister—Quentin Bell says: ". . . it is clear to the modern reader, though it was not at all clear to Virginia, that she was in love and that her love was returned." What is even clearer is that it is possible to be too "modern," if that is what enables one to read a sensual character into every exuberant or sympathetic friendship between women. Vita Sackville-West, of course, whom Virginia Woolf knew when both writers were already celebrated, was an established sapphist, and was plainly in pursuit of Virginia. Virginia, she wrote, "dislikes the quality of masculinity," but that was the view of one with a vested interest in believing it. As for Virginia, she "felt," according to her biographer, "as a lover feels—she desponded when she fancied herself neglected, despaired when Vita was away, waited anxiously for letters, needed Vita's company and lived in that strange mixture of elation and despair which lovers—and one would have supposed only lovers—can experience." But all this is Quentin Bell. Virginia herself, reporting a three-day visit from Sackville-West, appears erotically detached: "These Sapphists *love* women; friendship is never untinged with amorosity. . . . I like her and being with her and the splendour—she shines in the grocer's shop . . . with a candle lit radiance." She acknowledged what she readily called Vita's "glamour," but the phrase "these Sapphists" is too mocking to be lover's language. And she was quick to criticize Vita (who was married to Harold Nicolson) as a mother: ". . . she is a little cold and off-hand with her boys." Virginia Woolf's biographer nevertheless supposes—he admits all this is conjecture—"some caressing, some bedding together." Still, in the heart of this love, if it was love, was the ultimate withdrawal: "In brain and insight," Virginia remarked in her diary, "she is not as highly organised as I am." Vita was splendid but "not reflective." She wrote "with a pen of brass." And: "I have no enormous opinion of her poetry." Considering all of which, Quentin Bell notes persuasively that "she could not really love without feeling that she was in the presence of a superior intellect." Sackville-West, for her part, insisted that not only did Virginia not like the quality of masculinity, but also the "possessiveness and love of domination in men."

Yet Leonard Woolf dominated Virginia Woolf overwhelmingly—nor did she resist—not so much because his braininess impressed her (his straightforwardly thumping writing style must have claimed her loyalty more than her admiration), but because he possessed her in the manner of—it must be said again—a strong-minded nurse with obsessive jurisdiction over a willful patient. The issue of Virginia Woolf's tentative or potential lesbianism becomes reduced, at this point, to the merest footnote of possibility. Sackville-West called her "inviolable"; and the fact is she was conventionally married, and had conventional expectations of marriage. She wanted children. For a wedding present Violet Dickinson sent her a cradle. "My baby shall sleep in [it]," she said at thirty. But it stood empty, and she felt, all her life, the ache of the irretrievable. "I don't like the physicalness of having children of my own," she wrote at forty-five, recording how "the little creatures"—Vanessa's children—"moved my infinitely sentimental throat." But then, with a lurch of candor: "I can dramatise myself a parent, it is true. And perhaps I have killed the feeling instinctively; or perhaps nature does." Two years after declaring the feeling killed, during a dinner party full of worldly conversation with the Webbs and assorted eminences, she found herself thinking: "L. and myself . . . the pathos, the symbolical quality of the childless couple."

The feeling was not killed; it had a remarkable durability. There is no record of her response to the original decision not to have children. That decision was Leonard's, and it was "medical." He consulted three or four people variously qualified, including Vanessa's doctor and the nurse who ran the home to which Virginia was sent when most dangerously disturbed (and to whom, according to Bell, Leonard ascribed "an unconscious but violent homosexual passion for Virginia"—which would, one imagines, make one wonder about the disinterestedness of her advice). Leonard also requested the opinion of Dr. George Savage, Virginia's regular physician, whom he disliked, and was heartily urged to have babies; soon after we find him no longer in consultation with Dr. Savage. Bell tells us that "in the end Leonard decided and persuaded Virginia to agree that, although they both wanted children, it would be too dangerous for her to have them." The "too dangerous" is left unexplained; we do not even know Leonard's ostensible reason. Did he think she could not withstand pregnancy and delivery? She was neither especially frail nor without energy, and was a zealous walker, eight miles at a time, over both London and countryside; she hefted piles of books and packed them for the Hogarth Press; she had no organic impediments. Did he believe she could not have borne the duties of rearing? But in that class there was no household without its nanny (Vanessa had two), and just as she never had to do a housekeeping chore (she never laid a fire, or made a bed, or washed a sock), she need not have been obliged to take physical care of a child. Did he, then, fear an inherited trait—diseased offspring? Or did he intend to protect the phantom child from distress by preventing its birth into a baleful household? Or did he mean, out of some curious notion of intellectual purity, not to divide the strength of Virginia's available sanity, to preserve her undistracted for her art?

Whatever the reason, and to spare her—or himself—what pains we can only guess at, she was in this second instance released from "normality." Normality is catch-as-catch-can. Leonard, in his deliberateness, in his responsibility, was more serious than that, and surrendered her to a program of omissions. She would be spared the tribulations both of the conjugal bed and of childbed. She need not learn ease in the one; she need not, no, must not, venture into the other. In forbidding Virginia maternity, Leonard abandoned her to an unparalleled and unslakable envy. Her diary again and again records the pangs she felt after visits with Vanessa's little sons—pangs, defenses, justifications: she suffered. Nor was it a social suffering—she did not feel deprived of children because she was expected to. The name "Virginia Woolf" very soon acquired the same resonance for her contemporaries ("this celebrity business is quite chronic," she wrote) as it has for us—after which she was expected to be only Virginia Woolf. She learned, after a while, to be only that (which did not, however, prevent her from being an adored and delightful aunt), and to mock at Vanessa's mothering, and to call it obsessive and excessive. She suffered the envy of the childless for the fruitful, precisely this, and nothing societally imposed; and she even learned to transmute maternal envy into a more manageable variety—literary begrudging. This was directed at Vanessa's second son, Julian Bell, killed in the Spanish Civil War, toward whose literary ambitions Virginia Woolf was always ungenerous, together with Leonard; a collection of Julian's essays, prepared after his death, Leonard dubbed "Vanessa's necrophily." Vanessa-envy moved on into the second generation. It was at bottom a rivalry of creatureliness, in which Virginia was always the loser. Vanessa was on the side of "normality," the placid mother of three, enjoying all the traditional bourgeois consolations; she was often referred to as a madonna; and at the same time she was a thorough-going bohemian. Virginia was anything but placid, yet lived a sober sensible domestic life in a marriage stable beyond imagining, with no trace of bohemianism. Vanessa the bohemian madonna had the best of both hearth-life and free life. Virginia was barred from both.

Without the authoritative domestic role maternity would have supplied, with no one in the household dependent on her (for years she quarreled with her maid on equal or inferior terms), and finding herself always—as potential patient—in submission, Virginia Woolf was by degrees nudged into a position of severe dependency. It took odd forms: Leonard not only prescribed milk at eleven in the morning, but also topics for conversation in the evening. Lytton Strachey's sister-in-law recalls how among friends Leonard would work up the "backbone" of a subject "and then be happy to let [Virginia] ornament it if she wanted to." And he gave her pocket money every week. Her niece Angelica reports that "Leonard kept Virginia on very short purse-strings," which she exercised through the pleasures of buying "coloured string and sealing-wax, notebooks and pencils." When she came to the end of writing a book, she trembled until Leonard read it and gave his approval. William Plomer remembers how Leonard would grow alarmed if, watching Virginia closely, he saw her laugh a little too convulsively. And once she absent-mindedly began to flick bits of meat off her dinner plate; Leonard hushed the company and led her away.*

—All of which has given Leonard his reputation for saintliness. A saint who successively secures acquiescence to frigidity, childlessness, dependency? Perhaps; probably; of course. These are, after all, conventual vows—celibacy, barrenness, obedience. But Leonard Woolf was a socialist, not an ascetic; he had a practical political intelligence; he was the author of books called *Empire and Commerce in Africa* and *Socialism and Co-operation;* he ran the Hogarth Press like a good businessman; at the same time he edited a monthly periodical, *The International Review;* he was literary editor of *The Nation.* He had exactly the kind of common-sensical temperament that scorns, and is repelled by, religious excess. And of Virginia he made a shrine; of himself, a monk. On the day of her death Virginia walked out of the house down to the river Ouse and drowned herself; not for nothing was that house called Monk's House. The letter she left for Leonard was like almost every other suicide note, horribly banal, not a writer's letter at all, and rich with guilt—"I feel certain I am going mad again. I feel we can't go through another of those terrible times. . . . I can't go on spoiling your life any longer." To Vanessa she wrote, "All I want to say is that Leonard has been so astonishingly good, every day, always; I can't imagine that anyone could have done more for me than he has. . . . I feel he has so much to do that he will go on, better without me. . . ."

Saints make guilt—especially when they impose monkish values; there is nothing new in that. And it was the monk as well as her madness she was fleeing when she walked into the Ouse, though it was the saint she praised. "I don't think two people could have been happier than we have been," the note to Leonard ended. A tragic happiness—such a thing is possible: cheerful invalids are a commonplace, and occasionally one hears of happy inmates. A saintly monk, a monkish nurse? All can be taken together, and all are true together. But the drive toward monkishness was in Leonard. What was natural for himself he prescribed for Virginia, and to one end only: to prevent her ongoing nervous crises from reaching their extreme state; to keep her sane. And to keep her sane was, ultimately, to keep her writing. It is reasonable to imagine that without Leonard Woolf there would have been very little of that corpus the name Virginia Woolf calls to mind—there would have been no *Mrs. Dalloway,* no *To the Lighthouse,* no *The Waves,* no *Common Reader.* And it may be that even the word Bloomsbury—the redolence, the signal—would not have survived, since she was its center. "She would not have been the symbol" of Bloomsbury, T. S. Eliot said, "if she had not been the maintainer of it." For Bloomsbury as an intellectual "period" to have escaped oblivion, there had to be at least one major literary voice to carry it beyond datedness. That voice was hers.

The effort to keep her sane was mammoth. Why did Leonard think it was worth it? The question, put here for the second time, remains callous but inevitable. Surely it would have been relieving at last (and perhaps to both of them) to let her slide away into those rantings, delusions, hallucinations; she might or might not have returned on her own. It is even possible that the nursing was incidental, and that she recovered each time because she still had the capacity to recover. But often enough Leonard—who knew the early symptoms intimately—was able to prevent

*Joan Russell Noble, ed., *Recollections of Virginia Woolf by Her Contemporaries* (William Morrow & Company, Inc., 1972).

her from going under; each pulling-back from that brink of dementia gained her another few months of literary work. Again and again he pulled her back. It required cajolery, cunning, mastery, agility, suspiciousness, patience, spoon-feeding, and an overwhelming sensitiveness to every flicker of her mood. Obviously it drained him; obviously he must have been tempted now and then to let it all go and give up. Almost anyone else would have. Why did he not? Again the answer must be manifold. Because she was his wife; because she was the beloved one to whom he had written during their courtship, "You don't know what a wave of happiness comes over me when I see you smile";* because his conscience obliged him to; because she suffered; because—this before much else—it was in his nature to succor suffering. And also: because of her gift; because of her genius; for the sake of literature; because she was unique. And because she had been a Miss Stephen; because she was Thoby Stephen's sister; because she was a daughter of Leslie Stephen; because she was, like Leonard's vision of Cambridge itself, "compounded of . . . the atmosphere of long years of history and great traditions and famous names [and] a profoundly civilized life"; because she was Bloomsbury; because she was England.

For her sake, for art's sake, for his own sake. Perhaps above all for his own sake. In her he had married a kind of escutcheon; she represented the finest grain of the finest stratum in England. What he shored up against disintegration was the life he had gained—a birthright he paid for by spooning porridge between Virginia Woolf's resisting lips.

Proust is right to tell us to go to a writer's books, not to his loyalties. Wherever Leonard Woolf is, there Virginia Woolf is not. The more Leonard recedes or is not present, the more Virginia appears in force. Consequently Quentin Bell's biography—the subversive strength of which is Leonard—demands an antidote. The antidote is, of course, in the form of a reminder—that Virginia Woolf was a woman of letters as well as a patient; that she did not always succumb but instead could be an original fantasist and fashioner of an unaccustomed way of seeing; that the dependency coincided with a vigorous intellectual autonomy; that together with the natural subordination of the incapacitated she possessed the secret confidence of the innovator.

Seen through Leonard's eyes, she is, in effect, always on the verge of lunacy. "I am quite sure," he tells us in his autobiography, "that Virginia's genius was closely connected with what manifested itself as mental instability and insanity. The creative imagination in her novels, her ability to 'leave the ground' in conversation, and the voluble delusions of the breakdown all came from the same place in her mind— she 'stumbled after her own voice' and followed 'the voices that fly ahead.' " At the same time her refusal to eat was associated with guilt—she talked of her "faults"— and Leonard insists that "she remained all through her illness, even when most insane, terribly sane in three-quarters of her mind. The point is that her insanity was in her premises, in her beliefs. She believed, for instance, that she was not ill. . . ."

Seen through the books, she is never "ill," never lunatic. Whether it was mental

*From an unpublished letter in the Berg Collection. Quoted in *The New York Times*, June 14, 1973.

instability or a clear-sighted program of experiment in the shape of the novel that unhinged her prose from the conventional margins that had gone before is a question not worth speculating over. Leonard said that when mad she heard the birds sing in Greek. The novels are not like that: it is not the data that are altered, but the sequence of things. When Virginia Woolf assaulted the "old" fiction in her famous *Mr. Bennett and Mrs. Brown,* she thought she was recommending getting rid of the habit of data; she thought this was to be her fictive platform. But when she grappled with her own inventions, she introduced as much data as possible and strained to express it all under the pressure of a tremendous simultaneity. What she was getting rid of was consecutiveness; precisely the habit of premises. If clinging to premises was the sanity of her insanity, then the intent of her fiction was not an extension of her madness, as Leonard claimed, but its calculated opposite. The poetry of her prose may have been like the elusive poetry of her dementia, but its steadfast design was not. "The design," she wrote of *Mrs. Dalloway,* "is so queer and so masterful"; elated, she saw ahead. She was an artist; she schemed, and not through random contractions or inflations of madness, but through the usual methods of art: inspired intellection, the breaking down of expectation into luminous segments of shock.

A simpler way of saying all this is that what she achieved as a stylist cannot really be explained through linking it with madness. The diaries give glimpses of rationalized prefigurations; a letter from Vanessa suggests moths, which metamorphosed into *The Moths,* which became *The Waves.* She knew her destination months before she arrived; she was in control of her work, she did what she meant to do. If the novels are too imaginatively astonishing to be persuasive on this point, the essays will convince. They are read too little, and not one of them is conceptually stale, or worn in any other way. In them the birds do not sing in Greek either, but the Greek—the sign of a masterly nineteenth-century literary education—shows like a spine. In the essays the control of brilliant minutiae is total—historical and literary figures, the particulars of biography, society, nationality, geography. She is a courier for the past. In Volume III of the *Collected Essays,* for instance, the range is from Chaucer through Montaigne through some Elizabethans major and minor, through Swift and Sterne and Lord Chesterfield, Fanny Burney and Cowper. She was interested also in the lives of women, especially writers. She studied Sara Coleridge, the poet's daughter; Harriette Wilson, the mistress of the Earl of Craven; Dr. Johnson's Mrs. Thrale; and Dorothy Osborne, a talented letter-writer of the seventeenth century. The language and scope of the essays astound. If they are "impressionistic," they are not self-indulgent; they put history before sensibility. When they are ironic, it is the kind of irony that enlarges the discriminatory faculty and does not serve the cynical temper. They mean to interpret other lives by the annihilation of the crack of time: they are after what the novels are after, a compression of then and now into the simultaneity of a singular recognition and a single comprehension. They mean to make every generation, and every instant, contemporaneous with every other generation and instant. And yet—it does not contradict—they are, taken all together, the English Essay incarnate.

The autonomous authority of the fiction, the more public authority of the essays, are the antidotes to Bell's Woolf, to Leonard's Virginia. But there is a third antidote implicit in the whole of the work, and in the drive behind the work, and that is Virginia Woolf's feminism. It ought to be said at once that it was what can now be called "classical" feminism. The latter-day choice of Virginia Woolf, on the style of Sylvia Plath, as a current women's-movement avatar is inapposite and mistaken. Classical feminism is inimical to certain developing strands of "liberation." Where feminism repudiates the conceit of the "gentler sex," liberation has come to reaffirm it. Where feminism asserts a claim on the larger world, liberation shifts to separatism. Where feminism scoffs at the plaint of "sisters under the skin," and maintains individuality of condition and temperament, liberation reinstates sisterhood and sameness. Where feminism shuns self-preoccupation, liberation experiments with self-examination, both psychic and medical. Classical feminism as represented by Virginia Woolf meant one thing only: access to the great world of thinking, being, and doing. The notion of "male" and "female" states of intellect and feeling, hence of prose, ultimately of culture, would have been the occasion of a satiric turn for Virginia Woolf; so would the idea of a politics of sex. Clive Bell reports that she licked envelopes once or twice for the Adult Suffrage League, but that she "made merciless fun of the flag-waving fanaticism" of the activists. She was not political— or, perhaps, just political enough, as when Chekhov notes that "writers should engage themselves in politics only enough to protect themselves from politics." Though one of her themes was women in history (several of her themes, rather; she took her women one by one, not as a race, species, or nation), presumably she would have mocked at the invention of a "history of women"—what she cared for, as *A Room of One's Own* both lucidly and passionately lays out, was access to a unitary culture. Indeed, *Orlando* is the metaphorical expression of this idea. History as a record of division or exclusion was precisely what she set herself against: the Cambridge of her youth kept women out, and all her life she preserved her resentment by pronouncing herself undereducated. She studied at home, Greek with Janet Case, literature and mathematics with her father, and as a result was left to count on her fingers forever—but for people who grow up counting on their fingers, even a Cambridge education cannot do much. Nevertheless she despised what nowadays is termed "affirmative action," granting places in institutions as a kind of group reparation; she thought it offensive to her own earned prestige, and once took revenge on the notion. In 1935 Forster, a member of the Committee of the London Library, informed her that a debate was under way concerning the admission of women members. No women were admitted. Six years later Virginia Woolf was invited to serve; she said she would not be a "sop"—she ought to have been invited years earlier, on the same terms as Forster, as a writer; not in 1941, when she was already fifty-nine, as a woman.

Nor will she do as martyr. Although Cambridge was closed to her, literary journalism was not; although she complains of being chased off an Oxbridge lawn forbidden to the feet of women, no one ever chased her off a page. Almost immediately she began to write for the *Times Literary Supplement* and for *Cornhill;* she was then twenty-two. She was, of course, Leslie Stephen's daughter, and it is doubtful whether any other young writer, male or female, could have started off so auspiciously: still, we speak here not of "connections" but of experience. At about the same time she was summoned to teach at Morley, a workers' college for men and women. One of her reports survives, and Quentin Bell includes it as an appendix. "My four women," she writes, "can hear eight lectures on the French Revolution if they wish to continue their historical learning"—and these were working-class women, in 1905. By 1928, women had the vote, and full access to universities, the liberal professions, and the civil service. As for Virginia Woolf, in both instances, as writer and teacher, she was solicited—and this cannot be, after all, only because she was Leslie Stephen's daughter. She could use on the spot only her own gifts, not the rumor of her father's. Once she determined to ignore what Bell calls the "matrimonial market" of upper-class partying, into which for a time her half-brother George dragooned her, she was freed to her profession. It was not true then, it is not true now, that a sublime and serious pen can be circumscribed.

Virginia Woolf was a practitioner of her profession from an early age; she was not deprived of an education, rather of a particular college; she grew rich and distinguished; she developed her art on her own line, according to her own sensibilities, and was acclaimed for it; though insane, she was never incarcerated. She was an elitist, and must be understood as such. What she suffered from, aside from the abysses of depression which characterized her disease, was not anything like the condition of martyrdom—unless language has become so flaccid that being on occasion patronized begins to equal death for the sake of an ideal. What she suffered from really was only the minor inflammations of the literary temperament. And she was not often patronized: her fame encouraged her to patronize others. She could be unkind, she could be spiteful, she could envy—her friendship with Katherine Mansfield was always unsure, being founded on rivalry. Mansfield and her husband, the journalist John Middleton Murry, "work in my flesh," Virginia Woolf wrote, "after the manner of the jigger insect. It's annoying, indeed degrading, to have these bitternesses." She was bitter also about James Joyce; she thought him, says Bell, guilty of "atrocities." Her diary speaks of "the damned egotistical self; which ruins Joyce," and she saw *Ulysses* as "insistent, raw, striking and ultimately nauseating." But she knew Joyce to be moving in the same direction as herself; it was a race that, despite her certainty of his faults, he might win. By the time of her death she must have understood that he *had* won. Still, to be outrun in fame is no martyrdom. And her own fame was and is in no danger, though, unlike Joyce, she is not taken as a fact of nature. Virginia Woolf's reputation in the thirty and more years since her death deepens; she becomes easier to read, more complex to consider.

To Charlotte Brontë, born sixty-six years before Virginia Woolf, Robert Southey, then Poet Laureate, had written, "Literature cannot be the business of a woman's life, and it ought not to be." No one addressed Virginia Woolf of Bloomsbury in this fashion; she was sought out by disciples, editors, litterateurs; in the end Oxford and Cambridge asked her to lecture before their women's colleges. If the issue of martyrdom is inappropriate (implying as it does that a woman who commits suicide is by definition a martyr), what of heroism? Virginia Woolf's death was or was not heroic, depending on one's view of suicide by drowning. The case for Leonard's heroism is more clear-cut: a saint is noble on behalf of others, a hero on behalf of himself. But if Virginia Woolf is to be seen as a heroine, it must be in those modes outside the manner of her death and even the manner of her life as a patient in the house.

If she is to be seen as a heroine, it must be in the conjuring of yet another of those Bloomsbury photographs—this time one that does not exist. The picture is of a woman sitting in an old chair holding a writing board; the point of her pen touches a half-filled page. To gaze at her bibliography is, in a way, to conjure this picture that does not exist—hour after hour, year after year, a life's accumulation of stupendous visionary toil. A writer's heroism is in the act of writing; not in the finished work, but in the work as it goes.

Vanessa's son gives us no heroine: only this stubborn and sometimes querulous self-starving madwoman, with so stoic, so heroic a male nurse. And when she runs away from him to swallow the Ouse, the heroism of both of them comes to an end.

On Excellence

In my Depression childhood, whenever I had a new dress, my cousin Sarah would get suspicious. The nicer the dress was, and especially the more expensive it looked, the more suspicious she would get. Finally she would lift the hem and check the seams. This was to see if the dress had been bought or if my mother had sewed it. Sarah could always tell. My mother's sewing had elegant outsides, but there was something catch-as-catch-can about the insides. Sarah's sewing, by contrast, was as impeccably finished inside as out; not one stray thread dangled.

My uncle Jake built meticulous grandfather clocks out of rosewood; he was a perfectionist, and sent to England for the clockworks. My mother built serviceable radiator covers and a serviceable cabinet, with hinged doors, for the pantry. She built a pair of bookcases for the living room. Once, after I was grown and in a house of my own, she fixed the sewer pipe. She painted ceilings, and also landscapes; she reupholstered chairs. One summer she planted a whole yard of tall corn. She thought herself capable of doing anything, and did everything she imagined. But nothing was perfect. There was always some clear flaw, never visible head-on. You had to look underneath where the seams were. The corn thrived, though not in rows. The stalks elbowed one another like gossips in a dense little village.

"Miss Brrrroooobaker," my mother used to mock, rolling her Russian rs, whenever I crossed a t she had left uncrossed, or corrected a word she had misspelled, or became impatient with a v that had tangled itself up with a w in her speech. ("Vvventriloquist," I would say. "Vvventriloquist," she would obediently repeat. And the next time it would come out "wiolinist.") Miss Brubaker was my high school English teacher, and my mother invoked her name as an emblem of raging finical obsession. "Miss Brrrroooobaker," my mother's voice hoots at me down the years, as I go on casting and recasting sentences in a tiny handwriting on monomaniacally uniform paper. The loops of my mother's handwriting—it was the Palmer Method—were as big as hoops, spilling generous splashy ebullience. She could pull off, at five minutes' notice, a satisfying dinner for 10 concocted out of nothing more than originality and panache. But the napkin would be folded a little off-center, and the spoon might be on the wrong side of the knife. She was an optimist who ignored trifles; for her, God was not in the details but in the intent. And all these culinary and agricultural efflorescences were extracurricular, accomplished in the crevices and niches of a 14-hour business day. When she scribbled out her family memoirs, in heaps of dog-eared notebooks, or on the backs of old bills, or on the margins of last year's calendar, I would resist typing them; in the speed of the chase she often omitted words like "the," "and," "will." The same flashing and bountiful hand fashioned and fired ceramic pots, and painted brilliant autumn views and vases of imaginary flowers and ferns, and decorated ordinary Woolworth platters with lavish enameled gardens. But bits of the painted petals would chip away.

Lavish: my mother was as lavish as nature. She woke early and saturated the hours with work and inventiveness, and read late into the night. She was all profusion, abundance, fabrication. Angry at her children, she would run after us whirling the cord of the electric iron, like a lasso or a whip; but she never caught us. When, in the seventh grade, I was afraid of failing the Music Appreciation final exam because I could not tell the difference between "To a Wild Rose" and "Barcarolle," she got the idea of sending me to school with a gauze sling rigged up on my writing arm, and an explanatory note that was purest fiction. But the sling kept slipping off. My mother gave advice like mad—she boiled over with so much passion for the predicaments of strangers that they turned into permanent cronies. She told intimate stories about people I had never heard of.

Despite the gargantuan Palmer loops (or possibly because of them), I have always known that my mother's was a life of—intricately abashing word!—excellence: insofar as excellence means ripe generosity. She burgeoned, she proliferated; she was endlessly leafy and flowering. She wore red hats, and called herself a gypsy. In her girlhood she marched with the suffragettes and for Margaret Sanger* and called herself a Red. She made me laugh, she was so varied: like a tree on which lemons, pomegranates, and prickly pears absurdly all hang together. She had the comedy of prodigality.

My own way is a thousand times more confined. I am a pinched perfectionist, the ultimate fruition of Miss Brubaker; I attend to crabbed minutiae and am self-trammeled through taking pains. I am a kind of human snail, locked in and condemned by my own nature. The ancients believed that the moist track left by the snail as it crept was the snail's own essence, depleting its body little by little; the farther the snail toiled, the smaller it became, until it finally rubbed itself out. That is how perfectionists are. Say to us Excellence, and we will show you how we use up our substance and wear ourselves away, while making scarcely any progress at all. The fact that I am an exacting perfectionist in a narrow strait only, and nowhere else, is hardly to the point, since nothing matters to me so much as a comely and muscular sentence. It is my narrow strait, this snail's road: the track of the sentence I am writing now; and when I have eked out the wet substance, ink or blood, that is its mark, I will begin the next sentence. Only in reading out sentences am I perfectionist; but then there is nothing else I know how to do, or take much interest in. I miter every pair of abutting sentences as scrupulously as Uncle Jake fitted one strip of rosewood against another. My mother's worldly and bountiful hand has escaped me. The sentence I am writing is my cabin and my shell, compact, self-sufficient. It is the burnished horizon—a merciless planet where flawlessness is the single standard, where even the inmost seams, however hidden from a laxer eye, must meet perfection. Here "excellence" is not strewn casually from a tipped cornucopia, here disorder does not account for charm, here trifles rule like tyrants.

I measure my life in sentences, and my sentences are superior to my mother's, pressed out, line by line, like the lustrous ooze on the underside of the snail, the snail's secret open seam, its wound, leaking attar. My mother was too mettlesome to feel the force of a comma. She scorned minutiae. She measured her life according

---

*(1883–1966) American leader in the birth control movement.

to what poured from the horn of plenty, which was her ample, cascading, elastic, susceptible, inexact heart. My narrower heart rides between the tiny horns of the snail, dwindling as it goes.

And out of this thinnest thread, this ink-wet line of words, must rise a visionary fog, a mist, a smoke, forging cities, histories, sorrows, quagmires, entanglements, lives of sinners, even the life of my furnace-hearted mother: so much wilderness, waywardness, plentitude on the head of the precise and impeccable snail, between the horns.

Justice (Again) to Edith Wharton

Nearly forty years ago, Edmund Wilson wrote a little essay about an underrated American novelist and called it "Justice to Edith Wharton." She was in need of justice, he claimed, because "the more commonplace work of her later years had had the effect of dulling the reputation of her earlier and more serious work." During this last period—a stretch of about seventeen years, from (roughly) 1920 to her death in 1937—Edith Wharton's novels were best sellers, her short stories commanded thousands of dollars; but both in mode and motivation she remained, like so many others in the twenties and thirties, a nineteenth-century writer. She believed in portraying character, her characters displayed the higher values, her prose was a platform for her own views. In 1937, when Wilson undertook to invigorate her reputation, the machinery of nineteenth-century fiction was beginning to be judged not so much as the expression of a long tradition, or (as nowadays we seem to view it) as the exhausted practice of a moribund convention, but more bluntly as a failure of talent. Wilson accounted for that apparent failure in Edith Wharton by speculating on the psychological differences between male and female writers:

> It is sometimes true of women writers—less often, I believe, of men—that a manifestation of something like genius may be stimulated by some exceptional emotional strain, but will disappear when the stimulus has passed. With a man, his professional, his artisan's life is likely to persist and evolve as a partially independent organism through the vicissitudes of his emotional experience. Henry James in a virtual vacuum continued to possess and develop his *métier*. But Mrs. Wharton had no *métier* in this sense.

What sort of "justice" is this? A woman typically writes best when her emotions are engaged; the barren female heart cannot seize the writer's trade? Only a decade ago, such a declaration would have been derided by old-fashioned feminists as a passing insolence. But even the satiric reader, contending in one fashion or another with this passage, would have been able, ten years ago, to pluck the offending notion out as a lapse in the texture of a measured and generally moderating mind.

No longer. Wilson's idea returns only to hold, and it holds nowhere so much as among the literary proponents of the current women's movement: Wilson's lapse is exalted to precept. The idea of Edith Wharton as a "woman writer" in need of constantly renewable internal stimuli, whose gifts are best sustained by "exceptional emotional strain"—all this suits the newest doctrine of sexual exclusiveness in literature. Indeed, one of the outstanding tenets of this doctrine embraces Wilson unrelentingly. "Rarely in the work now being written by women," according to an article called "Toward a Definition of the Female Sensibility,"

> does one feel the presence of writers genuinely penetrating their own experience, risking emotional humiliation and the facing-down of secret fears, unbearable wisdoms. . . . There are works, however, . . . in which one feels the heroic effort stirring,*

and there follow numerous examples of women writing well because of the stimulus of some exceptional emotional strain.

Restitution, then (one supposes), is to come to Edith Wharton not from the old-fashioned feminists, but from the newer sort, who embrace the proposition that strong emotion in women, emotion uniquely female, is what will best nourish a female literature. What we are to look for next, it follows, is an ambitious new-feminist critical work studying Wharton's "vicissitudes of . . . emotional experience" and correlating the most fevered points with the most accomplished of the fictions.

Such a work, it turns out, more extensive and more supple than Wilson's pioneer brief would suggest, has just made its appearance: Ellen Moers's *Literary Women.* Like other new feminists, Moers believes that there is such an entity as the "history of women," that there are poetic images uniquely female, and even "landscapes charged with female privacy." She writes of "how much the freedom and tactile sensations of near-naked sea bathing has meant to modern women," and insists that a scene recounting the sensation of walking through a field of sea-like grass provides that "moment when Kate Chopin reveals herself most truly a woman writer." Edith Wharton's life—a buried life—ought, properly scrutinized, to feed such a set of sympathies, and to lure the attention of restitution. *Literary Women,* after all, is conceived of in part as a rescue volume, as a book of rehabilitation and justice: a number of writers, Moers explains, "came to life for me as women writers as they had not done before. Mrs. Gaskell and Anne Brontë had once bored me; Emily Dickinson was an irritating puzzle, as much as a genius; I could barely read Mary Shelley and Mrs. Browning. Reading them anew as women writers taught me how to get excited about these five, and others as well."

Others as well. But Edith Wharton is omitted from *Literary Women.* Her name appears only once, as an entry in an appendix. Only *The House of Mirth* is mentioned there, along with a reference, apparently by way of explanation of the larger omission, to the chapter on Edith Wharton in Alfred Kazin's *On Native Grounds.* Pursuing the citation, one discovers that Kazin, like Wilson, like the new feminists, speaks of "the need that drove her to literature." Whatever the need, it does not engage Moers; or Kazin. He advances the notion that "to Edith Wharton, whose very career as a novelist was the tenuous product of so many personal maladjustments, the novel became an involuted expression of self." Unlike the new feminists, Kazin will not celebrate this expression; it represents for him a "failure to fulfill herself in art." Wharton, he concludes, "remains not a great artist but an unusual American, one who brought the weight of her personal experience to bear upon a modern American literature to which she was spiritually alien."

Justice to Edith Wharton: where, then, is it to come from? Not taken seriously by the dominant criticism, purposefully ignored by the radical separatist criticism

---

*Vivian Gornick, *The Village Voice,* May 31, 1973.

of the new feminists*—she represents an antagonism. The antagonism is not new. Wharton describes it herself in her memoir, *A Backward Glance:*

> My literary success puzzled and embarrassed my old friends far more than it impressed them, and in my own family it created a kind of constraint which increased with the years. None of my relations ever spoke to me of my books, either to praise or blame—they simply ignored them; and among the immense tribe of my cousins, though it included many with whom I was on terms of affectionate intimacy, the subject was avoided as if it were a kind of family disgrace, which might be condoned but could not be forgotten. Only one eccentric widowed cousin, living a life of lonely invalidism, turned to my novels for occasional distraction, and had the courage to tell me so.

She continues: "At first I felt this indifference acutely; but now I no longer cared, for my recognition as a writer had transformed my life."

So it is here—in this uplifting idea, "my life," this teleological and novelistic idea above all—that one will finally expect to look for Wharton's restitution "as a writer." The justice that criticism perversely fails to bring, biography will achieve.

Perhaps. The biography of a novelist contains a wonderful advantage: it accomplishes, when well executed, a kind of mimicry. A good biography is itself a kind of novel. Like the classic novel, a biography believes in the notion of "a life"—a life as a triumphal or tragic story with a shape, a story that begins at birth, moves on to a middle part, and ends with the death of the protagonist.

Despite the reliable pervasiveness of birth and death, hardly any "real" life is like that. Most simply unfold, or less than that, dream-walk themselves out. The middle is missing. What governs is not pattern but drift. Most American lives, moreover, fail to recognize that they are sticks in a stream, and are conceived of as novels-of-progress, as purposeful *Bildungsromane* saturated with an unending hopefulness, with the notion of infinite improvement on the way toward a salubrious goal; the frontier continues to inhabit the American mentality unfailingly.

And most American biographies are written out of this same source and belief. A biography that is most like a novel is least like a life. Edith Wharton's life, though much of it was pursued outside of America, is an American life in this sense: that, despite certain disciplines, it was predicated on drift, and fell out, rather than fell into place. If other American lives, less free than hers, drift less luckily between the Scylla and Charybdis of obligation and crisis, hers drifted in a setting all horizon, in a perpetual noncircumstance clear of external necessity. She had to invent her own environment and its conditions, and while this may seem the reverse of rudderlessness, what it signifies really is movement having to feign a destination. A life with a "shape" is occasioned by what is present in that life; drift grows out of what is absent. For Edith Wharton there was—outside the writing—no destination, and no obligation to get there. She had houses, she had wealth; she chose, rather than "had," friends. She had no family (she was estranged from her brothers, and we hear nothing further about the affectionate cousins), she had no husband (though she was married to one for more than half her life), she had no children. For a long time she resented and disliked children, and was obsessed by a love for small dogs. She was Henry James's ideal American heroine: she was indeed his very heiress of all the

---

*Though, to be fair, I have heard of at least one new-feminist literature class that has studied *The House of Mirth*—evidently because it is so easy to interpret its heroine as the ideal victim.

ages, she was "free," she was cultivated both in the conventional and the spiritual sense, she was gifted, acute, mobile; she appeared to be mistress of her destiny.

The destiny of such freedom is drift, and though her life was American in this, it was European in its resignation: she had no illusion that—outside the writing—she was doing more than "filling in." Her one moment of elevated and secure purpose occurred when, inspired by the model of Walt Whitman in the hospitals of the Civil War, she founded war relief agencies in France during the First World War. She supervised brilliantly: she supervised her friendships, her gardeners, her guests, the particulars of her dinner parties, her households; she even, to a degree, supervised the insurmountable Henry James—she took him for long rides in her car, she demanded hours in London and tea at Lamb House, she finagled with his publisher to provide him with a handsome advance (she herself was the secret philanthropist behind the scenes), she politicked to try to get him the Nobel Prize for Literature. She supervised and commanded, but since no one demanded anything of *her* (with a single exception, which, like the Gorgon's head, was not to be gazed at), she was captain, on an uncharted deep, of a ship without any imaginable port. She did everything on her own, to no real end; no one ever asked her to accommodate to any pressure of need, she had no obligations that she did not contrive or duty that she did not devise. Her necessities were self-imposed. Her tub went round and round in a sea of self-pleasing.

All this was outside the writing. One learns it from R. W. B. Lewis's prize-winning biography,* which is, like a posthumously uncovered Wharton novel, sustained by the idea of "a life." It has the fecund progression, the mastery of incident, the affectionate but balanced devotion to its protagonist, the power of suspenseful development, even the unraveling of a mysterious love story, that the "old" novel used to deliver—the novel before it became a self-referring "contemporary" art-object. In its own way it is a thesis novel: it is full of its intention to bring justice to Edith Wharton. A massive biography, almost by its weight, insists on the importance of its subject. Who would dare pass that writer by to whom a scholar-writer has dedicated, as Lewis has, nearly a decade of investigation and discovery? "They are among the handsomest achievements in our literature," he remarks of her major fictions. And adds: "I have wondered, with other admirers of Edith Wharton, whether her reputation might today stand even higher if she had been a man."

If the last statement has overtones of the new feminism—glory but for the impediment of sex—the book does not. Lewis sets out to render the life of an artist, not of a "woman artist." Unexpectedly, though it is the artist he is after, what he succeeds chiefly in giving us is the life of a woman. The "chiefly" is no small thing: it is useful to have a documented narrative of an exceptional upper-class woman of a certain American period. Still, without romanticizing what is meant by the phrase "an artist's life," there is a difference between the biography of a writer and the mode of living of a narrow American class.

Can the life justify the writer then? Or, to put it otherwise, can biography take the place of literary judgment? Lewis's book is a straightforward "tale," not a critical biography. Nor is it "psychobiography": though it yields new and revealing information about Edith Wharton's sexual experience, it does not propose to illumine the

---

*Edith Wharton: A Biography (Harper & Row, 1975). The prizes are the Pulitzer, the National Book Critics Circle Award, and Columbia University's Bancroft Prize.

hidden chambers of the writer's sentience—as, for example, Ruby V. Redinger's recent inquiry into George Eliot's relationship to her brother Isaac, with its hunches and conjectures, purports to do, or Quentin Bell's half-study, half-memoir of Virginia Woolf. Lewis has in common with these others the revelation of a secret. In the case of Quentin Bell, it is the exact extent of Virginia Woolf's insanity; in the volume on George Eliot, the secret is the dense burden of humiliation imposed by an adored brother more cruel and rigid than society itself. And in Lewis, the secret is an undreamed-of, now minutely disclosed, adulterous affair with a journalist. In all three accounts, the writer is on the whole not there. It is understandable that the writer is mainly absent for the psychobiographer; something else is being sought. It is even more understandable that the writer should be absent for a nephew-biographer, whose preoccupation is with confirming family stories.

But if, for Lewis, the writer is not there, it is not because he fails to look for her but because she is very nearly invisible. What, through luck and diligence, he causes to become visible is almost not the point, however unpredictable and startling his discoveries are. And they are two: the surprising place of Morton Fullerton in Edith Wharton's middle years, and the appearance of a candid manuscript, written in her seventies, describing, with the lyrical explicitness of an enraptured anatomist, a fictional incestuous coupling. The manuscript and the love affair are so contrary to the established Wharton legend of cold propriety that they go far to make us look again—but only at the woman, not at the writer.

The real secret in Lewis's biography is devoid of sex, lived or imagined, though its centerpiece is a bed; and it concerns not the woman but the writer. The secret is divulged on page 353, when Wharton is fifty-one, and occupies ten lines in a volume of nearly six hundred pages. The ten lines recount a perplexing incident—"a minor fit of hysterics." The occasion is mysterious: Edith Wharton and Bernard Berenson, touring the great cities and museums of Europe together, arrive at the Hotel Esplanade in Berlin. They check into their respective rooms, and Edith Wharton, ignoring the view of the city though she has never been there before, begins to rage

> because the bed in her hotel room was not properly situated; not until it had been moved to face the window did she settle down and begin to find Berlin "incomparable." Berenson thought this an absurd performance; but because Edith never harped upon the physical requirements of her literary life, he did not quite realize that she worked in bed every morning and therefore needed a bed which faced the light. It had been her practice for more than twenty years; and for a woman . . . who clung so tenaciously to her daily stint, the need was a serious one.

The fit and its moment pass; the ensuing paragraphs tell of German politics snubbed and German music imbibed—we are returned, in short, to the life of an upper-class American expatriate tourist, privileged to travel in the company of a renowned connoisseur. But the plangent moment—an outcry over the position of a bed—dominates the book: dominates what has gone before and what is to come, and recasts both. Either the biographer can stand up to this moment—the woman revealed *as writer*—or the book falls into the drifting ash of "a life."

It falls, but it is not the biographer's fault; or not his fault alone. Edith Wharton—as writer—is to blame. She put a veil over the bed that was her workplace, and screened away the real life that was lived in it. What moves like a long afterimage in the wake of reading Lewis is a procession of stately majesties: Edith Wharton always standing, always regal, always stiffly dressed and groomed, standing with her wonderfully vertical spine in the hall of one of her great houses, or in the drawing room of her Paris apartment, with her fine hand out to some equally resplendent guest, or in her gardens, not so much admiring her flowers as instructing or reprimanding the servants of her flowers; or else "motoring" through the dust of some picturesque lane in the French countryside, her chauffeur in peaked hat and leather goggles, like blinders, on a high seat in front of her, indistinguishable from the horse that still headed most vehicles on the road.

If this is the Wharton myth, she made it; she wove it daily. It winds itself out like a vivid movie, yet darkly; it leaves out the window-lit bed. What went on outside the bed does not account for what went on in it. She frequented literary salons, and on a smaller scale held them (after dinner, Henry James reading aloud in the library); she talked bookishly, and with fervor; she was an intellectual. But she was not the only brilliant woman of her time and status; all of that, in the biography of a writer, weighs little.

Visualize the bed: she used a writing board. Her breakfast was brought to her by Gross, the housekeeper, who almost alone was privy to this inmost secret of the bedchamber. (A secretary picked up the pages from the floor for typing.) Out of bed, she would have had to be, according to her code, properly dressed, and this meant stays. In bed, her body was free, and freed her pen.

There is a famous photograph of Edith Wharton seated at a desk; we know now, thanks to the "minor fit of hysterics" at the Hotel Esplanade, how the camera lies—even though it shows us everything we might want to know about a way of life. The time is in the 1890s, the writer is in her early thirties. The desk is vast, shining, with a gold-tooled leather top; at the rear of its far surface is a decorated rack holding half a dozen books, but these are pointless—not only because anyone using this desk would need an impossibly long reach, but because all the volumes are faced away from the writer, with their backs and titles to the open room. Two tall electrified candlestick-lamps (the wire drags awkwardly) stand sentinel over two smaller candlesticks; there is a single letter, already stamped; otherwise the desk is clear, except for a pair of nervous ringed hands fiddling with a bit of paper.

The hands belong to a young woman got up, to our eyes, as theatrically as some fanciful notion of royalty: she is plainly a lady of fashion, with a constricted waist and a constricting tall collar; her dress is of the whitest fabric, all eyeleted, embroidered, sashed; her hair is elaborately rolled and ringleted; an earring makes a white dot below the high dark eave of her hair: her back is straight, even as she leans forward with concentrated mouth and lost eyes, in the manner of a writer in trance. Mellifluous folds hide her feet; a lady has no legs. She is sitting on a graceful chair with whorled feet—rattan framed by the most beautiful carved and burnished wood. (A rattan chair with not a single hole? No one could ever have *worked* in such a chair; the photographer defrauds us—nothing more important than a letter will ever be written at this desk.) The Oriental carpet, with its curious and dense figures, is most explicitly in focus, and over the edge of it a tail of skirt spills, reflected white on a floor as sleek as polished glass. In the background, blurred to the camera's lens but instructive to ours: a broad-shouldered velvet chair, a marble bust on an ebony pedestal, a table with a huge porcelain sculpture, a lofty shut oak or walnut door.—In short, an "interior," reminding us that the woman at the unused desk has under-taken, as her first writing venture, a collaborative work called *The Decoration of Houses.*

There are other portraits in this vein, formal, posed, poised, "intellectual" (mean-ing the subject muses over a seeming letter or book), all jeweled clips and chokers and pearls in heavy rows, pendants, feathered hats, lapdogs, furs, statuesque burdens of flounced bosom and grand liquescent sleeve, queenly beyond our bourgeois ima-ginings. And the portraits of houses: multiple chimneys, balconies, cupolas, soaring Romanesque windows, immense stone staircases, summer awnings of palatial breadth, shaped ivy, topiary like oversized chess pieces, walks, vistas, clouds of flower beds.

What are we (putting aside Marxist thoughts) to make of this avalanche of privilege? It is not enough to say: money. The class she derived from never talked of money; the money was invisible, like the writing in bed, and just as secret, and just as indispensable. The "love of beauty," being part of class habit, does not explain it; perhaps the class habit does. It was the class habit that kept her on the move: the class habit that is restlessness and drift. She wore out houses and places, or else her spirit wore out in them: New York, Newport, Lenox—finally America. In France there was the Paris apartment in the Rue de Varenne, then a small estate in St Brice-sous-Forêt, in the country north of Paris, then an old château in Hyères, on the warm Mediterranean coast. Three times in her life she supervised the total renovation of a colossal mansion and its grounds, in effect building and furnishing and landscaping from scratch; and once, in Lenox, she bought a piece of empty land and really did start from scratch, raising out of the earth an American palace called The Mount. All of this exacted from her the energy, attentiveness, and insatiable governing impulses of a corporation chief executive; or the head of a small state.

In an architectural lull, she would travel. All her life she traveled compulsively, early in her marriage with her husband, touring Europe from February to June, afterward with various male companions, with the sense, and with the propriety, of leading a retinue. Accumulating "scenes"—hotels, landscapes, seascapes, museums, villages, ruins—she saw all the fabled cities of Europe, the islands of the Aegean, Tunis, Algiers, Carthage, the Sahara.

And all the while she was surrounded by a crowd. Not simply while traveling: the crowd was part of the daily condition of her houses and possessions. She had a household staff consisting of maids ("housemaids" and "chambermaids"—there appears to be a difference), a chief gardener and several under-gardeners, cook, housekeeper, major-domo, chauffeur, personal maid, "traveling" maid, secretary, "general agent," footmen. (One of the latter, accompanying her to I Tatti, the Berenson villa in Italy, inconveniently fell in love with a Berenson maid, and had to be surrendered.) These "establishments," Lewis remarks, "gave her what her bountiful nature desired: an ordered life, a carefully tended beauty of surroundings, and above all, total privacy." The "above all" engenders skepticism. Privacy? Survey-ing that mob of servants, even imagining them crossing silent carpets on tiptoe, one takes the impression, inevitably, of a hive. Her solitude was the congested solitude of a monarch; she was never, like other solitary-minded American writers (one thinks of Poe, or of course Emily Dickinson, or even Scott Fitzgerald), completely alone in the house. But these hectic movements of the hive were what she required; perhaps she would not have known how to do without them. Chekhov could sit at a table in the middle of the din of a large impoverished family, ignoring voices and footsteps in order to concentrate on the scratch of his pen. Edith Wharton sat up in bed with her writing board, in the middle of the active business of a house claiming her attention, similarly shutting out the only family she had. A hired family, an invented one. When she learned that her older brother Freddy, living not far away in Paris, had suffered a stroke, she was "unresponsive"; but when Gross, her housekeeper of long standing, and Elise, her personal maid, both grew fatally ill within a short space, she wrote in her diary, "All my life goes with those two dying women."

Nicky Mariano, in her memoir of her life as secretary-companion to Berenson, recalls how Edith Wharton treated her with indifference—until one day, aboard a yacht near Naples, she happened to ask after Elise. She was at once dispatched to the cabin below to visit with the maid. "From then on I became aware of a complete change in Edith's manner to me. There was a warmth, a tone of intimacy that I had never heard before." And again, describing how Wharton "looked after her servants with affectionate zeal and took a lively interest in all their joys and sorrows," she produces another anecdote:

> I remember how once during one of our excursions with her, she was deeply hurt and angry when on leaving a villa near Siena after a prolonged visit she discovered that neither her maid nor her chauffeur had been asked into the house.

What is the effect on a writer of being always encircled by servants? What we are to draw from this is not so much the sadness of purchased affections, or even the parasitism (once, left without much help for a brief period, she was bewildered about her daily survival), but something more perplexing: the moment-by-moment influence of continuous lower-class companionship. Room ought to be given to considering this; it took room in Wharton's life: she was with her servants all the time, she was with her friends and peers only some of the time. E. M. Forster sought out the common people in the belief that too much education atrophies the senses; in life and in art he went after the lower orders because he thought them the embodiment of the spontaneous gods of nature. In theory, at least—perhaps it was only literary theory—Forster wanted to become "instinctual," and instinct was with the working class. But Edith Wharton kept her distance even as she drew close; she remained mistress always. It made her a kind of double exile. As an expatriate settled in France, she had cut herself off from any direct infusion of the American sensibility and the American language. Through her attachment to her servants, she became intimately bound to illiterate lives remote from her mentality, preoccupations, habitual perceptions—a second expatriation as deliberate as the more obvious one. Nor did her servants give her access to "ordinary" life (she was no Lady Chatterley, there was no gamekeeper for her)—no one is "ordinary" while standing before the monarch of the house. Still, she fussed over her army of hirelings; it was a way of inventing claims. For her servants she provided pensions; she instituted a trust fund as a private charity for three Belgian children; she sent regular checks to her sister-in-law, divorced from her brother a quarter of a century and therefore clearly not to be taken for family. For family, in short, she substituted claims indisputably of her own making. She could feel responsible for servants and acquired dependents as others feel responsible for parents, brothers, children: but there was a tether made of money, and the power-end of the tether was altogether in her hand. With servants, there is no murkiness—as there sometimes is in friendship—about who is beholden to whom.

With her friends it was more difficult to invent claims; friendship has a way of resisting purchase, and she had to resort to ruses. When she wanted to release Morton Fullerton from the entangling blackmail of his former French mistress, she arranged with Henry James to make it seem as if the money were coming impersonally from a publisher. Fullerton having been, however briefly, her lover, it was hardly possible to hand over one hundred pounds and call it a "pension"; the object was not so much to keep Fullerton's friendship free as to establish the illusion of such freedom. It was enough for the controlling end of the money tether to know the tether was there; and anyhow the tether had a witness and an accomplice. "Please consider," James wrote, entering into the plot, "that I will play my mechanical part in your magnificent combination with absolute piety, fidelity, and punctuality."

But when it was James himself who came to be on the receiving end of the golden tether, he thundered against the tug of opulence, and the friendship was for a while impaired. The occasion was a proposal for his seventieth birthday: Edith Wharton, enlisting about forty moneyed Americans, thought to raise "not less than $5000," the idea being "that he should choose a fine piece of old furniture, or something of the kind"—but to James it all smelled blatantly of charity, meddling, pity, and cash. Once he got wind of the plan he called it a "reckless and indiscreet undertaking," and announced in a cable that he was beginning "instant prohibitive action. Please express to individuals approached my horror. Money absolutely returned."

It was returned, but within a few months James was hooked anyhow on that same line—hooked like Morton Fullerton, without being aware of it. This time the accomplice was Charles Scribner, who forwarded to James a phoney "advance" of eight thousand dollars intended to see him through the writing of *The Ivory Tower*—but the money was taken out of Wharton's own advance, from another publisher, of fifteen thousand dollars. The reluctant agent of the scheme, far from celebrating "your magnificent combination," saw it rather as "our fell purpose." "I feel rather mean and caddish and must continue so to the end of my days," Charles Scribner grumbled. "Please never give me away." In part this sullenness may have been guilt over not having himself volunteered, as James's publisher, to keep a master artist free from money anxiety, but beyond that there was a distaste for manipulation and ruse.

This moral confusion about proprieties—whom it is proper to tip, and whom not—expressed itself in other strange substitutions. It was not only that she wanted to pay her lover and her friend for services rendered, sexual or literary—clearly she had little overt recognition of the *quid pro quo* uses of philanthropy. It was not only that she loved her maid Gross more than her mother, and Arthur White her "man" more than her brother—it is understood that voluntary entanglements are not really entanglements at all. But there were more conspicuous replacements. Lacking babies, she habitually fondled small dogs: there is an absurd photograph of Edith Wharton as a young woman of twenty-eight, by then five years into her marriage, with an angry-looking Pekingese on each mutton-leg shoulder; the animals, pressed against her cheeks, nearly obscure her face; the face is cautious and contemplative, as of one not wanting to jar precious things. A similar photograph shows her husband gazing straight out at us with rather empty pale eyes over a nicely trimmed mustache and a perfect bow tie—on his lap, with no special repugnance, he is holding three small dogs, two of them of that same truculent breed, and though the caption reads "Teddy Wharton with his dogs," somehow we know better whose dogs they are. His body is detached; his expression, very correct and patient, barely hides—though Lewis argues otherwise—how he is being put upon by such a pose.

Until late in life, she never knew a child. Effie, the little girl in *The Reef,* is a child observed from afar—she runs, she enters, she departs, she is sent, she is summoned, at one moment she is presented as very young, at another she is old enough to be having lessons in Latin. She is a figment of a child. But the little dogs, up to the end of Edith Wharton's life, were always understood, always thought to have souls, always in her arms and in her bed; they were, Lewis says, "among the main joys of her being." Drawing up a list of her "ruling passions" at forty-four, she put "Dogs" second after "Justice and Order." At sixty-two she wrote in her journal of "the *us* ness" in the eyes of animals, "with the underlying *not-us* ness which belies it," and meditated on their "eternal inarticulateness and slavery. Why? their eyes seem to ask us."

The fellow feeling she had for the *not-us* ness of her Pekingese she did not have for her husband, who was, from her point of view, also *"not-us."* He too was inarticulate and mired in the slavery of a lesser intellect. He was a good enough man, interested (like his wife) in being perfectly clothed, vigorous and humorous and kind and compliant (so compliant that he once actually tried to make his way through James's *The Golden Bowl*)—undistinguished in any jot, the absolute product of his class. He had no work to do, and sought none. One of Edith Wharton's friends—a phrase instantly revealing, since her friends were practically never his; the large-hearted Henry James was nearly the only one to cross this divide—observed that Teddy Wharton's "idleness was busy and innocent." His ostensible employment was the management of his wife's trust funds, but he filled his days with sports and hunting, and his glass with fine wine. Wine was the one thing he had a connoisseur's familiarity with; and, of all the elegant good things of the world, wine was the one thing his wife disliked. When he was fifty-three he began to go mad, chiefly, it would seem, because he had married the wrong wife, with no inkling that she would turn out to be the wrong wife. Edith Newbold Jones at twenty-three was exactly what Edward Wharton, a dozen years older, had a right to expect for himself: she had heritage (her ancestor, Ebenezer Stevens, was an enterprising artillery officer in the Revolutionary War), she had inheritance (the Joneses owned the Chemical Bank of New York and much of the West Side). In brief, family and money. The dominant quality—what he had married her for, with that same idle innocence that took note only of the pleasantly obvious—was what Edith Wharton was afterward to call "tribe." The Whartons and the Joneses were of the same tribe—old Protestant money—and he could hardly predict that his wife would soon replace him in the nuptial bed with a writing board. At first he was perplexed but proud: Louis Auchincloss quotes a description of Teddy Wharton from Consuelo Vanderbilt's memoirs as "more of an equerry than an equal, walking behind [his wife] and carrying whatever paraphernalia she happened to discard," and once (Lewis tells us), walking as usual behind her, Teddy exclaimed to one of her friends, "Look at that waist! No one would ever guess that she had written a line of poetry in her life." She, meanwhile, was driven to writing in her journal, "Oh, Gods of derision! And you've given me over twenty years of it!" This outcry occurred immediately after she had shown her husband, during a wearing train journey, "a particularly interest-ing passage" in a scientific volume called *Heredity and Variation.* His response was not animated. "I heard the key turn in my prison-lock," she recorded, in the clear metaphorical style of her fiction.

A case can be made that it was she who turned the key on him. His encroaching madness altered him—he began to act oddly, out of character; or, rather, more in character than he had ever before dared. The equerry of the paraphernalia undertook to behave as if he were master of the paraphernalia—in short, he embezzled a part of the funds it had been his duty to preserve and augment. And, having been replaced in bed by a writing board, he suddenly confessed to his wife (or perhaps feverishly bragged) that he had recently gone to live with a prostitute in a Boston apartment, filling its remaining rooms with chorus girls; the embezzled funds paid for the apartment. The story was in the main confirmed. His madness had the crucial sanity of needs that are met.

His wife, who—granted that philanthropy is not embezzlement—was herself capable of money ruse, and who had herself once rapturously fallen from merely spiritual friendship, locked him up for it. Against his protestations, and those of his sister and brother, he was sent to a sanitorium. Teddy had stolen, Teddy had fallen; he was an adulterer. She had never stolen (though there is a robust if mistaken critical tradition that insists she stole her whole literary outlook from Henry James); but she had fallen, she was an adulteress. Teddy's sexual disgrace was public; hers went undivulged until her biographer came upon it more than three decades after her death. But these sardonic parallels and opposites illumine little beyond the usual ironies of the pot and the kettle. What had all at once happened in Edith Wharton's life was that something *bad* happened. Necessity intervened, her husband was irrefutably a manic-depressive. He had hours of excitement and accusation; more often he was in a state of self-castigation. He begged her for help, he begged to be taken back and to be given a second chance. ". . . when you came back last year," she told him, "I was ready to overlook everything you had done, and to receive you as if nothing had happened." This referred to the Boston apartment; she herself had been in a London hotel with Fullerton at nearly the same time. In the matter of her money she was more unyielding. Replying to his plea to be allowed to resume the management of her trusts and property, she took the tone of a mistress with a servant who has been let go, and who is now discovered still unaccountably loitering in the house. "In order that no further questions of this kind should come up, the only thing left for me to do is to suggest that you should resign your Trusteeship. . . . Your health unfortunately makes it impossible for you to take any active part in the management of my affairs." Gradually, over months, she evolved a policy: she did everything for him that seemed sensible, as long as it was cold-hearted. He was removed, still uncured, from the sanitorium, and subjected to a regime of doctors, trips, traveling companions, scoldings. In the end, when he was most sick and most desperate, she discarded him, handing him over to the doctors the way one hands over impeding paraphernalia to an equerry. She discarded him well before she divorced him; divorce, at that period and in her caste, took deliberation. She discarded him because he impeded, he distracted, he was a nuisance, he drained her, he wore her out. As a woman she was contemptuous of him, as a writer she fought off his interruptions. The doctors were more polite than Henry James, who charac-terized Teddy Wharton as able to "hold or follow no counter-proposal, no plan of opposition, of his own, for as much as a minute or two; he is immediately *off*—irrelevant and childish . . . one's pity for her is at the best scarce bearable."

She too pitied herself, and justly, though she forgot to pity *him*. He had lost all trust in himself, whatever he said he timidly or ingratiatingly or furiously took back. He was flailing vainly after the last flashes of an autonomy his wife had long ago stripped from him. And during all that angry space, when she was bitterly engaged in fending off the partisan ragings of his family, and coldly supervising his medical and traveling routines, she, in the stern autonomy of her morning bed, was writing *Ethan Frome*, finishing *The Reef*, bringing off short stories. She could do all this because she did not look into her husband's eyes and read there, as she had read in the eyes of her little dogs, the helpless pathos of "Why?" It was true that she did not and could not love him, but her virtue was always according to principle, not passion. Presumably she also did not love the French soldiers who were sick with tuberculosis contracted in the trenches of the First World War; nevertheless for them she organized a cure program, which she termed "the most vital thing that can be done in France now." Whatever the most vital thing for Teddy might have been—perhaps there was nothing—she relinquished it at last. The question of the tubercular soldiers was, like all the claims on her spirit that she herself initiated, volitional and opportune. She had sought out these tragedies, they were not implicated in the conditions of her own life, that peculiar bed she had made for herself—"such a great big uncompromising 4-poster," James called it. For the relief of tubercular soldiers and other good works, she earned a French medal, and was made a Chevalier of the Legion of Honor. An arena of dazzling public exertion. But in the lesser frame of private mess she did nothing to spare her husband the humiliation of his madness. It is one thing to go mad, it is another to be humiliated for it. The one time in her life drift stopped dead in its trackless spume, and a genuine claim made as if to seize her—necessity, redder in tooth and claw than any sacrifice one grandly chooses for oneself—she turned away. For her, such a claim was the Gorgon's head, to gaze on which was death.

Writer's death. This is something most writers not only fear but sweat to evade, though most do not practice excision with as clean a knife-edge as cut away "irrelevant and childish" Teddy from Edith Wharton's life. "Friend, client, child, sickness, fear, want, charity, all knock at once at thy closet door and say—'Come out unto us.' But keep thy state," Emerson advised, "come not into their confusion." And Mann's Tonio Kröger declaims that "one must die to life to be utterly a creator." This ruthless romantic idea—it cannot be lived up to by weaklings who succumb to conscience, let alone to love—is probably at bottom less romantic than pragmatic. But it is an idea very nearly the opposite of Wilson's and Kazin's more affecting view of Edith Wharton: that joylessness was her muse, that her troubles energized her for fiction—the stimulus of "some exceptional emotional strain," according to Wilson, "so many personal maladjustments," according to Kazin, which made the novelist possible. If anything made the novelist possible, it was the sloughing off of the sources of emotional strain and personal maladjustment. As for the parallel new-feminist opinion that a woman writes best when she risks "unbearable wisdoms," it does not apply: what wisdom Edith Wharton found unbearable she chose not to bear.

The rest was chatter. Having turned away from the Gorgon's head, she spent the

remainder of her life—indeed, nearly the whole of it—in the mainly insipid, sometimes inspired, adventure of elevated conversation. She had her friends. There were
few women—whether because she did not encounter her equals among women, or
because she avoided them, her biographer yields no hint. The majority were men
(one should perhaps say "gentlemen")—Lapsley, Lubbock, Berenson, Fullerton,
Simmons, James, Bourget, D'Humières, Berry, Sturgis, Hugh-Smith, Maynard,
Gregory, Grant, Scott . . . the list is longer still. Lewis fleshes out all these names
brilliantly, particularly Berry and Fullerton; the great comic miraculous James needs
no fleshing out. James was in a way afraid of her. She swooped down on him to pluck
him away for conversation or sightseeing, and he matched the "commotion and
exhaustion" of her arrivals against the vengeance of Bonaparte, Attila, and Tamer-
lane. "Her powers of devastation are ineffable," he reported, and got into the habit
of calling her the Angel of Devastation. She interrupted his work with the abrupt-
ness of a natural force (she might occur at any time) and at her convenience (she
had particular hours for her work, he had all hours for his). He read her novels and
dispatched wondrous celebrating smokescreens of letters ("I applaud, I mean I value,
I egg you on") to hide the insufficiency of his admiration. As for her "life," it was
a spectacle that had from the beginning upset him: her "desolating, ravaging,
burning and destroying energy." And again: "such a nightmare of perpetually
renewable choice and decision, such a luxury of bloated alternatives." "*What* an
incoherent life!" he summed it up. Lewis disagrees, and reproaches James for partial
views and a probable fear of strong women; but it may be, on all the lavish evidence
Lewis provides, that the last word will after all lie with drift, exactly as James
perceived it in her rushing aimlessness aimed at him.

Before Lewis's landmark discovery of the Wharton-Fullerton liaison, Walter Van
Rensselaer Berry—Wharton's distant cousin, an international lawyer and an aristocrat—was commonly regarded as the tender center and great attachment of her life.
Lewis does not refute this connection, though he convincingly drains it of sexual
particularity, and gives us the portrait of a conventionally self-contained dry-hearted
lifelong bachelor, a man caught, if not in recognizable drift, then in another sort
of inconclusiveness. But Walter Berry was Edith Wharton's first literary intellectual—a lightning bolt of revelation that, having struck early, never lost its electrical
sting. Clearly, she fed on intellectuals—but in a withdrawn and secretive way: she
rarely read her work aloud, though she rejoiced to hear James read his. She brooded
over history and philosophy, understood everything, but was incapable in fiction or
elsewhere of expressing anything but the most commonplace psychology. This was,
of course, her strength: she knew how human beings behave, she could describe and
predict and surprise. Beyond that, she had a fertile capacity for thinking up stories.
Plots and permutations of plots teemed. She was scornful of writers who agonized
after subject matter. Subjects, she said, swarmed about her "like mosquitoes," until
she felt stifled by their multiplicity and variety.

The truth is she had only one subject, the nineteenth century's unique European
literary subject: society. Standard American criticism, struggling to "place" Edith
Wharton in a literary environment unused to her subject, has contrived for her the
role of a lesser Henry James. This has served to indict her as an imitative figure. But
on no significant level is the comparison with James pertinent, except to say that
by and large they wrote about the same kinds of people, derived from the same class.

Otherwise the difference can be seized in a breath: James was a genius, Wharton not. James invented an almost metaphysical art, Wharton's insights lay close against their molds: what she saw she judged. James became an American in the most ideal sense, Wharton remained an estranged New Yorker. James was an uncanny moralist, Wharton a canny realist. James scarcely ever failed—or, at least, his few failures when they occurred were nevertheless glorious in aspiration and seamless in execution. When Wharton failed, she fell into an embarrassing triteness of language and seeing.

It is a pity that her name is attached so unrelentingly—thanks to the American high school!—to *Ethan Frome,* a desolate, even morbid, narrow, soft-at-the-center and at the last unsurprising novella not at all typical of her range. It is an outdoor book that ends mercilessly indoors; she was an indoor novelist. She achieved two permanent novels, one—*The House of Mirth*—a spoiled masterpiece, a kind of latterday reverse *Scarlet Letter,* very direct yet eerie, the other *The Age of Innocence,* a combination of ode and elegy to the New York of her childhood, affirmation and repudiation both. A good many of her short stories and some of the novellas ("The Old Maid," for instance) are marvels of shapeliness and pointedness. This applies also to stories written during her late period, when she is widely considered to have debased her gift. The common accusation—Wilson makes it—is that her prose finally came to resemble women's-magazine fiction. One can venture that she did not so much begin to sound like the women's magazines as that they began to sound like her, a condition that obtains until this moment. No one has explored Wharton's ongoing subliminal influence on current popular fiction (see almost any issue of *Redbook*); such an investigation would probably be striking in its disclosure of the strength of her legacy. Like any hokey imitation long after the model is lost to consciousness, it is not a bad compliment, though it may be awkward to admit it. (One of the least likely tributes to the Roman Empire, after all, is the pervasiveness of nineteenth-century American civic architecture.) But *The House of Mirth* and *The Age of Innocence* are, like everything unsurpassable because deeply idiosyncratic, incapable of spawning versions of themselves; in these two novels she is in command of an inwardness commensurate with structure. In them she does not simply grab hold of society, or judge it merely; she turns society into an exulting bird of prey, with blood on its beak, steadily beating its wings just over our heads; she turns society into an untamable *idea.* The reader, apprehensive, yet lured by the bird's lyric form, covers his face.

She could do all that; she had that power. Lewis, writing to justify and defend, always her sympathetic partisan, nevertheless hedges. Having acknowledged that she had "begun to locate herself—with a certain assurance, though without vanity—in the developing course of American literature," he appends a doubt:

> But in another part of her, there remained something of the conviction drilled into her in old New York that it was improper for a lady to write fiction. One could do so only if one joked about it—if one treated it, to borrow Lubbock's word, as "an amusement." She sometimes sounded as if her writing were her entertainingly guilty secret, and in her memoirs she referred to it (borrowing the title of a popular children's book of her own New York youth) as her "secret garden."
>
> But in the winter of 1911 [she was then at work on *The Reef*], as on perhaps half a dozen other occasions, it was the believing artist that was in the ascendancy during the hard-driving morning hours.

Somehow it is easy to doubt that she had this doubt—or, if she once had it, that she held it for long. To believe in her doubt is to make the bad case of the orthodox critics who, unlike Lewis, have shrunk from taking her seriously as an artist because as an American aristocrat she was born shockingly appurtenanced, and therefore deserves to be patronized for her sorrows. To believe in her doubt is to make the bad case of the new feminists, for whom female sex is, always and everywhere, an impediment difficult to transcend—even when, for an obsessed writer of talent, there is nothing to transcend. To believe in her doubt is to reverse the terms of her life and her work. Only "half a dozen other occasions" when Wharton was a "believing artist"? Only so few? This would mean that the life outside her bed—the dressed life of conversation and travel, the matchstick life of drift—was the primary life, and the life with her writing board—the life of the believing artist—the deviation, the anomaly, the distraction.

But we know, and have always known (Freud taught us only how to reinforce this knowledge), that the secret self is the true self, that obsession is confession. For Edith Wharton that is the only acceptable evaluation, the only possible justice. She did not doubt her allegiance. The writing came first. That she kept it separate from the rest was a misrepresentation and a mistake, but it may also have been a species of holy instinct—it was the one uncontaminated zone of her being: the place unprofaned. Otherwise she can be defined only by the horrific gyrations of "a life"—by the spiraling solipsism and tragic drift that led her to small dogs instead of babies, servants instead of family, high-minded male distance instead of connubial friendship, public virtue instead of private conscience, infatuation instead of the love that sticks. Only the writing board could justify these ugly substitutions. And some would say—myself not among them—that not even the writing board justified them.

Considerations for Thinking and Writing

1. Consider Ozick's "Riddle of the Ordinary" alongside Dillard's "Heaven and Earth in Jest." How do these two essays deal with the notion of paradox? Would you call their respective essays philosophical? Religious? Spiritual? Mystical? How do these authors compare in their notions of determinism and authority?

2. In "On Being Raised by a Daughter," Mairs quotes Nancy Chodorow, Nancy Friday, Julia Kristeva, and Virginia Woolf. In "The Riddle of the Ordinary," Ozick quotes Walter Pater, W. B. Yeats, the Kotzker Rebbe (Rabbi) and an anonymous "Buddhist sage." What do we learn about a writer from her choice of quotations? Does *whom* she quotes matter as much as *what* she quotes? How do writers use quotations to authorize their own writing?

3. In Ozick's "Mrs. Virginia Woolf: A Madwoman and Her Nurse," the nurse's story is arguably more central than the madwoman's. What does Ozick accomplish by giving Leonard Woolf's story such careful consideration? Consider Woolf's own retelling of the Carlyle story from the perspective of Jane Carlyle and Geraldine Jewsbury. Can you link these efforts with Angela Y. Davis's retelling of the history of reproductive rights in America?

4. Ozick's account of Leonard and Virginia Woolf dwells on a paradox: The more "free" of domestic chores Virginia became, the more dependent she became on Leonard. Ozick's essay on Edith Wharton also portrays freedom in a negative light: It turns into "drift." In what sense might a woman writer's freedom from domesticity be problematical? Does an alternative notion of freedom emerge from Ozick's essays?

5. "A writer's heroism," Ozick notes, "is in the act of writing: not in the finished work, but in the work as it goes." How does Ozick develop her notion of writers as heroes? What

do you make of her insistence that the work "as it goes," not the finished work, suffices as the writer's heroism?

6. Linger over Ozick's snail analogy in "On Excellence." How does she exploit this analogy throughout the essay? Compare Ozick's snail to Woolf's image of thinking as fishing in *A Room of One's Own*. Do these analogies help you to read Ehrlich's "Looking for a Lost Dog" as an allegory, a narrative that tells a more abstract story even as it tells a literal one?

7. In "Justice (Again) to Edith Wharton," Ozick addresses herself to the problems of reading Wharton as a "woman writer." What do her observations have in common with Margaret Atwood's in "On Being a 'Woman Writer,' " in Part II? How do they differ from Atwood's?

ADRIENNE RICH
(b. 1929)

For nearly forty years now Adrienne Rich's voice has been heard in poems, speeches, essays, reviews, and book-length studies of literary, social, and cultural ideas. Hers is a powerful voice, one that demands attention, an earnest and engaging voice passionately committed to the liberation of women and men from a prejudice that blinds perception and stunts the mind.

Although known first and perhaps best as a fine poet, Rich has become a spokeswoman for feminist consciousness, especially lesbianism. For Rich lesbianism is considerably more than a matter of sexual preference. In seeing it as "a sense of desiring oneself, choosing oneself," Rich associates lesbianism with the formation of identity, with the power of the self to discover and define itself. But it is also, as she has remarked, "a primary intensity between women," which energizes them, propels them toward one another, both challenging and charging their imaginations. Lesbianism is Rich's source of strength—literary, political, and personal.

And yet even though Rich has become associated with radical feminist ideology, she is not readily constrained by it. Her prose and poetry, while rooted in ideological concerns, nonetheless dramatize a self discovering freedom in language and art. In her best writing, Rich is less a polemi-

cist and publicist than an artist who challenges our preconceptions about women, especially their relationships with men and their responsibilities to one another. Her best work dramatically enacts the way she sees herself, perhaps most memorably described in these lines from her poem "Planetarium":

I am an instrument in the shape
of a woman trying to translate pulsations
into images for the relief of the body
and the reconstruction of the mind.

One place to see Rich's own reconstruction of the mind is in her autobiographical writing. In an essay not included in this book largely because it has been so often reprinted elsewhere, "When We Dead Awaken: Writing as Re-vision," Rich charts the changing perception of herself as woman and poet. She describes how she needed to change the images that represented, for her, ideals of both woman and poet, since her images of them had been dominated by men.

Change thus became the lodestone of Rich's life and work. The title of her first book of poems, *A Change of World* (1951), ironically forecasts the driving impulse in Rich's life, an impulse manifested even more vigorously by the title of a later poetry collection, *The Will to Change* (1971), in which she celebrates power and self-determination as agents of that necessary change. Between these two volumes Rich revised both her life and her poetry. In 1953 she married Alfred Conrad, a Harvard economist, and she bore three sons in four years. In her book *Of Woman Born* (1976) she describes her seventeen years of marriage and motherhood as "a radicalizing experience." She writes: "I knew I had to remake my life; I did not then understand that we [middle-class women] were expected to fill both the part of the Victorian Lady of Leisure, the Angel in the House, and also of the Victorian cook, scullery maid, laundress, governess, and nurse."

Rich's prose pieces range widely in tone, structure, manner, and style. The shifts in her focus are due partly to the varying occasions that called these pieces into being, partly to their differing purposes and intentions. "What Does a Woman Need to Know?"—a commencement address Rich delivered at Smith College in 1979—raises questions many college-educated women might ask themselves. Rich quickly arrives at her central concern: the issue of power, especially the relationship of knowledge and power, power and privilege. Rich is concerned that women be granted real power rather than token recognition, and that they settle for nothing less. Her tone is urgent without being strident, authoritative and provocative without being radically polemical. As in much of her work, she urges that women acquire the power of self-determination and the power to ensure equitable social change.

Her essay on Emily Dickinson "Vesuvius at Home: The Power of Emily Dickinson," performs a similar act of re-vision. Rich's fresh and influential reading of Dickinson opened the way for subsequent feminist approaches to Dickinson's work. Rich's essay is a strong piece of liberating criticism infused with cultural analysis and fueled by personal passion. Stressing the psychic energy of Dickinson's verse, its emotional depth and bold originality, Rich's analysis is a triumph of imaginative reconstruction of Dickinson's mind.

Also widely reprinted elsewhere, "When We Dead Awaken: Writing as Re-vision" (1972, 1976) explores the concept of re-vision, which Rich describes as "the act of looking back, of seeing with fresh eyes." It is an act essential for writers, both amateur and professional. It is also an essential act for readers if they don't want to see a paralyzed and ossified literary tradition. And as Rich insists, her version of re-vision is essential for women living in a male-dominated society. Re-vision is thus, as she notes, more than a mere chapter of cultural or literary history; "it is an act of survival." Rich uses her own experience as reader, poet, and woman to illustrate how such re-vision can and must occur.

In each of these prose pieces and in the many poems she has published, Rich writes out of an impassioned conviction that women's value lies not in their being mere appendages to men, whether those men are father and sons, husbands or colleagues or bosses. Women's value resides in themselves as individuals who differ from men and from one another even while they share a sense of communal sisterhood. Her writing is urgent, forceful, occasionally angry in its denunciation of women's subjugation and humiliation. It is also assertive, even annunciatory, in its insistence that conditions for living, working, and writing must be improved. Through its anger and critical passion, however, sounds a note of optimism, a belief that both men and women are listening and are ready for change.

What Does a Woman Need to Know?

I have been very much moved that you, the class of 1979, chose me for your commencement speaker. It is important to me to be here, in part because Smith is one of the original colleges for women, but also because she has chosen to continue identifying herself as a women's college. We are at a point in history where this fact has enormous potential, even if that potential is as yet unrealized. The possibilities for the future education of women that haunt these buildings and grounds are enormous, when we think of what an independent women's college might be: a college dedicated both to teaching women what women need to know and, by the same token, to changing the landscape of knowledge itself. The germ of those possibilities lies symbolically in The Sophia Smith Collection, an archive much in need of expansion and increase, but which by its very existence makes the statement that women's lives and work are valued here and that our foresisters, buried and diminished in male-centered scholarship, are a living presence, necessary and precious to us.

Suppose we were to ask ourselves simply: What does a woman need to know to become a self-conscious, self-defining human being? Doesn't she need a knowledge of her own history, of her much-politicized female body, of the creative genius of women of the past—the skills and crafts and techniques and visions possessed by women in other times and cultures, and how they have been rendered anonymous, censored, interrupted, devalued? Doesn't she, as one of that majority who are still denied equal rights as citizens, enslaved as sexual prey, unpaid or underpaid as workers, withheld from her own power—doesn't she need an analysis of her condition, a knowledge of the women thinkers of the past who have reflected on it, a knowledge, too, of women's world-wide individual rebellions and organized movements against economic and social injustice, and how these have been fragmented and silenced?

Doesn't she need to know how seemingly natural states of being, like heterosexuality, like motherhood, have been enforced and institutionalized to deprive her of power? Without such education, women have lived and continue to live in ignorance of our collective context, vulnerable to the projections of men's fantasies about us as they appear in art, in literature, in the sciences, in the media, in the so-called humanistic studies. I suggest that not anatomy, but enforced ignorance, has been a crucial key to our powerlessness.

There is—and I say this with sorrow—there is no women's college today which is providing young women with the education they need for survival as whole persons in a world which denies women wholeness—that knowledge which, in the words of Coleridge, "returns again as power." The existence of Women's Studies courses offers at least some kind of life line. But even Women's Studies can amount simply to compensatory history; too often they fail to challenge the intellectual and political structures that must be challenged if women as a group are ever to come into collective, nonexclusionary freedom. The belief that established science and scholarship—which have so relentlessly excluded women from their making—are "objective" and "value-free" and that feminist studies are "unscholarly," "biased," and "ideological" dies hard. Yet the fact is that all science, and all scholarship, and all art are ideological; there is no neutrality in culture. And the ideology of the education you have just spent four years acquiring in a women's college has been largely, if not entirely, the ideology of white male supremacy, a construct of male subjectivity. The silences, the empty spaces, the language itself, with its excision of the female, the methods of discourse tell us as much as the content, once we learn to watch for what is left out, to listen for the unspoken, to study the patterns of established science and scholarship with an outsider's eye. One of the dangers of a privileged education for women is that we may lose the eye of the outsider and come to believe that those patterns hold for humanity, for the universal, and that they include us.

And so I want to talk today about privilege and about tokenism and about power. Everything I can say to you on this subject comes hard-won, from the lips of a woman privileged by class and skin color, a father's favorite daughter, educated at Radcliffe, which was then casually referred to as the Harvard "Annex." Much of the first four decades of my life was spent in a continuous tension between the world the Fathers taught me to see, and had rewarded me for seeing, and the flashes of insight that came through the eye of the outsider. Gradually those flashes of insight, which at times could seem like brushes with madness, began to demand that I struggle to connect them with each other, to insist that I take them seriously. It was only when I could finally affirm the outsider's eye as the source of a legitimate and coherent vision that I began to be able to do the work I truly wanted to do, live the kind of life I truly wanted to live, instead of carrying out the assignments I had been given as a privileged woman and a token.

For women, all privilege is relative. Some of you were not born with class or skin-color privilege; but you all have the privilege of education, even if it is an education which has largely denied you knowledge of yourselves as women. You have, to begin with, the privilege of literacy; and it is well for us to remember that, in an age of increasing illiteracy, 60 percent of the world's illiterates are women. Between 1960 and 1970, the number of illiterate men in the world rose by 8 million, while the number of illiterate women rose by 40 million.* And the number of illiterate women is increasing. Beyond literacy, you have the privilege of training and tools which can allow you to go beyond the content of your education and re-educate yourselves—to debrief yourselves, we might call it, of the false messages of your education in this culture, the messages telling you that women have not really cared about power or learning or creative opportunities because of a psychobiological need to serve men and produce children; that only a few atypical women have been exceptions to this rule; the messages telling you that woman's experience is neither normative nor central to human experience. You have the training and the tools to do independent research, to evaluate data, to criticize, and to express in language and visual forms what you discover. This is a privilege, yes, but only if you do not give up in exchange for it the deep knowledge of the unprivileged, the knowledge that, as a woman, you have historically been viewed and still are viewed as existing, not in your own right, but in the service of men. And only if you refuse to give up your capacity to think as a woman, even though in the graduate schools and professions to which many of you will be going you will be praised and rewarded for "thinking like a man."

*United Nations, Department of International Economic and Social Affairs, Statistical Office, *1977 Compendium of Social Statistics* (New York: United Nations, 1980).

The word *power* is highly charged for women. It has been long associated for us with the use of force, with rape, with the stockpiling of weapons, with the ruthless accrual of wealth and the hoarding of resources, with the power that acts only in its own interest, despising and exploiting the powerless—including women and children. The effects of this kind of power are all around us, even literally in the water we drink and the air we breathe, in the form of carcinogens and radioactive wastes. But for a long time now, feminists have been talking about redefining power, about that meaning of power which returns to the root—*posse, potere, pouvoir*: to be able, to have the potential, to possess and use one's energy of creation—*transforming power*. An early objection to feminism—in both the nineteenth and twentieth centuries—was that it would make women behave like men—ruthlessly, exploitatively, oppressively. In fact, radical feminism looks to a transformation of human relationships and structures in which power, instead of a thing to be hoarded by a few, would be released to and from within the many, shared in the form of knowledge, expertise, decision making, access to tools, as well as in the basic forms of food and shelter and health care and literacy. Feminists—and many nonfeminists—are, and rightly so, still concerned with what power would mean in such a society, and with the relative differences in power among and between women here and now.

Which brings me to a third meaning of power where women are concerned: the false power which masculine society offers to a few women, on condition that they use it to maintain things as they are, and that they essentially "think like men." This is the meaning of female tokenism: that power withheld from the vast majority of women is offered to a few, so that it appears that any "truly qualified" woman can gain access to leadership, recognition, and reward; hence, that justice based on merit actually prevails. The token woman is encouraged to see herself as different from most other women, as exceptionally talented and deserving, and to separate herself from the wider female condition; and she is perceived by "ordinary" women as separate also, perhaps even as stronger than themselves.

Because you are, within the limits of all women's ultimate outsiderhood, a privileged group of women, it is extremely important for your future sanity that you understand the way tokenism functions. Its most immediate contradiction is that, while it seems to offer the individual token woman a means to realize her creativity, to influence the course of events, it also, by exacting of her certain kinds of behavior and style, acts to blur her outsider's eye, which could be her real source of power and vision. Losing her outsider's vision, she loses the insight which both binds her to other women and affirms her in herself. Tokenism essentially demands that the token deny her identification with women as a group, especially with women less privileged than she: if she is a lesbian, that she deny her relationships with individual women; that she perpetuate rules and structures and criteria and methodologies which have functioned to exclude women; that she renounce or leave undeveloped the critical perspective of her female consciousness. Women unlike herself—poor women, women of color, waitresses, secretaries, housewives in the supermarket, prostitutes, old women—become invisible to her; they may represent too acutely what she has escaped or wished to flee.

President Conway tells me that ever-increasing numbers of you are going on from Smith to medical and law schools. The news, on the face of it, is good: that, thanks to the feminist struggle of the past decade, more doors into these two powerful professions are open to women. I would like to believe that any profession would be better for having more women practicing it, and that any woman practicing law or medicine would use her knowledge and skill to work to transform the realm of health care and the interpretations of the law, to make them responsive to the needs of all those—women, people of color, children, the aged, the dispossessed—for whom they function today as repressive controls. I would like to believe this, but it will not happen even if 50 percent of the members of these professions are women, unless those women refuse to be made into token insiders, unless they zealously preserve the outsider's view and the outsider's consciousness.

For no woman is really an insider in the institutions fathered by masculine consciousness. When we allow ourselves to believe we are, we lose touch with parts of ourselves defined as unacceptable by that consciousness; with the vital toughness and visionary strength of the angry grandmothers, the shamanesses, the fierce marketwomen of the Ibo Women's War, the marriage-resisting women silkworkers of prerevolutionary China, the millions of widows, midwives, and women healers tortured and burned as witches for three centuries in Europe, the Beguines of the twelfth century, who formed independent women's orders outside the domination of the Church, the women of the Paris Commune who marched on Versailles, the uneducated housewives of the Women's Cooperative Guild in England who memorized poetry over the washtub and organized against their oppression as mothers, the women thinkers discredited as "strident," "shrill," "crazy," or "deviant" whose courage to be heretical, to speak their truths, we so badly need to draw upon in our own lives. I believe that every woman's soul is haunted by the spirits of earlier women who fought for their unmet needs and those of their children and their tribes and their peoples, who refused to accept the prescriptions of a male church and state, who took risks and resisted, as women today—like Inez Garcia, Yvonne Wanrow, Joan Little, Cassandra Peten—are fighting their rapists and batterers. Those spirits dwell in us, trying to speak to us. But we can choose to be deaf; and tokenism, the myth of the "special" woman, the unmothered Athena sprung from her father's brow, can deafen us to their voices.

In this decade now ending, as more women are entering the professions (though still suffering sexual harassment in the workplace, though still, if they have children, carrying two full-time jobs, though still vastly outnumbered by men in upper-level and decision-making jobs), we need most profoundly to remember that early insight of the feminist movement as it evolved in the late sixties: *that no woman is liberated until we all are liberated.* The media flood us with messages to the contrary, telling us that we live in an era when "alternate life styles" are freely accepted, when "marriage contracts" and "the new intimacy" are revolutionizing heterosexual relationships, that shared parenting and the "new fatherhood" will change the world. And we live in a society leeched upon by the "personal growth" and "human potential" industry, by the delusion that individual self-fulfillment can be found in thirteen weeks or a weekend, that the alienation and injustice experienced by women, by Black and Third World people, by the poor, in a world ruled by white males, in a society which fails to meet the most basic needs and which is slowly poisoning itself, can be mitigated or dispersed by Transcendental Meditation. Perhaps the most succinct expression of this message I have seen is the appearance of a magazine for women called *Self.* The insistence of the feminist movement, that each woman's selfhood is precious, that the feminine ethic of self-denial and self-sacrifice must give way to a true woman identification, which would affirm our connectedness with all women, is perverted into a commercially profitable and politically debilitating narcissism. It is important for each of you, toward whom many of these messages are especially directed, to discriminate clearly between "liberated life style" and feminist struggle, and to make a conscious choice.

It's a cliché of commencement speeches that the speaker ends with a peroration telling the new graduates that however badly past generations have behaved, their generation must save the world. I would rather say to you, women of the class of 1979: Try to be worthy of your foresisters, learn from your history, look for inspiration to your ancestresses. If this history has been poorly taught to you, if you do not know it, then use your educational privilege to learn it. Learn how some women of privilege have compromised the greater liberation of women, how others have risked their privileges to further it; learn how brilliant and successful women have failed to create a more just and caring society, precisely because they have tried to do so on terms that the powerful men around them would accept and tolerate. Learn to be worthy of the women of every class, culture, and historical age who did otherwise, who spoke boldly when women were jeered and physically harassed for speaking in public, who—like Anne Hutchinson, Mary Wollstonecraft, the Grimké sisters, Abby Kelley, Ida B. Wells-Barnett, Susan B. Anthony, Lillian Smith, Fannie Lou Hamer—broke taboos, who resisted slavery—their own and other people's. To become a token woman—whether you win the Nobel prize or merely get tenure at the cost of denying your sisters—is to become something less than a man indeed, since men are loyal at least to their own world view, their laws of brotherhood and male self-interest. I am not suggesting that you imitate male loyalties; with the philosopher Mary Daly, I believe that the bonding of women must be utterly different and for an utterly different end: not the misering of resources and power, but the release, in each other, of the yet unexplored resources and transformative power of women, so long despised, confined, and wasted. Get all the knowledge and skill you can in whatever professions you enter; but remember that most of your education must be self-education, in learning the things women need to know and in calling up the voices we need to hear within ourselves.

Compulsory Heterosexuality and Lesbian Existence

I

Biologically men have only one innate orientation—a sexual one that draws them to women,—while women have two innate orientations, sexual toward men and reproductive toward their young.[1]

I was a woman terribly vulnerable, critical, using femaleness as a sort of standard or yardstick to measure and discard men. Yes—something like that. I was an Anna who invited defeat from men without ever being conscious of it. (But I am conscious of it. And being conscious of it means I shall leave it all behind me and become—but what?) I was stuck fast in an emotion common to women of our time, that can turn them bitter, or Lesbian, or solitary. Yes, that Anna during that time was . . .

[Another blank line across the page:][2]

The bias of compulsory heterosexuality, through which lesbian experience is perceived on a scale ranging from deviant to abhorrent or simply rendered invisible, could be illustrated from many texts other than the two just preceding. The assumption made by Rossi, that women are "innately" sexually oriented only toward men, and that made by Lessing, that the lesbian is simply acting out of her bitterness toward men, are by no means theirs alone; these assumptions are widely current in literature and in the social sciences.

I am concerned here with two other matters as well: first, how and why women's choice of women as passionate comrades, life partners, co-workers, lovers, community has been crushed, invalidated, forced into hiding and disguise; and second, the virtual or total neglect of lesbian existence in a wide range of writings, including feminist scholarship. Obviously there is a connection here. I believe that much feminist theory and criticism is stranded on this shoal.

My organizing impulse is the belief that it is not enough for feminist thought that specifically lesbian texts exist. Any theory or cultural/political creation that treats lesbian existence as a marginal or less "natural" phenomenon, as mere "sexual preference," or as the mirror image of either heterosexual or male homosexual relations is profoundly weakened thereby, whatever its other contributions. Feminist theory can no longer afford merely to voice a toleration of "lesbianism" as an "alternative life style" or make token allusion to lesbians. A feminist critique of compulsory heterosexual orientation for women is long overdue. In this exploratory paper, I shall try to show why.

I will begin by way of examples, briefly discussing four books that have appeared in the last few years, written from different viewpoints and political orientations, but all presenting themselves, and favorably reviewed, as feminist.[3] All take as a basic assumption that the social relations of the sexes are disordered and extremely problematic, if not disabling, for women; all seek paths toward change. I have learned more from some of these books than from others, but on this I am clear: each one might have been more accurate, more powerful, more truly a force for change had the author dealt with lesbian existence as a reality and as a source of knowledge and power available to women, or with the institution of heterosexuality itself as a beachhead of male dominance.[4] In none of them is the question ever raised as to whether, in a different context or other things being equal, women would *choose* heterosexual coupling and marriage; heterosexuality is presumed the "sexual preference" of "most women," either implicitly or explicitly. In none of these books, which concern themselves with mothering, sex roles, relationships, and societal prescriptions for women, is compulsory heterosexuality ever examined as an institution powerfully affecting all these, or the idea of "preference" or "innate orientation" even indirectly questioned.

In *For Her Own Good: 150 Years of the Experts' Advice to Women* by Barbara Ehrenreich and Deirdre English, the authors' superb pamphlets *Witches, Midwives and Nurses: A History of Women Healers* and *Complaints and Disorders: The Sexual Politics of Sickness* are developed into a provocative and complex study. Their thesis in this book is that the advice given to American women by male health professionals, particularly in the areas of marital sex, maternity, and child care, has echoed the dictates of the economic marketplace and the role capitalism has needed women to play in production and/or reproduction. Women have become the consumer victims of various cures, therapies, and normative judgments in different periods (including the prescription to middle-class women to embody and preserve the sacredness of the home—the "scientific" romanticization of the home itself). None of the "experts' " advice has been either particularly scientific or women-oriented; it has reflected male needs, male fantasies about women, and male interest in controlling women—particularly in the realms of sexuality and motherhood—fused with the requirements of industrial capitalism. So much of this book is so devastatingly informative and is written with such lucid feminist wit that I kept waiting as I read for the basic proscription against lesbianism to be examined. It never was.

This can hardly be for lack of information. Jonathan Katz's *Gay American History*[5] tells us that as early as 1656 the New Haven Colony prescribed the death penalty for lesbians. Katz provides many suggestive and informative documents on the "treatment" (or torture) of lesbians by the medical profession in the nineteenth and twentieth centuries. Recent work by the historian Nancy Sahli documents the crackdown on intense female friendships among college women at the turn of the present century.[6] The ironic title *For Her Own Good* might have referred first and foremost to the economic imperative to heterosexuality and marriage and to the sanctions imposed against single women and widows—both of whom have been and still are viewed as deviant. Yet, in this often enlightening Marxist-feminist overview of male prescriptions for female sanity and health, the economics of prescriptive heterosexuality go unexamined.[7]

Of the three psychoanalytically based books, one, Jean Baker Miller's *Toward a New Psychology of Women*, is written as if lesbians simply do not exist, even as marginal beings. Given Miller's title, I find this astonishing. However, the favorable reviews the book has received in feminist journals, including *Signs* and *Spokeswoman*, suggest that Miller's heterocentric assumptions are widely shared. In *The Mermaid and the Minotaur: Sexual Arrangements and the Human Malaise*, Dorothy Dinnerstein makes an impassioned argument for the sharing of parenting between women and men and for an end to what she perceives as the male/female symbiosis of "gender arrangements," which she feels are leading the species further and further into violence and self-extinction. Apart from other problems that I have with this book (including her silence on the institutional and random terrorism men have practiced on women—and children—throughout history,[8] and her obsession with psychology to the neglect of economic and other material realities that help to create psychological reality), I find Dinnerstein's view of the relations between women and men as "a collaboration to keep history mad" utterly ahistorical. She means by this a collaboration to perpetuate social relations which are hostile, exploitative, and destructive to life itself. She sees women and men as equal partners in the making of "sexual arrangements," seemingly unaware of the repeated struggles of women to resist oppression (their own and that of others) and to change their condition. She ignores, specifically, the history of women who—as witches, *femmes seules*, marriage resisters, spinsters, autonomous widows, and/or lesbians—have managed on varying levels *not* to collaborate. It is this history, precisely, from which feminists have so much to learn and on which there is overall such blanketing silence. Dinnerstein acknowledges at the end of her book that "female separatism," though "on a large scale and in the long run wildly impractical," has something to teach us: "Separate, women could in principle set out to learn from scratch—undeflected by the opportunities to evade this task that men's presence has so far offered—what intact self-creative humanness is."[9] Phrases like "intact self-creative humanness" obscure the question of what the many forms of female separatism have actually been addressing. The fact is that women in every culture and throughout history *have* undertaken the task of independent, nonheterosexual, woman-connected existence, to the extent made possible by their context, often in the belief that they were the "only ones" ever to have done so. They have undertaken it even though few women have been in an economic position to resist marriage altogether, and even though attacks against unmarried women have ranged from aspersion and mockery to deliberate gynocide, including the burning and torturing of millions of widows and spinsters during the witch persecutions of the fifteenth, sixteenth, and seventeenth centuries in Europe.

Nancy Chodorow does come close to the edge of an acknowledgment of lesbian existence. Like Dinnerstein, Chodorow believes that the fact that women, and women only, are responsible for child care in the sexual division of labor has led to an entire social organization of gender inequality, and that men as well as women must become primary carers for children if that inequality is to change. In the process of examining, from a psychoanalytic perspective, how mothering by women affects the psychological development of girl and boy children, she offers documentation that men are "emotionally secondary" in women's lives, that "women have a richer, ongoing inner world to fall back on . . . men do not become as emotionally important to women as women do to men."[10] This would carry into the late twentieth century Smith-Rosenberg's findings about eighteenth- and nineteenth-century women's emotional focus on women. "Emotionally important" can, of course, refer to anger as well as to love, or to that intense mixture of the two often found in women's relationships with women—one aspect of what I have come to call the "double life of women" (see below). Chodorow concludes that because women have women as mothers, "the mother remains a primary internal object [*sic*] to the girl, so that heterosexual relationships are on the model of a nonexclusive, second relationship for her, whereas for the boy they re-create an exclusive, primary relationship." According to Chodorow, women "have learned to deny the limitations of masculine lovers for both psychological and practical reasons."[11]

But the practical reasons (like witch burnings, male control of law, theology, and science, or economic nonviability within the sexual division of labor) are glossed over. Chodorow's account barely glances at the constraints and sanctions which historically have enforced or ensured the coupling of women with men and obstructed or penalized women's coupling or allying in independent groups with other women. She dismisses lesbian existence with the comment that "lesbian relationships do tend to re-create mother-daughter emotions and connections, but most women are heterosexual" (implied: more mature, having developed beyond the mother-daughter connection?). She then adds: "This heterosexual preference and taboos on homosexuality, in addition to objective economic dependence on men, make the option of primary sexual bonds with other women unlikely—though more prevalent in recent years."[12] The significance of that qualification seems irresistible, but Chodorow does not explore it further. Is she saying that lesbian existence has become more *visible* in recent years (in certain groups), that economic and other pressures have changed (under capitalism, socialism, or both), and that consequently more women are rejecting the heterosexual "choice"? She argues that women want children because their heterosexual relationships lack richness and intensity, that in having a child a woman seeks to re-create her own intense relationship with her mother. It seems to me that on the basis of her own findings, Chodorow leads us implicitly to conclude that heterosexuality is *not* a "preference" for women, that, for one thing, it fragments the erotic from the emotional in a way that women find impoverishing and painful. Yet her book participates in mandating it. Neglecting the covert socializations and the overt forces which have channeled women into marriage and heterosexual romance, pressures ranging from the selling of daughters to the silences of literature to the images of the television screen, she, like Dinnerstein, is stuck with trying to reform a man-made institution—compulsory heterosexuality—as if, despite profound emotional impulses and complementarities drawing women toward women, there is a mystical/biological heterosexual inclination, a "preference" or "choice" which draws women toward men.

Moreover, it is understood that this "preference" does not need to be explained unless through the tortuous theory of the female Oedipus complex or the necessity for species reproduction. It is lesbian sexuality which (usually, and incorrectly, "included" under male homosexuality) is seen as requiring explanation. This assumption of female heterosexuality seems to me in itself remarkable: it is an enormous assumption to have glided so silently into the foundations of our thought.

The extension of this assumption is the frequently heard assertion that in a world of genuine equality, where men are nonoppressive and nurturing, everyone would be bisexual. Such a notion blurs and sentimentalizes the actualities within which women have experienced sexuality; it is a liberal leap across the tasks and struggles of here and now, the continuing process of sexual definition which will generate its own possibilities and choices. (It also assumes that women who have chosen women have done so simply because men are oppressive and emotionally unavailable, which still fails to account for women who continue to pursue relationships with oppressive and/or emotionally unsatisfying men.) I am suggesting that heterosexuality, like motherhood, needs to be recognized and studied as a *political institution*—even, or especially, by those individuals who feel they are, in their personal experience, the precursors of a new social relation between the sexes.

II

If women are the earliest sources of emotional caring and physical nurture for both female and male children, it would seem logical, from a feminist perspective at least, to pose the following questions: whether the search for love and tenderness in both sexes does not originally lead toward women; *why in fact women would ever redirect that search;* why species survival, the means of impregnation, and emotional/erotic relationships should ever have become so rigidly identified with each other; and why such violent strictures should be found necessary to enforce women's total emotional, erotic loyalty and subservience to men. I doubt that enough feminist scholars and theorists have taken the pains to acknowledge the societal forces which wrench women's emotional and erotic energies away from themselves and other women and from woman-identified values. These forces, as I shall try to show, range from literal physical enslavement to the disguising and distorting of possible options.

I do not assume that mothering by women is a "sufficient cause" of lesbian existence. But the issue of mothering by women has been much in the air of late, usually accompanied by the view that increased parenting by men would minimize antagonism between the sexes and equalize the sexual imbalance of power of males over females. These discussions are carried on without reference to compulsory heterosexuality as a phenomenon, let alone as an ideology. I do not wish to psychologize here, but rather to identify sources of male power. I believe large numbers of men could, in fact, undertake child care on a large scale without radically altering the balance of male power in a male-identified society.

In her essay "The Origin of the Family," Kathleen Gough lists eight characteristics of male power in archaic and contemporary societies which I would like to use as a framework: "men's ability to deny women sexuality or to force it upon them; to command or exploit their labor to control their produce; to control or rob them of their children; to confine them physically and prevent their movement; to use them as objects in male transactions; to cramp their creativeness; or to withhold from them large areas of the society's knowledge and cultural attainments."[13] (Gough does not perceive these power characteristics as specifically enforcing heterosexuality, only as producing sexual inequality.) Below, Gough's words appear in italics; the elaboration of each of her categories, in brackets, is my own.

Characteristics of male power include *the power of men*

1. *to deny women* [their own] *sexuality*—[by means of clitoridectomy and infibulation; chastity belts; punishment, including death, for female adultery; punishment, including death, for lesbian sexuality; psychoanalytic denial of the clitoris; strictures against masturbation; denial of maternal and postmenopausal sensuality; unnecessary hysterectomy; pseudolesbian images in the media and literature; closing of archives and destruction of documents relating to lesbian existence]

2. *or to force it* [male sexuality] *upon them*—[by means of rape (including marital rape) and wife beating; father-daughter, brother-sister incest; the socialization of women to feel that male sexual "drive" amounts to a right;[14] idealization of heterosexual romance in art, literature, the media, advertising, etc.; child marriage; arranged marriage; prostitution; the harem; psychoanalytic doctrines of frigidity and vaginal orgasm; pornographic depictions of women responding pleasurably to sexual violence and humiliation (a subliminal message being that sadistic heterosexuality is more "normal" than sensuality between women)]

3. *to command or exploit their labor to control their produce*—[by means of the institutions of marriage and motherhood as unpaid production; the horizontal segregation of women in paid employment; the decoy of the upwardly mobile token woman; male control of abortion, contraception, sterilization, and childbirth; pimping; female infanticide, which robs mothers of daughters and contributes to generalized devaluation of women]

4. *to control or rob them of their children*—[by means of father right and "legal kidnaping";[15] enforced sterilization; systematized infanticide; seizure of children from lesbian mothers by the courts; the malpractice of male obstetrics; use of the mother as "token torturer"[16] in genital mutilation or in binding the daughter's feet (or mind) to fit her for marriage]

5. *to confine them physically and prevent their movement*—[by means of rape as terrorism, keeping women off the streets; purdah; foot binding; atrophying of women's athletic capabilities; high heels and "feminine" dress codes in fash-

ion; the veil; sexual harassment on the streets; horizontal segregation of women in employment; prescriptions for "full-time" mothering at home; enforced economic dependence of wives]

6. *to use them as objects in male transactions*—[use of women as "gifts"; bride price; pimping; arranged marriage; use of women as entertainers to facilitate male deals—e.g., wife-hostess, cocktail waitress required to dress for male sexual titillation, call girls, "bunnies," geisha, *kisaeng* prostitutes, secretaries]

7. *to cramp their creativeness*—[witch persecutions as campaigns against midwives and female healers, and as pogrom against independent, "unassimilated" women;[17] definition of male pursuits as more valuable than female within any culture, so that cultural values become the embodiment of male subjectivity; restriction of female self-fulfillment to marriage and motherhood; sexual exploitation of women by male artists and teachers; the social and economic disruption of women's creative aspirations;[18] erasure of female tradition][19]

8. *to withhold from them large areas of the society's knowledge and cultural attainments*—[by means of noneducation of females; the "Great Silence" regarding women and particularly lesbian existence in history and culture;[20] sex-role tracking which deflects women from science, technology, and other "masculine" pursuits; male social/professional bonding which excludes women; discrimination against women in the professions]

These are some of the methods by which male power is manifested and maintained. Looking at the schema, what surely impresses itself is the fact that we are confronting not a simple maintenance of inequality and property possession, but a pervasive cluster of forces, ranging from physical brutality to control of consciousness, which suggests that an enormous potential counterforce is having to be restrained.

Some of the forms by which male power manifests itself are more easily recognizable as enforcing heterosexuality on women than are others. Yet each one I have listed adds to the cluster of forces within which women have been convinced that marriage and sexual orientation toward men are inevitable—even if unsatisfying or oppressive—components of their lives. The chastity belt; child marriage; erasure of lesbian existence (except as exotic and perverse) in art, literature, film; idealization of heterosexual romance and marriage—these are some fairly obvious forms of compulsion, the first two exemplifying physical force, the second two control of consciousness. While clitoridectomy has been assailed by feminists as a form of woman torture,[21] Kathleen Barry first pointed out that it is not simply a way of turning the young girl into a "marriageable" woman through brutal surgery. It intends that women in the intimate proximity of polygynous marriage will not form sexual relationships with each other, that—from a male, genital-fetishist perspective—female erotic connections, even in a sex-segregated situation, will be literally excised.[22]

The function of pornography as an influence on consciousness is a major public issue of our time, when a multibillion-dollar industry has the power to disseminate increasingly sadistic, women-degrading visual images. But even so-called soft-core pornography and advertising depict women as objects of sexual appetite devoid of emotional context, without individual meaning or personality—essentially as a sexual commodity to be consumed by males. (So-called lesbian pornography, created for the male voyeuristic eye, is equally devoid of emotional context or individual person-ality.) The most pernicious message relayed by pornography is that women are natural sexual prey to men and love it, that sexuality and violence are congruent, and that for women sex is essentially masochistic, humiliation pleasurable, physical abuse erotic. But along with this message comes another, not always recognized: that enforced submission and the use of cruelty, if played out in heterosexual pairing, is sexually "normal," while sensuality between women, including erotic mutuality and respect, is "queer," "sick," and either pornographic in itself or not very exciting compared with the sexuality of whips and bondage.[23] Pornography does not simply create a climate in which sex and violence are interchangeable; *it widens the range of behavior considered acceptable from men in heterosexual intercourse*—behavior which reiteratively strips women of their autonomy, dignity, and sexual potential, including the potential of loving and being loved by women in mutuality and integrity.

In her brilliant study *Sexual Harassment of Working Women: A Case of Sex Discrimination,* Catharine A. MacKinnon delineates the intersection of compulsory heterosexuality and economics. Under capitalism, women are horizontally segre-gated by gender and occupy a structurally inferior position in the workplace. This is hardly news, but MacKinnon raises the question why, even if capitalism "requires some collection of individuals to occupy low-status, low-paying positions . . . such persons must be biologically female," and goes on to point out that "the fact that male employers often do not hire qualified women, *even when they could pay them less than men* suggests that more than the profit motive is implicated" [emphasis added].[24] She cites a wealth of material documenting the fact that women are not only segregated in low-paying service jobs (as secretaries, domestics, nurses, typists, telephone operators, child-care workers, waitresses), but that "sexualization of the woman" is part of the job. Central and intrinsic to the economic realities of women's lives is the requirement that women will "market sexual attractiveness to men, who tend to hold the economic power and position to enforce their predilections." And MacKinnon documents that "sexual harassment perpetuates the interlocked struc-ture by which women have been kept sexually in thrall to men at the bottom of the labor market. Two forces of American society converge: men's control over women's sexuality and capital's control over employees' work lives."[25] Thus, women in the workplace are at the mercy of sex as power in a vicious circle. Economically disadvan-taged, women—whether waitresses or professors—endure sexual harassment to keep their jobs and learn to behave in a complaisantly and ingratiatingly heterosexual manner because they discover this is their true qualification for employment, what-ever the job description. And, MacKinnon notes, the woman who too decisively resists sexual overtures in the workplace is accused of being "dried up" and sexless, or lesbian. This raises a specific difference between the experiences of lesbians and homosexual men. A lesbian, closeted on her job because of heterosexist prejudice, is not simply forced into denying the truth of her outside relationships or private life. Her job depends on her pretending to be not merely heterosexual, but a heterosexual *woman* in terms of dressing and playing the feminine, deferential role required of "real" women.

MacKinnon raises radical questions as to the qualitative differences between sexual harassment, rape, and ordinary heterosexual intercourse. ("As one accused rapist put it, he hadn't used 'any more force than is usual for males during the preliminaries.' ") She criticizes Susan Brownmiller[26] for separating rape from the mainstream of daily life and for her unexamined premise that "rape is violence, intercourse is sexuality," removing rape from the sexual sphere altogether. Most crucially she argues that "taking rape from the realm of 'the sexual,' placing it in the realm of 'the violent,' allows one to be against it without raising any questions about the extent to which the institution of heterosexuality has defined force as a normal part of 'the preliminaries.' "[27] "Never is it asked whether, under conditions of male supremacy, the notion of 'consent' has any meaning."[28]

The fact is that the workplace, among other social institutions, is a place where women have learned to accept male violation of their psychic and physical boundaries as the price of survival; where women have been educated—no less than by romantic literature or by pornography—to perceive themselves as sexual prey. A woman seeking to escape such casual violations along with economic disadvantage may well turn to marriage as a form of hoped-for protection, while bringing into marriage neither social nor economic power, thus entering that institution also from a disadvantaged position. MacKinnon finally asks:

> What if inequality is built into the social conceptions of male and female sexuality, of masculinity and femininity, of sexiness and heterosexual attractiveness? Incidents of sexual harassment suggest that male sexual desire itself may be aroused by female vulnerability. . . . Men feel they can take advantage, so they want to, so they do. Examination of sexual harassment, precisely because the episodes appear commonplace, forces one to confront the fact that sexual intercourse normally occurs between economic (as well as physical) unequals . . . the apparent legal requirement that violations of women's sexuality appear out of the ordinary before they will be punished helps prevent women from defining the ordinary conditions of their own consent.[29]

Given the nature and extent of heterosexual pressures—the daily "eroticization of women's subordination," as MacKinnon phrases it[30]—I question the more or less psychoanalytic perspective (suggested by such writers as Karen Horney, H. R. Hayes, Wolfgang Lederer, and, most recently, Dorothy Dinnerstein) that the male need to control women sexually results from some primal male "fear of women" and of women's sexual insatiability. It seems more probable that men really fear not that they will have women's sexual appetites forced on them or that women want to smother and devour them, but that women could be indifferent to them altogether, that men could be allowed sexual and emotional—therefore economic—access to women *only* on women's terms, otherwise being left on the periphery of the matrix.

The means of assuring male sexual access to women have recently received searching investigation by Kathleen Barry.[31] She documents extensive and appalling evidence for the existence, on a very large scale, of international female slavery, the institution once known as "white slavery" but which in fact has involved, and at this very moment involves, women of every race and class. In the theoretical analysis derived from her research, Barry makes the connection between all enforced conditions under which women live subject to men: prostitution, marital rape, father-daughter and brother-sister incest, wife beating, pornography, bride price, the selling of daughters, purdah, and genital mutilation. She sees the rape paradigm—where the victim of sexual assault is held responsible for her own victimization—as leading to the rationalization and acceptance of other forms of enslavement where the woman is presumed to have "chosen" her fate, to embrace it passively, or to have courted it perversely through rash or unchaste behavior. On the contrary, Barry maintains, "female sexual slavery is present in ALL situations where women or girls cannot change the conditions of their existence; where regardless of how they got into those conditions, e.g., social pressure, economic hardship, misplaced trust or the longing for affection, they cannot get out; and where they are subject to sexual violence and exploitation."[32] She provides a spectrum of concrete examples, not only as to the existence of a widespread international traffic in women, but also as to how this operates—whether in the form of a "Minnesota pipeline" funneling blonde, blue-eyed midwestern runaways to Times Square, or the purchasing of young women out of rural poverty in Latin America or Southeast Asia, or the providing of *maisons d'abattage* for migrant workers in the eighteenth arrondissement of Paris. Instead of "blaming the victim" or trying to diagnose her presumed pathology, Barry turns her floodlight on the pathology of sex colonization itself, the ideology of "cultural sadism" represented by the pornography industry and by the overall identification of women primarily as "sexual beings whose responsibility is the sexual service of men."[33]

Barry delineates what she names a "sexual domination perspective" through whose lens sexual abuse and terrorism of women by men has been rendered almost invisible by treating it as natural and inevitable. From its point of view, women are expendable as long as the sexual and emotional needs of the male can be satisfied. To replace this perspective of domination with a universal standard of basic freedom for women from gender-specific violence, from constraints on movement, and from male right of sexual and emotional access is the political purpose of her book. Like Mary Daly in *Gyn/Ecology,* Barry rejects structuralist and other cultural-relativist rationalizations for sexual torture and anti-woman violence. In her opening chapter, she asks of her readers that they refuse all handy escapes into ignorance and denial. "The only way we can come out of hiding, break through our paralyzing defenses, is to know it all—the full extent of sexual violence and domination of women. . . . In *knowing,* in facing directly, we can learn to chart our course out of this oppression, by envisioning and creating a world which will preclude sexual slavery."[34]

"Until we name the practice, give conceptual definition and form to it, illustrate its life over time and in space, those who are its most obvious victims will also not be able to name it or define their experience."

But women are all, in different ways and to different degrees, its victims; and part of the problem with naming and conceptualizing female sexual slavery is, as Barry clearly sees, compulsory heterosexuality.[35] Compulsory heterosexuality simplifies the task of the procurer and pimp in world-wide prostitution rings and "eros centers," while, in the privacy of the home, it leads the daughter to "accept" incest/rape by her father, the mother to deny that it is happening, the battered wife to stay on with an abusive husband. "Befriending or love" is a major tactic of the procurer, whose job it is to turn the runaway or the confused young girl over to the pimp for seasoning. The ideology of heterosexual romance, beamed at her from childhood out of fairy tales, television, films, advertising, popular songs, wedding pageantry, is a tool ready to the procurer's hand and one which he does not hesitate to use, as Barry documents. Early female indoctrination in "love" as an emotion may be largely a Western concept; but a more universal ideology concerns the primacy and uncontrollability of the male sexual drive. This is one of many insights offered by Barry's work:

> As sexual power is learned by adolescent boys through the social experience of their sex drive, so do girls learn that the locus of sexual power is male. Given the importance placed on the male sex drive in the socialization of girls as well as boys, early adolescence is probably the first significant phase of male identification in a girl's life and development. . . . As a young girl becomes aware of her own increasing sexual feelings . . . she turns away from her heretofore primary relationships with girlfriends. As they become secondary to her, recede in importance in her life, her own identity also assumes a secondary role and she grows into male identification.[36]

We still need to ask why some women never, even temporarily, turn away from "heretofore primary relationships" with other females. And why does male identification—the casting of one's social, political, and intellectual allegiances with men—exist among lifelong sexual lesbians? Barry's hypothesis throws us among new questions, but it clarifies the diversity of forms in which compulsory heterosexuality presents itself. In the mystique of the overpowering, all-conquering male sex drive, the penis-with-a-life-of-its own, is rooted the law of male sex right to women, which justifies prostitution as a universal cultural assumption on the one hand, while defending sexual slavery within the family on the basis of "family privacy and cultural uniqueness" on the other.[37] The adolescent male sex drive, which, as both young women and men are taught, once triggered cannot take responsibility for itself or take no for an answer, becomes, according to Barry, the norm and rationale for adult male sexual behavior: a condition of *arrested sexual development.* Women learn to accept as natural the inevitability of this "drive" because they receive it as dogma. Hence, marital rape; hence, the Japanese wife resignedly packing her husband's suitcase for a weekend in the *kisaeng* brothels of Taiwan; hence, the psychological as well as economic imbalance of power between husband and wife, male employer and female worker, father and daughter, male professor and female student.

The effect of male identification means

> internalizing the values of the colonizer and actively participating in carrying out the colonization of one's self and one's sex. . . . Male identification is the act whereby women place men above women, including themselves, in credibility, status, and importance in most situations, regardless of the comparative quality the women may bring to the situation. . . . Interaction with women is seen as a lesser form of relating on every level.[38]

What deserves further exploration is the doublethink many women engage in and from which no woman is permanently and utterly free: However woman-to-woman relationships, female support networks, a female and feminist value system are relied on and cherished, indoctrination in male credibility and status can still create synapses in thought, denials of feeling, wishful thinking, a profound sexual and intellectual confusion.[39] I quote here from a letter I received the day I was writing this passage: "I have had very bad relationships with men—I am now in the midst of a very painful separation. I am trying to find my strength through women—without my friends, I could not survive." How many times a day do women speak words like these or think them or write them, and how often does the synapse reassert itself?

Barry summarizes her findings:

> Considering the arrested sexual development that is understood to be normal in the male population, and considering the numbers of men who are pimps, procurers, members of slavery gangs, corrupt officials participating in this traffic, owners, operators, employees of brothels and lodging and entertainment facilities, pornography purveyors, associated with prostitution, wife beaters, child molesters, incest perpetrators, johns (tricks) and rapists, one cannot but be momentarily stunned by the enormous male population engaging in female sexual slavery. The huge number of men engaged in these practices should be cause for declaration of an international emergency, a crisis in sexual violence. But what should be cause for alarm is instead accepted as normal sexual intercourse.[40]

Susan Cavin, in a rich and provocative, if highly speculative, dissertation, suggests that patriarchy becomes possible when the original female band, which includes children but ejects adolescent males, becomes invaded and outnumbered by males; that not patriarchal marriage, but the rape of the mother by the son, becomes the first act of male domination. The entering wedge, or leverage, which allows this to happen is not just a simple change in sex ratios; it is also the mother-child bond, manipulated by adolescent males in order to remain within the matrix past the age of exclusion. Maternal affection is used to establish male right of sexual access, which, however, must ever after be held by force (or through control of consciousness) since the original deep adult bonding is that of woman for woman.[41] I find this hypothesis extremely suggestive, since one form of false consciousness which serves compulsory heterosexuality is the maintenance of a mother-son relationship between women and men, including the demand that women provide maternal solace, nonjudgmental nurturing, and compassion for their harassers, rapists, and batterers (as well as for men who passively vampirize them).

But whatever its origins, when we look hard and clearly at the extent and elaboration of measures designed to keep women within a male sexual purlieu, it becomes an inescapable question whether the issue feminists have to address is not simple "gender inequality" nor the domination of culture by males nor mere "taboos against homosexuality," but the enforcement of heterosexuality for women as a means of assuring male right of physical, economic, and emotional access.[42] One of many means of enforcement is, of course, the rendering invisible of the lesbian possibility, an engulfed continent which rises fragmentedly into view from time to time only to become submerged again. Feminist research and theory that contribute to lesbian invisibility or marginality are actually working against the liberation and empowerment of women as a group.[43]

The assumption that "most women are innately heterosexual" stands as a theoretical and political stumbling block for feminism. It remains a tenable assumption partly because lesbian existence has been written out of history or catalogued under disease, partly because it has been treated as exceptional rather than intrinsic, partly because to acknowledge that for women heterosexuality may not be a "preference" at all but something that has had to be imposed, managed, organized, propagandized, and maintained by force is an immense step to take if you consider yourself freely and "innately" heterosexual. Yet the failure to examine heterosexuality as an institution is like failing to admit that the economic system called capitalism or the caste system of racism is maintained by a variety of forces, including both physical violence and false consciousness. To take the step of questioning heterosexuality as a "preference" or "choice" for women—and to do the intellectual and emotional work that follows—will call for a special quality of courage in heterosexually identified feminists, but I think the rewards will be great: a freeing-up of thinking, the exploring of new paths, the shattering of another great silence, new clarity in personal relationships.

III

I have chosen to use the terms *lesbian existence* and *lesbian continuum* because the word *lesbianism* has a clinical and limiting ring. *Lesbian existence* suggests both the fact of the historical presence of lesbians and our continuing creation of the meaning of that existence. I mean the term *lesbian continuum* to include a range—through each woman's life and throughout history—of woman-identified experience, not simply the fact that a woman has had or consciously desired genital sexual experience with another woman. If we expand it to embrace many more forms of primary intensity between and among women, including the sharing of a rich inner life, the bonding against male tyranny, the giving and receiving of practical and political support, if we can also hear it in such associations as *marriage resistance* and the "haggard" behavior identified by Mary Daly (obsolete meanings: "intractable," "willful," "wanton," and "unchaste," "a woman reluctant to yield to wooing"),[44] we begin to grasp breadths of female history and psychology which have lain out of reach as a consequence of limited, mostly clinical, definitions of *lesbianism*.

Lesbian existence comprises both the breaking of a taboo and the rejection of a compulsory way of life. It is also a direct or indirect attack on male right of access to women. But it is more than these, although we may first begin to perceive it as a form of naysaying to patriarchy, an act of resistance. It has, of course, included isolation, self-hatred, breakdown, alcoholism, suicide, and intrawoman violence; we romanticize at our peril what it means to love and act against the grain, and under heavy penalties; and lesbian existence has been lived (unlike, say, Jewish or Catholic existence) without access to any knowledge of a tradition, a continuity, a social underpinning. The destruction of records and memorabilia and letters documenting the realities of lesbian existence must be taken very seriously as a means of keeping heterosexuality compulsory for women, since what has been kept from our knowledge is joy, sensuality, courage, and community, as well as guilt, self-betrayal, and pain.[45]

Lesbians have historically been deprived of a political existence through "inclusion" as female versions of male homosexuality. To equate lesbian existence with male homosexuality because each is stigmatized is to erase female reality once again. Part of the history of lesbian existence is, obviously, to be found where lesbians, lacking a coherent female community, have shared a kind of social life and common cause with homosexual men. But there are differences: women's lack of economic and cultural privilege relative to men; qualitative differences in female and male relationships—for example, the patterns of anonymous sex among male homosexuals, and the pronounced ageism in male homosexual standards of sexual attractiveness. I perceive the lesbian experience as being, like motherhood, a profoundly *female* experience, with particular oppressions, meanings, and potentialities we cannot comprehend as long as we simply bracket it with other sexually stigmatized existences. Just as the term *parenting* serves to conceal the particular and significant reality of being a parent who is actually a mother, the term *gay* may serve the purpose of blurring the very outlines we need to discern, which are of crucial value for feminism and for the freedom of women as a group.[46]

As the term *lesbian* has been held to limiting, clinical associations in its patriarchal definition, female friendship and comradeship have been set apart from the erotic, thus limiting the erotic itself. But as we deepen and broaden the range of what we define as lesbian existence, as we delineate a lesbian continuum, we begin to discover the erotic in female terms: as that which is unconfined to any single part of the body or solely to the body itself; as an energy not only diffuse but, as Audre Lorde has described it, omnipresent in "the sharing of joy, whether physical, emotional, psychic," and in the sharing of work; as the empowering joy which "makes us less willing to accept powerlessness, or those other supplied states of being which are not native to me, such as resignation, despair, self-effacement, depression, self-denial."[47] In another context, writing of women and work, I quoted the autobiographical passage in which the poet H. D. described how her friend Bryher supported her in persisting with the visionary experience which was to shape her mature work:

> I knew that this experience, this writing-on-the-wall before me, could not be shared with anyone except the girl who stood so bravely there beside me. This girl said without hesitation, "Go on." It was she really who had the detachment and integrity of the Pythoness of Delphi. But it was I, battered and dissociated . . . who was seeing the pictures, and who was reading the writing or granted the inner vision. Or perhaps, in some sense, we were "seeing" it together, for without her, admittedly, I could not have gone on.[48]

If we consider the possibility that all women—from the infant suckling at her mother's breast, to the grown woman experiencing orgasmic sensations while suckling her own child, perhaps recalling her mother's milk smell in her own, to two women, like Virginia Woolf's Chloe and Olivia, who share a laboratory,[49] to the woman dying at ninety, touched and handled by women—exist on a lesbian continuum, we can see ourselves as moving in and out of this continuum, whether we identify ourselves as lesbian or not.

We can then connect aspects of woman identification as diverse as the impudent, intimate girl friendships of eight or nine year olds and the banding together of those women of the twelfth and fifteenth centuries known as Beguines who "shared houses, rented to one another, bequeathed houses to their room-mates . . . in cheap subdivided houses in the artisans' area of town," who "practiced Christian virtue on their own, dressing and living simply and not associating with men," who earned their livings as spinsters, bakers, nurses, or ran schools for young girls, and who managed—until the Church forced them to disperse—to live independent both of marriage and of conventual restrictions.[50] It allows us to connect these women with the more celebrated "Lesbians" of the women's school around Sappho of the seventh century B.C., with the secret sororities and economic networks reported among African women, and with the Chinese marriage-resistance sisterhoods—communities of women who refused marriage or who, if married, often refused to consummate their marriages and soon left their husbands, the only women in China who were not footbound and who, Agnes Smedley tells us, welcomed the births of daughters and organized successful women's strikes in the silk mills.[51] It allows us to connect and compare disparate individual instances of marriage resistance: for example, the strategies available to Emily Dickinson, a nineteenth-century white woman genius, with the strategies available to Zora Neale Hurston, a twentieth-century Black woman genius. Dickinson never married, had tenuous intellectual friendships with men, lived self-convented in her genteel father's house in Amherst, and wrote a lifetime of passionate letters to her sister-in-law Sue Gilbert and a smaller group of such letters to her friend Kate Scott Anthon. Hurston married twice but soon left each husband, scrambled her way from Florida to Harlem to Columbia University to Haiti and finally back to Florida, moved in and out of white patronage and poverty, professional success, and failure; her survival relationships were all with women, beginning with her mother. Both of these women in their vastly different circumstances were marriage resisters, committed to their own work and selfhood, and were later characterized as "apolitical." Both were drawn to men of intellectual quality; for both of them women provided the ongoing fascination and sustenance of life.

If we think of heterosexuality as *the* natural emotional and sensual inclination for women, lives such as these are seen as deviant, as pathological, or as emotionally and sensually deprived. Or, in more recent and permissive jargon, they are banalized as "life styles." And the work of such women, whether merely the daily work of individual or collective survival and resistance or the work of the writer, the activist, the reformer, the anthropologist, or the artist—the work of self-creation—is undervalued, or seen as the bitter fruit of "penis envy" or the sublimation of repressed eroticism or the meaningless rant of a "man-hater." But when we turn the lens of vision and consider the degree to which and the methods whereby heterosexual "preference" has actually been imposed on women, not only can we understand differently the meaning of individual lives and work, but we can begin to recognize a central fact of women's history: that women have always resisted male tyranny. A feminism of action, often though not always without a theory, has constantly re-emerged in every culture and in every period. We can then begin to study women's struggle against powerlessness, women's radical rebellion, not just in male-defined "concrete revolutionary situations"[52] but in all the situations male ideologies have not perceived as revolutionary—for example, the refusal of some women to produce children, aided at great risk by other women;[53] the refusal to produce a higher standard of living and leisure for men (Leghorn and Parker show how both are part of women's unacknowledged, unpaid, and ununionized economic contribution). We can no longer have patience with Dinnerstein's view that women have simply collaborated with men in the "sexual arrangements" of history. We begin to observe behavior, both in history and in individual biography, that has hitherto been invisible or misnamed, behavior which often constitutes, given the limits of the counterforce exerted in a given time and place, radical rebellion. And we can connect these rebellions and the necessity for them with the physical passion of woman for woman which is central to lesbian existence: the erotic sensuality which has been, precisely, the most violently erased fact of female experience.

Heterosexuality has been both forcibly and subliminally imposed on women. Yet everywhere women have resisted it, often at the cost of physical torture, imprisonment, psychosurgery, social ostracism, and extreme poverty. "Compulsory heterosexuality" was named as one of the "crimes against women" by the Brussels International Tribunal on Crimes against Women in 1976. Two pieces of testimony from two very different cultures reflect the degree to which persecution of lesbians is a global practice here and now. A report from Norway relates:

> A lesbian in Oslo was in a heterosexual marriage that didn't work, so she started taking tranquillizers and ended up at the health sanatorium for treatment and rehabilitation. . . . The moment she said in family group therapy that she believed she was a lesbian, the doctor told her she was not. He knew from "looking into her eyes," he said. She had the eyes of a woman who wanted sexual intercourse with her husband. So she was subjected to so-called "couch therapy." She was put into a comfortably heated room, naked, on a bed, and for an hour her husband was to . . . try to excite her sexually. . . . The idea was that the touching was always to end with sexual intercourse. She felt stronger and stronger aversion. She threw up and sometimes ran out of the room to avoid this "treatment." The more strongly she asserted that she was a lesbian, the more violent the forced heterosexual intercourse became. This treatment went on for about six months. She escaped from the hospital, but she was brought back. Again she escaped. She has not been there since. In the end she realized that she had been subjected to forcible rape for six months.

And from Mozambique:

> I am condemned to a life of exile because I will not deny that I am a lesbian, that my primary commitments are, and will always be to other women. In the new Mozambique, lesbianism is considered a left-over from colonialism and decadent Western civilization. Lesbians are sent to rehabilitation camps to learn through self-criticism the correct line about themselves. . . . If I am forced to denounce my own love for women, if I therefore denounce myself, I could go back to Mozambique and join forces in the exciting and hard struggle of rebuilding a nation, including the struggle for the emancipation of Mozambiquan women. As it is, I either risk the rehabilitation camps, or remain in exile.[54]

Nor can it be assumed that women like those in Carroll Smith-Rosenberg's study, who married, stayed married, yet dwelt in a profoundly female emotional and passional world, "preferred" or "chose" heterosexuality. Women have married because it was necessary, in order to survive economically, in order to have children who would not suffer economic deprivation or social ostracism, in order to remain respectable, in order to do what was expected of women, because coming out of "abnormal" childhoods they wanted to feel "normal" and because heterosexual romance has been represented as the great female adventure, duty, and fulfillment. We may faithfully or ambivalently have obeyed the institution, but our feelings— and our sensuality—have not been tamed or contained within it. There is no statistical documentation of the numbers of lesbians who have remained in heterosexual marriages for most of their lives. But in a letter to the early lesbian publication *The Ladder,* the playwright Lorraine Hansberry had this to say:

> I suspect that the problem of the married woman who would prefer emotional-physical relationships with other women is proportionally much higher than a similar statistic for men. (A statistic surely no one will ever really have.) This because the estate of woman being what it is, how could we ever begin to guess the numbers of women who are not prepared to risk a life alien to what they have been taught all their lives to believe was their "natural" destiny—AND—their only expectation for ECONOMIC security. It seems to be that

this is why the question has an immensity that it does not have for male homosexuals. . . . A woman of strength and honesty may, if she chooses, sever her marriage and marry a new male mate and society will be upset that the divorce rate is rising so—but there are few places in the United States, in any event, where she will be anything remotely akin to an "outcast." Obviously this is not true for a woman who would end her marriage to take up life with another woman.[55]

This *double life*—this apparent acquiescence to an institution founded on male interest and prerogative—has been characteristic of female experience: in mother-hood and in many kinds of heterosexual behavior, including the rituals of courtship; the pretense of asexuality by the nineteenth-century wife; the simulation of orgasm by the prostitute, the courtesan, the twentieth-century "sexually liberated" woman.

Meridel LeSueur's documentary novel of the depression, *The Girl,* is arresting as a study of female double life. The protagonist, a waitress in a St. Paul working-class speakeasy, feels herself passionately attracted to the young man Butch, but her survival relationships are with Clara, an older waitress and prostitute, with Belle, whose husband owns the bar, and with Amelia, a union activist. For Clara and Belle and the unnamed protagonist, sex with men is in one sense an escape from the bedrock misery of daily life, a flare of intensity in the gray, relentless, often brutal web of day-to-day existence:

It was like he was a magnet pulling me. It was exciting and powerful and frightening. He was after me too and when he found me I would run, or be petrified, just standing in front of him like a zany. And he told me not to be wandering with Clara to the Marigold where we danced with strangers. He said he would knock the shit out of me. Which made me shake and tremble, but it was better than being a husk full of suffering and not knowing why.[56]

Throughout the novel the theme of double life emerges; Belle reminisces about her marriage to the bootlegger Hoinck:

You know, when I had that black eye and said I hit it on the cupboard, well he did it the bastard, and then he says don't tell anybody. . . . He's nuts, that's what he is, nuts, and I don't see why I live with him, why I put up with him a minute on this earth. But listen kid, she said, I'm telling you something. She looked at me and her face was wonderful. She said, Jesus Christ, Goddam him I love him that's why I'm hooked like this all my life, Goddam him I love him.[57]

After the protagonist has her first sex with Butch, her women friends care for her bleeding, give her whiskey, and compare notes.

My luck, the first time and I got into trouble. He gave me a little money and I come to St. Paul where for ten bucks they'd stick a huge vet's needle into you and you start it and then you were on your own. . . . I never had no child. I've just had Hoinck to mother, and a hell of a child he is.[58]

Later they made me go back to Clara's room to lie down. . . . Clara lay down beside me and put her arms around me and wanted me to tell her about it but she wanted to tell about herself. She said she started it when she was twelve with a bunch of boys in an old shed. She said nobody had paid any attention to her before and she became very popular. . . . They like it so much, she said, why shouldn't you give it to them and get presents and attention? I never cared anything for it and neither did my mama. But it's the only thing you got that's valuable.[59]

Sex is thus equated with attention from the male, who is charismatic though brutal, infantile, or unreliable. Yet it is the women who make life endurable for each other, give physical affection without causing pain, share, advise, and stick by each other. *(I am trying to find my strength through women—without my friends, I could not survive.)* LeSueur's *The Girl* parallels Toni Morrison's remarkable *Sula,* another revelation of female double life:

> Nel was the one person who had wanted nothing from her, who had accepted all aspects of her. . . . Nel was one of the reasons Sula had drifted back to Medallion. . . . The men . . . had merged into one large personality: the same language of love, the same entertainments of love, the same cooling of love. Whenever she introduced her private thoughts into their rubbings and goings, they hooded their eyes. They taught her nothing but love tricks, shared nothing but worry, gave nothing but money. She had been looking all along for a friend, and it took her a while to discover that a lover was not a comrade and could never be—for a woman.

But Sula's last thought at the second of her death is "Wait'll I tell Nel." And after Sula's death, Nel looks back on her own life:

> "All that time, all that time, I thought I was missing Jude." And the loss pressed down on her chest and came up into her throat. "We was girls together," she said as though explaining something. "O Lord, Sula," she cried, "Girl, girl, girlgirlgirl!" It was a fine cry—loud and long—but it had no bottom and it had no top, just circles and circles of sorrow.[60]

The Girl and *Sula* are both novels which examine what I am calling the lesbian continuum, in contrast to the shallow or sensational "lesbian scenes" in recent commercial fiction.[61] Each shows us woman identification untarnished (till the end of LeSueur's novel) by romanticism; each depicts the competition of heterosexual compulsion for women's attention, the diffusion and frustration of female bonding that might, in a more conscious form, reintegrate love and power.

IV

Woman identification is a source of energy, a potential springhead of female power, curtailed and contained under the institution of heterosexuality. The denial of reality and visibility to women's passion for women, women's choice of women as allies, life companions, and community, the forcing of such relationships into dissimulation and their disintegration under intense pressure have meant an incalculable loss to the power of all women *to change the social relations of the sexes, to liberate ourselves and each other.* The lie of compulsory female heterosexuality today afflicts not just feminist scholarship, but every profession, every reference work, every curriculum, every organizing attempt, every relationship or conversation over which it hovers. It creates, specifically, a profound falseness, hypocrisy, and hysteria in the heterosexual dialogue, for every heterosexual relationship is lived in the queasy strobe light of that lie. However we choose to identify ourselves, however we find ourselves labeled, it flickers across and distorts our lives.[62]

The lie keeps numberless women psychologically trapped, trying to fit mind, spirit, and sexuality into a prescribed script because they cannot look beyond the parameters of the acceptable. It pulls on the energy of such women even as it drains the energy of "closeted" lesbians—the energy exhausted in the double life. The lesbian trapped in the "closet," the woman imprisoned in prescriptive ideas of the "normal" share the pain of blocked options, broken connections, lost access to self-definition freely and powerfully assumed.

The lie is many-layered. In Western tradition, one layer—the romantic—asserts that women are inevitably, even if rashly and tragically, drawn to men; that even when that attraction is suicidal (e.g., *Tristan and Isolde,* Kate Chopin's *The Awakening*), it is still an organic imperative. In the tradition of the social sciences it asserts that primary love between the sexes is "normal"; that women *need* men as social and economic protectors, for adult sexuality, and for psychological completion; that the heterosexually constituted family is the basic social unit; that women who do not attach their primary intensity to men must be, in functional terms, condemned to an even more devastating outsiderhood than their outsiderhood as women. Small wonder that lesbians are reported to be a more hidden population than male homosexuals. The Black lesbian-feminist critic Lorraine Bethel, writing on Zora Neale Hurston, remarks that for a Black woman—already twice an outsider—to choose to assume still another "hated identity" is problematic indeed. Yet the lesbian continuum has been a life line for Black women both in Africa and the United States.

> Black women have a long tradition of bonding together . . . in a Black/women's community that has been a source of vital survival information, psychic and emotional support for us. We have a distinct Black woman-identified folk culture based on our experiences as Black women in this society; symbols, language and modes of expression that are specific to the realities of our lives. . . . Because Black women were rarely among those Blacks and females who gained access to literary and other acknowledged forms of artistic expression, this Black female bonding and Black woman-identification has often been hidden and un-recorded except in the individual lives of Black women through our own memories of our particular Black female tradition.[63]

Another layer of the lie is the frequently encountered implication that women turn to women out of hatred for men. Profound skepticism, caution, and righteous paranoia about men may indeed be part of any healthy woman's response to the misogyny of male-dominated culture, to the forms assumed by "normal" male sexuality, and to *the failure even of "sensitive" or "political" men to perceive or find these troubling.* Lesbian existence is also represented as mere refuge from male abuses, rather than as an electric and empowering charge between women. One of the most frequently quoted literary passages on lesbian relationship is that in which Colette's Renée, in *The Vagabond,* describes "the melancholy and touching image of two weak creatures who have perhaps found shelter in each other's arms, there to sleep and weep, safe from man who is often cruel, and there to taste *better than any pleasure, the bitter happiness of feeling themselves akin, frail and forgotten* [emphasis added]."[64] Colette is often considered a lesbian writer. Her popular reputation has, I think, much to do with the fact that she writes about lesbian existence as if for a male audience; her earliest "lesbian" novels, the Claudine series, were written under compulsion for her husband and published under both their names. At all events, except for her writings on her mother, Colette is a less reliable source on the lesbian continuum than, I would think, Charlotte Brontë, who understood that while women may, indeed must, be one another's allies, mentors, and comforters in the female struggle for survival, there is quite extraneous delight in each other's company and attraction to each other's minds and character, which attend a recognition of each other's strengths.

By the same token, we can say that there is a *nascent* feminist political content in the act of choosing a woman lover or life partner in the face of institutionalized heterosexuality.[65] But for lesbian existence to realize this political content in an ultimately liberating form, the erotic choice must deepen and expand into conscious woman identification—into lesbian feminism.

The work that lies ahead, of unearthing and describing what I call here "lesbian existence," is potentially liberating for all women. It is work that must assuredly move beyond the limits of white and middle-class Western Women's Studies to examine women's lives, work, and groupings within every racial, ethnic, and political structure. There are differences, moreover, between "lesbian existence" and the "lesbian continuum," differences we can discern even in the movement of our own lives. The lesbian continuum, I suggest, needs delineation in light of the "double life" of women, not only women self-described as heterosexual but also of self-described lesbians. We need a far more exhaustive account of the forms the double life has assumed. Historians need to ask at every point how heterosexuality as institution has been organized and maintained through the female wage scale, the enforcement of middle-class women's "leisure," the glamorization of so-called sexual liberation, the withholding of education from women, the imagery of "high art" and popular culture, the mystification of the "personal" sphere, and much else. We need an economics which comprehends the institution of heterosexuality, with its doubled workload for women and its sexual divisions of labor, as the most idealized of economic relations.

The question inevitably will arise: Are we then to condemn all heterosexual relationships, including those which are least oppressive? I believe this question, though often heartfelt, is the wrong question here. We have been stalled in a maze of false dichotomies which prevents our apprehending the institution as a whole: "good" versus "bad" marriages; "marriage for love" versus arranged marriage; "liberated" sex versus prostitution; heterosexual intercourse versus rape; *Liebeschmerz* versus humiliation and dependency. Within the institution exist, of course, qualitative differences of experience; but the absence of choice remains the great unacknowledged reality, and in the absence of choice, women will remain dependent upon the chance or luck of particular relationships and will have no collective power to determine the meaning and place of sexuality in their lives. As we address the institution itself, moreover, we begin to perceive a history of female resistance which has never fully understood itself because it has been so fragmented, miscalled, erased. It will require a courageous grasp of the politics and economics, as well as the cultural propaganda, of heterosexuality to carry us beyond individual cases or diversified group situations into the complex kind of overview needed to undo the power men everywhere wield over women, power which has become a model for every other form of exploitation and illegitimate control.

Notes

1. Alice Rossi, "Children and Work in the Lives of Women," paper delivered at the University of Arizona, Tucson, February 1976.

2. Doris Lessing, *The Golden Notebook,* 1962 (New York: Bantam, 1977), p. 480.

3. Nancy Chodorow, *The Reproduction of Mothering* (Berkeley: University of California Press, 1978); Dorothy Dinnerstein, *The Mermaid and the Minotaur: Sexual Arrangements and the Human Malaise* (New York: Harper & Row, 1976); Barbara Ehrenreich and Deirdre English, *For Her Own Good; 150 Years of the Experts' Advice to Women* (Garden City, N.Y.: Doubleday, Anchor, 1978); Jean Baker Miller, *Toward a New Psychology of Women* (Boston: Beacon, 1976).

4. I could have chosen many other serious and influential recent books, including anthologies, which would illustrate the same point: e.g., *Our Bodies, Ourselves,* the Boston Women's Health Book Collective's best seller (New York: Simon and Schuster, 1976), which devotes a separate (and inadequate) chapter to lesbians, but whose message is that heterosexuality is most women's life preference; Berenice Carroll, ed., *Liberating Women's History: Theoretical and Critical Essays* (Urbana: University of Illinois Press, 1976), which does not include even a token essay on the lesbian presence in history, though an essay by Linda Gordon, Persis Hunt, *et al.* notes the use by male historians of "sexual deviance" as a category to discredit and dismiss Anna Howard Shaw, Jane Addams, and other feminists ("Historical Phallacies: Sexism in American Historical Writing"); and Renate Bridenthal and Claudia Koonz, eds., *Becoming Visible: Women in European History* (Boston: Houghton Mifflin, 1977), which contains three mentions of male homosexuality but no materials that I have been able to locate on lesbians. Gerda Lerner, ed., *The Female Experience: An American Documentary* (Indianpolis: Bobbs-Merrill, 1977), contains an abridgement of two lesbian-feminist–position papers from the contemporary movement but no other documentation of lesbian existence. Lerner does note in her preface, however, how the charge of deviance has been used to fragment women and discourage women's resistance. Linda Gordon, in *Woman's Body, Woman's Right: A Social History of Birth Control in America* (New York: Viking, Grossman, 1976), notes accurately that "it is not that feminism has produced more lesbians. There have always been many lesbians, despite the high levels of repression; and most lesbians experience their sexual preference as innate" (p. 410).

[A.R., 1986: I am glad to update the first annotation in this footnote. *"The New" Our Bodies, Our-* *selves* (New York: Simon and Schuster, 1984) contains an expanded chapter on "Loving Women: Lesbian Life and Relationships" and furthermore emphasizes *choices* for women through-out—in terms of sexuality, health care, family, politics, etc.]

5. Jonathan Katz, ed., *Gay American History: Lesbians and Gay Men in the U.S.A.* (New York: Thomas Y. Crowell, 1976).

6. Nancy Sahli, "Smashing Women's Relationships before the Fall," *Chrysalis: A Magazine of Women's Culture* 8 (1979): 17–27.

7. This is a book which I have publicly endorsed. I would still do so, though with the above caveat. It is only since beginning to write this article that I fully appreciated how enormous is the unasked question in Ehrenreich and English's book.

8. See, for example, Kathleen Barry, *Female Sexual Slavery* (Englewood Cliffs, N.J.: Prentice-Hall, 1979); Mary Daly, *Gyn/Ecology: The Meta-ethics of Radical Feminism* (Boston: Beacon, 1978); Susan Griffin, *Woman and Nature: The Roaring inside Her* (New York: Harper & Row, 1978); Diana Russell and Nicole van de Ven, eds., *Proceedings of the International Tribunal of Crimes against Women* (Millbrae, Calif.: Les Femmes, 1976); and Susan Brownmiller, *Against Our Will: Men, Women and Rape* (New York: Simon and Schuster, 1975); *Aegis: Magazine on Ending Violence against Women* (Feminist Alliance against Rape, P.O. Box 21033, Washington, D.C. 20009).

[A.R., 1986: Work on both incest and woman battering has appeared in the 1980s which I did not cite in the essay. See Florence Rush, *The Best-Kept Secret* (New York: McGraw-Hill, 1980); Louise Armstrong, *Kiss Daddy Goodnight: A Speakout on Incest* (New York: Pocket Books, 1979); Sandra Butler, *Conspiracy of Silence: The Trauma of Incest* (San Francisco: New Glide, 1978); F. Delacoste and F. Newman, eds., *Fight Back!: Feminist Resistance to Male Violence* (Minneapolis: Cleis Press, 1981); Judy Freespirit, *Daddy's Girl: An Incest Survivor's Story* (Langlois, Ore.: Diaspora Distribution, 1982); Judith Herman, *Father-Daughter Incest* (Cambridge, Mass.: Harvard University Press, 1981); Toni McNaron and Yarrow Morgan, eds., *Voices in the Night: Women Speaking about Incest* (Minneapolis: Cleis Press, 1982); and Betsy Warrior's richly informative, multipurpose compilation of essays, statistics, listings, and facts, the *Battered Women's Directory* (formerly entitled *Working on Wife Abuse*), 8th ed. (Cambridge, Mass.; 1982).]

9. Dinnerstein, p. 272.

10. Chodorow, pp. 197–198.

11. *Ibid.,* pp. 198–199.

12. *Ibid.*, p. 200.

13. Kathleen Gough, "The Origin of the Family," in *Toward an Anthropology of Women*, ed. Rayna [Rapp] Reiter (New York: Monthly Review Press, 1975), pp. 69–70.

14. Barry, pp. 216–219.

15. Anna Demeter, *Legal Kidnapping* (Boston: Beacon, 1977), pp. xx, 126–128.

16. Daly, pp. 139–141, 163–165.

17. Barbara Ehrenreich and Deirdre English, *Witches, Midwives and Nurses: A History of Women Healers* (Old Westbury, N.Y.: Feminist Press, 1973); Andrea Dworkin, *Woman Hating* (New York: Dutton, 1974), pp. 118–154; Daly, pp. 178–222.

18. See Virginia Woolf, *A Room of One's Own* (London: Hogarth, 1929), and *id.*, *Three Guineas* (New York: Harcourt Brace, [1938] 1966); Tillie Olsen, *Silences* (Boston: Delacorte, 1978); Michelle Cliff, "The Resonance of Interruption," *Chrysalis: A Magazine of Women's Culture* 8 (1979): 29–37.

19. Mary Daly, *Beyond God the Father* (Boston: Beacon, 1973), pp. 347–351; Olsen, pp. 22–46.

20. Daly, *Beyond God the Father*, p. 93.

21. Fran P. Hosken, "The Violence of Power: Genital Mutilation of Females," *Heresies: A Feminist Journal of Art and Politics* 6 (1979): 28–35; Russell and van de Ven, pp. 194–195.

[A.R., 1986: See especially "Circumcision of Girls," in Nawal El Saadawi, *The Hidden Face of Eve: Women in the Arab World* (Boston: Beacon, 1982), pp. 33–43.]

22. Barry, pp. 163–164.

23. The issue of "lesbian sadomasochism" needs to be examined in terms of dominant cultures' teachings about the relation of sex and violence. I believe this to be another example of the "double life" of women.

24. Catharine A. MacKinnon, *Sexual Harassment of Working Women: A Case of Sex Discrimination* (New Haven, Conn.: Yale University Press, 1979), pp. 15–16.

25. *Ibid.*, p. 174.

26. Brownmiller, *op. cit.*

27. MacKinnon, p. 219. Susan Schecter writes: "The push for heterosexual union at whatever cost is so intense that . . . it has become a cultural force of its own that creates battering. The ideology of romantic love and its jealous possession of the partner as property provide the masquerade for what can become severe abuse" (*Aegis: Magazine on Ending Violence against Women* [July–August 1979]: 50–51).

28. MacKinnon, p. 298.

29. *Ibid.*, p. 220.

30. *Ibid.*, p. 221.

31. Barry, *op. cit.*

[A.R., 1986: See also Kathleen Barry, Charlotte Bunch, and Shirley Castley, eds., *International Feminism: Networking against Female Sexual Slavery* (New York: International Women's Tribune Center, 1984).]

32. Barry, p. 33.

33. *Ibid.*, p. 103.

34. *Ibid.*, p. 5.

35. *Ibid.*, p. 100.

[A.R., 1986: This statement has been taken as claiming that "all women are victims" purely and simply, or that "all heterosexuality equals sexual slavery." I would say, rather, that all women are affected, though differently, by dehumanizing attitudes and practices directed at women as a group.]

36. *Ibid.*, p. 218.

37. *Ibid.*, p. 140.

38. *Ibid.*, p. 172.

39. Elsewhere I have suggested that male identification has been a powerful source of white women's racism and that it has often been women already seen as "disloyal" to male codes and systems who have actively battled against it (Adrienne Rich, "Disloyal to Civilization: Feminism, Racism, Gynephobia," in *On Lies, Secrets, and Silence: Selected Prose, 1966–1978* [New York: W. W. Norton, 1979]).

40. Barry, p. 220.

41. Susan Cavin, "Lesbian Origins" (Ph.D. diss., Rutgers University, 1978), unpublished, ch. 6.

[A.R., 1986: This dissertation was recently published as *Lesbian Origins* (San Francisco: Ism Press, 1986).]

42. For my perception of heterosexuality as an economic institution I am indebted to Lisa Leghorn and Katherine Parker, who allowed me to read the unpublished manuscript of their book *Woman's Worth: Sexual Economics and the World of Women* (London and Boston: Routledge & Kegan Paul, 1981).

43. I would suggest that lesbian existence has been most recognized and tolerated where it has resembled a "deviant" version of heterosexuality— e.g., where lesbians have, like Stein and Toklas, played heterosexual roles (or seemed to in public) and have been chiefly identified with male culture. See also Claude E. Schaeffer, "The Kuterai Female Berdache: Courier, Guide, Prophetess and Warrior," *Ethnohistory* 12, no. 3 (Summer 1965): 193–236. (Berdache: "an individual of a definite physiological sex [m. or f.] who assumes the role and status of the opposite sex and who is viewed by the community as being of one sex physiologically but as having assumed the role and status of the opposite sex" [Schaeffer, p. 231].) Lesbian existence has also been relegated to an upper-class phenomenon, an elite decadence (as in the fascination with Paris salon lesbians such as Renée Vivien and Natalie Clifford Barney), to the obscuring of

such "common women" as Judy Grahn depicts in her *The Work of a Common Woman* (Oakland, Calif.: Diana Press, 1978) and *True to Life Adventure Stories* (Oakland, Calif.: Diana Press, 1978).

44. Daly, *Gyn/Ecology*, p. 15.

45. "In a hostile world in which women are not supposed to survive except in relation with and in service to men, entire communities of women were simply erased. History tends to bury what it seeks to reject" (Blanche W. Cook, " 'Women Alone Stir My Imagination': Lesbianism and the Cultural Tradition," *Signs: Journal of Women in Culture and Society* 4, no. 4 [Summer 1979]: 719–720). The Lesbian Herstory Archives in New York City is one attempt to preserve contemporary documents on lesbian existence—a project of enormous value and meaning, working against the continuing censorship and obliteration of relationships, networks, communities in other archives and elsewhere in the culture.

46. [A.R., 1986: The shared historical and spiritual "crossover" functions of lesbians and gay men in cultures past and present are traced by Judy Grahn in *Another Mother Tongue: Gay Words, Gay Worlds* (Boston: Beacon, 1984). I now think we have much to learn both from the uniquely female aspects of lesbian existence and from the complex "gay" identity we share with gay men.]

47. Audre Lorde, "Uses of the Erotic: The Erotic as Power," in *Sister Outsider* (Trumansburg, N.Y.: Crossing Press, 1984).

48. Adrienne Rich, "Conditions for Work: The Common World of Women," in *On Lies, Secrets, and Silence*, p. 209; H. D., *Tribute to Freud* (Oxford: Carcanet, 1971), pp. 50–54.

49. Woolf, *A Room of One's Own*, p. 126.

50. Gracia Clark, "The Beguines: A Mediaeval Women's Community," *Quest: A Feminist Quarterly* 1, no. 4 (1975): 73–80.

51. See Denise Paulmé, ed., *Women of Tropical Africa* (Berkeley: University of California Press, 1963), pp. 7, 266–267. Some of these sororities are described as "a kind of defensive syndicate against the male element," their aims being "to offer concerted resistance to an oppressive patriarchate," "independence in relation to one's husband and with regard to motherhood, mutual aid, satisfaction of personal revenge." See also Audre Lorde, "Scratching the Surface: Some Notes on Barriers to Women and Loving," in *Sister Outsider*, pp. 45–52; Marjorie Topley, "Marriage Resistance in Rural Kwangtung," in *Women in Chinese Society*, ed. M. Wolf and R. Witke (Stanford, Calif.: Stanford University Press, 1978), pp. 67–89; Agnes Smedley, *Portraits of Chinese Women in Revolution*, ed. J. MacKinnon and S. MacKinnon (Old Westbury, N.Y.: Feminist Press, 1976), pp. 103–110.

52. See Rosalind Petchesky, "Dissolving the Hyphen: A Report on Marxist-Feminist Groups 1–5," in *Capitalist Patriarchy and the Case for Socialist Feminism*, ed. Zillah Eisenstein (New York: Monthly Review Press, 1979), p. 387.

53. [A.R., 1986: See Angela Davis, *Women, Race and Class* (New York: Random House, 1981), p. 102; Orlando Patterson, *Slavery and Social Death: A Comparative Study* (Cambridge: Harvard University Press, 1982), p. 133.]

54. Russell and van de Ven, pp. 42–43, 56–57.

55. I am indebted to Jonathan Katz's *Gay American History (op. cit.)* for bringing to my attention Hansberry's letters to *The Ladder* and to Barbara Grier for supplying me with copies of relevant pages from *The Ladder*, quoted here by permission of Barbara Grier. See also the reprinted series of *The Ladder*, ed. Jonathan Katz *et al.* (New York: Arno, 1975), and Deirdre Carmody, "Letters by Eleanor Roosevelt Detail Friendship with Lorena Hickok," *New York Times* (October 21, 1979).

56. Meridel LeSueur, *The Girl* (Cambridge, Mass.: West End Press, 1978), pp. 10–11. LeSueur describes, in an afterword, how this book was drawn from the writings and oral narrations of women in the Workers Alliance who met as a writers' group during the depression.

57. *Ibid.*, p. 20.

58. *Ibid.*, pp. 53–54.

59. *Ibid.*, p. 55.

60. Toni Morrison, *Sula* (New York: Bantam, 1973), pp. 103–104, 149. I am indebted to Lorraine Bethel's essay " 'This Infinity of Conscious Pain': Zora Neale Hurston and the Black Female Literary Tradition," in *All the Women Are White, All the Blacks Are Men, but Some of Us Are Brave: Black Women's Studies*, ed. Gloria T. Hull, Patricia Bell Scott, and Barbara Smith (Old Westbury, N.Y.: Feminist Press, 1982).

61. See Maureen Brady and Judith McDaniel, "Lesbians in the Mainstream: The Image of Lesbians in Recent Commercial Fiction," *Conditions* 6 (1979): 82–105.

62. See Russell and van de Ven, p. 40: "Few heterosexual women realize their lack of free choice about their sexuality, and few realize how and why compulsory heterosexuality is also a crime against them."

63. Bethel, " 'This Infinity of Conscious Pain,' " *op. cit.*

64. Dinnerstein, the most recent writer to quote this passage, adds ominously: "But what has to be added to her account is that these 'women enlaced' are sheltering each other not just from what men want to do to them, but also from what they want to do to each other" (Dinnerstein, p. 103). The fact is, however, that woman-to-woman violence is a minute grain in the universe of male-against-female violence perpetuated and rationalized in every social institution.

65. Conversation with Blanche W. Cook, New York City, March 1979.

Vesuvius at Home:
The Power of Emily Dickinson

I am traveling at the speed of time, along the Massachusetts Turnpike. For months, for years, for most of my life, I have been hovering like an insect against the screens of an existence which inhabited Amherst, Massachusetts, between 1830 and 1886. The methods, the exclusions, of Emily Dickinson's existence could not have been my own; yet more and more, as a women poet finding my own methods, I have come to understand her necessities, could have been witness in her defense.

"Home is not where the heart is," she wrote in a letter, "but the house and the adjacent buildings." A statement of New England realism, a directive to be followed. Probably no poet ever lived so much and so purposefully in one house; even, in one room. Her niece Martha told of visiting her in her corner bedroom on the second floor at 280 Main Street, Amherst, and of how Emily Dickinson made as if to lock the door with an imaginary key, turned, and said: "Matty: here's freedom."

I am traveling at the speed of time, in the direction of the house and buildings.

Western Massachusetts: the Connecticut Valley: a countryside still full of reverberations: scene of Indian uprisings, religious revivals, spiritual confrontations, the blazing-up of the lunatic fringe of the Puritan coal. How peaceful and how threatened it looks from Route 91, hills gently curled above the plain, the tobacco barns standing in fields sheltered with white gauze from the sun, and the sudden urban sprawl: ARCO, McDonald's, shopping plazas. The country that broke the heart of Jonathan Edwards, that enclosed the genius of Emily Dickinson. It lies calmly in the light of May, cloudy skies breaking into warm sunshine, light-green spring softening the hills, dogwood and wild fruit-trees blossoming in the hollows.

From Northampton bypass there's a four-mile stretch of road to Amherst—Route 9—between fruit farms, steakhouses, supermarkets. The new University of Massachusetts rears its skyscrapers up from the plain against the Pelham Hills. There is new money here, real estate, motels. Amherst succeeds on Hadley almost without notice. Amherst is green, rich-looking, secure; we're suddenly in the center of town, the crossroads of the campus, old New England college buildings spread around two village greens, a scene I remember as almost exactly the same in the dim past of my undergraduate years when I used to come there for college weekends.

Left on Seelye Street, right on Main; driveway at the end of a yellow picket fence. I recognize the high hedge of cedars screening the house, because twenty-five years ago I walked there, even then drawn toward the spot, trying to peer over. I pull into the driveway behind a generous nineteenth-century brick mansion with wings and porches, old trees and green lawns. I ring at the back door—the door through which Dickinson's coffin was carried to the cemetery a block away.

For years I have been not so much envisioning Emily Dickinson as trying to visit, to enter her mind, through her poems and letters, and through my own intimations of what it could have meant to be one of the two mid–nineteenth-century American geniuses, and a woman, living in Amherst, Massachusetts. Of the other genius, Walt Whitman, Dickinson wrote that she had heard his poems were "disgraceful." She knew her own were unacceptable by her world's standards of poetic convention, and of what was appropriate, in particular, for a woman poet. Seven were published in her lifetime, all edited by other hands; more than a thousand were laid away in her bedroom chest, to be discovered after her death. When her sister discovered them, there were decades of struggle over the manuscripts, the manner of their presentation to the world, their suitability for publication, the poet's own final intentions. Narrowed-down by her early editors and anthologists, reduced to quaintness or spinsterish oddity by many of her commentators, sentimentalized, fallen-in-love with like some gnomic Garbo, still unread in the breadth and depth of her full range of work, she was, and is, a wonder to me when I try to imagine myself into that mind.

I have a notion that genius knows itself; that Dickinson chose her seclusion, knowing she was exceptional and knowing what she needed. It was, moreover, no hermetic retreat, but a seclusion which included a wide range of people, of reading and correspondence. Her sister Vinnie said, "Emily is always looking for the rewarding person." And she found, at various periods, both women and men: her sister-in-law Susan Gilbert, Amherst visitors and family friends such as Benjamin Newton, Charles Wadsworth, Samuel Bowles, editor of the Springfield *Republican,* and his wife; her friends Kate Anthon and Helen Hunt Jackson, the distant but significant figures of Elizabeth Barrett, the Brontës, George Eliot. But she carefully selected her society and controlled the disposal of her time. Not only the "gentlewomen in plush" of Amherst were excluded; Emerson visited next door but she did not go to meet him; she did not travel or receive routine visits; she avoided strangers. Given her vocation, she was neither eccentric nor quaint; she was determined to survive, to use her powers, to practice necessary economies.

Suppose Jonathan Edwards had been born a woman; suppose William James, for that matter, had been born a woman? (The invalid seclusion of his sister Alice is suggestive.) Even from men, New England took its psychic toll; many of its geniuses seemed peculiar in one way or another, particularly along the lines of social intercourse. Hawthorne, until he married, took his meals in his bedroom, apart from the family. Thoreau insisted on the values both of solitude and of geographical restriction, boasting that "I have traveled much in Concord." Emily Dickinson—viewed by her bemused contemporary Thomas Higginson as "partially cracked," by the twentieth century as fey or pathological—has increasingly struck me as a practical woman, exercising her gift as she had to, making choices. I have come to imagine her as somehow too strong for her environment, a figure of powerful will, not at all frail or breathless, someone whose personal dimensions would be felt in a household. She was her father's favorite daughter though she professed being afraid of him. Her sister dedicated herself to the everyday domestic labors which would free Dickinson to write. (Dickinson herself baked the bread, made jellies and gingerbread, nursed her mother through a long illness, was a skilled horticulturalist who grew pomegranates, calla lilies, and other exotica in her New England greenhouse.)

Upstairs at last: I stand in the room which for Emily Dickinson was "freedom." The best bedroom in the house, a corner room, sunny, overlooking the main street of Amherst in front, the way to her brother Austin's house on the side. Here, at a small table with one drawer, she wrote most of her poems. Here she read Elizabeth Barrett's *Aurora Leigh,* a woman poet's narrative poem of a woman poet's life; also George Eliot; Emerson; Carlyle; Shakespeare; Charlotte and Emily Brontë. Here I become, again, an insect, vibrating at the frames of windows, clinging to panes of glass, trying to connect. The scent here is very powerful. Here in this white-curtained, high-ceilinged room, a red-haired woman with hazel eyes and a contralto voice wrote poems about volcanoes, deserts, eternity, suicide, physical passion, wild beasts, rape, power, madness, separation, the daemon, the grave. Here, with a darning needle, she bound these poems—heavily emended and often in variant versions—into booklets, secured with darning thread, to be found and read after her death. Here she knew "freedom," listening from above-stairs to a visitor's piano-playing, escaping from the pantry where she was mistress of the household bread and puddings, watching, you feel, watching ceaselessly, the life of sober Main Street below. From this room she glided downstairs, her hand on the polished bannister, to meet the complacent magazine editor, Thomas Higginson, unnerve him while claiming she herself was unnerved. "Your scholar," she signed herself in letters to him. But she was an independent scholar, used his criticism selectively, saw him rarely and always on *her* premises. It was a life deliberately organized on her terms. The terms she had been handed by society—Calvinist Protestantism, Romanticism, the nineteenth-century corseting of women's bodies, choices, and sexuality—could spell insanity to a woman genius. What this one had to do was retranslate her own unorthodox, subversive, sometimes volcanic propensities into a dialect called metaphor: her native language. "Tell all the Truth—but tell it Slant—." It is always what is under pressure in us, especially under pressure of concealment—that explodes in poetry.

The women and men in her life she equally converted into metaphor. The masculine pronoun in her poems can refer simultaneously to many aspects of the "masculine" in the patriarchal world—the god she engages in dialogue, again on *her* terms; her own creative powers, unsexing for a woman, the male power-figures in her immediate environment—the lawyer Edward Dickinson, her brother Austin, the preacher Wadsworth, the editor Bowles—it is far too limiting to trace that "He" to some specific lover, although that was the chief obsession of the legend-mongers for more than half a century. Obviously, Dickinson was attracted by and interested in men whose minds had something to offer her; she was, it is by now clear, equally attracted by and interested in women whose minds had something to offer. There are many poems to and about women, and some which exist in two versions with alternate sets of pronouns. Her latest biographer, Richard Sewall, rejecting an earlier Freudian biographer's theory that Dickinson was essentially a psychopathological case, the by-product of which happened to be poetry, creates a context in which the importance, and validity, of Dickinson's attachments to women may now, at last, be seen in full. She was always stirred by the existences of women like George Eliot or Elizabeth Barrett, who possessed strength of mind, articulateness, and energy. (She once characterized Elizabeth Fry and Florence Nightingale as "holy"—one suspects she merely meant "great.")

But of course Dickinson's relationships with women were more than intellectual. They were deeply charged, and the sources of both passionate joy and pain. We are only beginning to be able to consider them in a social and historical context. The historian Carroll Smith Rosenberg has shown that there was far less taboo on intense, even passionate and sensual relationships between women in the American nineteenth-century "female world of love and ritual," as she terms it, than there was later in the twentieth century. Women expressed their attachments to other women both physically and verbally; a marriage did not dilute the strength of a female friendship, in which two women often shared the same bed during long visits, and wrote letters articulate with both physical and emotional longing. The nineteenth-century close woman friend, according to the many diaries and letters Smith Rosen-berg has studied, might be a far more important figure in a woman's life than the nineteenth-century husband. None of this was perceived or condemned as "lesbian-ism."[1] We will understand Emily Dickinson better, read her poetry more percep-tively, when the Freudian imputation of scandal and aberrance in women's love for women has been supplanted by a more informed, less misogynistic attitude toward women's experiences with each other.

But who, if you read through the seventeen hundred and seventy-five poems—who—woman or man—could have passed through that imagination and not come out transmuted? Given the space created by her in that corner room, with its window-light, its potted plants and work-table, given that personality, capable of imposing its terms on a household, on a whole community, what single theory could hope to contain her, when she'd put it all together in that space?

"Matty: here's freedom," I hear her saying as I speed back to Boston along the turnpike, as I slip the ticket into the toll-collector's hand. I am thinking of a confined space in which the genius of the nineteenth-century female mind in America moved, inventing a language more varied, more compressed, more dense with implications, more complex of syntax, than any American poetic language to date; in the trail of that genius my mind has been moving, and with its language and images my mind still has to reckon, as the mind of a woman poet in America today.

In 1971, a postage stamp was issued in honor of Dickinson; the portrait derives from the one existing daguerreotype of her, with straight, center-parted hair, eyes staring somewhere beyond the camera, hands poised around a nosegay of flowers, in correct nineteenth-century style. On the first-day-of-issue envelope sent me by a friend there is, besides the postage stamp, an engraving of the poet as popular fancy has preferred her, in a white lace ruff and with hair as bouffant as if she had just stepped from a Boston beauty-parlor. The poem chosen to represent her work to the American public is engraved, alongside a dew-gemmed rose, below the portrait:

> If I can stop one heart from breaking
> I shall not live in vain
> If I can ease one life the aching
> Or cool one pain
> Or help one fainting robin
> Unto his nest again
> I shall not live in vain.

Now, this is extremely strange. It is a fact that, in 1864, Emily Dickinson wrote this verse; and it is a verse which a hundred or more nineteenth-century versifiers could have written. In its undistinguished language, as in its conventional sentiment, it is remarkably untypical of the poet. Had she chosen to write many poems like this one we would have no "problem" of nonpublication, of editing, of estimating the poet at her true worth. Certainly the sentiment—a contented and unambiguous altruism—is one which even today might in some quarters be accepted as fitting from a female versifier—a kind of Girl Scout prayer. But we are talking about the woman who wrote:

[1]"The Female World of Love and Ritual: Relations between Women in Nineteenth-Century Amer-ica," *Signs*, vol. 1, no. 1.

He fumbles at your Soul
As Players at the Keys
Before they drop full Music on—
He stuns you by degrees—
Prepares your brittle Nature
For the Ethereal Blow
By fainter Hammers—further heard—
Then nearer—Then so slow
Your breath has time to straighten—
Your brain—to bubble Cool—
Deals—One—imperial—Thunderbolt—
That scalps your naked Soul—

When Winds take Forests in their Paws—
The Universe—is still—

(#315)

Much energy has been invested in trying to identify a concrete, flesh-and-blood male lover whom Dickinson is supposed to have renounced, and to the loss of whom can be traced the secret of her seclusion and the vein of much of her poetry. But the real question, given that the art of poetry is an art of transformation, is how this woman's mind and imagination may have used the masculine element in the world at large, or those elements personified as masculine—including the men she knew; how her relationship to this reveals itself in her images and language. In a patriarchal culture, specifically the Judeo-Christian, quasi-Puritan culture of nineteenth-century New England in which Dickinson grew up, still inflamed with religious revivals, and where the sermon was still an active, if perishing, literary form, the equation of divinity with maleness was so fundamental that it is hardly surprising to find Dickinson, like many an early mystic, blurring erotic with religious experience and imagery. The poem I just read has intimations of both seduction and rape merged with the intense force of a religious experience. But are these metaphors for each other, or for something more intrinsic to Dickinson? Here is another:

He put the Belt around my life—
I heard the Buckle snap—
And turned away, imperial,
My Lifetime folding up—
Deliberate, as a Duke would do
A Kingdom's Title Deed—
Henceforth, a Dedicated sort—
A member of the Cloud.

Yet not too far to come at call—
And do the little Toils
That make the Circuit of the Rest—
And deal occasional smiles
To lives that stoop to notice mine—
And kindly ask it in—
Whose invitation, know you not
For Whom I must decline?

(#273)

These two poems are about possession, and they seem to me a poet's poems—that is, they are about the poet's relationship to her own power, which is exteriorized in masculine form, much as masculine poets have invoked the female Muse. In writing at all—particularly an unorthodox and original poetry like Dickinson's—women have often felt in danger of losing their status as women. And this status has always been defined in terms of relationship to men—as daughter, sister, bride, wife, mother, mistress, Muse. Since the most powerful figures in patriarchal culture have been men, it seems natural that Dickinson would assign a masculine gender to that in herself which did not fit in with the conventional ideology of womanliness. To recognize and acknowledge our own interior power has always been a path mined with risks for women; to acknowledge that power and commit oneself to it as Emily Dickinson did was an immense decision.

Most of us, unfortunately, have been exposed in the schoolroom to Dickinson's "little-girl" poems, her kittenish tones, as in "I'm Nobody! Who Are You?" (a poem whose underlying anger translates itself into archness) or

> I hope the Father in the skies
> Will lift his little girl—
> Old fashioned—naughty—everything—
> Over the stile of "Pearl."
>
> (#70)

or the poems about bees and robins. One critic—Richard Chase—has noted that in the nineteenth century "one of the careers open to women was perpetual child-hood." A strain in Dickinson's letters and some—though by far a minority—of her poems was a self-diminutivization, almost as if to offset and deny—or even dis-guise—her actual dimensions as she must have experienced them. And this emphasis on her own "littleness," along with the deliberate strangeness of her tactics of seclusion, have been, until recently, accepted as the prevailing character of the poet: the fragile poetess in white, sending flowers and poems by messenger to unseen friends, letting down baskets of gingerbread to the neighborhood children from her bedroom window; writing, but somehow naively. John Crowe Ransom, arguing for the editing and standardization of Dickinson's punctuation and typography, calls her "a little home-keeping person" who, "while she had a proper notion of the final destiny of her poems . . . was not one of those poets who had advanced to that later stage of operations where manuscripts are prepared for the printer, and the poet's diction has to make concessions to the publisher's style-book." (In short, Emily Dickinson did not wholly know her trade, and Ransom believes a "publisher's style-book" to have the last word on poetic diction.) He goes on to print several of her poems, altered by him "with all possible forbearance." What might, in a male writer—a Thoreau, let us say, or a Christopher Smart or William Blake—seem a legitimate strangeness, a unique intention, has been in one of our two major poets devalued into a kind of naiveté, girlish ignorance, feminine lack of professionalism, just as the poet herself has been made into a sentimental object. ("Most of us are half in love with this dead girl," confesses Archibald MacLeish. Dickinson was fifty-five when she died.)

It is true that more recent critics, including her most recent biographer, have gradually begun to approach the poet in terms of her greatness rather than her littleness, the decisiveness of her choices instead of the surface oddities of her life or the romantic crises of her legend. But unfortunately anthologists continue to plagiarize other anthologies, to reprint her in edited, even bowdlerized versions; the popular image of her and of her work lags behind the changing consciousness of scholars and specialists. There still does not exist a selection from her poems which depicts her in her fullest range. Dickinson's greatness cannot be measured in terms of twenty-five or fifty or even five hundred "perfect" lyrics; it has to be seen as the accumulation it is. Poets, even, are not always acquainted with the full dimensions of her work, or the sense one gets, reading in the one-volume complete edition (let alone the three-volume variorum edition) of a mind engaged in a lifetime's musing on essential problems of language, identity, separation, relationship, the integrity of the self; a mind capable of describing psychological states more accurately than any poet except Shakespeare. I have been surprised at how narrowly her work, still, is known by women who are writing poetry, how much her legend has gotten in the way of her being repossessed, as a source and a foremother.

I know that for me, reading her poems as a child and then as a young girl already seriously writing poetry, she was a problematic figure. I first read her in the selection heavily edited by her niece which appeared in 1937; a later and fuller edition appeared in 1945 when I was sixteen, and the complete, unbowdlerized edition by Johnson did not appear until fifteen years later. The publication of each of these editions was crucial to me in successive decades of my life. More than any other poet, Emily Dickinson seemed to tell me that the intense inner event, the personal and psychological, was inseparable from the universal; that there was a range for psychological poetry beyond mere self-expression. Yet the legend of the life was troubling, because it seemed to whisper that a woman who undertook such explorations must pay with renunciation, isolation, and incorporeality. With the publication of the *Complete Poems,* the legend seemed to recede into unimportance beside the unquestionable power and importance of the mind revealed there. But taking possession of Emily Dickinson is still no simple matter.

The 1945 edition, entitled *Bolts of Melody,* took its title from a poem which struck me at the age of sixteen and which still, thirty years later, arrests my imagination:

> I would not paint—a picture—
> I'd rather be the One
> Its bright impossibility
> To dwell—delicious—on—
> And wonder how the fingers feel
> Whose rare—celestial—stir
> Evokes so sweet a Torment—
> Such sumptuous—Despair—
>
> I would not talk, like Cornets—
> I'd rather be the One
> Raised softly to the Ceilings—
> And out, and easy on—
> Through Villages of Ether
> Myself endured Balloon
> By but a lip of Metal
> The pier to my Pontoon—

Nor would I be a Poet—
It's finer—own the Ear—
Enamored—impotent—content—
The License to revere,
A privilege so awful
What would the Dower be,
Had I the Art to stun myself
With Bolts of Melody!

(#505)

This poem is about choosing an orthodox "feminine" role: the receptive rather than the creative; viewer rather than painter, listener rather than musician; acted-upon rather than active. Yet even while ostensibly choosing this role she wonders "how the fingers feel / whose rare-celestial—stir— / Evokes so sweet a Torment—" and the "feminine" role is praised in a curious sequence of adjectives: "Enamored—*impotent*—content—." The strange paradox of this poem—its exquisite irony—is that it is about choosing not to be a poet, a poem which is gainsaid by no fewer than one thousand seven hundred and seventy-five poems made during the writer's life, including itself. Moreover, the images of the poem rise to a climax (like the Balloon she evokes) but the climax happens as she describes, not what it is to be the receiver, but the maker and receiver at once: "A Privilege so awful / What would the Dower be / Had I the Art to stun myself / With Bolts of Melody!"—a climax which recalls the poem: "He fumbles at your Soul / As Players at the Keys / Before they drop full Music on—" And of course, in writing those lines she possesses herself of that privilege and that Dower. I have said that this is a poem of exquisite ironies. It is, indeed, though in a very different mode, related to Dickinson's "little-girl" strategy. The woman who feels herself to be Vesuvius at home has need of a mask, at least, of innocuousness and of containment.

On my volcano grows the Grass
A meditative spot—
An acre for a Bird to choose
Would be the General thought—

How red the Fire rocks below—
How insecure the sod
Did I disclose
Would populate with awe my solitude.

(#1677)

Power, even masked, can still be perceived as destructive.

A still—Volcano—Life—
That flickered in the night—
When it was dark enough to do
Without erasing sight—

A quiet—Earthquake style—
Too subtle to suspect
By natures this side Naples—
The North cannot detect

> The Solemn—Torrid—Symbol—
> The lips that never lie—
> Whose hissing Corals part—and shut—
> And Cities—ooze away—
>
> (#601)

Dickinson's biographer and editor Thomas Johnson has said that she often felt herself possessed by a daemonic force, particularly in the years 1861 and 1862, when she was writing at the height of her drive. There are many poems besides "He put the Belt around my Life" which could be read as poems of possession by the daemon—poems which can also be, and have been, read as poems of possession by the deity, or by a human lover. I suggest that a woman's poetry about her relationship to her daemon—her own active, creative power—has in patriarchal culture used the language of heterosexual love or patriarchal theology. Ted Hughes tells us that

> the eruption of [Dickinson's] imagination and poetry followed when she shifted her passion, with the energy of desperation, from [the] lost man onto his only possible substitute,—the Universe in its Divine aspect. . . . Thereafter, the marriage that had been denied in the real world went forward in the spiritual . . . just as the Universe in its Divine aspect became the mirror-image of her "husband," so the whole religious dilemma of New England, at that most critical moment in history, became the mirror-image of her relationship to him, of her "marriage" in fact.[2]

This seems to me to miss the point on a grand scale. There are facts we need to look at. First, Emily Dickinson did not marry. And her nonmarrying was neither a pathological retreat, as John Cody sees it, nor probably even a conscious decision; it was a fact in her life as in her contemporary Christina Rossetti's; both women had more primary needs. Second: unlike Rossetti, Dickinson did not become a religiously dedicated woman; she was heretical, heterodox, in her religious opinions, and stayed away from church and dogma. What, in fact, *did* she allow to "put the Belt around her Life"—what *did* wholly occupy her mature years and possess her? For "Whom" did she decline the invitations of other lives? The writing of poetry. Nearly two thousand poems. Three hundred and sixty-six poems in the year of her fullest power. What was it like to be writing poetry you knew (and I am sure she did know) was of a class by itself—to be fueled by the energy it took first to confront, then to condense that range of psychic experience into that language; then to copy out the poems and lay them in a trunk, or send a few here and there to friends or relatives as occasional verse or as gestures of confidence? I am sure she knew who she was, as she indicates in this poem:

> Myself was formed—a Carpenter—
> An unpretending time
> My Plane—and I, together wrought
> Before a Builder came—
>
> To measure our attainments
> Had we the Art of Boards
> Sufficiently developed—He'd hire us
> At Halves—

[2]Hughes, ed., *A Choice of Emily Dickinson's Verse* (London: Faber & Faber, 1968), p. 11.

> My Tools took Human—Faces—
> The Bench, where we had toiled—
> Against the Man—persuaded—
> We—Temples Build—I said—
>
> (#488)

This is a poem of the great year 1862, the year in which she first sent a few poems to Thomas Higginson for criticism. Whether it antedates or postdates that occasion is unimportant; it is a poem of knowing one's measure, regardless of the judgments of others.

There are many poems which carry the weight of this knowledge. Here is another one:

> I'm ceded—I've stopped being Theirs—
> The name They dropped upon my face
> With water, in the country church
> Is finished using, now,
> And They can put it with my Dolls,
> My childhood, and the string of spools,
> I've finished threading—too—
>
> Baptized before, without the choice,
> But this time, consciously, of Grace—
> Unto supremest name—
> Called to my Full—The Crescent dropped—
> Existence's whole Arc, filled up,
> With one small Diadem.
>
> My second Rank—too small the first—
> Crowned—Crowing—on my Father's breast—
> A half unconscious Queen—
> But this time—Adequate—Erect—
> With Will to choose, or to reject—
> And I choose, just a Crown—
>
> (#508)

Now, this poem partakes of the imagery of being "twice-born" or, in Christian liturgy, "confirmed"—and if this poem had been written by Christina Rossetti I would be inclined to give more weight to a theological reading. But it was written by Emily Dickinson, who used the Christian metaphor far more than she let it use her. This is a poem of great pride—not pridefulness, but *self*-confirmation—and it is curious how little Dickinson's critics, perhaps misled by her diminutives, have recognized the will and pride in her poetry. It is a poem of movement from childhood to womanhood, of transcending the patriarchal condition of bearing her father's name and "crowing—on my Father's breast—." She is now a conscious Queen "Adequate—Erect / With Will to choose, or to reject—."

There is one poem which is the real "onlie begetter" of my thoughts here about Dickinson; a poem I have mused over, repeated to myself, taken into myself over many years. I think it is a poem about possession by the daemon, about the dangers and risks of such possession if you are a woman, about the knowledge that power in a woman can seem destructive, and that you cannot live without the daemon once it has possessed you. The archetype of the daemon as masculine is beginning to change, but it has been real for women up until now. But this woman poet also perceives herself as a lethal weapon:

> My life had stood—a Loaded Gun—
> In Corners—till a Day
> The Owner passed—identified—
> And carried Me away—
>
> And now We roam in Sovereign Woods—
> And now We hunt the Doe—
> And every time I speak for Him—
> The Mountains straight reply—
>
> And do I smile, such cordial light
> Upon the Valley glow—
> It is as a Vesuvian face
> Had let its pleasure through—
>
> And when at Night—Our good Day done—
> I guard My Master's Head—
> 'Tis better than the Eider-Duck's
> Deep Pillow—to have shared—
>
> To foe of His—I'm deadly foe—
> None stir the second time—
> On whom I lay a Yellow Eye—
> Or an emphatic Thumb—
>
> Though I than He—may longer live
> He longer must—than I—
> For I have but the power to kill,
> Without—the power to die—
>
> (#754)

Here the poet sees herself as split, not between anything so simple as "masculine" and "feminine" identity but between the hunter, admittedly masculine, but also a human person, an active, willing being, and the gun—an object, condemned to remain inactive until the hunter—the *owner*—takes possession of it. The gun contains an energy capable of rousing echoes in the mountains and lighting up the valleys; it is also deadly, "Vesuvian"; it is also its owner's defender against the "foe." It is the gun, furthermore, who *speaks for him*. If there is a female consciousness in this poem it is buried deeper than the images: it exists in the ambivalence toward power, which is extreme. Active willing and creation in women are forms of aggression, and aggression is both "the power to kill" and punishable by death. The union of gun with hunter embodies the danger of identifying and taking hold of her forces, not least that in so doing she risks defining herself—and being defined—as aggressive, as unwomanly ("and now we hunt the Doe"), and as potentially lethal. That which she experiences in herself as energy and potency can also be experienced as pure destruction. The final stanza, with its precarious balance of phrasing, seems a desperate attempt to resolve the ambivalence; but, I think, it is no resolution, only a further extension of ambivalence.

> Though I than He—may longer live
> He longer must—than I—
> For I have but the power to kill,
> Without—the power to die—

The poet experiences herself as loaded gun, imperious energy; yet without the Owner, the possessor, she is merely lethal. Should that possession abandon her—but the thought is unthinkable: "He longer *must* than I." The pronoun is masculine; the antecedent is what Keats called "The Genius of Poetry."

I do not pretend to have—I don't even wish to have—explained this poem, accounted for its every image; it will reverberate with new tones long after my words about it have ceased to matter. But I think that for us, at this time, it is a central poem in understanding Emily Dickinson, and ourselves, and the condition of the woman artist, particularly in the nineteenth century. It seems likely that the nineteenth-century woman poet, especially, felt the medium of poetry as dangerous, in ways that the woman novelist did not feel the medium of fiction to be. In writing even such a novel of elemental sexuality and anger as *Wuthering Heights*, Emily Brontë could at least theoretically separate herself from her characters; they were, after all, fictitious beings. Moreover, the novel is or can be a construct, planned and organized to deal with human experiences on one level at a time. Poetry is too much rooted in the unconscious; it presses too close against the barriers of repression; and the nineteenth-century woman had much to repress. It is interesting that Elizabeth Barrett tried to fuse poetry and fiction in writing *Aurora Leigh*—perhaps apprehending the need for fictional characters to carry the charge of her experience as a woman artist. But with the exception of *Aurora Leigh* and Christina Rossetti's "Goblin Market"—that extraordinary and little-known poem drenched in oral eroticism—Emily Dickinson's is the only poetry in English by a woman of that century which pierces so far beyond the ideology of the "feminine" and the conventions of womanly feeling. To write it at all, she had to be willing to enter chambers of the self in which

> Ourself behind ourself, concealed—
> Should startle most—

and to relinquish control there, to take those risks, she had to create a relationship to the outer world where she could feel in control.

It is an extremely painful and dangerous way to live—split between a publicly acceptable persona and a part of yourself that you perceive as the essential, the creative and powerful self, yet also as possibly unacceptable, perhaps even monstrous.

> Much Madness is divinest Sense—
> To a discerning Eye—
> Much Sense—the starkest Madness—
> 'Tis the Majority
> In this, as All, prevail—
> Assent—and you are sane—
> Demur—you're straightway dangerous—
> And handled with a Chain—

> (#435)

For many women the stresses of this splitting have led, in a world so ready to assert our innate passivity and to deny our independence and creativity, to extreme consequences: the mental asylum, self-imposed silence, recurrent depression, suicide, and often severe loneliness.

Dickinson is *the* American poet whose work consisted in exploring states of psychic extremity. For a long time, as we have seen, this fact was obscured by the kinds of selections made from her work by timid if well-meaning editors. In fact, Dickinson was a great psychologist; and like every great psychologist, she began with the material she had at hand: herself. She had to possess the courage to enter, through language, states which most people deny or veil with silence.

> The first Day's Night had come—
> And grateful that a thing
> So terrible—had been endured—
> I told my Soul to sing—
>
> She said her Strings were snapt—
> Her Bow—to Atoms blown—
> And so to mend her—gave me work
> Until another Morn—
>
> And then—a Day as huge
> As Yesterdays in pairs,
> Unrolled its horror in my face—
> Until it blocked my eyes—
>
> My Brain—begun to laugh—
> I mumbled—like a fool—
> And tho' 'tis Years ago—that Day—
> My Brain keeps giggling—still.
>
> And Something's odd—within—
> That person that I was—
> And this One—do not feel the same—
> Could it be Madness—this?
>
> (#410)

Dickinson's letters acknowledge a period of peculiarly intense personal crisis; her biographers have variously ascribed it to the pangs of renunciation of an impossible love, or to psychic damage deriving from her mother's presumed depression and withdrawal after her birth. What concerns us here is the fact that she chose to probe the nature of this experience in language:

> The Soul has Bandaged moments—
> When too appalled to stir—
> She feels some ghastly Fright come up
> And stop to look at her—
>
> Salute her—with long fingers—
> Caress her freezing hair—
> Sip, Goblin, from the very lips
> The Lover—hovered—o'er—
> Unworthy, that a thought so mean
> Accost a Theme—so—fair—

> The soul has moments of Escape—
> When bursting all the doors—
> She dances like a Bomb, abroad,
> And swings upon the Hours. . . .
>
> The Soul's retaken moments—
> When, Felon led along,
> With shackles on the plumed feet,
> And staples, in the Song,
>
> The Horror welcomes her, again,
> These, are not brayed of Tongue—
>
> (#512)

In this poem, the word "Bomb" is dropped, almost carelessly, as a correlative for the soul's active, liberated states—it occurs in a context of apparent euphoria, but its implications are more than euphoric—they are explosive, destructive. The Horror from which in such moments the soul escapes has a masculine, "Goblin" form, and suggests the perverse and terrifying rape of a "Bandaged" and powerless self. In at least one poem, Dickinson depicts the actual process of suicide:

> He scanned it—staggered—
> Dropped the Loop
> To Past or Period—
> Caught helpless at a sense as if
> His mind were going blind—
>
> Groped up, to see if God was there—
> Groped backward at Himself—
> Caressed a Trigger absently
> And wandered out of Life.
>
> (#1062)

The precision of knowledge in this brief poem is such that we must assume that Dickinson had, at least in fantasy, drifted close to that state in which the "Loop" that binds us to "Past or Period" is "Dropped" and we grope randomly at what remains of abstract notions of sense, God, or self, before—almost absent-mindedly—reaching for a solution. But it's worth noting that this is a poem in which the suicidal experience has been distanced, refined, transformed through a devastating accuracy of language. It is not suicide that is studied here, but the dissociation of self and mind and world which precedes.

Dickinson was convinced that a life worth living could be found within the mind and against the grain of external circumstance: "Reverse cannot befall / That fine prosperity / Whose Sources are interior—" (#395). The horror, for her, was that which set "Staples in the Song"—the numbing and freezing of the interior, a state she describes over and over:

> There is a Languor of the Life
> More imminent than Pain—
> 'Tis Pain's Successor—When the Soul
> Has suffered all it can—

A Drowsiness—diffuses—
A Dimness like a Fog
Envelopes Consciousness—
As Mists—obliterate a Crag.

The Surgeon—does not blanch—at pain—
His Habit—is severe—
But tell him that it ceased to feel—
The creature lying there—

And he will tell you—skill is late—
A Mightier than He—
Has ministered before Him—
There's no Vitality.

(#396)

I think the equation surgeon-artist is a fair one here; the artist can work with the materials of pain; she cuts to probe and heal; but she is powerless at the point where

After great pain, a formal feeling comes—
The Nerves sit ceremonious, like Tombs—
The stiff Heart questions was it He, that bore,
And Yesterday, or Centuries before?

The Feet, mechanical, go round—
Of Ground, or Air, or Ought—
A Wooden way
Regardless grown,
A Quartz contentment, like a stone—

This is the Hour of Lead
Remembered, if outlived
As Freezing persons, recollect the Snow—
First—Chill—then Stupor—then the letting go—

(#341)

For the poet, the terror is precisely in those periods of psychic death, when even the possibility of work is negated; her "occupation's gone." Yet she also describes the unavailing effort to numb emotion:

Me from Myself—to banish—
Had I Art—
Impregnable my Fortress
Unto All Heart—

But since Myself—assault Me—
How have I peace
Except by subjugating
Consciousness?

And since We're mutual Monarch
How this be
Except by Abdication—
Me—of Me?

(#642)

The possibility of abdicating oneself—of ceasing to be—remains.

Severer Service of myself
I—hastened to demand
To fill the awful Longitude
Your life had left behind—

I worried Nature with my Wheels
When Hers had ceased to run—
When she had put away Her Work
My own had just begun.

I strove to weary Brain and Bone—
To harass to fatigue
The glittering Retinue of nerves—
Vitality to clog

To some dull comfort Those obtain
Who put a Head away
They knew the Hair to—
And forget the color of the Day—

Affliction would not be appeased—
The Darkness braced as firm
As all my stratagem had been
The Midnight to confirm—

No Drug for Consciousness—can be—
Alternative to die
Is Nature's only Pharmacy
For Being's Malady—

(#786)

Yet consciousness—not simply the capacity to suffer, but the capacity to experience intensely at every instant—creates of death not a blotting-out but a final illumination:

This Consciousness that is aware
Of Neighbors and the Sun
Will be the one aware of Death
And that itself alone

Is traversing the interval
Experience between
And most profound experiment
Appointed unto Men—

How adequate unto itself
Its properties shall be
Itself unto itself and none
Shall make discovery.

Adventure most unto itself
The Soul condemned to be—
Attended by a single Hound
Its own identity.

(#822)

The poet's relationship to her poetry has, it seems to me—and I am not speaking only of Emily Dickinson—a twofold nature. Poetic language—the poem on paper— is a concretization of the poetry of the world at large, the self, and the forces within the self; and those forces are rescued from formlessness, lucidified, and integrated in the act of writing poems. But there is a more ancient concept of the poet, which is that she is endowed to speak for those who do not have the gift of language, or to see for those who—for whatever reasons—are less conscious of what they are living through. It is as though the risks of the poet's existence can be put to some use beyond her own survival.

> The Province of the Saved
> Should be the Art—To save—
> Through Skill obtained in Themselves—
> The Science of the Grave
>
> No Man can understand
> But He that hath endured
> The Dissolution—in Himself—
> That Man—be qualified
>
> To qualify Despair
> To Those who failing new—
> Mistake Defeat for Death—Each time—
> Till acclimated—to—
>
> (#539)

The poetry of extreme states, the poetry of danger, can allow its readers to go further in our own awareness, take risks we might not have dared; it says, at least: "Someone has been here before."

> The Soul's distinct Connection
> With immortality
> Is best disclosed by Danger
> Or quick Calamity—
>
> As Lightning on a Landscape
> Exhibits Sheets of Place—
> Not yet suspected—but for Flash—
> And Click—and Suddenness.
>
> (#974)

> Crumbling is not an instant's Act
> A fundamental pause
> Dilapidation's processes
> Are organized Decays.
>
> 'Tis first a Cobweb on the Soul
> A Cuticle of Dust
> A Borer in the Axis
> An Elemental Rust—
>
> Ruin is formal—Devil's work
> Consecutive and slow—

Fail in an instant—no man did
Slipping—is Crash's law.

(#997)

I felt a Cleaving in my Mind
As if my Brain had split—
I tried to match it—Seam by Seam—
But could not make them fit.

The thought behind, I strove to join
Unto the thought before—
But Sequence ravelled out of Sound
Like Balls—upon a Floor.

(#937)

There are many more Emily Dickinsons than I have tried to call up here. Wherever you take hold of her, she proliferates. I wish I had time here to explore her complex sense of Truth; to follow the thread we unravel when we look at the numerous and passionate poems she wrote to or about women; to probe her ambivalent feelings about fame, a subject pursued by many male poets before her; simply to examine the poems in which she is directly apprehending the natural world. No one since the seventeenth century had reflected more variously or more probingly upon death and dying. What I have tried to do here is follow through some of the origins and consequences of her choice to be not only a poet but a woman who explored her own mind, without any of the guidelines of orthodoxy. To say "yes" to her powers was not simply a major act of nonconformity in the nineteenth century; even in our own time it has been assumed that Emily Dickinson, not patriarchal society, was "the problem." The more we come to recognize the unwritten and written laws and taboos underpinning patriarchy, the less problematical, surely, will seem the methods she chose.

Considerations for Thinking and Writing

1. If you have access to Rich's essay "When We Dead Awaken," compare her discussion of her own poetry with her discussion of Emily Dickinson's poems in "Vesuvius at Home." Comment on important similarities and differences. Explain.

2. Select two or three of Dickinson's poems and write a paper analyzing them. You may choose to include some discussion of how Rich herself sees the poems, and you may also want to note how the poems impinge on your own experience.

3. Respond to Rich's argument in "What Does a Woman Need to Know?" If you find her argument inadequate, explain why. If you agree with it, support Rich's position with additional evidence, perhaps from your personal experience. Also consider writing your own very different essay on the same topic. That is, steal Rich's title and take off in your own direction.

4. Read Nancy Mairs's essay "On Not Liking Sex." Notice how Mairs includes in that piece a revision of her earlier written views. Consider her revision, both its manner and its matter, in light of Rich's notion of re-vision as described in the headnote to Rich.

5. Compare Rich's celebration of Emily Dickinson with Didion's of Georgia O'Keeffe or Alice Walker's tribute to Zora Neale Hurston. How does each writer see her subject? What

relationship exists between writer and subject? What relationship does the writer establish between herself and the reader? Between her subject and the reader?

6. Compare the way Rich speaks of her Jewish identity with Cynthia Ozick's treatment of her own Jewish roots. Or compare the way Rich or Ozick uses her cultural identity with the ways Alice Walker or June Jordan uses her identity as a Black woman.

PHYLLIS ROSE
(b. 1942)

Phyllis Rose writes frequently about women. Her essays range from the half-dozen paragraphs of a syndicated newspaper column (the "Hers" column of *The New York Times*, for which she has written ten brief essays) to two book-length biographical studies. The pieces anthologized here, like Rose's work overall, spring from two related enthusiasms: a revaluation of women writers and a penchant for biography. "New beliefs," Rose has noted, require new facts, "with the political ferment of feminism beginning to change the way we look at 'fact,' at what is worth discussing and what is not."

Phyllis Rose was educated at Radcliffe College (B.A.), Yale University (M.A.), and Harvard University (Ph.D.). She has written essays and reviews for *The Atlantic, Vogue,* and *The Washington Post,* as well as *The New York Times.* A collection of her literary essays appeared in 1985 under the title *Writing about Women: Essays in a Renaissance.* Before that collection Rose published *Woman of Letters: A Life of Virginia Woolf* (1978) and *Parallel Lives: Five Victorian Marriages* (1984).

Rose began to read the works of women writers when she was a child. At the time she made no distinction between male and female authors, lumping together, for example, Austen and Kipling, Dumas and the Brontës. She graduated from college before "Women's Studies" courses existed. In fact, while an undergraduate English major, Rose was required to read only two women writers in four years: Jane Austen and George Eliot. Both writers, she points out, were considered masculine, Eliot for her "manly" style and Austen for her subject: power. Rose began to read the works of women writers systematically at twenty-eight, when she sought connections between her own life and mind and the lives and minds of others. She read female psychology, finding especially useful the works of Judith Bardwick and David McClelland. With the aid of these and other works, especially Virginia Woolf's *Three Guineas,* she decided that "female nature was not nature at all but a style created by cultural circumstance and historical experience." Rose explored such questions as: "Do women have a separate nature from men which should be celebrated and perpetuated? Should we aim to integrate women . . . into the structures of power: Or should we aim to cultivate their separateness?" And she realized that her own temperament tends toward the integrationist impulse—what she calls "classical feminism" as opposed to the separatist impulse of its more radical counterpart.

"Mothers and Fathers," one of Rose's "Hers" columns, provides a brief sketch of her mother, who at seventy-five still retains her blonde, blue-eyed beauty. And if she lost much of her vision to glaucoma, she nonetheless retained her power as a mother, authoritatively telling her grown-up daughter to eat her pancakes before tackling the eggs. Phyllis Rose doesn't protest. She knows that her mother, like other mothers, simply assumes it is her right to tell her daughter how to do things. She also knows that this telling is part of the unchanging order of things. More important than these brief glimpses into the dynamics of the mother-daughter relationship, however, are the feelings and memories Rose explores in the essay: guilt feelings about not doing enough along with happy memories of good times shared. Memories surface and fade, feelings rise and fall, and Rose segues from both via the essay's associative logic into a folk tale concerned with relations between parents and children in youth and old age. The tale's tart moral lingers; its reversal of roles neatly encapsulates Rose's experience.

If "Mothers and Fathers" reveals the personal side of Rose, "Nora Astorga" suggests something of her political and moral consciousness. The late Nora Astorga became a heroine of the Sandinistas by luring one of Anastasio Somoza's chief officials to his death with a promise of sexual surrender. Rose raises questions about the justifiability of Astorga's actions. Is political murder to be lauded, condoned, condemned? How is our answer influenced by our own politics? And how important is the fact of Astorga's gender? Rose suggests, through analogous situations in history and the Bible, that Astorga succeeded because she played on male expectations of female behavior. In upsetting those expectations, Astorga broke the stereotype of the female, but only temporarily, for as Rose demonstrates, stereotypes die hard. The piece, overall, shares with "Mothers and Fathers" a rather casual associative structure. It lacks the personal tone of the other essay, relying instead on literary and historical allusions coupled with social and psychological analysis to illuminate a prevalent cultural attitude.

"Tools of Torture" combines the personal narrative mode of "Mothers" with the more public and analytical discourse of "Nora Astorga." Its structure is tighter; its details are more numerous and better connected. In tone it is less bemused than "Mothers" and more ironically detached than "Nora Astorga." And perhaps in the same way as Nora Astorga's murderous behavior, Rose's graphic descriptions of torture instruments are uncharacteristic of a woman. Here, as elsewhere in her writing, Rose is self-consciously provocative. The essay derives its bite from the analogies Rose develops, especially that between torture and French cuisine. To the imagination of both torturer and chef, "nothing is unthinkable." Equally provocative is Rose's connection of pleasure with pain: the exquisite pleasure of experiencing physical pampering is made analogous to the lovingly detailed attentions torturers express toward the physical pain of their victims. But neither of these notions forms the centerpiece of her essay. That honor is reserved for a pair of ideas, one political and one personal: first, that "wherever people believe strongly in some cause, they will justify torture"; and second, that "nothing leads you less wrong than your awareness of your own pleasure." Like "Mothers" and "Nora Astorga," "Tools of Torture" reveals a tenacious mind, one that explores relationships and seizes connections, a mind that is not afraid to describe unpleasant subjects and investigate unpalatable experiences.

The prologue to *Parallel Lives* is a much more ambitious essay than the others. Written as the introduction to Rose's illuminating analysis of five Victorian marriages, the essay-prologue is concerned less with the specifically marital than with the imaginative. Rose explores the notion that "certain imaginative patterns—call them mythologies or ideologies—determine the shape of marital lives." Happy and unhappy marriages, in other words, involve respectively compatible and disjunctive imaginative reorderings of shared experience. Rose puts it this way: "Every marriage seems to me a subjectivist fiction with two points of view often deeply in conflict, sometimes fortuitously congruent."

As in her briefer essays, Rose's approach in the prologue to *Parallel Lives* is literary, sociocultural, and political, the political dimension concerned most particularly with marital power. For Rose, love is not the mortar that either holds marriages together or allows them to crumble. Neither is money or sex of supreme importance. And although religious ideals and moral concerns assume a degree of prominence, the crux of the matter is power—the balance of power, the management of power, the relative priority of desires—and along with them, exploitation, understanding, and strength.

Throughout the Prologue to *Parallel Lives* Rose explores ways in which power is negotiated in marriage. Her analytical armory includes personal experience (but only implicitly), social and cultural analysis, psychological explanation, literary and historical analogy, and philosophical speculation. At her best she manipulates these strategies in lucid prose that provokes her readers to think about what they feel, how they feel, and why.

Parallel Lives

Prologue

I believe, first of all, that living is an act of creativity and that, at certain moments of our lives, our creative imaginations are more conspicuously demanded than at others. At certain moments, the need to decide upon the story of our own lives becomes particularly pressing—when we choose a mate, for example, or embark upon a career. Decisions like that make sense, retroactively, of the past and project a meaning onto the future, knit past and future together, and create, suspended between the two, the present. Questions we have all asked of ourselves, such as Why am I doing this? or the even more basic What am I doing? suggest the way in which living forces us to look for and forces us to find a design within the primal stew of data which is our daily experience. There is a kind of arranging and telling and choosing of detail—of narration, in short—which we must do so that one day will prepare for the next day, one week prepare for the next week. In some way we all decide when we have grown up and what event will symbolize for us that state of maturity—leaving home, getting married, becoming a parent, losing our parents, making a million, writing a book. To the extent that we impose some narrative form onto our lives, each of us in the ordinary process of living is a fitful novelist, and the biographer is a literary critic.

Marriages, or parallel lives as I have chosen to call them, hold a particular fascination for the biographer-critic because they set two imaginations to work constructing narratives about experience presumed to be the same for both. In using the word *parallel*, however, I hope to call attention to the gap between the narrative lines as well as to their similarity.

An older school of literary biography was concerned to show how "life" had influenced an author's work. My own assumption is that certain imaginative patterns—call them mythologies or ideologies—determine the shape of a writer's life as well as his or her work. I therefore look for connections between the two without assuming that reality is the template for fiction—assuming, if anything, the reverse.

In first approaching this material, I looked for evidence that what people read helped form their views of their own experience. Some emerged. Jane Welsh, for example, being courted by Thomas Carlyle, derived her view of their relationship from reading *La Nouvelle Héloïse*. Dickens's management of his separation from his wife seemed influenced by the melodramas in which he was fond of acting. But what came to interest me more was the way in which every marriage was a narrative construct—or two narrative constructs. In unhappy marriages, for example, I see two versions of reality rather than two people in conflict. I see a struggle for imaginative dominance going on. Happy marriages seem to me those in which the two partners agree on the scenario they are enacting, even if, as was the case with Mr. and Mrs. Mill, their own idea of their relationship is totally at variance with the facts. I speak with great trepidation about "facts" in such matters, but, speaking loosely, the facts in the Mills' case—that a woman of strong and uncomplicated will dominated a guilt-ridden man—were less important than their shared imaginative view of the facts, that their marriage fitted their shared ideal of a marriage of equals. I assume, then, as little objective truth as possible about these parallel lives, for every marriage seems to me a subjectivist fiction with two points of view often deeply in conflict, sometimes fortuitously congruent.

That, sketchily, is the ground of my literary interest in parallel lives, but there is a political dimension as well. On the basis of family life, we form our expectations about power and powerlessness, about authority and obedience in other spheres, and in that sense the family is, as has so often been insisted, the building block of society. The idea of the family as a school for civil life goes back to the ancient Romans, and feminist criticism of the family as such a school—the charge that it is a school for despots and slaves—goes back at least to John Stuart Mill. I cite this tradition to locate, in part, my own position: like Mill, I believe marriage to be the primary political experience in which most of us engage as adults, and so I am interested in the management of power between men and women in that microcosmic relationship. Whatever the balance, every marriage is based upon some understanding, articulated or not, about the relative importance, the priority of desires, between its two partners. Marriages go bad not when love fades—love can modulate into affection without driving two people apart—but when this understanding about the balance of power breaks down, when the weaker member feels exploited or the stronger feels unrewarded for his or her strength.

People who find this a chilling way to talk about one of our most treasured human bonds will object that "power struggle" is a flawed circumstance into which relationships fall when love fails. (For some people it is impossible to discuss power without adding the word *struggle*.) I would counter by pointing out the human tendency to invoke love at moments when we want to disguise transactions involving power. Like the aged Lear handing over his kingdom to his daughters, when we resign power, or assume new power, we insist it is not happening and demand to be talked to about love. Perhaps that is what love is—the momentary or prolonged refusal to think of another person in terms of power. Like an enzyme which blocks momentarily a normal biological process, what we call love may inhibit the process of power negotiation—from which inhibition comes the illusion of equality so characteristic of lovers. If the impulse to abjure measurement and negotiation comes from within, unbidden, it is one of life's graces and blessings. But if it is culturally induced, and more particularly desired of one segment of humanity than another, then we may perhaps find it repugnant and call it a mask for exploitation. Surely, in regard to marriage, love has received its fair share of attention, power less than its share. For every social scientist discussing the family as a psychopolitical structure, for every John Stuart Mill talking about "subjection" in marriage, how many pieties are daily uttered about love? Who can resist the thought that love is the ideological bone thrown to women to distract their attention from the powerlessness of their lives? Only millions of romantics can resist it—and other millions who might see it as the bone thrown to men to distract them from the bondage of *their* lives.

In unconscious states, as we know from Freud, the mind is astonishingly fertile and inventive in its fiction-making, but in conscious states this is not so. The plots we choose to impose on our own lives are limited and limiting. And in no area are they so banal and sterile as in this of love and marriage. Nothing else being available to our imaginations, we will filter our experience through the romantic clichés with which popular culture bombards us. And because the callowness and conventionality of the plots we impose on ourselves are a betrayal of our inner richness and complexity, we feel anxious and unhappy. We may turn to therapy for help, but the plots *it* evokes, if done less than expertly, are also fairly limiting.

Easy stories drive out hard ones. Simple paradigms prevail over complicated ones. If, within marriage, power is the ability to impose one's imaginative vision and make it prevail, then power is more easily obtained if one has a simple and widely accepted paradigm at hand. The patriarchal paradigm has long enforced men's power within marriage: a man works hard to make himself worthy of a woman; they marry; he heads the family; she serves him, working to please him and care for him, getting protection in return. This plot regularly generates its opposite, the plot of female power through weakness: the woman, somehow wounded by family life, needs to be cared for and requires an offering of guilt. Mrs. Rochester, the madwoman in the attic in *Jane Eyre,* is a fairly spectacular example. The suffering female demanding care has often proved stronger than the conquering male deserving care—a dialectic of imaginative visions of which the Carlyles provide a good example—but neither side of the patriarchal paradigm seems to bring out the best in humanity. In regard to marriage, we need more and more complex plots. I reveal my literary bias in saying I believe we need literature, which, by allowing us to experience more fully, to imagine more fully, enables us to live more freely. In a pragmatic way, we can profit from an immersion in the nineteenth-century novel which took the various stages of marriage as its central subject.

We tend to talk informally about other people's marriages and to disparage our own talk as gossip. But gossip may be the beginning of moral inquiry, the low end of the platonic ladder which leads to self-understanding. We are desperate for information about how other people live because we want to know how to live ourselves, yet we are taught to see this desire as an illegitimate form of prying. If marriage is, as Mill suggested, a political experience, then discussion of it ought to be taken as seriously as talk about national elections. Cultural pressure to avoid such talk as "gossip" ought to be resisted, in a spirit of good citizenship. In that spirit, then, I offer some private lives for examination and discussion. I will try to tell these stories in such a way as to raise questions about the role of power and the nature of equality within marriage, for I assume a connection between politics and sex. In the interests of objectivity, I offer the joint lives of some Victorian men and women for whom the rules of the game were perhaps clearer than they are for us.

To many people the word *Victorian* means prudish, repressive, asexual, and little more. This popular understanding has been wholly unaffected by over two decades of scholarship which have tried to destroy the notion of a monolithic Victorian culture in Britain, pointing out, to begin with, that a span of over sixty years (Victoria ruled from 1837 to 1901) is highly resistant to responsible generalization. It has also been unaffected by a surge of memoirs, biographies, and scholarly studies, led off by Steven Marcus's *The Other Victorians,* whose goal as a group has been, speaking crudely, to show the kinky side of Victorian life. (More accurately, I'd describe Marcus's study of pornography and sexuality as aiming to suggest the tremendous amount of sexual energy which the Victorians were sublimating in the interests of civilization.) Strange and marvelous stories have come to light, a remarkable number having to do with double or hidden lives. Arthur Munby *(Munby: Man of Two Worlds),* a respectable barrister, was obsessed with working-class women, collected their life stories and photographs, and was secretly married to his household servant for many years. J. R. Ackerley *(My Father and Myself)* discovered that his father, another person of seemingly irreproachable respectability, had maintained a separate household, with second wife and children, a few blocks from the family home. But even more important to Ackerley, a homosexual, was the discovery that his father, like many other Guardsmen, had been enthusiastically homosexual in his youth.

Such books (I have mentioned a couple I found particularly absorbing) get talked about now in the amused or astonished tones children use for discussing evidence of their parents' sexuality. The comparison is appropriate, since the Victorians—or more precisely our imagined condensation of Victorian culture—still constitute our parental generation in the largest sense and we rebel against a partly real, partly invented nineteenth-century sexual code. But we are the flip side of the same pancake. If Marcus began the process of resexualizing the Victorians by suggesting the power of what they repressed, Foucault has more recently and from a more radical perspective attacked the whole notion of Victorian prudery. Whether one talks about sex encouragingly (as we do) or discouragingly (as the Victorians did) is of no significance to Foucault; the Victorians, like every generation since the eighteenth century, participated in the transformation of sex into "discourse."

When I said that the rules of the game were somewhat clearer for the Victorians than for us, I had in mind primarily the difficulty of divorce. Before the Matrimonial Causes Act of 1857, divorce was possible in England only by Act of Parliament, a process so expensive and unusual as to place it virtually out of reach of the middle class, although, in special cases such as non-consummation, annulments were possible through the ecclesiastical courts. Even after 1857, when secular courts were established to grant divorces, relatively few people could bring themselves to submit to the scandalous procedure: adultery had invariably to be one of the grounds. So these unions, however haphazardly undertaken, were intended to last for life. Comparatively, our easy recourse to divorce seems—to adopt Robert Frost's image—like playing tennis without the net. John Stuart Mill, who advocated divorce, nevertheless believed that re-marriage was an inefficient remedy for certain kinds of marital distress, those caused by the human tendency to grow unhappy in the course of years and to blame this unhappiness on one's spouse. The sufferer, after the initial elation brought by change, would reach the same point eventually with a second mate, said Mill, and at what a cost of disrupted life! It has become a story familiar enough today. But the Victorians, with no easy escape from difficult domestic situations, were forced to be more inventive.

Few were more inventive than Mill's eventual wife, Harriet Taylor, who, for twenty years, arranged to live in a virtual *ménage à trois* with her husband and Mill, a companion to both, lover to neither. Her inventiveness depended on a de-emphasis of sexual fulfillment which it requires effort to perceive as useful rather than merely pinched. But I think the effort must be made. Of the five marriages I discuss, at least two of them, and possibly a third, were sexless, and it will not do just to say "How bizarre."

In fact, scholars in our own post-liberated age who interest themselves in innovative living arrangements are beginning to discover that people a hundred years ago may have had *more* flexibility than we do now. Lillian Faderman, for example, has described with great sympathy the nineteenth-century American practice of the "Boston marriage," a long-term monogamous relationship between two women who are otherwise unmarried. The emotional and even financial advantages of such a relationship are immediately evident, whether or not—and this is something we shall never know—sex was involved. The important point is that such relationships were seen as healthy and useful. Henry James, for one, was delighted that his sister Alice had some joy in her life, in the form of her Boston marriage to Katherine Loring. But what seemed healthy and useful to the nineteenth century suddenly became "abnormal" after the impact, in the early twentieth century, of popular Freudianism. With all experience sexualized, living arrangements such as those Boston marriages could not be so easily entered upon or easily discussed; they became outlaw, suppressed, matters to hide. By the mid-1920s, it was no longer possible to mention a Boston marriage without embarrassment. By sexualizing experience, popular Freudianism had the moralistic result of limiting possibilities.

I prefer to see the sexless marriages I discuss as examples of flexibility rather than of abnormality. Some people might say they are not really marriages because they are sexless; it's a point I'd want to argue. There must be other models of marriage— of long-term association between two people—than the very narrow one we are all familiar with, beginning with a white wedding gown, leading to children, and ending in death, or, these days increasingly often, in divorce.

Many cultural circumstances worked against the likelihood of sexual satisfaction within Victorian marriages. The inflexible taboo on pre-marital sex for middle-class women meant, among other things, that it was impossible to determine sexual compatibility before marriage. The law then made the wife absolute property of her husband and sexual performance one of her duties. Imagine a young woman married to a man she finds physically repulsive. She is in the position of being raped nightly—and with the law's consent. The legendary Victorian advice about sex, "Lie back and think of England," may be seen as not entirely comical if we realize that in many cases a distaste for sex developed from a distaste for the first sexual partner and from sexual performance which was essentially forced. In addition, the absence of birth control made it impossible to separate sex from its reproductive function, so that to be sexually active meant also the discomforts of pregnancy, the pain of childbirth, and the burden of children. For men, the middle-class taboo on pre-marital sex meant sexual experience could be obtained only with prostitutes or working-class women, an early conditioning which Freud said breeds dangers in the erotic life, by encouraging a split between objects of desire and objects of respect.

We would seem to have a greater chance of happiness now. Theoretically, men and women can get to know each other in casual, relaxed circumstances before marrying. More young people feel free to sleep together, to live together before marriage. They do not have to wait until they are irrevocably joined to discover they are incompatible. Nor are they so irrevocably joined. If we discover, as we seem to, early and late, that despite all our opportunity to test compatibility, we have married someone with whom we are not compatible, we can disconnect ourselves and try again. Perhaps most important, women can hold jobs, earn a living, own property, thereby gaining a chance for some status in the family. Birth control is reliable and available, so women needn't be, quite so much as formerly, the slaves of children. Nor need men be so oppressed by the obligation of supporting large and expensive families. We can separate sex from reproduction; it can be purely a source of pleasure. If all this does not ensure that, cumulatively, we are happier in our domesticity than the Victorians, then perhaps we expect even more of our marriages than the Victorians did—perhaps we place too much of a burden on our personal relationships, as Christopher Lasch, among others, has suggested. Or perhaps the deep tendency of human nature to unhappiness is even harder to reach by legislation and technology than one might have thought.

Neither in novels nor in biographical material can I find much evidence that people of the last century placed less emphasis on their personal relationships than we do. Romantic expectations seem to know no season, except the season of life. Dickens and Carlyle offer examples of one connubial dream: that an idealized woman will reward the young man for his professional labors. Of the five Victorian couples I have written about, the Mills and the Leweses, for various reasons, expected less out of marriage and found greater satisfaction in it than the others. Temperament and ideological bent seem more important in determining happiness than whether one lived in the nineteenth or the twentieth century.

We should remind ourselves, I think, of the romantic bias in Anglo-American attitudes towards marriage, whether of the nineteenth or the twentieth century. Effie Ruskin, travelling in Italy, discovered how much more comfortable Continental ways of being married were than English. For the English assumed you loved your husband and were loved by him and wanted to be with him as much as possible, whereas the Europeans made no such extraordinary assumption. They knew they were making the best of a difficult situation often arranged by people other than the participants and for reasons quite apart from love, and so they gave each other considerable latitude. One hardly knows whether the Victorians suffered more from their lack of easy recourse to divorce or from the disappearance of the brisk assumptions of arranged marriages. At least when marriages were frankly arrangements of property, no one expected them to float on an unceasing love-tide, whereas we and the Victorians have been in the same boat on that romantic flood.

In general, the similarities between marriages then and now seem to me greater than the differences. Then as now certain problems of adjustment, focussing usually on sex or relatives, seem typical of early stages of marriage, and others, for example absence of excitement, seem typical of later stages. In good marriages then as now shared experience forms a bond increasingly important with time, making discontents seem minor. And then as now, love also tends to walk out the door when poverty flies in the window. Conditions I would have thought unreproducible today—Ruskin's total innocence of the female nude and consequent shock when confronted by one—turn out to have been reproduced in the lives of people I know. I have been reminded continually in these Victorian marriages of marriages of friends: strong women still adopt a protective coloring of weakness as George Eliot did; earnest men with strongly egalitarian politics are still subject to domination by shrews, as John Mill was; men like Dickens still divorce in middle age the wives they have used up and outdistanced; clever women like Jane Carlyle still solace themselves for their powerlessness by mocking their husbands. Moreover, attitudes towards marriage which I would have thought outdated prove not to be. Apparently it is still possible to assume that the man is without question the more important partner in a marriage. That is, the patriarchal paradigm still prevails. Indeed, as fundamentalist religion and morality revive in contemporary America's ethical vacuum, we are likely to find ourselves fighting the nineteenth-century wars of personal morality all over again. Since we have not come so far as some of us fear and some of us hope we have, people who want to legislate morality back to an imagined ideal should, at the least, learn some humility in the face of the conservatism of human nature.

Nora Astorga

Nora Astorga is a heroine of the Sandinista revolution. In 1978, when the dictator Somoza was still in power, she attracted one of his chief officials, the notoriously brutal Gen. Reynaldo Pérez Vega, second in command of the National Guard. General Pérez pursued her and she resisted until one day she called his office and left the message that something the general was very interested in and had long been asking for could be his that day. She would be at home. When he showed up she had him send away his bodyguards. In her bedroom he took off his firearms. Then he was set upon and killed by Sandinista guerrillas who had been hiding there. Later Nora Astorga sent a photo of herself in guerrilla fatigues to the newspaper *La Prensa* and took full credit for her role.

In March 1984 the Government of Nicaragua decided to appoint its Deputy Foreign Minister, Nora Astorga, as Ambassador to the United States. Last week the nomination was rejected by the State Department as inappropriate. Is she an accomplice to murder or a savior of her country? Was the action slaughter or revolutionary justice? We are willing to acknowledge that murder is sometimes justified by politics, otherwise war would be impossible. But political killing off the battlefield is morally ambiguous in the extreme. On the verge of assassinating Julius Caesar, Brutus—as imagined by Shakespeare—announces that he should be seen as a "sacrificer," not a "butcher." The ambiguity remains, however. You know the figure that from one angle looks like a vase and from another a witch? Same with Brutus: from one angle a noble idealist willing to assume the terrible guilt of murder to rid his country of a tyrant; from another a self-indulgent fool who deludes himself into thinking there is an excuse for murder.

Still, however uncomfortable we are with political murder, we recognize that it exists in a different moral category from murder for personal gain or murder from passion. How you feel about it—whether you can imagine it as justified—tends to depend on two things: how long ago it happened and whether you agree with the killer's politics. The two are connected. If the assassination took place long enough ago, you are more willing to sympathize with the assassin's cause.

In Nora Astorga's case there is another important element: She is a woman. Political murder may be more than usually problematic when a woman is implicated. Two crimes are being committed—a murder and a betrayal of expectations about female behavior.

The Bible tells the story of Jael, wife of a nomad chief, who killed the Canaanite general Sisera. After a battle in which his forces were routed by the Israelites, Sisera took shelter in the camp of Jael's husband, officially neutral but allied to the Israelites. Jael made Sisera at home in her tent, covered him with a blanket and soothed his jangled nerves with a drink of milk. When he was asleep she drove a wooden tent peg through his forehead. The next day she proudly acknowledged what she had done, and she is praised in the Book of Judges for her righteousness.

Charlotte Corday went to Paris from the provinces with the firm intention of killing Marat and thereby (she hoped) ending the Reign of Terror. She kept sending Marat requests for an appointment. He did not answer. She persevered and finally gained entry to his apartment. Marat, hearing a woman's voice, allowed her to be brought in to him. Because of an illness, he had to keep his body under water, so he was in the bath when she killed him, with a dinner knife bought the previous day. Charlotte Corday was tried for murder; when asked what she had to say in her defense she replied, "Nothing, except that I have succeeded." Composedly, she met her death by guillotine. She looked forward, she had said, to happiness with Brutus in the Elysian fields.

What is strikingly similar in the stories of Charlotte Corday, the biblical Jael and Nora Astorga is their pride in what they have done and their insistence that they be given credit for their daring. All three also play on the fact that they seem harmless to their enemies. Nora Astorga and Jael used female "hospitality" to entrap. Having played on notions of what woman is like to disarm her enemy, the revolutionary heroine involved in murder defies our notions of what a woman is. She uses stereotypes of female behavior to succeed and in succeeding overthrows the stereotypes.

Despite one's moral repugnance at any murder, the woman who murders for a cause demands respect in a way that Delilah, for example, that sneaky seductress, does not. The revolutionary murderess puts her life and her soul on the line. She fascinates because of her daring and aggressiveness. At some level many women, I believe, look for such stereotype-defying heroines, even—perhaps especially—murderesses. That is how I would explain all the interest in Jean Harris. We wanted to see her as a heroine-murderess, but she kept slipping out of the role into something much smaller, and what is ultimately interesting about the Harris case is not Mrs. Harris but the public's response—its fascination.

A Freudian would say that we are fascinated with female assassins because they represent our deepest fears. I would amend that to say "men's deepest fears." Men—the more macho, the more innocent—go into sexual encounters assuming the harmlessness and passivity of their partners. Women are trained to be wary of them. An aggressive sexual partner is no more than most women expect. An aggressive—even murderously aggressive—female is no deep fear of most women. Men have much more to fear from aggressive women than women do.

As we also know from Freud, the things we fear most we tend to joke about the most. Perhaps this explains the extraordinary levity with which the American press has tended to treat the appointment of Nora Astorga. *Time* captioned its picture of her "experienced hostess" and ended an article on her appointment with a quotation from a United States diplomat: "There's a limit to how close I'd get to her." A *New York Times* editorial titled "Femme Fatale" compared her to Marlene Dietrich in several film roles and expressed regret that Josef von Sternberg was not around to direct her.

A woman warrior takes up an enemy general's offer to go to bed with him and helps kill him instead. To some people that's the stuff of which legends are made, to others jokes. I, for one, wonder if a male version of Nora Astorga—a former revolutionary terrorist appointed Ambassador to the United States—would be treated with such levity.

Mothers and Fathers

My mother has always said: "The daughters come back to you eventually. When the sons go they're gone." She has other favorite sayings—"A father's not a mother," "The beginning is the half of all things," and "De gustibus non disputandum est," which she translated as "That's what makes horse races"—all of which have become increasingly meaningful to me with time. Recently I told her that she was right in a fight we had twenty-seven years ago about which language I should study in high school. This came up because I had just had the same discussion with my son and took the side my mother took then (French). She laughed when I told her that she was right twenty-seven years ago. There have been more and more nice moments like that with my mother as we both grow older.

She is seventy-five, ash blond, blue-eyed, a beauty. When my father died three years ago she suddenly developed glaucoma and lost a lot of her vision. She says she literally "cried her eyes out." She can read only very slowly, with the help of a video enhancer supplied by the Lighthouse for the Blind. Nevertheless, her lipstick is always perfect. She doesn't use a mirror. She raises her hand to her lips and applies it. When I praise her for this, she says, "By now I should know where my mouth is."

She doesn't walk alone at night and during the day rarely gets beyond the area she can reach on foot, between 50th and 60th streets, First Avenue and Fifth. She loves to transgress those boundaries, so when I come in from Connecticut I usually pick her up in my car and drive her to distant parts of Manhattan: the Lower East Side, the Seaport, TriBeCa, SoHo, the Village. One of our favorite things to do together is to have Sunday brunch at a restaurant on West Broadway near Houston Street. We go there especially for the pecan pancakes and the scrambled eggs with salmon and dill.

One day this winter we went there for Sunday brunch. It was a particularly cold day and I was suffering from a pulled muscle in my neck. I walked with one shoulder higher than the other. My mother walked slowly and with a slight stoop. But as soon as we entered the door, the restaurant buoyed us up. We were patrons, to be pampered. We had a reservation. We could share in the general atmosphere of youth, energy, chic, competence, success. The waiters were stylishly dressed with an accent of the 1940's. This was SoHo.

One young man, wearing a plaid shirt and pinch-pleated trousers, showed us to a table in a bright front section overlooking the sidewalk. This was excellent for my mother, who often finds restaurants too dark and carries a spelunker's light to read menus by. But we didn't need a menu; we ordered pecan pancakes and scrambled eggs with salmon and dill. When they arrived we split them and I began with the eggs. "Eat the pancakes first," my mother said. I didn't ask why. She's my mother. She has to tell me how to do things.

Three beautiful women dressed in black who were eating lunch at a table nearby finished eating, cleared their table and moved it aside. From the corner they took a cello, a violin and a flute, removed their covers and positioned themselves to play. They started with Schubert and went on to a medley of Strauss waltzes. My spirits soared. I looked at my mother to see if she was listening to the music. She was. I could see she was as ravished by it as I was, and for the same reason. Without exchanging a word both of us moved simultaneously thirty years backward in our minds and to another place.

"Palm Beach," I said.

My mother nodded. "Hoops, crinolines, strapless dresses with net skirts, white fox stoles. Each of us took three suitcases. Those days are gone forever."

In the 1950's my father, in his proud and powerful middle age, took my mother, my brother, my sister and me to Palm Beach for two weeks every winter until just after New Year's Day. We stayed at a hotel called the Whitehall; its core was originally the mansion of Henry F. Flagler, the railroad man and Florida pioneer. The lobby had floors of inlaid marble and variegated marble pillars.

The Whitehall dining room was a gigantic sunken area that, family legend said, was Mr. Flagler's indoor swimming pool. Whether it was or not didn't matter then, doesn't now. It was a magical place. The families as they came in for dinner and took their usual places were brilliantly dressed: fathers in the light-colored raw silk jackets appropriate for the South; mothers in strapless dresses with wide skirts supported by hoops and crinolines; children, after a day on the beach and the tennis courts, scraped, peeling, but burnished for dinner. Nothing was casual. The hotel hairdresser was heavily booked. Elaborate sets and comb-outs several times a week were not unusual. Jewelry was not left in the vault at home. The room sparkled. There was general splendor, the result of all that effort and the discipline of dressing for dinner. And at the center of the room a quintet in black formal clothes played music throughout the four-course meal. Every night, usually during the clear consommé, they played a medley of Strauss waltzes.

* * *

My mother and I are tied together because we share the same memories. My brother and sister share them, too. We are a family because the Whitehall, a certain dude ranch in the Great Smokies, the layout of our house on Central Avenue and other recondite geographies exist in our minds and no others. We move in the same mental spaces. In some of our dreams we wander the same streets, trying to get back to the same house. One form of loneliness is to have a memory and no one to share it with. If, in twenty years, I want to reminisce about Sunday brunch in a certain SoHo restaurant I may have nobody to reminisce with. That will be lonely.

Often I feel I do not do enough for my mother. When I read *King Lear* I realize that I'd be flattering myself to identify with Cordelia. I have the awful suspicion that I am much more like Regan or Goneril—from Lear's point of view monsters of ingratitude; from their own just two women taking their turn at the top, enjoying their middle-aged supremacy. When these guilty thoughts afflict me a folk tale comes to mind.

There once was a bird with three young to carry across a river. She put the first on her back and, halfway across, asked, "Will you care for me in my old age as I have cared for you?" "Yes, Mama," said the first bird, and the mother dumped him in the river, calling him a liar. Second bird, same result. "Will you care for me in my old age as I have cared for you?" "Yes." "Liar." But the third bird, asked if he would care for his mother in her old age as she had cared for him, answered: "I can't promise that. I can only promise to care for my own children as you have cared for me."

It's a truthful response and it satisfied the mother bird, a philosophic spirit if ever there was one. But when I imagine my son saying the same thing to me—"I can only promise to care for my own children as you have cared for me"—I don't seem to find much comfort in it.

Tools of Torture: An Essay on Beauty and Pain

In a gallery off the rue Dauphine, near the *parfumerie* where I get my massage, I happened upon an exhibit of medieval torture instruments. It made me think that pain must be as great a challenge to the human imagination as pleasure. Otherwise there's no accounting for the number of torture instruments. One would be quite enough. The simple pincer, let's say, which rips out flesh. Or the head crusher, which breaks first your tooth sockets, then your skull. But in addition I saw tongs, thumbscrews, a rack, a ladder, ropes and pulleys, a grill, a garrote, a Spanish horse, a Judas cradle, an iron maiden, a cage, a gag, a strappado, a stretching table, a saw, a wheel, a twisting stork, an inquisitor's chair, a breast breaker, and a scourge. You don't need complicated machinery to cause incredible pain. If you want to saw your victim down the middle, for example, all you need is a slightly bigger than usual saw. If you hold the victim upside down so the blood stays in his head, hold his legs apart, and start sawing at the groin, you can get as far as the navel before he loses consciousness.

Even in the Middle Ages, before electricity, there were many things you could do to torment a person. You could tie him up in an iron belt that held the arms and legs up to the chest and left no point of rest, so that all his muscles went into spasm within minutes and he was driven mad within hours. This was the twisting stork, a benign-looking object. You could stretch him out backward over a thin piece of wood so that his whole body weight rested on his spine, which pressed against the sharp wood. Then you could stop up his nostrils and force water into his stomach through his mouth. Then, if you wanted to finish him off, you and your helper could jump on his stomach, causing internal hemorrhage. This torture was called the rack. If you wanted to burn someone to death without hearing him scream, you could use a tongue lock, a metal rod between the jaw and collarbone that prevented him from opening his mouth. You could put a person in a chair with spikes on the seat and arms, tie him down against the spikes, and beat him, so that every time he flinched from the beating he drove his own flesh deeper onto the spikes. This was the inquisitor's chair. If you wanted to make it worse, you could heat the spikes. You could suspend a person over a pointed wooden pyramid and whenever he started to fall asleep, you could drop him onto the point. If you were Ippolito Marsili, the inventor of this torture, known as the Judas cradle, you could tell yourself you had invented something humane, a torture that worked without burning flesh or breaking bones. For the torture here was supposed to be sleep deprivation.

The secret of torture, like the secret of French cuisine, is that nothing is unthinkable. The human body is like a foodstuff, to be grilled, pounded, filleted. Every opening exists to be stuffed, all flesh to be carved off the bone. You take an ordinary wheel, a heavy wooden wheel with spokes. You lay the victim on the ground with blocks of wood at strategic points under his shoulders, legs, and arms. You use the wheel to break every bone in his body. Next you tie his body onto the wheel. With all its bones broken, it will be pliable. However, the victim will not be dead. If you want to kill him, you hoist the wheel aloft on the end of a pole and leave him to starve. Who would have thought to do this with a man and a wheel? But, then, who would have thought to take the disgusting snail, force it to render its ooze, stuff it in its own shell with garlic butter, bake it, and eat it?

Not long ago I had a facial—only in part because I thought I needed one. It was research into the nature and function of pleasure. In a dark booth at the back of the beauty salon, the aesthetician put me on a table and applied a series of ointments to my face, some cool, some warmed. After a while she put something into my hand, cold and metallic. "Don't be afraid, madame," she said. "It is an electrode. It will not hurt you. The other end is attached to two metal cylinders, which I roll over your face. They break down the electricity barrier on your skin and allow the moisturizers to penetrate deeply." I didn't believe this hocus-pocus. I didn't believe in the electricity barrier or in the ability of these rollers to break it down. But it all felt very good. The cold metal on my face was a pleasant change from the soft warmth of the aesthetician's fingers. Still, since Algeria it's hard to hear the word "electrode" without fear. So when she left me for a few minutes with a moist, refreshing cheesecloth over my face, I thought, What if the goal of her expertise had been pain, not moisture? What if the electrodes had been electrodes in the Algerian sense? What if the cheesecloth mask were dipped in acid?

In Paris, where the body is so pampered, torture seems particularly sinister, not because it's hard to understand but because—as the dark side of sensuality—it seems so easy. Beauty care is among the glories of Paris. *Soins esthétiques* include makeup, facials, massages (both relaxing and reducing), depilations (partial and complete), manicures, pedicures, and tanning, in addition to the usual run of *soins* for the hair: cutting, brushing, setting, waving, styling, blowing, coloring, and streaking. In Paris the state of your skin, hair, and nerves is taken seriously, and there is little of the puritanical thinking that tries to persuade us that beauty comes from within. Nor do the French think, as Americans do, that beauty should be offhand and low-maintenance. Spending time and money on *soins esthétiques* is appropriate and necessary, not self-indulgent. Should that loving attention to the body turn malevolent, you have torture. You have the procedure—the aesthetic, as it were—of torture, the explanation for the rich diversity of torture instruments, but you do not have the cause.

Historically torture has been a tool of legal systems, used to get information needed for a trial or, more directly, to determine guilt or innocence. In the Middle Ages confession was considered the best of all proofs, and torture was the way to produce a confession. In other words, torture didn't come into existence to give vent to human sadism. It is not always private and perverse but sometimes social and institutional, vetted by the government and, of course, the Church. (There have been few bigger fans of torture than Christianity and Islam.) Righteousness, as much as viciousness, produces torture. There aren't squads of sadists beating down the doors to the torture chambers begging for jobs. Rather, as a recent book on torture by Edward Peters says, the institution of torture creates sadists; the weight of a culture, Peters suggests, is necessary to recruit torturers. You have to convince people that they are working for a great goal in order to get them to overcome their repugnance to the task of causing physical pain to another person. Usually the great goal is the preservation of society, and the victim is presented to the torturer as being in some way out to destroy it.

From another point of view, what's horrifying is how easily you can persuade someone that he is working for the common good. Perhaps the most appalling psychological experiment of modern times, by Stanley Milgram, showed that ordinary, decent people in New Haven, Connecticut, could be brought to the point of inflicting (as they thought) severe electric shocks on other people in obedience to an authority and in pursuit of a goal, the advancement of knowledge, of which they approved. Milgram used—some would say abused—the prestige of science and the university to make his point, but his point is chilling nonetheless. We can cluck over torture, but the evidence at least suggests that with intelligent handling most of us could be brought to do it ourselves.

In the Middle Ages, Milgram's experiment would have had no point. It would have shocked no one that people were capable of cruelty in the interest of something they believed in. That was as it should be. Only recently in the history of human thought has the avoidance of cruelty moved to the forefront of ethics. "Putting cruelty first," as Judith Shklar says in *Ordinary Vices,* is comparatively new. The belief that the "pursuit of happiness" is one of man's inalienable rights, the idea that "cruel and unusual punishment" is an evil in itself, the Benthamite notion that behavior should be guided by what will produce the greatest happiness for the greatest number—all these principles are only two centuries old. They were born with the eighteenth-century democratic revolutions. And in two hundred years they have not been universally accepted. Wherever people believe strongly in some cause, they will justify torture—not just the Nazis, but the French in Algeria.

Many people who wouldn't hurt a fly have annexed to fashion the imagery of torture—the thongs and spikes and metal studs—hence reducing it to the frivolous and transitory. Because torture has been in the mainstream and not on the margins of history, nothing could be healthier. For torture to be merely kinky would be a big advance. Exhibitions like the one I saw in Paris, which presented itself as educational, may be guilty of pandering to the tastes they deplore. Solemnity may be the wrong tone. If taking one's goals too seriously is the danger, the best discouragement of torture may be a radical hedonism that denies that any goal is worth the means, that refuses to allow the nobly abstract to seduce us from the sweetness of the concrete. Give people a good croissant and a good cup of coffee in the morning. Give them an occasional facial and a plate of escargots. Marie Antoinette picked a bad moment to say "Let them eat cake," but I've often thought she was on the right track.

All of which brings me back to Paris, for Paris exists in the imagination of much of the world as the capital of pleasure—of fun, food, art, folly, seduction, gallantry, and beauty. Paris is civilization's reminder to itself that nothing leads you less wrong than your awareness of your own pleasure and a genial desire to spread it around. In that sense the myth of Paris constitutes a moral touchstone, standing for the selfish frivolity that helps keep priorities straight.

Considerations for Thinking and Writing

1. Compare Phyllis Rose's views on power in marriage, as expressed in the prologue to *Parallel Lives* and in "Mothers and Fathers," with Adrienne Rich's perspective on power in "What Does a Woman Need to Know?"

2. Compare Rose's remarks on pleasure and pain with the perspective offered by Angela Carter in her essay on body tattooing, "People as Pictures."

3. Read the end of Rose's "Tools of Torture," especially her comments on torture as a political weapon. Relate Rose's comments to Didion's description of San Salvador.

4. Compare Rose's comments on mothers and fathers with two of the following: Carter's "Mother Lode"; Dillard's "Mother" from *An American Childhood*"; Ozick's "On Excellence"; and Walker's "In Search of Our Mothers' Gardens."

5. Given a continuum of political perspectives from ultraconservative to radical feminist, where would you place Phyllis Rose, and why?

6. Enter the debate Rose describes in her essay on Nora Astorga. Consider what Astorga did and how she accomplished it. After considering Rose's argument about this event, develop your own set of reflections on the issue.

7. Discuss Rose's idea that every marriage is a fictionalized reconstruction of a shared past. To what extent can her idea be applied to the lives of individuals? If you agree that we tend to make up or remake our past to form a coherent image of ourselves, perhaps even a myth of our lives, do you see this tendency as something useful or destructive, something avoidable or inevitable? Explain.

SUSAN SONTAG
(b. 1933)

Susan Sontag is generally recognized as one of America's leading intellectuals. She has a reputation for writing and lecturing with incisive analysis. Her essays, crafted less as works of literary art than as engaging forays into thought, exemplify Francis Bacon's distinction between probative and magistral thinking. Probative thought is thought unfinished, thought still being formulated. Magistral thinking is finished thought, thought that provides a sense of certainty and conclusiveness. Although Sontag's writing includes quotable aphoristic statements, it is designed more to provoke thought than to conclude it, to explore ideas rather than explain them. The forms of her essays, moreover, often reflect her restlessly inquiring mind.

Her essay "A Woman's Beauty" provides an opportunity to watch her mind at work and to listen to her distinctive voice. First, there is the historical perspective that Sontag frequently provides. In her consideration of beauty—in her argument against the dangerous and limiting ideals to which women have been subjected through the backhanded praise of their beauty—Sontag touches on Greek and Christian perspectives. To recognize this historical interest, however, is not to suggest that this is a historical essay. It is not. Sontag does not trace, for example, the historical development of the idea of beauty in Western culture. She does not explain the various subspecies of beauty that emerged in the history of Western art. Instead she seizes on an important attitude toward beauty reflected in Greek and Christian perspectives—an attitude that can be used to comment on women's beauty today. Sontag is concerned not with the past in and of itself but with how the past can help us understand the present. Her concern is with the way ideas affect the modern world.

A second important characteristic of this essay and of Sontag's writing in general is its lack of autobiographical impulse. Whereas Joan Didion, Nancy Mairs, or Alice Walker would almost certainly discuss her own physical appearance, importing personal experience directly into her essay, Sontag assiduously avoids the personal note. To include it even without dwelling on it would be to distract us from her primary concern: how the current conception of "woman's beauty" skews our perception of women in culturally significant and socially destructive ways.

While not all of Sontag's characteristic habits of thinking in writing appear in "A Woman's Beauty," one additional feature does: her thoughtfulness. Even in such a brief essay (written originally, by the way, for readers of *Vogue* magazine) Sontag writes for the thinking reader. She is concerned with ideas, especially with their effects on present cultural perspectives. Neither aesthetician, philosopher, nor historian, Susan Sontag measures and evaluates the impact of ideas on contemporary life; she examines their force, their significance, and their influence. Such concerns give her cultural criticism its intellectual edge.

Susan Sontag was born in 1933 in New York City. After studying at the University of California at Berkeley, she earned a B.A. in philosophy from the University of Chicago (1951) at the age of eighteen. Four years later, after studying religion at Union Theological Seminary, she was awarded two master's degrees, one in English in 1954 and another in philosophy in 1955, both from Harvard University. She continued her studies abroad at St. Anne's College, Oxford, and at the Sorbonne in Paris. From the other side of the desk, her intellectual experience has included extensive lecturing and the teaching of religion, writing, and philosophy at Columbia and Rutgers universities and at the City University of New York. Her reputation as a formidable polemicist and rigorous intellectual has been augmented by her many articles and reviews in such publications as *Harper's, The Atlantic, Partisan Review,* and the *New York Review of Books.*

Sontag is a writer with a taste for ideas. In the same way that writers and readers demonstrate a proclivity toward particular kinds of fashions, films, literature, music, and art, and as they incline toward certain forms of politics, morality, or behavior, so may they possess a love for ideas. Sontag's most persistent writerly trait seems to be just this pronounced taste for ideas, which—as she suggested in one of her early essays, "Notes on Camp"—is really a form of intelligence. Sontag's taste in ideas, moreover, runs both wide and deep, and her intellectual interests are clearly reflected in the scope of her writing. Her three collections of essays, *Against Interpretation* (1966), *Styles of Radical Will* (1969), and *Under the Sign of Saturn* (1980), include essays about science fiction, disaster films, and contemporary theater; Marxism, fascism, and revolutionary politics; pornography and violence; and recent European intellectual fashions. She has written book-length essays on the Vietnam war (*Trip to Hanoi,* 1969), on photography (*On Photography,* 1976), and on disease (*Illness as Metaphor,* 1978; *AIDS and Its Metaphors,* 1989). She has also written two novels—*The Benefactor* (1963) and *Death Kit* (1967)—and a volume of short stories, *I etcetera* (1978). In addition, she has directed three films and several theatrical productions.

To enter Susan Sontag's intellectual world, we can attend to the way she talks about the writers and thinkers she admires. One promising place to begin is with the title of Sontag's essay on Elias Canetti, a modern Bulgarian-born writer and intellectual who wrote in German. Sontag titled her tribute to Canetti "Mind as Passion," partly because Canetti, at sixteen, decided to try to learn everything possible, something Sontag herself may give the impression she has also attempted; perhaps also because the word "passion" conveys Sontag's as well as Canetti's absorption in the act of thinking and the fate of ideas. "Passion," furthermore, suggests both the thinker alive in a state of excitement and the thinker as intellectual sensualist, as someone whose thinking is also a kind of feeling, whose interest in ideas also reveals an intense excitement about them. Conversely, Sontag believes that when a writer celebrates sensation as feeling, he or she should not betray the mind. For Sontag, Roland Barthes was such a writer. Like Canetti and Barthes, and like Paul Goodman, another of her intellectual heroes, Susan Sontag has cast a wide intellectual net and pulled it deeply through the seas of thought. But lest this image give the impression that her writing or thinking is overly academic or intellectually precious, we adduce her own words attesting to her affection for the work of Paul Goodman:

> There is no living American writer for whom I have felt the same simple curiosity to read as quickly as possible anything he wrote, on any subject. That I mostly agreed with what he thought was not the main reason; there are other writers I agree with who are not so loyal. It was his voice that seduced me. . . . It was his voice . . . his intelligence and the poetry of his intelligence incarnated, which kept me a loyal and passionate addict. . . . His writing and his mind were touched with grace.

This passionate tribute evokes Sontag's desire to write in a distinctive voice that conveys the power of the mind at work in the world of ideas. At her most eloquent Susan Sontag achieves this desire, thereby earning the praise she accords Paul Goodman. In the process her own mind and writing are similarly touched with grace.

In Plato's Cave

Humankind lingers unregenerately in Plato's cave, still reveling, its age-old habit, in mere images of the truth. But being educated by photographs is not like being educated by older, more artisanal images. For one thing, there are a great many more images around, claiming our attention. The inventory started in 1839 and since then just about everything has been photographed, or so it seems. This very insatiability of the photographing eye changes the terms of confinement in the cave, our world. In teaching us a new visual code, photographs alter and enlarge our notions of what is worth looking at and what we have a right to observe. They are a grammar and, even more important, an ethics of seeing. Finally, the most grandiose result of the photographic enterprise is to give us the sense that we can hold the whole world in our heads—as an anthology of images.

To collect photographs is to collect the world. Movies and television programs light up walls, flicker, and go out; but with still photographs the image is also an object, lightweight, cheap to produce, easy to carry about, accumulate, store. In Godard's *Les Carabiniers* (1963), two sluggish lumpen-peasants are lured into join-ing the King's Army by the promise that they will be able to loot, rape, kill, or do whatever else they please to the enemy, and get rich. But the suitcase of booty that Michael-Ange and Ulysse triumphantly bring home, years later, to their wives turns out to contain only picture postcards, hundreds of them, of Monuments, Depart-ment Stores, Mammals, Wonders of Nature, Methods of Transport, Works of Art, and other classified treasures from around the globe. Godard's gag vividly parodies the equivocal magic of the photographic image. Photographs are perhaps the most mysterious of all the objects that make up, and thicken, the environment we recognize as modern. Photographs really are experience captured, and the camera is the ideal arm of consciousness in its acquisitive mood.

To photograph is to appropriate the thing photographed. It means putting oneself into a certain relation to the world that feels like knowledge—and, therefore, like power. A now notorious first fall into alienation, habituating people to abstract the world into printed words, is supposed to have engendered that surplus of Faustian energy and psychic damage needed to build modern, inorganic societies. But print seems a less treacherous form of leaching out the world, of turning it into a mental object, than photographic images, which now provide most of the knowledge people have about the look of the past and the reach of the present. What is written about a person or an event is frankly an interpretation, as are handmade visual statements, like paintings and drawings. Photographed images do not seem to be statements about the world so much as pieces of it, miniatures of reality that anyone can make or acquire.

Photographs, which fiddle with the scale of the world, themselves get reduced, blown up, cropped, retouched, doctored, tricked out. They age, plagued by the usual ills of paper objects; they disappear; they become valuable, and get bought and sold; they are reproduced. Photographs, which package the world, seem to invite packag-ing. They are stuck in albums, framed and set on tables, tacked on walls, projected as slides. Newspapers and magazines feature them; cops alphabetize them; museums exhibit them; publishers compile them.

For many decades the book has been the most influential way of arranging (and usually miniaturizing) photographs, thereby guaranteeing them longevity, if not immortality—photographs are fragile objects, easily torn or mislaid—and a wider public. The photograph in a book is, obviously, the image of an image. But since it is, to begin with, a printed, smooth object, a photograph loses much less of its essential quality when reproduced in a book than a painting does. Still, the book is not a wholly satisfactory scheme for putting groups of photographs into general circulation. The sequence in which the photographs are to be looked at is proposed by the order of pages, but nothing holds readers to the recommended order or indicates the amount of time to be spent on each photograph. Chris Marker's film, *Si j'avais quatre dromadaires* (1966), a brilliantly orchestrated meditation on photographs of all sorts and themes, suggests a subtler and more rigorous way of packaging (and enlarging) still photographs. Both the order and the exact time for looking at each photograph are imposed; and there is a gain in visual legibility and emotional impact. But photographs transcribed in a film cease to be collectable objects, as they still are when served up in books.

Photographs furnish evidence. Something we hear about, but doubt, seems proven when we're shown a photograph of it. In one version of its utility, the camera record incriminates. Starting with their use by the Paris police in the murderous roundup of Communards in June 1871, photographs became a useful tool of modern states in the surveillance and control of their increasingly mobile populations. In another version of its utility, the camera record justifies. A photograph passes for incontrovertible proof that a given thing happened. The picture may distort; but there is always a presumption that something exists, or did exist, which is like what's in the picture. Whatever the limitations (through amateurism) or pretensions (through artistry) of the individual photographer, a photograph—any photograph—seems to have a more innocent, and therefore more accurate, relation to visible reality than do other mimetic objects. Virtuosi of the noble image like Alfred Stieglitz and Paul Strand, composing mighty, unforgettable photographs decade after decade, still want, first of all, to show something "out there," just like the Polaroid owner for whom photographs are a handy, fast form of note-taking, or the shutterbug with a Brownie who takes snapshots as souvenirs of daily life.

While a painting or a prose description can never be other than a narrowly selective interpretation, a photograph can be treated as a narrowly selective transparency. But despite the presumption of veracity that gives all photographs authority, interest, seductiveness, the work that photographers do is no generic exception to the usually shady commerce between art and truth. Even when photographers are most concerned with mirroring reality, they are still haunted by tacit imperatives of taste and conscience. The immensely gifted members of the Farm Security Administration photographic project of the late 1930s (among them Walker Evans, Dorothea Lange, Ben Shahn, Russell Lee) would take dozens of frontal pictures of one of their sharecropper subjects until satisfied that they had gotten just the right look on film—the precise expression on the subject's face that supported their own notions about poverty, light, dignity, texture, exploitation, and geometry. In deciding how a picture should look, in preferring one exposure to another, photographers are always imposing standards on their subjects. Although there is a sense in which the camera does indeed capture reality, not just interpret it, photographs are as much an interpretation of the world as paintings and drawings are. Those occasions when the taking of photographs is relatively undiscriminating, promiscuous, or self-effacing do not lessen the didacticism of the whole enterprise. This very passivity—and ubiquity—of the photographic record is photography's "message," its aggression.

Images which idealize (like most fashion and animal photography) are no less aggressive than work which makes a virtue of plainness (like class pictures, still lifes of the bleaker sort, and mug shots). There is an aggression implicit in every use of the camera. This is as evident in the 1840s and 1850s, photography's glorious first two decades, as in all the succeeding decades, during which technology made possible an ever increasing spread of that mentality which looks at the world as a set of potential photographs. Even for such early masters as David Octavius Hill and Julia Margaret Cameron, who used the camera as a means of getting painterly images, the point of taking photographs was a vast departure from the aims of painters. From its start, photography implied the capture of the largest possible number of subjects. Painting never had so imperial a scope. The subsequent industrialization of camera technology only carried out a promise inherent in photography from its very beginning: to democratize all experiences by translating them into images.

That age when taking photographs required a cumbersome and expensive contraption—the toy of the clever, the wealthy, and the obsessed—seems remote indeed from the era of sleek pocket cameras that invite anyone to take pictures. The first cameras, made in France and England in the early 1840s, had only inventors and buffs to operate them. Since there were then no professional photographers, there could not be amateurs either, and taking photographs had no clear social use; it was a gratuitous, that is, an artistic activity, though with few pretensions to being an art. It was only with its industrialization that photography came into its own as art. As industrialization provided social uses for the operations of the photographer, so the reaction against these uses reinforced the self-consciousness of photography-as-art.

Recently, photography has become almost as widely practiced an amusement as sex and dancing—which means that, like every mass art form, photography is not practiced by most people as an art. It is mainly a social rite, a defense against anxiety, and a tool of power.

Memorializing the achievements of individuals considered as members of families (as well as of other groups) is the earliest popular use of photography. For at least a century, the wedding photograph has been as much a part of the ceremony as the prescribed verbal formulas. Cameras go with family life. According to a sociological study done in France, most households have a camera, but a household with children is twice as likely to have at least one camera as a household in which there are no children. Not to take pictures of one's children, particularly when they are small, is a sign of parental indifference, just as not turning up for one's graduation picture is a gesture of adolescent rebellion.

Through photographs, each family constructs a portrait-chronicle of itself—a portable kit of images that bears witness to its connectedness. It hardly matters what activities are photographed so long as photographs get taken and are cherished. Photography becomes a rite of family life just when, in the industrializing countries of Europe and America, the very institution of the family starts undergoing radical surgery. As that claustrophobic unit, the nuclear family, was being carved out of a much larger family aggregate, photography came along to memorialize, to restate symbolically, the imperiled continuity and vanishing extendedness of family life. Those ghostly traces, photographs, supply the token presence of the dispersed relatives. A family's photograph album is generally about the extended family—and, often, is all that remains of it.

As photographs give people an imaginary possession of a past that is unreal, they also help people to take possession of space in which they are insecure. Thus, photography develops in tandem with one of the most characteristic of modern activities: tourism. For the first time in history, large numbers of people regularly travel out of their habitual environments for short periods of time. It seems positively unnatural to travel for pleasure without taking a camera along. Photographs will offer indisputable evidence that the trip was made, that the program was carried out, that fun was had. Photographs document sequences of consumption carried on outside the view of family, friends, neighbors. But dependence on the camera, as the device that makes real what one is experiencing, doesn't fade when people travel more. Taking photographs fills the same need for the cosmopolitans accumulating photograph-trophies of their boat trip up the Albert Nile or their fourteen days in China as it does for lower-middle-class vacationers taking snapshots of the Eiffel Tower or Niagara Falls.

A way of certifying experience, taking photographs is also a way of refusing it—by limiting experience to a search for the photogenic, by converting experience into an image, a souvenir. Travel becomes a strategy for accumulating photographs. The very activity of taking pictures is soothing, and assuages general feelings of disorientation that are likely to be exacerbated by travel. Most tourists feel compelled to put the camera between themselves and whatever is remarkable that they encounter. Unsure of other responses, they take a picture. This gives shape to experience: stop, take a photograph, and move on. The method especially appeals to people handicapped by a ruthless work ethic—Germans, Japanese, and Americans. Using a camera appeases the anxiety which the work-driven feel about not working when they are on vacation and supposed to be having fun. They have something to do that is like a friendly imitation of work: they can take pictures.

People robbed of their past seem to make the most fervent picture takers, at home and abroad. Everyone who lives in an industrialized society is obliged gradually to give up the past, but in certain countries, such as the United States and Japan, the break with the past has been particularly traumatic. In the early 1970s, the fable of the brash American tourist of the 1950s and 1960s, rich with dollars and Babbittry, was replaced by the mystery of the group-minded Japanese tourist, newly released from his island prison by the miracle of overvalued yen, who is generally armed with two cameras, one on each hip.

Photography has become one of the principal devices for experiencing something, for giving an appearance of participation. One full-page ad shows a small group of people standing pressed together, peering out of the photograph, all but one looking stunned, excited, upset. The one who wears a different expression holds a camera to his eye; he seems self-possessed, is almost smiling. While the others are passive, clearly alarmed spectators, having a camera has transformed one person into something active, a voyeur: only he has mastered the situation. What do these people see? We don't know. And it doesn't matter. It is an Event: something worth seeing—and therefore worth photographing. The ad copy, white letters across the dark lower third of the photograph like news coming over a teletype machine, consists of just six words: ". . . Prague . . . Woodstock . . . Vietnam . . . Sapporo . . . Londonderry . . . LEICA." Crushed hopes, youth antics, colonial wars, and winter sports are alike—are equalized by the camera. Taking photographs has set up a chronic voyeuristic relation to the world which levels the meaning of all events.

A photograph is not just the result of an encounter between an event and a photographer; picture-taking is an event in itself, and one with ever more peremptory rights—to interfere with, to invade, or to ignore whatever is going on. Our very sense of situation is now articulated by the camer's interventions. The omnipresence of cameras persuasively suggests that time consists of interesting events, events worth photographing. This, in turn, makes it easy to feel that any event, once under way, and whatever its moral character, should be allowed to complete itself—so that something else can be brought into the world, the photograph. After the event has ended, the picture will still exist, conferring on the event a kind of immortality (and importance) it would never otherwise have enjoyed. While real people are out there killing themselves or other real people, the photographer stays behind his or her camera, creating a tiny element of another world: the image-world that bids to outlast us all.

Photographing is essentially an act of non-intervention. Part of the horror of such memorable coups of contemporary photojournalism as the pictures of a Vietnamese bonze reaching for the gasoline can, of a Bengali guerrilla in the act of bayoneting a trussed-up collaborator, comes from the awareness of how plausible it has become, in situations where the photographer has the choice between a photograph and a life, to choose the photograph. The person who intervenes cannot record; the person who is recording cannot intervene. Dziga Vertov's great film, *Man with a Movie Camera* (1929), gives the ideal image of the photographer as someone in perpetual movement, someone moving through a panorama of disparate events with such agility and speed that any intervention is out of the question. Hitchcock's *Rear Window* (1954) gives the complementary image: the photographer played by James Stewart has an intensified relation to one event, through his camera, precisely because he has a broken leg and is confined to a wheelchair; being temporarily immobilized prevents him from acting on what he sees, and makes it even more important to take pictures. Even if incompatible with intervention in a physical sense, using a camera is still a form of participation. Although the camera is an observation station, the act of photographing is more than passive observing. Like sexual voyeurism, it is a way of at least tacitly, often explicitly, encouraging whatever is going on to keep on happening. To take a picture is to have an interest in things as they are, in the status quo remaining unchanged (at least for as long as it takes to get a "good" picture), to be in complicity with whatever makes a subject interesting, worth photographing—including, when that is the interest, another person's pain or misfortune.

"I always thought of photography as a naughty thing to do—that was one of my favorite things about it," Diane Arbus wrote, "and when I first did it I felt very perverse." Being a professional photographer can be thought of as naughty, to use

Arbus's pop word, if the photographer seeks out subjects considered to be disreputable, taboo, marginal. But naughty subjects are harder to find these days. And what exactly is the perverse aspect of picture-taking? If professional photographers often have sexual fantasies when they are behind the camera, perhaps the perversion lies in the fact that these fantasies are both plausible and so inappropriate. In *Blowup* (1966), Antonioni has the fashion photographer hovering convulsively over Verushka's body with his camera clicking. Naughtiness, indeed! In fact, using a camera is not a very good way of getting at someone sexually. Between photographer and subject, there has to be distance. The camera doesn't rape, or even possess, though it may presume, intrude, trespass, distort, exploit, and, at the farthest reach of metaphor, assassinate—all activities that, unlike the sexual push and shove, can be conducted from a distance, and with some detachment.

There is a much stronger sexual fantasy in Michael Powell's extraordinary movie *Peeping Tom* (1960), which is not about a Peeping Tom but about a psychopath who kills women with a weapon concealed in his camera, while photographing them. Not once does he touch his subjects. He doesn't desire their bodies; he wants their presence in the form of filmed images—those showing them experiencing their own death—which he screens at home for his solitary pleasure. The movie assumes connections between impotence and aggression, professionalized looking and cruelty, which point to the central fantasy connected with the camera. The camera as phallus is, at most, a flimsy variant of the inescapable metaphor that everyone unselfconsciously employs. However hazy our awareness of this fantasy, it is named without subtlety whenever we talk about "loading" and "aiming" a camera, about "shooting" a film.

The old-fashioned camera was clumsier and harder to reload than a brown Bess musket. The modern camera is trying to be a ray gun. One ad reads:

> The Yashica Electro-35 GT is the spaceage camera your family will love. Take beautiful pictures day or night. Automatically. Without any nonsense. Just aim, focus and shoot. The GT's computer brain and electronic shutter will do the rest.

Like a car, a camera is sold as a predatory weapon—one that's as automated as possible, ready to spring. Popular taste expects an easy, an invisible technology. Manufacturers reassure their customers that taking pictures demands no skill or expert knowledge, that the machine is all-knowing, and responds to the slightest pressure of the will. It's as simple as turning the ignition key or pulling the trigger.

Like guns and cars, cameras are fantasy-machines whose use is addictive. However, despite the extravagances of ordinary language and advertising, they are not lethal. In the hyperbole that markets cars like guns, there is at least this much truth: except in wartime, cars kill more people than guns do. The camera/gun does not kill, so the ominous metaphor seems to be all bluff—like a man's fantasy of having a gun, knife, or tool between his legs. Still, there is something predatory in the act of taking a picture. To photograph people is to violate them, by seeing them as they never see themselves, by having knowledge of them they can never have; it turns people into objects that can be symbolically possessed. Just as the camera is a sublimation of the gun, to photograph someone is a sublimated murder—a soft murder, appropriate to a sad, frightened time.

Eventually, people might learn to act out more of their aggressions with cameras and fewer with guns, with the price being an even more image-choked world. One situation where people are switching from bullets to film is the photographic safari that is replacing the gun safari in East Africa. The hunters have Hasselblads instead of Winchesters; instead of looking through a telescopic sight to aim a rifle, they look through a viewfinder to frame a picture. In end-of-the-century London, Samuel Butler complained that "there is a photographer in every bush, going about like a roaring lion seeking whom he may devour." The photographer is now charging real beasts, beleaguered and too rare to kill. Guns have metamorphosed into cameras in this earnest comedy, the ecology safari, because nature has ceased to be what it always had been—what people needed protection from. Now nature—tamed, endangered, mortal—needs to be protected from people. When we are afraid, we shoot. But when we are nostalgic, we take pictures.

It is a nostalgic time right now, and photographs actively promote nostalgia. Photography is an elegiac art, a twilight art. Most subjects photographed are, just by virtue of being photographed, touched with pathos. An ugly or grotesque subject may be moving because it has been dignified by the attention of the photographer. A beautiful subject can be the object of rueful feelings, because it has aged or decayed or no longer exists. All photographs are *memento mori*. To take a photograph is to participate in another person's (or thing's) mortality, vulnerability, mutability. Precisely by slicing out this moment and freezing it, all photographs testify to time's relentless melt.

Cameras began duplicating the world at that moment when the human landscape started to undergo a vertiginous rate of change: while an untold number of forms of biological and social life are being destroyed in a brief span of time, a device is available to record what is disappearing. The moody, intricately textured Paris of Atget and Brassaï is mostly gone. Like the dead relatives and friends preserved in the family album, whose presence in photographs exorcises some of the anxiety and remorse prompted by their disappearance, so the photographs of neighborhoods now torn down, rural places disfigured and made barren, supply our pocket relation to the past.

A photograph is both a pseudo-presence and a token of absence. Like a wood fire in a room, photographs—especially those of people, of distant landscapes and faraway cities, of the vanished past—are incitements to reverie. The sense of the unattainable that can be evoked by photographs feeds directly into the erotic feelings of those for whom desirability is enhanced by distance. The lover's photograph hidden in a married woman's wallet, the poster photograph of a rock star tacked up over an adolescent's bed, the campaign-button image of a politician's face pinned on a voter's coat, the snapshots of a cabdriver's children clipped to the visor—all such talismanic uses of photographs express a feeling both sentimental and implicitly magical: they are attempts to contact or lay claim to another reality.

Photographs can abet desire in the most direct, utilitarian way—as when someone collects photographs of anonymous examples of the desirable as an aid to masturbation. The matter is more complex when photographs are used to stimulate the moral impulse. Desire has no history—at least, it is experienced in each instance as all foreground, immediacy. It is aroused by archetypes and is, in that sense, abstract. But moral feelings are embedded in history, whose personae are concrete, whose situations are always specific. Thus, almost opposite rules hold true for the use of the photograph to awaken desire and to awaken conscience. The images that mobilize conscience are always linked to a given historical situation. The more general they are, the less likely they are to be effective.

A photograph that brings news of some unsuspected zone of misery cannot make a dent in public opinion unless there is an appropriate context of feeling and attitude. The photographs Matthew Brady and his colleagues took of the horrors of the battlefields did not make people any less keen to go on with the Civil War. The photographs of ill-clad, skeletal prisoners held at Andersonville inflamed Northern public opinion—against the South. (The effect of the Andersonville photographs must have been partly due to the very novelty, at that time, of seeing photographs.) The political understanding that many Americans came to in the 1960s would allow them, looking at the photographs Dorothea Lange took of Nisei on the West Coast being transported to internment camps in 1942, to recognize their subject for what it was—a crime committed by the government against a large group of American citizens. Few people who saw those photographs in the 1940s could have had so unequivocal a reaction; the grounds for such a judgment were covered over by the pro-war consensus. Photographs cannot create a moral position, but they can reinforce one—and can help build a nascent one.

Photographs may be more memorable than moving images, because they are a neat slice of time, not a flow. Television is a stream of underselected images, each of which cancels its predecessor. Each still photograph is a privileged moment, turned into a slim object that one can keep and look at again. Photographs like the one that made the front page of most newspapers in the world in 1972—a naked South Vietnamese child just sprayed by American napalm, running down a highway toward the camera, her arms open, screaming with pain—probably did more to increase the public revulsion against the war than a hundred hours of televised barbarities.

One would like to imagine that the American public would not have been so unanimous in its acquiescence to the Korean War if it had been confronted with photographic evidence of the devastation of Korea, an ecocide and genocide in some respects even more thorough than those inflicted on Vietnam a decade later. But the supposition is trivial. The public did not see such photographs because there was, ideologically, no space for them. No one brought back photographs of daily life in Pyongyang, to show that the enemy had a human face, as Felix Greene and Marc Riboud brought back photographs of Hanoi. Americans did have access to photographs of the suffering of the Vietnamese (many of which came from military sources and were taken with quite a different use in mind) because journalists felt backed in their efforts to obtain those photographs, the event having been defined by a significant number of people as a savage colonialist war. The Korean War was understood differently—as part of the just struggle of the Free World against the Soviet Union and China—and, given that characterization, photographs of the cruelty of unlimited American firepower would have been irrelevant.

Though an event has come to mean, precisely, something worth photographing, it is still ideology (in the broadest sense) that determines what constitutes an event. There can be no evidence, photographic or otherwise, of an event until the event itself has been named and characterized. And it is never photographic evidence which can construct—more properly, identify—events; the contribution of photography always follows the naming of the event. What determines the possibility of being affected morally by photographs is the existence of a relevant political consciousness. Without a politics, photographs of the slaughter-bench of history will most likely be experienced as, simply, unreal or as a demoralizing emotional blow.

The quality of feeling, including moral outrage, that people can muster in response to photographs of the oppressed, the exploited, the starving, and the massacred also depends on the degree of their familiarity with these images. Don McCullin's photographs of emaciated Biafrans in the early 1970s had less impact for some people than Werner Bischof's photographs of Indian famine victims in the early 1950s because those images had become banal, and the photographs of Tuareg families dying of starvation in the sub-Sahara that appeared in magazines everywhere in 1973 must have seemed to many like an unbearable replay of a now familiar atrocity exhibition.

Photographs shock insofar as they show something novel. Unfortunately, the ante keeps getting raised—partly through the very proliferation of such images of horror. One's first encounter with the photographic inventory of ultimate horror is a kind of revelation, the prototypically modern revelation: a negative epiphany. For me, it was photographs of Bergen-Belsen and Dachau which I came across by chance in a bookstore in Santa Monica in July 1945. Nothing I have seen—in photographs or in real life—ever cut me as sharply, deeply, instantaneously. Indeed, it seems plausible to me to divide my life into two parts, before I saw those photographs (I was twelve) and after, though it was several years before I understood fully what they were about. What good was served by seeing them? They were only photographs— of an event I had scarcely heard of and could do nothing to affect, of suffering I could hardly imagine and could do nothing to relieve. When I looked at those photographs, something broke. Some limit had been reached, and not only that of horror; I felt irrevocably grieved, wounded, but a part of my feelings started to tighten; something went dead; something is still crying.

To suffer is one thing; another thing is living with the photographed images of suffering, which does not necessarily strengthen conscience and the ability to be compassionate. It can also corrupt them. Once one has seen such images, one has started down the road of seeing more—and more. Images transfix. Images anesthetize. An event known through photographs certainly becomes more real than it would have been if one had never seen the photographs—think of the Vietnam War. (For a counter-example, think of the Gulag Archipelago, of which we have no photographs.) But after repeated exposure to images it also becomes less real.

The same law holds for evil as for pornography. The shock of photographed atrocities wears off with repeated viewings, just as the surprise and bemusement felt the first time one sees a pornographic movie wear off after one sees a few more. The sense of taboo which makes us indignant and sorrowful is not much sturdier than the sense of taboo that regulates the definition of what is obscene. And both have been sorely tried in recent years. The vast photographic catalogue of misery and injustice throughout the world has given everyone a certain familiarity with atrocity, making the horrible seem more ordinary—making it appear familiar, remote ("it's only a photograph"), inevitable. At the time of the first photographs of the Nazi camps, there was nothing banal about these images. After thirty years, a saturation point may have been reached. In these last decades, "concerned" photography has done at least as much to deaden conscience as to arouse it.

The ethical content of photographs is fragile. With the possible exception of photographs of those horrors, like the Nazi camps, that have gained the status of ethical reference points, most photographs do not keep their emotional charge. A photograph of 1900 that was affecting then because of its subject would, today, be more likely to move us because it is a photograph taken in 1900. The particular qualities and intentions of photographs tend to be swallowed up in the generalized pathos of time past. Aesthetic distance seems built into the very experience of looking at photographs, if not right away, then certainly with the passage of time. Time eventually positions most photographs, even the most amateurish, at the level of art.

The industrialization of photography permitted its rapid absorption into rational— that is, bureaucratic—ways of running society. No longer toy images, photographs became part of the general furniture of the environment—touchstones and confirmations of that reductive approach to reality which is considered realistic. Photographs were enrolled in the service of important institutions of control, notably the family and the police, as symbolic objects and as pieces of information. Thus, in the bureaucratic cataloguing of the world, many important documents are not valid unless they have, affixed to them, a photograph-token of the citizen's face.

The "realistic" view of the world compatible with bureaucracy redefines knowl-edge—as techniques and information. Photographs are valued because they give information. They tell one what there is; they make an inventory. To spies, meteorologists, coroners, archaeologists, and other information professionals, their value is inestimable. But in the situations in which most people use photographs, their value as information is of the same order as fiction. The information that photographs can give starts to seem very important at that moment in cultural history when everyone is thought to have a right to something called news. Photographs were seen as a way of giving information to people who do not take easily to reading. The *Daily News* still calls itself "New York's Picture Newspaper," its bid for populist identity. At the opposite end of the scale, *Le Monde,* a newspaper designed for skilled, well-informed readers, runs no photographs at all. The presumption is that, for such readers, a photograph could only illustrate the analysis contained in an article.

A new sense of the notion of information has been constructed around the photographic image. The photograph is a thin slice of space as well as time. In a world ruled by photographic images, all borders ("framing") seem arbitrary. Anything can be separated, can be made discontinuous, from anything else: all that is necessary is to frame the subject differently. (Conversely, anything can be made adjacent to anything else.) Photography reinforces a nominalist view of social reality as consisting of small units of an apparently infinite number—as the number of photographs that could be taken of anything is unlimited. Through photographs, the world becomes a series of unrelated, freestanding particles; and history, past and present, a set of anecdotes and *faits divers.* The camera makes reality atomic, manageable, and opaque. It is a view of the world which denies interconnectedness, continuity, but which confers on each moment the character of a mystery. Any photograph has multiple meanings; indeed, to see something in the form of a photograph is to encounter a potential object of fascination. The ultimate wisdom of the photographic image is to say: "There is the surface. Now think—or rather feel, intuit—what is beyond it, what the reality must be like if it looks this way." Photographs, which cannot themselves explain anything, are inexhaustible invitations to deduction, speculation, and fantasy.

Photography implies that we know about the world if we accept it as the camera records it. But this is the opposite of understanding, which starts from *not* accepting the world as it looks. All possibility of understanding is rooted in the ability to say no. Strictly speaking, one never understands anything from a photograph. Of course, photographs fill in blanks in our mental pictures of the present and the past: for example, Jacob Riis's images of New York squalor in the 1880s are sharply instructive to those unaware that urban poverty in late-nineteenth-century America was really that Dickensian. Nevertheless, the camera's rendering of reality must always hide more than it discloses. As Brecht points out, a photograph of the Krupp works reveals virtually nothing about that organization. In contrast to the amorous relation, which is based on how something looks, understanding is based on how it functions. And functioning takes place in time, and must be explained in time. Only that which narrates can make us understand.

The limit of photographic knowledge of the world is that, while it can goad conscience, it can, finally, never be ethical or political knowledge. The knowledge gained through still photographs will always be some kind of sentimentalism, whether cynical or humanist. It will be a knowledge at bargain prices—a semblance of knowledge, a semblance of wisdom; as the act of taking pictures is a semblance of appropriation, a semblance of rape. The very muteness of what is, hypothetically, comprehensible in photographs is what constitutes their attraction and provocativeness. The omnipresence of photographs has an incalculable effect on our ethical sensibility. By furnishing this already crowded world with a duplicate one of images, photography makes us feel that the world is more available than it really is.

Needing to have reality confirmed and experience enhanced by photographs is an aesthetic consumerism to which everyone is now addicted. Industrial societies turn their citizens into image-junkies; it is the most irresistible form of mental pollution. Poignant longings for beauty, for an end to probing below the surface, for a redemption and celebration of the body of the world—all these elements of erotic feeling are affirmed in the pleasure we take in photographs. But other, less liberating feelings are expressed as well. It would not be wrong to speak of people having a *compulsion* to photograph: to turn experience itself into a way of seeing. Ultimately, having an experience becomes identical with taking a photograph of it, and participating in a public event comes more and more to be equivalent to looking at it in photographed form. That most logical of nineteenth-century aesthetes, Mallarmé, said that everything in the world exists in order to end in a book. Today everything exists to end in a photograph.

A Woman's Beauty:
Put-Down or Power Source?

For the Greeks, beauty was a virtue: a kind of excellence. Persons then were assumed to be what we now have to call—lamely, enviously—*whole* persons. If it did occur to the Greeks to distinguish between a person's "inside" and "outside," they still expected that inner beauty would be matched by beauty of the other kind. The well-born young Athenians who gathered around Socrates found it quite paradoxical that their hero was so intelligent, so brave, so honorable, so seductive—and so ugly. One of Socrates' main pedagogical acts was to be ugly—and teach those innocent, no doubt splendid-looking disciples of his how full of paradoxes life really was.

They may have resisted Socrates' lesson. We do not. Several thousand years later, we are more wary of the enchantments of beauty. We not only split off—with the greatest facility—the "inside" (character, intellect) from the "outside" (looks); but we are actually surprised when someone who is beautiful is also intelligent, talented, good.

It was principally the influence of Christianity that deprived beauty of the central place it had in classical ideals of human excellence. By limiting excellence (*virtus* in Latin) to *moral* virtue only, Christianity set beauty adrift—as an alienated, arbitrary, superficial enchantment. And beauty has continued to lose prestige. For close to two centuries it has become a convention to attribute beauty to only one of the two sexes: the sex which, however Fair, is always Second. Associating beauty with women has put beauty even further on the defensive, morally.

A beautiful woman, we say in English. But a handsome man. "Handsome" is the masculine equivalent of—and refusal of—a compliment which has accumulated certain demeaning overtones, by being reserved for women only. That one can call a man "beautiful" in French and in Italian suggests that Catholic countries—unlike those countries shaped by the Protestant version of Christianity—still retain some vestiges of the pagan admiration for beauty. But the difference, if one exists, is of degree only. In every modern country that is Christian or post-Christian, women *are* the beautiful sex—to the detriment of the notion of beauty as well as of women.

To be called beautiful is thought to name something essential to women's character and concerns. (In contrast to men—whose essence is to be strong, or effective, or competent.) It does not take someone in the throes of advanced feminist awareness to perceive that the way women are taught to be involved with beauty encourages narcissism, reinforces dependence and immaturity. Everybody (women and men) knows that. For it is "everybody," a whole society, that has identified being feminine with caring about how one *looks.* (In contrast to being masculine—which is identified with caring about what one *is* and *does* and only secondarily, if at all, about how one looks.) Given these stereotypes, it is no wonder that beauty enjoys, at best, a rather mixed reputation.

It is not, of course, the desire to be beautiful that is wrong but the obligation to be—or to try. What is accepted by most women as a flattering idealization of their sex is a way of making women feel inferior to what they actually are—or normally grow to be. For the ideal of beauty is administered as a form of self-oppression. Women are taught to see their bodies in *parts,* and to evaluate each part separately. Breasts, feet, hips, waistline, neck, eyes, nose, complexion, hair, and so on—each in turn is submitted to an anxious, fretful, often despairing scrutiny. Even if some pass muster, some will always be found wanting. Nothing less than perfection will do.

In men, good looks is a whole, something taken in at a glance. It does not need to be confirmed by giving measurements of different regions of the body, nobody encourages a man to dissect his appearance, feature by feature. As for perfection, that is considered trivial—almost unmanly. Indeed, in the ideally good-looking man a small imperfection or blemish is considered positively desirable. According to one movie critic (a woman) who is a declared Robert Redford fan, it is having that cluster of skin-colored moles on one cheek that saves Redford from being merely a "pretty face." Think of the depreciation of women—as well as of beauty—that is implied in that judgment.

"The privileges of beauty are immense," said Cocteau. To be sure, beauty is a form of power. And deservedly so. What is lamentable is that it is the only form of power that most women are encouraged to seek. This power is always conceived in relation to men; it is not the power to do but the power to attract. It is a power that negates itself. For this power is not one that can be chosen freely—at least, not by women—or renounced without social censure.

To preen, for a woman, can never be just a pleasure. It is also a duty. It is her work. If a woman does real work—and even if she has clambered up to a leading position in politics, law, medicine, business, or whatever—she is always under pressure to confess that she still works at being attractive. But in so far as she is keeping up as one of the Fair Sex, she brings under suspicion her very capacity to be objective, professional, authoritative, thoughtful. Damned if they do—women are. And damned if they don't.

One could hardly ask for more important evidence of the dangers of considering persons as split between what is "inside" and what is "outside" than that interminable half-comic half-tragic tale, the oppression of women. How easy it is to start off by defining women as caretakers of their surfaces, and then to disparage them (or find them adorable) for being "superficial." It is a crude trap, and it has worked for too long. But to get out of the trap requires that women get some critical distance from that excellence and privilege which is beauty, enough distance to see how much beauty itself has been abridged in order to prop up the mythology of the "feminine." There should be a way of saving beauty *from* women—and *for* them.

Simone Weil

The culture-heroes of our liberal bourgeois civilization are anti-liberal and anti-bourgeois; they are writers who are repetitive, obsessive, and impolite, who impress by force—not simply by their tone of personal authority and by their intellectual ardor, but by the sense of acute personal and intellectual extremity. The bigots, the hysterics, the destroyers of the self—these are the writers who bear witness to the fearful polite time in which we live. Mostly it is a matter of tone: it is hardly possible to give credence to ideas uttered in the impersonal tones of sanity. There are certain eras which are too complex, too deafened by contradictory historical and intellectual experiences, to hear the voice of sanity. Sanity becomes compromise, evasion, a lie. Ours is an age which consciously pursues health, and yet only believes in the reality of sickness. The truths we respect are those born of affliction. We measure truth in terms of the cost to the writer in suffering—rather than by the standard of an objective truth to which a writer's words correspond. Each of our truths must have a martyr.

What revolted the mature Goethe in the young Kleist, who submitted his works to the elder statesman of German letters "on the knees of his heart"—the morbid, the hysterical, the sense of the unhealthy, the enormous indulgence in suffering out of which Kleist's plays and tales were mined—is just what we value today. Today Kleist gives pleasure, most of Goethe is a classroom bore. In the same way, such writers as Kierkegaard, Nietzsche, Dostoevsky; Kafka, Baudelaire, Rimbaud, Genet—and Simone Weil—have their authority with us precisely because of their air of unhealthiness. Their unhealthiness is their soundness, and is what carries conviction.

Perhaps there are certain ages which do not need truth as much as they need a deepening of the sense of reality, a widening of the imagination. I, for one, do not doubt that the sane view of the world is the true one. But is that what is always wanted, truth? The need for truth is not constant; no more than is the need for repose. An idea which is a distortion may have a greater intellectual thrust than the truth; it may better serve the needs of the spirit, which vary. The truth is balance, but the opposite of truth, which is unbalance, may not be a lie.

Thus I do not mean to decry a fashion, but to underscore the motive behind the contemporary taste for the extreme in art and thought. All that is necessary is that we not be hypocritical, that we recognize why we read and admire writers like Simone Weil. I cannot believe that more than a handful of the tens of thousands of readers she has won since the posthumous publication of her books and essays really share her ideas. Nor is it necessary—necessary to share Simone Weil's anguished and unconsummated love affair with the Catholic Church, or accept her gnostic theology of divine absence, or espouse her ideals of body denial, or concur in her violently unfair hatred of Roman civilization and the Jews. Similarly, with Kierkegaard and Nietzsche; most of their modern admirers could not and do not embrace their ideas. We read writers of such scathing originality for their personal authority, for the example of their seriousness, for their manifest willingness to sacrifice themselves for their truths, and—only piecemeal—for their "views." As the corrupt Alcibiades followed Socrates, unable and unwilling to change his own life, but moved, enriched, and full of love, so the sensitive modern reader pays his respect to a level of spiritual reality which is not, could not, be his own.

Some lives are exemplary, others not; and of exemplary lives, there are those which invite us to imitate them, and those which we regard from a distance with a mixture of revulsion, pity, and reverence. It is, roughly, the difference between the hero and the saint (if one may use the latter term in an aesthetic, rather than a religious sense). Such a life, absurd in its exaggerations and degree of self-mutilation—like Kleist's, like Kierkegaard's—was Simone Weil's. I am thinking of the fanatical asceticism of Simone Weil's life, her contempt for pleasure and for happiness, her noble and ridiculous political gestures, her elaborate self-denials, her tireless courting of affliction; and I do not exclude her homeliness, her physical clumsiness, her migraines, her tuberculosis. No one who loves life would wish to imitate her dedication to martyrdom, or would wish it for his children or for anyone else whom he loves. Yet so far as we love seriousness, as well as life, we are moved by it, nourished by it. In the respect we pay to such lives, we acknowledge the presence of mystery in the world—and mystery is just what the secure possession of the truth, an objective truth, denies. In this sense, all truth is superficial; and some (but not all) distortions of the truth, some (but not all) insanity, some (but not all) unhealthiness, some (but not all) denials of life are truth-giving, sanity-producing, health-creating, and life-enhancing.

The Aesthetics of Silence

1

Every era has to reinvent the project of "spirituality" for itself. (Spirituality = plans, terminologies, ideas of deportment aimed at resolving the painful structural contradictions inherent in the human situation, at the completion of human consciousness, at transcendence.)

In the modern era, one of the most active metaphors for the spiritual project is "art." The activities of the painter, the musician, the poet, the dancer, once they were grouped together under that generic name (a relatively recent move), have proved a particularly adaptable site on which to stage the formal dramas besetting consciousness, each individual work of art being a more or less astute paradigm for regulating or reconciling these contradictions. Of course, the site needs continual refurbishing. Whatever goal is set for art eventually proves restrictive, matched against the widest goals of consciousness. Art, itself a form of mystification, endures a succession of crises of demystification; older artistic goals are assailed and, ostensibly, replaced; outworn maps of consciousness are redrawn. But what supplies all these crises with their energy—an energy held in common, so to speak—is the very unification of numerous, quite disparate activities into a single genus. At the moment when "art" comes into being, the modern period of art begins. From then on, any of the activities therein subsumed becomes a profoundly *problematic* activity, all of whose procedures and, ultimately, whose very right to exist can be called into question.

From the promotion of the arts into "art" comes the leading myth about art, that of the absoluteness of the artist's activity. In its first, more unreflective version, the myth treated art as an *expression* of human consciousness, consciousness seeking to know itself. (The evaluative standards generated by this version of the myth were fairly easily arrived at: some expressions were more complete, more ennobling, more informative, richer than others.) The later version of the myth posits a more complex, tragic relation of art to consciousness. Denying that art is mere expression, the later myth rather relates art to the mind's need or capacity for self-estrangement. Art is no longer understood as consciousness expressing and therefore, implicitly, affirming itself. Art is not consciousness per se, but rather its antidote—evolved from within consciousness itself. (The evaluative standards generated by this version of the myth proved much harder to get at.)

The newer myth, derived from a post-psychological conception of consciousness, installs within the activity of art many of the paradoxes involved in attaining an absolute state of being described by the great religious mystics. As the activity of the mystic must end in a *via negativa*, a theology of God's absence, a craving for the cloud of unknowing beyond knowledge and for the silence beyond speech, so art must tend toward anti-art, the elimination of the "subject" (the "object," the "image"), the substitution of chance for intention, and the pursuit of silence.

In the early, linear version of art's relation to consciousness, a struggle was discerned between the "spiritual" integrity of the creative impulses and the distracting "materiality" of ordinary life, which throws up so many obstacles in the path of authentic sublimation. But the newer version, in which art is part of a dialectical transaction with consciousness, poses a deeper, more frustrating conflict. The "spirit" seeking embodiement in art clashes with the "material" character of art itself. Art is unmasked as gratuitous, and the very concreteness of the artist's tools (and, particularly in the case of language, their historicity) appears as a trap. Practiced in a world furnished with second-hand perceptions, and specifically confounded by the treachery of words, the artist's activity is cursed with mediacy. Art becomes the enemy of the artist, for it denies him the realization—the transcendence—he desires.

Therefore, art comes to be considered something to be overthrown. A new element enters the individual artwork and becomes constitutive of it: the appeal (tacit or overt) for its own abolition—and, ultimately, for the abolition of art itself.

2

The scene changes to an empty room.

Rimbaud has gone to Abyssinia to make his fortune in the slave trade. Wittgenstein, after a period as a village schoolteacher, has chosen menial work as a hospital orderly. Duchamp has turned to chess. Accompanying these exemplary renunciations of a vocation, each man has declared that he regards his previous achievements in poetry, philosophy, or art as trifling, of no importance.

But the choice of permanent silence doesn't negate their work. On the contrary, it imparts retroactively an added power and authority to what was broken off— disavowal of the work becoming a new source of its validity, a certificate of unchallengeable seriousness. That seriousness consists in not regarding art (or philosophy practiced as an art form: Wittgenstein) as something whose seriousness lasts forever, an "end," a permanent vehicle for spiritual ambition. The truly serious attitude is one that regards art as a "means" to something that can perhaps be achieved only by abandoning art; judged more impatiently, art is a false way or (the word of the Dada artist Jacques Vaché) a stupidity.

Though no longer a confession, art is more than ever a deliverance, an exercise in asceticism. Through it, the artist becomes purified—of himself and, eventually, of his art. The artist (if not art itself) is still engaged in a progress toward "the good." But whereas formerly the artist's good was mastery of and fulfillment in his art, now the highest good for the artist is to reach the point where those goals of excellence become insignificant to him, emotionally and ethically, and he is more satisfied by being silent than by finding a voice in art. Silence in this sense, as termination, proposes a mood of ultimacy antithetical to the mood informing the self-conscious artist's traditional serious use of silence (beautifully described by Valéry and Rilke): as a zone of meditation, preparation for spiritual ripening, an ordeal that ends in gaining the right to speak.

So far as he is serious, the artist is continually tempted to sever the dialogue he has with an audience. Silence is the furthest extension of that reluctance to communicate, that ambivalence about making contact with the audience which is a leading motif of modern art, with its tireless commitment to the "new" and/or the "esoteric." Silence is the artist's ultimate other-worldly gesture: by silence, he frees himself from servile bondage to the world, which appears as patron, client, consumer, antagonist, arbiter, and distorter of his work.

Still, one cannot fail to perceive in this renunciation of "society" a highly social gesture. The cues for the artist's eventual liberation from the need to practice his vocation come from observing his fellow artists and measuring himself against them. An exemplary decision of this sort can be made only after the artist has demonstrated that he possesses genius and exercised that genius authoritatively. Once he has surpassed his peers by the standards which he acknowledges, his pride has only one place left to go. For, to be a victim of the craving for silence is to be, in still a further sense, superior to everyone else. It suggests that the artist has had the wit to ask more questions than other people, and that he possesses stronger nerves and higher standards of excellence. (That the artist *can* persevere in the interrogation of his art until he or it is exhausted scarcely needs proving. As René Char has written, "No bird has the heart to sing in a thicket of questions.")

3

The exemplary modern artist's choice of silence is rarely carried to this point of final simplification, so that he becomes literally silent. More typically, he continues speaking, but in a manner that his audience can't hear. Most valuable art in our time has been experienced by audiences as a move into silence (or unintelligibility or invisibility or inaudibility); a dismantling of the artist's competence, his responsible sense of vocation—and therefore as an aggression against them.

Modern art's chronic habit of displeasing, provoking, or frustrating its audience can be regarded as a limited, vicarious participation in the ideal of silence which has been elevated as a major standard of "seriousness" in contemporary aesthetics.

But it is also a contradictory form of participation in the ideal of silence. It is contradictory not only because the artist continues making works of art, but also because the isolation of the work from its audience never lasts. With the passage of time and the intervention of newer, more difficult works, the artist's transgression becomes ingratiating, eventually legitimate. Goethe accused Kleist of having written his plays for an "invisible theatre." But eventually the invisible theatre becomes "visible." The ugly and discordant and senseless become "beautiful." The history of art is a sequence of successful transgressions.

The characteristic aim of modern art, to be *unacceptable* to its audience, inversely states the unacceptability to the artist of the very presence of an audience—audience in the modern sense, an assembly of voyeuristic spectators. At least since Nietzsche observed in *The Birth of Tragedy* that an audience of spectators as we know it, those present whom the actors ignore, was unknown to the Greeks, a good deal of contemporary art seems moved by the desire to eliminate the audience from art, an enterprise that often presents itself as an attempt to eliminate "art" altogether. (In favor of "life"?)

Committed to the idea that the power of art is located in its power to *negate,* the ultimate weapon in the artist's inconsistent war with his audience is to verge closer and closer to silence. The sensory or conceptual gap between the artist and his audience, the space of the missing or ruptured dialogue, can also constitute the grounds for an ascetic affirmation. Beckett speaks of "my dream of an art unresentful of its insuperable indigence and too proud for the farce of giving and receiving." But there is no abolishing a minimal transaction, a minimal exchange of gifts—just as there is no talented and rigorous asceticism that, whatever its intention, doesn't produce a gain (rather than a loss) in the capacity for pleasure.

And none of the aggressions committed intentionally or inadvertently by modern artists has succeeded in either abolishing the audience or transforming it into something else, a community engaged in a common activity. They cannot. As long as art is understood and valued as an "absolute" activity, it will be a separate, elitist one. Elites presuppose masses. So far as the best art defines itself by essentially "priestly" aims, it presupposes and confirms the existence of a relatively passive, never fully initiated, voyeuristic laity that is regularly convoked to watch, listen, read, or hear—and then sent away.

The most the artist can do is to modify the different terms in this situation vis-à-vis the audience and himself. To discuss the idea of silence in art is to discuss the various alternatives within this essentially unalterable situation.

4

How literally does silence figure in art?

Silence exists as a *decision*—in the exemplary suicide of the artist (Kleist, Lautréamont), who thereby testifies that he has gone "too far"; and in the already cited model renunciations by the artist of his vocation.

Silence also exists as a *punishment*—self-punishment, in the exemplary madness of artists (Hölderlin, Artaud) who demonstrate that sanity itself may be the price of trespassing the accepted frontiers of consciousness; and, of course, in penalties (ranging from censorship and physical destruction of artworks to fines, exile, prison for the artist) meted out by "society" for the artist's spiritual nonconformity or subversion of the group sensibility.

Silence doesn't exist in a literal sense, however, as the *experience* of an audience. It would mean that the spectator was aware of no stimulus or that he was unable to make a response. But this can't happen; nor can it even be induced programmatically. The non-awareness of any stimulus, the inability to make a response, can result only from a defective presence on the part of the spectator, or a misunderstanding of his own reactions (misled by restrictive ideas about what would be a "relevant" response). As long as audiences, by definition, consist of sentient beings in a "situation," it is impossible for them to have no response at all.

Nor can silence, in its literal state, exist as the *property* of an artwork—even of works like Duchamp's readymades or Cage's *4'33"*, in which the artist has ostentatiously done no more to satisfy any established criteria of art than set the object in a gallery or situate the performance on a concert stage. There is no neutral surface, no neutral discourse, no neutral theme, no neutral form. Something is neutral only with respect to something else—like an intention or an expectation. As a property of the work of art itself, silence can exist only in a cooked or nonliteral sense. (Put otherwise: if a work exists at all, its silence is only one element in it.) Instead of raw or achieved silence, one finds various moves in the direction of an ever receding horizon of silence—moves which, by definition, can never be fully consummated. One result is a type of art that many people characterize pejoratively as dumb, depressed, acquiescent, cold. But these privative qualities exist in a context of the artist's objective intention, which is always discernible. Cultivating the metaphoric silence suggested by conventionally lifeless subjects (as in much of Pop Art) and constructing "minimal" forms that seem to lack emotional resonance are in themselves vigorous, often tonic choices.

And, finally, even without imputing objective intentions to the artwork, there remains the inescapable truth about perception: the positivity of all experience at every moment of it. As Cage has insisted, "There is no such thing as silence. Something is always happening that makes a sound." (Cage has described how, even in a soundless chamber, he still heard two things: his heartbeat and the coursing of the blood in his head.) Similarly, there is no such thing as empty space. As long as a human eye is looking, there is always something to see. To look at something which is "empty" is still to be looking, still to be seeing something—if only the ghosts of one's own expectations. In order to perceive fullness, one must retain an acute sense of the emptiness which marks it off; conversely, in order to perceive emptiness, one must apprehend other zones of the world as full. (In *Through the Looking Glass,* Alice comes upon a shop "that seemed to be full of all manner of curious things—but the oddest part of it all was that whenever she looked hard at any shelf, to make out exactly what it had on it, that particular shelf was always quite empty, though the others round it were crowded full as they could hold.")

"Silence" never ceases to imply its opposite and to depend on its presence: just as there can't be "up" without "down" or "left" without "right," so one must acknowledge a surrounding environment of sound or language in order to recognize silence. Not only does silence exist in a world full of speech and other sounds, but any given silence has its identity as a stretch of time being perforated by sound. (Thus, much of the beauty of Harpo Marx's muteness derives from his being surrounded by manic talkers.)

A genuine emptiness, a pure silence are not feasible—either conceptually or in fact. If only because the artwork exists in a world furnished with many other things, the artist who creates silence or emptiness must produce something dialectical: a full void, an enriching emptiness, a resonating or eloquent silence. Silence remains, inescapably, a form of speech (in many instances, of complaint or indictment) and an element in a dialogue.

5

Programs for a radical reduction of means and effects in art—including the ultimate demand for the renunciation of art itself—can't be taken at face value, undialectically. Silence and allied ideas (like emptiness, reduction, the "zero degree") are boundary notions with a very complex set of uses, leading terms of a particular spiritual and cultural rhetoric. To describe silence as a rhetorical term is, of course, not to condemn this rhetoric as fraudulent or in bad faith. In my opinion, the myths of silence and emptiness are about as nourishing and viable as might be devised in an "unwholesome" time—which is, of necessity, a time in which "unwholesome" psychic states furnish the energies for most superior work in the arts. Yet one can't deny the pathos of these myths.

This pathos appears in the fact that the idea of silence allows, essentially, only two types of valuable development. Either it is taken to the point of utter self-negation (as art) or else it is practiced in a form that is heroically, ingeniously inconsistent.

6

The art of our time is noisy with appeals for silence.

A coquettish, even cheerful nihilism. One recognizes the imperative of silence, but goes on speaking anyway. Discovering that one has nothing to say, one seeks a way to say *that.*

Beckett has expressed the wish that art would renounce all further projects for disturbing matters on "the plane of the feasible," that art would retire, "weary of puny exploits, weary of pretending to be able, of being able, of doing a little better the same old thing, of going further along a dreary road." The alternative is an art consisting of "the expression that there is nothing to express, nothing from which to express, no power to express, no desire to express, together with the obligation to express." From where does this obligation derive? The very aesthetics of the death wish seems to make of that wish something incorrigibly lively.

Apollinaire says, "J'ai fait des gestes blancs parmi les solitudes." But he *is* making gestures.

Since the artist can't embrace silence literally and remain an artist, what the rhetoric of silence indicates is a determination to pursue his activity more deviously than before. One way is indicated by Breton's notion of the "full margin." The artist is enjoined to devote himself to filling up the periphery of the art space, leaving the central area of usage blank. Art becomes privative, anemic—as suggested by the title of Duchamp's only effort at film-making "Anemic Cinema," a work from 1924–26. Beckett projects the idea of an "impoverished painting," painting which is "authentically fruitless, incapable of any image whatsoever." Jerzy Grotowski's manifesto for his Theatre Laboratory in Poland is called "Plea for a Poor Theatre." These programs for art's impoverishment must not be understood simply as terroristic admonitions to audiences, but rather as strategies for improving the audience's experience. The notions of silence, emptiness, and reduction sketch out new prescriptions for looking, hearing, etc.—which either promote a more immediate, sensuous experience of art or confront the artwork in a more conscious, conceptual way.

7

Consider the connection between the mandate for a reduction of means and effects in art, whose horizon is silence, and the faculty of attention. In one of its aspects, art is a technique for focusing attention, for teaching skills of attention. (While the whole of the human environment might be so described—as a pedagogic instrument—this description particularly applies to works of art.) The history of the arts is tantamount to the discovery and formulation of a repertory of objects on which to lavish attention. One could trace exactly and in order how the eye of art has panned over our environment, "naming," making its limited selection of things which people then become aware of as significant, pleasurable, complex entities. (Oscar Wilde pointed out that people didn't see fogs before certain nineteenth-century poets and painters taught them how to; and surely, no one saw as much of the variety and subtlety of the human face before the era of the movies.)

Once the artist's task seemed to be simply that of opening up new areas and objects of attention. That task is still acknowledged, but it has become problematic.

The very faculty of attention has come into question, and been subjected to more rigorous standards. As Jasper Johns says: "Already it's a great deal to see anything *clearly,* for we don't see *anything* clearly."

Perhaps the quality of the attention one brings to bear on something will be better (less contaminated, less distracted), the less one is offered. Furnished with impoverished art, purged by silence, one might then be able to begin to transcend the frustrating selectivity of attention, with its inevitable distortions of experience. Ideally, one should be able to pay attention to everything.

The tendency is toward less and less. But never has "less" so ostentatiously advanced itself as "more."

In the light of the current myth, in which art aims to become a "total experience," soliciting total attention, the strategies of impoverishment and reduction indicate the most exalted ambition art could adopt. Underneath what looks like a strenuous modesty, if not actual debility, is to be discerned an energetic secular blasphemy: the wish to attain the unfettered, unselective, total consciousness of "God."

8

Language seems a privileged metaphor for expressing the mediated character of art-making and the artwork. On the one hand, speech is both an immaterial medium (compared with, say, images) and a human activity with an apparently essential stake in the project of transcendence, of moving beyond the singular and contingent (all words being abstractions, only roughly based on or making reference to concrete particulars). On the other hand, language is the most impure, the most contaminated, the most exhausted of all the materials out of which art is made.

This dual character of language—its abstractness, and its "fallenness" in history—serves as a microcosm of the unhappy character of the arts today. Art is so far along the labyrinthine pathways of the project of transcendence that one can hardly conceive of it turning back, short of the most drastic and punitive "cultural revolution." Yet at the same time, art is foundering in the debilitating tide of what once seemed the crowning achievement of European thought: secular historical consciousness. In little more than two centuries, the consciousness of history has transformed itself from a liberation, an opening of doors, blessed enlightenment, into an almost insupportable burden of self-consciousness. It's scarcely possible for the artist to write a word (or render an image or make a gesture) that doesn't remind him of something already achieved.

As Nietzsche says: "Our pre-eminence: we live in the age of comparison, we can verify as has never been verified before." Therefore "we enjoy differently, we suffer differently: our instinctive activity is to compare an unheard number of things."

Up to a point, the community and historicity of the artist's means are implicit in the very fact of intersubjectivity: each person is a being-in-a-world. But today, particularly in the arts using language, this normal state of affairs is felt as an extraordinary, wearying problem.

Language is experienced not merely as something shared but as something corrupted, weighed down by historical accumulation. Thus, for each conscious artist, the creation of a work means dealing with two potentially antagonistic domains of meaning and their relationships. One is his own meaning (or lack of it); the other is the set of second-order meanings that both extend his own language and encumber, compromise, and adulterate it. The artist ends by choosing between two inherently limiting alternatives, forced to take a position that is either servile or insolent. Either he flatters or appeases his audience, giving them what they already know, or he commits an aggression against his audience, giving them what they don't want.

Modern art thus transmits in full the alienation produced by historical consciousness. Whatever the artist does is in (usually conscious) alignment with something else already done, producing a compulsion to be continually checking his situation, his own stance against those of his predecessors and contemporaries. To compensate for this ignominious enslavement to history, the artist exalts himself with the dream of a wholly ahistorical, and therefore unalienated, art.

9

Art that is "silent" constitutes one approach to this visionary, ahistorical condition.

Consider the difference between *looking* and *staring.* A look is voluntary; it is also mobile, rising and falling in intensity as its foci of interest are taken up and then exhausted. A stare has, essentially, the character of a compulsion; it is steady, unmodulated, "fixed."

Traditional art invites a look. Art that is silent engenders a stare. Silent art allows—at least in principle—no release from attention, because there has never, in principle, been any soliciting of it. A stare is perhaps as far from history, as close to eternity, as contemporary art can get.

10

Silence is a metaphor for a cleansed, non-interfering vision, appropriate to artworks that are unresponsive before being seen, unviolable in their essential integrity by human scrutiny. The spectator would approach art as he does a landscape. A landscape doesn't demand from the spectator his "understanding," his imputations of significance, his anxieties and sympathies; it demands, rather, his absence, it asks that he not add anything to *it.* Contemplation, strictly speaking, entails self-forgetfulness on the part of the spectator: an object worthy of contemplation is one which, in effect, annihilates the perceiving subject.

Toward such an ideal plenitude to which the audience can add nothing, analogous to the aesthetic relation to nature, a great deal of contemporary art aspires—through various strategies of blandness, of reduction, of deindividuation, of alogicality. In principle, the audience may not even add its thought. All objects, rightly perceived, are already full. This is what Cage must mean when, after explaining that there is no such thing as silence because something is always happening that makes a sound, he adds, "No one can have an idea once he starts really listening."

Plenitude—experiencing all the space as filled, so that ideas cannot enter—means impenetrability. A person who becomes silent becomes opaque for the other; somebody's silence opens up an array of possibilities for interpreting that silence, for imputing speech to it.

The way in which this opaqueness induces spiritual vertigo is the theme of

Bergman's *Persona*. The actress's deliberate silence has two aspects: Considered as a decision apparently relating to herself, the refusal to speak is apparently the form she has given to the wish for ethical purity; but it is also, as behavior, a means of power, a species of sadism, a virtually inviolable position of strength from which she manipulates and confounds her nurse-companion, who is charged with the burden of talking.

But the opaqueness of silence can be conceived more positively, as free from anxiety. For Keats, the silence of the Grecian urn is a locus of spiritual nourishment: "unheard" melodies endure, whereas those that pipe to "the sensual ear" decay. Silence is equated with arresting time ("slow time"). One can stare endlessly at the Grecian urn. Eternity, in the argument of Keats' poem, is the only interesting stimulus to thought and also the sole occasion for coming to the end of mental activity, which means interminable, unanswered questions ("Thou, silent form, dost tease us out of thought/ As doth eternity"), in order to arrive at a final equation of ideas ("Beauty is truth, truth beauty") which is both absolutely vacuous and completely full. Keats' poem quite logically ends in a statement that will seem, if the reader hasn't followed his argument, like empty wisdom, a banality. As time, or history, is the medium of definite, determinate thought, the silence of eternity prepares for a thought beyond thought, which must appear from the perspective of traditional thinking and the familiar uses of the mind as no thought at all—though it may rather be the emblem of new, "difficult" thinking.

11

Behind the appeals for silence lies the wish for a perceptual and cultural clean slate. And, in its most hortatory and ambitious version, the advocacy of silence expresses a mythic project of total liberation. What's envisaged is nothing less than the liberation of the artist from himself, of art from the particular artwork, of art from history, of spirit from matter, of the mind from its perceptual and intellectual limitations.

As some people know now, there are ways of thinking that we don't yet know about. Nothing could be more important or precious than that knowledge, however unborn. The sense of urgency, the spiritual restlessness it engenders, cannot be appeased, and continues to fuel the radical art of this century. Through its advocacy of silence and reduction, art commits an act of violence upon itself, turning art into a species of auto-manipulation, of conjuring—trying to bring these new ways of thinking to birth.

Silence is a strategy for the transvaluation of art, art itself being the herald of an anticipated radical transvaluation of human values. But the success of this strategy must mean its eventual abandonment, or at least its significant modification.

Silence is a prophecy, one which the artist's actions can be understood as attempting both to fulfill and to reverse.

As language points to its own transcendence in silence, silence points to its own transcendence—to a speech beyond silence.

But can the whole enterprise become an act of bad faith if the artist knows *this*, too?

12

A famous quotation: "Everything that can be thought at all can be thought clearly. Everything that can be said at all can be said clearly. But not everything that can be thought can be said."

Notice that Wittgenstein, with his scrupulous avoidance of the psychological issue, doesn't ask why, when, and in what circumstances someone would *want* to put into words "everything that can be thought" (even if he could), or even to utter (whether clearly or not) "everything that could be said."

13

Of everything that's said, one can ask: *why?* (Including: why should I say *that?* And: why should I say anything at all?)

Moreover, strictly speaking, nothing that's *said* is true. (Though a person can *be* the truth, one can't ever say it.)

Still, things that are said can sometimes be helpful—which is what people ordinarily mean when they regard something *said* as being true. Speech can enlighten, relieve, confuse, exalt, infect, antagonize, gratify, grieve, stun, animate. While language is regularly used to inspire to action, some verbal statements, either written or oral, are themselves the performing of an action (as in promising, swearing, bequeathing). Another use of speech, if anything more common than that of provoking actions, is to provoke further speech. But speech can silence, too. This indeed is how it must be: without the polarity of silence, the whole system of language would fail. And beyond its generic function as the dialectical opposite of speech, silence—like speech—also has more specific, less inevitable uses.

One use for silence: certifying the absence or renunciation of thought. Silence is often employed as a magical or mimetic procedure in repressive social relationships, as in the Jesuit regulations about speaking to superiors and in the disciplining of children. (This should not be confused with the practice of certain monastic disciplines, such as the Trappist order, in which silence is both an ascetic act and bears witness to the condition of being perfectly "full.")

Another, apparently opposed, use for silence: certifying the completion of thought. In the words of Karl Jaspers, "He who has the final answers can no longer speak to the other, breaking off genuine communication for the sake of what he believes in."

Still another use for silence: providing time for the continuing or exploring of thought. Notably, speech closes off thought. (An example: the enterprise of criticism, in which there seems no way for a critic not to assert that a given artist is *this*, he's *that*, etc.) But if one decides an issue isn't closed, it's not. This is presumably the rationale behind the voluntary experiments in silence that some contemporary spiritual athletes, like Buckminster Fuller, have undertaken, and the element of wisdom in the otherwise mainly authoritarian, philistine silence of the orthodox Freudian psychoanalyst. Silence keeps things "open."

Still another use for silence: furnishing or aiding speech to attain its maximum integrity or seriousness. Everyone has experienced how, when punctuated by long silences, words weigh more; they become almost palpable. Or how, when one talks less, one begins feeling more fully one's physical presence in a given space. Silence undermines "bad speech," by which I mean dissociated speech—speech dissociated from the body (and, therefore, from feeling), speech not organically informed by the sensuous presence and concrete particularity of the speaker and by the individual occasion for using language. Unmoored from the body, speech deteriorates. It becomes false, inane, ignoble, weightless. Silence can inhibit or counteract this tendency, providing a kind of ballast, monitoring and even correcting language when it becomes inauthentic.

Given these perils to the authenticity of language (which doesn't depend on the character of any isolated statement or even group of statements, but on the relation of speaker, utterance, and situation), the imaginary project of saying clearly "everything that can be said" suggested by Wittgenstein's remarks looks fearfully complicated. (How much time would one have? Would one have to speak quickly?) The philosopher's hypothetical universe of clear speech (which assigns to silence only "that whereof one cannot speak") would seem to be a moralist's, or a psychiatrist's, nightmare—at the least a place no one should lightheartedly enter. Is there anyone who *wants* to say "everything that could be said"? The psychologically plausible answer would seem to be no. But yes is plausible, too—as a rising ideal of modern culture. Isn't that what many people *do* want today—to say everything that can be said? But this aim cannot be maintained without inner conflict. In part inspired by the spread of the ideals of psychotherapy, people are yearning to say "everything" (thereby, among other results, further undermining the crumbling distinction between public and private endeavors, between information and secrets). But in an overpopulated world being connected by global electronic communication and jet travel at a pace too rapid and violent for an organically sound person to assimilate without shock, people are also suffering from a revulsion at any further proliferation of speech and images. Such different factors as the unlimited "technological reproduction" and near universal diffusion of printed language and speech as well as images (from "news" to "art objects"), and the degeneration of public language within the realms of politics and advertising and entertainment, have produced, especially among the better-educated inhabitants of modern mass society, a devaluation of language. (I should argue, contrary to McLuhan, that a devaluation of the power and credibility of images has taken place no less profound than, and essentially similar to, that afflicting language.) And, as the prestige of language falls, that of silence rises.

I am alluding, at this point, to the sociological context of the contemporary ambivalence toward language. The matter, of course, goes much deeper than this. In addition to the specific sociological determinants, one must recognize the operation of something like a perennial discontent with language that has been formulated in each of the major civilizations of the Orient and Occident, whenever thought reaches a certain high, *excruciating* order of complexity and spiritual seriousness.

Traditionally, it has been through the religious vocabulary, with its meta-absolutes of "sacred" and "profane," "human" and "divine," that the disaffection with language itself has been charted. In particular, the antecedents of art's dilemmas and strategies are to be found in the radical wing of the mystical tradition. (Cf., among Christian texts, the *Mystica Theologia* of Dionysius the Areopagite, the anonymous *Cloud of Unknowing*, the writings of Jakob Boehme and Meister Eckhart; and parallels in Zen, Taoist, and Sufi texts.) The mystical tradition has always recognized, in Norman Brown's phrase, "the neurotic character of language." (According to Boehme, Adam spoke a language different from all known languages. It was "sensual speech," the unmediated expressive instrument of the senses, proper to beings integrally part of sensuous nature—that is, still employed by all the animals except that sick animal, man. This, which Boehme calls the only "natural language," the sole language free from distortion and illusion, is what man will speak again when he recovers paradise.) But in our time, the most striking developments of such ideas have been made by artists (and certain psychotherapists) rather than by the timid legatees of the religious traditions.

Explicitly in revolt against what is deemed the desiccated, categorized life of the ordinary mind, the artist issues his own call for a revision of language. A good deal of contemporary art is moved by this quest for a consciousness purified of contaminated language and, in some versions, of the distortions produced by conceiving the world exclusively in conventional verbal (in their debased sense, "rational" or "logical") terms. Art itself becomes a kind of counterviolence, seeking to loosen the grip upon consciousness of the habits of lifeless, static verbalization, presenting models of "sensual speech."

If anything, the volume of discontent has been turned up since the arts inherited the problem of language from religious discourse. It's not just that words, ultimately, are inadequate to the highest aims of consciousness; or even that they get in the way. Art expresses a double discontent. We lack words, and we have too many of them. It raises two complaints about language. Words are too crude. And words are also too busy—inviting a hyperactivity of consciousness that is not only dysfunctional in terms of human capacities of feeling and acting, but actively deadens the mind and blunts the senses.

Language is demoted to the status of an event. Something takes place in time, a voice speaking which points to the before and to what comes after an utterance: silence. Silence, then, is both the precondition of speech and the result or aim of properly directed speech. On this model, the artist's activity is the creating or establishing of silence; the efficacious artwork leaves silence in its wake. Silence, administered by the artist, is part of a program of perceptual and cultural therapy, often on the model of shock therapy rather than of persuasion. Even if the artist's medium is words, he can share in this task: language can be employed to check language, to express muteness. Mallarmé thought it was the job of poetry, using words, to clean up our word-clogged reality—by creating silences around things. Art must mount a full-scale attack on language itself, by means of language and its surrogates, on behalf of the standard of silence.

14

In the end, the radical critique of consciousness (first delineated by the mystical tradition, now administered by unorthodox psychotherapy and high modernist art) always lays the blame on language. Consciousness, experienced as a burden, is conceived of as the memory of all the words that have ever been said.

Krishnamurti claims that we must give up psychological, as distinct from factual, memory. Otherwise, we keep filling up the new with the old, closing off experience by hooking each experience onto the last.

We must destroy continuity (which is insured by psychological memory), by going to the *end* of each emotion or thought.

And after the end, what supervenes (for a while) is silence.

15

In his Fourth Duino Elegy, Rilke gives a metaphoric statement of the problem of language and recommends a procedure for approaching as near the horizon of silence as he considers feasible. A prerequisite of "emptying out" is to be able to perceive what one is "full of," what words and mechanical gestures one is stuffed with, like a doll; only then, in polar confrontation with the doll, does the "angel" appear, a figure representing an equally inhuman though "higher" possibility, that of an entirely unmediated, translinguistic apprehension. Neither doll nor angel, human beings remain situated within the kingdom of language. But for nature, then things, then other people, then the textures of ordinary life to be experienced from a stance other than the crippled one of mere spectatorship, language must regain its chastity. As Rilke describes it in the Ninth Elegy, the redemption of language (which is to say, the redemption of the world through its interiorization in consciousness) is a long, infinitely arduous task. Human beings are so "fallen" that they must start with the simplest linguistic act: the naming of things. Perhaps no more than this minimal function can be preserved from the general corruption of discourse. Language may very well have to remain within a permanent state of reduction. Though perhaps, when this spiritual exercise of confining language to naming is perfected, it may be possible to pass on to other, more ambitious uses of language, nothing must be attempted which will allow consciousness to become reestranged from itself.

For Rilke the overcoming of the alienation of consciousness is conceivable; and not, as in the radical myths of the mystics, through transcending language altogether. It suffices to cut back drastically the scope and use of language. A tremendous spiritual preparation (the contrary of "alienation") is required for this deceptively simple act of naming. It is nothing less than the scouring and harmonious sharpening of the senses (the very opposite of such violent projects, with roughly the same end and informed by the same hostility to verbal-rational culture, as "systematically deranging the senses").

Rilke's remedy lies halfway between exploiting the numbness of language as a gross, fully installed cultural institution and yielding to the suicidal vertigo of pure silence. But this middle ground of reducing language to naming can be claimed in quite another way than his. Contrast the benign nominalism proposed by Rilke (and proposed and practiced by Francis Ponge) with the brutal nominalism adopted by many other artists. The more familiar recourse of modern art to the aesthetics of the inventory is not made—as in Rilke—with an eye to "humanizing" things, but rather to confirming their inhumanity, their impersonality, their indifference to and separateness from human concerns. (Examples of the "inhumane" preoccupation with naming: Roussel's *Impressions of Africa;* the silk-screen paintings and early films of Andy Warhol; the early novels of Robbe-Grillet, which attempt to confine the function of language to bare physical description and location.)

Rilke and Ponge assume that there *are* priorities: rich as opposed to vacuous objects, events with a certain allure. (This is the incentive for trying to peel back language, allowing the "things" themselves to speak.) More decisively, they assume that if there are states of false (language-clogged) consciousness, there are also authentic states of consciousness—which it's the function of art to promote. The alternative view denies the traditional hierarchies of interest and meaning, in which some things have more "significance" than others. The distinction between true and false experience, true and false consciousness is also denied: in principle, one should desire to pay attention to everything. It's this view, most elegantly formulated by Cage though its practice is found everywhere, that leads to the art of the inventory, the catalogue, surfaces; also "chance." The function of art isn't to sanction any specific experience, except the state of being open to the multiplicity of experience—which ends in practice by a decided stress on things usually considered trivial or unimportant.

The attachment of contemporary art to the "minimal" narrative principle of the catalogue or inventory seems almost to parody the capitalist world-view, in which the environment is atomized into "items" (a category embracing things and persons, works of art and natural organisms), and in which every item is a commodity—that is, a discrete, portable object. A general leveling of value is encouraged in the art of inventory, which is itself only one of the possible approaches to an ideally uninflected discourse. Traditionally, the effects of an artwork have been unevenly distributed, to induce in the audience a certain sequence of experience: first arousing, then manipulating, and eventually fulfilling emotional expectations. What is proposed now is a discourse without emphases in this traditional sense. (Again, the principle of the stare as opposed to the look.)

Such art could also be described as establishing great "distance" (between spectator and art object, between the spectator and his emotions). But, psychologically, distance often is linked with the most intense state of feeling, in which the coolness or impersonality with which something is treated measures the insatiable interest that thing has for us. The distance that a great deal of "anti-humanist" art proposes is actually equivalent to obsession—an aspect of the involvement in "things" of which the "humanist" nominalism of Rilke has no intimation.

16

"There is something strange in the acts of writing and speaking," Novalis wrote in 1799. "The ridiculous and amazing mistake people make is to believe they use words in relation to things. They are unaware of the nature of language—which is to be its own and only concern, making it so fertile and splendid a mystery. When someone talks just for the sake of talking he is saying the most original and truthful thing he can say."

Novalis' statement may help explain an apparent paradox: that in the era of the widespread advocacy of art's silence, an increasing number of works of art babble. Verbosity and repetitiveness are particularly noticeable in the temporal arts of prose fiction, music, film, and dance, many of which cultivate a kind of ontological stammer—facilitated by their refusal of the incentives for a clean, anti-redundant discourse supplied by linear, beginning-middle-and-end construction. But actually, there's no contradiction. For the contemporary appeal for silence has never indicated merely a hostile dismissal of language. It also signifies a very high estimate of language—of its powers, of its past health, and of the current dangers it poses to a free consciousness. From this intense and ambivalent valuation proceeds the impulse for a discourse that appears both irrepressible (and, in principle, interminable) and strangely inarticulate, painfully reduced. Discernible in the fictions of Stein, Burroughs, and Beckett is the subliminal idea that it might be possible to out-talk language, or to talk oneself into silence.

This is not a very promising strategy, considering what results might reasonably be anticipated from it. But perhaps not so odd, when one observes how often the aesthetic of silence appears alongside a barely controlled abhorrence of the void.

Accommodating these two contrary impulses may produce the need to fill up all the spaces with objects of slight emotional weight or with large areas of barely modulated color or evenly detailed objects, or to spin a discourse with as few possible inflections, emotive variations, and risings and fallings of emphasis. These procedures seem analogous to the behavior of an obsessional neurotic warding off a danger. The acts of such a person must be repeated in the identical form, because the danger remains the same; and they must be repeated endlessly, because the danger never seems to go away. But the emotional fires feeding the art-discourse analogous to obsessionalism may be turned down so low one can almost forget they're there. Then all that's left to the ear is a kind of steady hum or drone. What's left to the eye is the neat filling of a space with things, or, more accurately, the patient transcription of the surface detail of things.

In this view, the "silence" of things, images, and words is a prerequisite for their proliferation. Were they endowed with a more potent, individual charge, each of the various elements of the artwork would claim more psychic space and then their total number might have to be reduced.

17

Sometimes the accusation against language is not directed against all of language but only against the written word. Thus Tristan Tzara urged the burning of all books and libraries to bring about a new era of oral legends. And McLuhan, as everyone knows, makes the sharpest distinction between written language (which exists in "visual space") and oral speech (which exists in "auditory space"), praising the psychic and cultural advantages of the latter as the basis for sensibility.

If written language is singled out as the culprit, what will be sought is not so much the reduction as the metamorphosis of language into something looser, more intuitive, less organized and inflected, non-linear (in McLuhan's terminology) and—noticeably—more verbose. But, of course, it is just these qualities that characterize many of the great prose narratives of our time. Joyce, Stein, Gadda, Laura Riding, Beckett, and Burroughs employ a language whose norms and energies come from oral speech, with its circular repetitive movements and essentially first-person voice.

"Speaking for the sake of speaking is the formula of deliverance," Novalis said. (Deliverance from what? From speaking? From art?)

In my opinion, Novalis has succinctly described the proper approach of the writer to language and offered the basic criterion for literature as an art. But to what extent oral speech is the privileged model for the speech for literature as an art is still an open question.

18

A corollary of the growth of this conception of art's language as autonomous and self-sufficient (and, in the end, self-reflective) is a decline in "meaning" as traditionally sought in works of art. "Speaking for the sake of speaking" forces us to relocate the meaning of linguistic or para-linguistic statements. We are led to abandon meaning (in the sense of references to entities outside the artwork) as the criterion for the language of art in favor of "use." (Wittgenstein's famous thesis, "the meaning is the use," can and should be rigorously applied to art.)

"Meaning" partially or totally converted into "use" is the secret behind the widespread strategy of *literalness,* a major development of the aesthetics of silence. A variant on this: hidden literality, exemplified by such different writers as Kafka and Beckett. The narratives of Kafka and Beckett seem puzzling because they appear to invite the reader to ascribe high-powered symbolic and allegorical meanings to them and, at the same time, repel such ascriptions. Yet when the narrative is examined, it discloses no more than what it literally means. The power of their language derives precisely from the fact that the meaning is so bare.

The effect of such bareness is often a kind of anxiety—like the anxiety produced when familiar things aren't in their place or playing their accustomed role. One may be made as anxious by unexpected literalness as by the Surrealists' "disturbing" objects and unexpected scale and condition of objects conjoined in an imaginary landscape. Whatever is wholly mysterious is at once both psychically relieving and anxiety-provoking. (A perfect machine for agitating this pair of contrary emotions: the Bosch drawing in a Dutch museum that shows trees furnished with two ears at the sides of their trunks, as if they were listening to the forest, while the forest floor is strewn with eyes.) Before a fully conscious work of art, one feels something like the mixture of anxiety, detachment, pruriency, and relief that a physically sound person feels when he glimpses an amputee. Beckett speaks favorably of a work of art which would be a "total object, complete with missing parts, instead of partial object. Question of degree."

But exactly what is a totality and what constitutes completeness in art (or anything else)? That problem is, in principle, unresolvable. Whatever way a work of art is, it could have been—could be—different. The necessity of *these* parts in this order is never given; it is conferred.

The refusal to admit this essential contingency (or openness) is what inspires the audience's will to confirm the closedness of a work by interpreting it, and what creates the feeling common among reflective artists and critics that the artwork is always somehow in arrears of or inadequate to its "subject." But unless one is committed to the idea that art "expresses" something, these procedures and attitudes are far from inevitable.

19

This tenacious concept of art as "expression" has given rise to the most common, and dubious, version of the notion of silence—which invokes the idea of "the ineffable." The theory supposes that the province of art is "the beautiful," which implies effects of unspeakableness, indescribability, ineffability. Indeed, the search to express the inexpressible is taken as the very criterion of art; and sometimes becomes the occasion for a strict—and to my mind untenable—distinction between prose literature and poetry. It is from this position that Valéry advanced his famous argument (repeated in a quite different context by Sartre) that the novel is not, strictly speaking, an art form at all. His reason is that since the aim of prose is to communicate, the use of language in prose is perfectly straightforward. Poetry, being an art, should have quite different aims: to express an experience which is essentially ineffable; using language to express muteness. In contrast to prose writers, poets are engaged in subverting their own instrument and seeking to pass beyond it.

This theory, so far as it assumes that art is concerned with beauty, is not very interesting. (Modern aesthetics is crippled by its dependence upon this essentially vacant concept. As if art were "about" beauty, as science is "about" truth!) But even if the theory dispenses with the notion of beauty, there is still a more serious objection. The view that expressing the ineffable is an essential function of poetry (considered as a paradigm of all the arts) is naïvely unhistorical. The ineffable, while surely a perennial category of consciousness, has certainly not always made its home in the arts. Its traditional shelter was in religious discourse and, secondarily (as Plato relates in his 7th Epistle), in philosophy. The fact that contemporary artists are concerned with silence—and, therefore, in one extension, with the ineffable—must be understood historically, as a consequence of the prevailing contemporary myth of the "absoluteness" of art. The value placed on silence doesn't arise by virtue of the *nature* of art, but derives from the contemporary ascription of certain "absolute" qualities to the art object and to the activity of the artist.

The extent to which art *is* involved with the ineffable is more specific, as well as contemporary: art, in the modern conception, is always connected with systematic transgressions of a formal sort. The systematic violation of older formal conventions practiced by modern artists gives their work a certain aura of the unspeakable—for instance, as the audience uneasily senses the negative presence of what else could be, but isn't being, said; and as any "statement" made in an aggressively new or difficult form tends to seem equivocal or merely vacant. But these features of ineffability must not be acknowledged at the expense of one's awareness of the positivity of the work of art. Contemporary art, no matter how much it has defined itself by a taste for negation, can still be analyzed as a set of assertions of a formal kind.

For instance, each work of art gives us a form or paradigm or model of *knowing* something, an epistemology. But viewed as a spiritual project, a vehicle of aspirations toward an absolute, what any work of art supplies is a specific model for meta-social or meta-ethical *tact*, a standard of decorum. Each artwork indicates the unity of certain preferences about what can and cannot be said (or represented). At the same time that it may make a tacit proposal for upsetting previously consecrated rulings on what can be said (or represented), it issues its own set of limits.

20

Contemporary artists advocate silence in two styles: loud and soft.

The loud style is a function of the unstable antithesis of "plenum" and "void." The sensuous, ecstatic, translinguistic apprehension of the plenum is notoriously fragile: in a terrible, almost instantaneous plunge it can collapse into the void of negative silence. With all its awareness of risk-taking (the hazards of spiritual nausea, even of madness), this advocacy of silence tends to be frenetic and overgeneralizing. It is also frequently apocalyptic and must endure the indignity of all apocalyptic thinking: namely, to prophesy the end, to see the day come, to outlive it, and then to set a new date for the incineration of consciousness and the definitive pollution of language and exhaustion of the possibilities of art-discourse.

The other way of talking about silence is more cautious. Basically, it presents itself as an extension of a main feature of traditional classicism: the concern with modes of propriety, with standards of seemliness. Silence is only "reticence" stepped up to the nth degree. Of course, in the translation of this concern from the matrix of traditional classical art, the tone has changed—from didactic seriousness to ironic openmindedness. But while the clamorous style of proclaiming the rhetoric of silence may seem more passionate, its more subdued advocates (like Cage, Johns) are saying something equally drastic. They are reacting to the same idea of art's absolute aspirations (by programmatic disavowals of art); they share the same disdain for the "meanings" established by bourgeois-rationalist culture, indeed for culture itself in the familiar sense. What is voiced by the Futurists, some of the Dada artists, and Burroughs as a harsh despair and perverse vision of apocalypse is no less serious for being proclaimed in a polite voice and as a sequence of playful affirmations. Indeed, it could be argued that silence is likely to remain a viable notion for modern art and consciousness only if deployed with a considerable, near systematic irony.

21

It is in the nature of all spiritual projects to tend to consume themselves—exhausting their own sense, the very meaning of the terms in which they are couched. (This is why "spirituality" must be continually reinvented.) All genuinely ultimate projects of consciousness eventually become projects for the unraveling of thought itself.

Art conceived as a spiritual project is no exception. As an abstracted and fragmented replica of the positive nihilism expounded by the radical religious myths, the serious art of our time has moved increasingly toward the most excruciating inflections of consciousness. Conceivably, irony is the only feasible counterweight to this grave use of art as the arena for the ordeal of consciousness. The present prospect is that artists will go on abolishing art, only to resurrect it in a more retracted version. As long as art bears up under the pressure of chronic interrogation, it would seem desirable that some of the questions have a certain playful quality.

But this prospect depends, perhaps, on the viability of irony itself.

From Socrates on, there are countless witnesses to the value of irony for the private individual: as a complex, serious method of seeking and holding one's truth, and as a means of saving one's sanity. But as irony becomes the good taste of what is, after all, an essentially collective activity—the making of art—it may prove less serviceable.

One need not judge as categorically as Nietzsche, who thought the spread of irony throughout a culture signified the floodtide of decadence and the approaching end of that culture's vitality and powers. In the post-political, electronically connected cosmopolis in which all serious modern artists have taken out premature citizenship, certain organic connections between culture and "thinking" (and art is certainly now, mainly, a form of thinking) appear to have been broken, so that Nietzsche's diagnosis may need to be modified. But if irony has more positive resources than Nietzsche acknowledged, there still remains a question as to how far the resources of irony can be stretched. It seems unlikely that the possibilities of continually undermining one's assumptions can go on unfolding indefinitely into the future, without being eventually checked by despair or by a laugh that leaves one without any breath at all.

Considerations for Thinking and Writing

1. After reading Sontag's "Woman's Beauty," Walker's "Beauty," and Carter's "Wound in the Face," discuss how contemporary film, television, or advertising reflects the views of one or more of these writers. Consider especially Sontag's notion that to celebrate women's beauty is really to disenfranchise them and limit their power.

2. Compare Sontag's "Aesthetics of Silence" with Audre Lorde's essay "The Transformation of Silence into Language and Action." Before developing your own thoughts on the power of speech and silence, read Tillie Olsen's essay in Part II: "Silences: One Out of Twelve." Consider what light Olsen's perspective sheds on Sontag's and Lorde's.

3. Apply the insights of Sontag's essay on photography ("In Plato's Cave") to images from contemporary advertising, modern art, or the history of photography. You might look at and into the photographs of Edward Steichen, Eugène Atget, Walker Evans, or W. Eugene Smith.

4. Compare Sontag's discussion of Simone Weil with Joyce Carol Oates's view of Weil. Which essay do you find more convincing? Why? Can you find a way to accommodate both Sontag's and Oates's views, or are their perspectives utterly contradictory? Explain.

5. Compare Susan Sontag as a critic of culture and society with Angela Carter, Joan Didion, or Audre Lorde. Consider the way each writer approaches her subject, the voice she establishes, and the perspective from which she makes her judgments.

6. Sontag is not ashamed to pay tribute to her intellectual heroes, to writers and thinkers she admires. After reading what she says of Elias Canetti and Paul Goodman (see the headnote), pay tribute to a writer who represents for you an example to be admired or emulated.

ALICE WALKER
(b. 1944)

Alice Walker's prose has been highly acclaimed for its passion, its honesty, and its beauty. She has published two collections of short stories and three novels, one of which, *The Color Purple*, won both the Pulitzer Prize and the American Book Award. Her essays, from which the selections that follow were taken, are collected in her 1983 volume *In Search of Our Mothers' Gardens*.

Walker's nonfiction prose ranges over such subjects as family relations, race relations, and the relations between the sexes. Some of her essays concern family relationships, which she has described as "sacred." Crucial for the survival of the family (especially the Black family), according to Walker, are "love, cohesion, and support." Also crucial are the devotion and creative energies of mothers, grandmothers, aunts—the real mainstays of families, who ensure their survival and continuity. Walker's most powerful and enduring prose, in fact, is about the women in her life.

Walker has paid tribute to Zora Neale Hurston, a writer she believes is woefully undervalued as both artist and influence. For Walker, Hurston has been a model of artistic integrity, exemplifying the career of a talented artist who suffered double neglect, since she was both a woman and a Black at a time when neither was much valued. And although Walker has written of other women artists, perhaps her most important tribute to women has been the celebration of her mother and grandmother. Despite suffering prejudice and oppression, these women nevertheless found outlets for their considerable artistic talent—Walker's grandmother with quilting and her mother with gardening.

Writing as a Black feminist, Walker reveals the tremendous suffering, frustration, and waste in the lives of the poor Black women she considers to be "among America's greatest heroes." Yet while she makes the lives of such women her most frequent subject, she occasionally expands her view to explore questions about our common humanity. On such occasions the impact of her writing is felt across boundaries of race, sex, and social class, largely because Walker offers us a vision of survival, suggesting, as one of her reviewers has observed, the capacity of human beings "to live in spiritual health and beauty" in such a way that "their inner selves can blossom."

Born in Georgia in 1944, Alice Walker is the youngest of eight children of Black sharecroppers. She attended Spellman College and Sarah Lawrence, from which she graduated with a B.A. During her college years she became deeply involved in the civil rights movement and participated in a variety of social programs, working for voter registration, welfare rights, and Head Start. She has taught at Jackson State College, Wellesley College, Brandeis University, and the University of California at Berkeley. Throughout her life Walker has exhibited a confidence that will not be shaken by discouragement. This confidence Walker learned from her mother, whose faith was weapon enough to combat any form of fear or discouragement.

Walker is a model of writerly determination. She has described how she was discouraged from pursuing a literary vocation by those who felt that as a Black woman she had little chance to succeed. This discouragement, however, only strengthened Walker's resolve to be the writer she has since become. And if she was disqualified by virtue of her race, sex, and education from becoming "a young Keats," as she put it, she could become another kind of poet, one less classically allusive and more immediately concerned with her history as a Black woman. And yet, ironically, there are ways in which Walker's writing reveals Keatsian concerns. Like Keats, she is a poet, perhaps as much a poet in her prose as in her verse. Like Keats also, Walker forges a self in her writing. And if Keats formed himself on the poetry of his great male British poetic precursors, Walker forms herself from her equally important and comparably creative female precursors. These connections, surprising as they may seem, accentuate the kinship of these writers in their capacity for empathy. And they further accentuate a shared desire to subject ideas to the proof of experience. As Keats put it in one of his famous letters, "axioms in philosophy are not axioms until they are proved upon our pulses." Walker's writing gives every indication that her ideas spring from deeply felt experience.

If Walker can be compared in these and perhaps other ways with so different a writer as Keats, she can be seen as even more closely linked to writers closer to home—to her sister writers of whatever race and color, especially to Black American writers both male and female, such as James Baldwin and Zora Neale Hurston. The writings of both Baldwin and Hurston serve as precedent and counterpoint for Walker's own. But whereas Baldwin achieved wide public prominence and acclaim, winning prizes for his essays and fiction, Hurston was assiduously neglected. Walker's appreciative essays about Hurston attempt to correct this unhappy state of affairs, one that we have inherited as a result of the undervaluation of the Black and female experience that was Hurston's central writerly preoccupation. With Hurston, who as a Black folklorist recorded and preserved a rich oral tradition, Walker shares a love for spoken language and a strong desire to see it survive. Like Hurston, Walker is a recorder of stories, her own life stories, the stories of her mother and grandmother, and the stories of women of earlier generations, both those who recorded them, as Hurston did, and those who never had the chance.

Throughout her work—as poet, novelist, editor, essayist, speaker, teacher—Walker has revealed an ability to see things fresh and to see them whole. She has also demonstrated an ability to identify and appreciate the many voices she has heard and to value their distinctiveness. Her own voice captures the essence of her vision in language at once beautiful and true.

Beauty: When the Other Dancer Is the Self

It is a bright summer day in 1947. My father, a fat, funny man with beautiful eyes and a subversive wit, is trying to decide which of his eight children he will take with him to the county fair. My mother, of course, will not go. She is knocked out from getting most of us ready: I hold my neck stiff against the pressure of her knuckles as she hastily completes the braiding and then beribboning of my hair.

My father is the driver for the rich old white lady up the road. Her name is Miss Mey. She owns all the land for miles around, as well as the house in which we live. All I remember about her is that she once offered to pay my mother thirty-five cents for cleaning her house, raking up piles of her magnolia leaves, and washing her family's clothes, and that my mother—she of no money, eight children, and a chronic earache—refused it. But I do not think of this in 1947. I am two and a half years old. I want to go everywhere my daddy goes. I am excited at the prospect of riding in a car. Someone has told me fairs are fun. That there is room in the car for only three of us doesn't faze me at all. Whirling happily in my starchy frock, showing off my biscuit-polished patent-leather shoes and lavender socks, tossing my head in a way that makes my ribbons bounce, I stand, hands on hips, before my father. "Take me, Daddy," I say with assurance; "I'm the prettiest!"

Later, it does not surprise me to find myself in Miss Mey's shiny black car, sharing the back seat with the other lucky ones. Does not surprise me that I thoroughly enjoy the fair. At home that night I tell the unlucky ones all I can remember about the merry-go-round, the man who eats live chickens, and the teddy bears, until they say: that's enough, baby Alice. Shut up now, and go to sleep.

It is Easter Sunday, 1950. I am dressed in a green, flocked, scalloped-hem dress (handmade by my adoring sister, Ruth) that has its own smooth satin petticoat and tiny hot-pink roses tucked into each scallop. My shoes, new T-strap patent leather, again highly biscuit-polished. I am six years old and have learned one of the longest Easter speeches to be heard that day, totally unlike the speech I said when I was two: "Easter lilies / pure and white / blossom in / the morning light." When I rise to give my speech I do so on a great wave of love and pride and expectation. People in the church stop rustling their new crinolines. They seem to hold their breath. I can tell they admire my dress, but it is my spirit, bordering on sassiness (womanish-ness), they secretly applaud.

"That girl's a little *mess*," they whisper to each other, pleased.

Naturally I say my speech without stammer or pause, unlike those who stutter, stammer, or, worst of all, forget. This is before the word "beautiful" exists in people's vocabulary, but "Oh, isn't she the *cutest* thing!" frequently floats my way. "And got so much sense!" they gratefully add . . . for which thoughtful addition I thank them to this day.

It was great fun being cute. But then, one day, it ended.

I am eight years old and a tomboy. I have a cowboy hat, cowboy boots, checkered shirt and pants, all red. My playmates are my brothers, two and four years older than I. Their colors are black and green, the only difference in the way we are dressed. On Saturday nights we all go to the picture show, even my mother; Westerns are her favorite kind of movie. Back home, "on the ranch," we pretend we are Tom Mix, Hopalong Cassidy, Lash LaRue (we've even named one of our dogs Lash LaRue); we chase each other for hours rustling cattle, being outlaws, delivering damsels from distress. Then my parents decide to buy my brothers guns. These are not "real" guns. They shoot "BBs," copper pellets my brothers say will kill birds. Because I am a girl, I do not get a gun. Instantly I am relegated to the position of Indian. Now there appears a great distance between us. They shoot and shoot at everything with their new guns. I try to keep up with my bow and arrows.

One day while I am standing on top of our makeshift "garage"—pieces of tin nailed across some poles—holding my bow and arrow and looking out toward the fields, I feel an incredible blow in my right eye. I look down just in time to see my brother lower his gun.

Both brothers rush to my side. My eye stings, and I cover it with my hand. "If you tell," they say, "we will get a whipping. You don't want that to happen, do you?" I do not. "Here is a piece of wire," says the older brother, picking it up from the roof; "say you stepped on one end of it and the other flew up and hit you." The pain is beginning to start. "Yes," I say. "Yes, I will say that is what happened." If I do not say this is what happened, I know my brothers will find ways to make me wish I had. But now I will say anything that gets me to my mother.

Confronted by our parents we stick to the lie agreed upon. They place me on a bench on the porch and I close my left eye while they examine the right. There is a tree growing from underneath the porch that climbs past the railing to the roof. It is the last thing my right eye sees. I watch as its trunk, its branches, and then its leaves are blotted out by the rising blood.

I am in shock. First there is intense fever, which my father tries to break using lily leaves bound around my head. Then there are chills: my mother tries to get me to eat soup. Eventually, I do not know how, my parents learn what has happened. A week after the "accident" they take me to see a doctor. "Why did you wait so long to come?" he asks, looking into my eye and shaking his head. "Eyes are sympathetic," he says. "If one is blind, the other will likely become blind too."

This comment of the doctor's terrifies me. But it is really how I look that bothers me most. Where the BB pellet struck there is a glob of whitish scar tissue, a hideous cataract, on my eye. Now when I stare at people—a favorite pastime, up to now—they will stare back. Not at the "cute" little girl, but at her scar. For six years I do not stare at anyone, because I do not raise my head.

Years later, in the throes of a mid-life crisis, I ask my mother and sister whether I changed after the "accident." "No," they say, puzzled. "What do you mean?"

What do I mean?

I am eight, and, for the first time, doing poorly in school, where I have been something of a whiz since I was four. We have just moved to the place where the "accident" occurred. We do not know any of the people around us because this is a different county. The only time I see the friends I knew is when we go back to our old church. The new school is the former state penitentiary. It is a large stone building, cold and drafty, crammed to overflowing with boisterous, ill-disciplined children. On the third floor there is a huge circular imprint of some partition that has been torn out.

"What used to be here?" I ask a sullen girl next to me on our way past it to lunch.

"The electric chair," says she.

At night I have nightmares about the electric chair, and about all the people reputedly "fried" in it. I am afraid of the school, where all the students seem to be budding criminals.

"What's the matter with your eye?" they ask, critically.

When I don't answer (I cannot decide whether it was an "accident" or not), they shove me, insist on a fight.

My brother, the one who created the story about the wire, comes to my rescue. But then brags so much about "protecting" me, I become sick.

After months of torture at the school, my parents decide to send me back to our old community, to my old school. I live with my grandparents and the teacher they board. But there is no room for Phoebe, my cat. By the time my grandparents decide there *is* room, and I ask for my cat, she cannot be found. Miss Yarborough, the boarding teacher, takes me under her wing, and begins to teach me to play the piano. But soon she marries an African—a "prince," she says—and is whisked away to his continent.

At my old school there is at least one teacher who loves me. She is the teacher who "knew me before I was born" and bought my first baby clothes. It is she who makes life bearable. It is her presence that finally helps me turn on the one child at the school who continually calls me "one-eyed bitch." One day I simply grab him by his coat and beat him until I am satisfied. It is my teacher who tells me my mother is ill.

My mother is lying in bed in the middle of the day, something I have never seen. She is in too much pain to speak. She has an abscess in her ear. I stand looking down on her, knowing that if she dies, I cannot live. She is being treated with warm oils and hot bricks held against her cheek. Finally a doctor comes. But I must go back to my grandparents' house. The weeks pass but I am hardly aware of it. All I know is that my mother might die, my father is not so jolly, my brothers still have their guns, and I am the one sent away from home.

"You did not change," they say.

Did I imagine the anguish of never looking up?

I am twelve. When relatives come to visit I hide in my room. My cousin Brenda, just my age, whose father works in the post office and whose mother is a nurse, comes to find me. "Hello," she says. And then she asks, looking at my recent school picture, which I did not want taken, and on which the "glob," as I think of it, is clearly visible, "You still can't see out of that eye?"

"No," I say, and flop back on the bed over my book.

That night, as I do almost every night, I abuse my eye. I rant and rave at it, in front of the mirror. I plead with it to clear up before morning. I tell it I hate and despise it. I do not pray for sight. I pray for beauty.

"You did not change," they say.

I am fourteen and baby-sitting for my brother Bill, who lives in Boston. He is my favorite brother and there is a strong bond between us. Understanding my feelings of shame and ugliness he and his wife take me to a local hospital, where the "glob" is removed by a doctor named O. Henry. There is still a small bluish crater where the scar tissue was, but the ugly white stuff is gone. Almost immediately I become a different person from the girl who does not raise her head. Or so I think. Now that I've raised my head I win the boyfriend of my dreams. Now that I've raised my head I have plenty of friends. Now that I've raised my head classwork comes from my lips as faultlessly as Easter speeches did, and I leave high school as valedictorian, most popular student, and *queen,* hardly believing my luck. Ironically, the girl who was voted most beautiful in our class (and was) was later shot twice through the chest by a male companion, using a "real" gun, while she was pregnant. But that's another story in itself. Or is it?

"You did not change," they say.

It is now thirty years since the "accident." A beautiful journalist comes to visit and to interview me. She is going to write a cover story for her magazine that focuses on my latest book. "Decide how you want to look on the cover," she says. "Glamorous, or whatever."

Never mind "glamorous," it is the "whatever" that I hear. Suddenly all I can think of is whether I will get enough sleep the night before the photography session: if I don't, my eye will be tired and wander, as blind eyes will.

At night in bed with my lover I think up reasons why I should not appear on the cover of a magazine. "My meanest critics will say I've sold out," I say. "My family will now realize I write scandalous books."

"But what's the real reason you don't want to do this?" he asks.

"Because in all probability," I say in a rush, "my eye won't be straight."

"It will be straight enough," he says. Then, "Besides, I thought you'd made your peace with that."

And I suddenly remember that I have.

I remember:

I am talking to my brother Jimmy, asking if he remembers anything unusual about the day I was shot. He does not know I consider that day the last time my father, with his sweet home remedy of cool lily leaves, chose me, and that I suffered and raged inside because of this. "Well," he says, "all I remember is standing by the side of the highway with Daddy, trying to flag down a car. A white man stopped, but when Daddy said he needed somebody to take his little girl to the doctor, he drove off."

I remember:

I am in the desert for the first time. I fall totally in love with it. I am so overwhelmed by its beauty, I confront for the first time, consciously, the meaning of the doctor's words years ago: "Eyes are sympathetic. If one is blind, the other will likely become blind too." I realize I have dashed about the world madly, looking at this, looking at that, storing up images against the fading of the light. *But I might have missed seeing the desert!* The shock of that possibility—and gratitude for over twenty-five years of sight—sends me literally to my knees. Poem after poem comes—which is perhaps how poets pray.

On Sight

I am so thankful I have seen
The Desert
And the creatures in the desert
And the desert Itself.

The desert has its own moon
Which I have seen
With my own eye.
There is no flag on it.

Trees of the desert have arms
All of which are always up
That is because the moon is up
The sun is up
Also the sky
The stars
Clouds
None with flags.

If there *were* flags, I doubt
the trees would point.
Would you?

But mostly, I remember this:

I am twenty-seven, and my baby daughter is almost three. Since her birth I have worried about her discovery that her mother's eyes are different from other people's. Will she be embarrassed? I think. What will she say? Every day she watches a television program called "Big Blue Marble." It begins with a picture of the earth as it appears from the moon. It is bluish, a little battered-looking, but full of light, with whitish clouds swirling around it. Every time I see it I weep with love, as if it is a picture of Grandma's house. One day when I am putting Rebecca down for her nap, she suddenly focuses on my eye. Something inside me cringes, gets ready to try to protect myself. All children are cruel about physical differences, I know from experience, and that they don't always mean to be is another matter. I assume Rebecca will be the same.

But no-o-o-o. She studies my face intently as we stand, her inside and me outside her crib. She even holds my face maternally between her dimpled little hands. Then, looking every bit as serious and lawyerlike as her father, she says, as if it may just possibly have slipped my attention: "Mommy, there's a *world* in your eye." (As in, "Don't be alarmed, or do anything crazy.") And then, gently, but with great interest: "Mommy, where did you *get* that world in your eye?"

For the most part, the pain left then. (So what, if my brothers grew up to buy even more powerful pellet guns for their sons and to carry real guns themselves. So what, if a young "Morehouse man" once nearly fell off the steps of Trevor Arnett Library because he thought my eyes were blue.) Crying and laughing I ran to the bathroom, while Rebecca mumbled and sang herself off to sleep. Yes indeed, I realized, looking into the mirror. There *was* a world in my eye. And I saw that it was possible to love it: that in fact, for all it had taught me of shame and anger and inner vision, I *did* love it. Even to see it drifting out of orbit in boredom, or rolling up out of fatigue, not to mention floating back at attention in excitement (bearing witness, a friend has called it), deeply suitable to my personality, and even characteristic of me.

That night I dream I am dancing to Stevie Wonder's song "Always" (the name of the song is really "As," but I hear it as "Always"). As I dance, whirling and joyous, happier than I've ever been in my life, another bright-faced dancer joins me. We dance and kiss each other and hold each other through the night. The other dancer has obviously come through all right, as I have done. She is beautiful, whole and free. And she is also me.

Motheroot

Creation often
needs two hearts
one to root
and one to flower
One to sustain
in time of drouth
and hold fast
against winds of pain
the fragile bloom
that in the glory
of its hour
affirms a heart
unsung, unseen.

—MARILOU AWIAKTA,
Abiding Appalachia

In Search of Our Mothers' Gardens

> I described her own nature and temperament. Told how they needed a larger life for their expression. . . . I pointed out that in lieu of proper channels, her emotions had overflowed into paths that dissipated them. I talked, beautifully I thought, about an art that would be born, an art that would open the way for women the likes of her. I asked her to hope, and build up an inner life against the coming of that day. . . . I sang, with a strange quiver in my voice, a promise song.
>
> —*Jean Toomer, "Avey," Cane*

The poet speaking to a prostitute who falls asleep while he's talking—

When the poet Jean Toomer walked through the South in the early twenties, he discovered a curious thing: black women whose spirituality was so intense, so deep, so *unconscious*, that they were themselves unaware of the richness they held. They stumbled blindly through their lives: creatures so abused and mutilated in body, so dimmed and confused by pain, that they considered themselves unworthy even of hope. In the selfless abstractions their bodies became to the men who used them, they became more than "sexual objects," more even than mere women: they became "Saints." Instead of being perceived as whole persons, their bodies became shrines: what was thought to be their minds became temples suitable for worship. These crazy Saints stared out at the world, wildly, like lunatics—or quietly, like suicides; and the "God" that was in their gaze was as mute as a great stone.

Who were these Saints? These crazy, loony, pitiful women?

Some of them, without a doubt, were our mothers and grandmothers.

In the still heat of the post-Reconstruction South, this is how they seemed to Jean Toomer: exquisite butterflies trapped in an evil honey, toiling away their lives in an era, a century, that did not acknowledge them, except as "the *mule* of the world." They dreamed dreams that no one knew—not even themselves, in any coherent fashion—and saw visions no one could understand. They wandered or sat about the countryside crooning lullabies to ghosts, and drawing the mother of Christ in charcoal on courthouse walls.

They forced their minds to desert their bodies and their striving spirits sought to rise, like frail whirlwinds from the hard red clay. And when those frail whirlwinds fell, in scattered particles, upon the ground, no one mourned. Instead, men lit candles to celebrate the emptiness that remained, as people do who enter a beautiful but vacant space to resurrect a God.

Our mothers and grandmothers, some of them: moving to music not yet written. And they waited.

They waited for a day when the unknown thing that was in them would be made known; but guessed, somehow in their darkness, that on the day of their revelation they would be long dead. Therefore to Toomer they walked, and even ran, in slow motion. For they were going nowhere immediate, and the future was not yet within their grasp. And men took our mothers and grandmothers, "but got no pleasure from it." So complex was their passion and their calm.

To Toomer, they lay vacant and fallow as autumn fields, with harvest time never in sight: and he saw them enter loveless marriages, without joy; and become prostitutes, without resistance; and become mothers of children, without fulfillment.

For these grandmothers and mothers of ours were not Saints, but Artists; driven to a numb and bleeding madness by the springs of creativity in them for which there was no release. They were Creators, who lived lives of spiritual waste, because they were so rich in spirituality—which is the basis of Art—that the strain of enduring their unused and unwanted talent drove them insane. Throwing away this spirituality was their pathetic attempt to lighten the soul to a weight their work-worn, sexually abused bodies could bear.

What did it mean for a black woman to be an artist in our grandmothers' time? In our great-grandmothers' day? It is a question with an answer cruel enough to stop the blood.

Did you have a genius of a great-great-grandmother who died under some ignorant and depraved white overseer's lash? Or was she required to bake biscuits for a lazy backwater tramp, when she cried out in her soul to paint watercolors of sunsets, or the rain falling on the green and peaceful pasturelands? Or was her body broken and forced to bear children (who were more often than not sold away from her)—eight, ten, fifteen, twenty children—when her one joy was the thought of modeling heroic figures of rebellion, in stone or clay?

How was the creativity of the black woman kept alive, year after year and century after century, when for most of the years black people have been in America, it was a punishable crime for a black person to read or write? And the freedom to paint, to sculpt, to expand the mind with action did not exist. Consider, if you can bear to imagine it, what might have been the result if singing, too, had been forbidden by law. Listen to the voices of Bessie Smith, Billie Holiday, Nina Simone, Roberta Flack, and Aretha Franklin, among others, and imagine those voices muzzled for life. Then you may begin to comprehend the lives of our "crazy," "Sainted" mothers and grandmothers. The agony of the lives of women who might have been Poets, Novelists, Essayists, and Short-Story Writers (over a period of centuries), who died with their real gifts stifled within them.

And, if this were the end of the story, we would have cause to cry out in my paraphrase of Okot p'Bitek's great poem:

> O, my clanswomen
> Let us all cry together!
> Come,
> Let us mourn the death of our mother,
> The death of a Queen
> The ash that was produced
> By a great fire!
> O, this homestead is utterly dead
> Close the gates
> With *lacari* thorns,
> For our mother
> The creator of the Stool is lost!
> And all the young women
> Have perished in the wilderness!

But this is not the end of the story, for all the young women—our mothers and grandmothers, *ourselves*—have not perished in the wilderness. And if we ask ourselves why, and search for and find the answer, we will know beyond all efforts to erase it from our minds, just exactly who, and of what, we black American women are.

One example, perhaps the most pathetic, most misunderstood one, can provide a backdrop for our mothers' work: Phillis Wheatley, a slave in the 1700s.

Virginia Woolf, in her book *A Room of One's Own,* wrote that in order for a woman to write fiction she must have two things, certainly: a room of her own (with key and lock) and enough money to support herself.

What then are we to make of Phillis Wheatley, a slave, who owned not even herself? This sickly, frail black girl who required a servant of her own at times—her health was so precarious—and who, had she been white, would have been easily considered the intellectual superior of all the women and most of the men in the society of her day.

Virginia Woolf wrote further, speaking of course not of our Phillis, that "any woman born with a great gift in the sixteenth century [insert "eighteenth century," insert "black woman," insert "born or made a slave"] would certainly have gone crazed, shot herself, or ended her days in some lonely cottage outside the village, half witch, half wizard [insert "Saint"], feared and mocked at. For it needs little skill and psychology to be sure that a highly gifted girl who had tried to use her gift for poetry would have been so thwarted and hindered by contrary instincts [add "chains, guns, the lash, the ownership of one's body by someone else, submission to an alien religion"], that she must have lost her health and sanity to a certainty."

The key words, as they relate to Phillis, are "contrary instincts." For when we read the poetry of Phillis Wheatley—as when we read the novels of Nella Larsen or the oddly false-sounding autobiography of that freest of all black women writers, Zora Hurston—evidence of "contrary instincts" is everywhere. Her loyalties were completely divided, as was, without question, her mind.

But how could this be otherwise? Captured at seven, a slave of wealthy, doting whites who instilled in her the "savagery" of the Africa they "rescued" her from . . . one wonders if she was even able to remember her homeland as she had known it, or as it really was.

Yet, because she did try to use her gift for poetry in a world that made her a slave, she was "so thwarted and hindered by . . . contrary instincts, that she . . . lost her health. . . ." In the last years of her brief life, burdened not only with the need to express her gift but also with a penniless, friendless "freedom" and several small children for whom she was forced to do strenuous work to feed, she lost her health, certainly. Suffering from malnutrition and neglect and who knows what mental agonies, Phillis Wheatley died.

So torn by "contrary instincts" was black, kidnapped, enslaved Phillis that her description of "the Goddess"—as she poetically called the Liberty she did not have—is ironically, cruelly humorous. And, in fact, has held Phillis up to ridicule for more than a century. It is usually read prior to hanging Phillis's memory as that of a fool. She wrote:

> The Goddess comes, she moves divinely fair,
> Olive and laurel binds her *golden* hair.
> Wherever shines this native of the skies,
> Unnumber'd charms and recent graces rise. [My italics]

It is obvious that Phillis, the slave, combed the "Goddess's" hair every morning; prior, perhaps, to bringing in the milk, or fixing her mistress's lunch. She took her imagery from the one thing she saw elevated above all others.

With the benefit of hindsight we ask, "How could she?"

But at last, Phillis, we understand. No more snickering when your stiff, struggling, ambivalent lines are forced on us. We know now that you were not an idiot or a traitor; only a sickly little black girl, snatched from your home and country and made a slave; a woman who still struggled to sing the song that was your gift, although in a land of barbarians who praised you for your bewildered tongue. It is not so much what you sang, as that you kept alive, in so many of our ancestors, *the notion of song.*

Black women are called, in the folklore that so aptly identifies one's status in society, "the *mule* of the world," because we have been handed the burdens that everyone else—*everyone* else—refused to carry. We have also been called "Matriarchs," "Superwomen," and "Mean and Evil Bitches." Not to mention "Castraters" and "Sapphire's Mama." When we have pleaded for understanding, our character has been distorted; when we have asked for simple caring, we have been handed empty inspirational appellations, then stuck in the farthest corner. When we have asked for love, we have been given children. In short, even our plainer gifts, our labors of fidelity and love, have been knocked down our throats. To be an artist and a black woman, even today, lowers our status in many respects, rather than raises it: and yet, artists we will be.

Therefore we must fearlessly pull out of ourselves and look at and identify with our lives the living creativity some of our great-grandmothers were not allowed to know. I stress *some* of them because it is well known that the majority of our great-grandmothers knew, even without "knowing" it, the reality of their spirituality, even if they didn't recognize it beyond what happened in the singing at church—and they never had any intention of giving it up.

How they did it—those millions of black women who were not Phillis Wheatley, or Lucy Terry or Frances Harper or Zora Hurston or Nella Larsen or Bessie Smith; or Elizabeth Catlett, or Katherine Dunham, either—brings me to the title of this essay, "In Search of Our Mothers' Gardens," which is a personal account that is yet shared, in its theme and its meaning, by all of us. I found, while thinking about the far-reaching world of the creative black woman, that often the truest answer to a question that really matters can be found very close.

In the late 1920s my mother ran away from home to marry my father. Marriage, if not running away, was expected of seventeen-year-old girls. By the time she was twenty, she had two children and was pregnant with a third. Five children later, I was born. And this is how I came to know my mother: she seemed a large, soft, loving-eyed woman who was rarely impatient in our home. Her quick, violent temper was on view only a few times a year, when she battled with the white landlord who had the misfortune to suggest to her that her children did not need to go to school.

She made all the clothes we wore, even my brothers' overalls. She made all the towels and sheets we used. She spent the summers canning vegetables and fruits. She spent the winter evenings making quilts enough to cover all our beds.

During the "working" day, she labored beside—not behind—my father in the fields. Her day began before sunup, and did not end until late at night. There was never a moment for her to sit down, undisturbed, to unravel her own private thoughts; never a time free from interruption—by work or the noisy inquiries of her many children. And yet, it is to my mother—and all our mothers who were not famous—that I went in search of the secret of what has fed that muzzled and often mutilated, but vibrant, creative spirit that the black woman has inherited, and that pops out in wild and unlikely places to this day.

But when, you will ask, did my overworked mother have time to know or care about feeding the creative spirit?

The answer is so simple that many of us have spent years discovering it. We have constantly looked high, when we should have looked high—and low.

For example: in the Smithsonian Institution in Washington, D.C., there hangs a quilt unlike any other in the world. In fanciful, inspired, and yet simple and identifiable figures, it portrays the story of the Crucifixion. It is considered rare, beyond price. Though it follows no known pattern of quilt-making, and though it is made of bits and pieces of worthless rags, it is obviously the work of a person of powerful imagination and deep spiritual feeling. Below this quilt I saw a note that says it was made by "an anonymous Black woman in Alabama, a hundred years ago."

If we could locate this "anonymous" black woman from Alabama, she would turn out to be one of our grandmothers—an artist who left her mark in the only materials she could afford, and in the only medium her position in society allowed her to use.

As Virginia Woolf wrote further, in *A Room of One's Own:*

> Yet genius of a sort must have existed among women as it must have existed among the working class. [Change this to "slaves" and "the wives and daughters of sharecroppers."] Now and again an Emily Brontë or a Robert Burns [change this to "a Zora Hurston or a Richard Wright"] blazes out and proves its presence. But certainly it never got itself on to paper. When, however, one reads of a witch being ducked, of a woman possessed by devils [or "Sainthood"], of a wise woman selling herbs [our root workers), or even a very remarkable man who had a mother, then I think we are on the track of a lost novelist, a suppressed poet, of some mute and inglorious Jane Austen. . . . Indeed, I would venture to guess that Anon, who wrote so many poems without signing them, was often a woman. . . .

And so our mothers and grandmothers have, more often than not anonymously, handed on the creative spark, the seed of the flower they themselves never hoped to see: or like a sealed letter they could not plainly read.

And so it is, certainly, with my own mother. Unlike "Ma" Rainey's songs, which retained their creator's name even while blasting forth from Bessie Smith's mouth, no song or poem will bear my mother's name. Yet so many of the stories that I write, that we all write, are my mother's stories. Only recently did I fully realize this: that through years of listening to my mother's stories of her life, I have absorbed not only the stories themselves, but something of the manner in which she spoke, something of the urgency that involves the knowledge that her stories—like her life—must be recorded. It is probably for this reason that so much of what I have written is about characters whose counterparts in real life are so much older than I am.

But the telling of these stories, which came from my mother's lips as naturally as breathing, was not the only way my mother showed herself as an artist. For stories, too, were subject to being distracted, to dying without conclusion. Dinners must be started, and cotton must be gathered before the big rains. The artist that was and is my mother showed itself to me only after many years. This is what I finally noticed:

Like Mem, a character in *The Third Life of Grange Copeland,* my mother adorned with flowers whatever shabby house we were forced to live in. And not just your typical straggly country stand of zinnias, either. She planted ambitious gardens—and still does—with over fifty different varieties of plants that bloom profusely from early March until late November. Before she left home for the fields, she watered her flowers, chopped up the grass, and laid out new beds. When she returned from the fields she might divide clumps of bulbs, dig a cold pit, uproot and replant roses, or prune branches from her taller bushes or trees—until night came and it was too dark to see.

Whatever she planted grew as if by magic, and her fame as a grower of flowers spread over three counties. Because of her creativity with her flowers, even my memories of poverty are seen through a screen of blooms—sunflowers, petunias, roses, dahlias, forsythia, spirea, delphiniums, verbena . . . and on and on.

And I remember people coming to my mother's yard to be given cuttings from her flowers; I hear again the praise showered on her because whatever rocky soil she landed on, she turned into a garden. A garden so brilliant with colors, so original in its design, so magnificent with life and creativity, that to this day people drive by our house in Georgia—perfect strangers and imperfect strangers—and ask to stand or walk among my mother's art.

I notice that it is only when my mother is working in her flowers that she is radiant, almost to the point of being invisible—except as Creator: hand and eye. She is involved in work her soul must have. Ordering the universe in the image of her personal conception of Beauty.

Her face, as she prepares the Art that is her gift, is a legacy of respect she leaves to me, for all that illuminates and cherishes life. She has handed down respect for the possibilities—and the will to grasp them.

For her, so hindered and intruded upon in so many ways, being an artist has still been a daily part of her life. This ability to hold on, even in very simple ways, is work black women have done for a very long time.

This poem is not enough, but it is something, for the woman who literally covered the holes in our walls with sunflowers:

> They were women then
> My mama's generation
> Husky of voice—Stout of
> Step
> With fists as well as
> Hands
> How they battered down
> Doors
> And ironed
> Starched white
> Shirts
> How they led

Armies
Headragged Generals
Across mined
Fields
Booby-trapped
Kitchens
To discover books
Desks
A place for us
How they knew what we
Must know
Without knowing a page
Of it
Themselves.

Guided by my heritage of a love of beauty and a respect for strength—in search of my mother's garden, I found my own.

And perhaps in Africa over two hundred years ago, there was just such a mother; perhaps she painted vivid and daring decorations in oranges and yellows and greens on the walls of her hut; perhaps she sang—in a voice like Roberta Flack's—*sweetly* over the compounds of her village; perhaps she wove the most stunning mats or told the most ingenious stories of all the village storytellers. Perhaps she was herself a poet—though only her daughter's name is signed to the poems that we know.

Perhaps Phillis Wheatley's mother was also an artist.

Perhaps in more than Phillis Wheatley's biological life is her mother's signature made clear.

Zora Neale Hurston:
A Cautionary Tale and a Partisan View

I became aware of my need of Zora Neale Hurston's work some time before I knew her work existed. In late 1970 I was writing a story that required accurate material on voodoo practices among rural Southern blacks of the thirties; there seemed none available I could trust. A number of white, racist anthropologists and folklorists of the period had, not surprisingly, disappointed and insulted me. They thought blacks inferior, peculiar, and comic, and for me this undermined, no, *destroyed,* the relevance of their books. Fortunately, it was then that I discovered *Mules and Men,* Zora's book on folklore, collecting, herself, and her small, all-black community of Eatonville, Florida. Because she immersed herself in her own culture even as she recorded its "big old lies," i.e., folk tales, it was possible to see how she and it (even after she had attended Barnard College and become a respected writer and apprentice anthropologist) fit together. The authenticity of her material was verified by her familiarity with its context, and I was soothed by her assurance that she was exposing not simply an adequate culture but a superior one. That black people can be on occasion peculiar and comic was knowledge she enjoyed. That they could be racially or culturally inferior to whites never seems to have crossed her mind.

The first time I heard Zora's *name,* I was auditing a black-literature class taught by the great poet Margaret Walker, at Jackson State College in Jackson, Mississippi. The reason this fact later slipped my mind was that Zora's name and accomplishments came and went so fast. The class was studying the usual "giants" of black literature: Chesnutt, Toomer, Hughes, Wright, Ellison, and Baldwin, with the hope of reaching LeRoi Jones very soon. Jessie Fauset, Nella Larsen, Ann Petry, Paule Marshall (unequaled in intelligence, vision, craft by anyone of her generation, to put her contributions to our literature modestly), and Zora Neale Hurston were names appended, like verbal footnotes, to the illustrious all-male list that paralleled them. As far as I recall, none of their work was studied in the course. Much of it was out of print, in any case, and remains so. (Perhaps Gwendolyn Brooks and Margaret Walker herself were exceptions to this list; both poets of such obvious necessity it would be impossible to overlook them. And their work—owing to the political and cultural nationalism of the sixties—was everywhere available.)

When I read *Mules and Men* I was delighted. Here was this perfect book! The "perfection" of which I immediately tested on my relatives, who are such typical black Americans they are useful for every sort of political, cultural, or economic survey. Very regular people from the South, rapidly forgetting their Southern cultural inheritance in the suburbs and ghettos of Boston and New York, they sat around reading the book themselves, listening to me read the book, listening to each other read the book, and a kind of paradise was regained. For what Zora's book did was this: it gave them back all the stories they had forgotten or of which they had grown ashamed (told to us years ago by our parents and grandparents—not one of whom could *not* tell a story to make you weep, or laugh) and showed how marvelous, and, indeed, priceless, they are. This is not exaggerated. No matter how they read the stories Zora had collected, no matter how much distance they tried to maintain between themselves, as new sophisticates, and the lives their parents and grandparents lived, no matter how they tried to remain cool toward all Zora revealed, in the end they could not hold back the smiles, the laughter, the joy over who she was showing them to be: descendants of an inventive, joyous, courageous, and outrageous people; loving drama, appreciating wit, and, most of all, relishing the pleasure of each other's loquacious and *bodacious* company.

This was my first indication of the quality I feel is most characteristic of Zora's work: racial health; a sense of black people as complete, complex, *undiminished* human beings, a sense that is lacking in so much black writing and literature. (In my opinion, only Du Bois showed an equally consistent delight in the beauty and spirit of black people, which is interesting when one considers that the angle of his vision was completely the opposite of Zora's.) Zora's pride in black people was so pronounced in the ersatz black twenties that it made other blacks suspicious and perhaps uncomfortable (after all, *they* were still infatuated with things European). Zora was interested in Africa, Haiti, Jamaica, and—for a little racial diversity (Indians)—Honduras. She also had a confidence in herself as an individual that few people (anyone?), black or white, understood. This was because Zora grew up in a community of black people who had enormous respect for themselves and for their ability to govern themselves. Her own father had written the Eatonville town laws. This community affirmed her right to exist, and loved her as an extension of its self. For how many other black Americans is this true? It certainly isn't true for any that I know. In her easy self-acceptance, Zora was more like an uncolonized African than she was like her contemporary American blacks, most of whom believed, at least during their formative years, that their blackness was something wrong with them.

On the contrary, Zora's early work shows she grew up pitying whites because the ones she saw lacked "light" and soul. It is impossible to imagine Zora envying anyone (except tongue in cheek), and least of all a white person for being white. Which is, after all, if one is black, a clear and present calamity of the mind.

Condemned to a desert island for life, with an allotment of ten books to see me through, I would choose, unhesitatingly, two of Zora's: *Mules and Men,* because I would need to be able to pass on to younger generations the life of American blacks as legend and myth; and *Their Eyes Were Watching God,* because I would want to enjoy myself while identifying with the black heroine, Janie Crawford, as she acted out many roles in a variety of settings, and functioned (with spectacular results!) in romantic and sensual love. *There is no book more important to me than this one* (including Toomer's *Cane,* which comes close, but from what I recognize is a more perilous direction).

Having committed myself to Zora's work, loving it, in fact, I became curious to see what others had written about her. This was, for the young, impressionable, barely begun writer I was, a mistake. After reading the misleading, deliberately belittling, inaccurate, and generally irresponsible attacks on her work and her life by almost everyone, I became for a time paralyzed with confusion and fear. For if a woman who had given so much of obvious value to all of us (and at such risks: to health, reputation, sanity) could be so casually pilloried and consigned to a sneering oblivion, what chance would someone else—for example, myself—have? I was aware that I had much less gumption than Zora.

For a long time I sat looking at this fear, and at what caused it. Zora was a woman who wrote and spoke her mind—as far as one could tell, practically always. People who knew her and were unaccustomed to this characteristic in a woman, who was, moreover, a. sometimes in error, and b. successful, for the most part, in her work, attacked her as meanly as they could. Would I also be attacked if I wrote and spoke my mind? And if I dared open my mouth to speak, must I always be "correct"? And by whose standards? Only those who have read the critics' opinions of Zora and her work will comprehend the power of these questions to riddle a young writer with self-doubt.

Eventually, however, I discovered that I repudiate and despise the kind of criticism that intimidates rather than instructs the young; and I dislike fear, especially in myself. I did then what fear rarely fails to force me to do: I fought back. I began to fight for Zora and her work; for what I knew was good and must not be lost to us.

Robert Hemenway was the first critic I read who seemed indignant that Zora's life ended in poverty and obscurity; that her last days were spent in a welfare home and her burial paid for by "subscription." Though Zora herself, as he is careful to point out in his book *Zora Neale Hurston: A Literary Biography,* remained gallant and unbowed until the end. It was Hemenway's efforts to define Zora's legacy and his exploration of her life that led me, in 1973, to an overgrown Fort Pierce, Florida, graveyard in an attempt to locate and mark Zora's grave. Although by that time I considered her a native American genius, there was nothing grand or historic in my mind. It was, rather, a duty I accepted as naturally mine—as a black person, a woman, and a writer—because Zora was dead and I, for the time being, was alive.

*   *   *

Zora was funny, irreverent (she was the first to call the Harlem Renaissance literati the "niggerati"), good-looking, sexy, and once sold hot dogs in a Washington park just to record accurately how the black people who bought the hot dogs talked. (A letter I received a month ago from one of her old friends in D.C. brought this news.) She would go anywhere she had to go: Harlem, Jamaica, Haiti, Bermuda, to find out anything she simply had to know. She loved to give parties. Loved to dance. Would wrap her head in scarves as black women in Africa, Haiti, and everywhere else have done for centuries. On the other hand, she loved to wear hats, tilted over one eye, and pants and boots. (I have a photograph of her in pants, boots, and broadbrim that was given to me by her brother, Everette. She has her foot up on the running board of a car—presumably hers, and bright red—and looks racy.) She would light up a fag—which wasn't done by ladies then (and, thank our saints, as a young woman she was never a lady) on the street.

Her critics disliked even the "rags" on her head. (They seemed curiously incapable of telling the difference between an African-American queen and Aunt Jemima.) They disliked her apparent sensuality: the way she tended to marry or not marry men, but enjoyed them anyway—while never missing a beat in her work. They hinted slyly that Zora was gay, or at least bisexual—how else could they account for her drive? Though there is not, perhaps unfortunately, a shred of evidence that this was true. The accusation becomes humorous—and of course at all times irrelevant—when one considers that what she *did* write was one of the sexiest, most "healthily" rendered heterosexual love stories in our literature. In addition, she talked too much, got things from white folks (Guggenheims, Rosenwalds, and footstools) much too easily, was slovenly in her dress, and appeared maddeningly indifferent to other people's opinions of her. With her easy laughter and her Southern drawl, her belief in doing "cullud" dancing authentically, Zora seemed—among these genteel "New Negroes" of the Harlem Renaissance—*black*. No wonder her presence was always a shock. Though almost everyone agreed she was a delight, not everyone agreed such audacious black delight was permissible, or, indeed, quite the proper image for the race.

Zora was before her time, in intellectual circles, in the life style she chose. By the sixties everyone understood that black women could wear beautiful cloths on their beautiful heads and care about the authenticity of things "cullud" *and* African. By the sixties it was no longer a crime to receive financial assistance—in the form of grants and fellowships—for one's work. (Interestingly, those writers who complained that Zora "got money from white folks" were often themselves totally supported, down to the food they ate—or, in Langston Hughes's case, *tried* to eat, after his white "Godmother" discarded him—by white patrons.) By the sixties, nobody cared that marriage didn't last forever. No one expected it to. And I do believe that now, in the seventies, we do not expect (though we may wish and pray) every black person who speaks *always* to speak *correctly* (since this is impossible): and if we *do* expect it, we deserve all the silent leadership we are likely to get.

During the early and middle years of her career Zora was a cultural revolutionary simply because she was always herself. Her work, so vigorous among the rather pallid productions of many of her contemporaries, comes from the essence of black folk life. During her later life she became frightened of the life she had always dared bravely before. Her work too became reactionary, static, shockingly misguided and timid. (This is especially true of her last novel, *Seraphs on the Sewannee,* which is not even about black people, which is no crime, but *is* about white people for whom it is impossible to care, which is.)

A series of misfortunes battered Zora's spirit and her health. And she was broke. *Being broke made all the difference.*

Without money of one's own in a capitalist society, there is no such thing as independence. This is one of the clearest lessons of Zora's life, and why I consider the telling of her life "a cautionary tale." We must learn from it what we can.

Without money, an illness, even a simple one, can undermine the will. Without money, getting into a hospital is problematic and getting out without money to pay for the treatment is nearly impossible. Without money, one becomes dependent on other people, who are likely to be—even in their kindness—erratic in their support and despotic in their expectations of return. Zora was forced to rely, like Tennessee Williams's Blanche, "on the kindness of strangers." Can anything be more dangerous, if the strangers are forever in control? Zora, who worked so hard, was never able to make a living from her work.

She did not complain about not having money. She was not the type. (Several months ago I received a long letter from one of Zora's nieces, a bright ten-year-old, who explained to me that her aunt was so proud that the only way the family could guess she was ill or without funds was by realizing they had no idea where she was. Therefore, none of the family attended either Zora's sickbed or her funeral.) Those of us who have had "grants and fellowships from 'white folks' " know this aid is extended in precisely the way welfare is extended in Mississippi. One is asked, *curtly,* more often than not: How much do you need *just to survive?* Then one is—if fortunate—given a third of that. What is amazing is that Zora, who became an orphan at nine, a runaway at fourteen, a maid and manicurist (because of necessity and not from love of the work) before she was twenty—with one dress—managed to become Zora Neale Hurston, author and anthropologist, at all.

For me, the most unfortunate thing Zora ever wrote is her autobiography. After the first several chapters, it rings false. One begins to hear the voice of someone whose life required the assistance of too many transitory "friends." A Taoist proverb states that *to act sincerely with the insincere is dangerous.* (A mistake blacks as a group have tended to make in America.) And so we have Zora sincerely offering gratitude and kind words to people one knows she could not have respected. But this unctuousness, so out of character for Zora, is also a result of dependency, a sign of her powerlessness, her inability to pay back her debts with anything but words. They must have been bitter ones for her. In her dependency, it should be remembered, Zora was not alone—because it is quite true that America does not support or honor us as human beings, let alone as blacks, women, and artists. We have taken help where it was offered because we are committed to what we do and to the survival of our work. Zora was committed to the survival of her people's cultural heritage as well.

In my mind, Zora Neale Hurston, Billie Holiday, and Bessie Smith form a sort of unholy trinity. Zora *belongs* in the tradition of black women singers, rather than among "the literati," at least to me. There were the extreme highs and lows of her life, her undaunted pursuit of adventure, passionate emotional and sexual experience, and her love of freedom. Like Billie and Bessie she followed her own road, believed in her own gods, and pursued her own dreams, and refused to separate herself from "common" people. It would have been nice if the three of them had had one another to turn to, in times of need. I close my eyes and imagine them: Bessie would be in charge of all the money; Zora would keep Billie's masochistic tendencies in check and prevent her from singing embarrassing anything-for-a-man songs, thereby preventing Billie's heroin addiction. In return, Billie could be, along with Bessie, the family that Zora felt she never had.

We are a people. A people do not throw their geniuses away. And if they are thrown away, it is our duty *as artists and as witnesses for the future* to collect them again for the sake of our children, and, if necessary, bone by bone.

The Civil Rights Movement: What Good Was It?

[I wrote the following essay in the winter of 1966–67 while sharing one room above Washington Square Park in New York with a struggling young Jewish law student who became my husband. It was my first published essay and won the three-hundred-dollar first prize in the annual *American Scholar* essay contest. The money was almost magically reassuring to us in those days of disaffected parents, outraged friends, and one-item meals, and kept us in tulips, peonies, daisies, and lamb chops for several months.]

Someone said recently to an old black lady from Mississippi, whose legs had been badly mangled by local police who arrested her for "disturbing the peace," that the Civil Rights Movement was dead, and asked, since it was dead, what she thought about it. The old lady replied, hobbling out of his presence on her cane, that the Civil Rights Movement was like herself, "if it's dead, it shore ain't ready to lay down!"

This old lady is a legendary freedom fighter in her small town in the Delta. She has been severely mistreated for insisting on her rights as an American citizen. She has been beaten for singing Movement songs, placed in solitary confinement in prisons for talking about freedom, and placed on bread and water for praying aloud to God for her jailers' deliverance. For such a woman the Civil Rights Movement will never be over as long as her skin is black. It also will never be over for twenty million others with the same "affliction," for whom the Movement can never "lay down," no matter how it is killed by the press and made dead and buried by the white American public. As long as one black American survives, the struggle for equality with other Americans must also survive. This is a debt we owe to those blameless hostages we leave to the future, our children.

Still, white liberals and deserting Civil Rights sponsors are quick to justify their disaffection from the Movement by claiming that it is all over. "And since it is over," they will ask, "would someone kindly tell me what has been gained by it?" They then list statistics supposedly showing how much more advanced segregation is now than ten years ago—in schools, housing, jobs. They point to a gain in conservative politicians during the last few years. They speak of ghetto riots and of the survey that shows that most policemen are admittedly too anti-Negro to do their jobs in ghetto areas fairly and effectively. They speak of every area that has been touched by the Civil Rights Movement as somehow or other going to pieces.

They rarely talk, however, about human attitudes among Negroes that have undergone terrific changes just during the past seven to ten years (not to mention all those years when there was a Movement and only the Negroes knew about it). They seldom speak of changes in personal lives because of the influence of people in the Movement. They see general failure and few, if any, individual gains.

They do not understand what it is that keeps the Movement from "laying down" and Negroes from reverting to their former *silent* second-class status. They have apparently never stopped to wonder why it is always the white man—on his radio and in his newspaper and on his television—who says that the Movement is dead. If a Negro were audacious enough to make such a claim, his fellows might hanker to see him shot. The Movement is dead to the white man because it no longer interests him. And it no longer interests him because he can afford to be uninterested: he does not have to live by it, with it, or for it, as Negroes must. He can take a rest from the news of beatings, killings, and arrests that reach him from North and South—if his skin is white. Negroes cannot now and will never be able to take a rest from the injustices that plague them, for they—not the white man—are the target.

Perhaps it is naïve to be thankful that the Movement "saved" a large number of individuals and gave them something to live for, even if it did not provide them with everything they wanted. (Materially, it provided them with precious little that they wanted.) When a movement awakens people to the possibilities of life, it seems unfair to frustrate them by then denying what they had thought was offered. But what was offered? What was promised? What was it all about? What good did it do? Would it have been better, as some have suggested, to leave the Negro people as they were, unawakened, unallied with one another, unhopeful about what to expect for their children in some future world?

I do not think so. If knowledge of my condition is all the freedom I get from a "freedom movement," it is better than unawareness, forgottenness, and hopelessness, the existence that is like the existence of a beast. Man only truly lives by knowing; otherwise he simply performs, copying the daily habits of others, but conceiving nothing of his creative possibilities as a man, and accepting someone else's superiority and his own misery.

When we are children, growing up in our parents' care, we await the spark from the outside world. Sometimes our parents provide it—if we are lucky—sometimes it comes from another source far from home. We sit, paralyzed, surrounded by our anxiety and dread, hoping we will not have to grow up into the narrow world and ways we see about us. We are hungry for a life that turns us on; we yearn for a knowledge of living that will save us from our innocuous lives that resemble death. We look for signs in every strange event; we search for heroes in every unknown face.

It was just six years ago that I began to be alive. I had, of course, been living before—for I am now twenty-three—but I did not really know it. And I did not know it because nobody told me that I—a pensive, yearning, typical high-school senior, but Negro—existed in the minds of others as I existed in my own. Until that time my mind was locked apart from the outer contours and complexion of my body as if it and the body were strangers. The mind possessed both thought and spirit—I wanted to be an author or a scientist—which the color of the body denied. I had never seen myself and existed as a statistic exists, or as a phantom. In the white world I walked, less real to them than a shadow; and being young and well hidden among the slums, among people who also did not exist—either in books or in films or in the government of their own lives—I waited to be called to life. And, by a miracle, I was called.

There was a commotion in our house that night in 1960. We had managed to buy our first television set. It was battered and overpriced, but my mother had gotten used to watching the afternoon soap operas at the house where she worked as maid, and nothing could satisfy her on days when she did not work but a continuation of her "stories." So she pinched pennies and bought a set.

I remained listless throughout her "stories," tales of pregnancy, abortion, hypocrisy, infidelity, and alcoholism. All these men and women were white and lived in houses with servants, long staircases that they floated down, patios where liquor was served four times a day to "relax" them. But my mother, with her swollen feet eased out of her shoes, her heavy body relaxed in our only comfortable chair, watched each movement of the smartly coiffed women, heard each word, pounced upon each innuendo and inflection, and for the duration of these "stories" she saw herself as one of them. She placed herself in every scene she saw, with her braided hair turned blond, her two hundred pounds compressed into a sleek size-seven dress, her rough dark skin smooth and *white*. Her husband became "dark and handsome," talented, witty, urbane, charming. And when she turned to look at my father sitting near her in his sweat shirt with his smelly feet raised on the bed to "air," there was always a tragic look of surprise on her face. Then she would sigh and go out to the kitchen looking lost and unsure of herself. My mother, a truly great woman who raised eight children of her own and half a dozen of the neighbors' without a single complaint, was convinced that she did not exist compared to "them." She subordinated her soul to theirs and became a faithful and timid supporter of the "Beautiful White People." Once she asked me, in a moment of vicarious pride and despair, if I didn't think that "they" were "jest naturally smarter, prettier, better." My mother asked this: a woman who never got rid of any of her children, never cheated on my father, was never a hypocrite if she could help it, and never even tasted liquor. She could not even bring herself to blame "them" for making her believe what they wanted her to believe: that if she did not look like them, think like them, be sophisticated and corrupt-for-comfort's-sake like them, she was a nobody. Black was not a color on my mother; it was a shield that made her invisible.

Of course, the people who wrote the soap-opera scripts always made the Negro maids in them steadfast, trusty, and wise in a home-remedial sort of way; but my mother, a maid for nearly forty years, never once identified herself with the scarcely glimpsed black servant's face beneath the ruffled cap. Like everyone else, in her daydreams at least, she thought she was free.

Six years ago, after half-heartedly watching my mother's soap operas and wondering whether there wasn't something more to be asked of life, the Civil Rights Movement came into my life. Like a good omen for the future, the face of Dr. Martin Luther King, Jr., was the first black face I saw on our new television screen.

And, as in a fairy tale, my soul was stirred by the meaning for me of his mission—at the time he was being rather ignominiously dumped into a police van for having led a protest march in Alabama—and I fell in love with the sober and determined face of the Movement. The singing of "We Shall Overcome"—that song betrayed by nonbelievers in it—rang for the first time in my ears. The influence that my mother's soap operas might have had on me became impossible. The life of Dr. King, seeming bigger and more miraculous than the man himself, because of all he had done and suffered, offered a pattern of strength and sincerity I felt I could trust. He had suffered much because of his simple belief in nonviolence, love, and brotherhood. Perhaps the majority of men could not be reached through these beliefs, but because Dr. King kept trying to reach them in spite of danger to himself and his family, I saw in him the hero for whom I had waited so long.

What Dr. King promised was not a ranch-style house and an acre of manicured lawn for every black man, but jail and finally freedom. He did not promise two cars for every family, but the courage one day for all families everywhere to walk without shame and unafraid on their own feet. He did not say that one day it will be us chasing prospective buyers out of our prosperous well-kept neighborhoods, or in other ways exhibiting our snobbery and ignorance as all other ethnic groups before us have done; what he said was that we had a right to live anywhere in this country we chose, and a right to a meaningful well-paying job to provide us with the upkeep of our homes. He did not say we had to become carbon copies of the white American middle class; but he did say we had the right to become whatever we wanted to become.

Because of the Movement, because of an awakened faith in the newness and imagination of the human spirit, because of "black and white together"—for the first time in our history in some human relationship on and off TV—because of the beatings, the arrests, the hell of battle during the past years, I have fought harder for my life and for a chance to be myself, to be something more than a shadow or a number, than I had ever done before in my life. Before, there had seemed to be no real reason for struggling beyond the effort for daily bread. Now there was a chance at that other that Jesus meant when He said we could not live by bread alone.

I have fought and kicked and fasted and prayed and cursed and cried myself to the point of existing. It has been like being born again, literally. Just "knowing" has meant everything to me. Knowing has pushed me out into the world, into college, into places, into people.

Part of what existence means to me is knowing the difference between what I am now and what I was then. It is being capable of looking after myself intellectually as well as financially. It is being able to tell when I am being wronged and by whom. It means being awake to protect myself and the ones I love. It means being a part of the world community, and being *alert* to which part it is that I have joined, and knowing how to change to another part if that part does not suit me. To know is to exist: to exist is to be involved, to move about, to see the world with my own eyes. This, at least, the Movement has given me.

The hippies and other nihilists would have me believe that it is all the same whether the people in Mississippi have a movement behind them or not. Once they have their rights, they say, they will run all over themselves trying to be just like everybody else. They will be well fed, complacent about things of the spirit, emotionless, and without that marvelous humanity and "soul" that the Movement has seen them practice time and time again. "What has the Movement done," they ask, "with the few people it has supposedly helped?" "Got them white-collar jobs, moved them into standardized ranch houses in white neighborhoods, given them nondescript gray flannel suits?" "What are these people now?" they ask. And then they answer themselves, "Nothings!"

I would find this reasoning—which I have heard many, many times from hippies and nonhippies alike—amusing if I did not also consider it serious. For I think it is a delusion, a cop-out, an excuse to disassociate themselves from a world in which they feel too little has been changed or gained. The real question, however, it appears to me, is not whether poor people will adopt the middle-class mentality once they are well fed; rather, it is whether they will ever be well fed enough to be able to choose whatever mentality they think will suit them. The lack of a movement did not keep my mother from *wishing* herself bourgeois in her daydreams.

There is widespread starvation in Mississippi. In my own state of Georgia there are more hungry families than Lester Maddox would like to admit—or even see fed. I went to school with children who ate red dirt. The Movement has prodded and pushed some liberal senators into pressuring the government for food so that the hungry may eat. Food stamps that were two dollars and out of the reach of many families not long ago have been reduced to fifty cents. The price is still out of the reach of some families, and the government, it seems to a lot of people, could spare enough free food to feed its own people. It angers people in the Movement that it does not; they point to the billions in wheat we send free each year to countries abroad. Their government's slowness while people are hungry, its unwillingness to believe that there are Americans starving, its stingy cutting of the price of food stamps, make many Civil Rights workers throw up their hands in disgust. But they do not give up. They do not withdraw into the world of psychedelia. They apply what pressure they can to make the government give away food to hungry people. They do not plan so far ahead in their disillusionment with society that they can see these starving families buying identical ranch-style houses and sending their snobbish children to Bryn Mawr and Yale. They take first things first and try to get them fed.

They do not consider it their business, in any case, to say what kind of life the people they help must lead. How one lives is, after all, one of the rights left to the individual—when and if he has opportunity to choose. It is not the prerogative of the middle class to determine what is worthy of aspiration. There is also every possibility that the middle-class people of tomorrow will turn out ever so much better than those of today. I even know some middle-class people of today who are not *all* bad.

I think there are so few Negro hippies because middle-class Negroes, although well fed, are not careless. They are required by the treacherous world they live in to be clearly aware of whoever or whatever might be trying to do them in. They are middle class in money and position, but they cannot afford to be middle class in complacency. They distrust the hippie movement because they know that it can do nothing for Negroes as a group but "love" them, which is what all paternalists claim to do. And since the only way Negroes can survive (which they cannot do, unfortunately, on love alone) is with the support of the group, they are wisely wary and stay away.

A white writer tried recently to explain that the reason for the relatively few Negro hippies is that Negroes have built up a "super-cool" that cracks under LSD and makes them have a "bad trip." What this writer doesn't guess at is that Negroes are needing drugs less than ever these days for any kind of trip. While the hippies are "tripping," Negroes are going after power, which is so much more important to their survival and their children's survival than LSD and pot.

Everyone would be surprised if the Israelis ignored the Arabs and took up "tripping" and pot smoking. In this country we are the Israelis. Everybody who can do so would like to forget this, of course. But for us to forget it for a minute would be fatal. "We Shall Overcome" is just a song to most Americans, *but we must do it.* Or die.

What good was the Civil Rights Movement? If it had just given this country Dr. King, a leader of conscience, for once in our lifetime, it would have been enough. If it had just taken black eyes off white television stories, it would have been enough. If it had fed one starving child, it would have been enough.

If the Civil Rights Movement is "dead," and if it gave us nothing else, it gave us each other forever. It gave some of us bread, some of us shelter, some of us knowledge and pride, all of us comfort. It gave us our children, our husbands, our brothers, our fathers, as men reborn and with a purpose for living. It broke the pattern of black servitude in this country. It shattered the phony "promise" of white soap operas that sucked away so many pitiful lives. It gave us history and men far greater than Presidents. It gave us heroes, selfless men of courage and strength, for our little boys and girls to follow. It gave us hope for tomorrow. It called us to life.

Because we live, it can never die.

Considerations for Thinking and Writing

1. Compare the urgent plea and implicit advice in Walker's "In Search of Our Mothers' Gardens" with June Jordan's "Where Is the Love?" and with Chapter One of Virginia Woolf's *A Room of One's Own.* What do these essays share in vision, values, attitude, and idea?

2. Compare Walker's tribute to Zora Neale Hurston with Didion's to Georgia O'Keeffe and Cynthia Ozick's to Edith Wharton. What does each writer see in the woman she celebrates? Why is each of these women valued by the writers? Consider how the approaches of Walker, Didion, and Ozick are similar and how they differ.

3. Compare Walker's discussion of the Civil Rights movement with June Jordan's "Many Rivers to Cross" and Audre Lorde's "Feminism & Black Liberation: The Great American Disease." Which writer seems to you most urgent and impassioned? Which seems the most convincing? Why?

4. Compare Walker's discussion of her physical disfigurement in "Beauty" with Nancy Mairs's essay "On Being a Cripple" and Audre Lorde's piece on breast cancer, "Breast Cancer: Power vs. Prosthesis." Explain what each writer contributes to your understanding of how disfigurement affects identity, empowerment, self-determination, and self-image.

5. In another essay not included in this book Walker has written that "all partisan movements add to the fullness of our understanding of our society as a whole." In what sense do you think this statement may or may not be true, whether you think of women's liberation or of any other movement or ideology?

6. Compare Walker's voice and vision with those of the other two Black women writers in Part I, June Jordan and Audre Lorde. After identifying the distinctive features of each writer, explain whose voice and vision most appeal to you and why.

VIRGINIA WOOLF
(1882-1941)

A child born in England in 1882 could hardly have found a home more hospitable to letters than that into which Adeline Virginia Stephen was born. Her father, Leslie Stephen, was the editor of *The Cornhill Magazine* and a writer of biographies and essays on literature and philosophy. Her mother, Julia Stephen, had become a nurse after the death of her first husband, and was shortly to publish a book on nursing. In their literate and animated household resided Julia Stephen's three children from her previous marriage; Leslie Stephen's retarded child from his previous marriage; the four children of Julia and Leslie: Vanessa, Thoby, Virginia, and Adrian; various and illustrious house guests; and a voluminous library.

Virginia Stephen learned early that being a woman disqualified her from membership in this civilized and intellectual elite. It was her fate to be, as she later said, among "the daughters of educated men." These stinging words document Woolf's struggle against the infantilizing consequences of being denied (unlike her two brothers) a university education. A revealing journal entry links her emergence as a writer to her father's death in 1904, the same year in which she published her first essay in *The Guardian*: "His life would have entirely ended mine. . . . No writing, no books:—inconceivable." Inconceivable also to those who know her as the author of ten novels, several of them brilliant, bold, and innovative experiments in narrative technique; two canny and challenging books of feminist criticism, *A Room of One's Own* and *Three Guineas*; and six volumes of essays ranging confidently across eight centuries of people and their books. Her letters fill six volumes; her diaries, five more.

Though her career as a writer did not begin with her father's death, Virginia Woolf's association with the so-called Bloomsbury set did. Moving with her brothers and sister to the vicinity of the British Museum, Virginia left behind with the Victorian decor a way of life she no longer wanted: "We were full of experiments and reforms. We were going to do without table napkins . . . ; we were going to paint; to write; to have coffee after dinner instead of tea at nine o'clock. Everything was going to be new; everything was going to be different. Everything was on trial." In the nightly company of her brothers' Cambridge friends—including Lytton Strachey, the future novelist E. M. Forster, and the future economist John Maynard Keynes—Virginia joined the talk about politics, writing, art, psychology, and sexuality. Another member of the company was the socialist writer Leonard Woolf, described by Virginia as "that violent trembling misanthropic Jew who had already shaken his fist at civilisation and was about to disappear into the tropics." Leonard and Virginia Woolf were married in 1912; they never had children. Cynthia Ozick's "Mrs. Virginia Woolf," a circumspect account of Leonard Woolf's devotion to his wife during her many struggles with mental illness and throughout her intense involvement with the bisexual writer Vita Sackville-West, appears elsewhere in this volume. During the cold wartime spring of 1941, fearing the onset of another psychotic episode and a German invasion of England, Woolf took her own life in the river Ouse.

In her essay on Mary Wollstonecraft, Virginia Woolf observes "how much influence circumstances have upon opinions." Woolf saw herself as dwelling among contradictory circumstances: she was heir to a culture that did not hesitate to disinherit her when it saw fit. Perhaps because of the "severances and oppositions in [her] mind," Woolf's undogmatic and asystematic feminism wanders restlessly between two destinations in *A Room of One's Own*. On the one hand, she imagines the ideal creative mind as "androgynous," or, as she called a mind undimmed by anger and bitterness, "incandescent." This ideal suggests that once a woman conquers the forces that impoverish her, refuse to educate her, sexually objectify her, and entrap her in housekeeping—once she has "money and a room of her own"—she will (like men) produce art of the first order. Woolf surmises that Shakespeare's (hypothetical) sister, left to flourish, might well have been another Shakespeare.

On the other hand, Woolf candidly announces her alienation from patriarchal culture and institutions: "Again if one is a woman one is often surprised by a sudden splitting off of consciousness, say in walking down Whitehall, when from being the natural inheritor of that civilisation, she becomes, on the contrary, outside of it, alien and critical." Woolf's sense that her own mind was, far from being androgynous, deeply influenced by her experience as a woman led her to articulate a distinctive literary tradition created, revised, and esteemed by women. Woolf seems indeed to have realized that Shakespeare's sister, under the most favorable of circumstances, would have become the writer *Judith* Shakespeare, not simply another William Shakespeare.

Woolf's parable of Shakespeare's sister in *A Room of One's Own* brings to mind her promise to use "all the liberties and licences of a novelist" in explaining her "opinions" on women and fiction. While Woolf clearly has an argument to make in *A Room of One's Own*, she makes it by presenting vividly and convincingly the texture of women's lives in a patriarchal culture. In Chapter One, reprinted here, Woolf's narrative of a day spent at an English university includes elegant and precise descriptions of a luncheon at a men's college and a dinner at a women's college. Woolf's diction and tone ask the reader

both to compare the two meals and to demand an accounting for the glaring differences between them. Determining to find answers to hard questions, Woolf becomes the reader's surrogate and ally. Thus her unusual argumentative strategy proves shrewdly disarming.

In her second long essay on feminism, *Three Guineas* (a selection from which appears in Part II), Woolf again offers a search for answers rather than dogmatic assertions. Having been solicited by three organizations—one determined to stop war, one fostering women in the professions, and one building a women's college—Woolf considers what demands she might make of each organization in exchange for her donation. Her own situation proves emblematic of the situation of women generally. Woolf demonstrates in *Three Guineas* that women newly empowered to participate in the public domain must take seriously their responsibility for reshaping and humanizing patriarchal institutions.

It is important that the institution with which Woolf was professionally linked was not the academy but the press. It was Woolf's singular talent as a critic to wed intellectual rigor to journalistic spontaneity. She directed her essays toward "the common reader," writing cleanly and clearly and avoiding scholarly jargon and prejudice. And yet she was seldom prosaic. We find in her essays what she found in those of the Romantic essayist Charles Lamb: "that wild flash of imagination, that lightning crack of genius in the middle of them which leaves them flawed and imperfect, but starred with poetry." It is perhaps Woolf's burning need to get to the heart of things that lights up her essays, however complex, peripheral, or obscure their subjects.

Woolf did not hesitate to retrieve writers from complete obscurity or to illumine shadowy moments in otherwise well-known histories. In "Geraldine and Jane" Woolf explores an obscure friendship between "two incompatible but deeply attached" Victorian women. Keeping Jane Carlyle's illustrious husband, Thomas Carlyle, in the background, Woolf speculates boldly on what each friend offered the other. The two figures become animated and striking; only Geraldine Jewsbury's characters remain "stuffed figures moldering on their perches." In her portrait of Mary Wollstonecraft, Woolf focuses not on Wollstonecraft's theories but on the energy and wisdom with which she adjusted her theories to accommodate her experience. The dense, brief narrative, while strictly chronological, is crafted to reflect Wollstonecraft's intensity. When Wollstonecraft dies shortly after childbirth, Woolf abruptly stops her narra-

tive in mid-sentence before resuming it.

Though Virginia Woolf is rarely described as a personal essayist, her essays show us in how tight an embrace the private and the public are locked. Her deep sympathy for her subject, her commitment to ideas, and her profound devotion to her craft suggest that she learned much from the sixteenth-century French essayist Montaigne, "that great master of the art of life." With Montaigne, Woolf realized that "beyond the difficulty of communicating oneself, there is the supreme difficulty of being oneself." It must have helped her to know that, like Montaigne and a very few others, it was in her power to be herself in the world of the page.

A Room of One's Own

Chapter One

But, you may say, we asked you to speak about women and fiction—what has that got to do with a room of one's own? I will try to explain. When you asked me to speak about women and fiction I sat down on the banks of a river and began to wonder what the words meant. They might mean simply a few remarks about Fanny Burney; a few more about Jane Austen; a tribute to the Brontës and a sketch of Haworth Parsonage under snow; some witticisms if possible about Miss Mitford; a respectful allusion to George Eliot; a reference to Mrs. Gaskell and one would have done. But at second sight the words seemed not so simple. The title women and fiction might mean, and you may have meant it to mean, women and what they are like; or it might mean women and the fiction that they write; or it might mean women and the fiction that is written about them; or it might mean that somehow all three are inextricably mixed together and you want me to consider them in that light. But when I began to consider the subject in this last way, which seemed the most interesting, I soon saw that it had one fatal drawback. I should never be able to come to a conclusion. I should never be able to fulfil what is, I understand, the first duty of a lecturer—to hand you after an hour's discourse a nugget of pure truth to wrap up between the pages of your notebooks and keep on the mantelpiece for ever. All I could do was to offer you an opinion upon one minor point—a woman must have money and a room of her own if she is to write fiction; and that, as you will see, leaves the great problem of the true nature of woman and the true nature of fiction unsolved. I have shirked the duty of coming to a conclusion upon these two questions—women and fiction remain, so far as I am concerned, unsolved problems. But in order to make some amends I am going to do what I can to show you how I arrived at this opinion about the room and the money. I am going to develop in your presence as fully and freely as I can the train of thought which led me to think this. Perhaps if I lay bare the ideas, the prejudices, that lie behind this statement you will find that they have some bearing upon women and some upon fiction. At any rate, when a subject is highly controversial—and any question about sex is that—one cannot hope to tell the truth. One can only show how one came to hold whatever opinion one does hold. One can only give one's audience the chance of drawing their own conclusions as they observe the limitations, the prejudices, the idiosyncrasies of the speaker. Fiction here is likely to contain more truth than fact. Therefore I propose, making use of all the liberties and licences of a novelist, to tell you the story of the two days that preceded my coming here—how, bowed down by the weight of the subject which you have laid upon my shoulders, I pondered it, and made it work in and out of my daily life. I need not say that what I am about to describe has no existence; Oxbridge is an invention; so is Fernham; "I" is only a convenient term for somebody who has no real being. Lies will flow from my lips, but there may perhaps be some truth mixed up with them; it is for you to seek out this truth and to decide whether any part of it is worth keeping. If not, you will of course throw the whole of it into the wastepaper basket and forget all about it.

Here then was I (call me Mary Beton, Mary Seton, Mary Carmichael or by any name you please—it is not a matter of any importance) sitting on the banks of a river a week or two ago in fine October weather, lost in thought. That collar I have spoken of, women and fiction, the need of coming to some conclusion on a subject that raises all sorts of prejudices and passions, bowed my head to the ground. To the right and left bushes of some sort, golden and crimson, glowed with the colour, even it seemed burnt with the heat, of fire. On the further bank the willows wept in perpetual lamentation, their hair about their shoulders. The river reflected whatever it chose of sky and bridge and burning tree, and when the undergraduate had oared his boat through the reflections they closed again, completely, as if he had never been. There one might have sat the clock round lost in thought. Thought—to call it by a prouder name than it deserved—had let its line down into the stream. It swayed, minute after minute, hither and thither among the reflections and the weeds, letting the water lift it and sink it, until—you know the little tug—the sudden conglomeration of an idea at the end of one's line: and then the cautious hauling of it in, and the careful laying of it out? Alas, laid on the grass how small, how insignificant this thought of mine looked; the sort of fish that a good fisherman puts back into the water so that it may grow fatter and be one day worth cooking and eating. I will not trouble you with that thought now, though if you look carefully you may find it for yourselves in the course of what I am going to say.

But however small it was, it had, nevertheless, the mysterious property of its kind—put back into the mind, it became at once very exciting, and important; and as it darted and sank, and flashed hither and thither, set up such a wash and tumult of ideas that it was impossible to sit still. It was thus that I found myself walking with extreme rapidity across a grass plot. Instantly a man's figure rose to intercept me. Nor did I at first understand that the gesticulations of a curious-looking object, in a cut-away coat and evening shirt, were aimed at me. His face expressed horror and indignation. Instinct rather than reason came to my help; he was a Beadle; I was a woman. This was the turf; there was the path. Only the Fellows and Scholars are allowed here; the gravel is the place for me. Such thoughts were the work of a moment. As I regained the path the arms of the Beadle sank, his face assumed its usual repose, and though turf is better walking than gravel, no very great harm was done. The only charge I could bring against the Fellows and Scholars of whatever the college might happen to be was that in protection of their turf, which has been rolled for 300 years in succession, they had sent my little fish into hiding.

What idea it had been that had sent me so audaciously trespassing I could not now remember. The spirit of peace descended like a cloud from heaven, for if the spirit of peace dwells anywhere, it is in the courts and quadrangles of Oxbridge on a fine October morning. Strolling through those colleges past those ancient halls the roughness of the present seemed smoothed away; the body seemed contained in a miraculous glass cabinet through which no sound could penetrate, and the mind, freed from any contact with facts (unless one trespassed on the turf again), was at liberty to settle down upon whatever meditation was in harmony with the moment. As chance would have it, some stray memory of some old essay about revisiting Oxbridge in the long vacation brought Charles Lamb to mind—Saint Charles, said Thackeray, putting a letter of Lamb's to his forehead. Indeed, among all the dead (I give you my thoughts as they came to me), Lamb is one of the most congenial; one to whom one would have liked to say, Tell me then how you wrote your essays? For his essays are superior even to Max Beerbohm's, I thought, with all their perfection, because of that wild flash of imagination, that lightning crack of genius in the middle of them which leaves them flawed and imperfect, but starred with poetry. Lamb then came to Oxbridge perhaps a hundred years ago. Certainly he wrote an essay—the name escapes me—about the manuscript of one of Milton's poems which he saw here. It was *Lycidas* perhaps, and Lamb wrote how it shocked him to think it possible that any word in *Lycidas* could have been different from what it is. To think of Milton changing the words in that poem seemed to him a sort of sacrilege. This led me to remember what I could of *Lycidas* and to amuse myself with guessing which word it could have been that Milton had altered, and why. It then occurred to me that the very manuscript itself which Lamb had looked at was only a few hundred yards away, so that one could follow Lamb's footsteps across the quadrangle to that famous library where the treasure is kept. Moreover, I recollected, as I put this plan into execution, it is in this famous library that the manuscript of Thackeray's *Esmond* is also preserved. The critics often say that *Esmond* is Thackeray's most perfect novel. But the affectation of the style, with its imitation of the eighteenth century, hampers one, so far as I remember; unless indeed the eighteenth-century style was natural to Thackeray—a fact that one might prove by looking at the manuscript and seeing whether the alterations were for the benefit of the style or of the sense. But then one would have to decide what is style and what is meaning, a question which—but here I was actually at the door which leads into the library itself. I must have opened it, for instantly there issued, like a guardian angel barring the way with a flutter of black gown instead of white wings, a deprecating, silvery, kindly gentleman, who regretted in a low voice as he waved me back that ladies are only admitted to the library if accompanied by a Fellow of the College or furnished with a letter of introduction.

That a famous library has been cursed by a woman is a matter of complete indifference to a famous library. Venerable and calm, with all its treasures safe locked within its breast, it sleeps complacently and will, so far as I am concerned, so sleep for ever. Never will I wake those echoes, never will I ask for that hospitality again,

I vowed as I descended the steps in anger. Still an hour remained before luncheon, and what was one to do? Stroll on the meadows? sit by the river? Certainly it was a lovely autumn morning; the leaves were fluttering red to the ground; there was no great hardship in doing either. But the sound of music reached my ear. Some service or celebration was going forward. The organ complained magnificently as I passed the chapel door. Even the sorrow of Christianity sounded in that serene air more like the recollection of sorrow than sorrow itself; even the groanings of the ancient organ seemed lapped in peace. I had no wish to enter had I the right, and this time the verger might have stopped me, demanding perhaps my baptismal certificate, or a letter of introduction from the Dean. But the outside of these magnificent buildings is often as beautiful as the inside. Moreover, it was amusing enough to watch the congregation assembling, coming in and going out again, busying themselves at the door of the chapel like bees at the mouth of a hive. Many were in cap and gown; some had tufts of fur on their shoulders; others were wheeled in bath-chairs; others, though not past middle age, seemed creased and crushed into shapes so singular that one was reminded of those giant crabs and crayfish who heave with difficulty across the sand of an aquarium. As I leant against the wall the University indeed seemed a sanctuary in which are preserved rare types which would soon be obsolete if left to fight for existence on the pavement of the Strand. Old stories of old deans and old dons came back to mind, but before I had summoned up courage to whistle—it used to be said that at the sound of a whistle old Professor _____ instantly broke into a gallop—the venerable congregation had gone inside. The outside of the chapel remained. As you know, its high domes and pinnacles can be seen, like a sailing-ship always voyaging never arriving, lit up at night and visible for miles, far away across the hills. Once, presumably, this quadrangle with its smooth lawns, its massive buildings, and the chapel itself was marsh too, where the grasses waved and the swine rooted. Teams of horses and oxen, I thought, must have hauled the stone in wagons from far countries, and then with infinite labour the grey blocks in whose shade I was now standing were poised in order one on top of another, and then the painters brought their glass for the windows, and the masons were busy for centuries up on that roof with putty and cement, spade and trowel. Every Saturday somebody must have poured gold and silver out of a leathern purse into their ancient fists, for they had their beer and skittles presumably of an evening. An unending stream of gold and silver, I thought, must have flowed into this court perpetually to keep the stones coming and the masons working; to level, to ditch, to dig and to drain. But it was then the age of faith, and money was poured liberally to set these stones on a deep foundation, and when the stones were raised, still more money was poured in from the coffers of kings and queens and great nobles to ensure that hymns should be sung here and scholars taught. Lands were granted; tithes were paid. And when the age of faith was over and the age of reason had come, still the same flow of gold and silver went on; fellowships were founded; lectureships endowed; only the gold and silver flowed now, not from the coffers of the king, but from the chests of merchants and manufacturers, from the purses of men who had made, say, a fortune from industry, and returned, in their wills, a bounteous share of it to endow more chairs, more lectureships, more fellowships in the university where they had learnt their craft. Hence the libraries and laboratories; the observatories; the splendid equipment of costly and delicate instruments which now stands on glass shelves, where centuries ago the grasses waved and the swine rooted.

Certainly, as I strolled round the court, the foundation of gold and silver seemed deep enough; the pavement laid solidly over the wild grasses. Men with trays on their heads went busily from staircase to staircase. Gaudy blossoms flowered in window-boxes. The strains of the gramophone blared out from the rooms within. It was impossible not to reflect—the reflection whatever it may have been was cut short. The clock struck. It was time to find one's way to luncheon.

It is a curious fact that novelists have a way of making us believe that luncheon parties are invariably memorable for something very witty that was said, or for something very wise that was done. But they seldom spare a word for what was eaten. It is part of the novelist's convention not to mention soup and salmon and ducklings, as if soup and salmon and ducklings were of no importance whatsoever, as if nobody ever smoked a cigar or drank a glass of wine. Here, however, I shall take the liberty to defy that convention and to tell you that the lunch on this occasion began with soles, sunk in a deep dish, over which the college cook had spread a counterpane of the whitest cream, save that it was branded here and there with brown spots like the spots on the flanks of a doe. After that came the partridges, but if this suggests a couple of bald, brown birds on a plate you are mistaken. The partridges, many and various, came with all their retinue of sauces and salads, the sharp and the sweet, each in its order; their potatoes, thin as coins but not so hard; their sprouts, foliated as rosebuds but more succulent. And no sooner had the roast and its retinue been done with than the silent serving-man, the Beadle himself perhaps in a milder manifestation, set before us, wreathed in napkins, a confection which rose all sugar from the waves. To call it pudding and so relate it to rice and tapioca would be an insult. Meanwhile the wineglasses had flushed yellow and flushed crimson; had been emptied; had been filled. And thus by degrees was lit, halfway down the spine, which is the seat of the soul, not that hard little electric light which we call brilliance, as it pops in and out upon our lips, but the more profound, subtle and subterranean glow, which is the rich yellow flame of rational intercourse. No need to hurry. No need to sparkle. No need to be anybody but oneself. We are all going to heaven and Vandyck is of the company—in other words, how good life seemed, how sweet its rewards, how trivial this grudge or that grievance, how admirable friendship and the society of one's kind, as, lighting a good cigarette, one sunk among the cushions in the window-seat.

If by good luck there had been an ash-tray handy, if one had not knocked the ash out of the window in default, if things had been a little different from what they were, one would not have seen, presumably, a cat without a tail. The sight of that abrupt and truncated animal padding softly across the quadrangle changed by some fluke of the subconscious intelligence the emotional light for me. It was as if some one had let fall a shade. Perhaps the excellent hock was relinquishing its hold. Certainly, as I watched the Manx cat pause in the middle of the lawn as if it too questioned the universe, something seemed lacking, something seemed different. But what was lacking, what was different, I asked myself, listening to the talk. And to answer that question I had to think myself out of the room, back into the past, before the war indeed, and to set before my eyes the model of another luncheon party held in rooms not very far distant from these; but different. Everything was different. Meanwhile the talk went on among the guests, who were many and young, some of this sex, some of that; it went on swimmingly, it went on agreeably, freely, amusingly. And as it went on I set it against the background of that other talk, and as I matched the two together I had no doubt that one was the descendant, the legitimate heir of the other. Nothing was changed; nothing was different save only—here I listened with all my ears not entirely to what was being said, but to the murmur or current behind it. Yes, that was it—the change was there. Before the war at a luncheon party like this people would have said precisely the same things but they would have sounded different, because in those days they were accompanied by a sort of humming noise, not articulate, but musical, exciting, which changed the value of the words themselves. Could one set that humming noise to words? Perhaps with the help of the poets one could. A book lay beside me and, opening it, I turned casually enough to Tennyson. And here I found Tennyson was singing:

> There has fallen a splendid tear
>   From the passion-flower at the gate.
> She is coming, my dove, my dear;
>   She is coming, my life, my fate;
> The red rose cries, "She is near, she is near";
>   And the white rose weeps, "She is late";
> The larkspur listens, "I hear, I hear";
>   And the lily whispers, "I wait."

Was that what men hummed at luncheon parties before the war? And the women?

> My heart is like a singing bird
>   Whose nest is in a water'd shoot;
> My heart is like an apple tree
>   Whose boughs are bent with thick-set fruit;
> My heart is like a rainbow shell
>   That paddles in a halcyon sea;
> My heart is gladder than all these
>   Because my love is come to me.

Was that what women hummed at luncheon parties before the war?

There was something so ludicrous in thinking of people humming such things even under their breath at luncheon parties before the war that I burst out laughing, and had to explain my laughter by pointing at the Manx cat, who did look a little absurd, poor beast, without a tail, in the middle of the lawn. Was he really born so, or had he lost his tail in an accident? The tailless cat, though some are said to exist in the Isle of Man, is rarer than one thinks. It is a queer animal, quaint rather than beautiful. It is strange what a difference a tail makes—you know the sort of things one says as a lunch party breaks up and people are finding their coats and hats.

This one, thanks to the hospitality of the host, had lasted far into the afternoon. The beautiful October day was fading and the leaves were falling from the trees in the avenue as I walked through it. Gate after gate seemed to close with gentle finality behind me. Innumerable beadles were fitting innumerable keys into well-oiled locks; the treasure-house was being made secure for another night. After the avenue one comes out upon a road—I forget its name—which leads you, if you take the right turning, along to Fernham. But there was plenty of time. Dinner was not till half-past seven. One could almost do without dinner after such a luncheon. It is strange how a scrap of poetry works in the mind and makes the legs move in time to it along the road. Those words—

> There has fallen a splendid tear
>   From the passion-flower at the gate.
> She is coming, my dove, my dear—

sang in my blood as I stepped quickly along towards Headingley. And then, switching off into the other measure, I sang, where the waters are churned up by the weir:

> My heart is like a singing bird
>   Whose nest is in a water'd shoot;
> My heart is like an apple tree . . .

What poets, I cried aloud, as one does in the dusk, what poets they were!

In a sort of jealousy, I suppose, for our own age, silly and absurd though these comparisons are, I went on to wonder if honestly one could name two living poets now as great as Tennyson and Christina Rossetti were then. Obviously it is impossible, I thought, looking into those foaming waters, to compare them. The very reason why the poetry excites one to such abandonment, such rapture, is that it celebrates some feeling that one used to have (at luncheon parties before the war perhaps), so that one responds easily, familiarly, without troubling to check the feeling, or to compare it with any that one has now. But the living poets express a feeling that is actually being made and torn out of us at the moment. One does not recognize it in the first place; often for some reason one fears it; one watches it with keenness and compares it jealously and suspiciously with the old feeling that one knew. Hence the difficulty of modern poetry; and it is because of this difficulty that one cannot remember more than two consecutive lines of any good modern poet. For this reason—that my memory failed me—the argument flagged for want of material. But why, I continued, moving on towards Headingley, have we stopped humming under our breath at luncheon parties? Why has Alfred ceased to sing

> She is coming, my dove, my dear?

Why has Christina ceased to respond

> My heart is gladder than all these
> Because my love is come to me?

Shall we lay the blame on the war? When the guns fired in August 1914, did the faces of men and women show so plain in each other's eyes that romance was killed? Certainly it was a shock (to women in particular with their illusions about education, and so on) to see the faces of our rulers in the light of the shell-fire. So ugly they looked—German, English, French—so stupid. But lay the blame where one will, on whom one will, the illusion which inspired Tennyson and Christina Rossetti to sing so passionately about the coming of their loves is far rarer now than then. One has only to read, to look, to listen, to remember. But why say "blame"? Why, if it was an illusion, not praise the catastrophe, whatever it was, that destroyed illusion and put truth in its place? For truth . . . those dots mark the spot where, in search of truth, I missed the turning up to Fernham. Yes indeed, which was truth and which was illusion, I asked myself. What was the truth about these houses, for example, dim and festive now with their red windows in the dusk, but raw and red and squalid, with their sweets and their boot-laces, at nine o'clock in the morning? And the willows and the river and the gardens that run down to the river, vague now with the mist stealing over them, but gold and red in the sunlight—which was the truth, which was the illusion about them? I spare you the twists and turns of my cogitations, for no conclusion was found on the road to Headingley, and I ask you to suppose that I soon found out my mistake about the turning and retraced my steps to Fernham.

As I have said already that it was an October day, I dare not forfeit your respect and imperil the fair name of fiction by changing the season and describing lilacs hanging over garden walls, crocuses, tulips and other flowers of spring. Fiction must stick to facts, and the truer the facts the better the fiction—so we are told. Therefore it was still autumn and the leaves were still yellow and falling, if anything, a little faster than before, because it was now evening (seven twenty-three to be precise) and a breeze (from the south-west to be exact) had risen. But for all that there was something odd at work:

> My heart is like a singing bird
> > Whose nest is in a water'd shoot;
> My heart is like an apple tree
> > Whose boughs are bent with thick-set fruit—

perhaps the words of Christina Rossetti were partly responsible for the folly of the fancy—it was nothing of course but a fancy—that the lilac was shaking its flowers over the garden walls, and the brimstone butterflies were scudding hither and thither, and the dust of the pollen was in the air. A wind blew, from what quarter I know not, but it lifted the half-grown leaves so that there was a flash of silver grey in the air. It was the time between the lights when colours undergo their intensification and purples and golds burn in window-panes like the beat of an excitable heart; when for some reason the beauty of the world revealed and yet soon to perish (here I pushed into the garden, for, unwisely, the door was left open and no beadles seemed about), the beauty of the world which is so soon to perish, has two edges, one of laughter, one of anguish, cutting the heart asunder. The gardens of Fernham lay before me in the spring twilight, wild and open, and in the long grass, sprinkled and carelessly flung, were daffodils and bluebells, not orderly perhaps at the best of times, and now wind-blown and waving as they tugged at their roots. The windows of the building, curved like ships' windows among generous waves of red brick, changed from lemon to silver under the flight of the quick spring clouds. Somebody was in a hammock, somebody, but in this light they were phantoms only, half guessed, half seen, raced across the grass—would no one stop her?—and then on the terrace, as if popping out to breathe the air, to glance at the garden, came a bent figure, formidable yet humble, with her great forehead and her shabby dress—could it be the famous scholar, could it be J——— H——— herself? All was dim, yet intense too, as if the scarf which the dusk had flung over the garden were torn asunder by star or sword—the flash of some terrible reality leaping, as its way is, out of the heart of the spring. For youth ———

Here was my soup. Dinner was being served in the great dining-hall. Far from being spring it was in fact an evening in October. Everybody was assembled in the big dining-room. Dinner was ready. Here was the soup. It was a plain gravy soup. There was nothing to stir the fancy in that. One could have seen through the transparent liquid any pattern that there might have been on the plate itself. But there was no pattern. The plate was plain. Next came beef with its attendant greens and potatoes—a homely trinity, suggesting the rumps of cattle in a muddy market, and sprouts curled and yellowed at the edge, and bargaining and cheapening, and women with string bags on Monday morning. There was no reason to complain of human nature's daily food, seeing that the supply was sufficient and coal-miners doubtless were sitting down to less. Prunes and custard followed. And if any one complains that prunes, even when mitigated by custard, are an uncharitable vegetable (fruit they are not), stringy as a miser's heart and exuding a fluid such as might run in misers' veins who have denied themselves wine and warmth for eighty years and yet not given to the poor, he should reflect that there are people whose charity embraces even the prune. Biscuits and cheese came next, and here the water-jug was liberally passed round, for it is the nature of biscuits to be dry, and these were biscuits to the core. That was all. The meal was over. Everybody scraped their chairs back; the swing-doors swung violently to and fro; soon the hall was emptied of every sign of food and made ready no doubt for breakfast next morning. Down corridors and up staircases the youth of England went banging and singing. And was it for a guest, a stranger (for I had no more right here in Fernham than in Trinity or Somerville or Girton or Newnham or Christchurch), to say, "The dinner was not good," or to say (we were now, Mary Seton and I, in her sitting-room), "Could we not have dined up here alone?" for if I had said anything of the kind I should have been prying and searching into the secret economies of a house which to the stranger wears so fine a front of gaiety and courage. No, one could say nothing of the sort. Indeed, conversation for a moment flagged. The human frame being what it is, heart, body and brain all mixed together, and not contained in separate compartments as they will be no doubt in another million years, a good dinner is of great importance to good talk. One cannot think well, love well, sleep well, if one has not dined well. The lamp in the spine does not light on beef and prunes. We are all *probably* going to heaven, and Vandyck is, we *hope,* to meet us round the next corner—that is the dubious and qualifying state of mind that beef and prunes at the end of the day's work breed between them. Happily my friend, who taught science, had a cupboard where there was a squat bottle and little glasses—(but there should have been sole and partridge to begin with)—so that we were able to draw up to the fire and repair some of the damages of the day's living. In a minute or so we were slipping freely in and out among all those objects of curiosity and interest which form in the mind in the absence of a particular person, and are naturally to be discussed on coming together again—how somebody has married, another has not; one thinks this, another that; one has improved out of all knowledge, the other most amazingly gone to the bad—with all those speculations upon human nature and the character of the amazing world we live in which spring naturally from such beginnings. While these things were being said, however, I became shamefacedly aware of a current setting in of its own accord and carrying everything forward to an end of its own. One might be talking of Spain or Portugal, of book or racehorse, but the real interest of whatever was said was none of those things, but a scene of masons on a high roof some five centuries ago. Kings and nobles brought treasure in huge sacks and poured it under the earth. This scene was for ever coming alive in my mind and placing itself by another of lean cows and a muddy market and withered greens and the stringy hearts of old men—these two pictures, disjointed and disconnected and nonsensical as they were, were for ever coming together and combating each other and had me entirely at their mercy. The best course, unless the whole talk was to be distorted, was to expose what was in my mind to the air, when with good luck it would fade and crumble like the head of the dead king when they opened the coffin at Windsor. Briefly, then, I told Miss Seton about the masons who had been all those years on the roof of the chapel, and about the kings and queens and nobles bearing sacks of gold and silver on their shoulders, which they shovelled into the earth; and then how the great financial magnates of our own time came and laid cheques and bonds, I suppose, where the others had laid ingots and rough lumps of gold. All that lies beneath the colleges down there, I said; but this college, where we are now sitting, what lies beneath its gallant red brick and the wild unkempt grasses of the garden? What force is behind the plain china off which we dined, and (here it popped out of my mouth before I could stop it) the beef, the custard and the prunes?

Well, said Mary Seton, about the year 1860— Oh, but you know the story, she said, bored, I suppose, by the recital. And she told me—rooms were hired. Committees met. Envelopes were addressed. Circulars were drawn up. Meetings were held; letters were read out; so-and-so has promised so much; on the contrary, Mr. ———— won't give a penny. The *Saturday Review* has been very rude. How can we raise a fund to pay for offices? Shall we hold a bazaar? Can't we find a pretty girl to sit in the front row? Let us look up what John Stuart Mill said on the subject. Can any one persuade the editor of the ———— to print a letter? Can we get Lady ———— to sign it? Lady ———— is out of town. That was the way it was done, presumably, sixty years ago, and it was a prodigious effort, and a great deal of time was spent on it. And it was only after a long struggle and with the utmost difficulty that they got thirty thousand pounds together.[1] So obviously we cannot have wine and partridges and servants carrying tin dishes on their heads, she said. We cannot have sofas and separate rooms. "The amenities," she said, quoting from some book or other, "will have to wait."[2]

At the thought of all those women working year after year and finding it hard to get two thousand pounds together, and as much as they could do to get thirty thousand pounds, we burst out in scorn at the reprehensible poverty of our sex. What had our mothers been doing then that they had no wealth to leave us? Powdering their noses? Looking in at shop windows? Flaunting in the sun at Monte Carlo? There were some photographs on the mantel-piece. Mary's mother—if that was her picture—may have been a wastrel in her spare time (she had thirteen

---

[1]"We are told that we ought to ask for £30,000 at least. . . . It is not a large sum, considering that there is to be but one college of this sort for Great Britain, Ireland and the Colonies, and considering how easy it is to raise immense sums for boys' schools. But considering how few people really wish women to be educated, it is a good deal."—Lady Stephen, *Life of Miss Emily Davies.*

[2]Every penny which could be scraped together was set aside for building, and the amenities had to be postponed.—R. Strachey, *The Cause.*

children by a minister of the church), but if so her gay and dissipated life had left too few traces of its pleasures on her face. She was a homely body; an old lady in a plaid shawl which was fastened by a large cameo; and she sat in a basket-chair, encouraging a spaniel to look at the camera, with the amused, yet strained expression of one who is sure that the dog will move directly the bulb is pressed. Now if she had gone into business; had become a manufacturer of artificial silk or a magnate on the Stock Exchange; if she had left two or three hundred thousand pounds to Fernham, we could have been sitting at our ease tonight and the subject of our talk might have been archaelogy, botany, anthropology, physics, the nature of the atom, mathematics, astronomy, relativity, geography. If only Mrs. Seton and her mother and her mother before her had learnt the great art of making money and had left their money, like their fathers and their grandfathers before them, to found fellowships and lectureships and prizes and scholarships appropriated to the use of their own sex, we might have dined very tolerably up here alone off a bird and a bottle of wine; we might have looked forward without undue confidence to a pleasant and honourable lifetime spent in the shelter of one of the liberally endowed professions. We might have been exploring or writing; mooning about the venerable places of the earth; sitting contemplative on the steps of the Parthenon, or going at ten to an office and coming home comfortably at half-past four to write a little poetry. Only, if Mrs. Seton and her like had gone into business at the age of fifteen, there would have been—that was the snag in the argument—no Mary. What, I asked, did Mary think of that? There between the curtains was the October night, calm and lovely, with a star or two caught in the yellowing trees. Was she ready to resign her share of it and her memories (for they had been a happy family, though a large one) of games and quarrels up in Scotland, which she is never tired of praising for the fineness of its air and the quality of its cakes, in order that Fernham might have been endowed with fifty thousand pounds or so by a stroke of the pen? For, to endow a college would necessitate the suppression of families altogether. Making a fortune and bearing thirteen children—no human being could stand it. Consider the facts, we said. First there are nine months before the baby is born. Then the baby is born. Then there are three or four months spent in feeding the baby. After the baby is fed there are certainly five years spent in playing with the baby. You cannot, it seems, let children run about the streets. People who have seen them running wild in Russia say that the sight is not a pleasant one. People say, too, that human nature takes its shape in the years between one and five. If Mrs. Seton, I said, had been making money, what sort of memories would you have had of games and quarrels? What would you have known of Scotland, and its fine air and cakes and all the rest of it? But it is useless to ask these questions, because you would never have come into existence at all. Moreover, it is equally useless to ask what might have happened if Mrs. Seton and her mother and her mother before her had amassed great wealth and laid it under the foundations of college and library, because, in the first place, to earn money was impossible for them, and in the second, had it been possible, the law denied them the right to possess what money they earned. It is only for the last forty-eight years that Mrs. Seton has had a penny of her own. For all the centuries before that it would have been her husband's property—a thought which, perhaps, may have had its share in keeping Mrs. Seton and her mothers off the Stock Exchange. Every penny I earn, they may have said, will be taken from me and disposed of according to my husband's wisdom—perhaps to found a scholarship or to endow a fellowship in Balliol or Kings, so that to earn money, even if I could earn money, is not a matter that interests me very greatly. I had better leave it to my husband.

At any rate, whether or not the blame rested on the old lady who was looking at the spaniel, there could be no doubt that for some reason or other our mothers had mismanaged their affairs very gravely. Not a penny could be spared for "amenities"; for partridges and wine, beadles and turf, books and cigars, libraries and leisure. To raise bare walls out of the bare earth was the utmost they could do.

So we talked standing at the window and looking, as so many thousands look every night, down on the domes and towers of the famous city beneath us. It was very beautiful, very mysterious in the autumn moonlight. The old stone looked very white and venerable. One thought of all the books that were assembled down there; of the pictures of old prelates and worthies hanging in the panelled rooms; of the painted windows that would be throwing strange globes and crescents on the pavement; of the tablets and memorials and inscriptions; of the fountains and the grass; of the quiet rooms looking across the quiet quadrangles. And (pardon me the thought) I thought, too, of the admirable smoke and drink and the deep armchairs and the pleasant carpets: of the urbanity, the geniality, the dignity which are the offspring of luxury and privacy and space. Certainly our mothers had not provided us with anything comparable to all this—our mothers who found it difficult to scrape together thirty thousand pounds, our mothers who bore thirteen children to ministers of religion at St. Andrews.

So I went back to my inn, and as I walked through the dark streets I pondered this and that, as one does at the end of the day's work. I pondered why it was that Mrs. Seton had no money to leave us; and what effect poverty has on the mind; and what effect wealth has on the mind; and I thought of the queer old gentlemen I had seen that morning with tufts of fur upon their shoulders; and I remembered how if one whistled one of them ran; and I thought of the organ booming in the chapel and of the shut doors of the library; and I thought how unpleasant it is to be locked out; and I thought how it is worse perhaps to be locked in; and, thinking of the safety and prosperity of the one sex and of the poverty and insecurity of the other and of the effect of tradition and of the lack of tradition upon the mind of a writer, I thought at last that it was time to roll up the crumpled skin of the day, with its arguments and its impressions and its anger and its laughter, and cast it into the hedge. A thousand stars were flashing across the blue wastes of the sky. One seemed alone with an inscrutable society. All human beings were laid asleep—prone, horizontal, dumb. Nobody seemed stirring in the streets of Oxbridge. Even the door of the hotel sprang open at the touch of an invisible hand—not a boots was sitting up to light me to bed, it was so late.

Mary Wollstonecraft*

Great wars are strangely intermittent in their effects. The French Revolution took some people and tore them asunder; others it passed over without disturbing a hair of their heads. Jane Austen, it is said, never mentioned it; Charles Lamb ignored

*Mary Wollstonecraft (1759–1797); William Godwin (1756–1836).

it; Beau Brummell never gave the matter a thought. But to Wordsworth and to Godwin it was the dawn; unmistakably they saw

> France standing on the top of golden hours,
> And human nature seeming born again.

Thus it would be easy for a picturesque historian to lay side by side the most glaring contrasts—here in Chesterfield Street was Beau Brummell letting his chin fall carefully upon his cravat and discussing in a tone studiously free from vulgar emphasis the proper cut of the lapel of a coat; and here in Somers Town was a party of ill-dressed, excited young men, one with a head too big for his body and a nose too long for his face, holding forth day by day over the tea-cups upon human perfectibility, ideal unity, and the rights of man. There was also a woman present with very bright eyes and a very eager tongue, and the young men, who had middle-class names, like Barlow and Holcroft and Godwin, called her simply 'Wollstonecraft', as if it did not matter whether she were married or unmarried, as if she were a young man like themselves.

Such glaring discords among intelligent people—for Charles Lamb and Godwin, Jane Austen and Mary Wollstonecraft were all highly intelligent—suggest how much influence circumstances have upon opinions. If Godwin had been brought up in the precincts of the Temple and had drunk deep of antiquity and old letters at Christ's Hospital, he might never have cared a straw for the future of man and his rights in general. If Jane Austen had lain as a child on the landing to prevent her father from thrashing her mother, her soul might have burnt with such a passion against tyranny that all her novels might have been consumed in one cry for justice.

Such had been Mary Wollstonecraft's first experience of the joys of married life. And then her sister Everina had been married miserably and had bitten her wedding ring to pieces in the coach. Her brother had been a burden on her; her father's farm had failed, and in order to start that disreputable man with the red face and the violent temper and the dirty hair in life again she had gone into bondage among the aristocracy as a governess—in short, she had never known what happiness was, and, in its default, had fabricated a creed fitted to meet the sordid misery of real human life. The staple of her doctrine was that nothing mattered save independence. 'Every obligation we receive from our fellow-creatures is a new shackle, takes from our native freedom, and debases the mind.' Independence was the first necessity for a woman; not grace or charm, but energy and courage and the power to put her will into effect, were her necessary qualities. It was her highest boast to be able to say, 'I never yet resolved to do anything of consequence that I did not adhere readily to it'. Certainly Mary could say this with truth. When she was a little more than thirty she could look back upon a series of actions which she had carried out in the teeth of opposition. She had taken a house by prodigious efforts for her friend Fanny, only to find that Fanny's mind was changed and she did not want a house after all. She had started a school. She had persuaded Fanny into marrying Mr Skeys. She had thrown up her school and gone to Lisbon alone to nurse Fanny when she died. On the voyage back she had forced the captain of the ship to rescue a wrecked French vessel by threatening to expose him if he refused. And when, overcome by a passion for Fuseli, she declared her wish to live with him and been refused flatly by his wife, she had put her principle of decisive action instantly into effect, and had gone to Paris determined to make her living by her pen.

The Revolution thus was not merely an event that had happened outside her; it was an active agent in her own blood. She had been in revolt all her life—against tyranny, against law, against convention. The reformer's love of humanity, which has so much of hatred in it as well as love, fermented within her. The outbreak of revolution in France expressed some of her deepest theories and convictions, and she dashed off in the heat of that extraordinary moment those two eloquent and daring books—the *Reply to Burke* and the *Vindication of the Rights of Woman*, which are so true that they seem now to contain nothing new in them—their originality has become our commonplace. But when she was in Paris lodging by herself in a great house, and saw with her own eyes the King whom she despised driving past surrounded by National Guards and holding himself with greater dignity than she expected, then, 'I can scarcely tell you why', the tears came to her eyes. 'I am going to bed,' the letter ended, 'and, for the first time in my life, I cannot put out the candle.' Things were not so simple after all. She could not understand even her own feelings. She saw the most cherished of her convictions put into practice—and her eyes filled with tears. She had won fame and independence and the right to live her own life—and she wanted something different. 'I do not want to be loved like a goddess,' she wrote, 'but I wish to be necessary to you.' For Imlay, the fascinating American to whom her letter was addressed, had been very good to her. Indeed, she had fallen passionately in love with him. But it was one of her theories that love should be free—'that mutual affection was marriage and that the marriage tie should not bind after the death of love, if love should die'. And yet at the same time that she wanted freedom she wanted certainty. 'I like the word affection,' she wrote, 'because it signifies something habitual.'

The conflict of all these contradictions shows itself in her face, at once so resolute and so dreamy, so sensual and so intelligent, and beautiful into the bargain with its great coils of hair and the large bright eyes that Southey thought the most expressive he had ever seen. The life of such a woman was bound to be tempestuous. Every day she made theories by which life should be lived; and every day she came smack against the rock of other people's prejudices. Every day too—for she was no pedant, no cold-blooded theorist—something was born in her that thrust aside her theories and forced her to model them afresh. She acted upon her theory that she had no legal claim upon Imlay; she refused to marry him; but when he left her alone week after week with the child she had borne him her agony was unendurable.

Thus distracted, thus puzzling even to herself, the plausible and treacherous Imlay cannot be altogether blamed for failing to follow the rapidity of her changes and the alternate reason and unreason of her moods. Even friends whose liking was impartial were disturbed by her discrepancies. Mary had a passionate, an exuberant, love of Nature, and yet one night when the colours in the sky were so exquisite that Madeleine Schweizer could not help saying to her, 'Come, Mary—come, nature-lover—and enjoy this wonderful spectacle—this constant transition from colour to colour', Mary never took her eyes off the Baron de Wolzogen. 'I must confess,' wrote Madame Schweizer, 'that this erotic absorption made such a disagreeable impression on me, that all my pleasure vanished.' But if the sentimental Swiss was disconcerted by Mary's sensuality, Imlay, the shrewd man of business, was exasperated by her intelligence. Whenever her saw her he yielded to her charm, but then her quickness, her penetration, her uncompromising idealism harassed him. She saw through his excuses; she met all his reasons; she was even capable of managing his business. There was no peace with her—he must be off again. And then her letters followed him, torturing him with their sincerity and their insight. They were so outspoken; they pleaded so passionately to be told the truth; they showed such a contempt for soap and alum and wealth and comfort; they repeated, as he suspected, so truthfully that he had only to say the word, 'and you shall never hear of me more', that he could not endure it. Tickling minnows he had hooked a dolphin, and the creature rushed him through the waters till he was dizzy and only wanted to escape. After all, though he had played at theory-making too, he was a business man, he depended upon soap and alum; 'the secondary pleasures of life', he had to admit, 'are very necessary to my comfort'. And among them was one that for ever evaded Mary's jealous scrutiny. Was it business, was it politics, was it a woman, that perpetually took him away from her? He shillied and shallied; he was very charming when they met; then he disappeared again. Exasperated at last, and half insane with suspicion, she forced the truth from the cook. A little actress in a strolling company was his mistress, she learnt. True to her own creed of decisive action, Mary at once soaked her skirts so that she might sink unfailingly, and threw herself from Putney Bridge. But she was rescued; after unspeakable agony she recovered, and then her 'unconquerable greatness of mind', her girlish creed of independence, asserted itself again, and she determined to make another bid for happiness and to earn her living without taking a penny from Imlay for herself or their child.

It was in this crisis that she again saw Godwin, the little man with the big head, whom she had met when the French Revolution was making the young men in Somers Town think that a new world was being born. She met him—but that is a euphemism, for in fact Mary Wollstonecraft actually visited him in his own house. Was it the effect of the French Revolution? Was it the blood she had seen spilt on the pavement and the cries of the furious crowd that had rung in her ears that made it seem a matter of no importance whether she put on her cloak and went to visit Godwin in Somers Town, or waited in Judd Street West for Godwin to come to her? And what strange upheaval of human life was it that inspired that curious man, who was so queer a mixture of meanness and magnanimity, of coldness and deep feeling—for the memoir of his wife could not have been written without unusual depth of heart—to hold the view that she did right—that he respected Mary for trampling upon the idiotic convention by which women's lives were tied down? He held the most extraordinary views on many subjects, and upon the relations of the sexes in particular. He thought that reason should influence even the love between men and women. He thought that there was something spiritual in their relationship. He had written that 'marriage is a law, and the worst of all laws . . . marriage is an affair of property, and the worst of all properties'. He held the belief that if two people of the opposite sex like each other, they should live together without any ceremony, or, for living together is apt to blunt love, twenty doors off, say, in the same street. And he went further; he said that if another man liked your wife 'this will create no difficulty. We may all enjoy her conversation, and we shall all be wise enough to consider the sensual intercourse a very trivial object.' True, when he wrote those words he had never been in love; now for the first time he was to experience that sensation. It came very quietly and naturally, growing 'with equal advances in the mind of each' from those talks in Somers Town, from those discussions upon everything under the sun which they had held so improperly alone in his rooms. 'It was friendship melting into love . . .', he wrote. 'When, in the course of things, the disclosure came, there was nothing in a manner for either party to disclose to the other.' Certainly they were in agreement upon the most essential points; they were both of opinion, for instance, that marriage was unnecessary. They would continue to live apart. Only when Nature again intervened, and Mary found herself with child, was it worth while to lose valued friends, she asked, for the sake of a theory? She thought not, and they were married. And then that other theory—that it is best for husband and wife to live apart—was not that also incompatible with other feelings that were coming to birth in her? 'A husband is a convenient part of the furniture of the house', she wrote. Indeed, she discovered that she was passionately domestic. Why not, then, revise that theory too, and share the same roof. Godwin should have a room some doors off to work in; and they should dine out separately if they liked—their work, their friends, should be separate. Thus they settled it, and the plan worked admirably. The arrangement combined 'the novelty and lively sensation of a visit with the more delicious and heart-felt pleasures of domestic life'. Mary admitted that she was happy; Godwin confessed that, after all one's philosophy, it was 'extremely gratifying' to find that 'there is someone who takes an interest in one's happiness'. All sorts of powers and emotions were liberated in Mary by her new satisfaction. Trifles gave her an exquisite pleasure—the sight of Godwin and Imlay's child playing together; the thought of their own child who was to be born; a day's jaunt into the country. One day, meeting Imlay in the New Road, she greeted him without bitterness. But, as Godwin wrote, 'Ours is not an idle happiness, a paradise of selfish and transitory pleasures'. No, it too was an experiment, as Mary's life had been an experiment from the start, an attempt to make human conventions conform more closely to human needs. And their marriage was only a beginning; all sorts of things were to follow after. Mary was going to have a child. She was going to write a book to be called *The Wrongs of Women*. She was going to reform education. She was going to come down to dinner the day after her child was born. She was going to employ a midwife and not a doctor at her confinement— but that experiment was her last. She died in child-birth. She whose sense of her own existence was so intense, who had cried out even in her misery, 'I cannot bear to think of being no more—of losing myself—nay, it appears to me impossible that I should cease to exist', died at the age of thirty-six. But she has her revenge. Many millions have died and been forgotten in the hundred and thirty years that have passed since she was buried; and yet as we read her letters and listen to her arguments and consider her experiments, above all, that most fruitful experiment, her relation with Godwin, and realise the high-handed and hot-blooded manner in which she cut her way to the quick of life, one form of immortality is hers undoubtedly: she is alive and active, she argues and experiments, we hear her voice and trace her influence even now among the living.

Montaigne*

Once at Bar-le-Duc Montaigne saw a portrait which René, King of Sicily, had painted of himself, and asked, 'Why is it not, in like manner, lawful for every one to draw himself with a pen, as he did with a crayon?' Off-hand one might reply, Not only is it lawful, but nothing could be easier. Other people may evade us, but our own features are almost too familiar. Let us begin. And then, when we attempt the task, the pen falls from our fingers; it is a matter of profound, mysterious, and overwhelming difficulty.

After all, in the whole of literature, how many people have succeeded in drawing themselves with a pen? Only Montaigne and Pepys and Rousseau perhaps. The *Religio Medici* is a coloured glass through which darkly one sees racing stars and a strange and turbulent soul. A bright polished mirror reflects the face of Boswell peeping between other people's shoulders in the famous biography. But this talking of oneself, following one's own vagaries, giving the whole map, weight, colour, and circumference of the soul in its confusion, its variety, its imperfection—this art belonged to one man only: to Montaigne. As the centuries go by, there is always a crowd before that picture, gazing into its depths, seeing their own faces reflected in it, seeing more the longer they look, never being able to say quite what it is that they see. New editions testify to the perennial fascination. Here is the Navarre Society in England reprinting in five fine volumes Cotton's translation; while in France the firm of Louis Conard is issuing the complete works of Montaigne with the various readings in an edition to which Dr Armaingaud has devoted a long lifetime of research.

To tell the truth about oneself, to discover oneself near at hand, is not easy.

> We hear of but two or three of the ancients who have beaten this road [said Montaigne]. No one since has followed the track; 'tis a rugged road, more so than it seems, to follow a pace so rambling and uncertain, as that of the soul; to penetrate the dark profundities of its intricate internal windings; to choose and lay hold of so many little nimble motions; 'tis a new and extraordinary undertaking, and that withdraws us from the common and most recommended employments of the world.

There is, in the first place, the difficulty of expression. We all indulge in the strange, pleasant process called thinking, but when it comes to saying, even to some one opposite, what we think, then how little we are able to convey! The phantom is through the mind and out of the window before we can lay salt on its tail, or slowly sinking and returning to the profound darkness which it has lit up momentarily with a wandering light. Face, voice, and accent eke out our words and impress their feebleness with character in speech. But the pen is a rigid instrument; it can say very little; it has all kinds of habits and ceremonies of its own. It is dictatorial too: it is always making ordinary men into prophets, and changing the natural stumbling trip of human speech into the solemn and stately march of pens. It is for this reason that Montaigne stands out from the legions of the dead with such irrepressible vivacity. We can never doubt for an instant that his book was himself. He refused to teach; he refused to preach; he kept on saying that he was just like other people.

*Michel de Montaigne (1533–1592).

All his effort was to write himself down, to communicate, to tell the truth, and that is a 'rugged road, more than it seems'.

For beyond the difficulty of communicating oneself, there is the supreme difficulty of being oneself. This soul, or life within us, by no means agrees with the life outside us. If one has the courage to ask her what she thinks, she is always saying the very opposite to what other people say. Other people, for instance, long ago made up their minds that old invalidish gentlemen ought to stay at home and edify the rest of us by the spectacle of their connubial fidelity. The soul of Montaigne said, on the contrary, that it is in old age that one ought to travel, and marriage, which, rightly, is very seldom founded on love, is apt to become, towards the end of life, a formal tie better broken up. Again with politics, statesmen are always praising the greatness of Empire, and preaching the moral duty of civilising the savage. But look at the Spanish in Mexico, cried Montaigne in a burst of rage. 'So many cities levelled with the ground, so many nations exterminated . . . and the richest and most beautiful part of the world turned upside down for the traffic of pearl and pepper! Mechanic victories!' And then when the peasants came and told him that they had found a man dying of wounds and deserted him for fear lest justice might incriminate them, Montaigne asked:

> What could I have said to these people? 'Tis certain that this office of humanity would have brought them into trouble. . . . There is nothing so much, nor so grossly, nor so ordinarily faulty as the laws.

Here the soul, getting restive, is lashing out at the more palpable forms of Montaigne's great bug-bears, convention and ceremony. But watch her as she broods over the fire in the inner room of that tower which, though detached from the main building, has so wide a view over the estate. Really she is the strangest creature in the world, far from heroic, variable as a weathercock, 'bashful, insolent; chaste, lustful; prating, silent; laborious, delicate; ingenious, heavy; melancholic, pleasant; lying, true; knowing, ignorant; liberal, covetous, and prodigal'—in short, so complex, so indefinite, corresponding so little to the version which does duty for her in public, that a man might spend his life merely in trying to run her to earth. The pleasure of the pursuit more than rewards one for any damage that it may inflict upon one's worldly prospects. The man who is aware of himself is henceforward independent; and he is never bored, and life is only too short, and he is steeped through and through with a profound yet temperate happiness. He alone lives, while other people, slaves of ceremony, let life slip past them in a kind of dream. Once conform, once do what other people do because they do it, and a lethargy steals over all the finer nerves and faculties of the soul. She becomes all outer show and inward emptiness; dull, callous, and indifferent.

Surely then, if we ask this great master of the art of life to tell us his secret, he will advise us to withdraw to the inner room of our tower and there turn the pages of books, pursue fancy after fancy as they chase each other up the chimney, and leave the government of the world to others. Retirement and contemplation—these must be the main elements of his prescription. But no; Montaigne is by no means explicit. It is impossible to extract a plain answer from that subtle, half smiling, half melancholy man, with the heavy-lidded eyes and the dreamy, quizzical expression. The truth is that life in the country, with one's books and vegetables and flowers, is often

extremely dull. He could never see that his own green peas were so much better than
other people's. Paris was the place he loved best in the whole world—'jusques à ses
verrues et à ses taches'. As for reading, he could seldom read any book for more than
an hour at a time, and his memory was so bad that he forgot what was in his mind
as he walked from one room to another. Book learning is nothing to be proud of,
and as for the achievements of science, what do they amount to? He had always
mixed with clever men, and his father had a positive veneration for them, but he
had observed that, though they have their fine moments, their rhapsodies, their
visions, the cleverest tremble on the verge of folly. Observe yourself: one moment
you are exalted; the next a broken glass puts your nerves on edge. All extremes are
dangerous. It is best to keep in the middle of the road, in the common ruts, however
muddy. In writing choose the common words; avoid rhapsody and eloquence—yet,
it is true, poetry is delicious; the best prose is that which is most full of poetry.

It appears, then, that we are to aim at a democratic simplicity. We may enjoy
our room in the tower, with the painted walls and the commodious bookcases, but
down in the garden there is a man digging who buried his father this morning, and
it is he and his like who live the real life and speak the real language. There is
certainly an element of truth in that. Things are said very finely at the lower end
of the table. There are perhaps more of the qualities that matter among the ignorant
than among the learned. But again, what a vile thing the rabble is! 'the mother of
ignorance, injustice, and inconstancy. Is it reasonable that the life of a wise man
should depend upon the judgment of fools?' Their minds are weak, soft and without
power of resistance. They must be told what it is expedient for them to know. It
is not for them to face facts as they are. The truth can only be known by the
well-born soul—'l'âme bien née'. Who, then, are these well-born souls, whom we
would imitate if only Montaigne would enlighten us more precisely?

But no. 'Je n'enseigne poinct; je raconte.' After all, how could he explain other
people's souls when he could say nothing 'entirely simply and solidly, without
confusion or mixture, in one word', about his own, when indeed it became daily
more and more in the dark to him? One quality or principle there is perhaps—that
one must not lay down rules. The souls whom one would wish to resemble, like
Etienne de La Boétie, for example, are always the supplest. 'C'est estre, mais ce n'est
pas vivre, que de se tenir attaché et obligé par necessité a un seul train.' The laws
are mere conventions, utterly unable to keep touch with the vast variety and turmoil
of human impulses; habits and customs are a convenience devised for the support
of timid natures who dare not allow their souls free play. But we, who have a private
life and hold it infinitely the dearest of our possessions, suspect nothing so much
as an attitude. Directly we begin to protest, to attitudinise, to lay down laws, we
perish. We are living for others, not for ourselves. We must respect those who
sacrifice themselves in the public service, load them with honours, and pity them
for allowing, as they must, the inevitable compromise; but for ourselves let us fly
fame, honour, and all offices that put us under an obligation to others. Let us simmer
over our incalculable cauldron, our enthralling confusion, our hotch-potch of impulses, our perpetual miracle—for the soul throws up wonders every second. Movement and change are the essence of our being; rigidity is death; conformity is death:
let us say what comes into our heads, repeat ourselves, contradict ourselves, fling out
the wildest nonsense, and follow the most fantastic fancies without caring what the
world does or thinks or says. For nothing matters except life; and, of course, order.

This freedom, then, which is the essence of our being, has to be controlled. But it is difficult to see what power we are to invoke to help us, since every restraint of private opinion or public law has been derided, and Montaigne never ceases to pour scorn upon the misery, the weakness, the vanity of human nature. Perhaps, then, it will be well to turn to religion to guide us? 'Perhaps' is one of his favourite expressions; 'perhaps' and 'I think' and all those words which qualify the rash assumptions of human ignorance. Such words help one to muffle up opinions which it would be highly impolitic to speak outright. For one does not say everything; there are some things which at present it is advisable only to hint. One writes for a very few people, who understand. Certainly, seek the Divine guidance by all means, but meanwhile there is, for those who live a private life, another monitor, an invisible censor within, 'un patron au dedans', whose blame is much more to be dreaded than any other because he knows the truth; nor is there anything sweeter than the chime of his approval. This is the judge to whom we must submit; this is the censor who will help us to achieve that order which is the grace of a well-born soul. For 'C'est une vie exquise, celle qui se maintient en ordre jusques en son privé'. But he will act by his own light; by some internal balance will achieve that precarious and everchanging poise which, while it controls, in no way impedes the soul's freedom to explore and experiment. Without other guide, and without precedent, undoubtedly it is far more difficult to live well the private life than the public. It is an art which each must learn separately, though there are, perhaps, two or three men, like Homer, Alexander the Great, and Epaminondas among the ancients, and Etienne de La Boétie among the moderns, whose example may help us. But it is an art; and the very material in which it works is variable and complex and infinitely mysterious—human nature. To human nature we must keep close. '. . . il faut vivre entre les vivants'. We must dread any eccentricity or refinement which cuts us off from our fellow-beings. Blessed are those who chat easily with their neighbours about their sport or their buildings or their quarrels, and honestly enjoy the talk of carpenters and gardeners. To communicate is our chief business; society and friendship our chief delights; and reading, not to acquire knowledge, not to earn a living, but to extend our intercourse beyond our own time and province. Such wonders there are in the world; halcyons and undiscovered lands, men with dogs' heads and eyes in their chests, and laws and customs, it may well be, far superior to our own. Possibly we are asleep in this world; possibly there is some other which is apparent to beings with a sense which we now lack.

Here then, in spite of all contradictions and all qualifications, is something definite. These essays are an attempt to communicate a soul. On this point at least he is explicit. It is not fame that he wants; it is not that men shall quote him in years to come; he is setting up no statue in the market-place; he wishes only to communicate his soul. Communication is health; communication is truth; communication is happiness. To share is our duty; to go down boldly and bring to light those hidden thoughts which are the most diseased; to conceal nothing; to pretend nothing; if we are ignorant to say so; if we love our friends to let them know it.

'. . . car, comme je scay par une trop certaine expérience, il n'est aucune si douce consolation en la perte de nos amis que celle que nous aporte la science de n'avoir rien oublié a leur dire et d'avoir eu avec eux une parfaite et entière communication.'

There are people who, when they travel, wrap themselves up, 'se défendans de la contagion d'un air incogneu' in silence and suspicion. When they dine they must have the same food they get at home. Every sight and custom is bad unless it resembles those of their own village. They travel only to return. That is entirely the wrong way to set about it. We should start without any fixed idea where we are going to spend the night, or when we propose to come back; the journey is everything. Most necessary of all, but rarest good fortune, we should try to find before we start some man of our own sort who will go with us and to whom we can say the first thing that comes into our heads. For pleasure has no relish unless we share it. As for the risks—that we may catch cold or get a headache—it is always worth while to risk a little illness for the sake of pleasure. 'Le plaisir est des principales espèces du profit.' Besides if we do what we like, we always do what is good for us. Doctors and wise men may object, but let us leave doctors and wise men to their own dismal philosophy. For ourselves, who are ordinary men and women, let us return thanks to Nature for her bounty by using every one of the senses she has given us; vary our state as much as possible; turn now this side, now that, to the warmth, and relish to the full before the sun goes down the kisses of youth and the echoes of a beautiful voice singing Catullus. Every season is likeable, and wet days and fine, red wine and white, company and solitude. Even sleep, that deplorable curtailment of the joy of life, can be full of dreams; and the most common actions—a walk, a talk, solitude in one's own orchard can be enhanced and lit up by the association of the mind. Beauty is everywhere, and beauty is only two fingers'-breadth from goodness. So, in the name of health and sanity, let us not dwell on the end of the journey. Let death come upon us planting our cabbages, or on horseback, or let us steal away to some cottage and there let strangers close our eyes, for a servant sobbing or the touch of a hand would break us down. Best of all, let death find us at our usual occupations, among girls and good fellows who make no protests, no lamentations; let him find us 'parmy les jeux, les festins, faceties, entretiens communs et populaires, et la musique, et des vers amoureux'. But enough of death; it is life that matters.

It is life that emerges more and more clearly as these essays reach not their end, but their suspension in full career. It is life that becomes more and more absorbing as death draws near, one's self, one's soul, every fact of existence: that one wears silk stockings summer and winter; puts water in one's wine; has one's hair cut after dinner; must have glass to drink from; has never worn spectacles; has a loud voice; carries a switch in one's hand; bites one's tongue; fidgets with one's feet; is apt to scratch one's ears; likes meat to be high; rubs one's teeth with a napkin (thank God, they are good!); must have curtains to one's bed; and, what is rather curious, began by liking radishes, then disliked them, and now likes them again. No fact is too little to let it slip through one's fingers, and besides the interest of facts themselves there is the strange power we have of changing facts by the force of the imagination. Observe how the soul is always casting her own lights and shadows; makes the substantial hollow and the frail substantial; fills broad daylight with dreams; is as much excited by phantoms as by reality; and in the moment of death sports with a trifle. Observe, too, her duplicity, her complexity. She hears of a friend's loss and sympathises, and yet has a bitter-sweet malicious pleasure in the sorrows of others. She believes; at the same time she does not believe. Observe her extraordinary susceptibility to impressions, especially in youth. A rich man steals because his father kept him short of money as a boy. This wall one builds not for oneself, but because one's father loved building. In short, the soul is all laced about with nerves and sympathies which affect her every action, and yet, even now in 1580, no one has any clear knowledge—such cowards we are, such lovers of the smooth conventional ways—how she works or what she is except that of all things she is the most mysterious, and one's self the greatest monster and miracle in the world. '. . . plus je me hante et connois, plus ma difformité m'estonne, moins je m'entens en moy.' Observe, observe perpetually, and, so long as ink and paper exist, 'sans cesse et sans travail' Montaigne will write.

But there remains one final question which, if we could make him look up from his enthralling occupation, we should like to put to this great master of the art of life. In these extraordinary volumes of short and broken, long and learned, logical and contradictory statements, we have heard the very pulse and rhythm of the soul, beating day after day, year after year, through a veil which, as time goes on, fines itself almost to transparency. Here is some one who succeeded in the hazardous enterprise of living; who served his country and lived retired; was landlord, husband, father; entertained kings, loved women, and mused for hours alone over old books. By means of perpetual experiment and observation of the subtlest he achieved at last a miraculous adjustment of all these wayward parts that constitute the human soul. He laid hold of the beauty of the world with all his fingers. He achieved happiness. If he had had to live again, he said, he would have lived the same life over. But, as we watch with absorbed interest the enthralling spectacle of a soul living openly beneath our eyes, the question frames itself, Is pleasure the end of all? Whence this overwhelming interest in the nature of the soul? Why this overmastering desire to communicate with others? Is the beauty of this world enough, or is there, elsewhere, some explanation of the mystery? To this what answer can there be? There is none. There is only one more question: 'Que scais-je?'

Geraldine and Jane*

Geraldine Jewsbury would certainly not have expected anybody at this time of day to bother themselves about her novels. If she had caught one pulling them down from the shelf in some library she would have expostulated. 'They're such nonsense, my dear', she would have said. And then one likes to fancy that she would have burst out in that irresponsible, unconventional way of hers against libraries and literature and love and life and all the rest of it with a 'Damn it all!' or a 'Confound it!' for Geraldine was fond of swearing.

The odd thing about Geraldine Jewsbury, indeed, was the way in which she combined oaths and endearments, sense and effervescence, daring and gush: '. . . defenceless and tender on the one hand, and strong enough to cleave the very rocks on the other'—that is how Mrs. Ireland, her biographer, puts it; or again: 'Intellectually she was a man, but the heart within her was as womanly as ever daughter of Eve could boast'. Even to look at there was, it would seem, something incongruous, queer, provocative about her. She was very small and yet boyish; very

*Geraldine Jewsbury (1812–1880); Jane Welsh Carlyle (1801–1866); Thomas Carlyle (1795–1881).

ugly yet attractive. She dressed very well, wore her reddish hair in a net, and ear-rings made in the form of miniature parrots swung in her ears as she talked. There, in the only portrait we have of her, she sits reading, with her face half-turned away, defenceless and tender at the moment rather than cleaving the very rocks.

But what had happened to her before she sat at the photographer's table reading her book it is impossible to say. Until she was twenty-nine we know nothing of her except that she was born in the year 1812, was the daughter of a merchant, and lived in Manchester, or near it. In the first part of the nineteenth century a woman of twenty-nine was no longer young; she had lived her life or she had missed it. And though Geraldine, with her unconventional ways, was an exception, still it cannot be doubted that something very tremendous had happened in those dim years before we know her. Something had happened in Manchester. An obscure male figure looms in the background—a faithless but fascinating creature who had taught her that life is treacherous, life is hard, life is the very devil for a woman. A dark pool of experience had formed in the back of her mind into which she would dip for the consolation or for the instruction of others. 'Oh! it is too frightful to talk about. For two years I lived only in short respites from this blackness of darkness', she exclaimed from time to time. There had been seasons 'like dreary, calm November days when there is but one cloud, but that one covers the whole heaven'. She had struggled, 'but struggling is no use'. She had read Cudworth through. She had written an essay upon materialism before giving way. For, though the prey to so many emotions, she was also oddly detached and speculative. She liked to puzzle her head with questions about 'matter and spirit and the nature of life' even while her heart was bleeding. Upstairs there was a box full of extracts, abstracts, and conclusions. Yet what conclusion could a woman come to? Did anything avail a woman when love had deserted her, when her lover had played her false? No. It was useless to struggle; one had better let the wave engulf one, the cloud close over one's head. So she meditated, lying often on a sofa with a piece of knitting in her hands and a green shade over her eyes. For she suffered from a variety of ailments—sore eyes, colds, nameless exhaustion; and Greenheys, the suburb outside Manchester, where she kept house for her brother, was very damp. 'Dirty, half-melted snow and fog, a swampy meadow, set off by a creeping cold damp'—that was the view from her window. Often she could hardly drag herself across the room. And then there were incessant interruptions: somebody had come unexpectedly for dinner; she had to jump up and run into the kitchen and cook a fowl with her own hands. That done, she would put on her green shade and peer at her book again, for she was a great reader. She read metaphysics, she read travels, she read old books and new books— and especially the wonderful books of Mr. Carlyle.

Early in the year 1841 she came to London and secured an introduction to the great man whose works she so much admired. She met Mrs Carlyle. They must have become intimate with great rapidity. In a few weeks Mrs Carlyle was 'dearest Jane'. They must have discussed everything. They must have talked about life and the past and the present, and certain 'individuals' who were sentimentally interested or were not sentimentally interested in Geraldine. Mrs Carlyle, so metropolitan, so brilliant, so deeply versed in life and scornful of its humbugs, must have captivated the young woman from Manchester completely, for directly Geraldine returned to Manchester she began writing long letters to Jane which echo and continue the intimate conversations of Cheyne Row. 'A man who has had *le plus grand succès* among women, and who was the most passionate and poetically refined lover in his manners and conversation you would wish to find, once said to me . . .' So she would begin. Or she would reflect:

> It may be that we women are made as we are in order that they may in some sort fertilise the world . . . We shall go on loving, they [the men] will go on struggling and toiling, and we are all alike mercifully allowed to die—after a while. I don't know whether you will agree to this, and I cannot see to argue, for my eyes are very bad and painful.

Probably Jane agreed to very little of all this. For Jane was eleven years the elder. Jane was not given to abstract reflections upon the nature of life. Jane was the most caustic, the most concrete, the most clear-sighted of women. But it is perhaps worth noting that when she first fell in with Geraldine she was beginning to feel those premonitions of jealousy, that uneasy sense that old relationships had shifted and that new ones were forming themselves, which had come to pass with the establishment of her husband's fame. No doubt, in the course of those long talks in Cheyne Row, Geraldine had received certain confidences, heard certain complaints, had drawn certain conclusions. For besides being a mass of emotion and sensibility, Geraldine was a clever, witty woman who thought for herself and hated what she called 'respectability' as much as Mrs Carlyle hated what she called 'humbug'. In addition, Geraldine had from the first the strangest feelings about Mrs Carlyle. She felt 'vague undefined yearnings to be yours in some way'. 'You will let me be yours and think of me as such, will you not?' she urged again and again. 'I think of you as Catholics think of their saints', she said: '. . . you will laugh, but I feel towards you much more like a lover than a female friend!' No doubt Mrs Carlyle did laugh, but also she could scarcely fail to be touched by the little creature's adoration.

Thus when Carlyle himself early in 1843 suggested unexpectedly that they should ask Geraldine to stay with them, Mrs Carlyle, after debating the question with her usual candour, agreed. She reflected that a little of Geraldine would be 'very enlivening', but, on the other hand, much of Geraldine would be very exhausting. Geraldine dropped hot tears on to one's hands; she watched one; she fussed one; she was always in a state of emotion. Then 'with all her good and great qualities' Geraldine had in her 'a born spirit of intrigue' which might make mischief between husband and wife, though not in the usual way, for, Mrs Carlyle reflected, her husband 'had the habit' of preferring her to other women, 'and habits are much stronger in him than passions'. On the other hand, she herself was getting lazy intellectually; Geraldine loved talk and clever talk; with all her aspirations and enthusiasms it would be a kindness to let the young woman marooned in Manchester come to Chelsea; and so she came.

She came on the 1st or 2nd of February, and she stayed till the Saturday, the 11th of March. Such were visits in the year 1843. And the house was very small, and the servant was inefficient. Geraldine was always there. All the morning she scribbled letters. All the afternoon she lay fast asleep on the sofa in the drawing-room. She dressed herself in a low-necked dress to receive visitors on Sunday. She talked too much. As for her reputed intellect, 'she is sharp as a meat axe, but as narrow'. She flattered. She wheedled. She was insincere. She flirted. She swore. Nothing would make her go. The charges against her rose in a crescendo of irritation. Mrs Carlyle almost had to turn her out of the house. At last they parted; and Geraldine, as she got into the cab, was in floods of tears, but Mrs Carlyle's eyes were dry. Indeed, she was immensely relieved to see the last of her visitor. Yet when Geraldine had driven off and she found herself alone she was not altogether easy in her mind. She knew that her behaviour to a guest whom she herself had invited had been far from perfect. She had been 'cold, cross, ironical, disobliging'. Above all, she was angry with herself for having taken Geraldine for a *confidante*. 'Heaven grant that the consequences may be only *boring*—not *fatal*', she wrote. But it is clear that she was very much out of temper; and with herself as much as with Geraldine.

Geraldine, returned to Manchester, was well aware that something was wrong. Estrangement and silence fell between them. People repeated malicious stories which she half believed. But Geraldine was the least vindictive of women—'very noble in her quarrels', as Mrs Carlyle herself admitted—and, if foolish and sentimental, neither conceited nor proud. Above all, her love for Jane was sincere. Soon she was writing to Mrs Carlyle again 'with an assiduity and disinterestedness that verge on the superhuman', as Jane commented with a little exasperation. She was worrying about Jane's health and saying that she did not want witty letters, but only dull letters telling the truth about Jane's state. For—it may have been one of those things that made her so trying as a visitor—Geraldine had not stayed for four weeks in Cheyne Row without coming to conclusions which it is not likely that she kept entirely to herself. 'You have no one who has any sort of consideration for you', she wrote. 'You have had patience and endurance till I am sick of the virtues, and what have they done for you? Half-killed you.' 'Carlyle', she burst out, 'is much too grand for everyday life. A sphinx does not fit in comfortably to our parlour life arrangements.' But she could do nothing. 'The more one loves, the more helpless one feels', she moralised. She could only watch from Manchester the bright kaleidoscope of her friend's existence and compare it with her own prosaic life, all made up of little odds and ends; but somehow, obscure though her own life was, she no longer envied Jane the brilliance of her lot.

So they might have gone on corresponding in a desultory way at a distance—and 'I am tired to death of writing letters into space', Geraldine exclaimed; 'one only writes after a long separation, to oneself, instead of one's friend'—had it not been for the Mudies. The Mudies and Mudieism, as Geraldine called it, played a vast, if almost unrecorded, part in the obscure lives of Victorian gentlewomen. In this case the Mudies were two girls, Elizabeth and Juliet: 'flary, staring, and conceited, stolid-looking girls', Carlyle called them, the daughters of a Dundee schoolmaster, a respectable man who had written books on natural history and died, leaving a foolish widow and little or no provision for his family. Somehow the Mudies arrived in Cheyne Row inconveniently, if one may hazard a guess, just as dinner was on the table. But the Victorian lady never minded that—she put herself to any inconvenience to help the Mudies. The question at once presented itself to Mrs Carlyle, what could be done for them? Who knew of a place? who had influence with a rich man? Geraldine flashed into her mind. Geraldine was always wishing she could be of use. Geraldine might fairly be asked if there were situations to be had for the Mudies in Manchester. Geraldine acted with a promptitude that was much to her credit. She 'placed' Juliet at once. Soon she had heard of another place for Elizabeth. Mrs Carlyle, who was in the Isle of Wight, at once procured stays, gown, and petticoat for Elizabeth, came up to London, took Elizabeth all the way across London to Euston Square at half past seven in the evening, put her in charge of a benevolent-looking, fat old man, saw that a letter to Geraldine was pinned to her stays, and returned home, exhausted, triumphant, yet, as happens often with the devotees of Mudieism, a prey to secret misgivings. Would the Mudies be happy? Would they thank her for what she had done? A few days later the inevitable bugs appeared in Cheyne Row, and were ascribed, with or without reason, to Elizabeth's shawl. What was far worse, Elizabeth herself appeared four months later, having proved herself 'wholly inapplicable to any practical purpose', having 'sewed a *black* apron with *white* thread', and, on being mildly scolded, having 'thrown herself on the kitchen floor and kicked and screamed'. 'Of course, her immediate dismissal is the result.' Elizabeth vanished—to sew more black aprons with white thread, to kick and scream and be dismissed—who knows what happened eventually to poor Elizabeth Mudie? She disappears from the world altogether, swallowed up in the dark shades of her sisterhood. Juliet, however, remained. Geraldine made Juliet her charge. She superintended and advised. The first place was unsatisfactory. Geraldine engaged herself to find another. She went off and sat in the hall of a 'very stiff old lady' who wanted a maid. The very stiff old lady said she would want Juliet to clear-starch collars, to iron cuffs, and to wash and iron petticoats. Juliet's heart failed her. All this clear-starching and ironing, she exclaimed, were beyond her. Off went Geraldine again, late in the evening, and saw the old lady's daughter. It was arranged that the petticoats should be 'put out' and only the collars and frills left for Juliet to iron. Off went Geraldine and arranged with her own milliner to give her lessons in quilling and trimming. And Mrs Carlyle wrote kindly to Juliet and sent her a packet. So it went on with more places and more bothers, and more old ladies, and more interviews till Juliet wrote a novel, which a gentleman praised very highly, and Juliet told Miss Jewsbury that she was annoyed by another gentleman who followed her home from church; but still she was a very nice girl, and everybody spoke well of her until the year 1849, when suddenly, without any reason given, silence descends upon the last of the Mudies. It covers, one cannot doubt, another failure. The novel, the stiff old lady, the gentleman, the caps, the petticoats, the clear-starching—what was the cause of her downfall? Nothing is known. 'The wretched stalking blockheads', wrote Carlyle, 'stalked fatefully, in spite of all that could be done and said, steadily downwards towards perdition and sank altogether out of view.' For all her endeavours, Mrs Carlyle had to admit that Mudieism was always a failure.

But Mudieism had unexpected results. Mudieism brought Jane and Geraldine together again. Jane could not deny that 'the fluff of feathers' whom she had served up, as her way was, in so many a scornful phrase for Carlyle's amusement, had 'taken up the matter with an enthusiasm even surpassing my own'. She had grit in her as well as fluff. Thus when Geraldine sent her the manuscript of her first novel, *Zoe*, Mrs Carlyle bestirred herself to find a publisher ('for', she wrote, 'what is to become of her when she is old without ties, without purpose?') and with surprising success. Chapman & Hall at once agreed to publish the book, which, their reader reported, 'had taken hold of him with a grasp of iron'. The book had been long on the way. Mrs Carlyle herself had been consulted at various stages of its career. She had read the first sketch 'with a feeling little short of terror! So much power of genius rushing so recklessly into unknown space.' But she had also been deeply impressed.

Geraldine in particular shows herself here a far more profound and daring speculator than ever I had fancied her. I do not believe there is a woman alive at the present day, not even

Georges Sand herself, that could have written some of the best passages in this book . . . but they must not publish it—decency forbids!

There was, Mrs Carlyle complained, an indecency or 'want of reserve in the spiritual department', which no respectable public would stand. Presumably Geraldine consented to make alterations, though she confessed that she 'had no vocation for propriety as such', the book was rewritten, and it appeared at last in February 1845. The usual buzz and conflict of opinion at once arose. Some were enthusiastic, others were shocked. The 'old and young roués of the Reform Club almost go off into hysterics over—its *indecency*'. The publisher was a little alarmed; but the scandal helped the sale, and Geraldine became a lioness.

And now, of course, as one turns the pages of the three little yellowish volumes, one wonders what reason there was for approval or disapproval, what spasm of indignation or admiration scored that pencil mark, what mysterious emotion pressed violets, now black as ink, between the pages of the love scenes. Chapter after chapter glides amiably, fluently past. In a kind of haze we catch glimpses of an illegitimate girl called Zoe; of an enigmatic Roman Catholic priest called Everhard; of a castle in the country; of ladies lying on sky-blue sofas; of gentlemen reading aloud; of girls embroidering hearts in silk. There is a conflagration. There is an embrace in a wood. There is incessant conversation. There is a moment of terrific emotion when the priest exclaims, 'Would that I had never been born!' and proceeds to sweep a letter from the Pope asking him to edit a translation of the principal works of the Fathers of the first four centuries and a parcel containing a gold chain from the University of Göttingen into a drawer because Zoe has shaken his faith. But what indecency there was pungent enough to shock the roués of the Reform Club, what genius there was brilliant enough to impress the shrewd intellect of Mrs Carlyle, it is impossible to guess. Colours that were fresh as roses eighty years ago have faded to a feeble pink; nothing remains of all those scents and savours but a faint perfume of faded violets, of stale hair-oil, we know not which. What miracles, we exclaim, are within the power of a few years to accomplish! But even as we exclaim, we see, far away, a trace perhaps of what they meant. The passion, in so far as it issues from the lips of living people, is completely spent. The Zoes, the Clothildes, the Everhards moulder on their perches; but, nevertheless, there is somebody in the room with them; an irresponsible spirit, a daring and agile woman, if one considers that she is cumbered with crinoline and stays; an absurd sentimental creature, languishing, expatiating, but for all that still strangely alive. We catch a sentence now and then rapped out boldly, a thought subtly conceived. 'How much better to do right without religion!' 'Oh! if they really believed all they preach, how would any priest or preacher be able to sleep in his bed!' 'Weakness is the only state for which there is no hope.' 'To love rightly is the highest morality of which mankind is capable.' Then how she hated the 'compacted, plausible theories of men'! And what is life? For what end was it given us? Such questions, such convictions, still hurtle past the heads of the stuffed figures mouldering on their perches. They are dead, but Geraldine Jewsbury herself still survives, independent, courageous, absurd, writing page after page without stopping to correct, and coming out with her views upon love, morality, religion, and the relations of the sexes, whoever may be within hearing, with a cigar between her lips.

Some time before the publication of *Zoe*, Mrs Carlyle had forgotten, or overcome, her irritation with Geraldine, partly because she had worked so zealously in the cause of the Mudies, partly also because by Geraldine's painstaking she was 'almost over-persuaded back into my old illusion that she has some sort of strange, passionate . . . incomprehensible *attraction* towards me'. Not only was she drawn back into correspondence—after all her vows to the contrary she again stayed under the same roof with Geraldine, at Seaforth House near Liverpool, in July 1844. Not many days had passed before Mrs Carlyle's 'illusion' about the strength of Geraldine's affection for her proved to be no illusion but a monstrous fact. One morning there was some slight tiff between them: Geraldine sulked all day; at night Geraldine came to Mrs Carlyle's bedroom and made a scene which was 'a revelation to me, not only of Geraldine, but of human nature! Such mad, lover-like jealousy on the part of one woman towards another it had never entered into my heart to conceive.' Mrs Carlyle was angry and outraged and contemptuous. She saved up a full account of the scene to entertain her husband with. A few days later she turned upon Geraldine in public and sent the whole company into fits of laughter by saying, 'I wondered she should expect me to behave decently to her after she had for a whole evening been making love before my very face to *another man*!' The trouncing must have been severe, the humiliation painful. But Geraldine was incorrigible. A year later she was again sulking and raging and declaring that she had a right to rage because 'she loves me better than all the rest of the world'; and Mrs Carlyle was getting up and saying, 'Geraldine, until you can behave like a gentlewoman . . .' and leaving the room. And again there were tears and apologies and promises to reform.

Yet though Mrs Carlyle scolded and jeered, though they were estranged, and though for a time they ceased to write to each other, still they always came together again. Geraldine, it is abundantly clear, felt that Jane was in every way wiser, better, stronger than she was. She depended on Jane. She needed Jane to keep her out of scrapes; for Jane never got into scrapes herself. But though Jane was so much wiser and cleverer than Geraldine, there were times when the foolish and irresponsible one of the two became the counsellor. Why, she asked, waste your time in mending old clothes? Why not work at something that will really employ your energies? Write, she advised her. For Jane, who was so profound, so far-seeing, could, Geraldine was convinced, write something that would help women in 'their very complicated duties and difficulties'. She owed a duty to her sex. But, the bold woman proceeded, 'do not go to Mr Carlyle for sympathy, do not let him dash you with cold water. You must respect your own work, and your own motives'—a piece of advice that Jane, who was afraid to accept the dedication of Geraldine's new novel *The Half Sisters,* lest Mr Carlyle might object, would have done well to follow. The little creature was in some ways the bolder and the more independent of the two.

She had, moreover, a quality that Jane with all her brilliancy lacked—an element of poetry, a trace of the speculative imagination. She browsed upon old books and copied out romantic passages about the palm trees and cinnamon of Arabia and sent them to lie, incongruously enough, upon the breakfast table in Cheyne Row. Jane's genius, of course, was the very opposite; it was positive, direct, and practical. Her imagination concentrated itself upon people. Her letters owe their incomparable brilliancy to the hawk-like swoop and descent of her mind upon facts. Nothing escapes her. She sees through clear water down to the rocks at the bottom. But the intangible eluded her; she dismissed the poetry of Keats with a sneer; something of the narrowness and something of the prudery of a Scottish country doctor's daughter clung to her. Though infinitely the less masterly, Geraldine was sometimes the broader minded.

Such sympathies and antipathies bound the two women together with an elasticity that made for permanence. The tie between them could stretch and stretch indefinitely without breaking. Jane knew the extent of Geraldine's folly; Geraldine had felt the full lash of Jane's tongue. They had learnt to tolerate each other. Naturally, they quarrelled again; but their quarrels were different now; they were quarrels that were bound to be made up. And when after her brother's marriage in 1854 Geraldine moved to London, it was to be near Mrs Carlyle at Mrs Carlyle's own wish. The woman who in 1843 would never be a friend of hers again was now the most intimate friend she had in the world. She was to lodge two streets off; and perhaps two streets off was the right space to put between them. The emotional friendship was full of misunderstandings at a distance; it was intolerably exacting under the same roof. But when they lived round the corner their relationship broadened and simplified; it became a natural intercourse whose ruffles and whose calms were based upon the depths of intimacy. They went about together. They went to hear *The Messiah*; and, characteristically, Geraldine wept at the beauty of the music and Jane had much ado to prevent herself from shaking Geraldine for crying and from crying herself at the ugliness of the chorus women. They went to Norwood for a jaunt, and Geraldine left a silk handkerchief and an aluminium brooch ('a love token from Mr Barlow') in the hotel and a new silk parasol in the waiting-room. Also Jane noted with sardonic satisfaction that Geraldine, in an attempt at economy, bought two second-class tickets, while the cost of a return ticket first class was precisely the same.

Meanwhile Geraldine lay on the floor and generalised and speculated and tried to formulate some theory of life from her own tumultuous experience. 'How loathsome' (her language was always apt to be strong—she knew that she 'sinned against Jane's notions of good taste' very often), how loathsome the position of women was in many ways! How she herself had been crippled and stunted! How her blood boiled in her at the power that men had over women! She would like to kick certain gentlemen—'the lying hypocritical beggars! Well, it's no good swearing—only, I am angry and it eases my mind.'

And then her thoughts turned to Jane and herself and to the brilliant gifts—at any rate, Jane had brilliant gifts—which had borne so little visible result. Nevertheless, except when she was ill,

> I do not think that either you or I are to be called failures. We are indications of a development of womanhood which as yet is not recognised. It has, so far, no ready-made channels to run in, but still we have looked and tried, and found that the present rules for women will not hold us—that something better and stronger is needed. . . . There are women to come after us, who will approach nearer the fullness of the measure of the stature of a woman's nature. I regard myself as a mere faint indication, a rudiment of the idea, of certain higher qualities and possibilities that lie in women, and all the eccentricities and mistakes and miseries and absurdities I have made are only the consequences of an imperfect formation, an immature growth.

So she theorised, so she speculated; and Mrs Carlyle listened, and laughed, and contradicted, no doubt, but with more of sympathy than of derision: she could have wished that Geraldine were more precise; she could have wished her to moderate her language. Carlyle might come in at any moment; and if there was one creature that Carlyle hated, it was a strong-minded woman of the Georges Sand species. Yet she could not deny that there was an element of truth in what Geraldine said; she had always thought that Geraldine 'was born to spoil a horn or make a spoon'. Geraldine was no fool in spite of appearances.

But what Geraldine thought and said; how she spent her mornings; what she did in the long evenings of the London winter—all, in fact, that constituted her life at Markham Square—is but slightly and doubtfully known to us. For, fittingly enough, the bright light of Jane extinguished the paler and more flickering fire of Geraldine. She had no need to write to Jane any more. She was in and out of the house—now writing a letter for Jane because Jane's fingers were swollen, now taking a letter to the post and forgetting, like the scatter-brained romantic creature she was, to post it. A crooning domestic sound like the purring of a kitten or the humming of a tea-kettle seems to rise, as we turn the pages of Mrs Carlyle's letters, from the intercourse of the two incompatible but deeply attached women. So the years passed. At length, on Saturday, 21st April 1866, Geraldine was to help Jane with a tea-party. Mr Carlyle was in Scotland, and Mrs Carlyle hoped to get through some necessary civilities to admirers in his absence. Geraldine was actually dressing for the occasion when Mr Froude appeared suddenly at her house. He had just had a message from Cheyne Row to say that 'something had happened to Mrs Carlyle'. Geraldine flung on her cloak. They hastened together to St George's Hospital. There, writes Froude, they saw Mrs Carlyle, beautifully dressed as usual,

> as if she had sat upon the bed after leaving the brougham, and had fallen back upon it asleep . . . The brilliant mockery, the sad softness with which the mockery alternated, both were alike gone. The features lay composed in a stern majestic calm . . . [Geraldine] could not speak.

Nor indeed can we break that silence. It deepened. It became complete. Soon after Jane's death she went to live at Sevenoaks. She lived there alone for twenty-two years. It is said that she lost her vivacity. She wrote no more books. Cancer attacked her and she suffered much. On her deathbed she began tearing up Jane's letters, as Jane had wished, and she had destroyed all but one before she died. Thus, just as her life began in obscurity, so it ended in obscurity. We know her well only for a few years in the middle. But let us not be too sanguine about 'knowing her well'. Intimacy is a difficult art, as Geraldine herself reminds us.

> Oh, my dear [she wrote to Mrs Carlyle], if you and I are drowned, or die, what would become of us if any superior person were to go and write our 'life and errors'? What a precious mess a 'truthful person' would go and make of us, and how very different to what we really are or were!

The echo of her mockery, ungrammatical, colloquial, but as usual with the ring of truth in it, reaches us from where she lies in Lady Morgan's vault in the Brompton cemetery.

Considerations for Thinking and Writing

1. Why does Woolf begin *A Room of One's Own* so abruptly? Who is the "you" and why is Woolf speaking on behalf of her audience?

2. "Lies will flow from my lips," promises Woolf at the start of *A Room of One's Own*. What fictional techniques does Woolf employ to argue that "a woman must have money and

a room of her own if she is to write fiction"? Why does she seem to stray so far from her subject in this first chapter? What does a comparison of Woolf's "lies" with Kingston's "suppositions" suggest?

3. How do mundane events in *A Room of One's Own* take on symbolic significance? Why, for example, does trespassing occur so close to the beginning of the book? What does Woolf suggest by observing "what a difference a tail makes" on a cat? Compare the meticulously detailed accounts of meals at a men's and a women's college. Why does Woolf discuss the meals in this order?

4. Of Mary Wollstonecraft, Woolf writes, "The Revolution thus was not merely an event that had happened outside her; it was an active agent in her own blood." How does Wollstonecraft's life merge the public and the private? Look back to *A Room of One's Own* and speculate on the role that education plays in bringing women into the public realm.

5. "Mary's life," Woolf remarks, "had been an experiment from the start." Woolf repeatedly described her own life and work as "experimental." In what way do Woolf's essays represent experimentation? How do they experiment with the reader's expectations?

6. Pause over this excerpt from Woolf's essay on Montaigne: "But the pen is a rigid instrument; it can say very little; it has all kinds of habits and ceremonies of its own. It is dictatorial too: it is always making ordinary men into prophets, and changing the natural stumbling trip of human speech into the solemn and stately march of pens. It is for this reason that Montaigne stands out from the legions of the dead with such irrepressible vivacity." Feminist critics such as Sandra M. Gilbert and Susan Gubar have observed that our culture traditionally links pen and penis, making writing seem a male prerogative. Why might Woolf wish to dissociate Montaigne from the "rigidity" of the pen; from "habits and ceremonies"; from dictatorship and prophecy; from "solemn and stately" marching? Is she suggesting that Montaigne is engaged in a type of writing that is nonmasculinist? How do Montaigne's essays, as she describes them, compare with the essays of Woolf which you are reading?

7. While most readers are probably unfamiliar with both Jane Carlyle and Geraldine Jewsbury, we feel that "Geraldine and Jane" provides an important account of friendship between women. Woolf writes, "Such sympathies and antipathies bound the two women together with an elasticity that made for permanence." How does Woolf render the complementarity of these two very different women? How does Woolf's version of their relationship compare with Rose's discussion of marriage in the Prologue to *Parallel Lives*? How might Rich's notion of a "lesbian continuum" ("Compulsory Heterosexuality and Lesbian Existence") inform a reading of this essay?

Part II

INTRODUCTION:
Positions and Perspectives

Of us
not much is known.
Our lives were not
extraordinary.
Our silence seals
a deeper silence.

. . . .

Not at all easy, this, to speak
of love. And to survive. Our skin
grows red with passion in reserve.
Unbridled, it would deaden every
nerve. Feeling—the reins, the check,
restraint, repose, out of whose thousand
fragments we are restored. Loving
each other even after death. As if
life were not, had not been, enough.

We touch, we hold, we keep
one another free.
—Rika Lesser, "Degli Sposi"

You have probably realized by now that there is wordplay in the title of this book, *Women's Voices.* On the one hand, we have been asking you to think of a woman's writing as it represents her "voice." The questions we pose in Part I urge you to consider how these voices engage in dialogues with the reader and with one another. At the same time, the voices you are hearing in Part I speak not only to you and to one another but to themselves. In other words, we have designed Part I of *Women's Voices* to suggest that one woman writer may speak in multiple voices, and that she may think about her voices partly in terms of gender.

In Part II we have chosen a different approach, representing a larger number of women writers by a single selection apiece (in most cases). This change in strategy is just that: strategic. Our purpose is to foreground the distinctive position from which each writer speaks, her point of view, her ideas. Many of the writers featured in Part II might have appeared in Part I; Woolf, in fact, does appear there. (As you will see, some writers in Part II, writers as different as Luce Irigaray and Tillie Olsen, deliberately attempt to speak with several voices within a single essay.) In Part II you will hear voices that try to persuade you to change your mind, or at least to know your mind. We invite you now to consider and explore a vast range of ideas, arguments,

439

speculations, opinions, and intuitions about women's lives, women's writing, and women's thinking.

Cynthia Ozick writes that Virginia Woolf "took her women one by one." While we think this description applies to our procedure in Part II, we do see some common themes and issues among these diverse writings. We begin with selections by six feminist forerunners: Mary Wollstonecraft, Margaret Fuller, Elizabeth Cady Stanton, Olive Schreiner, Virginia Woolf, and Simone de Beauvoir. Wollstonecraft runs before the forerunners, leaving them a legacy of feminist analysis, arguments, and demands that even today retains its value and force. While the material conditions of women's lives have vastly improved in the two centuries since the publication of Wollstonecraft's *Vindication of the Rights of Woman* (1791), the cultural context for those improvements has remained startlingly the same. Wollstonecraft's most enduring insight is that the position of women in a given culture is not natural but is produced by that culture. The enduring feminist focus on gender—a culturally produced sexual identity—rather than on biologically determined sexual identity owes a profound debt to Wollstonecraft. An experienced teacher who had run her own school, Wollstonecraft maintained that women should be educated not for marriage but for a self-respecting life of moral judgment and social participation. Fuller (1845) echoes this position, proclaiming a general need for a new curriculum, "a new whole for the wants of the time."

Like Stanton (1860), Schreiner (1911), and Woolf (1938), Wollstonecraft uses slavery as a metaphor for the oppression of women in marriage. In England, until well into the reign of Victoria, the laws of coverture effectively permitted the husband's legal status to cover or efface the wife's. Wollstonecraft's plea for "a civil existence within the state" is most simply a plea for legal personhood, but it was readily extended by Stanton, for example, to a de-

mand for suffrage and representation. Like Schreiner and Woolf after her, Wollstonecraft imagined a world in which a vast spectrum of occupations and employments were open to women. All three realized that such access would also gain a wider ear for feminist critiques of patriarchal culture—particularly of militarism—and empower women's activism.

Simone de Beauvoir's famous statement that "one is not born a woman; one becomes a woman" both restates Wollstonecraft's powerful insight about gender and revises it in the light of psychoanalysis and structuralism. The introduction to *The Second Sex* (1949) expresses the disenfranchisement of women as the very structure of patriarchal thinking: "self" as male and "Other" as female. Freud's notion of the Oedipus complex, in which the child renounces the mother to accept and identify with the father's authority, has offered feminists a compelling narrative of how patriarchal culture perpetuates itself. Where, then, do feminists intervene in this self-perpetuating cycle?

Two rather different answers emerge. Hélène Cixous (a feminist theorist) and Luce Irigaray (a practicing psychoanalyst) both refocus the psychoanalytic story on the pre-Oedipal stage, that is, the stage before the child renounces the mother. Following the insights of the French psychoanalyst Jacques Lacan, who recasts the Oedipal story as the child's entry into the language of the father, these women theorize a "feminine" way of writing and speaking which differs from the way women have been taught by patriarchal culture. *"L'écriture féminine"*—writing woman, writing the body—is a notion that entails such bold rhetorical experiments as Cixous's "Laugh of the Medusa" and Irigaray's "When Our Two Lips Speak Together."

The other answer is offered by the American feminist theorist Nancy Chodorow. Chodorow's psychoanalysis is not that of Lacan but that of Anglo-American object-relations theory. As its name suggests, object-relations theory concerns itself with the conscious and unconscious factors governing object choice—the self's choice of an "other." Chodorow uses this theory to assert that mothers produce daughters who have the capacity to mother, and sons "whose nurturant capacities . . . have been systematically curtailed and repressed." For this reason, Chodorow advocates shared parenting as a means of alleviating sexual inequality.

To complement these feminist commentaries on psychoanalytic insights we have included Patricia Berry's Jungian alternative to the myth of Oedipus. Berry's mythmaking focuses on an image, not a narrative, presenting a dialectical rather than a developmental view of the psyche. Finally, Jane Gallop's essay on psychoanalytic feminist criticism (written while she was expecting her first child) offers a canny critique of the notion of the pre-Oedipal mother.

While psychoanalysis has had a great influence on feminist literary and social theory in both France and the United States, American feminist literary criticism owes its enormous impact on higher education to its pragmatism. In the early 1970s Tillie Olsen's *Silences* raised probing questions about the reception and fate of women writers. Olsen asks why the work of so few women writers is read, taught, and discussed. Olsen's "One Out of Twelve" became a watchword for feminists who devoted themselves to recovering lost and neglected works of women writers. In Annette Kolodny's "Dancing through the Minefield" we find a coherent and controversial program for feminist criticism. Kolodny advocates a three-part agenda: introducing women writers into the curriculum; reading women's writing in the context of a distinct female countertradition; and rereading men's writing with a new sensitivity to issues of gender. The pioneering works of Sandra M. Gilbert and Susan Gubar *(The Madwoman in the Attic)* and Elaine Showalter *(A Literature of Their Own)* argue on behalf of a female literary tradition. In "The Parables of the Cave," Gilbert and Gubar read the "Author's Introduction" to Mary Shelley's neglected novel *The Last Man* as a parable of female authorship. Showalter's essay suggests a feminist skepticism about "high" and "low" culture. One of the premises she shares with many feminist critics is that literature is not self-contained but rather both represents and interrogates culture at large. To balance the writing of feminist critics, we have included two essays by writers of fiction— Nadine Gordimer and Margaret Atwood—which address the relationship between imagination and ideology.

As Nancy F. Cott's essay "Feminist Theory and Feminist Movements" makes clear, American feminism historically proclaims both women's "sameness" and their "difference" with respect to men. The enormous strides that women have taken toward full equality in our society have empowered women to explore the meanings of difference—both difference between women and men and differences among women. The difference it makes to be different—this is a theme shared by such diverse essays as Zora Neale Hurston's "How It Feels to Be Colored Me" and Evelyn Fox Keller's study of the biologist Barbara McClintock, "A World of Difference." The difference of women's voices is the explicit subject of Gloria Steinem's "Men and Women Talking." Steinem exposes the masculinist bias of research that studies talking without studying *listening*: Such a bias portrays women as silent, not different. Steinem studies the verbal interactions of men and women in the hope of providing "a much wider range of alternatives for women *and* for men." What a wider range of alternatives might mean for women in the workplace is the subject of Mary Anne Dolan's "When Feminism Failed."

The notion of alternatives—of choice itself—becomes far more complex when we are dealing not with women's words and careers but with women's bodies.

Rape, childbirth, and reproductive rights are issues that remind us of the difference it makes to have a woman's body. Kate Simon's autobiographical "Birthing" recalls a moment in history before legal abortions and before the systematic relocation of birthing to hospitals. We can better appreciate how fortunate Simon's mother was in her competent abortionist when we read "Racism, Birth Control and Reproductive Rights." Angela Y. Davis narrates the history of the birth control movement in the United States from the point of view of a woman of color, knowing well that the story she has to tell differs radically from that told by white feminists. Susan Brownmiller's *Against Our Will* (which has been criticized by Davis and others for reviving "the myth of the black rapist") analyzes rape in America in feminist terms. Her analysis suggests that women are oppressed not only by rape but by their very vulnerability to rape.

While Davis demonstrates that one's identity as a woman may be in tension with one's racial or ethnic identity, Hurston suggests a more fluid notion of identity: To Hurston, one may be exuberantly different in different ways at different moments. Like Hurston's novel *Their Eyes Were Watching God*, Paule Marshall's "Poets in the Kitchen" celebrates the vigor and resourcefulness with which Black women have survived their double oppression. You may also wish to reread Adrienne Rich's "Compulsory Heterosexuality and Lesbian Existence" in Part I. This essay advocates a view of relations between women that is flexible enough to admit the sameness within the lesbian difference.

The final three essayists in Part II all take up the question of a cultural identification between women and nature. In "Is Gender Necessary Redux (1976–1987)," Ursula K. Le Guin describes her novel *The Left Hand of Darkness* as a "thought-experiment": "I eliminated gender, to find out what was left." While her experiment with the idea of bisexual beings had mixed results, Le Guin registers shrewdly how gender may shape both a writer's and a reader's life in a genderless world. The implicitly masculinist bias of scientific thinking is the subject of Evelyn Fox Keller's "World of Difference." Keller argues that Barbara McClintock's unorthodox way of thinking about nature—her "feeling for the organism"—Keller argues, presents an alternative to the prevailing scientific view of nature as "other." Finally, Leslie Marmon Silko's "Landscape, History, and the Pueblo Imagination" meditates on a culture that identifies culture itself with nature. Among the Pueblos, an affinity to nature lies at the heart of human experience, and is not the prerogative of either sex. We close Part II with Silko's meditative essay, inviting you to listen closely to a voice in which the familiar words of difference, separation, and identity subside, enabling rarer words of accommodation, harmony, and inclusion to resonate within us.

MARY WOLLSTONECRAFT

A Vindication of the Rights of Woman

[On Love]

To speak disrespectfully of love is, I know, high treason against sentiment and fine feelings; but I wish to speak the simple language of truth, and rather to address the head than the heart. To endeavour to reason love out of the world would be to out-Quixote Cervantes, and equally offend against common sense; but an endeavour to restrain this tumultuous passion, and to prove that it should not be allowed to dethrone superior powers, or to usurp the sceptre which the understanding should ever coolly wield, appears less wild.

Youth is the season for love in both sexes; but in those days of thoughtless enjoyment provision should be made for the more important years of life, when reflection takes place of sensation. But Rousseau, and most of the male writers who have followed his steps, have warmly indicated that the whole tendency of female education ought to be directed to one point—to render them pleasing.

Let me reason with the supporters of this opinion who have any knowledge of human nature. Do they imagine that marriage can eradicate the habitude of life? The woman who has only been taught to please will soon find that her charms are oblique sunbeams, and that they cannot have much effect on her husband's heart when they are seen every day, when the summer is passed and gone. Will she then have sufficient native energy to look into herself for comfort, and cultivate her dormant faculties? or is it not more rational to expect that she will try to please other men, and, in the emotions raised by the experience of new conquests, endeavour to forget the mortification her love or pride has received? When the husband ceases to be a lover, and the time will inevitably come, her desire of pleasing will then grow languid, or become a spring of bitterness; and love, perhaps, the most evanescent of all passions, gives place to jealousy or vanity.

I now speak of women who are restrained by principle or prejudice. Such women, though they would shrink from an intrigue with real abhorrence, yet, nevertheless, wish to be convinced by the homage of gallantry that they are cruelly neglected by their husbands; or, days and weeks are spent in dreaming of the happiness enjoyed by congenial souls, till their health is undermined and their spirits broken by discontent. How then can the great art of pleasing be such a necessary study? it is only useful to a mistress. The chaste wife and serious mother should only consider her power to please as the polish of her virtues, and the affection of her husband as one of the comforts that render her task less difficult, and her life happier. But, whether she be loved or neglected, her first wish should be to make herself respectable, and not to rely for all her happiness on a being subject to like infirmities with herself. . . .

[Women in Society]

. . . The preposterous distinctions of rank, which render civilization a curse, by dividing the world between voluptuous tyrants and cunning envious dependents, corrupt, almost equally, every class of people, because respectability is not attached to the discharge of the relative duties of life, but to the station, and when the duties are not fulfilled the affections cannot gain sufficient strength to fortify the virtue of which they are the natural reward. Still there are some loop-holes out of which a man may creep, and dare to think and act for himself; but for a woman it is an herculean task, because she has difficulties peculiar to her sex to overcome, which require almost superhuman powers.

A truly benevolent legislator always endeavours to make it the interest of each individual to be virtuous; and thus private virtue becoming the cement of public happiness, an orderly whole is consolidated by the tendency of all the parts towards a common centre. But the private or public virtue of woman is very problematical, for Rousseau, and a numerous list of male writers, insist that she should all her life be subjected to a severe restraint, that of propriety. Why subject her to propriety—blind propriety—if she be capable of acting from a nobler spring, if she be an heir of immortality? Is sugar always to be produced by vital blood? Is one half of the human species, like the poor African slaves, to be subjected to prejudices that brutalize them, when principles would be a surer guard, only to sweeten the cup of man? Is not this indirectly to deny woman reason? for a gift is a mockery, if it be unfit for use.

Women are, in common with men, rendered weak and luxurious by the relaxing pleasures which wealth procures; but added to this they are made slaves to their persons, and must render them alluring that man may lend them his reason to guide their tottering steps aright. Or should they be ambitious, they must govern their tyrants by sinister tricks, for without rights there cannot be any incumbent duties. The laws respecting woman . . . make an absurd unit of a man and his wife; and then, by the easy transition of only considering him as responsible, she is reduced to a mere cipher.

The being who discharges the duties of its station is independent; and, speaking of women at large, their first duty is to themselves as rational creatures, and the next, in point of importance, as citizens, is that, which includes so many, of a mother. The rank in life which dispenses with their fulfilling this duty, necessarily degrades them by making them mere dolls. Or should they turn to something more important than merely fitting drapery upon a smooth block, their minds are only occupied by some soft platonic attachment; or the actual management of an intrigue may keep their thoughts in motion; for when they neglect domestic duties, they have it not in their power to take the field and march and counter-march like soldiers, or wrangle in the senate to keep their faculties from rusting.

I know that, as a proof of the inferiority of the sex, Rousseau has exultingly exclaimed, How can they leave the nursery for the camp! And the camp has by some moralists been proved the school of the most heroic virtues; though I think it would puzzle a keen casuist to prove the reasonableness of the greater number of wars that have dubbed heroes. I do not mean to consider this question critically; because, having frequently viewed these freaks of ambition as the first natural mode of civilization, when the ground must be torn up, and the woods cleared by fire and sword, I do not choose to call them pests; but surely the present system of war has little connection with virtue of any denomination, being rather the school of *finesse* and effeminacy than of fortitude.

Yet, if defensive war, the only justifiable war, in the present advanced state of society, where virtue can show its face and ripen amidst the rigours which purify the air on the mountain's top, were alone to be adopted as just and glorious, the true heroism of antiquity might again animate female bosoms. But fair and softly, gentle reader, male or female, do not alarm thyself, for though I have compared the character of a modern soldier with that of a civilized woman, I am not going to advise them to turn their distaff into a musket, though I sincerely wish to see the bayonet converted into a pruning-hook. I only re-created an imagination, fatigued by contemplating the vices and follies which all proceed from a feculent stream of wealth that has muddied the pure rills of natural affection, by supposing that society will some time or other be so constituted, that man must necessarily fulfil the duties of a citizen, or be despised, and that while he was employed in any of the departments of civil life, his wife, also an active citizen, should be equally intent to manage her family, educate her children, and assist her neighbours.

But to render her really virtuous and useful, she must not, if she discharge her civil duties, want individually the protection of civil laws; she must not be dependent on her husband's bounty for her subsistence during his life, or support after his death; for how can a being be generous who has nothing of its own? or virtuous who is not free? The wife, in the present state of things, who is faithful to her husband, and neither suckles nor educates her children, scarcely deserves the name of a wife, and has no right to that of a citizen. But take away natural rights, and duties become null.

Women then must be considered as only the wanton solace of men, when they become so weak in mind and body that they cannot exert themselves unless to pursue some frothy pleasure, or to invent some frivolous fashion. What can be a more melancholy sight to a thinking mind, than to look into the numerous carriages that drive helter-skelter about this metropolis in a morning full of pale-faced creatures who are flying from themselves! I have often wished, with Dr Johnson, to place some of them in a little shop with half a dozen children looking up to their languid countenances for support. I am much mistaken, if some latent vigour would not soon give health and spirit to their eyes, and some lines drawn by the exercise of reason on the blank cheeks, which before were only undulated by dimples, might restore lost dignity to the character, or rather enable it to attain the true dignity of its nature. Virtue is not to be acquired even by speculation, much less by the negative supineness that wealth naturally generates.

Besides, when poverty is more disgraceful than even vice, is not morality cut to the quick? Still to avoid misconstruction, though I consider that women in the common walks of life are called to fulfil the duties of wives and mothers, by religion and reason, I cannot help lamenting that women of a superior cast have not a road open by which they can pursue more extensive plans of usefulness and independence. I may excite laughter, by dropping a hint, which I mean to pursue, some future time, for I really think that women ought to have representatives, instead of being arbitrarily governed without having any direct share allowed them in the deliberations of government.

But, as the whole system of representation is now, in this country, only a convenient handle for despotism, they need not complain, for they are as well represented as a numerous class of hard-working mechanics, who pay for the support of royalty when they can scarcely stop their children's mouths with bread. How are they represented whose very sweat supports the splendid stud of an heir-apparent, or varnishes the chariot of some female favourite who looks down on shame? Taxes on the very necessaries of life, enable an endless tribe of idle princes and princesses to pass with stupid pomp before a gaping crowd, who almost worship the very parade which costs them so dear. This is mere gothic grandeur, something like the barbarous useless parade of having sentinels on horseback at Whitehall, which I could never view without a mixture of contempt and indignation.

How strangely must the mind be sophisticated when this sort of state impresses it! But, till these monuments of folly are levelled by virtue, similar follies will leaven the whole mass. For the same character, in some degree, will prevail in the aggregate of society; and the refinements of luxury, or the vicious repinings of envious poverty, will equally banish virtue from society, considered as the characteristic of that society, or only allow it to appear as one of the stripes of the harlequin coat, worn by the civilized man.

In the superior ranks of life, every duty is done by deputies, as if duties could ever be waived, and the vain pleasures which consequent idleness forces the rich to pursue, appear so enticing to the next rank, that the numerous scramblers for wealth sacrifice everything to tread on their heels. The most sacred trusts are then considered as sinecures, because they were procured by interest, and only sought to enable a man to keep *good company*. Women, in particular, all want to be ladies. Which is simply to have nothing to do, but listlessly to go they scarcely care where, for they cannot tell what.

But what have women to do in society? I may be asked, but to loiter with easy grace; surely you would not condemn them all to suckle fools and chronicle small beer! No. Women might certainly study the art of healing and be physicians as well as nurses. And midwifery, decency seems to allot to them though I am afraid the word midwife, in our dictionaries, will soon give place to *accoucheur,* and one proof of the former delicacy of the sex be effaced from the language.

They might also study politics, and settle their benevolence on the broadest basis; for the reading of history will scarcely be more useful than the perusal of romances, if read as mere biography; if the character of the times, the political improvements, arts, etc., be not observed. In short, if it be not considered as the history of man; and not of particular men, who filled a niche in the temple of fame, and dropped into the black rolling stream of time, that silently sweeps all before it into the shapeless void called—eternity.—For shape, can it be called, 'that shape hath none'?

Business of various kinds, they might likewise pursue, if they were educated in a more orderly manner, which might save many from common and legal prostitution. Women would not then marry for a support, as men accept of places under Government, and neglect the implied duties; nor would an attempt to earn their own subsistence, a most laudable one! sink them almost to the level of those poor abandoned creatures who live by prostitution. For are not milliners and mantua-makers reckoned the next class? The few employments open to women, so far from being liberal, are menial; and when a superior education enables them to take charge of the education of children as governesses, they are not treated like the tutors of sons, though even clerical tutors are not always treated in a manner calculated to render them respectable in the eyes of their pupils, to say nothing of the private comfort of the individual. But as women educated like gentlewomen, are never designed for the humiliating situation which necessity sometimes forces them to fill; these situations are considered in the light of a degradation; and they know little of the human heart, who need to be told, that nothing so painfully sharpens sensibility as such a fall in life.

Some of these women might be restrained from marrying by a proper spirit of delicacy, and others may not have had it in their power to escape in this pitiful way from servitude; is not that Government then very defective, and very unmindful of the happiness of one-half of its members, that does not provide for honest, independent women, by encouraging them to fill respectable stations? But in order to render their private virtue a public benefit, they must have a civil existence in the State, married or single; else we shall continually see some worthy woman, whose sensibility has been rendered painfully acute by undeserved contempt, droop like 'the lily broken down by a plowshare'.

It is a melancholy truth; yet such is the blessed effect of civilization! the most respectable women are the most oppressed; and, unless they have understandings far superior to the common run of understandings, taking in both sexes, they must, from being treated like contemptible beings, become contemptible. How many women thus waste life away the prey of discontent, who might have practised as physicians, regulated a farm, managed a shop, and stood erect, supported by their own industry, instead of hanging their heads surcharged with the dew of sensibility, that consumes the beauty to which it at first gave lustre; nay, I doubt whether pity and love are so near akin as poets feign, for I have seldom seen much compassion excited by the helplessness of females, unless they were fair; then, perhaps, pity was the soft handmaid of love, or the harbinger of lust.

How much more respectable is the woman who earns her own bread by fulfilling any duty, than the most accomplished beauty!—beauty did I say!—so sensible am I of the beauty of moral loveliness, or the harmonious propriety that attunes the passions of a well-regulated mind, that I blush at making the comparison; yet I sigh to think how few women aim at attaining this respectability by withdrawing from the giddy whirl of pleasure, or the indolent calm that stupefies the good sort of women it sucks in.

Proud of their weakness, however, they must always be protected, guarded from care, and all the rough toils that dignify the mind. If this be the fiat of fate, if they will make themselves insignificant and contemptible, sweetly to waste 'life away', let them not expect to be valued when their beauty fades, for it is the fate of the fairest flowers to be admired and pulled to pieces by the careless hand that plucked them. In how many ways do I wish, from the purest benevolence, to impress this truth on my sex; yet I fear that they will not listen to a truth that dear bought experience has brought home to many an agitated bosom, nor willingly resign the privileges of rank and sex for the privileges of humanity, to which those have no claim who do not discharge its duties.

Those writers are particularly useful, in my opinion, who make man feel for man, independent of the station he fills, or the drapery of factitious sentiments. I then would fain convince reasonable men of the importance of some of my remarks; and prevail on them to weigh dispassionately the whole tenor of my observations. I appeal to their understandings; and, as a fellow-creature, claim, in the name of my sex, some interest in their hearts. I entreat them to assist to emancipate their companion, to make her a *helpmeet* for them.

Would men but generously snap our chains, and be content with rational fellowship instead of slavish obedience, they would find us more observant daughters, more affectionate sisters, more faithful wives, more reasonable mothers—in a word, better citizens. We should then love them with true affection, because we should learn to respect ourselves; and the peace of mind of a worthy man would not be interrupted by the idle vanity of his wife, nor the babes sent to nestle in a strange bosom, having never found a home in their mother's.

MARGARET FULLER

Woman in the Nineteenth Century

A Woman at Forty

But to return to the thread of my subject.

Another sign of the times is furnished by the triumphs of Female Authorship. These have been great, and are constantly increasing. Women have taken possession of so many provinces for which men had pronounced them unfit, that, though these still declare there are some inaccessible to them, it is difficult to say just *where* they must stop.

The shining names of famous women have cast light upon the path of the sex, and many obstructions have been removed. When a Montague could learn better than her brother, and use her lore afterwards to such purpose as an observer, it seemed amiss to hinder women from preparing themselves to see, or from seeing all they could, when prepared. Since Somerville has achieved so much, will any young girl be prevented from seeking a knowledge of the physical sciences, if she wishes it? De Stael's name was not so clear of offense; she could not forget the Woman in the thought; while she was instructing you as a mind, she wished to be admired as a Woman; sentimental tears often dimmed the eagle glance. Her intellect, too, with all its splendor, trained in a drawing-room, fed on flattery, was tainted and flawed; yet its beams make the obscurest school-house in New England warmer and lighter to the little rugged girls who are gathered together on its wooden bench. They may never through life hear her name, but she is not the less their benefactress.

The influence has been such, that the aim certainly is, now, in arranging school instruction for girls, to give them as fair a field as boys. As yet, indeed, these arrangements are made with little judgment or reflection; just as the tutors of Lady Jane Grey, and other distinguished women of her time, taught them Latin and Greek, because they knew nothing else themselves, so now the improvement in the education of girls is to be made by giving them young men as teachers, who only teach what has been taught themselves at college, while methods and topics need revision for these new subjects, which could better be made by those who had experienced the same wants. Women are, often, at the head of these institutions; but they have, as yet, seldom been thinking women, capable of organizing a new whole for the wants of the time, and choosing persons to officiate in the departments. And when some portion of instruction of a good sort is got from the school, the far greater proportion which is infused from the general atmosphere of society contradicts its purport. Yet books and a little elementary instruction are not furnished in vain. Women are better aware how great and rich the universe is, not so easily blinded by narrowness or partial views of a home circle. "Her mother did so before her" is no longer a sufficient excuse. Indeed, it was never received as an excuse to mitigate the severity of censure, but was adduced as a reason, rather, why there should be no effort made for reformation.

Whether much or little has been done, or will be done,—whether women will add to the talent of narration the power of systematizing,—whether they will carve marble, as well as draw and paint,—is not important. But that it should be acknowledged that they have intellect which needs developing—that they should not be considered complete, if beings of affection and habit alone—is important.

Yet even this acknowledgment, rather conquered by Woman than proffered by Man, has been sullied by the usual selfishness. Too much is said of women being better educated, that they may become better companions and mothers *for men.* They should be fit for such companionship, and we have mentioned, with satisfaction, instances where it has been established. Earth knows no fairer, holier relation than that of a mother. It is one which, rightly understood, must both promote and require the highest attainments. But a being of infinite scope must not be treated with an exclusive view to any one relation. Give the soul free course, let the organization, both of body and mind, be freely developed, and the being will be fit for any and every relation to which it may be called. The intellect, no more than the sense of hearing, is to be cultivated merely that Woman may be a more valuable companion to Man, but because the Power who gave a power, by its mere existence signifies that it must be brought out toward perfection.

In this regard of self-dependence, and a greater simplicity and fulness of being, we must hail as a preliminary the increase of the class contemptuously designated as "old maids."

We cannot wonder at the aversion with which old bachelors and old maids have been regarded. Marriage is the natural means of forming a sphere, of taking root in the earth; it requires more strength to do this without such an opening; very many have failed, and their imperfections have been in every one's way. They have been more partial, more harsh, more officious and impertinent, than those compelled by severer friction to render themselves endurable. Those who have a more full experience of the instincts have a distrust as to whether the unmarried can be thoroughly human and humane, such as is hinted in the saying, "Old maids' and bachelors' children are well cared for," which derides at once their ignorance and their presumption.

Yet the business of society has become so complex, that it could now scarcely be carried on without the presence of these despised auxiliaries; and detachments from the army of aunts and uncles are wanted to stop gaps in every hedge. They rove about, mental and moral Ishmaelites, pitching their tents amid the fixed and ornamented homes of men.

In a striking variety of forms, genius of late, both at home and abroad, has paid its tribute to the character of the Aunt and the Uncle, recognizing in these personages the spiritual parents, who have supplied defects in the treatment of the busy or careless actual parents.

They also gain a wider, if not so deep experience. Those who are not intimately and permanently linked with others, are thrown upon themselves; and, if they do not there find peace and incessant life, there is none to flatter them that they are not very poor, and very mean.

A position which so constantly admonishes, may be of inestimable benefit. The person may gain, undistracted by other relationships, a closer communion with the one. Such a use is made of it by saints and sibyls. Or she may be one of the lay sisters of charity, a canoness, bound by an inward vow,—or the useful drudge of all men, the Martha, much sought, little prized,—or the intellectual interpreter of the varied life she sees; the Urania of a half-formed world's twilight.

Or she may combine all these. Not "needing to care that she may please a husband," a frail and limited being, her thoughts may turn to the centre, and she may, by steadfast contemplation entering into the secret of truth and love, use it for the good of all men, instead of a chosen few, and interpret through it all the forms of life. It is possible, perhaps, to be at once a priestly servant and a loving muse.

Saints and geniuses have often chosen a lonely position, in the faith that if, undisturbed by the pressure of near ties, they would give themselves up to the inspiring spirit, it would enable them to understand and reproduce life better than actual experience could.

How many "old maids" take this high stand we cannot say: it is an unhappy fact that too many who have come before the eye are gossips rather, and not always good-natured gossips. But if these abuse, and none make the best of their vocation, yet it has not failed to produce some good results. It has been seen by others, if not by themselves, that beings, likely to be left alone, need to be fortified and furnished within themselves; and education and thought have tended more and more to regard these beings as related to absolute Being, as well as to others. It has been seen that, as the breaking of no bond ought to destroy a man, so ought the missing of none to hinder him from growing. And thus a circumstance of the time, which springs rather from its luxury than its purity, has helped to place women on the true platform.

Perhaps the next generation, looking deeper into this matter, will find that contempt is put upon old maids, or old women, at all, merely because they do not use the elixir which would keep them always young. Under its influence, a gem brightens yearly which is only seen to more advantage through the fissures Time makes in the casket. No one thinks of Michael Angelo's Persican Sibyl, or St. Theresa, or Tasso's Leonora, or the Greek Electra, as an old maid, more than of Michael Angelo or Canova as old bachelors, though all had reached the period in life's course appointed to take that degree.

See a common woman at forty; scarcely has she the remains of beauty, of any soft poetic grace which gave her attraction as Woman, which kindled the hearts of those who looked on her to sparkling thoughts, or diffused round her a roseate air of gentle love. See her, who was, indeed, a lovely girl, in the coarse, full-blown dahlia flower of what is commonly matron-beauty, "fat, fair, and forty," showily dressed, and with manners as broad and full as her frill or satin cloak. People observe, "How well she is preserved!" "She is a fine woman still," they say. This woman, whether as a duchess in diamonds, or one of our city dames in mosaics, charms the poet's heart no more, and would look much out of place kneeling before the Madonna. She "does well the honors of her house,"—"leads society,"—is, in short, always spoken and thought of upholstery-wise.

Or see that care-worn face, from which every soft line is blotted,—those faded eyes, from which lonely tears have driven the flashes of fancy, the mild white beam of a tender enthusiasm. This woman is not so ornamental to a tea-party; yet she would please better, in picture. Yet surely she, no more than the other, looks as a human being should at the end of forty years. Forty years! have they bound those brows with no garland? shed in the lamp no drop of ambrosial oil?

Not so looked the Iphigenia in Aulis. Her forty years had seen her in anguish, in sacrifice, in utter loneliness. But those pains were borne for her father and her country; the sacrifice she had made pure for herself and those around her. Wandering alone at night in the vestal solitude of her imprisoning grove, she has looked up through its "living summits" to the stars, which shed down into her aspect their own lofty melody. At forty she would not misbecome the marble.

Not so looks the Persica. She is withered; she is faded; the drapery that enfolds her has in its dignity an angularity, too, that tells of age, of sorrow, of a stern resignation to the *must.* But her eye, that torch of the soul, is untamed, and, in the intensity of her reading, we see a soul invincibly young in faith and hope. Her age is her charm, for it is the night of the past that gives this beacon-fire leave to shine. Wither more and more, black Chrysalid! thou dost but give the winged beauty time to mature its splendors!

Not so looked Victoria Colonna, after her life of a great hope, and of true conjugal fidelity. She had been, not merely a bride, but a wife, and each hour had helped to plume the noble bird. A coronet of pearls will not shame her brow; it is white and ample, a worthy altar for love and thought.

Even among the North American Indians, a race of men as completely engaged in mere instinctive life as almost any in the world, and where each chief, keeping many wives as useful servants, of course looks with no kind eye on celibacy in Woman, it was excused in the following instance mentioned by Mrs. Jameson. A woman dreamt in youth that she was betrothed to the Sun. She built her a wigwam apart, filled it with emblems of her alliance, and means of an independent life. There she passed her days, sustained by her own exertions, and true to her supposed engagement.

In any tribe, we believe, a woman, who lived as if she was betrothed to the Sun, would be tolerated, and the rays which made her youth blossom sweetly, would crown her with a halo in age.

There is, on this subject, a nobler view than heretofore, if not the noblest, and improvement here must coincide with that in the view taken of marriage. "We must have units before we can have union," says one of the ripe thinkers of the times.
. . .

ELIZABETH CADY STANTON

From Address to the New York State Legislature, 1860

You who have read the history of nations, from Moses down to our last election, where have you ever seen one class looking after the interests of another? Any of you can readily see the defects in other governments, and pronounce sentence against those who have sacrificed the masses to themselves; but when we come to our own case, we are blinded by custom and self-interest. Some of you who have no capital can see the injustice which the laborer suffers; some of you who have no slaves, can see the cruelty of his oppression; but who of you appreciate the galling humiliation, the refinements of degradation, to which women (the mothers, wives, sisters, and daughters of freemen) are subject, in this the last half of the nineteenth century? How many of you have ever read even the laws concerning them that now disgrace your statute-books? In cruelty and tyranny, they are not surpassed by any slaveholding code in the Southern states; in fact they are worse, by just so far as woman, from her social position, refinement, and education, is on a more equal ground with the oppressor.

Allow me just here to call the attention of that party now so much interested in the slave of the Carolinas, to the similarity in his condition and that of the mothers, wives, and daughters of the Empire State. The Negro has no name. He is Cuffy Douglas or Cuffy Brooks, just whose Cuffy he may chance to be. The woman has no name. She is Mrs. Richard Roe or Mrs. John Doe, just whose Mrs. she may chance to be. Cuffy has no right to his earnings; he can not buy or sell, or lay up anything that he can call his own. Mrs. Roe has no right to her earnings; she can neither buy nor sell, make contracts, nor lay up anything that she can call her own. Cuffy has no right to his children; they can be sold from him at any time. Mrs. Roe has no right to her children; they may be bound out to cancel a father's debts of honor. The unborn child, even, by the last will of the father, may be placed under the guardianship of a stranger and a foreigner. Cuffy has no legal existence; he is subject to restraint and moderate chastisement. Mrs. Roe has no legal existence; she has not the best right to her own person. The husband has the power to restrain, and administer moderate chastisement.

Blackstone declares that the husband and wife are one, and learned commentators have decided that that one is the husband. In all civil codes, you will find them classified as one. Certain rights and immunities, such and such privileges are to be secured to white male citizens. What have women and Negroes to do with rights? What know they of government, war, or glory?

The prejudice against color, of which we hear so much, is no stronger than that against sex. It is produced by the same cause, and manifested very much in the same way. The Negro's skin and the woman's sex are both *prima facie* evidence that they were intended to be in subjection to the white Saxon man. The few social privileges which the man gives the woman, he makes up to the Negro in civil rights. The woman may sit at the same table and eat with the white man; the free Negro may hold property and vote. The woman may sit in the same pew with the white man in church; the free Negro may enter the pulpit and preach. Now, with the black man's right to suffrage, the right unquestioned, even by Paul, to minister at the altar, it is evident that the prejudice against sex is more deeply rooted and more unreasonably maintained than that against color. . . .

Just imagine an inhabitant of another planet entertaining himself some pleasant evening in searching over our great national compact, our Declaration of Independence, our Constitutions, or some of our statute-books; what would he think of those "women and Negroes" that must be so fenced in, so guarded against? Why, he would certainly suppose we were monsters, like those fabulous giants or Brobdingnagians of olden times, so dangerous to civilized man, from our size, ferocity, and power. Then let him take up our poets, from Pope down to Dana; let him listen to our Fourth of July toasts, and some of the sentimental adulations of social life, and no logic could convince him that this creature of the law, and this angel of the family altar, could be one and the same being. Man is in such a labyrinth of contradictions with his marital and property rights; he is so befogged on the whole question of maidens, wives, and mothers, that from pure benevolence we should relieve him from this troublesome branch of legislation. We should vote, and make laws for ourselves. Do not be alarmed, dear ladies! You need spend no time reading Grotius, Coke, Puffendorf, Blackstone, Bentham, Kent, and Story to find out what you need. We may safely trust the shrewd selfishness of the white man, and consent to live under the same broad code where he has so comfortably ensconced himself. Any legislation that will do for man, we may abide by most cheerfully. . . .

Now do not think, gentlemen, we wish you to do a great many troublesome things for us. We do not ask our legislators to spend a whole session in fixing up a code of laws to satisfy a class of most unreasonable women. We ask no more than the poor devils in the Scripture asked, "Let us alone." In mercy, let us take care of ourselves, our property, our children, and our homes. True, we are not so strong, so wise, so crafty as you are, but if any kind friend leaves us a little money, or we can by great industry earn fifty cents a day, we would rather buy bread and clothes for our children than cigars and champagne for our legal protectors. There has been a great deal written and said about protection. We, as a class, are tired of one kind of protection, that which leaves us everything to do, to dare, and to suffer, and strips us of all means for its accomplishment. We would not tax man to take care of us. No, the Great Father has endowed all his creatures with the necessary powers for self-support, self-defense, and protection. We do not ask man to represent us; it is hard enough in times like these for man to carry backbone enough to represent himself. So long as the mass of men spend most of their time on the fence, not knowing which way to jump, they are surely in no condition to tell us where we had better stand. In pity for man, we would no longer hang like a mill-stone round his neck. Undo what man did for us in the Dark Ages, and strike out all special legislation for us; strike the words "white male" from all your constitutions, and then, with fair sailing, let us sink or swim, live or die, survive or perish together.

Declaration of Sentiments and Resolutions

Adopted by the Seneca Falls Convention, July 19–20, 1848

When, in the course of human events, it becomes necessary for one portion of the family of man to assume among the people of the earth a position different from that which they have hitherto occupied, but one to which the laws of nature and of nature's God entitle them, a decent respect to the opinions of mankind requires that they should declare the causes that impel them to such a course.

We hold these truths to be self-evident: that all men and women are created equal; that they are endowed by their Creator with certain inalienable rights; that among these are life, liberty, and the pursuit of happiness; that to secure these rights governments are instituted, deriving their just powers from the consent of the governed. Whenever any form of government becomes destructive of these ends, it is the right of those who suffer from it to refuse allegiance to it, and to insist upon the institution of a new government, laying its foundation on such principles, and organizing its powers in such form, as to them shall seem most likely to effect their safety and happiness. Prudence, indeed, will dictate that governments long established should not be changed for light and transient causes; and accordingly all experience hath shown that mankind are more disposed to suffer, while evils are sufferable, than to right themselves by abolishing the forms to which they were accustomed. But when a long train of abuses and usurpations, pursuing invariably the same object, evinces a design to reduce them under absolute despotism, it is their duty to throw off such government, and to provide new guards for their future security. Such has been the patient sufferance of the women under this government, and such is now the necessity which constrains them to demand the equal station to which they are entitled.

The history of mankind is a history of repeated injuries and usurpations on the part of man toward woman, having in direct object the establishment of an absolute tyranny over her. To prove this, let facts be submitted to a candid world.

He has never permitted her to exercise her inalienable right to the elective franchise.

He has compelled her to submit to laws, in the formation of which she had no voice.

He has withheld from her rights which are given to the most ignorant and degraded men—both natives and foreigners.

Having deprived her of this first right of a citizen, the elective franchise, thereby leaving her without representation in the halls of legislation, he has oppressed her on all sides.

He has made her, if married, in the eye of the law, civilly dead.

He has taken from her all right in property, even to the wages she earns.

He has made her, morally, an irresponsible being, as she can commit many crimes with impunity, provided they be done in the presence of her husband. In the covenant of marriage, she is compelled to promise obedience to her husband, he becoming to all intents and purposes, her master—the law giving him power to deprive her of her liberty, and to administer chastisement.

He has so framed the laws of divorce, as to what shall be the proper causes, and in case of separation, to whom the guardianship of the children shall be given, as to be wholly regardless of the happiness of women—the law, in all cases, going upon a false supposition of the supremacy of man, and giving all power into his hands.

After depriving her of all rights as a married woman, if single, and the owner of property, he has taxed her to support a government which recognizes her only when her property can be made profitable to it.

He has monopolized nearly all the profitable employments, and from those she is permitted to follow, she receives but a scanty remuneration. He closes against her all the avenues to wealth and distinction which he considers most honorable to himself. As a teacher of theology, medicine, or law, she is not known.

He has denied her the facilities for obtaining a thorough education, all colleges being closed against her.

He allows her in Church, as well as State, but a subordinate position, claiming Apostolic authority for her exclusion from the ministry, and, with some exceptions, from any public participation in the affairs of the Church.

He has created a false public sentiment by giving to the world a different code of morals for men and women, by which moral delinquencies which exclude women from society, are not only tolerated, but deemed of little account in man.

He has usurped the prerogative of Jehovah himself, claiming it as his right to assign for her a sphere of action, when that belongs to her conscience and to her God.

He has endeavored, in every way that he could, to destroy her confidence in her own powers, to lessen her self-respect, and to make her willing to lead a dependent and abject life.

Now, in view of this entire disfranchisement of one-half the people of this country, their social and religious degradation—in view of the unjust laws above mentioned, and because women do feel themselves aggrieved, oppressed, and fraudulently deprived of their most sacred rights, we insist that they have immediate admission to all the rights and privileges which belong to them as citizens of the United States.

In entering upon the great work before us, we anticipate no small amount of misconception, misrepresentation, and ridicule; but we shall use every instrumentality within our power to effect our object. We shall employ agents, circulate tracts, petition the State and National legislatures, and endeavor to enlist the pulpit and the press in our behalf. We hope this Convention will be followed by a series of Conventions embracing every part of the country.

[The following resolutions were discussed by Lucretia Mott, Thomas and Mary Ann McClintock, Amy Post, Catharine A. F. Stebbins, and others, and were adopted:]

WHEREAS, The great precept of nature is conceded to be, that "man shall pursue his own true and substantial happiness." Blackstone in his Commentaries remarks, that this law of Nature being coeval with mankind, and dictated by God himself, is of course superior in obligation to any other. It is binding over all the globe, in all countries and at all times; no human laws are of any validity if contrary to this, and such of them as are valid, derive all their force, and all their validity, and all their authority, mediately and immediately, from this original; therefore,

Resolved, That such laws as conflict, in any way, with the true and substantial happiness of woman, are contrary to the great precept of nature and of no validity, for this is "superior in obligation to any other."

Resolved, That all laws which prevent woman from occupying such a station in society as her conscience shall dictate, or which place her in a position inferior to that of man, are contrary to the great precept of nature, and therefore of no force or authority.

Resolved, That woman is man's equal—was intended to be so by the Creator, and the highest good of the race demands that she should be recognized as such.

Resolved, That the women of this country ought to be enlightened in regard to the laws under which they live, that they may no longer publish their degradation by declaring themselves satisfied with their present position, nor their ignorance, by asserting that they have all the rights they want.

Resolved, That inasmuch as man, while claiming for himself intellectual superiority, does accord to woman moral superiority, it is pre-eminently his duty to encourage her to speak and teach, as she has an opportunity, in all religious assemblies.

Resolved, That the same amount of virtue, delicacy, and refinement of behavior that is required of woman in the social state, should also be required of man, and the same transgressions should be visited with equal severity on both man and woman.

Resolved, That the objection of indelicacy and impropriety, which is so often brought against woman when she addresses a public audience, comes with a very ill-grace from those who encourage, by their attendance, her appearance on the stage, in the concert, or in feats of the circus.

Resolved, That woman has too long rested satisfied in the circumscribed limits which corrupt customs and a perverted application of the Scriptures have marked out for her, and that it is time she should move in the enlarged sphere which her great Creator has assigned her.

Resolved, That it is the duty of the women of this country to secure to themselves their sacred right to the elective franchise.

Resolved, That the equality of human rights results necessarily from the fact of the identity of the race in capabilities and responsibilities.

Resolved, therefore, That, being invested by the Creator with the same capabilities, and the same consciousness of responsibility for their exercise, it is demonstrably the right and duty of woman, equally with man, to promote every righteous cause by every righteous means; and especially in regard to the great subjects of morals and religion, it is self-evidently her right to participate with her brother in teaching them, both in private and in public, by writing and by speaking, by any instrumentalities proper to be used, and in any assemblies proper to be held; and this being a self-evident truth growing out of the divinely implanted principles of human nature, any custom or authority adverse to it, whether modern or wearing the hoary sanction of antiquity, is to be regarded as a self-evident falsehood, and at war with mankind.

[At the last session Lucretia Mott offered and discussed the following resolution:]

Resolved, That the speedy success of our cause depends upon the zealous and untiring efforts of both men and women, for the overthrow of the monopoly of the pulpit, and for the securing to woman an equal participation with men in the various trades, professions, and commerce.

OLIVE SCHREINER

Woman and War

It may be said, 'Granting fully that you are right, that, as woman's old fields of labour slip from her, she must grasp the new, or must become wholly dependent on her sexual function alone, all the other elements of human nature in her becoming atrophied and arrested through lack of exercise: and, granting that her evolution being arrested, the evolution of the whole race will be also arrested in her person: granting all this to the full, and allowing that the bulk of human labour tends to become more and more intellectual and less and less purely mechanical, as perfected machinery takes the place of crude human exertion; and that therefore if woman is to be saved from degeneration and parasitism, and the body of humanity from arrest, she must receive a training which will cultivate all the intellectual and all the physical faculties with which she is endowed, and be allowed freely to employ them; nevertheless, would it not be possible, and perhaps be well, that a dividing line of some kind should be drawn between the occupations of men and of women? Would it not, for example, be possible that woman should retain agriculture, textile manufacture, trade, domestic management, the education of youth, and medicine, in addition to child-bearing, as her exclusive fields of toil; while to the male should be left the study of abstract science, law, and war, and statecraft; as of old, man took war and the chase, and woman absorbed the further labours of life? Why should there not be again a fair and even division in the field of social labour?"

Superficially, this suggestion appears rational, having at least this to recommend it—that it appears to harmonize with the course of human evolution in the past; but closely examined, it will, we think, be found to have no practical or scientific basis, and to be out of harmony with the conditions of modern life. In ancient and primitive societies, the mere larger size and muscular strength of man, and woman's incessant physical activity in child-bearing and suckling and rearing the young, made almost inevitable a certain sexual division of labour in almost all countries, save perhaps in ancient Egypt. Woman naturally took the heavy agricultural and domestic labours, which were yet more consistent with the continual dependence of infant life on her own, than those of man in war and the chase. There was nothing artificial in such a division; it threw the heaviest burden of the most wearying and unexciting forms of social labour on woman, but under it both sexes laboured in a manner essential to the existence of society, and each transmitted to the other, through inheritance, the fruit of its slowly expanding and always exerted powers; and the race progressed.

Individual women might sometimes, and even often, become the warrior chief of a tribe; the King of Ashantee might train his terrible regiment of females; and men might now and again plant and weave for their children: but in the main, and in most societies, the division of labour was just, natural, beneficial; and it was inevitable that such a division should take place. Were to-day a band of civilized men, women, and infants thrown down absolutely naked and defenceless in some desert, and cut off hopelessly from all external civilized life, undoubtedly very much of the old division of labour would, at least for a time, reassert itself; men would look about for stones and sticks with which to make weapons to repel wild beasts and enemies, and would go a-hunting meat and fighting savage enemies and tend the beasts when tamed: women would suckle their children, cook the meat men brought, build shelters, look for roots and if possible cultivate them; there certainly would be no parasite in the society; the woman who refused to labour for her offspring, and the man who refused to hunt or defend society, would not be supported by their fellows, would soon be extinguished by want. As wild beasts were extinguished and others tamed and the materials for war improved, fewer men would be needed for hunting and war; then they would remain at home and aid in building and planting; many women would retire into the house to perfect domestic toil and handicrafts, and on a small scale the common ancient evolution of society would practically repeat itself. But for the present, we see no such natural and spontaneous division of labour based on natural sexual distinctions in the new fields of intellectual or delicately skilled manual labour, which are taking the place of the old.

It is possible, though at present there is nothing to give indication of such a fact, and it seems highly improbable, that, in some subtle manner now incomprehensible, there might tend to be a subtle correlation between that condition of the brain and nervous system which accompanies ability in the direction of certain modern forms of mental, social labour, and the particular form of reproductive function possessed by an individual. It may be that, inexplicable as it seems, there may ultimately be found to be some connection between that condition of the brain and nervous system which fits the individual for the study of the higher mathematics, let us say, and the nature of their sex attributes. The mere fact that, of the handful of women who, up to the present, have received training and been allowed to devote themselves to abstract study, several have excelled in the higher mathematics, proves of necessity no pre-eminent tendency on the part of the female sex in the direction of mathematics, as compared to labour in the fields of statesmanship, administration, or law; as into these fields there has been practically no admittance for women. It is sometimes stated, that as several women of genius in modern times have sought to find expression for their creative powers in the art of fiction, there must be some inherent connection in the human brain between the ovarian sex function and the art of fiction. The fact is, that modern fiction being merely a description of human life in any of its phases, and being the only art that can be exercised without special training or special appliances, and produced in the moments stolen from the multifarious, brain-destroying occupations which fill the average woman's life, they have been driven to find this outlet for their powers as the only one presenting itself. How far otherwise might have been the directions in which their genius would naturally have expressed itself can be known only partially even to the women themselves; what the world has lost by that compulsory expression of genius, in a form which may not have been its most natural form of expression, or only one of its forms, no one can ever know. Even in the little third-rate novelist whose works cumber the ground, we see often a pathetic figure, when we recognize that beneath that failure in a complex and difficult art, may lie buried a sound legislator, an able architect, an original scientific investigator, or a good judge. Scientifically speaking, it is as unproven that there is any organic relation between the brain of the female and the production of art in the form of fiction, as that there is an organic relation between the hand of woman and a typewriting machine. Both the creative writer and the typist, in their respective spheres, are merely finding outlets for their powers in the direction of least resistance. The tendency of women at the present day to undertake certain forms of labour, proves only that in the crabbed, walled-in, and bound conditions surrounding woman at the present day, these are the lines along which action is most possible to her.

It may possibly be that in future ages, when the male and female forms have been placed in like intellectual conditions, with like stimuli, like training, and like rewards, that some aptitudes may be found running parallel with the line of sex function when humanity is viewed as a whole. It may possibly be that, when the historian of the future looks back over the history of the intellectually freed and active sexes for countless generations, that a decided preference of the female intellect for mathematics, engineering, or statecraft may be made clear; and that a like marked inclination in the male to excel in acting, music, or astronomy may by careful and large comparison be shown. But, for the present, we have no adequate scientific data from which to draw any conclusion, and any attempt to divide the occupations in which male and female intellects and wills should be employed, must be to attempt a purely artificial and arbitrary division: a division not more rational and scientific than an attempt to determine by the colour of his eyes and the shape and strength of his legs, whether a lad should be an astronomer or an engraver. Those physical differences among mankind which divide races and nations—not merely those differences, enormously greater as they are generally, than any physical differences between male and female of the same race, which divide the Jew and the Swede, the Japanese and the Englishman, but even those subtle physical differences which divide closely allied races such as the English and German—often appear to be allied with certain subtle differences in intellectual aptitudes. Yet even with regard to these differences, it is almost impossible to determine scientifically in how far they are the result of national traditions, environment, and education, and in how far the result of real differences in organic conformation.

No study of the mere physical differences between individuals of different races would have enabled us to arrive at any knowledge of their mental aptitude; nor does the fact that certain individuals of a given human variety have certain aptitudes form a rational ground for compelling all individuals of that variety to undertake a certain form of labour.

No analysis, however subtle, of the physical conformation of the Jew could have suggested *a priori,* and still less could have proved, apart from ages of practical experience, that, running parallel with any physical characteristics which may distinguish him from his fellows, was an innate and unique intellectual gift in the direction of religion. The fact that, during three thousand years, from Moses to Isaiah, through Jesus and Paul, on to Spinoza, the Jewish race has produced men who have given half the world its religious faith and impetus, proves that, somewhere and somehow, whether connected organically with that physical organization that marks the Jew, or as the result of his traditions and training, there does go this gift in the matter of religion. Yet, on the other hand, we find millions of Jews who are totally and markedly deficient in it, and to base any practical legislation for the individual even on this proven intellectual aptitude of the race as a whole would be manifestly as ridiculous as abortive. Yet more markedly, with the German—no consideration of his physical peculiarities, though it proceeded to the subtlest analysis of nerve, bone, and muscle, could in the present stage of our knowledge have proved to us what generations of experience appear to have proved, that, with that organization which constitutes the German, goes an unique aptitude for music. There is always the possibility of mistaking the result of training and external circumstance for inherent tendency, but when we consider the passion for music which the German has shown, and when we consider that the greatest musicians the world has seen, from Bach, Beethoven, and Mozart to Wagner, have been of that race, it appears highly probable that such a correlation between the German organization and the intellectual gift of music does exist. Similar intellectual peculiarities seem to be connoted by the external differences which mark off other races from each other. Nevertheless, were persons of all of these nationalities gathered in one colony, any attempt to legislate for their restriction to certain forms of intellectual labour on the ground of their apparently proved national aptitudes or disabilities, would be regarded as insane. To insist that all Jews, and none but Jews, should lead and instruct in religious matters; that all Englishmen, and none but Englishmen, should engage in trade; that each German should make his living by music, and none but a German allowed to practise it, would drive to despair the unfortunate individual Englishman, whose most marked deficiency might be in the direction of finance and bartering trade power; the Jew, whose religious instincts might be entirely rudimentary; or the German, who could not distinguish one note from another; and the society as a whole would be an irremediable loser, in one of the heaviest of all forms of social loss—the loss of the full use of the highest capacities of all its members.

It may be that with sexes as with races, the subtlest physical differences between them may have their fine mental correlatives; but no abstract consideration of the human body in relation to its functions of sex can, in the present state of our knowledge, show us what intellectual capacities tend to vary with sexual structure, and nothing in the present or past condition of male and female give us more than the very faintest possible indication of the relation of their intellectual aptitudes and their sexual functions. And even were it proved by centuries of experiment that with the possession of the uterine function of sex tends to go exceptional intellectual capacity in the direction of mathematics rather than natural history, or an inclination for statecraft rather than for mechanical invention; were it proved that, generally speaking and as a whole, out of twenty thousand women devoting themselves to law and twenty thousand to medicine, they tended to achieve relatively more in the field of law than of medicine, there would yet be no possible healthy or rational ground for restricting the activities of the individual female to that line in which the average female appeared rather more frequently to excel.

That even one individual in a society should be debarred from undertaking that form of social toil for which it is most fitted, makes an unnecessary deficit in the general social assets. That one male Froebel should be prohibited or hampered in his labour as an educator of infancy, on the ground that infantile instruction was the field of the female; that one female with gifts in the direction of state administration, should be compelled to instruct an infants' school, perhaps without the slightest gift for so doing, is a running to waste of social life-blood.

Free trade in labour and equality of training, intellectual or physical, is essential if the organic aptitudes of a sex or class are to be determined. And our demand to-day is that natural conditions inexorably, but beneficently, may determine the labours of each individual, and not artificial restrictions.

As there is no need to legislate that Hindus, being generally supposed to have a natural incapacity for field sports, shall not betake themselves to them—for, if they have no capacity, they will fail; and, as in spite of the Hindus' supposed general incapacity for sport, it is possible for an individual Hindu to become the noted batsman of his age; so, also, there is no need to legislate that woman should be restricted in her choice of fields of labour; for the organic incapacity of the individual, if it exist, will legislate far more powerfully than any artificial, legal, or social obstruction can do; and it may be that the one individual in ten thousand who selects a field not generally sought by his fellows will enrich humanity by the result of an especial genius. Allowing all to start from the one point in the world of intellectual culture and labour, with our ancient Mother Nature sitting as umpire, distributing the prizes and scratching from the lists the incompetent, is all we demand, but we demand it determinedly. Throw the puppy into the water; if it swims, well; if it sinks, well; but do not tie a rope round its throat and weight it with a brick, and then assert its incapacity to keep afloat.

For the present our cry is, *'We take all labour for our province!'*

From the judge's seat to the legislator's chair; from the statesman's closet to the merchant's office; from the chemist's laboratory to the astronomer's tower, there is no post or form of toil for which it is not our intention to attempt to fit ourselves; and there is no closed door we do not intend to force open; and there is no fruit in the garden of knowledge it is not our determination to eat. Acting in us, and through us, nature we know will mercilessly expose to us our deficiencies in the field of human toil, and reveal to us our powers. *And, for to-day, we take all labour for our province!*

But, it may then be said: 'What of war, that struggle of the human creature to attain its ends by physical force and at the price of the life of others: will you take part in that also?' We reply: Yes; more particularly in that field we intend to play our part. We have always borne part of the weight of war, and the major part. It is not merely that in primitive times we suffered from the destruction of the fields we tilled and the houses we built; or that in later times as domestic labourers and producers, though unwaged, we, in taxes and material loss and additional labour, paid as much as our males towards the cost of war; nor is it that in a comparatively insignificant manner, as nurses of the wounded in modern times, or now and again as warrior chieftainesses and leaders in primitive and other societies, we have borne our part; nor is it even because the spirit of resolution in its women, and their willingness to endure, has in all ages again and again largely determined the fate of a race that goes to war, that we demand our controlling right where war is concerned. Our relation to war is far more intimate, personal, and indissoluble than this. Men have made boomerangs, bows, swords, or guns with which to destroy one another; we have made the men who destroyed and were destroyed! We have in all ages produced, at an enormous cost, the primal munition of war, without which no other would exist. There is no battlefield on earth, nor ever has been, howsoever covered with slain, which it has not cost the women of the race more in actual bloodshed and anguish to supply, than it has cost the men who lie there. *We pay the first cost on all human life.*

In supplying the men for the carnage of a battlefield, women have not merely lost actually more blood, and gone through a more acute anguish and weariness, in the long months of bearing and in the final agony of child-birth, than has been experienced by the men who cover it; but, in the long months and years of rearing that follow, the women of the race go through a long, patiently endured strain which no knapsacked soldier on his longest march has ever more than equalled; while, even in the matter of death, in all civilized societies, the probability that the average woman will die in child-birth is immeasurably greater than the probability that the average male will die in battle.

There is, perhaps, no woman, whether she have borne children, or be merely potentially a child-bearer, who could look down upon a battlefield covered with slain, but the thought would rise in her, 'So many mothers' sons! So many bodies brought into the world to lie there! So many months of weariness and pain while bones and muscles were shaped within; so many hours of anguish and struggle that breath might be; so many baby mouths drawing life at woman's breasts;—all this, that men might lay with glazed eyeballs, and swollen bodies, and fixed, blue, unclosed mouths, and great limbs tossed—this, that an acre of ground might be manured with human flesh, that next year's grass or poppies or karoo bushes may spring up greener and redder, where they have lain, or that the sand of a plain may have a glint of white bones!' And we cry, 'Without an inexorable cause, this should not be!' No woman who is a woman says of a human body, 'It is nothing!'

On that day, when the woman takes her place beside the man in the governance and arrangement of external affairs of her race will also be that day that heralds the death of war as a means of arranging human differences. No tinsel of trumpets and flags will ultimately seduce women into the insanity of recklessly destroying life, or gild the wilful taking of life with any other name than that of murder, whether it be the slaughter of the million or of one by one. And this will be, not because with the sexual function of maternity necessarily goes in the human creature a deeper moral insight, or a loftier type of social instinct than that which accompanies the paternal. Men have in all ages led as nobly as women in many paths of heroic virtue, and toward the higher social sympathies; in certain ages, being freer and more widely cultured, they have led further and better. The fact that woman has no inherent all-round moral superiority over her male companion, or naturally on all points any higher social instinct, is perhaps most clearly exemplified by one curious very small fact: the two terms signifying intimate human relationships which in almost all human languages bear the most sinister and antisocial significance are both terms which have as their root the term 'mother', and denote feminine relationships—the words 'mother-in-law' and 'step-mother.'

In general humanity, in the sense of social solidarity, and in magnanimity, the male has continually proved himself at least the equal of the female.

Nor will women shrink from war because they lack courage. Earth's women of every generation have faced suffering and death with an equanimity that no soldier on a battlefield has ever surpassed and few have equalled; and where war has been to preserve life, or land, or freedom, unparasitized and labouring women have in all ages known how to bear an active part, and die.

Nor will woman's influence militate against war because in the future woman will not be able physically to bear her part in it. The smaller size of her muscle, which would severely have disadvantaged her when war was conducted with a battle-axe or sword and hand to hand, would now little or at all affect her. If intent on training for war, she might acquire the skill for guiding a Maxim or shooting down a foe with a Lee-Metford at four thousand yards as ably as any male; and undoubtedly, it has not been only the peasant girl of France, who has carried latent and hid within her person the gifts that make the supreme general. If our European nations should continue in their present semi-civilized condition, which makes war possible, for a few generations longer, it is highly probable that as financiers, as managers of the commissariat department, as inspectors of provisions and clothing for the army, women will play a very leading part; and that the nation which is the first to employ its women so may be placed at a vast advantage over its fellows in time of war. It is not because of woman's cowardice, incapacity, nor, above all, because of her general superior virtue, that she will end war when her voice is fully, finally, and clearly heard in the governance of states—it is because, on this one point, and on this point almost alone, the knowledge of woman, simply as woman, is superior to that of man; she knows the history of human flesh; she knows its cost; he does not.

In a besieged city, it might well happen that men in the streets might seize upon statues and marble carvings from public buildings and galleries and hurl them in to stop the breaches made in their ramparts by the enemy, unconsideringly and merely because they came first to hand, not valuing them more than had they been paving-stones. But one man could not do this—the sculptor! He, who, though there might be no work of his own chisel among them, yet knew what each of these works of art had cost, knew by experience the long years of struggle and study and the infinitude of toil which had gone to the shaping of even one limb, to the carving of even one perfected outline, *he* could never so use them without thought or care. Instinctively he would seek to throw in household goods, even gold and silver, all the city held, before he sacrificed its works of art!

Men's bodies are our woman's works of art. Given to us power of control, we will never carelessly throw them in to fill up the gaps in human relationships made by international ambitions and greeds. The thought would never come to us as woman, 'Cast in men's bodies; settle the thing so!' Arbitration and compensation would as naturally occur to her as cheaper and simpler methods of bridging the gaps in national relationships, as to the sculptor it would occur to throw in anything rather than statuary, though he might be driven to that at last!

This is one of those phases of human life, not very numerous, but very important, towards which the man as man, and the woman as woman, on the mere ground of their different sexual function with regard to reproduction, stand, and must stand, at a somewhat differing angle. The physical creation of human life, which, in as far as the male is concerned, consists in a few moments of physical pleasure; to the female must always signify months of pressure and physical endurance, crowned with danger to life. To the male, the giving of life is a laugh; to the female, blood, anguish, and sometimes death. Here we touch one of the few yet important differences between man and woman as such.

The twenty thousand men prematurely slain on a field of battle, mean, to the women of their race, twenty thousand human creatures to be borne within them for months, given birth to in anguish, fed from their breasts and reared with toil, if the numbers of the tribe and the strength of the nation are to be maintained. In nations continually at war, incessant and unbroken child-bearing is by war imposed on all women if the state is to survive; and whenever war occurs, if numbers are to be maintained, there must be an increased child-bearing and rearing. This throws upon woman as woman a war tax, compared with which all that the male expends in military preparations is comparatively light.

The relations of the female towards the production of human life influences undoubtedly even her relation towards animal and all life. 'It is a fine day, let us go out and kill something!' cries the typical male of certain races, instinctively. 'There is a living thing, it will die if it is not cared for,' says the average woman, almost equally instinctively. It is true, that the woman will sacrifice as mercilessly, as cruelly, the life of a hated rival or an enemy, as any male; *but she always knows what she is doing, and the value of the life she takes!* There is no lighthearted, careless enjoyment in the sacrifice of life to the normal woman; her instinct, instructed by practical experience, steps in to prevent it. She always knows what life costs; and that it is more easy to destroy than create it.

It is also true, that, from the loftiest standpoint, the condemnation of war which has arisen in the advancing human spirit, is in no sense related to any particular form of sex function. The man and the woman alike, who with Isaiah on the hills of Palestine, or the Indian Buddha under his bo-tree, have seen the essential unity of all sentient life; and who therefore see in war but a symptom of that crude discoordination of life on earth, not yet at one with itself, which affects humanity in these early stages of its growth: and who are compelled to regard as the ultimate goal of the race, though yet perhaps far distant across the ridges of innumerable coming ages, that harmony between all forms of conscious life, metaphorically prefigured by the ancient Hebrew, when he cried, 'The wolf shall dwell with the lamb; and the leopard shall lie down with the kid; and the calf and the young lion and the fatling together and a little child shall lead them!'—to that individual, whether man or woman, who has reached this standpoint, there is no need for enlightenment from the instincts of the child-bearers of society as such; their condemnation of war, rising not so much from the fact that it is a wasteful destruction of human flesh, as that it is an indication of the non-existence of that co-ordination, the harmony which is summed up in the cry, 'My little children, love one another.'

But for the vast bulk of humanity, probably for generations to come, the instinctive antagonism of the human child-bearer to reckless destruction of that which she has at so much cost produced, will be necessary to educate the race to any clear conception of the bestiality and insanity of war.

War will pass when intellectual culture and activity have made possible to the female an equal share in the control and governance of modern national life; it will probably not pass away much sooner; its extinction will not be delayed much longer.

It is especially in the domain of war that we, the bearers of men's bodies, who supply its most valuable munition, who, not amid the clamour and ardour of battle, but singly, and alone, with a three-in-the-morning courage, shed our blood and face death that the battlefield may have its food, a food more precious to us than our heart's blood; it is we especially, who in the domain of war, have our word to say, a word no man can say for us. It is our intention to enter into the domain of war and to labour there till in the course of generations we have extinguished it.

If to-day we claim all labour for our province, yet more especially do we claim those fields in which the difference in the reproductive function between man and woman may place male and female at a slightly different angle with regard to certain phases of human life.

VIRGINIA WOOLF

Three Guineas

The Daughters of Educated Men

". . . Since your* expression is decidedly downcast, it seems as if these quotations about the nature of professional life have brought you to some melancholy conclusion. What can it be? Simply, you reply, that we, daughters of educated men, are between the devil and the deep sea. Behind us lies the patriarchal system; the private house, with its nullity, its immorality, its hypocrisy, its servility. Before us lies the public world, the professional system, with its possessiveness, its jealousy, its pugnacity, its greed. The one shuts us up like slaves in a harem; the other forces us to circle, like caterpillars head to tail, round and round the mulberry tree, the sacred tree, of property. It is a choice of evils. Each is bad. Had we not better plunge off the bridge into the river; give up the game; declare that the whole of human life is a mistake and so end it?

"But before you take that step, Madam, a decisive one, unless you share the opinion of the professors of the Church of England that death is the gate of life—*Mors Janua Vitae* is written upon an arch in St. Paul's—in which case there is, of course, much to recommend it, let us see if another answer is not possible.

"Another answer may be staring us in the face on the shelves of your own library, once more in the biographies. Is it not possible that by considering the experiments that the dead have made with their lives in the past we may find some help in answering the very difficult question that is now forced upon us? At any rate, let us try. The question that we will now put to biography is this: For reasons given above we are agreed that we must earn money in the professions. For reasons given above those professions seem to us highly undesirable. The question we put to you, lives of the dead, is how can we enter the professions and yet remain civilized human beings; human beings, that is, who wish to prevent war?

"This time let us turn to the lives not of men but of women in the nineteenth century—to the lives of professional women. But there would seem to be a gap in your library, Madam. There are no lives of professional women in the nineteenth century. A Mrs. Tomlinson, the wife of a Mr. Tomlinson, F.R.S., F.C.S., explains the reason. This lady, who wrote a book 'advocating the employment of young ladies as nurses for children,' says: '. . . it seemed as if there were no way in which an unmarried lady could earn a living but by taking a situation as governess, for which post she was often unfit by nature and education, or want of education.' That was written in 1859—less than 100 years ago. That explains the gap on your shelves. There were no professional women, except governesses, to have lives written of them. And the lives of governesses, that is the written lives, can be counted on the fingers of one hand. What then can we learn about the lives of professional women from studying the lives of governesses? Happily old boxes are beginning to give up their old secrets. Out the

*Woolf is replying to a previous hypothetical speaker.

465

other day crept one such document written about the year 1811. There was, it appears, an obscure Miss Weeton, who used to scribble down her thoughts upon professional life among other things when her pupils were in bed. Here is one such thought. 'Oh! how I have burned to learn Latin, French, the Arts, the Sciences, anything rather than the dog trot way of sewing, teaching, writing copies, and washing dishes every day. . . . Why are not females permitted to study physics, divinity, astronomy, etc., etc., with their attendants, chemistry, botany, logic, mathematics, &c.?' That comment upon the lives of governesses, that question from the lips of governesses, reaches us from the darkness. It is illuminating, too. But let us go on groping; let us pick up a hint here and a hint there as to the professions as they were practised by women in the nineteenth century. Next we find Anne Clough, the sister of Arthur Clough, pupil of Dr. Arnold, Fellow of Oriel, who, though she served without a salary, was the first principal of Newnham, and thus may be called a professional woman in embryo—we find her training for her profession by 'doing much of the housework' . . . 'earning money to pay off what had been lent by their friends,' 'pressing for leave to keep a small school,' reading books her brother lent her, and exclaiming, 'If I were a man, I would not work for riches, to make myself a name or to leave a wealthy family behind me. No, I think I would work for my country, and make its people my heirs.' The nineteenth-century women were not without ambition it seems. Next we find Josephine Butler, who, though not strictly speaking a professional woman, led the campaign against the Contagious Diseases Act to victory, and then the campaign against the sale and purchase of children 'for infamous purposes'—we find Josephine Butler refusing to have a life of herself written, and saying of the women who helped her in those campaigns: 'The utter absence in them of any desire for recognition, of any vestige of egotism in any form, is worthy of remark. In the purity of their motives they shine out "clear as crystal." ' That, then, was one of the qualities that the Victorian woman praised and practised—a negative one, it is true; not to be recognized; not to be egotistical; to do the work for the sake of doing the work. An interesting contribution to psychology in its way. And then we come closer to our own time; we find Gertrude Bell, who, though the diplomatic service was and is shut to women, occupied a post in the East which almost entitled her to be called a pseudo-diplomat—we find rather to our surprise that 'Gertrude could never go out in London without a female friend or, failing that, a maid. . . . When it seemed unavoidable for Gertrude to drive in a hansom with a young man from one tea party to another, she feels obliged to write and confess it to my mother.' So they were chaste, the women pseudo-diplomats of the Victorian Age? And not merely in body; in mind also. Gertrude 'was not allowed to read Bourget's *The Disciple*' for fear of contracting whatever disease that book may disseminate. Dissatisfied but ambitious, ambitious but austere, chaste yet adventurous—such are some of the qualities that we have discovered. But let us go on looking—if not at the lines, then between the lines of biography. And we find, between the lines of their husbands' biographies, so many women practising—but what are we to call the profession that consists in bringing nine or ten children into the world, the profession which consists in running a house, nursing an invalid, visiting the poor and the sick, tending here an old father, there an old mother?—there is no name and there is no pay for that profession; but we find so many mothers, sisters and daughters of educated men practising it in the nineteenth century that we must lump them and their lives together behind their husbands' and brothers', and leave them to deliver their message to those who have the time to extract it and the imagination with which to decipher it. Let us ourselves, who as you hint are pressed for time, sum up these random hints and reflections upon the professional life of women in the nineteenth century by quoting once more the highly significant words of a woman who was not a professional woman in the strict sense of the word, but had some nondescript reputation as a traveller nevertheless—Mary Kingsley:

'I don't know if I ever revealed the fact to you that being allowed to learn German was *all* the paid-for education I ever had. £2,000 was spent on my brother's. I still hope not in vain.'

"That statement is so suggestive that it may save us the bother of groping and searching between the lines of professional men's lives for the lives of their sisters. If we develop the suggestions we find in that statement, and connect it with the other hints and fragments that we have uncovered, we may arrive at some theory or point of view that may help us to answer the very difficult question, which now confronts us. For when Mary Kingsley says, '. . . being allowed to learn German was *all* the paid-for education I ever had,' she suggests that she had an unpaid-for education. The other lives that we have been examining corroborate that suggestion. What then was the nature of that 'unpaid-for education' which, whether for good or for evil, has been ours for so many centuries? If we mass the lives of the obscure behind four lives that were not obscure, but were so successful and distinguished that they were actually written, the lives of Florence Nightingale, Miss Clough, Mary Kingsley and Gertrude Bell, it seems undeniable that they were all educated by the same teachers. And those teachers, biography indicates, obliquely, and indirectly, but emphatically and indisputably none the less, were poverty, chastity, derision, and—what word however covers 'lack of rights and privileges'? Shall we press the old word 'freedom' once more into service? 'Freedom from unreal loyalties,' then, was the fourth of their teachers; that freedom from loyalty to old schools, old colleges, old churches, old ceremonies, old countries which all those women enjoyed, and which, to a great extent, we still enjoy by the law and custom of England. We have no time to coin new words, greatly though the language is in need of them. Let 'freedom from unreal loyalties' then stand as the fourth great teacher of the daughters of educated men.

"Biography thus provides us with the fact that the daughters of educated men received an unpaid-for education at the hands of poverty, chastity, derision and freedom from unreal loyalties. It was this unpaid-for education, biography informs us, that fitted them, aptly enough, for the unpaid-for professions. And biography also informs us that those unpaid-for professions had their laws, traditions, and labours no less certainly than the paid-for professions. Further, the student of biography cannot possibly doubt from the evidence of biography that this education and these professions were in many ways bad in the extreme, both for the unpaid themselves and for their descendants. The intensive childbirth of the unpaid wife, the intensive money-making of the paid husband in the Victorian age had terrible results, we cannot doubt, upon the mind and body of the present age. To prove it we need not quote once more the famous passage in which Florence Nightingale denounced that education and its results; nor stress the natural delight with which she greeted the Crimean war; nor illustrate from other sources—they are, alas, innumerable—the inanity, the pettiness, the spite, the tyranny, the hypocrisy, the immorality which it engendered as the lives of both sexes so abundantly testify. Final proof of its harshness upon one sex at any rate can be found in the annals of our 'great war,' when hospitals, harvest fields and munition works were largely staffed by refugees flying from its horrors to their comparative amenity.

"But biography is many-sided; biography never returns a single and simple answer to any question that is asked of it. Thus the biographies of those who had biographies—say Florence Nightingale, Anne Clough, Emily Brontë, Christina Rossetti, Mary Kingsley—prove beyond a doubt that this same education, the unpaid for, must have had great virtues as well as great defects, for we cannot deny that these, if not educated, still were civilized women. We cannot, when we consider the lives of our uneducated mothers and grandmothers, judge education simply by its power to 'obtain appointments,' to win honour, to make money. We must, if we are honest, admit that some who had no paid-for education, no salaries and no appointments were civilized human beings—whether or not they can rightly be called 'English' women is matter for dispute; and thus admit that we should be extremely foolish if we threw away the results of that education or gave up the knowledge that we have obtained from it for any bribe or decoration whatsoever. Thus biography, when asked the question we have put to it—how can we enter the professions and yet remain civilized human beings, human beings who discourage war, would seem to reply: If you refuse to be separated from the four great teachers of the daughters of educated men— poverty, chastity, derision and freedom from unreal loyalties—but combine them with some wealth, some knowledge, and some service to real loyalties then you can enter the professions and escape the risks that make them undesirable.

"Such being the answer of the oracle, such are the conditions attached to this guinea. You shall have it, to recapitulate, on condition that you help all properly qualified people, of whatever sex, class or colour, to enter your profession; and further on condition that in the practise of your profession you refuse to be separated from poverty, chastity, derision and freedom from unreal loyalties. Is the statement now more positive, have the conditions been made more clear and do you agree to the terms? You hesitate. Some of the conditions, you seem to suggest, need further discussion. Let us take them, then, in order. By poverty is meant enough money to live upon. That is, you must earn enough to be independent of any other human being and to buy that modicum of health, leisure, knowledge and so on that is needed for the full development of body and mind. But no more. Not a penny more.

"By chastity is meant that when you have made enough to live on by your profession you must refuse to sell your brain for the sake of money. That is you must cease to practise your profession, or practise it for the sake of research and experiment; or, if you are an artist, for the sake of the art; or give the knowledge acquired professionally to those who need it for nothing. But directly the mulberry tree begins to make you circle, break off. Pelt the tree with laughter.

"By derision—a bad word, but once again the English language is much in need of new words—is meant that you must refuse all methods of advertising merit, and hold that ridicule, obscurity and censure are preferable, for psychological reasons, to fame and praise. Directly badges, orders, or degrees are offered you, fling them back in the giver's face.

"By freedom from unreal loyalties is meant that you must rid yourself of pride of nationality in the first place; also of religious pride, college pride, school pride, family pride, sex pride and those unreal loyalties that spring from them. Directly the seducers come with their seductions to bribe you into captivity, tear up the parchments; refuse to fill up the forms.

"And if you still object that these definitions are both too arbitrary and too general, and ask how anybody can tell how much money and how much knowledge are needed for the full development of body and mind, and which are the real loyalties which we must serve and which the unreal which we must despise, I can only refer you—time presses—to two authorities. One is familiar enough. It is the psychometer that you carry on your wrist, the little instrument upon which you depend in all personal relationships. If it were visible it would look something like a thermometer. It has a vein of quicksilver in it which is affected by any body or soul, house or society in whose presence it is exposed. If you want to find out how much wealth is desirable, expose it in a rich man's presence; how much learning is desirable expose it in a learned man's presence. So with patriotism, religion and the rest. The conversation need not be interrupted while you consult it; nor its amenity disturbed. But if you object that this is too personal and fallible a method to employ without risk of mistake, witness the fact that the private psychometer has led to many unfortunate marriages and broken friendships, then there is the other authority now easily within the reach even of the poorest of the daughters of educated men. Go to the public galleries and look at pictures; turn on the wireless and rake down music from the air; enter any of the public libraries which are now free to all. There you will be able to consult the findings of the public psychometer for yourself. To take one example, since we are pressed for time. The *Antigone* of Sophocles has been done into English prose or verse by a man whose name is immaterial. Consider the character of Creon. There you have a most profound analysis by a poet, who is a psychologist in action, of the effect of power and wealth upon the soul. Consider Creon's claim to absolute rule over his subjects. That is a far more instructive analysis of tyranny than any our politicians can offer us. You want to know which are the unreal loyalties which we must despise, which the real loyalties which we must honour? Consider Antigone's distinction between the laws and the Law. That is a far more profound statement of the duties of the individual to society than any our sociologists can offer us. Lame as the English rendering is, Antigone's five words are worth all the sermons of all the archbishops. But to enlarge would be impertinent. Private judgment is still free in private; and that freedom is the essence of freedom. . . ."

SIMONE DE BEAUVOIR

The Second Sex

Introduction

Translated by H. M. Parshley

For a long time I have hesitated to write a book on woman. The subject is irritating, especially to women; and it is not new. Enough ink has been spilled in quarrelling over feminism, and perhaps we should say no more about it. It is still talked about, however, for the voluminous nonsense uttered during the last century seems to have done little to illuminate the problem. After all, is there a problem? And if so, what is it? Are there women, really? Most assuredly the theory of the eternal feminine still has its adherents who will whisper in your ear: 'Even in Russia women still are *women*'; and other erudite persons—sometimes the very same—say with a sigh: 'Woman is losing her way, woman is lost.' One wonders if women still exist, if they will always exist, whether or not it is desirable that they should, what place they occupy in this world, what their place should be. 'What has become of women?' was asked recently in an ephemeral magazine.

But first we must ask: what is a woman? *'Tota mulier in utero'*, says one, 'woman is a womb'. But in speaking of certain women, connoisseurs declare that they are not women, although they are equipped with a uterus like the rest. All agree in recognizing the fact that females exist in the human species; today as always they make up about one half of humanity. And yet we are told that femininity is in danger; we are exhorted to be women, remain women, become women. It would appear, then, that every female human being is not necessarily a woman; to be so considered she must share in that mysterious and threatened reality known as femininity. Is this attribute something secreted by the ovaries? Or is it a Platonic essence, a product of the philosophic imagination? Is a rustling petticoat enough to bring it down to earth? Although some women try zealously to incarnate this essence, it is hardly patentable. It is frequently described in vague and dazzling terms that seem to have been borrowed from the vocabulary of the seers, and indeed in the times of St Thomas it was considered an essence as certainly defined as the somniferous virtue of the poppy.

But conceptualism has lost ground. The biological and social sciences no longer admit the existence of unchangeably fixed entities that determine given characteristics, such as those ascribed to woman, the Jew, or the Negro. Science regards any characteristic as a reaction dependent in part upon a *situation*. If today femininity no longer exists, then it never existed. But does the word *woman*, then, have no specific content? This is stoutly affirmed by those who hold to the philosophy of the enlightenment, of rationalism, of nominalism; women, to them, are merely the human beings arbitrarily designated by the word *woman*. Many American women particularly are prepared to think that there is no longer any place for woman as such; if a backward individual still takes herself for a woman, her friends advise her to be psychoanalysed and thus get rid of this obsession. In regard to a work, *Modern Woman: The Lost Sex*, which in other respects has its irritating features, Dorothy Parker has written: 'I cannot be just to books which treat of woman as woman. . . . My idea is that all of us, men as well as women, should be regarded as human beings.' But nominalism is a rather inadequate doctrine, and the anti-feminists have had no trouble in showing that women simply *are not* men. Surely woman is, like man, a human being; but such a declaration is abstract. The fact is that every concrete human being is always a singular, separate individual. To decline to accept such notions as the eternal feminine, the black soul, the Jewish character, is not to deny that Jews, Negroes, women exist today—this denial does not represent a liberation for those concerned, but rather a flight from reality. Some years ago a well-known woman writer refused to permit her portrait to appear in a series of photographs especially devoted to women writers; she wished to be counted among the men. But in order to gain this privilege she made use of her husband's influence!

Women who assert that they are men lay claim none the less to masculine consideration and respect. I recall also a young Trotskyite standing on a platform at a
boisterous meeting and getting ready to use her fists, in spite of her evident fragility.
She was denying her feminine weakness; but it was for love of a militant male whose
equal she wished to be. The attitude of defiance of many American women proves
that they are haunted by a sense of their femininity. In truth, to go for a walk with
one's eyes open is enough to demonstrate that humanity is divided into two classes
of individuals whose clothes, faces, bodies, smiles, gaits, interests, and occupations
are manifestly different. Perhaps these differences are superficial, perhaps they are
destined to disappear. What is certain is that they do most obviously exist.

If her functioning as a female is not enough to define woman, if we decline also
to explain her through 'the eternal feminine', and if nevertheless we admit, provisionally, that women do exist, then we must face the question: what is a woman?

To state the question is, to me, to suggest, at once, a preliminary answer. The
fact that I ask it is in itself significant. A man would never set out to write a book
on the peculiar situation of the human male. But if I wish to define myself, I must
first of all say: 'I am a woman'; on this truth must be based all further discussion.
A man never begins by presenting himself as an individual of a certain sex; it goes
without saying that he is a man. The terms *masculine* and *feminine* are used
symmetrically only as a matter of form, as on legal papers. In actuality the relation
of the two sexes is not quite like that of two electrical poles, for man represents both
the positive and the neutral, as is indicated by the common use of *man* to designate
human beings in general; whereas woman represents only the negative, defined by
limiting criteria, without reciprocity. In the midst of an abstract discussion it is
vexing to hear a man say: 'You think thus and so because you are a woman'; but
I know that my only defence is to reply: 'I think thus and so because it is true,'
thereby removing my subjective self from the argument. It would be out of the
question to reply: 'And you think the contrary because you are a man', for it is
understood that the fact of being a man is no peculiarity. A man is in the right in
being a man; it is the woman who is in the wrong. It amounts to this: just as for
the ancients there was an absolute vertical with reference to which the oblique was
defined, so there is an absolute human type, the masculine. Woman has ovaries, a
uterus: these peculiarities imprison her in her subjectivity, circumscribe her within
the limits of her own nature. It is often said that she thinks with her glands. Man
superbly ignores the fact that his anatomy also includes glands, such as the testicles,
and that they secrete hormones. He thinks of his body as a direct and normal
connection with the world, which he believes he apprehends objectively, whereas
he regards the body of woman as a hindrance, a prison, weighed down by everything
peculiar to it. 'The female is a female by virtue of a certain *lack* of qualities,' said
Aristotle; 'we should regard the female nature as afflicted with a natural defective-
ness.' And St Thomas for his part pronounced woman to be an 'imperfect man', an
'incidental' being. This is symbolized in Genesis where Eve is depicted as made from
what Bossuet called 'a supernumerary bone' of Adam.

Thus humanity is male and man defines woman not in herself but as relative to
him; she is not regarded as an autonomous being. Michelet writes: 'Woman, the
relative being . . .' And Benda is most positive in his *Rapport d'Uriel*: 'The body
of man makes sense in itself quite apart from that of woman, whereas the latter
seems wanting in significance by itself. . . . Man can think of himself without

woman. She cannot think of herself without man.' And she is simply what man decrees; thus she is called 'the sex', by which is meant that she appears essentially to the male as a sexual being. For him she is sex—absolute sex, no less. She is defined and differentiated with reference to man and not he with reference to her; she is the incidental, the inessential as opposed to the essential. He is the Subject, he is the Absolute—she is the Other.[1]

The category of the *Other* is as primordial as consciousness itself. In the most primitive societies, in the most ancient mythologies, one finds the expression of a duality—that of the Self and the Other. This duality was not originally attached to the division of the sexes; it was not dependent upon any empirical facts. It is revealed in such works as that of Granet on Chinese thought and those of Dumézil on the East Indies and Rome. The feminine element was at first no more involved in such pairs as Varuna-Mitra, Uranus-Zeus, Sun-Moon, and Day-Night than it was in the contrasts between Good and Evil, lucky and unlucky auspices, right and left, God and Lucifer. Otherness is a fundamental category of human thought.

Thus it is that no group ever sets itself up as the One without at once setting up the Other over against itself. If three travellers chance to occupy the same compartment, that is enough to make vaguely hostile 'others' out of all the rest of the passengers on the train. In small-town eyes all persons not belonging to the village are 'strangers' and suspect; to the native of a country all who inhabit other countries are 'foreigners'; Jews are 'different' for the anti-Semite, Negroes are 'inferior' for American racists, aborigines are 'natives' for colonists, proletarians are the 'lower class' for the privileged.

Lévi-Strauss, at the end of a profound work on the various forms of primitive societies, reaches the following conclusion: 'Passage from the state of Nature to the state of Culture is marked by man's ability to view biological relations as a series of contrasts; duality, alternation, opposition, and symmetry, whether under definite or vague forms, constitute not so much phenomena to be explained as fundamental and immediately given data of social reality.'[2] These phenomena would be incomprehensible if in fact human society were simply a *Mitsein* or fellowship based on solidarity and friendliness. Things become clear, on the contrary, if, following Hegel, we find in consciousness itself a fundamental hostility towards every other consciousness; the subject can be posed only in being opposed—he sets himself up as the essential, as opposed to the other, the inessential, the object.

But the other consciousness, the other ego, sets up a reciprocal claim. The native travelling abroad is shocked to find himself in turn regarded as a 'stranger' by the natives of neighbouring countries. As a matter of fact, wars, festivals, trading, treaties, and contests among tribes, nations, and classes tend to deprive the concept *Other* of its absolute sense and to make manifest its relativity; willy-nilly, individuals and groups are forced to realize the reciprocity of their relations. How is it, then, that this reciprocity has not been recognized between the sexes, that one of the contrasting terms is set up as the sole essential, denying any relativity in regard to its correlative and defining the latter as pure otherness? Why is it that women do not dispute male sovereignty? No subject will readily volunteer to become the object, the inessential; it is not the Other who, in defining himself as the Other, establishes the One. The Other is posed as such by the One in defining himself as the One. But if the Other is not to regain the status of being the One, he must be submissive enough to accept this alien point of view. Whence comes this submission in the case of woman?

There are, to be sure, other cases in which a certain category has been able to dominate another completely for a time. Very often this privilege depends upon inequality of numbers—the majority imposes its rule upon the minority or persecutes it. But women are not a minority, like the American Negroes or the Jews; there are as many women as men on earth. Again, the two groups concerned have often been originally independent; they may have been formerly unaware of each other's existence, or perhaps they recognized each other's autonomy. But a historical event has resulted in the subjugation of the weaker by the stronger. The scattering of the Jews, the introduction of slavery into America, the conquests of imperialism are examples in point. In these cases the oppressed retained at least the memory of former days; they possessed in common a past, a tradition, sometimes a religion or a culture.

The parallel drawn by Bebel between women and the proletariat is valid in that neither ever formed a minority or a separate collective unit of mankind. And instead of a single historical event it is in both cases a historical development that explains their status as a class and accounts for the membership of *particular individuals* in that class. But proletarians have not always existed, whereas there have always been women. They are women in virtue of their anatomy and physiology. Throughout history they have always been subordinated to men,[3] and hence their dependency is not the result of a historical event or a social change—it was not something that *occurred*. The reason why otherness in this case seems to be an absolute is in part that it lacks the contingent or incidental nature of historical facts. A condition brought about at a certain time can be abolished at some other time, as the Negroes of Haiti and others have proved; but it might seem that a natural condition is beyond the possibility of change. In truth, however, the nature of things is no more immutably given, once for all, than is historical reality. If woman seems to be the inessential which never becomes the essential, it is because she herself fails to bring about this change. Proletarians say 'We'; Negroes also. Regarding themselves as subjects, they transform the bourgeois, the whites, into 'others'. But women do not say 'We', except at some congress of feminists or similar formal demonstration; men say 'women', and women use the same word in referring to themselves. They do not authentically assume a subjective attitude. The proletarians have accomplished the revolution in Russia, the Negroes in Haiti, the Indo-Chinese are battling for it in Indo-China; but the women's effort has never been anything more than a symbolic agitation. They have gained only what men have been willing to grant; they have taken nothing, they have only received.

The reason for this is that women lack concrete means for organizing themselves into a unit which can stand face to face with the correlative unit. They have no past, no history, no religion of their own; and they have no such solidarity of work and interest as that of the proletariat. They are not even promiscuously herded together in the way that creates community feeling among the American Negroes, the ghetto Jews, the workers of Saint-Denis, or the factory hands of Renault. They live dispersed among the males, attached through residence, housework, economic condition, and social standing to certain men—fathers or husbands—more firmly than they are to other women. If they belong to the bourgeoisie, they feel solidarity with men of that class, not with proletarian women; if they are white, their allegiance is to white men, not to Negro women. The proletariat can propose to massacre the ruling class, and a sufficiently fanatical Jew or Negro might dream of getting sole possession of the atomic bomb and making humanity wholly Jewish or black; but woman cannot even dream of exterminating the males. The bond that unites her to her oppressors is not comparable to any other. The division of the sexes is a biological fact, not an event in human history. Male and female stand opposed within a primordial *Mitsein,* and woman has not broken it. The couple is a fundamental unity with its two halves riveted together, and the cleavage of society along the line of sex is impossible. Here is to be found the basic trait of woman: she is the Other in a totality of which the two components are necessary to one another.

One could suppose that this reciprocity might have facilitated the liberation of woman. When Hercules sat at the feet of Omphale and helped with her spinning, his desire for her held him captive; but why did she fail to gain a lasting power? To revenge herself on Jason, Medea killed their children; and this grim legend would seem to suggest that she might have obtained a formidable influence over him through his love for his offspring. In *Lysistrata* Aristophanes gaily depicts a band of women who joined forces to gain social ends through the sexual needs of their men; but this is only a play. In the legend of the Sabine women, the latter soon abandoned their plan of remaining sterile to punish their ravishers. In truth woman has not been socially emancipated through man's need—sexual desire and the desire for offspring—which makes the male dependent for satisfaction upon the female.

Master and slave, also, are united by a reciprocal need, in this case economic, which does not liberate the slave. In the relation of master to slave the master does not make a point of the need that he has for the other; he has in his grasp the power of satisfying this need through his own action; whereas the slave, in his dependent condition, his hope and fear, is quite conscious of the need he has for his master. Even if the need is at bottom equally urgent for both, it always works in favour of the oppressor and against the oppressed. That is why the liberation of the working class, for example, has been slow.

Now, woman has always been man's dependant, if not his slave; the two sexes have never shared the world in equality. And even today woman is heavily handicapped, though her situation is beginning to change. Almost nowhere is her legal status the same as man's, and frequently it is much to her disadvantage. Even when her rights are legally recognized in the abstract, long-standing custom prevents their full expression in the mores. In the economic sphere men and women can almost be said to make up two castes; other things being equal, the former hold the better jobs, get higher wages, and have more opportunity for success than their new competitors. In industry and politics men have a great many more positions and they monopolize the most important posts. In addition to all this, they enjoy a traditional prestige that the education of children tends in every way to support, for the present enshrines the past—and in the past all history has been made by men. At the present time, when women are beginning to take part in the affairs of the world, it is still a world that belongs to men—they have no doubt of it at all and women have scarcely any. To decline to be the Other, to refuse to be a party to the deal—this would be for women to renounce all the advantages conferred upon them by their alliance with the superior caste. Man-the-sovereign will provide woman-the-liege with material protection and will undertake the moral justification of her existence; thus she can evade at once both economic risk and the metaphysical risk of a liberty in which ends and aims must be contrived without assistance. Indeed, along with the ethical urge of each individual to affirm his subjective existence, there is also the temptation to forgo liberty and become a thing. This is an inauspicious road, for he who takes it—passive, lost, ruined—becomes henceforth the creature of another's will, frustrated in his transcendence and deprived of every value. But it is an easy road; on it one avoids the strain involved in undertaking an authentic existence. When man makes of woman the *Other,* he may, then, expect to manifest deep-seated tendencies towards complicity. Thus, woman may fail to lay claim to the status of subject because she lacks definite resources, because she feels the necessary bond that ties her to man regardless of reciprocity, and because she is often very well pleased with her role as the *Other.*

But it will be asked at once: how did all this begin? It is easy to see that the duality of the sexes, like any duality, gives rise to conflict. And doubtless the winner will assume the status of absolute. But why should man have won from the start? It seems possible that women could have won the victory; or that the outcome of the conflict might never have been decided. How is it that this world has always belonged to the men and that things have begun to change only recently? Is this change a good thing? Will it bring about an equal sharing of the world between men and women?

These questions are not new, and they have often been answered. But the very fact that woman *is the Other* tends to cast suspicion upon all the justifications that men have ever been able to provide for it. These have all too evidently been dictated by men's interest. A little-known feminist of the seventeenth century, Poulain de la Barre, put it this way: 'All that has been written about women by men should be suspect, for the men are at once judge and party to the lawsuit.' Everywhere, at all times, the males have displayed their satisfaction in feeling that they are the lords of creation. 'Blessed be God . . . that He did not make me a woman,' say the Jews in their morning prayers, while their wives pray on a note of resignation: 'Blessed be the Lord, who created me according to His will.' The first among the blessings for which Plato thanked the gods was that he had been created free, not enslaved; the second, a man, not a woman. But the males could not enjoy this privilege fully unless they believed it to be founded on the absolute and the eternal; they sought to make the fact of their supremacy into a right. 'Being men, those who have made and compiled the laws have favoured their own sex, and jurists have elevated these laws into principles', to quote Poulain de la Barre once more.

Legislators, priests, philosophers, writers, and scientists have striven to show that the subordinate position of woman is willed in heaven and advantageous on earth. The religions invented by men reflect this wish for domination. In the legends of Eve and Pandora men have taken up arms against women. They have made use of philosophy and theology, as the quotations from Aristotle and St Thomas have shown. Since ancient times satirists and moralists have delighted in showing up the weaknesses of women. We are familiar with the savage indictments hurled against women throughout French literature. Montherlant, for example, follows the tradition of Jean de Meung, though with less gusto. This hostility may at times be well founded, often it is gratuitous; but in truth it more or less successfully conceals a desire for self-justification. As Montaigne says, 'It is easier to accuse one sex than to excuse the other'. Sometimes what is going on is clear enough. For instance, the Roman law limiting the rights of woman cited 'the imbecility, the instability of the sex' just when the weakening of family ties seemed to threaten the interests of male heirs. And in the effort to keep the married woman under guardianship, appeal was made in the sixteenth century to the authority of St Augustine, who declared that 'woman is a creature neither decisive nor constant', at a time when the single woman was thought capable of managing her property. Montaigne understood clearly how arbitrary and unjust was woman's appointed lot: 'Women are not in the wrong when they decline to accept the rules laid down for them, since the men make these rules without consulting them. No wonder intrigue and strife abound.' But he did not go so far as to champion their cause.

It was only later, in the eighteenth century, that genuinely democratic men began to view the matter objectively. Diderot, among others, strove to show that woman is, like man, a human being. Later John Stuart Mill came fervently to her defence. But these philosophers displayed unusual impartiality. In the nineteenth century the feminist quarrel became again a quarrel of partisans. One of the consequences of the industrial revolution was the entrance of women into productive labour, and it was just here that the claims of the feminists emerged from the realm of theory and acquired an economic basis, while their opponents became the more aggressive. Although landed property lost power to some extent, the bourgeoisie clung to the old morality that found the guarantee of private property in the solidity of the family. Woman was ordered back into the home the more harshly as her emancipation became a real menace. Even within the working class the men endeavoured to restrain woman's liberation, because they began to see the women as dangerous competitors—the more so because they were accustomed to work for lower wages.

In proving woman's inferiority, the anti-feminists then began to draw not only upon religion, philosophy, and theology, as before, but also upon science—biology, experimental psychology, etc. At most they were willing to grant 'equality in difference' to the *other* sex. That profitable formula is most significant; it is precisely like the 'equal but separate' formula of the Jim Crow laws aimed at the North American Negroes. As is well known, this so-called equalitarian segregation has resulted only in the most extreme discrimination. The similarity just noted is in no way due to chance, for whether it is a race, a caste, a class, or a sex that is reduced to a position of inferiority, the methods of justification are the same. 'The eternal feminine' corresponds to 'the black soul' and to 'the Jewish character'. True, the Jewish problem is on the whole very different from the other two—to the anti-Semite the Jew is not so much an inferior as he is an enemy for whom there is to be granted no place on earth, for whom annihilation is the fate desired. But there are deep similarities between the situation of woman and that of the Negro. Both are being emancipated today from a like paternalism, and the former master class wishes to 'keep them in their place'—that is, the place chosen for them. In both cases the former masters lavish more or less sincere eulogies, either on the virtues of 'the good Negro' with his dormant, childish, merry soul—the submissive Negro—or on the merits of the woman who is 'truly feminine'—that is, frivolous, infantile, irresponsible—the submissive woman. In both cases the dominant class bases its argument on a state of affairs that it has itself created. As George Bernard Shaw puts it, in substance, 'The American white relegates the black to the rank of shoeshine boy; and he concludes from this that the black is good for nothing but shining shoes.' This vicious circle is met with in all analogous circumstances; when an individual (or a group of individuals) is kept in a situation of inferiority, the fact is that he *is* inferior. But the significance of the verb *to be* must be rightly understood here;

it is in bad faith to give it a static value when it really has the dynamic Hegelian sense of 'to have become'. Yes, women on the whole *are* today inferior to men; that is, their situation affords them fewer possibilities. The question is: should that state of affairs continue?

Many men hope that it will continue; not all have given up the battle. The conservative bourgeoisie still see in the emancipation of women a menace to their morality and their interests. Some men dread feminine competition. Recently a male student wrote in the *Hebdo-Latin:* 'Every woman student who goes into medicine or law robs us of a job.' He never questioned his rights in this world. And economic interests are not the only ones concerned. One of the benefits that oppression confers upon the oppressors is that the most humble among them is made to *feel* superior; thus, a 'poor white' in the South can console himself with the thought that he is not a 'dirty nigger'—and the more prosperous whites cleverly exploit this pride.

Similarly, the most mediocre of males feels himself a demigod as compared with women. It was much easier for M. de Montherlant to think himself a hero when he faced women (and women chosen for his purpose) than when he was obliged to act the man among men—something many women have done better than he, for that matter. And in September 1948, in one of his articles in the *Figaro littéraire,* Claude Mauriac—whose great originality is admired by all—could[4] write regarding woman: '*We* listen on a tone [*sic!*] of polite indifference . . . to the most brilliant among them, well knowing that her wit reflects more or less luminously ideas that come from *us.*' Evidently the speaker referred to is not reflecting the ideas of Mauriac himself, for no one knows of his having any. It may be that she reflects ideas originating with men, but then, even among men there are those who have been known to appropriate ideas not their own; and one can well ask whether Claude Mauriac might not find more interesting a conversation reflecting Descartes, Marx, or Gide rather than himself. What is really remarkable is that by using the questionable *we* he identifies himself with St Paul, Hegel, Lenin, and Nietzsche, and from the lofty eminence of their grandeur looks down disdainfully upon the bevy of women who make bold to converse with him on a footing of equality. In truth, I know of more than one woman who would refuse to suffer with patience Mauriac's 'tone of polite indifference'.

I have lingered on this example because the masculine attitude is here displayed with disarming ingenuousness. But men profit in many more subtle ways from the otherness, the alterity of woman. Here is a miraculous balm for those afflicted with an inferiority complex, and indeed no one is more arrogant towards women, more aggressive or scornful, than the man who is anxious about his virility. Those who are not fear-ridden in the presence of their fellow men are much more disposed to recognize a fellow creature in woman; but even to these the myth of Woman, the Other, is precious for many reasons.[5] They cannot be blamed for not cheerfully relinquishing all the benefits they derive from the myth, for they realize what they would lose in relinquishing woman as they fancy her to be, while they fail to realize what they have to gain from the woman of tomorrow. Refusal to pose oneself as the Subject, unique and absolute, requires great self-denial. Furthermore, the vast majority of men make no such claim explicitly. They do not *postulate* woman as inferior, for today they are too thoroughly imbued with the ideal of democracy not to recognize all human beings as equals.

In the bosom of the family, woman seems in the eyes of childhood and youth to be clothed in the same social dignity as the adult males. Later on, the young man, desiring and loving, experiences the resistance, the independence of the woman desired and loved; in marriage, he respects woman as wife and mother, and in the concrete events of conjugal life she stands there before him as a free being. He can therefore feel that social subordination as between the sexes no longer exists and that on the whole, in spite of differences, woman is an equal. As, however, he observes some points of inferiority—the most important being unfitness for the professions—he attributes these to natural causes. When he is in a co-operative and benevolent relation with woman, his theme is the principle of abstract equality, and he does not base his attitude upon such inequality as may exist. But when he is in conflict with her, the situation is reversed: his theme will be the existing inequality, and he will even take it as justification for denying abstract equality.

So it is that many men will affirm as if in good faith that women *are* the equals of man and that they have nothing to clamour for, while *at the same time* they will say that women can never be the equals of man and that their demands are in vain. It is, in point of fact, a difficult matter for man to realize the extreme importance of social discriminations which seem outwardly insignificant but which produce in woman moral and intellectual effects so profound that they appear to spring from her original nature. The most sympathetic of men never fully comprehend woman's concrete situation. And there is no reason to put much trust in the men when they rush to the defence of privileges whose full extent they can hardly measure. We shall not, then, permit ourselves to be intimidated by the number and violence of the attacks launched against women, nor to be entrapped by the self-seeking eulogies bestowed on the 'true woman', nor to profit by the enthusiasm for woman's destiny manifested by men who would not for the world have any part of it.

We should consider the arguments of the feminists with no less suspicion, however, for very often their controversial aim deprives them of all real value. If the 'woman question' seems trivial, it is because masculine arrogance has made of it a 'quarrel'; and when quarrelling one no longer reasons well. People have tirelessly sought to prove that woman is superior, inferior, or equal to man. Some say that, having been created after Adam, she is evidently a secondary being; others say on the contrary that Adam was only a rough draft and that God succeeded in producing the human being in perfection when He created Eve. Woman's brain is smaller; yes, but it is relatively larger. Christ was made a man; yes, but perhaps for his greater humility. Each argument at once suggests its opposite, and both are often fallacious. If we are to gain understanding, we must get out of these ruts; we must discard the vague notions of superiority, inferiority, equality which have hitherto corrupted every discussion of the subject and start afresh.

Very well, but just how shall we pose the question? And, to begin with, who are we to propound it at all? Man is at once judge and party to the case; but so is woman. What we need is an angel—neither man nor woman—but where shall we find one? Still, the angel would be poorly qualified to speak, for an angel is ignorant of all the basic facts involved in the problem. With a hermaphrodite we should be no better off, for here the situation is most peculiar; the hermaphrodite is not really the combination of a whole man and a whole woman, but consists of parts of each and thus is neither. It looks to me as if there are, after all, certain women who are best qualified to elucidate the situation of woman. Let us not be misled by the sophism that because Epimenides was a Cretan he was necessarily a liar; it is not a mysterious essence that compels men and women to act in good or in bad faith, it is their situation that inclines them more or less towards the search for truth. Many of today's women, fortunate in the restoration of all the privileges pertaining to the estate of the human being, can afford the luxury of impartiality—we even recognize its necessity. We are no longer like our partisan elders; by and large we have won the game. In recent debates on the status of women the United Nations has persistently maintained that the equality of the sexes is now becoming a reality, and already some of us have never had to sense in our femininity an inconvenience or an obstacle. Many problems appear to us to be more pressing than those which concern us in particular, and this detachment even allows us to hope that our attitude will be objective. Still, we know the feminine world more intimately than do the men because we have our roots in it, we grasp more immediately than do men what it means to a human being to be feminine; and we are more concerned with such knowledge. I have said that there are more pressing problems, but this does not prevent us from seeing some importance in asking how the fact of being women will affect our lives. What opportunities precisely have been given us and what withheld? What fate awaits our younger sisters, and what directions should they take? It is significant that books by women on women are in general animated in our day less by a wish to demand our rights than by an effort towards clarity and understanding. As we emerge from an era of excessive controversy, this book is offered as one attempt among others to confirm that statement.

But it is doubtless impossible to approach any human problem with a mind free from bias. The way in which questions are put, the points of view assumed, presuppose a relativity of interest; all characteristics imply values, and every objective description, so called, implies an ethical background. Rather than attempt to conceal principles more or less definitely implied, it is better to state them openly, at the beginning. This will make it unnecessary to specify on every page in just what sense one uses such words as *superior, inferior, better, worse, progress, reaction,* and the like. If we survey some of the works on woman, we note that one of the points of view most frequently adopted is that of the public good, the general interest; and one always means by this the benefit of society as one wishes it to be maintained or established. For our part, we hold that the only public good is that which assures the private good of the citizens; we shall pass judgement on institutions according to their effectiveness in giving concrete opportunities to individuals. But we do not confuse the idea of private interest with that of happiness, although that is another common point of view. Are not women of the harem more happy than women voters? Is not the housekeeper happier than the working-woman? It is not too clear just what the word *happy* really means and still less what true values it may mask. There is no possibility of measuring the happiness of others, and it is always easy to describe as happy the situation in which one wishes to place them.

In particular those who are condemned to stagnation are often pronounced happy on the pretext that happiness consists in being at rest. This notion we reject, for our perspective is that of existentialist ethics. Every subject plays his part as such specifically through exploits or projects that serve as a mode of transcendence; he achieves liberty only through a continual reaching out towards other liberties. There is no justification for present existence other than its expansion into an indefinitely open future. Every time transcendence falls back into immanence, stagnation, there is a degradation of existence into the *'en-soi'*—the brutish life of subjection to given conditions—and of liberty into constraint and contingence. This downfall represents a moral fault if the subject consents to it; if it is inflicted upon him, it spells frustration and oppression. In both cases it is an absolute evil. Every individual concerned to justify his existence feels that his existence involves an undefined need to transcend himself, to engage in freely chosen projects.

Now, what peculiarly signalizes the situation of woman is that she—a free and autonomous being like all human creatures—nevertheless finds herself living in a world where men compel her to assume the status of the Other. They propose to stabilize her as object and to doom her to immanence since her transcendence is to be overshadowed and for ever transcended by another ego *(conscience)* which is essential and sovereign. The drama of woman lies in this conflict between the fundamental aspirations of every subject (ego)—who always regards the self as the essential—and the compulsions of a situation in which she is the inessential. How can a human being in woman's situation attain fulfilment? What roads are open to her? Which are blocked? How can independence be recovered in a state of dependency? What circumstances limit woman's liberty and how can they be overcome? These are the fundamental questions on which I would fain throw some light. This means that I am interested in the fortunes of the individual as defined not in terms of happiness but in terms of liberty.

Quite evidently this problem would be without significance if we were to believe that woman's destiny is inevitably determined by physiological, psychological, or economic forces. Hence I shall discuss first of all the light in which woman is viewed by biology, psychoanalysis, and historical materialism. Next I shall try to show exactly how the concept of the 'truly feminine' has been fashioned—why woman has been defined as the Other—and what have been the consequences from man's point of view. Then from woman's point of view I shall describe the world in which women must live; and thus we shall be able to envisage the difficulties in their way as, endeavouring to make their escape from the sphere hitherto assigned them, they aspire to full membership in the human race.

Notes

1. E. Lévinas expresses this idea most explicitly in his essay *Temps et l'Autre*. 'Is there not a case in which otherness, alterity [*altérité*], unquestionably marks the nature of a being, as its essence, an instance of otherness not consisting purely and simply in the opposition of two species of the same genus? I think that the feminine represents the contrary in its absolute sense, this contrariness being in no wise affected by any relation between it and its correlative and thus remaining absolutely other. Sex is not a certain specific difference . . . no more is the sexual difference a mere contradiction. . . . Nor does this difference lie in the duality of two complementary terms, for two complementary terms imply a pre-existing whole. . . . Otherness reaches its full flowering in the feminine, a term of the same rank as consciousness but of opposite meaning.'

I suppose that Lévinas does not forget that woman, too, is aware of her own consciousness, or ego. But it is striking that he deliberately takes a man's point of view, disregarding the reciprocity of subject and object. When he writes that woman is mystery, he implies that she is mystery for man. Thus his description, which is intended to be objective, is in fact an assertion of masculine privilege.

2. See C. Lévi-Strauss, *Les Structures élémentaires de la parenté*.

3. With rare exceptions, perhaps, like certain matriarchal rulers, queens, and the like.—Tr.

4. Or at least he thought he could.

5. A significant article on this theme by Michel Carrouges appeared in No. 292 of the *Cahiers du Sud*. He writes indignantly: 'Would that there were no woman-myth at all but only a cohort of cooks, matrons, prostitutes, and blue-stockings

serving functions of pleasure or usefulness!' That is to say, in his view woman has no existence in and for herself; he thinks only of her *function* in the male world. Her reason for existence lies in man. But then, in fact, her poetic 'function' as a myth might be more valued than any other. The real problem is precisely to find out why woman should be defined with relation to man.

HÉLÈNE CIXOUS

The Laugh of the Medusa

TRANSLATED BY KEITH COHEN AND PAULA COHEN

I shall speak about women's writing: about *what it will do*. Woman must write her self: must write about women and bring women to writing, from which they have been driven away as violently as from their bodies—for the same reasons, by the same law, with the same fatal goal. Woman must put herself into the text—as into the world and into history—by her own movement.

The future must no longer be determined by the past. I do not deny that the effects of the past are still with us. But I refuse to strengthen them by repeating them, to confer upon them an irremovability the equivalent of destiny, to confuse the biological and the cultural. Anticipation is imperative.

Since these reflections are taking shape in an area just on the point of being discovered, they necessarily bear the mark of our time—a time during which the new breaks away from the old, and, more precisely, the (feminine) new from the old (*la nouvelle de l'ancien*). Thus, as there are no grounds for establishing a discourse, but rather an arid millenial ground to break, what I say has at least two sides and two aims: to break up, to destroy; and to foresee the unforeseeable, to project.

I write this as a woman, toward women. When I say "woman," I'm speaking of woman in her inevitable struggle against conventional man; and of a universal woman subject who must bring women to their senses and to their meaning in history. But first it must be said that in spite of the enormity of the repression that has kept them in the "dark"—that dark which people have been trying to make them accept as their attribute—there is, at this time, no general woman, no one typical woman. What they have *in common* I will say. But what strikes me is the infinite richness of their individual constitutions: you can't talk about *a* female sexuality, uniform, homogeneous, classifiable into codes—any more than you can talk about one unconscious resembling another. Women's imagination is inexhaustible, like music, painting, writing: their stream of phantasms is incredible.

I have been amazed more than once by a description a woman gave me of a world all her own which she had been secretly haunting since early childhood. A world of searching, the elaboration of a knowledge, on the basis of a systematic experimentation with the bodily functions, a passionate and precise interrogation of her erotogeneity. This practice, extraordinarily rich and inventive, in particular as concerns masturbation, is prolonged or accompanied by a production of forms, a veritable aesthetic activity, each stage of rapture inscribing a resonant vision, a composition, something beautiful. Beauty will no longer be forbidden.

I wished that that woman would write and proclaim this unique empire so that other women, other unacknowledged sovereigns, might exclaim: I, too, overflow; my desires have invented new desires, my body knows unheard-of songs. Time and again I, too, have felt so full of luminous torrents that I could burst—burst with forms much more beautiful than those which are put up in frames and sold for a stinking fortune. And I, too, said nothing, showed nothing; I didn't open my mouth, I didn't repaint my half of the world. I was ashamed. I was afraid, and I swallowed my shame and my fear. I said to myself: You are mad! What's the meaning of these waves, these floods, these outbursts? Where is the ebullient, infinite woman who, immersed as she was in her naiveté, kept in the dark about herself, led into self-disdain by the great arm of parental-conjugal phallocentrism, hasn't been ashamed of her strength? Who, surprised and horrified by the fantastic tumult of her drives (for she was made to believe that a well-adjusted normal woman has a . . . divine composure), hasn't accused herself of being a monster? Who, feeling a funny desire stirring inside her (to sing, to write, to dare to speak, in short, to bring out something new), hasn't thought she was sick? Well, her shameful sickness is that she resists death, that she makes trouble.

And why don't you write? Write! Writing is for you, you are for you; your body is yours, take it. I know why you haven't written. (And why I didn't write before the age of twenty-seven.) Because writing is at once too high, too great for you, it's reserved for the great—that is for "great men"; and it's "silly." Besides, you've written a little, but in secret. And it wasn't good, because it was in secret, and because you punished yourself for writing, because you didn't go all the way, or because you wrote, irresistibly, as when we would masturbate in secret, not to go further, but to attenuate the tension a bit, just enough to take the edge off. And then as soon as we come, we go and make ourselves feel guilty—so as to be forgiven; or to forget, to bury it until the next time.

Write, let no one hold you back, let nothing stop you: not man; not the imbecilic capitalist machinery, in which publishing houses are the crafty, obsequious relayers of imperatives handed down by an economy that works against us and off our backs; and not *yourself*. Smug-faced readers, managing editors, and big bosses don't like the true texts of women—female-sexed texts. That kind scares them.

I write woman: woman must write woman. And man, man. So only an oblique consideration will be found here of man; it's up to him to say where his masculinity and femininity are at: this will concern us once men have opened their eyes and seen themselves clearly.[1]

Now women return from afar, from always: from "without," from the heath where witches are kept alive; from below, from beyond "culture"; from their childhood which men have been trying desperately to make them forget, condemning it to "eternal rest." The little girls and their "ill-mannered" bodies immured, well-preserved, intact unto themselves, in the mirror. Frigidified. But are they ever seething underneath! What an effort it takes—there's no end to it—for the sex cops to bar their threatening return. Such a display of forces on both sides that the struggle has for centuries been immobilized in the trembling equilibrium of a deadlock.

* * *

Here they are, returning, arriving over and again, because the unconscious is impregnable. They have wandered around in circles, confined to the narrow room in which they've been given a deadly brainwashing. You can incarcerate them, slow them down, get away with the old Apartheid routine, but for a time only. As soon as they begin to speak, at the same time as they're taught their name, they can be taught that their territory is black: because you are Africa, you are black. Your continent is dark. Dark is dangerous. You can't see anything in the dark, you're afraid. Don't move, you might fall. Most of all, don't go into the forest. And so we have internalized this horror of the dark.

Men have committed the greatest crime against women. Insidiously, violently, they have led them to hate women, to be their own enemies, to mobilize their immense strength against themselves, to be the executants of their virile needs. They have made for women an antinarcissism! A narcissism which loves itself only to be loved for what women haven't got! They have constructed the infamous logic of antilove.

We the precocious, we the repressed of culture, our lovely mouths gagged with pollen, our wind knocked out of us, we the labyrinths, the ladders, the trampled spaces, the bevies—we are black and we are beautiful.

We're stormy, and that which is ours breaks loose from us without our fearing any debilitation. Our glances, our smiles, are spent; laughs exude from all our mouths; our blood flows and we extend ourselves without ever reaching an end; we never hold back our thoughts, our signs, our writing; and we're not afraid of lacking.

What happiness for us who are omitted, brushed aside at the scene of inheritances; we inspire ourselves and we expire without running out of breath, we are everywhere!

From now on, who, if we say so, can say no to us? We've come back from always.

It is time to liberate the New Woman from the Old by coming to know her—by loving her for getting by, for getting beyond the Old without delay, by going out ahead of what the New Woman will be, as an arrow quits the bow with a movement that gathers and separates the vibrations musically, in order to be more than her self.

I say that we must, for, with a few rare exceptions, there has not yet been any writing that inscribes femininity; exceptions so rare, in fact, that, after plowing through literature across languages, cultures, and ages,[2] one can only be startled at this vain scouting mission. It is well known that the number of women writers (while having increased very slightly from the nineteenth century on) has always been ridiculously small. This is a useless and deceptive fact unless from their species of female writers we do not first deduct the immense majority whose workmanship is in no way different from male writing, and which either obscures women or reproduces the classic representations of women (as sensitive—intuitive—dreamy, etc.).[3]

Let me insert here a parenthetical remark. I mean it when I speak of male writing. I maintain unequivocally that there is such a thing as *marked* writing; that, until now, far more extensively and repressively than is ever suspected or admitted, writing has been run by a libidinal and cultural—hence political, typically masculine— economy; that this is a locus where the repression of women has been perpetuated, over and over, more or less consciously, and in a manner that's frightening since it's often hidden or adorned with the mystifying charms of fiction; that this locus has grossly exaggerated all the signs of sexual opposition (and not sexual difference), where woman has never *her* turn to speak—this being all the more serious and unpardonable in that writing is precisely *the very possibility of change,* the space that can serve as a springboard for subversive thought, the precursory movement of a transformation of social and cultural structures.

Nearly the entire history of writing is confounded with the history of reason, of which it is at once the effect, the support, and one of the privileged alibis. It has been one with the phallocentric tradition. It is indeed that same self-admiring, self-stimulating, self-congratulatory phallocentrism.

With some exceptions, for there have been failures—and if it weren't for them, I wouldn't be writing (I-woman, escapee)—in that enormous machine that has been operating and turning out its "truth" for centuries. There have been poets who would go to any lengths to slip something by at odds with tradition—men capable of loving love and hence capable of loving others and of wanting them, of imagining the woman who would hold out against oppression and constitute herself as a superb, equal, hence "impossible" subject, untenable in a real social framework. Such a woman the poet could desire only by breaking the codes that negate her. Her appearance would necessarily bring on, if not revolution—for the bastion was supposed to be immutable—at least harrowing explosions. At times it is in the fissure caused by an earthquake, through that radical mutation of things brought on by a material upheaval when every structure is for a moment thrown off balance and an ephemeral wildness sweeps order away, that the poet slips something by, for a brief span, of woman. Thus did Kleist expend himself in his yearning for the existence of sister-lovers, maternal daughters, mother-sisters, who never hung their heads in shame. Once the palace of magistrates is restored, it's time to pay: immediate bloody death to the uncontrollable elements.

But only the poets—not the novelists, allies of representationalism. Because poetry involves gaining strength through the unconscious and because the unconscious, that other limitless country, is the place where the repressed manage to survive: women, or as Hoffmann would say, fairies.

She must write her self, because this is the invention of a *new insurgent* writing which, when the moment of her liberation has come, will allow her to carry out the indispensable ruptures and transformations in her history, first at two levels that cannot be separated.

a) Individually. By writing her self, woman will return to the body which has been more than confiscated from her, which has been turned into the uncanny stranger on display—the ailing or dead figure, which so often turns out to be the nasty companion, the cause and location of inhibitions. Censor the body and you censor breath and speech at the same time.

Write your self. Your body must be heard. Only then will the immense resources of the unconscious spring forth. Our naphtha will spread, throughout the world, without dollars—black or gold—nonassessed values that will change the rules of the old game.

To write. An act which will not only "realize" the decensored relation of woman to her sexuality, to her womanly being, giving her access to her native strength; it will give her back her goods, her pleasures, her organs, her immense bodily territories which have been kept under seal; it will tear her away from the superegoized structure in which she has always occupied the place reserved for the guilty (guilty of everything, guilty at every turn: for having desires, for not having any; for being frigid, for being "too hot"; for not being both at once; for being too motherly and not enough; for having children and for not having any; for nursing and for not nursing . . .)—tear her away by means of this research, this job of analysis and illumination, this emancipation of the marvelous text of her self that she must urgently learn to speak. A woman without a body, dumb, blind, can't possibly be a good fighter. She is reduced to being the servant of the militant male, his shadow. We must kill the false woman who is preventing the live one from breathing. Inscribe the breath of the whole woman.

b) An act that will also be marked by woman's *seizing* the occasion to *speak*, hence her shattering entry into history, which has always been based *on her suppression*. To write and thus to forge for herself the antilogos weapon. To become *at will* the taker and initiator, for her own right, in every symbolic system, in every political process.

It is time for women to start scoring their feats in written and oral language.

Every woman has known the torment of getting up to speak. Her heart racing, at times entirely lost for words, ground and language slipping away—that's how daring a feat, how great a transgression it is for a woman to speak—even just open her mouth—in public. A double distress, for even if she transgresses, her words fall almost always upon the deaf male ear, which hears in language only that which speaks in the masculine.

It is by writing, from and toward women, and by taking up the challenge of speech which has been governed by the phallus, that women will confirm women in a place other than that which is reserved in and by the symbolic, that is, in a place other than silence. Women should break out of the snare of silence. They shouldn't be conned into accepting a domain which is the margin or the harem.

Listen to a woman speak at a public gathering (if she hasn't painfully lost her wind). She doesn't "speak," she throws her trembling body forward; she lets go of herself, she flies; all of her passes into her voice, and it's with her body that she vitally supports the "logic" of her speech. Her flesh speaks true. She lays herself bare. In fact, she physically materializes what she's thinking; she signifies it with her body. In a certain way she *inscribes* what she's saying, because she doesn't deny her drives the intractable and impassioned part they have in speaking. Her speech, even when "theoretical" or political, is never simple or linear or "objectified," generalized: she draws her story into history.

There is not that scission, that division made by the common man between the logic of oral speech and the logic of the text, bound as he is by his antiquated relation—servile, calculating—to mastery. From which proceeds the niggardly lip service which engages only the tiniest part of the body, plus the mask.

In women's speech, as in their writing, that element which never stops resonating, which, once we've been permeated by it, profoundly and imperceptibly touched by it, retains the power of moving us—that element is the song: first music from the first voice of love which is alive in every woman. Why this privileged relationship with the voice? Because no woman stockpiles as many defenses for countering the drives as does a man. You don't build walls around yourself, you don't forgo pleasure as "wisely" as he. Even if phallic mystification has generally contaminated good relationships, a woman is never far from "mother" (I mean outside her role functions: the "mother" as nonname and as source of goods). There is always within her at least a little of that good mother's milk. She writes in white ink.

Woman for women.—There always remains in woman that force which produces/is produced by the other—in particular, the other woman. *In* her, matrix, cradler; herself giver as her mother and child; she is her own sister-daughter. You might object, "What about she who is the hysterical offspring of a bad mother?" Everything will be changed once woman gives woman to the other woman. There is hidden and always ready in woman the source; the locus for the other. The mother, too, is a metaphor. It is necessary and sufficient that the best of herself be given to woman by another woman for her to be able to love herself and return in love the body that was "born" to her. Touch me, caress me, you the living no-name, give me my self as myself. The relation to the "mother," in terms of intense pleasure and violence, is curtailed no more than the relation to childhood (the child that she was, that she is, that she makes, remakes, undoes, there at the point where, the same, she mothers herself). Text: my body—shot through with streams of song; I don't mean the overbearing, clutchy "mother" but, rather, what touches you, the equi-voice that affects you, fills your breast with an urge to come to language and launches your force; the rhythm that laughs you; the intimate recipient who makes all metaphors possible and desirable; body (body? bodies?), no more describable than god, the soul, or the Other; that part of you that leaves a space between yourself and urges you to inscribe in language your woman's style. In women there is always more or less of the mother who makes everything all right, who nourishes, and who stands up against separation; a force that will not be cut off but will knock the wind out of the codes. We will rethink womankind beginning with every form and every period of her body. The Americans remind us, "We are all Lesbians"; that is, don't denigrate woman, don't make of her what men have made of you.

Because the "economy" of her drives is prodigious, she cannot fail, in seizing the occasion to speak, to transform directly and indirectly *all* systems of exchange based on masculine thrift. Her libido will produce far more radical effects of political and social change than some might like to think.

Because she arrives, vibrant, over and again, we are at the beginning of a new history, or rather of a process of becoming in which several histories intersect with one another. As subject for history, woman always occurs simultaneously in several places. Woman un-thinks[4] the unifying, regulating history that homogenizes and channels forces, herding contradictions into a single battlefield. In woman, personal history blends together with the history of all women, as well as national and world history. As a militant, she is an integral part of all liberations. She must be farsighted, not limited to a blow-by-blow interaction. She foresees that her liberation will do more than modify power relations or toss the ball over to the other camp; she will bring about a mutation in human relations, in thought, in all praxis: hers is not simply a class struggle, which she carries forward into a much vaster movement. Not that in order to be a woman-in-struggle(s) you have to leave the class struggle or repudiate it; but you have to split it open, spread it out, push it forward, fill it with the fundamental struggle so as to prevent the class struggle, or any other struggle for the liberation of a class or people, from operating as a form of repression, pretext for postponing the inevitable, the staggering alteration in power relations and in the production of individualities. This alteration is already upon us—in the United States, for example, where millions of night crawlers are in the process of undermining the family and disintegrating the whole of American sociality.

The new history is coming; it's not a dream, though it does extend beyond men's imagination, and for good reason. It's going to deprive them of their conceptual orthopedics, beginning with the destruction of their enticement machine.

It is impossible to *define* a feminine practice of writing, and this is an impossibility that will remain, for this practice can never be theorized, enclosed, coded—which doesn't mean that it doesn't exist. But it will always surpass the discourse that regulates the phallocentric system; it does and will take place in areas other than those subordinated to philosophico-theoretical domination. It will be conceived of only by subjects who are breakers of automatisms, by peripheral figures that no authority can ever subjugate.

Hence the necessity to affirm the flourishes of this writing, to give form to its movement, its near and distant byways. Bear in mind to begin with (1) that sexual opposition, which has always worked for man's profit to the point of reducing writing, too, to his laws, is only a historico-cultural limit. There is, there will be more and more rapidly pervasive now, a fiction that produces irreducible effects of femininity. (2) That it is through ignorance that most readers, critics, and writers of both sexes hesitate to admit or deny outright the possibility or the pertinence of a distinction between feminine and masculine writing. It will usually be said, thus disposing of sexual difference: either that all writing, to the extent that it materializes, is feminine; or, inversely—but it comes to the same thing—that the act of writing is equivalent to masculine masturbation (and so the woman who writes cuts herself out a paper penis); or that writing is bisexual, hence neuter, which again does away with differentiation. To admit that writing is precisely working (in) the in-between, inspecting the process of the same and of the other without which nothing can live, undoing the work of death—to admit this is first to want the two, as well as both, the ensemble of the one and the other, not fixed in sequences of struggle and expulsion or some other form of death but infinitely dynamized by an incessant process of exchange from one subject to another. A process of different subjects knowing one another and beginning one another anew only from the living boundaries of the other: a multiple and inexhaustible course with millions of encounters and transformations of the same into the other and into the in-between, from which woman takes her forms (and man, in his turn; but that's his other history).

In saying "bisexual, hence neuter," I am referring to the classic conception of bisexuality, which, squashed under the emblem of castration fear and along with the fantasy of a "total" being (though composed of two halves), would do away with the difference experienced as an operation incurring loss, as the mark of dreaded sectility.

To this self-effacing, merger-type bisexuality, which would conjure away castration (the writer who puts up his sign: "bisexual written here, come and see," when the odds are good that it's neither one nor the other), I oppose the *other bisexuality* on which every subject not enclosed in the false theater of phallocentric representationalism has founded his/her erotic universe. Bisexuality: that is, each one's location in self (*repérage en soi*) of the presence—variously manifest and insistent according to each person, male or female—of both sexes, nonexclusion either of the difference or of one sex, and, from this "self-permission," multiplication of the effects of the inscription of desire, over all parts of my body and the other body.

Now it happens that at present, for historico-cultural reasons, it is women who are opening up to and benefiting from this vatic bisexuality which doesn't annul differences but stirs them up, pursues them, increases their number. In a certain way, "woman is bisexual"; man—it's a secret to no one—being poised to keep glorious phallic monosexuality in view. By virtue of affirming the primacy of the phallus and of bringing it into play, phallocratic ideology has claimed more than one victim. As a woman, I've been clouded over by the great shadow of the scepter and been told: idolize it, that which you cannot brandish. But at the same time, man has been handed that grotesque and scarcely enviable destiny (just imagine) of being reduced to a single idol with clay balls. And consumed, as Freud and his followers note, by a fear of being a woman! For, if psychoanalysis was constituted from woman, to repress femininity (and not so successful a repression at that—men have made it clear), its account of masculine sexuality is now hardly refutable; as with all the "human" sciences, it reproduces the masculine view, of which it is one of the effects.

Here we encounter the inevitable man-with-rock, standing erect in his old Freudian realm, in the way that, to take the figure back to the point where linguistics is conceptualizing it "anew," Lacan preserves it in the sanctuary of the phallos (ϕ) "sheltered" from *castration's lack!* Their "symbolic" exists, it holds power—we, the sowers of disorder, know it only too well. But we are in no way obliged to deposit our lives in their banks of lack, to consider the constitution of the subject in terms of a drama manglingly restaged, to reinstate again and again the religion of the father. Because we don't want that. We don't fawn around the supreme hole. We have no womanly reason to pledge allegiance to the negative. The feminine (as the poets suspected) affirms: ". . . And yes," says Molly, carrying *Ulysses* off beyond any book and toward the new writing; "I said yes, I will Yes."

The Dark Continent is neither dark nor unexplorable.—It is still unexplored only because we've been made to believe that it was too dark to be explorable. And because they want to make us believe that what interests us is the white continent, with its monuments to Lack. And we believed. They riveted us between two horrifying myths: between the Medusa and the abyss. That would be enough to set half the world laughing, except that it's still going on. For the phallologocentric sublation[5] is with us, and it's militant, regenerating the old patterns, anchored in the dogma of castration. They haven't changed a thing: they've theorized their desire for reality! Let the priests tremble, we're going to show them our sexts!

Too bad for them if they fall apart upon discovering that women aren't men, or that the mother doesn't have one. But isn't this fear convenient for them? Wouldn't the worst be, isn't the worst, in truth, that women aren't castrated, that they have only to stop listening to the Sirens (for the Sirens were men) for history to change its meaning? You only have to look at the Medusa straight on to see her. And she's not deadly. She's beautiful and she's laughing.

Men say that there are two unrepresentable things: death and the feminine sex. That's because they need femininity to be associated with death; it's the jitters that give them a hard-on! for themselves! They need to be afraid of us. Look at the trembling Perseuses moving backward toward us, clad in apotropes. What lovely backs! Not another minute to lose. Let's get out of here.

Let's hurry: the continent is not impenetrably dark. I've been there often. I was overjoyed one day to run into Jean Genet. It was in *Pompes funèbres*. [6] He had come there led by his Jean. There are some men (all too few) who aren't afraid of femininity.

Almost everything is yet to be written by women about femininity: about their sexuality, that is, its infinite and mobile complexity, about their eroticization, sudden turn-ons of a certain minuscule-immense area of their bodies; not about destiny, but about the adventure of such and such a drive, about trips, crossings, trudges, abrupt and gradual awakenings, discoveries of a zone at one time timorous and soon to be forthright. A woman's body, with its thousand and one thresholds of ardor—once, by smashing yokes and censors, she lets it articulate the profusion of meanings that run through it in every direction—will make the old single-grooved mother tongue reverberate with more than one language.

We've been turned away from our bodies, shamefully taught to ignore them, to strike them with that stupid sexual modesty; we've been made victims of the old fool's game: each one will love the other sex. I'll give you your body and you'll give me mine. But who are the men who give women the body that women blindly yield to them? Why so few texts? Because so few women have as yet won back their body. Women must write through their bodies, they must invent the impregnable language that will wreck partitions, classes, and rhetorics, regulations and codes, they must submerge, cut through, get beyond the ultimate reserve-discourse, including the one that laughs at the very idea of pronouncing the word "silence," the one that, aiming for the impossible, stops short before the word "impossible" and writes it as "the end."

Such is the strength of women that, sweeping away syntax, breaking that famous thread (just a tiny little thread, they say) which acts for men as a surrogate umbilical cord, assuring them—otherwise they couldn't come—that the old lady is always right behind them, watching them make phallus, women will go right up to the impossible.

When the "repressed" of their culture and their society returns, it's an explosive, *utterly* destructive, staggering return, with a force never yet unleashed and equal to the most forbidding of suppressions. For when the Phallic period comes to an end, women will have been either annihilated or borne up to the highest and most violent incandescence. Muffled throughout their history, they have lived in dreams, in bodies (though muted), in silences, in aphonic revolts.

And with such force in their fragility; a fragility, a vulnerability, equal to their incomparable intensity. Fortunately, they haven't sublimated; they've saved their skin, their energy. They haven't worked at liquidating the impasse of lives without futures. They have furiously inhabited these sumptuous bodies: admirable hysterics who made Freud succumb to many voluptuous moments impossible to confess, bombarding his Mosaic statue with their carnal and passionate body words, haunting him with their inaudible and thundering denunciations, dazzling, more than naked underneath the seven veils of modesty. Those who, with a single word of the body, have inscribed the vertiginous immensity of a history which is sprung like an arrow from the whole history of men and from biblico-capitalist society, are the women, the supplicants of yesterday, who come as forebears of the new women, after whom no intersubjective relation will ever be the same. You, Dora, you the indomitable, the poetic body, you are the true "mistress" of the Signifier. Before long your efficacity will be seen at work when your speech is no longer suppressed, its point turned in against your breast, but written out over against the other.

In body.—More so than men who are coaxed toward social success, toward sublimation, women are body. More body, hence more writing. For a long time it has been in body that women have responded to persecution, to the familial-conjugal enterprise of domestication, to the repeated attempts at castrating them. Those who have turned their tongues 10,000 times seven times before not speaking are either dead from it or more familiar with their tongues and their mouths than anyone else. Now, I-woman am going to blow up the Law: an explosion henceforth possible and ineluctable; let it be done, right now, *in* language.

Let us not be trapped by an analysis still encumbered with the old automatisms. It's not to be feared that language conceals an invincible adversary, because it's the language of men and their grammar. We mustn't leave them a single place that's any more theirs alone than we are.

If woman has always functioned "within" the discourse of man, a signifier that has always referred back to the opposite signifier which annihilates its specific energy and diminishes or stifles its very different sounds, it is time for her to dislocate this "within," to explode it, turn it around, and seize it; to make it hers, containing it, taking it in her own mouth, biting that tongue with her very own teeth to invent for herself a language to get inside of. And you'll see with what ease she will spring forth from that "within"—the "within" where once she so drowsily crouched—to overflow at the lips she will cover the foam.

Nor is the point to appropriate their instruments, their concepts, their places, or to begrudge them their position of mastery. Just because there's a risk of identification doesn't mean that we'll succumb. Let's leave it to the worriers, to masculine anxiety and its obsession with how to dominate the way things work—knowing "how it works" in order to "make it work." For us the point is not to take possession in order to internalize or manipulate, but rather to dash through and to "fly."[7]

Flying is woman's gesture—flying in language and making it fly. We have all learned the art of flying and its numerous techniques; for centuries we've been able to possess anything only by flying; we've lived in flight, stealing away, finding, when desired, narrow passageways, hidden crossovers. It's no accident that *voler* has a double meaning, that it plays on each of them and thus throws off the agents of sense. It's no accident: women take after birds and robbers just as robbers take after women and birds. They (*illes*)[8] go by, fly the coop, take pleasure in jumbling the order of space, in disorienting it, in changing around the furniture, dislocating things and values, breaking them all up, emptying structures, and turning propriety upside down.

What woman hasn't flown/stolen? Who hasn't felt, dreamt, performed the gesture that jams sociality? Who hasn't crumbled, held up to ridicule, the bar of separation? Who hasn't inscribed with her body the differential, punctured the system of couples and opposition? Who, by some act of transgression, hasn't overthrown successiveness, connection, the wall of circumfusion?

A feminine text cannot fail to be more than subversive. It is volcanic; as it is written it brings about an upheaval of the old property crust, carrier of masculine investments; there's no other way. There's no room for her if she's not a he. If she's a her-she, it's in order to smash everything, to shatter the framework of institutions, to blow up the law, to break up the "truth" with laughter.

For once she blazes *her* trail in the symbolic, she cannot fail to make of it the chaosmos of the "personal"—in her pronouns, her nouns, and her clique of referents. And for good reason. There will have been the long history of gynocide. This is known by the colonized peoples of yesterday, the workers, the nations, the species off whose backs the history of men has made its gold; those who have known the ignominy of persecution derive from it an obstinate future desire for grandeur; those who are locked up know better than their jailers the taste of free air. Thanks to their history, women today know (how to do and want) what men will be able to conceive of only much later. I say woman overturns the "personal," for if, by means of laws, lies, blackmail, and marriage, her right to herself has been extorted at the same time as her name, she has been able, through the very movement of mortal alienation, to see more closely the inanity of "propriety," the reductive stinginess of the masculine-conjugal subjective economy, which she doubly resists. On the one hand she has constituted herself necessarily as that "person" capable of losing a part of herself without losing her integrity. But secretly, silently, deep down inside, she grows and multiplies, for, on the other hand, she knows far more about living and about the relation between the economy of the drives and the management of the ego than any man. Unlike man, who holds so dearly to his title and his titles, his pouches of value, his cap, crown, and everything connected with his head, woman couldn't care less about the fear of decapitation (or castration), adventuring, without the masculine temerity, into anonymity, which she can merge with, without annihilating herself: because she's a giver.

I shall have a great deal to say about the whole deceptive problematic of the gift. Woman is obviously not that woman Nietzsche dreamed of who gives only in order to.[9] Who could ever think of the gift as a gift-that-takes? Who else but man, precisely the one who would like to take everything?

If there is a "propriety of woman," it is paradoxically her capacity to depropriate unselfishly, body without end, without appendage, without principal "parts." If she is a whole, it's a whole composed of parts that are wholes, not simple partial objects but a moving, limitlessly changing ensemble, a cosmos tirelessly traversed by Eros, an immense astral space not organized around any one sun that's any more of a star than the others.

This doesn't mean that she's an undifferentiated magma, but that she doesn't lord it over her body or her desire. Though masculine sexuality gravitates around the penis, engendering that centralized body (in political anatomy) under the dictatorship of its parts, woman does not bring about the same regionalization which serves the couple head/genitals and which is inscribed only within boundaries. Her libido is cosmic, just as her unconscious is worldwide. Her writing can only keep going, without ever inscribing or discerning contours, daring to make these vertiginous crossings of the other(s) ephemeral and passionate sojourns in him, her, them, whom she inhabits long enough to look at from the point closest to their unconscious from the moment they awaken, to love them at the point closest to their drives; and then further, impregnated through and through with these brief, identificatory embraces, she goes and passes into infinity. She alone dares and wishes to know from within, where she, the outcast, has never ceased to hear the resonance of fore-language. She lets the other language speak—the language of 1,000 tongues which knows neither enclosure nor death. To life she refuses nothing. Her language does not contain, it carries; it does not hold back, it makes possible. When id is ambiguously uttered— the wonder of being several—she doesn't defend herself against these unknown women whom she's surprised at becoming, but derives pleasure from this gift of alterability. I am spacious, singing flesh, on which is grafted no one knows which I, more or less human, but alive because of transformation.

Write! and your self-seeking text will know itself better than flesh and blood, rising, insurrectionary dough kneading itself, with sonorous, perfumed ingredients, a lively combination of flying colors, leaves, and rivers plunging into the sea we feed. "Ah, there's her sea," he will say as he holds out to me a basin full of water from the little phallic mother from whom he's inseparable. But look, our seas are what we make of them, full of fish or not, opaque or transparent, red or black, high or smooth, narrow or bankless; and we are ourselves sea, sand, coral, seaweed, beaches, tides, swimmers, children, waves. . . . More or less wavily sea, earth, sky—what matter would rebuff us? We know how to speak them all.

Heterogeneous, yes. For her joyous benefits she is erogenous; she is the erotogeneity of the heterogeneous: airborne swimmer, in flight, she does not cling to herself; she is dispersible, prodigious, stunning, desirous and capable of others, of the other woman that she will be, of the other woman she isn't, of him, of you.

Woman be unafraid of any other place, of any same, or any other. My eyes, my tongue, my ears, my nose, my skin, my mouth, my body-for-(the)-other—not that I long for it in order to fill up a hole, to provide against some defect of mine, or because, as fate would have it, I'm spurred on by feminine "jealousy"; not because I've been dragged into the whole chain of substitutions that brings that which is substituted back to its ultimate object. That sort of thing you would expect to come straight out of "Tom Thumb," out of the *Penisneid* whispered to us by old grand-mother ogresses, servants to their father-sons. If they believe, in order to muster up some self-importance, if they really need to believe that we're dying of desire, that we are this hole fringed with desire for their penis—that's their immemorial busi-ness. Undeniably (we verify it at our own expense—but also to our amusement), it's their business to let us know they're getting a hard-on, so that we'll assure them (we the maternal mistresses of their little pocket signifier) that they still can, that it's still there—that men structure themselves only by being fitted with a feather. In the child it's not the penis that the woman desires, it's not that famous bit of skin around which every man gravitates. Pregnancy cannot be traced back, except within the historical limits of the ancients, to some form of fate, to those mechanical substitutions brought about by the unconscious of some eternal "jealous woman"; not to penis envies; and not to narcissism or to some sort of homosexuality linked to the ever-present mother! Begetting a child doesn't mean that the woman or the man must fall ineluctably into patterns or must recharge the circuit of reproduction. If there's a risk there's not an inevitable trap: may women be spared the pressure, under the guise of consciousness-raising, of a supplement of interdictions. Either you want a kid or you don't—*that's your business.* Let nobody threaten you; in satisfying your desire, let not the fear of becoming the accomplice to a sociality succeed the old-time fear of being "taken." And man, are you still going to bank on everyone's blindness and passivity, afraid lest the child make a father and, consequently, that in having a kid the woman land herself more than one bad deal by engendering all at once child—mother—father—family? No; it's up to you to break the old circuits. It will be up to man and woman to render obsolete the former relationship and all its consequences, to consider the launching of a brand-new subject, alive, with defamilialization. Let us demater-paternalize rather than deny woman, in an effort to avoid the cooptation of procreation, a thrilling era of the body. Let us defetishize. Let's get away from the dialectic which has it that the only good father is a dead one, or that the child is the death of his parents. The child is the other, but the other without violence, bypassing loss, struggle. We're fed up with the reuniting of bonds forever to be severed, with the litany of castration that's handed down and genealogized. We won't advance backward anymore; we're not going to repress something so simple as the desire for life. Oral drive, anal drive, vocal drive—all these drives are our strengths, and among them is the gestation drive—just like the desire to write: a desire to live self from within, a desire for the swollen belly, for language, for blood. We are not going to refuse, if it should happen to strike our fancy, the unsurpassed pleasures of pregnancy which have actually been always exaggerated or conjured away—or cursed—in the classic texts. For if there's one thing that's been repressed, here's just the place to find it: in the taboo of the pregnant woman. This says a lot about the power she seems invested with at the time, because it has always been suspected that, when pregnant, the woman not only doubles her market value, but—what's more important—takes on intrinsic value as a woman in her own eyes and, undeniably, acquires body and sex.

There are thousands of ways of living one's pregnancy; to have or not to have with that still invisible other a relationship of another intensity. And if you don't have that particular yearning, it doesn't mean that you're in any way lacking. Each body distributes in its own special way, without model or norm, the nonfinite and changing totality of its desires. Decide for yourself on your position in the arena of contradictions, where pleasure and reality embrace. Bring the other to life. Women know how to live detachment; giving birth is neither losing nor increasing. It's adding to life an other. Am I dreaming? Am I misrecognizing? You, the defenders of "theory," the sacrosanct yes-men of Concept, enthroners of the phallus (but not of the penis):

Once more you'll say that all this smacks of "idealism," or what's worse, you'll splutter that I'm a "mystic."

And what about the libido? Haven't I read the "Signification of the Phallus"? And what about separation, what about that bit of self for which, to be born, you undergo an ablation—an ablation, so they say, to be forever commemorated by your desire?

Besides, isn't it evident that the penis gets around in my texts, that I give it a place and appeal? Of course I do. I want all. I want all of me with all of him. Why should I deprive myself of a part of us? I want all of us. Woman of course has a desire for a "loving desire" and not a jealous one. But not because she is gelded; not because she's deprived and needs to be filled out, like some wounded person who wants to console herself or seek vengeance. I don't want a penis to decorate my body with. But I do desire the other for the other, whole and entire, male or female; because living means wanting everything that is, everything that lives, and wanting it alive. Castration? Let others toy with it. What's a desire originating from a lack? A pretty meager desire.

The woman who still allows herself to be threatened by the big dick, who's still impressed by the commotion of the phallic stance, who still leads a loyal master to the beat of the drum: that's the woman of yesterday. They still exist, easy and numerous victims of the oldest of farces: either they're cast in the original silent versions in which, as titanesses lying under the mountains they make with their quivering, they never see erected that theoretic monument to the golden phallus looming, in the old manner, over their bodies. Or, coming today out of their *infans* period and into the second, "enlightened" version of their virtuous debasement, they see themselves suddenly assaulted by the builders of the analytic empire and, as soon as they've begun to formulate the new desire, naked, nameless, so happy at making an appearance, they're taken in their bath by the new old men, and then, whoops! Luring them with flashy signifiers, the demon of interpretation—oblique, decked out in modernity—sells them the same old handcuffs, baubles, and chains. Which castration do you prefer? Whose degrading do you like better, the father's or the mother's? Oh, what pwetty eyes, you pwetty little girl. Here, buy my glasses and you'll see the Truth-Me-Myself tell you everything you should know. Put them on your nose and take a fetishist's look (you are me, the other analyst—that's what I'm telling you) at your body and the body of the other. You see? No? Wait, you'll have everything explained to you, and you'll know at last which sort of neurosis you're related to. Hold still, we're going to do your portrait, so that you can begin looking like it right away.

Yes, the naives to the first and second degree are still legion. If the New Women, arriving now, dare to create outside the theoretical, they're called in by the cops of the signifier, fingerprinted, remonstrated, and brought into the line of order that they are supposed to know; assigned by force of trickery to a precise place in the chain that's always formed for the benefit of a privileged signifier. We are pieced back to the string which leads back, if not to the Name-of-the-Father, then, for a new twist, to the place of the phallic-mother.

Beware, my friend, of the signifier that would take you back to the authority of a signified! Beware of diagnoses that would reduce your generative powers. "Common" nouns are also proper nouns that disparage your singularity by classifying it into species. Break out of the circles; don't remain within the psychoanalytic closure. Take a look around, then cut through!

And if we are legion, it's because the war of liberation has only made as yet a tiny breakthrough. But women are thronging to it. I've seen them, those who will be neither dupe nor domestic, those who will not fear the risk of being a woman; will not fear any risk, any desire, any space still unexplored in themselves, among themselves and others or anywhere else. They do not fetishize, they do not deny, they do not hate. They observe, they approach, they try to see the other woman, the child, the lover—not to strengthen their own narcissism or verify the solidity or weakness of the master, but to make love better, to invent.

Other love.—In the beginning are our differences. The new love dares for the other, wants the other, makes dizzying, precipitous flights between knowledge and invention. The woman arriving over and over again does not stand still; she's everywhere, she exchanges, she is the desire-that-gives. (Not enclosed in the paradox of the gift that takes nor under the illusion of unitary fusion. We're past that.) She comes in, comes-in-between herself me and you, between the other me where one is always infinitely more than one and more than me, without the fear of ever reaching a limit; she thrills in our becoming. And we'll keep on becoming! She cuts through defensive loves, motherages, and devourations: beyond selfish narcissism, in the moving, open, transitional space, she runs her risks. Beyond the struggle-to-the-death that's been removed to the bed, beyond the love-battle that claims to represent exchange, she scorns at an Eros dynamic that would be fed by hatred. Hatred: a heritage, again, a reminder, a duping subservience to the phallus. To love, to watch-think-seek the other in the other, to despecularize, to unhoard. Does this seem difficult? It's not impossible, and this is what nourishes life—a love that has no commerce with the apprehensive desire that provides against the lack and stultifies the strange; a love that rejoices in the exchange that multiplies. Wherever history still unfolds as the history of death, she does not tread. Opposition, hierarchizing exchange, the struggle for mastery which can end only in at least one death (one master—one slave, or two nonmasters ≠ two dead)—all that comes from a period in time governed by phallocentric values. The fact that this period extends into the present doesn't prevent woman from starting the history of life somewhere else. Elsewhere, she gives. She doesn't "know" what she's giving, she doesn't measure it; she gives, though, neither a counterfeit impression nor something she hasn't got. She gives more, with no assurance that she'll get back even some unexpected profit from what she puts out. She gives that there may be life, thought, transformation. This is an "economy" that can no longer be put in economic terms. Wherever she loves, all the old concepts of management are left behind. At the end of a more or less conscious computation, she finds not her sum but her differences. I am for you what you want me to be at the moment you look at me in a way you've never seen me before: at every instant. When I write, it's everything that we don't know we can be that is written out of me, without exclusions, without stipulation, and everything we will be calls us to the unflagging, intoxicating, unappeasable search for love. In one another we will never be lacking.

Notes

1. Men still have everything to say about their sexuality, and everything to write. For what they have said so far, for the most part, stems from the opposition activity/passivity from the power relation between a fantasized obligatory virility meant to invade, to colonize, and the consequential phantasm of woman as a "dark continent" to penetrate and to "pacify." (We know what "pacify" means in terms of scotomizing the other and misrecognizing the self.) Conquering her, they've made haste to depart from her borders, to get out of sight, out of body. The way man has of getting out of himself and into her whom he takes not for the other but for his own, deprives him, he knows, of his own bodily territory. One can understand how man, confusing himself with his penis and rushing in for the attack, might feel resentment and fear of being "taken" by the woman, of being lost in her, absorbed or alone.

2. I am speaking here only of the place "reserved" for women by the Western world.

3. Which works, then, might be called feminine? I'll just point out some examples: one would have to give them full readings to bring out what is pervasively feminine in their significance.

Which I shall do elsewhere. In France (have you noted our infinite poverty in this field?—the Anglo-Saxon countries have shown resources of distinctly greater consequence), leafing through what's come out of the twentieth century—and it's not much—the only inscriptions of femininity that I have seen were by Colette, Marguerite Duras, . . . and Jean Genet.

4. *Dé-pense,* a neologism formed on the verb *penser,* hence "unthinks," but also "spends" (from *dépenser*).—Tr.

5. Standard English term for the Hegelian *Aufhebung,* the French *la relève.*

6. Jean Genet, *Pompes funèbres* (Paris, 1948), p. 185 [privately published].

7. Also, "to steal." Both meanings of the verb *voler* are played on, as the text itself explains in the following paragraph.—Tr.

8. *Illes* is a fusion of the masculine pronoun *ils,* which refers back to birds and robbers, with the feminine pronoun *elles,* which refers to women.—Tr.

9. Reread Derrida's text, "Le style de la femme," in *Nietzsche aujourd'hui* (Union Générale d'Editions, Coll. 10/18), where the philoso-

pher can be seen operating an *Aufhebung* of all philosophy in its systematic reducing of woman to the place of seduction: she appears as the one who is taken for; the bait in person, all veils unfurled, the one who doesn't give but who gives only in order to (take).

==========

LUCE IRIGARAY

When Our Lips Speak Together

Translated by Carolyn Burke

If we continue to speak the same language to each other, we will reproduce the same story. Begin the same stories all over again. Don't you feel it? Listen: men and women around us all sound the same. Same arguments, same quarrels, same scenes. Same attractions and separations. Same difficulties, the impossibility of reaching each other. Same . . . same. . . . Always the same.

If we continue to speak this sameness, if we speak to each other as men have spoken for centuries, as they taught us to speak, we will fail each other. Again. . . . Words will pass through our bodies, above our heads, disappear, make us disappear. Far. Above. Absent from ourselves, we become machines that are spoken, machines that speak. Clean skins[1] envelop us, but they are not our own. We have fled into proper names, we have been violated by them.[2] Not yours, not mine. We don't have names. We change them as men exchange us, as they use us. It's frivolous to be so changeable so long as we are a medium of exchange.

How can I touch you if you're not there? Your blood is translated into their senses.[3] They can speak to each other and about us. But "us"? Get out of their language. Go back through all the names they gave you. I'm waiting for you, I'm waiting for myself. Come back. It's not so hard. Stay right here, and you won't be absorbed into the old scenarios, the redundant phrases, the familiar gestures, bodies already encoded in a system. Try to be attentive to yourself. To me. Don't be distracted by norms or habits.

Now normally or habitually, "I love you" is said to an enigma: an "other." An other body, an other sex. I love you: but I don't quite know who or what. "I love"

---

1. The two definitions of *propre*—"clean" and "proper"—suggest that female meanings are cleaned up and closed off by patriarchal naming systems.

2. Irigaray creates a neologism, *env(i)olées,* to suggest that women's lives *(vie)* and desires *(envie)* are violated *(violées)* and made to vanish *(envolées)* through the imposition upon them of proper names.

3. The play on *sang* ("blood") and *sens* ("meaning," "sense") extends the analogy between sexuality and writing. Blood is at once metaphorical and literal, a source of female sense and sexuality.

slips away, it is swallowed up, drowns, burns, disappears into nothingness. We must wait for the return of "I love." Perhaps for a long time, perhaps forever. What has become of "I love"? What has become of me? "I love" lies in wait for the other. Has he swallowed me? Spat me out? Taken me or left me? Shut me up or thrown me out? How is he now? No longer (part of) me? When he tells me, "I love you," does he give me back myself? Or does he give himself in this form? His? Mine? The same? Another? But then what have *I* become?

When you say I love you—right here, close to me, to you—you also say I love myself. Neither you nor I need wait for anything to be returned. I owe you nothing, you owe me nothing. This "I love you" is neither a gift nor a debt. You don't "give" me anything when you touch yourself, when you touch me: you touch yourself through me. You don't give yourself. What could I do with these selves, yours and mine, wrapped up like a gift? You keep both of us as much as you open us up. We find ourselves as we entrust ourselves to each other. This currency of alternatives and oppositions, choices and negotiations, has no value for us. Unless we remain in their order and reenact their system of commerce, where "we" has no place.

I love you: body shared, undivided. Neither you nor I severed. There is no need for blood spilt between us. No need for a wound to remind us that blood exists. It flows within us, from us. It is familiar, close. You are quite red, and still so white.[4] Both at once. You don't lose your candor as you become ardent. You are pure because you have stayed close to the blood. Because we are both white and red, we give birth to all the colors: pinks, browns, blonds, greens, blues. . . . For this whiteness is no sham, it is neither dead blood nor black blood. Sham is black: it absorbs everything, closes up and tries to come alive, but in vain. . . . The whiteness of this red appropriates nothing. It gives back as much as it receives, in luminous mutuality.

We are luminous. Beyond "one" or "two." I never knew how to count up to you. In their calculations, we count as two. Really, two? Doesn't that make you laugh? A strange kind of two, which isn't one, especially not one. Let them have oneness,[5] with its prerogatives, its domination, its solipsisms: like the sun. Let them have their strange division by couples, in which the other is the image of the one, but an image only. For them, being drawn to the other means a move toward one's mirage: a mirror[6] that is (barely) alive. Glacial, mute, the mirror is all the more faithful. Our vital energies are spent in this wearisome labor of doubling and miming. We have been destined to reproduce—that sameness in which, for centuries, we have been the other.

4. Irigaray's use of "red" and "white" differs consciously from the traditional Western opposition of these terms as symbolic of passion and purity. In general, she tries to create a locus in writing where such "opposites" may coexist, in a new way.

5. "Oneness," like "sameness," refers to the masculine standard that takes itself as a universal and collapses sexual difference.

6. Irigaray claims that man uses woman as a mirror in which he narcissistically seeks his own reflection. Her "speculum" would permit a different mode of "specula(riza)tion," curved to the female (see Irigaray, *Speculum of the Other Woman*, trans. Gillian C. Gill [Ithaca, N.Y.: Cornell University Press, 1985], pp. 136–46).

* * *

But how can I say "I love you" differently? I love you, my indifferent one? That would mean containing ourselves within their language. They have left us only absences, defects, negatives to name ourselves. We should be—it's already saying too much—indifferent, detached.[7]

Indifferent one, keep still. If you move, you disturb their order. You cause everything to fall apart. You break the circle of their habits, the circularity of their exchanges, their knowledge, their desire: their world. Indifferent one, you must not move or be moved unless they call you. If they say "come," then you may go forward, ever so slightly. Measure your steps according to their need—or lack of need—for their own image. One or two steps, no more, without exuberance or turbulence. Otherwise, you will smash everything, their mirror, their earth, their mother. And what about your life? You must pretend to receive it from them. You are only a small, insignificant receptacle, subject to their power alone.

So, we could be indifferent. Doesn't that make you laugh? At least, here, right now? We, indifferent? (If you roar with laughter always, everywhere, we will never talk to each other. And we will continue to be violated by their words. Instead, let's reappropriate our mouth and try to speak.) *Not* different, that's true. Still—that would be too easy. And that "not" would separate us again in order to define. Thus separated, "we" does not exist. Are we alike? If you will, but that's rather abstract. I don't really understand "alike." Do you? Alike from whose point of view? In respect to what, what standard or third term? I touch you, that's enough to know that you are my body.

I love you: our two lips cannot part to let *one* word pass. One single word that would say "you" or "me." Or, "equals": she who loves, she who is loved. Open or closed, for one never excludes the other, our lips say that both love each other. Together. To articulate one precise word, our lips would have to separate and be distant from each other. Between them, *one word*.

But where would such a word come from? A word correct, enclosed, wrapped around its meaning? Without a crack, faultless.[8] "You." "Me." Go on, laugh. . . . Without an opening, that would no longer be you or me. Without lips, it is no longer us. The unity, truth, and propriety of words come from their lack of lips, their forgetting of lips. Words are mute, when they have been uttered once and for all, neatly tied up so that their sense—their blood—can't escape. Like the children of men. But not ours. Besides, do we need or desire a child? Here and now, in our

7. Here, Irigaray plays with the various meanings of *indifférente*. At first, the loved one is seen as "detached," and this "masculine" sense of female indifference is used ironically. Then, *indifférente* comes to mean "nondifferent," or "undifferentiated" from each other. The force and consequences of the lovers' detachment from the old systems of language and sexuality are described in the following paragraphs.

8. *Sans faille* plays the masculine demand for univocal speech, in which the female is seen as "fault" or "lack," against the feminine desire for an open mode of signification. The text will enact the multiple meanings of *faille:* geographical fault or opening and sexual/linguistic/philosophical experience of duality. *Faille* also restates the central figure—the female lips, oral and vaginal, which are simultaneously open and closed.

closeness? Men and women have children to embody their closeness and their distance. But we?

I love you, childhood. I love you who are neither mother (pardon me, mother, for I prefer a woman) nor sister, neither daughter nor son. I love you—and there, where I love you, I don't care about the lineage of our fathers and their desire for imitation men. And their genealogical institutions. Let's be neither husband nor wife, do without the family, without roles, functions, and their laws of reproduction. I love you: your body, here, there, now. I/you touch you/me; it's quite enough for us to feel alive.

Open your lips, but do not open them simply. I do not open them simply. We—you/I—are never open nor closed. Because we never separate simply, *a single word* can't be pronounced, produced by, emitted from our mouths. From your/my lips, several songs, several ways of saying echo each other. For one is never separable from the other. You/I are always several at the same time. How could one dominate the other? Impose her voice, her tone, her meaning? They are not distinct, which does not mean that they are blurred. You don't understand a thing? No more than they understand you.[9]

Speak just the same. Because your language doesn't follow just one thread, one course, or one pattern, we are in luck. You speak from everywhere at the same time. You touch me whole at the same time. In all senses. Why only one song, one discourse, one text at a time? To seduce, satisfy, fill one of my "holes"? I don't have any, with you. We are not voids, lacks which wait for sustenance, fulfillment, or plenitude from an other. That our lips make us women does not mean that consuming, consummating, or being filled is what matters to us.

Kiss me. Two lips kiss two lips, and openness is ours again. Our "world." Between us, the movement from inside to outside, from outside to inside, knows no limits. It is without end. These are exchanges that no mark, no mouth[10] can ever stop. Between us, the house has no walls, the clearing no enclosure, language no circularity. You kiss me, and the world enlarges until the horizon vanishes. Are we unsatisfied? Yes, if that means that we are never finished. If our pleasure consists of moving and being moved by each other, endlessly. Always in movement, this openness is neither spent nor sated.

They neither taught us nor allowed us to say our multiplicity. That would have been improper speech. Of course, we were allowed—we had to?—display one truth

9. At this point in the text, the speaker addresses not *toi*, the loved one, but *vous*, the men whose language shows no comprehension of these new female speakers, who, in turn, cannot grasp their discourse.

10. Irigaray plays on *boucle* ("buckle") and *bouche* ("mouth"), to suggest that the female buccal exchanges are endless, their circularity open.

even as we sensed but muffled, stifled another. Truth's other side—its complement? its remainder?—stayed hidden. Secret. Inside and outside, we were not supposed to be the same. That doesn't suit their desires. Veiling and unveiling, isn't that what concerns them, interests them? Always repeating the same operation—each time, on each woman.

You/I then become two to please them. But once we are divided in two—one outside, the other inside—you no longer embrace yourself or me. On the outside, you attempt to conform to an order which is alien to you. Exiled from yourself, you fuse with everything that you encounter. You mime whatever comes near you. You become whatever you touch. In your hunger to find yourself, you move indefinitely far from yourself, from me. Assuming one model after another, one master after another, changing your face, form, and language according to the power that dominates you. Sundered. By letting yourself be abused, you become an impassive travesty. You no longer return as the indifferent one. You return: closed and impenetrable.

Speak to me. Can't you? Don't you want to any longer? Do you want to keep to yourself? Remain silent, white, virginal? Preserve the inner self? But it doesn't exist without the other. Don't tear yourself apart with choices that have been imposed on you. *Between us,* there is no rupture between virginal and nonvirginal. No event that makes us women. Long before your birth, you touched yourself, innocently. Your/my body does not acquire a sex by some operation, by the act of some power, function, or organ. You are already a woman; you don't need any special modification or intervention. You don't have to have an "outside," since "the other" already affects you, it is inseparable from you. You have been altered forever, everywhere. This is the crime that you never committed: you disturb their love of property.

How can I tell you that your sexual pleasure is in no way evil, you stranger to goods? There can be no fault until they rob you of your openness and close you up to brand you as their possession; practice their transgressions, infractions, and play other games with the law. When they—and you? speculate with your whiteness. If we play this game, we let ourselves be abused, damaged. We are alienated from ourselves to support the pursuit of their ends. That would be our role. If we submit to their reasoning, we are guilty. Their strategy—deliberate or not—is to make us guilty.

You have come back, divided: "we" are no more. You are split into red and white, black and white. How can we find each other again? Touch each other? We are cut into pieces, finished: our pleasure is trapped in their system, where "virgin" means one as yet unmarked by them, for them. Not yet a woman in their terms. Not yet imprinted with their sex, their language. Not yet penetrated or possessed by them. Still inhabiting that candor which is an awaiting, a nothing without them, a void without them. A virgin is but the future for their exchanges, their commerce, and their transports. A kind of reserve for their explorations, consummations, and exploitations—the future coming of their desires. But not ours.

How can I say it? That we are women from the start. That we don't need to be produced by them, named by them, made sacred or profane by them. That this has always already happened, without their labors. And that their history constitutes the locus of our exile. It's not that we have our own territory, but that their nation, family, home, and discourse imprison us in enclosures where we can no longer move—or live as "we." Their property is our exile. Their enclosures, the death of our love. Their words, the gag upon our lips.

How can we speak to escape their enclosures, patterns, distinctions and oppositions: virginal/deflowered, pure/impure, innocent/knowing. . . . How can we shake off the chains of these terms, free ourselves from their categories, divest ourselves of their names? Disengage ourselves, *alive,* from their concepts? Without reserve, without the immaculate whiteness which keeps their systems going. You know that we are never completed, but that we can only embrace each other whole. That "part by part"—of the body, of space, of time—interrupts our blood flow. Paralyzes us, petrifies us, immobilizes us. Makes us very pale, all but frigid.

Wait. My blood is coming back from their senses. It's getting warmer inside us, between us. Their words are becoming empty, bloodless, dead skins. While our lips are becoming red again. They're stirring, they're moving, they want to speak. What do you want to say? Nothing. Everything. Yes. Be patient. You will say it all. Begin with what you feel, here, right away. The female "all"[11] will come.

But you can't anticipate it, predict or fit it into a program. This "all" can't be schematized or mastered. It's the total movement of our body. No surface holds: no figures, lines, and points; no ground subsists. But there is no abyss. For us, depth does not mean a chasm. Where the earth has no solid crust, there can be no precipice. Our depth is the density of our body, in touch "all" over. There is no above/below, back/front, right side/wrong side, top/bottom in isolation, separate, out of touch. Our "all" intermingles. Without breaks or gaps.

If you/I are reluctant to speak, isn't it because we are afraid of not speaking well? But what is "well" or "badly"? What model could we use to speak "well"? What system of mastery and subordination could persecute us there[12] and break our spirits? Why aspire to the heights of a worthier discourse? Erection doesn't interest us: we're fine in the lowlands. We have so many spaces to share. Because we are always open, the horizon will never be circumscribed. Stretching out, never ceasing to unfold ourselves, we must invent so many different voices to speak all of "us," including our cracks and faults, that forever won't be enough time. We will never travel all the way round our periphery: we have so many dimensions. If you wish to speak "well" you constrict yourself, become narrower as you rise. Stretching, reaching higher, you leave behind the limitless realm of your body. Don't make yourself erect, you abandon us. The sky isn't up there: it's between us.

11. The syntactically startling *le toute* here is probably an oblique reference to Lacan's designation of women as *pas-toutes* ("not-alls") in *Le Séminaire XX: Encore* (Paris: Editions du Seuil, 1975). See "Così fan tutti" (*This Sex Which Is Not One,* trans. Catherine Porter [Ithaca, N.Y.: Cornell University Press, 1985], pp. 86–105), in which Irigaray asserts that psychoanalysis, in the voice of Lacan, excludes female expression from its discourse. The present text converts the *pas-toutes* into *toute,* a female mode of speaking "whole" and "all."
12. "There" refers to the locus of language as an ideological space whose geography is explored in this paragraph.

Don't fret about the "right" word. There is none. No truth between our lips. Everything has the right to be. Everything is worth exchanging, without privileges or refusals. Exchange? Everything can be exchanged when nothing is bought. Between us, there are no owners and no purchasers, no determinable objects and no prices. Our bodies are enriched by our mutual pleasure. Our abundance is inexhaustible: it knows neither want nor plenty. When we give ourselves "all," without holding back or hoarding, our exchanges have no terms. How to say this? The language we know is so limited. . . .

You'll say to me, why talk? We feel the same thing at the same time. Aren't my hands, my eyes, my mouth, my lips, my body enough for you? Isn't what they say to you sufficient? I could say yes, but that would be too easy. It has been said too often to reassure you/us.

If we don't invent a language, if we don't find our body's language, its gestures will be too few to accompany our story. When we become tired of the same ones, we'll keep our desires secret, unrealized. Asleep again, dissatisfied, we will be turned over to the words of men—who have claimed to "know" for a long time. But *not our body*. Thus seduced, allured, fascinated, ecstatic over our becoming, we will be paralyzed. Deprived of *our movements*. Frozen, although we are made for endless change. Without leaps or falls, and without repetition.

Continue, don't run out of breath. Your body is not the same today as yesterday. Your body remembers. *You* don't need to remember, to store up yesterday like capital in your head. Your memory? Your body reveals yesterday in what it wants today. If you think: yesterday I was, tomorrow I will be, you are thinking: I have died a little. Be what you are becoming, without clinging to what you could have been, might be. Never settle. Let's leave definitiveness to the undecided; we don't need it. Right here and now, our body gives us a very different certainty. Truth is necessary for those who are so distanced from their body that they have forgotten it. But their "truth" makes us immobile, like statues, if we can't divest ourselves of it. If we don't annul its power by trying to say, here, now, right away, how we are moved.

You are moving. You never stay still. You never stay. You never "are." How can I say you, who are always other? How can I speak you, who remain in a flux that never congeals or solidifies? How can this current pass into words? It is multiple, devoid of "causes" and "meanings," simple qualities; yet it is not decomposable. These movements can't be described as the passage from a beginning to an end. These streams don't flow into one, definitive sea; these rivers have no permanent banks; this body, no fixed borders. This unceasing mobility, this life. Which they might describe as our restlessness, whims, pretenses, or lies. For all this seems so strange to those who claim "solidity"[13] as their foundation.

13. See "La Mécanique des fluides" (*This Sex,* pp. 106–18), in which Irigaray suggests that Western discourse takes "solidity" and "solids" as bases for the determination of meaning, thereby neglecting the "fluids" that more appropriately express the female.

Speak, nevertheless. Between us, "hardness" is not the rule. We know the contours of our bodies well enough to appreciate fluidity. Our density can do without the sharp edges of rigidity. We are not attracted to dead bodies.

Yet how do we stay alive when far from each other? That's the danger. How can I await your return if we don't remain close when you are far away? If something palpable, here and now, doesn't evoke the touch of our bodies? How can we continue to live as ourselves if we are open to the infinity of our separation, closed upon the intangible sensation of absence? Let's not be ravished by their language again: let's not embody mourning. We must learn how to speak to each other so that we can embrace across distances. Surely, when I touch myself, I remember you. But so much is said, and said of us, that separates us.

Let's quickly invent our own phrases, so that everywhere and always, we continue to embrace. We are so subtle that nothing can stand in our way; nothing will keep us from reaching each other, even fleetingly,[14] as long as we find means of communication which have *our* density. We will walk through obstacles imperceptibly, without damage, to find each other. No one will see a thing. Our lack of resistance is our strength. For a long time, they have appreciated our suppleness for their embraces, their impressions. Why not use it for ourselves? Rather than let ourselves be branded by the—settled, stabilized, immobilized. Separated.

Don't weep. One day we will learn to say ourselves. And what we say will be far more beautiful than our tears, totally fluent.

Already, I carry you with me, everywhere. Not as a child, a burden, or a weight, no matter how loved or precious. You are not *within me*. I do not contain you or retain you in my stomach, my arms, or my head. Nor in my memory, my mind, or my language. You are just there, like my skin. A certainty that exists beyond all appearances, all disguises, all designations. I know that I live because you duplicate my life. Which doesn't mean that you subordinate your life to mine. Because you live, I feel alive, so long as you are neither my reply nor my imitation.

How can I say in another way: "We exist only as two?" We live as two beyond images, mirages, and mirrors. Between us, one is not the "real" and the other, her imitation; one is not the original and the other, her copy. Although we can be perfect dissemblers within their system, we relate to each other without simulation. Our resemblance does without semblances: in our bodies, already the same. Touch yourself, touch me, you'll "see."

No need to fashion a mirror image to be "a pair," or to repeat ourselves a second time. We are two, long before any representation of us exists. Let these two which your blood has made, which my body evokes for you, come together alive. You will always have the touching beauty of "the first time," if you are not congealed in

14. *Même fugitives* also hints that the lovers will meet as runaways or fugitives from the enclosures of the old order.

recreations. You will always be moved for the first time, if you are not immobilized in any form of repetition.

Let's do without models, standards, and examples. Let's not give ourselves orders, commands, or prohibitions. May our only demand be a call to move and be moved, together. Let's not dictate, moralize, or war with each other. Let's not want to be right, or have the right to criticize each other. If you/I sit in judgment, our existence comes to a stop. And what I love in you, in myself, no longer takes place for us: the birth that is never completed, the body never created once and for all time, the face and form never definitively finished, always still to be molded. The lips never opened or closed upon one single truth.

Light is not violent or deadly for us. The sun does not rise or set simply. Night and day are mingled in our gazes, our gestures, our bodies. Strictly speaking, we cast no shadow. There is no chance that one might become the darker double of the other. I want to remain nocturnal and find again in you my softly luminous night. Don't think that I love you as a bright beacon, lording it over everything around you. If we separate light from night, we give up the lightness of our mixture, we solidify all those differences that make us so simultaneously whole. We build walls between us, break off into parts, cut ourselves into two, and more. Although we are always one and the other, at the same time. If we separate ourselves that way, we "all" stop being born: without limits or shores other than those of our moving bodies.

And we won't stop speaking to each other until the limiting effects of time intervene. Don't worry. I can continue. Despite all the manufactured constraints of time and space, I still embrace you unceasingly. If others make of us fetishes to separate us, that's their business. Let's not become immobilized in these borrowed concepts.

If I say again and again: *not, nor, without* . . . , it's to remind you, to remind us, that we can touch each other only when naked. And that to find ourselves and each other, we have a great deal to take off. So many images and appearances separate us, one from another. They decked us out according to their desires for so long, and we adorned ourselves so often to please them, that we forgot the feel of our skin. Removed from our own skin, we remain distant. You and I, divided.

You? I? That's still saying too much. It cuts too sharply between us: "all."

NANCY CHODOROW

The Reproduction of Mothering

Afterword: Women's Mothering and Women's Liberation

Women's mothering perpetuates itself through social-structurally induced psychological mechanisms. It is not an unmediated product of physiology. Women come to mother because they have been mothered by women. By contrast, that men are mothered by women reduces their parenting capacities.

My account explains the reproduction of mothering. But it is not intended to demonstrate that this process is unproblematic or without contradictions. Women's mothering has created daughters as maternal, and this has ensured that parenting gets done. Yet the processes through which mothering is reproduced generate tensions and strains that undermine the sex-gender system even while reproducing it. The forms that these tensions and strains take depend in part on the internal development of the sex-gender system, in part on external historical conditions. In specific historical periods, such as the present, contradictions within the sex-gender system fuse with forces outside it, and lead to a situation in which resistance is widespread and often explicitly political.

Those very capacities and needs which create women as mothers create potential contradictions in mothering. A mother's sense of continuity with her infant may shade into too much connection and not enough separateness. Empathy and primary identification, enabling anticipation of an infant's or child's needs, may become an unconscious labeling of what her child ought to need, or what she thinks it needs. The development of a sense of autonomous self becomes difficult for children and leads to a mother's loss of sense of self as well. That women turn to children to complete a relational triangle, or to recreate a mother-child unity, means that mothering is invested with a mother's often conflictual, ambivalent, yet powerful need for her own mother. That women turn to children to fulfill emotional and even erotic desires unmet by men or other women means that a mother expects from infants what only another adult should be expected to give.

These tendencies take different forms with sons and daughters. Sons may become substitutes for husbands, and must engage in defensive assertion of ego boundaries and repression of emotional needs. Daughters may become substitutes for mothers, and develop insufficiently individuated senses of self.

Although these outcomes are potential in those personality characteristics which go into parenting and the psychological outcomes that women's mothering produces in children, their manifestation depends on how the family and women's mothering are situated socially. In a society where women do meaningful productive work, have ongoing adult companionship while they are parenting, and have satisfying emotional relationships with other adults, they are less likely to overinvest in children.

505

But these are precisely the conditions that capitalist industrial development has limited.

Beginning in the 1940s, studies began to claim that mothers in American society were "overprotecting" their children and not allowing them to separate. The mothers these studies describe are mothers of the 1920s. These mothers were rearing children when the new psychology was emphasizing maternal responsibility for children's development, when women were putting more time into child care even as there were fewer children to care for, when family mobility and the beginnings of suburbanization were removing women from daily contact with female kin. Women were expected to mother under precisely those conditions which, according to cross-cultural research, make it hardest to care for children and feel unambivalently affectionate toward them: as full-time mothers, with exclusive responsibility for children, in isolated homes. Most of the studies were not concerned with the lives of the mothers, but only with how their children were affected.

As women have turned for psychological sustenance to children, their overinvestment has perpetuated itself. Girls who grow up in family settings which include neither other women besides their mother nor an actively present father tend to have problems establishing a sufficiently individuated and autonomous sense of self. They in turn have difficulties in experiencing themselves as separate from their own children.

The exclusive responsibility of women for children exacerbates conflicts about masculinity in men. As long as women mother, a stable sense of masculine self is always more problematic than a stable sense of feminine self. Yet cross-culturally, the more father-absence (or absence of adult men) in the family, the more severe are conflicts about masculinity and fear of women.

When people have extreme needs for emotional support, and a few very intense relationships (whose sole basis is emotional connection, ungrounded in cooperative activity or institutionalized nonemotional roles) to provide for these needs, these relationships are liable to be full of conflict. For instance, heterosexual relationships based on idealized expectations of romantic love and total emotional sustenance, without the economic and political basis that marriage once had, often founder, as the present divorce rate testifies. Mother-son relationships in which the mother is looking for a husband create problems and resentments in both. Mother-daughter relationships in which the mother is supported by a network of women kin and friends, and has meaningful work and self-esteem, produce daughters with capacities for nurturance and a strong sense of self. Mother-daughter relationships in which the mother has no other adult support or meaningful work and remains ambivalently attached to her own mother produce ambivalent attachment and inability to separate in daughters. Those aspects of feminine personality which reproduce mothering become distorted.

Contemporary problems in mothering emerge from potential internal contradictions in the family and the social organization of gender—between women's mothering and heterosexual commitment, between women's mothering and individuation in daughters, between emotional connection and a sense of masculinity in sons. Changes generated from outside the family, particularly in the economy, have sharpened these contradictions.

At present, new strains emerge as women enter the paid labor force while continuing to mother. Women today are expected to be full-time mothers and to work in the paid labor force, are considered unmotherly if they demand day-care centers, greedy and unreasonable if they expect help from husbands, and lazy if they are single mothers who want to receive adequate welfare payments in order to be able to stay home for their children.

Women's mothering also affects men. In response to alienation and domination in the paid work world, many men are coming to regret their lack of extended connection with children. They feel that they are missing what remains one of the few deep personal experiences our society leaves us.

Until the contemporary feminist movement, social and psychological commentators put the burden of solution for these problems onto the individual and did not recognize that anything was systematically wrong. They described both the potential contradictions in mothering and their actual expression—mothers on a balancing wire of separation and connection, merging and loss of ego while maintaining a firm sense of autonomous self, drawing from and using the relation to their own mother while not letting this relationship overwhelm the relation to their child. They described the production of heterosexual contradictions and problems of masculinity as a routine product of women's mothering. To overcome these difficulties, mothers were to learn their balancing act better, and fathers were to be more seductive toward daughters and more of a model to sons.

Psychoanalytically oriented psychologists and social psychologists with whom I have talked about this book have argued that there is nothing inherently *wrong* with a sexual division of functions or roles—with the sexual division of labor. They argue that only inequality and differential valuation are wrong. But historically and cross-culturally we cannot separate the sexual division of labor from sexual inequality. The sexual division of labor and women's responsibility for child care are linked to and generate male dominance. Psychologists have demonstrated unequivocally that the very fact of being mothered by a woman generates in men conflicts over masculinity, a psychology of male dominance, and a need to be superior to women. Anthropologists argue that women's child-care responsibilities required that the earliest men hunt, giving them, and not women, access to the prestige and power that come from control over extradomestic distribution networks. They show that women's continued relegation to the domestic, "natural" sphere, as an extension of their mothering functions, has ensured that they remain less social, less cultural, and also less powerful than men.

Thus the social organization of parenting produces sexual inequality, not simply role differentiation. It is politically and socially important to confront this organization of parenting. Even though it is an arrangement that seems universal, directly rooted in biology, and inevitable, it can be changed. The possibility of change is indicated not only by a theoretical critique of biological determinism, but by the contradictory aspects of the present organization of parenting. Even as the present forms reproduce mothering, they help to produce a widespread dissatisfaction with their own limitations among women (and sometimes men).

If our goal is to overcome the sexual division of labor in which women mother, we need to understand the mechanisms which reproduce it in the first place. My account points precisely to where intervention should take place. Any strategy for change whose goal includes liberation from the constraints of an unequal social organization of gender must take account of the need for a fundamental reorganization of parenting, so that primary parenting is shared between men and women.

*   *   *

Some friends and colleagues have said that my account is too unqualified. In fact, *all* women *do not* mother or want to mother, and *all* women are not "maternal" or nurturant. *Some* women are far more nurturant than others, and want children far more. Some *men* are more nurturant than some women. I agree that all claims about gender differences gloss over important differences within genders and similarities between genders. I hope that this book leads people to raise questions about such variations, and to engage in the research that will begin to answer them.

Still, I believe that the intergender differences are socially and politically most significant. It is important to explore intragender differences and intergender similarities in order to argue against views of natural or biological gender differences, but it is crucial to take full account of structural and statistical truths about male-female differences. What is important is not to confuse these truths with prescription.

Some have suggested that I imply that there has been no change in the organization of parenting—that my account is "ahistorical." This criticism strikes at the heart of a problem. The sex-gender system is continually changing, as it responds to and affects other aspects of social and economic organization. Yet it stays the same in fundamental ways. It does not help us to deny the social and psychological rootedness of women's mothering nor the extent to which we participate, often in spite of our conscious intentions, in contemporary sex-gender arrangements. We know almost nothing about historical changes in parenting practices, and little about differences within contemporary society either—about the effects of class differences and of whether a mother works in the paid labor force or not. We know little about the effects of variations in family structure, such as whether a single mother lives with small children or with older ones as well, or if children grow up in a large or small household. We certainly need to know more about the effects of these differences and about historical changes in parenting.

Nor can we assume that the processes I discuss are unchanging. My account relies on psychoanalytic findings that, if we start from the childhood of Freud's first patients, span at least the past hundred years. But even during this period, parenting practices and the organization of parenting have changed. In the past hundred years there have been enormous changes in the availability of contraception and a growth of smaller, more isolated families. Child-rearing activities have become more and more isolated as well. Women spend much less of their lives bearing and rearing children. In the last twenty years, women with children have entered the paid labor force in great numbers, so that, as of 1974, about 46 percent of mothers with children under eighteen were in the labor force—over half of the mothers with school-age children and over a third of those with children under six. These changes have doubtless affected mother-child relationships and the content of mothering, but we do not know how. We do not know when cumulative slight shifts in parenting practices become qualitative, and indicate that we are no longer talking about the same system.

At the same time, women continue to be primary parents, both within the family and in alternate child-care settings. Even when we look at contemporary societies where nonfamilial child care is widespread—Israel, China, the Soviet Union, Cuba—women still perform this care.

My account does not concern the reproduction of mothering for all time. But it is probable that the issues I discuss are relevant in all societies. Many factors have gone into the reproduction of mothering in different societies and different historical periods. The factors I discuss are central to the reproduction of mothering today. If they were less significant in other times and places, this does not take away from my conclusions but points to more we need to know.

Those who suggest that my view does not allow for change often also suggest that I am pessimistic and make the current situation seem inevitable. A seeming inevitability comes first from language which refers to primary parenting activities as "mothering." It is hard for us to separate women from the parenting functions they perform, and to separate the care children need from the question of who performs it. We can and should separate these things, however.

My account also seems to make the processes it explains appear inevitable because I, like others who rely on psychoanalytic modes of explanation, describe things which happen to people by the time they are five. Psychoanalysis does show that we are formed in crucial ways by the time we are five, but it allows for change, either from life experiences or through the analytic process itself. In fact, psychoanalysis was developed not only to explain our early psychic formation but to show us how to overcome its limitations. Psychoanalysis, moreover, argues against a unilateral model of social determination, and for the variation and creativity in what people make of their early childhood experiences and their later experiences as well. In the present case, I show how parenting qualities are created in women through specific social and psychological processes. By implication, I show how these qualities could be created in men, if men and women parented equally.

We can draw on recent psychological theory and research to demonstrate the possibility of change. The earliest psychoanalytic theory stressed the importance of the biological feeding relationship in personality formation. Much recent theory, by contrast, suggests that infants require the whole parenting relationship of warmth, contact, and reliable care, and not the specific feeding relationship itself. This theory has been used to keep mothers in the home, now that biological imperatives are less persuasive. But it also indicates that people other than biological mothers can provide adequate care. Similarly, traditional child development theory has often held that children need parenting from one person only. But recent research suggests that children need consistency of care and the ability to relate to a small number of people stably over time. They do not require an exclusive relationship to one person. Historically, children have rarely been cared for exclusively by a biological mother, and recent studies of day care suggest that what is important is the quality of the day care and of the time spent with parents.

It is true that children grow up differently without exclusive mothering, but not necessarily in ways that are undesirable. Studies of more collective childrearing situations (the kibbutzim, China, Cuba) suggest that children develop more sense of solidarity and commitment to the group, less individualism and competitiveness, are less liable to form intense, exclusive adult relationships, than children reared in Western nuclear families. My view is that exclusive single parenting is bad for mother and child alike. As I point out earlier, mothers in such a setting are liable to overinvest in and overwhelm the relationship. Similarly, I think, children are better off in situations where love and relationship are not a scarce resource controlled and manipulated by one person only.

The current organization of parenting separates children and men. Most commentators claim that children should spend some time with men, but most are hesitant to suggest that this time should be of equivalent emotional quality to time spent with women. Because they are concerned with children's adoption of appropriate gender roles, they assume a different role for the father. Fathers must be primarily masculine role models for boys, and heterosexual objects for girls, because traditional gender roles and heterosexual orientation are necessary and desirable. These roles have been functional, but for a sex-gender system founded on sexual inequality, and not for social survival or free human activity. Fathers are supposed to help children to individuate and break their dependence on their mothers. But this dependence on her, and this primary identification, would not be created in the first place if men took primary parenting responsibilities.

Children could be dependent from the outset on people of both genders and establish an individuated sense of self in relation to both. In this way, masculinity would not become tied to denial of dependence and devaluation of women. Feminine personality would be less preoccupied with individuation, and children would not develop fears of *maternal* omnipotence and expectations of *women's* unique self-sacrificing qualities. This would reduce men's needs to guard their masculinity and their control of social and cultural spheres which treat and define women as secondary and powerless, and would help women to develop the autonomy which too much embeddedness in relationship has often taken from them.

Equal parenting would not threaten anyone's primary sense of gendered self (nor do we know what this self would look like in a nonsexist society). As Stoller has pointed out, men's primary sense of gendered self may be threatened with things as they are anyway. But this sense of self does not best come from role adoption. When it does, it is reactive and defensive rather than secure and flexible. Personal connection to and identification with both parents would enable a person to choose those activities she or he desired, without feeling that such choices jeopardized their gender identity.

My expectation is that equal parenting would leave people of both genders with the positive capacities each has, but without the destructive extremes these currently tend toward. Anyone who has good primary relationships has the foundation for nurturance and love, and women would retain these even as men would gain them. Men would be able to retain the autonomy which comes from differentiation without that differentiation being rigid and reactive, and women would have more opportunity to gain it. People's sexual choices might become more flexible, less desperate.

I would like to think we could simply initiate these transformations on a society-wide scale. However, women's mothering is tied to many other aspects of our society, is fundamental to our ideology of gender, and benefits many people. It is a major feature of the sex-gender system. It creates heterosexual asymmetries which reproduce the family and marriage, but leave women with needs that lead them to care for children, and men with capacities for participation in the alienated work world. It creates a psychology of male dominance and fear of women in men. It forms a basis for the division of the social world into unequally valued domestic and public spheres, each the province of people of a different gender.

Women's mothering is also a crucial link between the contemporary organization of gender and organization of production. It produces men with personality characteristics and psychic structure appropriate to participation in the capitalist work world. An ideology of women as mothers extends to women's responsibilities as maternal wives for emotional reconstitution and support of their working husbands. Assumptions that the social organization of parenting is natural and proper (that women's child *care* is indistinguishable from their child*bearing,* that women are for biological reasons better parents than men, moral arguments that women ought to mother) have continued to serve as grounds for arguments against most changes in the social organization of gender. Certainly resistance to changes in the sex-gender system is often strongest around women's maternal functions.

We live in a period when the demands of the roles defined by the sex-gender system have created widespread discomfort and resistance. Aspects of this system are in crisis internally and conflict with economic tendencies. Change will certainly occur, but the outcome is far from certain. The elimination of the present organization of parenting in favor of a system of parenting in which both men and women are responsible would be a tremendous social advance. This outcome is historically possible, but far from inevitable. Such advances do not occur simply because they are better for "society," and certainly not simply because they are better for some (usually less powerful) people. They depend on the conscious organization and activity of all women and men who recognize that their interests lie in transforming the social organization of gender and eliminating sexual inequality.

PATRICIA BERRY

What's the Matter with Mother?

If there is any concept that we in psychology have overused, it is that of the mother. And we have blamed her extensively. At one time or another, in one way or another, we have used her to explain each of our pathological syndromes: our schizophrenia as a double-binding by her; paranoia, an inability to trust because of her (a need to tie our thoughts into rigid systems, in compensation for her lack of order); hysteria, a tendency to over-sensitize without feeling, because of the wandering womb (*her* womb) in our bodies.

In light of the frequency of these explanations, I began to ask myself—so what's the matter with mother? What's the matter that makes her so useful particularly in psychology's explanations?

In order to explore this question, let us begin by turning it slightly to what mother's matter is—what the content of mother is. And let us focus on the Great Mother of our Western mythological tradition, as described by Hesiod in his *Theogony.* In the *Theogony* Hesiod honors the Great Mother Gaia, Earth, as the original divinity and progenitor of all the other divinities—all those many forms of our psychic possibilities, forms of psychic awareness. For all these, Gaia lays the original ground.

According to Hesiod, first there was Chaos, a formlessness, a nothingness. Then there was Gaia, Earth: the first form, the first principle, a something, a given.

But inasmuch as Creation takes place continuously—every day our psychic experience is created, our emotions and moods are given form—rather than tell Hesiod's creation tale in the past tense, we might more accurately tell it in the present: first there *is* Chaos, and then there is Mother Earth. Within our experiences of chaos, at the same moment there is contained a specific possibility of form. Or, each chaos mothers itself into form.

Now this view of chaos is different from our traditional linear notions, in which form is imposed later upon chaos from without or down from above, conquering and replacing the chaos.

To view this tale, however, as I am attempting, would be to see it as an image—i.e., more as a picture than as a narrative—so that the facets of the event (the chaos and forms or earth) are given all at once. Some interesting things turn up in this image picture that don't show up in sequential narrative. For example, this way of looking sees chaos and the forms as co-present: within chaos there are inherent forms. Each moment of chaos has shapes within it, and each form or shape embodies a specific chaos.

Of course, this way of looking at things also has implications therapeutically. For example, here it implies that one must not rid oneself too quickly of chaotic feelings (by abreacting or primal screaming them), because then one would also lose the forms. Better would be to contain, and even to nurture, the chaos so that its shapes may exist as well. (The image further suggests that our forms cannot rid us of chaos, for where the forms are is also where chaos is.)

I can support what I have just said with matter. For mother, this mothering ground of our lives, is connected with the word "matter." Mother and matter *(mater)* are cognates. And matter has been viewed in two ways—almost as though there were basically two sorts, or levels, of matter.

One level is considered as a universal substrate. And as such it exists only in abstraction. In itself, this matter is unknowable, invisible, and incorporeal. Matter in this sense is itself a kind of chaos or, as Augustine describes it, an absence of light, a deprivation of being.[1] So this view of matter holds it to be nothingness, a negativity, a lacking. Now the second view builds upon this first view.

The second sort of matter is not only the most nothing, but in addition the most something—the most concrete, tangible, visible, bodily. Augustine calls this matter "the earth as we know it" and contrasts the heaven, which is nearest to God, with this earth that though most concrete is nevertheless nearest to nothing.[2]

There is within the idea of matter a paradox. Matter (and by extension mother earth) is both the most something *and* the most nothing, the most necessary (in order that something can happen) and at the same time the most lacking. With this combination of qualities, matter and mother have of course had a rather hard time of it in our Western spiritual tradition. Mother/matter is the ground of existence and yet doesn't count—she is nothing. Archetypally, she is our earth and at the same time is always lacking.[3]

When we get close to our "matter," our lower substrates, our roots, our past, the ground from which we came, our lower physical nature, our cruder emotions, it is not surprising that we feel something unsettling, something inferior, chaotic, soiled perhaps. But these feelings are given with the very nature of mother's matter.

Let me tell you of an experience Hesiod had. In the beginning of the *Theogony*, Hesiod tells of his conversion to poet, to a man who praised the Gods. As he tells it, he was out tending his flocks when suddenly the Muses appeared and berated him for his lowly state. They evoked in him a sense of shame for being only a man of the earth. Hesiod became then a poet who praised the Muses, but he never gave up being a man of the earth (a farmer) nor the earth as his subject. He became instead a more complicated farmer, one who now sang the praises of an earth that felt to him shameful.

Now this would seem peculiar: that a man who was shamed, who was called a fool for being merely of the earth, would turn now to praise this very earth for which he felt shame. Or is it that the experience of shame is connected with the experience of earth, and perhaps shame is a way that may even lead one to the experience of earth?

Shame is a deep bodily reaction that cannot be controlled (at least very effectively) by the mind. And so shame points to something beyond the will—something of power beyond the human, which we might call the divine. Hesiod was led to experience the earth as a psychic earth that though shamefully of himself was yet, because of his very shame, more than himself. Within this psychic movement, earth became a divinity. No longer a mere flat expanse on which to pasture his sheep, as a Goddess she became an earth of many levels upon which his soul (his Muses) pastured as well. For Hesiod she was no longer "nothing-but" a physical ground, a neutral ground without quality; because she was experienced as a divinity she was experienced psychically, so that her matter mattered to and in the psyche.

Had it not been the experience of earth that the Muses wished to evoke in Hesiod, they might have approached him in another way. They could have brought about his conversion through a visionary experience of great beauty in the distance; they could have asked him in an uplifting moment to lay down his staff and follow them, or whatever. But what was given was the experience of earth—for Hesiod was to be a poet of the earth, and from this earth the entire *Theogony,* in praise of all the Gods and Goddesses, was to be sung.

Let me read you a Navajo chant that expresses something of the connection between shame and earth. It goes:

> I am ashamed before earth;
> I am ashamed before heavens;
> I am ashamed before dawn;
> I am ashamed before evening twilight;
> I am ashamed before blue sky;
> I am ashamed before darkness;
> I am ashamed before sun;
> I am ashamed before that standing within me which speaks with me.
> Some of these things are always looking at me.
> I am never out of sight.
> Therefore I must tell the truth.
> I hold my word tight to my breast.[4]

"I am ashamed"—who has not had that feeling when faced with the wonder of earth? But this sense of shame occurs too when other aspects of 'earthy' feeling appear. This happens in analysis when the 'chthonic' is constellated: the bug-eyed, toady, twisted, grotesque, slimy, or hulking creatures that bring us startling recognition of ugliness and deformity. Strange that we should feel these creatures as *de*formed, arising as they do from such natural, earthy levels of the psyche.

We generally try to repress these creatures. If that doesn't work we try second best: to rush them through their transformations as quickly as possible. With a kind of desperation we paint, model, and carry on active imaginations. The principal difficulty is that—in the hurry—we may lose the experience. Because these shameful creatures of the earth carry the experience of earth, we lose something of the very earth we are seeking when we transform them too smoothly. It is a funny psychological fact that being soiled is intimately connected with the experience and benefits of soil.

Fortunately for our mythological tradition, Hesiod's shame connects him to this earthy sustenance and generativity, so that out of her—out of Gaia—proceeds his *Theogony.* Out of her comes the starry sky, the mountains, the depths, the sea.

Strangely enough, all of those so-called masculine regions (starry sky; mountains– Olympos; depths–Hades; sea–Okeanos, Poseidon) have come out of her and are part of her basic matrix. Moreover she creates her own mate, Uranos. As this Uranos sky is a phallic force proceeding out of earth, we can see it as earth's original hermaphroditism. Within the feminine as void, within her as passive, lies a sky-like potentiality. Hence to get in touch with earth is also to connect with a sky that proceeds from earth, and the seeds that drop create a kind of original self-fertilization. Not one without problems. But for the moment it is enough to note that sky, mountains, depths, and generations all have their beginnings in primal earth.

In early worship black animals were sacrificed to Gaia Earth.[5] Let us speak for a moment about sacrifice. The very word *sacrifice* means "to make sacred." Thus it is the "black" that is sacred to Gaia and may help keep her sacred. Black: the dark, the depressed, grieving over losses, the inexplicable, the shadowy, the sinful (we might now say).

We now have another hint as to how we may get in touch with Gaia Earth, i.e., through feelings of depression, black moods, losses, and lostness. As shame is a way into the experience of mother earth, a related way is the feeling of one's darkest nature and hopelessness—limitations that do not change, complexes that have marked one's personality and will always be as they are, since they are the *ground* of personality, unique and individual. To attempt to lighten these experiences, to get away from these complexes, or to whitewash them with explanations, to rationalize them, would then also be to lose one's possibilities for psychic body, for earth. These limitations in fact *are* psychic earth.

Depth psychology serves this ground of the mother in many ways. One is by giving support to the human sense of shame and infirmity, the incomprehensible, the rejected. Psychology not only draws support from the mother's dark depths but in turn worships these depths by creating of them a theogony of phenomenological descriptions, systems, and pathological classifications, much as Hesiod created his theogony.

And this sense we have of something as pathological cannot be explained away as only due to society, or only because of our parents or the faulty interaction in our families. An idea of pathology, of something amiss, exists in every society. So it would seem to be an archetypal, primary experience. Though of course the designation of *what* is pathological may vary, nevertheless the archetypal fact of it remains constant, through the ages and from culture to culture.

By deepening the experience of pathology, we may deepen our recognition of the

Mother, the Earth. By this I do not mean experiencing pathology in projection, as something out there. If pathology is archetypal, then by definition we must experience it in ourselves, much as we would any other archetypal quality—anima, animus, child. . . . As meanings they begin in ourselves.

Another of the qualities of mother Gaia is that of immovability. Gaia made things stick. She was the goddess of marriage.[6] One swore oaths by her and they were binding.[7] Mother/matter as the inert becomes now mother as the settler, the stabilizer, the binder.

In psychotherapy we still can find this idea of Earth, earth as that which will settle down a youth who is too high-flying, or a woman who doesn't take responsibility for her home, or a man who is too intellectual. What these people need is earth, we say. The young man we may send off to work on a farm for the summer or urge him to marry. The housewife we may tell to pay more attention to her homelike activities, to put up her own preserves, or work in the garden, or take up knitting. The intellectual we tell to get down to the practical and live life, even at the expense of his 'bright ideas' and fantasies.

What we are attempting to cultivate in the psyche of all these people is some ground in which things "matter," happen, become substantial—something into which their life experiences may etch. We are trying to develop the mother within them, their prima materia, into a supporting matrix, some basic substrate in which psychic movements may take form and gather body.

The curious thing is how literal these therapeutic prescriptions for earth become. The analysand must actually, literally, do some concrete activity that everybody would agree is "earthy." And yet we all know that when people are even physically involved with the earth, they haven't necessarily what we mean by psychic earth. A person can grow his own grains and at the same time spin in a mental and emotional space with very little psychic grounding. So it isn't really just physical earth that connects us to the divinity of Mother Gaia, but psychic earth, earth that has become ensouled with divinity, psychically complicated and, like Hesiod's, touched by the metaphorical Muses of soul.

But there is this apparent difficulty in speaking of any kind of earth, because something about the nature of earth makes us take it more literally than we take the other elements. If a person lacked air, we would never send him off to learn to fly an airplane.[8] Or if a person's dreams showed that he lacked water, fluidity, we would hardly send him off to learn actually to swim. But when a person is lacking in earth, we tend to prescribe something rather obviously connected with the earth, like taking a cottage in the country, making a garden, or chopping firewood. . . .

Don't get me wrong. I'm not saying that the Muses of metaphor cannot appear in these activities. I'm only saying that they needn't necessarily. The more we insist on enjoining these quite literal earthy activities, the more we may be blocking the appearance of the Muses and a genuine metaphorical earth arising from within the person, where it makes matter (substance, containment) psychologically.

Depth psychology would seem a discipline in which this reworked and more metaphorical sense of earth is quite pronounced. It is a field in which we work a good deal for the benefit of, and in keeping with, the metaphorical ladies of soul. And yet even we find ourselves caught in the trap of earth literalisms. Perhaps it appears in the feeling that our particular orientation is *the* way—and certainly it begins with our persuasion as to what is most 'real.' For what's 'grounded' and what's 'real' tend to be habitually interrelated.

In Jungian psychology some of us see as most real our personal mother, our childhood, the breasts we actually nursed from as infants. Others of us see what is empirical as most real—those grounds that can be measured and tested. Still others see the social as most real, and so we strive for 'genuine' personal interaction and require group therapy. Others may see synchronistic events as most real.

But whatever we take as most real (and partly dependent as Jungians upon whether we inhabit the earth of London, San Francisco, New York, or Zürich) is what we are using as our mothering ground. And this grounding is extremely important: it is that which gives our thoughts fertility and substance, our therapies, body and results. It is what nourishes our psychological endeavors and makes them matter.

Yet we must not forget the other side of mother's nature (her archetypal being as lack, absence, deprivation). So however hard we work at grounding, each in his own way, we never feel this grounding complete. Always hidden in the very ground we are working is a gnawing sense of lack.

In other words, what we assume as most real, as our mother, is at the same time that which gives us a feeling of unsureness. And so we compensate this unsureness with insistence. We insist that one *must* go back and re-experience childhood, relive the good and bad breast dilemma, for this would give the grounding and the body that is needed. Or we say, if Jungian psychology is not to be lacking, it must be tested and proven to the world. Or, enough of all this flying around in the air talking about synchronicities, we must get down to where people really live with others, in personal emotions and real-life entanglements.

When one orientation fights another, the dispute is fairly serious, for each of us is defending the incompleteness we depend upon as our mother—the ground that has given, and is giving, our activities sustenance. But because we fear her nature as lack, we strive for more support by substantiating her ever more surely. As a solar hero, one fights for the death of the mother's ambiguity by fighting to the death for this increased grounding and substantiation of the mother. Thus identified, one casts aside other, less heroic, modes that would allow the incompleteness of mothering ground to connect with the Muses of metaphor, for whom lacking ground is fertile ground indeed. Metaphor depends upon this sense of lack, this sense of the "is not" with every "is."[9]

We must ask how it is that this literalizing tends to occur with earth. One explanation lies within the myth. We have mentioned how Gaia created out of herself not only the world but even her own spouse, Uranos. Every night Uranos, the sky, spread himself down over Gaia in mating. But the children thereby engendered he kept imprisoned in the earth, which gave Gaia, earth, great pain, the more so with each additional child, so that by the time the twelfth child arrived (twelve being the completion of a cycle), she plotted an end to this ever-increasing burden. And so she crafted a sickle to castrate Uranos.

This motif of the child trapped in the earth suggests a way of looking at the problem of literalization. A child, a new possibility, is born but then this child is trapped in matter. It is imprisoned in the earth (making this earth only physical, only literal matter). So the spirit of the new offspring, or the psyche or soul of it, is buried in an earth that is merely material. Interestingly enough, according to the tale, this materialism gives the mother Gaia herself great pain. She is burdened with each successive offspring buried within her. She is forced to carry what has been projected into her (as literal plans, goals, whatever), thereby losing her more metaphorical possibilities, that part of herself that is insubstantial.

In the myth the mother eases her burden by turning her destructive potential against this concretism. We might call her in this role the negative mother. She plots castration and devises the means for it. The sickle she invents, however, is fashioned of iron, that metal so important to the building of civilization. So her destructive act is not without benefit and expresses her pain over the way she as earth is being used.

It could be that when we put too many of our children, our possibilities, into concrete explanations and literal programs, burying their meanings for the soul by living them materially, we are not at all propitiating the mother. We are offending her and causing her great pain. We might, therefore, re-examine some of the negative mother phenomena that appear in dreams and fantasies to see if the negative mother, the castrating mother, isn't attempting (with her belittlement of us, the insecurity and inadequacy she makes us feel) to relieve herself of the concrete demand, the materialistic burden we have placed upon her. What we experience as 'castration' of our powers in the world might be that which can move us into a more psychic view of matter. In a curious sense, the effect of the mother's negativity may be to return us to soul. By destroying the superficial surface of that earth upon which we stand, our literal projections into and upon earth (achieving more and more, establishing ever more solidly—our materialism), perhaps she is giving opportunity for a deeper ground, a psychic earth beneath the level of appearance and in touch with the Muses.

Now let us look at the children trapped in the earth in another way. Let us see them as the children 'in us' who wish to remain as children buried within the mother, within the concrete. There seem several ways we could do this.

One way would be to identify with the child and then project a goodness, an all-embracing lovingness upon mother nature. Then because mother nature is all good, I-the-child am also good, innocent, helpless, without shadow and indeed without much body. I feel no shame—there *is* no such thing as shame—I am innocent. This state might resemble Hesiod's state before the Muses, and before he was called upon through his experience of awkwardness, separation, and shamefulness to worship the mother. Insofar as a child feels no shame, he is also unable to worship.

Another possibility would be for the child to reinforce his state as child by seeing the mother as all bad. This would be the nihilist perspective and just the converse of seeing the mother as all good. It too would deny the mother's possibilities as psychic, complex, worked earth. This child, scarred by the world's harshness, remains forever the unloved child, but nevertheless still the child.

Another way in which to remain as children buried in the earth is by dividing experience of the mother into two separate mothers: good mother/bad mother, good breast/bad breast. Although the opposing aspects of the mother are expressed, they have been separated and literalized, seen as nothing-but good here and bad there. And because they are literalized, they tend to be projected into the world as realities out there. This substantiation and projection give them extraordinary power so that I-as-child find myself overwhelmed. Unable to cope in a world so loaded with goods and bads, rights and wrongs, the child languishes ineffectually. Because the world is so important, the child becomes unable; the world's ambiguity becomes the child's ambivalence.

Most often, however, our child abandons his pattern at this point and moves into the neighboring one of hero. Then the darker attributes of the mother appear as the dragon to be heroically slain. Child-turned-hero now girds himself and charges off to do (what turns out to be a rather continuous) battle with the dark mother now become monster.

When heroically opposed, the mother turns monster. The religious sense of her is lost. Her nature as non-being, absence, lack is no longer part of her mystery—that which makes her greater than our own narrow senses of life and achievement. Rather she becomes a contrary force to rule over and conquer. Her earth becomes replaced by our ego-centricity, our illusions of competence, self-sufficiency, ego capability. We deny the earth's divinity and exchange her ground with its complexities, its twisted chthonic creatures, and shame for our goal-directed, clean, ever self-bettering fantasies of goodness, health, and achievement.

The nature of the hero is to take literally the mother's negativity. Her nature as lack, non-being, becomes a real something, an enemy to be fought; her femininity and passivity become a succubus to that heroic life fixed upon progressive achievement. The result is a heroic over-achievement and over-production, which must be countered by equally literal prophecies of doom and destruction. The mother as lack, as negative, returns in prophecies of ultimate, literal catastrophe. Because the earth is taken so literally, its negative reappears in the forebodings of an equally literal destruction.

The hero's mother complex is characterized by his struggles to be up and out, and above her. And because of his heroic labors to free himself from her, it is he who is most surely bound to her. Better service to the earth mother might be to assist her movement down to the deepest regions of her depths. For the mother's depths are the underworld. Gaia's original realm included both the upper realm of growth, nurturance, and life and the underworld realm of death, limitation, and ending.

We must describe a bit of this underworld to appreciate how astounding it is that this realm was once part of our mother's earth.

The underworld was a pneumatic, airy realm. The beings there, called shades *(skiai)* or images *(eidola)*, were insubstantial like the wind.[10] It is a realm in which objects cannot be grasped naturally, i.e., taken literally, but only felt in their emotional essence. Ulysses, for example, in his visit to the underworld, yearns for his mother, but when he attempts physically to embrace her finds she is only an immaterial shade. It is a realm of the non-concrete, the intangible.

And yet an essence of personality is preserved. Cerberus is said to strip away the flesh of persons who enter, leaving only their skeletal structures, those essential forms on which the flesh of each life has been modeled. This sense of essence is also shown by the repetitions that some shades enact (Ixion on his wheel, Sisyphus and his stone, Tantalos and his everlasting hunger and thirst). These repetitions may be viewed symbolically as the characteristic pattern of each individual personality.

The underworld is colorless.[11] Even the shade of black does not appear except in the upperworld sacrifices to it,[12] hence we emphasize the experience of blackness in connection with Gaia, for black is our upperworld experience of the underworld, our way into it. But once there, one is, so to speak, deeper than one's emotion. One is beneath the depression, the black mood, by having gone down through it to the point where it no longer is. When we no longer cling to the light, blackness loses its darkness.

In the underworld one is among the essences, the invisible aspects of the upperworld. The word "Hades" means the invisible or the "invisibility-giving."[13] It is that realm deep beneath the concrete world and yet somehow within it, in the same way that the seed is within the full-grown plant and yet is its inherent limitation, its structure, its telos.

But there came to be a split between the upperworld aspect of Gaia's earth and its underworld aspect. Her upper realm became Ge-Demeter while the under realm became Ge-chthonia and relegated to Persephone.[14] The upperworld became a Demeter realm of concrete, daily life, devoid of the spiritual values, the sense of essence and the dark (and beneath the dark) carried by her underworld daughter, Persephone. For reunion with this underworld daughter, Demeter suffers inconsolably. And we without a religious sense that includes and connects us with the earth's depths and essential insubstantiality suffer as well.

In our efforts to establish a solid 'real' world and make the mother carry our concreteness, we have lost an aspect of her grounding—a grounding that has not so much to do with growth in any of the more concrete senses of upperworld development. More psychologically futile is our invisible mother in the underworld: the Persephone who rules over the soul in its essential, limiting, and immaterial patterns; and that original mother of all—Gaia—she who is Earth, and yet without contradiction, that deeper ground of support beneath the earth's physical appearance, the non-being beneath and within being. Our fruitfulness—our fecundity, our sense of what 'matters'—has its roots in our very unsureness, in our sense of lack.

Notes

1. Augustine, *Confessions*, XII, 3.

2. Ibid., XII, 7.

3. It is interesting to note in this regard that Theophrastus describes green, the color of nature, as "composed of both the solid and the void. . . ." Cf. G. M. Stratton, "Theophrastus on the Senses," in *Theophrastus* (Amsterdam: E. J. Bonset, 1964), p. 135.

4. Told by Torlino, trans. Washington Matthews, 1894.

5. L. R. Farnell, *The Cults of the Greek States*, III (Oxford: Clarendon Press, 1907), p. 2. This sacrifice of the black animal (in Gaia's case the ewe) was typical for Hades and other Gods in their chthonic, underworld forms. So we must realize that Earth Gaia is as much at home with the dead and the underworld as she is with the seemingly more life-sustaining activities of agriculture and vegetation. For her there is no real contradiction between life and death, daily world and underworld.

6. Farnell, p. 15; cf. also W. Fowler, *The Religious Experience of the Roman People* (London: Macmillan, 1933), p. 121.

7. Farnell, p. 2.

8. From James Hillman, *The Dream and the Underworld* (New York: Harper & Row, 1979), p. 77.

9. As pointed out by Robert Romanyshyn, Conference for Archetypal Psychology, University of Dallas, 1977.

10. F. Cumont, *After Life in Roman Paganism* (New York: Dover Press, 1922), p. 166.

11. C. Kerényi, *The Gods of the Greeks* (London: Thames & Hudson, 1961), p. 247.

12. Cumont, p. 166.

13. Kerényi, p. 230. Cf. also H. J. Rose, *A Handbook of Greek Mythology* (London: Methuen, 1965), p. 78, where he suggests that the name Hades may also be derived phonetically from "the Unseen."

14. Whereas Demeter, like Gaia, appeared imagistically as the ripened or ripening corn, she never appeared in connection with the seed in the ground or with underworld figures as did Gaia; cf. Fowler, p. 121. This absence of Demeter's underworld aspect makes an underworld Persephone "necessary."

JANE GALLOP

Reading the Mother Tongue: Psychoanalytic Feminist Criticism

In the early seventies, American feminist literary criticism had little patience for psychoanalytic interpretation, dismissing it along with other forms of what Mary Ellmann called "phallic criticism."[1] Not that psychoanalytic literary criticism was a specific target of feminist critics, but Freud and his science were viewed by feminism in general as prime perpetrators of patriarchy. If we take Kate Millett's *Sexual Politics*[2] as the first book of modern feminist criticism, let us remark that she devotes ample space and energy to attacking Freud, not of course as the forerunner of any school of literary criticism, but as a master discourse of our, which is to say masculinist, culture. But, although Freud may generally have been a target for feminism, feminist literary critics of the early seventies expended more of their energy in the attack on New Criticism. The era was, after all, hardly a heyday for American psychoanalytic criticism; formalist modes of reading enjoyed a hegemony in the literary academy in contrast with which psychoanalytic interpretation was a rather weak arm of patriarchy.

Since then, there have been two changes in this picture. In the last decade, psychoanalytic criticism has grown in prestige and influence, and a phenomenon we can call psychoanalytic feminist criticism has arisen.[3] I would venture that two major factors have contributed to this boom in American psychoanalytic criticism. First, the rise of feminist criticism, in its revolt against formalism, has rehabilitated thematic and psychological criticism, the traditional mainstays of psychoanalytic interpretation. Because feminism has assured the link between psychosexuality and the sociohistorical realm, psychoanalysis is now linked to major political and cultural questions. Glistening on the horizon of sociopolitical connection, feminism promises to save psychoanalysis from its ahistorical and apolitical doldrums.

The second factor that makes psychoanalytic reading a growth industry in the United States is certainly more widely recognized: it is the impact of French post-structuralist thought on the American literary academy. There is, of course, the direct influence of Lacanian psychoanalysis which promotes language to a principal role in the psychoanalytic drama and so naturally offers fertile ground for crossing psychoanalytic and literary concerns. Yet I think, in fact, the wider effect in this country has come from Derridean deconstruction. Although deconstruction is not strictly psychoanalytic, Freud's prominent place in Derridean associative networks promises a criticism that is, finally, respectably textual and still, in some recognizable way, Freudian. Although this second, foreign factor in the growth of American psychoanalytic criticism seems far away from the realm of homespun feminist criticism, I would contend that there is a powerful if indirect connection between the two. I would speculate that the phenomenal spread of deconstruction in American departments of English is in actuality a response to the growth of feminist criticism. At a moment when it was no longer possible to ignore feminist criticism's challenge to the critical establishment, deconstruction appeared offering a perspective that was not in opposition to but rather beyond feminism, offering to sublate feminism into something supposedly "more radical."

Thus, feminist criticism has, both directly and indirectly, given new viability to psychoanalytic criticism. Central to this viability has been the burgeoning new field of psychoanalytic feminist criticism. Again, I see two major factors accounting for this growth. One is actually another effect of French post-structuralism—likewise stemming from Lacan and Derrida but, significantly, passing through those women thinkers we Americans have come to call the "French feminists."[4] Through writers like Luce Irigaray, Hélène Cixous, and Julia Kristeva, we have seen a way of thinking that appears to be at once feminist and psychoanalytic, and also highly literary. The second factor has been the enormous impact made by Nancy Chodorow's study of mothering.[5] Chodorow has taken an object-relations view centered on the pre-Oedipal relation to the early mother and set it in a feminist framework cognizant of the sociohistorical determinants of the institution of mothering. This particular mix of mother-centered psychoanalysis and American social scientific feminism has proven especially suggestive for feminist literary critics.

Psychoanalytic feminist criticsm thus provides the vehicle which allows two heretofore unlikely couples to meet. In this vehicle, we not only find feminism joining hands with psychoanalysis but, behind that more obvious couple in what constitutes a theoretical double date, we might possibly glimpse the coming together of post-structuralism and American feminist social science, a pair that has rarely been known to speak.

A historic year for American psychoanalytic criticism, 1985 saw the appearance of a major monument in the field: the first anthology of psychoanalytic feminist criticism, *The (M)other Tongue,* edited by Shirley Nelson Garner, Claire Kahane, and Madelon Sprengnether.[6] The coupling of psychoanalysis and feminism is clearly conducive to good reading, writing, and thinking. The anthology is excellent: a collection of first-rate pieces of feminist interpretation. As an attempt to survey this field, I would like to do a reading of this monument, at the very least of the inscription on its face.

The heroine in this book is surely the mother. The story progresses from "father-based" Oedipal structures to "mother-based" pre-Oedipal models and finally to an insistence that even in pre-Oedipal theories we attend not only to the child but to the mother.[7] At the beginning of the book, in a critical survey of Freud's Oedipal scripts for girls, the mother is silent, ignored, invisible; by the end, in Susan Suleiman's strong statement, the mother is coming into her own, coming to writing. Our heroine would seem to be the ideal figure to bless the marriage of psychoanalysis and feminism. A powerful figure in familiosexual configurations of subjectivity, the mother is, of course, also a woman.

When I read this paper aloud, I said that the title of the anthology was "The Mother Tongue," but that in fact was *telling* not *reading* the title, for the title is, above all, a piece of writing not easily transcribed into oral language. Since the second word is actually written "(M)other," the title is both "The Mother Tongue" and "The Other Tongue," or perhaps not quite both but neither. Not quite the mother tongue nor quite the other tongue. The title itself is no longer quite in *our* mother tongue (plain English), although it is not in any other. It brings out the other in the mother.

The play on mother and other reminds us that in psychoanalytic theory the mother is the subject's first other, the other in opposition to which the self constitutes itself. Or rather, as becomes clear in object-relations theory and particularly in Chodorow, the mother is the site of something which is both other and not quite other, of the other as self and the self as other.[8] Thus the monstrous word— "Mother-other"—in its fluid, double identity could be said to body forth the borderline status of the powerful, early mother, so central to psychoanalytic feminist theory.

Yet the title of the book is not "The (M)other" but "The (M)other Tongue." The book would appear to be not just about Mother but about language. The title phrase is nowhere glossed, or even used in the book, at least not with the *M* in parentheses. But we do find the simpler phrase, "The Mother Tongue" (without parentheses). In fact, the editors' introduction concludes on that more familiar phrase: "Feminists working from a number of critical approaches are concluding that it is time to learn, to begin to speak our mother tongue" (p. 29).

Although not marked or marred in any way by unseemly, unpronounceable punctuation, the phrase "mother tongue" in this sentence clearly does not mean what it usually means in *our* mother tongue, in the idiomatic English we know so well. If it is only now time "to learn, to *begin* to speak" this language, then this is not what we usually refer to as our native language. It may look familiar on the page, but this is not the same old mother tongue, but precisely an other mother tongue.

However "other" we can imagine this tongue to be, in this unmarked version it still looks like the idiomatic phrase. No mark forces the reader to see the otherness in this "mother tongue." This lack of marking may be part of a larger tendency, in this concluding sentence, to cover over an alterity that is, elsewhere, carefully noted. In this last sentence of the introduction, "feminists working from a number of critical approaches are" jointly, in a plural, inclusive verb, "concluding." In the "mother tongue," we are not divided. Yet the triumphant conclusion forgets a difference articulated earlier in the introduction between two "critical approaches," between the Chodorovians and the post-structuralists.

In the vicinity of the "mother" there is perhaps a tendency to cover over difference. Something about the figure of the mother seems to bless marriage and frown upon separation. From object-relations theory we learn that, for the infant, differentiation *is* differentiation *from the mother*. Imagining that the mother demands symbiosis, the infant experiences the drive toward separation as a guilty betrayal of the mother. Guilty to see the mother as other, to see the other in the mother; guilty thus to differentiate within the oceanic symbiosis. According to Chodorow, this atmosphere particularly characterizes the daughter's relation to the mother, long past infancy, and finally carries over into adult relations between women. This special feminine lack of rigid separation has been celebrated by feminists, but let us not forget the corollary uneasiness that attends the drive toward differentiation, never wholly absent from this complex. I would speculate that the tendency within feminist criticism to glorify the figure of the mother might often occur along with a concomitant pressure to cover over differences between feminists.[9] "Feminists working from a number of critical approaches are concluding that it is time . . . to speak our mother tongue." In "the mother" we are not divided.

The conclusion of the editors' introduction quoted above, with its lack of marked alterity, might be read as a happy ending. Given generic conventions, comedy concludes with the resolution of previous differences in a festive joining of all parties. But earlier in the narrative when the pressure of triumphant conclusion does not yet weigh so heavily, the differences between critical approaches can be delineated. In rehearsing the history of psychoanalytic feminism, the introduction finds that the French feminists have, like their American sisters, "turned to the preoedipal relation." The editors then carefully add: "Although this shift to the mother has brought some degree of rapprochement between this line of French feminist concern and Anglo-American theory, the French detour though Lacan results in a difference. The insertion of the question of language introduces the notion of a form of expressivity outside the dominant discourse" (pp. 22–23).

"The mother" brings us some rapprochement, a lessening of difference; but "the question of language," "the mother *tongue*" comprises difference. The question of the mother tongue inserts itself in the very reading of this passage. The word "rapprochement" can be found in an English dictionary, yet it is still pronounced in such a manner as not to let us forget that it is a French import. Not quite the mother nor quite the other tongue, it brings out the other in the mother. The French and English versions of the word remain close, so that "rapprochement" itself may be said to function as a point of rapprochement between the two languages. The appearance of this word in the text wishfully enacts a closing of the difference between the French and the Anglo-Americans.[10] The book itself represents a wish to close up that gap, to be able to speak the mother tongue and the other tongue simultaneously, hence the title. But however ardent that wish, it is also true that the relation between the mother tongue and the other tongue involves us with real material difference so that the book's title cannot simply be pronounced.

Chodorow is everywhere in this book, appearing in three-quarters of the essays and providing its theoretical framework and coherence. But Chodorow's theory, however useful for feminism and psychoanalysis, remains, as the editors point out (p. 20), solidly within the traditional American paradigm for social science and has nothing to say about "the question of language," a question that remains crucial for literary critics, for us feminists reading texts.

Yet this book also partakes of the "difference" of the "French detour":[11] "the insertion of the question of language [which] introduces the notion of a form of expressivity outside the dominant discourse." The title of the book is an attempt to write beyond dominant discourse. The play of its parenthesis, using the material of the language to reflect on the language, resembles the stylistic devices of post-structuralist writers such as Derrida and Irigaray as well as American feminists such as Mary Daly. The feminists and the post-structuralists are trying to find a mode of expressivity which is not already shackled by the ideological weight of standard language, the dominant discourse. Standard language might be called the mother tongue, so the attempt to write outside the dominant discourse could be construed as a try for the other rather than the mother tongue. But as the title of our anthology makes us see, "the other" is already inscribed *in* "the mother tongue." These feminist and post-structuralist attempts at new expressivity do not really go outside the dominant discourse but rather bring out what deconstructionists such as Barbara Johnson have called "the difference within."[12] We are not looking for a new language, a radical outside, but for "the other within," the alterity that has always lain silent, unmarked and invisible within the mother tongue.

Another name—a more specifically feminist name—for dominant discourse is "patriarchal discourse," and that phrase appears at the beginning of the book's preface where the editors write: "Oedipally organized narrative . . . that is based on the determining role of the father and of patriarchal discourse tells a different story from preoedipal narrative, which locates the source of movement and conflict in the figure of the mother" (p. 10).

The Oedipal is associated with the father; the pre-Oedipal with the mother. Psychoanalytic feminists valorize the pre-Oedipal because the mother is a woman and she is suppressed in Oedipally organized narrative. But there is a fifth term that intrudes upon the two couples. Whereas the pre-Oedipal finds its source uniquely in "the figure of the mother," the Oedipal is based not just on the father but also on "patriarchal discourse." The use of that phrase here bespeaks "the French detour through Lacan" where the Oedipal father, the third term that intrudes upon the dyad, is the symbolic father, representing the order of language and law. As the editors will later say, "the French detour through Lacan results in a difference." From the very beginning of the book, "the insertion of the question of language introduces" a disruption into psychoanalytic feminism's tendency to polarize into mother vs. father, pre-Oedipal vs. Oedipal. Words like "narrative" and "story" in the sentence from the preface remind us that we are still very much in the realm of literary criticism. And no "story," however primal, however familial, psychoanalytic, or basic to our culture, can forgo the question of discourse. If, like the Oedipal, the pre-Oedipal is "narrative," then it must be transmitted in some sort of discourse. Patriarchal discourse determines Oedipal narrative, but what sort of language would be associated with the pre-Oedipal?

One answer provided in this book is what Naomi Schor calls "the myth of a sort of prelapsarian preoedipus": the pre-Oedipal is an Edenic world of immediacy before the advent of language (p. 223).[13] Such an answer retains the purity of the polar opposition between the golden pre-Oedipal and the fallen Oedipal, but in that case—rather than the new fertile topos for literary criticism announced by the book—the pre-Oedipal would be beyond narrative, beyond the reach of the literary critic.

Another answer, certainly the most prominent in the anthology, is of course "the mother tongue" itself, which sounds like it would be the language spoken by the figure who dominates the pre-Oedipal. In the introduction, the editors write: "At this juncture . . . the tendency of Anglo-American psychoanalytic feminism to focus on the drama of the preoedipal relationship between mother and daughter intersects with French feminist dreams of another mode of discourse, another side of language whose authority is the mother" (p. 24). A mode of language where mother not father is authority—matriarchal discourse—is not an object of focus but a dream, that is to say, in psychoanalytic terms, the fulfillment of a wish. *Another* mode, *another* side: the mother tongue as other tongue, a dream devoutly to be wished.

Anglo-Americans focus; French dream. On one side, "the drama of the preoedipal relationship"; across, "another mode of discourse." The only term repeated on both sides: "mother." Hitching the "expressivity outside the dominant discourse" to the mother seems to promise a lessening of difference, a rapprochement on various fronts. This "juncture," this "intersection": paths that seemed to run parallel on either side of a gap are crossing. In "mother," we are not divided.

If "French feminist dreams" come down to the mother tongue, then perhaps we can ignore the differences between "focus" and "dream," "drama" and "language." For those terms represent other differences between Anglo-American and French "critical approaches." To focus (telescope or microscope) is the classic mode of empiricist scientific investigation. The drama of the pre-Oedipal is treated as a classic object of positivist study. That it is then, figuratively, a "drama" renders the pre-Oedipal relationship (figuratively) literary and preps it for use in analogical operations on literary works.

On the other side, to dream is to become, oneself, the classic object of psychoanalytic study, the dreamer's psyche. If Freud invented psychoanalysis through interpreting his own dreams, then psychoanalysis may be the locus of an uncanny self-knowledge where subject and object are neither identical nor different, where the subject and object of knowledge are aspects of "the same person" separated by the opaque materiality of the dream. Such study no longer partakes of the positivist objectivity of the focusing lens, but rather inevitably implicates the subject's desires and defenses in the investigation.[14]

In *The Interpretation of Dreams,* Freud provides us with a method of interpretation that involves attention to marginal specificity, to details we overlook when we reduce a story to its central drama. That aspect of Freud's work has influenced a different sort of literary criticism, one indebted to psychoanalysis for its interpretive methods rather than its dramatic analogies. This sort of dream-reading is more typical of psychoanalytic criticism deriving from French post-structuralism.

Focus on narrative structure ("drama" and "relationship") in the anthology has led us to the "figure of the mother," central to the book. But this other sort of psychoanalytic reading might be applied to our dream of the mother tongue. For example, the word "patriarchal" is actually spelled five different ways in this book: aside from its standard spelling, we can read "partriarchial" (p. 16), "patriarchial" (p. 22), "partiarchal" (p. 105), and "partrarchal" (p. 264 n. 11). Presumably these are typographical errors, yet no other word in the book is so frequently misspelled, as if some unconscious (editors'? typist's? typesetter's?) was insistently trying to alter patriarchal discourse in one way or another, trying to speak something other than patriarchal.[15] This is not a language "whose authority is the mother," not matriarchal, but other than patriarchal. This is clearly no one's mother tongue, but it may be the other tongue, perhaps what Lacan calls the discourse of the Other, that speaks in and through the mother tongue.[16]

The mother tongue, the language we learn at our mother's breast, *is* patriarchal language. That is where we learned the language which feminism has taught us to see as full of masculinist bias. In trying to move beyond the father, the mother looks like an alternative, but if we are trying to move beyond patriarchy, the mother is not outside. As Chodorow—among others[17]—has shown us, the institution of motherhood is a cornerstone of patriarchy. Although the father may be absent from the pre-Oedipal, patriarchy constitutes the very structure of the mother-child dyad.[18] The early mother may appear to be outside patriarchy, but that very idea of the mother (and the woman) as outside of culture, society, and politics is an essential ideological component of patriarchy.

There is a drive in this book to speak outside of patriarchal discourse. But to the extent that drive fixes on "the figure of the mother" and/or glorifies the pre-Oedipal, the book risks losing its title to diacritical marks and settling for a mother tongue which is not recognizably an other tongue.

In their preface, the editors of the anthology write: "It is clear that fascination by the preoedipal period and a corresponding focus on the figure of the mother in theories of human development have had a profound impact on the discipline of psychoanalysis and on the feminist interpretation of literature" (p. 10). "The discipline of psychoanalysis" and "the feminist interpretation of literature" are two widely separated realms, with apparently little in common. The opposition here is not only between Freudian and feminist ways of thinking but also between a quasi-medical practice of healing and a mode of literary interpretation. And yet these widely divergent domains are simply conjoined under the aegis of the pre-Oedipal period and the figure of the mother. Perhaps, since the pre-Oedipal is the realm of fusion and indifferentiation, its "impact" might include a preference for merger over distinction.

Or rather I should say, not the impact of the pre-Oedipal, but the impact of the "fascination by the preoedipal." Coppélia Kahn, in her contribution to the anthology, speaks of the "charmed preoedipal dyad" (p. 74). From the preface, we might infer that the pre-Oedipal period not only is a magical moment for infant and early mother but exercises a charm over those who contemplate it, who study and theorize. "Fascinate": "1. To be an object of intense interest to; attract irresistibly. 2. To hold motionless; to spellbind or mesmerize. 3. *Obsolete.* To bewitch; cast under a spell. [Latin *fascināre*, to enchant, bewitch, from *fascinus*, a bewitching, amulet in the shape of a phallus.]"[19] The pre-Oedipal fascinates, attracts us irresistibly and holds us motionless, and in place of the phallic amulet, we are bewitched by the figure of the mother. The maternal having replaced the phallic, the early seventies' opposition between psychoanalysis and feminism can give way to a charmed union.

But, in fact, all charms, dreams, and wishes aside, what is the status of this marriage blessed by the mother? How mutual is the fascination?

The editors' introduction to *The (M)other Tongue* is comprised of two sections: its last four pages briefly summarize the articles to be found in the book; but the bulk of the introduction is a history of the encounters between psychoanalysis and feminism. The last paragraph of that history begins: "So far we have traced the ways in which feminism has reacted to psychoanalysis. . . . But there may be another story here, that of the response of psychoanalysis to feminism" (p. 25). For ten pages they have traced feminism's response to psychoanalysis, and now with but one paragraph left, they are just beginning to imagine the other side ("there *may be* another story"). This relationship seems far too one-sided; psychoanalytic feminism is simply the influence of psychoanalysis on feminism. One party has done all the talking; the other all the listening. Not a very good model for a marriage.

In the psychoanalytic context, however, we know of another relationship in which the one who does all the listening is not necessarily in the subordinate position, in which knowledge and authority in certain ways derive from the one who does all the listening. Perhaps, after all, psychoanalysis has been doing all its talking in relation to the knowledge it presumes feminism (or women) to have. That may be why feminism has been so willing to listen. But that other story, the influence of feminism on psychoanalysis, remains to be told.

That story would have to begin with what the other story has left out, what psychoanalysis for all its talking could not say. For if feminism, in its listening posture, is in the place of the analyst, then when we speak we will intervene in response to some marked gap in the story of the one who does all the talking. In the last paragraph of the historical introduction, the editors start to imagine that story: "Psychoanalysis, whether it posits in the beginning maternal presence or absence, has yet to develop a story of the mother as other than the object of the infant's desire or the matrix from which he or she develops an infant subjectivity" (p. 25). "Whether it posits in the beginning maternal presence or absence": that is, whether we are dealing with object-relations theory or Lacanian theory. Finally, even these two opposing schools of psychoanalysis are united in their common lack. In Lacanian models she is the prohibited object of desire; in object-relations she is the mirror where the infant can find his or her subjectivity. In either case her only role is to complement the infant's subjectivity; in neither story is she ever a subject. It is not mother that is lacking from psychoanalytic accounts, but precisely mother as other ("Psychoanalysis . . . has yet to develop a story of the mother as other").

In *The Reproduction of Mothering,* Chodorow begins to notice this blind spot in psychoanalysis, but she too quickly attributes it to the gender of the theorists: "male theorists . . . ignore the mother's involvements outside her relationship to her infant and her possible interest in mitigating its intensity. Instead, they contrast the infant's moves toward differentiation and separation to the mother's attempts to retain symbiosis" (*RM,* p. 87). Since the subject of both sentences is "male theorists," we might infer that now that women are theorizing they will not make the same mistake. Such a supposition about female theorists is equivalent to the assumption that the mother is outside patriarchy.

Susan Suleiman's essay in *The (M)other Tongue* begins with an account of the same syndrome in psychoanalytic theory ("It is as if, for psychoanalysis, the only self worth worrying about in the mother-child relationship were that of the child" [p. 356]). Although explicitly following Chodorow's lead, Suleiman's examples (from Helene Deutsch, Melanie Klein, Alice Balint, and Karen Horney) expose this bias not (merely) in the fathers but in the mothers of psychoanalytic theory. Toward the end of her exposé of the mother's position in psychoanalysis—entitled "The Psychoanalytic Projection"—Suleiman remarks in a footnote: "It will certainly be noticed that almost all of the analysts I have been quoting are women" (p. 356 n. 8).

Only remarking this in a footnote, Suleiman makes no serious or prolonged attempt to understand why these women might perpetrate such patriarchal bias. It might be argued that, although women, these theorists are not, strictly speaking, feminists, or at least are not in a position to benefit from the work done in the contemporary field of psychoanalytic feminism. It might also be argued that they are all practicing analysts and therefore have an investment in the discipline of psychoanalysis that a literary critic, for example, need not share. Yet I think the problem might be more pervasive, that the maternal figure may move many of us to wish for an embrace that obliterates otherness. And those of us who are attracted to psychoanalytic theory may be particularly susceptible to the mother's charming figure, the dream of the mother without otherness.

I want to cite just one example of the bias against maternal alterity in contemporary psychoanalytic feminist criticism. My example comes not from this anthology
but from an article by Ronnie Scharfman published in the 1981 issue of *Yale French
Studies* entitled *Feminist Readings*. That volume shares many traits with *The
(M)other Tongue:* in particular, a lot of psychoanalytic feminist theory and an
attempt to bring together American and French feminisms.[20] Scharfman's text is
an example of a feminist literary application of object-relations theory as it has come
down through Chodorow. Scharfman writes: "Winnicott . . . asks what a baby sees
upon looking at the mother's face. . . . 'Ordinarily, what the baby sees is himself
or herself.' " Again drawing on Winnicott, Scharfman describes an "unsuccessful
mirroring bond": "When a mother reflects her own mood or the 'rigidity of her own
defenses,' rather than her child's, what the baby sees is the mother's face, and the
'mother's face is not then a mirror.' The consequences are tragic."[21] Scharfman does
not critique Winnicott's position but simply produces a very agile literary application
of it. Tragedy here remains the consequence of seeing the mother's subjectivity,
seeing the mother as other.

By focusing on the women theorists, Suleiman goes beyond Chodorow to show
us a problem that stems not from the theorists' gender but from a bias in psychoanalytic theory itself: "Psychoanalysis is nothing if not a theory of childhood. We should
not be surprised if it locates . . . every . . . aspect of adult personality in the child
the adult once was, and often continues to be" (p. 358). Psychoanalysis is "a theory
of childhood," that is, not merely about childhood, but a childhood theory, theorized
from the child's point of view. That is its great strength: it has given us access to
what is denied by any psychology that assumes that the child simply becomes an
adult, rational, civilized. But the child's particular blind spot is an inability to have
any realistic notion of the mother as an other subjectivity.[22]

Chodorow, drawing on Alice Balint's work, focuses on this aspect of the relation
to the mother, pointing to its continuation in adults and its determining role in
ideology. In *The Reproduction of Mothering* she writes that "people continue not
to recognize their mother's interests while developing capacities for 'altruistic love'
in the process of growing up. They support their egoism, moreover, by idealizing
mothers and by the creation of social ideology" (*RM,* p. 81). The child the adult
continues to be cannot tolerate the mother's otherness. And that child is the source
of psychoanalytic theory. If one of the major goals of feminism has been to put a
stop to women's self-sacrifice, their exploitation through the ideology of maternal
altruism, then it must counter every adult child's wish for the mother to be the
perfect selfless mirror. That is where psychoanalysis and feminism may find themselves on opposite sides, one taking the child's wishes into account, the other
defending the mother's side of the story.

Pointing us toward this opposition between psychoanalysis and feminism, Suleiman's essay stands out from the rest of the texts in the anthology, representing so
to speak the internal alterity, the other within *The (M)other Tongue*. She goes
beyond "the figure of the mother"—object for the infant's psyche—in search of the
mother's subjectivity. In fact, Suleiman's text is not an example of psychoanalytic
feminism but rather a feminist reading of psychoanalysis, which ultimately rejects
psychoanalysis. Her essay is the last one in the anthology. Thus by the time we reach
the end of the first anthology of psychoanalytic feminist criticism, we have in some
way gone beyond the boundaries of the new field into a critique of its very possibility.

That such an essay should be included and positioned last suggests that perhaps such a move is finally inevitable. If this collection is the first to celebrate the alliance of feminism and psychoanalysis, then it also bears within it a sense of the limitations of such an alliance. *The (M)other Tongue* would be very different if it did not end with Suleiman's text. Since it does, we are, in some ways, forced to rethink what has come before.

Earlier, in looking at the editors' introduction, I said that *The (M)other Tongue* seemed to follow the generic code for comedy, culminating in a procession of couples marching hand in hand (psychoanalysis with feminism, Anglo-American theory with French feminism, the discipline of psychoanalysis with the feminist interpretation of literature). But an editors' introduction is always a secondary revision (in the psychoanalytic sense of the term)[23] of the unruly material of an anthology. Ending with Suleiman's text, *The (M)other Tongue* actually concludes not with marriage but divorce.

And the accusations we hear typify the contemporary subgenre of the feminist divorce tale. Psychoanalysis does not allow mother her selfhood, makes her an object of service, and expects her to sacrifice herself to her partner's fantasies about her.[24] If "the figure of the mother" blesses the marriage of psychoanalysis and feminism, the mother as other presides over their divorce.

The anthology thus indeed leads us from the mother (fantasy figure and ideological construction) to the (m)other. . . . But what of the (m)other tongue? In this book, it seems that the question of language is always tied to that other tongue, French, and to those "French feminists." As we have also seen, the other tongue, the "expressivity outside the dominant discourse," is usually construed as a mother tongue. On this question, Suleiman's essay is no exception. She discusses a less well-known French woman writer, Chantal Chawaf, who "has tied the practice of feminine writing to the biological fact of motherhood" (p. 370). Like other women of the French school, Chawaf is trying to practice *écriture féminine* (feminine writing), but more explicitly than with the other practitioners, her "expressivity outside" would be a mother tongue. ("Chawaf has stated in interviews and in commentaries on her work that for her motherhood is the only access to literary creation" [p. 370].)

Yet even here in this exemplary instance of a mother tongue, we can find the intrusion of an other tongue. Suleiman is discussing in particular a novel by Chawaf entitled *Maternité* (French cognate for "maternity"). When she quotes from the novel (p. 370), the footnote reads: "42. Chantal Chawaf, *Manternité* (Paris, 1979), 20." In the text, the title reads correctly, *Maternité,* but there at the bottom of the page we find an alien within the mother tongue. Perhaps the monstrous word "manternité" includes the English word "man" in the French word, producing a composite that is in no one's mother tongue, that can only be read in two languages at once, that cannot simply be pronounced.[25] Not quite the mother tongue nor quite the other tongue; that errant *n* brings out the other in the mother.

In the classic psychoanalytic story, the "man" comes to disrupt the charmed pre-Oedipal dyad. As Janet Adelman puts it in another footnote in the anthology, this Oedipal intrusion of the man is but a late form, a repetition of an otherness already there in the early mother: "For the infant, the mother's separateness constitutes the first betrayal; insofar as she is not merely his, she is promiscuously other.

I suspect that this sense of otherness itself as promiscuous betrayal antedates the more specific oedipal jealousies and is retrospectively sexualized by them" (p. 134 n. 17). Those of us under the fascination of the pre-Oedipal often see the man's entry as the fall from Eden. In a Lacanian version of that story, the man's intrusion saves us from symbiotic fusion, from the mother's engulfment. Adelman (and Chodorow and Suleiman) remind us however that both the positive and the negative valuations of the pre-Oedipal equally ignore the fact that the pre-Oedipal mother is already other.

The disruptive appearance of the word "man" within maternity may also remind us that maternity may not be simply a form of feminine writing. The masculine is inscribed in motherhood; patriarchal discourse structures the institution and the experience of motherhood as we know it. In any case, whether suppressed wish for separation or unauthorized critique, the *n* in Suleiman's footnote continues the legacy of the title's parentheses, interrupting the mother tongue by an other tongue.

Although there may be a wish to link French feminine writing with the pre-Oedipal, at the specific point in the editors' introduction where they remark that the question of language results in a difference, they make it clear that the other tongue is not pre-Oedipal. "The insertion of the question of language introduces a notion of a form of expressivity outside the dominant discourse . . . an *'écriture féminine.'* . . . Such French feminists as Cixous and Irigaray seek to formulate a female poetics that would allow mother and daughter, once locked in a symbiotic fusion and plenitude, to become women and subjects, in and through language" (p. 23). Symbiotic fusion and plenitude lock women in, pre-Oedipal fascination holds them motionless.[26] The question of language must be inserted as the wedge to break the hold of the figure of the mother. *Ecriture féminine* must not be arrested by the plenitude of the mother tongue, but must try to be always and also an other tongue.

The other tongue is hard to pronounce, but those of us who have learned critical interpretation from psychoanalysis and from feminism are learning how to read it. At its best, psychoanalytic feminist criticism is teaching us not how to speak the mother tongue, not *only* how to see the mother as other and not mirror, but how to read the other within the mother tongue.

Notes

1. See Mary Ellmann, *Thinking about Women* (New York, 1968), pp. 27–54.

2. See Kate Millett, *Sexual Politics* (Garden City, N.Y., 1970).

3. This paper was originally written to be read at a 1985 MLA Convention Forum entitled "Psychoanalytic Criticism: Its Place and Potential." The forum was sponsored by the Division for Psychological Approaches to Literature and included four ancillary workshops exploring the meaning, impact, and future of this recent growth in psychoanalytic criticism. I would like to thank Claire Kahane and David Willbern for their invitation which led me to write the present paper. The central panel, chaired by Willbern, included Peter Brooks, Murray Schwartz, Cary Nelson, and my-

self. The workshop on psychoanalysis and feminism, chaired by Kahane, included Marianne Hirsch, Judith Kegan Gardiner, and Jerry Aline Flieger and provided excellent examples of psychoanalytic feminist criticism. I would particularly draw attention to Hirsch's paper—"Why Didn't I Recognize My Mother (or, Why Didn't My Mother Recognize Me?): Psychoanalytic Theories and Maternal Silence"—where the focus and concerns intersect with those of the present paper.

4. For an introduction to the French feminists, see *New French Feminisms: An Anthology,* ed. Elaine Marks and Isabelle de Courtivron (Amherst, Mass., 1980).

5. See Nancy Chodorow, *The Reproduction of Mothering: Psychoanalysis and the Sociology of*

Gender (Berkeley and Los Angeles, 1978); all further references to this work, abbreviated *RM,* will be included in the text.

6. See *The (M)other Tongue: Essays in Feminist Psychoanalytic Interpretation,* ed. Shirley Nelson Garner, Claire Kahane, and Madelon Sprengnether (Ithaca, N.Y., 1985); all further references to this work will be included in the text.

7. The phrases "father-based" and "mother-based" come from the preface to *The (M)other Tongue,* pp. 9–10.

8. I owe the phrases "other as self" and "self as other" to a related use by Naomi Schor, *"Eugénie Grandet:* Mirrors and Melancholia," in *The (M)other Tongue,* p. 218 n. 2.

9. For a similar discussion of the relation of pre-Oedipal psychology to feminism, see Jane Flax, "The Conflict between Nurturance and Autonomy in Mother-Daughter Relationships and within Feminism," *Feminist Studies* 4 (June 1978): 171–91.

10. In this context let us remark the phrase "Anglo-American." It is not at all obvious that English and American feminists share a theory. For example, British psychoanalytic feminists tend to be Lacanian. Of course one could say that object-relations theory is an English movement. But then Chodorow has not been very influential in Britain. Perhaps the phrase stems rather from the fact that the English and Americans more or less share a "mother tongue." The contrast between the French and the Anglo-Americans is thus a difference between two language groups.

11. For a similar appearance of the concept of the "French detour," see Jane Gallop, *The Daughter's Seduction: Feminism and Psychoanalysis* (Ithaca, N.Y., 1982), pp. 139–40. In her essay "Enforcing Oedipus: Freud and Dora" in *The (M)other Tongue,* Sprengnether makes reference to this passage from *The Daughter's Seduction* (p. 61 n. 15).

12. See, for example, Barbara Johnson, *The Critical Difference: Essays in the Contemporary Rhetoric of Reading* (Baltimore, 1981), p. 4.

13. For examples in *The (M)other Tongue* of this myth at work, see Dianne Hunter, "Hysteria, Psychoanalysis, and Feminism: The Case of Anna O.," pp. 98–99, and Jim Swan, "Difference and Silence: John Milton and the Question of Gender," p. 168.

14. For exemplary instances of critical self-implication in *The (M)other Tongue,* see Schor, *"Eugénie Grandet,"* pp. 236–37, and Kahane, "The Gothic Mirror," p. 340.

15. In *The Psychopathology of Everyday Life,* Freud opens the possibility of treating mistakes by copyists and compositors as psychologically motivated, that is, interpretable; see Freud, *The Standard Edition of the Complete Psychological Works*

of Sigmund Freud, ed. and trans. James Strachey, 24 vols. (London, 1953–74), 6:129.

16. According to Jacques Lacan, "the unconscious is the discourse of the Other." See Lacan, *Ecrits* (Paris, 1966), pp. 265, 379, 469, 549, 628, 632–34, 654, 814–15, 830, and 839.

17. See, principally, Dorothy Dinnerstein, *The Mermaid and the Minotaur: Sexual Arrangements and Human Malaise* (New York, 1976), and Adrienne Rich, *Of Woman Born: Motherhood as Experience and Institution* (New York, 1976).

18. Schor makes the same point in *The (M)other Tongue:* "What Eugénie begins to understand is that even as she enjoyed the shelter of the symbiotic mother-daughter relationship, even then she lived under the sway of the Symbolic, the order in which she was inscribed before her birth" (*"Eugénie Grandet,"* p. 227).

19. *The American Heritage Dictionary of the English Language,* new college ed., s.v. "fascinate."

20. I have done a reading of this volume which explores many of the same themes as the present paper, "The Monster in the Mirror: The Feminist Critic's Psychoanalysis," which will be published in an anthology on psychoanalysis and feminism, edited by Richard Feldstein and Judith Roof.

21. Ronnie Scharfman, "Mirroring and Mothering in Simone Schwartz-Bart's *Pluie et vent sur Télumée Miracle* and Jean Rhys' *Wide Sargasso Sea,"* *Yale French Studies* 62 (1981): 91, 99. Scharfman is quoting from D. W. Winnicott, "Mirror-role of Mother and Family in Child Development," *Playing and Reality* (New York, 1971), pp. 111–18.

22. According to Chodorow, "Alice Balint argues that the essence of 'love for the mother' is that it is not under the sway of the reality principle" (*RM,* p. 79). Chodorow's source here is Alice Balint, "Love for the Mother and Mother Love," in *Primary Love and Psycho-Analytic Technique,* ed. Michael Balint (New York, 1965), pp. 91–108.

23. "Secondary revision" is the "rearrangement of a dream so as to present it in the form of a relatively consistent and comprehensible scenario." This definition is taken from J. Laplanche and J.-B. Pontalis, *The Language of Psycho-analysis,* trans. Donald Nicholson-Smith (London, 1973), p. 412.

24. The phrase "object of service" is taken from the editors' introduction to *The (M)other Tongue,* p. 19.

25. In the month following my writing of the present essay, I find myself regularly making a certain typo: "materity" for "maternity." It is as if I felt there was an *n* that did not belong in "maternity."

26. Kahane uses the same image of being "locked into a symbiotic relation" in her essay in *The (M)other Tongue,* pp. 336, 337.

TILLIE OLSEN

Silences

One Out of Twelve:
Writers Who Are Women in Our Century

It is the women's movement, part of the other movements of our time for a fully human life, that has brought this forum into being; kindling a renewed, in most instances a first-time, interest in the writings and writers of our sex.

Linked with the old, resurrected classics on women, this movement in three years has accumulated a vast new mass of testimony, of new comprehensions as to what it is to be female. Inequities, restrictions, penalties, denials, leechings have been painstakingly and painfully documented; damaging differences in circumstances and treatment from that of males attested to; and limitations, harms, a sense of wrong, voiced.

It is in the light and dark of this testimony that I examine my subject today: the lives and work of writers, women, in our century (though I speak primarily of those writing in the English language—and in prose).

Compared to the countless centuries of the silence of women, compared to the century preceding ours—the first in which women wrote in any noticeable numbers—ours has been a favorable one.

The road was cut many years ago, as Virginia Woolf reminds us:

> by Fanny Burney, by Aphra Behn, by Harriet Martineau, by Jane Austen, by George Eliot, many famous women and many more unknown and forgotten. . . . Thus, when I came to write . . . writing was a reputable and harmless occupation.

Predecessors, ancestors, a body of literature, an acceptance of the right to write: each in themselves an advantage.

In this second century we have access to areas of work and of life experience previously denied; higher education; longer, stronger lives; for the first time in human history, freedom from compulsory childbearing; freer bodies and attitudes toward sexuality; a beginning of technological easing of household tasks; and—of the greatest importance to those like myself who come from generations of illiterate women—increasing literacy, and higher degrees of it. *Each one of these a vast gain.* *

And the results?

Productivity: books of all manner and kind. My own crude sampling, having to be made without benefit of research assistants, secretary, studies (nobody's made them), or computer (to feed the entire *Books in Print* and *Contemporary Authors*

---

*These are measured phrases, enormously compressed. Each asks an entire book or books, to indicate its enabling relationship to literature written by women in this century—including the very numbers of women enabled to write.

into, for instance) indicates that at present four to five books are published by men to every one by a woman.*

Comparative earnings: no authoritative figures available.

Achievement: as gauged by what supposedly designates it: appearance in twentieth-century literature courses, required reading lists, textbooks, quality anthologies, the year's best, the decade's best, the fifty years' best, consideration by critics or in current reviews—*one woman writer for every twelve men* (8 percent women, 92 percent men). For a week or two, make your own survey whenever you pick up an anthology, course bibliography, quality magazine or quarterly, book review section, book of criticism.

What weights my figures so heavily toward the one-out-of-twelve ratio are twentieth-century literature course offerings, and writers decreed worthy of critical attention in books and articles. Otherwise my percentage figures would have come closer to one out of seven.

But it would not matter if the ratio had been one out of six or five. Any figure but one to one would insist on query: Why? What, not true for men but only for women, makes this enormous difference? (Thus, class—economic circumstance—and color, those other traditional silencers of humanity, can be relevant only in the special ways that they affect the half of their numbers who are women.)

Why are so many more women silenced than men? Why, when women do write (one out of four or five works published) is so little of their writing known, taught, accorded recognition? What is the nature of the critical judgments made throughout that (along with the factors different in women's lives) steadily reduce the ratio from one out of three in anthologies of student work to one out of seventeen in course offerings?

This talk, originally intended to center on the writing, the achievement of women writers in our century, became instead these queryings. Yet—in a way sadder, angrier, prouder—it still centers on the writing, the achievement. †

One woman writer of achievement for every twelve men writers so ranked. Is this proof again—and in this so much more favorable century—of women's innately inferior capacity for creative achievement?

Only a few months ago (June 1971), during a Radcliffe-sponsored panel on "Women's Liberation, Myth or Reality," Diana Trilling, asking why it is that women

have not made even a fraction of the intellectual, scientific or artistic-cultural contributions which men have made,

*Richard Altick in his "Sociology of Authorship" found the proportion of women writers to men writers in Britain a fairly constant one for the years 1800 to 1935: 20 percent. This was based on books published, not on recognized achievement.

†Added to text, 1976.

came again to the traditional conclusion that

> it is not enough to blame women's place in culture or culture itself, because that leaves
> certain fundamental questions unanswered . . . necessarily raises the question of the
> biological aspects of the problem.

Biology: that difference.* Evidently unknown to or dismissed by her and the
others who share her conclusion are the centuries of prehistory during which biology
did not deny equal contribution; and *the other determining difference—not* biology—between male and female in the centuries after; the *differing past of women—*
that should be part of every human consciousness, certainly every woman's
consciousness (in the way that the 400 years of bondage, colonialism, the slave
passage, are to black humans).
Work first:

> Within our bodies we bore the race. Through us it was shaped, fed and clothed. . . . Labour
> more toilsome and unending than that of man was ours. . . . No work was too hard, no
> labour too strenuous to exclude us.†

True for most women in most of the world still.
    Unclean; taboo. The Devil's Gateway. The three steps behind; the girl babies
drowned in the river; the baby strapped to the back. Buried alive with the lord,
burned alive on the funeral pyre, burned as witch at the stake. Stoned to death for
adultery. Beaten, raped. Bartered. Bought and sold. Concubinage, prostitution,
white slavery. The hunt, the sexual prey, "I am a lost creature, O the poor Clarissa."
Purdah, the veil of Islam, domestic confinement. Illiterate. Denied vision. Excluded,
excluded, excluded from council, ritual, activity, learning, language, when there was
neither biological nor economic reason to be excluded.
    Religion, when all believed. In sorrow shalt thou bring forth children. May thy
wife's womb never cease from bearing. Neither was the man created for the woman
but the woman for the man. Let the woman learn in silence and in all subjection.
Contrary to biological birth fact: Adam's rib. The Jewish male morning prayer:
thank God I was not born a woman. Silence in holy places, seated apart, or not
permitted entrance at all; castration of boys because women too profane to sing in
church.
    And for the comparative handful of women born into the privileged class; being,
not doing; man does, woman is; to you the world says work, to us it says seem. God
is thy law, thou mine. Isolated. Cabin'd, cribb'd, confin'd; the private sphere. Bound
feet: corseted, cosseted, bedecked; denied one's body. Powerlessness. Fear of rape,
male strength. Fear of aging. Subject to. Fear of expressing capacities. Soft attractive
graces; the mirror to magnify man. Marriage as property arrangement. The vices of
slaves:‡ dissembling, flattering, manipulating, appeasing.

---

*Biologically, too, the change for women now is enormous: life expectancy (USA) seventy-eight
years—as contrasted with forty-eight years in 1900. Near forty-eight years of life before and after one
is "a woman," that is: "capable of conceiving and bearing young." (And childbearing more and more
voluntary.)
    †Olive Schreiner. *Women and Labour.*
    ‡Elizabeth Barrett Browning's phrase; other phrases throughout from the Bible, John Milton, Rich-
ardson's *Clarissa,* Matthew Arnold, Elizabeth Cady Stanton, Virginia Woolf, Viola Klein, Mountain
Wolf Woman.

Bolstering. Vicarious living, infantilization, trivialization. Parasitism, individualism, madness. Shut up, you're only a girl. O Elizabeth, why couldn't you have been born a boy? For twentieth-century woman: roles, discontinuities, part-self, part-time; conflict; imposed "guilt"; "a man can give full energy to his profession, a woman cannot."

How is it that women have not made a fraction of the intellectual, scientific, or artistic-cultural contributions that men have made?

Only in the context of this punitive difference in circumstance, in history, between the sexes; this past, hidden or evident, that (though objectively obsolete—yes, even the toil and the compulsory childbearing obsolete) *continues so terribly, so determiningly to live on, only in this context can the question be answered or my subject here today—the women writer in our century; one out of twelve—be understood.*

How much it takes to become a writer. Bent (far more common than we assume), circumstances, time, development of craft—but beyond that: how much conviction as to the importance of what one has to say, one's right to say it. And the will, the measureless store of belief in oneself to be able to come to, cleave to, find the form for one's own life comprehensions. Difficult for any male not born into a class that breeds such confidence. Almost impossible for a girl, a woman.

The leeching of belief, of will, the damaging of capacity begin so early. Sparse indeed is the literature on the way of denial to small girl children of the development of their endowment as born human: active, vigorous bodies; exercise of the power to do, to make, to investigate, to invent, to conquer obstacles, to resist violations of the self; to think, create, choose; to attain community, confidence in self. Little has been written on the harms of instilling constant concern with appearance; the need to please, to support; the training in acceptance, deferring. Little has been added in our century to George Eliot's *The Mill on the Floss* on the effect of the differing treatment—"climate of expectation"—for boys and for girls.

But it is there if one knows how to read for it, and indelibly there in the resulting damage. One—out of twelve.

In the vulnerable girl years, unlike their sisters in the previous century, women writers go to college.* The kind of experience it may be for them is stunningly documented in Elaine Showalter's pioneering "Women and the Literary Curriculum."† Freshman texts in which women have little place, if at all; language itself, all achievement, anything to do with the human in male terms—*Man in Crises, The Individual and His World.* Three hundred thirteen male writers taught; seventeen

---

*True almost without exception among the writers who are women in *Twentieth Century Authors* and *Contemporary Authors.*

†*College English,* May 1971. A year later (October 1972), *College English* published an extensive report, "Freshman Textbooks," by Jean Mullens. In the 112 most used texts, she found 92.47 percent (5,795) of the selections were by men; 7.53 percent (472) by women (One Out of Twelve). Mullens deepened Showalter's insights as to the subtly undermining effect on freshman students of the texts' contents and language, as well as the minuscule proportion of women writers.

women writers: That classic of adolescent rebellion, *A Portrait of the Artist as a Young Man*; and sagas (male) of the quest for identity (but then Erikson, the father of the concept, propounds that identity concerns girls only insofar as making themselves into attractive beings for the right kind of man).* Most, *not all,* of the predominantly male literature studied, written by men whose understandings are not universal, but restrictively male (as Mary Ellmann, Kate Millett, and Dolores Schmidt have pointed out); in our time more and more surface, hostile, one-dimensional in portraying women.

In a writer's young years, susceptibility to the vision and style of the great is extreme. Add the aspiration-denying implication, consciously felt or not (although reinforced daily by one's professors and reading) that (as Virginia Woolf noted years ago) women writers, women's experience, and literature written by women are by definition minor. (Mailer will not grant even the minor: "the one thing a writer has to have is balls.") No wonder that Showalter observes:

> Women [students] are estranged from their own experience and unable to perceive its shape and authenticity, in part because they do not see it mirrored and given resonance in literature. . . . They are expected to identify with masculine experience, which is presented as the human one, and have no faith in the validity of their own perceptions and experiences, rarely seeing them confirmed in literature, or accepted in criticism. . . . [They] notoriously lack the happy confidence, the exuberant sense of the value of their individual observations which enables young men to risk making fools of themselves for the sake of an idea.

Harms difficult to work through. Nevertheless, some young women (others are already lost) maintain their ardent intention to write—fed indeed by the very glories of some of this literature that puts them down.

But other invisible worms are finding out the bed of crimson joy.† Self-doubt; seriousness, also questioned by the hours agonizing over appearance; concentration shredded into attracting, being attractive; the absorbing real need and love for working with words felt as hypocritical self-delusion ("I'm not truly dedicated"), for what seems (and is) esteemed is being attractive to men. High aim, and accomplishment toward it, discounted by the prevalent attitude that, as girls will probably marry (attitudes not applied to boys who will probably marry), writing is no more than an attainment of a dowry to be spent later according the needs and circumstances within the true vocation: husband and family. The growing acceptance that going on will threaten other needs, to love and be loved ("a woman has to sacrifice all claims to femininity and family to be a writer").‡

And the agony—peculiarly mid-century, escaped by their sisters of pre-Freudian, pre-Jungian times—that "creation and femininity are incompatible."§ Anaïs Nin's words.

---

*In keeping with his 1950s–60s thesis of a distinctly female "biological, evolutionary need to fulfill self through serving others."

> †O Rose thou art sick./The invisible worm,
> That flies in the night/In the howling storm:
>
> Has found out thy bed/Of crimson joy:
> And his dark secret love/Does thy life destroy.
> —William Blake

‡Plath. A letter when a graduate student.
§*The Diary of Anaïs Nin*, Vol. III, 1939–1944.

The aggressive act of creation; the guilt for creating. I did not want to rival man; to steal man's creation, his thunder. I must protect them, not outshine them.*

The acceptance—against one's experienced reality—of the sexist notion that the act of creation is not as inherently natural to a woman as to a man, but rooted instead in unnatural aggression, rivalry, envy, or thwarted sexuality.

And in all the usual college teaching—the English, history, psychology, sociology courses—little to help that young woman understand the source or nature of this inexplicable draining self-doubt, loss of aspiration, of confidence.

It is all there in the extreme in Plath's *Bell Jar*—that (inadequate)† portrait of the artist as young woman (significantly, one of the few that we have)—from the precarious sense of vocation to the paralyzing conviction that (in a sense different from what she wrote years later)

> Perfection is terrible. It cannot have children.
> It tamps the womb.

And indeed, in our century as in the last, until very recently almost all distinguished achievement has come from childless women: Willa Cather, Ellen Glasgow, Gertrude Stein, Edith Wharton, Virginia Woolf, Elizabeth Bowen, Katherine Mansfield, Isak Dinesen, Katherine Anne Porter, Dorothy Richardson, Henry Handel Richardson, Susan Glaspell, Dorothy Parker, Lillian Hellman, Eudora Welty, Djuna Barnes, Anaïs Nin, Ivy Compton-Burnett, Zora Neale Hurston, Elizabeth Madox Roberts, Christina Stead, Carson McCullers, Flannery O'Connor, Jean Stafford, May Sarton, Josephine Herbst, Jessamyn West, Janet Frame, Lillian Smith, Iris Murdoch, Joyce Carol Oates, Hannah Green, Lorraine Hansberry.

Most never questioned or at least accepted (a few sanctified) this different condition for achievement, not imposed on men writers. Few asked the fundamental human equality question regarding it that Elizabeth Mann Borghese, Thomas Mann's daughter, asked when she was eighteen and sent to a psychiatrist for help in getting over an unhappy love affair (revealing also a working ambition to become a great musician although "women cannot be great musicians"). "You must choose between your art and fulfillment as a woman," the analyst told her, "between music and family life." "Why?" she asked. "Why must I choose? No one said to Toscanini or to Bach or my father that they must choose between their art and personal, family life; fulfillment as a man. . . . Injustice everywhere." Not where it is free choice. But where it is forced because of the circumstances for the sex into which one is born—a choice men of the same class do not have to make in order to do their work—that is not choice, that is a coercive working of sexist oppression.‡

What possible difference, you may ask, does it make to literature whether or not a woman writer remains childless—free choice or not—especially in view of the marvels these childless women have created?

---

*A statement that would have baffled Austen, the Brontës, Mrs. Gaskell, Eliot, Stowe, Alcott, etc. The strictures were felt by them in other ways.

†Inadequate, for the writer-being ("muteness is sickness for me") is not portrayed. By contrast, how present she is in Plath's own *Letters Home.*

‡"Them lady poets must not marry, pal," is how John Berryman, poet (himself oft married) expressed it. The old patriarchal injunction: "Woman, this is man's realm. If you insist on invading it, unsex yourself—and expect the road to be made difficult." Furthermore, this very unmarriedness and childlessness has been used to discredit women as unfulfilled, inadequate, somehow abnormal.

Might there not have been other marvels as well, or other dimensions to these marvels? Might there not have been present profound aspects and understandings of human life as yet largely absent in literature?

More and more women writers in our century, primarily in the last two decades, are assuming as their right fullness of work *and* family life.* Their emergence is evidence of changing circumstances making possible for them what (with rarest exception) was not possible in the generations of women before. I hope and I fear for what will result. I hope (and believe) that complex new richness will come into literature; I fear because almost certainly their work will be impeded, lessened, partial. For the fundamental situation remains unchanged. Unlike men writers who marry, most will not have the societal equivalent of a wife—nor (in a society hostile to growing life) anyone but themselves to mother their children. Even those who can afford help, good schools, summer camps, may *(may)* suffer what seventy years ago W. E. B. Du Bois called "The Damnation of Women": "that only at the sacrifice of the chance to do their best work can women bear and rear children."†

Substantial creative achievement demands time . . . and with rare exceptions only full-time workers have created it.‡

I am quoting myself from "Silences," a talk nine years ago. In motherhood, as it is structured,

circumstances for sustained creation are almost impossible. Not because the capacities to create no longer exist, or the need (though for a while as in any fullness of life the need may be obscured), but . . . the need cannot be first. It can have at best only part self, part time. . . . Motherhood means being instantly interruptible, responsive, responsible. Children need one *now* (and remember, in our society, the family must often try to be the center for love and health the outside world is not). The very fact that these are needs of love, not duty, that one feels them as one's self; *that there is no one else to be responsible*

*Among those with children: Harriette Arnow, Mary Lavin, Mary McCarthy, Tess Slesinger, Eleanor Clark, Nancy Hale, Storm Jameson, Janet Lewis, Jean Rhys, Kay Boyle, Ann Petry, Dawn Powell, Meridel LeSueur, Evelyn Eaton, Dorothy Canfield Fisher, Pearl Buck, Josephine Johnson, Caroline Gordon, Shirley Jackson; and a sampling in the unparalleled last two decades: Doris Lessing, Nadine Gordimer, Margaret Laurence, Grace Paley, Hortense Calisher, Edna O'Brien, Sylvia Ashton-Warner, Pauli Murray, Françoise Mallet-Joris, Cynthia Ozick, Joanne Greenberg, Joan Didion, Penelope Mortimer, Alison Lurie, Hope Hale Davis, Doris Betts, Muriel Spark, Adele Wiseman, Lael Wertenbaker, Shirley Ann Grau, Maxine Kumin, Margaret Walker, Gina Barriault, Mary Gray Hughes, Maureen Howard, Norma Rosen, Lore Segal, Alice Walker, Nancy Willard, Charlotte Painter, Sallie Bingham. (I would now add Clarice Lispector, Ruth Prawer Jhabvala, June Arnold, Ursula Le Guin, Diane Johnson, Alice Munro, Helen Yglesias, Susan Cahill, Rosellen Brown, Alta, and Susan Griffin.) Some wrote before children, some only in the middle or later years. Not many have directly used the material open to them out of motherhood as central source for their work.

†*Darkwater: Voices from within the Veil.*

‡This does not mean that these full-time writers were hermetic or denied themselves social or personal life (think of James, Turgenev, Tolstoy, Balzac, Joyce, Gide, Colette, Yeats, Woolf, etc. etc.); nor did they, except perhaps at the flood, put in as many hours daily as those doing more usual kinds of work. Three to six hours daily have been the norm ("the quiet, patient, generous mornings will bring it"). Zola and Trollope are famous last-century examples of the four hours; the *Paris Review* interviews disclose many contemporary ones.

Full-timeness consists not in the actual number of hours at one's desk, but in that writing is one's major profession, practiced habitually, in freed, protected, undistracted time as needed, when it is needed.

for these needs, gives them primacy. It is distraction, not meditation, that becomes habitual; interruption, not continuity; spasmodic, not constant, toil. Work interrupted, deferred, postponed makes blockage—at best, lesser accomplishment. Unused capacities atrophy, cease to be.

There are other vulnerabilities to loss, diminishment. Most women writers (being women) have had bred into them the "infinite capacity"; what Virginia Woolf named (after the heroine of a famous Victorian poem) *The Angel in the House,* who "must charm . . . sympathize . . . flatter . . . conciliate . . . be extremely sensitive to the needs and moods and wishes of others before her own . . . excel in the difficult arts of family life. . . ."

> It was she who used to come between me and my paper . . . who bothered me and wasted my time and so tormented me that at last I killed her . . . or she would have plucked out my heart as a writer.*

There is another angel, so lowly as to be invisible, although without her no art, or any human endeavor, could be carried on for even one day—the essential angel, with whom Virginia Woolf (and most women writers, still in the privileged class) did not have to contend—the angel who must assume the physical responsibilities for daily living, for the maintenance of life.

Almost always in one form or another (usually in the wife, two-angel form) she has dwelt in the house of men. She it was who made it possible for Joseph Conrad to "wrestle with the Lord for his creation":

> Mind and will and conscience engaged to the full, hour after hour, day after day . . . never aware of the even flow of daily life made easy and noiseless for me by a silent, watchful, tireless affection.

The angel who was "essential" to Rilke's "great task":

> like a sister who would run the house like a friendly climate, there or not there as one wished . . . and would ask for nothing except just to be there working and warding at the frontiers of the invisible.

Men (even part-time writers who must carry on work other than writing)† have had and have this inestimable advantage toward productivity. I cannot help but notice how curiously absent both of these angels, these watchers and warders at the frontiers of the invisible, are from the actual contents of most men's books, except perhaps on the dedication page:

To my wife, without whom . . .

I digress, and yet I do not; the disregard for the essential angel, the large absence of any sense of her in literature or elsewhere, has not only cost literature great contributions from those so occupied or partially occupied, but by failing to help create an arousing awareness (as literature has done in other realms) has contributed to the agonizingly slow elimination of this technologically and socially obsolete, human-wasting drudgery: Virginia Woolf's dream of a long since possible "economi-

---

*Professions for Women.
†As must many women writers.

cal, powerful and efficient future when houses will be cleaned by a puff of hot wind."

Sometimes the essential angel is present in women's books,* though still most "heroines are in white dresses that never need washing" (Rebecca Harding Davis's phrase of a hundred years ago). Some poets admit her as occasional domestic image; a few preen her as femininity; Sylvia Plath could escape her only by suicide:

> . . . flying . . .
> Over the engine that killed her——
> The mausoleum, the wax house.

For the first time in literary history, a woman poet of stature, accustomed through years to the habits of creation, began to live the life of most of her sex: the honey drudgers: the winged unmiraculous two-angel, whirled mother-maintenance life, that most women, not privileged, know. A situation without help or husband and with twenty-four hours' responsibility for two small human lives whom she adored and at their most fascinating and demanding. The world was blood-hot and personal. Creation's needs at its height. She had to get up at

> four in the morning, that still blue almost eternal hour before the baby's cry,

to write at all.† After the long expending day, tending, caring, cleaning, enjoying, laundering, feeding, marketing, delighting, outing; being

> a very efficient tool or weapon, used and in demand from moment to moment. . . . Nights [were] no good [for writing]. I'm so flat by then that all I can cope with is music and brandy and water.

The smog of cooking, the smog of hell floated in her head. The smile of the icebox annihilated. There was a stink of fat and baby crap; viciousness in the kitchen! And the blood jet poetry (for which there was never time and self except in that still blue hour before the baby's cry) there was no stopping it:‡

> It is not a question in these last weeks of the conflict in a woman's life between the claims of the feminine and the agonized work of art

Elizabeth Hardwick, a woman, can say of Sylvia Plath's suicide,

> Every artist is either a man or woman, and the struggle is pretty much the same for both.

A comment as insensible of the two-angel realities ("so lowly as to be invisible") as are the oblivious masculine assumptions, either that the suicide was because of

---

*Among them: Harriette Arnow, Willa Cather, Dorothy Canfield Fisher, H. H. Richardson (of *Ultima Thule*), Ruth Suckow, Elizabeth Madox Roberts, Sarah Wright, Agnes Smedley; Emily Dickinson, pre-eminently; Sylvia Plath, sometimes Christina Stead, Doris Lessing. (I would now add Edith Summers Kelley [*Weeds* and *The Devil's Hand*], the Marge Piercy of *Small Changes*, and my own fiction.)

†In the long tradition of early rising, an hour here and there, or late-night mother-writers from Mrs. Trollope to Harriette Arnow to this very twenty-four hours—necessarily fitting in writing time in accordance with maintenance of life, and children's, needs.

‡Phrases, lines, throughout from Plath's *Ariel*, letters, BBC broadcasts.

Daddy's death twenty-three years before, revived and compounded by her husband's desertion; or else a real-life *Story of O* (that elegant pornography), sacramental culmination of being used up by ecstasy (poetry in place of sex this time):

> the pride of an utter and ultimate surrender, like the pride of O, naked and chained in her owl mask as she asks Sir Stephen for death. . . .*

If in such an examined extremity, the profound realities of woman's situation are ignored, how much less likely are they—particularly the subtler ones—to be seen, comprehended, taken into account, as they affect lesser-known women writers in more usual circumstances.

In younger years, confidence and vision leeched, aspiration reduced. In adult years, sporadic effort and unfinished work; women made "mediocre caretakers of their talent": that is, writing is not first. The angel in the house situation; probably also the essential angel, maintenance-of-life necessity; increasingly in our century, work on a paid job as well; and for more and more women writers, the whirled expending motherhood years. Is it so difficult to account for the many occasional-fine-story or one-book writers; the distinguished but limited production of others (Janet Lewis, Ann Petry, for example); the years and years in getting one book done (thirty years for Margaret Walker's *Jubilee,* twenty for Marguerite Young's *Miss Macintosh My Darling*); the slowly increasing numbers of women who not until their forties, fifties, sixties, publish for the first time (Dorothy Richardson, Hortense Calisher, Theodora Kroeber, Linda Hoyer—John Updike's mother); the women who start with children's, girls' books (Maxine Kumin), some like Cid Ricketts Sumner *(Tammy)* seldom or never getting to adult fiction that would encompass their wisdom for adults; and most of all, the unsatisfactory quality of book after book that evidences the marks of part-time, part-self authorship, and to whose authors Sarah Orne Jewett's words to the part-time, part-self young Willa Cather still apply, seventy years after:

> If you don't keep and mature your force and above all have time and quiet to perfect your work, you will be writing things not much better than you did five years ago. . . . Otherwise, what might be strength is only crudeness, and what might be insight is only observation. You will write about life, but never life itself.†

Yes, the loss in quality, the minor work, the hidden silences, are there in woman after woman writer in our century.‡ We will never have the body of work that we were capable of producing. Blight, said Blake, never does good to a tree:

> And if a blight kill not a tree but it still bear fruit, let none say that the fruit was in consequence of the blight.

*Richard Howard, in *The Art of Sylvia Plath,* edited by Charles Newman.
†*Letters of Sarah Orne Jewett,* edited by Annie Fields.
‡Compared to men writers of like distinction and years of life, few women writers have had lives of unbroken productivity, or leave behind a "body of work." Early beginnings, then silence; or clogged late ones (foreground silences); long periods between books (hidden silences) characterize most of us. A Colette, Wharton, Glasgow, Millay, Lessing, Oates are the exceptions.

As for myself, who did not publish a book until I was fifty, who raised children without household help or the help of the "technological sublime" (the atom bomb was in manufacture before the first automatic washing machine); who worked outside the house on everyday jobs as well (as nearly half of all women do now, though a woman with a paid job, except as a maid or prostitute, is still rarest of any in literature); who could not kill the essential angel (there was no one else to do her work); would not—if I could—have killed the caring part of the Woolf angel; as distant from the world of literature most of my life as literature is distant (in content too) from my world:

The years when I should have been writing, my hands and being were at other (inescapable) tasks. Now, lightened as they are, when I must do those tasks into which most of my life went, like the old mother, grandmother in my *Tell Me a Riddle* who could not make herself touch a baby, I pay a psychic cost: "the sweat beads, the long shudder begins." The habits of a lifetime when everything else had to come before writing are not easily broken, even when circumstances now often make it possible for writing to be first; habits of years—response to others, distractibility, responsibility for daily matters—stay with you, mark you, become you. The cost of "discontinuity" (that pattern still imposed on women) is such a weight of things unsaid, an accumulation of material so great, that everything starts up something else in me; what should take weeks. takes me sometimes months to write; what should take months, takes years.

I speak of myself to bring here the sense of those others to whom this is in the process of happening (unnecessarily happening, for it need not, must not continue to be) and to remind us of those (I so nearly was one) who never come to writing at all.

We must not speak of women writers in our century (as we cannot speak of women in any area of recognized human achievement) without speaking also of the invisible, the as-innately-capable: the born to the wrong circumstances—diminished, excluded, foundered, silenced.

We who write are survivors, *"only's."** One-out-of-twelve.*

I must go very fast now, telescope and omit (there has already been so much telescoping and omitting), move to work, professional circumstances.

Devaluation: Still in our century, women's books of great worth suffer the death of being unknown, or at best a peculiar eclipsing, far outnumbering the similar fate of the few such books by men. I think of the writers Kate Chopin, Mary Austin, Dorothy Richardson, Henry Handel Richardson *(Ultima Thule),* Susan Glaspell

---

*For myself, "survivor" contains its other meaning: one who must bear witness for those who foundered; try to tell how and why it was that they, also worthy of life, did *not* survive. And pass on ways of surviving; and tell our chancy luck, our special circumstances.

"Only's" is an expression out of the 1950s Civil Rights time: the young Ralph Abernathy reporting to his Birmingham church congregation on his trip up north for support:

I go to Seattle and they tell me, "Brother, you got to meet so and so, why he's the only Negro Federal Circuit Judge in the Northwest"; I go to Chicago and they tell me, "Brother, you've got to meet so and so, why he's the only full black professor of Sociology there is"; I go to Albany and they tell me, "Brother, you *got* to meet so and so, why he's the only black senator in the state legislature . . ." [long dramatic pause] . . . WE DON'T WANT NO ONLY'S.

Only's are used to rebuke ("to be models"); to imply the unrealistic "see, it can be done, all you need is capacity and will." Accepting a situation of "only's" means: "let inequality of circumstance continue to prevail."

(Jury of Her Peers), Elizabeth Madox Roberts *(Time of Man)*, Janet Lewis, Ann Petry, Harriette Arnow *(The Dollmaker)*, Agnes Smedley *(Daughter of Earth)*, Christina Stead, Kay Boyle, Jean Rhys—every one of them absorbing, and some with the stamp of enduring.* Considering their acknowledged stature, how comparatively unread, untaught, are Edith Wharton, Ellen Glasgow, Elizabeth Bowen, Dorothy Parker, Gertrude Stein, Katherine Mansfield—even Virginia Woolf, Willa Cather, and Katherine Anne Porter.†

Critical attitudes: Two centuries later, still what Cynthia Ozick calls "the *perpetual* dancing dog phenomenon,"‡ the injurious reacting to a book, not for its quality or content, but on the basis of its having been written by a woman—with consequent misreading, mistreatment. §

One addition to the "she writes like a man" "with masculine power" kind of "praise." Power is seldom recognized as the power it is at all, if the subject matter is considered woman's: it is minor, moving, evocative, instinctive, delicate. "As delicate as a surgeon's scalpel," says Katherine Anne Porter of such a falsifying description for Katherine Mansfield's art. Instinctive?

> I judge her work to have been to a great degree a matter of intelligent use of her faculties, a conscious practice of a hard won craftsmanship, a triumph of discipline. . . .**

Climate in literary circles for those who move in them:†† Writers know the importance of being taken seriously, with respect for one's vision and integrity; of comradeship with other writers; of being dealt with as a writer on the basis of one's work and not for other reasons; and how chancy is recognition and getting published. There is no time to speak of this today; but nearly all writers who are women are at a disadvantage here.

Restriction: For all our freer life in this century, our significantly greater access to work, education, travel, varied experience, there is still limitation of circumstances for scope, subject, social context, the kind of comprehensions which come only in situations beyond the private. (What Charlotte Brontë felt so keenly 125 years ago as a denial of "facilities for observation . . . a knowledge of the world" which gives other writers "Thackeray, Dickens . . . an importance, variety, depth greatly beyond what I can offer.")‡‡ "Trespass vision" cannot substitute.

Constriction: not always recognized as constriction. The age-old coercion of women toward one dimension continues to be "terribly, determiningly" present. Women writers are still suspect as unnatural if they concern themselves with aspects of their experience, interests, being, beyond the traditionally defined women's sphere. Hortense Calisher is troubled that women writers

---

*1976: At least some of these writers are now coming out of eclipse. But Glaspell, Mary Austin, Roberts, and H. H. Richardson are still out of print. So is most of Christina Stead.

†Eclipsing, devaluation, neglect are the result of critical judgments, a predominantly male domain. The most damaging, and still prevalent, critical attitude remains "that women's experience and literature written by women are, by definition, minor." Indeed, for a sizable percentage of male writers, critics, academics, writer-women are eliminated from consideration (consciousness) altogether.

‡"Women and Creativity," *Motive*, April 1969.

§Savor Mary Ellmann's inimitable *Thinking about Women*.

**"The Art of Katherine Mansfield," *The Collected Essays of Katherine Anne Porter*.

††See Carolyn Kizer's "Pro Femina" in her *Knock upon Silence*.

‡‡Letter to her publisher, W. S. Williams, 1849.

straining toward a world sensibility, or one equivalent to the roaming consciences of the men . . . or dispens[ing] with whatever was clearly female in their sensibility or experience . . . flee from the image society projects on [them].*

But conscience and world sensibility are as natural to women as to men; men have been freer to develop and exercise them, that is all. Indeed, one of the most characteristic strains in literature written by women (however dropped out of sight, or derided) *is* conscience, concern with wrongs to human beings in their time—from the first novel in our language by a woman, Aphra Behn's *Oroonoko,* that first by anyone against slavery, through Harriet Martineau, Elizabeth Gaskell, George Sand, Harriet Beecher Stowe, Elizabeth Barrett Browning, Rebecca Harding Davis, Helen Hunt Jackson, Olive Schreiner, Ethel Voynich, Charlotte Perkins Gilman—to our own century's Gabriela Mistral, Virginia Woolf (the essays), Nelly Sachs, Anna Seghers, Rachel Carson, Lillian Hellman, Lorraine Hansberry, Theodora Kroeber *(Ishi),* Agnes Smedley, Harriette Arnow, Doris Lessing, Nadine Gordimer, Sylvia Ashton-Warner.

In contradiction to the compass of her own distinguished fiction, Calisher defines the "basic female experience from puberty on through childbed" as women's natural subject:

For myself the feminism that comes straight from the belly, from the bed, and from childbed. A sensibility trusting itself for what it is, as the *other* half of basic life.

Constriction to the stereotypic biological-woman (breeder, sex-partner) sphere. Not only leaving out (what men writers usually leave out) ongoing motherhood, the maintenance-of-life, and other angel in the house so determiningly the experience of most women once they get out of bed and up from childbed, but other common female realities as well.†

And it leaves out the rest of women's biological endowment as born human (including the creative capacity out of which women and men write). *It was the denial of this endowment to live the whole of human life,* the confinement of woman to a sphere, that brought the Women's Rights movement into being in the last century—feminism born of humanism (and that prevented our Calishers from writing throughout centuries).

The acceptance of these age-old constrictive definitions of woman at a time when they are less true than ever to the realities of most women's lives—and need not be true at all—remains a complex problem for women writing in our time. (Mary Wollstonecraft defined it as "the consciousness of being always female which degrades our sex.")

So Anaïs Nin: accepting the constriction to a "feminine sensibility that would not

*"No Important Woman Writer . . . ," *Mademoiselle,* February 1970. These excerpts and my exceptions to them are not wholly fair to this superb essay, which I read originally and quoted from in a copy with an important page (unnoticed) missing. My abashed apologies to Calisher.
†Among them: ways in which innate human drives and capacities (intellect; art; organization; invention; sense of justice; love of beauty, life; courage; resilience, resistance; need for community) denied development and scope, nevertheless struggle to express themselves and function; what goes on in jobs; penalties for aging; the profound experience of children—and the agonizing having to raise them in a world not yet fit for human life; what it is to live as a single woman; having to raise children alone; going on; causes besides the accepted psychiatric ones, of breakdown in women. The list goes on and on.

threaten man." Dwelling in the private, the inner; endless vibrations of mood; writing what was muted, exquisite, sensuous, subterranean. That is, in her fiction. In her *Diaries* (along with the narcissistic), the public, the social; power of characterization, penetrating observation, hard intellect, range of experience and relationship; different beauties. Qualities and complexities not present in her fiction—to its impoverishment.

The Bold New Women, to use another example (this from the title of a recent anthology), are the old stereotypic women, depicting themselves within the confines of the sexual-creature, biological-woman literary ghetto; mistaking themselves as new because the sex is explicit as in current male genre; the style and conception of female sexuality, out of Lawrence or Miller. "Whole areas of me are made by the kind of experience women haven't had before," reminds Doris Lessing. "Liberty is the right not to lie," says Camus.

These pressures toward censorship, self-censorship; toward accepting, abiding by entrenched attitudes, thus falsifying one's own reality, range, vision, truth, voice, are extreme for women writers (indeed have much to do with the fear, the sense of powerlessness that pervades certain of our books, the "above all, amuse" tone of others). Not to be able to come to one's truth or not to use it in one's writing, even in telling the truth having to "tell it slant," robs one of drive, of conviction; limits potential stature; results in loss to literature and the comprehensions we seek in it.*

My time is up.

You who teach, read writers who are women. There is a whole literature to be re-estimated, revalued. Some works will prove to be, like the lives of their human authors, mortal—speaking only to their time. Others now forgotten, obscured, ignored, will live again for us.

Read, listen to, living women writers; our new as well as our established, often neglected ones. Not to have audience is a kind of death.

Read the compass of women writers in our infinite variety. Not only those who tell us of ourselves as "the other half," but also those who write of the other human dimensions, realms.

Teach women's lives through the lives of the women who wrote the books, as well as through the books themselves; and through autobiography, biography, journals, letters. Because most literature concerns itself with the lives of the few, know and teach the few books closer to the lives of the many. It should not be that Harriette Arnow's *The Dollmaker,* Elizabeth Madox Robert's *Time of Man,* Grace Paley's *Little Disturbances* are out of paperback print; that a Zora Neale Hurston is reprinted for the first time; that Agnes Smedley's classic *Daughter of Earth* † has been out of print, unread, unknown, for forty years—a book of the greatest meaning, too, for those many students who are the first generation of their families to come into college.

Be critical. Women have the right to say: this is surface, this falsifies reality, this degrades.

Help create writers, perhaps among them yourselves. There is so much unwritten that needs to be written. There are others besides the silenced eleven-out-of-twelve

---

*Compounding the difficulty is that experiences and comprehensions not previously admitted into literature—especially when at variance with the canon—are exceedingly hard to come to, validate, establish as legitimate material for literature—let alone shape into art.

† In 1976 these books are all back in print.

who could bring into literature what is not there now. That first generation of their families to come into college, who come from my world which (in Camus's words) gives "emotion without measure," are a special hope. It does not matter if in its beginning what emerges is not great, or even (as ordinarily defined) "good" writing.

Whether that is literature, or whether that is not literature, I will not presume to say,

wrote Virginia Woolf in her preface to *Life as We Have Known It, Memoirs of the Working Women's Guild,*

but that it explains much and tells much, that is certain.

The greatness of literature is not only in the great writers, the good writers; it is also in that which explains much and tells much* (the soil, too, of great literature).

Soil or blossom, the hope and intention is that before the end of our second writing century, we will begin to have writers who are women in numbers equal to our innate capacity—at least twelve for every one writer-woman of recognized achievement now.†

<hr>

ANNETTE KOLODNY

<hr>

Dancing through the Minefield: Some Observations on the Theory, Practice, and Politics of a Feminist Literary Criticism

Had anyone the prescience, ten years ago, to pose the question of defining a "feminist" literary criticism, she might have been told, in the wake of Mary Ellmann's *Thinking about Women,* [1] that it involved exposing the sexual stereotyping of women in both our literature and our literary criticism and, as well, demonstrating the inadequacy of established critical schools and methods to deal fairly or sensitively

*Lessing's description of the novel (in her afterword to Schreiner's *Story of an African Farm*) pertains to this writing which "explains much and tells much": "com[ing] out of a part of the human consciousness which is trying to understand itself, to come into the light. Not on the level where poetry works, or music, or mathematics, the high arts; no, but on the rawest and most workaday level, like earthworms making new soil where things can grow." But there are other forms of expression which can do this, and more: the journal, letters, memoirs, personal utterances—for they come more natural for most, closer to possibility of use, of shaping—and, *in one's own words,* become source, add to the authentic store of human life, human experience. The inestimable value of this, its emergence as a form of literature, is only beginning to be acknowledged. As yet, there is no place in literature analogous to the honored one accorded "folk" and "primitive" expression in art and in music.

†And for every twelve enabled to come to recognized achievement, remember: there would still remain countless others still lessened or silenced—as long as the other age-old silencers of humanity, class and/or color prevail.

with works written by women. In broad outline, such a prediction would have stood well the test of time, and, in fact, Ellmann's book continues to be widely read and to point us in useful directions. What could not have been anticipated in 1969, however, was the catalyzing force of an ideology that, for many of us, helped to bridge the gap between the world as we found it and the world as we wanted it to be. For those of us who studied literature, a previously unspoken sense of exclusion from authorship, and a painfully personal distress at discovering whores, bitches, muses, and heroines dead in childbirth where we had once hoped to discover ourselves, could—for the first time—begin to be understood as more than "a set of disconnected, unrealized private emotions."[2] With a renewed courage to make public our otherwise private discontents, what had once been "felt individually as personal insecurity" came at last to be "viewed collectively as structural inconsistency"[3] within the very disciplines we studied. Following unflinchingly the full implications of Ellmann's percipient observations, and emboldened by the liberating energy of feminist ideology—in all its various forms and guises—feminist criticism very quickly moved beyond merely "expos[ing] sexism in one work of literature after another,"[4] and promised, instead, that we might at last "begin to record new choices in a new literary history."[5] So powerful was that impulse that we experienced it, along with Adrienne Rich, as much "more than a chapter in cultural history": it became, rather, "an act of survival."[6] What was at stake was not so much literature or criticism as such, but the historical, social, and ethical consequences of women's participation in, or exclusion from, either enterprise.

The pace of inquiry these last ten years has been fast and furious—especially after Kate Millett's 1970 analysis of the sexual politics of literature[7] added a note of urgency to what had earlier been Ellmann's sardonic anger—while the diversity of that inquiry easily outstripped all efforts to define feminist literary criticism as either a coherent system or a unified set of methodologies. Under its wide umbrella, everything has been thrown into question: our established canons, our aesthetic criteria, our interpretative strategies, our reading habits, and, most of all, ourselves as critics and as teachers. To delineate its full scope would require nothing less than a book—a book that would be outdated even as it was being composed. For the sake of brevity, therefore, let me attempt only a summary outline.

Perhaps the most obvious success of this new scholarship has been the return to circulation of previously lost or otherwise ignored works by women writers. Following fast upon the initial success of the Feminist Press in reissuing gems such as Rebecca Harding Davis's 1861 novella, *Life in the Iron Mills,* and Charlotte Perkins Gilman's 1892 *The Yellow Wallpaper,* published in 1972 and 1973, respectively,[8] commercial trade and reprint houses vied with one another in the reprinting of anthologies of lost texts and, in some cases, in the reprinting of whole series. For those of us in American literature especially, the phenomenon promised a radical reshaping of our concepts of literary history and, at the very least, a new chapter in understanding the development of women's literary traditions. So commercially successful were these reprintings, and so attuned were the reprint houses to the political attitudes of the audiences for which they were offered, that many of us found ourselves wooed to compose critical introductions, which would find in the pages of nineteenth-century domestic and sentimental fictions some signs of either muted rebellions or overt radicalism, in anticipation of the current wave of "new feminism." In rereading with our students these previously lost works, we inevitably raised perplexing questions as to the reasons for their disappearance from the canons of "major works," and we worried over the aesthetic and critical criteria by which they had been accorded diminished status.

This increased availability of works by women writers led, of course, to an increased interest in what elements, if any, might comprise some sort of unity or connection among them. The possibility that women had developed either a unique or at least a related tradition of their own, especially intrigued those of us who specialized in one national literature or another, or in historical periods. Nina Baym's recent *Woman's Fiction: A Guide to Novels by and about Women in America, 1820–1870*[9] demonstrates the Americanists' penchant for examining what were once the "best sellers" of their day, the ranks of the popular fiction writers, among which women took a dominant place throughout the nineteenth century, while the feminist studies of British literature emphasized instead the wealth of women writers who have been regarded as worthy of canonization. Not so much building upon one another's work as clarifying, successively, the parameters of the questions to be posed, Sydney Janet Kaplan, Ellen Moers, Patricia Meyer Spacks, and Elaine Showalter, among many others, concentrated their energies on delineating an internally consistent "body of work" by women that might stand as a female countertradition. For Kaplan, in 1975, this entailed examining women writers' various attempts to portray feminine consciousness and self-consciousness, not as a psychological category, but as a stylistic or rhetorical device.[10] That same year, arguing essentially that literature publicizes the private, Spacks placed her consideration of a "female imagination" within social and historical frames, to conclude that, "for readily discernible historical reasons women have characteristically concerned themselves with matters more or less peripheral to male concerns," and she attributed to this fact an inevitable difference in the literary emphases and subject matters of female and male writers.[11] The next year, Moers's *Literary Women: The Great Writers* focused on the pathways of literary influence that linked the English novel in the hands of women.[12] And, finally, in 1977, Showalter took up the matter of a "female literary tradition in the English novel from the generation of the Brontës to the present day" by arguing that, because women in general constitute a kind of "subculture within the framework of a larger society," the work of women writers, in particular, would thereby demonstrate a unity of "values, conventions, experiences, and behaviors impinging on each individual" as she found her sources of "self-expression relative to a dominant [and, by implication, male] society."[13]

At the same time that women writers were being reconsidered and reread, male writers were similarly subjected to a new feminist scrutiny. The continuing result—to put ten years of difficult analysis into a single sentence—has been nothing less than an acute attentiveness to the ways in which certain power relations-usually those in which males wield various forms of influence over females—are inscribed in the texts (both literary and critical), that we have inherited, not merely as subject matter, but as the unquestioned, often unacknowledged *given* of the culture. Even more important than the new interpretations of individual texts are the probings into the consequences (for women) of the conventions that inform those texts. For example, in surveying selected nineteenth- and early twentieth-century British novels which employ what she calls "the two suitors convention," Jean E. Kennard sought to understand why and how the structural demands of the convention, even in the hands of women writers, inevitably work to imply "the inferiority and necessary subordination of women." Her 1978 study, *Victims of Convention,* points out that the symbolic nature of the marriage which conventionally concludes such novels "indicates the adjustment of the protagonist to society's values, a condition which is equated with her maturity." Kennard's concern, however, is with the fact that the structural demands of the form too often sacrifice precisely those "virtues of independence and individuality," or, in other words, the very "qualities we have been invited to admire in" the heroines.[14] Kennard appropriately cautions us against drawing from her work any simplistically reductive thesis about the mimetic relations between art and life. Yet her approach nonetheless suggests that what is important about a fiction is not whether it ends in a death or a marriage, but what the symbolic demands of that particular conventional ending imply about the values and beliefs of the world that engendered it.

Her work thus participates in a growing emphasis in feminist literary study on the fact of literature as a social institution, embedded not only within its own literary traditions, but also within the particular physical and mental artifacts of the society from which it comes. Adumbrating Millett's 1970 decision to anchor her "literary reflections" to a preceding analysis of the historical, social, and economic contexts of sexual politics,[15] more recent work—most notably Lillian Robinson's—begins with the premise that the process of artistic creation "consists not of ghostly happenings in the head but of a matching of the states and processes of symbolic models against the states and processes of the wider world."[16] The power relations inscribed in the form of conventions within our literary inheritance, these critics argue, reify the encodings of those same power relations in the culture at large. And the critical examination of rhetorical codes becomes, in their hands, the pursuit of ideological codes, because both embody either value systems or the dialectic of competition between value systems. More often than not, these critics also insist upon examining not only the mirroring of life in art, but also the normative impact of art on life. Addressing herself to the popular art available to working class women, for example, Robinson is interested in understanding not only "the forms it uses," but, more important, "the myths it creates, the influence it exerts." "The way art helps people to order, interpret, mythologize, or dispose of their own experience," she declares, may be "complex and often ambiguous, but it is not impossible to define."[17]

Whether its focus be upon the material or the imaginative contexts of literary invention; single texts or entire canons; the relations between authors, genres, or historical circumstances; lost authors or well-known names, the variety and diversity of all feminist literary criticism finally coheres in its stance of almost defensive rereading. What Adrienne Rich had earlier called "re-vision," that is, "the act of looking back, of seeing with fresh eyes, of entering an old text from a new critical direction,"[18] took on a more actively self-protective coloration in 1978, when Judith Fetterley called upon the woman reader to learn to "resist" the sexist designs a text might make upon her—asking her to identify against herself, so to speak, by manipulating her sympathies on behalf of male heroes, but against female shrew or bitch characters.[19] Underpinning a great deal of this critical rereading has been the not-unexpected alliance between feminist literary study and feminist studies in linguistics and language-acquisition. Tillie Olsen's commonsense observation of the danger of "perpetuating—by continued usage—entrenched, centuries-old oppressive power realities, early-on incorporated into language,"[20] has been given substantive analysis in the writings of feminists who study "language as a symbolic system closely tied to a patriarchal social structure." Taken together, their work demonstrates "the importance of language in establishing, reflecting, and maintaining an asymmetrical relationship between women and men."[21]

To consider what this implies for the fate of women who essay the craft of language is to ascertain, perhaps for the first time, the real dilemma of the poet who finds her most cherished private experience "hedged by taboos, mined with false-namings."[22] It also explains the dilemma of the male reader who, in opening the pages of a woman's book, finds himself entering a strange and unfamiliar world of symbolic significance. For if, as Nelly Furman insists, neither language use nor language acquisition are "gender-neutral," but are, instead, "imbued with our sex-inflected cultural values";[23] and if, additionally, reading is a process of "sorting out the structures of signification,"[24] in any text, then male readers who find themselves outside of and unfamiliar with the symbolic systems that constitute female experience in women's writings, will necessarily dismiss those systems as undecipherable, meaningless, or trivial. And male professors will find no reason to include such works in the canons of "major authors." At the same time, women writers, coming into a tradition of literary language and conventional forms already appropriated, for centuries, to the purposes of male expression, will be forced virtually to "wrestle" with that language in an effort "to remake it as a language adequate to our conceptual processes."[25] To all of this, feminists concerned with the politics of language and style have been acutely attentive. "Language conceals an invincible adversary," observes French critic Hélène Cixous, "because it's the language of men and their grammar."[26] But equally insistent, as in the work of Sandra M. Gilbert and Susan Gubar, has been the understanding of the need for *all* readers—male and female alike—to learn to penetrate the otherwise unfamiliar universes of symbolic action that comprise women's writings, past and present.[27]

To have attempted so many difficult questions and to have accomplished so much—even acknowledging the inevitable false starts, overlapping, and repetition—in so short a time, should certainly have secured feminist literary criticism an honored berth on that ongoing intellectual journey which we loosely term in academia, "critical analysis." Instead of being welcomed onto the train, however, we've been forced to negotiate a minefield. The very energy and diversity of our enterprise have rendered us vulnerable to attack on the grounds that we lack both definition and coherence; while our particular attentiveness to the ways in which literature encodes and disseminates cultural value systems calls down upon us imprecations echoing those heaped upon the Marxist critics of an earlier generation. If we are scholars dedicated to rediscovering a lost body of writings by women, then our finds are questioned on aesthetic grounds. And if we are critics, determined to practice revisionist readings, it is claimed that our focus is too narrow, and our results are only distortions or, worse still, polemical misreadings.

The very vehemence of the outcry, coupled with our total dismissal in some quarters,[28] suggests not our deficiencies, however, but the potential magnitude of our challenge. For what we are asking to be scrutinized are nothing less than shared cultural assumptions so deeply rooted and so long ingrained that, for the most part, our critical colleagues have ceased to recognize them as such. In other words, what is really being bewailed in the claims that we distort texts or threaten the disappearance of the great Western literary tradition itself[29] is not so much the disappearance of either text or tradition but, instead, the eclipse of that particular *form* of the text, and that particular *shape* of the canon, which previously reified male readers' sense of power and significance in the world. Analogously, by asking whether, as readers, we ought to be "really satisfied by the marriage of Dorothea Brooke to Will Ladislaw? of Shirley Keeldar to Louis Moore?" or whether, as Kennard suggests, we must reckon with the ways in which "the qualities we have been invited to admire in these heroines [have] been sacrificed to structural neatness,"[30] is to raise difficult and profoundly perplexing questions about the ethical implications of our otherwise unquestioned aesthetic pleasures. It is, after all, an imposition of high order to ask the viewer to attend to Ophelia's sufferings in a scene where, before, he'd always so comfortably kept his eye fixed firmly on Hamlet. To understand all this, then, as the real nature of the challenge we have offered and, in consequence, as the motivation for the often overt hostility we've aroused should help us learn to negotiate the minefield, if not with grace, then with at least a clearer comprehension of its underlying patterns.

The ways in which objections to our work are usually posed, of course, serve to obscure their deeper motivations. But this may, in part, be due to our own reticence at taking full responsibility for the truly radicalizing premises that lie at the theoretical core of all we have so far accomplished. It may be time, therefore, to redirect discussion, forcing our adversaries to deal with the substantive issues and pushing ourselves into a clearer articulation of what, in fact, we are about. Up until now, I fear, we have only piecemeal dealt with the difficulties inherent in challenging the authority of established canons and then justifying the excellence of women's traditions, sometimes in accord with standards to which they have no intrinsic relation.

At the very point at which we must perforce enter the discourse—that is, claiming excellence or importance for our "finds"—all discussion has already, we discover, long ago been closed. "If Kate Chopin were *really* worth reading," an Oxford-trained colleague once assured me, "she'd have lasted—like Shakespeare"; and he then proceeded to vote against the English department's crediting a women's studies seminar I was offering in American women writers. The canon, for him, conferred excellence; Chopin's exclusion demonstrated only her lesser worth. As far as he was concerned, I could no more justify giving English department credit for the study of Chopin than I could dare publicly to question Shakespeare's genius. Through hindsight, I've now come to view that discussion as not only having posed fruitless oppositions, but also as having entirely evaded the much more profound problem lurking just beneath the surface of our disagreement. That is, that the fact of canonization puts any work beyond questions of establishing its merit and, instead, invites students to offer only increasingly more ingenious readings and interpretations, the purpose of which is to validate the greatness already imputed by canonization.

Had I only understood it for what it was then, into this circular and self-serving set of assumptions I might have interjected some statement of my right to question why *any* text is revered and my need to know what it tells us about "how we live, how we have been living, how we have been led to imagine ourselves, [and] how our language has trapped as well as liberated us."[31] The very fact of our critical training within the strictures imposed by an established canon of major works and authors, however, repeatedly deflects us from such questions. Instead, we find ourselves endlessly responding to the *riposte* that the overwhelmingly male presence among canonical authors was only an accident of history—and never intentionally sexist—coupled with claims to the "obvious" aesthetic merit of those canonized texts. It is, as I say, a fruitless exchange, serving more to obscure than to expose the territory being protected and dragging us, again and again, through the minefield.

It is my contention that current hostilities might be transformed into a true dialogue with our critics if we at last made explicit what appear, to this observer, to constitute the three crucial propositions to which our special interests inevitably give rise. They are, moreover, propositions which, if handled with care and intelligence, could breathe new life into now moribund areas of our profession: (1) Literary history (and with that, the historicity of literature) is a fiction; (2) insofar as we are taught how to read, what we engage are not texts but paradigms; and, finally, (3) that since the grounds upon which we assign aesthetic value to texts are never infallible, unchangeable, or universal, we must reexamine not only our aesthetics but, as well, the inherent biases and assumptions informing the critical methods which (in part) shape our aesthetic responses. For the sake of brevity, I won't attempt to offer the full arguments for each but, rather, only sufficient elaboration to demonstrate what I see as their intrinsic relation to the potential scope of and present challenge implied by feminist literary study.

1. *Literary history (and, with that, the historicity of literature) is a fiction.* To begin with, an established canon functions as a model by which to chart the continuities and discontinuities, as well as the influences upon and the interconnections between works, genres, and authors. That model we tend to forget, however, is of our own making. It will take a very different shape, and explain its inclusions and exclusions in very different ways, if the reigning critical ideology believes that new literary forms result from some kind of ongoing internal dialectic within preexisting styles and traditions or if, by contrast, the ideology declares that literary change is dependent upon societal development and thereby determined by upheavals in the social and economic organization of the culture at large.[32] Indeed, whenever in the previous century of English and American literary scholarship one alternative replaced the other, we saw dramatic alterations in canonical "wisdom."

This suggests, then, that our sense of a "literary history" and, by extension, our confidence in a "historical" canon is rooted not so much in any definitive understanding of the past as it is in our need to call up and utilize the past on behalf of a better understanding of the present. Thus, to paraphrase David Couzens Hoy, it becomes "necessary to point out that the understanding of art and literature is such an essential aspect of the present's self-understanding that this self-understanding conditions what even gets taken" as comprising that artistic and literary past. To quote Hoy fully, "this continual reinterpretation of the past goes hand in hand with the continual reinterpretation by the present of itself."[33] In our own time, uncertain as to which, if any, model truly accounts for our canonical choices or accurately explains literary history, and pressured further by the feminists' call for some justification of the criteria by which women's writings were largely excluded from both that canon and history, we suffer what Harold Bloom has called "a remarkable dimming" of "our mutual sense of canonical standards."[34]

Into this apparent impasse, feminist literary theorists implicitly introduce the observation that our choices and evaluations of current literature have the effect either of solidifying or of reshaping our sense of the past. The authority of any established canon, after all, is reified by our perception that current work seems to grow, almost inevitably, out of it (even in opposition or rebellion), and is called into question when what we read appears to have little or no relation to what we recognize as coming before. So, were the larger critical community to begin to seriously attend to the recent outpouring of fine literature by women, this would surely be accompanied by a concomitant researching of the past, by literary histori- ans, in order to account for the present phenomenon. In that process, literary history would itself be altered: works by seventeenth-, eighteenth-, or nineteenth-century women, to which we had not previously attended, might be given new importance as "precursors" or as prior influences upon present-day authors; while selected male writers might also be granted new prominence as figures whom the women today, or even yesterday, needed to reject. I am arguing, in other words, that the choices we make in the present inevitably alter our sense of the past that led to them.

Related to this is the feminist challenge to that patently mendacious critical fallacy that we read the "classics" in order to reconstruct the past "the way it really was," and that we read Shakespeare and Milton in order to apprehend the meanings that they intended. Short of time machines or miraculous resurrections, there is simply no way to know, precisely or surely, what "really was," what Homer intended when he sang, or Milton when he dictated. Critics more acute than I have already pointed up the impossibility of grounding a reading in the imputation of authorial intention because the further removed the author is from us, so too must be her or his systems of knowledge and belief, points of view, and structures of vision (artistic and otherwise).[35] (I omit here the difficulty of finally either proving or disproving the imputation of intentionality because, inescapably, the only appropriate authority is unavailable: deceased.) What we have really come to mean when we speak of competence in reading historical texts, therefore, is the ability to recognize literary conventions which have survived through time—so as to remain operational in the mind of the reader—and, where these are lacking, the ability to translate (or perhaps transform?) the text's ciphers into more current and recognizable shapes. But we never really reconstruct the past in its own terms. What we gain when we read the "classics," then, is neither Homer's Greece nor George Eliot's England *as they knew it* but, rather, an approximation of an already fictively imputed past made available, through our interpretive strategies, for present concerns. Only by understanding this can we put to rest that recurrent delusion that the "continuing relevance" of the classics serves as "testimony to perennial features of human experience."[36] The only "perennial feature" to which our ability to read and reread texts written in previous centuries testifies is our inventiveness—in the sense that all of literary history is a fiction which we daily recreate as we reread it. What distinguishes feminists in this regard is their desire to alter and extend what we take as historically relevant from out of that vast storehouse of our literary inheritance and, further, feminists' recogni- tion of the storehouse for what it really is: a resource for remodeling our literary history, past, present, and future.

2. *Insofar as we are taught how to read, what we engage are not texts but paradigms.* To pursue the logical consequences of the first proposition leads, however uncom- fortably, to the conclusion that we appropriate meaning from a text according to what we need (or desire) or, in other words, according to the critical assumptions or predispositions (conscious or not) that we bring to it. And we appropriate different meanings, or report different gleanings, at different times—even from the same text—according to our changed assumptions, circumstances, and requirements. This, in essence, constitutes the heart of the second proposition. For insofar as literature is itself a social institution, so, too, reading is a highly socialized—or learned—activity. What makes it so exciting, of course, is that it can be constantly relearned and refined, so as to provide either an individual or an entire reading

community, over time, with infinite variations of the same text. It *can* provide that, but, I must add, too often it does not. Frequently our reading habits become fixed, so that each successive reading experience functions, in effect, normatively, with one particular kind of novel stylizing our expectations of those to follow, the stylistic devices of any favorite author (or group of authors) alerting us to the presence or absence of those devices in the works of others, and so on. "Once one has read his first poem," Murray Krieger has observed, "he turns to his second and to the others that will follow thereafter with an increasing series of preconceptions about the sort of activity in which he is indulging. In matters of literary experience, as in other experiences," Krieger concludes, "one is a virgin but once."[37]

For most readers, this is a fairly unconscious process, and not unnaturally, what we are taught to read well and with pleasure, when we are young, predisposes us to certain specific kinds of adult reading tastes. For the professional literary critic, the process may be no different, but it is at least more conscious. Graduate schools, at their best, are training grounds for competing interpretive paradigms or reading techniques: affective stylistics, structuralism, and semiotic analysis, to name only a few of the more recent entries. The delight we learn to take in the mastery of these interpretive strategies is then often mistakenly construed as our delight in reading specific texts, especially in the case of works that would otherwise be unavailable or even offensive to us. In my own graduate career, for example, with superb teachers to guide me, I learned to take great pleasure in *Paradise Lost,* even though as both a Jew and a feminist, I can subscribe neither to its theology nor to its hierarchy of sexual valuation. If, within its own terms (as I have been taught to understand them), the text manipulates my sensibilities and moves me to pleasure—as I will affirm it does—then, at least in part, that must be because, in spite of my real-world alienation from many of its basic tenets, I have been able to enter that text through interpretive strategies which allow me to displace less comfortable observations with others to which I have been taught pleasurably to attend. Though some of my teachers may have called this process "learning to read the text properly," I have now come to see it as learning to effectively manipulate the critical strategies which they taught me so well. Knowing, for example, the poem's debt to epic conventions, I am able to discover in it echoes and reworkings of both lines and situations from Virgil and Homer; placing it within the ongoing Christian debate between Good and Evil, I comprehend both the philosophic and the stylistic significance of Satan's ornate rhetoric as compared to God's majestic simplicity in Book III. But, in each case, an interpretative model, already assumed, had guided my discovery of the evidence for it.[38]

When we consider the implications of these observations for the processes of canon formation and for the assignment of aesthetic value, we find ourselves locked in a chicken-and-egg dilemma, unable easily to distinguish as primary the importance of *what* we read as opposed to *how* we have learned to read it. For, simply put, we read well, and with pleasure, what we already know how to read; and what we know how to read is to a large extent dependent upon what we have already read (works from which we've developed our expectations and learned our interpretive strategies). What we then choose to read—and, by extension, teach and thereby "canonize"—usually follows upon our previous reading. Radical breaks are tiring, demanding, uncomfortable, and sometimes wholly beyond our comprehension.

Though the argument is not usually couched in precisely these terms, a considerable segment of the most recent feminist rereadings of women writers allows the conclusion that, where those authors have dropped out of sight, the reason may be due not to any lack of merit in the work but, instead, to an incapacity of predominantly male readers to properly interpret and appreciate women's texts—due, in large part, to a lack of prior acquaintance. The fictions which women compose about the worlds they inhabit may owe a debt to prior, influential works by other women or, simply enough, to the daily experience of the writer herself or, more usually, to some combination of the two. The reader coming upon such fiction, with knowledge of neither its informing literary traditions nor its real-world contexts, will thereby find himself hard-pressed, though he may recognize the words on the page, to competently decipher its intended meanings. And this is what makes the recent studies by Spacks, Moers, Showalter, Gilbert and Gubar, and others so crucial. For, by attempting to delineate the connections and interrelations that make for a female literary tradition, they provide us invaluable aids for recognizing and understanding the unique literary traditions and sex-related contexts out of which women write.

The (usually male) reader who, both by experience and by reading, has never made acquaintance with those contexts—historically, the lying-in room, the parlor, the nursery, the kitchen, the laundry, and so on—will necessarily lack the capacity to fully interpret the dialogue or action embedded therein; for, as every good novelist knows, the meaning of any character's action or statement is inescapably a function of the specific situation in which it is embedded.[39] Virginia Woolf therefore quite properly anticipated the male reader's dispostion to write off what he could not understand, abandoning women's writings as offering "not merely a difference of view, but a view that is weak, or trivial, or sentimental because it differs from his own." In her 1929 essay on "Women and Fiction," Woolf grappled most obviously with the ways in which male writers and male subject matter had already preempted the language of literature. Yet she was also tacitly commenting on the problem of (male) audience and conventional reading expectations when she speculated that the woman writer might well "find that she is perpetually wishing to alter the established values [in literature]—to make serious what appears insignificant to a man, and trivial what is to him important."[40] "The 'competence' necessary for understanding [a] literary message . . . depends upon a great number of codices," after all; as Cesare Segre has pointed out, to be competent, a reader must either share or at least be familiar with, "in addition to the code language . . . the codes of custom, of society, and of conceptions of the world"[41] (what Woolf meant by "values"). Males ignorant of women's "values" or conceptions of the world will necessarily, thereby, be poor readers of works that in any sense recapitulate their codes.

The problem is further exacerbated when the language of the literary text is largely dependent upon figuration. For it can be argued, as Ted Cohen has shown, that while "in general, and with some obvious qualifications . . . all literal use of language is accessible to all whose language it is . . . figurative use can be inaccessible to all but those who share information about one another's knowledge, beliefs, intentions, and attitudes."[42] There was nothing fortuitous, for example, in Charlotte Perkins Gilman's decision to situate the progressive mental breakdown and increasing incapacity of the protagonist of *The Yellow Wallpaper* in an upstairs room that had once served as a nursery (with barred windows, no less). But the reader unacquainted with the ways in which women traditionally inhabited a household might not have taken the initial description of the setting as semantically relevant; and the progressive infantilization of the adult protagonist would thereby lose some of its symbolic implications. Analogously, the contemporary poet who declares, along with

Adrienne Rich, the need for "a whole new poetry beginning here" is acknowledging
that the materials available for symbolization and figuration from women's contexts
will necessarily differ from those that men have traditionally utilized:

> Vision begins to happen in such a life
> as if a woman quietly walked away
> from the argument and jargon in a room
> and sitting down in the kitchen, began turning in her lap
> bits of yarn, calico and velvet scraps,
>
> . . . .
>
> pulling the tenets of a life together
> with no mere will to mastery,
> only care for the many-lived, unending
> forms in which she finds herself.[43]

What, then, is the fate of the woman writer whose competent reading community
is composed only of members of her own sex? And what, then, the response of the
male critic who, on first looking into Virginia Woolf or Doris Lessing, finds all of
the interpretative strategies at his command inadequate to a full and pleasurable
deciphering of their pages? Historically, the result has been the diminished status
of women's products and their consequent absence from major canons. Nowadays,
however, by pointing out that the act of "interpreting language is no more sexually
neutral than language use or the language system itself," feminist students of
language, like Nelly Furman, help us better understand the crucial linkage between
our gender and our interpretive, or reading, strategies. Insisting upon "the contribution of the . . . reader [in] the active attribution of significance to formal signifiers,"[44]
Furman and others promise to shake us all—female and male alike—out of our
canonized and conventional aesthetic assumptions.

3. *Since the grounds upon which we assign aesthetic value to texts are never
infallible, unchangeable, or universal, we must reexamine not only our aesthetics but,
as well, the inherent biases and assumptions informing the critical methods which (in
part) shape our aesthetic responses.* I am, on the one hand, arguing that men will
be better readers, or appreciators, of women's books when they have read more of
them (as women have always been taught to become astute readers of men's texts).
On the other hand, it will be noted, the emphasis of my remarks shifts the act of
critical judgment from assigning aesthetic valuations to texts and directs it, instead,
to ascertaining the adequacy of any interpretive paradigm to a full reading of both
female and male writing. My third proposition—and, I admit, perhaps the most
controversial—thus calls into question that recurrent tendency in criticism to establish norms for the evaluation of literary works when we might better serve the cause
of literature by developing standards for evaluating the adequacy of our critical
methods.[45] This does not mean that I wish to discard aesthetic valuation. The
choice, as I see it, is not between retaining or discarding aesthetic values; rather, the
choice is between having some awareness of what constitutes (at least in part) the
bases of our aesthetic responses and going without such an awareness. For it is my
view that insofar as aesthetic responsiveness continues to be an integral aspect of
our human response system—in part spontaneous, in part learned and educated—we
will inevitably develop theories to help explain, formalize, or even initiate those
responses.

In challenging the adequacy of received critical opinion or the imputed excellence of established canons, feminist literary critics are essentially seeking to discover how aesthetic value is assigned in the first place, where it resides (in the text or in the reader), and, most important, what validity may really be claimed by our aesthetic "judgments." What ends do those judgments serve, the feminist asks; and what conceptions of the world or ideological stances do they (even if unwittingly) help to perpetuate? In so doing, she points out, among other things, that any response labeled "aesthetic" may as easily designate some immediately experienced moment or event as it may designate a species of nostalgia, a yearning for the components of a simpler past, when the world seemed known or at least understandable. Thus the value accorded an opera or a Shakespeare play may well reside in the viewer's immediate viewing pleasure, or it may reside in the play's nostalgic evocation of a once-comprehensible and ordered world. At the same time, the feminist confronts, for example, the reader who simply cannot entertain the possibility that women's worlds are symbolically rich, the reader who, like the male characters in Susan Glaspell's 1917 short story, "A Jury of Her Peers," has already assumed the innate "insignificance of kitchen things."[46] Such a reader, she knows, will prove himself unable to assign significance to fictions that attend to "kitchen things" and will, instead, judge such fictions as trivial and as aesthetically wanting. For her to take useful issue with such a reader, she must make clear that what appears to be a dispute about aesthetic merit is, in reality, a dispute about the *contexts of judgment;* and what is at issue, then, is the adequacy of the prior assumptions and reading habits brought to bear on the text. To put it bluntly: we have had enough pronouncements of aesthetic valuation for a time; it is now our task to evaluate the imputed norms and normative reading patterns that, in part, led to those pronouncements.

By and large, I think I've made my point. Only to clarify it do I add this coda: when feminists turn their attention to the works of male authors which have traditionally been accorded high aesthetic value and, where warranted, follow Olsen's advice that we assert our "right to say: this is surface, this falsifies reality, this degrades,"[47] such statements do not necessarily mean that we will end up with a diminished canon. To question the source of the aesthetic pleasures we've gained from reading Spenser, Shakespeare, Milton, and so on, does not imply that we must deny those pleasures. It means only that aesthetic response is once more invested with epistemological, ethical, and moral concerns. It means, in other words, that readings of *Paradise Lost* which analyze its complex hierarchal structures but fail to note the implications of gender within that hierarchy; or which insist upon the inherent (or even inspired) perfection of Milton's figurative language but fail to note the consequences, for Eve, of her specifically gender-marked weakness, which, like the flowers to which she attends, requires "propping up"; or which concentrate on the poem's thematic reworking of classical notions of martial and epic prowess into Christian (moral) heroism but fail to note that Eve is stylistically edited out of that process—all such readings, however useful, will no longer be deemed wholly adequate. The pleasures we had earlier learned to take in the poem will not be diminished thereby, but they will become part of an altered reading attentiveness.

These three propositions I believe to be at the theoretical core of most current feminist literary criticism, whether acknowledged as such or not. If I am correct in this, then that criticism represents more than a profoundly skeptical stance toward all other preexisting and contemporaneous schools and methods, and more than an impassioned demand that the variety and variability of women's literary expression be taken into full account, rather than written off as caprice and exception, the irregularity in an otherwise regular design. It represents that locus in literary study where, in unceasing effort, female self-consciousness turns in upon itself, attempting to grasp the deepest conditions of its own unique and multiplicitous realities, in the hope, eventually, of altering the very forms through which the culture perceives, expresses, and knows itself. For, if what the larger women's movement looks for in the future is a transformation of the structures of primarily male power which now order our society, then the feminist literary critic demands that we understand the ways in which those structures have been—and continue to be—reified by our literature and by our literary criticism. Thus, along with other "radical" critics and critical schools, though our focus remains the power of the word to both structure and mirror human experience, our overriding commitment is to a radical altera-tion—an improvement, we hope—in the nature of that experience.

What distinguishes our work from those similarly oriented "social consciousness" critiques, it is said, is its lack of systematic coherence. Pitted against, for example, psychoanalytic or Marxist readings, which owe a decisive share of their persuasive-ness to their apparent internal consistency as a system, the aggregate of feminist literary criticism appears woefully deficient in system, and painfully lacking in program. It is, in fact, from all quarters, the most telling defect alleged against us, the most explosive threat in the minefield. And my own earlier observation that, as of 1976, feminist literary criticism appeared "more like a set of interchangeable strategies than any coherent school or shared goal orientation" has been taken by some as an indictment, by others as a statement of impatience. Neither was in-tended. I felt then, as I do now, that this would "prove both its strength *and* its weakness,"[48] in the sense that the apparent disarray would leave us vulnerable to the kind of objection I've just alluded to; while the fact of our diversity would finally place us securely where, all along, we should have been: camped out, on the far side of the minefield, with the other pluralists and pluralisms.

In our heart of hearts, of course, most critics are really structuralists (whether or not they accept the label) because what we are seeking are patterns (or structures) that can order and explain the otherwise inchoate; thus, we invent, or believe we discover, relational patternings in the texts we read which promise transcendence from difficulty and perplexity to clarity and coherence. But, as I've tried to argue in these pages, to the imputed "truth" or "accuracy" of these findings, the feminist must oppose the painfully obvious truism that what is attended to in a literary work, and hence what is reported about it, is often determined not so much by the work itself as by the critical technique or aesthetic criteria through which it is filtered or, rather, read and decoded. All the feminist is asserting, then, is her own equivalent right to liberate new (and perhaps different) significances from these same texts; and, at the same time, her right to choose which features of a text she takes as relevant because she is, after all, asking new and different questions of it. In the process, she claims neither definitiveness nor structural completeness for her different readings and reading systems, but only their usefulness in recognizing the particular achieve-ments of woman-as-author and their applicability in conscientiously decoding woman-as-sign.

That these alternate foci of critical attentiveness will render alternate readings or interpretations of the same text—even among feminists—should be no cause for alarm. Such developments illustrate only the pluralist contention that "in approaching a text of any complexity . . . the reader must choose to emphasize certain aspects which seem to him crucial" and that, "in fact, the variety of readings which we have for many works is a function of the selection of crucial aspects made by the variety of readers." Robert Scholes, from whom I've been quoting, goes so far as to assert that "there is no single 'right' reading for any complex literary work," and, following the Russian formalist school, he observes that "we do not speak of readings that are simply true or false, but of readings that are more or less rich, strategies that are more or less appropriate."[49] Because those who share the term "feminist" nonetheless practice a diversity of critical strategies, leading, in some cases, to quite different readings, we must acknowledge among ourselves that sister critics, "having chosen to tell a different story, may in their interpretation identify different aspects of the meanings conveyed by the same passage."[50]

Adopting a "pluralist" label does not mean, however, that we cease to disagree; it means only that we entertain the possibility that different readings, even of the same text, may be differently useful, even illuminating, within different contexts of inquiry. It means, in effect, that we enter a dialectical process of examining, testing, even trying out the contexts—be they prior critical assumptions or explicitly stated ideological stances (or some combination of the two)—that led to the disparate readings. Not all will be equally acceptable to every one of us, of course, and even those prior assumptions or ideologies that are acceptable may call for further refinement and/or clarification. But, at the very least, because we will have grappled with the assumptions that led to it, we will be better able to articulate *why* we find a particular reading or interpretation adequate or inadequate. This kind of dialectical process, moreover, not only makes us more fully aware of what criticism is, and how it functions; it also gives us access to its future possibilities, making us conscious, as R. P. Blackmur put it, "of what we have done," "of what can be done next, or done again,"[51] or, I would add, of what can be done differently. To put it still another way: just because we will no longer tolerate the specifically sexist omissions and oversights of earlier critical schools and methods does not mean that, in their stead, we must establish our own "party line."

In my view, our purpose is not and should not be the formulation of any single reading method or potentially procrustean set of critical procedures nor, even less, the generation of prescriptive categories for some dreamed-of nonsexist literary canon.[52] Instead, as I see it, our task is to initiate nothing less than a playful pluralism, responsive to the possibilities of multiple critical schools and methods, but captive of none, recognizing that the many tools needed for our analysis will necessarily be largely inherited and only partly of our own making. Only by employing a plurality of methods will we protect ourselves from the temptation of so oversimplifying any text—and especially those particularly offensive to us—that we render ourselves unresponsive to what Scholes has called "its various systems of meaning and their interaction."[53] Any text we deem worthy of our critical attention is usually, after all, a locus of many and varied kinds of (personal, thematic, stylistic, structural, rhetorical, etc.) relationships. So, whether we tend to treat a text as a *mimesis*, in which words are taken to be recreating or representing viable worlds; or whether we prefer to treat a text as a kind of equation of communication, in which decipherable messages are passed from writers to readers; and whether we locate meaning as inherent in the text, the act of reading, or in some collaboration between reader and text—whatever our predilection, let us not generate from it a straitjacket that limits the scope of possible analysis. Rather, let us generate an ongoing dialogue of competing potential possibilities—among feminists and, as well, between feminist and nonfeminist critics.

The difficulty of what I describe does not escape me. The very idea of pluralism seems to threaten a kind of chaos for the future of literary inquiry while, at the same time, it seems to deny the hope of establishing some basic conceptual model which can organize all data—the hope which always begins any analytical exercise. My effort here, however, has been to demonstrate the essential delusions that inform such objections: If literary inquiry has historically escaped chaos by establishing canons, then it has only substituted one mode of arbitrary action for another—and, in this case, at the expense of half the population. And if feminists openly acknowledge ourselves as pluralists, then we do not give up the search for patterns of opposition and connection—probably the basis of thinking itself; what we give up is simply the arrogance of claiming that our work is either exhaustive or definitive. (It is, after all, the identical arrogance we are asking our nonfeminist colleagues to abandon.) If this kind of pluralism appears to threaten both the present coherence of and the inherited aesthetic criteria for a canon of "greats," then, as I have earlier argued, it is precisely that threat which, alone, can free us from the prejudices, the strictures, and the blind spots of the past. In feminist hands, I would add, it is less a threat than a promise.

What unites and repeatedly invigorates feminist literary criticism, then, is neither dogma nor method but, as I have indicated earlier, an acute and impassioned *attentiveness* to the ways in which primarily male structures of power are inscribed (or encoded) within our literary inheritance; the consequences of that encoding for women—as characters, as readers, and as writers; and, with that, a shared analytic *concern* for the implications of that encoding not only for a better understanding of the past, but also for an improved reordering of the present and future as well. If that *concern* identifies feminist literary criticism as one of the many academic arms of the larger women's movement, then that *attentiveness*, within the halls of academe, poses no less a challenge for change, generating, as it does, the three propositions explored here. The critical pluralism that inevitably follows upon those three propositions, however, bears little resemblance to what Robinson has called "the greatest bourgeois theme of all, the myth of pluralism, with its consequent rejection of ideological commitment as 'too simple' to embrace the (necessarily complex) truth."[54] Only ideological commitment could have gotten us to enter the minefield, putting in jeopardy our careers and our livelihood. Only the power of ideology to transform our conceptual worlds, and the inspiration of that ideology to liberate long-suppressed energies and emotions, can account for our willingness to take on critical tasks that, in an earlier decade, would have been "abandoned in despair or apathy."[55] The fact of differences among us proves only that, despite our shared commitments, we have nonetheless refused to shy away from complexity, preferring rather to openly disagree than to give up either intellectual honesty or hard-won insights.

Finally, I would argue, pluralism informs feminist literary inquiry not simply as a description of what already exists but, more importantly, as the only critical stance consistent with the current status of the larger women's movement. Segmented and variously focused, the different women's organizations neither espouse any single system of analysis nor, as a result, express any wholly shared, consistently articulated ideology. The ensuing loss in effective organization and political clout is a serious one, but it has not been paralyzing; in spite of our differences, we have united to *act* in areas of clear mutual concern (the push for the Equal Rights Amendment is probably the most obvious example). The trade-off, as I see it, has made possible an ongoing and educative dialectic of analysis and proffered solutions, protecting us thereby from the inviting traps of reductionism and dogma. And so long as this dialogue remains active, both our politics and our criticism will be free of dogma— but never, I hope, of feminist ideology, in all its variety. For, "whatever else ideologies may be—projections of unacknowledged fears, disguises for ulterior motives, phatic expressions of group solidarity" (and the women's movement, to date, has certainly been all of these, and more)—whatever ideologies express, they are, as Geertz astutely observes, "most distinctively, maps of problematic social reality and matrices for the creation of collective conscience." And despite the fact that "ideological advocates . . . tend as much to obscure as to clarify the true nature of the problems involved," as Geertz notes, "they at least call attention to their existence and, by polarizing issues, make continued neglect more difficult. Without Marxist attack, there would have been no labor reform; without Black Nationalists, no deliberate speed."[56] Without Seneca Falls, I would add, no enfranchisement of women, and without "consciousness raising," no feminist literary criticism nor, even less, women's studies.

Ideology, however, only truly manifests its power by ordering the *sum* of our actions.[57] If feminist criticism calls anything into question, it must be that dog-eared myth of intellectual neutrality. For, what I take to be the underlying spirit, or message, of any consciously ideologically premised criticism—that is, that ideas are important *because* they determine the ways we live, or want to live, in the world—is vitiated by confining those ideas to the study, the classroom, or the pages of our books. To write chapters decrying the sexual sterotyping of women in our literature, while closing our eyes to the sexual harrassment of our women students and colleagues; to display Katharine Hepburn and Rosalind Russell in our courses on "The Image of the Independent Career Women in Film," while managing not to notice the paucity of female administrators on our own campus; to study the women who helped make universal enfranchisement a political reality, while keeping silent about our activist colleagues who are denied promotion or tenure; to include segments on "Women in the Labor Movement" in our American studies or women's studies courses, while remaining willfully ignorant of the department secretary fired for her efforts to organize a clerical workers' union; to glory in the delusions of "merit," "privilege," and "status" which accompany campus life in order to insulate ourselves from the millions of women who labor in poverty—all this is not merely hypocritical; it destroys both the spirit and the meaning of what we are about. It puts us, however unwittingly, in the service of those who laid the minefield in the first place. In my view, it is a fine thing for many of us, individually, to have traversed the minefield; but that happy circumstance will only prove of lasting importance if, together, we expose it for what it is (the male fear of sharing power and significance with women) and deactivate its components, so that others, after us, may literally dance through the minefield.

Notes

"Dancing through the Minefield" was the winner of the 1979 Florence Howe Essay Contest, which is sponsored by the Women's Caucus of the Modern Language Association.

Some sections of this essay were composed during the time made available to me by a grant from the Rockefeller Foundation, for which I am most grateful.

This essay intentionally deals with white feminist critics only, because it was originally conceived as the first of a two-essay dialogue with myself. The second essay, "Sharp-Shooting from the Outskirts of the Minefield: The Radical Critique by American Black and Third World Feminist Literary Critics," was to argue that black and Third World American feminist literary critics stand as a group apart from the whites, united by their far more probing analyses of the institutions which give rise to current literary tastes and by their angrier indictment of current critical practice and theory. Due to recurrent eye problems, however, and some difficulty in obtaining all the articles I sought, the second essay could not be completed along with the first and, as yet, remains in draft. Despite the omission of any discussion of the fine work done by black and Third World feminist critics, I decided to allow the first essay into print—for whatever discussion it may initiate; and I beg the reader's patience while I endeavor to complete its follow-up companion.

1. Mary Ellman, *Thinking about Women* (New York: Harcourt Brace Jovanovich, Harvest, 1968).
2. See Clifford Gertz, "Ideology as a Cultural System," in his *The Interpretation of Cultures: Selected Essays* (New York: Basic Books, 1973), p. 232.
3. Ibid., p. 204.
4. Lillian S. Robinson, "Cultural Criticism and the *Horror Vacui,*" *College English* 33, no. 1 (1972); reprinted as "The Critical Task" in her *Sex, Class, and Culture* (Bloomington: Indiana University Press, 1978), p. 51.
5. Elaine Showalter, *A Literature of Their Own: British Women Novelists from Brontë to Lessing* (Princeton: Princeton University Press, 1977), p. 36.
6. Adrienne Rich, "When We Dead Awaken: Writing as Re-Vision," *College English* 34, no. 1 (October 1972); reprinted in *Adrienne Rich's Poetry,* ed. Barbara Charlesworth Gelpi and Albert Gelpi (New York: W. W. Norton, 1975), p. 90.
7. Kate Millett, *Sexual Politics* (Garden City, N.Y.: Doubleday, 1970).
8. Rebecca Harding Davis, *Life in the Iron Mills,* originally published in *The Atlantic Monthly,* April 1861; reprinted with "A Biograph-

ical Interpretation" by Tillie Olsen (New York: Feminist Press, 1972). Charlotte Perkins Gilman, *The Yellow Wallpaper,* originally published in *The New England Magazine,* May 1892; reprinted with an afterword by Elaine R. Hedges (New York: Feminist Press, 1973).
9. Nina Baym, *Woman's Fiction: A Guide to Novels by and about Women in America, 1820–1870* (Ithaca: Cornell University Press, 1978).
10. In her *Feminine Consciousness in the Modern British Novel* (Urbana: University of Illinois Press, 1975), p. 3, Sydney Janet Kaplan explains that she is using the term "feminine consciousness" "not simply as some general attitude of women toward their own femininity, and not as something synonymous with a particular sensibility among female writers. I am concerned with it as a literary device: a method of characterization of females in fiction."
11. Patricia Meyer Spacks, *The Female Imagination* (New York: Avon Books, 1975), p. 6.
12. Ellen Moers, *Literary Women: The Great Writers* (Garden City, N.Y.: Doubleday, 1976).
13. Showalter, *A Literature of Their Own,* p. 11.
14. Jean E. Kennard, *Victims of Convention* (Hamden, Conn.: Archon Books, 1978), p. 164, 18, 14.
15. See Millett, *Sexual Politics,* pt. 3, "The Literary Reflection," pp. 235–361.
16. The phrase is Geertz's, "Ideology as a Cultural System," p. 214.
17. Lillian Robinson, "Criticism—and Self-Criticism," *College English* 36, no. 4 (1974), and "Criticism: Who Needs It?" in *The Uses of Criticism,* ed. A. P. Foulkes (Bern and Frankfurt: Lang, 1976); both reprinted in *Sex, Class, and Culture,* pp. 67, 80.
18. Rich, "When We Dead Awaken," p. 90.
19. Judith Fetterley, *The Resisting Reader: A Feminist Approach to American Fiction* (Bloomington: Indiana University Press, 1978).
20. Tillie Olsen, *Silences* (New York: Delacorte Press/Seymour Lawrence, 1978), pp. 239–240.
21. See Cheris Kramer, Barrie Thorne, and Nancy Henley, "Perspectives on Language and Communication," Review Essay in *Signs* 3, no. 3 (Summer 1978): 646.
22. See Adrienne Rich's discussion of the difficulty in finding authentic language for her experience as a mother in her *Of Woman Born* (New York: W. W. Norton, 1976), p. 15.
23. Nelly Furman, "The Study of Women and Language: Comment on Vol. 3, no. 3," *Signs* 4, no. 1 (Autumn 1978): 184.
24. Again, my phrasing comes from Geertz, "Thick Description: Toward an Interpretive Theory of Culture," in his *Interpretation of Cultures: Selected Essays* (New York: Basic Books, 1972), p. 9.

25. Julia Penelope Stanley and Susan W. Robbins, "Toward a Feminist Aesthetic," *Chrysalis*, no. 6 (1977): 63.

26. Hélène Cixous, "The Laugh of the Medusa," trans. Keith Cohen and Paula Cohen, *Signs* 1, no. 4 (Summer 1976): 87.

27. In *The Madwoman in the Attic: The Woman Writer and the Nineteenth-Century Literary Imagination* (New Haven: Yale University Press, 1979), Sandra M. Gilbert and Susan Gubar suggest that women's writings are in some sense "palimpsestic" in that their "surface designs conceal or obscure deeper, less accessible (and less socially acceptable) levels of meaning" (p. 73). It is, in their view, an art designed "both to express and to camouflage" (p. 81).

28. Consider, for example, Paul Boyers's reductive and inaccurate generalization that "what distinguishes ordinary books and articles about women from feminist writing is the feminist insistence on asking the same questions of every work and demanding ideologically satisfactory answers to those questions as a means of evaluating it," in his "A Case against Feminist Criticism," *Partisan Review* 43, no. 4 (1976): 602. It is partly as a result of such misconceptions, that we have the paucity of feminist critics who are granted a place in English departments which otherwise pride themselves on the variety of their critical orientations.

29. Ambivalent though he is about the literary continuity that begins with Homer, Harold Bloom nonetheless somewhat ominously prophesies "that the first true break . . . will be brought about in generations to come, if the burgeoning religion of Liberated Woman spreads from its clusters of enthusiasts to dominate the West," in his *A Map of Misreading* (New York: Oxford University Press, 1975), p. 33. On p. 36, he acknowledges that while something "as violent [as] a quarrel would ensue if I expressed my judgment" on Robert Lowell and Norman Mailer, "it would lead to something more intense than quarrels if I expressed my judgment upon . . . the 'literature of Women's Liberation.'"

30. Kennard, *Victims of Convention*, p. 14.

31. Rich, "When We Dead Awaken," p. 90.

32. The first is a proposition currently expressed by some structuralists and formalist critics; the best statement of the second probably appears in Georg Lukacs, *Writer and Critic* (New York: Grosset and Dunlap, 1970), p. 119.

33. David Couzens Hoy, "Hermeneutic Circularity, Indeterminacy, and Incommensurability," *New Literary History* 10, no. 1 (Autumn 1978): 166–67.

34. Bloom, *Map of Misreading*, p. 36.

35. John Dewey offered precisely this argument in 1934 when he insisted that a work of art "is recreated every time it is esthetically experienced. . . . It is absurd to ask what an artist 'really' meant by his product: he himself would find different meanings in it at different days and hours and in different stages of his own development." Further, he explained, "It is simply an impossibility that any one today should experience the Parthenon as the devout Athenian contemporary citizen experienced it, any more than the religious statuary of the twelfth century can mean, esthetically, even to a good Catholic today just what it meant to the worshipers of the old period," in *Art as Experience* (New York: Capricorn Books, 1958), pp. 108–9.

36. Charles Altieri, "The Hermeneutics of Literary Indeterminacy: A Dissent from the New Orthodoxy," *New Literary History* 10, no. 1 (Autumn 1978): 90.

37. Murray Krieger, *Theory of Criticism: A Tradition and Its System* (Baltimore: Johns Hopkins University Press, 1976), p. 6.

38. See Stanley E. Fish, "Normal Circumstances, Literal Language, Direct Speech Acts, the Ordinary, the Everyday, the Obvious, What Goes without Saying, and Other Special Cases," *Critical Inquiry* 4, no. 4 (Summer 1978): 627–28.

39. Ibid., p. 643.

40. Virginia Woolf, "Women and Fiction," *Granite and Rainbow: Essays* (London: Hogarth, 1958), p. 81.

41. Cesare Segre, "Narrative Structures and Literary History," *Critical Inquiry* 3, no. 2 (Winter 1976): 272–73.

42. Ted Cohen, "Metaphor and the Cultivation of Intimacy," *Critical Inquiry* 5, no. 1 (Autumn 1978): 9.

43. From Adrienne Rich's "Transcendental Etude" in her *The Dream of a Common Language: Poems, 1974–1977* (New York: W. W. Norton, 1978), pp. 76–77.

44. Furman, "The Study of Women and Language," p. 184.

45. "A recurrent tendency in criticism is the establishment of false norms for the evaluation of literary works," notes Robert Scholes in his *Structuralism in Literature: An Introduction* (New Haven: Yale University Press, 1974), p. 131.

46. For a full discussion of the Glaspell short story which takes this problem into account, please see my "A Map for Re-Reading: Or, Gender and the Interpretation of Literary Texts," in a Special Issue on Narrative, *New Literary History*, vol. XI, no. 3 (Spring 1980): 451–467.

47. Olsen, *Silences*, p. 45.

48. Annette Kolodny, "Literary Criticism," Review Essay in *Signs* 2, no. 2 (Winter 1976): 420.

49. Scholes, *Structuralism in Literature*, pp. 144–45. These comments appear within his explication of Tzvetan Todorov's theory of reading.

50. I borrow this concise phrasing of pluralistic modesty from M. H. Abrams's "The Deconstructive Angel," *Critical Inquiry* 3, no. 3 (Spring 1977): 427. Indications of the pluralism that was to mark feminist inquiry were to be found in the diversity of essays collected by Susan Koppelman Cornillon for her early and ground-breaking anthology, *Images of Women in Fiction: Feminist*

Perspectives (Bowling Green, Ohio: Bowling Green University Popular Press, 1972).

51. R. P. Blackmur, "A Burden for Critics," *The Hudson Review* 1 (1948): 171. Blackmur, of course, was referring to the way in which criticism makes us conscious of how art functions; I use his wording here because I am arguing that that same awareness must also be focused on the critical act itself. "Consciousness," he avers, "is the way we feel the critic's burden."

52. I have earlier elaborated my objection to prescriptive categories for literature in "The Feminist as Literary Critic," Critical Response in *Critical Inquiry* 2, no. 4 (Summer 1976): 827–28.

53. Scholes, *Structuralism in Literature*, pp. 151–52.

54. Lillian Robinson, "Dwelling in Decencies: Radical Criticism and the Feminist Perspective," *College English* 32, no. 8 (May 1971); reprinted in *Sex, Class, and Culture*, p. 11.

55. "Ideology bridges the emotional gap between things as they are and as one would have them be, thus insuring the performance of roles that might otherwise be abandoned in despair or apathy," comments Geertz in "Ideology as a Cultural System," p. 205.

56. Ibid., pp. 220, 205.

57. I here follow Frederic Jameson's view in *The Prison-House of Language: A Critical Account of Structuralism and Russian Formalism* (Princeton, N.J.: Princeton University Press, 1974), p. 107, that: "Ideology would seem to be that grillwork of form, convention, and belief which orders our actions."

SANDRA M. GILBERT AND SUSAN GUBAR

The Madwoman in the Attic

The Parables of the Cave

"Next then," I said, "take the following parable of education and ignorance as a picture of the condition of our nature. Imagine mankind as dwelling in an underground cave . . ."
—PLATO

Where are the songs I used to know,
Where are the notes I used to sing?
I have forgotten everything
I used to know so long ago.
—CHRISTINA ROSSETTI

. . . there came upon me an overshadowing bright Cloud, and in the midst of it the figure of a Woman, most richly adorned with transparent Gold, her Hair hanging down, and her Face as the terrible Crystal for brightness [and] immediately this Voice came, saying, Behold I am God's Eternal Virgin-Wisdom . . . I am to unseal the Treasures of God's deep Wisdom unto thee, and will be as Rebecca was unto Jacob, a true Natural Mother; for out of my Womb thou shalt be brought forth after the manner of a Spirit, Conceived and Born again.
—JANE LEAD

Although Plato does not seem to have thought much about this point, a cave is—as Freud pointed out—a female place, a womb-shaped enclosure, a house of earth, secret and often sacred. To this shrine the initiate comes to hear the voices of darkness, the wisdom of inwardness. In this prison the slave is immured, the virgin sacrificed, the priestess abandoned. "We have put her living in the tomb!" Poe's paradigmatic exclamation of horror, with its shadow of solipsism, summarizes the Victorian shudder of disgust at the thought of cavern confrontations and the evils they might reveal—the suffocation, the "black bat airs," the vampirism, the chaos of what Victor Frankenstein calls "filthy creation." But despite its melodrama, Poe's remark summarizes too (even if unintentionally) the plight of the woman in patriarchal culture, the woman whose cave-shaped anatomy is her destiny. Not just, like Plato's cave-dweller, a prisoner of Nature, this woman is a prisoner of her own nature, a prisoner in the "grave cave" of immanence which she transforms into a vaporous Cave of Spleen.

In this regard, an anecdote of Simone de Beauvoir's forms a sort of counter-parable to Plato's:

> I recall seeing in a primitive village of Tunisia a subterranean cavern in which four women were squatting: the old one-eyed and toothless wife, her face horribly devastated, was cooking dough on a small brazier in the midst of an acrid smoke; two wives somewhat younger, but almost as disfigured, were lulling children in their arms—one was giving suck; seated before a loom, a young idol magnificently decked out in silk, gold, and silver was knotting threads of wool. As I left this gloomy cave—kingdom of immanence, womb, and tomb—in the corridor leading upward toward the light of day I passed the male, dressed in white, well groomed, smiling, sunny. He was returning from the marketplace, where he had discussed world affairs with other men; he would pass some hours in this retreat of his at the heart of the vast universe to which he belonged, from which he was not separated. For the withered old women, for the young wife doomed to the same rapid decay, there was no universe other than the smoky cave, whence they emerged only at night, silent and veiled.

Destroyed by traditional female activities—cooking, nursing, needling, knotting—which ought to have given them life as they themselves give life to men, the women of this underground harem are obviously buried in (and by) patriarchal definitions of their sexuality. Here is immanence with no hope of transcendence, nature seduced and betrayed by culture, enclosure without any possibility of escape. Or so it would seem.

Yet the womb-shaped cave is also the place of female power, the *umbilicus mundi*, one of the great antechambers of the mysteries of transformation. As herself a kind of cave, every woman might seem to have the cave's metaphorical power of annihilation, the power—as de Beauvoir puts it elsewhere—of "night in the entrails of the earth," for "in many a legend," she notes, "we see the hero lost forever as he falls back into the maternal shadows—cave, abyss, hell." At the same time, as herself a fated inhabitant of that earth-cave of immanence in which de Beauvoir's Tunisian women were trapped, every woman might seem to have metaphorical access to the dark knowledge buried in caves. Summarizing the characteristics of those female "great weavers" who determine destiny—Norns, Fates, priestesses of Demeter, prophetesses of Gaea—Helen Diner points out that "all knowledge of Fate comes from the female depths; none of the surface powers knows it. Whoever wants to know about Fate must go down to the woman," meaning the Great Mother, the Weaver Woman who weaves "the world tapestry out of genesis and demise" in her cave of power. Yet individual women are imprisoned in, not empowered by, such caves, like Blake's symbolic worms, "Weaving to Dreams the Sexual strife/And

weeping over the Web of life." How, therefore, does any woman—but especially
a literary woman, who thinks in images—reconcile the cave's negative metaphoric
potential with its positive mythic possibilities? Immobilized and half-blinded in
Plato's cave, how does such a woman distinguish what she is from what she sees,
her real creative essence from the unreal cutpaper shadows the cavern-master claims
as reality?

In a fictionalized "Author's Introduction" to *The Last Man* (1826) Mary Shelley
tells another story about a cave, a story which implicitly answers these questions and
which, therefore, constitutes yet a third parable of the cave. In 1818, she begins,
she and "a friend" visited what was said to be "the gloomy cavern of the Cumaean
Sibyl." Entering a mysterious, almost inaccessible chamber, they found "piles of
leaves, fragments of bark, and a white filmy substance resembling the inner part of
the green hood which shelters the grain of the unripe Indian corn." At first, Shelley
confesses, she and her male companion (Percy Shelley) were baffled by this discovery, but "At length, my friend . . . exclaimed 'This *is* the Sibyl's cave; these are
sibylline leaves!' " Her account continues as follows.

> On examination, we found that all the leaves, bark, and other substances were traced with
> written characters. What appeared to us more astonishing, was that these writings were
> expressed in various languages: some unknown to my companion . . . some . . . in modern
> dialects. . . . We could make out little by the dim light, but they seemed to contain
> prophecies, detailed relations of events but lately passed; names . . . and often exclamations
> of exultation or woe . . . were traced on their thin scant pages. . . . We made a hasty
> selection of such of the leaves, whose writing one, at least of us could understand, and then
> . . . bade adieu to the dim hypaethric cavern. . . . Since that period . . . I have been employed
> in deciphering these sacred remains. . . . I present the public with my latest discoveries
> in the slight Sibylline pages. Scattered and unconnected as they were, I have been obliged
> to . . . model the work into a consistent form. But the main substance rests on the divine
> intuitions which the Cumaean damsel obtained from heaven.

Every feature of this cave journey is significant, especially for the feminist critic who
seeks to understand the meaning not just of male but also of female parables of the
cave.

To begin with, the sad fact that not Mary Shelley but her male companion is able
to recognize the Sibyl's cave and readily to decipher some of the difficult languages
in which the sibylline leaves are written suggests the woman writer's own anxieties
about her equivocal position in a patriarchal literary culture which often seems to
her to enact strange rituals and speak in unknown tongues. The woman may *be* the
cave, but—so Mary Shelley's hesitant response suggests—it is the man who knows
the cave, who analyzes its meaning, who (like Plato) authors its primary parables,
and who even interprets its language, as Gerard Manley Hopkins, that apostle of
aesthetic virility, was to do more than half a century after the publication of *The
Last Man*, in his sonnet "Spelt from Sibyl's Leaves."

Yet the cave is a female space and it belonged to a female hierophant, the lost
Sibyl, the prophetess who inscribed her "divine intuitions" on tender leaves and
fragments of delicate bark. For Mary Shelley, therefore, it is intimately connected
with both her own artistic authority and her own power of self-creation. A male poet
or instructor may guide her to this place, but, as she herself realizes, she and she

alone can effectively reconstruct the scattered truth of the Sibyl's leaves. Literally the daughter of a dead and dishonored mother—the powerful feminist Mary Woll-stonecraft—Mary Shelley portrays herself in this parable as figuratively the daughter of the vanished Sybil, the primordial prophetess who mythically conceived all women artists.

That the Sibyl's leaves are now scattered, fragmented, barely comprehensible is thus the central problem Shelley faces in her own art. Earlier in her introduction, she notes that finding the cave was a preliminary problem. She and her companion were misled and misdirected by native guides, she tells us; left alone in one chamber while the guides went for new torches, they "lost" their way in the darkness; ascending in the "wrong" direction, they accidentally stumbled upon the true cave. But the difficulty of this initial discovery merely foreshadows the difficulty of the crucial task of reconstruction, as Shelley shows. For just as the path to the Sibyl's cave has been forgotten, the coherent truth of her leaves has been shattered and scattered, the body of her art dismembered, and, like Anne Finch, she has become a sort of "Cypher," powerless and enigmatic. But while the way to the cave can be "remembered" by accident, the whole meaning of the sibylline leaves can only be re-membered through painstaking labor: translation, transcription, and stitchery, re-vision and re-creation.

The specifically sexual texture of these sibylline documents, these scattered leaves and leavings, adds to their profound importance for women. Working on leaves, bark, and "a white filmy substance," the Sibyl literally wrote, and wrote *upon*, the Book of Nature. She had, in other words, a goddess's power of maternal creativity, the sexual/artistic strength that is the female equivalent of the male potential for literary paternity. In her "dim hypaethric cavern"—a dim sea-cave that was never-theless *open* to the sky—she received her "divine intuitions" through "an aperture" in the "arched dome-like roof" which "let in the light of heaven." On her "raised seat of stone, about the size of a Grecian couch," she *conceived* her art, inscribing it on leaves and bark from the green world outside. And so fierce are her verses, so truthful her "poetic rhapsodies," that even in deciphering them Shelley exclaims that she feels herself "taken . . . out of a world, which has averted its once benignant face from me, to one glowing with imagination and power." For in recovering and reconstructing the Sibyl's scattered artistic/sexual energy, Shelley comes to recog-nize that she is discovering and creating—literally *de-ciphering*—her own creative power. "Sometimes I have thought," she modestly confesses, "that, obscure and chaotic as they are, [these translations from the Sibyl's leaves] owe their present form to me, their decipherer. As if we should give to another artist, the painted fragments which form the mosaic copy of Raphael's Transfiguration in St. Peter's; he would put them together in a form, whose mode would be fashioned by his own peculiar mind and talent."

Given all these implications and overtones, it seems to us that the submerged message of Shelley's parable of the cave forms in itself a fourth parable in the series we have been discussing. This last parable is the story of the woman artist who enters the cavern of her own mind and finds there the scattered leaves not only of her own power but of the tradition which might have generated that power. The body of her precursor's art, and thus the body of her own art, lies in pieces around her, dismembered, dis-remembered, disintegrated. How can she remember it and become a member of it, join it and rejoin it, integrate it and in doing so achieve her own integrity, her own selfhood? Surrounded by the ruins of her own tradition, the leavings and unleavings of her spiritual mother's art, she feels—as we noted earlier—like someone suffering from amnesia. Not only did she fail to recognize— that is, to remember—the cavern itself, she no longer knows its languages, its messages, its forms. With Christina Rossetti, she wonders once again "Where are the songs I used to know,/Where are the notes I used to sing?" Bewildered by the incoherence of the fragments she confronts, she cannot help deciding that "I have forgotten everything/I used to know so long ago."

But it is possible, as Mary Shelley's introduction tells us, for the woman poet to reconstruct the shattered tradition that is her matrilineal heritage. Her trip into the cavern of her own mind, despite (or perhaps because of) its falls in darkness, its stumblings, its anxious wanderings, begins the process of re-membering. Even her dialogue with the Romantic poet who guides her (in Mary Shelley's version of the parable) proves useful, for, as Northrop Frye has argued, a revolutionary "mother-goddess myth" which allows power and dignity to women—a myth which is anti-hierarchical, a myth which would liberate the energy of all living creatures—"gained ground" in the Romantic period. Finally, the sibylline messages themselves speak to her, and in speaking to her they both enable her to speak for herself and empower her to speak for the Sibyl. Going "down to the woman" of Fate whom Helen Diner describes, the woman writer recovers herself as a woman of art. Thus, where the traditional male hero makes his "night sea journey" to the center of the earth, the bottom of the mere, the belly of the whale, to slay or be slain by the dragons of darkness, the female artist makes her journey into what Adrienne Rich has called "the cratered night of female memory" to revitalize the darkness, to retrieve what has been lost, to regenerate, reconceive, and give birth.

What she gives birth to is in a sense her own mother goddess and her own mother land. In this parable of the cave it is not the male god Osiris who has been torn apart but his sister, Isis, who has been dismembered and destroyed. Similarly, it is not the male poet Orpheus whose catastrophe we are confronting but his lost bride, Eury-dice, whom we find abandoned in the labyrinthine caverns of Hades. Or to put the point another way, this parable suggests that (as the poet H. D. knew) the traditional figure of Isis in search of Osiris is really a figure of Isis in search of herself, and the betrayed Eurydice is really (like Virginia Woolf's "Judith Shakespeare") the woman poet who never arose from the prison of her "grave cave." Reconstructing Isis and Eurydice, then, the woman artist redefines and recovers the lost Atlantis of her literary heritage, the sunken continent whose wholeness once encompassed and explained all those figures on the horizon who now seem "odd," fragmentary, incomplete—the novelists historians call "singular anomalies," the poets critics call "poetesses," the revolutionary artists patriarchal poets see as "unsexed," monstrous, grotesque. Remembered by the community of which they are and were members, such figures gain their full authority, and their visions begin to seem like conceptions as powerful as the Sibyl's were. Emily Brontë's passionate A. G. A., Jane Lead's Sophia, H. D.'s *bona dea* all have a place in this risen Atlantis which is their mother country, and Jane Eyre's friendship for Diana and Mary Rivers, Aurora Leigh's love of her Italian mother land together with her dream of a new Jerusalem, Emily Dickinson's "mystic green" where women "live aloud," and George Eliot's concept of sisterhood—all these visions and re-visions help define the utopian boundaries of the resurrected continent.

That women have translated their yearnings for motherly or sisterly precursors into visions of such a land is as clear as it is certain that this metaphoric land, like the Sibyl's leaves and the woman writer's power, has been shattered and scattered. Emily Dickinson, a woman artist whose own carefully sewn together "packets" of poetry were—ironically enough—to be fragmented by male editors and female heirs, projected her yearning for this lost female home into the figure of a caged (and female) leopard. Her visionary nostalgia demonstrates that at times the memory of this Atlantis could be as painful for women writers as amnesia about it often was. "Civilization—spurns—the Leopard!" she noted, commenting that "Deserts— never rebuked her Satin—. . . [for] This was the Leopard's nature—Signor—/ Need—a keeper—frown?" and adding, poignantly, that we should

> Pity—the Pard—that left her Asia—
> Memories—of Palm—
> Cannot be stifled—with Narcotic—
> Nor suppressed—with Balm—

Similarly, though she was ostensibly using the symbolism of traditional religion, Christina Rossetti described her pained yearning for a lost, visionary continent like Dickinson's "Asia" in a poem whose title—"Mother Country"—openly acknowledges the real subject:

> Oh what is that country
>   And where can it be
> Not mine own country,
>   But dearer far to me?
>
> Yet mine own country,
>   If I one day may see
> Its spices and cedars,
>   Its gold and ivory.
>
> As I lie dreaming
>   It rises, that land;
> There rises before me
>   Its green golden strand,
> With the bowing cedars
>   And the shining sand;
> It sparkles and flashes
>   Like a shaken brand.

The ambiguities with which Rossetti describes her own relationship to this land ("Not mine own . . . But dearer far") reflect the uncertainty of the self-definition upon which her vision depends. Is a woman's *mother* country her "own"? Has Mary Shelley a "right" to the Sibyl's leaves? Through what structure of definitions and qualifications can the female artist claim her matrilineal heritage, her birthright of that power which, as Annie Gottlieb's dream asserted, is important to her *because of* her mother? Despite these implicit questions, Rossetti admits that "As I lie dreaming/It rises that land"—rises, significantly, glittering and flashing "like a shaken brand," rises from "the cratered night of female memory," setting fire to the darkness, dispersing the shadows of the cavern, destroying the archaic structures which enclosed it in silence and gloom.

There is a sense in which, for us, this book is a dream of the rising of Christina Rossetti's "mother country." And there is a sense in which it is an attempt at reconstructing the Sibyl's leaves, leaves which haunt us with the possibility that if we can piece together their fragments the parts will form a whole that tells the story of the career of a single woman artist, a "mother of us all," as Gertrude Stein would put it, a woman whom patriarchal poetics dismembered and whom we have tried to remember. Detached from herself, silenced, subdued, this woman artist tried in the beginning, as we shall see, to write like an angel in the house of fiction: with Jane Austen and Maria Edgeworth, she concealed her own truth behind a decorous and ladylike facade, scattering her real wishes to the winds or translating them into incomprehensible hieroglyphics. But as time passed and her cave-prison became more constricted, more claustrophobic, she "fell" into the gothic/Satanic mode and, with the Brontës and Mary Shelley, she planned mad or monstrous escapes, then dizzily withdrew—with George Eliot and Emily Dickinson—from those open spaces where the scorching presence of the patriarchal sun, whom Dickinson called "the man of noon," emphasized her vulnerability. Since "Creation seemed a mighty Crack" to make her "visible," she took refuge again in the safety of the "dim hypaethric cavern" where she could be alone with herself, with a truth that was hers even in its fragmentation.

Yet through all these stages of her history this mythic woman artist dreamed, like her sibylline ancestress, of a visionary future, a utopian land in which she could be whole and energetic. As tense with longing as the giant "korl woman," a metal sculpture the man named Wolfe carves from flesh-colored pig "refuse" in Rebecca Harding Davis's *Life in the Iron Mills,* she turned with a "wild, eager face," with "the mad, half-despairing gesture of drowning," toward her half-conscious imagination of that future. Eventually she was to realize, with Adrienne Rich, that she was "reading the Parable of the Cave/while living in the cave"; with Sylvia Plath she was to decide that "I am a miner" surrounded by "tears/The earthen womb/Exudes from its dead boredom"; and like Plath she was to hang her cave "with roses," transfiguring it—as the Sibyl did—with artful foliage. But her vision of self-creation was consistently the same vision of connection and resurrection. Like the rebirth of the drowned Atlantans in Ursula Le Guin's utopian "The New Atlantis," this vision often began with an awakening in darkness, a dim awareness of "the whispering thunder from below," and a sense that even if "we could not answer, we knew because we heard, because we felt, because we wept, we knew that we were; and we remembered other voices." Like Mary Shelley's piecing together of the Sibil's leaves, the vision often entailed a subversive transfiguration of those female arts to which de Beauvoir's cave-dwelling seamstresses were condemned into the powerful arts of the underground Weaver Woman, who uses her magical loom to weave a distinctively female "Tapestr[y] of Paradise." And the fact that the cave is and was a place where such visions were possible is itself a sign of the power of the cave and a crucial message of the parable of the cave, a message to remind us that the cave is not just the place from which the past is retrieved but the place where the future is conceived, the "earthen womb"—or, as in Willa Cather's *My Antonia,* the "fruit cave"—from which the new land rises.

Elizabeth Barrett Browning expressed this final point for the later nineteenth century, as if to carry Mary Shelley's allegorical narrative one step further. Describing a utopian island paradise in which all creatures are "glad and safe. . . . No guns nor springes in my dream," she populated this peaceful land with visionary poets who have withdrawn to a life in dim sea caves—"I repair/To live within the caves:/And near me two or three may dwell,/Whom dreams fantastic please as well," she wrote, and then described her paradise more specifically:

> Long winding caverns, glittering far
>   Into a crystal distance!
> Through clefts of which, shall many a star
>   Shine clear without resistance!
> And carry down its rays the smell
> Of flowers above invisible.

Here, she declared, her poets—implicitly female or at least matriarchal rather than patriarchal, worshipers of the Romantic mother goddess Frye describes—would create their own literary tradition through a re-vision of the high themes their famous "masculinist" counterparts had celebrated.

> . . . often, by the joy without
>   And in us overcome,
> We, through our musing, shall let float
>   Such poems—sitting dumb—
> As Pindar might have writ if he
>   Had tended sheep in Arcady;
> Or Aeschylus—the pleasant fields
>   He died in, longer knowing;
> Or Homer, had men's sins and shields
>   Been lost in Meles flowing;
> Or poet Plato, had the undim
> Unsetting Godlight broke on him.

Poet Plato revised by a shining woman of noon, a magical woman like Jane Lead's "Eternal Virgin-Wisdom," with "her Face as the terrible Crystal for brightness!" In a sense that re-vision is the major subject of our book, just as it was the theme of Barrett Browning's earnest, female prayer:

> Choose me the cave most worthy choice,
>   To make a place for prayer,
> And I will choose a praying voice
>   To pour our spirits there.

And the answer to Barrett Browning's prayer might have been given by the sibylline voice of Jane Lead's Virgin-Wisdom, or Sophia, the true goddess of the cave: "for out of my Womb thou shalt be brought forth after the manner of a Spirit, Conceived and Born again."

ELAINE SHOWALTER

Rethinking the Seventies: Women Writers and Violence

"A lot of women get killed," he says.
"Yes, I know, they look for it."
—MURIEL SPARK, *THE DRIVER'S SEAT*

Fighting back. On a multiplicity of levels, that is the activity we must engage in together if we—women—are to redress the imbalance and rid ourselves and men of the ideology of rape.
—SUSAN BROWNMILLER, *AGAINST OUR WILL*

Being violent is what triggers many rapes. The girl I raped began screaming at me. Now she's dead.
—WILLIAM MOSBACH, CONVICTED RAPIST AND MURDERER

Inhibition of sexual pleasure in women is often associated with two complementary themes. The first is a fear of loss of control over the insides of one's body. . . . The second theme is an anxious and obsessive concern with men as cruel intruders and rapists.
—ROBERT MAY, *SEX AND FANTASY* (1980)

According to police reports, 4,814 women were murdered in the United States in 1979, an increase of 10% over the previous year. Rapes had gone up by an even higher 13 percentage points, totalling 75,989 reported cases in 1979.
—*CONGRESSIONAL RECORD,* 8 December 1980

When I wrote about women writers for the *Antioch Review* in 1972, we seemed to be at the beginning of an exciting new phase, "a female Renaissance, a new Golden Age, an era of eros and anger." Women writers seemed at last to be able to express anger and passion, to confront their own raging emotions instead of burying them or sublimating them into madness. They were ready to risk the abuse of male critics by dealing honestly with the full range of female experience. Reclaiming their own experience, women writers were also reasserting control over it. Moreover, in the liberating aftermath of Philip Roth's *Portnoy's Complaint* (1969) and with the support of a young women's movement, women writers were insisting on their access to a complete—if "unladylike"—language of the body. The Angel in the House, that phantom of feminine perfection who haunted Virginia Woolf and her literary descendents, who stood at the shoulder of women writers and urged them to be sympathetic, tender, and pure, seemed to have perished at last: "No more arts and wiles, no more fun and games. Today women writers are involved in a fierce encounter with the physical and sexual and social facts of their lives, and given women's experience the encounter is bound to be bloody."

The encounter has been bloodier than I expected. In retrospect, the seventies seem to have been a feminist Camelot, the one brief shining moment when it seemed as if women had real choices; in the name of *autonomy* and *control* we were taking back our bodies, taking back the night. As Elizabeth Fox-Genovese wrote in the *Antioch Review* (Spring 1980), "Women appeared to have a great deal to gain, to have someplace to go. The illusion of possibility runs through this literature like a silver thread." But if, in 1981, the Angel in the House is dead, she has been replaced by another spectre who is more difficult to kill, for he *is* the killer, the Ripper, Mr. Goodbar, the Midnight Rambler himself. Control, autonomy, possibility are mocked by the avenger's fist, or phallus, or knife. Whereas the woman's novel of the 1950s and 1960s too often ended in the heroine's madness or suicide, it now ends in her rape, assault, or murder. Today's heroines fear dying, not flying.

These violent plots obviously reflect both the social reality of rape and women's intense concern with rape as a sexual problem in American culture. Susan Brownmiller's *Against Our Will: Men, Women, and Rape* (1975) was a pivotal book of the decade, one which made a strong case for the politicization of rape as a feminist issue; and Brownmiller described a violence against women that was confirmed by each day's newspaper, each night's TV news. If women's lives have expanded during the 1970s, we have also become more imprisoned and paralyzed by the fear of male violence. As Brownmiller observes, "The ultimate effect of rape upon the woman's mental and emotional health has been accomplished *even without the act.* For to accept a special burden of self-protection is to reinforce the concept that women must live and move about in fear and can never expect to achieve the personal freedom, independence, and self-assurance of men."

No one seems to know how to account for the staggering increase (about 15 percent every year) in reported cases of rape during the 1970s—cases estimated moreover to be only a small percentage of the total actual occurrences. Some think that reporting has increased rather than rape itself, that women who previously would have been afraid or ashamed to tell the police are now more conscious of their rights and more likely to find support in rape centers, in police departments, and in court. Others, including many radical feminists, believe that rape is not an aberration, but a point on the continuum of male-aggressive, female-passive sexual behavior, and that it reflects the fundamental oppression of women in a patriarchal society. It has also been suggested that both the crime of rape and its depiction have increased as a direct result of the women's movement. In her review of *Against Our Will* in the *New York Review of Books* (11 December 1975), Diane Johnson wondered whether "it is even female anger that is affecting an increase in rape itself, as if whatever is at stake in this ancient hostility, it is now the rapist who has his back to the wall." More recently, the film critic Gene Siskel, discussing several hit films featuring the rape and stabbing of young women, suggested that "film-makers are picking up on the notion that a lot of men are angry at women, don't know how to cope with women."

We might take the new plots of women's fiction as further evidence of backlash, a warning that breaking the rules, challenging the ideology of feminine subservience and trying to live a more independent life inevitably puts a woman in jeopardy; many readers have experienced the books this way. But I think more complex concerns than these topical and pragmatic ones are at stake. Women's novels are testing the limits of the liberated will and the metaphysics of violence. What are the irrational forces of evil and violence that collide with control of one's life? Are they outside the self, in male society? Or are they also within the self, in fantasy, guilt, and hate? The phantom killer is obviously a monitory figure; he may also be a projection of female violence, the extreme form of an anger women have only recently begun to imagine and explore. Although its fictional forms are more disturbing than we might have predicted, violence as a fantasy was an undercurrent of feminist thought during the decade.

The Violence Meeting and Other Fantasies

In 1970, at the Second Congress to Unite Women in New York, I purchased for twenty cents (even the price seems unreal) a mimeographed story called "The Twig Benders" by "Wilda Chase." Presented as "a pornographic study of pornography," it was sold by The Feminists, one of the angriest and most radical of the early women's liberation groups; unlike their political analyses, which were printed on pink paper, "The Twig Benders" was mimeo'd on the back of flyers for a pro-abortion rally at St. Patrick's Cathedral.

The notion of feminist pornography quite interested many men at the time; as I noted in my earlier article for the *Antioch Review,* sex from the woman's point of view seemed especially provocative and titillating. One editor of a literary quarterly was eager to do a piece on feminist pornography. The women's movement, which had bored and puzzled him before (why would any woman want to join? asked this rebel of the thirties), now throbbed with erotic potential. He called several times asking to see "The Twig Benders." After I sent it, he never called again; it must have come as a shock. "The Twig Benders" is about women raping, mutilating, humiliating, and murdering men: "Just over the county line they passed a boy on his way home with a bag of groceries, and they offered him a lift. Then stopping on a side road, they gang-raped him, mutilating him psychically and physically to such a degree that they knew he would never be able to function again. Afraid of being caught, they dragged him back into the car and when they were on the highway at full speed they opened the door and pushed him out." I assume that the point was role-reversal, a rhetorical device to startle us into awareness of the porno-graphic imagination that routinely tortures and kills women. But maybe not. The Feminists were a hostile group (one pamphlet was called "Man-hating") and "Wilda Chase" may have meant every word.

There were other signs, other bent twigs pointing to a violent feminist revenge, or the fantasy of such revenge, on male brutality. The media were constantly on the lookout for such possibilities. Valerie Solanis shot Andy Warhol, citing the mani-festo of SCUM (Society for Cutting Up Men), of which she was the sole member. Inez Garcia killed the man who raped her. The Red Witches of Italy, a group that specialized in shooting male gynecologists, firebombing cars, and attacking rapists, made the news in 1976 and 1977. Some observers thought they could connect the women's movement to an increase in female terrorism and the female crime rate, to the Weatherwomen, the Manson gang, the Baader-Meinhof gang, and the Symbionese Liberation Army. But most criminologists agreed that few women criminals had any connection with or understanding of feminism; they were instead much more likely to be the poorest and most isolated victims of oppression and brutality. Female terrorists too were typically recruited by men who had a decisive influence in persuading them to resort to violence.

There were moments, however, when even the gentlest women reacted to the constant barrage of *male* violence against women, in the news, in books, and in films, with the wish to retaliate in kind. Reviewing Hitchcock's *Frenzy* in the *New York Times* (1972), Victoria Sullivan noted that its underlying message is that "psychopathic rapists are basically nice guys screwed up by their mums." Considering the popularity of films about rape *(Clockwork Orange, Straw Dogs, Going Home)* Sullivan concluded: "I want to see films about men getting raped by women. . . . I want to see the camera linger on the look of terror in his eyes when he suddenly realizes that the woman is bigger, stronger, and far more brutal than he." No American filmmaker took Sullivan's sardonic invitation, of course; but the French feminist director Nelly Kaplan made three extraordinary films in the 1970s with the theme of women's revenge: *La Fiancée du Pirate, Papa les Petits Bateaux,* and *Néa.* None became popular; the last two were never even released in the United States, and *Néa* was booked into porn theatres in England under the title *A Young Emmanuelle.* Kaplan's vision is as merciless, if not as murderous, as that of Wilda Chase; her heroines Marie, Cookie, and Néa systematically destroy the small-minded, ugly, greedy, stupid, and exploitative men who try to rape/abduct/betray them. "Revenge," the glowing Kaplan remarked at the London Women's Film Festival, "is good for the complexion."

But women as a group are so conditioned to the victim's role, and so far from attempting any kind of violence, even in self-defense, that their expanded awareness of sex crimes only increases their sense of helplessness, vulnerability, and fear. Feminists, I think, realized very early that this was the case. On 4 August 1971, East Coast pioneers, organizers, and leaders of the women's movement were summoned by telephone to a secret discussion of violence as a strategy. Should we arm ourselves and train for some kind of violent confrontation? It seemed like a preposterous question to me, but I attended with friends from New Jersey N.O.W. The auditorium in New York's P.S. 41 was sweltering; paranoia ran high. There were rumors that bikers, Hell's Angels, hoodlums, and hardhats were planning to attack the Women's Equality Day March on August 26, to beat and rape the women demonstrators. Gloria Steinem and Kate Millett advocated peace and nonviolence, but the other star speakers—Flo Kennedy, Myrna Lamb, Anselma dell'Olio, Robin Morgan—were emotional and alarming: The FBI is training infiltrators for the women's movement. Turn the knife on the Man. Sisters are being killed, killing each other. Get guns. Piss up. Martha Shelley of the Radical Lesbians restored some sanity with her confession of feminine incompetence—how she failed to master karate (too weak); failed to buy a gun (too expensive); failed to join the Weathermen (too secret); and failed to make bombs from *The Anarchist's Cookbook* (too complicated).

But on the whole the evening had little laughter; at the end of the speeches we were frightened, tense, and uncertain. Then the swinging doors at the back of the auditorium opened, and there was Ti-Grace Atkinson, the perennial outlaw, all in black. Shootout at the OK Corral! At the podium, she began a low unintelligible harangue. Women began to shout from the audience; a few words and phrases drifted over: church . . . power . . . Mafia . . . violence . . . class. Was she cracking up? Unrolling a blow-up from the *Daily News* of the recently murdered reputed Mafia chieftain Joe Columbo, Atkinson mocked our talk of violence; we knew nothing about violence: "In fact, I truly believe the discussion of violence as a tactic for the women's movement is, at best, absurd. At worst, it is a feeble and somewhat flattering attempt by the CIA to flush out any potential firebrands. I think that the increasing discussion of violence as a tactic relevant for us is a case of 'militancy of the mouth.' " It later turned out that, in a scenario far more bizarre than anything Norman Mailer could have invented, Atkinson had become closely involved with the Italian-American Unity League and had been shattered by Joe Columbo's death. "For six months I did nothing but sit in my apartment and look at the picture of Columbo's bleeding face," she told a reporter. "That was violence, that was for real. I've been in a tremendous depression. I've started to rethink the whole women's movement."

The Violence Meeting, if it achieved nothing else, certainly ended any further feminist discussions of violence, and that was a good thing. It became a literary episode rather than a historical one, partly because it was stranger than fiction, and partly because it coincided with crises in the lives of several of the women who participated in it; Kate Millett's account of the Violence Meeting concluded her memoir/novel *Flying,* and Ti-Grace Atkinson later published her speech and her ferocious afterthoughts in her book *Amazon Odyssey.* In women's novels, meanwhile, violence continued to be a major theme. Men were the killers, women were the victims—but something was taking place within the familiar headlines. All the clichés about women, rape, and murder were being turned around and tried out; women writers could not discuss mass murders in cold blood, or sing the executioner's song.

Looking for It: Freedom and Death

The most ominous novels of the decade present death and rape (occurring in that order) as the goals or end-points of the heroine's plot. Whether the novelist or the heroine or fate spins the plot is ambiguous. Muriel Spark's *The Driver's Seat* (1970) is an icy tour de force about violence, sex, and power. The heroine, Lise, hunts for a psychopathic sex criminal and forces him to murder her in a ritual that seems like a religious sacrifice. Lise works in an office in Denmark that is a microcosm of the sexual power structure; she has "five girls under her and two men. Over her are two women and five men." To go on a holiday to an unidentified southern European city that appears to be Naples, she buys a garishly colored dress and a coat in clashing stripes. She is rude and loud; everyone remembers her, and that is her intention. She is constructing her own murder; she expects to be written about. At the airport duty-free shop, she buys her killer/boyfriend a knife shaped like a scimitar.

Spark tells us at the beginning of chapter 3 that Lise will "be found tomorrow morning dead from multiple stab-wounds"; throughout the book we are constantly reminded that Lise is the "victim." In her search for her killer, she rejects candidates who are primarily interested in the mechanism of sex: Carlo, the married Italian mechanic who tries to rape her, and Bill, the Enlightenment leader in the macrobiotic movement who needs her for his requisite orgasm (if he misses, "he has to fit in two the next day"). Lise wants only death, and she weeps in frustration when her "boyfriend" proves elusive. But she finds him at last, a sex criminal on parole from his asylum, who tries to run away from her, but is captured by her at last. She drives him to the park in Carlo's car, and instructs him how to kill her: "I'm going to lie down here. Then you tie my hands with my scarf; I'll put one hand over the other, it's the proper way. Then you'll tie my ankles together with your necktie. Then you strike."

The Driver's Seat has been admired but not very well understood by critics, and the movie version, with Elizabeth Taylor and Andy Warhol, was a commercial as well as a critical flop. Yet the world of the novel is weirdly comic, satiric, and clear in its macabre inversions of power and powerlessness. Even a minor character, the murderer's aunt Mrs. Fiedke, has no patience with the male sex:

> There was a time they would stand up and open the door for you. They would take their hat off. But they want their equality today. All I say is that if God had intended them to be as good as us he wouldn't have made them different from us to the naked eye. . . . With all due respect to Mr. Fiedke, may he rest in peace, the male sex is getting out of hand.

In *Communities of Women,* Nina Auerbach sees in this speech "a hidden Sparkian world in which women are in 'the driver's seat' of a mysterious metaphysical collusion that underlies the social world we see": the female community of the Fates. In Lise's careful selection of her death-dress, her patient hunt for her assassin, Spark gives us the devastated postulates of feminine wisdom: that a woman creates her identity by choosing her clothes, that she creates her history by choosing her man. Is "choice" in fact an illusion? Who is in the driver's seat, Spark mockingly asks— the man who strikes, or the woman who makes him her executioner? Is the power to choose her destroyer a form of female control, as the power to imagine violence is a form of fictional control?

Judith Rossner's 1975 best-seller, *Looking for Mr. Goodbar,* has many structural similarities to *The Driver's Seat.* It too suggests a disturbing and in this case unconscious collusion between male killer and female victim. In Rossner's novel, too, the conventions of the mystery novel are inverted; *Mr. Goodbar* begins with the murderer's confession. Such a beginning renounces more than suspense; it confuses the reader's sympathies, especially since this murderer, like Lise's, "had a very clear sense of himself as the victim of the woman he had murdered." Rossner's novel, however, is much more erotic, topical, and circumstantial than *The Driver's Seat* (apparently it was based on the double life of a murdered New York schoolteacher) and the movie version starring Diane Keaton was big box office; it climaxed with a long psychedelic murder scene, much admired by aficionados of film technique.

Most feminists read *Mr. Goodbar* as a warning to women against breaking the rules, sleeping around, and otherwise stepping out of line. But Theresa Dunn, the heroine, is by no means a liberated explorer. She is carefully placed historically and socially in the novel as the guilt-ridden product of an extremely repressive Catholic upbringing, who limps as the result of a severe case of adolescent scoliosis. Crippled by her experience and by her resistance to understanding it, Terry is also frightened by her brief contact with the nascent women's movement; consciousness-raising threatens her because she does not wish to confront her own buried rage and sexual guilt. She wants anonymity more than she wants sex; she wants the illusion of control that comes from choosing her own destruction. Less knowing than Lise, Terry nonetheless taunts her lover into violence. After the murder he discovers that he is limping; some kind of exchange or metamorphosis has occurred.

Mr. Goodbar is the gruesome contemporary version of O'Hara's *Appointment in Samarra* or one of those O. Henry stories where she sells her hair to buy him a watch-chain and he sells his watch to buy her a comb. Ironic destinies. Terry Dunn can't bear to have a man spend the night because she feels confined and strapped down as she did when she was a child in the hospital. Gary Cooper (!) White, the killer, needs to spend the night because he is exhausted, on the run, and uncertain of his masculinity. These characters fatally converge because both are looking for Mr. Goodbar, the escape through sexuality, but also the escape through a violent, omnipotent force (on the night of her murder Terry is reading *The Godfather*) that is the opposite of human will and decision. "Controlling your own destiny," Terry thinks. "There were huge limits after all. You couldn't control which men you met, or which ones liked you. . . . If you drove a car you could make fairly sure that you wouldn't smash into something else, but you could never control whether someone smashed into you." Perhaps it is the collision of fate, the smash-up beyond our control, that attracts women writers.

The Fear of the Intruder

It's not surprising that women should have "an anxious and obsessive" concern with rape, or that this fear should inhibit sexual pleasure. What does often surprise the reader of women's literature is the heroine's guilty analysis of her terror of being attacked, as if this fear were childish and neurotic. Perhaps psychologizing gives the illusion of control over an unfathomable and uncontrollable reality. In *Fear of Flying* (a novel, incidentally, that seems in even a short retrospect sunnily unconcerned about rape or other dangers), Isadora psychoanalyzes her own single moment of panic:

> I knew the man under my bed was partly my father. I thought of Groddeck's *Book of the It*. The fear of the intruder is the wish for the intruder. I thought of all my sessions with Dr. Happe in which we had spoken of my night terrors. I remembered my adolescent fantasy of being stabbed or shot by a strange man. I would be sitting at my desk writing and the man would always attack me from behind. Who was he? Why was my life populated by phantom men?

In contrast to other heroines of the seventies, Isadora is lucky that her phantoms are left over from adolescent fantasy. In novels by black women novelists, such as Toni Morrison's *The Bluest Eye* or Elleasse Sutherland's *Let the Lion Eat Straw*, the man under the bed may be *in fact* the father, or the uncle: sexual initiation as incest/rape. The fear of the intruder is a logical response to a society in which women are genuinely in danger; in my own placid university community, all of the violent crimes of the last decade have been committed against women: gang rapes, a torture murder, a decapitation (unsolved), a shooting. Two of my close women friends living in New York have been attacked by strange men—one stabbed, one shot. And yet one cannot live behind locked doors, even if the house were still a refuge.

Several women's novels during the seventies explore the ambiguity of fear, and look closely at powerlessness and vulnerability. In Gail Godwin's *The Odd Woman* (1974), Professor Jane Clifford, like Terry Dunn, fears loss of control: "If you called things by their name, you had more control of your life, and she liked to be in control." The absence of control in her life is symbolized by the Enema Bandit who preys on women and whose exploits are announced constantly by radio and TV. Single women are instructed "not to go out alone after dark and to lock all doors and windows." When she is alone, Jane is terrified of this potential intruder, full of sexual anxiety, and contemptuous of her own fear. By the end of the novel, when she is absolutely certain she hears him breaking into her house, Jane fantasizes a bargain with the Enema Bandit. She offers him her identity as a getaway disguise: "go in my closet and dress yourself in my warmest clothes; take my purse . . . and my credit cards and identification, and put a scarf over your head and start walking." Still hoping for control, Jane identifies with the Bandit as an obsessed and driven fellow-creature who can change his life as she hopes to change her own.

The psychic exchange between rapist/killer and woman hinted at in *The Odd Woman* and *Looking for Mr. Goodbar* is carried to its absolute extreme in Lois Gould's *A Sea-Change* (1976). In this haunting fantasy Jessie, who has been tied up and robbed—perhaps raped—by an intruder she calls "B.G." (Black Gunman) gradually becomes him. The transformation takes place during a storm—Hurricane Minerva—and the reader is forced to take this Jekyll-Hyde metamorphosis seriously; Jessie overcomes her fear of the intruder by becoming the intruder. B.G. is both her demon lover and her own repressed violent potentiality. We cannot even be sure whether the rape happened or was fantasized; the hurricane too is an emblem of female violence; but Jessie is certainly afraid of losing control over the inside of her body; she is afraid that B.G. will shoot a bullet into it.

The Shadow Knows (1974), by Diane Johnson, is the apotheosis of the intruder novels and the most subtle and terrifying study of female vulnerability and of the malign anonymous threat of modern life. (Stanley Kubrick took an option on the novel, but decided instead to have Johnson write the screenplay of *The Shining*, a "thriller" in which a woman and a child are menaced by a psychopathic man and by hints of the occult.) The heroine, N. (Nada?), is a divorced mother of four, living in a housing project; she is having an affair with a married man who may have abandoned her; she may be pregnant. N. believes that someone is trying to kill her, and she may be right. Anyone could do it: her ex-husband, her best friend, her lover, the detective. Who knows what evil lurks in the hearts of persons?

"You never know," the novel begins, and it teases us throughout. N. narrates her own story, and we don't know if she is reliable; she may indeed be cracking up. In fact, N. is not murdered; but at the end of the novel she is raped—a fate better than death—by a mysterious assailant. In some odd sense, the rape is N.'s punishment for breaking the rules, for protesting and making trouble, for having an affair, for going to graduate school instead of working for the telephone company. Johnson pulls us into complicity with this ending; it is a relief.

N.'s fears and her reasons for them seem genuine enough to me. The rape (I think) is part of the reality of the novel, as distinguished from its fantasy. But *The Shadow Knows* does not easily yield up its complexity to analysis; it is disturbing because it is finally so resistant to explication. In many respects, it is a contemporary example of the genre identified by the late Ellen Moers as Female Gothic—a psychological novel in which the isolated heroine is simultaneously persecuted and courageous. Modern Female Gothic deals in terror, cruelty, and monstrosity, all related to self-hatred. Considered in this tradition, *The Shadow Knows* can be read as a guilty encounter with female monstrosity, externalized as a character, but part of the heroine's own psyche. At the dark heart of the book is the relationship between N. and Osella, the enormously fat, crazy, evil ex-nursemaid who is her enemy and her double. Osella, insofar as we decipher the mystery, is the killer; at any rate, N. thinks so. N. goes to confront her at the Club Zanzibar where Osella does a strip-tease act, exposing a primitive and almost supernatural female power:

> She wore little trunks of purple satin and nothing else but a gold amulet around the expanse of her upper arm—a brilliant stroke, a rather Egyptian, goddess-like adornment, calling to mind one of those frightening and horrifying fertility goddesses with swollen bodies and timeless eyes and the same engulfing absorbing quality Osella radiated now. She seemed the embodiment of a principle, passive and patient, frightening to men, I guess, absorbing them into her immense proportions. She seemed a sort of super female needing only the puny seed of men and she would grow and grow and keep on growing.

The Shadow may be N. herself, or N.'s "shadow" Osella—Kali, the dark jungle queen, the fertility goddess, the man-eater. Osella is the bloated spectre of N.'s deepest fantasies—her own murderous anger, her sexuality, her wish for power. And it is perhaps for recognizing this truth that N. is raped by the faceless intruder, who is the secret agent of the male order. N. finally achieves a kind of tranquillity by accepting both the inner reality of her desires and her powerlessness in the world; she gets used to the dark, she joins the "spiritually sly." She is grateful to be alive.

Fighting Back

N.'s bargain is probably a wise one, because in fiction (and life?) raped women rarely fight back, and when they do, they lose. Women may be the jungle queens, but men still rule the jungle. In Marilyn French's *The Women's Room,* a young girl brutally raped by a black teen-ager cannot even fight back in court, where she is insulted and humiliated. The novel ends with a hopeless scenario of protest; a militant feminist group organizes around the case of Anita Morrow, a black woman convicted of murdering the white man who raped her. The militants plan to rescue her from prison and smuggle her out of the country; but the group has been infiltrated by the FBI and the police have been tipped off:

> On the day when Anita was to be transferred to the state prison . . . the women arrived singly, dressed in jeans or skirts, disguised as just women, and hung around the street until Morrow was brought out to the van. Then suddenly they mobilized in a circle, pulling guns out of skirts and coats.
>
> But the authorities expected them. Behind the brick wall was a policeman, two, three; they stepped out with machine guns—the women had only handguns—and mowed them down.

The women are massacred; the scene is an enactment not only of the darkest fantasies of the Violence Meeting, but also of Hollywood B-films. That this novel became a best-seller suggests that it tapped a very profound level of anger and fear in American women. (The television adaptation prudently omitted the rapes, substituting an optimistic conclusion of career success.)

There is an interesting and, I think, instructive contrast to the women's novels in another sensational best-seller by a male author, which is centrally and very oddly concerned with rape and with fighting back: John Irving's *The World According to Garp*. Irving is a writer fascinated with bloody violence, mutilation, and harsh destiny; his view of rape is not easy to understand. The presiding spirit of Garp's world is a minor character called Ellen James, who at the age of eleven was raped by two men who then cut out her tongue, like Lavinia in *Titus Andronicus*. She becomes the martyr-saint of a fanatical cult of feminists called the Ellen Jamesians, who amputate their own tongues and communicate with written notes and tracts. The Ellen Jamesians are a satirical invention; Irving makes them a grotesque and futile image of female self-mutilation. Even Ellen James deplores them and writes a sensational article called "Why I Am Not an Ellen Jamesian." At the end of the novel, Garp is shot by a maddened Ellen Jamesian.

Yet Irving feels outrage about rape, and in a long interpolated story, "The World According to Bensenhaver," he describes a violent rape and the victim's bloody and implausible revenge: she cuts her rapist's throat, stabs him repeatedly; he bleeds to death on top of her; the condom he has worn to protect himself against her female germs fills with blood to the size of a tennis ball. Is Irving recommending violence rather than protest? The Ellen Jamesians mutely protest a society in which women are silenced; "in a world of men they felt as if they had been shut up forever." The knife and the gun offer a universal language to women who have no political or social voice. But this offer, like Irving's outrage, is a fake. The real invitations of this novel are to voyeurism, cynicism, and vicarious thrills.

Literature and film offer women little support for fighting back and not much emotional catharsis. The vigilante violence acted out in movies like *Death Wish*, starring Charles Bronson, is offered to men avenging *their* women. Feminist vigilante action, like the Ellen Jamesians or Marilyn French's doomed militants, is seen as crazy, futile, and absurd. Political action by feminists, in the form of organized demonstrations, anti-pornography campaigns, and self-defense training, has also been ridiculed in the press by women writers as prominent as Margaret Drabble, who in an Op-Ed piece for the *New York Times* minimized the importance of rape as an issue: "Clearly there are women who suffer severe psychological as well as physical damage from rape. But equally, there are those who do not." Women, it is implied, should not over-react to this marginal problem. Violence triggers rape.

Violence is not, of course, a new subject for American literature; it may well be that rape is another metaphor for the apocalyptic sense of panic, uncertainty, and frustration that pervades contemporary life. If so, women's literature has joined the mainstream. The feminist fantasies of the liberated will characteristic of the seventies—the will towards autonomy, the will to change our lives, to release sexual and political force in a confrontation with confining institutions—have come up against an external limit, as have the expansive fantasies of other revolutionary movements in education, politics, and civil rights. To talk of controlling one's destiny in the face of the huge, impersonal, murderous shifts of the machinery of history is plainly hubristic in the eighties, a philosophy that may survive only behind the locked doors of EST seminars. For male writer-revolutionaries, disenchantment has taken the form of happy compromise (Jerry Rubin jogs and goes to work on Wall Street) combined with a continued delight in the violently amoral hero: Gary Gilmore or Jake LaMotta. For feminist writers, disenchantment is imagined as our own newly acknowledged sexuality and anger turned against us in the form of male violence, as if every movement by women pressing towards control engenders a more powerful and opposite reaction from men. The novels I have discussed are perhaps not the novels by which others will mark our literary progress in the seventies, but they seem to me to evoke with painful accuracy the spectres haunting the lives of many American women. In 1972, I thought that Virginia Woolf, much as she might have deplored the rage of this new generation, would have envied its freedom. In 1981, I'm not so sure.

NADINE GORDIMER

The Bolter and the Invincible Summer

My writing life began long before I left school, and I began to leave school (frequently) long before the recognised time came, so there is no real demarcation, for me, between school and "professional" life. The quotes are there because I think of professional life as something one enters by way of an examination, not as an obsessional occupation like writing for which you provide your own, often extraordinary or eccentric, qualifications as you go along. And I'm not flattered by the idea of being presented with a "profession," *honoris causa;* every honest writer or painter wants to achieve the impossible and needs no minimum standard laid down by an establishment such as a profession.

This doesn't mean that I think a writer doesn't need a good education in general, and that I don't wish I had had a better one. But maybe my own regrets arise out of the common impulse to find a justification, outside the limits of one's own talent, for the limits of one's achievement.

I was a bolter, from kindergarten age, but unlike most small children rapidly accustoming their soft, round selves to the sharp angles of desks and discipline, I went on running away from school, year after year. I was a day scholar at a convent in the Transvaal gold-mining town where we lived and when I was little I used to hide until I heard the hive of voices start up "Our Father" at prayers, and then I would walk out of the ugly iron gates and spend the morning on the strip of open veld that lay between the township where the school was and the township where my home was. I remember catching white butterflies there, all one summer morning, until, in the quiet when I had no shadow, I heard the school bell, far away, clearly, and I knew I could safely appear at home for lunch. When I was a little older, I took refuge for hours in the lavatory block, waiting in the atmosphere of Jeyes' Fluid for my opportunity to escape. By then I no longer lived from moment to moment, and could not enjoy the butterflies; the past, with the act of running away contained in it, and the future, containing discovery and punishment, made freedom impossible; the act of seizing it was merely a desperate gesture.

What the gesture meant, I don't know. I managed my school work easily; among the girls of the class I had the sort of bossy vitality that makes for popularity; yet I was overcome, from time to time, by what I now can at least label as anxiety states. Speculation about their cause hasn't much place here, which is lucky, for the people who were around me then are still alive. Autobiography can't be written until one is old, can't hurt anyone's feelings, can't be sued for libel, or, worse, contradicted.

There is just one curious aspect of my bolting that seems worth mentioning because it reveals a device of the personality that, beginning at that very time, perhaps, as a dream-defence, an escape, later became the practical subconscious cunning that enabled me to survive and grow in secret while projecting a totally different, camouflage image of myself. I ran away from school; yet there was another school, the jolly, competitive, thrillingly loyal, close-knit world of schoolgirl books, to which I longed to belong. (At one time I begged to go to boarding school, believing, no doubt, that I should find it there.) Of course, even had it existed, that "School Friend" world would have been the last place on earth for me. I should have found there, far more insistently, the walls, the smell of serge and floor polish, the pressure of uniformity and the tyranny of bell-regulated time that set off revolt and revulsion in me. What I did not know—and what a child never knows—is that there is more to the world than what is offered to him; more choices than those presented to him; more kinds of people than those (the only ones he knows) to which he feels but dares not admit he does not belong. I thought I *had* to accept school and the attitudes there that reflected the attitudes of home; therefore, in order to be a person I had to have *some* sort of picture of a school that would be acceptable to me—it didn't seem possible to live without it. The English novelist Stevie Smith once wrote that all children should be told of the possibility of committing suicide, to console them in case they believed there was no way out of the unbearable; it would be less dramatic but far more consoling if a child could be told that there is an aspect of himself he *does not know is permissible.*

The conclusion my bolting school drew from the grown-ups around me was that I was not the studious type and simply should be persuaded to reconcile myself to the minimum of learning. In our small town many girls left school at fifteen or even before. Then, after a six-weeks course at the local commercial college, a girl was ready for a job as a clerk in a shop or in the offices of one of the gold mines which had brought the town into being. And the typewriter itself merely tapped a mark-time for the brief season of glory, self-assertion and importance that came with the engagement party, the pre-nuptial linen "shower," and culminated not so much in the wedding itself as in the birth, not a day sooner than nine months and three weeks later, of the baby. There wasn't much point in a girl keeping her head stuck in books, anyway, even if she chose to fill the interim with one of the occupations that carried a slightly higher prestige, and were vaguely thought of as artistic—teaching tap-dancing, the piano, or "elocution."

I suppose I must have been marked out for one of these, because, although I had neither talent nor serious interest in drumming my toes, playing Czerny, or rounding my vowels, I enjoyed using them all as material in my talent for showing off. As I grew toward adolescence I stopped the home concerts and contented myself with mimicking, for the entertainment of one group of my parents' friends, other friends who were not present. It did not seem to strike those who were there that, in their absence, they would change places with the people they were laughing at; or perhaps it did (I do them an injustice) and they didn't mind.

All the time it was accepted that I was a candidate for home-dressmaking or elocution whom there was no point in keeping at school too long, I was reading and writing not in secret, but as one does, openly, something that is not taken into account. It didn't occur to anyone else that these activities were connected with learning, so why should it have occurred to me? And although I fed on the attention my efforts at impersonation brought me, I felt quite differently about any praise or comment that came when my stories were published in the children's section of a Sunday paper. While I was terribly proud to see my story in print—for only in print did it become "real," did I have proof of the miracle whereby the thing created has an existence of its own—I had a jealous instinct to keep this activity of mine from the handling that would pronounce it "clever" along with the mimicry and the home concerts. It was the beginning of the humble arrogance that writers and painters have, knowing that it is hardly likely that they will ever do anything really good, and not wanting to be judged by standards that will accept anything less. Is this too high-falutin' a motive to attribute to a twelve-year-old child? I don't think so. One can have a generalised instinct toward the unattainable long before one has actually met with it. When, not many years later, I read *Un Coeur Simple* or *War and Peace*—O, I knew this was *it*, without any guidance from the list of the World's Hundred Best Books that I once tried to read through.

I started writing at nine, because I was surprised by a poem I produced as a school exercise. The subject prescribed was "Paul Kruger" (President of the Transvaal Boer Republic), and although I haven't been asked to produce any juvenilia here, in view of what has happened between people like myself and our country since then, I can't resist quoting, just for the long-untasted patriotic flavour:

> Noble in heart,
> Noble in mind,
> Never deceitful,
> Never unkind . . .

It was the dum-de-de-dum that delighted me, rather than the sentiments or the subject. But soon I found that what I really enjoyed was making up a story, and that this was more easily done without the restrictions of dum-de-de-dum. After that I was always writing something, and from the age of twelve or thirteen, often publishing. My children's stories were anthropomorphic, with a dash of the Edwardian writers' Pan-cult paganism as it had been shipped out to South Africa in Kenneth Grahame's books, though already I used the background of mine dumps and veld animals that was familiar to me, and not the European one that provided my literary background, since there were no books about the world I knew. I wrote my elder sister's essays when she was a student at the Witwatersrand University, and kept up a fair average for her. I entered an essay in the literary section of the Eisteddfod run by the Welsh community in Johannesburg and bought with the prize chit *War and Peace, Gone With the Wind,* and an Arthur Ransome.

I was about fourteen then, and a happy unawareness of the strange combination of this choice is an indication of my reading. It was appetite rather than taste that I had; yet while it took in indiscriminately things that were too much for me, the trash tended to be crowded out and fall away. Some of the books I read in my early teens puzzle me, though. Why Pepys' Diary? And what made me plod through *The Anatomy of Melancholy?* Where did I hear of the existence of these books? (That list of the World's One Hundred Best, maybe.) And once I'd got hold of something like Burton, what made me go on from page to page? I think it must have been because although I didn't understand all that I was reading, and what I did understand was remote from my experience in the way that easily-assimilable romance was not, the half-grasped words dealt with the world of ideas, and so confirmed the recognition, somewhere, of that part of myself that I did not know was permissible.

All the circumstances and ingredients were there for a small-town prodigy, but, thank God, by missing the encouragement and practical help usually offered to "talented" children, I also escaped the dwarf status that is clapped upon the poor little devils before their time (if it ever comes). It did not occur to anyone that if I wanted to try to write I ought to be given a wide education in order to develop my mental powers and to give me some cultural background. But this neglect at least meant that I was left alone. Nobody came gawping into that private domain that was no dream-world but, as I grew up, the scene of my greatest activity and my only disciplines. When school-days finally petered out (I had stopped running away, but various other factors had continued to make attendance sketchy) I did have some sort of show of activity that passed for my life in the small town. It was so trivial that I wonder how family or friends can have accepted that any young person could expend vitality at such a low hum. It was never decided what I should "take up" and so I didn't have a job. Until, at twenty-two, I went to the Witwatersrand University, I led an outward life of sybaritic meagreness that I am ashamed of. In it I did not one thing that I wanted wholeheartedly to do; in it I attempted or gratified nothing (outside sex) to try out my reach, the measure of aliveness in me. My existential self was breathing but inert, like one of those unfortunate people who has had a brain injury in a motor accident and lies unhearing and unseeing, though he will eat when food comes and open his eyes to a light. I played golf, learnt to drink gin with the R.A.F. pupil pilots from the nearby air station during the Second World War, and took part in amateur theatricals, to show recognisable signs of life to the people around me. I even went to first aid and nursing classes because this was suggested as an "interest" for me; it did not matter to me what I did, since I could not admit that there was nothing, in the occupations and diversions offered, that really did interest me, and I was not sure—the only evidence was in books—that anything else was possible.

I am ashamed of this torpor, nevertheless, setting aside what I can now see as probable reasons for it, the careful preparation for it that my childhood constituted. I cannot understand why I did not free myself in the most obvious way, leave home and small town and get myself a job somewhere. No conditioning can excuse the absence of the simple act of courage that would resist it. My only overt rejection of my matchbox life was the fact that, without the slightest embarrassment or conscience, I let my father keep me. Though the needs provided for were modest, he was not a rich man. One thing at least I would not do, apparently—I would not work for the things I did not want. And the camouflage image of myself as a dilettantish girl, content with playing grown-up games at the end of my mother's apron strings—at most a Bovary in the making—made this possible for me.

When I was fifteen I had written my first story about adults, and had sent it off to a liberal weekly that was flourishing in South Africa at the time. They published it. It was about an old man who is out of touch with the smart, prosperous life he has secured for his sons, and who experiences a moment of human recognition where he least expects it—with one of their brisk young wives who is so unlike the wife he remembers. Not a bad theme, but expressed with the respectable bourgeois sentiment which one would expect. That was in 1939, two months after the war had broken out, but in the years that followed, the stories I was writing were not much influenced by the war. It occupied the news bulletins on the radio, taking place a long way off, in countries I had never seen; later, when I was seventeen or eighteen there were various boyfriends who went away to Egypt and Italy and sent back coral jewellery and leather bags stamped with the sphinx.

Oddly enough, as I became engaged with the real business of learning how to write, I became less prompt about sending my efforts off to papers and magazines. I was reading Maupassant, Chekhov, Maugham and Lawrence now, also discovering O. Henry, Katherine Anne Porter and Eudora Welty, and the stories in *Partisan Review, New Writing* and *Horizon.* Katherine Mansfield and Pauline Smith, although one was a New Zealander, confirmed for me that my own "colonial" background provided an experience that had scarcely been looked at, let alone thought about, except as a source of adventure stories. I had read "The Death of Ivan Ilyich" and "The Child of Queen Victoria"; the whole idea of what a story could do, be, swept aside the satisfaction of producing something that found its small validity in print. From time to time I sent off an attempt to one of the short-lived local politico-literary magazines—meant chiefly as platforms for liberal politics, they were the only publications that published poetry and stories outside the true-romance category—but these published stories were the easy ones. For the others I had no facility whatever, and they took months, even years, to cease changing shape before I found a way of getting hold of them in my mind, let alone nailing words down around them. And then most of them were too long, or too outspoken (not always in the sexual sense) for these magazines. In a fumbling way that sometimes slid home in an unexpected strike, I was looking for what people meant but didn't say, not only about sex, but also about politics and their relationship with the black people among whom we lived as people live in a forest among trees. So it was that I didn't wake up to blacks and the shameful enormity of the colour bar through a youthful spell in the Communist party, as did most of my contemporaries with whom I share the rejection of white supremacy, but through the apparently esoteric speleology of doubt, led by Kafka rather than Marx. And the "problems" of my country did not set me writing; on the contrary, it was learning to write that sent me falling, falling through the surface of "the South African way of life."

It was about this time, during a rare foray into the nursery bohemia of university students in Johannesburg, that I met a boy who believed that I was a writer. Just that; I don't mean that he saw me as Chosen for the Holy Temple of Art, or any presumptuous mumbo-jumbo of that kind. The cosmetic-counter sophistication I hopefully wore to disguise my stasis in the world I knew and my uncertainty of the possibility of any other, he ignored as so much rubbish. This aspect of myself, that everyone else knew, he did not; what he recognised was my ignorance, my clumsy battle to chip my way out of shell after shell of ready-made concepts and make my own sense of life. He was often full of scorn, and jeered at the way I was going about it; but he *recognised the necessity*. It was through him, too, that I roused myself sufficiently to insist on going to the university; not surprisingly, there was opposition to this at home, since it had been accepted so long that I was not the studious type, as the phrase went. It seemed a waste, spending money on a university at twenty-two (surely I should be married soon); it was suggested that (as distinct from the honourable quest for a husband) the real reason why I wanted to go was to look for men. It seems to me now that this would have been as good a reason as any. My one preoccupation, outside the world of ideas, was men, and I should have been prepared to claim my right to the one as valid as the other.

But my freedom did not come from my new life at university; I was too old, in many ways, had already gone too far, on my own scratched tracks, for what I might once have gained along the tarmac. One day a poet asked me to lunch. He was co-editor of yet another little magazine that was then halfway through the dozen issues that would measure its life. He had just published a story of mine and, like many editors when the contributor is known to be a young girl, was curious to meet its author. He was Uys Krige, an Afrikaans poet and playwright who wrote in English as well, had lived in France and Spain, spoke five languages, was familiar with their literature, and translated from three. He had been a swimming instructor on the Riviera, a football coach somewhere else, and a war correspondent with the International Brigade in Spain.

When the boy (that same boy) heard that I was taking the train to Johannesburg for this invitation—I still lived in the small town—he said: "I wouldn't go, if I were you, Nadine."

"For Pete's sake, why not?"

"Not unless you're prepared to change a lot of things. You may not feel the same, afterwards. You may never be able to go back."

"What on *earth* are you talking about?" I made fun of him: "I'll take the train back."

"No, once you see what a person like that is like, you won't be able to stand your ordinary life. You'll be miserable. So don't go unless you're prepared for this."

The poet was a small, sunburned, blond man. While he joked, enjoyed his food, had an animated discussion with the black waiter about the origin of the name of a fruit, and said for me some translations of Lorca and Eluard, first in Afrikaans and then, because I couldn't follow too well, in English, he had the physical brightness of a fisherman. It was true—I had never met anyone like this being before. I have met many poets and writers since, sick, tortured, pompous, mousy; I know the morning-after face of Apollo. But that day I had a glimpse of—not some spurious "artist's life," but, through the poet's person, the glint off his purpose—what we are all getting at, Camus' "invincible summer" that is there to be dug for in man beneath the grey of suburban life, the numbness of repetitive labour, and the sucking mud of politics.

Oh yes—not long after, a story of mine was published in an anthology, and a second publisher approached me with the offer to publish a collection. The following year I at last sent my stories where I had never been—across the seas to England

and America. They came back to me in due course, in hard covers with my name printed on the coloured jacket. There were reviews, and, even more astonishing, there was money. I was living alone in Johannesburg by then, and I was able to pay the rent and feed both myself and the baby daughter I had acquired. These things are a convenient marker for the beginning of working life. But mine really began that day at lunch. I see the poet occasionally. He's old now, of course; a bit seamed with disappointments, something of a political victim, since he doesn't celebrate his people's politics or the white man's colour bar in general. The truth isn't always beauty, but the hunger for it is.

MARGARET ATWOOD

On Being a "Woman Writer": Paradoxes and Dilemmas

I approach this article with a good deal of reluctance. Once having promised to do it, in fact, I've been procrastinating to such an extent that my own aversion is probably the first subject I should attempt to deal with. Some of my reservations have to do with the questionable value of writers, male or female, becoming directly involved in political movements of any sort: their involvement may be good for the movement, but it has yet to be demonstrated that it's good for the writer. The rest concern my sense of the enormous complexity not only of the relationships between Man and Woman, but also of those between those other abstract intangibles, Art and Life, Form and Content, Writer and Critic, etcetera.

Judging from conversations I've had with many other woman writers in this country, my qualms are not unique. I can think of only one writer I know who has any formal connection with any of the diverse organizations usually lumped together under the titles of Women's Liberation or the Women's Movement. There are several who have gone out of their way to disavow even any fellow-feeling; but the usual attitude is one of grudging admiration, tempered with envy: the younger generation, they feel, has it a hell of a lot better than they did. Most writers old enough to have a career of any length behind them grew up when it was still assumed that a woman's place was in the home and nowhere else, and that anyone who took time off for an individual selfish activity like writing was either neurotic or wicked or both, derelict in her duties to a man, child, aged relatives or whoever else was supposed to justify her existence on earth. I've heard stories of writers so consumed by guilt over what they had been taught to feel was their abnormality that they did their writing at night, secretly, so no one would accuse them of failing as housewives, as "women." These writers accomplished what they did by themselves, often at great personal expense; in order to write at all, they had to defy other women's as well as men's ideas of what was proper, and it's not finally all that comforting to have a phalanx of women—some younger and relatively unscathed, others from their own generation, the bunch that was collecting china, changing diapers and sneering at any female with intellectual pretensions twenty or even ten years ago—come breezing up now to tell them they were right all along. It's like being judged innocent after you've been hanged: the satisfaction, if any, is grim. There's a great temptation to say to Womens' Lib, "Where were you when I really needed you?" or "It's too late for me now." And you can see, too, that it would be fairly galling for these writers, if they have any respect for historical accuracy, which most do, to be hailed as products, spokeswomen, or advocates of the Women's Movement. When they were undergoing their often drastic formative years there *was* no Women's Movement. No matter that a lot of what they say can be taken by the theorists of the Movement as supporting evidence, useful analysis, and so forth: their own inspiration was not theoretical, it came from wherever all writing comes from. Call it experience and imagination. These writers, if they are honest, don't want to be wrongly identified as the children of a movement that did not give birth to them. Being adopted is not the same as being born.

A third area of reservation is undoubtedly a fear of the development of a one-dimensional Feminist Criticism, a way of approaching literature produced by women that would award points according to conformity or non-conformity to an ideological position. A feminist criticism is, in fact, already emerging. I've read at least one review, and I'm sure there have been and will be more, in which a novelist was criticized for not having made her heroine's life different, even though that life was more typical of the average woman's life in this society than the reviewer's "liberated" version would have been. Perhaps Women's Lib reviewers will start demanding that heroines resolve their difficulties with husband, kids, or themselves by stomping out to join a consciousness raising group, which will be no more satisfactory from the point of view of literature than the legendary Socialist Realist romance with one's tractor. However, a feminist criticism need not necessarily be one-dimensional. And—small comfort—no matter how narrow, purblind and stupid such a criticism in its lowest manifestations may be, it cannot possibly be *more* narrow, purblind and stupid than some of the non-feminist critical attitudes and styles that have preceded it.

There's a fourth possible factor, a less noble one: the often observed phenomenon of the member of a despised social group who manages to transcend the limitations imposed on the group, at least enough to become "successful." For such a person the impulse—whether obeyed or not—is to disassociate him/herself from the group and to side with its implicit opponents. Thus the Black millionaire who deplores the Panthers, the rich *Québecois* who is anti-Separatist, the North American immigrant who changes his name to an "English" one; thus, alas, the Canadian writer who makes it, sort of, in New York, and spends many magazine pages decrying provincial dull Canadian writers; and thus the women with successful careers who say *"I've* never had any problems, I don't know what they're talking about." Such a woman tends to regard herself, and to be treated by her male colleagues, as a sort of honorary man. It's the rest of them who are inept, brainless, tearful, self-defeating: not her. "You think like a man," she is told, with admiration and unconscious put-down. For both men and women, it's just too much of a strain to fit together the traditionally incompatible notions of "woman" and "good at something." And if you *are* good at something, why carry with you the stigma attached to that dismal category you've gone to such lengths to escape from? The only reason for rocking the boat is if you're still chained to the oars. Not everyone reacts like this, but this factor may explain some of the more hysterical opposition to Women's Lib on the part of a few woman writers, even though they may have benefitted from the Movement in the form of increased sales and more serious attention.

A couple of ironies remain; perhaps they are even paradoxes. One is that, in the development of modern Western civilization, writing was the first of the arts, before painting, music, composing, and sculpting, which it was possible for women to practice; and it was the fourth of the job categories, after prostitution, domestic service and the stage, and before wide-scale factory work, nursing, secretarial work, telephone operating and school teaching, at which it was possible for them to make any money. The reason for both is the same: writing as a physical activity is private. You do it by yourself, on your own time; no teachers or employers are involved, you don't have to apprentice in a studio or work with musicians. Your only business arrangements are with your publisher, and these can be conducted through the mails; your real "employers" can be deceived, if you choose, by the adoption of an assumed (male) name; witness the Brontës and George Eliot. But the private and individual nature of writing may also account for the low incidence of direct involvement by woman writers in the Movement now. If you are a writer, prejudice against women will affect you *as a writer* not directly but indirectly. You won't suffer from wage discrimination, because you aren't paid any wages; you won't be hired last and fired first, because you aren't hired or fired anyway. You have relatively little to complain of, and, absorbed in your own work as you are likely to be, you will find it quite easy to shut your eyes to what goes on at the spool factory, or even at the university. *Paradox:* reason for involvement then equals reason for non-involvement now.

Another paradox goes like this. As writers, woman writers are like other writers. They have the same professional concerns, they have to deal with the same contracts and publishing procedures, they have the same need for solitude to work and the same concern that their work be accurately evaluated by reviewers. There is nothing "male" or "female" about these conditions; they are just attributes of the activity known as writing. As biological specimens and as citizens, however, women are like other women: subject to the same discriminatory laws, encountering the same demeaning attitudes, burdened with the same good reasons for not walking through the park alone after dark. They too have bodies, the capacity to bear children; they eat, sleep and bleed, just like everyone else. In bookstores and publishers' offices and among groups of other writers, a woman writer may get the impression that she is "special"; but in the eyes of the law, in the loan office or bank, in the hospital and on the street she's just another woman. She doesn't get to wear a sign to the grocery store saying "Respect me, I'm a Woman Writer." No matter how good she may feel about herself, strangers who aren't aware of her shelf-full of nifty volumes with cover blurbs saying how gifted she is will still regard her as a nit.

We all have ways of filtering out aspects of our experience we would rather not think about. Woman writers can keep as much as possible to the "writing" end of their life, avoiding the less desirable aspects of the "woman" end. Or they can divide themselves in two, thinking of themselves as two different people: a "writer" and a "woman." Time after time, I've had interviewers talk to me about my writing for a while, then ask me, "As a woman, what do you think about—for instance—the Women's Movement," as if I could think two sets of thoughts about the same thing, one set as a writer or person, the other as a woman. But no one comes apart this easily; categories like Woman, White, Canadian, Writer are only ways of looking at a thing, and the thing itself is whole, entire and indivisible. *Paradox:* Woman and Writer are separate categories; but in any individual woman writer, they are inseparable.

One of the results of the paradox is that there are certain attitudes, some overt, some concealed, which women writers encounter *as* writers, but *because* they are women. I shall try to deal with a few of these, as objectively as I can. After that, I'll attempt a limited personal statement.

A. Reviewing and the Absence of an Adequate Critical Vocabulary

Cynthia Ozick, in the American magazine *Ms.*, says, "For many years, I had noticed that no book of poetry by a woman was ever reviewed without reference to the poet's sex. The curious thing was that, in the two decades of my scrutiny, there were *no* exceptions whatever. It did not matter whether the reviewer was a man or a woman; in every case, the question of the 'feminine sensibility' of the poet was at the center of the reviewer's response. The maleness of male poets, on the other hand, hardly ever seemed to matter."

Things aren't this bad in Canada, possibly because we were never fully indoctrinated with the Holy Gospel according to the distorters of Freud. Many reviewers manage to get through a review without displaying the kind of bias Ozick is talking about. But that it does occur was demonstrated to me by a project I was involved with at York University in 1971–72.

One of my groups was attempting to study what we called "sexual bias in reviewing," by which we meant not unfavourable reviews, but points being added or subtracted by the reviewer on the basis of the author's sex and supposedly associated characteristics rather than on the basis of the work itself. Our study fell into two parts: i) a survey of writers, half male, half female, conducted by letter: had they ever experienced sexual bias directed against them in a review? ii) the reading of a large number of reviews from a wide range of periodicals and newspapers.

The results of the writers' survey were perhaps predictable. Of the men, none said Yes, a quarter said Maybe, and three quarters said No. Half of the women said Yes, a quarter said Maybe and a quarter said No. The women replying Yes often wrote long, detailed letters, giving instances and discussing their own attitudes. All the men's letters were short.

This proved only that women were more likely to *feel* they had been discriminated against on the basis of sex. When we got around to the reviews, we discovered that they were sometimes justified. Here are the kinds of things we found.

I) Assignment of Reviews

Several of our letter writers mentioned this. Some felt books by women tended to be passed over by book-page editors assigning books for review; others that books by women tended to get assigned to women reviewers. When we started totting up reviews we found that most books in this society are written by men, and so are most reviews. Disproportionately often, books by women were assigned to women reviewers, indicating that books by women fell in the minds of those dishing out the reviews into some kind of "special" category. Likewise, woman reviewers tended to be reviewing books by women rather than by men (though because of the preponderance of male reviewers, there were quite a few male-written reviews of books by women).

II) The Quiller-Couch Syndrome

The heading of this one refers to the turn-of-the-century essay by Quiller-Couch, defining "masculine" and "feminine" styles in writing. The "masculine" style is, of course, bold, forceful, clear, vigorous, etc.; the "feminine" style is vague, weak, tremulous, pastel, etc. In the list of pairs you can include "objective" and "subjective," "universal" or "accurate depiction of society" versus "confessional," "personal," or even "narcissistic" and "neurotic." It's roughly seventy years since Quiller-Couch's essay, but the "masculine" group of adjectives is still much more likely to be applied to the work of male writers; female writers are much more likely to get hit with some version of "the feminine style" or "feminine sensibility," whether their work merits it or not.

III) The Lady Painter, or She Writes Like a Man

This is a pattern in which good equals male, and bad equals female. I call it the Lady Painter Syndrome because of a conversation I had about female painters with a male painter in 1960. "When she's good," he said, "we call her a painter; when she's bad, we call her a lady painter." "She writes like a man" is part of the same pattern; it's usually used by a male reviewer who is impressed by a female writer. It's meant as a compliment. See also "She thinks like a man," which means the author thinks, unlike most women, who are held to be incapable of objective thought (their province is "feeling"). Adjectives which often have similar connotations are ones such as "strong," "gutsy," "hard," "mean," etc. A hard-hitting piece of writing by a man is liable to be thought of as merely realistic; an equivalent piece by a woman is much more likely to be labelled "cruel" or "tough." The assumption is that women are by nature soft, weak and not very good, and that if a woman writer happens to be good, she should be deprived of her identity as a female and provided with higher (male) status. Thus the woman writer has, in the minds of such reviewers, two choices. She can be bad but female, a carrier of the "feminine sensibility" virus; or she can be "good" in male-adjective terms, but sexless. Badness seems to be ascribed then to a surplus of female hormones, whereas badness in a male writer is usually ascribed to nothing but badness (though a "bad" male writer is sometimes held, by adjectives implying sterility or impotence, to be deficient in maleness). "Maleness" is exemplified by the "good" male writer; "femaleness," since it is seen by such reviewers as a handicap or deficiency, is held to be transcended or discarded by the "good" female one. In other words, there is no critical vocabulary for expressing the concept "good/female." Work by a male writer is often spoken of by critics admiring it as having "balls"; ever hear anyone speak admiringly of work by a woman as having "tits"? *Possible antidotes:* Development of a "good/female" vocabulary ("Wow, has that ever got Womb . . ."); or, preferably, the development of a vocabulary that can treat structures made of words as though they are exactly that, not biological entities possessed of sexual organs.

IV) Domesticity

One of our writers noted a (usually male) habit of concentrating on domestic themes in the work of a female writer, ignoring any other topic she might have dealt with, then patronizing her for an excessive interest in domestic themes. We found several instances of reviewers identifying an author as a "housewife" and consequently dismissing anything she has produced (since, in our society, a "housewife" is viewed as a relatively brainless and talentless creature). We even found one instance in which the author was called a "housewife" and put down for writing like one when in fact she was no such thing.

For such reviewers, when a man writes about things like doing the dishes, it's realism; when a woman does, it's an unfortunate feminine genetic limitation.

V) Sexual Compliment–Put-Down

This syndrome can be summed up as follows;

SHE: "How do you like my (design for an airplane/mathematical formula/medical miracle)?"

HE: "You sure have a nice ass."

In reviewing it usually takes the form of commenting on the cute picture of the (female) author on the cover, coupled with dismissal of her as a writer.

VI) Panic Reaction

When something the author writes hits too close to home, panic reaction may set in. One of our correspondents noticed this phenomenon in connection with one of her books: she felt that the content of the book threatened male reviewers, who gave it much worse reviews than did any female reviewer. Their reaction seemed to be that if a character such as she'd depicted did exist, they didn't want to know about it. In panic reaction, a reviewer is reacting to content, not to technique or craftsmanship or a book's internal coherence or faithfulness to its own assumptions. (Panic reaction can be touched off in any area, not just male-female relationships.)

B. Interviewers and Media Stereotypes

Associated with the reviewing problem, but distinct from it, is the problem of the interview. Reviewers are supposed to concentrate on books, interviewers on the writer as a person, human being, or, in the case of women, woman. This means that an interviewer is ostensibly trying to find out what sort of person you are. In reality, he or she may merely be trying to match you up with a stereotype of "Woman Author" that pre-exists in her/his mind; doing it that way is both easier for the interviewer, since it limits the range and slant of questions, and shorter, since the interview can be practically written in advance. It isn't just women who get this treatment: all writers get it. But the range for male authors is somewhat wider, and usually comes from the literary tradition itself, whereas stereotypes for female authors are often borrowed from other media, since the ones provided by the tradition are limited in number.

In a bourgeois, industrial society, so the theory goes, the creative artist is supposed to act out suppressed desires and prohibited activities for the audience; thus we get certain Post-romantic male-author stereotypes, such as Potted Poe, Bleeding Byron, Doomed Dylan, Lustful Layton, Crucified Cohen, etc. Until recently the only personality stereotype of this kind was Elusive Emily, otherwise known as Recluse Rossetti: the woman writer as aberration, neurotically denying herself the delights of sex, kiddies and other fun. The Twentieth Century has added Suicidal Sylvia, a somewhat more dire version of the same thing. The point about these stereotypes is that attention is focused not on the actual achievements of the authors, but on their lives, which are distorted and romanticized; their work is then interpreted in the light of the distorted version. Stereotypes like these, even when the author becomes a cult object, do no service to anyone or anything, least of all the author's work. Behind all of them is the notion that authors must be more special, peculiar or weird than other people, and that their lives are more interesting than their work.

The following examples are taken from personal experience (mine, of interviewers); they indicate the range of possibilities. There are a few others, such as Earth Mother, but for those you have to be older.

I) Happy Housewife

This one is almost obsolete: it used to be for Woman's Page or programme. Questions were about what you liked to fix for dinner; attitude was, "Gosh, all the housework and you're a writer too!" Writing was viewed as a hobby, like knitting, one did in one's spare time.

II) Ophelia

The writer as crazy freak. Female version of Doomed Dylan, with more than a little hope on the part of the interviewer that you'll turn into Suicidal Sylvia and give them something to *really* write about. Questions like "Do you think you're in danger of going insane?" or "Are writers closer to insanity than other people?" No need to point out that most mental institutions are crammed with people who have never written a word in their life. "Say something interesting," one interviewer said to me. "Say you write all your poems on drugs."

III) Miss Martyr, or, Movie Mag

Read any movie mag on Liz Taylor and translate into writing terms and you've got the picture. The writer as someone who *suffers* more than others. Why does the writer suffer more? Because she's successful, and you all know Success Must Be Paid For. In blood and tears, if possible. If you say you're happy and enjoy your life and work, you'll be ignored.

IV) Miss Message

Interviewer incapable of treating your work as what it is, i.e. poetry and/or fiction. Great attempt to get you to say something about an Issue and then make you into an exponent, spokeswoman or theorist. (The two Messages I'm most frequently saddled with are Women's Lib and Canadian Nationalism, though I belong to no formal organization devoted to either.) Interviewer unable to see that putting, for instance, a nationalist into a novel doesn't make it a nationalistic novel, any more than putting in a preacher makes it a religious novel. Interviewer incapable of handling more than one dimension at a time.

What is Hard to Find is an interviewer who regards writing as a respectable profession, not as some kind of magic, madness, trickery or evasive disguise for a Message; and who regards an author as someone engaged in a professional activity.

C. Other Writers and Rivalry

Regarding yourself as an "exception," part of an unspoken quota system, can have interesting results. If there are only so many available slots for your minority in the medical school/law school/literary world, of course you will feel rivalry, not only with members of the majority for whom no quota operates, but especially for members of your minority who are competing with you for the few coveted places. And you will have to be better than the average Majority member to get in at all. But we're familiar with that.

Woman-woman rivalry does occur, though it is surprisingly less severe than you'd expect; it's likely to take the form of *wanting* another woman writer to be better than she is, expecting more of her than you would of a male writer, and being exasperated with certain kinds of traditional "female" writing. One of our correspondents discussed these biases and expectations very thoroughly and with great intelligence: her letter didn't solve any problems but it did emphasize the complexities of the situation. Male-male rivalry is more extreme; we've all been treated to media-exploited examples of it.

What a woman writer is often unprepared for is the unexpected personal attack on her by a jealous male writer. The motivation is envy and competitiveness, but the form is often sexual put-down. "You may be a good writer," one older man said to a young woman writer who had just had a publishing success, "but I wouldn't want to fuck you." Another version goes more like the compliment–put-down noted under Reviewing. In either case, the ploy diverts attention from the woman's achievement as a writer—the area where the man feels threatened—to her sexuality, where either way he can score a verbal point.

Personal Statement

I've been trying to give you a picture of the arena, or that part of it where being a "woman" and "writer," as concepts, overlap. But, of course, the arena I've been talking about has to do largely with externals: reviewing, the media, relationships with other writers. This, for the writer, may affect the tangibles of her career: how she is received, how viewed, how much money she makes. But in relationship to the writing itself, this is a false arena. The real one is in her head, her real struggle the daily battle with words, the language itself. The false arena becomes valid for writing itself only insofar as it becomes part of her material and is transformed into one of the verbal and imaginative structures she is constantly engaged in making. Writers, as writers, are not propagandists or examples of social trends or preachers or politicians. They are makers of books, and unless they can make books well they will be bad writers, no matter what the social validity of their views.

At the beginning of this article, I suggested a few reasons for the infrequent participation in the Movement of woman writers. Maybe these reasons were the wrong ones, and this is the real one: no good writer wants to be merely a transmitter of someone else's ideology, no matter how fine that ideology may be. The aim of propaganda is to convince, and to spur people to action; the aim of writing is to create a plausible and moving imaginative world, and to create it from words. Or, to put it another way, the aim of a political movement is to improve the quality of people's lives on all levels, spiritual and imaginative as well as material (and any political movement that doesn't have this aim is worth nothing). Writing, however, tends to concentrate more on life, not as it ought to be, but as it is, as the writer feels it, experiences it. Writers are eye-witnesses, I-witnesses. Political movements, once successful, have historically been intolerant of writers, even those writers who initially aided them; in any revolution, writers have been among the first to be lined up against the wall, perhaps for their intransigence, their insistence on saying what they perceive, not what, according to the ideology, ought to exist. Politicians, even revolutionary politicians, have traditionally had no more respect for writing as an activity valuable in itself, quite apart from any message or content, than has the rest of the society. And writers, even revolutionary writers, have traditionally been suspicious of anyone who tells them what they ought to write.

The woman writer, then, exists in a society that, though it may turn certain individual writers into revered cult objects, has little respect for writing as a profession, and not much respect for women either. If there were more of both, articles like this would be obsolete. I hope they become so. In the meantime, it seems to me that the proper path for a woman writer is not an all-out manning (or womaning) of the barricades, however much she may agree with the aims of the Movement. The proper path is to become better as a writer. Insofar as writers are lenses, condensers of their society, her work may include the Movement, since it is so palpably among the things that exist. The picture that she gives of it is altogether another thing, and will depend, at least partly, on the course of the Movement itself.

NANCY F. COTT

Feminist Theory and Feminist Movements: The Past before Us

Feminism is nothing if not paradoxical. It aims for individual freedoms by mobilizing sex solidarity. It acknowledges diversity among women while positing that women recognize their unity. It requires gender consciousness for its basis, yet calls for the elimination of prescribed gender roles. These paradoxes of feminism are rooted in women's actual situation, being the same (in a species sense) as men; being different, with respect to reproductive biology and gender construction, from men. In another complication, all women may be said to be 'the same', as distinct from all men with respect to reproductive biology, and yet 'not the same', with respect to the variance of gender construction. Both theory and practice in feminism historically have had to deal with the fact that women are the same as and different from men, and the fact that women's gender identity is not separable from the other factors that make up our selves: race, region, culture, class, age. How have past women's movements accommodated these realities? In both England and the United States from the mid–nineteenth century on, it can be seen that women's rights ideology has taken different forms and emphases depending on whether women's 'equality' or 'difference' comes to the fore; conflict or convergence between these themes has had bearing on the qualities and mass appeal of the women's movement. Until the 1960s and 1970s, feminist ideology did not take much cognizance of women's self-identification besides gender, but it has not been possible to marshal movements of women, in a practical sense, without attention to those factors. A look at the history of the greatest mobilization of women on their own political behalf before the 1960s—that is, in the woman suffrage movement—and its aftermath, provides a case in point. The following discussion focuses on the United States, though one need not go far to find parallels between the United States and England, despite differences in class and political structures between the two countries, as Olive Banks's overview has recently made clear.[1]

Women's rights advocates in the nineteenth and early twentieth centuries pursued long, often passionate struggles for individual autonomy and for women's access to all men's prerogatives in higher education, paid employment, the professions, and citizenship (meaning, of course, the ballot). Their arguments for women's advancement were grouped around two poles—two logically opposing poles, which I am going to call, for the sake of convenience, the 'sameness' and 'difference' arguments. That is, on the one hand women claimed that they had the same intellectual and spiritual endowment as men—were human beings equally with men—and therefore deserved equal or the same opportunities men had, to advance and develop themselves. On the other hand women argued that their sex differed from the male—that whether through natural endowment, environment or training, human females were moral, nurturant, pacific and philosophically disinterested, where males were competitive, aggrandizing, belligerent and self-interested; and that it therefore served the best interests of both sexes for women to have equal access to education, work and citizenship in order to represent themselves and to balance society with their characteristic contribution. For instance, one mid-nineteenth-century United States reformer and suffragist wrote in *The Agitator,* a paper she edited herself, 'Nothing less than admission in law, and in fact, to equality in all rights, political, civil and social, with the male citizens of the community, will answer the demands now being made for American women'; while a contemporary wrote in another journal, *The Lily,* 'It is woman's womanhood, her instinctive femininity, her highest morality that society now needs to counteract the excess of masculinity that is everywhere to be found in our unjust and unequal laws.' What is even more interesting, women could voice these two arguments almost in the same breath.[2]

Taking a slightly different slant on it, Aileen S. Kraditor, in her 1965 book *The Ideas of the Woman Suffrage Movement,* characterized these two approaches in the United States suffrage movement as the natural rights or 'justice' argument, and the argument from 'expediency'. She claimed that the former dominated among nineteenth-century women's rights advocates, and the latter after the turn of the century. Kraditor acknowledged the coexistence of both arguments all along the way, however, and recent historians of woman's rights and woman suffrage ideology, including William Leach, Carole Nichols, Steven Buechler, and the contributors to the volume on feminist theory edited by Dale Spender, have made clear that both kinds of arguments flourished during the whole long span between Mary Wollstonecraft's *Vindication* and the attainment of woman suffrage after World War I.[3]

Whether women framed their arguments principally around 'justice' (or, to put it another way, 'sameness', or, to put it yet another way, 'equal rights') or did not, it was clear both before and after 1900 that they were impelled by a strong sense of the *in*justice of existing circumstances for women. In reminiscences of women born in the 1850s to 1880s (whose energies fuelled the woman suffrage movement), one finds the genesis of their views in uncomplicated rage at male dominance and the arbitrariness of male privilege, and jealousy of male prerogatives, even when— perhaps because—one finds affirmation of female character. Writer Mary Austin's retrospect on small-town America's expectations in the 1880s suggests women's motivation to argue on grounds of *both* common humanity and sexual difference, to adopt (lawyer-like) every possible defence to meet resistance: as she experienced it, 'there was a human norm, and it was the average man. Whatever in woman differed from this norm was a *female weakness,* of intelligence, of character, of physique.'[4] The coexistent (logically contradictory) emphases, on women's full and equal human capacity, and yet on women's unique strengths and potential, reflected the fact that 'woman's sphere' was both the point of oppression and the point of departure for nineteenth-century feminists. 'Womanhood' was their hallmark and they insisted it should be a 'human norm' too.

Furthermore, woman's rights advocacy was always in dialogue with those hostile to its aims; if the 'antis' protested that women were 'unsexing' themselves and seeking identity with men, one kind of argument was called for; if the 'antis' said women were less competent than men in the public arena, another kind; if the antis said 'strong-minded' women sought to rule over men, another response—and so on. Through the long history of the woman's rights movement the two strands of argument, 'sameness' and 'difference', 'justice' and 'expediency', were not seen as mutually exclusive, but as juxtaposable. I do not mean to accord one side of these sets of terms greater value than another. Kraditor's term 'expediency' has a negative ring, especially in contrast to 'justice', but I mean it to be understood in its most neutral sense. The term should encompass all interpretations of the instrumentality of social rights to women, including social justice and self-protection as well as social control. American suffragist Harriet Burton Laidlaw captured the dual message most succinctly in her 1912 assertion that insofar as women were like men they deserved the same rights, and insofar as they differed they ought to represent themselves.[5]

At the time Laidlaw staked that two-pronged claim, a mass women's movement, which would at its height involve two million women, was cohering around the issue of woman suffrage in the United States. By the decade beginning in 1910 the demand for woman suffrage was a capacious umbrella under which a large diversity of beliefs and organizations could shelter, or (to use a more appropriate metaphor), an expansive platform on which they could all comfortably, if temporarily, stand. The nineteenth-century view of the ballot as symbol of the self-possessed individual's relation to the state was joined and to an extent superseded, in the early twentieth century, by new emphasis on the ballot as tool of group interests. Population growth, in-migration, industrialization and the rise of great cities were re-working the implications of the ballot, and compelling progressive reformers to re-envision the state as the arena in which group particularity and potential cooperation might be worked out. City and state 'machine' politics, though often deplored by suffragists, made one message especially clear: votes were a principal means for self-identified groups to have immediate needs answered, and/or to be manipulated. (The woman who would later become the victorious general of the campaign for the Nineteenth Amendment, which gave women the vote, Carrie Chapman Catt, in 1908 first successfully instituted in New York City so-called 'machine' methods of canvassing and recording of electoral districts in woman suffrage work.)

Several historians have given us the impression that American suffragists moved towards victory in the decade from 1910 only by relying on 'expedient' arguments (in Kraditor's words), by stressing what I have called 'difference' arguments, by accommodating their aims to the image of the maternal, nurturant, altruistic woman, and therefore becoming more 'conservative'.[6] Such emphases *were* visible in the decade after 1910, but it should not be assumed that because arguments from 'difference' or 'expedience' *could* be conservative, they necessarily were. On the contrary, claims for women's 'difference' could be turned to radical social goals. Mary Heaton Vorse, for instance, a labour agitator and partisan of the Industrial Workers of the World, socialist, suffragist, feminist, and editor of *The Masses*, believed that women as a group were best suited to work for the end of class exploitation and achievement of social justice.[7]

In the decade beginning in 1910 women from never-before-mobilized groups— blacks, new immigrants, political radicals, college students—joined the American woman suffrage movement, multiplying grass-roots organizations; women influenced by British suffragettes instigated 'militant' tactics. This was the first time that the word 'feminism' came into use, to denote, in Charlotte Perkins Gilman's words, 'the social awakening of the women of all the world', or, in Inez Milholland's, the 'significant' and 'profound' 'movement to readjust the social position of woman . . . in its largest general aspects'. Socialists moved in force into the movement for woman suffrage. As never before, men and women in discrete ethnic or racial or ideological groups saw the advantage of doubling their voting numbers if women obtained suffrage. Black suffragists, for example, whose numbers swelled in the decade following 1910, felt that the enfranchisement of black women would address, and help to redress, the forcible disfranchisement of black men in the South; they mobilized not only as a matter of gender justice but of race progress, despite their awareness that white racist arguments were simultaneously being raised on behalf of woman suffrage. The mass movement that gathered at this point was not, on the whole, conservative and accommodationist but, rather, encompassed the broadest spectrum of opinion in its history, from conservative to radical, from accommodationist to revolutionary.[8] At the same time, the extent to which reformers, men and women (although voteless), had worked to incorporate social welfare into the purview of government—the extent to which the modern state had assumed health, safety and welfare functions—domesticated the content of politics, helping to make votes for women more acceptable. What had been a radical threat to conventional ideology of 'woman's sphere' in the mid-nineteenth century came more into accord with conventional notions of woman's appropriate realm.[9] Just as important, the grass-roots activity building toward coalition in favour of woman suffrage was part and parcel, in the decade from 1910, of flux and creativity in American politics and society—these being years when urban politics elicited coalitions among members of the middle class, working class, and organized labour, when national politics brought forth a 'Progressive' third party, a 'New Freedom' among the Democrats, and the greatest-ever electoral success of socialists; years when cultural and social rebellion swirled and eddied along with the political.

The vote was not only a goal shared by women of divergent political leanings, it was a goal that, as understood by early twentieth-century suffragists in the United States, harmonized the two strands in foregoing women's rights advocacy: it was an equal rights goal that enabled women to make special contributions; it sought to give women the same capacity as men so they could express their differences; it was a just end in itself but it was also an expedient means to other ends. Suffragists in the decade from 1910 were as likely to argue that women deserved the vote because of their sex—because women as a group had relevant benefits to bring and values to defend in the polity—as to argue that women deserved the vote *despite* their sex. The demand for equal suffrage for women could be brought into accord with the notion that women differed from men, because the vote was recognized as a tool of group interests as well as a symbol of equal access of citizens to self-government. Indeed, the more that women's particular interests were stressed, while the premise of equal access was sustained, the better the argument for woman suffrage. Analogous arguments could be, and were, used about the particular interests of any self-identified sub-group of women—for instance, women industrial workers, who argued for reasons of class and sex their warrant for the ballot. Thus Mollie Schepps, a New York City garment maker, reasoned in the wake of the disastrous Triangle factory fire that killed over 140 women employed there, 'working women must use the ballot in order to abolish the burning and crushing of our bodies for the profit of a very few.'[10]

The mass movement assembled by a coalition of women of diverse racial, ethnic and political identities was successfully ambiguous, or inclusive, on the point whether women were most significantly the same as, or different from, men. Both 'sameness' and 'difference' arguments, both 'equal rights' and 'special contributions' arguments, both 'justice' and 'expediency' arguments existed side by side. Although the sexual 'differences' that were highlighted drew on traditional notions of women as nurturers and mothers, the implicit constraints of conventional stereotypes were minimized by turning stereotypes to serve goals of equal access and equal rights. Activists had a workable (if not logically coherent) understanding of the social construction of womanhood. True, they did not wholly repudiate biological or God-given grounding for what women had in common (i.e. motherhood and its said-to-be-attendant qualities). Many women activists, however, in the train of Darwin, and especially in the train of Charlotte Perkins Gilman's analysis of the 'sexuo-economic' relation between woman and man, had a social/evolutionary analysis of their 'differentness' from men (of their 'group'-ness) that led toward change even when it lent itself to conventional sentimentalization.

I assume here that feminism requires some extent of conceptualization of sexual difference, to generate identification with the group 'women'; and that such a conceptualization must build around the belief that gender—or, let us say, 'woman's condition'—is socially constructed and thus can be dismantled or changed. Until the national victory of woman suffrage, women had (if they looked for it) a convenient, reliable and in fact *profound* index and emblem of their socially constructed, humanly constructed gender difference: their common disfranchisement. Shared votelessness was a powerful reason why, despite all the social diversities among women, 'the cause of woman' could seem a reasonable cause, a spur to, rather than a rein on, whatever other identity or goals a woman might have. Just as Mary Ritter Beard, a municipal activist and early adherent to Alice Paul's militant Congressional Union (and later a historian of women), said in 1914 that she could not rank her commitment to suffrage and labour reform because the two were 'inseparable' in her interest, suffrage became for many women in the decade from 1910 inseparable from other, possibly divergent goals.[11]

The feminist conceptualization of women's solidarity, and motivation toward coalition of 'all women', lasted little beyond the goal of the ballot. Just a few years after the Nineteenth Amendment to the United States constitution was ratified, commentators observed, 'the American women's movement . . . is splintered into a hundred fragments under as many warring leaders'; 'the woman "bloc" does not tend to become more and more solidified but tends to become more and more disintegrated.'[12] The most palpable evidence of lack of a ruling consensus among women activists was division of opinion over the Equal Rights Amendment. The renewed National Woman's Party, born of the militant suffrage activists, developed that new proposal to bring full legal equality by constitutional amendment in the period immediately following the gain of suffrage; the amendment was first introduced into Congress in December 1923. Just as the Woman's Party, with its sole focus on the United States constitution, its efforts to create women's voting blocs, its constant lobbying of national political leaders, and its direct action techniques of picketing, demonstrating, and going to jail, had comprised a small and controversial, but highly effective minority within the suffrage movement, so it marshalled only a tiny minority of active women when it adopted the programme of the ERA. Once the National Woman's Party declared its policy of 'blanket' legislation for equal rights, its former allies for the ballot, the major women's voluntary organizations and the Women's Bureau of the United States Department of Labor, were arrayed against it. Differences between the 'militant' minority and other groups that had been tolerable in the suffrage coalition were tolerable no longer.

In the NWP's view the Equal Rights Amendment was the logical sequel to woman suffrage, the fulfilment of Susan B. Anthony's vision. The many differences in state codes and practices in sex discrimination made a constitutional amendment the most direct route to equal rights. Even so-called 'protective' legislation, if sex-based, the NWP claimed, kept women from equal opportunity: the laws, for instance, regulating hours, wages and conditions of work for women and minors, while none regulated men's, kept women classed with children as the industrial 'wards' of the state. Opponents of the ERA (among women who considered themselves feminists) were mainly concerned with keeping sex-based protective labour and welfare legislation in force. They were opposed to other sex discriminations in law, such as those affecting women's nationality, or jury service, but argued that those would be removed more appropriately and efficiently by attacking each specific case. They assumed that an ERA would invalidate protective labour legislation—the result of decades of women reformers' efforts—or at least throw it into the courts for protracted argument. Most women workers, they argued (with basis), appreciated protective legislation as a hedge against exploitation by employers. If protective laws hampered job opportunities for some small minority of working women, they reasoned, then the proper tactic was to exempt some occupations, not to undermine such laws altogether, in the way a constitutional amendment would.[13]

The ERA controversy was symptom rather than cause of divisions in the 1920s among a former united front of women. The National Woman's Party, supporters of the ERA, stressed the capacities women shared with men, as individuals in society, rather than how the two sexes differed by virtue of their reproductive or familial roles. They looked out on the social landscape and saw women who were (like themselves) vigorous and capable. They wanted to premise social policy on the equality of the sexes, since they saw sex equality as both possible and desirable. Opponents of the ERA (the great majority of politically active women) stressed instead women's biological and socially induced differences from men. They focused on the roles and identities of women as members of families more than as individuals. They premised *their* social policy on the observation that women were weak, or vulnerable; they believed one had to treat the world as it *was*, a world of sex inequality. 'So long as men cannot be mothers,' Florence Kelley wrote eloquently in this vein in 1921, 'so long legislation adequate for them can never be adequate for wage-earning women; and the cry Equality, Equality, where Nature has created Inequality, is as stupid and deadly as the cry Peace, Peace, where there is no Peace.'[14]

The division between advocates of 'equal rights' and 'special protections' for women in the United States was paralleled in England, though the legislative question was not precisely the same.[15] Individuals' positions on this issue depended on their priorities for social justice and social change, their political and class loyalties, and, just as clearly, on their views of woman's nature and purpose. The salutary ambiguity sustained by the suffrage coalition on the question of likening women to or distinguishing them from men was put under severe stress by the ERA debate; at the same time the ruling consensus on what women shared—on the social construction of womanhood—was shattered. The themes of 'sameness' and 'difference' were lodged on opposite sides of the controversy. The logical contradictions between the two poles of argument came to the fore. Women in the uneasy position of opposing 'equal rights' stressed how their sex differed from men to the extent of sounding anti-feminist. Those supporting 'equal rights' so bypassed the issue of difference that their clarion call to solidarity rang hollow in most women's ears.

The demobilization of the women's movement in the 1920s was a complex process, for the partisan differences that occurred among feminists were socially and ideologically situated in an era of exhaustion of optimism after World War I, an era of reaction against the Bolshevik Revolution and militant labour, an era of mass consumerism, and mass commercialization of sexual and family values. In such a situation, women's politics in the United States diverged on many different axes besides the question of 'equal rights' versus 'protection': women as individuals and in groups differed on questions such as public ownership, disarmament, Prohibition, women's role in political parties; they differed in increasingly noticeable ways on the political spectrum from left to right. There were also issues on which women's groups were able to work in concert: for instance, to eliminate discrimination in the laws governing married women's nationality, or to protect married women's employment (as the Depression set in). There were some new coalitions: an amalgam of peace groups in the mid-1920s, for instance, and an unprecedented, if tenuous, alliance between black women's and white women's groups in the South, both striving to end lynch law.[16] What one does not find in the 1920s is any overall shared conception of 'the woman question'—of what needed to be changed in the sexual structure and what equipped women together to create change—that could mobilize divergent groups of women as the goal of the ballot had.

In trying to understand and explain the disaggregation of the women's movement in the 1920s, or, for that matter, the different situation we face today as compared to the period 1967–74, it is too easy and mistaken to expect that women's interests are 'normally' a unity. One cannot take an extraordinary period of coalition building and common-ground sharing among women of differing needs and politics—for instance, 1912–19 and 1967–74—as the ordinary, the 'norm' from which the sequel is grievous decline. There is an element of inevitability or predictability in any fragmentation that follows a united front of women, for as much as women have common cause in gender issues, they are differentiated by political and cultural and sexual loyalties, and by racial, class and ethnic identities, which inform their experience of gender itself. Only women holding culturally hegemonic values and positions—that is, in the United States, women who are white, heterosexual, middle class, politically midstream—have the privilege (or deception) of seeing their condition as that of 'woman', glossing over their other characteristics. Such hegemonic understanding of womanhood has, historically, an essential strategic function in creating sex solidarity among women and in consciousness raising. Thus, at the turn of the century black women, or Jewish immigrants, or industrial workers, or socialists, shared in the galvanizing, malleable notion of women's social identity as mothers and caretakers of humanity, and yet also distinguished particular aspects of its relevance or irrelevance to them. The same dynamic that mobilizes women who see their lives as women as socially constructed leads them to name and particularize the attendant characteristics of their gender identity. What is crucial, of course, in developing or constricting a mass movement, is whether women's particular loyalties and gender identity work in tandem or against each other. That depends on the persuasiveness of prevailing notion(s) of feminism and who are its standardbearers. It depends in important ways on the political climate in general, too: political and cultural rebellion on many fronts characterized both the periods 1912–19 and 1967–74, in which there were mass movements of women.

The analogy between the decade following 1910 and the height of the women's liberation movement in our lifetimes is certainly not perfect. The overriding goal of the suffrage imposed a unity (even if specious) on the earlier decade that is not replicated even in the overlapping goals of many sectors of the recent women's movement—reproductive rights, for instance, or the ERA. The range of theories and of constituencies in recent feminism is wider and more differentiated than in the decade from 1910, and one must also consider new factors such as mass audio-visual media in the spread and impact of the movement. The political parallels can be instructive, nonetheless, especially now that divisions within the movement, younger women's 'postfeminist' attitudes, and rightwing backlash echo problems of the 1920s, and make the pattern of mobilization and demobilization around and after suffrage more understandable to us than it might have been ten years ago.

If there is a model here, looking back on two extraordinary periods of mass movement by women, it would have two conditions. One would be a conceptualiza-tion of the social construction of womanhood that does not bar simultaneity of feminist arguments for women's difference from and equality to men—a conceptual-ization with sufficient relevance and malleability to sustain coalition. If we look closely at even the extraordinary periods of 1912–19 and 1967–74, they exhibit not 'unity' but strategic coalition. Whether we see this as heroic, or lamentable, or merely human nature, it seems that mass movements of women have only been possible when women have instrumental or 'expedient' reasons for advancing gender interests—when, in other words, characteristics or aims besides gender grievances also motivate them. The vote, for instance, was pursued for different reasons by socialists and by members of the Daughters of the American Revolution, by black women and white racists; 'sexual politics' has been differently understood by, though equally central to, radical lesbians and middle-class wives.

In the recent women's movement there has never been one ruling version of woman's place, but a spectrum of conceptualizations from 'socialization' to 'oppres-sion' to 'patriarchy'. There has been a constant tension between the claim for the power of sisterhood—the viability of an analysis of 'all women'—and the voices of women of non-hegemonic groups, especially women of colour and lesbians. The definition of women as a sex/class, which is a major, perhaps the major, contribution of recent feminist theory, has been pulled in two directions: towards the elimination of gender roles ('sameness' argument) and toward the valorization of female being ('difference' argument).

The past eight to ten years have been characterized by what seem to be especially contradictory developments. The value accorded to 'sexual difference' in feminist theory has increased at the same time that the universality of the claim for sisterhood has been debunked. Ethnic, racial, and sexual diversity among women is stressed more than ever before in feminist theory, but so is the emphasis on how women (as a whole) differ from men (as a whole). Perhaps, though, these are not contradictory developments, nor even ironically related. Feminist stress on women's socially con-structed 'difference' from men can go along with recognition of diversity among women themselves, if we acknowledge the multifaceted entity—the patchwork quilt, so to speak—that is the group called women. That acknowledgement allows coalition building, the only realistic political 'unity' women have had or will have.

The second condition in this hypothetical model is the fertile ground provided by an era of political and cultural rebellion. 'There has always been a women's movement in this century'—agreed; but whether there will be mass movement or not, whether feminism will be a self-propagating or a sectarian ideology, has much to do with the predisposing ground. Feminism does not have a story discrete from the rest of historical process. As Ray Strachey, a leading British suffragist, wrote with regard to the rise of the women's movement in the nineteenth century, 'Nothing which occurred in those years could be irrelevant to the great social change which was going on, and nothing was without its share of influence upon it.'[17] Just as women are part of humanity, and yet have their own recognizable identity within any society's cultural construction of gender, feminism takes part in—comprises part of—the general cultural order, while it has its own tradition, logic and trajectory. Sole concentration on the internal evolution of feminist ideology and leadership will not read the past accurately, nor, alone, will the placement of feminist movements in overall political or cultural change, but the two together have something to teach us.

Notes

1. Olive Banks, *Faces of Feminism* (Oxford, 1981).

2. Mary Livermore in *Agitator* 1 (13 March 1869), 4; Jane Frohock in *Lily* 8:23 (1 December 1856).

3. Aileen S. Kraditor, *The Ideas of the Woman Suffrage Movement, 1890–1900* (New York, 1965), 38–43, 87–91; William Leach, *True Love and Perfect Union* (New York, 1980), esp. 8, 276–87; Carole Nichols, 'A New Force in Politics: The Suffragists' Experience in Connecticut' (MA essay, Sarah Lawrence College, Bronxville, NY, 1979), 15–16, 26–30, and 'Votes and More for Women: Suffrage and After in Connecticut', *Women and History*, 5 (Spring 1983), 29–30; Dale Spender (ed.), *Feminist Theorists* (New York, 1984), esp. Jenny Uglow, 'Josephine Butler: From Sympathy to Theory'; Steven M. Buechler, *The Transformation of the Woman Suffrage Movement: The Case of Illinois, 1850–1920* (New Brunswick, NJ, 1986).

4. Mary Austin, *Earth Horizon: Autobiography* (Boston, 1932), 156, 91–2, 128. See also E. S. Dummer, *Why I Think So* (Chicago, 1937), 10; Miriam Allen de Ford, 'Feminism, Cause or Effect?', typescript, 5 pp., de Ford Papers, Box 573, San Francisco Historical Society; C. C. Catt, 'Why I Have Found Life Worth Living,' 29 Mar. 1928, Catt Papers microfilm, Reel 9 (from Library of Congress, Washington, DC); Lorinne Pruette, 'The Evolution of Disenchantment', and Inez Haynes Irwin, 'The Making of a Militant', in Elaine Showalter, ed., *These Modern Women* (Old Westbury, NY, 1978), 71–72, 39; Rheta Childe Dorr, *A Woman of Fifty* (New York, 1924), 13.

5. Quoted in Kraditor, *Ideas*, 91.

6. E.g., Kraditor, *Ideas;* Richard Evans, *The Feminists: Women's Emancipation Movements in Europe, America, and Australasia, 1840–1920* (New York, 1977), 214–27; Carl N. Degler, *At*

Odds (New York, 1980), 357–60; Ronald Schaffer, 'The Montana Woman Suffrage Campaign, 1911–14', *Pacific Northwest Quarterly* 55 (January 1964), 12, and 'The Problem of Consciousness in the Woman Suffrage Movement: A California Perspective', *Pacific Historical Quarterly* 45 (November 1976), 490–92.

7. Mary Heaton Vorse, *Footnote to Folly* (New York, 1935), 168–69, and see her letters of the decade from 1910 in Vorse Collection, Walter Reuther Library of Labor History and Urban Affairs, Wayne State University, Detroit, Michigan.

8. C. P. Gilman, 'What Is Feminism?' *Boston Sunday Herald*, 3 September 1916; Inez Milholland, 'The Liberation of a Sex', *McClure's* 40:4 (February 1913), 181; Judith Schwarz, *The Radical Feminists of Heterodoxy* (New Lebanon, NH, 1983); Elinor Lerner, 'Jewish Involvement in the NY City Woman Suffrage Movement', *American Jewish History* LXX (1981), 442–61; Eleanor Flexner, *Century of Struggle*, 240–93; Rosalyn Terborg-Penn, 'Afro-Americans in the Struggle for Woman Suffrage' (unpublished PhD dissertation, Howard University, Washington, D.C., 1977), esp. 265, 275–76, and her 'Discontented Black Feminists', in Lois Scharf and Joan Jensen, eds, *Decades of Discontent* (Westport, CT, 1983), 261–66; MariJo Buhle, *Women and American Socialism* (Urbana, IL, 1981), 214–45; Sharon Hartman Strom, 'Leadership and Tactics in the American Woman Suffrage Movement: A New Perspective from Massachusetts', *Journal of American History* 62 (1975), 296–315; Ellen Dubois, 'Harriot Stanton Blatch and the Revival of American Suffragism', paper presented at the sixth Berkshire Conference on the History of Women, Smith College, Northampton, Mass., 2 June 1984.

9. Paula Baker, 'The Domestication of Politics: Women and American Political Society, 1780–1920', *American Historical Review* 89 (June 1984), 620–47; Ellen Dubois, 'The Radicalism of

the Woman Suffrage Movement', *Feminist Studies* 3 (1975), 63–71. The literature on Progressivism is vast: Richard McCormick, 'The Discovery that Business Corrupts Politics', *American Historical Review* 86 (April 1981), makes an interesting beginning.

10. From *Senators vs. Working Women*, pamphlet published by Wage Earners Suffrage League of NY (1912), excerpted in Rosalyn Baxandall et al. (eds.), *America's Working Women* (New York, 1976), 218.

11. Mary Beard to Alice Paul, letter of 1914 quoted in Barbara Turoff, *Mary Beard as Force in History* (Dayton, OH, 1979), 24.

12. Frances Kellor, 'Women in British and American Politics', *Current History* 17 (February 1923), 823; William Hard in 'What the American Man Thinks', *Woman Citizen* (September 8, 1923), 17, quoted in William O'Neill, *Everyone Was Brave* (Chicago, 1968), 264.

13. For fuller discussion of the ERA controversy, see my article 'Feminist Politics in the 1920s: The National Woman's Party', *Journal of American History* 71 (June 1984), 57–61.

14. Florence Kelley, 'The New Woman's Party,' *Survey* 47 (5 March 1921), 828.

15. Banks, *Faces of Feminism*, 103–17, 153–79.

16. See J. Stanley Lemons, *The Woman Citizen: Social Feminism in the 1920s* (Urbana, IL, 1973), 63–68; Lois Scharf, *To Work and to Wed* (Westport, CT, 1980); Joan Jensen, ' "All Pink Sisters": The War Department and the Feminist Movement in the 1920s', in Scharf and Jensen, *Decades;* Jacqueline Dowd Hall, *Revolt Against Chivalry: Jessie Daniel Ames and the Women's Campaign Against Chivalry* (New York, 1980).

17. See Dale Spender, *There Has Always Been a Women's Movement in This Century* (London, 1983); Ray Strachey, *The Cause* (London, 1928; repr. 1979), 5.

GLORIA STEINEM

Men and Women Talking

Once upon a time (that is, just a few years ago), psychologists believed that the way we chose to communicate was largely a function of personality. If certain conversational styles turned out to be more common to one sex than the other (more abstract and aggressive talk for men, for instance, more personal and equivocal talk for women), then this was just another tribute to the influence of biology on personality.

Consciously or otherwise, feminists have challenged this assumption from the beginning. Many of us learned a big lesson in the sixties when our generation spoke out on the injustices of war, as well as of race and class; yet women who used exactly the same words and style as our male counterparts were less likely to be listened to or to be taken seriously. When we tried to talk about this and other frustrations, the lack of listening got worse, with opposition and even ridicule just around every corner. Only women's own meetings and truth telling began to confirm what we had thought each of us was alone in experiencing. It was also those early consciousness-raising groups that began to develop a more cooperative, less combative way of talking, an alternative style that many women have maintained and been strengthened by ever since.

The problem is that this culturally different form has remained an almost totally female event. True, it has helped many, many women arrive at understanding each other and working out strategies for action. But as an influence on the culturally male style of public talking, it has remained almost as removed as its more domestic versions of the past.

One reason for our decade or so of delay in challenging existing styles of talking makes good tactical sense. Our first task was to change the words themselves. We did not feel included (and usage studies showed that, factually, we were not) in hundreds of such supposedly generic terms as *mankind* and *he, the brotherhood of man* and *statesman.* Nor could we fail to see the racial parallels to being identified as "girls" at advanced ages, or with first names only, or by our personal connection (or lack of one) to a member of the dominant group.

Hard as it was (and still is), this radical act of seizing the power to name ourselves and our experience was easier than taking on the politics of conversation. Documenting society-wide patterns of talking required expensive research and surveys. Documenting the sexism in words, and even conjuring up alternatives, took only one courageous woman scholar and a dictionary (for instance, *Guidelines for Equal Treatment of the Sexes,* the pioneering work of Alma Graham for McGraw-Hill). That was one good economic reason why such works were among the first and best by feminist scholars.

In retrospect, the second cause for delay makes less feminist sense—the long popularity of assertiveness training. Though most women needed to be more assertive (or even more aggressive, though that word was considered too controversial), many of these courses taught women how to play the existing game, not how to change the rules. Unlike the feminist assault on sexist language, which demanded new behavior from men, too, assertiveness training was more reformist than revolutionary. It pushed one-way change for women only, thus seeming to confirm masculine-style communication as the only adult model or the most effective one. Certainly, many individual women were helped, and many men were confronted with the educational experience of an assertive woman, but the larger impact was usually to flatter the existing masculine game of talk-politics by imitating it.

Since then, however, a few feminist scholars have had the time and resources to document conversational patterns of mixed- and single-sex groups, both here and in Europe. Traditional scholarship, influenced by feminism, has also begun to look at conversational styles as functions of power and environment. For instance, employees pursue topics raised by their employers more than the reverse, older people feel free to interrupt younger ones, and subordinates are more polite than bosses. Since women share all those conversational habits of the less powerful, even across the many lines of class and status that divide us, how accidental can that be?

Even the new feminist-influenced research has a long way to go in neutralizing the masculine bias of existing studies. For instance, *talking* is assumed to be the important and positive act, while *listening,* certainly a productive function, is the subject of almost no studies at all.

Nonetheless, there is enough new scholarship to document different styles, to point out some deficiencies in the masculine model of communicating, and to give us some ideas on how to create a synthesis of both that could provide a much wider range of alternatives for women *and* for men.

I

Have you assumed that women talk more than men—and thus may dominate in discussion if nowhere else? If so, you're not alone. Researchers of sex differences in language started out with that assumption. So did many feminists, who often explained women's supposedly greater penchant for talking as compensation for a lack of power to act.

In fact, however, when Dale Spender, an English feminist and scholar, surveyed studies of talkativeness for her recent book, *Man Made Language,* she concluded that "perhaps in more than any other research area, findings we~e in complete contradiction with the stereotype. . . . There has not been one study which provides evidence that women talk more than men, and there have been numerous studies which indicate that men talk more than women."

Her conclusion held true regardless of whether the study in question asked individuals to talk into a tape recorder with no group interaction; or compared men and women talking on television; or measured amounts of talk in mixed groups (even among male and female state legislators); or involved group discussions of a subject on which women might be expected to have more expertise. (At a London workshop on sexism and education, for instance, the five men present managed to talk more than their thirty-two female colleagues combined.)

Some studies of male silence in heterosexual couples might seem to counter these results, but Spender's research supports their conclusion that a major portion of female talk in such one-to-one situations is devoted to drawing the man out, asking questions, introducing multiple subjects until one is accepted by him, or demonstrating interest in the subjects he introduces. Clearly, male silence (or silence from a member of any dominant group) is not necessarily the same as listening. It might mean a rejection of the speaker, a refusal to become vulnerable through self-revelation, or a decision that this conversation is not worthwhile. Similarly, talking by the subordinate group is not necessarily an evidence of power. Its motive may be a Scheherazade-like need to intrigue and thus survive, or simply to explain and justify one's actions.

In addition to a generally greater volume of talk, however, men interrupt women more often than vice versa. This is true both in groups and in couples. Male interruptions of women also bring less social punishment than female interruptions of men. Men also interrupt women more often than women interrupt each other.

Moreover, males are more likely to police the subject matter of conversation in mixed-sex groups. One study of working-class families showed that women might venture into such "masculine" topics as politics or sports, and men might join "feminine" discussions of domestic events, but in both cases, it was the men who ridiculed or otherwise straightened out nonconformers who went too far. Even in that London workshop on sexism, for instance, the concrete experiences of the female participants were suppressed in favor of the abstract, general conclusions on sexism that were preferred by the men. The few males present set the style for all the females.

How did the myth of female talkativeness and conversational dominance get started? Why has this supposed female ability been so accepted that many sociologists, and a few battered women themselves, have even accepted it as a justification for some men's violence against their wives?

The uncomfortable truth seems to be that the amount of talk by women has been measured less against the amount of men's talk than against the expectation of female silence.

Indeed, women who accept and set out to disprove the myth of the talkative woman may pay the highest price of all. In attempting to be the exceptions, we silence ourselves. If that is so, measuring our personal behavior against real situations and real studies should come as a relief, a confirmation of unspoken feelings.

We are not crazy, for instance, if we feel that, when we finally do take the conversational floor in a group, we are out there in exposed verbal flight, like fearful soloists plucked from the chorus. We are not crazy to feel that years of unspoken thoughts are bottled up inside our heads, and come rushing out in a way that may make it hard to speak calmly, even when we finally have the chance.

Once we give up searching for approval by stifling our thoughts, or by imitating the male norm of abstract, assertive communicating, we often find it easier to simply say what needs to be said, and thus to earn respect and approval. Losing self-consciousness and fear allows us to focus on the content of what we are saying instead of on ourselves.

Women's well-developed skill as listeners, perhaps the real source of our much-vaunted "intuition," should not be left behind. We must retain it for ourselves and teach it to men by bringing it with us into our work and daily lives, but that will only happen if we affirm its value. Female culture does have a great deal to contribute to the dominant one. Furthermore, women might feel better about talking equally, selecting subjects, and even interrupting occasionally if we took the reasonable attitude that we are helping men to become attentive and retentive listeners, too. We are paying them the honor of communicating as honestly as we can and treating them as we would want to be treated. After all, if more men gained sensitive listening skills, they would have "intuition," too.

These are practical exercises for achieving a change in the balance of talk. Try tape-recording a dinner-table conversation or meeting (in the guise of recording facts, so participants don't become self-conscious about their talk politics), then play the tape back to the same group, and ask them to add up the number of minutes talked, interruptions, and subject introductions for each gender. Or give a dozen poker chips to each participant in a discussion, and require that one chip be given up each time a person speaks. Or break the silence barrier for those who rarely talk by going around the room once at the beginning of each meeting, consciousness-raising-style, with a question that each participant must answer personally, even if it's only a self-introduction. (It is said that the British Labour party was born only after representatives of its warring factions spent an hour moving their conference table into a larger room. That one communal act broke down individual isolation, just as one round of communal speaking helps break the ice.)

If such methods require more advance planning or influence on the group than you can muster, or if you're trying to sensitize just one person, try some individual acts. Discussing the results of studies on who talks more can produce some very healthy self-consciousness in both women and men. If one group member speaks rarely, try addressing more of your own remarks to her (or him) directly. On the other hand, if one man (or woman) is a domineering interrupter, try objecting directly, interrupting in return, timing the minutes of his or her talk, or just being inattentive. If someone cuts you off, say with humor, "That's one," then promise some conspicuous act when the interruptions get to three. Keep score on "successful" topic introductions, add them up by gender, and announce them at the discussion's end.

If questions and comments following a lecture come mostly from men, stand up and say so. It may be a learning moment for everyone. The prevalence of male speakers in mixed audiences has caused some feminist lecturers to reserve equal time for questions from women only.

To demonstrate the importance of listening as a positive act, try giving a quiz on the content of female and male speakers. Hopefully you *won't* discover the usual: that men often remember what male speakers say better than they remember female speakers' content; that women often remember male content better, too, but that women listen and retain the words of *both* sexes somewhat better than men do.

Check the talk politics concealed in your own behavior. Does your anxiety level go up (and your hostess instincts quiver) when women are talking and men are listening, but not the reverse? For instance, men often seem to feel okay about "talking shop" for hours while women listen, but women seem able to talk in men's presence for only a short time before feeling anxious, apologizing, and encouraging the men to speak. If you start to feel wrongly uncomfortable about making males listen, try this exercise: *keep on talking,* and encourage your sisters to do the same. Honor men by treating them as honestly as you treat women. You will be allowing them to learn.

II

Here are three popular assumptions: (1) Women talk about themselves, personalize, and gossip more than men do. (2) Men would rather talk to groups of men than to mixed groups, and women prefer mixed groups to all-female ones. (3) Women speakers and women's issues are hampered by the feminine style of their presentation. As you've probably guessed by now, most evidence is to the contrary of all three beliefs.

After recording the conversational themes of single-sex and mixed-sex groups, for instance, social psychologist Elizabeth Aries found that men in all-male groups were more likely to talk about themselves than were women in all-female ones. Men were also more likely to use self-mentions to demonstrate superiority or aggressiveness, while women used them to share an emotional reaction to what was being said by others.

Phil Donahue, one of the country's most experienced interviewers, capsulizes the cultural difference between men and women this way: "If you're in a social situation, and women are talking to each other, and one woman says, 'I was hit by a car today,' all the other women will say, 'You're kidding! What happened? Where? Are you all right?' In the same situation with males, one male says, 'I was hit by a car today.' I guarantee you that there will be another male in the group who will say, 'Wait till I tell you what happened to *me.*'"

If quantity of talking about oneself is a measure of "personalizing," and self-aggrandizement through invoking the weakness of others is one characteristic of gossip, then men may be far more "gossipy" than women—especially when one includes sexual bragging.

In addition, subjects introduced by males in mixed groups are far more likely to "succeed" than subjects introduced by women, and, as Aries concluded, women in mixed groups are more likely to interact with men than with other women. Thus, it's not unreasonable to conclude that mixed groups spend more time discussing the lives and interests of male participants than of female ones.

On the other hand, research by Aries and others shows that women are more likely to discuss human relationships. Since "relationships" often fall under "gossip" in men's view, this may account for the frequent male observation that women "personalize" everything. Lecturers often comment, for instance, that women in an audience ask practical questions about their own lives, while men ask abstract questions about groups or policies. When the subject is feminism, women tend to ask about practical problems. Men are more likely to say something like, "But how will feminism impact the American family?"

To quote Donahue, who deals with mostly female audiences: "I've always felt a little anxious about the possibility of a program at night with a male audience. The problem as I perceive it—and this is a generalization—is that men tend to give you a speech, whereas women will ask a question and then listen for the answer and make another contribution to the dialogue. In countless situations I have a male in my audience stand up and say in effect, 'I don't know what you're arguing about; here's the answer to this thing.' And then proceed to give a mini-speech."

Aries also documented the more cooperative, rotating style of talk and leadership in women-only groups: the conscious or unconscious habit of "taking turns." As a result, women actually prefer talking in their own single-sex groups for the concrete advantages of both having a conversational turn and being listened to. On the other hand, she confirmed research that shows male-only groups to have more stable hierarchies, with the same one or several talkers dominating most of the time.

As Aries points out, no wonder men prefer the variation and opportunity of mixed-sex audiences. They combine the seriousness of a male presence with more choice of styles—and, as Spender adds caustically, the assurance of at least some noncompetitive listeners.

Women's more gentle delivery, "feminine" choice of adjectives, and greater attention to grammar and politeness have been heavily criticized. Linguist Robin Lakoff pioneered the exposure of "ladylike" speech as a double bind that is both required of little girls, and used as a reason why, as adults, they may not be seen as forceful or serious. (Even Lakoff seems to assume, however, that female speech is to be criticized as the deficient form, while male speech is the norm and thus escapes equal comment.) Sociologist Arlie Hochschild also cites some survival techniques of racial minorities that women of all races seem to share: playing dumb and dissembling, for instance, or expressing frequent approval of others.

But whether this criticism of female speech patterns is justified or not, there is also evidence that a rejection of the way a woman speaks is often a way of blaming or dismissing her without dealing with the content of what she is saying.

For instance, women speakers are more likely to hear some version of "You have a good point, but you're not making it effectively," or "Your style is too aggressive/weak/loud/quiet." It is with such paternalistic criticisms that male politicians often dismiss the serious message of a female colleague, or that husbands turn aside the content of arguments made by their wives.

It is also such criticisms that allow women candidates to be rejected without dealing with the substance of the issues they raise. When Bella Abzug of New York and Gloria Schaeffer of Connecticut both ran for political office in one recent year, each was said to have a personal style that would prevent her from being an effective senator: Abzug because she was "too abrasive and aggressive," and Schaeffer because she was "too ladylike and quiet." Style was made the central issue by the press, and thus became one in the public-opinion polls. Both were defeated.

There are three anomalies that give away this supposedly "helpful" criticism. First, it is rarely used when a woman's message is not challenging to male power. (How often are women criticized for being too fierce in defense of their families? How often was Phyllis Schlafly criticized for being too aggressive in her opposition to the Equal Rights Amendment?) Second, the criticism is rarely accompanied by real support, even when the critic presents himself (or herself) as sympathetic. (Women political candidates say they often get critiques of their fund-raising techniques instead of cash, even from people who agree with them on issues.) Finally, almost everyone, regardless of status, feels a right to criticize. (Women professors report criticism of their teaching style from young students, as do women bosses from their employees.)

Just as there is a conversational topic that men in a group often find more compelling than any introduced by a woman (even when it's exactly the same topic, but *re*introduced by a man), or a political issue that is "more important" than any of concern to women, so there is usually a better, more effective style than the one a woman happens to be using.

Men *would* support us, we are told, if only we learned how to ask for their support in the right way. It's a subtle and effective way of blaming the victim.

What can we do to break through these stereotypes? Keeping notes for one meeting or one week on the male/female ratio of gossip or self-mentions could be educational. Declaring a day's moratorium on all words that end in "—tion" and all generalities might encourage men to state their personal beliefs *without* disguising them as general conclusions.

As a personal exercise, try countering slippery abstractions with tangible examples. When David Susskind and Germaine Greer were guests on the same television talk show, for instance, Susskind used general, pseudoscientific statements about women's monthly emotional changes as a way of excusing the injustices cited by this very intelligent woman. Finally, Greer turned politely to Susskind and said, "Tell me, David. Can you tell if I'm menstruating right now—or not?" She not only eliminated any doubts raised by Susskind's statements, but subdued his pugnacious style for the rest of the show.

Men themselves are working to break down the generalities and competitiveness that a male-dominant culture has imposed on them. Some are meeting in all-male consciousness-raising groups, learning how to communicate more openly and personally among themselves.

Many women are also trying to break down the barriers we ourselves maintain. For instance, women's preference for talking to one another has a great deal to do with the shorthand that shared experience provides. Furthermore, the less powerful group usually knows the powerful one much better than vice versa—blacks have had to understand whites in order to survive, women have had to know men—yet the powerful group can afford to regard the less powerful one as a mystery. Indeed, the idea of differentness and the Mysterious Other may be necessary justifications for the power imbalance and the lack of empathy it requires.

One result is that, even when the powerful group *wants* to listen, the other may despair of talking: it's just too much trouble to explain. Recognizing this unequal knowledge encourages women to talk about themselves to men, at least to match the time they spend talking about themselves. After all, they cannot read our minds.

On issues of style, role reversals are enlightening. For instance, ask a man who is critical of "aggressive" women to try to argue a serious political point while speaking "like a lady." A woman candidate might also ask critics to write a speech in the style they think she should use. Responding in kind can create a quick reversal. There's a certain satisfaction to saying, in the middle of a man's impassioned speech: "I suppose you have a point to make, but you're not expressing it well. Now, if you just used more personal examples. If you changed your language, your timing, and perhaps your suit. . . ."

Finally, if all talk fails, try putting the same message in writing. The point is to get your message across, whether or not the man in question can separate it from the medium.

III

Women's higher-pitched voices and men's lower ones are the result of physiology. Because deep voices are more pleasant and authoritative, women speakers will always have a problem. Besides, female facial expressions and gestures aren't as forceful . . . and so on. It's true that tone of voice is partly created by throat-construction and the resonance of bones. Though there is a big area of male-female overlap in voice tone, as well as in size, strength, and other physical attributes, we assume that all men will have a much deeper pitch than all women.

In fact, however, no one knows exactly how much of our speaking voices are imitative and culturally produced. Studies of young boys before puberty show that their vocal tones may deepen *even before physiological changes can account for it.* They are imitating the way the males around them speak. Dale Spender cites a study of males who were not mute, but who were born deaf and thus unable to imitate sound. Some of them never went through an adolescent voice change at all.

Whatever the mix of physiological and cultural factors, however, the important point is that the *acceptance* of vocal tone is definitely cultural and therefore subject to change.

In Japan, for instance, a woman's traditionally high-pitched, soft speaking voice is considered a very important sexual attribute. (When asked in a public-opinion poll what attribute they found most attractive in women, the majority of Japanese men said "voice.") Though trained to speak in upper registers, Japanese women, like many of their sisters around the world, often speak in lower tones when men are not present. They may even change their language as well. (A reporter's tapes of Japanese schoolgirls talking among themselves caused a scandal. They were using masculine word endings and verbs in a country where the language is divided into formally masculine and feminine forms.) Thus, Japanese men may find a high voice attractive not for itself but for its tribute to a traditional subservience.

Some American women also cultivate a high, childish, or whispery voice à la Marilyn Monroe. We may sense that a woman is talking to a man on the other end of the phone, or a man to a woman, because she lightens her normal tone and he deepens his.

A childlike or "feminine" vocal style becomes a drawback, however, when women try for any adult or powerful role. Female reporters were kept out of television and radio for years by the argument that their voices were too high, grating, or nonauthoritative to speak the news credibly. Even now, women's voices may be thought more suitable for human interest and "soft news," while men still announce "hard news." In the early days of television, women were allowed to do the weather reports—very sexily. When meteorology and weather maps became the vogue, however, most stations switched to men. Even now, 85 percent of all voice-overs on television ads, including those for women's products, are done by men. Even on floor wax and detergents, men are likely to be the voices of expertise and authority.

In the long run, however, men may suffer more from cultural restrictions on tone of voice than women do. Linguist Ruth Brend's study of male and female intonation patterns in the United States, for instance, disclosed four contrasting levels used by women in normal speech, but only three levels used by men. This isn't a result of physiology: men also have at least four levels available to them, but they rarely use the highest one. Thus, women may speak publicly in both high and low tones with some degree of social acceptability, but men must use their lower tones only. It's okay to flatter the ruling class with imitation, just as it's okay for women to wear pants or for blacks to speak and dress like Establishment whites, but it's less okay for men to wear feminine clothes, for whites to adopt black speech and street style, or for men to imitate or sound like women. (Such upper-class exceptions as the female-impersonating shows put on by the Hasty Pudding Club at Harvard or by the very rich men of the Bohemian Grove in California seem to indicate that even ridicule of women requires security. It's much less likely to happen at the working-class level of bowling clubs and bars.)

As the price of "masculinity," men as a group are losing variety in their speech and an ability to express a full range of emotions. The higher proportion of masculine monotones is also a penalty to the public ear.

In the same way, physical expressiveness may be viewed as "feminine." Women can be vivacious. We are allowed more varieties of facial expression and gestures. Men must be rocklike. Certainly, some emotive and expressive men are being imprisoned by that belief.

The down side is that women's greater range of expression is also used to ridicule females as emotionally unstable. That sad point is made by Nancy Henley in *Body Politics: Power, Sex, and Nonverbal Communication.* "Women's facial expressivity," she explains, "has been allowed a wider range than men's, encompassing within the sex stereotype not only pleasant expressions, but negative ones like crying." Since males are encouraged to leave crying and other emotional expression in their childhoods, females who retain this human ability are often compared to children.

Nonetheless, women's wider range also allows us to recognize more physical expression when we see it. Henley refers to a study showing that women of all races and black men usually do better than white men at identifying nonverbal emotional clues. We're both less imprisoned by the rocklike mask of being in control, and more needful of the survival skill of paying attention.

In short, women need to affirm and expand expressiveness, but men are also missing some major ways of signaling the world and getting signals back.

You can't change vocal cords (theirs or ours), but you can make sure they're being well used. Tape-record women talking together, then record the same people talking to men. It's a good way to find out whether we're sending out geishalike tonal clues. Some women are neglecting our lower range. Others, especially when trying to be taken seriously, are overcompensating for supposed emotionalism by narrowing to a "reasonable" monotone. Men may also change under pressure of taped evidence: for instance, the contrast between their dullness when talking with men and their expressiveness when talking to children. Many actors, female and male, are living testimonials to how much and how quickly—with effort, exercise, and freedom—a vocal range can change.

Most important, remember that there is nothing *wrong* with women's voices, and no subject or emotion they cannot convey. This is especially important for women who are lonely tokens. The first women in law and business schools, the board room, or the assembly line often report that the sound of their own voices comes as a shock—a major barrier to reciting in class, speaking up on policy, or arguing in union meetings. It may take a while for words said in a female voice to be taken seriously, but a head-turning response to the unusual sound is also a tribute to its owner as a courageous pioneer.

The advent of video recorders is a major breakthrough in understanding and changing our nonverbal expressions. Watching the incontrovertible evidence of how we come across to others can be more useful than years of psychiatry. Many men and boys could also benefit from such expressiveness exercises as a game of charades, or communicating with children. Women and girls can free body movements through sports, a conscious effort to take up more space when sitting or standing, and using body language we may now use only when relaxed with other women. Many of us could benefit from watching female impersonators and learning the many ways in which we have been trained to be female impersonators, too.

The point is not that one gender's cultural style is superior to the other's. The current "feminine" style of communicating may be better suited to, say, the performing arts, medical diagnosis, and conflict resolution. It has perfected emotional expressiveness, careful listening, and a way of leaving an adversary with dignity intact. The current "masculine" style may be better suited to, say, procedural instruction, surgical teams and other situations requiring hierarchical command, and job interviews. It has perfected linear and abstract thinking, quick commands, and a willingness to speak well of oneself or present views with assertiveness. But we will never achieve this full human circle of expression if women imitate the male "adult" style. We have to teach as well as learn.

A feminist assault on the politics of talking, and listening, is a radical act. It's a way of transforming the cultural vessel in which both instant communication and long-term anthropological change are carried. Unlike the written word, or visual imagery, or any form of communication divorced from our presence, talking and listening won't allow us to hide. There is no neutral page, image, sound, or even a genderless name to protect us. We are demanding to be accepted and understood by all the senses and for our whole selves.

That's precisely what makes the change so difficult. And so crucial.

KATE SIMON

Birthing

He looked so much like a story character—the gentled Scrooge of a *St. Nicholas Magazine* Christmas issue, a not-too-skeletal Ichabod Crane—that it is difficult to say how he really looked. And he was ephemeral, his visits timed for the hours we were in school so that we caught only occasional glimpses of him as he strode around a corner, immensely tall (something we were not accustomed to in our Mediterranean street) and thin, wearing a long, skinny black coat and a shapeless black hat, carrying a black doctor's satchel. We knew Dr. James had visited when we found our mothers in bed "resting," an odd word, an odd event. When we left for school, they had no symptoms of cold or cough or pain; preoccupied perhaps, but that was common among women who worried about getting the rent paid on time, about shoes for the children, about husbands who habitually came home late from work. There was never an explanation for Dr. James's visit, what he did, what he said; only the mother on the bed, a peculiar worrisome thing, like finding the library or school suddenly, without warning, closed. By suppertime the mothers would be chopping, cutting, cooking, sometimes more quiet than usual, sometimes more irritable, nothing more.

When I became a member of a medical family that had practiced in the Bronx for decades, I once mentioned Dr. James and his unexplained short visits to mothers only, and never to deliver babies. A spate of enthusiastic information poured over the dinner table. Dr. James was, even when I knew him as a child, quite an old man, retired from a prestigious and lucrative practice in Boston, they thought. His was a prosperous intellectual family, the famous New England Jameses that produced William and Henry, but to the older Bronx doctors, *the* James was the magnificent old driven scarecrow. Having educated his children and seen their arrival into respected professions, he dedicated himself to poor immigrant women for whom there was no sex information, no birth-control clinics, nothing but knitting needles, hat pins, lengths of wire, the drinking of noxious mixtures while they sat in scalding baths to prevent the birth of yet another child. At times one woman would inflict these well-meant injuries on a sister, a neighbor; sometimes they were solitary acts of desperation. Some women died of septicemia; some of those who could not kill the fetus had to wait out the nine months and the delivery to let the infant die of exposure or suffocation.

To prevent such suicides and murders, Dr. James went from one immigrant neighborhood to another, performing abortions. (How he was informed where he was needed no one seemed to know; there must have been one woman in each area who transmitted messages.) He lived to be quite old and, according to my informants, worked vigorously at his self-appointed job until he died, having performed thousands of abortions, the fee a dollar or two or nothing, depending on the degree of poverty he met. Every adult in his neighborhoods knew him and his function, including cops and Board of Health people, who usually let him be. It was during the periodic sweeps of new brooms in office that he was arrested and imprisoned. He succumbed to it all very calmly, didn't call lawyers or his family, nor offered bail. Apparently he got in touch with one or two colleagues who called others, who in turn called others, and together they stormed the court where he was being tried. They pleaded, they argued, they shouted; they accused the police and the court of ignorance and inhumanity, and had him released. This drama was repeated several times, memorable times for the doctors who could thus demonstrate their admiration for the old man with the courage and independence to act as they might, if they but could.

Dr. James was a careful gynecologist as well as a skilled abortionist. There were women he would not abort. My little sister was much more gently handled, more eagerly cosseted, than my brother and I were because, my mother told me when we had become close adult friends, the baby was unwanted and was allowed to be born only because Dr. James refused to perform another abortion; she had had too many and another could be hazardous. How many she had I found out when I checked her into a hospital a few years before she died. Thirteen. I asked her again when we were alone in her hospital room whether I had heard correctly. Thirteen? And three children besides? Yes, and that was by no means the neighborhood record, she said. How could I account for the fact that a number of our Italian neighbors, urged by the Catholic Church to produce large families, had no more than two or three children? Certainly it wasn't the abstinence of Italian husbands, no more controlled than Jewish husbands. It was the work of the blessed hands of that wonderful old *goy*.

When school started in September before I was quite eight, the walks with my swollen mother—watching her skirt so that she didn't stumble on the stairs, pacing my steps, skipping in place to her lumbering, rocking walk, like the elephant in the zoo—stopped. When we came home from school there was a quiet in the house that seemed to tremble against the walls, no lilting greetings, no apples and crackers on the table, in the sink a cold half cup of tea with milk. She was resting, and resting meant sick, like the times when Dr. James had come and gone. It also meant trouble. I kept glancing surreptitiously at her ankles to see if they were swollen. In scraps of eavesdropping I had accumulated something about women swelling and having convulsions before babies were born. My mother had swelled but didn't have convulsions when I was born, a difficult delivery, "with instruments" that dented my forehead. (Tracing the dent in my forehead, I wondered if it would squeeze my brains and someday make me crazy, like Mrs. Silverberg or my father's sister Surrele, whose name was thrown at me when I threw shoes and slammed doors.) "Instruments" were enormous black pincers, like those the iceman used to pull blocks of ice from his wagon, stuck in my mother's belly, ripping through the flesh and searching among her bleeding bowels until it hit my forehead and grabbed me, pulling up and out again through the red, messed flesh into the air, and dropped me, a doll covered with pee and shit, into hands that slapped to make me breathe. And now, in our house, a few paces from the kitchen, fewer from the dining room, it was probably all going to happen again; tonight, tomorrow night, the next night. It always happened late at night, a shameful, secret thing, too dark and terrible for open day.

One afternoon in early October we came home to find Mrs. Nagy and Mrs. Kaplan bustling around the kitchen and Fannie Herman standing in the hallway wringing her hands. Mrs. Nagy gave us a piece of strudel and told us brusquely to go down and stay in the street until our father came home. We hung around the stoop feeling uncomfortable, lost. We had to go to the toilet, we were getting cold in the falling light, we didn't feel like playing. Something was happening to our mother and why couldn't we see her? It had to do with her belly and the baby. I wanted to watch and at the same time wanted to be far, far away; to be someone else in another place, a girl who lived in a book.

When our father arrived and asked us what we were doing in the street so late, my brother mumbled something about the baby and we ran upstairs. We could hear Mrs. Kaplan's voice in the far big bedroom as my father walked into it and closed the door. Mrs. Nagy was in the kitchen putting stuffed cabbage and pieces of cornbread on the table. Our father called to us to eat and do our homework in the kitchen, he would eat later. We were to be quick and quiet and go to bed—and close the door—as soon as we were through. We didn't talk, as we often did, in bed; there was no point at which to start a discussion of something so large and forbidding, and words might betray our fear.

During the night we were awakened by a shriek and then another. Our door was pushed shut and we knew we were not to open it, not to get out of bed, not to see what was happening. People bustled in the hallway, to and from the kitchen, to and from the bathroom. Someone rang the doorbell and was admitted, probably the doctor. Through the sound of feet and the hushed voices, another scream and more, louder, more piercing, like ambulances. This I, too, had done to my mother, distorted her good-natured, singing person into a howling animal. I imagined her hair wild and swept across her staring green eyes, her pretty mouth torn by the screams, the doctor pushing the immense pincers into her belly and searching, searching for the baby, ripping her to pieces as my birth had done. My brother was asleep or pretended to be. I was alone in a guilt that made me want to disappear, to die.

Not knowing how to die, I separated myself from myself, one girl not there, one girl going through familiar actions in a dumbness and deafness like a thick rubber Halloween mask. I don't know who gave us breakfast; I ate it. I don't know what happened in school; I was there and managed to perform whatever was asked of me. I did my homework; it was correct. They told me I had a little sister; I didn't say anything. The women on the street asked me how my mother was; I said all right. This went on, the living in a cold, flat country, for several days, the guilt pushed down, out, away, and kept away. When my mother called to me from her bedroom to come and see the new baby, it was pretty, I called back, "Tomorrow," and ran to the street.

One of the days when my mother was still in her bed and we still fed by the neighbors, a monitor came into my classroom and handed a note to the teacher. We all sat up, eager for whatever news it might bring, an injunction from the principal about noise in the auditorium, an announcement of a shortened school day, possibly. My teacher called me to her and told me that I was wanted by my brother's teacher. All the kids stared as I walked awkwardly (was my skirt hitched up in back? my socks falling?) out of the room. When I reached his classroom, my brother was standing at her desk, looking shamefaced but not especially stricken. His teacher, Miss Sullivan, one of the smiling young ones, said she knew my mother had just had a baby but a big girl like myself could take care of a little brother almost as well as his mother could. But maybe I was too busy to notice that he didn't wash too well. Pulling his collar away from his neck, she showed me a broad band of dirt that began at a sharp edge just below his clean jaws. I had said every morning, "Wash your face," but forgot to mention his neck. Everything became hard and clear, as if it were cut out of metal, in that room, as deeply indelible as the painting of the boys listening to Sir Walter Raleigh's adventures in the auditorium: Miss Sullivan's blond lashes, her left eye a little bigger than the right, the spot of spit at the corner of her dry lips, the gray clouds of old chalk marks on the blackboard, the word cards, SENT, WENT, BENT, on the wall, the gluey tan wood of the windowsill, the pale afternoon sun streaking the floor, a red sweater and a brown sweater hanging crooked in the half-open wardrobe, the brown desks on iron legs, on each desk hands folded as for a somber occasion like a visit from the nurse, above each desk eyes staring at me.

I stood there leaden with shame until Miss Sullivan dismissed me with, "See that he washes better," and sent me back to my classroom. It was difficult to open the door and walk into those eyes that were going to stare at me and later, at three o'clock, come closer to ask what happened. I answered, "Oh, nothing. Miss Sullivan wanted me to check my brother's homework; he's careless, she said." I wanted to vomit, to stamp, to scream, to break, to kill: him, me, them, my mother, my father, everything, the whole world. But I had to walk him home. He searched my face as he ran across the playground toward me, hesitated, and attached himself to Jimmy, walking near me, as he had to, but a safe distance away, on the far side of Jimmy. As soon as he dropped his books on the floor of our bedroom he ran into my mother's room, where I heard them giggling together. She called to me, "Don't you want to come and see the baby?" I yelled back, "Tomorrow," still afraid of what I might see, a baby with a ditch in its head, a mother all rags of flesh, an exploded, splashed cartoon animal. All my fault. My brother came back into the kitchen where I was trying to peel an apple in one long coil, an especially delicate operation because I was using a big breadknife. He pushed my arm, breaking the coil, and ran toward the hallway, laughing. I threw the knife at him and saw it quivering in the wall where his head had been a second before. It fell from the wall. I picked it up and continued cutting the apple as I listened to him screaming to my mother, "She tried to kill me! She threw the knife, the big knife, at me! She's crazy! Send her away! Please, Mama, send her away! I'm afraid of her!" I heard her slippers patter down the hall, closed my eyes tight shut, and waited. She shook me. "Open your eyes. Look at me." I looked, I would have to sometime, and saw her as she was most mornings, in her thick brown bathrobe, her short hair not yet combed, her lips pale. "What's the matter with you? Do you know you could have killed him? Do you know that he would be dead, forever dead? Never talk again, never walk, never see, never hear?

Do you know that you would be locked away in an asylum for crazy people? And spend the rest of your life, many, many years, with other crazies?" I said nothing, tried not to be there. "I've got to go back to bed now and attend to the baby. This your father will hear about and I won't get in his way. Whatever punishment you get you'll deserve."

It rained that evening and my brother was granted the privilege, usually mine, of carrying the umbrella to the El station. It was a special pleasure, a special ceremony, to go out into the wet night as if on an emergency mission—a nurse, a doctor—to rescue our fathers. We clustered, at the bottom of the steep El stairs, admiring the dark shine of the trolley tracks, the rain bubbling the puddles like boiling black cereal, holding the handles tight as the wind fought our umbrellas, listening to the rumble and roar of the train, the screeching stop, the rush of feet down the stairs. For many of us, the big smile as we yelled, "Pa, here I am, here," and were recognized and patted on the arm or head was the only overt affection we knew from our fathers. The umbrellas, now taller and single, separated to walk on their two long legs and their two short up Tremont Avenue, down to Bathgate, or shadowed themselves under the struts and tracks of Third Avenue.

By the time my brother and father got home and the wet umbrella placed in the bathtub, the story of the knife had been told, so serious a matter that it came before supper. Asked why I had thrown the knife, I answered—and it seemed a feeble reason—"Because his neck was dirty and he made me ashamed in front of his whole class." I couldn't say, "Because I hate mothers and babies and screaming in the night and people being pulled out of bellies with instruments and brothers who jump around and play while I have to take care of them." I couldn't find the words or shape the sentence because they were truly crazy things to say, worse than throwing knives. There was no preliminary lecture, cause and effect clear and simple. With a few words to my mother about the *gilgul*, the restless, evil spirit I must have in me—although he didn't really believe in such superstitious things—my father pushed me into the bathroom and, while he carefully pulled his belt out of the trouser loops, told me to lie across the covered toilet, pick up my skirt, and pull down my bloomers.

I had been slapped, on the face, on the behind, punched by boys and pinched by girls; my knees were often scraped, my fingers blistered and cut, but there was no preparation for the pain beyond pain of this first beating, the swish of the strap becoming a burning scream through my whole body, my arms shaking as they clung to the edge of the bathtub, my fingers scratching at the squealing porcelain, my ribs crushed against the toilet lid. I shrieked and begged, "Papa, don't. Stop, please. Please stop. Please, Papa." He stopped when he was out of breath, his face red, his brown eyes bulging. Replacing his belt, he walked out of the bathroom, closing the door. I stood there for a long while, then splashed cold water on my behind, fixed my clothing, and stood some more, not knowing where to go. In time I heard fumbling at the doorknob and my mother's voice telling my brother to get away, to let me be. A few minutes later she opened the door to tell me it was time to eat. I slipped out of the bathroom and into my bedroom, pushed the big chair against the door that had no lock, piled my books, my brother's books, the wooden sewing machine cover, and the heavy coats that were in the closet on the chair, and got into bed, pushing myself way, way down under the featherbed, stroking and rubbing myself until I fell asleep.

The next morning my brother banged on the door for his books. As I pulled the heavy chair away so he could get in, I noticed his neck was clean. My mother was back in bed with the baby I had no intention of seeing. I grabbed a roll from the breadbox in the kitchen and ate it as I dressed, then left the house quickly, passing my brother, who stood on the third floor waiting at Jimmy's door. We avoided each other for the next day or two, he hanging on to Jimmy, I watching that they looked each way down the street before they crossed broad, busy 180th.

After my mother had spent her traditional ten days in bed, she put on the clothing she wore before the big belly and fixed us nice lunches: noodles, pot cheese, and raisins with cinnamon and sugar, radishes and cucumbers in sour cream, salami sandwiches. Ordinariness washed, day by day, over our lives except for the baby lying in my mother's lap in the kitchen. She looked unfinished and wandering, making strange faces, her eyes a milky blue and bobbling in her head, the tiny fingers reaching and curling toward everything, nothing. When her eyes turned to gold and steady, and some of the grimaces became smiles, I began to like her a little and let her pull at my fingers and hair.

MARY ANNE DOLAN

When Feminism Failed

The first tremor struck me at a meeting one early morning in 1983. I was sitting in my office at the large table where, as editor of the *Los Angeles Herald Examiner*, I planned daily editions with the news staff.

Gwen Jones, the fashion editor, had strolled in while I was reading that day's papers and asked if we could chat. She had been worrying about coming to me for a long time, she said. But we went back a ways together and trusted each other and, she'd determined, "I thought you should know."

Gwen, a young feminist-leaning journalist, was concerned about the women I'd put in charge of large departments of the paper, specifically hers. It was great to have female executives, she said, but not if they didn't listen and didn't support you and seemed only concerned about building their own bureaucracies. Things were changing at the newspaper, she said. Issues were being politicized, meetings were stultifying. In general, her department's morale was down and the writers were dispirited. It wasn't—I remember her words—"fun anymore."

Others—male and female—had tried to make the same point, this time, something caught in my heart.

But I forged ahead with what I thought of as an experiment in "management by family." It was my privilege and ultimately my duty.

I had come to the editorship of the *Herald* after nearly 10 years in executive newspaper jobs and after many more years working with colleagues to promote a greater role for women in journalism. In Washington, we had organized in Nora

Ephron's apartment house, we had changed the concept of "society pages," we had marched on the Gridiron. We had succeeded in getting women like me into newspaper training programs and onto national and foreign news desks.

I had begun as a clerk, answering telephones and carrying lunches for the women's department of the now-defunct *Washington Star*. In 1981, when I was touted as the first woman in America to rise through the ranks to the editorship of a major metropolitan newspaper, there was no way I was not going to bring other women with me.

This was a moment when the promise of the women's movement could be fulfilled. We had permission at last. The joint belonged to us! We would bring all those "female" qualities we had been boasting about on placards for years in through the front door, into the open of the newsroom. We would be a family. Between male and female would be respect and generosity and adaptability and warmth and comity and nurturing. Such an environment would make the most of our talents and, centrally, of our work. We would have honest conflict and competition, but also compromise and consensus and, therefore, success. We would make mincemeat of the male business model.

In no time, the *Herald* had what we believed was the first 50/50 male/female masthead in the country. We had the first female circulation director. We had a woman as sports columnist and a woman as editor of the editorial pages. There were many women in middle echelons, including the business editor. We were determined to show that women could do as well as men at running a big paper. By the time I left the paper five years later to return to writing, I still believed this to be true, but I also knew it would take a long time to get beyond the male models so many women had adopted.

Looking back, I can say that of the women I appointed to top-level positions, only one truly resisted the clichéd power traps and rose to the kind of heights Betty Friedan predicted when she wrote *The Feminine Mystique* 25 years ago. Only one learned to "compete not as a woman or a man but as a human being."

It wasn't that all the men at the *Herald* were wise and wonderful as leaders (though many of them were). Nor did all the women in positions of responsibility abuse their power. What happened was that, by and large, they took on the worst— sometimes hilarious—aspects of the stereotypical corporate ladder-climbing male. As soon as masthead status was achieved, the power grab began.

The number of formal meetings, with "boss" at the head of the table, quadrupled; there were premeetings and postmeetings. Words like "facilitate" and "strategize" came into vogue. Everyone was suddenly afraid that somebody else knew something she didn't. Or had a more impressive title.

Office geography became as important in what had once been our cranky *Citizen Kane* newsroom as it is in the West Wing of the White House. Secretaries began acting like palace guards.

There were memos everywhere, multicopied and held with brightly colored plastic paper clips representing various fiefdoms. If you didn't have a "record" of a conversation, the conversation hadn't taken place.

Where there was opportunity to deal with people openly and with ease, many female managers were wary. They acted out a script that was part Osgood Conklin, part J.R. Ewing, part M.B.A./One-Minute-Manager and a tiny bit Mom. Many spent a good deal of time seeking out the nearest male authority figures. A succession of male general managers was courted. Male executives from Hearst, the parent company in New York, who flew in on business were afforded a coquettish new brand of ancient pagan king-worship.

It took me a while to catch on to all this. For one thing, I hadn't expected it. For another, I didn't want to see it. To me, the women I had imported as managers and editors appeared wise, funny, mature. But to the staff they were brittle, conniving, power-hungry and unyielding. One after another, close friends of mine tried to convey to me what was happening; some even feared I would lose my job to one of the women they saw as plotting against me. (I guffawed at this notion, and in this, at least, I was right. After I left, none of these women were given a shot at the editorship and all but one have since left the paper.) At some point in all this, a male columnist and friend of many years' standing suggested I procure a new kind of bulletproof vest—for my back.

I can see now how my own background and my cheery belief in the accomplishments of the American women's movement may have impaired my vision. I can hear Germaine Greer snickering, but it seemed to me then, and it seems to me still, that we have much to applaud in our society's progress toward equality between the sexes. Thanks to brothers who always treated me as a peer, parents who admirably delivered roots and wings, and mentors—men and women both—I developed personal confidence and greater confidence in women as leaders.

At the *Herald*, I was criticized for being too strident on some matters (boycotting redundant meetings—with the general manager and business administration of the paper, for example) and too soft on others (spending too much time, emotion and money coaxing a series of stories out of a slow-producing correspondent in Nicaragua). But my working model was well-known: trying to build enthusiasm and excitement through the sheer creative spin of work. The challenge was daunting: the *Herald* was facing off day-to-day against the monolithic *Los Angeles Times.* We had fewer people and severely limited resources. I fought for staff and money but also for paint and library research equipment and, sometimes, flowers. I often wandered into the newsroom offering some treat or other, prompting some staffers to buzz: "Here comes Rosalynn Carter with cookies for the earthquake victims."

Bringing women to the center of this challenge was a simple, natural joy. They were experienced professionals who rightly demanded good titles and good salaries, and got them, just as I had. Not one had reason to feel financially insecure or psychologically threatened. Yet the fact was, many of these women were content to go along with a humanizing philosophy in the workplace as a diversion only. Their essential creed was an ancient one, the male one: power first.

In the newsroom, the effects of these conflicting creeds became obvious. It was, as Gwen had said, not good. Curiously, the sense of family that suffered was, I think, what had initially attracted the women I had hired.

In the end, the realization of how truly stymied we women still were by our lack of female models and our lack of confidence to do things differently left me as dispirited as many of us felt after the Vice Presidential campaign of Geraldine Ferraro.

The clearest thing I could say at the time was that women—or men—who have never felt empowered, whether by parents or teachers or mentors, cannot be expected to know how to handle this commodity, as hot and alien as some radioactive substance. No one wakes up in the morning and naturally knows what to do, or what not to do, with power—how to avoid addiction to it, how to protect it, how to give it away. By the time I wore "Editor" on my metaphoric green eyeshade, I had not learned it all, but I knew I had been excellently taught. And it troubled me that, somehow, I had not done enough.

A friend sent me back to Steven Spielberg's movie *Gremlins.* In it, she reminded me, the adventurer who brings the adorable little magwai out of an exotic China-town lair is advised by an Ancient One: never lead it to water and don't let it eat after midnight.

"When you brought women into a strange land," she said, "the same rules applied. You gave women water—power—and, optimistically, you left them alone. Like gremlins, they turned into monsters."

Surely that wasn't inevitable, was it?

Still, mine was only one case history, an experiment. It had been an exhausting and profoundly disappointing chapter in my career, but instructive. When I left the *Herald* in 1985, I tucked it under my arm until I could know how, or why, to pass it along.

My experiment came back to me with the full force of an earthquake almost three years later. I was having a conversation with Alexander Astin, a professor of higher education at the University of California at Los Angeles. As director of an annual national survey of college freshmen, Astin has for 22 years collected data on the hopes and dreams of the young. "Students are a pretty good barometer on society," he was saying, "and what they're teaching us is that society's values have shifted." Of 1987's roughly 290,000 freshmen, a record 75.6 percent said that "being very well off financially" was a top goal, considerably more than in 1986 and nearly twice the 1970 percentage.

That, in itself, was not what intrigued me. Rather, it was that during that same period—as female enrollment swelled to equal and, in some parts of the country, exceed male enrollment—the interest in "developing a meaningful philosophy of life" reached an all-time low. From a peak of 82.9 percent in the freshmen class of 1967, this interest has nose-dived to a 39.4 rating. The mind and matter values had virtually flip-flopped.

I asked Astin what he thought accounted for that extreme swing. He touched his fingertips together, paused, and answered: "The women's movement."

I knew what he meant. I thought about the fact that while I was seeing startlingly diminished evidence of a social conscience and benificence in my own age group, studies showed young people were turning to materialism like flies to butter. There had to be a deeper cause than the Reagan era and Wall Street. The most significant social movement of my lifetime—the women's movement—had to have played a key role.

"A large part of the thinking behind the women's movement said that the goodies in this society were disproportionately reserved for the men," Astin said, "and that there were obstacles to women having access to these goodies. . . . It was one thing to resent not being free to become a doctor or lawyer or business person because of an expectation that a woman should take care of a man and raise kids. But I think it was something else to emphasize women having an opportunity to go out and make a killing just like the guys. . . ."

Had the tangible goals of the movement survived, but without the philosophical underpinnings that had made them so supremely important? Had status, money, power become, in themselves, the rewards? "In every trend," Astin told me, "the men are now taking their leads from the women. . . . But, in one of the great ironies, the women have come to resemble the old male models."

I dragged myself back to my office in Westwood that afternoon, realizing as I walked along the sidewalk, somewhere between the U.C.L.A. Student Union and my Videotheque store, that if we were passing on to our children merely the values of power, money, and status, it was because those were what we were clinging to. What was missing in the "new" women I saw at the *Herald* and elsewhere was the joyful "I am." What remained was the fearful "I want."

The more time I've spent with female professionals in Los Angeles and other cities, the more I have noticed a shift away from the attitudes of the 60's and 70's—that talk of strength and sisterhood—to the hard-edged, glitzy patois of the 80's. Women's anger toward men is, I believe, even greater now than before. Devotion to success at the expense of personal well-being is rampant. Something is seriously askew.

What of the legacy of the women's movement? Some argue that we have, as a society, moved forward under its continuing influence. Others subscribe to the "critical mass" theory—that is, that only when enough women (or blacks or Hispanics or homosexuals) gain power does an evolutionary movement toward equality occur. I find that the latter theory is quickly embraced by those who prefer to ignore the negative female leadership styles they see around them. But many of those I interviewed for this article argued that both men and women are furthering the problem by refusing to deal with it honestly.

"Let's face it," said one man, "those of us who would like to learn management techniques from our female boss don't even know what to say when we see her hire and promote women and then set up rivalries with them. If we confront her, we're 'just being men'; if we don't, we're 'wimps.' "

Or this, from a woman, an entertainment executive in Hollywood: "I think women dress like men and act like men in the office because corporate males love it; it doesn't threaten their sexuality."

At a conclave held in February at the University of Southern California to examine the effects of the women's movement on the media, Anne Taylor Fleming, a writer and television commentator, addressed fellow panel members at the summary session of the meeting: "We talk a lot about women getting 'access' to male worlds—the power and the money—but a part of me is saying, 'Do I want that? Is that what we want? Didn't we want to redefine that terrain? Didn't we want to figure out a way to help men be more genteel, more gentle?' I don't see it happening. . . . What I worry about is that along with making the breakthroughs, we are acceding to the styles of male behavior. I think it bodes ill certainly for women, probably for men and for all our children."

Fleming's point, applauded by the audience, was not picked up by the moderator, Betty Friedan. It was significant, I thought, that the subject was being dodged. Others agreed. Said one frustrated conferee: "This is no time to be semi-honest."

"I will tell you exactly what I see and it's not good," said Judy Miller, vice president of marketing at Braun & Company, a Los Angeles public relations firm.

She is also president of the powerful Los Angeles Trusteeship for the Betterment of Women, a mother and a community leader.

"I see two types of women in the U.S. corporate culture—the young M.B.A. women and the 'super bitches.' The younger women come out of graduate schools with all the degrees, full of training and enthusiasm and no people skills. They figure they just do the job required, get paid big money fast and that's that. They have no ability to interact, no ability to work with teams, no talent at delegating and no willingness to give credit rather than hog it.

"The new generation of M.B.A.'s has been trained like men and they come in and act like little automatons, as if they've rejected their instinctive skills. Very, very few women are good all-round contributors. Most couldn't care less, refuse to play and then hit a ceiling and are not promoted. They blame the system or the men who, right now, are acting like better contributors than the women."

And the older workers?

"They used to be queen bees. Now, they're super bitches. They feel 'entitled'—to power, to huge salaries, to treating others, especially women, with disdain and an arrogance that says, 'I don't need anybody.' They all go off and tell dirty jokes with the guys, completely rejecting their own femininity and becoming sexist counterparts.

"I tell myself that we may be sensitive to this because any woman out there who makes it still represents every woman," Miller said. "Or I think, 'Maybe there are enough women doing things that we're just seeing universally held bad human traits coming out.' I don't know."

At the U.S.C. conference, entitled "Women, Men and Media: Breakthroughs and Backlash," Betty Friedan asked a distinguished group of national media figures the following question: "Are women going to move to money rather than social consciousness?"

Howard Rosenberg, the *Los Angeles Times* television critic, said: "If we labor under the assumption that women are somehow going to be of a higher consciousness than men, we are wrong."

Esther Shapiro, a television producer ("Dynasty"), said: "Well, women have an equal opportunity to be as ruthless as they want."

The question, to me, is not whether women can be as ruthless as men; we all know the answer to that. But is it so unreasonable to expect, as we did during the height of the women's movement, that women can be humanizers?

In the unique laboratory that was the *Herald,* women given large doses of power were transmogrified by it. Faced with the freedom to behave differently from the iconic male executive, the new women chose the course of least change.

Can we avoid imitating the very worst, rather than the best, of the male model? Can we spare our children our mistakes? The U.C.L.A. data would suggest that the next generation is patterning itself after women who, perhaps involuntarily, are helping to reinforce rather than reinvent the models of the past.

I am haunted by the ancient words of Euripides:

> The Gods
> Visit the sins of the fathers
> upon the children.

Of the many aftershocks I've felt since leaving the *Herald,* the strongest came on the day Gwen Jones died. She was 37, beautiful, wise and withered to death by cancer. On a February day, we gathered in a large church in Altadena, Calif., to mourn her.

A friend warned me that this occasion would be tough on many levels, not the least being that it was the first real "family reunion" of the old Heraldites: "Don't worry if it isn't there anymore. Offices really can't be families, you know."

But it was there all right.

We wept and sang and hugged and cheered Gwen for bringing us back together. Despite those who had tried to politicize us, fragment us, defeat us, it had happened. We were family. The younger female executives came excitedly to talk about their new babies and their husbands as well as their work.

Only one of the former "power women" showed up. Unsurprisingly, she created the only power pew in this most non-hierarchical of environments. She sat with the current and former publishers of the newspaper, both men, one at each elbow.

The women I have watched most carefully are those who richly deserved and won the opportunity to effect change. These are not downtrodden females. I cannot think of one out of the 40 or 50 who immediately march before my eyes who is not attractive, possessed of wit and capable of warmth.

No, this monster is within. Out of some ancient fear that the power is not truly ours, we set about destroying it. Like slaves who can't give up their masters, we cling either to male bosses or to male models. We are responsible for keeping alive the "He-Tarzan, Me-Jane" ethic, rendering ourselves powerless all over again. But somehow comfortable.

We ought to ask again: What do we want? If it is not to reach within ourselves and out to men, to humanize institutions and to pass on a different set of standards to our children, then what?

The "new female model" Betty Friedan called for in "The Second Stage"—the synthesis of "female experiences and female values"—has not yet formed. It is, perhaps, in the bulbs, as Eleanor Holmes Norton says, and will flower when the earth is warm enough. But it is time to be sure we are teaching the young well.

One can only hope that when Gwen's 6-year-old daughter, Jasmine, is ready, the garden will be in full bloom.

ANGELA Y. DAVIS

Racism, Birth Control and Reproductive Rights

When nineteenth-century feminists raised the demand for "voluntary motherhood," the campaign for birth control was born. Its proponents were called radicals and they were subjected to the same mockery as had befallen the initial advocates of woman suffrage. "Voluntary motherhood" was considered audacious, outrageous and outlandish by those who insisted that wives had no right to refuse to satisfy their husbands' sexual urges. Eventually, of course, the right to birth control, like women's right to vote, would be more or less taken for granted by U.S. public opinion. Yet in 1970, a full century later, the call for legal and easily accessible abortions was no less controversial than the issue of "voluntary motherhood" which had originally launched the birth control movement in the United States.

Birth control—individual choice, safe contraceptive methods, as well as abortions when necessary—is a fundamental prerequisite for the emancipation of women. Since the right of birth control is obviously advantageous to women of all classes and races, it would appear that even vastly dissimilar women's groups would have attempted to unite around this issue. In reality, however, the birth control movement has seldom succeeded in uniting women of different social backgrounds, and rarely have the movement's leaders popularized the genuine concerns of working-class women. Moreover, arguments advanced by birth control advocates have some-times been based on blatantly racist premises. The progressive potential of birth control remains indisputable. But in actuality, the historical record of this movement leaves much to be desired in the realm of challenges to racism and class exploitation.

The most important victory of the contemporary birth control movement was won during the early 1970s when abortions were at last declared legal. Having emerged during the infancy of the new Women's Liberation movement, the strug-gle to legalize abortions incorporated all the enthusiasm and the militancy of the young movement. By January, 1973, the abortion rights campaign had reached a triumphant culmination. In *Roe* v. *Wade* (410 U.S.) and *Doe* v. *Bolton* (410 U.S.), the U.S. Supreme Court ruled that a woman's right to personal privacy implied her right to decide whether or not to have an abortion.

The ranks of the abortion rights campaign did not include substantial numbers of women of color. Given the racial composition of the larger Women's Liberation movement, this was not at all surprising. When questions were raised about the absence of racially oppressed women in both the larger movement and the abortion rights campaign, two explanations were commonly proposed in the discussions and literature of the period: women of color were overburdened by their people's fight against racism; and/or they had not yet become conscious of the centrality of sexism. But the real meaning of the almost lily-white complexion of the abortion rights campaign was not to be found in an ostensibly myopic or underdeveloped conscious-ness among women of color. The truth lay buried in the ideological underpinnings of the birth control movement itself.

The failure of the abortion rights campaign to conduct a historical self-evaluation led to a dangerously superficial appraisal of Black people's suspicious attitudes toward birth control in general. Granted, when some Black people unhesitatingly equated birth control with genocide, it did appear to be an exaggerated—even paranoiac—reaction. Yet white abortion rights activists missed a profound message, for underly-ing these cries of genocide were important clues about the history of the birth control movement. This movement, for example, had been known to advocate involuntary sterilization—a racist form of mass "birth control." If ever women would enjoy the right to plan their pregnancies, legal and easily accessible birth control measures and abortions would have to be complemented by an end to sterilization abuse.

As for the abortion rights campaign itself, how could women of color fail to grasp its urgency? They were far more familiar than their white sisters with the murderously clumsy scalpels of inept abortionists seeking profit in illegality. In New York, for instance, during the several years preceding the decriminalization of abortions in that state, some 80 percent of the deaths caused by illegal abortions involved Black and Puerto Rican women.[1] Immediately afterward, women of color received close to half of all the legal abortions. If the abortion rights campaign of the early 1970s needed to be reminded that women of color wanted desperately to escape the back-room quack abortionists, they should have also realized that these same women were not about to express pro-abortion sentiments. They were in favor of *abortion rights,* which did not mean that they were proponents of abortion. When Black and Latina women resort to abortions in such large numbers, the stories they tell are not so much about their desire to be free of their pregnancy, but rather about the miserable social conditions which dissuade them from bringing new lives into the world.

Black women have been aborting themselves since the earliest days of slavery. Many slave women refused to bring children into a world of interminable forced labor, where chains and floggings and sexual abuse for women were the everyday conditions of life. A doctor practicing in Georgia around the middle of the last century noticed that abortions and miscarriages were far more common among his slave patients than among the white women he treated. According to the physician, either Black women worked too hard or

> . . . as the planters believe, the blacks are possessed of a secret by which they destroy the fetus at an early stage of gestation. . . . All country practitioners are aware of the frequent complaints of planters [about the] . . . unnatural tendency in the African female to destroy her offspring.[2]

Expressing shock that ". . . whole families of women fail to have any children,"[3] this doctor never considered how "unnatural" it was to raise children under the slave system. The . . . episode of Margaret Garner, a fugitive slave who killed her own daughter and attempted suicide herself when she was captured by slavecatchers, is a case in point.

> She rejoiced that the girl was dead—"now she would never know what a woman suffers as a slave"—and pleaded to be tried for murder. "I will go singing to the gallows rather than be returned to slavery!"[4]

Why were self-imposed abortions and reluctant acts of infanticide such common occurrences during slavery? Not because Black women had discovered solutions to their predicament, but rather because they were desperate. Abortions and infanticides were acts of desperation, motivated not by the biological birth process but by the oppressive conditions of slavery. Most of these women, no doubt, would have expressed their deepest resentment had someone hailed their abortions as a stepping stone toward freedom.

During the early abortion rights campaign it was too frequently assumed that legal abortions provided a viable alternative to the myriad problems posed by poverty. As if having fewer children could create more jobs, higher wages, better schools, etc., etc. This assumption reflected the tendency to blur the distinction between *abortion rights* and the general advocacy of *abortions*. The campaign often failed to provide a voice for women who wanted the *right* to legal abortions while deploring the social conditions that prohibited them from bearing more children.

The renewed offensive against abortion rights that erupted during the latter half of the 1970s has made it absolutely necessary to focus more sharply on the needs of poor and racially oppressed women. By 1977 the passage of the Hyde Amendment in Congress had mandated the withdrawal of federal funding for abortions, causing many state legislatures to follow suit. Black, Puerto Rican, Chicana and Native American Indian women, together with their impoverished white sisters, were thus effectively divested of the right to legal abortions. Since surgical sterilizations, funded by the Department of Health, Education and Welfare, remained free on demand, more and more poor women have been forced to opt for permanent infertility. What is urgently required is a broad campaign to defend the reproductive rights of all women—and especially those women whose economic circumstances often compel them to relinquish the right to reproduction itself.

Women's desire to control their reproductive system is probably as old as human history itself. As early as 1844 the *United States Practical Receipt Book* contained, among its many recipes for food, household chemicals and medicines, "receipts" for "birth preventive lotions." To make "Hannay's Preventive Lotion," for example,

> [t]ake pearlash, 1 part; water, 6 parts. Mix and filter. Keep it in closed bottles, and use it, with or without soap, immediately after connexion.[5]

For "Abernethy's Preventive Lotion,"

> [t]ake bichloride of mercury, 25 parts; milk of almonds, 400 parts; alcohol, 100 parts; rosewater, 1000 parts. Immerse the glands in a little of the mixture. . . . Infallible, if used in proper time.[6]

While women have probably always dreamed of infallible methods of birth control, it was not until the issue of women's rights in general became the focus of an organized movement that reproductive rights could emerge as a legitimate demand. In an essay entitled "Marriage," written during the 1850s, Sarah Grimke argued for a ". . . right on the part of woman to decide *when* she shall become a mother, how often and under what circumstances."[7] Alluding to one physician's humorous observation, Grimke agreed that if wives and husbands alternatively gave birth to their children, ". . . no family would ever have more than three, the husband bearing one and the wife two."[8] But, as she insists, ". . . the *right* to decide this matter has been almost wholly denied to woman."[9]

Sarah Grimke advocated women's right to sexual abstinence. Around the same time the well-known "emancipated marriage" of Lucy Stone and Henry Blackwell took place. These abolitionists and women's rights activists were married in a ceremony that protested women's traditional relinquishment of their rights to their persons, names and property. In agreeing that as husband, he had no right to the "custody of the wife's person,"[10] Henry Blackwell promised that he would not attempt to impose the dictates of his sexual desires upon his wife.

The notion that women could refuse to submit to their husbands' sexual demands eventually became the central idea of the call for "voluntary motherhood." By the 1870s, when the woman suffrage movement had reached its peak, feminists were publicly advocating voluntary motherhood. In a speech delivered in 1873, Victoria Woodhull claimed that

> [t]he wife who submits to sexual intercourse against her wishes or desires, virtually commits suicide; while the husband who compels it, commits murder, and ought just as much to be punished for it, as though he strangled her to death for refusing him.[11]

Woodhull, of course, was quite notorious as a proponent of "free love." Her defense of a woman's right to abstain from sexual intercourse within marriage as a means of controlling her pregnancies was associated with Woodhull's overall attack on the institution of marriage.

It was not a coincidence that women's consciousness of their reproductive rights was born within the organized movement for women's political equality. Indeed, if women remained forever burdened by incessant childbirths and frequent miscarriages, they would hardly be able to exercise the political rights they might win. Moreover, women's new dreams of pursuing careers and other paths of self-development outside marriage and motherhood could only be realized if they could limit and plan their pregnancies. In this sense, the slogan "voluntary motherhood" contained a new and genuinely progressive vision of womanhood. At the same time, however, this vision was rigidly bound to the lifestyle enjoyed by the middle classes and the bourgeoisie. The aspirations underlying the demand for "voluntary motherhood" did not reflect the conditions of working-class women, engaged as they were in a far more fundamental fight for economic survival. Since this first call for birth control was associated with goals which could only be achieved by women possessing material wealth, vast numbers of poor and working-class women would find it rather difficult to identify with the embryonic birth control movement.

Toward the end of the nineteenth century the white birth rate in the United States suffered a significant decline. Since no contraceptive innovations had been publicly introduced, the drop in the birth rate implied that women were substantially curtailing their sexual activity. By 1890 the typical native-born white woman was bearing no more than four children.[12] Since U.S. society was becoming increasingly urban, this new birth pattern should not have been a surprise. While farm life demanded large families, they became dysfunctional within the context of city life. Yet this phenomenon was publicly interpreted in a racist and anti-working-class fashion by the ideologues of rising monopoly capitalism. Since native-born white women were bearing fewer children, the specter of "race suicide" was raised in official circles.

In 1905 President Theodore Roosevelt concluded his Lincoln Day Dinner speech with the proclamation that "race purity must be maintained."[13] By 1906 he blatantly equated the falling birth rate among native-born whites with the impending threat of "race suicide." In his State of the Union message that year Roosevelt admonished the well-born white women who engaged in "willful sterility—the one sin for which the penalty is national death, race suicide."[14] These comments were made during a period of accelerating racist ideology and of great waves of race riots and lynchings on the domestic scene. Moreover, President Roosevelt himself was attempting to muster support for the U.S. seizure of the Philippines, the country's most recent imperialist venture.

How did the birth control movement respond to Roosevelt's accusation that their cause was promoting race suicide? The President's propagandistic ploy was a failure, according to a leading historian of the birth control movement, for, ironically, it led to greater support for its advocates. Yet, as Linda Gordon maintains, this controversy ". . . also brought to the forefront those issues that most separated feminists from the working class and the poor."[15]

> This happened in two ways. First, the feminists were increasingly emphasizing birth control as a route to careers and higher education—goals out of reach of the poor with or without birth control. In the context of the whole feminist movement, the race-suicide episode was an additional factor identifying feminism almost exclusively with the aspirations of the more privileged women of the society. Second, the pro-birth control feminists began to popularize the idea that poor people had a moral obligation to restrict the size of their families, because large families create a drain on the taxes and charity expenditures of the wealthy and because poor children were less likely to be "superior."[16]

The acceptance of the race-suicide thesis, to a greater or lesser extent, by women such as Julia Ward Howe and Ida Husted Harper reflected the suffrage movement's capitulation to the racist posture of Southern women. If the suffragists acquiesced to arguments invoking the extension of the ballot to women as the saving grace of white supremacy, then birth control advocates either acquiesced to or supported the new arguments invoking birth control as a means of preventing the proliferation of the "lower classes" and as an antidote to race suicide. Race suicide could be prevented by the introduction of birth control among Black people, immigrants and the poor in general. In this way, the prosperous whites of solid Yankee stock could maintain their superior numbers within the population. Thus class-bias and racism crept into the birth control movement when it was still in its infancy. More and more, it was assumed within birth control circles that poor women, Black and immigrant alike, had a "moral obligation to restrict the size of their families."[17] What was demanded as a "right" for the privileged came to be interpreted as a "duty" for the poor.

When Margaret Sanger embarked upon her lifelong crusade for birth control—a term she coined and popularized—it appeared as though the racist and anti-working-class overtones of the previous period might possibly be overcome. For Margaret Higgens Sanger came from a working-class background herself and was well acquainted with the devastating pressures of poverty. When her mother died, at the age of forty-eight, she had borne no less than eleven children. Sanger's later memories of her own family's troubles would confirm her belief that working-class women had a special need for the right to plan and space their pregnancies autonomously. Her affiliation, as an adult, with the Socialist movement was a further cause for hope that the birth control campaign would move in a more progressive direction.

When Margaret Sanger joined the Socialist party in 1912, she assumed the responsibility of recruiting women from New York's working women's clubs into the party.[18] *The Call*—the party's paper—carried her articles on the women's page. She wrote a series entitled "What Every Mother Should Know," another called "What Every Girl Should Know," and she did on-the-spot coverage of strikes involving women. Sanger's familiarity with New York's working-class districts was a result of her numerous visits as a trained nurse to the poor sections of the city. During these visits, she points out in her autobiography, she met countless numbers of women who desperately desired knowledge about birth control.

According to Sanger's autobiographical reflections, one of the many visits she made as a nurse to New York's Lower East Side convinced her to undertake a personal crusade for birth control. Answering one of her routine calls, she discovered that twenty-eight-year-old Sadie Sachs had attempted to abort herself. Once the crisis had passed, the young woman asked the attending physician to give her advice on birth prevention. As Sanger relates the story, the doctor recommended that she ". . . tell [her husband] Jake to sleep on the roof."[19]

I glanced quickly to Mrs. Sachs. Even through my sudden tears I could see stamped on her face an expression of absolute despair. We simply looked at each other, saying no word until the door had closed behind the doctor. Then she lifted her thin, blue-veined hands and clasped them beseechingly. "He can't understand. He's only a man. But you do, don't you? Please tell me the secret, and I'll never breathe it to a soul. Please!"[20]

Three months later Sadie Sachs died from another self-induced abortion. That night, Margaret Sanger says, she vowed to devote all her energy toward the acquisition and dissemination of contraceptive measures.

I went to bed, knowing that no matter what it might cost, I was finished with palliatives and superficial cures; I resolved to seek out the root of evil, to do something to change the destiny of mothers whose miseries were as vast as the sky.[21]

During the first phase of Sanger's birth control crusade, she maintained her affiliation with the Socialist party—and the campaign itself was closely associated with the rising militancy of the working class. Her staunch supporters included Eugene Debs, Elizabeth Gurley Flynn and Emma Goldman, who respectively represented the Socialist party, the International Workers of the World and the anarchist movement. Margaret Sanger, in turn, expressed the anti-capitalist commitment of her own movement within the pages of its journal, *Woman Rebel,* which was "dedicated to the interests of working women."[22] Personally, she continued to march on picket lines with striking workers and publicly condemned the outrageous assaults on striking workers. In 1914, for example, when the National Guard massacred scores of Chicano miners in Ludlow, Colorado, Sanger joined the labor movement in exposing John D. Rockefeller's role in this attack.[23]

Unfortunately, the alliance between the birth control campaign and the radical labor movement did not enjoy a long life. While Socialists and other working-class activists continued to support the demand for birth control, it did not occupy a central place in their overall strategy. And Sanger herself began to underestimate the centrality of capitalist exploitation in her analysis of poverty, arguing that too many children caused workers to fall into their miserable predicament. Moreover, ". . . women were inadvertently perpetuating the exploitation of the working class," she believed, "by continually flooding the labor market with new workers."[24] Ironically, Sanger may have been encouraged to adopt this position by the neo-Malthusian ideas embraced in some socialist circles. Such outstanding figures of the European socialist movement as Anatole France and Rosa Luxemburg had proposed a "birth strike" to prevent the continued flow of labor into the capitalist market.[25]

When Margaret Sanger severed her ties with the Socialist party for the purpose of building an independent birth control campaign, she and her followers became more susceptible than ever before to the anti-Black and anti-immigrant propaganda of the times. Like their predecessors, who had been deceived by the "race suicide" propaganda, the advocates of birth control began to embrace the prevailing racist ideology. The fatal influence of the eugenics movement would soon destroy the progressive potential of the birth control campaign.

During the first decades of the twentieth century the rising popularity of the eugenics movement was hardly a fortuitous development. Eugenic ideas were perfectly suited to the ideological needs of the young monopoly capitalists. Imperialist incursions in Latin America and in the Pacific needed to be justified, as did the intensified exploitation of Black workers in the South and immigrant workers in the North and West. The pseudoscientific racial theories associated with the eugenics campaign furnished dramatic apologies for the conduct of the young monopolies. As a result, this movement won the unhesitating support of such leading capitalists as the Carnegies, the Harrimans and the Kelloggs.[26]

By 1919 the eugenic influence on the birth control movement was unmistakably clear. In an article published by Margaret Sanger in the American Birth Control League's journal, she defined "the chief issue of birth control" as "more children from the fit, less from the unfit."[27] Around this time the ABCL heartily welcomed the author of *The Rising Tide of Color Against White World Supremacy* into its inner sanctum.[28] Lothrop Stodard, Harvard professor and theoretician of the eugenics movement, was offered a seat on the board of directors. In the pages of the ABCL's journal, articles by Guy Irving Birch, director of the American Eugenics Society, began to appear. Birch advocated birth control as a weapon to

> . . . prevent the American people from being replaced by alien or Negro stock, whether it be by immigration or by overly high birth rates among others in this country.[29]

By 1932 the Eugenics Society could boast that at least twenty-six states had passed compulsory sterilization laws and that thousands of "unfit" persons had already been surgically prevented from reproducing.[30] Margaret Sanger offered her public approval of this development. "Morons, mental defectives, epileptics, illiterates, paupers, unemployables, criminals, prostitutes and dope fiends" ought to be surgically sterilized, she argued in a radio talk.[31] She did not wish to be so intransigent as to leave them with no choice in the matter; if they wished, she said, they should be able to choose a lifelong segregated existence in labor camps.

Within the American Birth Control League, the call for birth control among Black people acquired the same racist edge as the call for compulsory sterilization. In 1939 its successor, the Birth Control Federation of America, planned a "Negro Project." In the Federation's words,

> [t]he mass of Negroes, particularly in the South, still breed carelessly and disastrously, with the result that the increase among Negroes, even more than among whites, is from that portion of the population least fit, and least able to rear children properly.[32]

Calling for the recruitment of Black ministers to lead local birth control committees, the Federation's proposal suggested that Black people should be rendered as vulnerable as possible to their birth control propaganda. "We do not want word to get out," wrote Margaret Sanger in a letter to a colleague,

> . . . that we want to exterminate the Negro population and the minister is the man who can straighten out that idea if it ever occurs to any of their more rebellious members.[33]

This episode in the birth control movement confirmed the ideological victory of the racism associated with eugenic ideas. It had been robbed of its progressive potential, advocating for people of color not the individual right to *birth control*, but rather the racist strategy of *population control*. The birth control campaign would be called upon to serve in an essential capacity in the execution of the U.S. government's imperialist and racist population policy.

The abortion rights activists of the early 1970s should have examined the history of their movement. Had they done so, they might have understood why so many of their Black sisters adopted a posture of suspicion toward their cause. They might have understood how important it was to undo the racist deeds of their predecessors, who had advocated birth control as well as compulsory sterilization as a means of eliminating the "unfit" sectors of the population. Consequently, the young white feminists might have been more receptive to the suggestion that their campaign for abortion rights include a vigorous condemnation of sterilization abuse, which had become more widespread than ever.

It was not until the media decided that the casual sterilization of two Black girls in Montgomery, Alabama, was a scandal worth reporting that the Pandora's box of sterilization abuse was finally flung open. But by the time the case of the Relf sisters broke, it was practically too late to influence the politics of the abortion rights movement. It was the summer of 1973 and the Supreme Court decision legalizing abortions had already been announced in January. Nevertheless, the urgent need for mass opposition to sterilization abuse became tragically clear. The facts surrounding the Relf sisters' story were horrifyingly simple. Minnie Lee, who was twelve years old, and Mary Alice, who was fourteen, had been unsuspectingly carted into an operating room, where surgeons irrevocably robbed them of their capacity to bear children.[34] The surgery had been ordered by the HEW-funded Montgomery Community Action Committee after it was discovered that Depo-Provera, a drug previously administered to the girls as a birth prevention measure, caused cancer in test animals.[35]

After the Southern Poverty Law Center filed suit on behalf of the Relf sisters, the girls' mother revealed that she had unknowingly "consented" to the operation, having been deceived by the social workers who handled her daughters' case. They had asked Mrs. Relf, who was unable to read, to put her "X" on a document, the contents of which were not described to her. She assumed, she said, that it authorized the continued Depo-Provera injections. As she subsequently learned, she had authorized the surgical sterilization of her daughters.[36]

In the aftermath of the publicity exposing the Relf sisters' case, similar episodes were brought to light. In Montgomery alone, eleven girls, also in their teens, had been similarly sterilized. HEW-funded birth control clinics in other states, as it turned out, had also subjected young girls to sterilization abuse. Moreover, individual women came forth with equally outrageous stories. Nial Ruth Cox, for example, filed suit against the state of North Carolina. At the age of eighteen—eight years before the suit—officials had threatened to discontinue her family's welfare payments if she refused to submit to surgical sterilization.[37] Before she assented to the operation, she was assured that her infertility would be temporary.[38]

Nial Ruth Cox's lawsuit was aimed at a state which had diligently practiced the theory of eugenics. Under the auspices of the Eugenics Commission of North Carolina, so it was learned, 7,686 sterilizations had been carried out since 1933. Although the operations were justified as measures to prevent the reproduction of "mentally deficient persons," about 5,000 of the sterilized persons had been Black.[39] According to Brenda Feigen Fasteau, the ACLU attorney representing Nial Ruth Cox, North Carolina's recent record was not much better.

> As far as I can determine, the statistics reveal that since 1964, approximately 65% of the women sterilized in North Carolina were Black and approximately 35% were white.[40]

As the flurry of publicity exposing sterilization abuse revealed, the neighboring state of South Carolina had been the site of further atrocities. Eighteen women from Aiken, South Carolina, charged that they had been sterilized by a Dr. Clovis Pierce during the early 1970s. The sole obstetrician in that small town, Pierce had consistently sterilized Medicaid recipients with two or more children. According to a nurse in his office, Dr. Pierce insisted that pregnant welfare women "will have to submit [sic!] to voluntary sterilization" if they wanted him to deliver their babies.[41] While he was ". . . tired of people running around and having babies and paying for them with my taxes,"[42] Dr. Pierce received some $60,000 in taxpayers' money for the sterilizations he performed. During his trial he was supported by the South Carolina Medical Association, whose members declared that doctors ". . . have a moral and legal right to insist on sterilization permission before accepting a patient, if it is done on the initial visit."[43]

Revelations of sterilization abuse during that time exposed the complicity of the federal government. At first the Department of Health, Education and Welfare claimed that approximately 16,000 women and 8,000 men had been sterilized in 1972 under the auspices of federal programs.[44] Later, however, these figures underwent a drastic revision. Carl Shultz, director of HEW's Population Affairs Office, estimated that between 100,000 and 200,000 sterilizations had actually been funded that year by the federal government.[45] During Hitler's Germany, incidentally, 250,000 sterilizations were carried out under the Nazis' Hereditary Health Law.[46] Is it possible that the record of the Nazis, throughout the years of their reign, may have been almost equaled by U.S. government-funded sterilizations in the space of a single year?

Given the historical genocide inflicted on the native population of the United States, one would assume that Native American Indians would be exempted from the government's sterilization campaign. But according to Dr. Connie Uri's testimony in a Senate committee hearing, by 1976 some 24 percent of all Indian women of childbearing age had been sterilized.[47] "Our blood lines are being stopped," the Choctaw physician told the Senate committee. "Our unborn will not be born. . . . This is genocidal to our people."[48] According to Dr. Uri, the Indian Health

Services Hospital in Claremore, Oklahoma, had been sterilizing one out of every four women giving birth in that federal facility.[49]

Native American Indians are special targets of government propaganda on sterilization. In one of the HEW pamphlets aimed at Indian people, there is a sketch of a family with *ten children* and *one horse* and another sketch of a family with *one child* and *ten horses.* The drawings are supposed to imply that more children mean more poverty and fewer children mean wealth. As if the ten horses owned by the one-child family had been magically conjured up by birth control and sterilization surgery.

The domestic population policy of the U.S. government has an undeniably racist edge. Native American, Chicana, Puerto Rican and Black women continue to be sterilized in disproportionate numbers. According to a National Fertility Study conducted in 1970 by Princeton University's Office of Population Control, 20 percent of all married Black women have been permanently sterilized.[50] Approximately the same percentage of Chicana women had been rendered surgically infertile.[51] Moreover, 43 percent of the women sterilized through federally subsidized programs were Black.[52]

The astonishing number of Puerto Rican women who have been sterilized reflects a special government policy that can be traced back to 1939. In that year President Roosevelt's Interdepartmental Committee on Puerto Rico issued a statement attributing the island's economic problems to the phenomenon of overpopulation.[53] This committee proposed that efforts be undertaken to reduce the birth rate to no more than the level of the death rate.[54] Soon afterward an experimental sterilization campaign was undertaken in Puerto Rico. Although the Catholic Church initially opposed this experiment and forced the cessation of the program in 1946, it was converted during the early 1950s to the teachings and practice of population control.[55] In this period over 150 birth control clinics were opened, resulting in a 20 percent decline in population growth by the mid-1960s.[56] By the 1970s over 35 percent of all Puerto Rican women of childbearing age had been surgically sterilized.[57] According to Bonnie Mass, a serious critic of the U.S. government's population policy,

> . . . if purely mathematical projections are to be taken seriously, if the present rate of sterilization of 19,000 monthly were to continue, then the island's population of workers and peasants could be extinguished within the next 10 or 20 years . . . [establishing] for the first time in world history a systematic use of population control capable of eliminating an entire generation of people.[58]

During the 1970s the devastating implications of the Puerto Rican experiment began to emerge with unmistakable clarity. In Puerto Rico the presence of corporations in the highly automated metallurgical and pharmaceutical industries had exacerbated the problem of unemployment. The prospect of an ever-larger army of unemployed workers was one of the main incentives for the mass sterilization program. Inside the United States today, enormous numbers of people of color—and especially racially oppressed youth—have become part of a pool of permanently unemployed workers. It is hardly coincidental, considering the Puerto Rican example, that the increasing incidence of sterilization has kept pace with the high rates of unemployment. As growing numbers of white people suffer the brutal consequences of unemployment, they can also expect to become targets of the official sterilization propaganda.

The prevalence of sterilization abuse during the latter 1970s may be greater than ever before. Although the Department of Health, Education and Welfare issued guidelines in 1974, which were ostensibly designed to prevent involuntary sterilizations, the situation has nonetheless deteriorated. When the American Civil Liberties Union's Reproductive Freedom Project conducted a survey of teaching hospitals in 1975, they discovered that 40 percent of those institutions were not even aware of the regulations issued by HEW.[59] Only 30 percent of the hospitals examined by the ACLU were even attempting to comply with the guidelines.[60]

The 1977 Hyde Amendment has added yet another dimension to coercive sterilization practices. As a result of this law passed by Congress, federal funds for abortions were eliminated in all cases but those involving rape and the risk of death or severe illness. According to Sandra Salazar of the California Department of Public Health, the first victim of the Hyde Amendment was a twenty-seven-year-old Chicana woman from Texas. She died as a result of an illegal abortion in Mexico shortly after Texas discontinued government-funded abortions. There have been many more victims—women for whom sterilization has become the only alternative to the abortions, which are currently beyond their reach. Sterilizations continue to be federally funded and free, to poor women, on demand.

Over the last decade the struggle against sterilization abuse has been waged primarily by Puerto Rican, Black, Chicana and Native American women. Their cause has not yet been embraced by the women's movement as a whole. Within organizations representing the interests of middle-class white women, there has been a certain reluctance to support the demands of the campaign against sterilization abuse, for these women are often denied their individual rights to be sterilized when they desire to take this step. While women of color are urged, at every turn, to become permanently infertile, white women enjoying prosperous economic conditions are urged, by the same forces, to reproduce themselves. They therefore sometimes consider the "waiting period" and other details of the demand for "informed consent" to sterilization as further inconveniences for women like themselves. Yet whatever the inconveniences for white middle-class women, a fundamental reproductive right of racially oppressed and poor women is at stake. Sterilization abuse must be ended.

Notes

1. Edwin M. Gold *et al.*, "Therapeutic Abortions in New York City: A Twenty-Year Review," in *American Journal of Public Health*, Vol. LV (July, 1965), pp. 964–972. Quoted in Lucinda Cisla, "Unfinished Business: Birth Control and Women's Liberation," in Robin Morgan, editor, *Sisterhood Is Powerful: An Anthology of Writings from the Women's Liberation Movement* (New York: Vintage Books, 1970), p. 261. Also quoted in Robert Staples, *The Black Woman in America* (Chicago: Nelson Hall, 1974), p. 146.

2. Herbert Gutman, *The Black Family in Slavery and Freedom, 1750–1925* (New York: Pantheon Books, 1976), pp. 80–81 (note).

3. *Ibid.*

4. Herbert Aptheker, "The Negro Woman," *Masses and Mainstream*, Vol. 11, No. 2 (February 1948), p. 12.

5. Quoted in Rosalyn Baxandall, Linda Gordon, Susan Reverby, editors, *America's Working Women: A Documentary History—1600 to the Present* (New York: Random House, 1976), p. 17.

6. *Ibid.*

7. Gerda Lerner, *The Female Experience: An American Documentary* (Indianapolis: Bobbs-Merrill, 1977), p. 91.

8. *Ibid.*

9. *Ibid.*

10. "Marriage of Lucy Stone under Protest" appeared in Elizabeth Cady Stanton, Susan B. Anthony and Matilda Joslyn Gage, *History of Woman Suffrage*, Vol. 1 (1848–1861) (New York: Fowler and Wells, 1881). Quoted in Miriam Schneir, *Feminism: The Essential Historical Writings* (New York: Vintage Books, 1972), p. 104.

11. Speech by Victoria Woodhull, "The Elixir of Life." Quoted in Schneir, *op. cit,* p. 153.

12. Mary P. Ryan, *Womanhood in America from Colonial Times to the Present* (New York: Franklin Watts, Inc., 1975), p. 162.

13. Melvin Steinfeld, *Our Racist Presidents* (San Ramon, California: Consensus Publishers, 1972), p. 212.

14. Bonnie Mass, *Population Target: The Political Economy of Population Control in Latin America* (Toronto, Canada: Women's Educational Press, 1977), p. 20.

15. Linda Gordon, *Woman's Body, Woman's Right: Birth Control in America* (New York: Penguin Books, 1976), p. 157.

16. *Ibid.,* p. 158.

17. *Ibid.*

18. Margaret Sanger, *An Autobiography* (New York: Dover Press, 1971), p. 75.

19. *Ibid.,* p. 90.

20. *Ibid.,* p. 91.

21. *Ibid.,* p. 92.

22. *Ibid.,* p. 106.

23. Mass, *op. cit.,* p. 27.

24. Bruce Dancis, "Socialism and Women in the United States, 1900–1912," *Socialist Revolution,* No. 27, Vol. VI, No. 1 (January–March 1976), p. 96.

25. David M. Kennedy, *Birth Control in America: The Career of Margaret Sanger* (New Haven and London: Yale University Press, 1976), pp. 21–22.

26. Mass, *op. cit.,* p. 20.

27. Gordon, *op. cit.,* p. 281.

28. Mass, *op. cit.,* p. 20.

29. Gordon, *op. cit.,* p. 283.

30. Herbert Aptheker, "Sterilization, Experimentation and Imperialism," *Political Affairs,* Vol. LIII, No. 1 (January 1974), p. 44.

31. Gena Corea, *The Hidden Malpractice* (New York: A Jove/HBJ Book, 1977), p. 149.

32. Gordon, *op. cit.,* p. 332.

33. *Ibid.,* pp. 332–333.

34. Aptheker, "Sterilization," p. 38. See also Anne Braden, "Forced Sterilization: Now Women Can Fight Back," *Southern Patriot,* September, 1973.

35. *Ibid.*

36. Jack Slater, "Sterilization, Newest Threat to the Poor," *Ebony,* Vol. XXVIII, No. 12 (October, 1973), p. 150.

37. Braden, *op. cit.*

38. Les Payne, "Forced Sterilization for the Poor?" *San Francisco Chronicle,* February 26, 1974.

39. Harold X., "Forced Sterilization Pervades South," *Muhammed Speaks,* October 10, 1975.

40. Slater, *op. cit.*

41. Payne, *op. cit.*

42. *Ibid.*

43. *Ibid.*

44. Aptheker, "Sterilization," p. 40.

45. Payne, *op. cit.*

46. Aptheker, "Sterilization," p. 48.

47. Arlene Eisen, "They're Trying to Take Our Future—Native American Women and Sterilization," *The Guardian,* March 23, 1972.

48. *Ibid.*

49. *Ibid.*

50. Quoted in a pamphlet issued by the Committee to End Sterilization Abuse, Box A244, Cooper Station, New York 10003.

51. *Ibid.*

52. *Ibid.*

53. Gordon, *op. cit.,* p. 338.

54. *Ibid.*

55. Mass, *op. cit.,* p. 92.

56. *Ibid.,* p. 91.

57. Gordon, *op. cit.,* p. 401. See also pamphlet issued by CESA.

58. Mass, *op. cit.,* p. 108.

59. Rahemah Aman, "Forced Sterilization," *Union Wage,* March 4, 1978.

60. *Ibid.*

SUSAN BROWNMILLER

Against Our Will

The Police-Blotter Rapist

The typical American rapist might be the boy next door. Especially if the boy next door happens to be about 19 years of age and the neighborhood you live in happens to fit the socioeconomic description of lower class or bears the appellation of "ghetto." That is what the statistics show.

One must approach all statistics with caution if one is going to make generalizations, particularly statistics regarding violent crime. Statisticians of crime are routine fact gatherers, and the raw material they work with is usually mined from police-precinct arrest records or from records of convictions. Since there are many acts of rape, few arrests and still fewer convictions, a huge gulf of unavailable information unfortunately exists.

Police in every town and city compile their figures based on those offenders they manage to catch: height, weight, age, race, *modus operandi,* previous arrest record, etc. These figures are forwarded yearly to Washington, fed into computers and ground out again as the most comprehensive national statistics on forcible rape that we have: the *Uniform Crime Reports* put out by the Federal Bureau of Investigation. The *Uniform Crime Reports* and a few intensive studies done by a handful of criminologists allow us to draw up a profile of the All-American rapist.

Before we go any further let us remember that we are traveling on a road marked with cautionary blinking lights. A feminist definition of rape goes beyond the legal, criminal definition with which the nation's system of jurisprudence concerns itself. . . . Then, according to the FBI itself, forcible rape is "one of the most under-reported crimes due primarily to fear and/or embarrassment on the part of the victim," and one in five rapes, or possibly one in twenty, may actually be reported, which skews all recordable statistics. Further, a provable bias by police and juries against the word of the female victim—and particularly the word of a black female victim—drastically cuts down on the number of cases available for study. On a national average, police say that 15 percent of all rape cases reported to them turn out on cursory investigation to be "unfounded"—in other words, they didn't believe the complainant. In reported rape cases where the police *do* believe the victim, only 51 percent of the offenders are actually apprehended, and of these, 76 percent are prosecuted, and of these, 47 percent are acquitted or have their case dismissed. (In some locales the conviction rate based on arrests is a shocking 3 percent.)

In 1973 the FBI reported 51,000 "founded" cases of forcible rape and attempted rape across the United States, a rise, it noted, of 10 percent over the previous year and a rise of 62 percent over a five-year period. Its figures did not include statutory rape offenses. Seventy-three percent of the FBI's reported cases were completed rapes and the remaining ones were assaults or attempts to commit rape that fell short of completion. If we say conservatively that only one in five rape incidents was actually reported, we arrive at a figure of 255,000 rapes and attempted rapes in these United

States in 1973, a figure that I consider to be an unemotional, rock-bottom minimum. For purposes of comparison we should note that during the same year the FBI reported 19,510 murders, 416,270 aggravated assaults and 382,680 robberies.

Murder, assault, rape and robbery are the Big Four of violent crimes, and rape is the fastest-rising. The volume of rapes has increased 62 percent over a five-year period as compared with a 45 percent rise for the other criminal acts. Not given to speculation, the FBI does not venture as to why. It might mean that there has been a rise in the reporting of rapes by victims who have gained courage to speak out from the women's movement—this is most likely—or it could mean a significant rise in hostility and violence directed at women. We simply cannot say for certain.

Of the 51,000 rape cases that the police believed and reported on to the FBI in 1973, they managed a "clearance"—in other words, they made an arrest—in 51 percent of the crimes. Comparatively, the police clearance rate was 79 percent for murder, 63 percent for aggravated assault and 27 percent for robbery offenses. In the field of violent crime, only robbery has a lower clearance rate than rape.

Who, then, are the police-blotter rapists who form the raw material for the *Uniform Crime Reports* analysis? Sixty-one percent are under the age of 25; the largest concentration of offenders is in the 16-to-24-year age range. According to the FBI, 47 percent are black and 51 percent are white, and "all other races comprised the remainder."

Evan Connell, a novelist of some repute, wrote a *tour de force* some years ago entitled *The Diary of a Rapist.* Connell's protagonist, Earl Summerfield, was a timid, white, middle-class civil-service clerk, age 27, who had an inferiority complex, delusions of intellectual brilliance, a wretched, deprived sex life, and an older, nagging, ambitious, "castrating" wife. Connell's book made gripping reading, but the portrait of Earl Summerfield was far from an accurate picture of an average real-life rapist. In fact, Connell's *Diary* contains almost every myth and misconception about rape and rapists that is held in the popular mind. From the no-nonsense FBI statistics and some intensive sociological studies that are beginning to appear, we can see that the typical American rapist is no weirdo, psycho schizophrenic beset by timidity, sexual deprivation, and a domineering wife or mother. Although the psycho rapist, whatever his family background, certainly does exist, just as the psycho murderer certainly does exist, he is the exception and not the rule. The typical American perpetrator of forcible rape is little more than an aggressive, hostile youth who chooses to do violence to women.

We may thank the legacy of Freudian psychology for fostering a totally inaccurate popular conception of rape. Freud himself, remarkable as this may seem, said nothing about rapists. His confederates were slightly more loquacious, but not by much. Jung mentioned rape only in a few of his mythological interpretations. Alfred Adler, a man who understood the power thrust of the male and who was a firm believer in equal rights for women, never mentioned rape in any of his writings. Deutsch and Horney, two brilliant women, looked at rape only from the psychology of the victim.

In the nineteen fifties a school of criminology arose that was decidedly pro-Freudian in its orientation and it quickly dominated a neglected field. But even among the Freudian criminologists there was a curious reluctance to tackle rape head on. The finest library of Freudian and Freudian-related literature, the A. A. Brill Collection, housed at the New York Psychoanalytic Institute, contains an impressive number of weighty tomes devoted to the study of exhibitionism (public exposure of the penis) yet no Freudian or psychoanalytic authority has ever written a major volume on rape. Articles on rape in psychology journals have been sparse to the point of nonexistence.

Why the Freudians could never come to terms with rape is a puzzling question. It would not be too glib to suggest that the male bias of the discipline, with its insistence on the primacy of the penis, rendered it incapable of seeing the forest for the trees. And then, the use of an intuitive approach based largely on analysis of idiosyncratic case studies allowed for no objective sampling. But perhaps most critically, the serious failure of the Freudians stemmed from their rigid unwillingness to make a moral judgment. The major psychoanalytic thrust was always to "understand" what they preferred to call "deviant sexual behavior," but never to condemn.

"Philosophically," wrote Dr. Manfred Guttmacher in 1951, "a sex offense is an act which offends the sex mores of the society in which the individual lives. And it offends chiefly because it generates anxiety among the members of that society. Moreover, prohibited acts generate the greatest anxiety in those individuals who themselves have strong unconscious desires to commit similar or related acts and who have suppressed or repressed them. These actions of others threaten our ego defenses."

This classic paragraph, I believe, explains most clearly the Freudian dilemma.

When the Freudian-oriented criminologists did attempt to grapple with rape they lumped the crime together with exhibitionism (their hands-down favorite!), homosexuality, prostitution, pyromania and even oral intercourse in huge, undigestible volumes that sometimes bore a warning notice on the flyleaf that the material contained herein might advisably be restricted to adults. Guttmacher's *Sex Offenses* and Benjamin Karpman's *The Sexual Offender and His Offenses* were two such products of the fifties. Reading through these and other volumes it is possible to stumble on a nugget of fact or a valuable insight, and we ought to keep in mind, I guess, how brave they must have seemed at the time. After all, they were dealing not only with s-e-x, but with aberrant s-e-x, and in their misguided way they were attempting to forge a new understanding. "Moral opprobrium has no place in medical work," wrote Karpman. A fine sentiment, indeed, yet one hundred pages earlier this same Karpman in this same book defined perversity as "a sexual act that defies the biological goal of procreation."

By and large the Freudian criminologists, who loved to quibble with one another, defined the rapist as a victim of an "uncontrollable urge" that was "infantile" in nature, the result of a thwarted "natural" impulse to have intercourse with his mother. His act of rape was "a neurotic overreaction" that stemmed from his "feelings of inadequacy." To sum up in the Freudian's favorite phrase, he was "a sexual psychopath." Rapists, wrote Karpman, were "victims of a disease from which many of them suffer more than their victims."

This, I should amend, was a picture of the Freudians' favorite rapist, the one they felt they might be able to treat. Dr. Guttmacher, for one, was aware that other types of rapists existed but they frankly bored him. Some, he said, were "sadistic," imbued with an exaggerated concept of masculine sexual activity, and some seemed "like the soldier of a conquering army." "Apparently," he wrote, "sexually well-adjusted youths have in one night committed a series of burglaries and, in the course of one of them, committed rape—apparently just as another act of plunder."

Guttmacher was chief medical officer for the Baltimore criminal courts. His chilling passing observation that rapists might be sexually well-adjusted youths was a reflection of his Freudian belief in the supreme rightness of male dominance and aggression, a common theme that runs through Freudian-oriented criminological literature. But quickly putting the "sexually well-adjusted youths" aside, Guttmacher dove into clinical studies of two rapists put at his disposal who were more to his liking. Both were nail-biters and both had "nagging mothers." One had an unde-scended testicle. In his dreary record of how frequently they masturbated and wet their beds, he never bothered to write down what they thought of women.

Perhaps the quintessential Freudian approach to rape was a 1954 Rorschach study conducted on the *wives* of eight, count 'em, eight, convicted rapists, which brought forth this sweeping indictment from one of the authors, the eminent psychoanalyst and criminologist Dr. David Abrahamsen:

> The conclusions reached were that the wives of the sex offenders on the surface behaved toward men in a submissive and masochistic way but latently denied their femininity and showed an aggressive masculine orientation; they unconsciously invited sexual aggression, only to respond to it with coolness and rejection. They stimulated their husbands into attempts to prove themselves, attempts which necessarily ended in frustration and in-creased their husbands' own doubts about their masculinity. In doing so, the wives unknow-ingly continued the type of relationship the offender had had with his mother. There can be no doubt that the sexual frustration which the wives caused is one of the factors motivating rape, which might be tentatively described as a displaced attempt to force a seductive but rejecting mother into submission.

In the nineteen sixties, leadership in the field of criminology passed to the sociologists, and a good thing it was.* Concerned with measuring the behavior of groups and their social values, instead of relying on extrapolation from individual case studies, the sociologists gave us charts, tables, diagrams, theories of social relevance, and, above all, hard, cold statistical facts about crime. (Let us give credit where credit is due. The rise of computer technology greatly facilitated this kind of research.)

In 1971 Menachem Amir, an Israeli sociologist and a student of Marvin E. Wolfgang, America's leading criminologist, published a study of rape in the city of

*Transitions are never clean. In 1965 a 900-page volume called *Sex Offenders* by Paul Gebhard and other members of the Institute for Sex Research founded by the late Alfred C. Kinsey put in an appearance. The Gebhard volume forms a sort of missing link between the idiosyncratic Freudians and the sociological approach. Suffering from the racial bias that marred the work of Dr. Kinsey, Gebhard's group tried to find meaningful differences—or similarities—among convicted rapists, child molesters and homosexuals but arbitrarily excluded blacks from their study because "their sexual behavior and attitudes differ to some degree." The spirit of Kinsey floats over this work. Gebhard tells us, "As Dr. Kinsey often said, the difference between a 'good time' and a 'rape' may hinge on whether the girl's parents were awake when she finally arrived home." Elsewhere Gebhard divines that the reason there are so few female sex offenders is because "the average woman has a weaker 'sex drive' than the average male." Perhaps the most usable observation to come out of this comparison study (of nocturnal emissions, masturbatory behavior, animal contact, and incidence of premarital, extramarital and postmarital coitus) is a remark that "the heterosexual adjustment" of rapists "is quantiatively well above average" when compared to a control group of church members and union men, which says as much about Gebhard's standards of heterosexual adjustment as it does about rapists. Another usable observation, but one that the reader must make, is that the incidence of nocturnal emission, masturbation, animal contact, and premarital, ex-tramarital and postmarital coitus has no relevance whatsoever to the study of why men rape. And perhaps a 900-page volume was necessary to prove it.

Philadelphia, begun ten years before. *Patterns in Forcible Rape,* a difficult book for those who choke on methodological jargon, was annoyingly obtuse about the culturally conditioned behavior of women in situations involving the threat of force, but despite its shortcomings the Philadelphia study was an eye-opener. It was the first pragmatic, in-depth statistical study of the nature of rape and rapists. Going far beyond the limited vision of the police and the *Uniform Crime Reports,* or the idiosyncratic concerns of the Freudians, Amir fed his computer such variables as *modus operandi,* gang rape versus individual rape, economic class, prior relationships between victim and offender, and both racial and interracial factors. For the first time in history the sharp-edged profile of the typical rapist was allowed to emerge. It turned out that he was, for the most part, an unextraordinary, violence-prone fellow.

Marvin Wolfgang, Amir's mentor at the University of Pennsylvania's school of criminology, deserves credit for the theory of "the subculture of violence," which he developed at length in his own work. An understanding of the subculture of violence is critical to an understanding of the forcible rapist. "Social class," wrote Wolfgang, "looms large in all studies of violent crime." Wolfgang's theory, and I must oversimplify, is that within the dominant value system of our culture there exists a subculture formed of those from the lower classes, the poor, the disenfranchised, the black, whose values often run counter to those of the dominant culture, the people in charge. The dominant culture can operate within the laws of civility because it has little need to resort to violence to get what it wants. The subculture, thwarted, inarticulate and angry, is quick to resort to violence; indeed, violence and physical aggression become a common way of life. Particularly for young males.

Wolfgang's theory of crime, and unlike other theories his is soundly based on statistical analysis, may not appear to contain all the answers, particularly the kind of answers desired by liberals who want to excuse crimes of violence strictly on the basis of social inequities in the system, but Wolfgang would be the first to say that social injustice is one of the root causes of the subculture of violence. His theory also would not satisfy radical thinkers who prefer to interpret all violence as the product of the governmental hierarchy and its superstructure of repression.

But there is no getting around the fact that most of those who engage in antisocial, criminal violence (murder, assault, rape and robbery) come from the lower socioeconomic classes; and that because of their historic oppression the majority of black people are contained within the lower socioeconomic classes and contribute to crimes of violence in numbers disproportionate to their population ratio in the census figures *but not disproportionate* to their position on the economic ladder.

We are not talking about Jean Valjean, who stole a loaf of bread in *Les Misérables,* but about physical aggression as "a demonstration of masculinity and toughness"— this phrase is Wolfgang's—the prime tenet of the subculture of violence. Or, to use a current phrase, the *machismo* factor. Allegiance or conformity to *machismo,* particularly in a group or gang, is the *sine qua non* of status, reputation and identity for lower-class male youth. Sexual aggression, of course, is a major part of *machismo.*

The single most important contribution of Amir's Philadelphia study was to place the rapist squarely within the subculture of violence. The rapist, it was revealed, had no separate identifiable pathology aside from the individual quirks and personality disturbances that might characterize any single offender who commits any sort of crime.

The patterns of rape that Amir was able to trace were drawn from the central files of the Philadelphia police department for 1958 and 1960, a total of 646 cases and 1,292 offenders.* One important fact that Amir's study revealed right off the bat was that in 43 percent of the Philadelphia cases, the rapists operated in pairs or groups, giving the lie to one of the more commonly held myths that the rapist is a secretive, solitary offender.

The median age of the Philadelphia rapist was 23, but the age group most likely to commit rape was the 15-to-19 bracket. A preponderant number of the Philadelphia rapists were not married, a status attributable to their youthful age. Ninety percent of the Philadelphia rapists "belonged to the lower part of the occupational scale," in descending order "from skilled workers to the unemployed." Half of the Philadelphia rapists had a prior arrest record, and most of these had the usual run of offenses such as burglary, robbery, disorderly conduct and assault. Only 9 percent of those with prior records had been previously arrested for rape. In other words, rapists were in the mold of the typical youthful offender.†

Not surprisingly, the Philadelphia rapist generally lived in one of those inner-city neighborhoods that according to the census tracts are known for a high degree of crime, and most particularly for "crime against the person." His victim *also* tended to live in the same neighborhood. Since Amir was studying a large Northern city with an extensive black ghetto population, the sociologist's proportion of black offenders was higher than the national average. The FBI, as I have mentioned, records that 47 percent of all arrested rapists are black. Amir in Philadelphia found that 82 percent of his reported rapists were black, as were 80 percent of the rapists' victims. He concluded, "Rape was found to be an intraracial event, especially between Negro men and women." In other words, forcible rape in Philadelphia was overwhelmingly black on black. Black men raped black women. In lesser numbers, white men raped white women. Most rapists, conveniently for them, raped women who lived in their neighborhood or close by. The percentage of interracial rape in the city of Philadelphia for the years 1958 and 1960, Amir discovered, was small. (More recent studies differ with Amir on this point. . . .)

"Contrary to past impression," Amir wrote, "analysis revealed that 71 percent of the rapes were planned." This observation was another of Amir's most significant contributions to the study of rape. Far from being a spontaneous explosion by an individual with pent-up emotions and uncontrollable lusts, he discovered the act was usually planned in advance and elaborately arranged by a single rapist or a group of buddies. In some cases the lone rapist or the gang had a particular victim in mind and coolly took the necessary steps to lure her into an advantageous position. In other cases the *decision* to rape was made in advance by a gang, a pair of cohorts or a lone-wolf rapist, but *selection* of the female was left to chance. Whoever

---

*Amir's raw material differed from the FBI's. The FBI releases data based on those men actually arrested for rape and attempted rape. Amir's data was based on statistical information about all reported rapes that the police felt were "founded." Amir did not include cases of attempted rape, but he did include profiles of "known" offenders who were never apprehended. The sociologist used "known" to mean "undeniably existing," not necessarily "known to the police." Of the 1,292 offenders that form the basis of Amir's study, only 845 men were actually arrested.

†The FBI's "Careers in Crime" file, using more current statistics, shows that nationally more than 70 percent of all arrested rapists have prior records. In addition, more than 85 percent go on to be repeaters in crime and show up on later police blotters, in descending order of frequency, for burglary, assault, robbery, rape and homicide.

happened by and could be seized, coerced or enticed to a favorable place became the victim. As might be expected, almost all group rapes in Philadelphia police files were found to have been planned. As a matter of fact, advance planning and coordination proved absolutely essential to the commission of gang rape. A "secure" place had to be located; precautions had to be taken to guarantee that the rape-in-progress would remain undetected by passers-by, police or neighbors; and selection of the victim had to be agreed upon by the group.

One-quarter of the single-offender rapes in Amir's study were *not* planned. In his words, the spontaneous offender had "no previous idea of committing the crime . . . but opportunities (place of meeting, victim's behavior, etc.) created the impulse, or the offender's judgment was impaired, usually by the consumption of alcohol before the event."

Further observations that Amir drew from his computer were these: Forcible rape in Philadelphia increased slightly during the hot summer months, but not by much. Rape was an all-year-round event, although group rape did show a noticeable summer increase. Friday night, Saturday and Sunday appeared to be the favored time for commission of the crime, giving rape—for the rapists—an interesting aspect of weekend conviviality and paycheck (or lack of paycheck) celebration. Nights in general were favored over days: The top-risk hours for women were between 8 P.M. and 2 A.M. In 85 percent of the 646 cases Amir examined, some form of physical force or the display of a weapon was required by the rapist or rapists to achieve their goal. In the remaining 15 percent, verbal intimidation or the sheer physical presence of the offenders sufficed to overcome a victim's resistance.

When other crimes of violence are compared statistically with rape, the profile of the forcible rapist falls at a point midway between the profile of the man who commits aggravated assault and the man who commits robbery.* Variables that go into a profile include age, race, occupation, spatial patterns of the crime, *modus operandi,* the role played by alcohol, prior arrest record, etc. When offender profiles for rape, robbery and assault are viewed side by side, the rapist emerges as the man in the middle. His is the least sharp image. His profile "borrows" characteristics from the others, so to speak. The rapist is slightly younger than the assaultive offender and slightly older than the robber or mugger. He uses less physical force than the average man arrested for aggravated assault, but he employs more force than the average robber. He drinks less alcohol before committing his crime than the man who is arrested for assault, but he drinks more alcohol prior to his crime than the man who goes out to rob. He commits his crime less in his own neighborhood than the average man picked up for assault, but he does not range so far afield as the man who commits armed robbery.

Two further comparisons are somewhat related: Rape is more frequently committed against a total stranger than assault, but less frequently committed against a total stranger than robbery. Finally, a case of rape stands a greater chance of being interracial than a case of assault, but the interracial element is more frequent in robbery.

---

*I owe this valuable insight to the sociologist Lynn Curtis, another protégé and student of Marvin Wolfgang's. The rapist as "man in the middle" is apparent from the FBI's *Uniform Crime Reports;* from Volumes 11 and 12 of *Crimes of Violence* (1969), the staff report submitted to the National Commission on the Causes and Prevention of Violence on which Curtis worked as assistant director; and from Curtis' own work on the Big Four of violent crimes, which I read in manuscript. The profile of the murderer, by the way, is distinctively set off from the three other types of violent offenders.

It seems likely that this "man in the middle" profile of the forcible rapist reflects the nature of his act, which "borrows" characteristics from the other two offenses. Like assault, rape is an act of physical damage to another person, and like robbery it is also an act of acquiring property: The intent is to "have" the female body in the acquisitory meaning of the term. A woman is perceived by the rapist both as hated person and desired property. Hostility *against* her and possession *of* her may be simultaneous motivations, and the hatred for her is expressed in the same act that is the attempt to "take" her against her will. In one violent crime, rape is an act against person and property.

Contrary to popular opinion, New York and Washington are not the rape capitals of the nation. That honor, bestowed yearly by the FBI as a sort of negative Oscar, usually goes to Los Angeles, but Denver, Little Rock, Memphis, San Francisco–Oakland, Las Vegas, Tallahassee and Albuquerque are right up there in the running, and a good student of rape must always keep in mind that police reporting procedures vary dramatically from city to city. The FBI does note emphatically that cities with populations in excess of a quarter of a million show higher rape rates per capita than suburban areas while rural areas lag far behind, so in this sense, rape can be said to be a big-city crime, although the rape rate in suburbia is noticeably rising. When rapes per capita are viewed geographically, the Southwestern states emerge as the champions. Southwestern states also lead the nation in rates for homicide and assault, so Southern and Western traditions of violence would appear to be an operative factor.

One statistical consideration that has received too much attention to the detriment of other aspects is the actual site of the crime. Brenda Brown's 1973 Memphis police department study reported that 34 percent of all rapes occurred in the victim's residence, usually by forced, illegal entry; 22 percent took place in automobiles; 26 percent occurred in "open spaces" (alleys, parks, roads, on the street, in the bushes, behind a building, etc.); 9 percent took place in the offender's residence; and the remaining 9 percent occurred indoors in a variety of places ranging from a church to an abandoned building.

The 17-city survey conducted by the task force of the National Commission on the Causes and Prevention of Violence reported that 52 percent of all rapes occurred in the home (most frequently in the bedroom); 23 percent occurred outside; 14 percent occurred in commercial establishments and other inside locations; and 11 percent occurred in automobiles.

Menachem Amir's Philadelphia study reported that 56 percent of all rapes occurred in the home; 18 percent occurred in open spaces; 11 percent occurred in other indoor locations; and 15 percent occurred in automobiles. Taking into account that an offender often *escorts* a victim, either by duress or through a ploy, to a propitious rape location, Amir was also concerned with what he called "the initial meeting place in a rape event." He found that in 48 percent of the cases, offenders first spotted their victims on the street.

According to these three sets of statistics, the street, the home and the automobile emerge as dangerous, high-risk places, so what is left? Good locks on doors and windows and admonitions against hitchhiking and walking alone at night in deserted places are the usual palliatives, but they do nothing to affect the rape ideology, or to increase our understanding of the crime.

Rape begins in the rapist's mind, and *place* may be irrelevant. A small comparison study of rape patterns in Boston and Los Angeles is interesting in this respect.

Densely packed Boston has a relatively low reported rape rate while vast, sprawling Los Angeles, where people need cars to get about, is a leader. Two sociologists who scrutinized police reports in these two cities discovered that the Boston rapist was more likely to break into an apartment and confront his victim while the Los Angeles rapist was more likely to pick up his victim while cruising about in an automobile. They also found that gang rape was more common in Los Angeles than it was in Boston, which seems directly related to a transportation and mobility problem that encourages the practice of hitchhiking. Weapons were more frequently employed by the Boston rapist, a phenomenon that seems reasonable since solitary offenders have more need for a show of force than gang rapists whose very number provides the display of power. . . .

ZORA NEALE HURSTON

How It Feels to Be Colored Me

I am colored but I offer nothing in the way of extenuating circumstances except the fact that I am the only Negro in the United States whose grandfather on the mother's side was *not* an Indian chief.

I remember the very day that I became colored. Up to my thirteenth year I lived in the little Negro town of Eatonville, Florida. It is exclusively a colored town. The only white people I knew passed through the town going to or coming from Orlando. The native whites rode dusty horses, the Northern tourists chugged down the sandy village road in automobiles. The town knew the Southerners and never stopped cane chewing when they passed. But the Northerners were something else again. They were peered at cautiously from behind curtains by the timid. The more venturesome would come out on the porch to watch them go past and got just as much pleasure out of the tourists as the tourists got out of the village.

The front porch might seem a daring place for the rest of the town, but it was a gallery seat for me. My favorite place was atop the gate-post. Proscenium box for a born first-nighter. Not only did I enjoy the show, but I didn't mind the actors knowing that I liked it. I usually spoke to them in passing. I'd wave at them and when they returned my salute, I would say something like this: "Howdy-do-well-I-thank-you-where-you-goin'?" Usually automobile or the horse paused at this, and after a queer exchange of compliments, I would probably "go a piece of the way" with them, as we say in farthest Florida. If one of my family happened to come to the front in time to see me, of course negotiations would be rudely broken off. But even so, it is clear that I was the first "welcome-to-our-state" Floridian, and I hope the Miami Chamber of Commerce will please take notice.

During this period, white people differed from colored to me only in that they rode through town and never lived there. They liked to hear me "speak pieces" and sing and wanted to see me dance the parse-me-la, and gave me generously of their small silver for doing these things, which seemed strange to me for I wanted to do them so much that I needed bribing to stop. Only they didn't know it. The colored people gave no dimes. They deplored any joyful tendencies in me, but I was their Zora nevertheless. I belonged to them, to the nearby hotels, to the county—everybody's Zora.

But changes came in the family when I was thirteen, and I was sent to school in Jacksonville. I left Eatonville, the town of the oleanders, as Zora. When I disembarked from the river-boat at Jacksonville, she was no more. It seemed that I had suffered a sea change. I was not Zora of Orange County any more, I was now a little colored girl. I found it out in certain ways. In my heart as well as in the mirror, I became a fast brown—warranted not to rub nor run.

But I am not tragically colored. There is no great sorrow dammed up in my soul, nor lurking behind my eyes. I do not mind at all. I do not belong to the sobbing school of Negrohood who hold that nature somehow has given them a lowdown dirty deal and whose feelings are all hurt about it. Even in the helter-skelter skirmish that is my life, I have seen that the world is to the strong regardless of a little pigmentation more or less. No, I do not weep at the world—I am too busy sharpening my oyster knife.

Someone is always at my elbow reminding me that I am the granddaughter of slaves. It fails to register depression with me. Slavery is sixty years in the past. The operation was successful and the patient is doing well, thank you. The terrible struggle that made me an American out of a potential slave said "On the line!" The Reconstruction said "Get set!"; and the generation before said "Go!" I am off to a flying start and I must not halt in the stretch to look behind and weep. Slavery is the price I paid for civilization, and the choice was not with me. It is a bully adventure and worth all that I have paid through my ancestors for it. No one on earth ever had a greater chance for glory. The world to be won and nothing to be lost. It is thrilling to think—to know that for any act of mine, I shall get twice as much praise or twice as much blame. It is quite exciting to hold the center of the national stage, with the spectators not knowing whether to laugh or to weep.

The position of my white neighbor is much more difficult. No brown specter pulls up a chair beside me when I sit down to eat. No dark ghost thrusts its leg against mine in bed. The game of keeping what one has is never so exciting as the game of getting.

I do not always feel colored. Even now I often achieve the unconscious Zora of Eatonville before the Hegira. I feel most colored when I am thrown against a sharp white background.

For instance at Barnard. "Beside the waters of the Hudson" I feel my race. Among the thousand white persons, I am a dark rock surged upon, and overswept, but through it all, I remain myself. When covered by the waters, I am; and the ebb but reveals me again.

Sometimes it is the other way around. A white person is set down in our midst, but the contrast is just as sharp for me. For instance, when I sit in the drafty basement that is The New World Cabaret with a white person, my color comes. We enter chatting about any little nothing that we have in common and are seated by the jazz waiters. In the abrupt way that jazz orchestras have, this one plunges into a number. It loses no time in circumlocutions, but gets right down to business. It constricts the thorax and splits the heart with its tempo and narcotic harmonies. This orchestra grows rambunctious, rears on its hind legs and attacks the tonal veil with primitive fury, rending it, clawing it until it breaks through to the jungle beyond. I follow those heathen—follow them exultingly. I dance wildly inside myself; I yell within, I whoop; I shake my assegai above my head, I hurl it true to the mark *yeeeeooww!* I am in the jungle and living in the jungle way. My face is painted red and yellow and my body is painted blue. My pulse is throbbing like a war drum. I want to slaughter something—give pain, give death to what, I do not know. But the piece ends. The men of the orchestra wipe their lips and rest their fingers. I creep back slowly to the veneer we call civilization with the last tone and find the white friend sitting motionless in his seat, smoking calmly.

"Good music they have here," he remarks, drumming the table with his fingertips.

Music. The great blobs of purple and red emotion have not touched him. He has only heard what I felt. He is far away and I see him but dimly across the ocean and the continent that have fallen between us. He is so pale with his whiteness then and I am *so* colored.

At certain times I have no race, I am *me*. When I set my hat at a certain angle and saunter down Seventh Avenue, Harlem City, feeling as snooty as the lions in front of the Forty-Second Street Library, for instance. So far as my feelings are concerned, Peggy Hopkins Joyce on the Boule Mich with her gorgeous raiment, stately carriage, knees knocking together in a most aristocratic manner, has nothing on me. The cosmic Zora emerges. I belong to no race nor time. I am the eternal feminine with its string of beads.

I have no separate feeling about being an American citizen and colored. I am merely a fragment of the Great Soul that surges within the boundaries. My country, right or wrong.

Sometimes, I feel discriminated against, but it does not make me angry. It merely astonishes me. How *can* any deny themselves the pleasure of my company? It's beyond me.

But in the main, I feel like a brown bag of miscellany propped against a wall. Against a wall in company with other bags, white, red and yellow. Pour out the contents, and there is discovered a jumble of small things priceless and worthless. A first-water diamond, an empty spool, bits of broken glass, lengths of string, a key to a door long since crumbled away, a rusty knife-blade, old shoes saved for a road that never was and never will be, a nail bent under the weight of things too heavy for any nail, a dried flower or two still a little fragrant. In your hand is the brown bag. On the ground before you is the jumble it held—so much like the jumble in the bags, could they be emptied, that all might be dumped in a single heap and the bags refilled without altering the content of any greatly. A bit of colored glass more or less would not matter. Perhaps that is how the Great Stuffer of Bags filled them in the first place—who knows?

PAULE MARSHALL

The Poets in the Kitchen

Some years ago, when I was teaching a graduate seminar in fiction at Columbia University, a well known male novelist visited my class to speak on his development as a writer. In discussing his formative years, he didn't realize it but he seriously endangered his life by remarking that women writers are luckier than those of his sex because they usually spend so much time as children around their mothers and their mothers' friends in the kitchen.

What did he say that for? The women students immediately forgot about being in awe of him and began readying their attack for the question and answer period later on. Even I bristled. There again was that awful image of women locked away from the world in the kitchen with only each other to talk to, and their daughters locked in with them.

But my guest wasn't really being sexist or trying to be provocative or even spoiling for a fight. What he meant—when he got around to explaining himself more fully—was that, given the way children are (or were) raised in our society, with little girls kept closer to home and their mothers, the woman writer stands a better chance of being exposed, while growing up, to the kind of talk that goes on among women, more often than not in the kitchen; and that this experience gives her an edge over her male counterpart by instilling in her an appreciation for ordinary speech.

It was clear that my guest lecturer attached great importance to this, which is understandable. Common speech and the plain, workaday words that make it up are, after all, the stock in trade of some of the best fiction writers. They are the principal means by which characters in a novel or story reveal themselves and give voice sometimes to profound feelings and complex ideas about themselves and the world. Perhaps the proper measure of a writer's talent is skill in rendering everyday speech—when it is appropriate to the story—as well as the ability to tap, to exploit, the beauty, poetry and wisdom it often contains.

"If you say what's on your mind in the language that comes to you from your parents and your street and friends you'll probably say something beautiful." Grace Paley tells this, she says, to her students at the beginning of every writing course.

It's all a matter of exposure and a training of the ear for the would-be writer in those early years of apprenticeship. And, according to my guest lecturer, this training, the best of it, often takes place in as unglamorous a setting as the kitchen.

He didn't know it, but he was essentially describing my experience as a little girl. I grew up among poets. Now they didn't look like poets—whatever that breed is supposed to look like. Nothing about them suggested that poetry was their calling. They were just a group of ordinary housewives and mothers, my mother included, who dressed in a way (shapeless housedresses, dowdy felt hats and long, dark, solemn coats) that made it impossible for me to imagine they had ever been young.

Nor did they do what poets were supposed to do—spend their days in an attic room writing verses. They never put pen to paper except to write occasionally to their relatives in Barbados. "I take my pen in hand hoping these few lines will find

651

you in health as they leave me fair for the time being," was the way their letters invariably began. Rather, their day was spent "scrubbing floor," as they described the work they did.

Several mornings a week these unknown bards would put an apron and a pair of old house shoes in a shopping bag and take the train or streetcar from our section of Brooklyn out to Flatbush. There, those who didn't have steady jobs would wait on certain designated corners for the white housewives in the neighborhood to come along and bargain with them over pay for a day's work cleaning their houses. This was the ritual even in the winter.

Later, armed with the few dollars they had earned, which in their vocabulary became "a few raw-mouth pennies," they made their way back to our neighborhood, where they would sometimes stop off to have a cup of tea or cocoa together before going home to cook dinner for their husbands and children.

The basement kitchen of the brownstone house where my family lived was the usual gathering place. Once inside the warm safety of its walls the women threw off the drab coats and hats, seated themselves at the large center table, drank their cups of tea or cocoa, and talked. While my sister and I sat at a smaller table over in a corner doing our homework, they talked—endlessly, passionately, poetically, and with impressive range. No subject was beyond them. True, they would indulge in the usual gossip: whose husband was running with whom, whose daughter looked slightly "in the way" (pregnant) under her bridal gown as she walked down the aisle. That sort of thing. But they also tackled the great issues of the time. They were always, for example, discussing the state of the economy. It was the mid and late 30's then, and the aftershock of the Depression, with its soup lines and suicides on Wall Street, was still being felt.

Some people, they declared, didn't know how to deal with adversity. They didn't know that you had to "tie up your belly" (hold in the pain, that is) when things got rough and go on with life. They took their image from the bellyband that is tied around the stomach of a newborn baby to keep the navel pressed in.

They talked politics. Roosevelt was their hero. He had come along and rescued the country with relief and jobs, and in gratitude they christened their sons Franklin and Delano and hoped they would live up to the names.

If F.D.R. was their hero, Marcus Garvey was their God. The name of the fiery, Jamaican-born black nationalist of the 20's was constantly invoked around the table. For he had been their leader when they first came to the United States from the West Indies shortly after World War I. They had contributed to his organization, the United Negro Improvement Association (UNIA), out of their meager salaries, bought shares in his ill-fated Black Star Shipping Line, and at the height of the movement they had marched as members of his "nurses' brigade" in their white uniforms up Seventh Avenue in Harlem during the great Garvey Day parades. Garvey: He lived on through the power of their memories.

And their talk was of war and rumors of wars. They raged against World War II when it broke out in Europe, blaming it on the politicians. "It's these politicians. They're the ones always starting up all this lot of war. But what they care? It's the poor people got to suffer and mothers with their sons." If it was *their* sons, they swore they would keep them out of the Army by giving them soap to eat each day to make their hearts sound defective. Hitler? He was for them "the devil incarnate."

Then there was home. They reminisced often and at length about home. The old country. Barbados—or Bimshire, as they affectionately called it. The little Caribbean island in the sun they loved but had to leave. "Poor—poor but sweet" was the way they remembered it.

And naturally they discussed their adopted home. America came in for both good and bad marks. They lashed out at it for the racism they encountered. They took to task some of the people they worked for, especially those who gave them only a hard-boiled egg and a few spoonfuls of cottage cheese for lunch. "As if anybody can scrub floor on an egg and some cheese that don't have no taste to it!"

Yet although they caught H in "this man country," as they called America, it was nonetheless a place where "you could at least see your way to make a dollar." That much they acknowledged. They might even one day accumulate enough dollars, with both them and their husbands working, to buy the brownstone houses which, like my family, they were only leasing at that period. This was their consuming ambition: to "buy house" and to see the children through.

There was no way for me to understand it at the time, but the talk that filled the kitchen those afternoons was highly functional. It served as therapy, the cheapest kind available to my mother and her friends. Not only did it help them recover from the long wait on the corner that morning and the bargaining over their labor, it restored them to a sense of themselves and reaffirmed their self-worth. Through language they were able to overcome the humiliations of the work-day.

But more than therapy, that freewheeling, wide-ranging, exuberant talk functioned as an outlet for the tremendous creative energy they possessed. They were women in whom the need for self-expression was strong, and since language was the only vehicle readily available to them they made of it an art form that—in keeping with the African tradition in which art and life are one—was an integral part of their lives.

And their talk was a refuge. They never really ceased being baffled and overwhelmed by America—its vastness, complexity and power. Its strange customs and laws. At a level beyond words they remained fearful and in awe. Their uneasiness and fear were even reflected in their attitude toward the children they had given birth to in this country. They referred to those like myself, the little Brooklyn-born Bajans (Barbadians), as "these New York children" and complained that they couldn't discipline us properly because of the laws here. "You can't beat these children as you would like, you know, because the authorities in this place will dash you in jail for them. After all, these is New York children." Not only were we different, American, we had, as they saw it, escaped their ultimate authority.

Confronted therefore by a world they could not encompass, which even limited their rights as parents, and at the same time finding themselves permanently separated from the world they had known, they took refuge in language. "Language is the only homeland," Czeslaw Milosz, the émigré Polish writer and Nobel Laureate, has said. This is what it became for the women at the kitchen table.

It served another purpose also, I suspect. My mother and her friends were after all the female counterpart of Ralph Ellison's invisible man. Indeed, you might say they suffered a triple invisibility, being black, female and foreigners. They really didn't count in American society except as a source of cheap labor. But given the kind of women they were, they couldn't tolerate the fact of their invisibility, their powerlessness. And they fought back, using the only weapon at their command: the spoken word.

Those late afternoon conversations on a wide range of topics were a way for them to feel they exercised some measure of control over their lives and the events that shaped them. "Soully-gal, talk yuh talk!" they were always exhorting each other. "In this man world you got to take yuh mouth and make a gun!" They were in control, if only verbally and if only for the two hours or so that they remained in our house.

For me, sitting over in the corner, being seen but not heard, which was the rule for children in those days, it wasn't only what the women talked about—the content—but the way they put things—their style. The insight, irony, wit and humor they brought to their stories and discussions and their poet's inventiveness and daring with language—which of course I could only sense but not define back then.

They had taken the standard English taught them in the primary schools of Barbados and transformed it into an idiom, an instrument that more adequately described them—changing around the syntax and imposing their own rhythm and accent so that the sentences were more pleasing to their ears. They added the few African sounds and words that had survived, such as the derisive suck-teeth sound and the word "yam," meaning to eat. And to make it more vivid, more in keeping with their expressive quality, they brought to bear a raft of metaphors, parables, Biblical quotations, sayings and the like:

"The sea ain' got no back door," they would say, meaning that it wasn't like a house where if there was a fire you could run out the back. Meaning that it was not to be trifled with. And meaning perhaps in a larger sense that man should treat all of nature with caution and respect.

"I has read hell by heart and called every generation blessed!" They sometimes went in for hyperbole.

A woman expecting a baby was never said to be pregnant. They never used that word. Rather, she was "in the way" or, better yet, "tumbling big." "Guess who I butt up on in the market the other day tumbling big again!"

And a woman with a reputation of being too free with her sexual favors was known in their book as a "thoroughfare"—the sense of men like a steady stream of cars moving up and down the road of her life. Or she might be dubbed "a free-bee," which was my favorite of the two. I liked the image it conjured up of a woman scandalous perhaps but independent, who flitted from one flower to another in a garden of male beauties, sampling their nectar, taking her pleasure at will, the roles reversed.

And nothing, no matter how beautiful, was ever described as simply beautiful. It was always "beautiful-ugly": the beautiful-ugly dress, the beautiful-ugly house, the beautiful-ugly car. Why the word "ugly," I used to wonder, when the thing they were referring to was beautiful, and they knew it. Why the antonym, the contradiction, the linking of opposites? It used to puzzle me greatly as a child.

There is the theory in linguistics which states that the idiom of a people, the way they use language, reflects not only the most fundamental views they hold of themselves and the world but their very conception of reality. Perhaps in using the term "beautiful-ugly" to describe nearly everything, my mother and her friends were expressing what they believed to be a fundamental dualism in life: the idea that a thing is at the same time its opposite, and that these opposites, these contradictions make up the whole. But theirs was not a Manichaean brand of dualism that sees matter, flesh, the body, as inherently evil, because they constantly addressed each other as "soully-gal"—soul: spirit; gal: the body, flesh, the visible self. And it was clear from their tone that they gave one as much weight and importance as the other. They had never heard of the mind/body split.

As for God, they summed up His essential attitude in a phrase. "God," they would say, "don' love ugly and He ain' stuck on pretty."

Using everyday speech, the simple commonplace words—but always with imagination and skill—they gave voice to the most complex ideas. Flannery O'Connor would have approved of how they made ordinary language work, as she put it, "double-time," stretching, shading, deepening its meaning. Like Joseph Conrad they were always trying to infuse new life in the "old old words worn thin . . . by . . . careless usage." And the goals of their oral art were the same as his: "to make you hear, to make you feel . . . to make you *see.*" This was their guiding esthetic.

URSULA K. LE GUIN

Is Gender Necessary Redux (1976–1987)

Is Gender Necessary? 1976

Reconsiderations 1987

In the mid-1960s the women's movement was just beginning to move again, after a fifty-year halt. There was a groundswell gathering. I felt it, but I didn't know it was a groundswell; I just thought it was something wrong with me. I considered myself a feminist; I didn't see how you could be a thinking woman and not be a feminist; but I had never taken a step beyond the ground gained for us by Emmeline Pankhurst and Virginia Woolf.°

Along about 1967, I began to feel a certain unease, a need to step on a little farther, perhaps, on my own. I began to want to define and understand the meaning of sexuality and the meaning of gender, in my life and in our society. Much had gathered in the unconscious—both personal and collective—which must either be brought up into consciousness, or else turn destructive. It was that same need, I think, that had led Beauvoir to write *The Second Sex,* and Friedan to write *The Feminine Mystique,* and that was, at the same time, leading Kate Millett and others to write their books, and to create the

°Feminism has enlarged its ground and strengthened its theory and practice immensely, and enduringly, in these past twenty years; but has anyone actually taken a step "beyond" Virginia Woolf? The image, implying an ideal of "progress," is not one I would use now.

new feminism. But I was not a theoretician, a political thinker or activist, or a sociologist. I was and am a fiction writer. The way I did my thinking was to write a novel. That novel, *The Left Hand of Darkness,* is the record of my consciousness, the process of my thinking.

Perhaps, now that we have all° moved on to a plane of heightened consciousness about these matters, it might be of some interest to look back on the book, to see what it did, what it tried to do, and what it might have done, insofar as it is a "feminist"° book. (Let me repeat that last qualification, once. The fact is that the real subject of the book is not feminism or sex or gender or anything of the sort; as far as I can see, it is a book about betrayal and fidelity. That is why one of its two dominant sets of symbols is an extended metaphor of winter, of ice, snow, cold: the winter journey. The rest of this discussion will concern only half, the lesser half, of the book.)°

It takes place on a planet called Gethen, whose human inhabitants differ from us in their sexual physiology. Instead of our continuous sexuality, the Gethenians have an oestrus period, called *kemmer.* When they are not in *kemmer,* they are sexually inactive and impotent; they are also androgynous. An observer in the book describes the cycle:

> In the first phase of *kemmer* [the individual] remains completely androgynous. Gender, and potency, are not attained in isolation. . . . Yet the sexual impulse is tremendously strong in this phase, controlling the entire personality. . . . When the individual finds a partner in *kemmer,* hormonal secretion is further stimulated (most importantly by touch—secretion? scent?) until in one partner either a male or female hormonal dominance is established. The genitals engorge or shrink accordingly, foreplay intensifies, and the partner, triggered by the change, takes on the other sexual role (apparently without exception). . . . Normal individuals have no predisposition to either sexual role in *kemmer;* they do not know whether they will be the male or the female, and have

°Well, quite a lot of us, anyhow.

°Strike the quotation marks from the word *feminist,* please.

°This parenthesis is overstated; I was feeling defensive, and resentful that critics of the book insisted upon talking only about its "gender problems," as if it were an essay not a novel. *"The fact is* that the *real* subject of the book is. . . ."* This is bluster. I had opened a can of worms and was trying hard to shut it. "The fact is," however, that there are other aspects to the book, which are involved with its sex/gender aspects quite inextricably.

no choice in the matter. . . . The culminant phase of *kemmer*. . . lasts from two to five days, during which sexual drive and capacity are at maximum. It ends fairly abruptly, and if conception has not taken place, the individual returns to the latent phase and the cycle begins anew. If the individual was in the female role and was impregnated, hormonal activity of course continues, and for the gestation and lactation periods this individual remains female. . . . With the cessation of lactation the female becomes once more a perfect androgyne. No physiological habit is established, and the mother of several children may be the father of several more.

Why did I invent these peculiar people? Not just so that the book could contain, halfway through it, the sentence, "The king was pregnant"—though I admit that I am fond of that sentence. Not, certainly not, to propose Gethen as a model for humanity. I am not in favor of genetic alteration of the human organism—not at our present level of understanding. I was not recommending the Gethenian sexual setup: I was using it. It was a heuristic device, a thought-experiment. Physicists often do thought-experiments. Einstein shoots a light-ray through a moving elevator; Schrödinger puts a cat in a box. There is no elevator, no cat, no box. The experiment is performed, the question is asked, in the mind. Einstein's elevator, Schrödinger's cat, my Gethenians, are simply a way of thinking. They are questions, not answers; process, not stasis. One of the essential functions of science fiction, I think, is precisely this kind of question-asking: reversals of an habitual way of thinking, metaphors for what our language has no words for as yet, experiments in imagination.

The subject of my experiment, then, was something like this: Because of our lifelong social conditioning, it is hard for us to see clearly what, besides purely physiological form and function, truly differentiates men and women. Are there real differences in temperament, capacity, talent, psychic processes, etc.? If so, what are they? Only comparative ethnology offers, so far, any solid evidence on the matter, and the evidence is incomplete and often contradictory. The only going social experiments that are truly relevant are the kibbutzim and the Chinese communes, and they too are inconclusive—and hard to get unbiased information about. How to find out? Well, one can always put a cat in a box. One can send an imaginary, but conventional, indeed rather stuffy, young man from Earth into an imaginary culture which is totally free of sex roles because there is no, absolutely no, physiological sex distinction. I eliminated gender, to find out what was left. Whatever was left would be, presumably, simply human. It would define the area that is shared by men and women alike.

I still think that this was a rather neat idea. But as an experiment, it was messy. All results were uncertain; a repetition of the experiment by someone else, or by myself seven years later, would probably° give quite different results. Scientifically, this is most disreputable. That's all right; I am not a scientist. I play the game where the rules keep changing.

°Strike the word *probably* and replace it with *certainly.*

Among these dubious and uncertain results, achieved as I thought, and wrote, and wrote, and thought, about my imaginary people, three appear rather interesting to me.

First: The absence of war. In the 13,000 years of recorded history on Gethen, there has not been a war. The people seem to be as quarrelsome, competitive, and aggressive as we are; they have fights, murders, assassinations, feuds, forays, and so on. But there have been no great invasions by peoples on the move, like the Mongols in Asia or the Whites in the New World: partly because Gethenian populations seem to remain stable in size, they do not move in large masses, or rapidly. Their migrations have been slow, no one generation going very far. They have no nomadic peoples, and no societies which live by expansion and aggression against other societies. Nor have they formed large, hierarchically governed nation-states, the mobilizable entity that is the essential factor in modern war. The basic social unit all over the planet is a group of from 200 to 800 people, called a "hearth," a structure founded less on economic convenience than on sexual necessity (there must be others in *kemmer* at the same time), and therefore more tribal than urban in nature, though overlaid and interwoven with a later urban pattern. The hearth tends to be communal, independent, and somewhat introverted. Rivalries between hearths, as between individuals, are channeled into a socially approved form of aggression called *shifgrethor*, a conflict without physical violence, involving one-upsmanship, the saving and losing of face—conflict ritualized, stylized, controlled. When *shifgrethor* breaks down there may be physical violence, but it does not become mass violence, remaining limited, personal. The active group remains small. The dispersive trend is as strong as the cohesive. Historically, when hearths gathered into a nation for economic reasons, the cellular pattern still dominated the centralized one. There might be a king and a parliament, but authority was not enforced so much by might as by the use of *shifgrethor* and intrigue, and was accepted as custom, without appeal to patriarchal ideals of divine right, patriotic duty, etc. Ritual and parade were far more effective agents of order than armies or police. Class structure was flexible and open; the value of the social hierarchy was less economic than aesthetic, and there was no great gap between rich and poor. There was no slavery or servitude. Nobody owned anybody. There were no chattels. Economic organization was rather communistic or syndicalistic than capitalistic, and was seldom highly centralized.

During the time span of the novel, however, all this is changing. One of the two large nations of the planet is becoming a genuine nation-state, complete with patriotism and bureaucracy. It has achieved state capitalism and the centralization of power, authoritarian government, and a secret police; and it is on the verge of achieving the world's first war.

Why did I present the first picture, and show it in the process of changing to a different one? I am not sure. I think it is because I was trying to show a balance—and the delicacy of a balance. To me the "female principle" is, or at least historically has been, basically anarchic. It values order without constraint, rule by custom not by force. It has been the male who enforces order, who constructs power-structures, who makes, enforces, and breaks laws. On Gethen, these two principles are in balance: the decentralizing against the centralizing, the flexible against the rigid, the circular against the linear. But balance is a precarious state, and at the moment of the novel the balance, which had leaned toward the "feminine," is tipping the other way.°

Second: The absence of exploitation. The Gethenians do not rape their world. They have developed a high technology, heavy industry, automobiles, radios, explosives, etc., but they have done so very slowly, absorbing their technology rather than letting it overwhelm them. They have no myth of Progress at all. Their calendar calls the current year always the Year One, and they count backward and forward from that.

In this, it seems that what I was after again was a balance: the driving linearity of the "male," the pushing forward to the limit, the logicality that admits no boundary—and the circularity of the "female," the valuing of patience, ripeness, practicality, livableness. A model for this balance, of course, exists on Earth: Chinese civilization over the past six millennia. (I did not know when I wrote the book that the parallel extends even to the calendar; the Chinese historically never had a linear dating system, such as ours that dates from the birth of Christ.)°

Third: The absence of sexuality as a continuous social factor. For four-fifths of the month, a Gethenian's sexuality plays no part at all in his social life (unless he's pregnant); for the other one-fifth, it dominates him absolutely. In *kemmer*, one must have a partner, it is imperative. (Have you ever lived in a small apartment with a tabby-cat in heat?) Gethenian society fully accepts this imperative. When a Gethenian has to make love, he does make love, and everybody expects him to, and approves of it.

But still, human beings are human beings, not cats. Despite our continuous sexuality

°At the very inception of the whole book, I was interested in writing a novel about people in a society that had never had a war. That came first. The androgyny came second. (Cause and effect? Effect and cause?) I would now rewrite this paragraph this way: The "female principle" has historically been anarchic; that is, anarchy has been historically identified as female. The domain allotted to women—"the family," for example—is the area of order without coercion, rule by custom not by force. Men have reserved the structures of social power to themselves (and those few women whom they admit to it on male terms, such as queens, prime ministers); men make the wars and peaces, men make, enforce, and break the laws. On Gethen, the two polarities we perceive through our cultural conditioning as male and female are neither, and are in balance: consensus with authority, decentralizing with centralizing, flexible with rigid, circular with linear, hierarchy with network. But it is not a motionless balance, there being no such thing in life, and at the moment of the novel, it is wobbling perilously.

°A better model might be some of the pre-Conquest cultures of the Americas, though not those hierarchical and imperialistic ones approvingly termed, by our hierarchical and imperialistic standards, "high." The trouble with the Chinese model is that their civilisation instituted and practiced male domination as thoroughly as the other "high" civilisations. I was thinking of a Taoist ideal, not of such practices as bride-selling and foot-binding, which we are trained to consider unimportant, nor of the deep misogyny of Chinese culture, which we are trained to consider normal.

and our intense self-domestication (domesticated animals tend to be promiscuous, wild animals pairbonding, familial, or tribal in their mating), we are very seldom truly promiscuous. We do have rape, to be sure—no other animal has equaled us there. We have mass rape, when an army (male, of course) invades; we have prostitution, promiscuity controlled by economics; and sometimes ritual abreactive promiscuity controlled by religion; but in general we seem to avoid genuine license. At most we award it as a prize to the Alpha Male, in certain situations; it is scarcely ever permitted to the female without social penalty. It would seem, perhaps, that the mature human being, male or female, is not satisfied by sexual gratification without psychic involvement, and in fact may be *afraid of it,* to judge by the tremendous variety of social, legal, and religious controls and sanctions exerted over it in all human societies. Sex is a great mana, and therefore the immature society, or psyche, sets great taboos about it. The maturer culture, or psyche, can integrate these taboos or laws into an internal ethical code, which, while allowing great freedom, does not permit the treatment of another person as an object. But, however irrational or rational, there is always a code.

Because the Gethenians cannot have sexual intercourse unless both partners are willing, because they cannot rape or be raped, I figured that they would have less fear and guilt about sex than we tend to have; but still it is a problem for them, in some ways more than for us, because of the extreme, explosive, imperative quality of the oestrous phase. Their society would have to control it, though it might move more easily than we from the taboo stage to the ethical stage. So the basic arrangement, I found, is that of the kemmerhouse, in every Gethenian community, which is open to anyone in kemmer, native or stranger, so that he can find a partner. Then there are various customary (not legal) institutions, such as the kemmering group, a group who choose to come together during kemmer as a regular thing; this is like the primate tribe, or group marriage. Or there is the possibility of vowing kemmering, which is marriage, pairbonding for life, a personal commitment without legal sanction. Such commitments have intense moral and psychic significance, but they are not controlled by Church or State. Finally, there are two forbidden acts, which might be taboo or illegal or simply considered contemptible, depending on which of the regions of Gethen you are in: first, you don't pair off with a relative of a different generation (one who might be your own parent or child); second, you may mate, but not vow kemmering, with your own sibling. These are the old incest prohibitions. They are so general among us—and with good cause, I think, not so much genetic as psychological—that they seemed likely to be equally valid on Gethen.

These three 'results,' then, of my experiment, I feel were fairly clearly and successfully worked out, though there is nothing definitive about them.

In other areas where I might have pressed for at least such plausible results, I see now a failure to think things through, or to express them clearly. For example, I think I took the easy way in using such familiar governmental structures as a feudal monarchy and a modern-style bureaucracy for the two Gethenian countries that are the scene of the novel. I doubt that Gethenian governments, rising out of the cellular "hearth," would resemble any of our own so closely. They might be better, they might be worse, but they would certainly be different.

I regret even more certain timidities or ineptnesses I showed in following up the psychic implications of Gethenian physiology.° Just for example, I wish I had known Jung's work, when I wrote the book: so that I could have decided whether a Gethenian had *no* animus or anima, or *both*, or an animum. . . . But the central failure in this area comes up in the frequent criticism I receive, that the Gethenians seem like *men*, instead of menwomen.

This rises in part from the choice of pronoun. I call Gethenians "he," because I utterly refuse to mangle English by inventing a

°For example (and Jung wouldn't have helped with this, more likely hindered) I quite unnecessarily locked the Gethenians into heterosexuality. It is a naively pragmatic view of sex that insists that sexual partners must be of opposite sex! In any kemmerhouse homosexual practice would, of course, be possible and acceptable and welcomed—but I never thought to explore this option; and the omission, alas, implies that sexuality is heterosexuality. I regret this very much.

pronoun for "he/she."° "He" is the generic pronoun, damn it, in English. (I envy the Japanese, who, I am told, do have a he/she pronoun.) But I do not consider this really very important.° The pronouns wouldn't matter at all if I had been cleverer at *showing* the "female" component of the Gethenian characters in *action.*° Unfortunately, the plot and structure that arose as I worked the book out cast the Gethenian protagonist, Estraven, almost exclusively into roles which we are culturally conditioned to perceive as "male"—a prime minister (it takes more than even Golda Meir and Indira Gandhi to break a stereotype), a political schemer, a fugitive, a prison-breaker, a sledge-hauler. . . . I think I did this because I was privately delighted at watching, not a man, but a man-woman, do all these things, and do them with considerable skill and flair. But, for the reader, I left out too much. One does not see Estraven as a mother, with his children, in any role which we automatically perceive as "female": and therefore, we tend to see him as a man. This is a real flaw in the book, and I can only be very grateful to those readers, men and women, whose willingness to participate in the experiment led them to fill in that omission with the work of their own imagination, and to see Estraven as I saw him, as man and woman, familiar and different, alien and utterly human.°

It seems to be men, more often than women, who thus complete my work for me: I think because men are often more willing to identify as they read with poor, confused, defensive Genly, the Earthman, and therefore to participate in his painful and gradual discovery of love.

Finally, the question arises, is the book a Utopia? It seems to me that it is quite clearly not; it poses no *practicable* alternative to contemporary society, since it is based on an imaginary, radical change in human anatomy. All it tries to do is open up an alternative viewpoint, to widen the imagination, without making any very definite suggestions as to what might be seen from that new viewpoint. The most it says is, I think, something

°This "utter refusal" of 1968 restated in 1976 collapsed, utterly, within a couple of years more. I still dislike invented pronouns, but I now dislike them less than the so-called generic pronoun he/him/his, which does in fact exclude women from discourse; and which was an invention of male grammarians, for until the sixteenth century the English generic singular pronoun was they/them/their, as it still is in English and American colloquial speech. It should be restored to the written language, and let the pedants and pundits squeak and gibber in the streets.

In a screenplay of *The Left Hand of Darkness* written in 1985, I referred to Gethenians not pregnant or in kemmer by the invented pronouns a/un/a's, modelled on a British dialect. These would drive the reader mad in print, I suppose; but I have read parts of the book aloud using them, and the audience was perfectly happy, except that they pointed out that the subject pronoun, "a" pronounced [ˆ], sounds too much like "I" said with a Southern accent.
°I now consider it very important.
°If I had realised how the pronouns I used shaped, directed, controlled my own thinking. I might have been "cleverer."

°I now see it thus: Men were inclined to be satisfied with the book, which allowed them a safe trip into androgyny and back, from a conventionally male viewpoint. But many women wanted it to go further, to dare more, to explore androgyny from a woman's point of view as well as a man's. In fact, it does so, in that it was written by a woman. But this is admitted directly only in the chapter "The Question of Sex," the only voice of a woman in the book. I think women were justified in asking more courage of me and a more rigorous thinking-through of implications.

like this: If we were socially ambisexual, if men and women were completely and genuinely equal in their social roles, equal legally and economically, equal in freedom, in responsibility, and in self-esteem, then society would be a very different thing. What our problems might be, God knows; I only know we would have them. But it seems likely that our central problem would not be the one it is now: the problem of exploitation—exploitation of the woman, of the weak, of the earth. Our curse is alienation, the separation of yang from yin.° Instead of a search for balance and integration, there is a struggle for dominance. Divisions are insisted upon, interdependence is denied. The dualism of value that destroys us, the dualism of superior/inferior, ruler/ruled, owner/owned, user/used, might give way to what seems to me, from here, a much healthier, sounder, more promising modality of integration and integrity.

°—and the moralisation of yang as good—of yin as bad.

EVELYN FOX KELLER

A World of Difference

O Lady! We receive but what we give,
And in our life alone does Nature live:
Ours is her wedding garment, ours her shroud!
SAMUEL TAYLOR COLERIDGE, "DEJECTION: AN ODE"

If we want to think about the ways in which science might be different, we could hardly find a more appropriate guide than Barbara McClintock. Known to her colleagues as a maverick and a visionary, McClintock occupies a place in the history of genetics at one and the same time central and peripheral—a place that, for all its eminence, is marked by difference at every turn.

Born in 1902, McClintock began in her twenties to make contributions to classical genetics and cytology that earned her a level of recognition few women of her generation could imagine. Encouraged and supported by many of the great men of classical genetics (including T. H. Morgan, R. A. Emerson, and Lewis Stadler), McClintock was given the laboratory space and fellowship stipends she needed to pursue what had quickly become the central goal of her life: understanding the secrets of plant genetics. She rejected the more conventional opportunities then available to women in science (such as a research assistantship or a teaching post at a woman's college)[1] and devoted herself to the life of pure research. By the mid-1930s, she had already made an indelible mark on the history of genetics. But the fellowships inevitably ran out. With no job on the horizon, McClintock thought she would have to leave science. Morgan and Emerson, arguing that "it would be a scientific tragedy if her work did not go forward" (quoted in Keller 1983, p. 74), prevailed upon the Rockefeller Foundation to provide two years' interim support. Morgan described her as "the best person in the world" in her field but deplored her "personality difficulties": "She is sore at the world because of her conviction that she would have a much freer scientific opportunity if she were a man" (p. 73). Not until 1942 was McClintock's professional survival secured: at that time, a haven was provided for her at the Carnegie Institution of Washington at Cold Spring Harbor, where she has remained ever since. Two years later she was elected to the National Academy of Science; in 1945 she became president of the Genetics Society of America.

This dual theme of success and marginality that poignantly describes the first stage of McClintock's career continues as the leitmotif of her entire professional life. Despite the ungrudging respect and admiration of her colleagues, her most important work has, until recently, gone largely unappreciated, uncomprehended, and almost entirely unintegrated into the growing corpus of biological thought. This was the work, begun in her forties, that led to her discovery that genetic elements can move, in an apparently coordinated way, from one chromosomal site to another—in short, her discovery of genetic transposition. Even today, as a Nobel laureate and deluged with other awards and prizes for this same work, McClintock regards herself as, in crucial respects, an outsider to the world of modern biology—not because she is a woman but because she is a philosophical and methodological deviant.

No doubt, McClintock's marginality and deviance are more visible—and seem more dramatic—to her than to others. During the many years when McClintock's professional survival seemed so precarious, even her most devoted colleagues seemed unaware that she had no proper job. "What do you mean?" many of them asked me. "She was so good! How could she not have had a job?" Indeed, as Morgan himself suggested, her expectation that she would be rewarded on the basis of merit, on the same footing as her male colleagues, was itself read as a mark of her ingratitude—of what he called her "personality difficulties."

When discussing the second stage of her career, during which her revolutionary work on genetic transposition earned her the reputation more of eccentricity than of greatness, her colleagues are likely to focus on the enduring admiration many of them continued to feel. She, of course, is more conscious of their lack of comprehension and of the dismissal of her work by other, less admiring colleagues. She is conscious, above all, of the growing isolation that ensued.

Today, genetic transposition is no longer a dubious or isolated phenomenon. As one prominent biologist describes it, "[Transposable elements] are everywhere, in bacteria, yeast, *Drosophila,* and plants. Perhaps even in mice and men." (Marx 1981, quoted in Keller 1983, p. 193). But the significance of transposition remains

1. For an excellent overview of the opportunities available to women scientists in the 1920s and 1930s, see Rossiter 1982.

in considerable dispute. McClintock saw transposable elements as a key to developmental regulation; molecular biologists today, although much more sympathetic to this possibility than they were twenty, or even ten, years ago, are still unsure. And in evolutionary terms, McClintock's view of transposition as a survival mechanism available to the organism in times of stress seems to most (although not to all) pure heresy.

My interest here, as it has been from the beginning, is less on who was "right" than on the differences in perceptions that underlay such a discordance of views. The vicissitudes of McClintock's career give those differences not only special poignancy but special importance. In *A Feeling for the Organism: The Life and Work of Barbara McClintock* (Keller 1983), I argued that it is precisely the duality of success and marginality that lends her career its significance to the history and philosophy of science. Her success indisputably affirms her legitimacy as a scientist, while her marginality provides an opportunity to examine the role and fate of dissent in the growth of scientific knowledge. This duality illustrates the diversity of values, methodological styles, and goals that, to varying degrees, always exists in science; at the same time, it illustrates the pressures that, to equally varying degrees, operate to contain that diversity.

In the preface to that book (p. xii), I wrote:

> The story of Barbara McClintock allows us to explore the condition under which dissent in science arises, the function it serves, and the plurality of values and goals it reflects. It makes us ask: What role do interests, individual and collective, play in the evolution of scientific knowledge? Do all scientists seek the same kinds of explanations? Are the kinds of questions they ask the same? Do differences in methodology between different subdisciplines even permit the same kinds of answers? And when significant differences do arise in questions asked, explanations sought, methodologies employed, how do they affect communication between scientists? In short, why could McClintock's discovery of transposition not be absorbed by her contemporaries? We can say that her vision of biological organization was too remote from the kinds of explanations her colleagues were seeking, but we need to understand what that distance is composed of, and how such divergences develop.

I chose, in effect, not to read the story of McClintock's career as a romance—neither as "a tale of dedication rewarded after years of neglect—of prejudice or indifference eventually routed by courage and truth" (p. xii), nor as a heroic story of the scientist, years "ahead of her time," stumbling on something approximating what we now know as "the truth." Instead, I read it as a story about the languages of science—about the process by which worlds of common scientific discourse become established, effectively bounded, and yet at the same time remain sufficiently permeable to allow a given piece of work to pass from incomprehensibility in one era to acceptance (if not full comprehensibility) in another.

In this essay, my focus is even more explicitly on difference itself. I want to isolate McClintock's views of nature, of science, and of the relation between mind and nature, in order to exhibit not only their departure from more conventional views but also their own internal coherence. If we can stand inside this world view, the questions she asks, the explanations she seeks, and the methods she employs in her pursuit of scientific knowledge will take on a degree of clarity and comprehensibility they lack from outside. And at the heart of this world view lies the same respect for difference that motivates us to examine it in the first place. I begin therefore with a discussion of the implications of respect for difference (and complexity) in the general philosophy expressed in McClintock's testimony, and continue by discussing its implications for cognition and perception, for her interests as a geneticist, and for the relation between her work and molecular biology. I conclude the essay with a brief analysis of the relevance of gender to any philosophy of difference, and to McClintock's in particular.

Complexity and Difference

To McClintock, nature is characterized by an a priori complexity that vastly exceeds the capacities of the human imagination. Her recurrent remark, "Anything you can think of you will find,"[2] is a statement about the capacities not of mind but of nature. It is meant not as a description of our own ingenuity as discoverers but as a comment on the resourcefulness of natural order; in the sense not so much of adaptability as of largesse and prodigality. Organisms have a life and an order of their own that scientists can only begin to fathom. "Misrepresented, not appreciated, . . . [they] are beyond our wildest expectations. . . . They do everything we [can think of], they do it better, more efficiently, more marvelously." In comparison with the ingenuity of nature, our scientific intelligence seems pallid. It follows as a matter of course that "trying to make everything fit into set dogma won't work. . . . There's no such thing as a central dogma into which everything will fit."

In the context of McClintock's views of nature, attitudes about research that would otherwise sound romantic fall into logical place. The need to "listen to the material" follows from her sense of the order of things. Precisely because the complexity of nature exceeds our own imaginative possibilities, it becomes essential to "let the experiment tell you what to do." Her major criticism of contemporary research is based on what she sees as inadequate humility. She feels that "much of the work done is done because one wants to impose an answer on it—they have the answer ready, and they [know what] they want the material to tell them, so anything it doesn't tell them, they don't really recognize as there, or they think it's a mistake and throw it out. . . . If you'd only just let the material tell you."

Respect for complexity thus demands from observers of nature the same special attention to the exceptional case that McClintock's own example as a scientist demands from observers of science: "If the material tells you, 'It may be this,' allow that. Don't turn it aside and call it an exception, an aberration, a contaminant. . . . That's what's happened all the way along the line with so many good clues." Indeed, respect for individual difference lies at the very heart of McClintock's scientific passion. "The important thing is to develop the capacity to see one kernel [of maize] that is different, and make that understandable," she says. "If [something] doesn't fit, there's a reason, and you find out what it is." The prevailing focus on classes and numbers, McClintock believes, encourages researchers to overlook difference, to "call it an exception, an aberration, a contaminant." The consequences of this seem to her very costly. "Right and left," she says, they miss "what is going on."

2. All quotations from Barbara McClintock are taken from private interviews conducted between September 24, 1978, and February 25, 1979; most of them appear in Keller 1983.

She is, in fact, here describing the history of her own research. Her work on transposition in fact began with the observation of an aberrant pattern of pigmentation on a few kernels of a single corn plant. And her commitment to the significance of this singular pattern sustained her through six years of solitary and arduous investigation—all aimed at making the difference she saw understandable.

Making difference understandable does not mean making it disappear. In McClintock's world view, an understanding of nature can come to rest with difference. "Exceptions" are not there to "prove the rule"; they have meaning in and of themselves. In this respect, difference constitutes a principle for ordering the world radically unlike the principle of division of dichotomization (subject–object, mind–matter, feeling–reason, disorder–law). Whereas these oppositions are directed toward a cosmic unity typically excluding or devouring one of the pair, toward a unified, all-encompassing law, respect for difference remains content with multiplicity as an end in itself.

And just as the terminus of knowledge implied by difference can be distinguished from that implied by division, so the starting point of knowledge can also be distinguished. Above all, difference, in this world view, does not posit division as an epistemological prerequisite—it does not imply the necessity of hard and fast divisions in nature, or in mind, or in the relation between mind and nature. Division severs connection and imposes distance; the recognition of difference provides a starting point for relatedness. It serves both as a clue to new modes of connectedness in nature and as an invitation to engagement with nature. For McClintock, certainly, respect for difference serves both these functions. Seeing something that does not appear to fit is, to her, a challenge to find the larger multidimensional pattern into which it does fit. Anomalous kernels of corn were evidence not of disorder or lawlessness, but of a larger system of order, one that cannot be reduced to a single law.

Difference thus invites a form of engagement and understanding that allows for the preservation of the individual. The integrity of each kernel (or chromosome or plant) survives all our own pattern-making attempts; the order of nature transcends our capacities for ordering. And this transcendence is manifested in the enduring uniqueness of each organism: "No two plants are exactly alike. They're all different, and as a consequence, you have to know that difference," she explains. "I start with the seedling, and I don't want to leave it. I don't feel I really know the story if I don't watch the plant all the way along. So I know every plant in the field. I know them intimately, and I find it a great pleasure to know them." From days, weeks, and years of patient observation comes what looks like privileged insight: "When I see things, I can interpret them right away." As one colleague described it, the result is an apparent ability to write the "autobiography" of every plant she works with.

McClintock is not here speaking of relations to other humans, but the parallels are nonetheless compelling. In the relationship she describes with plants, as in human relations, respect for difference constitutes a claim not only on our interest but on our capacity for empathy—in short on the highest form of love: love that allows for intimacy without the annihilation of difference. I use the word *love* neither loosely nor sentimentally, but out of fidelity to the language McClintock herself uses to describe a form of attention, indeed a form of thought. Her vocabulary is consistently a vocabulary of affection, of kinship, of empathy. Even with puzzles, she explains, "The thing was dear to you for a period of time, you really had an affection for it. Then after a while, it disappears and it doesn't bother you. But for a short time you feel strongly attached to that little toy." The crucial point for us is that McClintock can risk the suspension of boundaries between subject and object without jeopardy to science precisely because, to her, science is not premised on that division. Indeed, the intimacy she experiences with the objects she studies— intimacy born of a lifetime of cultivated attentiveness—is a wellspring of her powers as a scientist.

The most vivid illustration of this process comes from her own account of a breakthrough in one particularly recalcitrant piece of cytological analysis. She describes the state of mind accompanying the crucial shift in orientation that enabled her to identify chromosomes she had earlier not been able to distinguish: "I found that the more I worked with them, the bigger and bigger [the chromosomes] got, and when I was really working with them I wasn't outside, I was down there. I was part of the system. I was right down there with them, and everything got big. I even was able to see the internal parts of the chromosomes—actually everything was there. It surprised me because I actually felt as if I was right down there and these were my friends. . . . As you look at these things, they become part of you. And you forget yourself."

Cognition and Perception

In this world of difference, division is relinquished without generating chaos. Self and other, mind and nature survive not in mutual alienation, or in symbiotic fusion, but in structural integrity. The "feeling for the organism" that McClintock upholds as the sine qua non of good research need not be read as "participation mystique"; it is a mode of access—honored by time and human experience if not by prevailing conventions in science—to the reliable knowledge of the world around us that all scientists seek. It is a form of attention strongly reminiscent of the concept of "focal attention" developed by Ernest Schachtel to designate "man's [*sic*] capacity to *center* his attention on an object fully, so that he can perceive or understand it from *many sides,* as fully as possible" (p. 251). In Schachtel's language, "focal attention" is the principal tool that, in conjunction with our natural interest in objects per se, enables us to progress from mere wishing and wanting to thinking and knowing— that equips us for the fullest possible knowledge of reality in its own terms. Such "object-centered" perception presupposes "a temporary eclipse of all the perceiver's egocentric thoughts and strivings, of all preoccupation with self and self-esteem, and a full turning towards the object, . . . [which, in turn] leads not to a *loss* of self, but to a heightened feeling of aliveness" (p. 181). Object-centered perception, Schachtel goes on to argue, is in the service of a love "which wants to affirm others in their total and unique being . . . [which affirms objects as] part of the same world of which man is a part" (p. 226). It requires

an experiential realization of the kinship between oneself and the other . . . a realization [that] is made difficult by fear and by arrogance—by fear because then the need to protect oneself by flight, appeasement, or attack gets in the way; by arrogance because then the other is no longer experienced as akin, but as inferior to oneself. (p. 227)

The difference between Schachtel and McClintock is that what Schachtel grants to the poet's perceptual style in contrast to that of the scientist, McClintock claims equally for science. She enlists a "feeling for the organism"—not only for living organisms but for any object that fully claims our attention—in pursuit of the goal shared by all scientists: reliable (that is, shareable and reproducible) knowledge of natural order.

This difference is a direct reflection of the limitations of Schachtel's picture of science. It is drawn not from observation of scientists like McClintock but only from the more stereotypic scientist, who "looks at the object with one or more hypotheses . . . in mind and thus 'uses' the object to corroborate or disprove a hypothesis, but does not encounter the object as such, in its own fullness." For Schachtel,

> modern natural science has as its main goal prediction, i.e. the power to manipulate objects in such a way that certain predicted events will happen. . . . Hence, the scientist usually will tend to perceive the object merely from the perspective of [this] power. . . . That is to say that his view of the object will be determined by the ends which he pursues in his experimentation. . . . He may achieve a great deal in this way and add important data to our knowledge, but to the extent to which he remains within the framework of this perspective he will not perceive the object in its own right. (1959, p. 171)

To McClintock, science has a different goal: not prediction per se, but understanding; not the power to manipulate, but empowerment—the kind of power that results from an understanding of the world around us, that simultaneously reflects and affirms our connection to that world.

What Counts as Knowledge

At the root of this difference between McClintock and the stereotypic scientist lies that unexamined starting point of science: the naming of nature. Underlying every discussion of science, as well as every scientific discussion, there exists a larger assumption about the nature of the universe in which that discussion takes place. The power of this unseen ground is to be found not in its influence on any particular argument in science but in its framing of the very terms of argument—in its definition of the tacit aims and goals of science. . . . Scientists may spend fruitful careers, building theories of nature that are astonishingly successful in their predictive power, without ever feeling the need to reflect on these fundamental philosophical issues. Yet if we want to ask questions about that success, about the value of alternative scientific descriptions of nature, even about the possibility of alternative criteria of success, we can do so only by examining those most basic assumptions that are normally not addressed.

We have to remind ourselves that, although all scientists share a common ambition for knowledge, it does not follow that what counts as knowledge is commonly agreed upon. The history of science reveals a wide diversity of questions asked, explanations sought, and methodologies employed in this common quest for knowledge of the natural world; this diversity is in turn reflected in the kinds of knowledge acquired, and indeed in what counts as knowledge. To a large degree, both the kinds of questions one asks and the explanations that one finds satisfying depend on one's a priori relation to the objects of study. In particular, I am suggesting that questions asked about objects with which one feels kinship are likely to differ from questions asked about objects one sees as unalterably alien. Similarly, explanations that satisfy us about a natural world that is seen as "blind, simple and dumb," ontologically inferior, may seem less self-evidently satisfying for a natural world seen as complex and, itself, resourceful. I suggest that individual and communal conceptions of nature need to be examined for their role in the history of science, not as causal determinants but as frameworks upon which all scientific programs are developed. More specifically, I am claiming that the difference between McClintock's conception of nature and that prevailing in the community around her is an essential key to our understanding of the history of her life and work.

It provides, for example, the context for examining the differences between McClintock's interests *as a geneticist* and what has historically been the defining focus of both classical and molecular genetics—differences crucial to the particular route her research took. To most geneticists, the problem of inheritance is solved by knowing the mechanism and structure of genes. To McClintock, however, as to many other biologists, mechanism and structure have never been adequate answers to the question "How do genes work?" Her focus was elsewhere: on function and organization. To her, an adequate understanding would, by definition, have to include an account of how they function in relation to the rest of the cell, and of course, to the organism as a whole.

In her language, the cell itself is an organism. Indeed, "Every component of the organism is as much an organism as every other part." When she says, therefore, that "one cannot consider the [gene] as such as being all important—more important is the overall organism," she means the genome as a whole, the cell, the ensemble of cells, the organism itself. Genes are neither "beads on a string" nor functionally disjoint pieces of DNA. They are organized functional units, whose very function is defined by their position in the organization as a whole. As she says, genes function "only with respect to the environment in which [they are] found."

Interests in function and in organization are historically and conceptually related to each other. By tradition, both are primary preoccupations of developmental biology, and McClintock's own interest in development followed from and supported these interests. By the same tradition, genetics and developmental biology have been two separate subjects. But for a geneticist for whom the answer to the question of how genes work must include function and organization, the problem of heredity becomes inseparable from the problem of development. The division that most geneticists felt they had to live with (happily or not) McClintock could not accept. To her, development, as the coordination of function, was an integral part of genetics.

McClintock's views today are clearly fed by her work on transposition. But her work on transposition was itself fed by these interests. Her own account (see Keller 1983, pp. 115–17) of how she came to this work and of how she followed the clues she saw vividly illustrates the ways in which her interests in function and organization—and in development—focused her attention on the patterns she saw and framed the questions she asked about the significance of these patterns. I suggest that they also defined the terms that a satisfying explanation had to meet.

Such an explanation had to account not so much for how transposition occurred as for why it occurred. The patterns she saw indicated a programmatic disruption in normal developmental function. When she succeeded in linking this disruption to the location (and change in location) of particular genetic elements, that very link was what captured her interest. (She knew she was "on to something important.") The fact that transposition occurred—the fact that genetic sequences are not fixed—was of course interesting too, but only secondarily so. To her, the paramount interest lay in the meaning of its occurrence, in the clue that transposition provided for the relation between genetics and development. Necessarily, a satisfying account of this relation would have to take due note of the complexity of the regulation process.

Transposition and the Central Dogma

Just two years after McClintock's first public presentation of her work on transposition came the culminating event in the long search for the mechanism of inheritance. Watson and Crick's discovery of the structure of DNA enabled them to provide a compelling account of the essential genetic functions of replication and instruction. According to their account, the vital information of the cell is encoded in the DNA. From there it is copied onto the RNA, which, in turn, is used as a blueprint for the production of the proteins responsible for genetic traits. In the picture that emerged—DNA to RNA to protein (which Crick himself dubbed the "central dogma")—the DNA is posited as the central actor in the cell, the executive governor of cellular organization, itself remaining impervious to influence from the subordinate agents to which it dictates. Several years later, Watson and Crick's original model was emended by Jacques Monod and François Jacob to allow for environmental control of the rates of protein synthesis. But even with this modification, the essential autonomy of DNA remained unchallenged: information flowed one way, always from, and never to, the DNA.

Throughout the 1950s and 1960s, the successes of molecular genetics were dramatic. By the end of the 1960s, it was possible to say (as Jacques Monod did say), "The Secret of Life? But this is in large part known—in principle, if not in details" (quoted in Judson 1979, p. 216). A set of values and interests wholly different from McClintock's seemed to have been vindicated. The intricacies, and difficulties, of corn genetics held little fascination in comparison with the quick returns from research on the vastly simpler and seemingly more straightforward bacterium and bacteriophage. As a result, communication between McClintock and her colleagues grew steadily more difficult; fewer and fewer biologists had the expertise required even to begin to understand her results.

McClintock of course shared in the general excitement of this period, but she did not share in the general enthusiasm for the central dogma. The same model that seemed so immediately and overwhelmingly satisfying to so many of her colleagues did not satisfy her. Although duly impressed by its explanatory power, she remained at the same time acutely aware of what it did not explain. It neither addressed the questions that were of primary interest to her—bearing on the relation between genetics and development—nor began to take into account the complexity of genetic organization that she had always assumed, and that was now revealed to her by her work on transposition.

McClintock locates the critical flaw of the central dogma in its presumption: it claimed to explain too much. Baldly put, what was true of *E. coli* (the bacterium most commonly studied) was *not* true of the elephant, as Monod (and others) would have had it (Judson 1979, p. 613). Precisely because higher organisms are multicellular, she argued, they necessarily require a different kind of economy. The central dogma was without question inordinately successful as well as scientifically productive. Yet the fact that it ultimately proved inadequate even to the dynamics of *E. coli* suggests that its trouble lay deeper than just a too hasty generalization from the simple to the complex; its presumptuousness, I suggest, was built into its form of explanation.

The central dogma is a good example of what I have earlier called (following Nanney 1957) master-molecule theories (Keller 1982). In locating the seat of genetic control in a single molecule, it posits a structure of genetic organization that is essentially hierarchical, often illustrated in textbooks by organizational charts like those of corporate structures. In this model, genetic stability is ensured by the unidirectionality of information flow, much as political and social stability is assumed in many quarters to require the unidirectional exercise of authority.

To McClintock, transposition provided evidence that genetic organization is necessarily more complex, and in fact more globally interdependent, than such a model assumes. It showed that the DNA itself is subject to rearrangement and, by implication, to reprogramming. Although she did not make the suggestion explicit, the hidden heresy of her argument lay in the inference that such reorganization could be induced by signals external to the DNA—from the cell, the organism, even from the environment.

For more than fifty years, modern biologists had labored heroically to purge biological thought of the last vestiges of teleology, particularly as they surfaced in Lamarckian notions of adaptive evolution. But even though McClintock is not a Lamarckian, she sees in transposition a mechanism enabling genetic structures to respond to the needs of the organism. Since needs are relative to the environmental context and hence subject to change, transposition, by implication, indirectly allows for the possibility of environmentally induced and genetically transmitted change. To her, such a possibility is not heresy—it is not even surprising. On the contrary, it is in direct accord with her belief in the resourcefulness of natural order. Because she has no investment in the passivity of nature, the possibility of internally generated order does not, to her, threaten the foundations of science. The capacity of organisms to reprogram their own DNA implies neither vitalism, magic, nor a countermanding will. It merely confirms the existence of forms of order more complex than we have, at least thus far, been able to account for.

The renewed interest in McClintock's work today is a direct consequence of developments (beginning in the early 1970s) in the very research programs that had seemed so philosophically opposed to her position; genetic mobility was rediscovered within molecular biology itself. That this was so was crucial, perhaps even necessary, to establishing the legitimacy of McClintock's early work, precisely because the weight of scientific authority has now come to reside in molecular biology. As a by-product, this legitimization also lends McClintock's views of science and attitudes toward research somewhat more credibility among professional biologists. To observers of science, this same historical sequence serves as a sharp reminder that the languages of science, however self-contained they seem, are not closed. McClintock's eventual vindication demonstrates the capacity of science to overcome its own characteristic kinds of myopia, reminding us that its limitations do not reinforce themselves indefinitely. Their own methodology allows, even obliges, scientists to continually reencounter phenomena even their best theories cannot accommodate. Or—to look at it from the other side—however severely communication between science and nature may be impeded by the preconceptions of a particular time, some channels always remain open; and, through them, nature finds ways of reasserting itself. (Keller 1983, p. 197)

In this sense, the McClintock story is a happy one.

It is important, however, not to overestimate the degree of rapprochement that has taken place. McClintock has been abundantly vindicated: transposition is acknowledged, higher organisms and development have once again captured the interest of biologists, and almost everyone agrees that genetic organization is manifestly more complex than had previously been thought. But not everyone shares her conviction that we are in the midst of a revolution that "will reorganize the way we look at things, the way we do research." Many researchers remain confident that the phenomenon of transposition can somehow be incorporated, even if they do not yet see how, into an improved version of the central dogma. Their attachment to this faith is telling. Behind the continuing skepticism about McClintock's interpretation of the role of transposition in development and evolution, there remains a major gap between her underlying interests and commitments and those of most of her colleagues.

The Issue of Gender

How much of this enduring difference reflects the fact that McClintock is a woman in a field still dominated by men? To what extent are her views indicative of a vision of "what will happen to science," as Erik Erikson asked in 1964 (1965, p. 243), "if and when women are truly represented in it—not by a few glorious exceptions, but in the rank and file of the scientific elite?"

On the face of it, it would be tempting indeed to call McClintock's vision of science "a feminist science." Its emphasis on intuition, on feeling, on connection and relatedness, all seem to confirm our most familiar stereotypes of women. And to the extent that they do, we might expect that the sheer presence of more women in science would shift the balance of community sentiment and lead to the endorsement of that vision. However, there are both general and particular reasons that argue strongly against this simple view.

. . . To the extent that science is defined by its past and present practitioners, anyone who aspires to membership in that community must conform to its existing code. As a consequence, the inclusion of new members, even from a radically different culture, cannot induce immediate or direct change. To be a successful scientist, one must first be adequately socialized. For this reason, it is unreasonable to expect a sharp differentiation between women scientists and their male colleagues, and indeed, most women scientists would be appalled by such a suggestion.

McClintock is in this sense no exception. She would disclaim any analysis of her work as a woman's work, as well as any suggestion that her views represent a woman's perspective. To her, science is not a matter of gender, either male or female; it is, on the contrary, a place where (ideally at least) "the matter of gender drops away." Furthermore, her very commitment to science is of a piece with her lifelong wish to transcend gender altogether. Indeed, her adamant rejection of female stereotypes seems to have been a prerequisite for her becoming a scientist at all. (See Keller 1983, chaps. 2 and 3.) In her own image of herself, she is a maverick in all respects—as a woman, as a scientist, even as a woman scientist.

Finally, I want to reemphasize that it would be not only misleading but actually contradictory to suggest that McClintock's views of science were shared by none of her colleagues. Had that been so, she could not have had even marginal status as a scientist. It is essential to understand that, in practice, the scientific tradition is far more pluralistic than any particular description of it suggests, and certainly more pluralistic than its dominant ideology. For McClintock to be recognized as a scientist, the positions that she represents, however unrepresentative, had to be, and were, identifiable as belonging somewhere within that tradition.

But although McClintock is not a total outsider to science, she is equally clearly not an insider. And however atypical she is as a woman, what she is *not* is a man. Between these two facts lies a crucial connection—a connection signaled by the recognition that, as McClintock herself admits, the matter of gender never does drop away.

I suggest that the radical core of McClintock's stance can be located right here: Because she is not a man, in a world of men, her commitment to a gender-free science has been binding; because concepts of gender have so deeply influenced the basic categories of science, that commitment has been transformative. In short, the relevance of McClintock's gender in this story is to be found not in its role in her personal socialization but precisely in the role of gender in the construction of science.

Of course, not all scientists have embraced the conception of science as one of "putting nature on the rack and torturing the answers out of her." Nor have all men embraced a conception of masculinity that demands cool detachment and domination. Nor even have all scientists been men. But most have. And however variable the attitudes of individual male scientists toward science and toward masculinity, the metaphor of a marriage between mind and nature necessarily does not look the same to them as it does to women. And this is the point.

In a science constructed around the naming of object (nature) as female and the parallel naming of subject (mind) as male, any scientist who happens to be a woman is confronted with an a priori contradiction in terms. This poses a critical problem of identity: any scientist who is not a man walks a path bounded on one side by inauthenticity and on the other by subversion. Just as surely as inauthenticity is the cost a woman suffers by joining men in misogynist jokes, so it is, equally, the cost suffered by a woman who identifies with an image of the scientist modeled on the patriarchal husband. Only if she undergoes a radical disidentification from self can she share masculine pleasure in mastering a nature cast in the image of woman as passive, inert, and blind. Her alternative is to attempt a radical redefinition of terms. Nature must be renamed as not female, or, at least, as not an alienated object. By the same token, the mind, if the female scientist is to have one, must be renamed as not necessarily male, and accordingly recast with a more inclusive subjectivity.

This is not to say that the male scientist cannot claim similar redefinition (certainly many have done so) but, by contrast to the woman scientist, his identity does not require it.

For McClintock, given her particular commitments to personal integrity, to be a scientist, and not a man, with a nonetheless intact identity, meant that she had to insist on a different meaning of mind, of nature, and of the relation between them. Her need to define for herself the relation between subject and object, even the very terms themselves, came not from a feminist consciousness, or even from a female consciousness. It came from her insistence on her right to be a scientist— from her determination to claim science as a human rather than a male endeavor. For such a claim, difference makes sense of the world in ways that division cannot. It allows for the kinship that she feels with other scientists, without at the same time obligating her to share all their assumptions.

Looked at in this way, McClintock's stance is, finally, a far more radical one than that implied in Erikson's question. It implies that what could happen to science "when women are truly represented in it" is not simply, or even, "the addition, to the male kind of creative vision, of women's vision" (p. 243), but, I suggest, a thoroughgoing transformation of the very possibilities of creative vision, for everyone. It implies that the kind of change we might hope for is not a direct or readily apparent one but rather an indirect and subterranean one. A first step toward such a transformation would be the undermining of the commitment of scientists to the masculinity of their profession that would be an inevitable concomitant of the participation of large numbers of women.

However, we need to remember that, as long as success in science does not require self-reflection, the undermining of masculinist or other ideological commitments is not a sufficient guarantee of change. But nature itself is an ally that can be relied upon to provide the impetus for real change: nature's responses recurrently invite reexamination of the terms in which our understanding of science is constructed. Paying attention to those responses—"listening to the material"—may help us to reconstruct our understanding of science in terms born out of the diverse spectrum of human experience rather than out of the narrow spectrum that our culture has labeled masculine.

References

Erikson, Erik H. Concluding Remarks. In *Women in the Scientific Professions*, ed. J. Mattfeld and C. van Aiken, Cambridge, Mass.: MIT Press, 1965.

Judson, Horace. *The Eighth Day of Creation: Makers of the Revolution in Biology.* New York: Simon & Schuster, 1979.

Keller, Evelyn Fox. "Feminism and Science." *Signs: Journal of Women in Culture and Society* 7, no. 3 (1982), pp. 589–602.

Keller, Evelyn Fox. *A Feeling for the Organism: The Life and Work of Barbara McClintock.* New York: Freeman, 1983.

Marx, Jean. "A Movable Feast in the Eukaryotic Genome." *Science* 211 (1981), p. 153.

Nanney, David L. "The Role of the Cytoplasm in Heredity." In *The Chemical Basis of Heredity*, ed. W. D. McElroy and H. B. Glass. Baltimore: Johns Hopkins University Press, 1957.

Rossiter, Margaret W. *Women Scientists in America.* Baltimore: Johns Hopkins University Press, 1982.

Schachtel, Ernest. *Metamorphosis.* New York: Basic Books, 1959.

LESLIE MARMON SILKO

Landscape, History, and the Pueblo Imagination

From a High Arid Plateau in New Mexico

You see that after a thing is dead, it dries up. It might take weeks or years, but eventually if you touch the thing, it crumbles under your fingers. It goes back to dust. The soul of the thing has long since departed. With the plants and wild game the soul may have already been borne back into bones and blood or thick green stalk and leaves. Nothing is wasted. What cannot be eaten by people or in some way used must then be left where other living creatures may benefit. What domestic animals or wild scavengers can't eat will be fed to the plants. The plants feed on the dust of these few remains.

The ancient Pueblo people buried the dead in vacant rooms or partially collapsed rooms adjacent to the main living quarters. Sand and clay used to construct the roof make layers many inches deep once the roof has collapsed. The layers of sand and clay make for easy gravedigging. The vacant room fills with cast-off objects and debris. When a vacant room has filled deep enough, a shallow but adequate grave can be scooped in a far corner. Archaeologists have remarked over formal burials complete with elaborate funerary objects excavated in trash middens of abandoned rooms. But the rocks and adobe mortar of collapsed walls were valued by the ancient people. Because each rock had been carefully selected for size and shape, then chiseled to an even face. Even the pink clay adobe melting with each rainstorm had to be prayed over, then dug and carried some distance. Corn cobs and husks, the rinds and stalks and animal bones were not regarded by the ancient people as filth or garbage. The remains were merely resting at a midpoint in their journey back to dust. Human remains are not so different. They should rest with the bones and rinds where they all may benefit living creatures—small rodents and insects—until their return is completed. The remains of things—animals and plants, the clay and the stones—were treated with respect. Because for the ancient people all these things had spirit and being.

The antelope merely consents to return home with the hunter. All phases of the hunt are conducted with love. The love the hunter and the people have for the Antelope People. And the love of the antelope who agree to give up their meat and blood so that human beings will not starve. Waste of meat or even the thoughtless handling of bones cooked bare will offend the antelope spirits. Next year the hunters will vainly search the dry plains for antelope. Thus it is necessary to return carefully the bones and hair, and the stalks and leaves to the earth who first created them. The spirits remain close by. They do not leave us.

The dead become dust, and in this becoming they are once more joined with the Mother. The ancient Pueblo people called the earth the Mother Creator of all things in this world. Her sister, the Corn Mother, occasionally merges with her because all succulent green life rises out of the depths of the earth.

Rocks and clay are part of the Mother. They emerge in various forms, but at some time before, they were smaller particles or great boulders. At a later time they may again become what they once were. Dust.

A rock shares this fate with us and with animals and plants as well. A rock has being or spirit, although we may not understand it. The spirit may differ from the spirit we know in animals or plants or in ourselves. In the end we all originate from the depths of the earth. Perhaps this is how all beings share in the spirit of the Creator. We do not know.

From the Emergence Place

Pueblo potters, the creators of petroglyphs and oral narratives, never conceived of removing themselves from the earth and sky. So long as the human consciousness remains *within* the hills, canyons, cliffs, and the plants, clouds, and sky, the term *landscape,* as it has entered the English language, is misleading. "A portion of territory the eye can comprehend in a single view" does not correctly describe the relationship between the human being and his or her surroundings. This assumes the viewer is somehow *outside* or *separate from* the territory he or she surveys. Viewers are as much a part of the landscape as the boulders they stand on. There is no high mesa edge or mountain peak where one can stand and not immediately be part of all that surrounds. Human identity is linked with all the elements of Creation through the clan: you might belong to the Sun Clan or the Lizard Clan or the Corn Clan or the Clay Clan.* Standing deep within the natural world, the ancient Pueblo understood the thing as it was—the squash blossom, grasshopper, or rabbit itself could never be created by the human hand. Ancient Pueblos took the modest view that the thing itself (the landscape) could not be improved upon. The ancients did not presume to tamper with what had already been created. Thus *realism,* as we now recognize it in painting and sculpture, did not catch the imaginations of Pueblo people until recently.

The squash blossom itself is *one thing:* itself. So the ancient Pueblo potter abstracted what she saw to be the key elements of the squash blossom—the four symmetrical petals, with four symmetrical stamens in the center. These key elements, while suggesting the squash flower, also link it with the four cardinal directions. By representing only its intrinsic form, the squash flower is released from a limited meaning or restricted identity. Even in the most sophisticated abstract form, a squash flower or a cloud or a lightning bolt became intricately connected with a complex system of relationships which the ancient Pueblo people maintained with each other, and with the populous natural world they lived within. A bolt of lightning is itself, but at the same time it may mean much more. It may be a messenger of good fortune when summer rains are needed. It may deliver death, perhaps the result of manipulations by the Gunnadeyahs, destructive necromancers. Lightning may strike down an evil-doer. Or lightning may strike a person of good will. If the person survives, lightning endows him or her with heightened power.

Pictographs and petroglyphs of constellations or elk or antelope draw their magic in part from the process wherein the focus of all prayer and concentration is upon

*Clan—A social unit composed of families sharing common ancestors who trace their lineage back to the Emergence where their ancestors allied themselves with certain plants or animals or elements.

the thing itself, which, in its turn, guides the hunter's hand. Connection with the spirit dimensions requires a figure or form which is all-inclusive. A "lifelike" rendering of an elk is too restrictive. Only the elk *is* itself. A *realistic* rendering of an elk would be only one particular elk anyway. The purpose of the hunt rituals and magic is to make contact with *all* the spirits of the Elk.

The land, the sky, and all that is within them—the landscape—includes human beings. Interrelationships in the Pueblo landscape are complex and fragile. The unpredictability of the weather, the aridity and harshness of much of the terrain in the high plateau country explain in large part the relentless attention the ancient Pueblo people gave the sky and the earth around them. Survival depended upon harmony and cooperation not only among human beings, but among all things—the animate and the less animate, since rocks and mountains were known to move, to travel occasionally.

The ancient Pueblos believed the Earth and the Sky were sisters (or sister and brother in the post-Christian version). As long as good family relations are maintained, then the Sky will continue to bless her sister, the Earth, with rain, and the Earth's children will continue to survive. But the old stories recall incidents in which troublesome spirits or beings threaten the earth. In one story, a malicious ka'tsina, called the Gambler, seizes the Shiwana, or Rainclouds, the Sun's beloved children.* The Shiwana are snared in magical power late one afternoon on a high mountain top. The Gambler takes the Rainclouds to his mountain stronghold where he locks them in the north room of his house. What was his idea? The Shiwana were beyond value. They brought life to all things on earth. The Gambler wanted a big stake to wager in his games of chance. But such greed, even on the part of only one being, had the effect of threatening the survival of all life on earth. Sun Youth, aided by old Grandmother Spider, outsmarts the Gambler and the rigged game, and the Rainclouds are set free. The drought ends, and once more life thrives on earth.

Through the Stories We Hear Who We Are

All summer the people watch the west horizon, scanning the sky from south to north for rain clouds. Corn must have moisture at the time the tassels form. Otherwise pollination will be incomplete, and the ears will be stunted and shriveled. An inadequate harvest may bring disaster. Stories told at Hopi, Zuni, and at Acoma and Laguna describe drought and starvation as recently as 1900. Precipitation in west-central New Mexico averages fourteen inches annually. The western pueblos are located at altitudes over 5,600 feet above sea level, where winter temperatures at night fall below freezing. Yet evidence of their presence in the high desert plateau country goes back ten thousand years. The ancient Pueblo people not only survived in this environment, but many years they thrived. In A.D. 1100 the people at Chaco Canyon had built cities with apartment buildings of stone five stories high. Their sophistication as sky-watchers was surpassed only by Mayan and Inca astronomers. Yet this vast complex of knowledge and belief, amassed for thousands of years, was never recorded in writing.

Instead, the ancient Pueblo people depended upon collective memory through

---

*Ka'tsina—Ka'tsinas are spirit beings who roam the earth and who inhabit kachina masks worn in Pueblo ceremonial dances.

successive generations to maintain and transmit an entire culture, a world view complete with proven strategies for survival. The oral narrative, or "story," became the medium in which the complex of Pueblo knowledge and belief was maintained. Whatever the event or the subject, the ancient people perceived the world and themselves within that world as part of an ancient continuous story composed of innumerable bundles of other stories.

The ancient Pueblo vision of the world was inclusive. The impulse was to leave nothing out. Pueblo oral tradition necessarily embraced all levels of human experience. Otherwise, the collective knowledge and beliefs comprising ancient Pueblo culture would have been incomplete. Thus stories about the Creation and Emergence of human beings and animals into this World continue to be retold each year for four days and four nights during the winter solstice. The "humma-hah" stories related events from the time long ago when human beings were still able to communicate with animals and other living things. But, beyond these two preceding categories, the Pueblo oral tradition knew no boundaries. Accounts of the appearance of the first Europeans in Pueblo country or of the tragic encounters between Pueblo people and Apache raiders were no more and no less important than stories about the biggest mule deer ever taken or adulterous couples surprised in cornfields and chicken coops. Whatever happened, the ancient people instinctively sorted events and details into a loose narrative structure. Everything became a story.

Traditionally everyone, from the youngest child to the oldest person, was expected to listen and to be able to recall or tell a portion, if only a small detail, from a narrative account or story. Thus the remembering and retelling were a communal process. Even if a key figure, an elder who knew much more than others, were to die unexpectedly, the system would remain intact. Through the efforts of a great many people, the community was able to piece together valuable accounts and crucial information that might otherwise have died with an individual.

Communal storytelling was a self-correcting process in which listeners were encouraged to speak up if they noted an important fact or detail omitted. The people were happy to listen to two or three different versions of the same event or the same humma-hah story. Even conflicting versions of an incident were welcomed for the entertainment they provided. Defenders of each version might joke and tease one another, but seldom were there any direct confrontations. Implicit in the Pueblo oral tradition was the awareness that loyalties, grudges, and kinship must always influence the narrator's choices as she emphasizes to listeners this is the way *she* has always heard the story told. The ancient Pueblo people sought a communal truth, not an absolute. For them this truth lived somewhere within the web of differing versions, disputes over minor points, outright contradictions tangling with old feuds and village rivalries.

A dinner-table conversation, recalling a deer hunt forty years ago when the largest mule deer ever was taken, inevitably stimulates similar memories in listeners. But hunting stories were not merely after-dinner entertainment. These accounts contained information of critical importance about behavior and migration patterns of mule deer. Hunting stories carefully described key landmarks and locations of fresh water. Thus a deer-hunt story might also serve as a "map." Lost travelers, and lost piñon-nut gatherers, have been saved by sighting a rock formation they recognize only because they once heard a hunting story describing this rock formation.

The importance of cliff formations and water holes does not end with hunting stories. As offspring of the Mother Earth, the ancient Pueblo people could not conceive of themselves within a specific landscape. Location, or "place," nearly always plays a central role in the Pueblo oral narratives. Indeed, stories are most frequently recalled as people are passing by a specific geographical feature or the exact place where a story takes place. The precise date of the incident often is less important than the place or location of the happening. "Long, long ago," "a long time ago," "not too long ago," and "recently" are usually how stories are classified in terms of time. But the places where the stories occur are precisely located, and prominent geographical details recalled, even if the landscape is well-known to listeners. Often because the turning point in the narrative involved a peculiarity or special quality of a rock or tree or plant found only at that place. Thus, in the case of many of the Pueblo narratives, it is impossible to determine which came first: the incident or the geographical feature which begs to be brought alive in a story that features some unusual aspect of this location.

There is a giant sandstone boulder about a mile north of Old Laguna, on the road to Paguate. It is ten feet tall and twenty feet in circumference. When I was a child, and we would pass this boulder driving to Paguate village, someone usually made reference to the story about Kochininako, Yellow Woman, and the Estrucuyo, a monstrous giant who nearly ate her. The Twin Hero Brothers saved Kochininako, who had been out hunting rabbits to take home to feed her mother and sisters. The Hero Brothers had heard her cries just in time. The Estrucuyo had cornered her in a cave too small to fit its monstrous head. Kochininako had already thrown to the Estrucuyo all her rabbits, as well as her moccasins and most of her clothing. Still the creature had not been satisfied. After killing the Estrucuyo with their bows and arrows, the Twin Hero Brothers slit open the Estrucuyo and cut out its heart. They threw the heart as far as they could. The monster's heart landed there, beside the old trail to Paguate village, where the sandstone boulder rests now.

It may be argued that the existence of the boulder precipitated the creation of a story to explain it. But sandstone boulders and sandstone formations of strange shapes abound in the Laguna Pueblo area. Yet most of them do not have stories. Often the crucial element in a narrative is the terrain—some specific detail of the setting.

A high dark mesa rises dramatically from a grassy plain fifteen miles southeast of Laguna, in an area known as Swanee. On the grassy plain one hundred and forty years ago, my great-grandmother's uncle and his brother-in-law were grazing their herd of sheep. Because visibility on the plain extends for over twenty miles, it wasn't until the two sheepherders came near the high dark mesa that the Apaches were able to stalk them. Using the mesa to obscure their approach, the raiders swept around from both ends of the mesa. My great-grandmother's relatives were killed, and the herd lost. The high dark mesa played a critical role: the mesa had compromised the safety which the openness of the plains had seemed to assure. Pueblo and Apache alike relied upon the terrain, the very earth herself, to give them protection and aid. Human activities or needs were maneuvered to fit the existing surroundings and conditions. I imagine the last afternoon of my distant ancestors as warm and sunny for late September. They might have been traveling slowly, bringing the sheep closer to Laguna in preparation for the approach of colder weather. The grass was tall and only beginning to change from green to a yellow which matched the late-afternoon sun shining off it. There might have been comfort in the warmth and the sight of the sheep fattening on good pasture which lulled my ancestors into their fatal inattention. They might have had a rifle whereas the Apaches had only bows and arrows. But there would have been four or five Apache raiders, and the surprise attack would have canceled any advantage the rifles gave them.

Survival in any landscape comes down to making the best use of all available resources. On that particular September afternoon, the raiders made better use of the Swanee terrain than my poor ancestors did. Thus the high dark mesa and the story of the two lost Laguna herders became inextricably linked. The memory of them and their story resides in part with the high black mesa. For as long as the mesa stands, people within the family and clan will be reminded of the story of that afternoon long ago. Thus the continuity and accuracy of the oral narratives are reinforced by the landscape—and the Pueblo interpretation of that landscape is *maintained.*

The Migration Story: An Interior Journey

The Laguna Pueblo migration stories refer to specific places—mesas, springs, or cottonwood trees—not only locations which can be visited still, but also locations which lie directly on the state highway route linking Paguate village with Laguna village. In traveling this road as a child with older Laguna people I first heard a few of the stories from that much larger body of stories linked with the Emergence and Migration.* It may be coincidental that Laguna people continue to follow the same route which, according to the Migration story, the ancestors followed south from the Emergence Place. It may be that the route is merely the shortest and best route for car, horse, or foot traffic between Laguna and Paguate villages. But if the stories about boulders, springs, and hills are actually remnants from a ritual that retraces the creation and emergence of the Laguna Pueblo people as a culture, as the people they became, then continued use of that route creates a unique relationship between the ritual-mythic world and the actual, everyday world. A journey from Paguate to Laguna down the long incline of Paguate Hill retraces the original journey from the Emergence Place, which is located slightly north of the Paguate village. Thus the landscape between Paguate and Laguna takes on a deeper significance: the landscape resonates the spiritual or mythic dimension of the Pueblo world even today.

Although each Pueblo culture designates a specific Emergence Place—usually a small natural spring edged with mossy sandstone and full of cattails and wild watercress—it is clear that they do not agree on any single location or natural spring as the one and only true Emergence Place. Each Pueblo group recounts its own stories about Creation, Emergence, and Migration, although they all believe that all human beings, with all the animals and plants, emerged at the same place and at the same time.†

---

*The Emergence—All the human beings, animals, and life which had been created emerged from the four worlds below when the earth became habitable.

The Migration—The Pueblo people emerged into the Fifth World, but they had already been warned they would have to travel and search before they found the place they were meant to live.

†Creation—Tse'itsi'nako, Thought Woman, the Spider, thought about it, and everything she thought came into being. First she thought of three sisters for herself, and they helped her think of the rest of the Universe, including the Fifth World and the four worlds below. The Fifth World is the world we are living in today. There are four previous worlds below this world.

Natural springs are crucial sources of water for all life in the high desert plateau country. So the small spring near Paguate village is literally the source and continuance of life for the people in the area. The spring also functions on a spiritual level, recalling the original Emergence Place and linking the people and the spring water to all other people and to that moment when the Pueblo people became aware of themselves as they are even now. The Emergence was an emergence into a precise cultural identity. Thus the Pueblo stories about the Emergence and Migration are not to be taken as literally as the anthropologists might wish. Prominent geographical features and landmarks which are mentioned in the narratives exist for ritual purposes, not because the Laguna people actually journeyed south for hundreds of years from Chaco Canyon or Mesa Verde, as the archaeologists say, or eight miles from the site of the natural springs at Paguate to the sandstone hilltop at Laguna.

The eight miles, marked with boulders, mesas, springs, and river crossings, are actually a ritual circuit or path which marks the interior journey the Laguna people made: a journey of awareness and imagination in which they emerged from being within the earth and from everything included in earth to the culture and people they became, differentiating themselves for the first time from all that had surrounded them, always aware that interior distances cannot be reckoned in physical miles or in calendar years.

The narratives linked with prominent features of the landscape between Paguate and Laguna delineate the complexities of the relationship which human beings must maintain with the surrounding natural world if they hope to survive in this place. Thus the journey was an interior process of the imagination, a growing awareness that being human is somehow different from all other life—animal, plant, and inanimate. Yet we are all from the same source: the awareness never deteriorated into Cartesian duality, cutting off the human from the natural world.

The people found the opening into the Fifth World too small to allow them or any of the animals to escape. They had sent a fly out through the small hole to tell them if it was the world which the Mother Creator had promised. It was, but there was the problem of getting out. The antelope tried to butt the opening to enlarge it, but the antelope enlarged it only a little. It was necessary for the badger with her long claws to assist the antelope, and at last the opening was enlarged enough so that all the people and animals were able to emerge up into the Fifth World. The human beings could not have emerged without the aid of antelope and badger. The human beings depended upon the aid and charity of the animals. Only through interdependence could the human beings survive. Families belonged to clans, and it was by clan that the human being joined with the animal and plant world. Life on the high arid plateau became viable when the human beings were able to imagine themselves as sisters and brothers to the badger, antelope, clay, yucca, and sun. Not until they could find a viable relationship to the terrain, the landscape they found themselves in, could they *emerge*. Only at the moment the requisite balance between human and *other* was realized could the Pueblo people become a culture, a distinct group whose population and survival remained stable despite the vicissitudes of climate and terrain.

Landscape thus has similarities with dreams. Both have the power to seize terrifying feelings and deep instincts and translate them into images—visual, aural, tactile—into the concrete where human beings may more readily confront and channel the terrifying instincts or powerful emotions into rituals and narratives which reassure the individual while reaffirming cherished values of the group. The identity of the individual as a part of the group and the greater Whole is strengthened, and the terror of facing the world alone is extinguished.

Even now, the people at Laguna Pueblo spend the greater portion of social occasions recounting recent incidents or events which have occurred in the Laguna area. Nearly always, the discussion will precipitate the retelling of older stories about similar incidents or other stories connected with a specific place. The stories often contain disturbing or provocative material, but are nonetheless told in the presence of children and women. The effect of these inter-family or inter-clan exchanges is the reassurance for each person that she or he will never be separated or apart from the clan, no matter what might happen. Neither the worst blunders or disasters nor the greatest financial prosperity and joy will ever be permitted to isolate anyone from the rest of the group. In the ancient times, cohesiveness was all that stood between extinction and survival, and, while the individual certainly was recognized, it was always as an individual simultaneously bonded to family and clan by a complex bundle of custom and ritual. You are never the first to suffer a grave loss or profound humiliation. You are never the first, and you understand that you will probably not be the last to commit or be victimized by a repugnant act. Your family and clan are able to go on at length about others now passed on, others older or more experienced than you who suffered similar losses.

The wide deep arroyo near the Kings Bar (located acoss the reservation borderline) has over the years claimed many vehicles. A few years ago, when a Viet Nam veteran's new red Volkswagen rolled backwards into the arroyo while he was inside buying a six-pack of beer, the story of his loss joined the lively and large collection of stories already connected with that big arroyo. I do not know whether the Viet Nam veteran was consoled when he was told the stories about the other cars claimed by the ravenous arroyo. All his savings of combat pay had gone for the red Volkswagen. But this man could not have felt any worse than the man who, some years before, had left his children and mother-in-law in his station wagon with the engine running. When he came out of the liquor store his station wagon was gone. He found it and its passengers upside down in the big arroyo. Broken bones, cuts and bruises, and a total wreck of the car. The big arroyo has a wide mouth. Its existence needs no explanation. People in the area regard the arroyo much as they might regard a living being, which has a certain character and personality. I seldom drive past that wide deep arroyo without feeling a familiarity with and even a strange affection for this arroyo. Because as treacherous as it may be, the arroyo maintains a strong connection between human beings and the earth. The arroyo demands from us the caution and attention that constitute respect. It is this sort of respect the old believers have in mind when they tell us we must respect and love the earth.

Hopi Pueblo elders have said that the austere and, to some eyes, barren plains and hills surrounding their mesa-top villages actually help to nurture the spirituality of the Hopi *way*. The Hopi elders say the Hopi people might have settled in locations far more lush where daily life would not have been so grueling. But there on the high silent sandstone mesas that overlook the sandy arid expanses stretching to all horizons, the Hopi elders say the Hopi people must "live by their prayers" if they are to survive. The Hopi way cherishes the intangible: the riches realized from interaction and interrelationships with all beings above all else. Great abundances of material things, even food, the Hopi elders believe, tend to lure human attention away from what is most valuable and important. The views of the Hopi elders are not much different from those elders in all the Pueblos.

The bare vastness of the Hopi landscape emphasizes the visual impact of every plant, every rock, every arroyo. Nothing is overlooked or taken for granted. Each ant, each lizard, each lark is imbued with great value simply because the creature is there, simply because the creature is alive in a place where any life at all is precious. Stand on the mesa edge at Walpai and look west over the bare distances toward the pale blue outlines of the San Francisco peaks where the ka'tsina spirits reside. So little lies between you and the sky. So little lies between you and the earth. One look and you know that simply to survive is a great triumph, that every possible resource is needed, every possible ally—even the most humble insect or reptile. You realize you will be speaking with all of them if you intend to last out the year. Thus it is that the Hopi elders are grateful to the landscape for aiding them in their quest as spiritual people.

Out Under the Sky

My earliest memories are of being outside, under the sky. I remember climbing the fence when I was three years old, and heading for the plaza in the center of Laguna village because other children passing by had told me there were ka'tsinas there dancing with pieces of wood in their mouths. A neighbor woman retrieved me before I ever saw the wood-swallowing ka'tsinas, but from an early age I knew that I wanted to be outside. Outside walls and fences.

My father had wandered all the hills and mesas around Laguna when he was a child. Because the Indian School and the taunts of the other children did not set well with him. It had been difficult in those days to be part Laguna and part white, or *amedicana*. It was still difficult when I attended the Indian School at Laguna. Our full-blooded relatives and clanspeople assured us we were theirs and that we belonged there because we had been born and reared there. But the racism of the wider world we call America had begun to make itself felt years before. My father's response was to head for the mesas and hills with his older brother, their dog, and .22 rifles. They retreated to the sandstone cliffs and juniper forests. Out in the hills they were not lonely because they had all the living creatures of the hills around them, and, whatever the ambiguities of racial heritage, my father and my uncle understood what the old folks had taught them: the earth loves all of us regardlessly, because we are her children.

I started roaming those same mesas and hills when I was nine years old. At eleven I rode away on my horse, and explored places my father and uncle could not have reached on foot. I was never afraid or lonely, although I was high in the hills, many miles from home. Because I carried with me the feeling I'd acquired from listening to the old stories, that the land all around me was teeming with creatures that were related to human beings and to me. The stories had also left me with a feeling of familiarity and warmth for the mesas and hills and boulders where the incidents or action in the stories had taken place. I felt as if I had actually been to those places, although I had only heard stories about them. Somehow the stories had given a kind of being to the mesas and hills, just as the stories had left me with the sense of having spent time with the people in the stories, although they had long since passed on.

It is unremarkable to sense the presence of those long passed at the locations where their adventures took place. Spirits range without boundaries of any sort. Spirits may be called back in any number of ways. The method used in the calling also determines how the spirit manifests itself. I think a spirit may or may not choose to remain at the site of its passing or death. I think they might be in a number of places at the same time. Storytelling can procure fleeting moments to experience who they were and how life felt long ago. What I enjoyed most as a child was standing at the site of an incident recounted in one of the ancient stories Aunt Susie had told us as girls. What excited me was listening to old Aunt Susie tell us an old-time story and then for me to realize that I was familiar with a certain mesa or cave that figured as the central location of the story she was telling. That was when the stories worked best. Because then I could sit there listening and be able to visualize myself as being located *within* the story being told, within the landscape. Because the storytellers did not just tell the stories, they would in their way act them out. The storyteller would imitate voices for vast dialogues between the various figures in the story. So we sometimes say the moment is alive again within us, within our imaginations and our memory, as we listen.

Aunt Susie once told me how it had been when she was a child and her grandmother agreed to tell the children stories. The old woman would always ask the youngest child in the room to go open the door. "Go open the door," her grandmother would say. "Go open the door so our esteemed ancestors may bring us the precious gift of their stories." Two points seem clear: the spirits could be present and the stories were valuable because they taught us how we were the people we believed we were. The myth, the web of memories and ideas that create an identity, a part of oneself. This sense of identity was intimately linked with the surrounding terrain, to the landscape which has often played a significant role in a story or in the outcome of a conflict.

The landscape sits in the center of Pueblo belief and identity. Any narratives about the Pueblo people necessarily give a great deal of attention and detail to all aspects of a landscape. For this reason, the Pueblo people have always been extremely reluctant to relinquish their land for dams or highways. For this reason, Taos Pueblo fought from 1906 until 1973 to win back their sacred Blue Lake, which was illegally taken from them by the creation of Taos National Forest. For this reason, the decision in the early 1950s to begin open-pit mining of the huge uranium deposits north of Laguna, near Paguate village, has had a powerful psychological impact upon the Laguna people. Already a large body of stories has grown up around the subject of what happens to people who disturb or destroy the earth. I was a child when the mining began and the apocalyptic warning stories were being told. And I have lived long enough to begin hearing the stories which verify the earlier warnings.

All that remains of the gardens and orchards that used to grow in the sandy flats southeast of Paguate village are the stories of the lovely big peaches and apricots the people used to grow. The Jackpile Mine is an open pit that has been blasted out of the many hundreds of acres where the orchards and melon patches once grew. The Laguna people have not witnessed changes to the land without strong reactions. Descriptions of the landscape *before* the mine are as vivid as any description of the present-day destruction by the open-pit mining. By its very ugliness and by the violence it does to the land, the Jackpile Mine insures that from now on it, too, will be included in the vast body of narratives which make up the history of the Laguna people and the Pueblo landscape. And the description of what that landscape looked like *before* the uranium mining began will always carry considerable impact.

Landscape as a Character in Fiction

Drought or the disappearance of game animals may signal disharmony or even witchcraft. When the rain clouds fail to appear in time to help the corn plants, or the deer are suddenly scarce, then we know the very sky and earth are telling human beings that all is not well. A deep arroyo continues to claim victims.

When I began writing I found that the plots of my short stories very often featured the presence of elements out of the landscape, elements which directly influenced the outcome of events. Nowhere is landscape more crucial to the outcome than in my short story, "Storyteller." The site is southwest Alaska, near the village of Bethel, on the Kuskokwim River. Tundra country. Here the winter landscape can suddenly metamorphize into a seamless blank white so solid that pilots in aircraft without electronic instruments lose their bearings and crash their planes straight into the frozen tundra, believing down to be up. Here on the Alaska tundra, in mid-February, not all the space-age fabrics, electronics, or engines can ransom human beings from the restless shifting forces of the winter sky and winter earth.

The young Yupik Eskimo woman works out an elaborate yet subconscious plan to avenge the deaths of her parents. After months of baiting the trap, she lures the murderer onto the river ice where he falls through to his death. The murderer is a white man who operates the village trading post. For years the murderer has existed like a parasite, exploiting not only the fur-bearing animals and the fish, but the Yupik people themselves. When the Yupik woman kills him, the white trader has just finished cashing in on the influx of workers for the petroleum exploration and pipeline who have suddenly come to the tiny village. For the Yupik people, souls deserving punishment spend varying lengths of time in a place of freezing. The Yupik see the world's end coming with ice, not fire. Although the white trader possesses every possible garment, insulation, heating fuel, and gadget ever devised to protect him from the frozen tundra environment, he still dies, drowning under the freezing river ice. Because the white man had not reckoned with the true power of that landscape, especially not the power which the Yupik woman understood instinctively and which she used so swiftly and efficiently. The white man had reckoned with the young woman and determined he could overpower her. But the white man failed to account for the conjunction of the landscape with the woman. The Yupik woman had never seen herself as anything but a part of that sky, that frozen river, that tundra. The river ice and the blinding white are her accomplices, and yet the Yupik woman never for a moment misunderstands her own relationship with that landscape. After the white trader has crashed through the river ice, the young woman finds herself a great distance from either shore of the treacherous frozen river. She can see nothing but the whiteness of the sky swallowing the earth. But far away in the distance, on the side of her log and tundra sod cabin, she is able to see the spot of bright red. A bright red marker she had nailed up weeks earlier because she was intrigued by the contrast between all that white and the spot of brilliant red. The Yupik woman knows the appetite of the frozen river. She realizes that the ice and the fog, the tundra and the snow seek constantly to be reunited with the living beings which skitter across it. The Yupik woman knows that inevitably she and all things will one day lie in those depths. But the woman is young and her instinct is to live. The Yupik woman knows how to do this.

Inside the small cabin of logs and tundra sod, the old Storyteller is mumbling the last story he will ever tell. It is the story of the hunter stalking a giant polar bear the color of blue glacier ice. It is a story which the old Storyteller has been telling since the young Yupik woman began to arrange the white trader's death. But a sudden storm develops. The hunter finds himself on an ice floe off shore. Visibility is zero, and the scream of the wind blots out all sound. Quickly the hunter realizes he is being stalked. Hunted by all the forces, by all the elements of the sky and earth around him. When at last the hunter's own muscles spasm and cause the jade knife to fall and shatter the ice, the hunter's death in the embrace of the giant ice blue bear is the foretelling of the world's end. When humans have blasted and burned the last bit of life from the earth, an immeasurable freezing will descend with a darkness that obliterates the sun.

Contributors to Part II

MARGARET ATWOOD was born in 1939 in Ottawa, Ontario. Educated at the University of Toronto and Radcliffe College (M.A., 1962), she has received many awards, including Canada's Molson Prize and a Guggenheim Fellowship. Best known for her novels and collections of short stories, Atwood has also published poetry and nonfiction. Her essays and reviews are collected in *Second Words*.

SIMONE DE BEAUVOIR (1908–1986) was born in Paris and educated at the Sorbonne. Before devoting herself to writing, she taught philosophy at several colleges in France. Like her works of nonfiction, Beauvoir's novels explore philosophical perspectives on experience. Her best-known work is *The Second Sex* (1949), from which the excerpt in this book is taken.

PATRICIA BERRY was born in Long Beach, California, in 1943. She was educated at Ohio State University (B.A., 1966), St. John's College (M.A., 1971), the C. G. Jung Institute, Zurich (diploma, 1976), and the University of Dallas

(Ph.D., 1984). She is Head of Training for the Inter-Regional Society of Jungian Analysts. A practicing psychotherapist in Boston, she has published articles in *Spring* and *Chiron*. *Echo's Subtle Body*, her collected essays, contains her influential "An Approach to the Dream" as well as "What's the Matter with Mother?," the essay reprinted in this volume.

SUSAN BROWNMILLER, born in 1935, is a journalist who has contributed to many periodicals, including *Esquire*, *Newsweek*, and the *New York Times Magazine*. She has also been a staff reporter for the *Village Voice* and a news writer for the American Broadcasting Company. Her three books are *Against Our Will: Men, Women, and Rape; Femininity;* and *Waverly Place*, a novel.

NANCY CHODOROW was born in New York City in 1944. Educated at Radcliffe College (A.B., 1966) and Brandeis University (M.A., 1972; Ph.D., 1975), she also attended the London School of Economics and Harvard University. She has taught courses in women's studies at

Wellesley College and in sociology at the University of California, Santa Cruz. She won the American Sociological Association's Jessie Bernard Award in 1980 for *The Reproduction of Mothering.*

HÉLÈNE CIXOUS was born in Algeria in 1938. She teaches at the University of Paris VIII (Vincennes), where she founded the first research group on the theory of femininity. She is the author of books, essays, novels, plays, and articles, including *Prénoms de personne; L'Exil de James Joyce, ou L'Art du remplacement; Dedans; Sorties;* and *La Venue à l'écriture.* She is on the editorial board of *Poétique.*

NANCY F. COTT, born in 1945, is one of the leading historians of American feminism. She has taught United States history and women's studies at Yale University since 1975. She is the author of *Roots of Bitterness: Documents of the Social History of American Women* (1972), *Bonds of Womanhood: "Woman's Sphere" in New England, 1780–1835* (1977), and *The Grounding of American Feminism* (1987).

ANGELA Y. DAVIS, an activist and writer, was born in 1944. She teaches philosophy and women's studies at San Francisco State University. Her autobiography, *Angela Davis,* appeared in 1974. Her essays have been collected in *Women, Race and Class* (1981) and *Women, Culture, and Politics* (1989).

MARY ANNE DOLAN was born in Washington, D.C., and was educated at Marymount College (Tarrytown, New York), the London School of Economics, and Cambridge University. She worked briefly in politics in the mid-1960s, then joined the *Washington Star.* During her nine years there, she eventually became assistant managing editor. She was the editor of the *Los Angeles Herald Examiner* for seven years, winning the Women's Golden Flame Award in 1980. She is now a syndicated columnist and television commentator based in Los Angeles.

MARGARET FULLER (1810–1850) was born in Cambridgeport, Massachusetts. A child prodigy, she received an exceptionally rigorous education from her father, a Harvard-educated politician. Associated with the Transcendentalists (Ralph Waldo Emerson, Bronson Alcott, and William Henry Channing), Fuller organized a discussion group of women—her famous "conversations"—in Boston. From 1840 to 1844 she was editor of the *Dial,* New England's leading Transcendentalist journal; at the invitation of Horace Greeley she then joined the staff of his *New-York Tribune* as a literary critic. She continued to write for the *Tribune* as a correspondent after she settled in Italy, where she championed the cause of Italian independence. Returning for a visit with her family, Fuller died in a shipwreck along with her husband, the marchese Giovanni Angelo Ossoli, and their small son, within sight of Fire Island, New York.

JANE GALLOP, born in 1952, has taught French literature and literary theory at Miami University in Ohio and is now a professor of humanities at Rice University. She is the author of four books— *Intersections: A Reading of Sade with Bataille, Blanchot, and Klossowski* (1981), *The Daughter's Seduction: Feminism and Psychoanalysis* (1982), *Reading Lacan* (1985), and *Thinking Through the Body* (1988). She has written extensively on French feminists and psychoanalytic theory.

SANDRA M. GILBERT was born in New York City in 1936 and was educated at Cornell (A.B., 1957), New York University (M.A., 1961), and Columbia (Ph.D., 1968). A professor of English at Princeton, Gilbert is a poet, short-story writer, and literary critic whose major critical works include *The Madwoman in the Attic: The Woman Writer and the Nineteenth-Century Literary Imagination* (1979) and *No Man's Land: The Place of the Woman Writer in the Twentieth Century* (1988), both with Susan Gubar. She and Gubar are also editors of *Shakespeare's Sisters:*

Feminist Essays on Women Poets (1979) and *The Norton Anthology of Literature by Women* (1985). Her most recent book of poetry is *Blood Pressure* (1989). *The Madwoman in the Attic* was nominated for the Pulitzer Prize.

NADINE GORDIMER was born (in 1923) and raised in South Africa, where she lives today. A writer of short stories, novels, and reportage, she is best known for her novels *The Conservationist* (1974), *Burger's Daughter* (1979), *July's People* (1981), and *A Sport of Nature* (1987). Her stories and novels, widely acclaimed in Britain and the United States though periodically banned in her own country, examine the impact of *apartheid* on the private lives of white, Black, and "colored" (Indian, Asian, and racially mixed) South Africans.

SUSAN GUBAR, born in 1940, is professor of English at Indiana University. Her major critical works are *The Madwoman in the Attic: The Woman Writer and the Nineteenth Century Literary Imagination* (1979) and *No Man's Land: The Place of the Woman Writer in the Twentieth Century* (1988), both with Sandra M. Gilbert. She and Gilbert are also editors of *Shakespeare's Sisters: Feminist Essays on Women Poets* (1979) and *The Norton Anthology of Literature by Women* (1985).

ZORA NEALE HURSTON (1903–1960) was born in Eatonville, Florida, and educated at Howard University, Barnard College, and Columbia University. She wrote in a variety of genres, including the novel, short story, drama, and essay. She also edited important collections of folklore. A prominent figure of the Harlem Renaissance in the 1920s and 1930s, Hurston consistently affirmed the dignity and grace of Black culture. Among her many books are the novel *Their Eyes Were Watching God* and *Mules and Men,* a collection of Black folklore.

LUCE IRIGARAY, born in Belgium, holds two doctorates, one in linguistics and one in philosophy. As a result of the publication of her feminist book *Speculum, de l'autre femme* (1974), she was ousted from the Freudian school of Jacques Lacan, where she had been trained as a psychoanalyst, and from her teaching position at the University of Paris VIII at Vincennes. She now practices as a psychoanalyst, conducts research in the relationship of language and psychology, and continues to write. In addition to *Speculum* (which is available in English as *Speculum of the Other Woman,* 1985), she has published seven other books, including *Le Langage des déments* (The language of the mad, 1973), *Ce Sexe que n'en est pas un* (1977; available in English as *This Sex Which Is Not One,* 1985), and books on Nietzsche and Heidegger.

EVELYN FOX KELLER, born in 1936, is a mathematical biophysicist and writer. She teaches at Northeastern University. She is the author of *A Feeling for the Organism: The Life and Work of Barbara McClintock* (1983) and a volume of essays, *Reflections on Gender and Science* (1985).

ANNETTE KOLODNY, born in New York City in 1941, has taught at the University of California at Berkeley; Yale University; the University of British Columbia at Vancouver; and the University of New Hampshire at Durham. She is currently Professor of English at Rensselaer Polytechnic Institute. Her major works include *The Lay of the Land: Metaphor as Experience and History in Life and Letters* (1975) and *Westering Women: Fantasies of the American Frontier: 1630–1860* (1983). In 1979 she won the Modern Language Association's Florence Howe Essay Prize for "Dancing through the Minefield."

URSULA K. LE GUIN was born in 1929 and raised in Berkeley, California. The daughter of the anthropologist Alfred K. Kroeber and the writer and folklorist Theodora Kroeber, Le Guin studied literature at Harvard and Columbia universities.

She is the author of novels that have won critical recognition within the science fiction community and beyond it. Two of her novels, *The Left Hand of Darkness* (1969) and *The Dispossessed* (1974), won both the Hugo (from the World Science Fiction Convention) and Nebula (from the Science Fiction Writers of America, Inc.) awards. Her Earthsea trilogy has won awards for children's literature. She lives in Portland, Oregon.

PAULE MARSHALL was born in Brooklyn, New York, in 1929. Educated at Brooklyn and Hunter colleges, she has taught at Yale, Columbia, and Virginia Commonwealth universities. She has received numerous awards, including grants from the Guggenheim and Ford foundations and from the National Endowment for the Humanities. Her books include *Brown Girl, Brownstones* (1959), *Soul Clap Hands and Sing* (1961), *The Chosen Place, the Timeless People* (1969), and *Praisesong for the Widow* (1975).

TILLIE OLSEN was born in Omaha, Nebraska, in 1913. She dropped out of high school during the Depression to work at a succession of jobs as a typist and factory worker to support her growing family. The recipient of several prestigious awards, including a Ford Foundation Grant and an O. Henry Award, she has taught at Amherst, Stanford, the University of Massachussetts, and MIT. Her books include *Tell Me a Riddle* and *Silences.*

OLIVE SCHREINER (1855–1920) was born in South Africa to missionary parents. Early in life she rebelled against her strict upbringing and in her twenties wrote *The Story of an African Farm,* which was published in 1883 under the pseudonym Ralph Iron. In 1881 she traveled to London, where she was to spend long periods for the remainder of her life, and became an important figure in the city's radical intellectual circles. During her lifetime her most famous book was *Women and Labour* (1911). A foe of imperialism and rac-

ism and a supporter of conscientious objectors, she lived in London during World War I. She died shortly afterward in South Africa.

ELAINE SHOWALTER was born in Cambridge, Massachusetts, in 1941. She has taught English at Rutgers University and is now professor of English at Princeton University. Her first book, *A Literature of Their Own: Women Writers from Brontë to Lessing* (1977), brought dozens of neglected nineteenth-century women writers to critical attention. She is also the author of *The Female Malady: Women, Madness, and Culture* (1985) and the editor of three volumes of essays, including *The New Feminist Criticism* (1985).

LESLIE MARMON SILKO was born in Laguna, New Mexico, in 1948 and spent her childhood on the Laguna Pueblo Indian Reservation. She has taught at the University of Arizona and the University of New Mexico. Her major works are a novel, *Ceremony* (1977); a collection of poems, *Laguna Woman: Poems* (1974); and a collection of short fiction, *Storyteller* (1981). In 1981 she received a five-year MacArthur fellowship. She is at work on a long novel.

KATE SIMON was born in Warsaw and came to New York at age four. She grew up in the Bronx and majored in English at Hunter College. The author of nine travel books, including *New York: Places and Pleasures* (1959), *Italy: The Places in Between* (1970), and *England's Green and Pleasant Land* (1974), Kate Simon has published two volumes of her autobiography, *Bronx Primitive: Portraits in a Childhood* (1982) and *A Wider World* (1986).

ELIZABETH CADY STANTON (1815–1902) was born in Johnstown, New York. An early leader in the struggle for women's rights, in 1848 she helped organize the Seneca Falls Convention, which inaugurated the movement for woman suffrage. In 1869 she became the first president of the National Woman Suffrage Association, a post she held till 1890. Her writings include the three-volume *History of Woman's Suffrage* (1881–1886); *A Woman's Bible* (1895), later reissued as *The Original Feminist Attack on the Bible* (1974); and an autobiography, *Eighty Years and More* (1898).

GLORIA STEINEM was born in Toledo, Ohio, in 1934. Educated at Smith College (B.A., 1956), she has been an editor, lecturer, writer, and political activist. Founding editor of *New York* and *Ms.* magazines, Steinem has published numerous articles and three books, including *Outrageous Acts and Everyday Rebellions* (1983), in which "Men and Women Talking" earlier appeared.

MARY WOLLSTONECRAFT (1759–1797) was born in London to a financially insecure middle-class family. Self-educated, she started a school and worked as a governess before becoming a professional writer. In London she was associated with a group of radical writers, artists, and publishers who sympathized with the French Revolution, among them William Godwin, whom she lived with and later married. The author of two novels, *Mary, a Fiction* (1788) and *Maria: or, The Wrongs of Woman* (1797), she is best known for *A Vindication of the Rights of Woman* (1792), a revolutionary critique of the social forces that place and keep women in a position of inferiority. She died of complications resulting from the birth of her second daughter, who was to become the novelist Mary Wollstonecraft Shelley, author of *Frankenstein.*

VIRGINIA WOOLF (1882–1941) was born in London to an affluent and intellectual family. After her father's death in 1904, she moved with her sister and brothers to Bloomsbury, where their household became the center of the flamboyant and experimental "Bloomsbury Group." She married Leonard Woolf, who was to become a novelist and publisher, in 1912. By 1915, when she published her first novel, *The Voyage Out,* Woolf had become a seasoned essayist and reviewer with ten years of experience in writing to length and to deadlines. She was the author of ten novels, including *Mrs. Dalloway* (1925) and *To The Lighthouse* (1927), and six volumes of essays. Her famous journals and letters fill a dozen more volumes. Woolf is also known for sounding the keynote for feminist literary criticism in *A Room of One's Own* (1929). *Three Guineas* (1938), written on the eve of World War II, makes a more urgent and politically charged case for feminism. Having struggled with depression and other forms of mental illness for years, Woolf drowned herself in 1941.

Index of Authors and Titles

About the Editors

Pat C. Hoy II is a professor of English at the U.S. Military Academy, where he directs the freshman writing program and teaches British and American literature as well as composition. He has also been a visiting lecturer in the Harvard Expository Writing Program. He received his B.A. from the Military Academy and his Ph.D. from the University of Pennsylvania.

His publications include essays, articles, and reviews in *South Atlantic Review, Twentieth-Century Literature,* and *The Sewanee Review.* His textbooks include *Prose Pieces* (with Robert DiYanni) and *Writing and Reading Essays,* forthcoming from McGraw-Hill. Essays on theory and pedagogy appear in *Literary Nonfiction* and *How Writers Teach Writing* (forthcoming). He was the managing editor of the *Doris Lessing Newsletter* for five years.

Esther H. Schor is an assistant professor of English at Princeton University, where she teaches nineteenth-century British literature and Women's Studies. She received her B.A. and Ph.D. from Yale. She has published essays in *Nineteenth-Century Literature, Shakespeare Quarterly,* and *Philosophy and Literature.*

At Princeton, she is codirector of the Mellon Seminar on Gender and Feminist Theory. With Anne Mellor and Audrey Fisch, she is co-editor of *The Other Mary Shelley* (a volume of essays), and has recently completed a book entitled *Elegiac Discourse: Subjectivity and Romanticism.* Her poems have appeared in *Yale Review, Sequoia,* the *Times Literary Supplement,* and *London Magazine.*

Robert DiYanni is Professor of English at Pace University, Pleasantville, New York, where he teaches British and American literature and also serves as Director of Interdisciplinary Studies. He received his B.A. from Rutgers University and his Ph.D. from the City University of New York.

Professor DiYanni has written articles and reviews on various aspects of literature and pedagogy. His books include *Prose Pieces, The Art of Reading, The Act of Writing* (all collaborative ventures), *Literature,* and *Modern American Poets: Their Voices and Visions.* He is now working on a book that explores how current literary theory can be applied in actual classroom practice.